P9-BJR-479

Twentieth-Century Literary Criticism

Guide to Gale Literary Criticism Series

For criticism on	Consult these Gale series
Authors now living or who died after December 31, 1959	***CONTEMPORARY LITERARY CRITICISM (CLC)***
Authors who died between 1900 and 1959	***TWENTIETH-CENTURY LITERARY CRITICISM (TCLC)***
Authors who died between 1800 and 1899	***NINETEENTH-CENTURY LITERATURE CRITICISM (NCLC)***
Authors who died between 1400 and 1799	***LITERATURE CRITICISM FROM 1400 TO 1800 (LC)*** ***SHAKESPEAREAN CRITICISM (SC)***
Authors who died before 1400	***CLASSICAL AND MEDIEVAL LITERATURE CRITICISM (CMLC)***
Black writers of the past two hundred years	***BLACK LITERATURE CRITICISM (BLC)***
Authors of books for children and young adults	***CHILDREN'S LITERATURE REVIEW (CLR)***
Dramatists	***DRAMA CRITICISM (DC)***
Hispanic writers of the late nineteenth and twentieth centuries	***HISPANIC LITERATURE CRITICISM (HLC)***
Native North American writers and orators of the eighteenth, nineteenth, and twentieth centuries	***NATIVE NORTH AMERICAN LITERATURE (NNAL)***
Poets	***POETRY CRITICISM (PC)***
Short story writers	***SHORT STORY CRITICISM (SSC)***
Major authors from the Renaissance to the present	***WORLD LITERATURE CRITICISM, 1500 TO THE PRESENT (WLC)***

ISSN 0276-8178

Volume 60

Twentieth-Century Literary Criticism

Excerpts from Criticism of the Works of Novelists, Poets, Playwrights, Short Story Writers, and Other Creative Writers Who Lived between 1900 and 1960, from the First Published Critical Appraisals to Current Evaluations

Jennifer Gariepy
Editor

Pamela Willwerth Aue
Joann Cerrito
Laurie Di Mauro
Nancy Dziedzic
Kathleen J. Edgar
David M. Galens
Thomas Ligotti
Scot Peacock
Terrie M. Rooney
Associate Editors

An ITP Information/Reference Group Company

Changing the Way the World Learns

NEW YORK • LONDON • BONN • BOSTON • DETROIT
MADRID • MELBOURNE • MEXICO CITY • PARIS
SINGAPORE • TOKYO • TORONTO • WASHINGTON
ALBANY NY • BELMONT CA • CINCINNATI OH

STAFF

Jennifer Gariepy, *Editor*

Pamela Willwerth Aue, Joann Cerrito, Laurie Di Mauro, Nancy G. Dziedzic, Kathleen J. Edgar, David M. Galens, Thomas Ligotti, Scot Peacock, Terrie M. Rooney, *Associate Editors*

Stacy A. McConnell, *Assistant Editor*

Marlene S. Hurst, *Permissions Manager*
Margaret A. Chamberlain, Maria Franklin, *Permissions Specialists*
Susan Brohman, Diane Cooper, Michele Lonoconus, Maureen Puhl, Shalice Shah, Kimberly F. Smilay, Barbara A. Wallace, *Permissions Associates*
Sarah Chesney, Edna Hedblad, Margaret McAvoy-Amato, Tyra Y. Phillips, Lori Schoenenberger, Rita Velazquez, *Permissions Assistants*

Victoria B. Cariappa, *Research Manager*
Mary Beth McElmeel, Tamara C. Nott, Michele P. Pica, Tracie A. Richardson, Amy Steele, Norma Sawaya, *Research Associates*
Alicia Noel Biggers, Julia C. Daniel, *Research Assistants*

Mary Beth Trimper, *Production Director*
Deborah Milliken, *Production Assistant*

Barbara J. Yarrow, *Graphic Services Manager*
Sherrell Hobbs, *Macintosh Artist*
Randy Bassett, *Image Database Supervisor*
Robert Duncan, *Scanner Operator*
Pamela A. Hayes, *Photography Coordinator*

Library of Congress Catalog Card Number 76-46132
ISBN 0-8103-9305-0
ISSN 0276-8178

Printed in the United States of America

10 9 8 7 6 5 4 3 2 1

I(T)P™ Gale Research Inc., an International Thomson Publishing Company.
ITP logo is a trademark under license.

Contents

Preface

Since its inception more than fifteen years ago, *Twentieth-Century Literary Criticism* has been purchased and used by nearly 10,000 school, public, and college or university libraries. *TCLC* has covered more than 500 authors, representing 58 nationalities, and over 25,000 titles. No other reference source has surveyed the critical response to twentieth-century authors and literature as thoroughly as *TCLC*. In the words of one reviewer, "there is nothing comparable available." *TCLC* "is a gold mine of information—dates, pseudonyms, biographical information, and criticism from books and periodicals—which many libraries would have difficulty assembling on their own."

Scope of the Series

TCLC is designed to serve as an introduction to authors who died between 1900 and 1960 and to the most significant interpretations of these author's works. The great poets, novelists, short story writers, playwrights, and philosophers of this period are frequently studied in high school and college literature courses. In organizing and excerpting the vast amount of critical material written on these authors, *TCLC* helps students develop valuable insight into literary history, promotes a better understanding of the texts, and sparks ideas for papers and assignments. Each entry in *TCLC* presents a comprehensive survey of an author's career or an individual work of literature and provides the user with a multiplicity of interpretations and assessments. Such variety allows students to pursue their own interests; furthermore, it fosters an awareness that literature is dynamic and responsive to many different opinions.

Every fourth volume of *TCLC* is devoted to literary topics. These topic entries widen the focus of the series from individual authors to such broader subjects as literary movements, prominent themes in twentieth-century literature, literary reaction to political and historical events, significant eras in literary history, prominent literary anniversaries, and the literatures of cultures that are often overlooked by English-speaking readers.

TCLC is designed as a companion series to Gale's *Contemporary Literary Criticism,* which reprints commentary on authors now living or who have died since 1960. Because of the different periods under consideration, there is no duplication of material between *CLC* and *TCLC*. For additional information about *CLC* and Gale's other criticism titles, users should consult the Guide to Gale Literary Criticism Series preceding the title page in this volume.

Coverage

Each volume of *TCLC* is carefully compiled to present:

- criticism of authors, or literary topics, representing a variety of genres and nationalities
- both major and lesser-known writers and literary works of the period
- 8-15 authors or 4-6 topics per volume
- individual entries that survey critical response to each author's work or each topic in literary history, including early criticism to reflect initial reactions; later criticism to represent any rise or decline in reputation; and current retrospective analyses.

Organization of This Book

An author entry consists of the following elements: author heading, biographical and critical introduction, list of principal works, excerpts of criticism (each preceded by an annotation and a bibliographic citation), and a bibliography of further reading.

- The **Author Heading** consists of the name under which the author most commonly wrote, followed by birth and death dates. If an author wrote consistently under a pseudonym, the pseudonym will be listed in the author heading and the real name given in parentheses on the first line of the biographical and critical introduction. Also located at the beginning of the introduction to the author entry are any name variations under which an author wrote, including transliterated forms for authors whose languages use nonroman alphabets.

- The **Biographical and Critical Introduction** outlines the author's life and career, as well as the critical issues surrounding his or her work. References to past volumes of *TCLC* are provided at the beginning of the introduction. Additional sources of information in other biographical and critical reference series published by Gale, including *Short Story Criticism, Children's Literature Review, Contemporary Authors, Dictionary of Literary Biography,* and *Something about the Author,* are listed in a box at the end of the entry.

- Most *TCLC* entries include **Portraits** of the author. Many entries also contain reproductions of materials pertinent to an author's career, including manuscript pages, title pages, dust jackets, letters, and drawings, as well as photographs of important people, places, and events in an author's life.

- The **List of Principal Works** is chronological by date of first book publication and identifies the genre of each work. In the case of foreign authors with both foreign-language publications and English translations, the title and date of the first English-language edition are given in brackets. Unless otherwise indicated, dramas are dated by first performance, not first publication.

- Critical excerpts are prefaced by **Annotations** providing the reader with information about both the critic and the criticism that follows. Included are the critic's reputation, individual approach to literary criticism, and particular expertise in an author's works. Also noted are the relative importance of a work of criticism, the scope of the excerpt, and the growth of critical controversy or changes in critical trends regarding an author. In some cases, these annotations cross-reference excerpts by critics who discuss each other's commentary.

- A complete **Bibliographic Citation** designed to facilitate location of the original essay or book precedes each piece of criticism.

- **Criticism** is arranged chronologically in each author entry to provide a perspective on changes in critical evaluation over the years. All titles of works by the author featured in the entry are printed in boldface type to enable the user to easily locate discussion of particular works. Also for purposes of easier identification, the critic's name and the publication date of the essay are given at the beginning of each piece of criticism. Unsigned criticism is preceded by the title of the journal in which it appeared. Some of the excerpts in *TCLC* also contain translated material. Unless otherwise noted, translations in brackets are by the editors; translations in parentheses or continuous with the text are by the critic. Publication information (such as footnotes or page and line references to specific editions of works) have been deleted at the editor's discretion to provide smoother reading of the text.

- An annotated list of **Further Reading** appearing at the end of each author entry suggests secondary sources on the author. In some cases it includes essays for which the editors could not obtain reprint rights.

Cumulative Indexes

- Each volume of *TCLC* contains a cumulative **Author Index** listing all authors who have appeared in Gale's Literary Criticism Series, along with cross references to such biographical series as *Contemporary Authors* and *Dictionary of Literary Biography*. For readers' convenience, a complete list of Gale titles included appears on the first page of the author index. Useful for locating authors within the various series, this index is particularly valuable for those authors who are identified by a certain period but who, because of their death dates, are placed in another, or for those authors whose careers span two periods. For example, F. Scott Fitzgerald is found in *TCLC,* yet a writer often associated with him, Ernest Hemingway, is found in *CLC.*

- Each *TCLC* volume includes a cumulative **Nationality Index** which lists all authors who have appeared in *TCLC* volumes, arranged alphabetically under their respective nationalities, as well as Topics volume entries devoted to particular national literatures.

- Each new volume in Gale's Literary Criticism Series includes a cumulative **Topic Index,** which lists all literary topics treated in *NCLC, TCLC, LC 1400-1800,* and the *CLC* yearbook.

- Each new volume of *TCLC,* with the exception of the Topics volumes, includes a **Title Index** listing the titles of all literary works discussed in the volume. In response to numerous suggestions from librarians, Gale has also produced a **Special Paperbound Edition** of the *TCLC* title index. This annual cumulation lists all titles discussed in the series since its inception and is issued with the first volume of *TCLC* published each year. Additional copies of the index are available on request. Librarians and patrons will welcome this separate index; it saves shelf space, is easy to use, and is recyclable upon receipt of the following year's cumulation. Titles discussed in the Topics volume entries are not included *TCLC* cumulative index.

Citing *Twentieth-Century Literary Criticism*

When writing papers, students who quote directly from any volume in Gale's literary Criticism Series may use the following general forms to footnote reprinted criticism. The first example pertains to materials drawn from periodicals, the second to material reprinted from books.

[1]William H. Slavick, "Going to School to DuBose Heyward," *The Harlem Renaissance Re-examined,* (AMS Press, 1987); excerpted and reprinted in *Twentieth-Century Literary Criticism,* Vol. 59, ed. Jennifer Gariepy (Detroit: Gale Research, 1995), pp. 94-105.

[2]George Orwell, "Reflections on Gandhi," *Partisan Review,* 6 (Winter 1949), pp. 85-92; excerpted and reprinted in *Twentieth-Century Literary Criticism,* Vol. 59, ed. Jennifer Gariepy (Detroit: Gale Research, 1995), pp. 40-3.

Suggestions Are Welcome

In response to suggestions, several features have been added to *TCLC* since the series began, including annotations to excerpted criticism, a cumulative index to authors in all Gale literary criticism series, entries devoted to criticism on a single work by a major author, more extensive illustrations, and a title index listing all literary works discussed in the series since its inception.

Readers who wish to suggest authors or topics to appear in future volumes, or who have other suggestions, are cordially invited to write the editors.

Acknowledgments

The editors wish to thank the copyright holders of the excerpted criticism included in this volume and the permissions managers of many book and magazine publishing companies for assisting us in securing reprint rights. We are also grateful to the staffs of the Detroit Public Library, the Library of Congress, the University of Detroit Mercy Library, Wayne State University Purdy/Kresge Library Complex, and the University of Michigan Libraries for making their resources available to us. Following is a list of the copyright holders who have granted us permission to reprint material in this volume of *TCLC*. Every effort has been made to trace copyright, but if omissions have been made, please let us know.

COPYRIGHTED EXCERPTS IN *TCLC*, VOLUME 60, WERE REPRINTED FROM THE FOLLOWING PERIODICALS:

The Atlantic Monthly, v. 182, October, 1948 for "Fear Hath A Hundred Eyes" by Charles J. Rolo. Copyright 1948, renewed 1976, by The Atlantic Monthly Company, Boston, MA. Reprinted by permission of the author.—***Canadian Literature***, n. 63, Winter, 1975 for "Duncan's Web" by Carole Gerson; n. 132, Spring, 1992 for " 'The Simple Adventures of a Memsahib' and the Prisonhouse of Languages" by Jennifer Lawn. Both reprinted by permission of the author.—***Die Welt der Slaven: Halbjahresschrift fur Slavistik***, vs. XIX-XX, 1974-75. Reprinted by permission of Böhlau Verlag, Köln, Wien.—***Forum Italicum***, v. VIII, March, 1973. Copyright © 1973 by Forum Italicum. Reprinted by permission of the publisher.—***Japan Quarterly***, v. 19, 1972. © 1972, by the Asahi Shimbun. Reprinted by permission of the Asahi Shimbun Publishing Company.—***Journal of Canadian Fiction***, v. II, Summer, 1973; v. III, 1975. Both reprinted by permission from Journal of Canadian Fiction, 2050 Mackay St., Montreal, Quebec H3G 2J1, Canada.—***Journal of Canadian Studies***, v. 12, Spring, 1977. Reprinted by permission of the publisher.—***Journal of Canadian Studies,*** v. 20, Summer, 1985. Reprinted by permission of the publisher.—***Journal of Commonwealth Literature***, v. XXVI, 1991 for " 'This Little Outpost of Empire': Sara Jeannette Duncan and the Decolonization of Canada" by Ajay Heble. Copyright by the author. Reprinted by permission of Hans Zell Publishers, an imprint of Bowker-Saur Ltd.—***The New York Times Book Review***, April 19, 1925; August 8, 1926; April 20, 1930; June 17, 1962; September 10, 1989; May 27, 1990. Copyright 1925, 1926, 1930, 1962, 1989, 1990 by The New York Times Company. Reprinted by permission of the publisher.—***The New York Times Magazine***, May 5, 1957. Copyright © 1957 by The New York Times Company. Reprinted by permission of the publisher.—***Pacific Affairs***, v. XLIII, Fall, 1970. Copyright 1970, University of British Columbia. Reprinted by permission of the publisher.—***Poetry***, v. CXVIII, July, 1971 "Faces at the Bottom" by F.D. Reeve. © 1971 by the Modern Poetry Association. Reprinted by permission of the Editor of Poetry and the author.—***Publications of the English Goethe Society***, v. LVII, 1988. Reprinted by permission of the publisher.—***Revue Des Langues Vivantes***, v. XXXII, 1966 for "Conflict and Compromise: Tonio Kroger's Paradox" by J. R. McWilliams; v. XLII, 1976 for "Casting Out Nines: Structure, Parody and Myth in 'Tonio Kroger' " by Benjamin Bennett. Both reprinted by permission of the author.—***Romance Notes***, v. XXII, Winter, 1981. Reprinted by permission of the publisher.—***Russian Literature Triquarterly***, No. 1, Fall, 1971. © 1971 by Ardis Publishers. Reprinted by permission of the publisher.—***Slavic and East-European Journal***, v. 13, Spring, 1969; v. 21, Summer, 1977. © 1969, 1977 by AATSEL of the U.S., Inc. Both reprinted by permission of the publisher.—***Studies in Canadian Literature***, v. 9, 1984 for "Narrative Uncertainty in Duncan's 'The Imperialist'" by Peter Allen; v. 11, Spring, 1986 for "Religion in Elgin: A Re-evaluation of the Subplot of 'The Imperialist' by Sara Jeannette Duncan" by Elizabeth Morton. Copyright by the authors. Both reprinted by permission of the editors.—***The Times Literary Supplement***, n. 1284, September 9, 1926; n. 1698, August 16, 1934; n. 3618, July 2, 1971. © The Times Supplements Limited 1926, 1934, 1971. All reproduced from The Times Literary Supplement by permission.—***VLS***, n. 106, June, 1992 for a review of "Little Apple" by Dwight Garner. Copyright © 1992 News Group Publications, Inc. Reprinted by permission of The Village Voice and the author.—***World Literature Written in English***, v. 16, April, 1977 for "Sara Jeannette Duncan's Indian Fiction" by Frank Birbalsingh. © Copyright 1977 WLWE-World Literature Written in English. Reprinted by permission of the publisher and the author.—***The Yearbook of English Studies***, v. 13, 1983. © Modern Humanities Research Association 1983. All rights reserved.

Reprinted by permission of the Editor and the Modern Humanities Research Association.

COPYRIGHTED EXCERPTS IN *TCLC*, VOLUME 60, WERE REPRINTED FROM THE FOLLOWING BOOKS:

Atkinson, Brooks. From ***Broadway. Revised edition***. Macmillan, 1970. Copyright © 1970, 1974 by Brooks Atkinson. All rights reserved. Reprinted with the permission of Macmillan Publishing Company.—Babbitt, Irving. From ***On Being Creative and Other Essays***. Houghton Mifflin, 1932. Copyright 1932, by Irving Babbitt, renewed 1960 by Edward S. Babbitt and Esther Babbitt Howe. All rights reserved. Reprinted by permission of the National Humanities Institute.—Brown, John Mason. From ***Two on the Aisle: Ten Years of American Theatre in Performance.*** Norton, 1938. Copyright 1938 by W. W. Norton & Company, Inc. Renewed 1966 by John Mason Brown. Reprinted by permission of the Literary Estate of John Mason Brown.—Caffrey, Margaret M. From ***Ruth Benedict: Stranger in This Land***. University of Texas Press, 1989. Copyright © 1989 by Margaret Mary Caffrey. All rights reserved. Reprinted by permission of the author and the University of Texas Press.—Dean, Misao. From ***A Different Point of View: Sara Jeannette Duncan***. McGill-Queen's University Press, 1991. © McGill-Queen's University Press 1991. Reprinted by permission of the publisher.—Downs, Robert B. From ***Famous American Books***. McGraw-Hill, 1971. Copyright © 1971 by McGraw-Hill, Inc. All rights reserved. Reproduced with permission.—Elstun, Esther. From "Richard Beer-Hofmann: The Poet as 'exculpator dei'" in ***Protest—Form—Tradition***. Joseph P. Strelka, Robert F. Bell, and Eugene Dobson, eds. University of Alabama Press, 1979. Copyright © 1979 by The University of Alabama Press. All rights reserved. Reprinted by permission of the publisher.—Ewen, David. From ***Complete Book of the American Theater***. Henry Holt and Company, 1958. Copyright © 1958 by David Ewen. Renewed 1986, by Hannah Ewen. All rights reserved. Reprinted by permission of The Literary Estate of David Ewen.—Geertz, Clifford. From ***Works and Lives: The Anthropologist as Author***. Stanford University Press, 1988. Copyright © 1988 by the Board of Trustees of Leland Stanford Junior University. Reprinted with the permission of the publishers, Stanford University Press. UK and Commonwealth rights, Basil Blackwood Ltd.—Gray, Ronald. From ***The German Tradition in Literature, 1871-1945***. Cambridge at the University Press, 1965. © Cambridge University Press 1965. Reprinted with the permission of the publisher.—Gumilev, Nikolai. From ***Nikolai Gumilev on Russian Poetry***. Edited and translated by David Lapeza. Ardis, 1977. Copyright © 1977 by Ardis. Reprinted by permission of the publisher.—Handler, Richard. From "Ruth Benedict and the Modernist Sensibility" in ***Modernist Anthropology: From Filedwork to Text***. Edited by Marc Manganaro. Princeton University Press, 1990. Copyright © 1990 by Princeton University Press. Reprinted by permission of the publisher.—Hatch, Elvin. From ***Theories of Man and Culture***. Columbia University Press, 1973. Copyright © 1973 Columbia University Press, New York. All rights reserved. Reprinted with the permission of the publisher.—Kahn, Lothar. From ***Mirrors of the Jewish Mind: A Gallery of Portraits of European Jewish Writers of Our Time***. Thomas Yoseloff, 1968. Copyright © 1968 by A.S. Barnes & Company, Inc. All rights reserved. Reprinted by permission of the publisher.—Keene, David. From ***Dawn to the West, Japanese Literature of the Modern Era: Poetry, Drama, Criticism, Vol. 2***. Holt, Rinehart and Winston, 1984. Copyright © 1984 by Donald Keene. All rights reserved. Reprinted by permission of Henry Holt and Company.—Liptzin, Solomon. From ***Germany's Stepchildren***. The Jewish Publication Society of America, 1944. Copyright 1944, renewed 1971, by The Jewish Publication Society. All rights reserved. Used through the courtesy of the Jewish Publication Society.—Mead, Margaret. From ***An Anthropologist at Work: Writings of Ruth Benedict***. Houghton Mifflin, 1959. Copyright © 1959 by Margaret Mead. Renewed 1987, by Mary Catherine Bateson. All rights reserved. Reprinted by permission of The Literary Estate of Margaret Mead.—Mintz, Sidney. From "Ruth Benedict" in ***Totems and Teachers: Perspectives on the History of Anthropology***. Edited by Sydel Silverman. Columbia University Press, 1981. Copyright © 1981 Columbia University Press, New York. All rights reserved. Reprinted with the permission of the publisher.—Modell, Judith Schachter. From ***Ruth Benedict: Patterns of a Life***. University of Pennsylvania Press, 1983. Copyright © 1983 by the University of Pennsylvania Press. All rights reserved. Reprinted by permission of the author.—Monas, Sidney. From an introduction to ***Selected Works of Nikolai S. Gumilev***. Edited and translated by Burton Raffel and Alla Burago. State University of New York Press, 1972. Copyright © 1972 State University of New York. All rights reserved. Reprinted by permission of the author.—Nichols, Ray. From ***Treason, Tradition, and the Intellectual: Julien Benda and Political Discourse***. Regents Press of Kansas, 1978. © Copyright

1978 by The Regents Press of Kansas. Reprinted by permission of the publisher.—Niess, Robert J. From ***Julien Benda***. University of Michigan Press, 1956. Copyright © by the University of Michigan 1956. Renewed 1984, by Robert J. Niess. Reprinted by permission of the publisher.—Pacifici, Sergio. From ***The Modern Italian Novel: From Pea to Moravia***. Southern Illinois University Press, 1979. Copyright © 1979 by Southern Illinois University Press. All rights reserved. Reprinted by permission of the publisher.—Poggioli, Renato. From ***The Poets of Russia: 1890-1930***. Cambridge, Mass.: Harvard University Press, 1960. Copyright © 1960 by the President and Fellows of Harvard College. Renewed © 1988 by Sylvia Poggioli. Excerpted by permission of the publishers.—Ruhl, Arthur. From ***Second Nights***. Charles Scribner's Sons, 1914. Copyright 1914 by Charles Scribner's Sons; copyright renewed 1942 by Zinaida Ruhl. Reprinted by permission of Scribner, a division of Simon & Schuster Inc.—Schalk, David L. From ***The Spectrum of Political Engagement: Mounier, Benda, Nizan, Brasillach, Sartre***. Princeton University Press, 1979. Copyright © 1979 by Princeton University Press. All rights reserved. Reprinted by permission of the publisher.—Slonim, Marc. From ***Modern Russian Literature: From Chekhov to the Present***. Oxford University Press, 1953. Copyright 1953 by Oxford University Press, Inc. Renewed 1981 by Tatiana Slonim. Reprinted by permission of the publisher.—Struve, Gleb. From ***Russian Literature Under Lenin and Stalin, 1917-1953***. University of Oklahoma Press, 1971. Copyright 1971 by the University of Oklahoma Press, Publishing Division of the University. Reprinted by permission of the publisher.—Tausky, Thomas E. From ***Sara Jeannette Duncan: Novelist of Empire***. P.D. Meany Publishers, 1980. © 1980 Thomas E. Tausky. All rights reserved. Reprinted by permission of the publisher.—Thomson, Boris. From ***Lot's Wife and the Venus of Milo: Conflicting Attitudes to the Cultural Heritage in Modern Russia***. Cambridge University Press 1978. © Cambridge University Press, 1978. Reprinted with the permission of the publisher.—Ueda, Makoto. From ***Modern Japanese Poets and the Nature of Literature***. Stanford University Press, 1983. Copyright © 1983 by the Board of Trustees of the Leland Stanford Junior University. Reprinted with the permission of the publishers, Stanford University Press.—Wilkinson, E. M. From "Tonio Kroger: An Interpretation," in ***Thomas Mann: A Collection of Critical Essays***. Edited by Henry Hatfield. Prenctice-Hall, 1964. © 1964 by Prentice-Hall, Inc. Renewed 1992, by Henry Hatfield. All rights reserved. Used by permission of Henry Hatfield.—Wilson, Graeme. From an introduction to ***Face at the Bottom of the World, and Other Poems***. By Hagiwara Sakutaro, translated by Graeme Wilson. Tuttle, 1969. © 1969 by The Charles E. Tuttle Co., Inc. All rights reserved. Reprinted by permission of the publisher.

PHOTOGRAPHS AND ILLUSTRATIONS APPEARING IN *TCLC*, VOLUME 60, WERE RECEIVED FROM THE FOLLOWING SOURCES:

Italian Information Center: **p.1**; Bildarchiv der Österreichischen Nationalbibliothek, Wien: **p.22**; Arthur Muray: **p.92**.

Corrado Alvaro

1896-1956

Italian novelist, short-story writer, journalist, essayist, playwright, and poet.

INTRODUCTION

A prolific author of both fiction and journalism for nearly forty years, Corrado Alvaro distinguished himself as one of the foremost practitioners of *verismo,* an Italian movement of literary realism that paralleled French Naturalism. His first success came with *Gente in Aspromonte* (*Revolt in Aspromonte*), considered by most critics to be his masterpiece. Alvaro identified himself and was viewed by others as a writer who incorporated the differences and tensions between urbanized, wealthy northern Italy and rural, poverty-stricken, southern Italy into his work. A concern with moral questions, a sensitivity to the harsh life of the southern Italian underclass, and a belief in violence as a legitimate means for producing social change are hallmarks of his work.

Biographical Information

Born in San Luca, a small village in the southernmost region of the Italian province of Calabria, Alvaro was educated at Jesuit boarding schools in Rome and Umbria. While attending the University of Milan, from which he graduated with a degree in literature in 1919, Alvaro began work as a journalist and literary critic for two daily newspapers, *Il resto di carlino* of Bologna and *Il corriere della sera* of Milan. During World War I he served as an officer in the Italian army and wrote for the anti-Fascist paper *Il mondo.* Alvaro's politics made made him the target of surveillance and finally forced him to leave Italy. During the 1930s he traveled widely in western Europe, the Middle East, and Russia, journeys he later recounted in his travel essays. After World War II Alvaro returned to Italy, where he continued to work for prominent daily newspapers in various capacities, including special correspondent, theater and film critic, and editor. He was elected secretary of the Italian Association of Writers in 1947, a post he held until his death in 1956.

Major Works

Alvaro's initial literary efforts did not enjoy great popularity, though critics have praised his first novel *L'uomo nel labirinto* for its depiction of alienation as an aspect of individuals and society as a whole. Alvaro's subsequent works, *L'amata alla finestra, Gente in Aspromonte, La signora dell'isola,* and *Vent'anni* established him as an important figure in Italian literature and earned him a prize of 50,000 lire given by the periodical *La Stampa* at the recommendation of a jury that included noted Italian novelist and dramatist Luigi Pirandello. Gradually, Alvaro moved from works that treated individual lives to those that depicted the social and political plight of Italy's lower classes. In his later works, he broadened his focus to describe the effects of World War I on all levels of Italian society. Alvaro is noted for his skill in depicting the contrasts between a yearning for the simple, pastoral way of life, and the desire to achieve material success that lures people to urban areas. He is especially praised for his realistic, epic depictions of the Italian poor. The novels *L'età breve* and *L'uomo è forte* as well as the diary *Quasi una vita* are often considered by commentators to be among his best works.

Critical Reception

Alvaro's novels and essays have been well-received by both critics and the public. In addition to prizes for individual works, he earned the Italian Academy Prize for the entire body of his writings. While some critics have noted that Alvaro's characters are sometimes vague or little more than collections of attitudes, particularly in later works, most have praised his ability to depict the conflicts between the rural and urban regions of Italy. Sergio Pacifici has noted: "The society depiced by Alvaro in *Revolt in Aspromonte* is a closed one, permits no failures, respects only success. The equation is unacceptable to our writer: he looks for understanding and compassion, even though he knows how rarely society exhibits them."

PRINCIPAL WORKS

Poesie grigioverdi (poetry) 1917
La siepe e l'orto (novel) 1920
L'uomo nel labirinto (novel) 1926
L'amata alla finestra (novel) 1929
Gente in Aspromonte [*Revolt in Aspromonte*] (novel) 1930
Misteri e avventure (travel essay) 1930
La signora dell'isola (novel) 1930
Vent'anni (novel) 1930
Calabria (travel essay) 1931
Viaggio in Turchia (travel essay) 1932
Itinerario italiano (travel essay) 1933
Cronaca (o fantasia) (travel essay) 1934
Il mare (travel essay) 1934
I maestri del diluvio: Viaggio nella Russia Sovietica (travel essay) 1935
L'uomo è forte [*Man Is Strong*] (novel) 1938
Caffè dei naviganti (drama) 1939
Il viaggio (travel essay) 1942
**L'età breve* (novel) 1946
Lunga notte di Medea (drama) 1949
Quasi una vita: Giornale di uno scrittore (diary) 1950
Il nostro tempo e la speranza (essays) 1952
Settantacinque racconti (short stories) 1955
Ultimo diario (diary) 1959
**Mastrangelina* (novel) 1960
**Tutto è accaduto* (novel) 1961
La moglie e i quaranta racconti (short stories) 1963

*These three novels form the trilogy *Memorie del mondo sommerso.*

CRITICISM

Peter Michael Riccio (essay date 1938)

SOURCE: "Corrado Alvaro," in *Italian Authors of Today,* 1938. Reprint by Books for Libraries Press, 1970, pp. 167-69.

[*In the following essay, Riccio praises Alvaro's works for their depictions of the human spirit.*]

Gente in Aspromonte by Corrado Alvaro had the distinction recently of carrying off the coveted prize of 50,000 lire offered by *La Stampa* of Turin for the best novel of the year published in Italy. That this book of Corrado Alvaro is worthy of such recognition is not difficult to understand if we pause a moment to consider the work of this young writer who hails from Calabria and spends most of his time in Rome trying to eke out a living by the use of his pen.

Alvaro first caught the public eye by a series of short stories that contained interesting cross-sections of the primitive and rustic life of his native Calabria. In ***L'Amata alla Finestra,*** an earlier work, and in the prize volume ***Gente in Aspromonte,*** Alvaro offers a collection of Calabrian scenes colored with the sharp tints of an intense realism and of a deep melancholy which make the reading of them a delightful treat, especially if one compares these writings of Alvaro with those of the vast majority of his literary contemporaries. Furthermore, a perusal of Alvaro's work reveals a literary technique that is devoid of the superfluously decorative flourishes that have been the curse of so many Italian writers. The sharp, barren and rugged coast of Calabria and the hard, primitive and passionate life of the people are depicted in a style that enhances the beauty and charm of the literary pictures. And with what depth and effect does the pen of Alvaro dip into the very heart and soul of the Calabrian countryside and the Calabrian family life! The reader cannot help but feel an obvious subsequent effect on his own spiritual vision.

There are authors who write novels that are nothing more nor less than descriptions of the region or environment from which they have sprung. These are sometimes called regionalists and as such their work often appeals only to a limited few. On the other hand there are writers who use the region or environment in which they live to reveal and give expression to their own soul. These have naturally a more universal appeal and have something more substantial to offer in the way of spiritually stimulating substance. And Corrado Alvaro is among those who belong to this second category.

In ***Gente in Aspromonte,*** Alvaro does not describe Calabria so much as he describes himself—a humble, melancholy and extremely sensitive being, moulded by the poverty, the hardships and disappointments of life. When Alvaro takes us on his excursions through Calabria we find our guide equipped with an especially fine pair of spiritual field glasses. And it is with these field glasses that Alvaro makes us scan the horizon of life—a horizon saturated with a grey mist but whose outline is sufficiently distinguished by the few penetrating rays of sunlight.

There is in the work of Alvaro a good deal that is reminiscent of the atmosphere and thought of such writers as Proust and Freud. This may readily be noted in the passions, the sex problems, the emotional struggles of his characters who try to adapt themselves to a life and environment dominated by the power of the senses, the sentiment, the sensual.

We had the pleasure of making the personal acquaintance of Alvaro in Rome at a café. We shall never forget how disappointed we were when we first met him. The expectations and the actualities were so different. We imagined a tall, middle-aged individual with sharply intelligent features and a hardened expression of life on his countenance. Instead, we met a short stocky young man, very humble and modest in appearance and with an almost naîve expression on his face. We had just returned from a trip through Calabria and had expected to find a more representative physical exponent of the region.

Alvaro is very anxious to come to America to train his appraising eye on the *panorama* of American life, not so much with the intention of reproducing what he will see into literary form as with a view toward taking in new scenes and strengthening his own vision of life.

Jerome D. Ross (essay date 1948)

SOURCE: "Nightmare Life in Death under Police State," in *New York Herald Tribune Weekly Book Review,* August 29, 1948, p. 3.

[*In the following review, Ross faults* Man Is Strong *for its vague characters and lack of suspense, but commends Alvaro's treatment of modern man's alienation.*]

Nightly, in the dream state, the individual compounds his fears, guilts, and insecurity into installments of a shadowy autobiography. Corrado Alvaro makes use of this fact in his story of dictatorship's degradation of the individual. The modern police state thrives by instilling a thousand fears, ten thousand guilts, and the author has selected, as a device by which to present modern man as slave of the state, the half-world of tormented dreams.

This strange dream novel, ***Man Is Strong,*** has had a curious history. A bitter indictment of totalitarianism, the Fascist censor permitted its publication in Italy only after the author had made certain minor deletions and written a foreword explaining that the scene was laid in Soviet Russia. Nazi censorship, doubtless realizing that this red herring would fool no German reader, forbade its publication at all. Actually, from a geographical point of view, it lies in the realm of the mind. The setting is as vague as the streets we roam and the houses we explore in our dreams. The story can take place anywhere, wherever fear and mass hysteria exist. For us, it is timely. During the current onslaught against civil liberties, American readers will find certain chilling analogies to the home scene.

Explicitly, ***Man Is Strong*** deals with the return of a young engineer to his own country after years in the outside, democratic world. During his absence the country has become completely totalitarian. He returns, a naive latter-day Candide, eager at first to share in the new spirit which he saw exemplified in the heroic plaster figures atop his country's pavilion at an international exposition. (Shades of the Soviet pavilion in Paris; of buxom Italia in the Flushing Meadows.) Like Candide, he undergoes a series of fantastic adventures in political re-education, succumbing at times to the mass neuroses of his countrymen, eventually rediscovering the value of freedom. The story as such—his love affair, his crime against the state, his attempted flight—is without form, fluid, surrealist impressions dissolving one into another. Merely as story, it is a bewildering hodgepodge unless viewed in its broadest significance and unless accepted as the shapeless, disconnected incidents of a troubled dream.

Fear, corrosive and degrading to man's dignity, is the single dominant motif of this book, determining both its mood and style. The mood is muted, an atmosphere bathed in sepia tones and misty shadows. For here is no study of terror which sharpens the senses, but rather of constant, gnawing, ever-present fear which blunts them. Mr. Alvaro explores that curse of our age, mass fear, as it lurks in the subconscious and distorts all conscious experience. His characters are obsessed with it and the symbols it evokes, to a point where they become themselves imaginary symbols of anxiety, fugue, deception, corruption. Participants in a national danse macabre, they glide in and out of the hero's path, mere silhouettes, each manifesting a different phase of the disease.

This method of treating such a tenuous theme may be valid enough, but the result is none too successful. The book is prolix, as ordinary dreams are, at times needlessly wordy, elsewhere too abrupt. It lacks the climaxes of nightmares. Others before Alvaro, notably Franz Kafka, have made use of stark terror in portraying the police state of mind: the victim confronted by unknown accusers, accused of unnamed crimes. Such fundamental dilemmas immediately seize hold of the reader; he, too, is caught in the trap. But Mr. Alvaro's engineer, Dirck, endures no consuming agonies of mind and body. Throughout he remains an intellectual symbol, too bloodless for the reader to seek any identification. In consequence, the book lacks suspense.

The other characters are even more ectoplasmic, simply congealed attitudes. Their raison d'etre lies in what they can contribute to Dirck's education; each in turn defines some facet of regimentation. Barbara, with whom Dirck is in love, serves to illustrate the impossibility of any normal relationship. Guilt and anxiety blunt her passion, pervert her natural affection, until, at length, her only decisive action is to denounce Dirck as a traitor. There is the Investigator who pursues but does not arrest, content to wait until each individual commits the overt crime hatched in the deep recesses of his imagination. There is the Director of Technology, the skilled puppet, who understands the ultimate role expected of him: when Dirck murders him, he achieves a false martyrdom in the state's hate-propaganda campaign. These people are all abstractions, obscure and at times tedious.

But the book offers interesting illustrations of behavior patterns in the world of fear and tyranny. In the dream world, which has its own devices, tangible objects are substituted for thoughts and physical attributes replace traits of character. In ***Man Is Strong*** the author employs many such devices, eerie and exaggerated. Trivial souvenirs—watches, scarves, bits of food, bits of cloth—epitomize the last remaining vestiges of individuality, and these objects the characters hoard with childish greed. Conversely, remains of food, empty plates, empty bottles—telltale evidence of hidden, personal enjoyment—these they destroy. Every movement, every remark, acquires a forbidden meaning. A piece of paper with the penciled words "I love you," is hastily swallowed lest writer or recipient stand charged with a crime against the state. A love scene is conducted in nonsense syllables for fear of informers. A cab driver's casual "Where to?" is answered with a lengthy catechism of one's name, residence, background, political reliability.

"We no longer belong to ourselves," is how one of the shadow creatures describes their existence to Dirck, "Our dreams, our thoughts, our ambitions and our will have all been invaded." For all its faults this novel is an imaginative analysis, unique and certainly sincere, of man's soul and spirit in modern bondage.

Charles J. Rolo (essay date 1948)

SOURCE: "Fear Hath a Hundred Eyes," in *The Atlantic Monthly,* Vol. 182, No. 4, October, 1948, pp. 106-7.

[*Rolo was an Egyptian-born American investment broker, editor, and critic who wrote several studies on Aldous Huxley. In the following excerpt, he praises Alvaro's depiction of the fascist state in* Man Is Strong *for its "anguished climate of nightmare and baleful unreason."*]

Joseph Conrad's indictment of the tsarist autocracy—"the ruthless destruction of innumerable minds . . . of dignity, of truth, of rectitude, of all that is faithful in human nature"—sums up the ravages of modern fascism . . . Those ravages—that destruction of minds and human ties and the accompanying climate of "darkness at noon"—are dramatized in ***Man Is Strong***. The book was published in Italy in 1939, after Alvaro had added a foreword stating that the police state described was Russia.

Scourges as immense as fascism and war present the novelist with a knotty problem of ways and means. A Frenchman has aptly remarked that "a single man killed is a misfortune, a million is a statistic." How to encompass the emotional reality of that aggregate of horrors which so easily becomes "a statistic" or a remote abstraction—"war dead," "purge," "pogrom"? [Albert] Camus's answer in *The Plague* was vividly realistic allegory. Alvaro's is the symbolism and superrealism of [Franz] Kafka, with its dreamlike intensity. Many of his devices have their exact parallel in *The Trial*—the mysterious circumstance left unexplained, the sinister coincidence, the felt presence of unseen, omnipotent powers, and so on.

The story opens with the return of Dirck, an expatriate, to his native country, recently emerged from civil war. Instantly, the atmosphere is that of waking nightmare. People stare "with hate" at Dirck's good clothes. Strange officials know his name and face. His room is searched. Barbara, with whom he renews an old love affair (years earlier she had been abroad), is terrified that to be seen with him will "incriminate" her. Danger and senseless prohibition hang over everything, and Dirck is rapidly infected with the cringing anxiety which is the norm—the obsessive consciousness that "they" are watching, listening, condemning. He feels guilty of a nameless crime, which he has *not* committed—and is certain to commit. "My dear," says his superior, "often the mere appearance of guilt is a crime."

Dirck's initiation into this "mysticism of crime" comes from a chance meeting with "the investigator," who takes him to an office decorated with pictures of hanged men. "We must destroy everything private, personal, intimate; there lies the cause of all evils," says the investigator. "To have a secret is a crime." Execution of the guilty makes crime "as beneficial an example to society as that set by the most loyal citizen." The prospective criminal "interests us enormously. . . . We need him." Corrupters, too, are needed to keep society well supplied with the spectacle of educative punishment, and the man from abroad is ideal for this form of "public service." Everything about him incites the guilty. "To borrow a term from religion, he is the devil." Dirck now sees clearly that his love for Barbara *is* a criminal conspiracy against the state. And when eventually, crazed by fear, he commits' a real crime, he feels that some monstrous plan which "they" conceived has been accomplished.

Since I've seen the book criticized for the very thing it aims at, its surrealistic quality, I should perhaps say that if you insist on lifelike characterization and the other qualities of conventional realism, then Alvaro is decidedly not your man. What he is so successful in achieving is the anguished climate of nightmare and baleful unreason. His book has, too, something of that tension of ideas which distinguished *Darkness at Noon*. It is a thoroughly unusual novel, and, to my mind, a remarkable one.

Helene Cantarella (essay date 1962)

SOURCE: "Cornered in Calabria," in *The New York Times Book Review,* June 17, 1962, p. 5.

[*In the following review, Cantarella praises* Revolt in Aspromonte *for its compassionate portrayal of the struggles of Italy's peasants.*]

There are two Italys. There is the prosperous, elegant, buoyant Italy of "the Italian miracle" that one hears about so much today in press and films. Then there is the other—the painful, bitter, eternal Italy of the peasants, particularly of the Southern peasants, as different from the first as day is from night. No Italian writer has more succinctly expressed the elemental anguish and frustrations of that second Italy than Corrado Alvaro, whose masterpiece, ***Revolt in Aspromonte,*** comes at last to American readers in a sensitive translation by Frances Frenaye.

Alvaro, whose untimely death in 1956 put an end to his brilliant career as journalist, novelist, and essayist, is considered in contemporary Italian letters as the voice of Calabria, that dramatically beautiful but poverty-stricken land which lies at the tip of the Italian boot. In this he fulfills for his native region the function that [Giovanni] Verga and [Elio] Vittorini performed for Sicily, Ignazio Silone for the Abruzzi and Carlo Levi for Lucania.

Calabria's high mountains are peopled in large part by shepherds and peasants. Strong, silent and long-suffering, they eke out a bare living which provides them with few of the pleasures that most men consider their due in life. Yet they accept their lot with stoic resignation. It is only when they are driven beyond the bounds of despair that their long-nurtured resentments erupt in implacable vendettas which take on the awesome dimensions of Greek tragedy.

Two such men are the shepherd Argiro and his gentle oldest son, Antonello. As poor as Job and plagued like him by a ruthless fate, they struggle to keep body and soul together against the wanton persecution and oppression of the local feudal family that controls the destinies of their village. Courage, hard work and sacrifice all come to nothing. When Argiro fails for lack of money to educate his youngest son Benedetto for the priesthood as the only way out of what amounts to virtual serfdom, Antonello decides to take fate into his own hands. In an apocalyptic climax he avenges in one night the wrongs suffered for years by him, his family and his village.

As he surrenders to the *carabinieri* who come for him in the high hills of Aspromonte, he displays the serenity of the man who has realized himself. "At last," he says, "I have met Justice face to face. It's taken me long enough to catch up with Her and say what I have to say." As the book ends, it matters little to him that he, the victim, should become the accused.

Swift, powerful and compassionate, Alvaro's novella tells more in its brief 120 pages about the reasons behind the so-called "Southern problem" and "banditism" than many a full-size tome. Its characters, for all their simplicity, are not inarticulate primitives. Upright men caught up in the toils of a system geared since time immemorial to exploit them, they fight back in the only way that remains when they find all the forces of society stubbornly arrayed against them. Transcending time and space as they move against the somber, poetic grandeur of their forbidding mountains, they take on an almost legendary stature and become symbols of the age-old struggle that has kept Italy cleft in twain and all the poorer for it.

Alice Ellen Mayhew (essay date 1962)

SOURCE: "The Travail of an Indigent Shepherd," in *The Saturday Review,* New York, Vol. XLV, No. 26, June 30, 1962, p. 25.

[*In the following review, Mayhew hails* Revolt in Aspromonte *for its unsparing, passionate depiction of southern Italian peasant life.*]

This short book is a minor classic, written with great economy and understated ferocity. It is a product of the Italian South, which, like our own, has an extraordinarily rich literary heritage. An unusual number of talented writers (three of the four Italian Nobel Literature Prize-winners) have dramatized its social and economic predicament and have vividly portrayed the barren terrain with its decaying manor, ragged children, and docile peasants at the mercy of the landowners, the moneylenders, the elements, and every piece of bad luck. Alvaro has remarked that one could love this country only if one was born into it.

Revolt in Aspromonte describes a village in this poor and rocky land, and an indigent shepherd's struggle to free himself from the system that is throttling him. It was written in 1930, when the southern province of Calabria was literally still a feudal society, because the liberation of the Kingdom of the Two Sicilies with its supposed redistribution of the land had done nothing for the peasants and had simply increased the fortunes of the aristocracy. The village of Aspromonte was what it had always been, a cluster of tiny rustic houses built around the palace of the Mezzatesta family, who owned all the fields, farms, and animals by which the peasants eked out their living.

The struggle that takes place in this setting is between the shepherd Argiro, who has just lost his oxen, and the decadent members of that family, to whom he appeals for help. Alvaro masterfully pictures the plight of the shepherd as he stands before the fat, scornful *patrone,* head bowed, twisting his hat, answering the mocking questions respectfully. At last he stalks out, determined to fight back. This incident, which changes Argiro's life, makes an indelible impression on his young son, who has stood wondering by as his father is degraded and dismissed.

They visit the village moneylender, a crass and shrewd man who takes advantage of the uncomplaining peasants after the cruelty of the landowners has reduced them to desperation. With borrowed funds Argiro manages to get on his feet again, but he is still smarting under the blows of his oppressors, and his children's lives begin more and more to be shaped by their father's wish for revenge.

Argiro's eldest son, the gentle Antonello, goes away to work so that he can help to send the talented youngest son, Benedetto, to the seminary. The novel achieves its greatest poignance in the scene where Antonello, treated by his family with the kindness shown one about to start on a long, sad journey, realizes that he is a man.

We watch the family grow stronger in their hopes for Benedetto: Antonello, sweetly proud of him; the father, a trifle foolishly boastful; the mother, both afraid and trusting; the two deaf-mute little brothers, awed and respectful; and Benedetto himself, sure, ascetic, talking quietly, with his lids fluttering. For Argiro, Benedetto is to be the answer to centuries of oppression. The poor peasant is to have a spokesman. Then disaster strikes again. In a frivolous act of cruelty, three sons of Camillo Mezzatesta set fire to Argiro's barn; the mule is destroyed, and the entire support of Benedetto falls on Antonello, who collapses under the strain.

When Antonello finds out who has caused his family this final misery, he returns to Aspromonte as a kind of avenging god. At this point the tale becomes a parable, and Antonello is no longer the gentle son of a poor shepherd, but the spirit of the oppressed everywhere who sacrifices himself by a terrible vengeance to redeem his brothers. The last two chapters are saved from abstractness only by the author's passion, which raises his story to tragedy.

What Alvaro is stating is that there can be no dignity for man without justice. At the end, when Antonello goes down to meet the police, he says, "At last I have met Justice face to face. It has taken me long enough to catch up with Her and say what I have to say."

Anthony R. Terrizzi (essay date 1973)

SOURCE: "Another Look at Corrado Alvaro's *L'uomo nel labirinto,*" in *Forum Italicum,* Vol. VII, No. 1, March, 1973, pp. 23-9.

[*In the following excerpt, Terrizzi offers a reconsideration of* L'Uomo nel labirinto *in the context of Alvaro's subsequent work.*]

Only after a decade from the death of Corrado Alvaro in 1956 did a first monographic study of his works appear, followed by a number of others in quick succession. Until then the recognition that the author had received from literary critics, although constant and generous, consisted mostly of reviews, commemorations and essays, dealing either with his multifaceted personality, or just one book, or merely certain aspects of his complex work. However, the availability of Alvaro's entire work did not change the direction of criticism significantly, and the influence of previous piecemeal interpretations and misinterpretations has continued to cloud the understanding of this writer. Therefore, some of Alvaro's works, particularly among his novels, need to be looked at anew, to be reexamined from the vantage point of the entire opus of the author's fiction and non-fiction.

Alvaro had been writing for just over a decade when he published ***Gente in Aspromonte*** (1930) and already many critics had decided that his inspiration was being hurt by insistence on addressing itself to "both the world of the southern countryside and that of the city, to Verga on one side and Proust and Freud on the other, since it succeeded in being genuine and creative only when it allowed the rural Vergan, tender, instinctive vein to flow free," as stated by [L.] Tonelli, one of the first to perceive the untruthfulness of that accusation ["L'amata alla finestra e Vent'anni," *Il Martocco*, 1931].

This dichotomy does not exist in Alvaro's inspiration, which is, if anything, much richer and more complex. A seemingly rurally inspired novel like ***Gente in Aspromonte,*** if viewed from within the context of the author's entire work, does not focus on its lyrical evocation of both childhood memories and an even further removed, and at least equally idyllic, legendary past. Its real focus is the recurrent theme of *all* of Alvaro's novels, whether they be of Calabria or cast in an urban setting: the plight and struggle of the individual of our time in a certain society, or of an entire class under the strain of a stifling and oppressive environment. In the presentation of this theme Alvaro often uses a southern Italian as the main character (Sebastiano Babe, Antonello, Luca Fabio, Rinaldo Diacono) because he is the object of the author's immediate sympathy, but people from other regions or urban environments often share equally in the common struggles and defeats. Alienation and man's general bewilderment, as seen through these characters, are not merely the result of origins in a small town in southern Italy, but rather a malaise affecting modern society as a whole.

Among the novels that call most for reexamination is the very first ever written by Alvaro, the short novel ***L'uomo nel labirinto,*** originally published in serial form in 1922, and in its present form in 1926. It portrays the ever-increasing feeling of impotence that seized the bourgeoisie following the First World War, a theme also treated by such contemporaries of Alvaro as [Giuseppe Antonio] Borgese in *Rubè* (1921) and [Alberto] Moravia in *Gli indifferenti* (1929).

The opening paragraph of ***L'uomo nel labirinto,*** a description of a typical afternoon *passeggiata* in an Italian city shortly after the world conflict, immediately introduces the reader to the confused emotions and the crisis of society which is shared by every person in the novel. But it is most poignantly observed in Sebastiano Babe, to whose feeling of impotence and failure is added the extra burden of his origin in a small town in southern Italy. Although he has been living in the city since boyhood, and has lived the life of a local petit bourgeois for which he had prepared himself as a boy, he also lives with the feeling of never having gotten into the mainstream of city life. Like everyone in his society, he is a man of unfulfilled dreams; he is unnerved by his awareness of the meaningless passing of time and feels confined to the role of passive spectator of reality. He blames his failure on his inability to insert himself into life in the city and this in turn on his origin. An inventor of sorts, he attempts many things simultaneously but does not see any to its conclusion, neither in his work nor in his personal life. He constantly indulges in wishful thinking and confused dreams, and this becomes his way of evading reality, his particular fashion of living, the vicious circle of his frustrations.

Babe feels that life has been a bad dream and has treated him poorly, except for his childhood which now appears in a light of its own, "Io sono stato ingannato, e tutta la mia vita, meno l'infanzia, mi sembra un sogno." He attempts to recapture its happiness by returning to his home town with his companion May, hoping that she will provide meaning to his existence.

Shortly after their departure, however, they both realize the futility of their venture; May leaves and Babe reaches his home town alone. The novel ends with Babe's daily visit to a solitary place, once a palace of local aristocrats and now a sort of village dump, to read aloud letters he has written to May but never mailed.

Neither his wife's death, the numerous women, nor his final return home, which is only the last futile attempt to escape from himself in a life that has been a continuous escape, has made a difference for Babe. He cannot recapture the illusions of his childhood by returning home, and so here too Babe is doomed to failure. In the final scene where Babe is reading the letters his inability to accept reality is clear; the village dump becomes the palace of his childhood. At the close of the novel Babe is seen as passive and lost in his village as he had been in the city at the beginning.

The Italian literary world saw this first Alvarian novel as the work of a promising young writer, but widely criticized it for lack of character development and its excessively detailed descriptions. Indeed, the novel was the typical first work of a promising young writer, with the many faults of construction and of language of the type that in a successive edition an author who has matured might be able to correct. However, the two faults critics pointed to were not faults, but stylistic choices quite effective in creating the characters and the story Alvaro had in mind.

Let us consider first the absence of character development. Babe's existence, as well as that of the other characters, poignantly reflects the conditions and the psychological state of bourgeois society in a provincial capital of that time, often made up of people who, before the real move to the city could take place, had escaped from the country to fulfill a dream of betterment and success which had been nourished for generations. Sebastiano Babe is doomed from the beginning and his state of mind mirrors the uneventful life of the city. He does not evolve as a character because his development is precluded by the stagnant environment in which he exists, which is far from the one he imagined in those dreams that finally produced the move to the city. Herein, rather than in his small town origin, lies the cause of his solitude.

There is no place for character development in this book, only a certain degree of movement, a progression of events, each of which leaves the characters once again where they started, in a state of despair, in a blind alley. The progression is not towards a final climatic failure, but rather from one failure to the next. The novel ends with Babe back in his village (and rightly so, as far as the narrative structure of the novel is concerned) but this is not a point of arrival. From the point of view of Babe's spiritual history the novel could have gone on, one failure after another. And every conceivable element of Alvaro's language in this novel expresses the barrenness, the lifelessness, the lack of real movement, let alone development, of the protagonist's passage before our eyes, as seen in this typical cluster of imagery depicting his passive drifting through a meaningless life:

> Era già notte. La stanza era buia come una bara. Tremando di freddo accese il lume. La finestra era socchiusa e una farfalla batteva contro il vetro tentando di uscire. Attorno al lume qualche tarma volava, e la stanza, fra il dondolio della lampada, pareva una loggia aperta sul mare.

The image of Babe imprisoned in a closed room while life or a deceptive semblance of it is seen or dreamed of as being outside, "stava tappato nel suo studio e non si sapeva cosa facesse tutto il giorno," is dominant in the novel, and is established at its very beginning; the numerous descriptions also are mostly directed towards reflecting that feeling of barrenness and of lifeless desolation:

> Fuori il paesaggio, sotto la forza del sole, era scarnito e invecchiato. Il grano era senza incanto né forza, i paesi assolati erano come vasi aridi e incrinati. L'estate si stendeva su tutta la terra di cui pareva aver prosciugate le fontane e la matrice.

The same end is achieved with the evident slowness of the narrative rhythm as well as the tone of melancholy that is forcefully created during the first descriptive pages and is effectively maintained throughout, with the contrast between the reawakening of spring and the inactive role of observer to which Babe has condemned himself.

The choice of the short novel as the best form to express what Alvaro wanted to say in this work proves to be effective, if the subject is the characters' inability to change and evolve, their almost aimless drifting, their casual sinking in the stagnant waters of the bourgeois life and ideals of the time. Additional pages would detract from the impact of the work and would add nothing to either the characters or Alvaro's representation of that social crisis.

One might consider then that character development was outside the author's plan in this novel. Instead, it is conceivable that what Alvaro wanted to do with his characters was to probe into their psychological make-up and reveal their structural layers, the deadly complexity of their stratification, the labyrinthine tortuousness of their confused minds. This was to take the place of character development and to provide possibly as much interest. One of the effective ways in which Alvaro seeks to achieve such depth of insight and to create further dimensions in his characters is by interspersing feelings and experiences of the barren present with mostly contrasting recollections of the cheerful past:

> Parlava come a se stesso, e intanto vedeva intorno a sé la notte con le sue stelle, e il cielo, e l'ombra dei monti, e il mare gonfio, come li conosceva. L'oste aveva chiusa la sua bottega ed essi erano rimasti soli, sullo spiazzo, facendo parte degli astri che viaggiavano verso il sole. Si vedeva nell'ombra il petto di lei crescere nel respiro, e la stoffa bianca della veste chiara pareva abbandonata e inerte. Fissando gli occhi nell'ombra egli ritrovava gli occhi di lei lucidi e inquieti. Nell'armonia di tutti i mondi ella gli appariva come un piccolo mondo ed era meravigliosa la sua presenza là e a quell'ora. Bastava questo perché i suoi pensieri tornassero indietro alle cose abbandonate. Quella donna appariva ora come una pianta sradicata dalla sua terra con le radici aggrovigliate e grondanti. Immutabile e presente, il pensiero di lei non ritrovava nulla in quella nuova terra, né riconosceva nulla, se non un nuovo mutamento e una nuova stanchezza. E anche per lui il vecchio mondo non era interamente scomparso.
>
> Il suo pensiero, dopo le prime impressioni, era ricondotto agli atti e ai pensieri di prima.

Alvaro's literary apprenticeship had taken place in a time when the style of [Gabriele] D'Annunzio's poetry and prose was enormously fashionable. Critics pointed to the "*dannunzianesimo*" in ***L'uomo nel labirinto*** as an exclusively negative element:

> Neppure in questo romanzo la prosa di Alvaro riesce a liberarsi dal dorato magma del dannunzianesimo: così troppo spesso egli interrompe la narrazione per abbandonarsi a virtuosistici esercizi descrittivi, scrivendo pagine che stridono come pezzi di bravura del tutto esterni e gratuiti.
>
> [Armando Balduino, *Corrado Alvaro*]

However, what is much more relevant is that Babe and his contemporaries had derived their intellectual nourishment exclusively from D'Annunzio, and that the novels and poems of D'Annunzio had expressed the fatuous and escapist dreams of bourgeois society and implanted them in the minds of middle-class people like Babe and his acquaintances. Thus, it fell to writers like [Italo] Svevo (*La coscienza di Zeno*) and Borgese (*Rubè*) and Alvaro (***L'uomo nel labirinto***) to express the drama of impotence of those D'Annunzian dreamers as they came to grips with a life and a society that, far from being receptive and ideal as in the false world of D'Annunzio's novels, was instead unreceptive, philistine, and hostile. And Borgese, too, very successfully exploited the baroque quality of D'Annunzian prose in *Rubè*. In ***L'uomo nel labirinto*** Alvaro is more or less employing *"dannunzianesimo"* to the same end. The almost baroque richness of his style conveys the sense of surface richness which hides the empty and meaningless life beneath. Alvaro's use of *"dannunzianesimo"* enhances the representation of Babe's society and generation.

Babe's keen sensitivity and perceptive observation of detail,

> Oggi, invece, mentre restava immobile, scorgendo la luce diafana della stanza e undendo i rumori della strada stentava a ritrovare i pensieri assidui; del resto temeva di svegliarli e vi si aggirava attorno, sentendo solo la stessa pietà e lo stesso piacere di sentirsi sano. Cominciarono allora i noti rumori della casa in faccende; le parole bisbigliate, lo strisciare della scopa, l'acciottolĩo dei piatti. Gli si destarono tutti i sensi e sentì per primo l'odore chiuso della stanza, poi scorse la luce viva negli interstizi della porta. Si scorse come caduto in un abisso e divenuto gracile e debole. Non gli andava bene nessuno dei panni usati che avevano qualcosa di pesante e di umidiccio, e, appesi, conservavano l'atto dei suoi movimenti che riconobbe odiosamente.

is not mere *"dannunzianesimo."* Rather, it is a carefully used technique to portray a perceptive, intelligent individual, who for all his inherent attributes is incapable of finding significance in his existence.

This first novel by Corrado Alvaro already takes the course which all his other novels will. It represents a first chapter in his entire work which will all be dedicated to portraying and achieving a better understanding of the reality of his time, a time of crisis for the social class that had dominated Italian and European life for almost a century, a crisis further heightened by two world conflicts and years of totalitarian rule in Italy and so many other countries of Europe.

Sergio Pacifici (essay date 1979)

SOURCE: "The 'Southern' Novel," in *The Modern Italian Novel: From Pea to Moravia*, Southern Illinois University Press, 1979, pp. 47-78.

[*Pacifici is an American educator, translator, and critic specializing in Italian language and literature. In the following excerpt, he discusses Alvaro's adherence to the tenets of the "verismo" school.*]

The bulk of Alvaro's literary production, which ranges all the way from autobiography and poetry to essays and fiction, is often rooted in his native Calabria, particularly his own *paese,* the village where he grew up and which left such an impression on his sensibility. His more mature work, on the other hand, reveals a shift of emphasis to the meaning of the encounter of a Southern intellectual with the bureaucratic civilization of the North, more specifically, that of Baroque and decadent Rome—thus following a trajectory that moves in the opposite direction to that of Giovanni Verga's final and greatest phase of his literary creativity. Verga's masterworks, *I Malavoglia, Mastro-don Gesualdo,* and the unforgettable stories of *Vita dei campi* pervasively influenced the character and scope of Alvaro's Southern novels, with a major exception: the role the city plays in the development of the stories of the two writers, and the meanings and implications it acquires could hardly be more different. In Verga, the city is portrayed as a temptress that lures and finally corrupts the young generation, uprooting it from its home nest and ultimately contributing to its tragic downfall. In Alvaro's work, the city, with all its Babelian aspects, comes to represent the ultimate conquest for his characters, engaged in their special search for the pot of gold at the end of the rainbow. The difference in the vision of the two artists is larger than it may appear at first: in Verga's stories the choice between *paese* and *città* is made on sentimental and ethical grounds and becomes a matter of allegiance to the time-honored tradition of the "home." In Alvaro's stories, the choice is a telling sign that the world does not begin and end with our native town. The question is no longer a matter of belief in, and respect for, certain traditions, but a conscious realization of changing economic conditions and of the opportunities offered by the mushrooming industries in the northern regions of a politically united nation.

By general critical consensus, ***Gente in Aspromonte*** remains, despite the passing of time, Alvaro's masterpiece, the most persuasive, moving book he wrote in his four and one-half decades of literary creativity. Much like Verga's *I Malavoglia,* the story centers on the difficult life led by a small family in Calabria and on their constant struggle to survive the adversities that threaten, and ultimately destroy, their modest dreams. The opening of the book has a markedly muted almost tragic tone about it:

> It is no easy life, that of the shepherds of Aspromonte, in the dead of winter when swollen streams rush down to the sea and the earth seems to float on the water. The shepherds stay in huts built of mud and sticks and sleep beside the animals. They go about in long capes with triangular hoods over their shoulders such as might have been worn by an ancient Greek god setting out upon a winter pilgrimage. The torrential streams make a deafening noise and in the clearings, amid the white snow, big black tubs, set over wood fires, steam with boiling milk curdled by a greenish ferment and a handful of wild herbs. The men standing around in their black capes and black wool suits are the only living beings among the dark surrounding mountains and the stiffly frozen trees. But even in this icy cold the nuts are ripening under the oak bark for the future delight of rooting pigs.

To a considerable extent, the shepherds are at the mercy of nature; water is possibly one of the most important factors in their harsh existence, followed by the danger posed by the terrain to which the animals are exposed when grazing on the rocky mountains. It is not infrequently that some of the animals fall into a gully, and their meat must be sold at once by the shepherds so as to recover at least part of the loss sustained.

Protagonists of the story are Argirò and his son Antonello. One day, the two set out to try to get a bank loan that will permit them to purchase and till a small plot of land, while their other parcel is allowed to rest for a year. As fate would have it, on that very day four of the animals (whose co-owner is Filippo Mezzatesta) are lost when they fall into a gully. Filippo will have none of Argirò's explanations of the accident and serves notice that he expects to receive all the money realized from the sale of the meat, including what normally would be Argirò's share. This last indignity persuades Argirò that he will never work for someone else again. With the help of Camillo Mezzatesta (Filippo's brother), a well-known usurer, he purchases some land, but bad weather destroys its harvest. The one remaining hope for his family's future is to send his youngest son, Benedetto, away to school at a seminary, and prepare himself for the priesthood. Education is quite expensive and the oldest son, Antonello, is sent away to work with a construction gang: his earnings are sent to the family so that his father's dream may come true. After the tragedy of his farm, Argirò buys a mule and becomes a private carter. Just as he is getting back on his feet, thanks to his hard work, three children, youngsters of Pirria (Camillo Mezzatesta's mistress) set the stall where the mule is kept on fire, and the animal is burned alive. The motivation of this dastardly act is pure envy, as Argirò sees it: "Fortune is blind and envy has eyes to see. That is the way people are made—they can't bear to see someone else get on." To add insult to injury, Camillo's children, with Andreuccio as their leader, parade "about the square holding a mock mule's funeral, one of them pretending to be the tearful Argirò." "Argirò watched them without understanding, saying over and over to himself: 'Oh, the pain they've given me! Is there no end to man's cruelty!' "

The new misfortune adds more pressure to the already precarious economic situation of the family: Antonello now sends his whole salary to his father, but, physically weak and sickly, loses his job and returns home. Much matured by his experiences away from his village, he is no longer willing to accept the gross inequalities of the social system into which he was born. The stage is now set for the final act of the tragedy: only violence is seen as the instrument that can change the order of things:

> The evening was dark and gloomy, with signs of a coming storm. There were flashing red lights in the sky like those that usually came in September, and it looked as if the downpour would flood the newly sprouted wheat. In this part of the country the rain can be an enemy of man. The rain that began that night continued to fall for several days, as if to tell Argirò that even if his mule were still alive, the roads would be impassable. It seemed as if the rain would never stop, and its endlessness dulled the edge of Argirò's sorrow as he stared at it listlessly like a prisoner staring at the bars of his prison.

Antonello's days as an honest, hard-working person are over. He turns into a brigand who slaughters Filippo Mezzatesta's herds, gives away the animal's meat, pillages his harvests, burns his precious land—all this while most of the villagers, held at Filippo's mercy for so long, refuse to come to his aid and indeed enjoy the spectacle of the fire voraciously destroying what had been valuable property. Filippo Mezzatesta himself comes down from the mountains where he has waged a courageous but hopeless fight to save his property from total destruction, his eyes lost and two streams of blood rushing down his cheeks. Justice, or the kind of justice the villagers welcome because it appears in the guise of fair retribution for past wrongs, has been done. Now at last Antonello can meekly surrender to the authorities—his violence has satisfied the villagers' anger. "When he saw the gleam of the carabinieri's caps and their guns pointing at him from behind the trees, he threw down his only weapon and stepped forward to greet them. 'At last,' he said, 'I have met Justice face to face. It's taken me long enough to meet Her.' "

The English translation of the book makes an ideological point the title in the original did not make. Indeed, it is questionable whether Alvaro himself would have wanted the word "Revolt" to appear on the book's cover during a period when the Fascist regime was making so much of its ability to restore "law and order" in a nation beleagured by internal unrest and discontent. Yet, the novel's message is clear in proposing violence as the one effective instrument capable of changing an odious social order, and submit the values of the establishment to stringent tests challenging their fairness and justice. This notwithstanding, another central question is left begging: if we admit that changing the structure and values of an unjust society is a highly desirable goal, can such a goal be achieved by the terrorist acts of a lone individual, without arousing the consciousness of the peasantry (and the working class) to the point of making inevitable their becoming actively involved, rather than remaining silent spectators, in the struggle against the middle class and the landowners? What is the meaning of the villagers' willingness to accept as a gift the meat of the animals slaughtered by Antonello or killed in the fire that has devastated Mezzatesta's property?

By a remarkable coincidence, in another country, Switzerland, another writer, who was to achieve world prominence, was writing a book with a theme similar to that of ***Revolt in Aspromonte***. His name was Secondo Tranquilli, his nom de plume Ignazio Silone: his novel, *Fontamara,* was to appear in a German and English translation long before it could be published in the original Italian. *Fontamara* has been called a political novel: it tells of the exploitation and hardships endured for centuries by the inhabitants of a small town after which the book is titled, "Bitter Fountain." The novel, remarkable for the simplicity of its theme and form is framed in terms of the old struggle of the city (or landed gentry, the governments, and the bureaucratic apparatus through which the villagers' lives are controlled) and the *cafoni* (the peasants who till the soil, and who must submit to the injustices of the rich and the powerful). What happens in the course of the story produces an awareness that nothing will ever change unless the *cafoni* join forces with all dispossessed and working people to fight the miserable conditions they have endured for far too long. The goal, then, is the formation of a militant force capable of bringing about change—by violence, if necessary. Since politics is a way of life, life itself must be politicized: the masses must be educated politically, led (and this is a most important aspect) by leaders developed by the masses themselves, and not, as in the past, by the bourgeoisie. After all, is it not the bourgeoisie that has set up the standards, the values and the structure socio-political-economic the peasants are struggling to change?

None of these implications are part of the narrative or thematic fabric of Alvaro's novel, in which the central theme receives a conventional structural treatment. Once again, the landowners exploit the peasants and no amount of suffering seems to have any effect: things do not change at all, and when they do it is only as the result of the actions of a man gone berserk, actions that are ultimately unproductive, since the destruction of property brings only temporary relief to an anger that will be passed on from one generation to the next.

The novel is, in every respect, in the best tradition of "*verismo.*" Its language is simple, direct, and yet poetic. Southern society is painted in somber colors: the rich are presented as unmovable bastions of power, devoid of understanding of and compassion toward poverty; the others—the shepherds and the peasants—are hopelessly weak, silently accepting the traditional relationship with the landowners; the country is hard, the city a beautiful, enviable heaven filled with every comfort, even if it does not enjoy the pleasure of savouring the fruits of the land with quite the same joy as the peasants. But this is a small consolation indeed; injustice is evident everywhere: in the way the peasants are treated, in the hardships imposed on Antonello so that Benedetto can be educated and move up the social ladder, in the way he must struggle in the school he has entered without adequate preparation, in the exploitation of Pirria (Camillo Mezzatesta's mistress), in the many setbacks and sorrow (which include two deaf-mute sons) Argirò must endure, including the derogative nickname "Pumpkinhead." With all this, Argirò retains his dignity and pride, as does his family, even in the moments of disappointment and sadness. There are tears and cries to be sure, and there is pain that at times cannot be contained. But, as in Verga's *I Malavoglia,* there is strength and a stubborn resolve to persevere in the human search for a good, honest life—a dream that just will not be. As in Verga's *I Malavoglia,* once the first accident takes place, there is no way the tragedy can be stopped from unraveling: one remedy follows another, to no avail, for the end is predictable almost to its last detail. The fabric of the family unravels almost mercilessly: the departure of his son to school makes Argirò proud, but also avoided by his envious peers, and in the end rejected by his very son; Antonello, whose help makes possible thc financing of his younger brother's schooling, comes home only to take revenge on a cruel society by way of his violence. But, while the novel follows the pattern of events of Verga's masterpiece, it also offers a new insight into the ideological form and structure of Southern society. Antonello's brother is sent away to school, because, as Gramsci remarked apropos of Pirandello's theatre, "there is no 'mechanism' that can raise life from a provincial level to a collectively national and European one." The awareness is in sharp contrast with traditional thinking on this issue: in Alvaro's book, the school diploma is turned into the very weapon by which someday Benedetto (and, by extension, the educated peasant) "will be able to humiliate the powerful," as Giuliano Manacorda persuasively suggests in his essay on our novelist.

A passage early in the book reveals the depth of his understanding of the way in which historical developments have and will continue to change the South:

> Just as mummies fall into dust when they come into contact with the air, so this ancient way of life is breaking up as it comes into touch with something new. We have here a disappearing civilization. Let us not weep over its eclipse, but, if we were born into it, let us store up in our memory as much of it as we can. The liberation of the Kingdom of the Two Sicilies superseded an order of things that had been established for centuries, and the redistribution of feudal property not only increased some already swollen private fortunes. This village remained what it had been from time immemorial, a cluster of one-story rustic houses on earth foundations with fireplaces hewed out of natural rock—all built around one nobleman's palace, with its gates, stables, gardens, kitchen and servants. The common people's interests and struggles centered about this palace, near the church, for it was the focal point of all the wealth, all the good and evil of the village.

In the context of the tradition of the "regionalistic" novel, the novelty of the passage just quoted is undeniable: unlike Verga, Alvaro is capable of giving his work a more clearly explicit historical dimension, without making it a historical novel, as [Federico] De Roberto had done in *The Viceroys.* Alvaro's conceives the artist as "a man who has the power to write harmoniously about life," and adds: "Pain is for the artist the key that opens all doors." Thanks to his creativity and power of synthesis, the artist, having witnessed an important event, gives it life and meaning, preserving it on the printed page for posterity. The society depicted by Alvaro in ***Revolt in Aspromonte*** is a closed one, permits no failures, respects only success. The equation is unacceptable to our writer: he looks for understanding and compassion, even though he knows how rarely society exhibits them. "A primitive and at the same time an intellectual," wrote Emilio Cecchi many years ago, by which he meant, if I read him correctly, a man deeply rooted in the primitive character of civilization of his native Calabria and yet capable of understanding intellectually, as well as poetically, his "world."

Anthony R. Terrizzi (essay date 1981)

SOURCE: "Notes on Alvaro's *Gente in Aspromonte,*" in *Romance Notes,* Vol. XXII, No. 2, Winter, 1981, pp. 236-41.

[*In the following essay, Terrizzi examines the complex interweaving of realistic and mythic themes in* Gente in Aspromonte.]

The publication of ***Gente in Aspromonte*** in 1930 brought Corrado Alvaro acclaim as a young writer of national significance. The short novel was well-received by the critics and suggested to them a direct derivation from Giovanni Verga's "verismo" and particularly from *I Malavoglia*. Alvaro had been writing for over a decade, and many critics had already decided that his inspiration was primarily two-fold: the world of the countryside of his native Calabria, and that of the city, as seen in his first novel, ***L'uomo nel labirinto,*** published in 1926. . . . [L. Tonelli] had concluded also that this dual inspiration was an impairment, addressing itself to "both the world of the southern countryside and that of the city, to Verga on one side and Proust and Freud on the other, since it succeeded in being genuine and creative only when it allowed the rural Vergan, tender, instinctive vein to flow free" [*Il Marzocco,* January 11, 1931]. Closer study, however, suggests that this dichotomy between "strapaese" and "stracittà" does not characterize Alvaro's inspiration which is in fact richer and more complex.

The setting of ***Gente in Aspromonte*** is exclusively Alvaro's native region, while in his preceding work (***L'uomo nel labirinto***) and in the novels that followed (the trilogy of "memorie del mondo sommerso") the author's birthplace is present only as a place of departure in that the characters, having forfeited the possibility of functioning successfully in their native environment because of their education or for other reasons, leave Calabria for an urban environment, a world distinctly different from that of their native village. In ***Gente in Aspromonte,*** Alvaro focuses instead on the plight of those southern Italians who are not prepared to emigrate into the urban bourgeoisie but remain to bear the hardships that the emigrants seek to escape. Here, as in all his novels, Alvaro strives to understand and portray the reality of his time; the conditions of Aspromonte indeed constituted a large portion of that reality, both in Italy and wherever else feudal oppression was still heavy on the rural peasantry. The customs of his native Calabria were deeply rooted within the author, and the expression given to this world in ***Gente in Aspromonte*** is not mere sentimental nostalgia: "E una civiltà che scompare," declares Alvaro, "e su di essa non c'è da piangere, ma bisogna trarre, chi ci è nato, il maggior numero di memorie." ***Gente in Aspromonte*** affords a vivid portrayal of the life of its people, and particularly of their struggle for existence. Except for the few wealthy landowners, cruel poverty is the universal way of life, for the mountain shepherds and the peasants of the town alike. To these people no misery is unknown and no resignation too difficult. But the story is also a drama of vengeance for secular injustice. The author, in fact, set his portrayal against a legendary and timeless Calabria as well as against a real one: "da secoli questo paese si era cacciato nella valle e vi si era addormentato."

It is primarily through the shepherd Argirò and his son Antonello that the conditions of the poverty-stricken region are presented. Argirò is a shepherd for the Mezzatesta brothers whose family has dominated and exploited the people of Aspromonte for years.

> Dovunque ci si volgeva era terra di questa casa, dalle foreste sui monti agli orti acquatici presso il mare. Dovunque, comunque. Era loro la terra, loro le ulive che vi cadevano sopra, erano loro le foreste sui monti intorno, loro i campi tosati di luglio quando tutta la terra è gialla e i colli cretosi crepano aridi.

During a storm four oxen in the care of Argirò fall from a cliff and are killed. The power of the "signori" is absolute; Argirò is fired for this accident, which is to take on tragic dimensions for the elderly shepherd and his family. Having lost his job, Argirò becomes obsessed with his long-nourished desire to change his social position and to seek revenge from the repressive society that has caused him a lifetime of suffering and indignity. It is to this end that he devotes all his energies and thoughts. He sees his hope for revenge in his youngest son, Benedetto, whom he destines to study for the priesthood. Religion, as such, is not relevant to this choice. A son-priest signifies a position for the father and his family—someone who could address the ruling Mezzatestas as "ladri e birbanti." He calls on his eldest son Antonello to sacrifice himself totally so that together they may support Benedetto's studies. Argirò purchases a mule and transports goods from the town to the coast, while Antonello must leave the town to seek work as a laborer—and thus begins *his* life of suffering and humiliation.

Solidarity among the poor does not exist however, and Argirò's plan works against him. The envy he had hoped to generate among the townspeople instead isolates him as rich and poor alike despise him for attempting to elevate himself to or above their level of existence. In fact, the Mezzatesta children set fire to his stable, killing the mule, his only means of support. Well-accustomed to adversity, "la vita . . . piena di pietre e spine," Argirò is determined to overcome this new setback but now the burden of supporting Benedetto falls entirely on Antonello. Finally, ill and too weak to work, Antonello is fired and returns home:

> Mi hanno licenziato perché non potevo lavorare abbastanza. Non resistevo e stavo sempre malato. Io lo sapevo che cos'era: debolezza. Sono tanti anni che faccio questa vita. Come può campare di pane solo uno che lavora?

At home and witnessing again the local oppression and injustice, Antonello can no longer tolerate these conditions and lays down his own plan for revenge, a revenge different from his father's in that it is not only a blow to the rich but a help to the poor. He sets fire to the vast Mezzatesta property and distributes the meat of the livestock among the poor. Antonello's only recourse against the oppression of the societal structure of Aspromonte had to be an act of revolt, outside the law; the only "justice" possible is enacted on a personal level.

Gente in Aspromonte, as its early critics noted, calls to mind Verga's *I Malavoglia*. Luigi Russo points out a likeness in theme

> che non è certo pura derivazione letteraria, ma coincidenze storiche. Quello che è il carico di lupini per i Malavoglia, sono i quattro buoi per l'Argirò; la possibilità di continuare una magra vita, legata costantemente ad un filo che una

> volta spezzato sarà estremamente difficile riallacciare. È sufficiente che ne vada male una perchè, in una società che non permette recuperi, si metta in moto l'affannosa serie dei tentativi destinati a fallire. [*I narratori,* 1958]

The similarities that exist, however, are due mainly to the geographical proximity of the setting of the two novels. The two writers remain basically different in both style and purpose. While both strive to achieve a true, although lyrical, representation of the social reality of their respective environments, Verga in *I Malavoglia* does not analyze the thoughts of his characters, but rather lets them act and speak for themselves in their own Sicilianized Italian. Alvaro, on the other hand [according to Rocco Montano, *Lo spirite e le lettere,* 1971]

> si immedesima con il personaggio e ci dice lui le emozioni di quello, usa la propria lingua, estremamente scaltrita, per comunicarci il mondo del contadino calabrese. E una resa ricca, piena di sfumature, di note sottili, attenta a tutti i movimenti della natura e dell'atmosfera . . . noi possiamo percepire lo scrittore che evoca luoghi della sua terra, un senso di nostalgia.

Moreover, Alvaro succeeds in simultaneously giving his realistic depiction a mythical and epic dimension that is totally missing in Verga's novels: "la particolare poetica degli umili dell'Alvaro assimila l'insegnamento verghiano e lo traduce in un'evocazione mitico-lirica della realtà" [Ferndinando Virdia, in his "Corrado Alvaro," *Dizionario biografico degli italiani,* 1960].

This mythical-lyrical-epic quality is achieved through Alvaro's masterful use of language which strives to create at the same time the sense of [what Giovanni Sinicropi terms in his "Appunti sopra la lingua di Alvaro," *Uomo e immagini,* 1969] the historical and the atemporal "creando un vago e pregno senso di mistero o quel clima tipicamente mitico e favoloso."

> I ragazzi ascoltavano le fiabe immaginando che si svolgessero in quella casa, e in quelle scuderie pensavano che la Cenerentola avesse ballato col Reuccio.
>
> Ed ecco che in quel buio si levò una voce, alta e potente, che veniva dalla cima del colle soprastante il paese. Arrivava distinta come quella del banditore, scendeva a larghe spirali su quel buio d'uomini, e le parole ben sillabate si ricongiugevano in un senso meraviglioso.

His imagery results in a progression from the representation of a historical reality to a suggestion of fairy tale and myth. The sense of the *meraviglioso* embraces both the mythical world of a legendary regional past and the mythical world of the child's memory.

This simultaneous sense of the historical and atemporal is not an occasional intrusion; it is present in the *entire* novel and is an integral part of its development. The "clima mitico e favoloso" throughout suggests that it is "una funzione volutamente presente e agente . . . nella stessa struttura del racconto" reflecting the author's intent "di situare i suoi personaggi ed il suo passaggio in un'atmosfera allusiva contro la prospettiva del passato storico della terra" [according to Sinicropi].

Gente in Aspromonte is structured in two main parts. Its introductory section is predominantly descriptive, slow-paced and clearly designed "non solo a delineare lo sfondo su cui si svolgerà la vicenda ma anche e soprattutto a creare l'atmosfera in cui i personaggi vivono sentono e pensano" [Armando Balduino in his *Corrado Alvaro,* 1965]. The second half of the work is characterized by a faster rhythm and dominated by action and social intercourse, where people speak and react to and in accordance with the conditions described in the first part. The novel nevertheless has a linear development, from the first landscape description to its explosive conclusion. The introductory pages set the tone of the entire novel, in the quiet desperation of the human condition throughout the region, in the inevitable defeat awaiting those who are still too young to be desperate or who in spite of their age still nourish illusions. It reveals the character of the region and of its people through a lyrical representation of both. Antonello, for example, says little in the novel, a silence which is artistically effective and perfectly in tune with the character established in the opening section. He is presented almost exclusively through his intercourse with the speechless, yet mysteriously familiar nature that surrounds him.

> Tutte queste voci sentiva Antonello per la prima volta, dopo gli assorti silenzi delle montagne. Il mondo era un'onda sonora intorno alla sua casa, e il cielo e le montagne che lo sostengono con le loro cime e i loro alberi, come un baldacchino, ora pesava immenso sul paese e sulla valle.

The novel also fuses together the people and environs of Aspromonte to make the plight of Argirò and Antonello that of all of the people of the area. In the second part, a *coralità* is achieved in a manner recalling that of Verga, by letting people for the most part act and speak on their own, by direct speech as well as through free indirect discourse.

From Alvaro's first novel (***L'uomo nel labirinto***) to his last (***Belmoro***), his themes were the alienation of contemporary man, his degradation, dehumanization, oppression and the attempt to deprive him of his individuality and his right to a meaningful existence. Undoubtedly he was inspired by a moral compulsion but not by that alone. The feeling of nostalgia was also strong, and the attraction of childhood memories, the love for the beautiful harshness of the land, the lure of the legendary past. Alvaro had repeatedly stated that his intent as a writer was to offer an artistic representation of reality. His novels often achieve a beautiful balance between the importance of the representative character and that of his social background. The polemic tone thus remains more an undercurrent than an open presence. The mythical dimension of ***Gente in Aspromonte*** places its portrayal of contemporary reality beyond the confines of a mere political or polemical documentary.

FURTHER READING

Criticism

Heiney, Donald. "Emigration Continued: Levi, Alvaro, and Others." *America in Modern Italian Literature,* pp. 126-45. New Brunswick, N. J.: Rutgers University Press, 1964.

Discusses Alvaro's short story "The Ruby" as an example of the use of a jewel as the symbol of the emigrant's view of America and the Italy to which he returns.

Eduard Bagritsky

1895-1934

(Pseudonym of Eduard Georgievich Dzyubin) Russian poet.

INTRODUCTION

Although not well known or widely translated in the West, Bagritsky was a moderately successful poet of the early Soviet period following the Russian Revolution of 1917. He remains best known for *Duma pro Opanasa* (*Lay of Opanas*), a folk epic that describes the experiences of a peasant who becomes implicated in the civil warfare that followed the Bolshevik Party's seizure of power. While Soviet critics have hailed the *Lay of Opanas* as a masterpiece of Revolutionary Romanticism, Western critics tend to view Bagritsky's career as a passionate but not wholly successful attempt to anchor his Romantic conceptions of nature, freedom, and human potential in the political and social realities of the Soviet era.

Biographical Information

Bagritsky was born to a Jewish family in Odessa, a port city in the Ukraine. Although Soviet literary sources describe his background as impoverished, Bagritsky's father was a modestly prosperous tradesman. Bagritsky attended technical school, where he received a diploma in land surveying, a profession that he never practiced. Instead, he began publishing poetry in local periodicals and almanacs, which soon placed him at the forefront of the lively artistic culture of Odessa. Although his early revolutionary activities are not thought to have been extensive, Bagritsky twice joined the Communist Army during the civil war years of 1918-1920, first as a supply manager at the Persian front and then as a political propagandist composing pamphlets and proclamations. He also worked as a staff writer for the satirical magazines *Pero v spinu* (A Pen in the Back) and *Tablochko* (Apple). With the steady decline of Odessa as an intellectual and literary mecca after the civil wars, Bagritsky and most of his circle moved permanently to Moscow in 1925. There he was disappointed to find he could not publish without publicly declaring a political affiliation. Consequently, Bagritsky joined the Constructivists, a literary group whose main creed was that all elements of a work should be developed according to the work's central, usually political, theme. Bagritsky's poetry from the Moscow period reflects his growing disillusionment with the outcome of the Revolution. Frequently confined to his home due to chronic asthma, Bagritsky died in 1934.

Major Works

Bagritsky's major publication, *Yugozapad* (*Southwest*), followed upon his relocation to Moscow. This selection from the first decade of his work includes seventeen lyric poems and the *Lay of Opanas.* An eclectic and metrically varied volume, *Southwest* bears traces of folk poetry, British Romanticism, French Symbolism, and Russian Acmeism, among other artistic influences. The lyric poems are considered dramatic and sensuous, featuring such typically Romantic characters as minstrels and beggars. The *Lay of Opanas* adapts the form of a "duma," or folk ballad, and incorporates classical epic qualities. The poem describes the fate of Opanas, a simple Ukrainian peasant who becomes caught up in the struggle among the Red (Communist), White (Czarist), and Green (Agrarian Anarchist) political factions. As a Green soldier, Opanas is forced to shoot Kogan, a Jewish Communist official commissioned to procure wheat from the Ukraine. For this act, Opanas himself is ultimately executed by the Communists. Bagritsky's subsequent publications continued an ambiguous, sometimes critical, exploration of the ideals and ramifications of the Communist Revolution. *Poslednyaya noch* (*The Last Night*), published in 1932, contains three narrative poems: "The Last Night," "A Man from the Outskirts," and "The Death of the Pioneer Girl." *Pobediteli* (*The Victors*) also appeared in that year. Before his death in 1934, Bagritsky was in the process of completing *Fevral* (*February*), an autobiographical narrative poem. His wife, who was a political prisoner from 1937 to 1956, assisted in the publication of the most important posthumous collections of her husband's work: *Sobranie sochinenii* and *Stikhotvoreniya i poemy*.

PRINCIPAL WORKS

Duma pro Opanasa [*Lay of Opanas*] (poetry) 1925
Yugozapad [*Southwest*] (poetry) 1928
Pobediteli [*The Victors*] (poetry) 1932
Poslednyaya noch [*The Last Night*] (poetry) 1932
**Sobranie sochinenii.* 2 vols. (poetry and prose) 1938
Dnevniki, Pisma, Stikhi (diary, letters, and poetry) 1964
Stikhotvoreniya i poemy (poetry) 1964

*Volume 2 exists only in manuscript form in Bagritsky's archive at the Gorky Institute of World Literature in Moscow.

CRITICISM

Alexander Kaun (essay date 1943)

SOURCE: "Postsymbolists" in *Soviet Poets and Poetry,* University of California Press, 1943, pp. 35-97.

[*In the following excerpt, Kaun discusses the sources, plot, and stylistic features of the* Lay of Opanas, *praising Bagritsky's work for its passionate optimism.*]

Eduard Bagritsky was a member of the Constructivist Literary Center for some five years, but he bore no consistent allegiance to any school. His output, considerable for the short span of his life, is somewhat eclectic, showing traces of Robert Burns (a few of whose poems he lovingly translated) and other Western Europeans, as well as of a multitude of Russians, from Pushkin through the acmeists and futurists. Such traces, however, may be found in any well-read author, and it is futile to use them as a basis for any specific label. Bagritsky's verses vary in form, from regular meter (with a partiality for the amphibrach) to blank metric and free verse, futuristic broken lines, and arbitrary rhythms. As to subject, it ranges from Tyll Eulenspiegel and the romantic beggars of Burns to contemporary themes, the leading one being civil war episodes. His main work, on which his reputation stands, is ***Elegy on Opanas,*** a narrative poem, wherein epic mingles with ballad, and classic passages alternate with national motives from the ancient *Lay of Prince Igor* and from folk songs. The very name of the elegy, ***Duma,*** suggests Bagritsky's affinity with the celebrated Taras Shevchenko (1814-1861), author of numerous *dumy* (the name applied to Ukrainian folk epics and songs); the text reveals further signs of this kinship.

The poem is saturated with Ukrainian color, in both landscape and motives. Opanas is an Ukrainian peasant, unwittingly swept by the waves of revolution and civil wars into the camp of Makhno's "Greens," a variety of bandits midway between Reds and Whites, with anarchistic pretensions. Bagritsky conveys the gaudy romance of the strife by a variety of means, now by delicately suggestive images, now by Gargantuan revelry in gory detail. Woven into the large epic canvas is the personal drama of Opanas, the simpleton who was jolted out of his peaceful rusticity by a group of Bolshevik grain collectors led by the Jew Kogan. Resentful of the highhanded methods of the city chaps, Opanas joins the Makhno band, and is soon transformed into a picturesque brigand. His costume is an eloquent record of his exploits: a shaggy Cossack cap, a fur coat "taken off a dead rabbi near Gomel," a "French" military jacket of "English cut," stripped probably off some White officer, protégé of the Entente powers, lastly a revolver dangling from the chain of a church censer. Luck is with him, as his squad surprises at night Kogan and his company, and to Opanas falls the honor of executing the Bolshevik.

> Opanas moves back one leg,
> He stands, he flaunts:
>
> "How do you do, comrade Kogan?
> Shave? You're next!"

An improbable note, perhaps admissible in an epic ballad, is introduced when Opanas, leading his captive to the wall, is revolted by the thought of killing an unarmed man, and offers to let Kogan escape. Not more probable is Kogan's refusal to be saved. To be sure, he reasons that his chance for escape from a Makhno camp is extremely slim, but what he says to Opanas sounds like grand opera:

> "Opanas, work clean,
> Don't blink the aim.
>
> 'Tis unseemly for a communist
> To run like a wolfhound."

Bagritsky manages to avoid the impression of mock heroics, chiefly by means of colloquial dialogue. He likewise succeeds in suggesting the brooding mood of Opanas, after he shoots Kogan. Haunted by the image of the fearless Bolshevik, Opanas, captured by the Reds, confesses having executed Kogan, and pays with his life.

This skeleton of the poem can hardly give an approximate idea of its power and colorfulness. Bagritsky combines a gift for describing dramatic scenes, battles, surging crowds, executions, with the typical Ukrainian badinage that one finds in Gogol or Shevchenko. He tempers the pathos of fratricidal war and pitiless carnage by the contrasting tone of everydayness, by bits of homely colloquialism and banter, of folk song and folk wisdom. Above all, what makes Bagritsky dear to the Soviet reader is that in this ***Elegy,*** as in most of his poems, he is free from the allegedly Russian pessimism. Whatever the subject, even during the long torment of his dying days, Bagritsky expressed a passionate affirmation of life, an exuberant love for the sensuous, and an indestructible trust in man and mankind.

One of the most striking features of Bagritsky's poetry is the way in which many of his images migrate over a number of years from poem to poem, appearing in quite diverse contexts. Together these images form pictures which change, as time passes, according to the combinations of images composing them. Such are the concreteness and vividness of Bagritsky's poetry that it has become a commonplace for commentators to refer to its images as conjuring up a whole poetic world.

—Wendy Rosslyn, in her "The Path to Paradise: Recurrent Images in the Poetry of Eduard Bagritsky," **in The Modern Language Review,** ***January 1976.***

Renato Poggioli (essay date 1960)

SOURCE: "Poets of Today," in *The Poets of Russia 1890-1930,* Harvard University Press, 1960, pp. 316-42.

[*Poggioli was an Italian-born American critic and transla-*

tor. Much of his critical writing is concerned with Russian literature, including The Poets of Russia: 1890-1930, *which is one of the most important examinations of this literary era. In the following excerpt, he discusses Bagritsky's work, particularly the* Lay of Opanas, *as a politically compromised expression of Romantic escapism.*]

[Bagritsky's] early collection ***Southwest*** (1928) looks almost like the work of a jejune Pasternak. Like Sel'vinskij, he adopted the verse-tale form and produced the best work of this kind in the ***Lay of Opanas*** (1925), relating the adventures of a Ukrainian peasant who joins the Greens, the agrarian anarchists led by the rebel Makhno, who fought with the Red against the Whites, and with the Whites against the Red. The story ends with the death of the protagonist, executed for killing a commissar sent into the countryside to seize wheat. As indicated by its title ("lay" renders the *duma* of the original, which means "folk ballad" in Ukrainian), this poem is patterned after the heroic rhapsodies of old Little Russia, and it is quite significant that its author chose the form of the popular epos to sing of those who fought not for the Revolution, but against it. It is equally significant that Bagritskij was one of the many poets of his generation that were ultimately led to abandon these pure lyrical forms which, for giving expression to private feeling and personal experience, seemed to the regime even more dangerous than the semi-popular narrative poems by which the same poets were evoking the picturesque and pathetic figures of some of its defeated enemies. By choosing to sing of outlaws and outcasts, Bagritskij and his companions attempted the only kind of romantic escape which was still possible at that time; yet by doing so they reduced poetry to a picturesque fancy, episodic and anecdotal, superficial and fragmentary, in brief, almost to a parody of itself.

Gleb Struve (essay date 1971)

SOURCE: "The Poets," in *Russian Literature under Lenin and Stalin 1917-1953,* University of Oklahoma Press, 1971, pp. 178-97.

[*A Russian-born educator, Struve is internationally known for his critical studies of Slavic literature. In the following excerpt, he provides a brief overview of Bagritsky's works, focusing on the* Lay of Opanas.]

[Bagritsky's] first volume of poetry, ***Yugozapad*** (***South-West,*** 1928), in some points resembled Tikhonov's early romantic realism. It was possible to trace in it the same influences—of Gumilyov and the Acmeists, of the English ballads (which he translated), and of Kipling. One of his favorite heroes seems to have been Tyll Eulenspiegel. A decided romantic who looked at the Revolution from outside, Bagritsky saw it as something strange and alien but recognized its elemental, sweeping force. In one of his best lyric poems, in which one feels the winds of the Revolution blowing about, he speaks of "strange constellations rising above us," of "strange banners unfurling over us," and likens himself to "a rusty oak leaf" bound to follow in the wake of these strange banners. In some of his poems, however, he tried to draw closer to the Revolution and to portray it other than subjectively. Such is his famous ***Duma pro Opanasa*** (***The Lay About Opanas***), which for a long time was regarded by Soviet critics as one of the masterpieces of Soviet poetry. It is a long poem, in which the lyric and the narrative elements are intermingled, telling the story of a simple Ukrainian peasant, Opanas, who flees from a Communist food-requisitioning detachment commanded by Kogan, a Jew. While fleeing, Opanas encounters the "Green" anarchist band of Makhno and is forced to join it. When Kogan falls into the hands of Makhno, Opanas is ordered to shoot him. He decides to let Kogan escape, but Kogan refuses the offer and chooses death, which he faces with proud indifference. Later on, the Makhno bands are defeated by the Reds, and Opanas is taken prisoner. Questioned by the Red commander Kotovsky, he admits having shot Kogan and submits docilely to his own execution.

The Lay About Opanas is a heroic revolutionary poem. The underlying romanticism of its conception is unquestionable. In form it has been influenced by Ukrainian folk poetry and by Taras Shevchenko, the national poet of the Ukraine. Its free and quick-changing meter recalls Ukrainian folk songs. There are in it some beautiful evocations of the Ukrainian landscape. In its combination of naïve simplicity and romantic hyperbolism it also derives from folk poetry.

In his later poems, collected in ***Pobediteli*** (***The Victors***) and ***Poslednyaya noch*** (***The Last Night***), Bagritsky tried to identify himself even more closely with the Revolution and Socialism, but at heart he remained a romantic; his sense of life, and zest for it, saved him from becoming didactic or doctrinaire. In the autobiographical narrative poem **"Fevral" ("February")**, which was published posthumously, the romantic note is again sounded very clearly. But ***South-West*** (for which Bagritsky made a careful and small selection from the poems written during the first ten years of his poetic activity) remains, I think, his best book, full of genuinely spontaneous poetry and striking a distinct personal note. Such poems as **"Pigeons," "The Watermelon,"** and **"The Cigarette Box"** deserve a place in any anthology of modern Russian poetry.

***The Lay of Opanas* centres on the overlap between fact and fiction, the area where fact may be more legendary than legend and fiction create truth in the realm of typicality.**

—Wendy Rosslyn, in her "Bagritskii Duma Pro Opanasa: The Poem and Its Context," in* Canadian-American Slavic Studies, *1977.

Boris Thomson (essay date 1978)

SOURCE: "Bagritsky's 'February'," in *Lot's Wife and the Venus of Milo: Conflicting Attitudes to the Cultural Heri-*

tage in Modern Russia, Cambridge University Press, 1978, pp. 77-97.

[*In the following excerpt, which was originally published as a section of the chapter "The Secret of Art: Two Soviet Myths" in* Lot's Wife and the Venus of Milo, *Thomson argues that Bagritsky's autobiographical "February," his final work, expresses a surprisingly ambivalent attitude toward the pre-Revolutionary past.*]

In the early part of his career Bagritsky was known as an ardent advocate of the continuity of poetic culture, with a reputation for a detailed knowledge of even the most recondite and unfashionable poets of the preceding epoch. In his later years, however, partly as a consequence of his hardening political attitudes, he seems to have moved towards a total repudiation of the past. His last poem, **'February,'** presents a strange synthesis of these contradictory impulses.

The first indication of Bagritsky's changing attitude to the past occurs in his poem **'Cigarette Packet' ('Papirosnyy korobok',** 1927). The poet has been chain-smoking late into the night, and as he sinks into an uneasy sleep, a picture of the Decembrist poet Ryleyev on a cigarette-packet catches his eye. Gradually this casual impression turns into a monstrous nightmare, which spawns the figures of the other Decembrists. Bagritsky is terrified, and he tries to drive out the unwelcome visitors, but Ryleyev tells him:

> You are ours for ever! We are with you everywhere . . .
> Our solidarity is assured for all eternity.

As the nightmare continues, Bagritsky is forced to undergo the flogging which they underwent and to experience all the horrors of the Tsarist past. As dawn comes, however, the figures of the nightmare reveal themselves to have been only the trees and currant-bushes of his garden. Bagritsky calls in his son and tells him:

> Rise up then, Vsevolod, and possess everything, rise up under the autumn sun! I know: you are born with pure blood in your veins, and you stand on the threshold of great times! Listen to my bequest: when I am gone from song and the wind and my fatherland, you must cut down the pines in the garden, and leave no trace behind, and root out the bush of blackcurrant!

And on this uncompromising and problematical note the poem ends. The evils of the past have vanished with the coming of day; nothing but healthy fruits and vegetation remain in their place. But this is not the conventional image of the beneficent and progressive workings of history; for here the fruits are seen as contaminated by the roots. Where almost all other Soviet writers would proudly place themselves in the Decembrist tradition, Bagritsky sees only the horror and the demoralization; Russian history is a long nightmare that must be obliterated if a new and healthier race is ever to inherit the world.

Where [Velimir] Khlebnikov [in his poem *Night Search*] had punned on the name Vladimir—'vladey mirom' (possess the world), Bagritsky echoes him on the name Vsevolod—'vsem voloday' (possess everything), but gives it precisely the opposite meaning. Khlebnikov's words were addressed to the past—the dead can keep their culture; Bagritsky's are addressed to the future, which will contain everything but the past. Khlebnikov places the words near the beginning of his poem, and then proceeds to question them, before finally showing that the words contain an ironic truth: the past has taken with it something that the future wishes too late that it had acquired; in Bagritsky the episode occurs at the end of the poem as its climax and moral.

The poem is a startling one, but in the following poems, **'My Origins' ('Proiskhozhdeniye',** 1930), **'The Last Night,' ('Poslednyaya noch',** 1932), **'A Man of the Outskirts' ('Chelovek predmest'ya',** 1932) Bagritsky returns to this vision of the past as a loathsome nightmare which has no place in the future. It is in this context that the poem **'February'** makes its extraordinary bid to settle accounts once and for all with the past.

The poem is, strictly speaking, unfinished (the poet died of tuberculosis early in 1934) and it appears that he had intended to insert some 'lyrical interludes' into the work. It is hard to believe that these would have enriched the poem any further; if anything they would have diluted it. As it stands it is already a self-contained and unified work of art.

The poem is set in Odessa, where the unnamed narrator-hero has returned on leave in the middle of the Great War. The ensuing action falls into three distinct episodes. In the first the hero tries to gain the attention of a girl he has always dreamt of hopelessly, and is contemptuously rejected. The scene then shifts to the immediate aftermath of the February revolution; the hero takes part in the storming of a police-station, and soon becomes a military policeman himself under the new regime. In the final episode he leads a raid on a private house suspected of harbouring some bandits; it proves to be not only that but a brothel as well, where the hero discovers the girl of his dreams in bed with an unknown officer. He arrests him, sends his men out of the room, and then rapes the girl himself. The poem ends with the hero's attempts to explain his actions.

This final episode is an extraordinarily powerful one, and it is not altogether surprising that it was based on an event from Bagritsky's own life, that took place soon after the November revolution:

> All this actually happened to me, just as I describe it. Yes, the schoolgirl and the search. I hardly added anything at all, but what was essential for the idea. First, the bandits we were looking for, turned out not to be in the house.
>
> Second, when I saw this schoolgirl, with whom I had once been in love, and who had now become an officers' prostitute, well, in the poem I send everyone out, and jump on the bed on top of her. It was, so to say, a break with the past, a settling of accounts with it. In actual fact I was completely bewildered and couldn't get out of the room fast enough. That's all there was . . .

For all Bagritsky's disclaimers these changes are not minor ones. It is worth looking at the poem in some detail to see why they were 'essential'.

The poem combines two distinct themes, the hopeless and envious love of an adolescent boy, and his identification with the revolutions that will destroy the society that has frustrated his love; in the final episode these two motives are brought together as the two sides of a single coin. The connection between them is the compromised reputation of the culture of the past: apparently infinitely beautiful and desirable, the girl finally turns out to be only a prostitute in an officers' brothel, a Venus of the cities of the plain. The hero's attempt to 'possess' and 'master' her is an allegory of the revolution's attitudes to this dubious heritage.

From the start the narrator feels an outsider, desperately insecure and unsure of himself. He is a Jew, like Bagritsky, who changed his real name Dzyubin to something more suggestive of the Red revolution (the root 'bagr-' means 'crimson'). His childhood too, as so often in Bagritsky's autobiographical writings, is depicted as a time of deprivation without any happiness or freedom or love:

> I never loved as I should have done, a poor little Jewish boy.

But, as the self-pitying tone suggests, and as the narrator himself is uneasily aware, it is not just a matter of deprivation, but an inner flaw, a lack of any confidence and *savoir-faire,* both social and sexual, that cripples him. As he explains in a sour mixture of self-disgust and envy:

> I never spied like the others through the chinks of the bathing huts. I never tried to accidentally pinch the girls . . . Shyness and vertigo sapped my strength.

Shy and friendless as a boy he becomes a passionate ornithologist (again like Bagritsky himself), with an extensive library and a collection of singing-birds, and throughout the poem ornithological imagery stands for an easier, rosier existence where the difficulties of this life will no longer alarm or threaten. But, typically, when he tries to describe his ideal future, he can picture it only in terms of specific childhood details that are not imagined, but remembered:

> I must find a corner in this world, where a clean towel hangs on its nail and smells of mother, where the soap lies ready by the tap, and the sun streaming through the window does not scorch the face like a hot coal . . .

This atmosphere of homely comfort (and particularly the dislike of bright lights) recurs again and again as a criterion by which to evaluate the hero's state throughout the poem. One might have expected such values to be condemned as nostalgic or bourgeois or at least un-Communist; but no! this is what will one day be restored, with the difference that today's outsiders will then be the insiders, with all that that implies in the way of self-possession, power and authority.

Now returned from the front the hero sits on the Odessa boulevard in his military uniform, hoping that at last he will be admitted to the magic circle from which he has been excluded:

> And now I am like an equal among them. If I want I can sit, if I want I can stroll, if I want—and there isn't an officer close by—I can smoke . . .

His service at the front has earned him (at least in his own eyes) the right apparently to equality with these more fortunate citizens. But he is still not their 'equal', only 'like an equal'; and his backward glance for an officer casts doubt even on that.

So too his knowing appraisal of the girl's escorts serves only to emphasize his own isolation:

> I knew all her acquaintances by sight; I knew their mannerisms, smiles, gestures, the way they slowed their steps when, with your chest, your hips or your hands, you deliberately try to feel the disturbing softness of girls' skin through its fragile covering. I knew it all . . .

For he knows this only with the knowledgeability of jealousy. The use of the impersonal second person singular ('when you try') may seem for a moment to come from direct experience, but it is contradicted by '*their* steps'; and so the final 'I knew it all' creates instead the impression of second-hand knowledge, the knowledge of an observer, an outsider, not a participant.

All the frustrations of his adolescence, his unhappy childhood and his poor background, his sense of exclusion from the 'world in which people play tennis, drink orangeade and kiss women', seem to crystallize in the figure of this girl. Alien and hateful though this world is, the narrator still wants to become part of it. Finally he screws up the courage to address her:

> I salute her, as if she were my commanding officer. What can I say to her? My tongue mutters some drivel: 'Permit me . . . Don't run away . . . Please, may I accompany you? I have served in the trenches . . . '

In these lines Bagritsky conveys the insecurity of the speaker; even his mention of his time in the trenches is not a boast, but a pathetic plea for consideration: 'Surely I deserve a reward?' Not surprisingly she dismisses him:

> 'Go away at once', and with her hand she points to the crossroads . . . There he stands at the crossing for the maintenance of order, like a whole empire of ribbons, polished buttons and medals, wedged into his boots, and covered on top with a gendarme's cap, around which doves out of Holy Writ and stormclouds, whorled like snails, circle in the intolerable radiance, so yellow that it hurts—a potbellied policeman, gleaming with fatty sweat, stuffed full since breakfast of ham-fat and bulging with vodka . . .

For a moment the individual frustration of the narrator seems to have passed into a social protest. The unattainable world of beauty and luxury symbolized by the pretty girl is allied to a smug and apparently impregnable ruling caste; words such as 'Empire' and 'Holy Writ' turn the policeman into a symbol of the power and authority of Imperial Russia. The girl that he desires becomes identified with all that he hates. But what these lines contain is not so much social protest as frustration masquerading as social protest; it is the 'I' of the poem who describes the scene, and the last one and a half lines, deliberately set off from the rest, make no pretence at objectivity (the hero does not speak to the policeman or go any nearer to him); they are made to look like an afterthought, an insult hurled from a safe distance and under the breath. Here in a single image is the nub of the situation, the rebel and the culture he loves and hates.

The second episode moves to the historical and political plane. It opens with an enthusiastic political meeting:

> People come in from the February night, grimacing in the light, bumping into one another, shaking the frost off their coats; and now they're all in with us together, talking, shouting, raising their hands, cursing and weeping.

The outsiders seem to have become insiders at last (they have 'come in' from the 'night'); they feel confident, on the winning side, in the majority. The 'I' has become happily absorbed into the 'we', and the revolutionaries set off to attack the police-station. The timid, insecure hero can now feel himself a real man:

> My body floods with the blood of manhood, the wind of manhood blows around my shirt. Childhood is over. Maturity has begun. Bang your rifle-butt on the stones! Off with your caps!

The hero's body floods with 'manhood', not in the usual sense of the Russian word, 'manly stoicism', which is hardly applicable in this situation of aggression, but in the more basic meaning of virility. Yet the childish gestures with rifle-butt and cap contrive to undercut these claims of manhood and maturity. It is as if the hero were still looking over his shoulder for reassurance: 'Is this how real insiders behave?'.

The revolutionaries take over the police-station without meeting any resistance, and they demand to see the Inspector. When they meet him they are taken aback by his effusiveness:

> Smiling, melting, swooning with cordiality and graciousness and the sheer happiness of meeting the delegates from the committee . . . And we—we just stood there, shifting from one leg to the other, our heels muddying the fantastic horses and parrots embroidered on the carpet. Of course we were in no mood for smiles. That's enough, hand over the keys, and clear out of here. There's nothing to negotiate. Good-bye . . . We set about taking things over. We wandered around all the corridors. [. . .] We found a prisoner's teapot, tinny and rusty, and drank our first tea of victory, the tea of freedom, out of it, slurping and burning our lips.

In the face of the mocking courtesy of the Inspector the assurance of the new rulers crumples, as is suggested by the broken lines, the abrupt changes in tone, from the embarrassing sense of being out of place and dirtying the carpets to the peremptory commands and the peculiar aimlessness of their activities after the takeover. Somehow the old regime's secret has escaped them. They are insiders to all appearances, but the imagery still hints that they are not masters but captives; the doors are closed behind them, and they drink their tea from a prisoner's teapot. Society has been turned upside-down, and the former insiders have been evicted, but the new masters are depicted as squatters, without any sense of permanence, and the confident assertion of the last line reads ironically because of the triviality of the actual gesture—drinking tea. As at the end of *Night Search* the revolutionaries seem to have won everything except the one thing they desired most of all.

The new regime is installed, and the narrator becomes assistant to the local commissar. Surrounded by the visible trappings of power, he wishes that his down-trodden Jewish forebears could see him now in his hour of triumph. But this need to justify himself by a challenge to the past shatters all his pretensions to maturity and self-assurance. He has become an insider only to find himself once again a prisoner, looking out through the windows at the world continuing without him:

> Nights on end I sat in damp guard rooms, gazing out at the passing world, foreign to me like elements of an alien nature.

In the final and culminating episode the hero and his men raid a house which is suspected of harbouring bandits. The scene in which they burst into the house is in many ways parallel to their takeover of the police-station, a similar mixture of timidity, self-consciousness, bewildered admiration and brutal violence:

> I went up to the door on my own. The lads, gripping their carbines between their knees, squeezed themselves flat against the wall. Everything was just as in a nice decent house—a lamp with a deep blue shade over the family table [. . .] a bust of Tolstoy on the cupboard. All the solidity of domestic comfort in the warm air [. . .] everything was quite in order. We burst in like a tempest, like the breath of the black streets, not wiping our feet or taking off our coats . . .

One might have expected the hero and his revolutionary sailors to be enraged and extra-suspicious rather than impressed by this picture of bourgeois culture. Do they recognize it perhaps as an incarnation of the ideal culture towards which they too aspire?

> I entered and stopped in amazement. The devil take it! What a blunder! What sort of thieves' kitchen was this—just some friends sitting over a cup of tea. What was I doing interrupting them? I too would like to sit in comfort, converse about Gumilev, and not wander through the nights like a spy, bursting into respectable families in search of non-existent bandits.

Because of the reference to Gumilev this passage might seem to be ironic (as it would be in most Soviet writers), but it is difficult to see any irony here. There is none in the narrator's tone: he is still fascinated by these bourgeois ideals, and quite willing to accept their right to exist like this, provided they break no laws. He even feels guilty at interrupting this cultural idyll.

But at this point one of the sailors recognizes the officers as the bandits they were looking for and tells them to put their hands up. The revolutionaries then proceed to search the house, and discover that it is a brothel. In one room they find the supposedly inaccessible girl naked in bed, and a man in his underclothes beside her. For a moment he brandishes a gun, and then he winks: 'Oh, the whole fleet's come! This little cannon's not much good against them. I surrender.'

The two faces of the bourgeois world fuse into one: the glamorous and unattainable culture of the bourgeoisie proves to be no more than a den of bandits and prostitutes, yet it still retains all its glamour and superiority. There is a striking stylistic contrast between the easy capitulation of the winking officer and the clumsy and embarrassed manner of the victorious revolutionaries. As in *Night Search,* even in defeat and humiliation, the old class still possesses its secret intact. And as in *Night Search* the secret is in the eyes.

What is this secret? And how can it be acquired? And what is the justification for acquiring it? These questions are raised in the final lines of the poem. The hero challenges the girl:

> (1) 'Well, do you recognize me?' Silence. Then in anger I blurted out: 'How much do I pay you for a session?' Quietly, not moving her lips, she said: 'Take pity on me! I don't want any money . . . ' I threw some money at her. I plunged in, without pulling off my boots or taking off my holster, or unbuttoning my tunic. Straight into that abyss of down and blanket under which all my predecessors had struggled and panted—into a dark and phantasmagoric torrent of visions, yelps, shameless movements, darkness and fierce light.
>
> (2) I am taking you because my generation was timid, because I was shy, because of the shame of my homeless forebears, because of the twittering of a chance bird. I am taking you as vengeance on a world from which I couldn't escape.
>
> (3) Receive me into your empty depths, where even grass cannot take root. Perhaps my nocturnal seed will fructify your desert.
>
> Spring showers will come, and a wind from the South, and the love-calls of swans.

The three sections indicate the successive stages in the hero's interpretation of what has happened in the act of 'possession', and they recapitulate the main themes of the poem, and indeed the three main attitudes to the problem of the culture of the past.

In the first stage he is concerned simply to possess and humiliate; all the gestures are violent and brutal. If one's ideal turns out to have been a prostitute all along, one might as well treat her the same way oneself. There is no 'secret' to be sought or redeemed in this 'possession'. But the very crudity of his assault leads him into the same old trap. Far from possessing the past he begins to wonder if he has not been possessed by it; the imagery is of being sucked in and swallowed up by darkness. Is there any significant difference between his actions and those of his predecessors?

In the second stage the tone changes dramatically: from action to introspection, from self-assertion to self-justification, from aggression almost to apology. Even the word 'vengeance' is so modified by the 'shy' and the 'timid' of the first two lines that it sounds impotent. The transition is extraordinary: the unattainable ideal has been caught in the act of collusion with the class-enemy, and the hero finds himself apologizing for his anger. He addresses her for the first time as 'tu', and without any mockery or contempt.

In the final section the situation is reversed, or rather restored. The hero addresses the girl once again in the tones of a diffident lover: 'receive me', 'perhaps'. Hateful though this old world is, the hero still wants to renew its vitality. But why does he call *her* a desert? in that case she wouldn't be worth possessing. Surely throughout the poem this ideal has been depicted as a secret inaccessible garden of elegance and beauty, of self-assurance and good taste, into which the hero time and again brings his muddy boots. Culture, upper-class whore that she is, needs only to throw herself open to the masses, and all will be forgiven. Because, surely, the desert is the uncultured post-revolutionary society. The culture of the past does not need the present to bear its fruit; it is the present which needs the secret of the past.

Of course, Bagritsky did not actually behave like this, or think of these arguments at the time; in some embarrassment he ran straight out of the room. Wasn't this in fact the normal, healthy and correct response? If the whole episode was, 'so to say, a break with the past, a settling of accounts with it', it is strange that Bagritsky should have felt the need to rewrite it this way: to turn a non-event into a rape, a 'complete break' into a desperate plea for continuity. Why should one have any truck with 'mastering' and 'possessing' such social undesirables? In *Night Search* the revolutionaries had come gradually to a grudging admission of the merits of the class-enemy. In **'February'** the supposed merits of the girl are stripped away one after another, until nothing remains, but she still remains uniquely desirable.

If in the works of other Soviet writers the intellectual hero often seeks (in vain) for renewal through a union with an illiterate peasant-girl, in Bagritsky the homeless revolutionary tries to establish and legitimize his inheritance by raping a bourgeois girl in an officer's brothel. The successive arguments of the hero to the girl are metaphors for the changing attitudes of the revolutionary generation to the culture of the past: first, a violent and destructive assault, then the envious aspirations and self-justifications of the frustrated and deprived outsider, and finally the half-hearted suggestion that perhaps between them they could improve the genetic stock. Partly because of this the final two lines of the poem with their evocation of a springtime idyll, complete with birds and all, are so unconvincing. These images have throughout been associated with escapism and self-defence, not of a new understanding. The hopes of the final lines, as of the whole poem, remain a pathetic, unattainable vision.

FURTHER READING

Bibliography

Kowalski, Luba Halat. "Eduard Bagritsky: A Selected Bibliography." *Russian Literature Quarterly* 8 (Winter 1973-1974): 540-42.

Brief selected bibliography divided into five sections: Main Editions (annotated), Articles by Bagritsky, Biographical Sources, Criticism and Memoirs, and Sources in English.

Biography

Kuprianova, Nina. "Eduard Bagritsky [1895-1934]: On the 80th Anniversary of the Poet's Birth." *Soviet Literature* No. 12 (333): 146-48.

Anniversary sketch charts the development of Bagritsky's verse in relation to the poet's life.

Criticism

Cukierman, Walenty. "The Odessan Myth and Idiom in Some Early Works of Odessa Writers." *Canadian-American Slavic Studies [Revue Canadienne-Americaine D'Etudes Slaves]* 14, No. 1 (Spring 1980): 36-51.

Describing the Ukrainian city as colorful, anarchic, and linguistically idiosyncratic, Cukierman discusses Odessa's influence on Bagritsky and contemporary writers.

Rosslyn, Wendy. "The Path to Paradise: Recurrent Images in the Poetry of Eduard Bagritsky." *The Modern Language Review* 71, No. 1 (January 1976): 97-105.

Discussion of Bagritsky's use of imagery that quotes extensively in Russian characters.

———. "Bagritskii's *Duma pro Opanasa:* The Poem and Its Context." *Canadian-American Slavic Studies [Revue Canadienne-Americaine D'Etudes Slaves]* 11, No. 3 (Fall 1977): 388-405.

Arguing that the poem's political context extends beyond the 1918-20 civil war, Rosslyn concludes that Bagritsky subordinates historical fact to artistic intention.

Slonim, Marc. *Soviet Russian Literature: Writers and Problems, 1917-1977.* New York: Oxford University Press, 1977, 437 p.

Provides a brief overview of Bagritsky's work that stresses the evolving relationship between the poet's Romantic sensibility and his Revolutionary politics.

Richard Beer-Hofmann

1866-1945

Austrian playwright, novelist, short story writer, and poet.

INTRODUCTION

An influential member of a group of writers known as "Young Vienna," Beer-Hofmann produced a small body of works that are characterized by keen psychological insight as well as a preoccupation with art, love, and death—themes that were often explored by Young Vienna writers. One of Beer-Hofmann's most important contributions to Austrian literature was his early experimentation with stream-of-consciousness narrative technique in his novel *Der Tod Georgs* (*The Death of George*) and other works. In his later years Beer-Hofmann worked on a cycle of biblical dramas, most prominently *Jaákobs Traum* (*Jacob's Dream*), that combined his growing awareness of his Jewish heritage with his sense of artistic calling.

Biographical Information

Beer-Hofmann was born in Vienna to Hermann and Rose Beer. A few days after his birth his mother died, and he was subsequently placed in the care of his aunt and uncle, Berta and Alois Hofmann, who later adopted him and whose surname was added to his own. Beer-Hofmann was raised in upper middle-class Jewish milieus in Brünn and Vienna. He later attended the University of Vienna, where he received a doctorate in jurisprudence in 1890. Rather than practicing law, however, he overcame the resistance of his family and embarked upon a career as a writer. In the 1890s Beer-Hofmann became acquainted with a number of Austrian artists and writers who collectively became known as Young Vienna and whose most famous members included Arthur Schnitzler and Hugo von Hofmannsthal. Beer-Hofmann's first published work, the short story collection *Novellen,* and his subsequent novel, *The Death of George*, demonstrated that he was a writer of acute psychological insight. In 1895 Beer-Hofmann married Paula Lissy, and their loving marriage was the subject of his last major work, a book of reminiscences entitled *Paula, ein Fragment.* From the early 1900s until his death Beer-Hofmann worked on writing biblical dramas, the most famous of which is *Jacob's Dream*. He also received critical acclaim for adapting and directing plays for the Burgtheater in Vienna. In 1938, after the Nazis assumed power in Germany, Beer-Hofmann went into hiding with Paula, and in 1939 the couple fled to the United States. En route to New York, Paula suffered a fatal heart attack; after his wife's death, Beer-Hofmann lived in Manhattan, eventually becoming an American citizen. He died in 1945.

Major Works

Critics have noted that the hallmarks of Beer-Hofmann's most mature work—his inventive literary techniques, beautiful imagery, and psychological astuteness—are all evident in his first published book, *Novellen.* In his novel *The Death of George* Beer-Hofmann polished the stream-of-consciousness technique that he had begun to experiment with in *Novellen. The Death of George* is considered a representative example of Austrian fin-de-siècle literature for its rich imagery and symbolism, its aesthete hero, and its exploration of youth, beauty, and death. However, in a marked departure from other works chronicling late nineteenth-century decadence, Beer-Hofmann's hero ultimately chooses to become more deeply engaged with life, rather than remaining detached from it. During his lifetime Beer-Hofmann grew more aware of his Jewish identity, and his interest in Judaism is reflected in *Jacob's Dream* and the unfinished David cycle, which consists of *Der junge David* (*Young David*) and fragments and outlines published as *Das Vorspiel auf dem Theater zu "König David."* In *Jacob's Dream* Beer-Hofmann depicted his hero as suffering from profound doubt—Jacob rails against having been chosen as God's elect—before ultimately deciding to enter into a covenant with God. Commentators observe that *Jacob's Dream* functions on many levels at once: it is the retelling of a well-known Bible story, a chronicle of Israel and the fate of the Jewish people, and a parable about the writer's artistic calling. After the Nazis came to power, Beer-Hofmann fled Vienna and took up residence in New York; there, he wrote *Paula, ein Fragment*, a memoir about his marriage and his recently deceased wife. In this reminiscence he explores the dominant themes of his life and work in his characteristic stream-of-consciousness style.

Critical Reception

Beer-Hofmann is recognized as a literary innovator for having used experimental techniques like stream of consciousness and the interior monologue long before they were in vogue. Several critics have remarked that Beer-Hofmann's stylistic experimentation prefigures the work of better-known writers, including Marcel Proust, James Joyce, and Virginia Woolf. Although Beer-Hofmann's work is generally overlooked today, his lullaby for his daughter, "Schlaflied für Mirjam" ("Lullaby for Miriam"), has endured and is widely anthologized.

PRINCIPAL WORKS

Novellen (short stories) 1893
Der Tod Georgs [*The Death of George*] (novel) 1900
Gedenkrede auf Wolfgang Amadé Mozart [*Memorial Oration on Wolfgang Amadeus Mozart*] (essay) 1906
Der Graf von Charolais (drama) [first publication] 1906
**Jaákobs Traum* [*Jacob's Dream*] (drama) 1919
Schlaflied für Mirjam [*Lullaby for Miriam*] (poetry) 1919
**Der junge David* [*Young David*] (drama) [first publication] 1933
**Vorspiel auf dem Theater zu "König David"* (drama) [first publication] 1936
Verse (poetry) 1941
Paula, ein Fragment (reminiscences) 1949
Gesammelte Werke (novel, short stories, dramas, poetry, and nofiction) 1963

*These works are collectively referred to as *Die Historie von "König David."*

CRITICISM

Solomon Liptzin (essay date 1936)

SOURCE: "The Viennese Aesthete," in *Richard Beer-Hofmann,* Bloch Publishing, 1936, pp. 1-21.

[*In the following excerpt, Liptzin discusses the psychological insight that characterizes Beer-Hofmann's work, particularly his first published volume,* Novellen.]

German literature at the close of the nineteenth century seemed to center in the three metropolises: Berlin, Munich, and Vienna. Each of these cities had a physiognomy of its own which found expression in its literary life. The Prussian capital, that had been most violently affected by the triumph of science and industrialism, reacted by taking over in its literary products the technique of science and the subject-matter of industrialism. It sought to substitute keen observation for native inspiration, to speak of heredity and environment instead of God and fate, to vie with sociology in the interpretation of social phenomena and with psychology in the exact description and careful analysis of instincts and reflexes. Thus was born the militant naturalism of Holz and Schlaf and Young Hauptmann. The Bavarian capital, though acceding to Berlin political supremacy in the new empire, sought to retain for itself the literary ascendancy that Wagner and Geibel and Heyse had for a generation bestowed upon it. The attack upon the older Munich school, especially upon Heyse, in the columns of Michael Georg Conrad's organ *Die Gesellschaft,* was at the same time the rallying cry for a new literary group with Munich as its center. Yet, though perhaps more vociferous in its negative creed and though perhaps more amenable to French than to Slavic or Scandinavian influences, this group did not in its essential accomplishments differ from its Berlin allies.

Far from the din and turmoil of the struggle between German mid-Victorianism and German modernism, Viennese men-of-letters continued to write their tired and melancholy poems, tales, and dramas, even as their unwieldy empire continued to drag out a slow and unheroic existence waiting for its inevitable end and dissolution. Though statesmen, lured by a false sense of security, might fail to discern this end, poets sensed it and the typical Viennese writer at the turn of the century was without faith in the future of his country. He neither accepted nor did he violently oppose the unsavory political and social regime, but with a gentle, critical smile he turned from it to a dream-world which he called the pure world of art as distinct from the impure world of every-day life. Since Vienna was the capital of a vast empire to which wealth flowed from every province, its typical writers were members of well-to-do patrician families who were spared the bitter struggle for bread. They had the leisure and the means to travel and to assimilate influences from the leading European literary centers. They felt themselves drawn especially to Baudelaire and Verlaine, Maeterlinck and Jens Peter Jacobsen, Oscar Wilde and d'Annunzio, Symbolists and Decadents, but nevertheless they avoided associating their poetic efforts too closely with those of any school. They did not shout, as did the Munich and Berlin writers, that they were revolutionizing either the technique or the subject-matter of literature, nor did they feel the need of setting up elaborate theories to justify weak results. They had no organ about which to group themselves as had the Munich circle in *Die Gesellschaft* or the Berlin circle in *Die Freie Bühne,* later renamed *Neue Rundschau.* We can speak of them as a unit only because, born in the same metropolis of the same social class within a few years of each other and facing in their youth and manhood similar problems, similar stimuli, and similar frustrations, they gave expression in their literary products to parallel themes, like characters, closely allied philosophies, and all this in analogous language.

At times Vienna cafés were common meeting grounds for discussions of art, atheism, and politics. Café Grienstadl was especially famed as the literary café and there in the nineties one could encounter Hermann Bahr, Arthur Schnitzler, Hugo von Hofmannsthal, Peter Altenberg, Felix Salten, Richard Beer-Hofmann, Karl Kraus, Felix Dörmann, and many lesser lights. Hermann Bahr writes in his diary on January 1, 1921: "It is now thirty years since I came to Vienna after straggling through Berlin, Paris, Madrid, Tangier, again Paris, again Berlin, and finally St. Petersburg. I was at that time invited by a young man of Brünn, E. M. Kafka, the editor of *Moderne Dichtung,* to found the group *Young Vienna*. The available material consisted of a young physician, Dr. Arthur Schnitzler; a person famed about town because of the splendor of his neckties, Dr. Richard Beer-Hofmann; and a high school youth who wrote under the name Loris, Hugo von Hofmannsthal. I looked them over and took the risk of founding the school."

Of the three young writers who were soon known in the nineties as the Viennese aesthetes, two have become internationally famous: Schnitzler and Hofmannsthal. The third is not too well known even in his own country and almost unknown abroad. Yet he alone outgrew his early beginnings and though he wrote but very little, that little is unique and will undoubtedly take its place among the permanent treasures of German literature.

The world of these aesthetes was in the main the world of pleasures that palled, of comedies that ended tragically, of dreams superimposed on reality, that burst at the slightest pin-prick of fate. Death had but to knock at the gate of the villa inhabited by Hugo von Hofmannsthal's Claudio, the hero of *Der Tor und der Tod,* and this aesthete immediately realized that his existence had been that of a fool. Old age had but to approach Schnitzler's dandy Anatol and his ironic smile became bitter, and as Julian Fichtner or Marquis von Sala or Casanova, he had difficulty in masking his utter loneliness and misery. Beer-Hofmann's characters, though allied to those of Schnitzler and Hofmannsthal, nevertheless manage as a result of an inner catastrophe to recover their balance and to stride forth into a new life filled with a more substantial meaning.

It was in 1893 at the age of twenty-seven that the young lawyer Richard Beer-Hofmann first attracted public notice with a slender volume entitled ***Novellen***. This volume consisted of two short tales: **"Das Kind"** and **"Camelias."** Michael Georg Conrad, who as editor of *Die Gesellschaft* for a time occupied a dominant position in the field of criticism, immediately hailed Beer-Hofmann as a master of fine psychological portraiture, as an original artist who had struck out on a new path, and congratulated German literature upon the rise of another poetic star. Although the Viennese writer in later decades withdrew this volume from publication and spoke of it merely as a youthful product little worthy of note, nevertheless a careful analysis of its contents reveals in embryonic form many of the themes and problems with which Beer-Hofmann wrestled in his later and maturer works.

There is, on the one hand, the stressing of man's insignificance in the universal order and, on the other hand, the assertion of the guilt of the creator towards even the most insignificant of his created objects. Then there are questions raised as to the necessity of pain in this world, the responsibility of the individual towards fate, the relations of parents to children and of children to parents—questions that reappear in manifold variations throughout the poet's creative career.

These early tales betray the influence of Maupassant in subject-matter and of Flaubert in style. **"Camelias,"** the shorter and less significant of the two stories, was written in December 1891. Its central figure is a Viennese dandy, the handsome Freddy. What strikes one as most peculiar about this beau is that, unlike the dandies of Schnitzler and of Hofmannsthal, he is not a frivolous philanderer. Though this well-to-do bachelor of thirty-eight has nothing of the puritan or ascetic about him, he nevertheless does not roam from object to object in the realm of irresponsible amours. On the contrary, Beer-Hofmann confers upon this earliest and most ridiculous of his characters, as well as upon the latter's hired mistress, the same sense of responsibility and the same tender conscience which he is afterwards to bestow upon his later more serious heroes and heroines. Freddy has had an affair with Franzi. For thirteen years he has been faithful to her and she to him, although their illicit relationship has been the result not of ecstatic intoxication but rather of a convenient arrangement measured in terms of dollars and cents.

One Saturday night in early spring, as Freddy returns home from a ball, he recalls the beautiful girl he has danced with throughout the evening, a girl he has known since her third year and whom he now suddenly discovers to have grown up. The flattering thought that the seventeen year old Thea found him still attractive, even though he was more than twenty years her senior, leads him to contemplate the possibility of marrying her and of putting an end to his unworthy affair with Franzi. He determines to break immediately his long habit of sending a bouquet of camellias to Franzi every Sunday. He will instead order large Parma-violets to be delivered to Thea's address.

This decision is hardly reached when doubts begin to assail Freddy. What a complete transformation in his accustomed manner of living this step would involve! What havoc it would wreak with his well regulated habits, with his present daily routine! Thea was young. Theatres, balls, concerts, marriage, love were new experiences to her. She would surely want to enjoy them to their fullest extent at a time when he was already tiring of these experiences.

Yet, assuming that he, the man of thirty-eight, were willing and able to devote himself entirely to satisfying the extravagant demands of a girl of seventeen who was first entering upon life, could he possibly look forward with equanimity to later years when, for example, he would be an aging individual of fifty-one, fond of restful quiet, and she a woman of thirty, a woman in her most dangerous period, full of intense craving for the joy of life? With his knowledge of women, he was sure that he could never trust his wife. Even if she remained true to him, the thought would constantly torture him that she was merely more skillful than others of her sex in betraying her old husband behind his back. At his present age might it not be preferable to avoid dangerous experiments and innovations? Franzi was devoted to him. What if he did pay for her love! She had never betrayed him. With her he had spent his twenties and thirties, the best years of youth. She was not likely to become unfaithful. She would care for him when his looks faded. They would both become old together. She was good and kind, even moral, if one took into consideration her background. "She had sold herself, or rather she had been sold by her mother; but could he take it ill of those who had grown up in misery out there, if they wished to protect their old age against need? Virtue neither warms nor satiates!—Should she have stood at the washing-trough throughout a joyless life, if she saw that her beauty alone could elevate her at one stroke above all this misery? Why did one make special demands for such great, heroic, impossible virtue upon those who starved and froze?" No! Freddy will not order violets for Thea; he will continue his habit of sending camellias to Franzi.

In July 1893 Beer-Hofmann wrote the second of his early tales, **"Das Kind,"** and in the hero Paul he recreated the Freddy type and subjected this character to a more tragic experience. Paul is a well-to-do Viennese student who does not at first take life too seriously. His supersensitive nerves and his extreme refinement result in his becoming a plaything of every passing mood. Though gifted with an excellent aesthetic taste and a keen sense of propriety, he yet fails to resist the sweet lure of a May evening and enters into an affair with an insignificant and unintelligent chambermaid. He soon tires of her, however, and yearns to free himself from the degrading alliance, but finds his path to freedom blocked by the birth of a child. With each rendezvous his anger and chagrin mount and the chains he has forged for himself grow more burdensome, until one day the girl suddenly informs him that this child, which had been cared for by a peasant woman in the country since its birth, has died. At first he experiences merely a sense of liberation from guilt and responsibility. But soon an inexplicable desire comes over him to find out all he can about the child. Too late there awaken in him paternal feelings and the knowledge of the seriousness of life. As long as the child lived, he had been criminally indifferent to it and had only rarely given it a fleeting thought. Now that it was dead, pain and pity overcame him, as though he had lost a beloved creature. With horror he conjures up the child's final hours. "If it cried, because it was hungry or because it felt pain, a cloth, soaked with brandy, was put into its mouth, so that it fell asleep. Amidst dirt and filth, it lay in its cradle and no hand had caressed it, no mouth had whispered tender, flattering words—as only mothers invent—to make it smile. He saw the narrow, unaired peasant's hovel in which they shut in the child, when they went to work. There it lay, with buzzing flies about it, flies that tortured and frightened it, alone, moaning until its voice failed, and its helpless eyes stared up to the low ceiling, not knowing, not suspecting, not comprehending death—merely agape with fearful questioning like the eyes of any animal that is perishing."

Paul travels to the village and seeks out the cemetery where his child lies buried. An ineffable sadness comes over him at the sight of the nameless grave. This child, whose face he cannot imagine, was somehow a link that might have united him with all creation about him. What a meaningless existence was his, filled with frivolous pleasures that left him lonely and desolate! Schnitzler in his later dramas and novels often depicts the tragedy of the dandy who has just passed the peak of life and who is beginning to feel the horror of solitude, far from a domestic haven and from children that lisp the magic word father. Paul, the hero of Beer-Hofmann's tale, senses the possibility of such tragedy and determines to renounce all empty joys and to face human relations and human problems with due seriousness and reverence. For, "all things had not merely form and color but were irradiated by a secret sense; they no longer stood as strangers near each other but were bound together by a single, common thought."

The unity of all life, as symbolized in the relations between parent and child, forms also the theme of Beer-Hofmann's finest poem, his **"Schlaflied für Miriam."** Hermann Bahr in an outburst of enthusiasm called this song the finest lyric since Goethe's *Über allen Gipfeln*. Alfred Kerr wrote in 1905 that he could never read the few verses of the poem without his voice breaking before the end was reached and more than twenty years later he reaffirmed his conviction that this little masterpiece would live as long as the German tongue survived. Rainer Maria Rilke, the most sensitive of twentieth century German poets, wrote in 1922 that during a stay at a Swedish estate he was sent for from great distances, as one sends for a physician, in order that he might recite the few verses of this poem to strange people who had heard of its extraordinary loveliness.

The poem might best be characterized as a philosophic lullaby. Designed to be chanted by a father at the cradle of his child, it was composed by Beer-Hofmann when his first-born daughter Miriam was fourteen days old. In four exquisite stanzas, eternal chords are touched that continue to vibrate in us: the dark origin of life and its unknown end, the blind path that we tread throughout our days and our absolute loneliness here below, the impossibility of communicating our deepest experiences even to those nearest and dearest to us and the tragic necessity of each generation recapitulating the past with all its errors and suffering. Yet somehow behind the apparent chaotic structure of the universe there seem to loom a mysterious purpose and a definite continuity of existence. "We are but banks of a river and deep in us flows blood of the past streaming on to the future, blood of our fathers full of unrest and pride. All our ancestors are in us. Who can feel himself alone?"

Beer-Hofmann did not share the pessimism of the fin-de-siècle poets who conceived of man as an accidental creature without a God and without a hope of heaven, a creature who wandered down meaningless lonely years until death, sudden or slow, blotted out his instincts and intelligence.

—Solomon Liptzin

A similar idea is voiced by Beer-Hofmann a decade later in a poem written in 1907 and entitled **"Altern."** The poet, then in his forties, takes up the problem of old age. Not with fear or regret does he enter upon the second half of his life but rather with joyous submission to fate that grants to all created objects through their very transformations a share of immortality. It is as wrong to pray for eternal youth as it would be to ask that a tree blossom everlastingly. The young tree longs to bear fruit and the fruit yearns to open its seeds and the seed strains to bloom anew. "Blossom—fruit—and again seed! Which is beginning and which is end?" The single tree is important only as the expression of the species tree at a given time. The single human being is important only as the vessel through which courses for a brief moment the immortal human stream.

Beer-Hofmann did not a generation ago share the pessimism of the fin-de-siècle poets who conceived of man as an accidental creature without a God and without a hope of heaven, a creature who wandered down meaningless lonely years until death, sudden or slow, blotted out his instincts and intelligence. On the contrary, Beer-Hofmann never tired of asserting his faith in the necessity of all our being and doing. No matter what we are or how we act, we are constantly spinning the slender thread of our lives into the firm untearing thread of the super-individual life that glides down the generations from hand to hand. We are indissolubly linked with our ancestors and with our descendants even to the furthest reaches of time. We are embedded in fate. "Nobody may lead his life for himself. One speaks—and a wind grasps his word and carries it on and sinks it into a strange life where it sprouts and blossoms and may cause havoc or may bring forth rich fruits and blessings. One walks—and his shadow falls on the road and covers with darkness a jewel that might have lured others. One is silent—and voices become audible which the sound of his words might have drowned. One stands motionless—and beneath the soles of his feet buds are stifled and perish because he did not move on. One leaves the road in order to be alone—and at a predestined hour he finds a strange fate waiting for him, his appearance having been long foretold."

Our lives are not limited by the boundaries of birth and death. We inherit and fulfill the desires of countless predecessors and are ourselves treasure-houses for the thoughts and dreams of innumerable successors.

This knowledge comes to Paul, the hero of Beer-Hofmann's novel ***Der Tod Georgs*** and wrests him, as it wrested his namesake, the hero of the tale **"Das Kind,"** from the fruitless pursuit of empty pleasures. This novel, appearing in 1900, exposes the weakness and futility of the aesthetic, decadent type which was then flourishing in fiction and drama in manifold variations from Oscar Wilde's Dorian Gray and Hermann Conradi's Adam Mensch to Schnitzler's Anatol and Hofmannsthal's fool Claudio.

Paul is a proud and passive hero who disdains all contact with reality. A tired sceptic, incapable of strong passion, he plays with his delicate sensations and gentle nerves as though he were always on a stage. Human beings and their relations, physical objects and their actions are to him but stuff for dreams. This superfluous character suddenly finds himself face to face with a grim fact that he cannot explain: death casts its warning shadow upon his frivolous days. As early as 1892 Schnitzler had depicted in the tale "Sterben" the effect produced upon such a character by the sudden knowledge of his early certain death. A year later Hugo von Hofmannsthal in the play *Der Tor und der Tod* had exposed a similar character to the same problem. Yet, though these writers also voice dissatisfaction with the aesthetic type whose unhealthy dream-world collapses when faced with such an experience, it is Beer-Hofmann alone who makes the contemplation of death the starting point for the aesthete's spiritual rebirth.

The plot of ***Der Tod Georgs*** is extremely meager. The framework is barely able to support the multiplicity of ideas that crowd the book. While at Ischl, an Austrian summer resort, Paul is visited one late afternoon by his friend Georg, a dynamic personality who has faith in himself, a young man who is on the threshold of a magnificent career, having just been called to a professorship at the University of Heidelberg. On the following morning Georg is found dead. He has suffered a fatal heart-attack during the night, and now Paul must perform the unpleasant duty of conveying the body to Georg's relatives at Vienna.

This simple experience sets up a series of thoughts and dreams that leave Paul no rest until a complete transformation comes over him, until he subordinates himself to fate and thus finds an escape in submission to the universal law. Then he feels himself no longer alone but rather part of a great entity that includes man and beast and plant and stone. "His life did not fade away as a solitary tone in the void but, harmonizing with a vast solemn melody preordained since the birth of time, it swept on to the accompaniment of universal eternal laws. Nothing unjust could happen to him, pain was not expulsion nor did death mean severance from the all. As an inevitable part of a universal whole, every deed was perhaps a sacrament, pain perhaps an honor, and death perhaps a mission."

Paul, the tired and melancholy aesthete, is filled with a new faith, the faith in the absolute justice that must prevail in God's immense structure. He renounces his feeble dreams and takes up the burden that fate has allotted to him and his people, namely to be a witness of God's justice in this unbelieving sphere. For, at the end of the novel we learn that Paul is a Jew and that he recognizes his people's mission to be the teaching of divine justice to all the nations. "Over the life of those whose blood flowed in him, justice was ever present like a sun whose rays never warmed them, whose light never shone for them, and yet before whose dazzling splendor they reverently shielded their pain-covered forehead with trembling hands.—Ancestors, who wandered from land to land, ragged and disgraced, the dust of all the highways in their hair and beards, every man's hand against them, despised by the lowest yet never despising themselves, honoring God but not as a beggar honors an almsgiver, calling out in their suffering not to the Lord of Mercy but to the God of Justice."

A single jolt, the death of a friend has thus sufficed to tear the aesthete out of his complacent, egoistic dream-existence and to make him conscious of his relations to the all and of his responsibility towards fate. In the earlier tale, **"Das Kind,"** it is the death of a child that gives the impetus to a similar inner crisis. In Beer-Hofmann's first drama, ***Der Graf von Charolais,*** it is the death of a father that makes a delicately nerved cavalier aware of the undercurrent of fate which bears us on its billows, now hurling us to the stars and now swallowing us in its unfathomable depths. In Beer-Hofmann's latest drama, ***Der junge David,*** it is the death of a dearly beloved wife that leads the young king to abandon all personal desires and to dedicate his life to his people.

How differently do Schnitzler's characters react in such situations! Sylvester Thorn in *Der Gang zum Weiher* leaves the fresh graves of his child and its mother in order to woo anew at once, holding it a crime against life to waste even a single precious day in weeping and in abstaining from possible pleasures. Friedrich Hofreiter in *Das weite Land* comes from the funeral of his friend in order to hurl himself into new flirtations and to seek further satisfaction of personal desires. Even characters who are themselves about to die and who are aware of this fact, as in *Der Schleier der Beatrice* and in *Der Ruf des Lebens,* spend their last hours in bacchic orgies. Schnitzler, the sceptical physician, does not share Beer-Hofmann's conviction that life is purposeful and that there is a meaning to existence which is not destroyed by the individual's inevitable end and dissolution. Where Schnitzler doubts, Beer-Hofmann hopes. Where Schnitzler despairs, Beer-Hofmann finds refuge in faith. Schnitzler remains to the end an aesthete and an epicurean. Beer-Hofmann, on the other hand, early breaks with aestheticism and Epicureanism, he reverts to the severe traditions of the Old Testament prophets, he becomes the poetic spokesman of an ancient heritage.

Solomon Liptzin (essay date 1944)

SOURCE: "Richard Beer-Hoffman," in *Germany's Stepchildren,* The Jewish Publication Society of America, 1944, pp. 239-54.

[*In the following excerpt, Liptzin discusses how Beer-Hofmann's Jewish heritage influenced his religious dramas.*]

When Theodor Herzl, at the close of the last century, proposed his radical solution of the duality in which Jews of the Diaspora found themselves, assimilationists and Jewish Aryans mocked at his visions. The non-German Jews, who flocked to his banner, were primarily interested in the political consequences of his thought, the homeward march of a long exiled people. The Viennese aesthetes and epicureans, who were his early associates, dismissed his Zionist theories with a shrug of the shoulders and a sceptical smile. For many years the influential Viennese organ to which he was a contributor refused to print any news or comments about his messianic complex, and he was compelled to found and to finance a newspaper of his own in order to further the spread of his ideas. A single Viennese poet of Jewish origin sensed the motivating force that prompted Herzl's dignified reaction to the German-Jewish duality. Immediately after the appearance of Herzl's pamphlet, The Jewish State, Richard Beer-Hofmann wrote to him: "More sympathetic even than everything contained in your book was the personality behind it. At last, once again a human being who does not bear his Judaism resignedly as a burden or as a misfortune, but who, on the contrary, is proud to be among the legitimate heirs of an ancient culture." Beer-Hofmann recommended to Herzl that the Palestinian experiment should begin with the founding of a great medical university to which all Asia was to flock and which was at the same time to initiate the sanitation of the Orient.

Like Herzl and Schnitzler, Beer-Hofmann stems from a patrician Jewish family. But this family had not yet succumbed to the assimilationist currents of the Austro-Hungarian metropolises. While the well-to-do Jewish circles of Vienna and Budapest were abandoning the rich heritage of their past for the doubtful privilege of being accepted on terms of social equality by the dominant German and Hungarian nationalities, the Beer and the Hofmann families clung to orthodox observances and ancestral customs. Their way of life was still simple, reserved, old-fashioned, and puritanical. Rooted in the Bohemian-Moravian provincial communities, they did not fall victim to the enervating and corrupting influences that emanated from the Danubian capitals. Even when they moved to Vienna and could share in the achievements of this highly cultured city, they gratefully accepted the new rights bestowed by the emancipation but never sought to merge completely with the German bourgeoisie. They lacked the ambition to garner social laurels by sloughing off their Jewish characteristics. They remained modestly within their own fold.

Richard Beer-Hofmann, therefore, as the sole offspring of the Beer and the Hofmann families, never experienced Judaism as a problem and never questioned the value of this heritage. It was for him rather a precious privilege, an undeserved gift, a constant source of astonishment. It has remained for him throughout his life a wonder and a delight. In contrast to the partially emancipated children of the ghetto, who stood in the shadow of the tree of Judaism and who sought to escape to an imagined pure sunlight, Beer-Hofmann possessed the personal and social gifts which enabled him to be entirely immersed in the German world. But he refused to follow the path of assimilation trodden by so many of his associates. When his education and environment removed him far from the tree of Judaism, he looked back upon it and was filled with shudders of ecstasy as he caught sight of it. Distance lent enchantment. Distance rendered possible a grasping of its total aspect. How ancient and deep-rooted, how mighty and tall, how marvelously beautiful is this tree! he exclaimed. And he never forgot to voice his thanks to his Creator, who had accorded him a heritage granted to but a few million inhabitants on this earth, a heritage which linked him with a unique people and a rare faith.

Beer-Hofmann's soul is healthy. The duality—German and Jew—which troubled so many of his contemporaries does not trouble him.

—Solomon Liptzin

In his early novel, ***Der Tod Georgs,*** which appeared in 1900, Beer-Hofmann spoke through the mouth of his hero Paul and related his discovery of Judaism, a discovery which thrust him out of the artificial, unhealthy, self-centered world of dandies, aesthetes, and decadents into the community of a people which had a worth-while task to perform on earth. This task consisted in upholding both in faith and in deed, at the cost of pain and of death, the claim of justice in all ages, especially in generations beset by injustice. "Over the life of those whose blood flowed in him, justice was ever present like a sun, whose rays never warmed them, whose light never shone for them, and yet before whose dazzling splendor they reverently shielded their pain-covered forehead with trembling hands.—Ancestors, who wandered from land to land, ragged and disgraced, the dust of all the highways in their hair and beards, every man's hand against them, despised by the lowest yet never despising themselves, honoring God but not as a beggar honors an almsgiver, calling out in their suffering, not to the Lord of Mercy, but to the God of Justice.—And before them, many ancestors whose dying was a great festival prepared for others: round about them festive robes, the sparkle of noble jewels, fluttering flags and pomp and the sound of bells and the song of vesper hymns, and over all a reflection of the sinking sun and of flames kindled by royal hands—they themselves tied to stakes, awaiting the fire, in their innocence fabricating sins for themselves and calling their tortures punishment, solely in order that their God might remain a God whose justice is unquestioned.—And back of these ancestors, a people which did not beg for grace but wrestled fiercely for the blessing of its Deity, a people wandering through seas, unhindered by deserts, always as aware of a God of Justice as of the blood in its veins, calling its victory God's victory, its defeat God's judgment, selecting for itself the rôle of witness to God's power, a people of saviors, anointed for thorns and chosen for pain. And slowly releasing their God from sacrifices and burnt-offerings, these ancestors raised him high above their heads until he stood beyond all transitory suns and worlds, no longer a warrior God of herdsmen, but a guardian of all right, invisible, irradiating all.—And of their blood was he."

Beer-Hofmann's discovery of the supreme value of his ancestral heritage has led him to become immersed in the severe traditions of the Old Testament prophets. Biblical sparks kindle his poetic imagination. He writes religious dramas, which delve into the fundamental question of Israel's relation to God and man and which bring new courage to his down-hearted coreligionists.

Beer-Hofmann's soul is healthy. The duality—German and Jew—which troubled so many of his contemporaries does not trouble him. His plays deal with universal themes and are addressed to readers and auditors as human beings, irrespective of boundary lines or racial, religious, and national divisions. German is the medium of his expression, and it becomes in his hands a musical instrument of delicate fiber. Austrian is the atmosphere he breathes, and it is laden with the sweet melancholy of the Danubian landscape and the fragrance of the Salzkammergut with its green lakes, white-foaming brooks, gentle hills, and snow-covered mountains. So strong is the hold of this Austrian atmosphere upon his soul that even in his last biblical drama, ***Der junge David,*** the Palestinian scene is infused with the aroma wafted from the land of his birth. Jewish is, however, the philosophy he expounds. The wisdom he brings to modern man is a wisdom reminiscent of the ancient prophets, whose spirit interpenetrates both the Old and the New Testaments and whose approach to life has long since become the common property of mankind. Although Beer-Hofmann uses subjects selected from widely different sources, he attains his best effects as an artist with material from the Jewish Bible.

Just as Goethe gave to the Germans, in the character of Faust, the best symbol of their longing and aspiration, so Beer-Hofmann saw in the biblical figure of David the symbolic personification of the Jewish soul in all its contradictory moods. He therefore projected a trilogy centering about this legendary character. Furthermore, even as Goethe's philosophic drama is preceded by a prologue in heaven, in which God and the archangels speak, so likewise Beer-Hofmann composed a dramatic prelude, entitled ***Jacob's Dream,*** in which Jacob, the ancestor of David, holds converse with God and the angels.

Two biblical episodes are selected to form the plot of ***Jacob's Dream***. The first is the conflict between the brothers Jacob and Edom which resulted from the former's stealing of the parental blessing. The second is Jacob's vision during the memorable night at Beth-El when he made his covenant with God.

The two brothers are conceived as two contrasting figures, representatives of opposing fates. Both are, however, placed in a sympathetic light and their struggle is all the more pathetic since it is preordained and inevitable. Edom, the foe of Jacob, is not a wild pogrom chieftain, but rather the proud ancestor of kings and no less necessary in the universal order than his gentler brother, the dreamer of mystic dreams. Edom is the practical son. His feet are firmly planted on the earth. His glance surveys with pride his fields and flocks. Before his arrows the wild animals fall as booty and at his command slaves gather corn and honey and wine and oil. Nor does he fail to give his tithe to God or to obey unquestioningly the religious precepts of his tribe. Jacob, on the other hand, is the eternal seeker, the eternal doubter, hounded by visions of unearthy spheres and afflicted with overmuch sympathy. Man and beast, the very stones about him and the brooks below him moan their pain to him, and their suffering reverberates in his compassionate breast. The blessing of Abraham was meant for the offspring who bears so heavy a burden and not for his contented brother. Isaac, Abraham's son, would have preferred to hand down the family blessing to Edom, the powerful hunter; but Rebecca, interpreting correctly the spirit of the ancestors, substituted Jacob for Edom, and thus Jacob became the bearer of the fate decreed for the children of Abraham.

The drama takes place on the morning and evening after this memorable event. In Beer-Sheba, on the edge of the wilderness, the house of Isaac lies bathed in pale moonlight. Shamartu, the slave of Edom, crouches on the wall and looks out into the distance awaiting his master. Below him slumber Basmath and Oholibamah, the wives of Edom, strange women from the tribes of Hitti and Hori. The gray silence of dawn is broken by the whispered questions of the awakening Basmath, who hours earlier had sent a messenger to inform Edom of Jacob's theft of the parental blessing and who was now eagerly awaiting her husband's return. If only Edom would leave the hunt and hasten back! For Jacob was fleeing from Canaan and might escape to Laban at Haran before the hand of the avenging brother could overtake him. Again and again Basmath's sharp questions cut through the cold, cruel dawn: Edom? Edom? Finally, the long awaited hunter bursts upon the scene, foaming with anger. He seeks to make his way to his father, but already he is too late. Isaac is resting under the wings of the angel of death. Jacob must be reached and destroyed, if the effect of the blessing is to be undone. Rebecca, fearing for her favorite son, hurls herself in Edom's path, promising him all that his heart desires, absolute rule over the household, over slaves and cattle and land, if only he will leave Jacob the ancestral blessing. "You, my Edom, are sated with possession and food and drink and sleep and women, what need have you of the blessing? Your joy flourishes on earth. Take your earthly heritage." When Edom insists on knowing why Jacob was preferred, Rebecca proudly answers that Jacob was chosen "because he walks about full of mysterious questions, hearing within himself the doubts, dreams, longings, and imperative voices of his ancestors, while you rejoice in your certain knowledge and satiety; because he does not entomb his God in distant heavens as you do, but wrestles with Him day by day and breast to breast; because he does not hunt and sacrifice and murder as you do, but rather pales in the presence of all suffering creatures and speaks to all of them as they to him. That is why the blessing is his—and also the burden of the blessing." At these words Edom rushes forth in rage. He has sworn not to eat or drink until he has seen Jacob's blood before him. The dogs have picked up the trail and will guide him unerringly to the fugitive.

The day is drawing to an end. Jacob in his hurried flight has reached a cliff, afterwards called Beth-El, and here he prepares to camp for the night. His sole companion on the height is Idnibaal, who for forty years has faithfully served Isaac and whom Rebecca has sent along as the guardian of her favorite son. Master and slave speak in hushed tones of the mysterious land stretching below them towards the west. There lies the once prosperous city of Ajath, now a mass of ruins, its proud kings and their prouder conquerors faded from the memory of the living. Beyond the horizon lies Jerusalem, the citadel of the Jebusites, the future capital of David's realm. The entire land has been promised by God to the seed of Abraham. Jacob, however, has no desire for its possession. He does not want to carve out for himself a kingdom on this earth, comparable to those already in existence. "The Hitti, the Perizzi, and the Kadmoni are disputing the watering places and the pastures, the Kenaani hold the seaports, the Keni occupy the fortified heights, and all these childish struggles will last only as long as the mighty powers, Egypt, Babylon, and Phoenicia tolerate them." Surely it was not to such temporal rule that God referred when he blessed Abraham! From Jacob's lips stream words of kindness and of understanding. He who has just fled from home and who is threatened by danger and death now becomes vividly conscious of the pain of his own servant, who also was once torn from a native home and compelled for decades to obey a foreigner's commands. Jacob speaks to Idnibaal of home and love and fate. Then, having conversed with him as an equal, he can no longer look upon him as a slave and therefore sets him free. The liberated Idnibaal thereupon invokes the blessings of the gods upon the gentle, sympathetic youth and then descends from the hill.

In the nebulous light of the fast gathering dusk, the figure of Edom becomes visible. The two brothers are alone on the hill, the one prepared to kill and the other unwilling even to resist. With masterful skill the dramatist resolves their enmity into friendship, closing the scene with the rite of blood-brotherhood. This rite is to affirm the necessity of the eternal survival of both types, the unproblematic hero and the tormented dreamer, the successful man of affairs and the impractical poet. When Edom asks whether his brother regards him as in any way inferior because he finds his complete satisfaction on earth, Jacob answers in simple words that supply the solution to the entire conflict: "No! God needs me as I am, and He needs you otherwise! Only because you are Edom may I be Jacob!" Every people is a chosen people, but each is chosen in a different way and experiences a different fate. All beings are equally necessary to God and all live as they must.

Edom has disappeared in the evening mist. Jacob falls asleep and in his slumber he hears about him the voices of nature grown articulate. The brook murmurs to him and the stone whereon he lies sings of its longing and pain. Angels descend from the clouds and the presence of God fills the air. In this awe-inspiring hour, Jacob seeks an answer to the riddle of existence, seeks to discover the reason for the apparent necessity of suffering in this world. When the archangels repeat God's promise that to the offspring of Abraham will be given the fat of the earth, the dew of the heavens, corn, wine, and the cities of men, he proudly rejects their gifts and releases God from His promise. Such riches may make a person like Edom happy but not one like Jacob. "Is my blood good for nothing better than for kings?" he asks. "I do not want dominion! Doesn't God know it? Does He really think I am envious of Egypt, Babylon, or the Princes by the sea? I envy no one. I don't even envy you, archangels, your blessedness. Could I be blessed when all suffer, when all approach me by day and night, when man and beast and herb and stone moan to me with mute eyes, imploring an answer of me?" Jacob feels called upon to supply God's answer to all questions. He wants to act as God's emissary and mouthpiece. An archangel tells him that this wish may be granted. Long after Egypt shall have passed away and Babylon disappeared, the seed of Jacob will continue to wander on earth, an eternal miracle of God's eternal world. "The mighty nations will turn to dust and be blown away as dust. You alone will die a thousand deaths and will a thousand times re-arise from the dead." In a magnificent poetic vision, the Archangel Michael reveals to Jacob the future of his offspring, a people who will bear God's message to the nations and who will be the measure of all faith, hope, and pain. Samael, the angel of darkness, a defiant figure resembling Milton's Lucifer, warns Jacob against accepting such a destiny. "It is true that others will bow to your testimony, but they'll beat the mouth bloody that pronounced it. It is true that you may wander eternally. But rest? Never! And home? A word without meaning for you! Yours will be a people from which all fetch booty. To sin against you? Whom is it not permitted? . . . Every people to which you attach yourself will burn you out like a cancer. You, the beloved of God, will be hated more than a poisonous plant or a mad beast! . . . You fool, chosen to be God's whippingpost! . . . He sacrifices you. He needs you as an unbribable witness to whom He can point. Who will doubt, if you, bleeding and downtrodden, still praise Him as a just God!" Jacob, however, cannot leave God. He accepts the rôle of the Lord's chosen one with all its blessing and all its horror. Trusting in his strength, pride, and patience, Jacob is ready to help bear God's burden. Amid the wrangling of the archangels, the voice of the Lord is heard: "For my sake you may suffer unheard of pain and yet amidst tortures know that I never cast you off! I want to be so heavily indebted to you, O my son, that as atonement I may raise you up beyond all others."

Jacob's pain is his patent of nobility, the cause of his greatness and the source of his pride. Nations, weakened by excessive wealth and luxury, decay and disappear; but the sons of Jacob, whipped by ever new suffering, rise to ever new heights. And if ever they tire of their mission and are in danger of succumbing to misfortune, then new leaders arise to remind them of their rôle as God's witnesses on earth. In ages overwhelmed by materialistic ambitions, messianic heroes, such as Moses, Isaiah, Jesus, Spinoza, Herzl, born of Jacob's blood, proclaim the Jew's spiritual mission. In our day of Jewish martyrdom and deepening gloom, poets of hope are necessary to reawaken the will to live among the hundreds of thousands scattered along the world's highways. Beer-Hofmann aids in this task with his artistic apotheosis of the Jewish people.

Jacob's Dream, completed in 1915, during the First World War, was followed by ***Young David,*** completed in 1933, the year which witnessed the rise to power of Adolf Hitler. The burden, which God designed for the anointed and which Jacob once voluntarily took upon himself, David is again called upon to assume during the play.

The opening act takes place near the grave of Rachel, the wife of Jacob. The crossroads are alive with groups of people that come and go. Abiathar, the sole survivor of the priests of Nob who have been murdered by Saul, asks questions about Rachel and Ruth and David, about God's omnipotence and its limitations, about God's eternal justice and his apparent injustice in permitting the murder of the innocent priests of Nob. If mortals can supply no answer, Abiathar will demand one of God. But can heaven's reply be meaningful to him? "God's days are not the days of man. God measures with a different measure, and in distant days perhaps an astounded offspring hears and hardly comprehends God's answer to a question which an ancestor, moaning in pain and wild woe, once asked of heaven." May it not therefore be best for us, storm-tossed creatures, to seek a humble refuge in faith, since absolute knowledge is unattainable?

Through doubt to faith is the process by which Beer-Hofmann's characters are stabilized and matured. Abiathar's questioning of God's ways is a necessary step in his evolution as priest and religious leader. In the drama it serves as a prelude to David's more searching scepticism, which is an essential phase of his training before he can be fit for the assumption of royal power.

The testing of David forms the climax of the drama. In the war between Israel and the Philistines, he has to take sides and finds himself in a cruel dilemma. As the vassal of Achish of Gath, he receives the command to report at the Philistine headquarters in order to join in the campaign against Israel. To disobey this command would necessitate the breaking of his oath of allegiance, an impossibility for a person of his loyal temperament. And even if he could break his oath, who would ever trust him thereafter? What friend or foe would ever regard as sacred an agreement with a person who in a critical hour was himself unfaithful to his liege lord? But, on the other hand, how could he, the anointed of his people, the national hero of Israel, assist in the slaughter of his own kinsmen and in the destruction of his own future realm?

The resolution of this dilemma is the principal theme of the stirring fourth act of the drama. Since David has sworn allegiance to the Philistines, thereby unwittingly tying the strangling noose about his neck, he must under all circumstances keep his oath until released. He will therefore go to King Achish of Gath, even though this step probably means his death. His men, however, have sworn allegiance only to him personally, only to David of Bethlehem. He will release them of their pledge. They will then be free to go to the assistance of Saul's forces and to defend their fatherland against hostile invasion. The cunning and unprincipled Achitophel warns David against setting out to certain doom. "Why do you go?" he asks in ill-concealed chagrin. "Because faith and loyalty must be maintained!" answers David. "Faith—Loyalty! They are but two words! Don't take them so seriously!" interposes the diplomat. "Merely two words, it is true—but on these the world rests!" replies David. The tragic consequences of this final decision are, however, averted at the very last moment by the arrival of a messenger from the Philistines, dispensing with David's services on the ground that it would be too dangerous to have in the Philistine ranks an ally who was a potential foe. Relieved of his bondage to the enemies of Israel, David can now follow the call of his own people. He decides to aid Saul, though this may mean forfeiting all personal ambition for the throne. But already it is too late. The battle between Saul and the Philistines is fought and lost at Gilboa before David's men can arrive.

After the death of Saul and his sons, all hopes of the Hebrews are concentrated on David as the sole possible savior. Before he assumes the crown, however, he passes through profound tragedy in the loss of Maacha, his beloved wife, and realizes that he must renounce all thoughts of personal happiness if he is to be a blessing for others. His guardian ancestress, Ruth, who ushered in the play and who appeared at the climax in order to admonish him to be faithful to his truest self, now reappears at the end to encourage him to take on the responsible burden assigned to him by a superior power. In reply to his painful question: "What is to become of me now?" she calmly offers these words of wisdom: "What ultimately becomes of all of us: dung of the earth. Perhaps a song—this, too, is soon wafted away. And yet, until then, David, you must, like God's stars, complete your designated orbit, neither more eternal nor more transitory than they."

The blessing and the burden of the blessing, which was once accepted by Jacob at Beth-El, is bequeathed by Ruth to David. As the standard-bearer of the Jewish fate, David will now undertake his task. This task is outlined by him to his followers in language reminiscent of ***Jacob's Dream***. He does not want to fashion another empire comparable to Egypt or Babylon, an empire based on force and lasting only until overthrown by a mightier force. All he desires is a peaceful breathing-spell until he can implant among his people the seed of a new faith and until a generation can grow up which does not speak in terms of territorial expansion or enslavement of neighbors, but which, on the contrary, is unhappy if it knows others to be in pain, which cannot breathe if oppression exists in its midst, which does not throw itself away on such vain objectives as splendor or domination. Even as it does not pay for an individual to live merely for himself, so too it does not pay for a people to think solely of its own aggrandizement.

Through the mouth of David, Beer-Hofmann voices his opposition to the ultra-nationalism rampant in recent years. He is sickened by the excessive brutality of his time. He refuses to be a party to the racial conceit flourishing all about him. He is a Jew and holds that the Jews are primarily a community of fate rather than a race or a religion. Few scientists, outside of the Nazi fold, believe nowadays in purity of races, nor do religious observances form an essential part of Jewish daily life in the present generation. The Jews, Beer-Hofmann insists, are a historical community held together, on the one hand, by the acceptance of certain doctrines enunciated by their prophets from Hosea and Amos and Isaiah up to the present day, and, on the other hand, by the refusal of the majority population in every country to accept such doctrines, a refusal backed up by anti-Semitic measures, from social ostracism in the most cultured lands to pogroms and mass murder in less civilized states. The Jews, Beer-Hofmann claims, not only believe, for example, that it is better to be killed than to kill, to suffer injustice than to commit injustice, but they prove, by their continued existence down the millenniums, that nonresistance has greater survival value than the mightiest of armies or the strongest of navies. All empires of ancient days, which were based on force, have crumbled and disappeared, but the Jews still live on as an eternal rebuke to the nations that rely on the power of the sword, and will continue to exist until these nations grow tired of bloodshed and accept the message of peace and justice. Then perhaps there will no longer be any necessity for the existence of the Jews as a separate entity, because the faith of which they are the bearers will have become the faith of all men. Therein Beer-Hofmann echoes sentiments of biblical days, sentiments voiced by the prophet Isaiah in verses which the contemporary poet accepted as the motto for his religious play: "Yea, He saith: It is too light a thing that thou shouldst be My servant to raise up the tribes of Jacob, and to restore the offspring of Israel; I will also appoint thee for a light of the nations, that My salvation may be unto the end of the earth. Thus saith the Lord, the Redeemer of Israel, his Holy One, to him who is despised of men, to him who is abhorred of nations, to a servant of rulers: Kings shall see and arise, princes, and they shall prostrate themselves; because of the Lord that is faithful, even the Holy One of Israel, who hath chosen thee."

Erich Kahler (essay date 1946)

SOURCE: "Richard Beer-Hofmann," in *Commentary*, Vol. 1, No. 6, April, 1946, pp. 45-50.

[*In the following excerpt, Kahler discusses the religious themes in Beer-Hofmann's work.*]

Beer-Hofmann's first great book, ***Der Tod Georgs*** (***The Death of George***), published in 1900, has for its theme the chain of reflections that a friend's death gives rise to in a young man; death reveals to him the nature of life, of his own life and human life in general. "George was dead to him. Yet all searching into George's possible fate had only been an anxious questioning of his own. . . . Much of his own anguish and confusion had been tranquillized by verbalization; so that he had disburdened himself of his own restless and questioning thoughts by casting them upon George, whence they echoed back in altered form, strange only as some favorite song is that we sang just a moment ago, and which now returns to us familiarly from sounding strings in the distance . . . he had sought only himself in everything and had found only himself in everything. It was his fate alone that was realized, and whatever else happened, happened far away, as if on a stage, as though performed, and when it told of others it seemed only to tell of himself; it was worth only what it was able to yield him personally: dread and compassion and a fleeting smile. He had arrogantly kept himself apart from those others who performed for him. He had never imagined that life—a strong master—would some day come from behind and take hold of him and command, threateningly: 'Play your part!' "

What dawns upon the meditative youth is the recognition of how infinitely connected man is with everything around him, with everything out of which he comes and into which he passes; it is an involuntary, ineluctable connection imposed by the laws of an all-embracing fate. "No one may live his life only for himself. He spoke; and a wind seized his words, carried them off and deposited them in a stranger's being; there they took seed and grew up, bursting their vessel apart perhaps and dowering it perhaps with a rich harvest of blessings. . . . His life did not fade away like an isolated sound in the void. Swallowed up in an immense orbit measured and solemnal since primordial time, his life went forward, vibrating to the all-pervading clangor of eternal laws. He could meet no injustice, suffering implied no slight, and death was not all-dividing. For, linked as he was with everything-necessary and indispensable to everything-every action was perhaps a trust, suffering was perhaps a dignity, and death perhaps a mission. . . . He who divined this was able to walk through life a just man; not lost in self-contemplation but with his glance directed into the distance, still clear-eyed in old age, ready to wonder like a child. His body and soul were preserved for him like a holy thing, his feet sure, not mired with blood and dirt. A wall stood to his left and right wherever he passed. Fear was unknown; for wherever he struck—whether on things dumber than stone—right spouted forth for him like gushing water and justice like an inexhaustible stream."

The man Beer-Hofmann emerges from these lines in all his shining self-certainty and with the limitations that came from his inherited sense of detachment; in all his piety toward fate—which confirmed him in his own essence—and in all his aloofness from active participation in the turbulence of our world. This aloofness from the world was implied in his very connection with the world, a passive, innate connection enjoined merely by his being the one he was and, more particularly still, by his being a poet—by the supra-historical relation to the world which is inherent in the creation of art.

The sway of fate in private entanglements—between father and son, man and wife—was again and again shown in his dramas and his verse. ***Der Graf von Charolais*** (***The Count of Charolais***) is a modern tragedy of fate. A specific, supra-individual, communal relationship, however, emerges from the personal complex and comes gradually to fill the entire reach of Beer-Hofmann's work—his relationship to Judaism.

This relationship to Judaism also sprang from a very personal source: from pride in and reverence for his ancestors. His immediate progenitors, his family in all its branches, were already ever present to him through pictures, souvenirs and anecdotes. He deeply enjoyed the comfortable feeling that he stemmed from a group of superior and cultivated individuals. Very early, however, he passed beyond that into a more comprehensive awareness of his common ancestry—an ancestry formed by the exceptional people to which he belonged.

It may be that in the beginning it was simply defiant bravado that moved him to concentrate on the Jewish destiny—the defiance of a proud man who wishes to acknowledge with unmistakable emphasis an affiliation that in the social circles of that generation, Christian and Jewish alike, was passed over in embarrassed silence, where it was not entirely suppressed. This was the era in which it was thought possible to obscure the existence of Jewry by social exclusion on one side and complete self-betrayal on the other. To be sure, this period saw the first steps in the direction of active Zionism, but there was hardly a perceptible influence in the atmosphere and immediate surroundings in which young Beer-Hofmann grew up that might have stimulated him to put any stress on Judaism. In any case, it was by way of this acknowledgment of his Jewishness that he gradually arrived at the kernel substance of his whole work. It became the most profound interpretation of the Jewish idea in post-biblical poetry.

In the famous **"Schlaflied für Miriam"** (**"Lullaby for Miriam"**) written in 1891, the peculiar antinomy that marked his entire existence was expressed: his feeling of aloneness on one side, and his subterranean, existential sense of connection with the world on the other. This connection is felt here in a very definite respect—it is with the community of his ancestors:

Blinde—so gehn wir und gehen allein,
Keiner kann Keinem Gefährte hier sein . . .
Was ich gewonnen, gräbt mit mir man ein,
Keiner kann Keinem ein Erbe hier sein.

(Blind—so we go, and go alone,
No one has anyone for comrade here. . . .
What I have won is buried with me,
No one is heir to anyone here.)

And yet:

Blut von Gewesenen—zu Kommenden
rollts,
Blut unserer Väter, voll Unruh und Stolz.
In uns sind *Alle.* Wer fühlt sich allein? . .
Du bist ihr Leben—ihr Leben ist dein. . . .

(Blood of those who were flows to those
who are to be,
Blood of our fathers, full of unrest and
pride.
In us are *all.* Who feels himself alone?
Thou art their life and their life is
thine. . . .)

The decisive experience in ***Der Tod Georgs*** is the acknowledgment of the antinomy. It is this toward which George's complex feelings and reflections on the death of his friend lead. The book culminates not only in the celebration of his ancestors and in the comfort and security derived from the sense of a unity of generations that defies time and death; there also emerges the specific, missionary idea of the generations of Jews outlasting time and death: " . . . bound to the stake, awaiting the flames, innocent yet inventing sins for themselves, calling their torments 'punishment,' only that their God might remain an unquestioned and all-righteous one . . . just as much imbued at all times with their feeling of the righteousness of God as with the blood in their veins: their victories were God's victory, their defeats, God's judgment; self-appointed witnesses of his might, a nation of saviors, anointed for thorns and chosen to suffer."

This idea—the assumption by humans of the guilt of God—was for Beer-Hofmann the core of Judaism, of a Judaism that was one with primitive Christianity.

Israel offers itself as a sacrifice so that God may be faultlessly perfect, so that the principle of perfection and justice may prevail in the world, realize itself and triumph. This is the basic theme developed with extraordinary luxuriance and an oriental profusion of decorative motif in Beer-Hofmann's two Biblical dramas, ***Jaákobs Traum*** (1918) and ***Der Junge David*** (1933).

In ***Jaákobs Traum*** (***Jacob's Dream***), his greatest work, this idea is most purely expressed. Its profound dialectic between heaven and earth, and body and soul, is variously inflected: in the contrast of the earthly to the heavenly world; on earth itself, in the contrast of the worldly to the spiritual type of man (Edom and Jacob); and on the heavenly plane, in the contrast of the rebel angel Samáel, "King of the Earth," to the archangels who are the agents of God. The "Prologue in Heaven" is in this respect the core of the entire pray. The dialectics is finally concentrated in Jacob himself, in the resistance he offers to the mediatorship thrust upon him from below as well as from above by the powers of the earth, springs and stones, who unburden their sorrows upon him, and by God, who also needs an "eternal spokesman and surrogate" here below—or, as Samáel puts it, "a chosen whippingboy."

An Deinem Dulderleibe peitscht Er ewig
Sein Gottum allen andern Völkern ein. . . .
Ihn schaudert vor der Qual, die Er erschaffen,
Dich braucht Er, dass Du—gläubig durch die Zeiten
Dich schleppend—allen Völkern rings verkündest,
Schuldlos sei Er—und Strafe alles Leid!

(On thy patient body does He forever whip
His divinity into all other nations. . . .
He trembles before the torment he has caused.
He needs thee, gullibly dragging thyself through the ages,
That thou mayest inform all peoples roundabout
That He is innocent—and suffering is but merited punishment.)

Yet God prevails through his superior strength. The dialectic is resolved, or rather it is made corporeal and organic in Israel, the victim chosen for sacrifice, who arose from Jacob's dream-struggles.

The second work, ***Der Junge David*** (***The Young David***), takes place entirely within the earthly sphere and is provided—even weighed down—with an overflowing abundance of ethnic-historical themes. There are two points on which the drama hinges: the first part, dealing with the downfall of Saul and David's rise, revolves about the problem of blessedness, a problem which Thomas Mann plumbed in an entirely different way in his Joseph figure.

Grace—in the mundane sphere—is first of all magic, "glamor," charm of body and being, overflowing vitality that draws people effortlessly, blandishingly subdues them. Thus did the boy David win over the melancholy old king, thus did the youth win over the king's son, daughter, dependents and the people of Judah, who then elevated him to leader in the uprising against Saul, the ruler who came from the rival tribe of Benjamin.

Grace, however, is more than the gift of involuntary effect. It proclaims itself first of all in the manner in which a man makes use of and controls his effect. Grace is also illumination, knowledge—but not indeed that most extreme clarity of consciousness which destroys certainty and makes one's course difficult. Grace is what the Greeks called kairos, that instinct for the right step at the right time, for going along with the rhythm of external events so as always to keep on top. Everything that happens to one, even occasional misfortune, turns in the end to one's advantage—that is, develops according to the logic of one's own existence. Accordingly, grace is also an attitude of command, it is dignity, the gift of never being compromised by events.

And finally, grace is luck, the conjunction and happy confluence of the inner with the outer, in which one cannot determine to what extent circumstance is responsible and to what extent the mastery which exploits circumstance; for the one enhances the other.

Richard Beer-Hofmann wrote very little—one novel, two plays, a *Theatrical Prologue to King David,* a thin volume of verse, and the autobiographical fragment *Paula*—yet the world is greatly in his debt.

—Erich Kahler

David flees from Saul's jealous persecution to the Philistines and becomes the vassal of their king. Afterwards, when he has been raised to the leadership of Judah, Saul's war against the Philistines faces him with the alternative of violating his oath to the Philistine king or betraying his people and hereditary ruler. Loyalty and honor stand in the balance. They are rescued when the Philistine king himself rejects him and absolves him from his bond of fealty. David joins forces unconditionally with Israel's ruler. Saul still hates him but David is once again saved when the king falls in battle together with Jonathan, his heir apparent. David's way to the crown lies clear.

But now, in the second part of the play, the idea of grace veers back to the fundamental theme of ***Jaákobs Traum***. The reverse side of grace is revealed: its heavy obligation, its burden, its election for sacrifice. David symbolizes in the sphere of earthly majesty a second stage in Israel's destiny. The loss of his beloved wife, Maácha, has struck him to the core. He longs to retreat to his private life. He longs to refuse the crown and spurn all distinction—"A wounded animal is permitted to crawl off!" They do not let him. Like Jacob's mission, the kingship is thrust on him from below by the people and the army, from above by God through the priests and prophets and his ancestress, Ruth. A nameless old man in the crowd reproaches him:

> Hier stehen hundert Jahre deines Volks—
> Kein einziges ruhevoll, verstört ein jedes
> Von Plünderung, Brand, verschleppten Frauen, Kindern—
> Hier knieen hundert Jahre Bangen, Hoffen—
> Jagst du sie fort—weil heut dir Weh geschah?! . . .
> Du bist nicht dein!—ein Volk hat dich erträumt!—
> Erschaffen aus der Sehnsucht von Geschlechtern,
> Steigst du aus ihrem Traum. . . .
> Die Heimat rief dich, eh du warst—sie ruft dich—
> Lass deine Heimat, David, nicht allein!
>
> (A hundred years of thy nation stand before thee,
> No single one peaceful, each disturbed
> By rapine, arson, by women and children carried away.
> Here kneel one hundred years of fears and hopes—
> Dost thou drive them forth because thou hast suffered a hurt today? . . .
> Thou art not of thy own possessing. A Nation conjured thee forth!
> Created out of the longing of generations,
> Thou risest from their dreams . . .
> Thy native land called to thee ere thou wert—she calls to thee now.
> Abandon not your home, David!)

And Ruth, his ancestress, implores God:

> Herr, sieh: dies Herz klafft wund und will verbluten—
> Still du die Wunde, doch lass offen stehen
> Dies Herz. . . .
>
> Er ist erwählt!—so wird er einmal klagen:
> Wo blieb der Segen—welches Glück ward mein?!'
> Lass damn ihn ahnen: Uber allen Segen
> Thront noch ein Segen: Andern Segen sein!
>
> ("See, Lord: this heart gapes wounded and would bleed to death.
> Still thou the wound, but let this heart stay open. . . .
> He is chosen! And some day he will complain:
> 'What of the blessing—what good fortune was mine?'
> Let him then guess it: above all blessings
> One higher blessing is still enthroned:
> to be a blessing to others!")

Richard Beer-Hofmann wrote very little—one novel, two plays, a ***Theatrical Prologue to King David,*** a thin volume of verse, and the autobiographical fragment ***Paula***—yet the world is greatly in his debt.

The work of his youth, the novel ***Der Tod Georgs,*** though its colors may be somewhat faded and its atmosphere of fastidious self-indulgence no longer accord with our tougher conception of life, retains historically an important significance. It inaugurated a new form of narrative, the interior monologue, and in so doing introduced into fiction a new dimension of time. Time is no longer bound by the absolute measure of external events. Time becomes the subjective-relative extension of inner experience, capable of infinite prolongation, even into timelessness itself.

Der Tod Georgs is the first book of this kind and stands at the beginning of a line of development marked out by Proust, Joyce, Kafka, Virginia Woolf and Hermann Broch.

Beer-Hofmann's Biblical plays, apart from their poetic beauty, have exercised a special human influence in that they have confronted both the Jews and the rest of the world with the unique meaning and the historical role of Israel. Above all, they have given the Jews inestimable comfort in their terrible distress, and a message of cheer: the doctrine of their exalted legitimacy, which helps them rise above their sufferings. They have indicated the proper attitude for Jews: an attitude of dignity, pride and inner raptness. The pride of a wise humility that cleaves through all humiliation. The pride of an outlook that takes in different ages, different worlds and different experiences. The pride of a spiritual immunity gained through inner experience. And the pride, finally, of a people that from remotest antiquity has put the idea of justice and perfection above all else.

And Beer-Hofmann, the man, in his own person taught this doctrine of dignity and pride. And it did one good to see Judaism represented for once in the figure of a princely person. Much of his own Charolais, that fierce, uncompromising and impulsive knight, was in him, but much more of his David.

All those who met him will continue to see him before them—handsome and strong with his powerful buffalo's head (about which there was something of a Jovian disguise) and his self-confident and even imperious step; yet also the sweetness of his smile, the irresistible cheerfulness of his greeting. He exuded happiness, the beneficence of happiness and the inner security that happiness bestows. "His body and soul were preserved for him like an holy thing, his feet sure, not mired with blood and dirt. . . ."

Whatever his limitations, one had to love him with all the *défauts de ses vertus.* He was a great sheik, childlike, knowing and infinitely wise, "still clear-eyed in old age, ready to wonder," full of wilfulness, caprice and grace.

Stephen Spender (essay date 1948)

SOURCE: "A Heroic Drama," in *Commentary,* Vol. 5, No. 1, January, 1948, pp. 87-8.

[*In the following essay, Spender discusses the revival of interest in poetic dramas and favorably reviews* Jacob's Dream.]

Recent years have seen a revival of interest in the poetic drama. Although it cannot be said that the poetic form has achieved significant victories in the theater, it may be claimed that the modern poet can only express certain ideas in dramatic form and that some of the most important poetry written in this century has, in fact, been dramatic. That important poems should be written which depend for their realization on a theater which cannot interpret them adequately, is an unsatisfactory situation. Nevertheless this should not lead us to ignore the fact that some of the most effective poetic statements of our time have been made in the poetic plays of Claudel, *The Dynasts* of Thomas Hardy, *Murder in the Cathedral* of T. S. Eliot, *Der Turm* of Hofmannsthal, and in ***Jacob's Dream*** of Beer-Hofmann.

It is significant also that four plays by poets expressing ideas so different as Hardy in *The Dynasts,* Claudel in *L'Annonce Faite à Marie,* Eliot in *Murder in the Cathedral,* and Beer-Hofmann in ***Jacob's Dream,*** should yet have most important characteristics in common. All these plays are concerned with man in relation to the historic human destiny within the universe, and all emphasize the inevitability of suffering of the most extreme kind if redemption is to be possible. They are all, in their different ways, religious statements, and they are "tragic statements" rather than tragedies because they emphasize tragedy as the human condition, beside which the actual conflicts which result in suffering have only secondary importance.

The Jewish attitude to experience (that of a very old race), as expressed by Beer-Hofmann, has more in common with Hardy's fatalism than with the Christian mysticism of Claudel or Eliot. To both Hardy and Beer-Hofmann, there is a sense of the guilt of the creative forces of the universe towards man as well as of man towards God and his fellowman. In Hardy, man is the victim of forces predominantly malicious, projections of his own spirit which, weighing the scale of human destiny towards the sinister and evil, form a kind of democracy of the whole human spiritual life in which the bad forces are almost certain always to form a parliamentary majority. In Beer-Hofmann men are victims of their own personalities and God has guilt in having created men as they are—a point of view very similar to Hardy's.

These four plays must be described as "successful" quite apart from any success they might have on the stage, because it is impossible to imagine the human drama, invented on so large a scale, being created in any other form for our time than in a dramatic and poetic one. Only poetry—or a prose which borrows imagistic effects from poetry—can concentrate into a small space of action such widely diffused material drawn from the history of races and the distances between heaven and earth.

I have never seen ***Jacob's Dream*** performed (indeed I have only read it recently). Apparently it attracted large audiences in Berlin and Vienna before the time of Hitler. I can imagine people being deeply moved by it, as by an impressive religious ceremony, but it is not, by ordinary standards, good theater. The action, indeed, does not so much develop, as unfold and open into a vision that entirely dwarfs what would seem to be its natural center—the rivalry between Jacob and his brother Edom. The first act is concerned with Jacob receiving from Isaac on his deathbed the blessing that should be bestowed upon his brother Edom. This act is the tragedy of Rachel, torn between Edom's wrath, succeeded by the translucent wave of Jacob's vision. Rachel is submerged by the new emotion of the second act between her love for her two sons, seeking to appease Edom by offering him the whole inheritance of Isaac if he will renounce vengeance on Jacob for having stolen the blessing. The next act is the story of Jacob turning Edom from his wrath by gentleness, and the last act shows us Jacob alone with the angels.

This scenario has little unity of action. It is like a succession of three waves: the wave of Rachel's passion succeeded by the wave of the two brothers, and Edom is submerged by Jacob's vision. There is no real conflict between the characters: or, rather, the conflict is with a protagonist who does not appear—God.

At the same time, poetically, a wonderful unity of growth is achieved: of passion leading to reconciliation and reconciliation to supreme vision.

There is a beauty of invention in, for example, the conversation between the spring which flows at Jacob's feet and the stone pillow supporting his head, which recalls the spiritual fantasy of Shelley in *Prometheus Unbound* and perhaps also certain passages in James Joyce's *Finnegan's Wake.* Even in translation (and Ida Bension Wynn's translation is a model of its kind) the language rises easily to the heights demanded of it when the angels appear. And perhaps the strength of the play does not lie so much in the language itself as in the remarkable conviction of the dignity and nobility of life which enables Beer-Hofmann to inhabit a world where the Old Testament with its patriarchs and its angels is as real as the landscape of the Promised Land. The dramatic action which creates for us the distress of Rachel, the wrath of Edom, the reconciliation of the brothers, and the vision of Jacob has a sculptural quality resembling a procession of figures belonging to a nobler age portrayed on a marble frieze.

No poem could be more profoundly encouraging and heroic than this play which reminds us inescapably of the grandeur of man's tasks in life.

Esther Elstun (essay date 1979)

SOURCE: "Richard Beer-Hofmann: The Poet as *exculpator dei,*" in *Protest—Form—Tradition,* The University of Alabama Press, 1979, pp. 123-31.

[*In the following essay, Elstun discusses the effects of exile on Beer-Hofmann's later work, particularly* Paula, ein Fragment.]

The external facts of Richard Beer-Hofmann's exile can be recounted in a few brief sentences. On the evening of August 19, 1939, after a year of hiding, he and his wife

Paula left Vienna for the last time, en route to the United States via Switzerland. Beer-Hofmann was seventy-three years old; his wife, sixty. She was still convalescing from the near-fatal heart attack she had had the preceding winter; consequently they were traveling in slow stages and still in Switzerland when Paula suffered a complete collapse. After weeks in the hospital she died on October 30 and was buried in the Friesenberg Cemetery at Zurich on November 2. Unable to obtain permission to remain in Switzerland, Beer-Hofmann continued the journey alone, arriving in New York on November 23. During the first year and a half of his exile, he and his daughter Mirjam lived in a flat on Waverley Place. In 1941 they moved to an apartment on Cathedral Parkway, which remained Beer-Hofmann's home until his death on September 26, 1945.

Those are the skeletal facts, and there is, of course, much more that could be said. The biographical facts have been related very briefly here so that primary attention could be devoted to an exploration of some philosophical and artistic questions: What effect did exile have on Beer-Hofmann's inner life and thought? Did it alter his view of life and the world? His view of Künstlertum? How did exile affect the literary work he completed between 1940 and 1945?

In order to answer these questions we shall have to look first at Beer-Hofmann's earlier life and work. Quantitatively, his literary production was very sparse indeed: two short stories (**"Camelias"** and **"Das Kind,"** 1893), a novel (***Der Tod Georgs,*** 1900), a five-act play (***Der Graf von Charolais,*** 1904), a cycle of Biblical dramas (***Die Historie von König David***), a dozen or so lyric poems, best known among them the **"Schlaflied für Mirjam,"** a commemorative piece (***Gedenkrede auf Wolfgang Amadé Mozart,*** 1906), and a book of memoirs named for his wife (***Paula, ein Fragment,*** posthumously published in its entirety in 1949). Yet as an arbiter of artistic taste and a friend, confidant, and advisor to others (in particular Hofmannsthal and Schnitzler) Beer-Hofmann was unquestionably the most influential member of that circle of Viennese writers known as "Jung Wien." A study of his early work reveals why that was so: ***Der Tod Georgs*** is probably the most representative Jugendstil novel in the German language, and in it, moreover, Beer-Hofmann employed a narrative technique that no longer startles us, but which was still daringly experimental at the turn of the century—the stream-of-consciousness technique.

Paul, the protagonist of ***Der Tod Georgs,*** is a very typical representative of turn-of-the-century Viennese decadence: he is a young man of impeccable taste, refinement and aesthetic sensibility, also characterized by inordinately delicate nerves and a pervasive kind of tiredness that paralyzes his will to act. Though Paul is preoccupied with death, it would be a mistake to conclude that he wants to die. By the end of Part I, which is very brief, he has already emerged as a young man who wants to live, but aloof from the turmoil, strife, and ugliness of life, in a limbo of the spirit and the senses where he can enjoy aesthetic pleasures undisturbed.

William Eickhorst has said of the decadent heroes portrayed by Austrian writers of the turn of the century that "inevitably they reach the same conclusion—namely, that they have no free will and are mastered by their nerves or life or fate. They have reached the last stage of civilization and there is no tomorrow" [*Decadence in German Fiction*]. Beer-Hofmann's young hero definitely does not conform to this type by the time the novel reaches its conclusion, where the problem of detachment from life versus involvement in it is resolved in favor of involvement—not in vague generalities, but in specific relation to Paul and his future life. For him there is a tomorrow, and it will be very different from his past.

Paul's transformation and ensuing affirmation of life stem from his newly won conviction that the universal order, however unfathomable it may seem, is somehow purposeful, unifying, and abiding. He has traveled a long hard road of doubt and inner anguish to reach this position; once there, he considers the possibility that the universal order is also just. The possibility is first expressed in questions, but they are clearly rhetorical, and in the final pages of the novel Beer-Hofmann has his protagonist come to this conclusion: "All things traveled a just path, each fulfilling the law prescribed for it . . . And injustice could not occur, for the earthly was not empowered to bend laws that prevailed, splendid, clear and simple, in the colorfully tangled diversity of events." At this point, moreover, the theme of a just and purposeful universal order receives a new and unexpected dimension: Paul's view of it is linked to the Jewish tradition. At this very late point in the novel the reader learns for the first time that Paul is a Jew, convinced that his Jewish blood and heritage are what have led him to his new insight: "For above the life of those whose blood flowed in him, justice had stood like a sun whose rays did not warm them, whose light had never shone for them, yet before whose blinding radiance they nevertheless reverently shielded their suffering brows with trembling hands."

In the closing pages of this early novel, then, we find the two major elements of Beer-Hofmann's Weltanschauung: the affirmation of a just and purposeful universal order despite his acute awareness of suffering and evil in the world, and the affirmation of his Jewishness—and this at a time when social and political circumstances led many Jews to regard their Jewishness as a burden. In all of his subsequent work Beer-Hofmann was to treat these themes again and again, developing them most fully, of course, in the ***David***-cycle.

Having identified the principal elements of Beer-Hofmann's view of life and the world, we now need to ask what implications it had for his work as a writer, what effect it had on his view of *Künstlertum.* The answers are provided most fully by ***Jaákobs Traum,*** the first play in the ***David***-cycle. (Completed in 1915, the play had its premiere at Vienna's Burgtheater in 1919.) On one level ***Jaákobs Traum*** is a poetic statement of the election of Israel. As a result of Jacob's covenant with God, it is Israel's destiny to be the exculpator dei in every age and in every place. On another level, however ***Jaákobs Traum*** is unquestionably an allegory of the poet and his calling. Like Jacob, the poet is God's elect; and the purpose of his election, like Israel's, is to be the *exculpator dei.* Like Jacob, the poet lives in a state of grace, but this is a very mixed blessing at best. Infinitely more receptive, more sensitive than most men to every aspect and phenomenon of life, the poet experiences its joys to a correspondingly greater degree. But this same sensitivity also makes him doubly conscious of life's cruelty, suffering, and ugliness. Consequently his *Auserwähltsein* [state of being elect] includes so great a measure of anguish, recurring doubt, and spiritual suffering that the state of grace often appears to be more curse than blessing. This view of the poet and his activity also emerges in many of Beer-Hofmann's aphorisms and short prose pieces. In **"Die Beschenkten,"** for example, he says: "God's elect receive a bitter, hopeless world, and—to turn the knife in the wound—God grants them a deeper knowledge of the world's woe than others—and calmly, as though it were His due—God receives from them, these eternally unrewarded laborers of love, these eternally unpaid exculpators of God, a world in which woe appears only as an austerity of sweetness—suffering as a way, perhaps, to bliss—death as the breaking open of a gate to . . . life—a poet's world—in spite of all—full of hope, for which in this, His, world there is not much room." In the last years of his life Beer-Hofmann had a series of conversations with Werner Vordtriede in which he also expressed this view of the poet: "Again and again the poet must become the exculpator of God. The *advocatus dei* is a much more difficult office than that of the *advocatus diaboli.* Nothing is more difficult than to excuse and justify the course of events in the world."

Beer-Hofmann's affirmation of the universal order, despite God's unfathomable and apparently contradictory ways, has been traced now from ***Der Tod Georgs*** to ***Jaákobs Traum***. In the next play in the cycle, ***Der junge David,*** the poet—as before—presents the bitter suffering and doubt that precede such an affirmation and frequently assail it once it has been made. As before, he deals with *Auserwähltsein* as both a state of grace and an agonizing burden. But he carries his treatment of these themes a step further than in the earlier works: by far the most important motif of ***Der junge David*** is faithfulness. Once the resolution has been made to accept the universal order and to assume that God's ways are somehow ultimately just, then the logical consequence is this faithfulness, or *Treue.* And this aspect of the matter returns us to the question posed at the beginning: did exile alter Beer-Hofmann's view of life and the world or his view of the poet and his calling? Remarkably enough, the answer is no. Persecution and exile, the drastic reversal of his financial circumstances and pleasant life style, and above all, the loss of his wife—these experiences certainly substantiated Beer-Hofmann's view of suffering as the preponderant element of *Auserwähltsein,* but they did not cause him to renounce or abandon his belief in a just universal order or his sense of a mysterious destiny at work in his own life and in the lives of others. Indeed there is every reason to think that these views and his own faithfulness to them were what enabled him to bear his exile with an equanimity that many of his contemporaries found remarkable.

The most compelling evidence that Beer-Hofmann's views remained essentially the same is provided by ***Paula, ein Fragment,*** the literary work that occupied him almost exclusively during the last years of his life. The following discussion will focus upon two aspects of ***Paula***: first, its treatment of the themes we have identified in Beer-Hofmann's earlier works, and second, its use of literary techniques and devices that Beer-Hofmann had first employed in ***Der Tod Georgs*** some fifty years before.

An important part of Beer-Hofmann's belief in a just and purposeful order was his strong sense of destiny—not only with respect to himself, but in relation to all life, past as well as present. This sense of destiny is one of the two central themes of ***Paula;*** the other is love. Actually Beer-Hofmann fuses them into one motif: the reader has an overwhelming sense of destiny at work in the lives of these two people—in their meeting each other at all, in their love for each other and their marriage despite tremendous obstacles, in their life together. This is first suggested by the very title of Part I: although more than three-fourths of it deals with Beer-Hofmann's life before he met Paula, it is entitled "Donnerstag, der 5. Dezember 1895"—the date of their first (and entirely accidental) encounter. The author's conviction that he and Paula were destined to meet and to love each other is expressed more explicitly in the closing passages of Part I: "Everything before was a chaotically tangled skein that I did not understand—where was its meaning? I had lived from day to day—now everything made sense as the path to this moment."

Thematically, *Paula, ein Fragment* is a chronicle of fate and of love. Because these themes are treated primarily against the background of Europe before the First World War, *Paula* is also a vivid historical document that gives the modern reader considerable insight into an era which now seems very remote and difficult to understand.

— Esther Elston

Given the biographical content of the book, the motifs of love and destiny are treated, of course, on a very personal level. But they are also part of the broader theme of Jewish destiny, and interwoven throughout with Beer-Hofmann's affirmation of his own Jewishness. Paula came from an Alsatian-Austrian Catholic family, and was only sixteen years old when she and Beer-Hofmann first met. She not only married him despite the vehement opposition of her family, but converted to Judaism as well. The Biblical story of Ruth clearly had very special significance for Beer-Hofmann.

Thematically, then, ***Paula, ein Fragment*** is a chronicle of fate and of love. Because these themes are treated primarily against the background of Europe before the First World War, ***Paula*** is also a vivid historical document that gives the modern reader considerable insight into an era which now seems very remote and difficult to understand.

The discussion of Beer-Hofmann's literary techniques in ***Paula*** must begin with a confession: he himself would vigorously reject my view of the book as a work of fiction. In the foreword to ***Paula*** Beer-Hofmann says: "The creative writer may include in his work whatever his awakened phantasy brings him, form it—with the appearance of a beginning and an end—into an image of the whole, freely choose light, rhythm, color, the fateful interweaving of events. But this undertaking of mine has *nothing* to do with 'Dichtung,' in *nothing* did it have free choice." Despite this assertion (and others like it elsewhere in the work), ***Paula*** is certainly as much Dichtung as *Wahrheit,* even though its content is biographical. Regarding ***Paula*** as a work of fiction is justified first of all by the fact that Beer-Hofmann did indeed form it into "an image of the whole," even one with the "appearance of a beginning and an end," the fragmentary nature of the work notwithstanding. Beer-Hofmann acknowledges the book's fragmentary character in his foreword, noting that many things in it will seem insufficiently weighed, others unduly emphasized, some things blurred or submerged in darkness, others appearing in too bright or even in too harsh a light. But he himself defends this with the observation that the book is no more fragmentary than life itself. In any case, this is precisely the kind of selectivity and variation in emphasis that the writer of fiction exercises.

Paula is not a loose, haphazard collection of anecdotes held together only by virtue of being about the same people. The work reflects the same deliberate and very purposeful ordering of material that characterizes ***Der Tod Georgs***. The ***Paula*** fragments do, to be sure, derive their external unity from the fact that Beer-Hofmann and Paula are the central figures throughout. But as a literary work the fragments also have an internal unity, which stems from Beer-Hofmann's use of recurring motifs as an organizing principle. That, too, is a technique he had used very successfully in ***Der Tod Georgs***.

Paula also represents the final development of a narrative style that Beer-Hofmann had employed in ***Der Tod Georgs***. There he still maintained the convention of third-person narration, and the novel's stream-of-consciousness passages are *erlebte Rede.* In ***Paula, ein Fragment*** the stream-of-consciousness passages are even more convincing, not only because they are written in the first person, but also because their language and syntax are less formal, i.e., more like the processes of thought in "real" life. Such a passage is the one in which Beer-Hofmann conveys his impressions and emotions during the first encounter with ***Paula***: "Borne by this tide, all memory courses down—my youth, my childhood, I feel fear—but what is youth, what is childhood—something new has begun—what was before, was a chrysalis—this is my true birth . . . not the world, things, surrounding me—about me the universe. I—no longer pursuing a goal, no longer on a path that ends—included—accepted—circling in an orbit—a star among constellations, without beginning or end." In this passage, with its highly charged language, couched not in complete sentences but consisting for the most part of a wealter of phrases linked together by dashes, Beer-Hofmann comes very close to expressing the ineffable, "was sich nicht ausdrücken lässt."

One respect in which ***Paula*** differs from ***Der Tod Georgs*** is that in his last work Beer-Hofmann occupies a distinct place as narrator—not in the sense of the author who is nowhere and everywhere present in his work, but as a person whose own character and personality emerge in the course of the narration, and who interrupts his story from time to time to comment, explain, or otherwise orient the reader. At one point, for example, Beer-Hofmann interrupts the story to explain why he is describing his own childhood in considerable detail. However matter-of-fact this interruption appears to be, it is nevertheless a literary device that takes the reader from narrated time to the level of narrative time (cf. Günther Müller's distinction). Here, moreover, the author creates the impression of taking the reader into his confidence: by explaining the reasons for developing the story as he does, he gives the reader a glimpse of the creative process itself.

Occasionally the shift in time is used very effectively to introduce or set the scene for recollections of earlier events, and in these instances it has the quality of a film flashback. Elsewhere, as in the afterword to the fragment, **"Alcidor,"** the author shifts to narrative time in order to reemphasize one of his major themes, and here the transition has the effect of editorial comment. Though these shifts in time have somewhat different purposes in ***Paula,*** Beer-Hofmann's use of them is reminiscent of his very bold treatment of time in ***Der Tod Georgs***.

Beer-Hofmann's poetic license with his biographical material lies above all in the very lyrical language in which much of ***Paula*** is written. In addition, there are passages that may be called "exposition in disguise"—passages in which he undoubtedly exercised a certain amount of license for the reader's benefit. A good example is the fragment **"Vor dem Laden,"** in which Beer-Hofmann tells of eavesdropping on a conversation between Paula's brother and Fräulein Karolin, a girl with whom she worked. The conversation seems a bit contrived, i.e., it strikes one as unlikely that so many details of Paula's family history would have been mentioned in such a casual chat. This, too, must be regarded as a literary technique, a means of giving the reader information about Paula and her family.

The fact that Beer-Hofmann allowed himself these liberties is not really the important point. Poetic license, after all, is hardly something for which the writer need apologize. More important is the question of *why* Beer-Hofmann was so anxious to persuade the public that ***Paula*** was not *Dichtung* in any sense of the word. The answer, I think, lies in his intense desire that people believe what he had written and his fear that they would not. Writing in exile, in a strange environment, he must have been all the more keenly aware of the devastating changes the world had undergone—changes that had erased virtually every trace of the life and times about which he was writing. In addition, the conversations with Werner Vordtriede (which took place during the writing of ***Paula***) reveal that Beer-Hofmann had always been tormented by the question, "Who will ever again believe anything I say, if, as a writer, I excite myself here with imaginary situations?" He may indeed have felt that his love of phantasy and imagined situations had now come back to haunt him. One gains that impression from his description of the struggle to keep ***Paula*** free of fictitious elements: "I am doing nothing else but resisting inspiration with all my strength. In earlier times I only needed to close my eyes, and immediately the most diverse phantasies presented themselves. Now I have all I can do to ward them off." There is no reason to doubt these words, but one is reminded of Thomas Mann's perceptive observation that literary works have a will of their own. Beer-Hofmann did not succeed in his efforts to write a strictly factual biography—and from the literary point of view, ***Paula, ein Fragment*** is the better for his failure.

FURTHER READING

Bibliography

Harris, Kathleen and Sheirich, Richard M. "Richard Beer-Hofmann: A Bibliography." *Modern Austrian Literature* 15, No. 1 (1982): 1-60.

Comprehensive annotated bibliography of works by and about Beer-Hofmann; includes information about his correspondence and unpublished work, primarily from the personal collection of Beer-Hofmann's daughter, Miriam BeerHofmann-Lens.

Criticism

Bermann, Tamar. "Richard Beer-Hofmann, 1866-1945." *The Jewish Quarterly* 14, No. 2 (Summer 1966): 37-39.

Appreciation of Beer-Hofmann on the centenary of his birth. Bermann deplores the fact that Beer-Hofmann's works have declined in popularity and urges a revival of interest in him.

Liptzin, Solomon. *Richard Beer-Hofmann*. New York: Block, 1936, 114 p.

Critical study.

———. "Richard Beer-Hofmann: A Biographical Essay," in *Jacob's Dream: A Prologue,* by Richard Beer-Hofmann. Philadelphia: The Jewish Publication Society of America, 1946, 188 p.

Overview of Beer-Hofmann's life and works.

Sheirich, Richard. "*Frevel* and *der erhöhte Augenblick* in Richard Beer-Hofmann: Reflections on a Biographical Problem." *Modern Austrian Literature* 13, No. 2 (1980): 1-16.

Interprets Beer-Hofmann's literary career in terms of two major biographical "givens": that Beer-Hofmann considered himself a prophet-poet whose calling was ordained by God and that his love for his wife, Paula, was linked to his poetic calling.

Additional coverage of Beer-Hofmann's life and career is contained in the following source published by Gale Research: *Dictionary of Literary Biography*, Vol. 81.

Julien Benda

1867-1956

French philosopher and novelist.

INTRODUCTION

Benda is one of the most controversial figures in twentieth-century French philosophy. In his best-known work, *La trahison des clercs* (*Treason of the Intellectuals*), he harshly criticized modern thinkers who embraced political and social ideologies at the expense of reasoned and unbiased examination of cultural phenomena. Because of Benda's radical views and caustic personality, his works were often dismissed during his lifetime, and today he is remembered more for his well-publicized intellectual battles than for his writings.

Biographical Information

Benda was born in Paris to a middle-class Jewish family. He studied at the Lycée Condorcet—concentrating on the classics and mathematics—and prepared for admission to the Ecole Polytechnique. Dissatisfied with his studies in mathematics, Benda instead entered the Sorbonne as a history student. There he began his lifelong commitment to Greco-Roman rationalism. Granted his degree in 1894, Benda began a career in journalism at the *Revue blanche* and went on to write for the *Nouvelle revue française*, the *Mercure de France*, *Divan*, and *Le figaro*. In the late 1890s Benda was one of many artists and intellectuals to become involved in the Dreyfus Affair—the court case of a Jewish officer in the French army convicted of selling secrets to Germany and condemned to life imprisonment on Devil's Island. Both the evidence involved in the case and the motives of those who prosecuted Alfred Dreyfus were questionable, resulting in a decade-long schism in French society between a pro-Dreyfus faction, known as *Dreyfusards*, who protested his innocence, and those who upheld the French court's judgement, many of whom were avowed anti-Semites. Despite his aversion to ideological causes, Benda openly supported the *Dreyfusards* on the grounds that truth and justice were "eternal values" and did not obfuscate his commitment to reason. In 1900 Benda published his first book, *Dialogues à Byzance*, a collection of philosophical pieces on the Dreyfus Affair previously published in the *Revue blanche*. For the next decade Benda continued publishing in intellectual journals and periodicals. In 1912 his first novel, *L'ordination*, was denied the prestigious Prix Goncourt, ostensibly because of anti-Semitism among the judges. Later that year Benda published *Le Bergsonisme; ou, Une philosophie de la mobilité*, an attack on philosopher Henri Bergson that strengthened Benda's reputation as a thinker in the tradition of strict classicism and rationalism. In the late 1920s Benda began to segregate himself from the intellectual community even further with the publication of his most controversial work, *Treason of the Intellectuals*, in which he castigated romanticism and asserted that artists should rely solely on reason rather than emotion or commitment to social or political doctrines. Ten years later, disgusted with the rise of fascism in Europe, Benda reversed some of the ideas he had set out in *Treason of the Intellectuals* and joined the French Communist Party. During the German occupation of France in World War II, Benda was forced to wear the yellow star marking him as a Jew and eventually went into hiding until the end of the war. He died in 1956.

Major Works

While Benda achieved modest success with his novels and short stories, he is known primarily for his works of political and social philosophy. Beginning with *Dialogues à Byzance*, Benda sought to divorce what he considered overly emotional romanticism from rational intellectualism. In *Le Bergsonisme* and *Sur le succès du Bergsonisme* Benda characterized Bergson's humanist and quasi-mystical philosophy as no more than a doctrine of irrational sentimentalism that was destructive to the vitality and stability of the social order. In 1945 he published *La France byzantine; ou, Le triomphe de la littérature pure: Mallarmé, Gide, Proust, Valéry, Alain, Giraudoux, Suarès, les surréalistes*, in which he broadly accused many highly respected French intellectuals of self-indulgent sentimentality. In *Belphégor: Essai sur l'esthétique de la présente société français* Benda criticized what he regarded as widespread cultural degeneracy in France. His most contentious arguments are contained in *Treason of the Intellectuals*, a sustained excoriation of emotion-based devotion to social and political causes that Benda believed corrupted the true purpose of the intellectual's role in society.

Critical Reception

Upon its publication in 1927, *Treason of the Intellectuals* generated controversy when some commentators disputed its claim that intellectuals had betrayed their traditional calling as impartial and independent observers of the world around them. Others accused Benda of hypocrisy because of his own tenacity during the Dreyfus Affair and his occasional political pamphleteering. With his vitriolic critiques of Bergson—whose emphasis on subjectivity and intuition had elevated him to near cult status—Benda alienated much of the academic community. Benda did, however, gain adherents to his cause. As T. S. Eliot stated: "[Benda] puts a problem which confronts every man of letters, . . . the problem of the scope and direction which the activities of the artist and the man of letters should take today." Irving Babbitt concurred with Benda's indictment of modern intellectuals, declaring: "One finds in him a combination of keen analysis with honesty and courage that is rare at the present time, or indeed at any time."

PRINCIPAL WORKS

Dialogues à Byzance (philosophy) 1900
Mon premier testament (philosophy) 1910
Dialogue d'Eleuthère (novel) 1911
L'ordination. 2 vols. [*The Yoke of Pity*] (novel) 1911-12
Le Bergsonisme: ou, Une philosophie de la mobilité (philosophy) 1912
Sur le succès du Bergsonisme (philosophy) 1914
Les sentiments de critias (philosophy) 1917
Belphégor: Essai sur l'esthétique de la présente société français [*Belphegor*] (philosophy) 1918
Les amorandes (novel) 1922
La croix des roses (novel) 1923
Billets de Sirius (philosophy) 1925
Lettres à Melisande pour son education philosophique (philosophy) 1925
La trahison des clercs [*Treason of the Intellectuals*] (philosophy) 1927
Essai d'un discours cohérent sur les rapports de Dieu et du monde (philosophy) 1931
Esquisse d'un histoire des Français dans leur volonté d'être une nation (philosophy) 1932
Discours à la nation européenne (philosophy) 1933
Délice d'Eleuthère (philosophy) 1935
La jeunesse d'un clerc (autobiography) 1936
Précision (philosophy) 1937
La Grande Epreuve des démocraties (philosophy) 1942
Le rapport d'Uriel (philosophy) 1943
Un antisémite sincère (philosophy) 1944
La France byzantine; ou, Le triomphe de la littérature pure: Mallarmé, Gide, Proust, Valéry, Alain, Giraudoux, Suarès, les surréalistes (philosophy) 1945
Exercice d'un enterré vif (philosophy) 1946
Du poétique (philosophy) 1946
Tradition de l'existentialisme; ou, Les philosophies de la vie (philosophy) 1947
Trois idoles romantiques: le dynamisme, l'existentialisme, la dialectique matérialiste (philosophy) 1948
Les cahiers d'un clerc (1936-1949) (autobiography) 1949
Songe d'Eleuthère (philosophy) 1949
De quelques constantes de l'esprit humain: Critique du mobilisme contemporain (philosophy) 1950

CRITICISM

T. S. Eliot (essay date 1928)

SOURCE: "The Idealism of Julien Benda," in *The New Republic Anthology, 1915-1935,* edited by Groff Conklin, Dodge Publishing Company, 1936, pp. 293-300.

[*An American-born English poet, critic, essayist, and dramatist, Eliot was one of the most influential writers in English of the first half of the twentieth century. His work and thought are characterized by experimentation, formal complexity, artistic and intellectual eclecticism, and a classicist's view of the artist working at an emotional distance from his or her creation. In the following essay, which originally appeared in* The New Republic *on 12 December 1928, Eliot critiques Benda's theories about the responsibility of intellectuals as presented in* La trahison des clercs.]

M. Julien Benda is a critic who does not write often or too much. His ***Belphégor,*** which some of us recognized as an almost final statement of the attitude of contemporary society to art and the artist, was published in 1918 or 1919. ***La Trahison des Clercs*** is the first book of the same type that M. Benda has written since ***Belphégor***; it represents some years of meditation and study; we expected a book of the same importance. We are not disappointed. And just as ***Belphégor,*** although based upon an examination of French society alone, applied to the relation of society to the arts in all Europe and America, so is ***La Trahison des Clercs*** of general application. It is, indeed, more general; for M. Benda now draws his illustrations from England, Germany, Italy and America, as well as from France. In these illustrations I do not think that he has been altogether fair; and as he has cited William James and Kipling, we are entitled to cross-examine him on his examination.

M. Benda's thesis may be divided into two parts, upon which we may find that we give separate verdicts. The first part is a general criticism of the political passions of the present time. The second part is a scrutiny of the culpability of certain noted men of letters, and implies a rule of life which M. Benda would lay down for men of letters of our time. In the first general diagnosis, I am inclined to yield complete assent; in the second part, he does not seem to me to have carried his analysis of individuals far enough; and the ideal that he holds up to contemporary men of letters seems to me to be infected with romance. But he puts a problem which confronts every man of letters; the same problem which Mr. Wyndham Lewis has solved for himself in his own way by writing his recent books: the problem of the scope and direction which the activities of the artist and the man of letters should take today.

With the first part of M. Benda's thesis I cannot deal in this short paper. No one can disagree with his statement of the "modern consummation of political passions"; his classification of passions of race (e.g., the Nordic theory and the Latin theory), passions of nations (e.g., fascism) and passions of class (e.g., communism). I say that no one can disagree with the statement, which is made with all M. Benda's usual lucidity and concision; but the analysis could be carried much farther than M. Benda carries it. A new Remy de Gourmont could "dissociate" these ideas of Nationalism of Class, of Race into their local components; and there is also the Religious Idea (not discussed by M. Benda) to be dissociated (with special reference to an actual controversy in England) into components such as conviction, piety, prejudice and politics. Each of these subjects would take a chapter by itself. Let us merely accept M. Benda's general statement of the "perfection" of these passions in the modern world—in universality, in coherence, in homogeneity, in precision, in continuity and in condensation; and proceed to the question: what is the role of the man of letters; does he today involve himself in these passions, and if so, why; and what is his proper function?

M. Benda brings a grave accusation against the modern "man of letters," whom he calls the *"clerc."* The accusation is retrospective, for it applies to most of the nineteenth century. The *"clerc,"* instead of sticking to his business of pure thought or pure art, has descended into politics in the widest and sometimes the lowest sense. M. Benda's instances are mostly contemporary and mostly French. For the sake of completeness, no doubt, he has added a few foreigners, such as D'Annunzio, Kipling and William James. Among these three *"clercs"* I can see nothing in common. D'Annunzio is a brilliant prose artist of pseudo-decadence, who took up with Italian nationalism as a new excitement; Kipling (it seems to me) writes of the Empire because he was born in India instead of Sussex (and as Mr. Dobree has said, part of his interesting peculiarity is that he makes the deck of a P. and O. liner seem as much British soil as Sussex or Shropshire); James is included merely because he voiced a rather silly enthusiasm for the American war with Spain. M. Benda is more exact with his own compatriots. Two of those whom he accuses are Barrès and Péguy. But one asks the question: has he carried his analysis far enough? I dislike both of these writers as much as M. Benda does. But the question is: are these writers dangerous because they have concerned themselves with practical and political matters, or rather because their attitude, both in art, speculative thought and practical thought, was wrong? Let us undertake to consider what are the causes of the inclination of men of letters—including poets, novelists and even painters (there is as yet no instance of a musician)—to occupy themselves with social theories: and second, to distinguish the artists or men of letters who excel in their proper sphere, but fail in their public occupation, from those who exhibit the *same* faults in their art as in their public activity, and finally from those who (if there are such) excel and are right in both.

Ours is an unsettled age. No one is sure to what "class" of society he belongs; at no time has "class" been more uncertain, and yet at no time has the consciousness of "class" been greater. Everyone is now conscious of class, but no one is sure what class is; everyone is conscious of nationality and race (our very passports impress that upon us), but no one is sure who or which or what is what or which race, or whether race is divided north and south or east and west or horizontally, or whether any of us is anything but a mongrel, and we suspect that the more we know about race the more clearly we shall see that we are all merely mongrels. We are conscious of these questions as a man with indigestion is conscious of his stomach. It might almost be said that everybody is conscious of every question and no one knows any answers. This has been called an age of specialization, but it is very much the age of the amateur. Not long ago I attended, with some curiosity, a "religious convention"; I heard a popular novelist and a popular actor talk nonsense for half an hour each, and then I left. There is, in fact, very little respect for authority: by which I mean respect for the man who has special knowledge of some subject of which oneself is ignorant.

The causes are, of course, many; and I merely mention these things in order to point out that the meddling of men of letters in practical affairs, to which M. Benda objects, is only one phenomenon of a general confusion. The publicist who writes about everything on earth responds to the demand of a public which has a mild and transient interest in everything on earth. All this is perfectly commonplace, and I only mention it in order to point out that it is, in practice, extremely difficult to draw a line between the mere vulgarizer of knowledge and the "intellectual" of wide interests. It is furthermore fallacious to group all the intellectuals who may be accused of doing somebody else's business, or of pandering to popular political passions, into one category, as an examination of M. Benda's instances will show.

> Today, it is enough to mention the Mommsens, the Treitschkes, the Ostwalds, the Brunetières, the Barrès, the Lemaîtres, the Péguys, the Maurras, the D'Annunzios and the Kiplings, to agree that the intellectuals [*clercs*] exercise political passions with all the characteristics of passion: tendency towards action, craving for immediate results, indifference to everything but the end in view, contempt for argument, violence, hatreds and obsessions [*idée fixe*].

This classification seems to me rather summary. To take the historians first: it is quite true that certain German historians, and still more, certain philosophers of history, have exhibited a bias in favor of national passions. It is also true of several other historians, not all contemporary with ourselves. Sometimes, when an historian has exactly the same bias as ourselves, we have the optical illusion of no bias at all; to many people Gibbon or Mr. Lytton Strachey seems to possess the virtue of detachment, instead of the virtue of a pleasant bias. The judgment of any historian must depend both on the degree of his prejudice, and (I am afraid) upon our moral judgment of the prejudice itself. And the historians, I submit, are in a class by themselves.

Far different is the case of writers like Péguy and Barrès. If anyone has done more harm than Barrès, it is Péguy. What these two authors have in common is a gift for language, and a sensibility for the emotional values of words, completely unrestrained by either logic or common sense. Like Hugo and Swinburne, they had no gift whatever for thinking; but unlike those poets, they disguised their lyricism in a form which looks to many people like a form of thought. But the question about such writers as these is not whether they have abused their gifts by applying them to the wrong uses, but whether they had any right to exist at all. The faults of the political outbursts of Péguy and Barrès are the faults apparent in all of their work; and if they are pernicious in politics, they are still more pernicious in literature. These two writers, again, are in quite a different category from Kipling. To make this difference quite clear would require a separate essay on Kipling, so I can only say this much: there is, no doubt, a bit of political jingoism in Kipling, but it does not affect his best work. The imperialism which is in all of Kipling's work, and in the best of it, is not a political passion at all; it has no practical aim, but is merely the statement of a fact: and there is all the difference in the world between the vision of an Empire which exists, and the incitement to passion for an Empire in the future. On this point, M. Benda is perhaps no more unintelligent than any other Continental writer.

Benda holds up to the artist, to the critic, to the philosopher, an ideal of detachment from passions of class, race, nation and party, which, even though he does not clearly distinguish *passion* from *interest,* looks very admirable.

— *T. S. Eliot*

Another author of our time, whom M. Benda does not mention, is equally to the point, and cannot be classified with any of the preceding. It is Mr. Wells. Wells is nearer to Barrès and Péguy than to Kipling, but must be distinguished from them very sharply. For whereas, to my thinking, there is a hopeless confusion in Barrès and Péguy which was bound to vitiate everything they wrote, Wells has positive, self-contained gifts for one or two types of imaginative fiction which are peculiarly his own. His imagination is that of the Common Man raised to the highest power. But being that of the Common Man, and of the Common Man of our time, it does not know where to stop. Hence there is a sharp division. Mr. Wells has all of the Common Man's respect for facts and information, and his imagination depends upon facts. When he uses the facts for imaginative purposes he is superb; when he uses his imagination to expound facts, he is deplorable. He has the Common Man's habit of assuming that if you have enough facts, you can dispense with reasoning, for the reason is supposed to be in the facts, instead of in the human mind; he is the reverse of Mr. Belloc, who supposes that if you have reason behind you, you can do what you like with the facts. The expected happens; when Belloc deals with facts, he fits them into his reason; when Wells deals with facts, he hampers his magnificent imagination, and becomes the quite unconscious victim of his parish prejudices. What a pity that Belloc supposes himself to be an historian, and that Wells supposes himself to be a biologist!

Another case which M. Benda does not mention, very different from that of Wells, is that of Shaw. Shaw has this in common with Péguy, that some of his faults must be referred to his masters—though it be as reprehensible to choose a bad master as to be a bad master. Péguy owes much to the philosophy of Bergson, which he translated into his own muddy rhetoric; the philosophy of Bergson after all is at least a philosophy; but what can be said for a disciple of the amateur crankiness of Samuel Butler? I cannot go thoroughly into the case of Shaw, but would only point out that here is the case of a kind of *trahison* not discussed by M. Benda: Shaw, the master of a lucid and witty dialogue prose hardly equalled since Congreve, and of a certain power of observation, squandering these gifts in the service of worn-out, home-made theories, as in the lamentable *Methusaleh.*

Here then, in England alone, we have at least three instances of *clercs* who might incur M. Benda's displeasure: Kipling, Wells and Shaw, and no two of them in the same category, or doing the same thing for the same reasons. I do not say that there are not the same social circumstances behind them all to account for them all, but merely that you cannot pass the same judgment on any two of them as individuals. In France there is perhaps more uniformity, but great differences appear there too. The great weakness of Benda's argument is that you cannot pass directly from the criticism of an age to the criticism of the individuals who represent that age. It breaks down further when you recognize that for practical purposes there is not much difference between a *clerc* who excites popular passions himself, and a *clerc* who does so by his influence upon others. Bergson, one would say, fulfilled Benda's requirements for the pure philosopher; for, apart from one pardonable outburst in 1914, when, as I remember, he identified France with Life, and Germany with Machinery, he has written nothing but pure philosophy. Yet half of the most excitable authors of our time, in France at least, have been Bergsonians. Péguy himself is a conspicuous example; and Péguy is also the remarkable example of a writer who managed to influence many people, largely because he had so confused a mind that there was room for everything in it somehow. He was a nationalist, a Dreyfusist, a republican who went into rhapsodies over Napoleon's tomb, a Socialist and a Catholic of a rather doubtful sort. The influence of Bergson again, as well as that of Péguy and the ecstatic Léon Bloy, is strong upon the leader of the Catholic rationalists, M. Jacques Maritain. I have a warm personal admiration for M. Maritain, as much for his saintly character as for his intelligence; but I have never seen a more romantic classicist, or a Thomist whose methods of thought were less like those of Aquinas. His occasional intemperance of language, and his occasional sentiment, hardly qualify him for the philosophical crown which M. Benda is waiting to bestow upon someone.

And on the other hand, it is doubtful whether M. Benda himself deserves it. He holds up to the artist, to the critic, to the philosopher, an ideal of detachment from passions of class, race, nation and party, which, even though he does not clearly distinguish *passion* from *interest,* looks very admirable. But it implies a complete severance of the speculative from the practical which is itself impossible, and leads, in M. Benda's implications, to an isolation which may be itself a romantic excess. I must avoid entering upon any question which would require a definition of those terrible terms romanticism and classicism; but that is unnecessary, for we are concerned only with what is *called* romanticism. It is apparent, I mean, that when anyone nowadays attacks anything on the ground that it is romanticism, he is always himself in danger of falling into an opposite extreme which is also and equally romantic. M. Benda attacks Maurras and the "neo-classicists," for instance, on the ground that their neo-classicism is itself a phase of romanticism. I think he is right, though the charge does not seem to me to be nearly so deadly as he seems to suppose. What he does not see is that his own brand of classicism is just as romantic as anyone else's.

The only moral to be drawn, therefore, is that you cannot lay down any hard and fast rule of what interests the *clerc,* the intellectual, should or should not have. All you can have is a standard of intellect, reason and critical ability which is applicable to the whole of a writer's work. If there is a right relation of emotion to thought in practical affairs, so there is in speculation and art too. A good poem, for instance, is not an outburst of pure feeling, but is the result of a more than common power of controlling and manipulating feelings: the faults which made D'Annunzio, for instance, rather a deplorable politician made him a second-rate artist. The surest way, perhaps, of judging the work of an author who ventures into a new field, whether it be that of political controversy or some other, is to trace if we can the growth of his interests and their relations among each other. A man may be led, by the connections of things themselves, far from his starting point, just as Sainte-Beuve, as literary critic, was led to study the whole of social life. Where there is no vital connection, the man may be a brilliant virtuoso, but is probably nothing more. Even within one sphere of business, as in a novel or a play, the vital connection may be absent; and if it is absent, the novel or poem or play will not endure.

Leonard Woolf (essay date 1928)

SOURCE: "Just for the Riband to Stick in Their Coats," in *The Nation and the Athenaeum,* Vol. XLIV, No. 13, December 29, 1928, p. 468.

[*Woolf was an English essayist and critic best known for his leading role in the Bloomsbury Group of artists and thinkers in early twentieth-century London. Woolf and his wife, the renowned writer Virginia Woolf, founded the Hogarth Press in 1917. The Woolfs and other members of the Bloomsbury Group contributed greatly to the Modernist movement in literature and art. In the following review of the first English-language translation of* La trahison des clercs, *Woolf challenges Benda's thesis that the "treason of the intellectuals" is a strictly modern, or even widespread, phenomenon.*]

Last year intelligent people in France were reading and discussing M. Julien Benda's ***La Trahison des Clercs,*** indeed, my copy of the book has sixteenth edition on it (though that does not mean quite the same as it would here). It has now been translated by Mr. Aldington and published under the title ***The Great Betrayal,*** by Julien Benda. The book is clever and original, and its thesis, if true, is important. M. Benda means by "clercs" the thinkers, artists, and writers, and he defines them as "all those whose activity essentially is *not* the pursuit of practical aims, all those who seek their joy in the practice of an art or a science or metaphysical speculation, in short in the possession of non-material advantages, and hence in a certain manner say: 'My kingdom is not of this world.' " M. Benda maintains that in recent times, by which he apparently means the last fifty years or so, something has happened to the clerks that never before in the world's history happened to them as a body. They have collectively betrayed their trust; they have consistently gone over to the side of unreason, passion, and prejudice; instead of standing up before the world and testifying to truth, justice, and humanity, they have justified the world in its follies and cruelties. No modern clerk would drink the hemlock with Socrates or face the axe with Gentilis, or go to the stake with Servetus; if he were asked: "Art not thou also one of truth's disciples?" he would stand warming himself at the fire and reply: "I am not." The heathens had their Socrates, the Renaissance its Erasmus, the eighteenth century its Voltaire; our age has its Nietzsches and its Treitschkes, its Barrès, and its Kiplings. They are a solid company of lost leaders who have left us for the handful of silver or the riband to stick in their coats.

M. Benda not only asserts the truth of these facts; he also offers some explanation of the phenomenon. The nineteenth century undoubtedly effected a revolution in the communal psychology of groups. The racial, national, and social group attained a cohesion new to history. The perfecting of communications, the herding of the population into towns, universal education, and the modern printing machine made this cohesion possible. The most effective material for binding the groups together was political passion, national passion, or class passion. Before the nineteenth century the nation or the class was a very loosely knit group, and the number of people affected by political events or moved by political passions was always very small. A war, for instance, was the business of kings, statesmen, and soldiers, and ordinary people were hardly concerned with it, even though it were a world war. They had time to cultivate their gardens, and that is what they did rather than maintain the bourgeois or proletariat front in the class war or hate the Germans. But to-day the nation and the class are everybody's business, and political passions are broadcast and standardized. Patriotism becomes one kind of standardized hatred, and bourgeoisism or proletarianism another. The clerk, who stands for reason and truth, ought to testify against the unreason and hatred thus let loose over the world. But the modern clerk betrays his trust. The herd is too strong for him. He has not the courage to stand out against the canalized and standardized volume of public opinion, and what is, perhaps, more important, he cannot resist the enormous temptation of the silver and ribands which await the modern clerk who will put in his pen at the service of political passions.

This is what I take to be M. Benda's thesis. Obviously there is some truth in it. The cohesion and canalization of political passion, in nations and in classes, are facts. The Nietzschean glorification of force and the dissemination of political and social hatred are recognized symptoms of twentieth-century civilization. It is, I think, also true that the modern clerk for the most part cuts a sorry figure. M. Benda's book is full of instances, chiefly German and French, of clerks—clerical clerks in the Church and lay intellectuals—who, instead of speaking for reason, freedom, humanity, and peace, have become the champions and lackeys of patriotic passion, national and class hatred, reaction, barbarism, and war. M. Barrès in France and Mr. Kipling in England are not unique, they are only better known and more successful than their followers. Mr. Shaw's defence of Fascism is a typical instance of the modern clerk's worship of success and "efficiency." The record of the Churches during the war and the attitude of the clergy in all countries towards nationalist passions support M. Benda's thesis.

But there is one point, and an important one, on which I am not sure that M. Benda proves his case. It is impossible, as one reads his book, not to be in doubt occasionally whether this betrayal of reason and humanity by the clerks is after all a modern phenomenon. Of course, there were Socrates, Erasmus, Voltaire, but history can also show a very large number of intellectuals who, in the confessional, would have had to say that in theory they had followed Reason, but in practice had betrayed her. If Servetus was a clerk who was burnt for his opinions, Calvin, who hunted him to the stake, was also a clerk. And it should be remembered that the judicial murder of Servetus, which, to quote Hallam, "had perhaps as many circumstances of aggravation as any execution for heresy that ever took place," was applauded by practically all the clerks of the time. Indeed, it is said that only one eminent man of learning opposed or protested against it, and his reward has been oblivion, for I do not suppose that one person in a million has ever heard the name of Castellio. The political passions which M. Benda deplores to-day hardly existed before the nineteenth century, but their place was, admirably filled by religious passions. And before the eighteenth century nearly all the clerks found reasons for applauding persecution and intolerance, Erasmus almost alone speaks for reason and humanity. Coming down to later times, it is possible to say of Burke and Wordsworth exactly what M. Benda says of the modern clerk, while Zola and Mr. Bertrand Russell and Einstein have shown that even to-day the betrayal is not universal. I think therefore, that M. Benda rather exaggerates the standard of reason and humanity in the clerks of previous generations. There always have been lost leaders; indeed, for a leader to live over the age of forty usually means that he is lost. It is the result, I believe, of what the doctors call scleroma.

Irving Babbitt (essay date 1932)

SOURCE: "Julien Benda," in *On Being Creative and Other Essays,* Houghton Mifflin Company, 1932, pp. 187-200.

[*With Paul Elmer More, Babbitt was one of the founders of the New Humanism (or neo-humanism) movement that arose during the twentieth century's second decade. The New Humanists were strict moralists who adhered to traditional conservative values in reaction to an age of scientific and artistic innovation. In regard to literature, they believed that the aesthetic qualities of a work of art should be subordinate to its moral and ethical purpose. In the following essay, Babbitt analyzes what he calls Benda's "sweeping indictment of the modernists."*]

The present moment in French literature would seem to be unusually confused. As a first step in getting one's bearings in a somewhat chaotic situation, one may perhaps distinguish between the writers who are still in the main modern movement and those who are in more or less marked opposition to it. This movement has been in one of its most important aspects primitivistic. Rousseau, with his tendency to disparage intellect in favor of the unconscious felicities of instinct, is, though not the first, easily the most influential of the primitivists.

Among the more prominent living opponents of primitivism one may mention M. Ernest Seillière, who has been developing in numerous volumes the thesis that Rousseau's doctrine of man's natural goodness, in theory fraternal, results practically in an 'irrational imperialism'; likewise M. Charles Maurras and the group of *l'Action française,* who, seeing in Rousseauism an alien intrusion into the French tradition, seek to restore this tradition, classical, Catholic and monarchial, such as it existed, for example, in the Age of Louis XIV. The members of this group, it is important to note, are less interested in classicism and religion for their own sake than as necessary supports for what they term an 'integral nationalism.' There is again the neo-scholastic group of which M. Jacques Maritain is probably the most gifted member. This group parts company with the modern movement not merely from the eighteenth century but from the Renaissance. In his *Three Reformers* M. Maritain assails Luther and Descartes as well as Rousseau, finding no firm anchorage for the spirit short of the *Summa* of Saint Thomas Aquinas.

Finally M. Julien Benda is one of the most interesting of those who oppose, on various grounds, the modern movement. He is an isolated figure in the contemporary battle of ideas in France. Some might even say that he pushes his independence to a point that is slightly quixotic. He has taken issue not only with the modernists but with many of the enemies of modernism. He discovers, for instance, a temper unduly narrow and exclusive in the neo-scholastics, a proneness to look on themselves alone as true men and on all others, who are outside the circle of their orthodoxy, as 'dogs and swine.' He detects again romantic elements in the cult that M. Maurras renders to reason, and is unable to see that 'integral nationalism' of the type promoted by *l'Action française* is genuinely Catholic or classical. Rousseau would, as a matter of fact, have the right to say (in the words of Emerson's Brahma) of many of those who profess to be reacting from him: 'When me they fly, I am the wings.'

M. Benda has been concerned primarily, not with the older forms of the primitivistic movement, but with those it has assumed during the last thirty or forty years. He has been above all an implacable enemy of the form it has taken in the philosophy of Bergson, of the anti-intellectual trend of this philosophy and its tendency to present as a spiritual illumination what is at bottom only the latest refinement of Rousseauistic revery. As a sample of revery thus setting up as a 'mystic union with the essence of things' M. Benda cites the following passage from M. Edouard LeRoy, Bergson's disciple and successor at the Collège de France: 'Distinctions have disappeared. Words no longer have any value. One hears welling forth mysteriously the sources of consciousness, like an unseen trickling of living water through the darkness of a moss-grown grotto. I am dissolved in the joy of becoming. I give myself over to the delight of being an ever streaming reality. I no longer know whether I see perfumes, or breathe sounds or taste colors,' etc.

The point of view is related to that of the contemporary French group known as the *surréalistes* who hope to achieve creative spontaneity by diving into the depths of the subrational. The *surréalistes* in turn have much in common with the English and American writers who abandon themselves to the 'stream of consciousness.'

M. Benda has studied above all the ravages of Bergsonism in the polite circles of French society—the circles whose traditional rôle it has been to maintain the principle of leisure. The influence of women has always been marked in these circles—but with a difference. In the older French society there were still men of leisure who set the tone and to whom the women deferred. In an industrial society like our own, on the other hand, the men are taken up more and more with business and money-making. In the meanwhile the women have been encouraged in the belief that they are richer than men in the type of intuition that Bergson exalts above reason. Hence their growing contempt for the masculine point of view. Men themselves are inclined to grant them, at least in art and literature, this superiority.

Julien Benda is one of the most interesting of those who oppose, on various grounds, the modern movement. He is an isolated figure in the contemporary battle of ideas in France. Some might even say that he pushes his independence to a point that is slightly quixotic.

— Irving Babbitt

It would not be difficult to find an American parallel to M. Benda's picture in ***Belphégor*** of the great industrialist who bows down before his wife's superiority because she gets up at noon and plays a little Schumann on the piano. Men are even more absorbed in utilitarian pursuits in America than in France, and even more inclined to turn over to women the cultural values which have been a chief concern of the great civilizations of the past.

Belphégor, though it continues M. Benda's previous onslaughts on Bergsonism, has a somewhat wider scope. The tendency to grant the primacy to emotion that this work assails goes at least as far back as the sentimentalists of the eighteenth century. When Faust, for example, exclaims that 'feeling is all,' he sums up Rousseau in his essential aspect, on the one hand, and, on the other, looks forward to 'the greedy thirst for immediacy' that is the theme of ***Belphégor***. One may grant at most that this thirst has led in the case of certain contemporaries to a more complete sloughing off of the traditional disciplines than one usually finds in the earlier primitivists. The net result from the outset of the quest of sensation and emotional intensity for their own sake, has been, in Mr. Santayana's phrase, a 'red-hot irrationality.'

Himself a Jew, M. Benda attributes the decadence he describes in part to Jewish influence; but there have always been, he goes on to explain, two types of Jews—those who in ancient times worshiped Belphegor and those who worshiped Jehovah. As a modern example of the former type, he mentions Bergson; of the latter, Spinoza. Moreover, the Jew would not have been able to act thus deleteriously on the Gentile if the power of psychic resistance of the Gentile had not been seriously lowered. One reason for this lowered resistance, M. Benda surmises, has been the decline of classical study. It might be supposed in that case that one way to fortify the cultivated classes against an irrational surrender to their emotions would be a more humanistic type of education. But M. Benda has no hope of a return to the humanities. He anticipates a future even worse than the present—a sort of indefinite progression in unreason.

It may be, however, that M. Benda is unduly gloomy in his forebodings, that even this tree will not quite grow to heaven. It is an encouraging sign that the rightness of his analysis of the emotional excess has been widely recognized—so much so that the term 'Belphegorism' has entered into current French usage. One may profit by M. Benda's analysis without sharing what appears to be his fatalism. Confronted by tendencies which he believes to be at once bad and irresistible, he inclines at times to misanthropy. Moreover, this misanthropy seems to have its source less in his reason than in his emotions; so that certain critics have found a Belphegorian taint in his own writings.

In theory at all events, M. Benda is not only consistently on the side of reason but he protects the word with a Socratic dialectic. Bergson proclaims that one can escape from mechanism and at the same time become vital and dynamic only by a resort to intuition, and then proceeds to identify the intuitive with the instinctive and the subrational. But the abstract type of reason that is at the basis of the mechanistic view of life, M. Benda retorts, is not the only type. Reason may also be intuitive. Saint-Beuve, for example, is intuitive in this sense when, in his *Lundis,* he enters into the unique gift of a writer and renders it with the utmost delicacy of shading. Intuition of this kind has nothing in common with what is, according to Bergson, the ideally intuitive act—namely, that of the chick when it pecks its way through its shell.

One may admire M. Benda's perspicacity in such discriminations and yet ask if it is enough to oppose reason in any sense to the cult of a subrational intuition and the 'Belphegorism' to which it leads. According to Bergson, there are two traditions in French philosophy: on the one hand, a tradition which puts primary emphasis on intuition and derives from Pascal; on the other, a tradition which is primarily rationalistic and derives from Descartes. One would like to know what M. Benda thinks of Bergson's claim to be in the direct line of descent from Pascal. Does he suppose that when Pascal appeals from reason to something that he calls variously 'sentiment,' 'instinct,' 'heart,' these terms have the same meaning for him that they have come to have since Rousseau and the sentimentalists? The truth is that the terms refer to a superrational quality of will identified with the divine will in the form of grace, and that it is this quality of will that has been weakened by the decline of traditional religion. Faith in a higher will, as it appears in a Pascal, acted restrictively on the 'lusts' of the natural man. According to the familiar classification, the three main lusts (the 'three rivers of fire' of which Pascal speaks) are the lust of knowledge, of sensation, and of power.

The most subtle peril, according to the austere Christian, is that which arises from the lust of knowledge. M. Benda is too thorough-going an intellectual to be apprehensive of any such peril, much less to fall, as the Christian has done at times, into obscurantism. He has probably never asked himself seriously the question that seemed to Cardinal Newman the most essential of all: 'What must be the face-to-face antagonist by which to withstand and baffle. . . . the all-corroding, all-dissolving energy of the intellect?' As for the lust of feeling, the reader of ***Belphégor*** is scarcely likely to accuse M. Benda of not being sufficiently on his guard against it. He has, again, in a recent work, ***La Trahison des Clercs*** (1928), set forth the dangers of certain modern manifestations of the lust of domination. The epigraph of this work is taken from the philosopher Renouvier, a disciple of Kant: 'The world suffers from a lack of faith in a transcendent truth.' One is prompted to inquire at once whether one can secure this faith in a transcendent truth simply by an appeal to reason; whether a true transcendence does not call for the affirmation, either in the Christian or some other form, of a higher will. At all events M. Benda develops the thesis that every civilized society requires a body of 'clerks' (and by clerks he understands not merely the clergy in the narrower sense of the term, but thinkers, writers and artists) who are dedicated to the service of the something in man that transcends his material interests and animal appetites. Other ages and civilizations have had 'clerks' who were faithful to their high vocation, often at the cost of contumely and persecution. But in our own day the clerks have been guilty of a 'great betrayal.' They themselves have become secular in temper, and in consequence have, instead of resisting the egoistic passions of the laity, taken to flattering them. They have sided more and more with the centrifugal forces, the forces that array man against man, class against class, and finally nation against nation. They have encouraged in particular a type of patriotism that, besides supplying themes to the votaries of Belphegor, has stimulated the will to power in a form that, as M. Benda describes it, is close to the 'irrational imperialism' of M. Seillière. If the clerks had been true and not traitorous, they would, instead of helping to inbreed differences, have rallied to the defense of the disciplines that tend to draw men to a common center even across national frontiers. As a result of the clerical apostasy, M. Benda foresees wars of zoölogical extermination. He admits, however, another possibility: men may be induced to vent their fury of conquest not upon other men but upon physical nature. He enlarges upon this latter possibility in a vein that might have appealed to Swift: 'Henceforth, united in an immense army, an immense factory, . . . contemptuous of every free and disinterested activity, thoroughly cured of faith in any good beyond the real world, . . . humanity will attain to a really grandiose control of its material environment, to a really joyous consciousness of its own power and grandeur. And history will smile at the thought that Socrates and Jesus Christ died for that race.'

M. Benda's work may be defined in its total trend as a sweeping indictment of the modernists by a modern. Thus far, at least, he has refused to ally himself with the reactionaries. The position of the modern may turn out to be untenable in the long run, unless it can be shown to be truly constructive; and it is on the constructive side that M. Benda is the least satisfying. The charge has been brought against him that the 'clerk,' as he conceives him, is too aloof, too much 'above the mêlée.' The contemplative life, however, may have its own justification. Furthermore, he is willing that his clerk should, on occasion, be militant in the secular order. The real difficulty is that M. Benda does not give an adequate notion of the doctrine and discipline on which the clerk is to base his militancy; nor again of the type of effort that must be put forth in the contemplative life, if it is to be more than a retreat into some tower of ivory. His weakness as a philosopher would appear, as I have already hinted, to be his failure to recognize that the opposite of the subrational is not merely the rational but the superrational, and that this superrational and transcendent element in man is a certain quality of will. This quality of will may prove to be alone capable of supplying a sufficient counterpoise to the various 'lusts,' including the lust of feeling, that result from the free unfolding of man's natural will. M. Benda's inadequacy in dealing with the will is closely related to his drift towards fatalism and his occasional misanthropy. Any one who affirmed the higher will on psychological rather than dogmatic or theological grounds might perhaps aspire to the praise of being a constructive modern. In the meanwhile, a necessary preliminary to any valid construction, must be a sound diagnosis of existing evils. It is just here—as an acute diagnostician of the modern mind and its maladies—that M. Benda has put us under obligations to him. One finds in him a combination of keen analysis with honesty and courage that is rare at the present time, or indeed at any time.

George Santayana (essay date 1933)

SOURCE: "The Prestige of the Infinite," in *Some Turns of Thought in Modern Philosophy,* Cambridge at the University Press, 1933, pp. 102-121.

[*Santayana was a Spanish-born philosopher, poet, novelist, and literary critic who received his undergraduate and graduate degrees from Harvard University, where he later taught philosophy. Late in his life, Santayana stated that "reason and ideals arise in doing something that at bottom there is no reason for doing." "Chaos," he had written earlier, "is perhaps at the bottom of everything." In the following essay, Santayana critiques the ideas advanced in Benda's* Essai d'un discours cohérent sur les rapports de dieu et du monde.]

"The more complex the world becomes and the more it rises above the indeterminate, so much the farther removed it is from God; that is to say, so much the more impious it is." M. Julien Benda is not led to this startling utterance [in his ***Essai d'un Discours cohérent sur les Rapports de Dieu et du Monde***] by any political or sentimental grudge. It is not the late war, nor the peace of Versailles, nor the parlous state of the arts, nor the decay of morality and prosperity that disgusts him with our confused world. It is simply overmastering respect for the infinite. ***La Trahison des Clercs,*** or Treason of the Levites, with which he had previously upbraided the intellectuals of his time, now appears to consist precisely in coveting a part in this world's inheritance, and forgetting that the inheritance of the Levites is the Lord: which, being interpreted philosophically, means that a philosopher is bound to measure all things by the infinite.

This infinite is not rhetorical, as if we spoke of infinite thought or infinite love: it is physico-mathematical. Nothing but number, M. Benda tells us, seems to him intelligible. Time, space, volume, and complexity (which appears to the senses as quality) stretch in a series of units, positions, or degrees, to infinity, as number does: and in such homogeneous series, infinite in both directions, there will be no fixed point of origin for counting or surveying the whole and no particular predominant scale. Every position will be essentially identical with every other; every suggested structure will be collapsible and reversible; and the position and relations of every unit will be indistinguishable from those of every other. In the infinite, M. Benda says, the parts have no identity: each number in the scale, as we begin counting from different points of origin, bears also every other number.

This is no mere mathematical puzzle; the thought has a strange moral eloquence. Seen in their infinite setting, which we may presume to be their ultimate environment, all things lose their central position and their dominant emphasis. The contrary of what we first think of them or of ourselves—for instance that we are alive, while they are dead or unborn—is also true. Egotism becomes absurd; pride and shame become the vainest of illusions. If then it be repugnant to reason that the series of numbers, moments, positions, and volumes should be limited—and the human spirit has a great affinity to the infinite—all specific quality and variety in things must be superficial and deeply unreal. They are masks in the carnival of phenomena, to be observed without conviction, and secretly dismissed as ironical by those who have laid up their treasure in the infinite.

This mathematical dissolution of particulars is reinforced by moral considerations which are more familiar. Existence—any specific fact asserting itself in any particular place or moment—is inevitably contingent, arbitrary, gratuitous, and insecure. A sense of insecurity is likely to be the first wedge by which repentance penetrates into the animal heart. If a man did not foresee death and fear it, he might never come at all to the unnatural thought of renouncing life. In fact, he does not often remember death: yet his whole gay world is secretly afraid of being found out, of being foiled in the systematic bluff by which it lives as if its life were immortal; and far more than the brave young man fears death in his own person, the whole life of the world fears to be exorcised by self-knowledge, and lost in air. And with good reason: because, whether we stop to notice this circumstance or not, every fact, every laborious beloved achievement of man or of nature, has come to exist against infinite odds. In the dark grab-bag of Being, this chosen fact was surrounded by innumerable possible variations or contradictions of it; and each of those possibilities, happening not to be realised here and now, yet possesses intrinsically exactly the same aptitude or claim to existence. Nor are these claims and aptitudes merely imaginary and practically contemptible. The flux of existence is continually repenting of its choices, and giving everything actual the lie, by continually substituting something else, no less specific and no less nugatory. *This* world, *any* world, exists only by an unmerited privilege. Its glory is offensive to the spirit, like the self-sufficiency of some obstreperous nobody, who happens to have drawn the big prize in a lottery. "The world", M. Benda writes, "inspires me with a double sentiment. I feel it to be full of grandeur, because it has succeeded in asserting itself and coming to exist; and I feel it to be pitiful, when I consider how it hung on a mere nothing that this particular world should never have existed." And though this so accidental world, by its manifold beauties and excitements, may arouse our romantic enthusiasm, it is fundamentally an *unholy* world. Its creation, he adds in italics, "*is something which reason would wish had never taken place.*"

For we must not suppose that God, when God is defined as infinite Being, can be the creator of the world. Such a notion would hopelessly destroy that coherence in thought to which M. Benda aspires. The infinite cannot be selective; it cannot possess a particular structure (such, for instance, as the Trinity) nor a particular quality (such as goodness). It cannot exert power or give direction. Nothing can be responsible for the world except the world itself. It has created, or is creating, itself perpetually by its own arbitrary act, by a groundless self-assertion which may be called (somewhat metaphorically) will, or even original sin: the original sin of existence, particularity, selfishness, or separation from God. Existence, being absolutely contingent and ungrounded, is perfectly free: and if it ties itself up in its own habits or laws, and becomes a terrible nightmare to itself by its automatic monotony, that still is only its own work and, figuratively speaking, its own fault. Nothing save its own arbitrary and needless pressure keeps it going in that round. This fatality is impressive, and popular religion has symbolised it in the person of a deity far more often recognised and worshipped than infinite Being. This popular deity, a symbol for the forces of nature and history, the patron of human welfare and morality, M. Benda calls the imperial God.

> It is clear that these two Gods . . . have nothing to do with one another. The God whom Marshal de Villars, rising in his stirrups and pointing his drawn sword heavenwards, thanks on the evening of Denain, is one God: quite another is the God within whose bosom the author of the *Imitation,* in a corner of his cell, feels the nothingness of all human victories.

It follows from this, if we are coherent, that any "return to God" which ascetic philosophy may bring about cannot be a social reform, a transition to some better form of natural existence in a promised land, a renovated earth, or a material or temporal heaven. Nor can the error of creation be corrected violently by a second arbitrary act, such as suicide, or the annihilation of the universe by some ultimate general collapse. If such events happen, they still leave the door open to new creations and fresh errors. But the marvel is (I will return to this point presently) that the world, in the person of a human individual endowed with reason, may perceive the error of its ways and correct it ideally, in the sphere of estimation and worship. Such is the only possible salvation. Reason, in order to save us, and we, in order to be saved, must both subsist: we must both be incidents in the existing world. We may then, by the operation of reason in us, recover our allegiance to the infinite, for we are bone of its bone and flesh of its flesh: and by our secret sympathy with it we may rescind every particular claim and dismiss silently every particular form of being, as something unreal and unholy.

An even more cogent reason why M. Benda's God cannot have been the creator of the world is that avowedly this God has never existed. We are expressly warned that "if God is infinite Being he excludes existence, in so far as to exist means to be distinct. In the sense which everybody attaches to the word existence, God, as I conceive him, *does not exist.*" Of course, in the mind of a lover of the infinite, this fact is not derogatory to God, but derogatory to existence. The infinite remains the first and the ultimate term in thought, the fundamental dimension common to all things, however otherwise they may be qualified; it remains the eternal background against which they all are defined and into which they soon disappear. Evidently, in this divine—because indestructible and necessary—dimension, Being is incapable of making choices, adopting paths of evolution, or exercising power: it knows nothing of phenomena; it is not their cause nor their sanction. It is incapable of love, wrath, or any other passion. "I will add", writes M. Benda, "something else which theories of an impersonal deity have less often pointed out. Since infinity is incompatible with personal being, God is incapable of morality." Thus mere intuition and analysis of the infinite, since this infinite is itself passive and indifferent, may prove a subtle antidote to passion, to folly, and even to life.

I think M. Benda succeeds admirably in the purpose announced in his title of rendering his discourse coherent. If once we accept his definitions, his corollaries follow. Clearly and bravely he disengages his idea of infinity from other properties usually assigned to the deity, such as power, omniscience, goodness, and tutelary functions in respect to life, or to some special human society. But coherence is not completeness, nor even a reasonable measure of descriptive truth; and certain considerations are omitted from M. Benda's view which are of such moment that, if they were included, they might transform the whole issue. Perhaps the chief of these omissions is that of an organ for thought. M. Benda throughout is engaged simply in clarifying his own ideas, and repeatedly disclaims any ulterior pretensions. He finds in the panorama of his thoughts an idea of infinite Being, or God, and proceeds to study the relation of that conception to all others. It is a task of critical analysis and religious confession: and nothing could be more legitimate and, to some of us, more interesting. But whence these various ideas, and whence the spell which the idea of infinite Being in particular casts over the meditative mind? Unless we can view these movements of thought in their natural setting and order of genesis, we shall be in danger of turning autobiography into cosmology and inwardness into folly.

One of the most notable points in M. Benda's analysis is his insistence on the leap involved in passing from infinite Being to any particular fact or system of facts; and again the leap involved in passing, when the converted spirit "returns to God," from specific animal interests—no matter how generous, social, or altruistic these interests may be—to absolute renunciation and sympathy with the absolute. "That a will to return to God should arise in the phenomenal world seems to be a miracle no less wonderful (though it be less wondered at) than that the world should arise in the bosom of God." "Love of man, charity, humanitarianism are nothing but the selfishness of the race, by which each animal species assures its specific existence." "To surrender one's individuality for the benefit of a larger self is something quite different from disinterestedness; it is the exact opposite." And certainly, if we regarded infinite Being as a cosmological medium—say, empty space and time—there would be a miraculous break, an unaccountable new beginning, if that glassy expanse was suddenly wrinkled by something called energy. But in fact there need never have been such a leap, or such a miracle, because there could never have been such a transition. Infinite Being is not a material vacuum "in the bosom" of which a world might arise. It is a Platonic idea—though Plato never entertained it—an essence, nonexistent and immutable, not in the same field of reality at all as a world of moving and colliding things. Such an essence is not conceivably the seat of the variations that enliven the world. It is only in thought that we may pass from infinite Being to an existing universe; and when we turn from one to the other, and say that now energy has emerged from the bosom of God, we are turning over a new leaf, or rather picking up an entirely different volume. The natural world is composed of objects and events which theory may regard as transformations of a hypothetical energy; an energy which M. Benda—who when he comes down to the physical world is a good materialist—conceives to have condensed and distributed itself into matter, which in turn composed organisms and ultimately generated consciousness and reason. But in whatever manner the natural world may have evolved, it is found and posited by us in perception and action, not, like infinite Being, defined in thought. This contrast is ontological, and excludes any derivation of the one object from the other. M. Benda himself tells us so; and we may wonder why he introduced infinite Being at all into his description of the world. The reason doubtless is that he was not engaged in describing the world, except by the way, but rather in classifying and clarifying his ideas in view of determining his moral allegiance. And he arranged his terms, whether ideal or material, in a single series, because they were alike present to his intuition, and he was concerned to arrange them in a hierarchy, according to their moral dignity.

Not only is infinite Being an incongruous and obstructive term to describe the substance of the world (which, if it subtends the changes in the world and causes them, must evidently change with them), but even mathematical space and time, in their ideal infinity, may be very far from describing truly the medium and groundwork of the universe. That is a question for investigation and hypothesis, not for intuition. But in the life of intuition, when that life takes a mathematical turn, empty space and time and their definable structure may be important themes; while, when the same life becomes a discipline of the affections, we see by this latest example, as well as by many a renowned predecessor of M. Benda, that infinite Being may dominate the scene.

Nor is this eventual dominance so foreign to the natural mind, or such a miraculous conversion, as it might seem. Here, too, there is no derivation of object from object, but an alternative for the mind. As M. Benda points out, natural interests and sympathies may expand indefinitely, so as to embrace a family, a nation, or the whole animate universe; we might even be chiefly occupied with liberal pursuits, such as science or music; the more we laboured at these things and delighted in them, the less ready should we be for renunciation and detachment. Must conversion then descend upon us from heaven like a thunderbolt? Far from it. We need not look for the principle of spiritual life in the distance: we have it at home from the beginning. Even the idea of infinite Being, though unnamed, is probably familiar. Perhaps in the biography of the human race, or of each budding mind, the infinite or indeterminate may have been the primary datum. On that homogeneous sensuous background, blank at first but secretly plastic, a spot here and a movement there may gradually have become discernible, until the whole picture of nature and history had shaped itself as we see it. A certain sense of that primitive datum, the infinite or indeterminate, may always remain as it were the outstretched canvas on which every picture is painted. And when the pictures vanish, as in deep sleep, the ancient simplicity and quietness may be actually recovered, in a conscious union with Brahma. So sensuous, so intimate, so unsophisticated the "return to God" may be for the spirit, without excluding the other avenues, intellectual and ascetic, by which this return may be effected in waking life, though then not so much in act as in intent only and allegiance.

I confess that formerly I had some difficulty in sharing the supreme respect for infinite Being which animates so many saints: it seemed to me the dazed, the empty, the deluded side of spirituality. Why rest in an object which can be redeemed from blank negation only by a blank intensity? But time has taught me not to despise any form of vital imagination, any discipline which may achieve perfection after any kind. Intuition is a broadly based activity; it engages elaborate organs and sums up and synthesises accumulated impressions. It may therefore easily pour the riches of its ancestry into the image or the sentiment which it evokes, poor as this sentiment or image might seem if expressed in words. In rapt or ecstatic moments, the vital momentum, often the moral escape, is everything, and the achievement, apart from that blessed relief, little or nothing. Infinite Being may profit in this way by offering a contrast to infinite annoyance. Moreover, in my own way, I have discerned in pure Being the involution of all forms. As felt, pure Being may be indeterminate, but as conceived reflectively it includes all determinations: so that when deployed into the realm of essence, infinite or indeterminate Being truly contains entertainment for all eternity.

M. Benda feels this pregnancy of the infinite on the mathematical side; but he hardly notices the fact, proclaimed so gloriously by Spinoza, that the infinity of extension is only one of an infinity of infinites. There is an aesthetic infinite, or many aesthetic infinites, composed of all the forms which nature or imagination might exhibit; and where imagination fails, there are infinite remainders of the unimagined. The version which M. Benda gives us of infinite Being, limited to the mathematical dimension, is therefore unnecessarily cold and stark. His one infinity is monochrome, whereas the total infinity of essence, in which an infinity of outlines is only one item, is infinitely many-coloured. Phenomena therefore fall, in their essential variety, within and not without infinite Being: so that in "returning to God" we might take the whole world with us, not indeed in its blind movement and piecemeal illumination, as events occur, but in an after-image and panoramic portrait, as events are gathered together in the realm of truth.

On the whole I think M. Benda's two Gods are less unfriendly to one another than his aggrieved tone might suggest. This pregnant little book ends on a tragic note.

> Hitherto human self-assertion in the state or the family, while serving the imperial God, has paid some grudging honours, at least verbally, to the infinite God as well, under the guise of liberalism, love of mankind, or the negation of classes. But today this imperfect homage is retracted, and nothing is reverenced except that which gives strength. If anyone preaches human kindness, it is in order to establish a "strong" community martially trained, like a super-state, to oppose everything not included within it, and to become omnipotent in the art of utilising the non-human forces of nature. . . . The will to return to God may prove to have been, in the history of the phenomenal world, a sublime accident.

Certainly the will to "return to God", if not an accident, is an incident in the life of the world; and the whole world itself is a sublime accident, in the sense that its existence is contingent, groundless, and precarious. Yet so long as the imperial God continues successfully to keep our world going, it will be no accident, but a natural necessity, that many a mind should turn to the thought of the infinite with awe, with a sense of liberation, and even with joy. The infinite God owes all his worshippers, little as he may care for them, to the success of the imperial God in creating reflective and speculative minds. Or (to drop these mythological expressions which may become tiresome) philosophers owe to nature and to the discipline of moral life their capacity to look beyond nature and beyond morality. And while they may *look* beyond, and take comfort in the vision, they cannot *pass* beyond. As M. Benda says, the most faithful Levite can return to the infinite only in his thought; in his life he must remain a lay creature. Yet nature, in forming the human soul, unintentionally unlocked for the mind the doors to truth and to essence, partly by obliging the soul to attend to things which are outside, and partly by endowing the soul with far greater potentialities of sensation and invention than daily life is likely to call forth. Our minds are therefore naturally dissatisfied with their lot and speculatively directed upon an outspread universe in which our persons count for almost nothing. These insights are calculated to give our brutal wills some pause. Intuition of the infinite and recourse to the infinite for religious inspiration follow of themselves, and can never be suppressed altogether, so long as life is conscious and experience provokes reflection.

Spirit is certainly not one of the forces producing spirit, but neither is it a contrary force. It is the actuality of feeling, of observation, of meaning. Spirit has no unmannerly quarrel with its parents, its hosts, or even its gaolers: they know not what they do. Yet spirit belongs intrinsically to another sphere, and cannot help wondering at the world, and suffering in it. The man in whom spirit is awake will continue to live and act, but with a difference. In so far as he has become pure spirit he will have transcended the fear of death or defeat; for now his instinctive fear, which will subsist, will be neutralized by an equally sincere consent to die and to fail. He will live henceforth in a truer and more serene sympathy with nature than is possible to rival natural beings. Natural beings are perpetually struggling to live only, and not to die; so that their will is in hopeless rebellion against the divine decrees which they must obey notwithstanding. The spiritual man, on the contrary, in so far as he has already passed intellectually into the eternal world, no longer endures unwillingly the continual death involved in living, or the final death involved in having been born. He renounces everything religiously in the very act of attaining it, resigning existence itself as gladly as he accepts it, or even more gladly; because the emphasis which action and passion lend to the passing moment seems to him arbitrary and violent; and as each task or experience is dismissed in turn, he accounts the end of it more blessed than the beginning.

John Dewey (essay date 1948)

SOURCE: "William James' Morals and Julien Benda's: It Is Not Pragmatism That Is Opportunist," in *Commentary,* Vol. 5, No. 1, January, 1948, pp. 46-50.

[*Dewey was one of the most celebrated American philosophers of the twentieth century and the leading philosopher of Pragmatism after the death of William James. Dewey criticized the detached pursuit of truth for its own sake and advocated a philosophy with the specific aim of seeking improvements in various spheres of human life. In the following essay, he offers a response to Benda's criticism of the American philosophical school of Pragmatism.*]

In his article, **"The Attack on Western Morality"** (*Commentary,* November 1947), M. Julien Benda chose to include what he regards as pragmatic philosophy as a leading figure in that attack. In fact, he assigns to it, along with and by the side of Russian Bolshevist philosophy, a place in the very front rank of the intellectual forces engaged in undermining the morality of the Western world. This is a serious charge; none the less serious because those who call themselves pragmatists will be highly surprised to learn that the philosophy they profess has had any such extensive influence either for good or evil. One's first impression is that M. Benda is using the term "pragmatic" loosely to stand for all movements that tend to put immediate and narrow expediency—in the sense of profit, whether financial, political, or personal—above all other considerations. Since "pragmatism" is a specific philosophical term having a definite meaning that has nothing in common with the usage just mentioned, this loose use would indicate also a loose sense of intellectual responsibility. But M. Benda cannot claim even this protection, slight as it is.

For after saying in his main sectional heading, "The Socratic Christian Morality was the Only One Honored a Few Years Ago," and giving to his next main section the caption "Deliberate Assaults Against this Morality at the End of the 19th Century—the Preaching of Pragmatic Morals," he proceeds to make a specific identification of these "pragmatic morals" with the doctrines of William James—who published, toward the "end of the 19th century," his book entitled *Pragmatism.*

Here is what M. Benda writes—and I quote it because it is the one and only textual reference by which he even suggests the evidence for the specific charge leveled against pragmatic philosophy: "Cecil Rhodes had already declared at the time of the Boer War: 'This war is just because it is useful to my country.' To be sure, he was only a business man; but an intellectual, Kipling, took a similar attitude. Dare I say that it was close, almost violently close, *to that of William James* at the time the island of Cuba was grabbed by his compatriots?"

The italics are inserted by me in order to make clear beyond doubt just what M. Benda intended by reference to pragmatic philosophy and morality. As authority for his statement about James, he expressly refers to "his *Letters,* II, pp. 73-74." What James *actually* said we shall soon see. By a curious coincidence, James refers in a later letter to Kipling's attitude to American seizure of the Philippines, and what he says on that point will also be quoted.

Here is what James actually wrote in a letter to a French philosopher-friend, François Pillon, on June 15, 1898. (The treaty of peace in which the "compatriots" of M. Benda's account grabbed the Philippines and Porto Rico—but *not* Cuba—was not signed until six months after the date of the letter to which M. Benda refers as his authority.) "We now have the Cuban War. A curious episode of history, showing how a nation's ideals can be changed in the twinkling of an eye, by a succession of outward events partly accidental." After referring to the "persuasion on the part of the people that the cruelty and misrule of Spain in Cuba call for her expulsion," and after mentioning the explosion of the Maine as the "partly accidental outward event" that suddenly changed the nation's ideals, he proceeds as follows: "The actual declaration of war by Congress, however, was a case of *psychologie des foules,* a genuine hysteric stampede at the last moment. . . . The European nations of the continent cannot believe that our pretense of humanity, and our disclaiming of all ideas of conquest is sincere. It has been *absolutely* sincere." The force of the "has been" in this sentence comes out clearly in a passage that follows: "But here comes in the psychological factor; once the excitement of action gets loosed . . . the old human instincts will get into play with all their old strength, and the ambition and sense of mastery which our nation has will set up new demands. It shall never take Cuba; I imagine that to be very certain. . . . But Porto Rico, and even the Philippines, are not so sure. We had supposed ourselves (with all our crudity and barbarity in certain ways) a better nation morally than the rest, safe at home, etc. . . . Dreams! Human Nature is everywhere the same; and at the least temptation all the old military passions rise and sweep everything before them."

I do not quote this passage in defense of William James; he does not need it. Nor do I quote it for a reason which would be wholly relevant in another context: namely, an exhibition of the realistic quality of his vision based on a degree of intellectual integrity and clarity that unfortunately is not ordinary. I quote the passage as Exhibit "A" with respect to the quality of M. Benda's intellectual responsibility. It may well be that James believed that the undeniable "cruelty and misrule" in Cuba, if not ended by the action of Spain itself, would in the end justify resort to war in order to free Cuba. That, however, is a speculative surmise. The *actual war,* as it took place, he attributes to what was, relatively, an external accident resulting in a manifestation of the "psychology of crowds," in which deep-seated instincts temporarily overthrew control by intelligence. A few years later, returning to the theme, he wrote: "I think that the manner in which the McKinley administration railroaded the country into its policy of conquest was abominable, and the way the country pucked [sic] up its ancient soul at the first touch of temptation, and followed, was sickening." (*Letters,* Vol. II).

James was not an absolute pacifist; possibly M. Benda himself did not carry his absolutism to the point of finding evil in the fact that the United States joined in the last war. But in any case, all this is merely introductory to the matter of the irresponsibility of M. Benda's account of James' position—his account of "pragmatic morality" as a philosophy of cheap and base expediency.

For it is not merely that what James wrote was written six months before the treaty in which was grabbed the Philippines. It is not merely that James was as right in his *prediction* that we would not take Cuba, as M. Benda is wrong in his report, fifty years later, that we *did* take it. These things are of minor importance, compared with the fact that William James was one of the first, one of the most indignant, and one of the most persistent of the Americans who protested against our seizure of the Philippines—an episode now happily terminated. Nor did William James wait till the seizure was legally completed. The very letter to which M. Benda refers in support of his statement about James, contains the following statement: "I am going to a great popular meeting in Boston today where a lot of my friends are to protest against the new 'imperialism.' " (James was the vice-president of the Anti-Imperialist League.)

It is not for me to try to tell which horn of the dilemma M. Benda may prefer: either he had not read the letter, or he had read it and chose to suppress both it and the attempt to learn about the public and well-known record of James with reference to the war and to the taking of Philippines. It is enough that he transforms a "grab" of the Philippines which James opposed, into a grab of Cuba—which did not take place; he then makes this transformation the main—because the one and only—textual reference for what he goes on to make of pragmatic morality. Comment on M. Benda's moral standard of responsibility in intellectual matters does not seem to be needed beyond noting that this is an emphatic and more genuine instance of "the treason of the intellectuals" than any he himself has fumed against.

M. Benda's association of James with Kipling is a secondary matter. But it is possible to quote from the same volume of James' letters the facts on this point. In a letter written in February of the year following the letter just dealt with, we find this passage about Kipling: "I wish he would harken a bit more to his deeper human self and a bit less to his shallower jingo self. If the Anglo-Saxon race would drop its sniveling cant, it would have a good deal less of a 'burden' to carry." And then comes the passage with respect to the Philippines: "Kipling knows perfectly well that our camps in the tropics are not college settlements or our armies bands of philanthropists slumming it; and I think it is a shame he should represent us to ourselves in that light."

I doubt if it is mere coincidence that it was only a few short months after his reflections on the outbreak of the primitive in Americans, as in other men, that James wrote: "As for me, my bed is made: I am against bigness and greatness in all forms, and with the invisible molecular forces that work from individual to individual, stealing in through the crannies of the world like so many soft rootlets, or like the capillary oozing of water, and yet rending the hardest monuments of man's pride if you give them time. . . . So I am against all big organizations as such . . . all big successes . . . and in favor of the eternal forces of truth which always work in the individual and immediately unsuccessful way."

This quotation from the man who is presented by M. Benda as teaching a gospel of immediate "practical" success suffices, I believe, to show how "violently" M. Benda "dares" in his account of the pragmatism of William James. It is a typical specimen of how far he "dares" in his whole account of pragmatism. Although I am far from claiming that all of us who are named pragmatists measure up to either the intellectual or the moral stature of William James, I definitely do claim that the passage just quoted from him comes as close to the spirit of pragmatism as M. Benda's account is remote from it.

The culmination of what M. Benda "dares" is found in passages in which he affiliates pragmatism with the philosophy held and practiced by those in control of the Soviet Union. One of these passages is in the heading that reads: "Two Forms of Pragmatic Ethics Particularly Triumphant at Present," the second of the "two forms" being explicitly identified with the philosophy of Bolshevist Communism. This identity he "dares" to assert in the sentence reading "[pragmatism] tends to recognize no moral values—justice, truth, reason—except as determined by practical considerations—or, more exactly, by economic interest"—i.e., in the case of the triumphant Bolshevist version. Were I to say that M. Benda's account of the latter philosophy is no more accurate than his version of pragmatic philosophy and leave the matter there, he might use that remark as evidence of an attempt to defend Russian official philosophy. So I will say that Macaulay's schoolboy might well be aware of the fact that no practical considerations of any sort, not even those of "economic interest," are determining factors of Bolshevistic philosophy. On the contrary, it is as absolutistic as the philosophy with which M. Benda has allied himself, although the absolutism is that of "dialectical materialism" instead of what is presumably in the case of M. Benda a "spiritualist," possibly supernatural, variety. In any case the conflict of the two philosophies with one another is that of rival absolutisms. It is curious to observe that the absolutistic state philosophy of Bolshevist Russia interprets American pragmatism in pretty much the same fashion as the absolutistic M. Benda. Neither can "dare" to report pragmatism in its own terms as the systematic elaboration of the *logic and ethics of scientific inquiry*.

The ideological amalgam expressed in M. Benda's phrase, "Socratic-Christian," is, to say the least, perplexing. Socrates was put to death on the ground that his questioning of accepted moral and civic doctrines was subversive. According to all accounts, the one thing for which he stood, the one thing that caused his death at the hands of established and recognized authorities, was that he placed the right and authority of continued systematic inquiry in the search for truth above all other authorities that claimed the right to regulate the course of life. M. Benda presumably has reasons he does not disclose for substituting "Socratic-Christian" for the usual phrase, "Judeo-Christian." But as long as these reasons are kept occult, one can only say that it looks a good deal like an attempt to eat the cake of supernatural absolutism and at the same time keep some of it under the pretense of questioning absolute claims. In any case, it is pertinent to state that, on the face of known facts, those who still assert the rights and authority of *critical* systematic examination of all *received* teachings and belief from any source—among whom pragmatists are numbered in the first rank—have the prior claim to the title "followers of Socrates."

If M. Benda should decide to write a responsible account of pragmatic philosophy, including its bearings on morality (for the phrase "pragmatic morality" *taken by itself* is meaningless), the account might well take its point of departure from the one and only correct statement in his recent article: the profound aversion of pragmatic philosophy to absolutisms of any sort, whether of the reactionary Right or the reactionary Left. An account that started from that point might be led to consider the grounds on which this aversion is based. These grounds are as simple as they are sufficient. By its own nature, absolutism of any kind tends toward a dogmatic assurance that regards all questioning of its tenets as morally subversive, morally destructive, and hence to be suppressed. The course of history from Socrates and Galileo to the present day of Bolshevist Communism, shows that this outcome has been an actual consequence *in fact,* not merely an implication of absolutist theories. The intolerance which follows in theory and practice alike from the dogmatism accompanying absolutism in belief invites, indeed demands, the elimination of dissenters as morally and politically dangerous. Purges did not begin with Nazism or Bolshevism. They follow when absolutism becomes a dominant philosophy.

But even this persecution of dissenters by imprisonment and death is not its only serious moral consequence. The less overt and less obvious suppression and perversion of inquiry may be an equally damaging result. The most effective means of smothering free inquiry proceeds from creation of an intellectual and moral atmosphere of matter-of-course conformity to ways of belief and behavior which are given the status of "eternal truths" through the backing by institutions whose prestige rests upon the supposed possession of these truths fortified by the weight of sheer historic success. It is absolutism, not pragmatism, which rationalizes the success of the status quo by identifying the real with the rational and existence with the real. It is still absolutism, and not pragmatism, which makes success in accomplishing a specially devised result its ultimate and all-sanctifying goal at the price of any means. It is not pragmatism but the system of M. Benda, insofar as it is absolutistic, which has something deeply in common with Bolshevist Communism.

In this connection the words already quoted from William James are of deep significance. He does not speak of "eternal truths" but of "the eternal forces of truth which always work," although *immediately* without success, as rootlets of plants work because they are *alive*—not because of external authority. The worst thing morally that can be said about the claim to be already in possession of eternal and absolute truth is that it can choke the life which otherwise would everlastingly be active in discovery of those temporal, even quotidian, truths by which life itself develops, disclosing as it develops still more truths that are alive because they are not closed and finished—as every "truth" which claims absoluteness is bound to be.

As for the moral and intellectual responsibility of the account given by M. Benda of the pragmatism he attributes to James, I can hardly do better than cite a statement by the authentic William James of what he regarded as the chief vice of American life: "That extraordinary idealization of 'success' in the mere outward sense of 'getting there' and getting there on as big a scale as we can, which characterizes our present generation." It is probable that one of his best known phrases is "that bitch-goddess success." This man who everywhere and all the time attacked what M. Benda presents as "pragmatic morality" is the man the latter "dares" to align with the Cecil Rhodes who (allegedly) said that something was just because it was useful to his nation! I should almost be grateful to M. Benda if I could believe that the very distortion of his account might serve to recall the attention of the present generation to all we still need to learn from the spirit that animates our legacy from William James.

What that spirit is can best be grasped not by isolated passages but from the whole of his writings, which reveal his profound love of variation, freshness, and spontaneity, his pluralistic conception of an open universe and man's creative role in it, his experimental theory of meaning and truth, his unwavering hospitality to new insights, and his imaginative fertility. To lump James with men who have called themselves "pragmatists," many of whom show no familiarity with his writings, who make absolutes of their doctrines, and who substitute the authority of uncritical tradition or violence for the authority of continuous scientific inquiry, is to be victimized by words. All the large words and abstractions of our time have been abused. After all, Hitler called himself a "socialist," Stalin calls himself a "democrat," clerical authoritarians call themselves "humanists," and Franco calls himself a "Christian."

To look behind the words to the substance of a man's vision is the sign of the free and sensitive intelligence.

E. O. Siepmann (essay date 1948)

SOURCE: "Conversations in France-II, III: Benda on Democracy," in *The Nineteenth Century and After,* Vols. CXLIII and CXLIV, Nos. 852 and 853, February and March, 1948, pp. 107-12; 156-60.

[*In the following essay, which consists of the last two installments of a three-part article, Siepmann provides an account of some of his conversations with Benda and outlines the principal ideas in* La grande epreuve des démocraties.]

During the last few months [of 1944] I have made friends with M. Benda. He is an extraordinary old man.

M. Benda lives in a cell, a tiny room in an out-of-the-way quarter. During the war he lived at Carcassonne in the same asceticism. He lived, moreover, under the noses of the Germans after their occupation of the southern zone, without any of the precautions suggested by the fact that he was one of the world's leading anti-Nazi prophets.

He went further. He wrote, smuggled out of France, and had published in the United States a book which sounds like a trumpet-call in its challenge to totalitarian ideas [***La Grande Epreuve des Démocraties***].

When I heard that M. Benda was living in Toulouse, I asked the distinguished scientist Professor Soulla to arrange for me to meet him. Professor Soulla, like Benda, lives relatively unknown among the Toulouse bourgeoisie. He moves in a circle of intellectuals, mostly exiles from Paris, whom these respectable citizens regard with distrust. Yet, whenever any distinguished person, like Louis Jouvet the actor, or Negrin the Spanish ex-Premier comes to Toulouse, these interesting people are to be found at the house of Professor Soulla, and not among the respectable citizens.

One is apt to forget that there is just as strong a mistrust of talent and brilliance among the commercial bourgeoisie in France, as among our own Philistines.

It was to Professor Soulla, then, and not to the Cercle France-Grande Bretagne nor to the Rector of the University, that I addressed myself; and he was in a position very soon to ' produce ' M. Benda at luncheon, to my delight. This delight has increased with many subsequent meetings.

M. Benda has, in spite of a strong tendency to malicious and destructive small-talk, an endearing personality. I think with pleasure of the occasions on which we have sat on opposite sides of a small table, divided by fruit and wine, while I heard him chuckle, and listened to the lucid replies which this kind and courageous thinker made to my naïve questions.

But the most exciting thing of all, was to discover that M. Benda is an admirer of British institutions, of British democracy.

I recall my first meeting with M. Benda at Professor Soulla's house. In spite of his age, M. Benda has light fingers and he rose from a piano to greet me. I saw a tiny man, with dark, beady eyes and meshes of long grey hair. His face reminded me of Voltaire . . . a small, sallow Voltaire; but Benda is more bird-like.

The food was good, and there was some exceptional wine. (Mme. Soulla spoke interestingly of her journey to Russia, while she stacked my plate); but I turned eyes and ears towards the little sage, who was sitting on my left.

M. Benda was susceptible to my displaying a detailed knowledge of his book ***La Grande Epreuve des Démocraties***. This susceptibility was natural, as I discovered that M. Benda had not yet seen a copy of the book, which I had found in Algiers and in London, but which had not reached France. (He never, of course, saw proofs; so that the early edition contains many errors, about which I was able to inform him.)

M. Benda told me that he had written another book. He gave it to a friend in the Résistance, for transmission to London. The friend was arrested, and the manuscript disappeared. M. Benda, who is an intellectual *par excellence,* had kept no duplicate copy!

M. Benda sat near the end of the table, and chuckled. He chuckled, chiefly, at his own jokes; quoting some quip of his own and adding naïvely: *'C'était joli, n'est-ce-pas?'*

The effect was not at all of vanity, but of a touching simplicity.

Less child-like were M. Benda's comments on his contemporaries.

He said:

> French literature is in a period of decadence. That is, we have a *literature of nuances.* It is out of the main stream of our historic, literary traditions.

> This is partly due to the influence of *salons,* which have always had too much influence in French literature.
>
> Look at Aragon. Why write *lyrical* novels?
>
> Lyricists who are not poets *don't make you think.*
>
> The same applies to Giraudoux. Look, too, at André Gide. He claims *now* to defend himself as a sheer litérateur; that is, as a lyricist. But he set out to be a moralist!

M. Benda is a moralist, who set out to be a moralist; and who has not expressed himself in novels.

I asked him about the fashionable J. P. Sartre because, besides writing plays and stories, Sartre sets up to be a philosopher who, in Benda's words, 'makes you think.'

'Sheer froth,' said M. Benda.

I found M. Benda as unreassuring about political, as about literary trends in France. He complained (here I got my first sniff of his taste for provocative, unfashionable views) among other things, that the young are too influential.

> They lend themselves to anything, [said M. Benda]. For this reason, they are always exploited. Look at Pétain's appeal to youth! I want to found a League Against Youth and Art! The young are *not* 'naturally' in the right, as demagogues and Youth-führers imply.

I recalled that M. Benda in his book on Democracy had praised balance, and even a certain intolerance towards destructive extremism; and, on the strength of these remarks I asked if he did not deplore the growth of extremism in France.

> France [said M. Benda] must fall into extremism because, unlike England (my book was fairly pro-English, you noticed, eh?) the Right is unworthy.
>
> Neither Sir Stafford Cripps nor Mr. Churchill want to change the English constitution! The Right-wing in France has waged open war on the republic itself, which it never accepted.

'By extremism,' I asked, 'do you mean that there will be a revolution in France?'

M. Benda prefers discussing principles to facts. He did not answer my question, except by definining his own rôle.

'My books,' he said, 'are clinical. I diagnose; but I do not prescribe treatment. I point out what is desirable.'

'What is desirable may not happen,' he added drily, cocking a beady eye at me.

Now that I know M. Benda better, I know that his conversation is less worthy (if, possibly, more entertaining) than his writing. In talk, M. Benda has a Father William-like quality and he likes to stand on his head; and he is frankly malicious. These qualities are strongly controlled as soon as he begins to write.

The value of Benda's thought for us is, I think, its unorthodoxy. Although Benda has affinities with the Left, even with the extreme Left, he is not content to buy his intellectual furniture ready-made. M. Benda does not hand out opinions in slabs, nor groups of ideas and assumptions. Each idea is examined separately. For this reason, he is a stimulating thinker in an age where lazy 'leftish' thinking tends to slop along taking for granted highly questionable 'axioms' because these cards—to vary my metaphor—belong to the pack.

Quite apart, then, from the fact that M. Benda is a scholar, a profound thinker and a moralist with a world-wide reputation, his views will be found especially significant in their variations from left-wing orthodoxy.

Benda's analysis of The Great Test, or Ordeal of Democracy falls into five parts: A. What Are Democratic Principles? B. Origins of these Principles. C. Abuses of these Principles. D. Attacks on these Principles, and E. Fallacies (arbitrarily and wrongly introduced into the definition of Democracy).

A. *What Are Democratic Principles?*

Of the basic principles of Democracy, according to Benda, the first is the respect of the human person, its 'inviolability' simply *qua* human person. This involves, of course, a reciprocal limitation of liberties among human beings; a limitation of what one French philosopher has called 'individual imperialism.' Living creatures have a natural tendency towards 'expansion,' and this tendency among individuals in a democracy must be limited by a recognition of others' rights: limited if necessary, says Benda, by force.

Democracy is based on a mutual contract: namely, that in return for his duties towards the State the citizen claims that the State has some duties towards him.

What is this respect of persons? It is a regard, above all, for the freedom of the human conscience; a notion which comes straight out of Christianity, because 'since Christianity supreme importance has been assigned to the realm of conscience, as opposed to the realm of public life' (to which classical civilisation gave first rank). In other words, Democracy honours what is free in Man; namely, his capacity to choose: *provided that liberty is not used to destroy Democracy itself.*

Democracy acknowledges the 'pursuit of happiness' as one of the rights of man (always with the same proviso); but the government does not guarantee happiness to men. The State guarantees only justice, and equal rights of opportunity; within that framework, the citizen may make himself happy or unhappy according to the use he makes of his liberty.

Now all this means that Democracy is based on certain *absolute values,* justice, truth and reason; as opposed to 'pragmatic' values, which are determined by circumstances and consequently variable.

The moral principles of Democracy are, therefore, *a priori* commandments of the conscience; and not, by any means, obedience to Nature or History. Democratic morality, says Benda, 'like all true morality *creates* its own object' and does not look for it in Nature (as the Nazis claimed).

'Nature, of course, can be made to serve Grace: but Nature does not justify,' said Malebranche.

Benda concludes by pointing out that democratic principles are *ascetic,* in so far as Democracy renounces expansion, and implies a certain statism as opposed to the much-vaunted dynamism of the 'younger' states.

B. *Origins.*

In so far as Democracy is based on absolute values, Benda says, its origins are Socratic. 'It was the sophists who defended "the morality of self-interest".'

In so far as Democracy proclaims the sacred character of the human person, independently of race, class or nation, and recognises the relation between State and individual as a contract, its origins are Christian.

British democracy is specifically protestant in origin; while the Christian inspiration of the French Revolution is well known.

Britain is defined by Benda as 'near-perfect' as an incarnation of democratic principles, but for the British attachment to custom, strictly practical outlook and inaptitude for abstract thought, which prevent the British from recognising the commands of pure reason, 'even if these commands are unhappily impossible to carry out.'

On France, Benda makes a much more severe reservation by asking if the establishment of democratic principles was 'not a pure accident,' contrary to the majority's wishes; so strong has been the boycotting of French democracy by the most powerful classes backed by some of its most brilliant intellectuals. Benda is referring to the Right; but his words are impressive, whatever their application, and he ends by asking if one must not give up the idea of seeing a durable democracy founded in such a country!

C. *Abuses of Democratic Principles.*

The chief abuses of genuinely democratic principles, according to Benda, are the abuse of individualism and the abuse of egalitarianism.

The most obvious abuse of individualism is to claim the material advantages of a free system, while refusing to make corresponding sacrifices. This is indeed 'individual imperialism.' This abuse may destroy a democracy; but it is important to point out (in view of anti-democratic propaganda) that only the abuse of individualism, and not individualism itself, bears the seeds of destruction.

The value of Benda's thought for us is, I think, its unorthodoxy. Although Benda has affinities with the Left, even with the extreme Left, he is not content to buy his intellectual furniture ready-made.

— E. O. Siepmann

The second, chief abuse of individualism is abuse of the right to criticise in times of crisis. Benda reminds us that 'a country shows its greatness in its readiness to suspend its own liberties (in times of a war or crisis), all the more because it thereby increases its own freedom.'

Another abuse (Benda wrote in time of war) by which individualism can ruin a democracy is by class or party conflict. If citizens, says Benda, cannot extinguish these conflicts at a time when the existence of the nation is endangered by some outside power, then it is practically certain to perish. This is all the more certain when one Party opens the gates to the attacking power, because it dislikes the internal opponents more than the external enemy. Democracy authorises party interests and even conflicts; but Democracy has never taught that such conflicts should persist when the nation was in danger.

Benda accepts, and never derides (as do so many 'fashionable' thinkers), the idea of 'nation.' He states specifically:—

> These remarks lose all meaning if one adopts another definition, which is admittedly accepted in some quarters, by which Democracy means the domination of the proletarian world, at the expense of all idea of nation and of all right to disagree. . . . One might say that the nation is the sum of forces which successfully resist class-passions. The end of the nation would therefore coincide with the end of such resistance.

The chief abuse of the 'egalitarian' principle lies in its claim that there should be equality not only in certain specified ways, but in *all* ways; in denying an *elite,* either real or decreed.

The source of such a claim is envy, and Benda—like Shaw—insists that any such 'levelling from the bottom' would be harmful to any community which adopted it. The claim is, indeed, a corruption of a democratic principle; Democracy demands equality only before the law, and of opportunity.

> A grave problem arises. Would it not be in the interest of any State not only to honour its élite as individuals, but to grant, as occurs in Great Britain, a certain pre-eminence to a class, whose pre-eminence would be hereditary, and to put up with the abuses which are inevitably associated with such an organism, as long as the abuses are eclipsed by the advantages to the community?

In France, says Benda, there is perhaps an endemic fanaticism for equality which may be positively anti-social.

'They want equality in liberty,' wrote Tocqueville, 'and, if they can't get it, they still want it under slavery'!

Benda, like Locke, asks if universal suffrage is not in itself an abuse of the truly democratic principle of egalitarianism; giving, as it does, an equal voice to the feeble-minded and to the Great Thinker. 'We are all equally Men,' said Voltaire, 'but not equal members of society.' Benda hastens to add that he does not propose a preponderance in voting for the rich or for the privileged; and he makes it clear that he is searching for some way in which Democracy, as a moral entity, could strengthen itself by strengthening the influence of *moral* eminence. The law of numbers, he recalls, is something like the law of force.

After the abuses of the individualist and egalitarian principles in democracy, Benda deals with abuse of its *spiritual* principles. This consists in calling upon the State to apply the absolute principles on which Democracy is based, even when this application appears to compromise the general interest. 'Perish the nation, rather than a principle!' is the mistaken war-cry which Benda, who is eminently practical and patriotic, denounces. He gives, as an instance, the outcry in favour of enforcing the rights of small states, even if the larger state or Democracy is admittedly not strong enough to intervene; although, in another part of his work, Benda argues that it is the duty of a Democracy (*when it is strong enough*) to intervene in the affairs of other states where democratic principles are flouted.

In ***La Grande Epreuve des Démocraties,*** M. Julien Benda gave his ideas on Democracy, and looked back on some of the factors which had endangered its survival. This book was written during the war, in clandestinity, smuggled abroad and published without M. Benda's even seeing the proofs. The result is that the book has not become as well known as ***La Trahison des Clercs,*** although it is—in my opinion—as important.

. . . . .

In my last article, I showed how Benda's analysis of the Great Ordeal of Democracy fell into five parts, of which I dealt with the first three: A. Principles, B. Origins, and C. Abuses.

We now come to D. Attacks, E. False Ideas, on Democracy; and we shall find Benda no less provocative in these sections, which suggest—among other ideas shocking to 'fashionable' thinkers—that the artist is, in some ways, an organic enemy of Democracy; and that a democracy is fully entitled to suppress its own internal opponents, without thereby ceasing to be democratic.

D. *Attacks on Democratic Principles* (as such, independently of their abuses).

Democratic principles, apart from their abuses, are sometimes attacked as such; although these attacks often identify the system with its abuses.

The chief attacks, says Benda, come from the spirit of conquest, from the 'sacerdotal' spirit, from the spirit of class, and from the 'artistic' spirit!

The glorification of *greatness,* instead of *happiness,* is one of the main points of the attack by the spirit of conquest. Benda remarks that such a spirit is bound to object to a system whose basis is the rights of the individual, his sacred character *qua* person, his capacity to discuss the acts of his chiefs, the equality of all before the law, and the elevation of certain values above the interests of any group.

Benda calls 'sacerdotal' the attack against Democracy constituted by the claim of a small group to have received the truth from God and a consequent right alone to govern humanity. This sacerdotal spirit, says Benda, comes fully into light in the catholic priest, and distinguishes him from the protestant minister who makes no claim to know the truth better than his flock, but searches for truth with them, and claims no right to give orders to his fellow citizens, but recognises their equality with him in the State.

Benda claims that the Catholic Church has opposed Democracy consistently, *e.g.,* by the Pope's protest against the Declaration of the Rights of Man, or by the insurrection of the French clergy against the establishment of the third republic.

The spirit of class, says Benda, easily allies itself with the spirit of conquest in its attack on Democracy; even—on occasion—if the conqueror comes from abroad. At Athens (not to look nearer home!) the propertied class connived with Sparta in the Peloponnesian War; and with Philip in the Macedonian War. Here Benda is manifestly denouncing the French collaborator with Germany who, *after Russia had been attacked,* came exclusively from the propertied class. But, with his usual integrity and clarity, he does not spare the Left. Benda denounces

> another attack against democratic principles in the name of class, that of the Marxist school against these principles in so far as they honour absolute static values, such as justice, truth, reason. According to the Marxist school, Man will only approach the Good when he gets rid of these 'abstractions,' of this 'divinism' (Marx) . . . in other words, when he admits a justice and a truth which are not transcendant over circumstances, but determined by his momentary economic circumstances, and changing as they do.

Formal declarations of such 'pragmatism' are found in Lenin and Stalin. Benda quotes Stalin's (speech on the Five-Year Plan) defence of 'contradiction' as a 'vital' value and as an 'instrument of combat.' He quotes Vichniac, an historian of Lenin, who tells us that the necessity which Lenin found, for the purposes of action, to call error what he had previously called truth (*e.g.,* the N.E.P.) was hugely facilitated by his contempt for all absolute values.

Finally, Benda draws attention to those artists, or so-called artists, who attack Democratic principles on æsthetic grounds. These 'intellectuals' militate, in the name of *immoralism,* against the democratic system as founded on 'moral truisms,' notably the 'Christian truisms' of justice and charity, which seem to them the negation of the artistic temperament.

Benda observes that it is indeed a new thing for men to call upon the tenets of morals or politics to supply them with the same emotions as a work of art; instead of grasping that the sole duty of such tenets is to be just, even if they are completely banal, and that those who are looking for the pleasures of sensibility must look for them elsewhere.

The artist, too, often blames Democracy for the success of mediocrity, and the general vulgarity of manners; which are by no means particular to Democracy. Benda goes so far as to add that the artist is in some ways an organic enemy of Democracy; whereas the philosopher (who does not regard a doctrine which honours universal rather than exceptional Man as a personal insult) is its natural ally.

Conquerors, castes, classes, artists (concludes Benda) all attack Democracy for the same reason: *from sensationalism*. The object of all four is *to feel a sensation*—to conquer, to rule, to repress, to 'feel.' They resent, in their *libido sentiendi,* the ascetic in Democracy.

E. *Fallacies*. (Ideas arbitrarily introduced into the concept of Democracy.)

Benda has some hard words to say on false liberalism, false pacifism, and false rationalism.

He considers that it is 'false liberalism' to think that Democracy owes freedom of action to all its members, including those who work openly to destroy it! The enemies of Democracy, he recalls, who nourish no such illusion themselves, are the first to use it as an argument against Democracy, when Democracy is striving to defend itself.

Benda is refreshingly unfashionable in pointing out that Democracy is not a celestial body, but a thing of this earth which must defend itself. 'Sire, your Kingdom is of *this* earth,' said Turgot to Louis XVI.

Democracy, says Benda, has a right to 'its share of intolerance,' where 'intolerance' means a democracy's right to curtail the liberty to destroy it—a liberty which Democracy never claimed to have created.

Supra-terrestrial notions of Democracy don't work. Democracy has the ordinary needs of 'something which wants to live,' and 'living is not always elegant.' To put ideas before survival may be 'elegant,' or even morally beautiful; but it is not, necessarily, Democratic.

As any ideas which are not strictly fashionable nowadays provoke such epithets as 'fascist,' Benda is careful to show the difference between (*a*) what may be justifiable in a Democracy's determination to forestall those who are working to destroy it, and (*b*) the reactions of a non-democratic state. There is a difference between (*a*) restricting the liberty of expression of citizens who are judged dangerous to the very existence of a régime; and (*b*) throwing them into gaol or sending them to hard labour or to a firing squad! Moreover, Democracy allows the accused to defend themselves, and even to exact reprisals if they have been falsely accused: which is rather different from the attitude of an autocracy in similar cases.

Within these limits, Benda insists on Democracy's right to suppress those of its internal opponents who are working to destroy it *qua* democracy.

He is equally searching in his detection of 'false pacifism.' True pacifism is the hatred but not the refusal of war, in all circumstances.

Benda shrewdly discovers the 'false pacifist,' or 'peace-at-any-price' citizen (even at the cost of liberty), behind the mask of those who argue that a defensive war is actually aggressive and that it has been plotted by 'industrialists or politicians.' Very often, says Benda, they refuse to accept the logical conclusion of their arguments, which is to consent to be molested from morning to night to the end of their days by an aggressor whom they decide not to resist.

Some, however, speak openly. 'Servitude rather than war,' was the motto of a group of French socialists before the war.

The error of all these 'false pacifists' is to suggest that the supreme value for Democracy is *human life,* whereas it is *human liberty*. Democracy condemns not the *fact* of war, but the *love* of war.

Moreover, there are two conceptions of peace. The first is that peace is founded on a contract between nations; this is the juridical conception.

The second expects peace to arise out of love among men; this is the sentimental conception of peace, and it is by far the most popular.

But the late Archbishop of Canterbury was not sentimental when, calling for sanctions against Mussolini's Italy, and being told that war might follow, he said: 'My ideal is not peace, but justice,' Nor was Christ, saying: 'I bring not peace, but a sword' (war against the wicked).

Benda laments that the Archbishop's words, whose harshness expresses the true democratic doctrine, should be antipathetic to a whole class of democrats.

Benda exposes a further *cliché* of false pacifism when he replies to those who complain that a defensive war, even if victorious, 'leads nowhere.' He recalls the innumerable cases in history where such wars—without ensuring a total security, which no people has ever known—have simply saved the liberty of peoples.

Such sophisms about war, says Benda, are a modern creation. Global condemnation of force, irrespective of motive, is moreover the unjust man's guarantee of impunity, and thus becomes one of the world's surest agents for immorality.

Democracy, in any case, contains no disarmament clause; on the contrary, by reason of its principle, the democratic state should be armed more than any other.

Another form of 'false pacifism' is the tendency among certain democrats to show a systematic hostility towards their own country's military institutions: a tendency to grudge its budget, the number of men under arms, or years of service, with the implication that by this 'anti-militarist' attitude they are expressing the true spirit of Democracy.

This Benda shows to be far from true.

The spirit of Democracy, he recalls, is to ensure that the military is subordinated to the civil power. Once this is achieved, Democracy—like all systems which mean to survive, and especially in the present state of the world—needs the organs of its defence to be strong.

Finally, Benda warns us of the danger of 'false rationalism.'

It is sometimes considered 'democratic,' he says, to consider that all our values are open to discussion, and that none of them may be elevated to a dogma, nor form part of a *mystique* (an error which is ably exploited by the enemies of democracy).

Benda says that 'the refusal to put any values beyond discussion is a guarantee of death for any organism.'

It is no law of Democracy to aim at a *total* rationalism, or to regard nothing as sacred. The law of Democracy is to put, like any other system which wants to survive, certain objects above and beyond examination. These objects are the right to criticise, the primacy of justice and liberty, national sovereignty, *i.e.,* all *democratic principles themselves.*

Yet, there are people who argue that Democracy should acknowledge no rules that do not arise from a rational process. Their gross error (common to a whole school of 'free-thinkers') is to think that *all* our perceptions must arise out of reason, instead of understanding that the adoption of political principles, being a moral process, must be fundamentally a matter of faith.

> It is surely easy to grasp that to attribute supreme value to liberty or justice is a moral position, whose excellence cannot be proved as one proves the accuracy of a geometrical proposition.

There is, of course, no implication that reason is not on the side of democratic principles. On the contrary, reason enters far further into the definition of justice than into any mystical faiths in race, etc. It remains true that Democracy, basing itself on pure reason, without the support of an element of passion, cannot successfully defend its principles in the temporal war. 'A passion,' said Spinoza, 'can only be defeated by another passion.'

For this reason, Benda suggests that Democracy may be stronger to defend itself in the United States and in Great Britain, where the adoption of democratic principles has a *religious basis,* than in France where it is based not on religion but on scepticism.

Such, says Benda, are the false notions or parasites which have crept into the democratic body to denature it. *All have the effect of preventing democracy from being strong.* M. Benda's epilogue on the fall of France in the last war, written under the enemy's occupation, may have a message for democrats of other nations.

> If a certain European democracy, recently overthrown, had not admitted these false notions, if it had refused liberty of action to those of its members whose only dream was to destroy it and who had for years preached a foreign policy with this aim, if it had rejected the dogma of peace at any price, if it had recognised that certain States which despised the Rights of Man must not be treated as its equals but constrained to respect, if it had understood its own need of a *mystique,* it would not have met the tragic destiny which befell it. Democracy, by expelling these agents of its own death, will show that it constitutes, like rival systems, an organism which intends to survive; without thereby ceasing to differ radically from those rival systems.

Robert J. Niess (essay date 1956)

SOURCE: "Of Literature," in *Julien Benda,* The University of Michigan Press, 1956, pp. 224-54.

[*Niess is an American writer and professor of French. In the following excerpt, he examines Benda's view of literature and literary artists.*]

"Avoir raison n'est pas littéraire."

That lapidary—and not completely unliterary—phrase from ***La France byzantine*** contains the essence of the long attack on the art of literature which Benda began in ***Dialogues à Byzance*** and which he has enormously developed in the books of the late years of his career. Clearly this antiliterary campaign has been his true favorite, for none of the others is either as old in his work or as continuously developed. But unfortunately for his reputation, it has also been the one which has served most to alienate from him large segments of that "bonne compagnie" to which he has never ceased addressing himself, whatever his opinion of that audience may be, since in it Benda has been doubly impolitic in his own particular way: he has been irritatingly right in some of his conclusions and so touched the sore spot, and, worse, he has also dared treat many of his most distinguished contemporaries with such violence—indeed, sometimes with such obvious injustice—that he has succeeded in discouraging almost everyone, even those best disposed toward his basic views. If unpopularity deliberately sought is the mark of purity, then Benda is the purest of the Levites.

Since its inception in ***Dialogues à Byzance*** the campaign has been of dual aspect: a prolonged effort to demonstrate the inanity of literary art, where Benda carries on and extends an antiliterary tradition that has as its guarantors Plato and Renouvier, among others; and a more original and violent attack on the creators of literature, the poets and novelists and dramatists, for certain moral and intellectual deficiencies he finds inherent in their status. Most of his critics, in thoroughly modern fashion, like to use his arguments as pretexts for amateur psychologizing and tend to ascribe his views to certain personal causes—his extreme age, his own comparative lack of success as a creator of fiction, his failure to win the Goncourt prize, a desire on his part for notoriety, envy, a natural perverseness and iconoclasm—but although all of them are doubtless partly right, none of their explanations touches on the true cause, Benda's experience in the Dreyfus Case. It is notable that his chief targets in ***Dialogues à Byzance,*** with the exception of one or two generals, are nearly all men of letters—Brunetière, Lavedan, Lemaitre, Coppée, Bourget, Hervieu, Barrès, Donnay—but obviously what most infuriated him in the Affaire was not simply the fact that an overwhelming proportion of prominent writers were on the wrong side of the question, that "poète" almost surely meant "patriotard," but that it marked the first time in French history that men of letters, *writing as men of letters,* were given a large voice in a purely judicial debate, were listened to by the public, and were given importance and influence in a matter which he contends was specifically beyond their competence. On a good many occasions after 1898 Benda was to complain bitterly and not completely unreasonably that the artist, merely because he is in the public eye, is given far too much credit in matters which cannot in the nature of things concern him and in which he cannot have important opinions, for after all the artist's merit lies, in Benda's view, in his sensibility and in his knowledge of worldly passions and in nothing more. It was the spectacle of the general weak-mindedness and muddleheadedness the poets displayed in debate in the Affaire, their passion for taking their own vibrations for reasons, their images for arguments, and their sonorities for ideas, that first made Benda conclude that the litterateur, dominated by his sensibility to emotion and sentiment, to metaphysical notions like "patrie," to pure sound and color, was the congenital opposite of the scientist or the philosopher, the intellectual properly speaking, who is dominated by sensibility to Idea alone.

In the course of his investigation of literature Benda has found that there are three main faults which seem to characterize the man of letters: he is essentially insincere, willing to corrupt his idea for the purpose of embellishing it and willing to give the public what it wants to hear at whatever cost to his own probity and integrity; he is essentially an "imperialist" and antidemocrat, loving to sing of war and hatred and violence; and he is essentially incapable of true intellectualism. Although Benda has never elucidated the point, the arguments and examples he adduces in support of these contentions make it clear that he regards the first of these faults as basic to the literary condition, as a universal vice of the litterateur in all climates and in all ages; the second would similarly appear to be a fundamental characteristic of the man of letters, though it has appeared chiefly in modern times, with the rise of egalitarian societies; while the third, if not quite a fault of the contemporary writer alone, is at least more widespread today than ever before.

The first of his criticisms, though perhaps the most fundamental, is not so much developed in the campaign as the other two. It does appear as early as ***Dialogues à Byzance*** and recurs not infrequently all through his discussion of the literary estate, but it is most stressed in the recent attacks on the contemporary man of letters, where the accusation of charlatanism is always present, implicitly or explicitly. The core of his opinion on this score is contained in one of the essays which appeared in *Les Nouvelles littéraires,* **"Péchés d'artistes"** (reprinted in ***Précision***). His basic theory here, undoubtedly an extension of Renouvier's remarks on the literary "dishonesty" Renan had demonstrated in the presentation of his ideas, is that it might be possible to show that literary talent, i.e., "l'art d'arranger des mots en vue d'un certain effet," necessarily implies a certain improbity. He is convinced that all free minds will concede his point that literature, in its essence, includes a certain "tricherie de l'esprit," since if they will take the time to look at the laws of writing they will immediately see that the author is compelled to make all kinds of concessions to his public, however sincere he may think himself.

For what are the rules of "good writing"? The author must not repeat the same word too soon on any page and so must seek synonyms where "la droite pensée" demands the same word; he must often substitute a feminine word for a masculine, when it is the masculine that he really wishes to employ; he must avoid harsh words, which are sometimes the very ones that tell his thought precisely; he must seek variety in a logical movement which asks only to be uniform. Now, all those who write "well" observe the laws, apparently without realizing that these are so many small betrayals; but it is unfortunately true that if they continue to observe them for very long their mental apparatus inevitably becomes twisted and impaired. Benda points out, justly enough, that a sentence which perfectly expresses a certain idea need not necessarily please or even hold the attention of the "honnête homme," the man interested in thought but at the same time a nonspecialist, for logic has no consideration at all for this man's tastes and preferences. If the writer attempts to arrange his sentence so that it will please the "honnête homme," therefore, he agrees to change it as the perfect expression of his idea. "Le dernier des humains, dit un verdict célèbre, est celui qui cheville. Risquerai-je: le dernier des humains est celui qui écrit bien." It seems to him that the philosophers who are outstanding for probity of mind, Kant, Comte, Renouvier, write badly, at least for the "honnête homme," but that the philosophers who are known for their literary talent are quite lacking in intellectual rigor—obviously, in thinking so much of Bergson and Renan he forgets Plato and Lucretius.

Benda's second charge, that the litterateur is essentially an imperialist and antidemocrat, a true reactionary, is both more original with him and more thoroughly developed in his work, this undoubtedly because of his tendency to see all of modern life as conditioned by political passion. This reproach is implicit all through ***Dialogues à Byzance,*** where it is constantly suggested that the poets were on Mercier's side because of their fundamental love of hierarchy, of "architectonic" social organization, and because of their equally fundamental detestation of any system looking to equality and justice. In ***Les Sentiments de Critias*** and ***Billets de Sirius,*** both written around the moral problems posed by the First World War, he argues that most French men of letters secretly bless the conflict, indeed bless war in general, for war always serves the ideas they love—militarism, clericalism, and the like—and provides them with their best, perhaps their only real source of lyricism. Peace would be a real catastrophe for many of them, he is sure, for with its coming all their inspiration would disappear: " . . . la guerre est la substance du lyrisme et de sa fortune. Oter la guerre aux lyriques, c'est leur ôter le pain de la bouche." In these books he is particularly bitter on the subject of the contemporary literary exaltation of the feudal and warlike soul, the praise of violence and scorn for peace and civilization in which so many *gens de letters* seem to indulge in times of stress. The litterateur is a man to whom falseness is very nearly the norm of conduct, but nowhere does he seem so false and base as when he depicts war in terms of heroism and pathos, for it is here that he most corrupts the naïve public mind and so renders conflict eternal.

But these early books were mere exercises in which Benda tried out his idea on the public. It was not until ***La Trahison des clercs*** and the works which followed it that he went at all deeply into the question of the litterateur's basic political and moral preferences, but once he had begun his investigation in earnest it yielded some highly provocative ideas.

One of the forms of clerkly betrayal to which Benda pays the keenest attention in ***La Trahison des clercs*** is the introduction of political passions into those works which had traditionally been mirrors of the disinterested intellect, the works of literary art. The process is not particularly surprising as a characteristic of the poets, he concedes, for the poetic document can scarcely be separated from its creator's passions, which in some instances, even in France, have always been political in nature. But certain modern poets have sounded a completely new and far more dangerous note, have indeed invented a whole new genre, "le lyrisme philosophique," in which the action of lyricism adds to itself the prestige of the spirit of abstraction:

> On ne saurait nier . . . que la passion politique, telle qu'elle s'exprime chez un Claudel ou un d'Annunzio, cette passion consciente et organisée, *exempte de toute naïveté,* froidement méprisante de l'adversaire, cette passion qui, chez le second de ces poètes, se montre si précisément politique, si savamment ajustée aux convoitises profondes de ses compatriotes, à la vulnérabilité exacte de l'étranger, ne soit quelque chose d'autre que les éloquentes généralités des *Tragiques* ou de l'*Année terrible.*

But the poets are not the only guilty ones; they may, in fact, be less guilty than some of their confreres, the novelists and dramatists. Here the situation is really more serious, for it is the function of these two types of litterateurs to depict the movements of the human soul in as objective a manner as possible. Where the modern novelist sins is not in sowing his work with tendentious reflections—Balzac did that—but in refusing to endow his fictional characters with sentiments and actions conformable to living reality and in insisting on making his personages the mirrors of his own passions. In some novels, for example, the traditionalist displays the only noble soul, in others it is the worker; in some only the Frenchman is admirable, in others only the foreign revolutionary:

> La malfaisance de ce procédé est double: non seulement il attise considérablement la passion politique dans le cœur du lecteur, mais il lui supprime un des effets les plus éminemment civilisateurs de l'oeuvre d'art, je veux parler de ce retour sur soi auquel tout spectateur est porté devant une représentation de l'être humain qu'il sent vraie et uniquement soucieuse du vrai. [***La Trahison des clercs***]

Such malpractice is the surest sign of a great decline in the artist himself and in the value of his activity, for his greatness lies precisely in the fact that he "plays" at human passions instead of living them and finds in his "game" the same joys as the common run of humanity finds in the pursuit of reality.

In Benda's investigation of the causes of the transformation of the *clerc,* the discussion very quickly turns to the *gens de lettres,* so quickly indeed that one suspects that the ***Trahison*** is fundamentally concerned with their defection alone. He points out that the new writers differ radically from their French predecessors in their stronger career interests; since for the past two centuries the highest literary success has gone, in France at least, only to those who have adopted clearly defined political attitudes, they quite understandably feel that if they wish to succeed they are obliged to adopt such an attitude. And if the attitude they adopt is so often authoritarian in nature, that is because all writers realize that the *bourgeoisie* is all-powerful now and that accordingly they must serve up to it the ideas it likes if they expect to reap the highest rewards. The writer is no longer a leader and guide of minds, he is a member of the flock. Then again, certain changes have taken place within the clerkly mind itself in recent times, especially in the mind of the literary *clerc.* He has, for instance, perfected his Romanticism, by which Benda here means the will to exploit only those themes which lend themselves readily to striking literary attitudes: the doctrines of authority, discipline, tradition, the scorn of the spirit of liberty, the affirmation of the morality of war and the necessity of some kind of human slavery are infinitely more likely to strike the minds of simple people than the sentimental effusions of liberals. When they are passed off as having their foundations in science and in "pure experience," as they so often are, these doctrines are even more effective. This development is the source of what Benda likes to call the "romantisme pessimiste" of the contemporary man of letters.

But the most profound change that has occurred in the clerkly mentality is indicated by the growing desire of artists to venerate only their "sensibilité artistique" and to find in it the basis of all their judgments:

> On peut dire que jusqu'à ces derniers trente ans les gens de lettres, du moins du monde latin, disciples en cela de la Grèce, se voulaient déterminés dans leurs jugements—même littéraires—incomparablement plus par la sensibilité à la raison que par la sensibilité artistique, dont, au reste, ils prenaient à peine conscience en tant que distincte de la première. [***La Trahison des clercs***]

Benda concedes that a weakening of sensibility to pure reason did take place around 1830, but scorn for intellectual sensibility is a completely new trait in the man of letters, a product of the other Romantic revolution of 1890. At about that time writers, enlightened by Bergsonian analysis, began to become clearly aware of the profound difference that separates "la sensibilité artistique" and "la sensibilité intellectuelle" and violently to choose in favor of the first. They began to declare, specifically, that a work is great if it is successful literarily, that its intellectual content is of no interest or importance, that all theses are equally defensible. This new reasoning inevitably had its effect on their political ideas, for if an object or a system is good only to the degree that it satisfies our artistic needs and desires, then it is evident that the authoritarian regimes alone are good:

> . . . la sensibilité artistique est autrement satisfaite par la vue d'un système qui tend à la réalisation de la force et de la grandeur que d'un système qui tend à l'établissement de la justice, le propre de la sensibilité artistique étant l'amour des réalités concrètes et la répugnance aux conceptions abstraites et de pure raison, dont l'idée de justice est le modèle; surtout la sensibilité artistique est éminemment flattée par la vue d'un

> ensemble d'éléments qui se subordonnent les uns aux autres jusqu'à un terme suprême qui les prime tous, tandis que la vue, qu'offre une démocratie, d'un ensemble d'éléments *dont aucun n'est le premier* frustre un des besoins fonciers de cette sensibilité. [***La Trahison des clercs***]

And there are psychological reasons, too, for this hatred, which Benda finds endemic in the literary type: the typical man of letters inclines by nature to regard as a kind of personal insult any doctrine which honors universal man, for the characteristic of all artists is precisely that they see themselves as exceptional beings, made to enjoy the world, not to serve it; again, the artist will detest any regime that limits his freedom of action by enforcing consideration of the rights of others, for as an artist he is tempted to believe that he has certain sovereign privileges, the familiar "rights of genius."

Benda's third charge against the litterateur—that he is fundamentally nonintellectual, even anti-intellectual, in character and mental conformation—stems as clearly as the other two from the Dreyfus Case, where day after day he witnessed the irritating spectacle of the public's insistence on giving the same value to the arguments of a Coppée or a Brunetière, even of a Zola or a France, as to the findings of the judicial experts themselves. His later work makes it quite apparent that he set out from that time to correct the situation, to bring the litterateur back to what he considers to be his true place in society, a place well below the scientist and the philosopher, and to demonstrate that the creator of fictions, whatever his pretentions and success with the intellectually naïve, has no real place in the corporation of thinkers. It is true that he never goes so far as to say specifically that literary talent excludes intellectual ability (as it seems to him to exclude probity), that style cancels thought, though he constantly implies exactly that; but he does admit, significantly, that even the masters who were able to join true thought to literary talent, Renan, Taine, Montesquieu, arouse in him a secret distrust which he does not at all experience when he reads the pages of such "untalented" thinkers as Descartes and Comte. Benda's paramount idea with respect to the artist is that, try as he will to make himself into an intellectual, he remains forever a "technicien de la jouissance"; the writer's sole function is to express his sensibility and by its expression to move the sensibility of others. It is this definition that allows him to repeat approvingly Comte's judgment that the litterateur in all ages is a false and superficial mind; it is by its terms that he can say quite seriously in ***La Jeunesse d'un clerc***: "Je garde une grande considération à l'érudit qui, s'il n'est que la valet de la grande intelligence synthétique, me semble une forme d'humanité meilleure et plus évoluée que le littérateur dont le propre est de se repaître de périodes agréables et d'affirmations creuses." And again, in ***Exercice d'un enterré vif***: "Je les [i.e., litterateurs] trouve volontiers enfantins et tiens un Kant ou un Descartes, voire un Fresnel ou un Darwin, pour des exemplaires humains supérieurs à Ronsard ou Baudelaire, voire à Dante ou Victor Hugo."

These ideas on the literary condition are most succinctly expressed in the second section of ***La France byzantine,*** entitled "Essai d'une psychologie originelle du littérateur," the point of departure of which is the argument that the litterateur represents a unique type on the face of the earth and that he was so long confounded with the intellectual because of an apostasy from his true nature as artist. Benda's first observation in this "psychologie originelle" is that the litterateur tends *by essence* to vagueness of ideas, since historically he has always wished to produce emotions, and vague ideas are far more suitable to that end than precise ideas, the characteristic of which is to inhibit emotion. The first states of consciousness to receive literary form, he observes, were stupor, terror, ecstasy, joy, sadness, hatred, fury, love, and all the earliest forms of literature express emotions, never ideas—epic, ode, elegy, tragedy, tale. The literature of observation and analysis arose only much later. Of course ideas began very early to accompany emotions in literature, but the ones which the litterateur found valid for his purpose—the creation of emotion—were vague ideas. And even those authors who in more recent times have taken philosophical systems as their subject matter offer no real contrast to their predecessors: they are still litterateurs because in the beginning they were *moved* by these ideas, and they were moved by them because they had stripped them of their precise outline and logical apparatus. The same must hold, of course, for those litterateurs who take science as their theme; Renan's works and the works that resemble them do not disprove his claim, he thinks, for they all depend on such terms as "peuple," "race," "classe," "nation," the very type of vague ideas and hence charged with a pathetic potential. "Le littérateur, en proscrivant l'idée nette et la rigueur logique, délétères de l'émotionnel, ne fait que prendre conscience d'une de ses raisons d'être" (***La France byzantine***).

Secondly, the litterateur, *by essence,* rejects general ideas, impersonal truth, objectivity. The earliest literature aimed at the expression of exterior reality alone, and only later in literary evolution did general types of humanity begin to appear. Perhaps because of his interest in individual beings and objects, the primitive litterateur always marked his work with his own personality; modesty and self-abnegation were not his characteristics, and here again he displays a sign of his basic unintellectualism, his flight from objectivity and impersonal truth—in which, Benda declares, the litterateur cannot believe. It is true, of course, that as he expresses his own soul and temperament the artist also gives expression to the souls of other men, but even as he thus gives voice to a kind of universal he does so in a *personal form* and therefore automatically rejects the judgment of the multitude, for sensibility to art is not characteristic of all men. And in this way again he is opposed to the intellectual, whose affirmations are in principle evident to all men, all men having the faculty of understanding.

Again, the litterateur *by essence* places form above matter:

> Le littérateur est celui qui, exprimant des sentiments, voire des idées, confère de l'importance à la matière verbale—la lettre, *littera, littera-tura*—par quoi il les exprime, et introduit de la beauté ou ce qu'il croit tel dans cette matière considérée *en soi,* c'est-à-dire indépendamment,

du moins pour une partie, de son rapport à la chose exprimée. [*La France byzantine*]

It is the search for verbal beauty that is the true hallmark of the litterateur, and the writer who would express his ideas without concern for beauty might be a great scientist, a great philosopher, a great psychologist, "il peut offrir le spectacle de l'émotion la plus profonde et la plus troublante" (*ibid.*), he still would not be a litterateur. And Benda insists: if a writer pursues only logical perfection he will not find what the litterateurs call beauty, for though there is clearly a kind of "ideological" beauty, the kind we find in a memoir of Fresnel or a page of Descartes, this is not beauty as the literary specialist sees it. But if the writer attempts to create beauty, even though he has nothing to say, then he is a litterateur: Guez de Balzac, Voiture are the type. "En somme, un des traits organiques du vrai littérateur est de porter au moins autant d'amour à la forme dont il vêt sa pensée qu'a cette pensée elle-même . . . ". And thus it is that the litterateur can be called congenitally insincere, since concern with form always implies willingness to compromise with truth.

Lastly, the litterateur has *by essence* the desire to please, and the man who would create literature only for himself would be a monster, contrary to nature. For literature in principle is an eminently social activity, and the man who practices it inevitably resembles the female in his desire to please, his coquettishness, his vanity, and his jealousy. And because he is "female"—Benda does not quite say "a prostitute"—with a basic desire to charm others, he has no scruple at all in "arranging" the truth, in disrespecting it. This "psychologie" is indeed an original one.

It is scarcely necessary to point out that these observations on the litterateur must inevitably apply to Benda himself, for there is simply no doubt at all that he is, in a certain sense at least, a litterateur too. There are, for example, his specific admissions that he regards himself as an *homme de lettres*. In ***Exercice d'un enterré vif*** he openly declares that much of his fury against his fellow writers came from his consciousness that he resembled them only too much and describes his long attraction to the novel as a very torment of his life, for each time he found himself in possession of a broad and powerful idea he was torn between his desire to incarnate it in fictional form and his consciousness that an essay would make a better vehicle. In ***Un Régulier dans le siècle*** he admits frankly that in writing ***Les Amorandes*** he had consciously tried to write a novel of life, of color, of concrete images, a novel capable of pleasing the *mondains* with whom he was then passing much of his time. If these admissions are not enough, there is the obvious fact of his literary practice itself—two novels, a volume of sketches, the constant and often successful search for a compelling personal style, as rhythmic and filled with what he calls "carnal" images as any of our time, his persistent effort toward the most dramatic form for his ideas, exemplified in his unusually numerous "dialogues" of Renanian type, his frequent and attractive "pensées détachées," the whole body of the Elutheriana, in which the literary intention is so evident. Taken in its mass, his work is clearly as much the product of the type of mentality he assails as of the kind he has always consciously tended toward. Here again is the basic struggle within the man between the forces of life and of idea, here again the secret of his interest. But, of course, the argument that his motives were all too frequently as literary as his contemporaries' has little real importance; it has no more validity than the argument that his criticism of the *bourgeoisie* is vitiated by his own bourgeois condition, or that his critique of nationalism is invalidated by his own chauvinistic temper. These observations serve only to demonstrate that this man who, by the estimate of some of his contemporaries, has made a career of injustice is courageous enough and honest and just enough to make an effort to look disinterestedly at the corporation to which his most fundamental inclinations bind him, whatever the dictates of his reasoning mind. If his conclusions are so exaggerated and so damning, that is undoubtedly because they are the product of an exaggerated desire to be fair.

Now, what of literature itself, what of the products of the literary mind? Almost the same ambivalence, in different terms, is evident in this context. All through Benda's works there are the most obvious signs of a wide literary knowledge and a real love of literary beauty, and almost equally frequent signs that literature holds a very high place in his scale of values because of the superior morality it connotes as one of the supreme "activités de luxe," one of the most beneficent because most disinterested agents of civilization. Indeed, it is this very regard for the philosophical and moral importance of literature that has served in part to keep Benda from whole-hearted devotion to the Communist principle of social organization, because, however much he may talk about the new reign of justice, it is clear that a society which would banish literature in its traditional Occidental sense could never have his complete support. For he is a *clerc,* a mandarin, and where does the mandarin find his pleasure but in the realm of the exquisite? It is apparent, too, that while he consistently regards science as the basis of intellectualism and while his preferences clearly go to it as the highest human activity, he also regards literature as the basis of culture, and much of his long career has been a struggle for the maintenance of culture in its traditional sense. The volume and frequency of his criticisms of the literary phenomenon, just as with Bergsonism, point to a long fascination. And even though these criticisms are often so violent and farfetched that they seem to justify the usual charge of philistinism brought against him, there are still good grounds for thinking that he does not mean all he says, that when he is most bitter about the faults of literature in general he is actually referring only to contemporary literature in its specifically "modern" aspects, and that he customarily pushes his expression beyond the bounds of reasonable acceptability because he is combating a popular fetish and because he is engaged in a polemic where nearly everyone is against him. He really cannot expect us always to take him seriously in the campaign, any more than in the campaign against Bergson; many of his most peremptory remarks, indeed, are obviously no more than the tactics of "la bonne guerre."

The criticisms he brings against the general nature of literature, i.e., literature in its eternal manifestations and not simply in its modern appearances, are two, and they reflect exactly two faults of the litterateur as Benda defines him: that literature is imperialism incarnated and that, far from being an agent of truth, it possesses no intrinsic intellectual value whatsoever. The first, the moral charge, is one of his favorite minor themes and as such is often discussed by Eleuthère in his musings on life and ideas [in ***Songe d'Eleuthère***]. The point he makes is obviously an extension of the passion for justice which Benda and Eleuthère share, the corollary of the belief that all existing things are evil by the mere fact of their existence, and a development of Benda's fixed opinion that it is in the nature of the artist to regard the world as made for his own uses alone. On more than one occasion, as Eleuthère regards the great artistic accomplishments of the past, his deep pleasure in them is somewhat tempered by the realization that art in all its forms is the most evident symbol of the oppression of the people by an elite. But now that societies have arisen which promise an end to oppression of the many by the few, societies whose principle is the guarantee of equality to all men, Eleuthère is somewhat baffled by the continuing existence of art, for it seems to him that it has become a real anomaly in the new world: such societies cannot, in the nature of things, produce art if they remain faithful to their basic principle. When democracy's authoritarian opponents tax it with inability to create beauty, democracy should cease its efforts to prove that its atmosphere is fully as favorable to artistic accomplishment as monarchy itself: it should simply and truthfully reply that its concern is not with beauty at all, but that it is in its nature to give mankind something far higher, justice. And when democracy's proponents argue that certain modern states have produced great artists, Eleuthère replies, in ***Songe d'Eleuthère,*** that they did not do so by observing their own principle, for democracy itself did not produce these great artists, they simply happened to be born under a democratic regime. No true artist can practice democracy in his capacity of artist, he is sure, and indeed an enormous number of artists seem to have detested the very word and very many still do; even Hugo and Michelet are not exceptions to his law, he believes, for although they took democracy as a theme of art and although their ideas were undeniably democratic, still their *temperament* was not: "Un tempérament démocratique ne passera jamais des heures à arranger des phrases par besoin de s'affirmer. Un tel besoin est souverainement impérialiste" (***Songe d'Eleuthère***). Inescapably, the work of art is impious:

> Elle naît d'une soif de dominer. L'ordre qu'elle insère au-dedans d'elle-même est un moyen d'accroître sa domination, de s'assurer contre l'extérieur qui veut la ramener au néant comme il y veut ramener toute chose. C'est un acte essentiellement militaire. Cela éclate dans l'art ordonné par essence: l'architecture. Tout le monde sent l'impérialisme d'une cathédrale.

Here, quite clearly, Eleuthère has gotten himself and his creator in a bit of trouble, for if organization and order are the primary sins of art, as they are of all life, then such literature as surrealism and Dadaism have produced would seem to be far holier than the art of the Greek, Roman, and French classics, "ordered" as it indisputably is. Yet surrealism and Dadaism and all their derivatives and congeners are anathema to Benda, and Eleuthère's preferences are for the classics. Eleuthère is not unconscious of the dilemma and in ***Songe d'Eleuthère*** does concede that the works which present a minimum of conscious organization are perhaps most aggreable to God. He quite prudently does not give his own opinion about them. It is interesting to speculate, all the same, that the theories of ***Essai d'un discours cohérent*** lead directly and inevitably to the most advanced esthetic thinking of our time and that, if circumstances had been slightly different, Benda might well have collaborated on the *Manifeste surréaliste.* Moreover, what of the question of the *clerc* who is an artist in the manner of a Baudelaire or a Verlaine? If his activity is essentially imperialistic in nature and gives other men the sensation of imperialism in action, how can he be a true *clerc*? For is not the *clerc*'s major duty to eradicate the very spirit of imperialism in mankind? Yet, by the definition of the ***Trahison*** itself, writing is one of the clerkly vocations and by no means the least honorable. Benda's discourse here is scarcely coherent.

Those not entirely unimportant points aside, however, it is Benda's final conclusion, expressed by Eleuthère in ***Délice d'Eleuthère,*** that art is intrinsically, basically evil: "Toute littérature est opposition, c'est-à-dire guerre. La non-opposition est silence, intelligence totale, *anti-littérature*" (italics mine). But perhaps there is more than a touch of Baudelairean attraction toward sin in him, for, evil or not, art has never ceased occupying him.

Benda's second criticism, that literature has no intellectual function and no intellectual value, is much more developed and much more seriously presented than the first; this is no mere metaphysical exercise but a long and reasoned attempt to prove by constant argument and example that modern society is in serious error when it looks to art for truth. Although as early as ***Dialogues à Byzance*** there are already clear evidences in his work that he considers literature a distinctly lower activity than science, even an infantile one, the campaign did not really begin in earnest until the opening of his attack on Bergson. It was very probably the "literary" character of Bergsonism that touched it off, the ideas advanced around the turn of the century by so many critics, more or less under the spell of the new belief, that philosophy and literature are sister activities with no clear line of demarcation between them, that the man of letters is frequently a better seer and guide to humanity than the pure intellectual in his library or his laboratory, and that accordingly literature can be a real agent for the discovery and dissemination of truth. It has always been Benda's intention to disprove this theory, to demonstrate that philosophy and science, with their essential rationality, are both organically different from literature and superior to it in moral value, that literature, raised by popular opinion to the level of highest human activity because it contains all the others, has in fact only one function, to please, to produce amusement, and that man's love of art is at bottom only a love of sensual delight.

The actual point of departure for the attack, the little phrase that can make Benda see red—and at the basis of every one of his campaigns there is probably such a phrase—is Anatole France's remark to the effect that if he had to choose between truth and beauty he would unhesitantingly choose beauty, sure that it bore within itself a truth higher than the truth itself. Time and again Benda has returned to the statement, always arguing in the same way: that the word "vérité," as Anatole employs it, is nothing but a play on words, that the "truth" of the frieze of the Parthenon or of Phryne's limbs—assuming that it exists at all—is a far different truth from the truth of Faraday's law or of Fermat's principle. Art is art, he will maintain, it is a product of human sensibility, not of human intellect—literature is not philosophy, much less science; literature, again as Anatole France had it, is the *Thousand and One Nights* of the Occident.

Yet the fact constantly arises to plague him that there is a good deal of literature, even poetry, which does contain valid valuable ideas and that he himself gave an excellent example of it in ***L'Ordination***. His answer, most succinctly expressed in ***Exercise d'un enterré vif,*** is that although real thought can be introduced into the forms of art, it is still *introduced* there, it is not there naturally: "La pensée, par sa nature, manque de style," that somewhat debatable argument of Valéry's, is his motto. For it is his conclusion, also to be found in the ***Exercise,*** that thought and artistic beauty are two *essentially distinct* qualities which, if they join at all, join only by accident.

This thought is considerably developed in ***Du Style d'idées,*** where Benda presents in the most ponderously reasoned form all the conclusions on the relationship of literature and ideas that he had reached during a lifetime of speculation. In the very first pages of the book he faces a crucial problem—one, incidentally, which he had already touched on in ***Discours à la nation européenne***—the relationship of idea and word. In the foreword he offers this specific statement of belief:

> Le style d'idées a . . . cela de particulier, *par quoi il diffère du style littéraire,* qu'il doit se mouler exactement sur la pensée, de même qu'en retour celle-ci lui demande de ne lui valoir qu'un vêtement transparent sans rechercher de beauté pour lui-même, sa beauté consistant dans le parfait de cette transparence. On pourrait observer à ce propos que les fameux vers de Boileau prêtent à l'esprit une action en deux temps, laquelle au vrai n'en présente qu'un. Il ne semble point que l'esprit commence par "concevoir bien," c'est-à-dire par former une idée claire et que ce soit ensuite que pour exprimer cette idée les mots "arrivent aisément." La vérité est que ces deux opérations n'en font qu'une et que, lorsque l'esprit forme vraiment une idée claire, les mots voulus sont là *dans le même moment,* par la raison que notre esprit est ainsi fait que la formation d'un concept et l'évocation d'un mot sont un seul et même acte. [first italics mine, second Benda's.]

It is not clear, unfortunately, why the process Benda attributes to the ideologist should not also be that of the litterateur, but in the distinction he makes between the two modes of composition lies the basis of his whole campaign, the argument that while the man of ideas expresses himself directly, that is honestly, the man of letters does not. It is the very difference he establishes between word and idea as employed by the artist that enables him to bring one of his most frequent charges: that the idea of the man of letters, when stripped of its garment of style, is more often than not reduced to a pure "misère." It is scarcely necessary to point out that changes in literary style imply quite as much difference in idea as do changes in the "ideological" style, and that the process he describes of "stripping" such and such an author's thought of its expression is not logical analysis at all but deliberate reduction in level of rhetoric.

This, however, is not the real interest of ***Du Style d'idées,*** which is to be found rather in its long discussion of the intellectual value of the various literary genres. Passing them in review—essay, novel, drama, poetry—he concludes that none of them has any real validity as expression of rational thought, because the inherent nature of literature makes it impossible for the writer, even if he were capable of straight thinking, to express any more than scattering and sporadic, personal views on humanity and on human passional movements. Literature has significance in the history of society; in the history of ideas it has absolutely none at all.

Nowhere is this opinion expressed with such pungency as it is concerning the poets, the writers who undoubtedly suffer from the most desperate case of "literaturism" and who represent the diametrical opposite of the "scientific" mind as Benda defines it. Simply because they are the most literary of litterateurs (and most foreign to his own kind of soul) they offer him one of those "cas-limites" he likes so well to discuss, and he finds them so interesting that he has lately been more and more drawn to contemplate their art, to attempt to discover the meaning and value of the contemporary movement, and to assay the human value of poetry, the poet's function in society.

It is in ***Du Poétique,*** an offshoot of ***La France byzantine,*** that Benda approaches the first of these subjects and tries to seek out the reasons why men apply the adjective "poetic" to certain groups of words. Unfortunately, however, his search results only in a very long listing of the ideas (he seems to confuse ideas with themes here) which to his mind have intrinsic poetic power and another, shorter list in which he includes those which do not seem to him to have this power. What is remarkable in these lists is not the ideas themselves (most of them are hackneyed and indicate a distinctly limited range of acceptance on his part), but the amazing claim that there are some ideas which have poetic virtue in themselves quite apart from any rendition by the poet and some which do not. He does not appear to realize that his ideas-poetic-in-themselves have already been treated by poets and so were endowed with poetic form when he encountered them. What he mistakes for their intrinsic poetry is the residue of that form lying deep in his subconscious, the remnants of the beauty which some poet's expression had given them. One has the impression, as this analysis unfolds, that Benda agrees with his classic master that "Tout est dit," but given the whole inclination of his mind to look backward for its truth and beauty, it is not surprising that he should fail to see that the domain of poetry lies limitlessly ahead.

Accompanying this list of ideas which have intrinsic poetic power is a series of quite surprising contrasts he draws between the poetic spirit and technique on the one hand and the scientific and philosophic spirit on the other, together with a number of provocative remarks on the general morality of the poetic exercise. Where Benda is most controversial, certainly, is in his discussion of the degree to which poetry is capable of interpenetrating the other forms of intellectual activity. Here he is obviously replying to the critics (and to the poets themselves) who profess to see the poetic manner and the poetic view in all kinds of exercises which lie outside the strict domain of verse, and to those numerous other intellectuals who would attempt to introduce the poet's ways into their own endeavors. As a good Kantian, he is shocked by such a tendency and so sets about writing a small "Critique of Pure Poetry" in which he attempts to draw up something like a delimitation of its proper sphere, his conclusion being that no other genre, so long as it continues to observe its own laws, can ever be properly poetic. Concerning philosophy, which both philosophers and poets are trying so hard to incorporate into the realm of poetry nowadays, he remarks:

> Pour autant qu'elle est science—psychologie objective, logique, morale expérimentale—elle ne nous donne aucun sentiment du poétique; elle nous le prodigue, au contraire, en tant qu'elle est métaphysique, qu'elle manie les idées d'infini, d'inconnaissable, d'ineffable, de nécessité, de liberté, d'immortalité, de création personnelle ou non du monde, et autres dont l'adéquation ou non au réel est indémontrable. C'est sur ce terrain, où elle ignore la science, qu'on a pu dire que la philosophie rejoint la poésie. [***Du Poétique***]

Just how unpoetic poetry can be when it treats a really philosophical concept and at the same time just how infantile it can be from the philosophical point of view is demonstrated, he thinks, by the verses of "Le Cimetière marin" which treat the ideas of Zeno. And with such poems as "Eloa" or "La Maison du berger," the philosophy consists in a description of the poet's sensibility in the face of the problem of evil, not in any treatment of the problem itself.

Benda is equally willing to give his views on what human movements cannot, in the nature of things, produce poetry. He considers that no written document is poetic when it takes on the guise of science or eloquence or oratory, or when it expresses a too-precise view of things—he finds no poetry, for instance, in the "Ballade des pendus" or "Montfaucon"—for the true sentiment of poetry is given by the ear, by "les mages du musical," i.e., by the symbolists, not by the Parnassians or the other masters of the picturesque. Poetry is much more likely to be produced by the floating contours drawn by a Loti or a Chateaubriand than by Hugo's firm and "cutting" visuality. It is possible to conclude, he thinks, that any idea that is too clear and distinct, even when expressed by the most beautiful image, is by the very fact of its clarity the negation of poetry. Nor does he feel that "le sentiment poétique" is created by the spectacle of the object limited to itself, for limitation is scientific, but rather by the object that allows us to understand more than it declares. Poetry is a product of "le prolongé," not of "l'arrêté," it comes only from the "extra-texte." This is why he finds no poetry in any expression of a soul state that is too precisely rendered: "ce qui, dans la chose écrite, me donne le sentiment du poétique est ce qui abolit en moi l'idée du déterminé et de l'explicable et y profuse le sens du rêve et du mystère" (***Du Poétique***). By this preference, he submits, the great line of French poets would be composed of Charles d'Orléans, Villon, Ronsard, La Fontaine, Lamartine, Musset, Verlaine, Fargue. "Baudelaire n'est plus esthétique que poétique" (*ibid.*).

In the last section of the book Benda faces the question which obviously has attracted him from the beginning, the moral value of poetry and of poetic sensibility. His general conclusion is that poetry would appear to be an immoral exercise, inasmuch as it addresses itself to the inner being and is thus the exact opposite of the most highly moral exercise, science, whose distinguishing characteristic is its tendency to envisage the world apart from any connection with man. Then too, since poetry is linked to the idea of mystery, of the unexplained, it seems to Benda to be the plaything of a humanity still in its infancy and thus devoid of real moral conceptions. It is serious that poetry should so often turn for its inspiration to the cruel forces of nature, to the shadowy, "fatal" past, to what is generally "military" in the world, but it is even more serious that the poetic spirit should flourish especially in those races which have remained nearest the state of nature and whose moral sense is correspondingly slight and that it should be weakest in those nations most open to the appeal of reason, for Benda is certain that the more man approaches true Christianity, the more insensitive he becomes to the appeal of poetry:

> Je situerai encore le statut moral du sentiment poétique en observant qu'en tant que lié au sens de l'épandu, non de l'arrêté, de l'estompé, non du précis, du musical, non du plastique, il est lié à la conscience du sensuel, non de l'intellectuel, du voluptueux, non du sévère. Sa conformation morale est femelle. Il est curieux de voir certaines personnes qui ne se nourrissent que de poésie soutenir qu'elles cultivent ainsi leur esprit et refuser de convenir qu'elles n'entendent satisfaire, au fond, que leur sensualité.
>
> Quant au sentiment du poétique en tant qu'il consiste à être charmé par des sons harmonieux, par un vocable évocateur, par une image belle ou gracieuse, il ne comporte aucune valeur morale. On le trouve au plus haut point chez des peuplades sauvages, dépourvues de toute moralité.
>
> En somme l'immoral l'emporte. [***Du Poétique***.]

So much for poetry as intellectual and spiritual exercise. Now what of it in its most specifically poetic form, modern poetry? The conclusions are even more damaging. Benda's general view is that while poetic sensibility evolved more rapidly in the nineteenth century than in all the two thousand years preceding the Romantics—he cites the fact of a whole new range of themes: progress, political freedom, the liberating power of science, the mystery of childhood, the Middle Ages, the Bible, the Eastern myths, and the introduction of new sensations and new associations of sensations—such enrichment has not been continued by the poets of our time. Some of the ideas discovered by the nineteenth century have inspired poems which are notable for their power of expression or their vigor of sentiment, but the evolutive process has actually stopped, he believes. Look, for example, at the surrealist doctrine that the two fundamental themes of poetry should be a mystic state in which the old separation of subject and object would be abolished, and the union of the individual soul to the "world soul"; it has produced a host of manifestoes and critical writings of all kinds, but not a single composition that gives him the sense of true poetry. Nor has the new attempt to create a poetry of words alone succeeded any better. "Le progrès de notre sensibilité poétique, qui va de l'action de Victor Hugo jusqu'à celle des symbolistes, semble depuis ce temps arrêté" (***Du Poétique***).

Benda is willing to go further: not only have our contemporaries failed to increase our range of poetic sensibility, for the most part they have not even touched it—and this because they seem to lack, nearly all of them, that quality which may loosely be called "naïveté" or "generosity." In their poems as well as in their doctrines they are all too much occupied by purely verbal techniques, by the desire to be "rare" and original, by the obligations of esthetic systems and theories of language, and so they never think of offering us emotions, never think of giving us human sympathy as we found it in "Le Lac" or the "Nuits." They are, in short: "plus occupés d'être les illustrateurs d'une poétique que des poètes" (***Du Poétique***).

It is perhaps true, he remarks, that no time ever saw so many doctrines but so little poetry—and is the profusion of doctrines not the surest sign of decadence in literature?

He is disturbed especially by two fundamental changes in the form of poetry (both, incidentally, stemming from the same new theory, that the poem must be spoken, not read): the suppression of meter in favor of pure rhythm and the elimination of punctuation. The first is the more serious of the two because it involves an important question concerning the acceptability of modern poetry to the public at large, implying as it does a distinct return to primitive modes of expression which the public, conditioned by thirty centuries of education, refuses to attempt. What the moderns are trying for here is a reconstitution of one form of the most primitive mode of existence, poetry molded to man in the state of nature. Humanity simply replies that it cannot take the step back: *"Non possumus."* But it is not only lack of punctuation and meter which exercises Benda, it is the deliberate unintelligibility of the modern poet that evokes his criticism. He is sure, to begin with, that the modern theorists are trying to pull the wool over the public's eyes when they declare that they are opposed only to "facile" intelligibility; at bottom, he thinks, they refuse *all* intelligibility, and this squarely on the ground that intelligibility of any kind comes from reason and the new poetry wishes to render only sensation:

> . . . elle toise non pas ceux qui ne comprennent que des truismes, mais tous ceux qui prétendent "comprendre," dès l'instant que ce mot veut dire autre chose que mobiliser des sensations et implique l'usage d'idées claires, si peu simples fussent-elles, mais qui ne désavouent pas l'intelligibilité cartésienne; en d'autres termes, l'obscurité n'est pas pour cette littérature une condition *relative,* variable suivant la qualité du lecteur et qu'il peut ne point ressentir grâce à un don spécial; elle en est un attribut *organique,* auquel elle est liée par essence et dont elle ne saurait se départir sous peine de se nier elle-même. [***Non Possumus***—italics Benda's.]

Nowhere, Benda thinks, is the basically antisocial nature of contemporary literature better illustrated than in this aspect of the new theories.

But why should the poets decree that they will no longer make themselves intelligible? Benda thinks their practice grows out of the contemporary philosophical movement: the will to express soul states different from the classic "formes arrêtées," i.e., the desire to seek out and render the states that lie below words; a new desire to commune with the nature of things, with the essence of the universe; the will to place themselves in the sphere of profound action, "pur devenir," dynamism and incessant mobility. And to this last intention his reply is an echo of his oldest arguments against his oldest enemy:

> . . . le sentiment du poétique ne nous est pas donné par la vue du mouvement, lequel, en tant que tel, est essentiellement inintelligible, mais par l'*idée* du mouvement, laquelle n'est pas un mouvement et est, elle, en tant qu'idée, une chose intelligible. Il ne nous est pas donné par le spectacle de la bataille de Waterloo, mais par l'idée, éminemment intelligible, que nous en proposent Victor Hugo ou Stendhal. [***Non Possumus***—italics Benda's.]

But whatever the motives of the new philosopher-poets, Benda is sure that their fundamental goal is everywhere and always to satisfy their *personal aspirations* by their art. And so they seem not to care at all what the *profanum vulgus* demands of poetry—though they may care more than a little that it does not buy their books.

Above all, Benda cannot agree with the doctrine that the reader must create his own sense for each poem he reads, because he is sure that the public will always demand some fixed meaning, not necessarily intellectual but at least "identical to itself," in what it reads. It is for this reason that he feels such deep frustration with those who would make of poetry only an arrangement of words, for in their refusal to construct patterns of sense he finds nothing but a colossal contempt for the public and for the whole business of art.

The feeling of a real divorce between public and poet becomes strongest, he observes, in the little magazines, where he finds all kinds of technical discussions, manifestoes, ukases, and decrees, but never a question as to whether the poets are satisfying the public. Nor indeed is the public even represented, for these magazines are edited by men who are all more or less poets, writing only for themselves and their specialized milieu. And if a new Hugo were to appear—but this is doubtful, for in the past four decades Benda has not seen a poet of value who was not esoteric—would the public have the courage to praise him after the jibes of the *chapelles*? For even in a democracy this is one situation where the majority does not rule and while the *chapelles* often intimidate the public, the opposite never happens.

Yet Benda considers that beneath the public's silence there is discernible a constant demand, an unchanging belief that it knows what it wants in poetry. He feels that the entire history of literature, with all its contradictions and enormous variations of taste, still indicates that mankind has ever sought two characteristics in poetry before it has declared itself satisfied: a certain universality based on intelligibility and a certain representative value, in which states of consciousness which are "identical to themselves" are proposed, for "tout poème qui nous touche, fût-il du plus abscons de nos aèdes, dans la mesure où il nous touche, nous propose *quelque chose,* ce quelque chose pouvant être un pur état sentimental, voire sensoriel" (***Non Possumus***—italics Benda's). It has always been true and always will remain true, he is sure, that the verse which refuses coherence and communication will touch the sensibilities of none but its author and his allies. But though he is as firmly convinced of this truth as of any in his canon, Benda is realistic enough at the same time to know that the new poetry is not doomed to extinction because it does not observe these fundamental laws; on the contrary, it seems, it is its opposite which is condemned.

It is sufficiently clear that poetry, far from being the queen of the arts, occupies a somewhat lower place in Benda's formal hierarchy. This being so, what is the poet's peculiar function, what does he do specifically that no other man can do so well? Not quite surprisingly, Benda seems disinclined to accept either the modern view that he is simply a *faber,* a worker in words, or the current revival, led by such prophets as Rolland de Renéville, Bertelé, Aragon, and Breton, of the Romantic argument that the poet is the true *vates.* On a good many occasions he has taken the opportunity to express quite a different opinion and to assign the muse's servant a humbler role than some of her modern worshipers would give him.

What most exercises Benda, and the point of view he expresses is certaintly not his alone, is the constant attribution of "discovery value" to poetry—the dominant theory that poetry is no longer simply a means of expression but a means of penetrating the secrets of the universe, the frequent preachment that we must "hearken to the poet" because he will lead us to the truth. Lead us to the truth indeed! In the first place, he thinks, we ordinary readers ask the poet to do no such thing; we ask him to move us, to charm us, and that is all. And even if we, the public, had such a view of the poet's capabilities, could he respond to our appeal? Surely not, for the restrictions of his art, as Benda sees them, permit him to discover neither intellectual truth, "scientific" truth, nor even mystic truth. In actual fact, Benda argues in ***Du Style d' idées,*** the poet is the very type of writer from whom it would be supremely impertinent to ask real thought, for his open and declared function is to express his own sensibility (and sometimes also, indirectly, the collective sensibility), not to discover its wellsprings or to cause us to advance in knowledge of its nature. He does not go so far as to claim that the poet cannot, on occasion, illuminate with a singularly piercing light certain of the components of his emotion, but at best such views on his part are scattered and secondary to his object. For his object is always and eternally to *live* his emotion, never to explain it in the abstract, independently of his personal coefficient, a mode of knowledge for which, Benda thinks, the poet has nothing but contempt. His role, by the argument of ***Du Style d'idées,*** is to offer us a description of his soul states in the face of the riddle of the world, the immensity of the sea, the charm of woman, the eternal suffering of mankind, but never to seek the true nature of religious sentiment, of sexual attraction, of the emotion of sympathy. If he gives expression to an idea at all, it must be in connection with a state of sensibility, surrounded by a kind of halo and never clear and distinct, for Valéry was right, according to Benda, when he observed that where clarity and distinctness begin, there poetry ends. Even if the poet is a Vigny and expresses a scientific or philosophic state, i.e., a soul state produced by a scientific or philosophical idea, he must still present it as a *state of sensibility,* never as a pure idea. And moreover, it has been Benda's experience that when the poet's ideas, given form as states of sensibility, are stripped of their "vêtement sensible" they become strangely banal or irritatingly gratuitous. What did we ever learn of the nature of religion from Louis Racine's poem or of justice from Sully Prudhomme's long meditation?

But there is one aspect of their activity wherein one might reasonably expect the poets to expound real ideas, and that is as theorists of the poetic activity itself. Yet even in the most famous of their pronouncements—Poe's *Poetical Principles,* Baudelaire's commentary on the same work, the preface to the *Odes et Ballades*—one is amazed to see that although there are many ingenious views on isolated points of technique, penetrating judgments of other poets, all kinds of precepts, resolutions, attacks, prohibitions, banishments, anathemas, there never is offered the slightest adequate or general idea of what the poet's function really is or of the special mechanism that governs it. Not one of the poets, he thinks, has produced anything so substantial as Renouvier's book on Victor Hugo. Here again, the poet remains still a poet, that is, incapable of the deliberate consideration of abstractions.

> . . . en effet, [Benda says in ***Du Poétique***] énoncer des idées qui vaillent par elles-mêmes, si l'on songe à la langue analytique qu'exigent de telles idées, est contraire à l'essence de la poésie; on pourrait même soutenir qu'il lui est contraire de les penser. Et peut-être certains poètes (encore que je n'en voie guère) ont-ils eu de telles idées. Mais les eurent-ils en tant que poètes?

But the poets will protest, and their words will be recorded in a score of little magazines, that of course they cannot give the kind of truth Benda speaks of; "scientific" truth; they are not illustrating concepts generated in a laboratory. But they will insist that they can give us another and higher kind of truth, a mystic truth, a spiritual transformation, a new soul, a new sense of life's meaning, a new innocence. And here again we, the public, differ: we do not want these things from them, Benda proclaims in his capacity as public interpreter, we do not even think they can give them. We ask of them emotions, the spectacle of a finer sensibility moving among the vicissitudes of life, and when the poet tells us of the somber or radiant revelations he will deliver before our eyes we "Lamoignons" cannot help thinking of the cock of the fable, with his pathetic demurrer: "Mais le moindre grain de mil / Ferait bien mieux mon affaire!" (***Non Possumus***).

And so at the end of all his discussion of the intellectual capabilities of the man of letters Benda comes to a pessimistic conclusion:

> En résumé, si l'on appelle littérateurs les moralistes d'anthologie, les critiques agréés du siècle, les romanciers, les dramaturges, les poètes, tous ceux chez qui domine l'élément littéraire, on peut dire que leur contribution à la connaissance de la réalité humaine consiste, dans le meilleur cas, en des observations perçantes mais éparses, ignorant la fécondation de l'une par l'autre que permettrait leur rapproachement et donc dénuées d'une avancée vraiment profonde dans cette réalité. . . . Unc histoire des idées vraiment fortes sur la réalité humaine peut négliger les littérateurs. Sur le sujet dont ils ont le plus traité, les passions, ce qui a été dit d'important, l'a été par certains philosophes ou savants, lesquels, d'ailleurs, forment eux-mêmes, dans leur corporation, une très infime minorité. [***Du Style d'idées***]

These then, are the reasons why Benda says that to be right is not literary and why he appends to Taine's remark that literary ideas are necessarily vague ideas the corollary that ideas, insofar as they strive to emerge from vagueness, are not literary at all:

> Ceux qui traitent la pensée selon un mode littéraire sont . . . les Alain et les Valéry, avec leurs affirmations non fondées, productrices d'étonnement, méprisantes de toute intention de persuader, qui contentent ces besoins si fréquents chez les raffinés: le goût du paradoxe, le sentiment de soufflet lancé au "sens commun;" affirmations vagues malgré leur ostentatoire précision, épargnant donc à l'attention du lecteur la fatigue de se fixer, la souffrance de se limiter; sibyllines et donc aguichantes; exprimées sous une forme qui avant tout se veut rare. [***Exercice d'un enterré vif***]

These are curious arguments indeed, although Benda is, historically, by no means the only one to represent this point of view. Yet perhaps no critic, at least in France, has ever pushed such conclusions quite so far as he, and certainly no recent student of French literature has gone to the extremes of ***Du Style d'idées*** or ***La France byzantine***. And it is again their exaggeration which renders them unacceptable, for it is difficult to deny some of his points a certain truth, especially when they are seen against the background of "Parisianism" which is their constant though unannounced context. It is clearly high time for someone to react vocally against the fantastic glorification of the artist which has become the stock in trade of too many of the more advanced magazines, and this is certainly the moment to recall that the writer does not hold the answer to all the questions and to protest against the advancement of political and moral opinion by men whose ideas are, in fact, not always better reasoned or more interesting than those of humbler condition.

But to concede a certain rightness—perhaps better, a certain justification—is not to concede that the attacks Benda has mounted are completely valid, for serious objections can be brought against every one of his major points. What does he mean, for instance, by the "littérateur"? Who is this man? Does Benda include in the class all writers, even the eternal geniuses, or is he referring only to such figures as Guez de Balzac or Maurice Dekobra? There is no way of knowing, and so Benda's "littérateur" becomes every writer—but he is also no writer, for even litterateurs are not mere figures on a chart any more than their critics are; they are men who differ radically among themselves in tastes and ideas, abilities and intentions, and to create out of any such heterogeneous human stock a mythical class of evildoers is a typical error of old-fashioned rationalism. Worse, the creation of such an imaginary class, all-inclusive as it seems to be, looks very much like an attempt on Benda's part to render the great guilty of the errors and deficiencies of the small, to make Homer and Dante and Shakespeare responsible for the faults of Upton Sinclair and Crébillon *père* and Paul de Kock, all for the greater glory of Comte and Darwin and Lamarck. If Benda meant to hurl his diatribes against literary hacks, then a good many of his points are sound and cogent, but nowhere in the campaign does he make any significant exceptions and by that error his whole argument becomes doubtful. There is more than a suspicion that he is directing his fire not at writers in general but at the moderns in particular, especially at Gide and Valéry and Alain, for a considerable part of his whole effort has gone to proving that the faults of modern literature are due in great measure to its abandonment of the classic standard. He would have troubled fewer readers if he had been more careful of his definitions.

And what of the writer's supposed insincerity? The whole argument here depends on what seems to be a basic error of observation, the belief that style and idea are separate for the artist but not for the intellectual, and that the writer's temperament and personality dominate his report on experience, while the intellectual's do not. But if Buffon's belief that style comes "de l'homme même" has any validity at all, then it would seem that the very stylistic deficiencies of the intellectual as Benda portrays him in ***Du Style d'idées,*** for instance, are in some way a measure of the man himself. Perhaps the public is not wholly wrong in refusing to pay so much honor to the pure intellectual as to the man of letters, in whom, perhaps, it unconsciously recognizes a higher human exemplar, or at least a more compelling temperament. And even though Benda's points were well taken, it is still difficult to see how the intrusion of a great personality can be construed as a defect and as grounds for bitter moral reproach.

As for the writer's "imperialism," the idea is ingenious and intriguing and possibly valid; only, it would seem that the same argument might also be brought against the work of philosophy and more especially against the work of moralistic intention, where the thinker's individual choices are implicitly or explicitly held up as a model for humanity. But Benda is silent on this kind of imperialism and by his silence betrays a disturbing prejudice.

Then, what of the litterateur's "anti-intellectualism"? Benda's theory depends on the fact—is it a fact?—that the contemporary author, because he seeks diversity and variety and because he refuses to "choose," does not conduct himself as a true intellectual should. But here Benda calls into question all of modern thought, not literature alone, since it may reasonably be argued that one of the primary characteristics of the contemporary intellectual movement is the very refusal to choose, to eliminate, to organize, and this squarely on intellectual grounds. Correspondingly, such failure to observe classic modes of thought, instead of representing nonintellectualism or anti-intellectualism, might well represent intellectualism of a higher order. The true weakness of Benda's position, however, is not his effort to prove that intellectualism must necessarily be Spinozist or Kantian in form and manner, but his insistence that the modern writer is morally inferior because he refuses to adhere to the older systems, and his even broader argument that in general the artist is inferior to the scientist or the philosopher. These are judgments that are difficult to defend, even though Plato and Renouvier might have approved them.

But the portion of the campaign in which Benda obviously lays himself most open to criticism is his long discussion of the relationship of literature and idea. There are, it would seem, two intentions here: an attempt to demonstrate that it is actually morally sounder and intellectually preferable to write badly than to write well, and a second attempt to demonstrate that literature is neither science nor rational philosophy. But of course this is not so, and it was scarcely necessary to write ***Du Style d'idées*** to prove it. Again, the whole conclusion rests on the most debatable premise—that truth, "rightness," can be found only in works of organized and developed ideas, only in works which are "scientific" in the wide sense. Perhaps Benda is right, but the modern world does not seem to agree. What is novel in this part of the attack is the constant resort to moral judgments of the broadest kind, the condemnation of literature for not giving what it cannot give. It is already a truism that good literature is not made with good sentiments; it could be added that good criticism is not made with sophistries.

On the whole, this is perhaps the most disappointing of Benda's campaigns, in spite of the fire and the élan and the real ingenuity with which it is conducted. In no other do his characteristics loom up so clearly, and in no other has he defined himself so thoroughly, for better or for worse. Unfair though it probably is, the suspicion keeps rising that it is in reality only a long plea *pro domo.* It may be of great help in assaying the value of Benda's career, but as "intellectual enrichment," what will the histories of criticism say?

Lothar Kahn (essay date 1968)

SOURCE: "Julien Benda: Assimilation with Self-Acceptance," in *Mirrors of the Jewish Mind: A Gallery of Portraits of European Jewish Writers of Our Time,* Thomas Yoseloff, 1968, pp. 52-67.

[Born in Rehlingen, Saar Territory, Kahn is an American educator and writer. In the following excerpt, he considers the influence of Benda's Jewish heritage on his opinions and works.]

Assimilation has been a much overused term in modern Jewish history. Like most such terms it has lost some of its meaning. As generally used it covers a broad range of attitudes which have but few beliefs in common. Assimilation implies a conscious desire to accept all of the ways and modes of the host people, and in the process to abandon, consciously or otherwise, one's ties to the Jewish heritage and people. André Maurois, it has been seen, has been silent on those ties. Emmanuel Berl, a lesser known contemporary, has largely rejected them. Julien Benda, one of France's foremost thinkers, has totally embraced the culture of France; very Cartesian and classicist in his thought, his work has been judged one of the most representative expressions of that culture. Yet Benda has retained and even nurtured what measure of Jewishness he sensed in himself.

The wide gap between the assimilationism of Emmanuel Berl and Julien Benda merits comparison. There is little Jewish awareness in Berl. In his many autobiographical works he never stoops to deny his Jewish origins. However, he does appear to look upon them as an evil trick of fate, one which it was futile to counteract. In 1925, he could write about his love for a Christian girl: . . . "I was perfectly happy to marry a young girl who was not Jewish. I abhor Zionism. I do not even understand this problem, considering myself as I do a Frenchman and a man. . . . My memory, in any case, does not extend further back than France. And Jerusalem evokes in me, above all, verses by Racine." In fact, Berl continues—after noting he was glad that Christiane, his girl, was Catholic—"I suffered from not belonging to any communion; for me the Synagogue was not one. I deplored seeing evaporate, for lack of a solid frame, the religious feeling which sometimes seemed to surge within me. . . . "

French in his political and cultural outlook, young Berl's religious yearnings—and they were few and spasmodic—turned toward Catholicism. He had grown up very Parisian, very sophisticated, with a Voltairian, irreligious upbringing that shied away from even the most simple of Jewish observances. Deprived in his youth of even a smattering of Jewish knowledge, and of any of those affective associations that are formed by habit, Berl appeased his later religious craving with an occasional and faint move toward the more accessible Church. Perhaps it was only the experience of Hitler which made him wish in 1952 that he had partaken in his youth of those great religious festivals "which shine with a quiet splendor in the memory of my co-religionists." Now, in the autumn of his life, after the shattering years of occupation, Berl describes with warmth and emotion the customs and rites of the holidays he missed.

But even after the liberation, Berl's distance from any position readily understandible to Jews was considerable.

One can still comprehend his wholehearted endorsement of the Munich Pact: Berl put his concern for humanity and peace above democratic loyalty and dread of Nazi expansion. But when his close friend and editorial associate, Pierre Drieu La Rochelle (1893-1945), became the Rosenberg—if not the Streicher—of France, Berl's failure to break with him became incomprehensible. With the collaborationist on trial after Auschwitz and Theresienstadt, all that Berl could say was that Drieu's antiSemitism, even in pre-war years, had sometimes been annoying to him. Since Hitler, Berl wrote, all anti-Semitism had become intolerable to him, that of Drieu not excluded. This detached view of a social disease that had cost so many lives permitted him to continue his relations with Drieu even after the vitriolic, racist pamphlets had appeared. Berl records this reaction, odd, to say the least: "How I would have liked to have it out with him, but it was already done." In *Prise de sang* (*Blood Test*) written after Drieu's trial and suicide, Berl strove hard to rehabilitate the anti-Semite's reputation. If this speaks well for Berl, the friend, it is a sad commentary on the humanity to which he professed loyalty.

But then, had Berl grasped the character and ravages of anti- Semitism? In 1925 he expressed himself in terms which clearly presaged his stand on the Drieu affair. *Méditations sur un amour défunt* (*Reflections on a Dead Love*) features a curious scapegoat theory in reverse. The worst effects of anti-Semitism, Berl held, was the excessive credence which Jews displayed toward it. Belief in anti-Semitism is the Jew's way of covering up personal inadequacies. "A Jew who is not invited to dinner believes that he would have been invited, were he not a Jew. A Jew, when someone shouts 'dirty Jew,' imagines that nothing would be said to him, were he not a Jew." Berl recalls a significant childhood experience. He was walking with his parents through an Algerian street when some rabble-rousers shouted *Mort aux Juifs* ("Death to the Jews"). Characteristically, Berl summarizes the experience as follows: "It wasn't the word 'Jews' which concerned me, but the word 'death.' "

Despite a softening in attitude toward his origins in the post-war years, Berl has on the whole looked upon the Jew as a Frenchman: not a Jewish Frenchman, but with the detachment of just any Frenchman. He remains the epitome of the fully assimilated Jew for whom "Jerusalem evokes only the verses of Racine."

Jerusalem evoked more, substantially more, for Julien Benda, one of the most controversial theorists of the intellectual's role in society. Benda was a much embattled man. At the time of his death in 1956, he had alienated much of the world which had once admired him. To some he appeared a heartless rationalist with little regard for the emotional makeup of people; to others he seemed intolerant and vicious toward those holding views distinct from his own. Little doubt that the philosopher's peculiar brand of unorthodoxy had the ill-starred quality of exasperating both sides of a question. He offended French nationalists by his determined espousal of Europeanism; he irritated internationalists with his venomous and often unreasoned anti-Germanism. French traditionalists never ceased to abuse him, but liberals also—especially after ***Belphégor***—voiced their displeasure. On most every question Benda's position was so rigidly independent that concurrence on broad points seldom signified approval of specifics. Benda had a predilection for dramatizing himself, often appearing ludicrous in the process. Finally, his fellow-intellectuals resented the strain which Benda's concept of *le clerc* (the cleric or monk) imposed on them. This concept has often been misinterpreted to mean that Benda wanted the intellectual to withdraw from the affairs of his time. Actually, Benda did not argue against participation as such, but that in participating the intellectual must remain an intellectual, considering issues from the standpoint of abstract truth and justice.

Benda, the cleric, worshipped at numerous shrines. He was a rapt member of the cult of intelligence, often mirrored in a Spinozan rationalism. He embraced with fervor the values of truth, justice and logic. He placed the scientific spirit considerably above the artistic frame of mind. He adhered to a "fixist," eternalist philosophy which required a strongly affirmative viewpoint. Methodologically, his "religion" revolved about the "dissociation of ideas," the love of systematization, the tendency to abstract thinking. He revered the memory of Spinoza, Descartes and Renouvier; he detested and battled against Bergsonism, Pragmatism and later Existentialism. Because the sentimental internationalism of Romain Rolland offended his calm rationalism, he bitterly fought it, although he was in sympathy with its overall objective. So rigid was Benda in the pursuit of his various "religions" that he was often accused of striking an intellectual pose.

Benda's Jewish attitudes should be viewed against the background of these intellectual tenets. A man with *so many* religions may not have *a* religion. Indeed, Julien Benda was never a Jew by religion. The Jewishness that was ingrained in him—and it was limited—was due to his sense of cultural and historical pride: partly the reaction to anti-Semitism, somewhat less by temperament, and very slightly by habit. Benda's writings were never chiefly concerned with Jewish themes, but he occasionally alluded to his Jewish heritage, commented on questions of Jewish interest, labeled his actions and thoughts as part of a Jewish mentality. Again and again he voiced an abiding affection and even admiration for the Jewish past. In fact, some of his superlatives concerning the Jewish record have been so un-Bendalike as to expose him to the charge of ethnocentrism, casting a long shadow of suspicion over his vaunted rationalism and sincerity.

The philosopher's thoughts on Jewish matters are found mostly in the autobiographical ***La Jeunesse d'un clerc*** (***The Youth of an Intellectual***), ***Un Régulier dans le siècle*** (***A Regulator of the Century***) and in Chapter VII of ***Le Rapport d'Uriel*** (***Uriel's Report***). His observations range from social and political issues to the character of anti-Semitism, from the meaning of the Jewish message to a description of classes and types of Jews.

Benda's childhood in a Parisian Jewish home of the 1870's was largely representative of the time and the place. He observed no Jewish ritual, being completely severed from all Jewish tradition, and for that matter all religious thought. In the years to come, this Voltairian climate sealed off his mind from even comprehending religious sentiment or emotion. The author recalls as his sole bit of religious instruction the negative lesson of being asked not to mock Catholic children walking to confession. The emancipated Bendas had little regard for Jewish culture and learning, which they judged primitive and even barbaric.

On the other hand, their socio-political thinking was largely governed by the fact of Jewishness. Thus, Benda's calm, impractical father—to whom he was more attached than to his lively, Parisian mother—kept eulogizing the French Revolution, which had freed the Jew and granted him civil rights. In fact, Camille Benda was wont to express dismay that there should be Jews who were not in accord with the Revolution or opposed to its achievements. Julien Benda asserts that the strong patriotism of French Jews of his father's generation could be traced back to their attachment to revolutionary ideas and the gratitude they felt toward these ideas. Jewish patriotism—including Benda's own—was different from that of other Frenchmen, because according to Benda it tended to stress the substance and meaning of the nation rather than the forms and symbols. It was equally distant from flags and uniforms on the one side and nationalist notions of earth, blood and instinct on the other. Instead, Jewish patriotism underscored appreciation of the values of liberty, equality and fraternity.

From his family Benda also gleaned the sources of Jewish ambition. Benda believed that devotion to the young and the full realization of their abilities had always been traditional in Jewish families. With the older generation having failed to produce the Messiah, all hope had to be centered on the younger one. But in the nineteenth century, for the first time, other factors entered into Jewish ambition. For the first time Jewish pride, individuality and self-esteem were given a chance to assert themselves. As though the restraints and humiliations of centuries were suddenly to be swept away with one mighty effort, Jews threw themselves headlong into the new careers open to them. What a challenge to disprove the old contention of Jewish inferiority! Benda recalls that, especially in bourgeois families, children were prodded into academic competition to demonstrate they could be first-rate people if they were only given a chance. They were to display at once their immense capacity for work and their intellectual endowment. As models to emulate, Jewish parents held up the Reinach brothers, who had walked off with every academic prize the French Academy could bestow. But in encouraging their children to exceptional effort, parents may have made a serious error. The Reinachs' triumphs, widely publicized, always struck Benda as one of the latent causes for the virulent anti-Semitism of the close of the century. In characteristically cynical fashion Benda wrote that *justice* may have demanded that the Reinachs receive *all* prizes, but political *interest*—and the self-interest of Jews—required that they receive only *some*. Benda himself was only a mediocre student, preferring other diversions to those of books. He claimed to have been intractable to his parents' entreaties and up to the time of his death was still resentful when Jews, as Jews, told him they were proud of him and his books.

Benda was to remember yet another intellectual condition peculiar to the Jews of his time. They knew but two political organisms, the individual and the state, with all linking bodies outside their mental orbit. Benda believed this a Jewish tendency because, as Jews, they thought of the social in a rational and abstract manner—as distinct from the concrete and historical thinking of others, which revolved about such institutions as church and army. Here again, Benda conceived of the Jews as steeped in the spirit of the Revolution, with its *a priori,* idealistic notions.

In his later years Benda was to claim that it was his parents, without deep roots in the soil of France, who unwittingly set the stage for his own non-historical thinking. Despite their fervent love for France, they did not instill in him a conscious respect for the whole of the French tradition. Undoubtedly, Benda surmised, their own past in France was too recent to lend any genuine meaning to a history-centered patriotism. Nor did his parents, as did non-Jewish parents, bind him to religious traditions or even moral teachings. Finally, his parents removed him from the continuum of history by failing to raise him in any particularist tradition, allowing for a universal rather than specific moral outlook. Benda later wondered about the influences which would explain his cult for values based on an eternal frame of reference and his aversion for those who would only consider them from an historical and transient viewpoint. "I am wondering if the true explanation resides not in the education [given him by his parents] and if God would not have recognized the author of ***La Trahison des clercs* [*Betrayal of the Intellectuals*]** in this little boy seated at the table between two adults who were praising the beauties of reason, work and science and never the particularities of his nation, ancestors and people."

If one is to believe Benda, the absence of firmly linked chains to the past was thus helpful in developing the individuality of his thought and did not harm him in his condition of being a Jew. Benda declared categorically that he was never at war with himself or with the Jew in him. There was, of course, only a limited Jewishness with which to reconcile other identities. But, in any case, and for whatever reason, he succeeded uncannily well in accepting himself as he saw himself. "I accepted my mathematical bent of mind, my Greco-Roman culture, my Jewish mentality with what limitations and non-inclusiveness these necessarily entail for a true understanding of the world and my feeling of solidarity with Man. I accepted the fact of my pure *intellectuality* [*ma nature de pur intellectuel*] with what it inevitably lacks in terms of loyal devotion, my love of the idea with what it suggests of the anti-social. I have accepted to be what I am and, above all, not to be what I am not."

Yet while accepting his Jewishness and even making some extraordinary claims for Jews, Benda was continually exasperated with some types of Jews. In his early years, he had often encountered *le snobisme des grands Juifs* and had little use for it; later he was to endure an equal aversion in the presence of strongly conscious or militant Jews who, he knew quite well, returned the compliment. Benda's religions would not tolerate traditionalist Jews, as they excluded traditionalists of any party or faith. His anti-particularism was also responsible for his scoffing at Zionism as a Jewish racism. Basically he regarded himself among *les juifs affranchis,* the assimilated Jews; although he was acutely yet painlessly aware they were detested by Jews and non-Jews alike.

Benda belongs to that rare species of Jewish writer who did not encounter until full manhood the phenomenon of anti-Semitism. To believe him, he did not recognize it until, at thirty, the Dreyfus Case suddenly and pungently drove home its meaning. But once familiar with it, he was never again to underestimate it. He relates in some detail an experience in prejudice. His novel ***L'Ordination*** had been presented to the Goncourt Academy (named after the Goncourt Brothers, whose name is tainted with anti-Semitism) for its annual prize—one of the most highly esteemed literary awards in France. Benda asserted that it was because of the anti-Jewish sentiment of two key members that the coveted prize was denied him on a late ballot. Paradoxically, this defeat marked the turn in his literary fortunes. Following this incident, after long years of relative obscurity, he found the doors of the publishing houses wide open to him. One may question the full accuracy of Benda's report and allegations, but one cannot doubt his sincerity when he wrote: "The hatred for Jews is one of the rare philosophies which, in this so strongly divided mankind, receives almost unanimous support."

Benda's reasoning here is externalized in ***Le Rapport d'Uriel,*** a work written in the mock-innocent, mildly satiric vein of Montesquieu's *Persian Letters* and some of Voltaire's short novels. Here Benda differentiates between conscious and subliminal charges against Jews. Among the voiced prejudices Benda lists first those coming under the heading of Jewish capitalism—i.e., theft, usury, exploitation, avarice—all at the expenses of the Christian masses and, especially, Christian workers. The second is that of Jew-based communism, an accusation entirely the antithesis of the former—but, adds Benda, in logic only. In emotion and passion, he maintains, they are one, with both striving to make the Jew odious. The third complaint he labels imperialism, a theory according to which the Jews care only for their own, have no love for the host nation, yet seek high office and power in it to gain control on behalf of the "chosen" people.

Benda's refutation of these accusations is more angry than original. It is interesting only in relation to the claims advanced for Jews. They are especially honest in business; they have a congenital fanaticism for justice which sometimes causes them to appear revolutionary. Jews above all others conceive commands of human conscience outside of the prejudices of historical and national factors and, more than others, treat them in their universal, absolute quality. Jews honor moral values in their eternal, everlasting aspects, independent of time and place and are thus an eminent factor of human liberation. In Benda's persistent equating of Jewish characteristics and values with those he espoused, one may indeed discern a considerable identification with things Jewish. He carried this identification further when he declared that, like himself, Jews have disdain for terrestial grandeur and—again like him—have a cult for the spiritually pure, and for rational intelligence. He quotes from the Psalms: "Other nations have their chariots and gilded arms; you, O Israel, you have your God."

In his exposition of hidden, "unconscious" reasons for anti-Semitism, Benda anticipated some of the psychological theories of prejudice which have come to hold sway in the United States in recent years. Benda realized that there were historical facts in the Jewish situation that were responsible for a particular brand of prejudice. But he astutely recognized that anti-Semitism, like all prejudice, would germinate mostly in those already predisposed for it. There were some who conferred upon themselves a certain superiority and primacy by despising others. By despising the Jew, by speaking and agitating against him, they bestowed upon themselves a patrician title, and also the ability, wealth and other status factors which they were actually lacking. "There seems to be a permanent element in the disdain for the Jew," he concludes, and adds these additional subliminal causes for the perennial disease: scapegoating, especially after a lost war; the need in many humans to discredit social justice and democratic ideals which they associate with the Jew (or does Benda?); the need of those governing to employ diversionary maneuvers when in difficulty.

Benda was no pacifist and strongly approved an army that would truly be in the service of a democratic republic. But the Dreyfus Affair apparently conditioned him forever against the military and the authoritarianism it represented. As a result, he was prone to equate anti-Semitism with the military, and his other personal philosophic and social villains, just as he had linked the Jews to his positive virtues. Benda predicted that anti-Semitism would rise and fall with the growth and decline of militarism. Conversely, he seemed to think the Jews would become apostles of a truly civil society because they were civil *par excellence.* This new society would opt for justice, human dignity, and the rights of the most humble. Above all, it would deny to any man the right to make a tool of another. Writing during the Nazi occupation, Benda pondered over the possible triumph of the military system and its effects upon Jewish survival. Any succeeding civil society, he feared, might come about only in time to honor the *memory* of the Jews.

In those gloomy days of World War II, spent in solitary exile in Carcassonne, writing book upon book, Benda appears to have moved somewhat closer to Judaism. ***Souvenirs d'un enterré vif*** (***Memories of One Buried Alive***), written when Benda was well over seventy, contains several passages in which he relates more than ever his values to those of Jews. Above all, he had discovered the Prophets and experienced for them a depth of sympathy which he had previously accorded to only a few religious writers—and these latter he now recognized as the spiritual heirs of the Prophets. The Prophets endowed him with a sentiment he had never known before: veneration for the people which had produced the Prophets and had thus borne into the world the idea of morality. It was their teaching and their message which the detractors of the Jews had always sought to stamp out. More than ever he conceived of the Jews as the representatives of the critical spirit in modern times; for less deeply mired in the nationalist ideas of blood and soil, they could interpret a problem more freely and independently. Now, too, he imputed to his "race" a special capacity for reflection and thought. He could only concur with the dictators of the thirties who had declared that "To think is to be Jewish." While Benda would not carry this notion to the extreme of claiming intellectuality for all Jews, or that they have a monopoly on it (he specifically denied this), he nevertheless credited them with a specificity in this area. He cited the disproportionate number of eminent Jewish scientists, philosophers, and men of letters. In his attic room, hidden away in safety, the aging philosopher was so overcome by compassion that he allowed his objectivity to forsake him. He imputed to Jews a virtual monopoly on justice. His statements were almost surely the result of powerful emotional reaction to the horrors outside his room. For an assimilated Jew, European and citizen of the world, a universalist rather than particularist thinker, his war-time statements suggest deeper attachment for the Jewish heritage than might have been expected.

Despite his mounting claims for the Jew and his heritage, Benda came closer to neither traditional Judaism nor Zionism. Here his Weltanschauung was in deadly conflict with either the irrational mysticism of the former and the politically oriented nationalism of the latter. The proclamation of Israel as a state evoked both traditional Judaism and Zionism, both areas in which he brooked no compromise.

Some critics have seen in Benda's isolation, his quarrelsomeness, his fundamental pessimism, less the result of reasoned intellectual conviction than of his personal and social heritage as a Jew. Some have even suspected the very concept of the cleric's role as a contemplative figure, apart from partisan strife, as a rationalization of his personal background. But it appears doubtful that this personal factor operated more potently in Benda's thinking than in that of other contemporaries. Benda, to be sure, saw himself as a Jew, but never exclusively as a Jew and certainly not even primarily as a Jew. The complete ease with which his family associated with Catholics in his youth, the perfectly natural manner in which he came to view such contacts, the absence of mainly Jewish associations, his ability to move in all Jewish circles but the most militant and nationalist make the hypothesis of an exceptional personal factor highly untenable. His intellectual formation had multiple origins and they all combined to shape the cleric that was Benda.

History is likely to remember Benda's plan for calm, detached reasoning, for the subordination of emotion to the intellect, for the quest for lasting values. All have struck a clear if unheeded note in a world gone awry with propaganda and emotive appeals to the human ear. History will also record his name for his persistent admonitions to intellectuals not to commit "treason" by over-valuing the temporal, by aspiring to power, influence, and prestige and thus neglect the truly clerical functions of searching for truth and justice. History will certainly not remember Benda as a Jew, for his Jewishness, though real, was minor and undistinguished. It cannot forget, however, the contribution which his Jewish background and the ethical values inherent in it added to his overall thinking. Benda was that rare species, the assimilated Jew, who yet fully accepted himself as a Jew.

Ray Nichols (essay date 1978)

SOURCE: "The 'Clerc' and the Intellectual," in *Treason, Tradition, and the Intellectual: Julien Benda and Political Discourse,* The Regents Press of Kansas, 1978, pp. 165-92.

[*In the following excerpt, Nichols articulates a distinction in Benda's work between the* clerc *and the intellectual.*]

"The intellectual": for Benda, this was a sort of sacred realm, a vocation, a clerkly ordination. And much of Benda's speech and action here remains pressingly alive, more so, indeed, today than at any time since the crises of the thirties. His concerns, his enemies, his hopes, his disillusionments, his career—all were quintessentially, representatively modern, in provocative and diverse ways. In practice, Benda was discriminating, pungent, wide-ranging, often valiant: there was much to respect in him. And there was much to learn through him. Most (if not, indeed, all) men find difficulty in living up to their professions at the best of times. Benda's times were not the best. Yet precisely because of this and because of his own articulate ardor, even the central problems with his clerkly stance were also potentials for our times.

The intellectual was a sacred realm. And Benda had indeed defended it, moving from the confident optimism of his earlier pronouncements to a more entrenched, more worried engagement with the modern world. He had always seen the territory of the *clerc* as a limited one. But increasingly, he had become concerned with another sort of limit, one imposed by the passions, the doctrines, the locations, the terms of contemporary existence. Diverse individuals and groups became increasingly engaged; and their engagements became ever more elemental, ever more threatening encroachments on the clerkly realm.

All this made Benda a controversialist. And it was a role in which he excelled, a concern, a bearing that itself both bore him up and bore with utmost point upon his own activities and the modern world. The core of the representative fascination he affords lies here, in his juxtaposition of austerely rationalistic professions with the skill and fervor of a pamphleteer. His polemic art could be searing, scorchingly apt, and bitingly insulting. (Perhaps the best example is his **"De Quelques avantages de l'écrivain conservateur."**) And his opponents often enough replied in kind. Calling him anarchistic, embittered, inhuman; a man without heart, a monster, an ogre of dialectics, a gnome of intellectualism, an intellectual reactionary—Benda's critics provided caustic characterizations of him. But if one seeks striking phrases for this portrait of the artist, surely the best is "l'idéologue passionné."

L'idéologue passionné: the man professing attachment to ideas, passionately involved, concerned in some sense to direct them to action, skillful at critique and polemic, and possessed of a zest for debunking. Much as he might condemn modern "ideologies," Benda himself accepted much of this characterization. In the ***Dialogues à Byzance*** he had referred to rationalism and its opponents as diverse species of religion, all needing their combatants and their martyrs. Later, he had treated ideological controversy as a matter of moral conflict, tantamount to war. Indeed, he admitted that he had wished death on General Mercier, Bergson, Kaiser Wilhelm, Maurras, and Mussolini—and he characterized this as "a true ideological fanaticism" on his part. Were men such as Maurras, Bergson, and Mussolini to be threatened by common assassins, he would endeavor to save them; but "for their ideas" he himself at times would willingly have killed them: his streak of cruelty here, said Benda, was "wholly ideological."

Here was the *clerc* militant, guided and goaded by passions of his own. "The world of my dreams. . . . It resembles an immense convent," silent, working under and in orders, with reverence for truth, reason, and justice, and hence without war. But that was *only* a dream of Benda's, not so clearly even an ideal. Benda might say the *clerc*'s role was purely speculative rather than a matter of living in the political battle; he might express contempt for action; he might praise the solitude of the infinite, reject the prostitution of the divine to the human, and scorn the material (even in the ***Trahison*** he sometimes used that word to cover both pragmatic interest and particularist pride); but he was himself engaged in battle, intent on his own mode of clerkly intellectual action, which he had gradually raised to equal status with—even to a higher place than—the purely speculative or contemplative or scholarly. With all his passion, zeal, and critical skill, he had never, himself, really been a pure Byzantine. For Benda's concern, his orientation, was with combat of a certain kind. His basic profession was of the eternal struggle of two realms, each with the other, through and in which civilization itself attained articulation, diffusion, and location. The sacred did not constitute the whole world. The clerkly realm existed in constant tension with that of the laymen. In a most important sense, what Benda had termed "ideological war" or "political quarrel" was both endemic and necessary. Here, as so often, the condemnation of ideology became self-referring; debunking became a two-edged sword.

Still, there are ideologies and ideologies. As with "the intellectual," the term signals (and itself enters) a field of problems rather than resolves them. Benda's own terms stressed "ideas" and the opposition of his own clerkly doctrines to those of his enemies, as well as the variety of passions. Benda's place in ideological controversy, his claims and charges, and his clerkly stance were intimately bound up together. Doctrines warred with passions; treason, with tradition; realism, with rationalism. Professions were multiple; and professing itself was crucial, not least because there was more involved in Benda's actual practices than in his own standard diagnoses and prognoses for them.

To reach an overall assessment of Benda and of the general bearing of the *clerc* on and for the intellectual, we must focus on these strains. We must first examine how adequately Benda's theory of passion was joined with his critique of doctrine in his charge of treason. And we must then examine the adequacy of Benda's rationalism proper—the ultimate nature and appropriateness of his intellectual ideal; the coherence of his practices; his pronouncements on moral conflict and social justice, on the rule of the concept, on civilization, and on political realism.

TREASON AND TRADITION

Cry "Treason!"—It is to conjure the most powerful of political impulses. Had Benda reckoned on this, for all his talk of political passion? Small wonder that his catalogue of false *clercs* and true ones occasioned much violent controversy and much special pleading, little of which was well directed. Too often the reaction was to a vague impression, a capsule conception, or a pet instance, not to the elaborate statement of the ***Trahison*** and its ancillary works. So, one of Benda's critics argued that Sorel was essentially a moralist (but this was precisely Benda's point). Another agreed to condemn Sorel—along with Spencer, Barrès, and Maurras—but not Nietzsche; a third defended Nietzsche, but not Péguy; a fourth took the side of Péguy and Barrès together and scolded Benda for his blindness to "divine truth." Such protests need neither be multiplied nor examined seriatim. For the most part they were superficial as well as partial, and their contradictory stances are more confusing than helpful. But they do serve to suggest that Benda's notion of treason was not self-evidently clear. They do direct attention to the basic problem: the nature and consistency of the general *criteria* whereby Benda had admitted some and excluded others from the kingdom of the *clercs*.

Clercs and others: this was the basic starting point. That there were two orders of men, two types of concern, two varieties of passion—this was Benda's fundamental conception. As we have seen, Benda's analysis of passion was a development of his general psychological approach to politics and culture. In large part, especially with its cognates ("passive"—suffering action from without, action as an attribute of the thing towards which action is directed; "pathos"—feeling as transient, in contrast to the permanent and the conceptual; suffering and "les souffrantes," "la vie pathétique"), it did aptly serve to designate Benda's characteristic treatment of human belief and behavior. And in large part, it was enlightening. Fixity of purpose and idea; need for immediate action and results; scorn for argument, hatred, and excess: this does seem a penetrating catalogue of characteristics—and characteristic dangers—associated with passion. Perhaps it would have been better to speak of lack of interest in, rather than of scorn for, argument. Perhaps "excess" was a somewhat loaded and question-begging term; but in context with Benda's other terms, it did identify something of substance. And one can agree that politics today appears to be a predominant concern. Transport and communications, urbanization, secularization, the organization of populations, disenchantment and reenchantments, all the familiar refrains of modern, even mass society, have perfected political commitment, in the sense that they bring more people into the public arena more rapidly and more directedly (if also more spasmodically). One can go further and agree that universality, coherence, contiguity, and even continuity are apt characterizations of modern political impulse. One can even grant that the term "political passions" aptly characterizes many of the impulses whereby men rise up against men. Passion does appear to possess (and to possess men with) a dynamic greater than does material interest per se, because it is less open to negotiation or mutuality and because it is more self-fueling, more direct, and more insatiable.

Yet, even given all this, Benda's theory of passion signaled troubles. Sometimes, irrationalism, for Benda, was sheer emotionalism and sometimes, romanticism; at other times it was the cult of activism (d'Annunzio), mystic vitalism (Péguy), intuitionism (Bergson), traditionalism (Barrès), movement (Bergsonism, orthodox Marxism, Existentialism); on still other occasions it was the more explicitly political doctrines of the strong state, nationalism, class, race, and pacifism. Were all these sins of passion in the same way and in the same degree? Benda's own prime masters, Kant and Spinoza, surely espoused no simple reason/emotion dichotomy. The Spinozan strand in Benda surely underlay his own acceptance of early (1830s) romanticism and his own articulations of the "passion of reason." His references to the coherence and homogeneity of belief and impulse and the contempt for individuals which supposedly underlay the doctrine of the strong state were developments of his earlier attacks on the metaphysical and primitive nature of group loyalties; they continued to suffer from the same problem of overgeneralization. He long remained ambiguous as to whether fearfulness or Alexandrine ecstasy was the basis of passionate devotion and over how one could distinguish between pure sentiment and the changing object of irrational desire. His talk of the greater purity of modern political passions rang oddly, given his repeated insistence on the extensive connections between politics and culture generally.

Clercs and others; true Dreyfusards and false ones; truly rational men and *les souffrantes*; *les aptes au bonheur* versus followers of *la vie pathétique*—was so strict a separation of passions possible? Were the distinctions here between true and treacherous *clercs* so clear and uniform? Might it not, rather, be the case that most men are microcosms of Benda's scheme, feeling within themselves the impulses of both *clerc* and *laïque?*

Benda's own comments on Nietzsche were especially apposite. He admitted that activism could be an end in itself and thus neither pragmatic nor in any obvious sense particularistic. He admitted that Nietzsche was no anti-Semite or nationalist and that his masters were quite unlike Hitler and Hitler's lieutenants. He noted approvingly that Nietzsche had condemned German brutalities against France. He even granted that Nietzsche had felt "no passion but the passion for thought," and he added: "Need I say that Nietzsche, who seems to me a bad 'clerk' from the nature of his teaching, seems to me one of the finest from his entire devotion to the passions of the spirit alone?"

Here Benda was offering *two* general criteria for irrationalist treason. And by his own testimony, the case of Nietzsche showed that these criteria need not coincide. Treacherous *clercs* might avidly embrace political passions as their own. (The avidness of the embrace was critical: Benda had said that even true *clercs* might feel the pull of political passions, but still remain faithful by resisting them.) Or they might espouse them doctrinally—apparently, as Nietzsche did, without necessarily feeling them as commanding interior impulses. And it was the latter of these two criteria that came increasingly to the fore in Benda's analyses. He spoke of the ideology and the self-consciousness of the intellectual organization of political passions at the start of the ***Trahison,*** and he stressed doctrines towards its end. In ***La Fin de l'éternel*** he focused on doctrines alone. Eventually, in the mid 1930s, he explicitly revised his earlier psychological theory, pronouncing political passions to be "intellectual passions . . . produced by political *ideas.*"

Benda was holding to a strict dichotomy between *clercs* and others. But by granting a separation between personal impulse *tout court* and doctrine, he was undermining his claim that *clercs* and *laïques* were of two distinct psychological types. More than that: he was blurring the grounds of his attack. For if a man can be an "irrationalist" in one dimension only, how is he to be classified as a traitor or a faithful *clerc?* And how is he to be compared with another whose "treason" is in a different dimension?

The point is of some importance. Consider its consequences for the one work that did try to grapple in a systematic fashion with Benda's charge of treason, that of R. J. Niess. Niess attempted to distinguish different *levels* of treasonable and near-treasonable activity. First, he claimed to identify, in addition to the traitors proper, "the effects of the philosophies and systems of another and vastly more important group, headed by Hegel, Marx, Comte, James, Bergson, and Nietzsche, a group which Benda does not even think of accusing of betrayal but who provided the philosophical grounds for the treason of the lesser men." Second, Niess asserted that men such as Dante and d'Aubigné were less culpable than others: "It seems to Benda that even these men were never guilty of the same kind of treason as their modern descendants, for in the midst of their political activity they succeeded in maintaining some generality of feeling and some attachment to abstract principles."

Now, the second of these assertions actually muddled together two separate comments by Benda. In fact, Benda explicitly condemned Dante and d'Aubigné as clerkly traitors; and when he spoke of generality of feeling and principle, he actually was referring to the basic distinction between doctrinal attachment and personal impulse. And the first of Niess's claims was simply incorrect. To make it was to ignore the fact that betrayal could consist in elevating the wrong beliefs into matters of basic principle. Nietzsche, Bergson, Hegel, Marx—Benda repeatedly condemned all of these figures on precisely this ground. Far from "not even thinking of accusing" them, Benda, as we have seen, listed them among his prime traitors. In the case of Comte, Benda moved to stronger condemnation with time. And as for James, Benda was forced to grant that philosophical pragmatism was different from crude distortion of truth for vulgar practical interests (or from James's own avid support for the American cause in Cuba, which Benda condemned in the ***Trahison***); but his basic opposition to doctrinal pragmatism, however elevated, never faltered.

And yet, if impulse and doctrine could be so disparate, confusion over Benda's notion of treason is understandable. The classification and comparison of individual figures became complex indeed. For that matter, the imputation of avidly embraced realist passion was itself a tricky enterprise, requiring much labor in many cases; and the very scale of Benda's attack ruled out so extended an undertaking. Small wonder that Benda increasingly tended to concentrate on doctrine. In Spinozan fashion, the link between passion and action was intellectualized. Even in the heat of controversy, doctrine was the focus and the ultimate desideratum.

But here, with doctrine, was a more fundamental source of confusion. For the most part, Benda clearly was concerned with doctrines themselves, in their original forms. Thus he commented that he was interested in theories alone. And thus he explained: "When I speak of a single 'clerk,' I am thinking of his work in its chief characteristics, i.e. in that part of his teaching which dominates all the rest, even if the remainder sometimes contradicts this dominant teaching." Malebranche, Benda noted by way of example, occasionally had written as though slavery were justifiable; and Nietzsche, as though he were a defender of human fraternity. Nevertheless, the whole of their works made Malebranche a master of liberal thought and Nietzsche a moralist of war. But Benda then added a quite different note. The "influence" of Malebranche and of Nietzsche, he contended, supported his interpretation of their "chief characteristics"—"and my subject is the influence which the 'clerks' have had in the world, and not what they were in themselves"; "my subject is not what the *clerc* venerates at the bottom of his heart, but what he exhorts other men to venerate."

The difficulty here was obvious. One may obtain two quite different judgments of a man by examining, respectively, the dominant characteristics of his writing or his later influence. And when one man is judged by his writings and another by his influence, the resulting classifications (and charges) are far from coherent. Indeed, Benda's judgments were even more muddied than this. For he meant more than one thing by "influence." Sometimes he was simply interested in the influence that had been produced by a man's doctrines in their full and original form. And sometimes he was concerned with the influence that a man's doctrines (especially those of Nietzsche and Hegel) had exercized when "deformed" by popular or party desires. With such multiple criteria, Benda all too easily (and all unconsciously) could shape his thesis to the case at hand and thus could readily contradict himself.

Three examples show this clearly. To Jean Paulhan, Benda's opposition to amnesty for wartime collaborators was the most reprehensible aspect of his immediate postwar stance. Did not such writers as Drieu la Rochelle, Motherlant, and Thérive, asked Paulhan, hold to that same "point de vue de Sirius" which Benda revered? They could not be condemned as traitors, for they had not foreseen the gas chamber and concentration camps to which their principles, in others' hands, would lead. In this case, the criticism missed the point: Benda had always been concerned to condemn doctrines such as those supported by the collaborators. But another case worked differently. Another of Benda's critics suggested that the standard of influence would lead one to "hold Christ responsible for the massacres of Saint Bartholomew, and the book-burnings so often kindled in his name." True, the parallel here was grossly exaggerated. As Benda himself noted, there were at least elements of Nietzsche's and Hegel's thought that supported the treasonable beliefs he condemned (and this hardly could be said of Jesus): "Certain philosophers have only themselves to blame for the misunderstanding of their true thought." But elements were not the same as chief characteristics. The real point was the problem posed by Benda's multiple criteria. And a third case shows graphically how these criteria could set even Benda's own examples to work against him. In his exchange with Daniel Halévy, Benda himself employed the very argument that has just been cited. He asserted that the writings of the *philosophes* could be taken to support political passions only when they had been *deformed* by later interpreters. And Voltaire and Rousseau themselves, he added sharply, were no more responsible for such deformation than Jesus was to blame for the Inquisition.

A painful gaffe—but not a surprising one. Benda's confusion of criteria was a potent source of trouble. And more trouble flowed from it. Above all was the appropriateness of Benda's central term of opprobrium, *trahison*. Treason (betrayal, perfidy, going over to the other side) implies responsibility—consciousness of one's actions and of their implications. Benda did often speak of the conscious efforts of men to influence others; and he occasionally distinguished between the characters of works and the aims of their authors. (Thus, for example, he condemned Valéry while praising Gide.) It was obviously inconsistent to level charges of treason without the same sort of analysis in all cases. Yet, even if Benda's intermittent efforts to identify motives are disregarded, the central difficulty with his charge of treason remains. There was a profound difference between *clercs* who consciously and intentionally involved themselves with the doctrinal defense of political passions and those who were unaware of the potential consequences of their pronouncements. At least some of the latter might well be accused, not of treason, but rather of error. And as in the case of "deformation," responsibility would surely lie—if anywhere—with those who extrapolated the implications. (If anywhere—for even here there are degrees of responsibility: i.e., deliberately taking from a work only what is wanted *à servir;* reading it superficially; not reading it at all, but merely accepting the claims of others about it.) Surely, "treason" was too strong a word to apply indiscriminately to all of these examples.

The problem with "treason," with the multiple senses of "influence," with the divergence between influence and original doctrine and between doctrine and personal impulse—clearly, all these flaws did seriously weaken Benda's case. They weakened it; but does that mean that nothing remained of it? Strip away the confusions, the incoherencies, and the apparent lapses; stick to Benda's central notions of realism and rationalism; and look to men's original (not deformed) doctrines—what then of the *clercs* and the world, both modern and past?

At times, Benda's clerkly stance gained strength from its opponents. It stood forth most persuasively, most clearly, and most brilliantly in contrast with the more shadowy, looming gods of others. Barrès, Sorel, Boulangism, Anti-Dreyfusism (and some Dreyfusism), the Bergsonian Left and the Maurrasian Right, the cult of fluid concepts, of refutation by historical movement alone, the fetishism of stimulation, of spontaneity, and of novelty—these were aptly enough deemed heresies of one sort or another. The French fascist "neosocialists" named Benda as a prime example of what they called the decadence of France: his abstract rationalism was to them a symbol of French decadence, of idealist flight from the concrete, of loss of "faith," of a diseased preference for analysis over engagement and for formal system over "instinctive and living" belief. ("La fuite devant la concrète, voilà la véritable trahison des clercs, celle dont la lâcheté menace la France et la monde.") Reviewing Drieu la Rochelle's *Socialisme fasciste,* Benda summed up this type succinctly: "He hates the *clerc.*" (Ironically, even Drieu was to seek to defend himself after the war by appropriating and twisting Benda's terms: "The intellectual, the *clerc,* the artist is not a citizen like others. He has duties and rights superior to those of others." Here, Drieu had come full circle from the original denunciations of a Barrès or a Brunetière.) In such contexts, Benda's own stance hardly can help but command sympathy. The horrors of nationalistic triumph, racism, and class war: Benda's prewar words on coming slaughter and barbarism were prophetic indeed. And much the same can be said of his prescience concerning the Belphégorean excesses of pop and happening in contemporary arts and letters, culture both immediately and mediately political.

But sympathy, like prophecy, is a tricky business. As Benda had himself so often warned, one may accept wrongly or for the wrong (or inadequate) reasons. And Benda's own reasons were problematical.

Benda's lists of clerkly traitors and loyalists give an indication of this. Ponder those lists, and a perplexing fact emerges. Few of the names that Benda cited on either side were those of social or political theorists. Plato, Aristotle, Hobbes, Voltaire, Montesquieu, Rousseau, Kant, and Proudhon among the faithful; Dante, Hegel, Comte, Marx, Nietzsche, Sorel, Barrès, and Maurras among the traitors—not even all of these are remembered primarily as political. And several of the most famous names here (Cicero, Augustine, Aquinas, Marsilius, Bodin, Grotius, Hooker, Locke, Burke, Mill) were missing altogether. To be sure, Benda's education had stressed the classics; both in education and in life he had been preoccupied with France. Perhaps it might be conceded that for a Frenchman of his time and situation only the omission of Cicero (and perhaps Aquinas) is really striking. Nonetheless, even those figures whom Benda did include were not discussed in much detail. Surely, social-political theorists would be those who most clearly could have served to explore the traditions of clerkly and lay callings. If anyone, they would have demarcated the lines between faithfulness and treachery. (Benda's perceptive but ambivalent comments on Machiavelli illustrated this.) Should not they have been considered at more length than any of the other figures of literature, philosophy, religion, the arts and sciences? Did they not deserve, even require, the most intensive scrutiny of all?

On reflection, some names in Benda's lists especially strike the eye. Benda's masters, Kant and Spinoza, both had warned against the philosopher-king (Kant, on the ground that ruling was dangerous for philosophy; Spinoza, on the ground that philosophy was dangerous for ruling). Benda had taken both these warnings to heart, distinguishing the concerns of *clercs* and *laïques,* insisting that the *clerc* should not rule. What, then, of Plato's presence in Benda's catalogue of clerkly loyalists? And what of Plato's advocacy of the noble pseudos as a way of gaining the support of both philosophers and subjects for the philosopher's rule? What, too, of Hobbes? His own theory of passion had an obvious affinity to Benda's and an understandable appeal to Benda. So with Hobbes's attacks on "insignificant speech." But for all that, Hobbes was the proponent of a modern, most un-Platonic reason, the advocate (for all its essentially negative purpose) of a strong state, and the reducer of ethics to emotive language, of justice to conventionally accepted words and laws backed by force, and of the *summum bonum* to mere "felicity," success in satisfying the continual flow of wordly, life-following desire.

Benda had said that he was concerned with the clerkly tradition taken "as a whole," in its "general characteristic." In the broadest and most general sense, one can talk of traditional defenses of truth, justice, and reason against the baser needs and demands of men. But the very breadth of such statements obscures critical differences, both social and conceptual, in the *meanings* (and connections) of these central terms.

As we have seen before, there are many traditions; and Benda's *clerc* was more than a purely historical figure. Indeed, we now can see that, as Benda employed them, the notions of treason and tradition were intimately linked. One was defined in terms of the other. Doubts about the grounds for one were also doubts about the grounds for the other. "Realism" and "rationalism"—these terms were at the core of Benda's clerkly analysis. Together with their associated terms ("political," "intellectual"; "barbaric," "civilized"; "romantic," "conceptual"; "worldly," "divine"; "pragmatist," "particularist"), they provided the focus of Benda's case. And even here—indeed, here above all—treason and tradition formed the critical context, critical both for Benda's proclaimed ideal and for his more specific practice. There was, in fact, a special irony in Benda's choice of these two terms. Here, social process, language, and conception were mordantly parallel; politics recapitulated etymology. For treason and tradition both spring from the same root (*tradere*—to place, to deliver up, to hand or give over). "To give over" to the other side is treason (*traditionem*); "to give over" to another generation is tradition (*traditio*). Now, each generation is just that—something both reproduced *and* reproductive, a development, a realignment, a new adaptation and selection. In contrast to "traditionalism," a tradition is neither static nor monolithic, but involves both continuity and innovation. And thus, the lines between betrayal and innovative adaptation, between giving over and moving along, may well be blurred. They may become battle lines. The nature of the change, in what manner and to what point the locus has been shifted, may become a central focus of controversy, not least among those devoted to "their tradition." And such controversy will revolve around the *significance* of the change—the *import* of the elements played up or down for the tradition "as a whole."

As one of Benda's more perceptive critics put it to him, some of those who became involved in the era could be said to be choosing rather than betraying. They acted, not for profit, but from duty; "they have only found, perhaps have founded, new gods." H. Stuart Hughes put it somewhat differently, somewhat better and more generally:

> It is important to distinguish between those who in scoffing at the Enlightenment were consciously attacking the humane values of the West, and those who, by probing more deeply the problem of human motivation and the structure of society, sought to restate that tradition in terms that would carry conviction to a skeptical generation.

It was in just such controversy, with gods old and new, that Benda played his own long role. And it was in just this context that Benda's own rationalism can be seen to be most problematical—and most productive—for "the intellectual" as a whole.

REALISM AND RATIONALISM

For all his endeavor to distinguish the realms of realism and rationalism, of *laïque* and *clerc,* Benda himself at least partly sensed a fundamental problem. His very career, his sense of his own vocation, his long concern to attack what he proclaimed to be modern heresies, his apotheosis of the conceptual, his defense of the ideal against the actual—all testified to deep and lingering gulfs between the devotion of mind to mind and other constraints of social existence. Realism and rationalism; treason, tradition, and controversy—by their very opposition, Benda's statements reflected on the irrational aspects of the modern world. By an extended encounter with Benda, we gain some deeper insights into the nature and meanings of this irrationalism, as well as of the rationalism that Benda defended throughout his long life.

Benda's era, like his career, was one of tumult, intellectual, cultural, and political. And it spawned a rich diversity of new movements and new creeds. Could anyone stand solidly abreast all these currents? Could even a self-avowed rationalism be born full-grown, and could it remain unmoved by them?

Benda had begun his clerkly offensive, in his *Revue blanche* articles, with a somewhat incoherent positivism, coupling together Descartes, Comte, and Spinoza. Incoherent—for even these earliest statements involved more than orthodox positivism of any brand. There were other strands here. Even when he turned to attack Maurrasian positivism and Comte himself, Benda adhered to his condemnation of littérateurs, his rejection of highly colored, imagistic, figurative language. (The matter is critical: we shall return to it below.) Call this, if one will, neoclassicist: it was partly in the line of seventeenth-century literary and philosophical theory. But only partly. Just as Benda was more than a positivist, so, as we have seen, was he more than a pure neoclassicist. And he was also more than a geometer. In his autobiographical writings of the 1930s, Benda could claim that his earliest training had instilled in him a love of the antiexperimental, the Jesuitical, the axiomatic, and the demonstrative; he could term himself a *régulier* and proclaim his devotion to order and rule; he could later add that consistency of actions with principles was admirable even if one disagreed with the principles; he could equate the rational with order (in the ***Discours*** and ***Trois Idoles romantiques***). But his concern with a theory of passion showed clearly enough that Benda was far from believing that all men, in all matters, were in a fundamental sense and manner rational. And not even order was a fundamentally consistent strand in Benda's own concerns: he also could defend "anarchy" and "the divine" *against* order (in the ***Dialogues à Byzance*** and the metaphysical ***Essai***), and he could grant that the realist world had its own inferior brand of coherent "rationality."

Science, mathematics, clarity and distinctness of letters, order and principle—none of these formed a coherent core for Benda's professions. Together, they constituted only a broad family of attachments, not a single, common orientation. As Benda put it in the ***Trahison,*** "reason" was above all the schools. And his concern for rational discourse and analysis came more and more to center on a neo-Kantian profession of the preeminence of the abstract concept whereby man moved from the brutally factual and immediate to the constructed and universal, from realist to intellectualist existence, from the already-actualized to the still-ideal.

Benda's rationalism altered with context, over time and place. And in this alteration, Benda did far more than attempt to settle accounts with his traditional philosophical conscience. In his confrontation of positivism, neoclassicism, a priori thought, scientism, and modern literature, Benda made a paradigmatic odyssey. Like many of his modern fellows, he sought to wrest from various creeds and movements some grounds for firm belief and action, grounds beyond mere existence, sheer faith, or blind activity.

Yet while Benda's rationalism was representative, even exemplary, in one way, it was far less so in another. Significantly, it was Gabriel Marcel who put the fundamental problem here. Rationalism, Marcel argued, traditionally had tried to attain knowledge of reality; and Benda's apparent slighting of this was tantamount to a misreading of the whole history of western philosophy. By identifying his own developed brand of neo-Kantian abstract rationalism with the supersensible and eternal (the nonrealist), Benda was committing "an abuse of language." Moreover, Marcel contended, it was an error to understand the universal in terms of the opposition between general and particular. The essence of universal knowledge was, rather, its "inner characteristic of harmony and intelligence." And thus understood, abstraction had only "the sovereignty of a form." It was "internally insufficient" and had no intrinsic value. Its worth could lie only in some epistemological function.

To be sure, Benda had a reply of sorts to this. (He granted that harmony and intelligibility were necessary as criteria for assessing abstractions. Nevertheless, he reiterated his charge that modern thought valued the particular as an end in itself; and this, he said, was at least as great an error—*if* that were indeed an error—as taking abstract conception to have an intrinsic value.) But this reply was hardly sufficient. A philosophical realist of Marcel's ilk could aptly enough characterize Benda's "rationalism" as the espousal of something less than that advanced by grand premodern traditions—and the same with Benda's treatment of "realism." In traditional terms, real and rational, actual and ideal, and practice and theory had been erected on notions of wholes; of unity; of a true universe, a true *cosmos;* and of correspondence between the ultimate order of things—physical and social and ethical—and the capacities of the human mind. Especially if one cannot now accept those traditional ontologies and epistemologies, what had Benda's alternative to offer in their place?

Benda's division between *clercs* and laymen echoed other divisions—pure and applied, detached and involved, spiritual and material, sacred and profane. But those echoes did not resound with a single voice. All these oppositions, for all that they have their places, become ambiguous. Developed in specific contexts, they move to others; moving, their uses multiply, blur, compound. For all Benda's condemnations of modern particularist and pragmatist heresies, his own stance itself embodied, was part of, and bore within it modern migrations—migrations across diverse terrains, not all of them obviously passable by the same routes. Benda's very attachment to a golden tradition and his mytho-poetic translation of that tradition into an ideal showed how far even he was from a monastic and monistic age or from a simple, unitary opposition of pure and impure.

Benda had advanced a terminology, but not one that provided a full-blown ontology. He was, after all and above all, a critic. His moral position, he finally saw, was "above all negative. It consists in defeating injustice." So with his other positions: operating negatively, he opposed the undemocratic, the anti-intellectual, the irrational. It was no accident that his major term of condemnation had been *trahison*—going away, departing. Active in opposition, in defense, and in critique, his positive stance was largely delimited negatively. In this sense, one might agree: "He thinks under the category of *No!*" And though "negation *of* negation" may lead to a positive stance, in Benda's case it took less than codified form, led to less than a "whole."

His talk of eternity and of the divine was especially significant, in ways that he did not seem to grasp. His opposition to the "lay world" smacked of old theological distinctions between grace and nature, but hardly fit his concern with science and erudition generally. As with many of his other terms, it became a figure, a malicious allusion, one that, carrying the burdens of past formations, blurred rather than illuminated his stance. Benda's god (the world thought of under the concept of the divine) revealed much about his pantheon. His neo-Kantianism, in fact, was founded upon a Ptolemaic revolution, whereby man's mind, his concepts, imposed intelligibility upon the raw world by a feat of intellectualization, rather than identifying any eternal and self-sufficient or actualizing essence. While no vulgar pragmatism, it was nonetheless itself a kind of higher instrumentalism. Benda's "sacred" rationalism was an attenuation of older, putatively universal human and philosophical stances. In this very attenuation, Benda revealed himself as a prime example of the modern erosion of old faiths.

And not just of faith. In Malraux's words: "The gods do not die because they lose their kingly power, but because they lose that property of belonging to the domain of the all-unknowable that was theirs. . . . The gods have no meaning if Olympus no longer has one." The meaning of Benda's Olympus; the power of the clerkly kingdom—how was so diminished, so formal a profession of mind's devotion to mind to provide adequate grounds and modes for intellectual action? For clearly, this was Benda's own chosen province, which was included in his theory of the *clerc* and was exemplified and stressed in his own life. Here was the full dimension of the political mind's modern plight, and here lay the ultimate test of Benda's claims.

Here, too, some of Benda's statements did less than justice to his stance. When the ideal becomes temporal, he proclaimed in a typical passage, it ceases to be ideal. The problem, of course, was the meaning and extent of "becoming temporal." The phrase was ambiguous: it could mean that the ideal had an impact on the temporal; that it derived from the temporal; or that it was equated with the temporal. The first of these was significantly different from both the others. Indeed, it approximated to what Benda himself had advocated, to his concern with the *clerc*'s import for civilization.

Because Benda's critics (then as now) often failed to explore such subtleties of his stance, Benda had little trouble in replying to them. More interesting were the comments of Jean-Paul Sartre. "Is it a matter," Sartre asked, "of acting as guardian of eternal values like Benda's clerk before the betrayal, or is it concrete, everyday freedom which must be protected by our taking sides in political and social struggles? . . . If the writer has chosen, as Benda has it, to talk drivel, he can speak in fine, rolling periods. . . . He won't disturb anybody; he won't address anybody." For, Sartre explained, "the [medieval] clerk . . . did not have to be concerned with the effects which his works would produce upon the masses, since he was assured in advance that they would have no knowledge of them. . . . He incessantly affirmed the Eternal's existence and demonstrated it precisely by the fact that his only concern was to regard it. In this sense, he realized, in effect, the ideal of Benda, but one can see under what conditions: spirituality and literature had to be alienated, a particular ideology had to triumph, a feudal pluralism had to make the isolation of the clerks possible." Indeed, Sartre concluded, "a clerk is always on the side of the oppressors.

A watchdog or a jester: it is up to him to choose. M. Benda has chosen the cap and bells and M. Marcel the kennel." True engagement, without oppression or alienation, would mean "the very notion of clerkship will appear inconceivable."

Part of this cut close to the bone. As we saw, Benda himself had granted, in the heat of the thirties, that were he forced to choose between maintaining the clerkly realm and ending social oppression, he would choose the former: the maintenance of oppression was preferable to the destruction of the kingdom of the *clercs*. But he had added that he did not believe such a choice was necessary. Moreover, even when he spoke of oppression, he had no concern for existential freedom in the Sartrean mode: he had explicitly criticized Existentialist notions of freedom and action, and had himself held to the importance of rationality as an *integral* aspect of both, if they were to be significant notions. In the same way, Benda would have nothing of Sartre's neo- or quasi-Marxist talk of ideological false consciousness, of bad faith or conscience, of clerkly alienation from other men and from basic social *praxis*. Implicit in Benda's whole profession and explicit in his talk of intellectual action were a rejection of general reduction to socioeconomic foundations, a denial that intellectual and material labor were in all fundamental ways the same, and a concentration on the different significances of men's diverse pronouncements, deeds, and roles. Here, at least, Benda was well aware of the genetic fallacy, of the pitfalls of debunking. Even "critical theory" depended on concepts and capacity and thereby in a sense transcended the era in which it claimed to be wholly engaged and of which it claimed to be a part. The call simply to "become engaged" (far more in Sartre and in vulgar Marxism than in Marx himself) begged the question of *what told one* to engage, and in what location, and in what mode—it begged the question of critical discrimination and analysis.

Still, much of this was more implicit than explicit. It was far from clear that Benda's brand of action was less formalistic or less troublesome than Sartre's. For all his talk of the divine, how did Benda grapple with incarnation? What sort of impact had the ideal upon the temporal in specific cases—Europe, France, the organized Left, social justice?

Regarding the first two instances, the verdict seems evident. Despite his proclamations about the idea of Europe and the ideal of France, Benda's supporting statements in both cases became increasingly ambiguous and, ultimately, realist. The case of democracy was somewhat more complex. One might well praise Benda for producing ***La Grande Epreuve des démocraties*** in the midst of the Occupation: "Benda deserves our respect: 'un clerc qui n'a pas trahi.' " But this confused the issue, confounding orthodox political treason towards the Third Republic with Benda's quite different doctrine. Certainly, Benda's general opposition to the Nazis and Vichy was perfectly consistent with his canons. And with regard to democracy itself, his distinctive emphasis was on the abstract and metaphysical. One could quarrel with this emphasis as somewhat esoteric and could consider that Benda had transferred many of his own clerkly canons to his ideal of democracy, yet still grant that it was clerkly. But the problem was that Benda was torn between the ideal and actuality. The way in which his use of the term "mystiques" altered was important. When he criticized them, he stressed the evils of dogmatism and passionate group spirit; but when he turned to praise democratic mystique, those evils vanished. Something more than vacillation was involved. Benda's condemnation of false rationalism—of adherence to principle at the expense of need—was a worry about what he earlier had termed the "treason of the laymen." (Nor was that an isolated reference: he repeated his condemnation of false rationalism, coupling it with lay treason, after the war.) In his treatment of false liberalism and abusive individualism as threats to stability and in his urging of a passion for democracy, which he admitted could produce injustice—in these, too, Benda was being severely realist. In his concern, he did at times subordinate the *clerc*-speculative to the *clerc*-militant, and he did laicize them both. Much the same could be said of his more extreme pronouncements on pacifism: by his own admission (and example), the doctrine of just cause could lead to passionate injustice and intemperance once battle was joined. The same was true regarding his support for *authoritarian* socialism: even if it were socialist and confronted by massive threats from the Right, a fundamental conflict still existed between authoritarianism and Benda's ideal of democracy. Again, the same was true regarding his concern for social justice: his calls here for bread and happiness for the poor seemed flatly to contradict his other statements, earlier and later, that justice was an ideal—something universal and abstract—and not at all a matter of happiness, humanitarianism, or material amelioration.

In part, these were relatively obvious matters of inconsistency between Benda's professed canons and some of his other public pronouncements. In large part they were the product and part of a phase in the life of a man by then in his late seventies, and perhaps they are not to be treated with the rigor due his more basic articulations. But only in part. These troubles around democracy indicated larger, more fundamental troubles. They pointed to a central problem, a problem lying at the heart of Benda's clerkly kingdom and, at the same time, pointing to the real potentials of that realm.

POLITICS AND DISCOURSE

From the time of his earliest public pronouncements, Benda consistently denounced the Right; he defended the Left alone. To argue that this in itself violated Benda's clerkly stance is to misread him. He defended the mystique as opposed to the politics of the Left; and he branded as treasonous certain doctrines of the Left (humanitarian sentimentalism, historicism, scientism, belief in the immediate efficacy of the ideal, and belief in purely material measures). Yet there was a problem here, posed by his continual use of the traditional terminology of the political spectrum. Benda commented on these terms explicitly once. "Left" and "Right," he granted, were abstractions; but so were all words. They were no less important for all that; and men took them seriously. Men took them seriously—indeed. This was the problem. By employing these terms himself, Benda was appropriating—and, by implication, was supporting—something realist in genesis and continued usage, a terminology that was far more clearly one of politics than of mystique. With Communism especially, this problem became more than implicit. Benda was careful to deny that he supported Communist politics as such, that he had joined the party, or even that he had accepted the Communist mystique; he endeavored to "guard his spirit." Having done all this, he chose to support some specific acts and positions. What was problematical, however, was the fact that he supported them in "realist" terminology, terminology that was often specifically redolent of Communist ideology. He said that the *clercs* must choose between Communist and Fascists, later between Communist authoritarians and bourgeois reactionary authoritarians. He said that the *clerc* must choose the side that at least promised bread to all—the side of the workers, of the revolutionary class. Perhaps Benda here was himself playing a simple layman's role. But such a distinction (as in the case of his World War I patriotism) was hard to draw in Benda's case. He had long proclaimed that his vocation was that of *clerc*. And when that proclamation is coupled with his insistence that he was concerned with how the *clerc* appeared in the modern world, how he was taken by modern society, the import of Benda's statements was powerful. Were Benda to be judged by the criterion of influence that he had used in identifying traitor-*clercs,* his own position would smack of treason. A man's public stance readily can be used to serve the cause with which, however hesitantly and with however many qualifications, he has identified himself. Despite his disclaimers, Benda failed to guard against (perhaps even to see) the uses to which a *clerc* could be put by politics when he engaged with mystiques.

There was a certain Manicheanism here. Ultimately, its terms were enshrined in Benda's division of the world into *clercs* and laymen.

In its way, Pierre Mauriac's caution about that division was apt enough. Mauriac distinguished two modes of politics: first, that of men who attempted to influence politics without illusions and who realized the dangers of compromise; second, that of Benda's *clercs,* who were to resist any contamination. Mauriac saw that the *clercs,* by virtue of their contempt for politics, would be more forcefully stricken by the need for political maneuvers when they found themselves driven to comment. "Necessity, urgency, is little favorable for reflection; emotion dominates and dictates their decisions; brusquely, and in a sort of disarray, they take part. And when, returning to their taste for analysis, they seek the reasons for their adherence, they arrive at unexpected confessions."

Had not Benda himself often enough confessed, *mea culpa*? "I wish neither to howl with the wolves' pack nor to bleat with the sheep," he had said. But he had also said: "The wolves have their beauty, not wolves disguised as shepherds." And his alter ego, Eleuthère, had admitted to a kind of love for "this Stalin . . . who has never read a novel or verse, but only political treatises." Yet Mauriac's caution did not touch the center of the problem here. By dividing the world between *clercs* and laymen, Benda reduced laymen to their lowest common denominator. He made politics *essentially* realist. Thus, realism subtly became a *standard for* politics—hence Benda's worries about the treason of the laymen, the harsh realism of some of his own pronouncements, and the distinctive beauty of undisguised, nonliterary wolves. Here again, "delimitation" is not neutral: the defining of "politics" is itself a political act of one kind or another, drawing boundaries, joining and distinguishing matters, establishing publicly authoritative structures, both conceptually and socially.

From the time of his earliest public pronouncements, Benda consistently denounced the Right; he defended the Left alone. To argue that this in itself violated Benda's clerkly stance is to misread him.

— *Ray Nichols*

Similarly with Benda's *clercs.* Sometimes Benda had advanced the notion of a divine element in laymen, whereby they could be partly raised from mere realist existence; sometimes he had located the divine solely within the realm of the *clercs.* These variations sprang from a deep ambivalence, a most critical aspect of Benda's problematic division of the world. It was an ambivalence that Benda's favorite term, *esprit* (with its dual connotations of "mind" and "spirit") did nothing to remove. In part, Benda here had reference to conceptual understanding generally; in part, to specifically moral ideals and critical intellectual action. How these two were "rationally" linked and how the *clerc* was to act consistently in terms of both of them were never fully specified.

Could they be? The *clercs,* Benda had said, were all those who "in a certain manner say: 'My kingdom is not of this world.' " But this did not show that all *clercs* shared another—a single—realm in common. The voice of the contemplative and the scholar; the voice of the critic and the prophet—these were instrumental in different ways, with different orientations and different bearings. They were different provinces, with diverse traditions—and different gods. And they might well call *clerc* away from *clerc,* rather than uniting into one kingdom.

Benda himself eventually glimpsed something of this problem as it arose within his stance. He came to recognize that his basic orientation, the core of his existence, was not the scientific gymnastics of speculative thought but active concern with moral critique. His Hellenic and Cartesian education, he said, led him to the former; his Jewish heritage, to the latter. Insomuch as it implied "respect for the truth," the worship of justice could fit with the worship of science. But not insomuch as justice was concerned with respect for the person and his rights as a person: then the two could "exist without one another, as one often enough has occasion to see."

"As one often enough has occasion to see": Benda himself had warned of the shipwreck of philosophy on the rocks of moralism. He had reflected that it was perhaps better to proclaim the laws of the mind than to proclaim justice; for the latter led to a social logomachy without end. He had commented, "Equivocation is the normal regime of political life." Equivocation was necessary to social peace; for without it there would be no debate, only murder. He had repeatedly characterized moral issues as central to political controversy because they were nonverifiable, nonscientific; they were matters of faith, of preference, and were essentially subjective. As he put it in a striking passage:

> Political quarrels take issue over interests of moral preferences, that is to say . . . things whose foundations are essentially undemonstrable. . . .
>
> Add that the "welfare of humanity" is an eminently subjective notion, under which everyone puts what he prefers. The same for "civilization," the rule of the "best," the right of the "elite". . . .
>
> What should be the coherent attitude of political passion?
>
> It should say: "My position is a preference, nothing other than a preference. . . ."
>
> But man will not accept this declaration.

Nor could Benda accept it. Morality—and social life—also has its shipwrecks, on the rocks of inadequate philosophy. And here Benda's own philosophy lacked, at least, coherence. His orientation, the thrust of his other pronouncements, had constantly been that civilization was not a matter of sheer feeling, of primitive sensibility, of barbaric, immediate desire, but was something far more, founded on the joint existence of men who stood for and articulated conceptual, intellectualized art, science, law, and justice. And these pronouncements themselves were no mere impulses, nor sheer moralism; they were elaborately articulated arguments, terms for man and society, which were diffused publicly, carrying within them the seeds of their own broader actualization, however partial or incomplete. Benda himself had said that these terms were maintained by speech and action. His own best example was exemplary.

Much of Benda's practice was better and more coherent (and when incoherent, more fruitfully provocative) than his attempted reconstructions of it. His assertions that there were specific conceptual "constants of human thought" may have been dubious, less than clear, and less than consistent. But he was surely correct when he said that there were other types of statements than empirical ones: statements that transformed the sensible into the intelligible, establishing meaning and providing richer views of "reality." And not just views: also social practices. Benda's own discourse represented more than his formalistic canons allowed him to grasp. Despite his insistence on clear and distinct discourse and his opposition to "literary" figure, Benda himself plunged deeply into figure at crucial points—and he showed thereby that this need not be superficial, not a matter of style in the sense of added ornamental, sensual flourish, but style in a profounder sense, a matter of fused form and content, a matter of fundamental significance. Once, late in life, he came close to seeing this. "True style," he said,

> must mold itself exactly onto the thought, even as in return the thought demands of the style no more than that it be a transparent vestment without seeking for any beauty for itself, its beauty consisting in the perfection of its transparency. . . . It does not appear that the mind commences by "conceiving well," that is to say by forming a clear idea and that it is afterwards that the words for expressing the idea "come easily." The truth is that these two operations are only one, for when the mind really forms a clear idea, the wished-for words are there at the identical moment, for the reason that our mind is so made that the formation of a concept and the evocation of a word are one single and identical act.

Though couched in a literary context, this statement may have resounded dimly from Benda's own political engagements. To be sure, even here Benda failed to grasp the implications—for himself and more generally. Some types of statements, providing general characterizations, are not readily identifiable as (or analyzable into) either "factual" or "evaluative." They may indeed set the terms *for* other simpler statements, made within their contexts, which can be so classified. This is not the place to develop these notions further. That Benda provokes them, and that he provokes us to develop them ourselves elsewhere, is a tribute to his endeavors. In *our* immediate context, Benda's "civilization" stands as an example. Here there was more than Benda's realism, more than sheer existence, and more than Benda's criticisms of orthodox Existentialism and Marxism led even him to see. There was a potential for politics of another sort, a process of juxtaposing, of bringing activities together, of rearticulating reciprocal transformations of tasks and culture, and of mutually tapping resources, both conceptually and socially. Civilization was more than formal. It had a mediating place and substance as complex as men's diverse projects of objectification and existence. Here, incarnate, was the clerkly problematic. Even if not an ancient *cosmos,* it was far more than utter fragmentation, and it was more than mere critique of critical criticism. Here, in a way, *clerc* was linked with *clerc*; and neither was subordinate to the other.

It was the *clercs* themselves who drew the boundaries, even among themselves—and in that very process, repeatedly brought themselves together, with the world.

In more ways than one, the clerkly stance was, and remains, representative. Benda's *clercs* were not depictions of the general social norms that "the intellectual" follows. They followed no ordinary, discrete professions. They were modes for emulation by some called intellectuals; they provided an alternative to talk (contemptuous, praising, worried) of "the intellectual class." At the least, we would demand of those who now call either for the separation or for the fusion of the intellectual and politics a sensitivity to the ambiguities of that call and of modes of responding to it, like that which Benda affords. The image of Benda the saboteur or of Benda manning the barricades, bare-breasted like Marianne, is too ludicrous to entertain. There are other modes of action. The *clerc,* in one of his persons, was the true scholar, the contemplative—the man "who writes, takes notes, reflects." We need such men, to defend the seriously gratuitous and to be aware of their own social practice and its bearing on and for others. We need them lest obsolescence consume everything, reducing it to commodity or utility, and men have no place or mode through which to discriminate. The *clerc,* in his other person, was the critic. And we need such men as this, lest brute fact triumph in all its sterile triviality. We need them, to remind us of the need for continuing activity. In Benda's own career as controversialist, he shows us much about the dynamics of ideological controversy and cultural exchange—of the significance of discourse generally as "intellectual action"; of how polemic is a path with a realism of its own, from which one cannot readily retreat once entered; of how even the most professedly "pure" discourse must move into figure (irony, analogy) to make its sallies and grasp for its own foundations.

History is for society as memory is for the individual. . . . Strangely reflected, we see our faces and are shocked by recognitions. Here lies Benda's ultimate significance. His creed was a diminished one; his practices were not always consistent with it. But others, promising more, have delivered far less. By clarifying whence we have come and where we are now, bearing and being born, Benda challenges us to move on. He contributes to a long multivoiced tradition of discourse, fruitful in its variations, its exchanges, and its modes of occurrence. Perhaps no whole ever has been more than this. Perhaps the discourse cannot be ended. Perhaps its continuation is critical in and for any sort of "civilization." In this location and in this manner, however aptly "the intellectual" may be delimited by analysis or by history, Benda's *clercs* will remain a problem. And that is as it must be.

David L. Schalk (essay date 1979)

SOURCE: "The Case against Engagement: Julien Benda and *La Trahison des Clercs,*" in *The Spectrum of Political Engagement: Mounier, Benda, Nizan, Brasillach, Sartre,* Princeton University Press, 1979, pp. 26-48.

[*Schalk is an American writer and educator. In the following excerpt, he considers Benda's views on political engagement and examines the critical reception of* The Treason of the Intellectuals, *as well as the practical understanding of Benda's ideas by various thinkers.*]

The idea of a treason or betrayal of the intellectuals has had an enormous success. This concept may be viewed as the reverse of the coin of engagement, or perhaps a slightly distorted mirror-image. It has become a commonplace in America and England. In France it may be traced back at least to the Dreyfus Affair, when intellectuals acquired along with their name a special critical function, and because of the victory signified by the revision of Dreyfus' first trial, gained "a *droit de cité* unknown in other countries." Both Dreyfusard and anti-Dreyfusard intellectuals accused each other of betraying their "true" functions. The explicit formulation of ***La Trahison des clercs*** did not, however, come until 1927, and in France at least the concept has become inseparably (and rightfully) identified with Julien Benda.

Though he has had a number of distinguished American admirers over the years, including T. S. Eliot, Julien Benda is not well known in this country. Specialists in French literature and intellectual history will recognize him as a polemicist and critic, a second-rank figure who throughout his very long life was overshadowed by several generations of brilliant contemporaries. He is remembered primarily for one book, though he wrote fifty and more than one thousand articles. ***La Trahison des clercs*** was first published in 1927, and translated into English in 1928 as ***The Treason of the Intellectuals.***

Benda's controversial attack on *certain types* of modern intellectuals has often been dismissed as unscholarly polemic. In his introduction to *The New Radicalism in America, 1889-1963,* Christopher Lasch states: ". . . I have not wished to write a tract, another ***Trahison des clercs,*** and I state my own prejudices here only in order to make it clear what they are, not because this book is intended to document them."

Even when Benda's contribution has been viewed positively, it has been rather badly misperceived. In April 1965 a symposium on "The Intellectual in Politics" was held at the University of Texas, and the proceedings were published in 1966 with a preface by H. Malcolm Macdonald. Macdonald felt that despite the divergencies of the views of the participants, a consensus did emerge, ". . . on the necessity of the intellectual, however defined, to remain true to his task of being what Julien Benda has called 'the conscience of humanity.' " In a vague and general sense that every intellectual from Ayn Rand to Herbert Marcuse could probably accept, Macdonald's assertion is correct. However, a close reading of the eight papers presented at the symposium reveals an almost total ignorance of the specifics of Benda's thought. Only one speaker, the Swedish political scientist and parliamentarian Gunnar Hecksher, refers specifically to ***La Trahison des clercs,*** but his brief remarks show little understanding of what Benda was advocating in that work. One other participant, the German historian Klaus Mehnert, does take a position close to that adopted by Benda in ***La Trahison des clercs,*** but he never mentions Benda by name.

Eugene McCarthy, at the time Senator from Wisconsin, was the last speaker at the symposium, and McCarthy made an eloquent plea for greater political involvement on the part of intellectuals. Without reference to Julien Benda, Senator McCarthy used the phrase "treason of the intellectuals" in *exactly* the opposite sense originally intended by Benda. No one would accuse Senator McCarthy, a man deeply steeped in Catholic theology and a talented poet and essayist in his own right, of lacking intellectual credentials. It is interesting to recall that two years after this speech was delivered McCarthy became the leader of the "Dump Johnson" movement, which attracted many American intellectuals and which appears to be a rare case of intellectuals having some demonstrable political influence, in that President Lyndon Johnson did not seek a second full term of office in 1968.

Senator McCarthy's "error" does suggest that while the notion of the "treason of the intellectuals" is very much a part of our political climate, there is no widespread awareness of the authorship of the term. Even when Benda's authorship is recognized, the precise meanings he attached to the concept of *la trahison des clercs* have long been forgotten, and there has been heated debate, since the Second World War at least, as to precisely what segment of the intellectual class is treasonous. One's own political predispositions clearly play a major role in determining whom one identifies as the betrayers.

To deal fully with the uses and misuses of Benda's concept of the betrayal of the intellectuals would require a long essay. As an illustration of the diversity of views, here are four examples chosen from a large number.

> Lawrence Stone defines the "ultimate *trahison des clercs*" as "the conscious denigration of the life of the mind."
>
> Robert Brustein says "We have been witnessing a modern *trahison des clercs*, signified by the surrender of men and women with great potential to America's hunger for personalities."
>
> Ferdinand Mount defines the treason of the clerks as "this prostration of mind before brutish might, not excluding that of Julien Benda, who coined the phrase. . . . "
>
> Richard Cobb defines the *trahison des clercs* as "intellectual commitment to political extremism."

A MAN WHO DETESTED CHAPELS

The controversy over *la trahison des clercs* continues and Benda remains relatively obscure. One reason for this apparent paradox is suggested by René Etiemble in his preface to the third edition of ***La Trahison des clercs*** (1958). Etiemble points out that for more than half a century Benda had obstinately refused every philosophical and political "mode." Benda produced polemics against Bergsonian intuition, Maurrassian sophism, and later intellectual "fads" such as surrealism and existentialism. Throughout his long life he had never received much except "hatred and sarcasm," had never reached many people, and had gained several thousand influential enemies with one work. ***La Trahison des clercs*** infuriated the literary people, who are especially "rancorous and vain." The media, Etiemble adds, which in a few weeks can make an "inoffensive imbecile" into a star, spent fifty years lowering Julien Benda into the image of a "fanatical, odious, and raging little man." Julien Benda was, as André Lwoff writes, a nonconformist, a man who "detested chapels." When he died in extreme old age his passing was barely noticed.

While Benda's technical mastery of French literary style has never been questioned, his methods of argumentation may also help to explain his lack of eminence. Readers who are familiar with ***La Trahison des clercs,*** even those in sympathy with Benda's fundamental positions, may well conclude that the imprecise knowledge of what Benda stood for is deserved. Raymond Aron, author of another, very different polemic against a large group of his fellow intellectuals, finds Benda's arguments often confused. Aron writes: ". . . if the betrayal consists in overvaluing the temporal and undervaluing the eternal, the intellectuals of our time are all traitors."

While Aron's formulation is persuasive, it is not a completely correct definition of what Benda came to view the betrayal to be. Benda would have been in full accord with Aron's assertion that " . . . the tendency to criticize the established order is, so to speak, the occupational disease of the intellectuals." Yet the matter is complicated because Benda would by no means claim that the criterion for discerning betrayal is criticism of the established order. In many cases it would be a betrayal *not* to challenge, and challenge publicly, the established order.

Pierre Chambat has shown, through a close examination of Benda's entire opus, that Benda was concerned with what he perceived as a "crisis of civilization." Even in ***La Trahison des clercs,*** Benda did not limit himself to the rather specific question of "Who betrayed?" He attempted to deal with many, if not all, facets of the intellectual's role in modern society. Such inquiries inevitably pose serious difficulties, since the individual commitment of the writer is so deeply enmeshed in the problem he is studying. Robert J. Niess, author of the definitive published biography of Julien Benda, recognizes these difficulties and proposes an interesting, if somewhat discouraging solution: "To discover the true role of the *clerc,* to learn whether or not he has betrayed, and to date the betrayal successfully would be the task of the perfect historian, that is, the unfalteringly alert mind, not only universally learned but completely impartial both politically and intellectually and strengthened by the most rigorous kind of philosophical training." Niess believes that Benda was especially weak as an historian. While Niess' judgment of Benda's skill as an historian may be disputed, his own analysis of the origins of ***La Trahison des clercs*** has been recognized as a masterful exercise in the history of ideas. The concept of the *clerc* is traced by Niess back to ***Dialogue à Byzance,*** published in 1900. Already Benda conceived of a body of *clercs* serving as the conscience of society, but it took him a long time to develop his central idea of a mass treason of the intellectuals. ***La Trahison des clercs*** is viewed as the essential document in Benda's intellectual life; at least with the hindsight we now possess he seems to have been progressing toward it all through his early and middle career, and after 1927 he constantly amplifies and defends it.

Niess' own judgment of ***La Trahison des clercs*** is quite ambivalent. There is a rather striking dichotomy between high praise and sharp criticism, which suggests that he was uncertain in his own evaluation. Niess points up many of the vagaries and inconsistencies in Benda's argumentation, the flagrant biases, and even finds examples of faulty reasoning. Yet he is convinced that in the future ***La Trahison des clercs*** will be seen as the one work which best combines Benda's passion and logic into a "brilliant system of social criticism." Niess is persuaded that it will hold up as "one of the most considerable books of our time." This dichotomy is again manifested in Niess' conclusions on Benda's entire career. He is quite severe; Benda made a "catastrophic intellectual error, the error of constant generalization without sufficient regard to facts. . . ." Yet Benda will someday be conceded an "honorable place in that brilliant line which he himself described, the line of St. Paul and Luther and Pascal, men who eternally prevent the world from slumbering in indolence and evil."

It seems unlikely that Benda will acquire this prominence (since he never had it during his lifetime) and retain it simply because he made people angry and kept them alert. Perhaps Niess felt that intellectuals reading Benda would sense intuitively that his message was an important one, reminding them of truths about their calling. H. Stuart Hughes, in his pathbreaking study of the intellectual history of Europe between 1890 and 1930, *Consciousness and Society,* selects ***La Trahison des clercs*** as one of three works of "intellectual summation," a "directional signpost" for the middle and late 1920s. On balance Hughes is even more critical than Niess, and he finds ***La Trahison des clercs*** a deeply flawed book. Hughes does, however, value the work as a "moral remonstrance," and a call to an "examination of conscience."

What is the nature of this "moral remonstrance" that both Niess and Hughes find in ***La Trahison des clercs?*** For Hughes it must be an important factor, since without it Benda's simplification of the issues, his "profoundly parochial outlook," his "narrowness of intellectual range," would hardly make the book worthy of mention.

THE ORIGINAL CONCEPTION OF LA TRAHISON DES CLERCS

Julien Benda never pretended to be a tolerant man; he hated his ideological and political enemies with an unremitting passion. Many readers will be annoyed by his stubborn refusal to consider opposing views, his digressions, his merciless hammering at the same points. Still the central line of his argument in ***La Trahison des clercs*** can be disentangled. A careful reformulation of this argument should serve three purposes. First, in viewing the strengths and weaknesses of the work in clearer focus, the reader will be able to evaluate its importance for himself or herself. Second, Benda's intellectual and political evolution after 1927 will be easier to comprehend, in particular the quite fascinating and apparently contradictory changes in his views on the political involvement of intellectuals. The common misconception of Benda as purely an "ivory-tower" theorist will be laid to rest definitively. I also hope to show that even in 1927 the question of political action of the *clerc,* and thus the question of engagement, posed the crucial paradox for Benda. Benda may have resolved it to his own satisfaction, though I doubt even that and find his ambivalence showing through in the very vehemence of his denials. The other ambivalence—that of the commentators—has, I believe, its roots in the same paradox. Benda touches painful nerves and reflects, in his own way, the doubts and hesitations felt by several generations of practicing intellectuals in Europe and America.

Benda opens ***La Trahison des clercs*** by formulating the essential qualities he finds in modern society at large. Both the intellectuals and humanity in general have been placing greater and greater emphasis on temporal concerns. This is an age of politics; political passions and those of race and class are now reaching almost everybody, even spreading to the Far East. (Benda may have been thinking of the Chinese Revolution of 1927, though as is almost always the case he makes no specific historical reference. He prefers to remain on a general, theoretical plane.) We know, Benda adds, precisely who our political enemies are, and thus we can hate them more bitterly. A "condensation" of political hatreds has developed, along with a greater uniformity of thought.

Julien Benda never pretended to be a tolerant man; he hated his ideological and political enemies with an unremitting passion.

— David L. Schalk

Again and again Benda stresses the growth of nationalist passion, the overweening concern with national glory and pride. He is horrified by new doctrines which advocate crushing enemy cultures totally, rather than incorporating the vanquished within the conquering society. Benda's distress at the rise of mystical nationalism cannot be overemphasized, and he frequently returns to the subject throughout his work. He devotes almost as much attention to the related issue of the rise of ideology in general. The passions of the past were precisely passions—that is, "naive explosions of instinct," with no theoretical grounding. However, a broad spectrum of intellectuals, from Karl Marx to Charles Maurras and their varied followers, have elaborated networks of doctrines designed to support political passions. These networks are effective and have increased the strength of political passions. Buttressed by a careful intellectual organization, each of the modern ideological systems argues that it is the "agent of good" in the world, and that its enemy represents the "genie of evil." Each system tries to be totalitarian, in the sense of covering all aspects of life, believing itself destined to succeed, and claiming that its ideology is founded on science.

Benda believes that these new, systematized passions arise from two fundamental desires: (1) temporal good, and (2) the wish to be separate and unique from other human groups. The former relates to class passion, the latter to racial passion, and nationalism unites the two. These passions are realist in that they relate to the world and are nonidealist, though they are so strong that one might term them "divinized realism." Men want to be in the real and practical world and not in the disinterested, metaphysical realm; no one would die now for "principles," for abstract universal values like justice. Older idealist passions, such as those motivating a "pure" crusader, have been absorbed by nationalism. The pragmatic behavior of a single localized state has become divinized—the state has become God and Mussolini's Italy admits it. Later in ***La Trahison des clercs*** Benda comments with disgust on the

Italian intellectuals' eulogy of warfare and scorn for civilian life, their praise of the morality of violence. He finds their apologies for the warlike instinct a "stupefaction of history."

The reader with some general knowledge of Benda's positions may be confused at this point, for he descends from the ivory tower into the heat of a polemic against a specific regime, even before he has elaborated his doctrine of the role of the *clerc*. Over the years his attacks on Italian fascism grew more vehement, especially after the invasion of Ethiopia.

Perhaps Benda realized that his remarks on Italy could lead him into a logical dilemma, for he makes the qualification that the *clerc* may become involved in external politics when an abstract injustice has been committed. (Of course, he can provide us with no universally applicable key to determine when an event may be classified as a true injustice, though he names Voltaire's role in the Calas Affair, and Zola's advocacy of Dreyfus' innocence as examples of justified involvement.) He could have cited his own participation in the Dreyfus Affair, which Pierre Chambat, in his judicious analysis of this aspect of Benda's career, does not hesitate to term "engagement." Only a decade later, in 1936, did Benda publicly admit and discuss his involvement in the Dreyfus Affair. This led Paul Nizan to remark that Benda "wanted to see in the Affair only a combat of eternal verities, when, in fact, it was simply a matter of an historical engagement."

Enough examples have been given to show that when Benda mentions specifics, it is easy to detect a leftist, or at least a liberal political inclination. I shall return to this important point later. Presumably Benda felt himself on surer ground in ***La Trahison des clercs*** when he added two *general* criteria for involvement. First, the true *clerc* never espouses causes for any personal gain. Also, if the *clerc* is really fulfilling his function he will be scorned and insulted by the layman.

Here, then, is the first mention of the problem of when and why the intellectual should enter the political arena. Benda's embarrassment is, I believe, evident to the reader. Probably because it is more difficult to prescribe contemporary behavior than to look to the past with the benefit of present knowledge, Benda devotes more attention in ***La Trahison des clercs*** to the question of how the intellectuals should have responded to the recent and dramatic changes in that part of humanity which he terms "lay" as opposed to clerical.

In the past the *clercs* had stood apart from the masses, were devoted to the metaphysical and the speculative, and scorned practical ends. This elite boasted a lineage of two thousand years and had always been in ". . . formal opposition to the realism of the multitudes." Thanks to the vigilance of these intellectual sentinels, humanity had at least ". . . done evil while honoring the good." This contradiction was the honor of humanity and kept civilization on its proper course until around 1890. At that time a sharp transition took place, and those who had been a "brake" on the realism of the masses began to stimulate that realism. To show that there is a qualitative difference in the contemporary period Benda cites individuals—Theodor Mommsen, Heinrich von Treitschke, Ferdinand Brunetière, Maurice Barrès, Charles Maurras, Gabriele d'Annunzio, Rudyard Kipling, and his former friend Charles Péguy, who had died during the first Battle of the Marne in 1914. The names of Georges Sorel and Friedrich Nietzsche are then added for good measure, and Benda finds everyone on the list to be equally evil. All are men of true political passion. (It is important to note that all of these intellectuals, with the possible exceptions of Péguy and Sorel, about whom there is heated scholarly debate, are strongly identified with the political Right. Had he been so inclined, Benda could have included in his first list of betrayers prominent, indeed internationally known, intellectuals who were active in left-wing causes, such as Romain Rolland and Henri Barbusse. The latter had been a member of the French Communist Party since 1923.)

The group of intellectuals Benda chose to denounce are condemned because they desire action and immediate results and have descended eagerly into the political forum. No disinterested group remains; the modern *clerc* is strongly xenophobic.

Benda does admit that external historical circumstances have played some role in this change in clerical attitudes, though he still wishes that the *clercs* had not acquiesced so joyfully. The historians, as guilty as the novelists and poets, are glorifying nationalism, producing pragmatic rather than disinterested work, and using history to strengthen political causes. The literary critics are unobjective and partisan; even the metaphysicians, supposedly the most abstract of all, are becoming political. The latter change is, Benda claims, totally without historical precedent.

"Intense" is a mild word to describe the degree of Benda's own French patriotism, and though he set forth an elaborate series of arguments to defend his loyalty to France, he is susceptible to the charge of xenophobia himself. His indictment of Germany, "the cancer of Europe," began in 1905 and persisted through his last published articles in 1954. As one might expect, he claims that the German philosophers, such as Fichte and Hegel, were the first to betray. Though the French have all too frequently heeded the siren song of their colleagues across the Rhine, "the nationalist *clerc* is essentially a German invention." Instead of honoring the abstract quality of what is uniquely human, the nineteenth-century German intellectuals began the trend of looking concretely at mankind so that differences become clearly visible. Even Christianity, and the agnostic Benda was always an admirer of the early Christians, has been subverted by the nationalists. Christ has been made a "professor of national egotism." Marxism in its guise as internationalist philosophy is not a valid substitute, Benda believes, since it has concrete aims and speaks in the name of one group, instead of all humanity.

The legacy of Hellenism, which for a time had been maintained by the classical French intellectuals, has at least been defeated. The modern *clerc* has the infantile wish to think of everything as "in time," never as outside or beyond time, and is concerned only with the contemporaneous, the immediate, present circumstances. One can see how appalled Benda would have been at the emphasis on "relevance," which was so important in American university curricula in the 1960s. The powerful new trend toward pragmatic career training which has surfaced in American (and European) colleges and universities in the 1970s would have equally distressed him. Benda finds all such new doctrines a reversal of Platonism, since they claim that real values are seen and concrete instead of "clouds" (*nuées*) of justice and temperance. For the first time in history *clercs* approve the judges of Socrates. Again and again Benda attacks the moral flavor the new *clercs* have given to realism, while stressing repeatedly that we are at a turning point in history. "The divinisation of the political" is the greatest and most evil work of the modern *clercs*. Even Machiavelli said that politics and morality were disassociated, and Charles Maurras now claims that "politics determine morality."

The new emphasis on man's natural violence especially distresses Benda, along with the preference for authoritarian regimes. When confronted with barbaric behavior, the *clercs* now invoke human nature and claim that nothing can be done. They have forgotten that the moralist is essentially a "utopian" and they derive a romantic pleasure from pessimism. The *clercs* even praise war for itself and not as a "sad necessity." Modern man is turning to Sparta for inspiration. The *clercs* have created and popularized a new honor—the honor of practical courage leading to the conquest of things. In Benda's view civilization is simply not possible unless functions are divided, and they are no longer divided when the *clercs* are laicized. Thus the general anti-intellectualism, the exalting of the man of arms over the man of study, the praise of action over thought, the unconscious over intellect, are to be expected.

Benda is convinced that despite all the pressures to conform it is possible for individual *clercs* to resist and remain independent. He clearly believes as strongly as does Noam Chomsky in the responsibility of intellectuals. If one is a real thinker, Benda states, he will be a universalist. However, today humanity wants its scholars to be "not guides but servants," and for the most part, that is what humanity gets. The general conclusion of ***La Trahison des clercs*** is that the political realism of the *clercs* is not a random fact but instead "linked to the essence of the modern world." The sceptic might accuse Benda of vast oversimplification and infer that he found the entire world to be treasonous, except himself, of course. Benda might have agreed with the second point, if pressed on the matter. He argues that because of the *clercs'* evasion of their duty, humanity now both perpetrates evil and honors it. Perhaps because of his deep-rooted pessimism, Benda was often an accurate prophet, and he predicts that civilization will move toward "the most total and perfect war that the world will have ever seen." It should be emphasized that these words were written in the relative calm of the mid-1920s, several years before the sense of living in a period "between two wars" became prevalent. Whether this new war is to be between nations or classes, Benda's diagnosis is somber. He sees little hope for peace and finds that most pacifist doctrines weaken the true cause of peace.

Benda pulls all his arguments together in a final summary, where he adopts a more inflexible position than he had earlier in the work. He now states that the true *clerc* must be *totally* disengaged from society. When the *clerc* declares to mankind that his "kingdom is not of this world," he may be crucified, ". . . but he is respected and his word haunts the memory of men." Yet in the real world of 1927 the betrayers dominate—Nietzsche, Sorel, Barrès, and their ilk, and Benda emphasizes again that this is no temporary aberration but rather a permanent trend in world historical development.

Benda wonders whether realism may not after all be the dominant force in human society. Coupled with the growing conquest of Nature, realism could easily produce a relapse into the worst forms of violence and cruelty—another striking prediction for 1933-1945. The best that one can hope for, Benda believes, is some form of union of nations and classes, though the "universal fraternity" which would emerge is not really desirable. It would merely be a higher form of nationalism, with the nation calling itself Man, and naming God as the enemy.

> And henceforth, unified into an immense army, into an immense factory, no longer aware of anything save heroism, discipline, inventions, scorning all free and disinterested activity, no longer placing the Good above the real world, and having for God only itself and its wishes, humanity will attain great things—that is, a really grandiose control over the matter which surrounds it, a really joyous consciousness of its power and its grandeur. And history will smile to think that Socrates and Jesus died for this species.

LA TRAHISON DES CLERCS AFTER 1927

There are hints in the original edition of ***La Trahison des clercs*** that under some circumstances Benda would allow the intellectuals to enter the political arena without betraying. In general, however, the correct way for the *clerc* to act in the modern world is to protest vocally, then submit and drink the hemlock when the State so orders. Any other action is treasonous. H. Stuart Hughes' criticism seems justified: "Had they followed to the letter the advice Benda offered, few European intellectuals would have survived the two decades subsequent to the publication of his book."

Doubtless to Benda's delight, ***La Trahison des clercs*** immediately stirred up passionate controversy, and Benda produced a great deal of polemical journalism in the decade after 1927. He collected some of his best articles and published them in a volume entitled ***Précision (1930-1937)***. Here we find a considerable evolution in Benda's thought on the subject of political involvement of the *clercs,* a movement not exactly toward compromise, but toward some recognition that the realities of modernity had to be faced in new ways. He tried to maintain continuity with his earlier positions by including a prefatory note explaining that he had chosen articles which dealt primarily with critiques of ***La Trahison des clercs***. These attacks had helped him to clarify his own positions, and he asserts that the articles selected were not mere sallies. The immediate subject was to serve as a pretext for more universal considerations.

The promised emphasis on universal problems in ***Précision*** is very hard to detect. Benda ranges widely, from discussions of educational policy and nationalism to a strong attack on marriage as one of the greatest betrayals of the modern *clerc,* since the *clerc* should reduce his "temporal surface" to a minimum. In some of the articles, however, the major themes of ***La Trahison des clercs*** are reexamined, first in a renewed attack on rightist *clercs* like Barrès, then in a more detailed treatment of the distinction between political speculation and immediate political action. Benda argues that there is a profound difference between the theoretical political analyses of the great *clercs* of the past and the conviction of many contemporary (1932) intellectuals that they are the "saviors" of society. The true task of the intellectuals remains ". . . to think correctly and to find truth, without concern for what will happen to the planet as a result."

Yet as the 1930s wore on, Benda participated in the general movement toward engagement which is such an important phenomenon in the intellectual history of that decade. He began to sign leftist manifestoes, becoming for a time a "fellow traveler," what the French call a *compagnon de route* of the French Communist Party. In ***Précision*** Benda tried to explain that he was not betraying by asserting that he would join such appeals only when they seemed to defend "eternal principles." The *clerc* must preach justice and truth without regard for the practical consequences of his position. Even in a totalitarian age Benda demands a strict idealism. It is natural to compromise, but the intellectual must ". . . *elevate himself above that which is natural.*" He retained enough optimism to believe that continuous pressure on political leaders can have some effect, can constrain them to be partially just. "History is made from shreds (*lambeaux*) of justice which the intellectual has torn from the politician."

Paul Nizan is surely correct when he describes the Benda of the mid-thirties as a *clerc de gauche*. Benda publicly stated that the *mystique de gauche* is acceptable for the *clerc,* as long as he does not descend into *la politique*. The leftist mystique is noble whereas that of the Right is ugly because it honors force. Yet in the articles published in the early 1930s Benda still emphasizes repeatedly that he will strictly limit his collaboration with the communists. In an article dating from 1934 entitled **"For Whom Do You Write?"** Benda professes a real inability to grasp the arguments of revolutionary writers—Paul Nizan is the example he cites—who claim that an intellectual who is reserved and withdrawn from society is really aiding capitalism. Benda cannot see how writers like Paul Valéry and Jean Giraudoux ". . . serve the *Comité des Forges* or the powerful banking interests. Even less that they serve them consciously."

The communist intellectuals attack the man "who meditates between his four walls" for not acting, even when his literary production "labors in the sense which is dear to them." The communists should recognize that there is an element in a writer which remains outside the social regime, that in France there exists a long tradition of literary independence, that French writers will not make good militants, whether communist or fascist. Benda follows this logic to the extreme of stating that he had written his polemical works ". . . with the perfect conviction that they would not change my contemporaries, . . . and [in any case] I care very little about this changing." In two hundred years some bibliophile—and he hopes that the species will still exist—might open his work and remark with surprise that in this universally pragmatic age here was one man who did not cooperate. Benda decides that he had been writing for such a judge.

Benda recognizes the power of Paul Nizan's arguments for a communist humanism. Nizan only made him see more clearly how different his conception of humanism is. It is, he proclaims, based on classical culture, and he holds strongly to the dichotomy between spiritual and material life. The reconciliation of intellectual and manual labor holds little attraction for him, since man is great only when he obeys his "divine part." He has no sympathy for those who "drink life through all their pores." Benda rejects contemporary left-leaning writers like Jean Guéhenno and Jean-Richard Bloch who call for humane rather than intellectual values. He prefers emaciated figures who lived the pure life of the spirit, and cites as examples Dante, Erasmus, Fénelon, and Pope Leo XIII. For Benda the Marxist-inspired religion of "total" man is merely a revitalized romanticism, venerating passion and action. There is no such creature as a "total" philosopher; one practices philosophy only "with the spirit." Spiritual and economic activities are totally distinct, and therefore his humanism demands the autonomy of the spiritual life, freedom for the spirit to escape society, even to act against society, to challenge any "established order." Benda realizes that he has the communists, the Hitlerians, and the *Action Française* against him, and the reader may perceive a certain nobility in his isolation, in his determination to retain his vision of classical humanism. It seems clear that if he had not been fettered by his idealism, if it were not for his adhesion to the classical (and in his view eternal) values of truth, justice, and reason, he would have gone the whole route and joined the Communist Party.

As the decade of the thirties progressed, "his scruples did fall away," though never completely. He felt obliged to confront a new question; how should the *clerc* respond in an extreme situation, when two equally brutal factions exist and are clashing with such violence that one must inevitably crush the other and dominate Europe if not the world? Benda phrased this question in a note first published in January 1937 in the *Nouvelle Revue française*. His response shows a substantial change since 1934 in his attitude toward communism and toward political involvement, though one can find a slender thread of continuity even with ***La Trahison des clercs*** (because, as we have seen, Benda admitted in the earlier work that the existence of absolute injustice validates involvement).

By 1937 Benda has actually become *critical* of the intellectual who remains in monastic isolation, pursuing his disinterested labor of science, poetry, or philosophy! In a very striking statement, which would not have sounded out of place had it appeared in Jean-Paul Sartre's *Les Temps modernes* after the Second World War, Benda wrote:

> I say that the *clerc* must now take sides. He must

> choose the side which, if it threatens liberty, at least threatens it in order to give bread to all men, and not for the benefit of wealthy exploiters. He will choose the side of which, if it must kill, will kill the oppressors and not the oppressed.
>
> The *clerc* must take sides with this group of violent men, since he has only the choice between their triumph or that of the others. He will give them [the communists] his signature. Perhaps his life. But he will retain the right to judge them. He will keep his critical spirit.

By 1938, Benda went as far as to claim that through their actions and the policies they advocated the communists were the only truly patriotic party in France. By keeping his critical spirit intact and not joining the French Communist Party, Benda probably spared himself a good deal of moral anguish when the Nazi-Soviet Pact was signed at the end of August 1939. Benda quickly denounced the pact as a *trahison* in an article dated September 1, 1939.

Despite suffering, exile, vicious anti-Semitic attacks by the fascist intellectual Robert Brasillach ("circumcized diplodocus" was one of Brasillach's more inventive and relatively mild insults), and extreme old age Julien Benda managed to survive the Second World War and retain his critical spirit. In June 1940 he fled Paris and barely escaped to Carcassonne in the Vichy zone. The Germans seized his Paris apartment in 1941, and all his notes and his library were taken and have never been recovered. Benda held an entry visa for the United States, where he had made a series of successful lecture tours in the years 1936-1938, but the Vichy government refused to allow him to leave. In May 1944, his friends warned him just in time and he escaped arrest by the Gestapo. He managed to get to Toulouse, where he stayed until the summer of 1945. During the Occupation his pen was of course silenced, except for a few pieces which appeared in clandestine resistance journals and a book published in New York in 1942. As soon as he was free to publish again, a flow of works that would have been impressive from a man half his age began to appear. (Chambat lists fourteen full-length books and the articles number in the hundreds.)

Neither the violent and terrible events of the two previous decades, nor his shifts of position in the 1930s, nor his willingness to offer "tactical support" to the communists from 1943 to 1950, could alter Benda's conviction that the initial thesis of ***La Trahison des clercs*** had lost none of its truth. He never saw, or at least never admitted, any contradiction between his passionate political commitment, which Paul Nizan and Pierre Chambat both categorize as "engagement," his vast journalistic output which dealt usually with day-to-day social and political issues, not "the eternal," and the fact that he is widely recognized as the leading spokesman in twentieth-century France "for the case against committed literature or thought." In ***Les Cahiers d'un clerc*** (1950), he stated: "I could rewrite my ***Trahison des clercs*** exactly as I wrote it twenty years ago."

When a new edition of ***La Trahison des clercs*** was published in 1947, Benda added an important introduction in which he emphasized that the *clercs* were still betraying their true function to the profit of practical interests. The practical interests he cites are the love of order, the monolithic state, the Communist Party (*sic*) or collaboration during the 1940-1944 period. No excuses were valid; any *clerc* was treasonous if his realism led him to accept fascism as a "fact" at the moment of Hitler's greatest triumphs. Benda eagerly joined the controversy over the "right to error," and was bitterly critical of intellectuals like François Mauriac who, even though they had impeccable resistance credentials, advocated the commutation of sentence for convicted collaborationist writers like Robert Brasillach. Benda believed that Brasillach's execution was completely justified. No alienation of individual liberty is to be tolerated; the clerical ideal remains "disinterested thought," and any intellectual who abandons that ideal must face the consequences. Thought must be "rigid" and adhere only to itself.

Thus two decades later Benda's theoretical opposition to most forms of engagement remains as firm as it was in 1927. He does at this time clarify his view on democracy. The *clerc* can adopt, even proselytize for, the democratic system and still remain loyal, because democracy has never existed: ". . . with its sovereign values of individual liberty, justice, and truth, *it is not practical.*" The duty of the *clerc* remains constant. "When injustice becomes master of the world, and the entire universe kneels before it, the *clerc* must remain standing and confront it with the human conscience."

THE FUTURE OF JULIEN BENDA AND LA TRAHISON DES CLERCS

Students of intellectual history are well aware of the pitfalls in trying to predict the influence of a scholar, artist, or other intellectual figure on future generations. One can never be certain that a forgotten author is really dead and buried, neatly in place with a paragraph in the literary histories. Because external conditions become propitious, or perhaps through the effort of a few scholarly defenders, an author can quite suddenly be found relevant, cited and reprinted, translated and talked about.

The first significant effort to pull Benda from oblivion was made two years after his death by the critic René Etiemble. In his preface to the third edition of ***La Trahison des clercs*** Etiemble emphasized Benda's belief that the true *clerc* will never say "my country right or wrong." Etiemble suggests that in 1958 more French artists and intellectuals are ready to struggle for universal values than in 1927. Etiemble mentions professors and journalists, priests, the Archbishop of Algiers, even a general. The opposition press took substantial risks to tell the truth about the Algerian War, and the Catholic daily *La Croix* rather belatedly published some articles which conferred upon it the "honor" of being seized in Algeria. There may be truth in the notion that in his native country Benda always retained what is best termed an "underground influence." The French intellectuals who became involved in the movement to end the war and grant Algeria independence were guided more by an outraged sense of justice than a desire for power and prestige.

As far as contemporary America is concerned, the ideas Benda championed may be traced to three distinct areas of our intellectual life, though his role in their formulation and advocacy is rarely recognized. First, there is the notion of professionalism, which is held by a substantial majority of the American academic community, and is quite close to the "pure" position advocated by Benda in ***La Trahison des clercs***. The sense of working within a discipline, of striving for the admittedly impossible goal of perfection within that discipline, the conviction that this unremitting labor is *the* important task for the scholar and intellectual, would not be foreign to Benda. Nor would the belief that outside involvement is painful, unnecessary, and to be avoided whenever possible, and that the university is a sacred place where the quest for pure, nonutilitarian knowledge should be pursued—though Benda himself was never part of the French university system.

Second, the vocal attacks during the 1960s by America's dissident academicians on the "Establishment Intellectuals"—holders of government contracts, cabinet advisors, consultants of all varieties, those who perform military research—remind one of Benda's denunciation of the new generation of realist *clercs.*

Finally, the political behavior of America's "Alienated Intellectual Elite," primarily in opposition to the Vietnam war, shows in its rationale a resemblance to the more activist strain in Benda's thought. . . . The evidence strongly suggests that Benda could not really resolve the contradiction between his commitment and his scholarly detachment. That dilemma was shared by many intellectuals during the period of engagement in the 1960s, and there is no reason to suspect that the tension is any less present now that the balance in America has swung sharply back toward detachment. It is perhaps significant that ***The Treason of the Intellectuals*** has been back in print since January 1969 in a paperback edition.

In France during the 1960s there was a steady flow of publications about Benda and several of his works were reprinted. A fourth edition of ***La Trahison des clercs*** was published in 1975, with an important new introduction by André Lwoff. Lwoff, interestingly enough not a *littérateur* but a scientist and the winner of the Nobel Prize in Medicine, believes that ***La Trahison des clercs*** has withstood "the dual trial of time and of history." Because of what Lwoff calls the "atemporal character" of Julien Benda's masterwork, it is safe to predict that Benda will continue to irritate, challenge, and enlighten future generations of intellectuals, in France and wherever his work is available.

FURTHER READING

Biography

Siepmann, Eric. "An Unorthodox Leftist." *The Twentieth Century* 160, No. 957 (November 1956): 452-56.

Posthumous personal and critical account of Benda.

Criticism

Gellner, Ernest. "La trahison de la trahison des clercs." In *The Political Responsibility of Intellectuals*, edited by Ian Maclean, Alan Montefiore, and Peter Winch, pp. 17-27. Cambridge: Cambridge University Press, 1990.

Contends that "*La trahison des clercs* was itself a case of 'la trahison des clercs' " because of what Gellner considers the "pragmatic" nature of Benda's argument.

Howarth, Herbert. "Some Gifts of France." In his *Notes on Some Figures behind T. S. Eliot*, pp. 150-98. Boston: Houghton Mifflin Company, 1964.

Summarizes Benda's influence on the work of T. S. Eliot.

Hughes, H. Stuart. "The Decade of the 1920s." In his *Consciousness and Society: The Reorientation of European Social Thought 1890-1930*, pp. 392-431. New York: Alfred A. Knopf, 1958.

Includes biographical and critical discussion of Benda.

Lewis, Wyndham. "Intuition versus the Intellect: or, Is There Such a Thing as an 'Intellectual'?" In his *Rude Assignment: A Narrative of My Career Up-to-Date*, pp. 29-42. London: Hutchinson & Co., n.d.

Discusses *The Treason of the Intellectuals* in relation to the works of other writers and philosophers of early twentieth-century France.

Pinkney, Tony. "Nationalism and the Politics of Style: Julien Benda and Samuel Beckett." *Literature and History* 14, No. 2 (Autumn 1988): 181-93.

Argues that Samuel Beckett was influenced by the works of Benda.

Additional coverage of Benda's life and career is contained in the following source published by Gale Research: *Contemporary Authors*, Vol. 120.

Ruth Benedict

1887-1948

(Full name Ruth Fulton Benedict; also wrote under the pseudonym Anne Singleton) American anthropologist, essayist, and poet.

INTRODUCTION

Benedict was a leading figure in the development of American anthropology. Her most famous works, *Patterns of Culture* and *The Chrysanthemum and the Sword,* are noted for applying concepts of psychology to anthropological studies. Both books greatly influenced later anthropologists and helped to popularize the subject of anthropology among the general public.

Biographical Information

Born in New York City and raised on a farm in upstate New York, Benedict attended Vassar College on a scholarship. Upon her graduation in 1909 she worked as a social worker and teacher. In 1914 she married biochemist Stanley Benedict (the couple later separated). In 1919 she returned to college and studied anthropology at the New School for Social Research. Benedict later enrolled at Columbia University to study with the German-born anthropologist Franz Boas, whose pioneering concept of "cultural relativity"—that is, the idea that a culture should be evaluated on its own terms rather than from an outside perspective—dominated anthropological thought of the time. She became Boas's teaching assistant in 1922; the following year she received her doctorate degree in anthropology. During this time she began doing fieldwork among Native American tribes of the West. Benedict taught at Columbia University until her death in 1948.

Major Works

Benedict's works relate the concept of culture to the psychological concept of personality. She asserted that just as personality determines the development of the individual, each culture contains a dominant mental pattern, "a personality writ large." In *Patterns of Culture,* based on her field experiences, Benedict compared several native cultures, including the Zuñi of New Mexico and the Kwakiutl of Vancouver Island. Influenced by the writings of German philosopher Friedrich Nietzsche, she attributed traits to each group that reflected the Apollonian-Dionysian dichotomy that Nietzsche articulated in his *The Birth of Tragedy*. She regarded the Zuñi, who valued a sober, orderly, and harmonious way of life, as having an Apollonian perspective of the world. Conversely, in the Kwakiutl Benedict saw a Dionysian pattern of thought and behavior characterized by excess and self-destructiveness. Throughout *Patterns of Culture,* Benedict questioned the concept of normality and proposed the theory that no culture is ethically or morally superior to another. She continued to explore this theory in *Race: Science and Politics* and *The Races of Mankind.* In 1946 Benedict published *The Chrysanthemum and the Sword,* an analysis of Japanese society. This book, which identifies and examines the central themes in Japanese culture, helped to shape America's policy toward Japan following World War II.

PRINCIPAL WORKS

The Concept of the Guardian Spirit in North America (nonfiction) 1923
Tales of the Cochiti Indians (folklore) 1931
Patterns of Culture (nonfiction) 1934
Zuñi Mythology. 2 vols. (folklore) 1935
Race: Science and Politics (nonfiction) 1940
The Races of Mankind [with Gene Weltfish] (nonfiction) 1943
The Chrysanthemum and the Sword (nonfiction) 1946

An Anthropologist at Work: Writings of Ruth Benedict (essays, journals, letters, and poetry) 1959

CRITICISM

Gordon Bowles (essay date 1947)

SOURCE: A review of *The Chrysanthemum and the Sword*, in *Harvard Journal of Asiatic Studies*, Vol. 10, No. 2, September, 1947, pp. 237-41.

[*In the following review, Bowles discusses Benedict's observations and analyses in* The Chrysanthemum and the Sword.]

It is difficult to judge fairly the merits and demerits of a descriptive analytical study when the author lacks first-hand acquaintance with his source material. In the present instance, the author has sought to meet the handicap by a threefold program of extensive reading, the generous use of well-qualified informants, and the employment of modern techniques of critical analysis. She has also attempted to turn this handicap into an advantage by using the data as a demonstration of what a trained observer can do with secondhand data at long range.

The reader cannot help being impressed by the orderly manner in which the data have been assembled and by the incisive phrasing and keen logic with which they have been presented. These speak for themselves and are a tribute not only to the author but to the entire study of society as a science. Dr. Benedict is certainly to be congratulated in having made available such an excellent study. The reader gets the impression, however, that the justification for such an experiment has been carried somewhat to excess. He feels that the study has sufficient merit in itself as not to have necessitated such a complete apologia as that contained in Chapter I, no matter how important and true its content.

The Chrysanthemum and the Sword is an interpretation of Japanese personality and character primarily during periods of response to emotional stress and, as Dr. Benedict points out, "All the ways in which the Japanese departed from Western conventions of war were data on their view of life and on their convictions of the whole duty of man."

By far the most valuable aspect of the study is the analysis of the Japanese sense of loyalty, especially as this involves the incurring of obligations and their repayment. A very useful table is given . . . which outlines schematically these obligations and their reciprocals.

The obligations or *on* of an individual are fivefold: those received from the emperor, from the parents, from one's lord, from one's teacher, and through the contacts of daily life. Each *on* has its reciprocal payment but the payment is of two kinds, those which have no limit in time or space and which can never be fully repaid (i.e., duty to the Emperor, to one's parents, and to one's work) and those which can and must be specifically repaid. The first is termed *gimu* and the latter *giri* or debts which are repaid "with mathematical equivalence." Such *giri* payments are of two types: *giri*-to-the-world, which involves duties to one's liege lord, duties to one's family, duties incurred as a result of gifts of money or favors, and finally duties to closely related kin such as aunts, uncles, nephews, nieces; the second type of *giri,* that to one's name, involves the clearing of "one's reputation of insult or imputation of failure." This *giri* involves also two other factors: "One's duty to admit no (professional) failure or ignorance" and "One's duty to fulfill the Japanese proprieties, e.g., observing all respect behavior, not living above one's station in life, curbing all displays of emotion on inappropriate occasions, etc."

Chapters 5 through 8, the heart of the book, are devoted to this summary of Japan's ethical code, to the sense of loyalty, and to the meaning and interpretation of obligation and to its repayment.

Useful as such a schematization may be, however, it should be borne in mind that in the minds of the Japanese the concepts of these virtues of *on, giri,* and *gimu* remain largely nebulous in character and are far less sharply defined than the author's scheme would lead one to suppose. The Japanese are not conscious of any such plan or outline of behavior nor would they all agree on the precise manner in which it has been presented.

Dr. Benedict has also brought together a number of observations, many of which, while not new, serve a very useful purpose in interpreting the reasons for given action. Among these observations probably the most cogent are the extreme sense of the importance of social hierarchy and the sense of compulsion to observe the conventions which such a hierarchy imposes, a greater sense of shame than guilt on occasions of mistake or failure, and the effect or result of such an attitude under conditions of strenuous competition, the preoccupation with this life rather than the next and the duty of the individual to master completely both mind and body, especially the control of the emotions.

The greatest single weakness of the study is probably the almost total disregard for the extent to which environment—and in particular Japan's weak and vulnerable economy—has been responsible for the development of those particular responses which are so typically Japanese.

The only reason given for Japan's policy of aggressive expansion, especially on the continental mainland, and for participation in World War II is the transfer of this extreme sense of social hierarchy from the national scene to that of East Asia. Japan's reasoning is explained as follows: "There was anarchy in the world as long as every nation had absolute sovereignty; it was necessary for her (Japan) to fight to establish a hierarchy—under Japan of course, since she alone represented a nation truly hierarchal from top to bottom and hence understood the necessity of taking 'one's proper place.' "

Such a thesis is suggested by Japanese traditions regarding the importance attached to social hierarchy itself but it does not represent the serious reasoning either of Japanese economists or of the people as a whole. It was essentially the rallying cry of the militant jingoists of the Greater East Asia Co-prosperity Sphere school of thought. This leads to a second point of weakness, the apparent or implied trust placed by Dr. Benedict upon the utterances of Japanese propagandists, as if these utterances were the real expression of the Japanese people rather than fuel to keep the home fires burning. The general propaganda line, certainly of the Japanese radio, was that Japan's lack of material resources could be more than compensated by the greatness of her spiritual resources. This again is in keeping with Japanese cultural tradition. It is very doubtful, however, if there was ever a time when there was not a lurking and probably a real fear of eventual defeat and of the consequences thereof.

It is too much to assume that the Government propaganda line was intended for more than those who had to have it in order to be convinced to carry on. There was grave doubt in the minds of a great many Japanese and especially those who were well educated. In the face of daily mounting destruction as the war progressed, the propaganda line was the only one the Government could consistently have followed. It did not, however, reflect the sober and considered opinion of informed Japanese.

Another weakness of the study is its failure to lay sufficient emphasis upon the shifting character or personality of the Japanese as expressed in terms of their response to changing circumstances. No one can question the author's realization that Western influences, economic competition, the stunning effects of defeat, and the completely changed outlook of the people have dimmed the external expressions of conventional cultural patterns. Apparently, however, the extent of this dimming process is not realized, for it is likely that the casual observer in Japan today would scarcely recognize the traditional code as outlined in ***The Chrysanthemum and the Sword***, so much have they been overshadowed by current forces and influences. To the trained observer, however, they would still be visible and still be active, but who can say how long some of them will survive?

There are numerous other points throughout the book which would have been greatly improved by more elaboration and by a greater emphasis upon environmental and especially economic causes. Thus considerable emphasis is placed upon the lack of mercy measures. Unless the statement, "Preoccupation with mercy toward the damaged rather than with other welfare measures . . . is certainly alien to the Japanese" is greatly qualified, it cannot be accepted as a fair statement.

This latter is only one of several instances in which the reader feels that only half the truth has been revealed, for it is often true of Japanese character that when there is a failure in one direction there is adequate or even over compensation in another:

Possibly then this reviewer would have to summarize his total impression as the feeling that, while the stuff was most beautiful and while it was most excellently tailored, somehow there was a lack of true fit in the garment finished for the Japanese.

Elgin Williams (essay date 1947)

SOURCE: "Anthropology for the Common Man," in *American Anthropologist,* Vol. 49, No. 1, 1947, pp. 84-90.

[*In the following essay, Williams reviews the mass-market edition of* Patterns of Culture, *providing an introduction to the methodology and principles that are central to this work.*]

Publication of Ruth Benedict's ***Patterns of Culture*** in a 25 cent edition is an extremely important event. What it means is no less than this: Anthropology has now become available to the man on the street.

What is it that has now become popularly available? Great interest will attach, for one thing, to Dr. Benedict's colorful and suggestive use of the concepts "Apollonian" and "Dionysian." People interested in their "complexes" (and that includes almost everybody!) will derive pleasure and profit from her shrewd application of psychoanalysis to anthropology. But there can be little doubt that overriding contribution of ***Patterns of Culture*** is the liberalizing tradition of the science, the tradition which has shown itself already powerful in dealing with race prejudice and hatred. The message of ***Patterns of Culture*** is that

> the possible human institutions and motives are legion, on every plane of cultural simplicity or complexity, and . . . wisdom consists in a greatly increased tolerance toward their divergences. No man can thoroughly participate in any culture unless he has been brought up and has lived according to its forms, but he can grant to other cultures the same significance to their participants which he recognizes in his own.

When Dr. Benedict asks for tolerance we know that she means tolerance toward Indians, Negroes, Jews, colonial peoples, and other minority groups now discriminated against (including infants and schoolchildren whose problems she knows so well). And this is probably what such statements as that quoted will be taken to mean. But it is important to note that, benevolent interpretations aside, this is *not* what she is saying, and this is not what anthropologists in general are saying. What they are saying is not only that we should tolerate feminism in females and homosexuality in homosexuals. They are saying that we should look upon *all* habits, *all* institutions (which are legion) with tolerance. We should "grant to other cultures the same significance to their participants which we recognize in our own."

Among professional students of man it is agreed to be an irresponsible pastime to discuss theoretical questions in terms and labels derived from the late war. But it is to be expected that the average citizen will be ignorant of this tabu and unconscious of his bad taste in violating it. For him the war experience has been a pervading thing, and this is an important fact to remember if ever the statements of anthropologists are taken literally. If these statements are ever read for a moment without an investment of benevolent meaning it is just possible that there will be a public hue-and-cry against anthropology.

For the war period has provided the greatest mass education in "cultural divergences" the world has so far witnessed. Large portions of the world's population have come to learn about "possible human institutions and motives" in exceedingly direct and searching fashion. And the Gold Star Mother (for instance) is going to be reluctant about granting significance to Hitler's culture, the surviving citizens of Hiroshima (for instance) are going to look for their wisdom elsewhere than in a "greatly increased tolerance" toward the divergences of American generals, and the remaining Jews of Europe (for instance) are going to be poor customers for gospels which hold that there are two sides to every question.

Although such a position follows from her theoretical premises it would be wrong to suppose that Dr. Benedict is asking for tolerance of war criminals and of war crimes. In fact on almost every page she denounces such culture-traits.

> War is, we have been forced to admit even in the face of its huge place in our own civilization, an asocial trait. . . . War in our own civilization is as good an illustration as one can take of the destructive lengths to which the development of a culturally selected trait may go. If we justify war, it is because all peoples always justify the traits of which they find themselves possessed, not because war will bear an objective examination of its merits.

And "warfare is not an isolated case." "Asocial elaborations" of cultural forms she knows to be frequent—"those cases are clearest where, as in dietary or mating regulations, for example, traditional usage runs counter to biological drives."

But that Dr. Benedict recognizes and condemns asocial traits which are destructive of human values is a tribute to her humanitarianism, not to her anthropological theory. The very existence of the category "asocial" is of course hotly denied in theory. Which brings to the fore again the question, What is anthropology *per se* trying to tell us? It is nothing new that war is bad and that women and children ought to be free. And to advocate "tolerance" of other ways of doing things must appear (to the naïve Common Man) as either irresponsible or foolish: other traits are either better or worse than our own—if better we ought to adopt them; if worse the least we can do is expose them. But it is just this tolerance which is anthropology's root and core. The conclusion is inescapable that the polemics against asocial habits are intrusions and the real message is Relativism. To the Common Man's question, What in this chaotic world is significant? comes the answer: Everything—and nothing. "The diversity of the possible combinations of culture-traits is endless, and adequate social orders can be built indiscriminately upon a great variety of . . . combinations." And in return for license to wallow in our own fatuity we grant this privilege to all other peoples. . . .

Thus speaks the theory. And probably everyone will admit it would be a bad thing for the race if anthropologists followed these dicta even half the time. But of course Dr. Benedict does not accept her theory any more than the other professors. Such an approach would tackle the problem of valuation not to solve it but to give it up entirely. The Common Man asks the question, How shall we straighten out our poor country and our chaotic world? and back comes the answer: You can't miss, so don't worry about it.

If this were the only answer given we should have to conclude that Dr. Benedict (and anthropologists generally) have taken the easy way out. The problem of significance and value is not even touched by "tolerance," by granting "to other cultures the same significance to their participants" which we recognize in our own (because we know that "all peoples always justify the traits of which they find themselves possessed"). On the contrary the problem of significance is a hard problem, to be solved not by shrugging the shoulders but, in Dr. Benedict's own words, by making "objective examinations of the merits" of culture-traits. And to an important degree, despite their theoretical banalities, Dr. Benedict and the rest of the anthropologists are already at work at this task.

A glance at some of this work in progress is instructive. Dr. Benedict offers objective examinations of the merits of many institutions and from these can be deduced her criterion of value. If the Common Man is not helped by her formal statements he *can* learn from what she does in practice. Take the critique of Zuñi marital customs:

> Marital jealousy [Dr. Benedict finds] is . . . soft-pedalled. They do not meet adultery with violence. A usual response on the Plains to the wife's adultery was to cut off the fleshy part of her nose. . . . But in Zuñi the unfaithfulness of the wife is no excuse for violence.

There are "no outbursts, no recriminations."

Can anyone read this and get the idea that Dr. Benedict regards Plains and Zuñi behavior as equally valid? Is she suggesting to the Common Man that it would be wisdom on his part to look on both modes of behavior (counting our own as Plains) with tolerance? Of course not. Dr. Benedict would be the last to suggest that we grant to the sensible Zuñi the same significance of their culture-trait as we recognize in our own, and thereby make ourselves out fools. She is definitely judging different ways of handling sex relations and we can set down her criterion tentatively: the presence or absence of violence. Violence is bad and non-violence good. Such a criterion of course provides a real answer to the Common Man's question, How should we run the country? The answer is something he can get his hands on, a recipe: Abjure violence, no matter what excuses for it you hear.

Take another example. Dr. Benedict has occasion to discuss the personal exercise of arbitrary authority and notes that among the Zuñi it is almost totally absent. The young in other cultures learn to walk the straight and narrow under penalty almost from birth, and in consequence tremble at authority all their lives. The initiation of boys

> is very often an uninhibited exercise of their prerogatives by those in authority; it is a hazing by those in power of those whom they must now admit to tribal status. . . . In South America the boys are herded under men with long sticks who use them freely on all occasions. They must

> run the gantlet with blows raining upon them, they must expect constant blows from behind accompanied by jeers.

But in Zuñi "not even the uncles" exercise authority because occasions are not tolerated which would demand it. In consequence,

> The child grows up without either the resentments or the compensatory day-dreams of ambition that have their roots in this familiar situation. When the child himself becomes an adult, he has not the motivations that lead him to imagine situations in which authority will be relevant.

Again the questions may be raised: Is Dr. Benedict here neutral as regards Zuñi practices *vs.* those of Africa, South America, and Australia? To her mind is Zuñi mildness and gentleness on a par with South American jeers and gantlets, one to be tolerated with the other? The answer is, Of course not. She is condemning ordeals which pave the way for status and authority. Again the Common Man is furnished with a recipe: Abjure authority, or your culture will be rotted to the core with neurotic personalities and compensatory day-dreams.

A third example will perhaps suffice. After noting that the Puritan attitude toward sex "flows from its identification with sin," Dr. Benedict remarks that the Zuñi have no sense of sin.

> Sin is unfamiliar to them, not only in sex but in any experience. They do not suffer guilt complexes, and they do not consider sex as a series of temptations to be resisted with painful efforts of the will. Chastity as a way of life is regarded with great disfavor, and no one in their folktales is criticized more harshly than the proud girls who resist marriage in their youth. They stay in and work, ignoring the occasions when they should legitimately be admired by the young men. But the gods do not take the steps they were supposed to take in Puritan ethics. They come down and contrive in spite of obstacles to sleep with them, and teach them delight and humility.

Surely Puritanism gets the worst of it here! No one can read this and still be tolerant of a social organization which produces guilt complexes, false pride, and the other sufferings so common in masochism and sadism. Again there is a maxim, a recipe for the Common Man: Despise not thy body.

Many more examples of this procedure could be cited. But those given should serve to show that in practice Dr. Benedict views the problem of significance in a totally different light from that which her formal statements would indicate. Other incisive critiques treat behavior at death, competition, attitudes toward homosexuals, the position of women. There is no room in the present account for an elaborate delineation of the theory of value which runs through all. But tentatively it can be said that the premiums on non-violence, on cooperation and equality, on life-affirming activity in general are all aspects of the same test: the test of consequences. Consequences, consequences for further living, is the bar of judgment to which Dr. Benedict's culture traits—both ends and means—repair.

Needless to say Dr. Benedict does not put the matter so explicitly. Formally she sticks to relativism. Her pragmatism is not so much at the tip of her tongue as bred in the bone. Try as she may to maintain the pose of relativism the test of consequences intrudes. This is most noticeable, as is fitting, in a theoretical confusion. It has been noted that Dr. Benedict—like anthropologists in general—holds to the doctrine of cultural uniqueness. ". . . Adequate social orders can be built indiscriminately upon a great variety of foundations. . . ." ". . . Ends and . . . means in one society cannot be judged in terms of those of another society, because essentially they are incommensurable." "No man can thoroughly participate in any culture unless he has been brought up and has lived according to its forms."

All this would seem to be clear enough. The statements are not equivocal. Yet we find the same writer judging these "incommensurable" ends and means, fussing at societies for their lack of discrimination, questioning wholesale the significance of cultures. She speaks of cultures combining "the most alien situations," traits which have "no intrinsic relation one with the other." Again and again one is told that "all cultures . . . have not sharpened their thousand items of behaviour to *a balanced and rhythmic pattern*." "If at one moment certain social orders seem to be pursuing certain ends, at another they are off *on some tangent apparently inconsistent with all that has gone before. . . .*" ". . . *Lack of integration* seems to be . . . characteristic of certain cultures. . . . " British Columbia tribal patterns are "un-coordinated," a "hodge-podge" of "contradictory bits." Some civilizations are "saner" than others.

Now in making these statements Dr. Benedict is plainly violating her canon of tolerance. It does not show much empathy with the British Columbian to tell him that his culture is a hodge-podge, un-coordinated and contradictory. After indiscriminatingly building a culture foreguaranteed to be adequate, the perplexed native finds its most striking characteristic to be "lack of integration." He is not likely to be convinced that one believes his ends and means cannot be judged when one proceeds to find his most cherished practices "off on some tangent" and "inconsistent with all that has gone before."

Happily, at least when talking to her own fellow-citizens, Dr. Benedict seems to recognize her inconsistency and urges the Common Man to forget the easygoing tolerance she has preached and adopt the stern self-criticism, the objective examination of ends and means she has practised. Attention has already been called to her indictment of Puritanism and of educational and child-rearing inanities. Similar indictments occur throughout the book. And in a passage near the end Dr. Benedict lays down her practising creed in words of such force that they deserve quoting at some length.

> There is [she writes] one difficult exercise to which we may accustom ourselves as we become increasingly culture-conscious. We may train ourselves to pass judgment upon the dominant

> traits of our own civilization. It is difficult enough for anyone brought up under their power to recognize them. It is still more difficult to discount, upon necessity, our predilection for them. They are as familiar as an old loved homestead. Any world in which they do not appear seems to us cheerless and untenable. Yet it is these very traits which by the operation of a fundamental cultural process are most often carried to extremes. They overreach themselves, and more than any other traits they are likely to get out of hand. Just at the very point where there is greatest likelihood of the need of criticism, we are bound to be less critical. Revision comes, but it comes by way of revolution or of breakdown. The possibility of orderly progress is shut off because the generation in question could not make any appraisal of its overgrown institutions. It could not cast them up in terms of profit and loss because it had lost its power to look at them objectively. The situation had to reach a breaking-point before relief was possible.
>
> Appraisal of our own dominant traits has so far waited till the trait in question was no longer a living issue. Religion was not objectively discussed till it was no longer the cultural trait to which our civilization was most deeply committed. Now for the first time the comparative study of religions is free to pursue any point at issue. It is not yet possible to discuss capitalism in the same way, and during wartime, warfare and the problems of international relations are similarly tabu. Yet the dominant traits of our civilization need special scrutiny. We need to realize that they are compulsive, not in proportion as they are basic and essential in human behaviour, but rather in the degree to which they are local and overgrown in our own culture. The one way of life which the Dobuan regards as basic in human nature is one that is fundamentally treacherous and safeguarded with morbid fears. The Kwakiutl similarly cannot see life except as a series of rivalry situations, wherein success is measured by the humiliation of one's fellows. Their belief is based on the importance of these modes of life in their civilization. But the importance of an institution in a culture gives no direct indication of its usefulness or its inevitability. The argument is suspect, and any cultural control which we may be able to exercise will depend upon the degree to which we can evaluate objectively the favoured and passionately fostered traits of our Western civilization.

Such advice the Common Man can get his teeth in. And the advice is complete in itself, requiring no additional dicta of "tolerance." The same resolutely objective examination and appraisal of institutional behavior which will make short work of Jim Crow and the business cycle will also stop this side of that nihilism which views what Nazis and Southerners do as "their own business" and "all right for them." The field-worker, like the citizen, "must be faithfully objective." But it is just such objectivity which condemns a great many institutions and behaviors and makes us careful in granting significance to our own or other cultures. For we *can* separate (in terms of their consequences) good and valid behavior from social exploitation, sadism, and that "endless ceremonialism not designed to serve major ends of human existence." It *is* possible, as Dr. Benedict has made so clear,

> to scrutinize different institutions and cast up their cost in terms of social capital, in terms of the less desirable behaviour traits they stimulate, and in terms of human suffering and frustration.

Such is Dr. Benedict's emphasis in a good half of her book. In the other half the emphasis, as we have seen, is on tolerance. This second emphasis is either superfluous or pernicious. Toward the conclusion of ***Patterns of Culture*** the well-documented and beautifully expressed plea for objective examination of cultures (including our own) is dominant. It is all the more sad, therefore, and all the more confusing for the Common Man, that the closing sentence again bids acceptance of "the coexisting and equally valid patterns of life which mankind has created for itself from the raw materials of existence."

A. L. Kroeber (essay date 1947)

SOURCE: A review of *The Chrysanthemum and the Sword*, in *American Anthropologist,* Vol. 49, No. 3, 1947, pp. 469-72.

[*Kroeber was a leading figure in American anthropology during the middle decades of the twentieth century and published numerous studies of Native American cultures. In the following review, he praises Benedict's treatment of the relationship between psychology and culture in* The Chrysanthemum and the Sword.]

This analysis of Japan [***The Chrysanthemum and the Sword***] is a book that makes one proud to be an anthropologist. It shows what can be done with orientation and discipline even without speaking knowledge of the language and residence in the country.

Dr. Benedict deals definitely with culture, and equally definitely with psychology. In her own manner the two are interfused; the cultural value standards are stated as such, and so too is it stated how normal individuals act under them. The skilful interweaving of the many facets of a large culture hardly lends itself to summary or to concept concentration, especially since the Japanese tend to view life as consisting of so many "circles" or departments. So a running series of her findings will be touched on here; as Dr. Benedict says, the tough-minded are content that differences should exist.

Japanese organization is hierarchical. Society still is aristocratic. Respect and its degrees and rules are learned in childhood, precisely within the face-to-face family. There is no extended family or large-scale filial piety; the family shrine is in the living room. Fundamental is finding one's place in the world; confusion exists when there is "neither elder brother nor younger brother." Proper placing of people allows dignity of behavior even in low station, such as cannot be attained under equality, the Japanese feel.

There is also a hierarchy of nations, and in this Japan senses strongly that the eyes of the world are upon her. By reason of this it is necessary that the Japanese soul be trained above matter, and that all contingencies be foreknown and planned for. The Emperor is inseparable from Japan, and therefore above criticism; but all others are expendable without salvage. Hence the standard of no surrender in war, but of full cooperation after peace.

The Meiji reform is sketched incisively as above all *maintaining* the hierarchy—with the explicit approval of Herbert Spencer. There was to be popular support, but no popular opinion; State Shinto as sign of respect to the order, but genuine religious freedom. Ceremonies are for the people, not by them. On the village level there is real democracy: the elders are not tax collectors for the State. But education is wholly under central authority. The Meiji Army and Navy promptly outlawed respect language; and promotion has been by merit in place of family, at any rate far more so than in civilian spheres. Why the State organized and built up the new basic industries only to turn them over at low price to the specially selected Zaibatsu oligarchy does not become wholly clear. The implication is that it was because planning was possible only in terms of hierarchical order. The proper station makes everyone feel safe. But export abroad of the hierarchical principle failed miserably elsewhere in Asia, no doubt because it was enforced.

The matter of obligations and reciprocations is gone into at length. *On* is obligation received, passively incurred, from superior, parents, lord, teacher, or others. About the latter there is ambivalence. Three phrases of thanks mean "this poisonous feeling," "difficult thing," "this does not end." The pre-Meiji phrase *katajikenai* meant both "I am insulted" and "grateful": that is, shame at receiving favor. It can be more generous to accept *on* than to tender it. One does not proffer it casually: that might be meddlesome. Repayment is of two main kinds: *gimu,* unstated in amount and kind, and due the emperor, parents, and one's work (called respectively *chu, ko,* and *nimmu*); and *giri,* which aims at exact equivalence, and may be unwilling at heart; it is hardest to bear, and one can be "cornered with *giri.*" Besides this *giri* to others, there is *giri* to one's own name, close to what we should call pride in honor. This leads to vendetta revenge, to non-admission of failure, but also to fulfillment of the properties. *Chu* was formerly due the shogun. Then the Japanese decided that European conflict of rulers and people was unworthy of Japan in history. *Giri* that clears one's name is outside the circle of *on;* "the world tips" while an insult is unrequited, and requiting it does not constitute aggression. To know *giri* is to be loyal for life, to repay *giri* is to offer one's life.

The Japanese have little sense of guilt, but a strong sense of shame. They avoid overt competition because the loser is shamed; they feel it as an aggression. Their hierarchical system naturally minimizes competition, much as the institution of the intermediary go-between cuts down shame if negotiations fail. Politeness is a means of preventing shame and the need of clearing one's name. Revenge for slight is "a kind of morning tub" by a people passionate about cleanliness. They are vulnerable to failures and slurs, and harry themselves over them, even to suicide. The latter is not specially common in fact, but all-important in fantasy. Suicide is played up vicariously in films and reading-matter as crime is in America. Milder manifestations of the vulnerability are lassitude and boredom. The constant goal is honor: commanding respect, a good name, privately and as a nation in the world. The means may change; the aim is constant.

The famous sincerity (*makoto, magokoro*), the basic virtue, the "soul" of the Emperor's Rescript, does not mean genuineness, but what makes other virtues "stick." It is the exponent of these to a higher power. Usually sincerity hallmarks or identifies the virtues most stressed: non-self-seeking, freedom from profit-making; self-discipline, freedom from passion; ability to lead, due to freedom from internal conflict. To wound another's feelings without intent is "insincere" because it is undisciplined; whereas to wound them deliberately in *giri* to one's name is justifiable. Self-respect, *jicho,* literally "self-weighty," implies circumspection, full self-control in order to control a situation. Again shame, *haji,* counts for more than guilt.

Due to the ever-present shame-preventing etiquette, "refined familiarity," as it is natural to well-bred Chinese or Americans, is killed off in childhood as being sauciness in Japanese girls, perhaps as "insincerity" in boys.

The Japanese are not puritanical. They cultivate sensory pleasures but keep them in their place: self-discipline is what is all-important. Soldiers "already know how to sleep; they need training in how to keep awake" by marching day and night. But when there is nothing at stake, sleeping is a favored indulgence. Love, both romantic and erotic, is fine, but as a "human feeling" it must be ruthlessly sacrificed to obligations. Strength to meet one's obligations is the most admired of all qualities. Hence the Japanese love the tragic ending. *Shuyo,* self-discipline, "enlarges life"; it polishes away "the rust of the body" and makes one like a sharp sword. Mental training (*muga* in Zen cult) promotes expertness of any kind by obliterating the "observing" or "interfering" self (self-consciousness, presumably), until there is "not even the thickness of a hair" between will and act, and the act is "one-pointed." This training, though the exercises were derived from China and perhaps ultimately from India, is not yoga, is not mystic, is not freedom from the flesh, does not lead to nirvana which the Japanese in general do not seek. They train for mastery of *this* life. They ask a great deal of themselves.

There is a chapter on "The Child Learns" and one on "The Japanese since VJ-Day." The one on learning comes at the end; it is full of facts on cultural practice, does not mention some of Gorer's allegations, and I think does not contain the word "socialization." As usual, Benedict has cut her own swath here.

So as not to seem wholly adulatory, I will mention—not in correction but in distinction—one point where emphasis might have been different. On the whole, Benedict stresses strongly those aspects of Japanese culture and character which are reciprocal, have to do with the interrelations of persons. She passes much more lightly over those which are primarily expressions of the self. Perhaps that is why there are only transient allusions to the obtrusive and compulsive Japanese cleanliness, neatness, frugality, economy of means, finish: these are primarily self-satisfying qualities, as shame, obligation, and hierarchy are turned toward others. This is not stricture—only a reminder that no book is completely perfect. This one eminently does enlarge understanding and polish away the rust of the mind.

Victor Barnouw (essay date 1949)

SOURCE: "Ruth Benedict: Apollonian and Dionysian," *The University of Toronto Quarterly,* Vol. XVIII, No. 3, April, 1949, pp. 241-53.

[*Barnouw is an American anthropologist and fiction writer. In the following essay, he provides an analysis of the underlying principles of* Patterns of Culture.]

"The Chippewa *can not kill the father!*" Ruth Benedict exclaimed to me one day, looking up gravely from my much blue-pencilled thesis and emphasizing each word separately. "They *can not kill the father!* Contrast with Eskimo!" My adviser turned her meditative eyes upon me and inquired, "Can't you fit that in somewhere?" As often happened, I felt that I almost saw her point, but not quite. However, I jotted a hurried note—"Chips don't kill father. . . . Esk.(?)"—and said that I would have to think about it.

Like most of Ruth Benedict's students, I looked up to her with a mixture of veneration and bewilderment. With her silvery aura of prestige, dignity, and charm, she seemed to be like a symbolic representative of the humanistic values of the Renaissance. Yet Ruth Benedict often seemed to have a kind of private language and way of thinking which made communication uncertain. She used unexpected verbal short-cuts, tangential observations, and symbols to convey her meaning; but these stratagems did not always succeed. In this particular case, I debated with myself for several days about her cryptic suggestion. Finally, I decided to insert a foot-note to the effect that while the Eskimos frequently killed their aged or incapacitated parents, the Chippewa had not resorted to this custom, although both groups were nomadic hunters who moved through an inhospitable environment in which care for the aged was difficult. Perhaps, I suggested, the Chippewa respected parental authority too much to be able to commit patricide. It is possible that I did not put my heart into that foot-note. At any rate, when Dr. Benedict came to re-read the manuscript, she deleted it with a dubious shake of the head, remarking that the idea was not convincing—and I did not contest the point.

Ruth Benedict sometimes had a way of talking about "primitive" peoples as if she could see an x-ray of their souls projected upon an invisible screen before her. "The Blackfeet always dance on a knife-edge," she would announce, as if seeing them there, balancing precariously along the blade. Then she would turn to her visitor with a charming smile. "*You* know," she would add with a nod of the head, implying that her consultant could also see the vision. This implicit confidence ushered the dazed neophyte into the company of Boas and the immortals. "The Pima like *slow* intoxication. That fits in perfectly with all of the rest about them, doesn't it? *You* know." One nodded, smiled, and tried hard to remember the information. ("Will they have that on the exams?") But perhaps Dr. Benedict assumed that her students had made their way through the same vast body of literature that she had read and come to the same vivid and original conclusions.

Ruth Benedict was thirty-two when she began to study anthropology—"to have something really to do," as she put it. Before then she had taught English in a girls' school and had written a great deal of poetry published under the name of Anne Singleton. Her devotion to poetry persisted through Ruth Benedict's later years. Even in the scholarly papers which began to appear in the nineteen-twenties when she was thoroughly steeped in the austere, almost military, intellectual discipline of Franz Boas, there was always some lyrical awareness of balance and phrase which went far above and beyond the normal call of academic duty.

Ruth Benedict also looked very like a tall and slender Platonic ideal of a poetess. The students who could not understand her lectures were at least able to derive something from the opportunity of looking at her. Her dreamily gazing eyes under the dark brows were most extraordinary, like the hooded grey eyes of an aristocratic eagle. In her face and manner there appeared to be a subtle blend of will and of trancelike reflection. She had an other-worldly look about her; yet she was resolute about the matters of this world. I used to feel that there were two sides to her complex character which were never completely fused. On the one hand, let us say, there was Anne Singleton, the Dionysian dreamer; and on the other hand there was Dr. Benedict, the disciplined Apollonian scholar. In one and the same individual there was an apparent juxtaposition of Sappho and Franz Boas, the chrysanthemum and the sword.

Archaeologically speaking, the earlier layer in this combination must have been Anne Singleton, who wrote lyrics about passion, love, and death, and lines like these:

> Only those
> Storm driven down the dark, see light arise,
> Her body broken for their rainbow bread,
> At late and shipwrecked close.

Anne Singleton, we may imagine, was youthfully responsive to the world of nature—mystical and Dionysian. Boas was a later force, an incarnation of will, discipline, and rationality. Call him an introjected "father figure," "animus," or what you will; his personal inspiration stamped the last thirty years of her life. On the walls of Ruth Benedict's office hung two framed photographs, one of a leathery old Blackfoot chieftain and one of Boas, two gnarled and weather-beaten old men who had evidently suffered and endured. It was Boas, one of the intellectual leaders of our time, who caught her loyalty, altered the direction of her life, and gave her "something really to do." His logic tempered her poetic intuition, which she evidently felt some need to chasten. Willingly Anne Singleton slipped on the rough hair shirt of discipline, took upon herself the exacting Boas regimen of hard work, read endlessly, endured the discomforts of ethnological field work, and finally emerged as "Dr. Benedict."

But it is a measure of her individuality that Ruth Benedict never became a mere rubber-stamp of the old man's thinking. In fact, her work represents a marked contrast to his. Boas had long ago rejected the "deep" intuitive plunges of German scholarship and philosophy; but in these same dubious sources Ruth Benedict now found inspiration. Under her master's perhaps somewhat jaundiced eye she turned to Nietzsche, Spengler, and Dilthey, whose ideas she somehow blended with the Boas tradition of intensive field work in a particular area. From this unexpected amalgam she managed to fashion her famous ***Patterns of Culture***. This book was originally a patchwork of separate articles and field studies, ingeniously stitched together into a more or less integrated whole and given force and dignity by a warm imagination and turn of phrase. In its pages Anne Singleton and Dr. Benedict came together and pooled their talents. The Dionysian poet and the Apollonian scholar were reconciled. This may explain the faults of the book; it also explains its charm. For, recently incarnated in a thirty-five cent Pelican edition, ***Patterns of Culture*** has become one of the most widely read medium-heavy books in the whole field of social science. In the next few pages we shall examine some of its doctrines.

One basic assertion in this treatise is to the effect that some human societies—not necessarily all—are characterized by a group ethos which is analogous to the personality of an individual, and that the essential values characteristic of a culture exert a selective influence upon all of the responses of the society to historical events. This idea was once stated with particular brilliance by Oswald Spengler in *The Decline of the West,* a book which greatly influenced Ruth Benedict. In his orchestral style, Spengler proclaimed that societies were guided by different metaphysical conceptions and that characteristic attitudes towards space and time were imbedded in every major facet of a particular culture. Scornful at his feeble contemporaries for having missed this discovery, Spengler exclaimed in a typical passage: "Who amongst them realizes that between the Differential Calculus and the dynastic principle of politics in the age of Louis XIV, between the Classical city-state and the Euclidean geometry, between the space-perspective of Western oil-painting and the conquest of space by railroad, telephone and long-range weapon, between contrapuntal music and credit economics, there are deep uniformities?"

Because of some guiding metaphysical attitudes, then, a given society is likely to reject any cultural innovations which appear to be out of harmony with its dominant *Weltanschauung*. Thus, the ancient Greeks, according to Spengler, were acquainted with the chronology and almanac-reckoning of the Babylonians and the Egyptians, but this did not alter their "shallow" conception of time. Spengler pointed out that neither Plato nor Aristotle had an observatory, and that, in "an act of the deepest symbolic significance," Pericles passed a decree directed against people who propagated astronomical theories. Moreover, according to Spengler, the Greeks had no sense of history. Even Thucydides claimed that before his time no events of importance had occurred in the world. Spengler contrasted the Greeks with the Egyptians in this respect. Egyptian culture was an embodiment of *care,* expressed in the use of granite and chiselled archives, in the elaborate administrative system and irrigation projects. Care for the past was expressed in chronological records and in the custom of mummification. But the a-historical Greeks burned their dead.

Spengler was one of the first theoreticians to deal with the problems of selective borrowing under acculturation and to turn for their solution to culture-and-personality characteristics rather than to economic or geographical determinants. Spengler also showed that borrowed items of culture usually undergo some kind of transformation in the new setting and are tailored to fit the culture into which they have been introduced. The rejections and refashionings which take place may be cited as evidence for the existence of a dominant attitude characteristic of the culture, if the same principle seems to be involved in each separate response to diffusion.

After she had absorbed this wisdom from Spengler, Ruth Benedict turned to the cultures of the south-western United States to see whether these groups were characterized by any guiding principles of this nature, and whether such central tendencies could explain the rejection, acceptance, or remodelling of diffused cultural items. In this area Dr. Benedict already had a predecessor. As early as 1916, H. K. Haeberlin had written a penetrating article which foreshadowed some of the themes in ***Patterns of Culture***. Haeberlin pointed out that many religious ceremonies and other aspects of culture could be found common to both the Hopi and Navajo, but that there were differences of emphasis in these societies. A ceremony designed to heal the sick among the Navajo was directed toward securing fertility for the fields among the Pueblo Indians. A game associated with the buffalo among the Plains tribes was associated with crops among the Hopi. Haeberlin explained this local refashioning as due to a psychological orientation. In the case of the Pueblo Indians this orientation could be designated under the heuristic catchword of "the idea of fertilization."

The integrating factor which Haeberlin therefore isolated as the ruling motivation in Pueblo culture was "the idea of fertilization." Ruth Benedict, following a similar line of thought, found a different focus of integration, and a different catchword or set of catchwords.

> The basic contrast between the Pueblos and the other cultures of North America is the contrast that is named and described by Nietzsche in his studies of Greek tragedy. He discusses two diametrically opposed ways of arriving at the values of existence. The Dionysian pursues them through "the annihilation of the ordinary bounds and limits of existence"; he seeks to attain in his most valued moments escape from the boundaries imposed upon him by his five senses, to break through into another order of experience. The desire of the Dionysian, in personal experience or in ritual, is to press through it toward a certain psychological state, to achieve excess. The closest analogy to the emotions he seeks is drunkenness, and he values the illuminations of frenzy. With Blake, he believes "the path of excess leads to the palace of wisdom." The Apollonian distrusts all this, and has often

> little idea of the nature of such experiences. He finds means to outlaw them from his conscious life. He "knows but one law, measure in the Hellenic sense." He keeps the middle of the road, stays within the known map, does not meddle with disruptive psychological states. In Nietzsche's fine phrase, even in the exaltation of the dance he "remains what he is, and retains his civic name." . . .
>
> It is not possible to understand Pueblo attitudes towards life without some knowledge of the culture from which they have detached themselves: that of the rest of North America. It is by the force of the contrast that we can calculate the strength of their opposite drive and the resistances that have kept out of the Pueblos the most characteristic traits of the American aborigines. For the American Indians as a whole, and including those of Mexico, were passionately Dionysian. They valued all violent experience, all means by which human beings may break through the usual sensory routine, and to all such experiences they attributed the highest value.

Ruth Benedict then provided illustrations of this widespread Dionysian tendency, such as fasting and self-torture in the vision quest and the ceremonial use of drugs, peyote, and alcohol to induce religious intoxication. These patterns were uniformly rejected by the Pueblo Indians, she explained, because they ran counter to the Apollonian values cherished by the people. The Hopi and Zuni had never brewed intoxicants or accepted drugs, although they were surrounded by Indian groups who did. Drinking was consequently no problem on Pueblo reservations. Self-torture was also incomprehensible to the Pueblos; and while whipping took place during the puberty ceremonies, this ordeal was merely a symbolic beating which drew no blood.

In a similar vein Dr. Benedict went on to delineate the rejection of the "Dionysian" Ghost Dance of the Great Plains, the shamanistic trance, the tradition of boasting, and other un-Apollonian patterns, such as: competition for prestige, punishment for adultery, frenzied lamentation at funerals, recourse to suicide, sense of sin, and dualism in cosmology.

This long list of items, so persuasively tied together, is cumulatively impressive and appears to be not only more convincing than Spengler's weird but stimulating linkage of bank-books and perspective in art, but also more exhaustive in its scope than Haeberlin's pioneer analysis of Pueblo culture. However, there are some dubious assertions in this original presentation for which proof would be difficult to secure. In particular, it is hard to accept her statement that "the American Indians as a whole, and including those of Mexico, were passionately Dionysian." This would presumably link together such varied cultures as the hunting bands of Labrador, the fishing communities of the North-West Coast, the caste societies of south-eastern North America, and the complex civilization of the Aztecs. In labelling them all "Dionysian" Dr. Benedict commits the very error for which she castigates the arm-chair anthropologists of the nineteenth century, who made facile generalizations about "primitives" and who failed to recognize the tremendous diversity of pre-literate cultures. Writers like Frazer, Dr. Benedict tells us, ignore all the aspects of cultural integration. "Mating or death practices are illustrated by bits of behaviour selected indiscriminately from the most different cultures, and the discussion builds up a kind of mechanical Frankenstein's monster with a right eye from Fiji, a left from Europe, one leg from Tierra del Fuego, and one from Tahiti, and all the fingers and toes from still different regions. Such a figure corresponds to no reality in the past or present. . . ."

Now, how does this erroneous procedure differ from that pursued by Dr. Benedict? To demonstrate the "Dionysian" bent of the American Indians, she selects a pierced tongue from Mexico, a chopped-off finger from the Plains, and a bitten-off nose from the Apache. These she somehow pieces together to suggest the ethos of "the culture from which they [the Pueblos] have detached themselves." Boas must have demurred at this heresy on the part of his favourite disciple.

A critic may also dissent from some of the specific items which illustrate the "Apollonian" nature of Pueblo culture. Drinking, for example, is probably not so rare, and initiation whippings are not so mild in Pueblo culture, to judge from some observations of other ethnologists. One trustworthy eye-witness described the floggings as being "very severe" and added that "pandemonium reigns in the kiva during this exciting half-hour"—which doesn't sound Apollonian. Sun Chief, who wrote his autobiography, confessed that he suffered permanent scars as the result of his initiation. We might question whether the Hopi snake dance is not more Dionysian than Dr. Benedict would have us believe; and perhaps the widespread Pueblo fear of witchcraft is indicative of a greater degree of conflict and tension than the amiable picture which can be derived from ***Patterns of Culture***.

One difficulty with the constructs utilized by Ruth Benedict seems to be that "Apollonian" peoples are not always as consistently Apollonian as they should be. Certainly, "Dionysian" peoples are not always Dionysian. Could a society exist in which everybody was engaged in pursuing ecstatic experiences, cutting off fingers, taking dope or hashish, getting drunk, and going into trances? Of course not. Some Apollonian core of sobriety and responsibility must be found in any culture, or else it will fall apart. At the same time, Dionysian elements can usually be discovered in any culture, no matter how "middle of the road" it may be. To be sure, one might still attempt to grade cultures and arrange them along an Apollonian-Dionysian continuum, but I should not like to try it. What are we in the United States, Apollonian or Dionysian? Is there an answer? I don't know. Perhaps most of us are Apollonian during the week and become more or less Dionysian from Saturday night to Monday morning, if Aldous Huxley is correct in his opinion that the average man's life alternates between senseless week-day routine and senseless week-end orgy.

In view of these difficulties, how are we to characterize forms of integration which exist outside of the Apollonian-Dionysian polarity? Should we have to find a new catchword for each culture (Babbittian? Confucian? Nanookian?) with each label representing a different principle of integration? Obviously, this is an unsatisfactory stratagem, as Dr. Benedict admitted in an almost self-disparaging paragraph: "It would be absurd to cut every culture down to the Procrustean bed of some catchword characterization. The danger of lopping off important facts that do not illustrate the main proposition is grave enough even at best. . . . We do not need a plank of configuration written into the platform of an ethnological school." Here she sounds more like Boas than like Spengler.

One important problem which Dr. Benedict did not pursue in ***Patterns of Culture*** concerns the means by which individuals are "Apollonianized." In other words, how do the Hopi manage to become such submissive, gentle people? And how were "Dionysian" attitudes cultivated among the Blackfeet in each new generation? In this book Ruth Benedict seemed to assume that the whole thing works by contagion. Thus, an individual born into an "Apollonian" culture and exposed to it long enough automatically becomes an "Apollonian" person, just as an Eskimo baby naturally learns to speak Eskimo rather than another language and eventually "takes over" Eskimo culture. But psychoanalysts and child psychologists would not consider such an answer satisfactory. They would like to know more specifically what typical childhood experiences condition the growing personality in this particular culture, leading to an Apollonian repression of hostile impulses, let us say. For if personality is formed to so large an extent in the earliest years of life, as these specialists assure us, one should know something about child-rearing patterns in such a society in order to determine how Apollonian mildness is actually cultivated. These psychodynamic problems were not Ruth Benedict's concern in ***Patterns of Culture*** any more than they were Spengler's concern in *The Decline of the West.* To be sure, there is a passing reference to the probable absence of the Oedipus complex among the Zuni, but beyond this there is little evidence of psychoanalytic orientation. In her later work, however, Dr. Benedict paid a greater degree of attention to childhood experiences and their relationship to adult personality.

It is interesting that in the meantime Dr. Benedict's work was instrumental in furthering the formation of a new school of psychoanalytic thought. Karen Horney paid her respects to the anthropologists (including Dr. Benedict) in *The Neurotic Personality of Our Time,* asserting that cultural factors had been understressed by Freud in his studies of the etiology of neuroses. Accordingly, Dr. Horney emphasized cultural conditions at the expense of the orthodox libidinal drives and infantile experiences.

In the course of her remarks Karen Horney touched on Ruth Benedict's Apollonian-Dionysian duality, describing the Dionysian tendency as a desire to lose the self.

> In our culture we are more aware of the opposite attitude toward the self, the attitude that emphasizes and highly values the particularities and uniqueness of individuality. Man in our culture feels strongly that his own self is a separate unity, distinguished from or opposite to the world outside. Not only does he insist on this individuality but he derives a great deal of satisfaction from it; he finds happiness in developing his special potentialities, mastering himself and the world in active conquest, being constructive and doing creative work. . . .
>
> But the opposite tendency that we have discussed—the tendency to break through the shell of individuality and be rid of its limitations and isolation—is an equally deep-rooted human attitude, and is also pregnant with potential satisfaction. Neither of these tendencies is in itself pathological; both the preservation and development of individuality and the sacrifice of individuality are legitimate goals in the solution of human problems.

This seems like a curious conclusion. But perhaps it is in keeping with the Spengler-Benedict tradition of cultural relativism. For after all, one cannot pass value-judgments (can one?) upon the incommensurable metaphysical assumptions and attitudes which underlie the destinies of cultures. Which is "better"—to be Apollonian or Dionysian?—or (to use Spengler's terms) to be Classical, Magian, or Faustian? But this is like asking: Is it better to be an oak-tree or a cow, a star-fish or Senator Vandenberg? There may be an answer, but one hardly knows where to begin.

Yet, there is a catch in this relativist position, at least for "reformers" like Benedict and Horney. Spengler was more consistent in his Olympian view, jeering sarcastically at "world-improvers" from his privileged position beyond space and time. But Ruth Benedict, whose books and pamphlets urgently combated racial prejudice, was a "world-improver" caught up in the issues of her day, passing value-judgments right and left upon the culture of her world. As for Karen Horney, it would seem that a psychoanalyst would also be debarred from a relativist position. The profession of psychoanalysis, which aims to "cure," assumes that there is some standard of emotional health which "neurotics" and "psychotics" do not meet. To be sure, in the wake of Benedict's book, much attention was paid to the variety in cultural standards of "normality." People were fond of pointing out, as Ruth Benedict had done, that trances or transvestism were accepted in other cultures, that therefore our ideas about normality were "ethnocentric," and that perhaps the only adequate concept of normality would have to be a statistical one based upon a particular society and carrying no cross-cultural implications. But this attitude is no longer so prevalent. A headache, after all, is a headache in any culture; a stomach ache is a stomach ache. People may eat different things, and a stomach ache may be brought about by a variety of causes; but all the same, some adequate cause-and-effect relations (transcending cultural differences) may be discovered which will account for, and perhaps cure, the stomach ache of a Hopi as well as the stomach ache of a New York business man. If this is feasible, why may not a psychosis be labelled a psychosis in any culture? Is it not possible that universally valid standards of human functioning are discoverable and that basic psychodynamic principles do not differ very much from one society to another?

Moreover, can we not say that in some societies people seem to be "happier" than in others, or that there are fewer mental and emotional disturbances in society A than in society B? From reading ***Patterns of Culture***, at least, one receives the very definite impression that the Pueblo tribes are "happier" than the Dobu. "Life in Dobu fosters extreme forms of animosity and malignancy which most societies have minimized by their institutions," Dr. Benedict tells us; while Pueblo culture is described as "a civilization whose forms are dictated by the typical choices of the Apollonian, all of whose delight is in formality and whose way of life is the way of measure and sobriety."

Now, in which society would you rather live? Or does it make no difference? I am sure that Ruth Benedict would much rather be a Zuni than a Dobu or Kwakiutl. Yet in the final paragraph of her book she speaks of the "coexisting and equally valid patterns of life which mankind has created for itself from the raw materials of existence." At the same time, at other points in ***Patterns of Culture***, she seems to approach absolute criteria for the evaluation of social systems. "It is possible," she suggests, "to scrutinize different institutions and cast up their cost in terms of social capital, in terms of the less desirable behaviour traits they stimulate, and in terms of human suffering and frustration." Here is an approach which can unite the disciplines of anthropology, sociology, and psychiatry, and one, moreover, which may also justify the activities of the liberal "world-improver." Yet Ruth Benedict was not consistent in this approach.

Elgin Williams has discussed the internal contradictions and inconsistencies in Ruth Benedict's work. "Formally she sticks to relativism," he observes. "Her pragmatism is not so much at the tip of her tongue as bred in the bone. Try as she may to maintain the pose of relativism, the test of consequences intrudes." He is aware of the fact that Dr. Benedict's concern for tolerance was expressed in her cultural relativism, but he inquires whether this relativism, if carried to a logical conclusion, would not lead to an acceptance of Jim Crow in the south and other manifestations of intolerance. These are stubborn old problems which may be phrased in a hundred different ways. Consider, for example, the Zuni and Apache, who of course have "equally valid patterns of life." Among these patterns the Zuni and Apache have remarkably contrasting solutions for the problem of adultery. In Zuni culture, the woman is not punished in any way, while among the Apache the injured husband bites off the end of his wife's nose. From an anthropological point of view, both patterns "function" successfully in their respective cultures. The one response is "Apollonian," the other "Dionysian." But is that all that we can say about them?

It seems to me that in a case like this, constructs such as "Apollonian" or "Dionysian" may obscure rather than enlighten the issue. Granted that group differences in "basic personality structure" and in culturally accepted values do exist, these do not in any way negate the essential psychic unity of mankind. An individual Hopi has a host of life-problems in common with an individual Apache, or Kwakiutl, or Dobu, however different may be the value-systems and metaphysical assumptions which underlie these cultures. Surely, some solutions to basic problems are more satisfactory than others. Very likely the Apache were happy to surrender their nose-biting practices, even if it meant giving up an important outlet for their Dionysian tendencies.

Ruth Benedict always stressed the extraordinary plasticity of man and the great diversity of his culture. To her, culture was a "superorganic" medium which was presumably linked by only the slenderest threads to its organic substratum.

—Victor Barnouw

However, there is one optimistic aspect in Ruth Benedict's view of culture, which should be congenial to the assumptions of a "world-improver." I refer to the absence of any cyclical fatalism like that of Spengler, or of any constitutional determinism like that of Sheldon. Nor does Dr. Benedict accept the philosophy of predestination that we find in the work of Kardiner, with its apparent assumption that adult life consists mainly of the working out of conflicts originating during infancy in response to childhood disciplines. The only determinism which Ruth Benedict stresses is a cultural determinism, but with the saving implication that man may develop some culture-consciousness and insight into the mould of his own culture and thereby change or transcend it in some way. Ruth Benedict always stressed the extraordinary plasticity of man and the great diversity of his culture. To her, culture was a "superorganic" medium which was presumably linked by only the slenderest threads to its organic substratum. According to this viewpoint, man has great potential freedom. But this free will does not seem to be particularly significant in a relativist framework, wherein whatever man does is equivalent. In this view, man is all dressed up with no place (or a thousand places) to go.

In the preceding pages we have examined some aspects of ***Patterns of Culture***. I have not attempted to deal with all of its sections, but mainly with the most challenging and original themes. The chapter on Dobu, to my mind, is an unfortunate inclusion because it is based entirely upon the work of one ethnologist who spent only six months among these islanders. Later, in the course of her official work in Washington during the war, Dr. Benedict made similar reconstructions on the basis of equally meagre evidence. To be sure, she had the excuse of war-time pressures and limitations; but all the same it seems rather rash, for example, to write a book about Japanese history, culture, and personality without ever having been to Japan, and after having interviewed only a few acculturated Japanese.

Our reflections about ***Patterns of Culture*** now lead us to two final questions. First of all, why did Ruth Benedict, who worked in close association with the highly critical Boas, develop a theme as questionable as her Apollonian-Dionysian duality appears to be? Secondly, what was Ruth Benedict's positive contribution to social science?

As to the first question, the answer lies partly in the fact that Dr. Benedict was exploring new territory and that her errors (if we can call them such) were those of a pioneer. But granted that this is so, why did Dr. Benedict elect the particular theme she chose for elaboration? Why, in spite of the flimsy evidence for such an assertion, did she insist upon branding all non-Pueblo Indians as "Dionysian"? If Dr. Benedict was a scholar (and she was), why did her scholarship turn soft at this particular point? What I am suggesting through these questions is that irrational factors may have helped to dictate Ruth Benedict's choice of theme. Let us take a leaf from Dr. Benedict's work and inquire into the factors behind her "selective borrowing" from *The Birth of Tragedy*.

Nietzsche's vague and chaotically rolling passages do not excite the imagination of every reader. If they did in Ruth Benedict's case, there must have been some tension within her own psyche which corresponded to the Apollonian-Dionysian conflict which Nietzsche described. This tension, whatever its source, seems to be particularly characteristic of Western culture and finds expression in various other terminologies, such as the conflict between classicism and romanticism, reason and emotion, bourgeois and bohemian, form and colour, ego and id. This internal conflict must have been particularly intense in the case of Nietzsche, for otherwise he would never have "discovered" the Apollonian-Dionysian antithesis among the ancient Greeks. My suggestion is that the same principle may be applicable to Ruth Benedict, and that in her case two conflicting tendencies were seeking some kind of integration. In her earlier years an integration was achieved under the aegis of the Dionysian Anne Singleton; in her later years under that of the Apollonian Dr. Benedict.

Perhaps it was some such inner duality which made Ruth Benedict so responsive to Nietzsche's nebulous dichotomy and led her to discover its manifestations among the cultures of aboriginal North America. As we have seen (in the case of Haeberlin), other guiding motivations besides the Apollonian can be deduced from a contrast of Pueblo with non-Pueblo cultures; so that Dr. Benedict's characterization is not the only and inevitable one. I am not suggesting that reason and deduction played no role in the application of Nietzsche's antithesis to Pueblo culture; but I do think it possible that irrational factors and "projection" were involved to some extent. Of course, I may be "projecting," myself, in making this analysis. However, it seems to me that the balance of forces between "emotion" and "reason" was remarkably even in Ruth Benedict's case. No faction got the upper hand altogether. Responsiveness to Spengler's intuition was balanced by respect for the rationality incarnated in Boas. Indeed, it may have been this very awareness of co-existing but "equally valid" approaches to life that led to the relativism which permeated Ruth Benedict's work.

But I have been Dionysian enough in throwing out such wild suggestions, and perhaps, like a Blackfoot Indian, I am balancing dangerously upon a thin knife-edge of speculation. So before I do any more damage, either to Dr. Benedict or to myself, let me turn to our final question: What was Ruth Benedict's positive contribution to social science?

It may sound paradoxical, in the light of what has gone before, but I think that Ruth Benedict made a very great contribution to present-day anthropology, not as a pamphleteer on race, not as a harried Washington bureaucrat answering too many telephone calls, not as the author of any particular book or article, but rather for the aims she pursued and the kinds of questions which she asked about ethnological material. Ruth Benedict's dignity lay in the fact that she went after important issues. Anthropologists who classified potsherds or measured skulls could afford to criticize her methodology. Their procedures, no doubt, were impeccable in comparison to hers, but the final value of their work still remains to be discovered. Too many of Boas's students got bogged down among the intricate details of kinship-systems or basket-weaves without having much understanding of why they worked so hard. When Franz Boas published page after page of blueberry-pie recipes in Kwakiutl, the old man probably knew what he was after; but when his students did the same kind of thing, they often lacked the driving central purpose which animated Boas. They mastered techniques and methods within their special fields, but often accomplished little more than that. It requires courage to stick to the important issues, and Ruth Benedict had that courage.

Like Boas, Ruth Benedict was very serious about her work in life. Time was short, she felt, and there was only room for the vital things. Her sense of dedication to a difficult and serious task marked everything she did. Her students immediately felt this and respected her essential dignity of spirit. In her later years, beset by phone calls, interruptions, manuscripts to read and refugees to interview, she moved through her book-lined office with a kind of sad, blurry nobility, overworked but always with a renewing buoyancy of spirit, kindliness, and deep sense of social responsibility. Perhaps the main thing about Ruth Benedict was the spiritual influence which she exerted upon her students and those who worked with her. Those who read her books may perhaps forget what they have learned; but those who knew Ruth Benedict in any way will always remember her as a symbol of spiritual and intellectual quest.

Margaret Mead (essay date 1959)

SOURCE: "Patterns of Culture: 1922-1934," in *An Anthropologist at Work: Writings of Ruth Benedict,* Houghton Mifflin Company, 1959, pp. 201-12.

[*Mead was a leading figure in American anthropology whose works, including* Coming of Age in Samoa *(1928) and* Sex and Temperament in Three Primitive Societies *(1935), emphasized a vital relevance between "primitive" and modern societies which she believed could illuminate contemporary social problems. In the following excerpt, she studies Benedict's defining methods and principles as an anthropologist.*]

Ruth Benedict stood midway between the older type of anthropology, in which theoreticians—men like Tylor or Frazer, Lang or Crawley—worked with materials gathered by others—with old documents, travelers' and missionaries' accounts, or with notes laboriously written down by native converts—and the kind of anthropology related to living cultures, which grew out of field work in the South Seas and in Africa. Because she wanted vivid materials, she valued old eyewitness accounts of American Indians, such as those found in the Jesuit Relations; because she wanted materials meticulously collected by the rigorous textual methods which Boas insisted upon, she herself was willing to spend long, grueling hours of work among Indians whose cultures, through the erosion of contact with cultures brought from Europe centuries before, had hardened in resistance or were disintegrating before her eyes.

She never had an opportunity to participate in a living culture where she could speak the language and get to know people well as individuals. In her work with North American Indians, she always had to work through interpreters and to seek out the particularly knowledgeable individual who was also amenable to the task of sitting and dictating while, with flying pencil and aching arm, she wrote down verbatim hundreds of pages of translated tales to be redictated when she returned to New York. The materials which she herself collected differed from the fragments which other students of North American Indians had collected in that she had seen the Indians who told the stories, had watched people whom she did not know go through a few ceremonies, and had learned to trust her knowledge of the shape and feel of a culture of which she was recording only a very small part.

Even when she was sitting in a pueblo day after day, she was always, because of the very nature of the problem, straining to see and hear a more coherent culture back of the broken phrases of the day. This made her field work more like reading the work of others and made it particularly easy for her to work over the field materials of her students. Back of their inadequate notes—as also back of her own partial ones and back of the partial insights of a Jesuit missionary, or a Grinnell camping with the Cheyenne, or a Sahagun recording the crumbling glory of the Aztecs—there was a whole, if one could but perceive it. She had begun her work by following separate themes and small items wherever they occurred, and in the conclusion to her study of the Guardian Spirit, she wrote:

> There is then no observed correlation between the vision-guardian-spirit concept, and the other traits with which it is associated, as it were organically, over the continent, and we have found no coalescence which we may regard as being other than fortuitous—an historical happening of definite time and place. The miscellaneous traits that enter in different centers into its make-up are none of them either the inevitable forerunner, the inevitable accompaniment of the concept, but have each an individual existence and a wider distribution outside this complex. In one region it has associated itself with puberty ceremonials, in another with totemism, in a third with secret societies, in a fourth with inherited rank, in a fifth with black magic. Among the Blackfoot, it is their economic system into which the medicine bundles have so insinuated themselves that the whole manner of it is unintelligible without taking into account the monetary value of the vision. Among the Kwakiutl, their social life and organization, their caste system, their concept of wealth, would be equally impossible of comprehension without a knowledge of those groups of individuals sharing the same guardian spirit by supernatural revelation. It is in every case a matter of social patterning—of that which cultural recognition has singled out and standardized.
>
> It is, so far as we can see, an ultimate fact of human nature that man builds up his culture out of disparate elements, combining and recombining them; and until we have abandoned the superstition that the result is an organism functionally interrelated, we shall be unable to see our cultural life objectively, or to control its manifestations.

This statement Radcliffe-Brown took as representing her ultimate position, namely, that she believed that cultures were made up of "rags and tatters." But she herself was working steadily to find some integrating principle that would explain both the disparate origins of the elements of which a culture was built and the wholeness which she felt was there in each culture.

Ruth Benedict stood midway between the older type of anthropology, in which theoreticians—men like Tylor or Frazer, Lang or Crawley—worked with materials gathered by others—with old documents, travelers' and missionaries' accounts, or with notes laboriously written down by native converts—and the kind of anthropology related to living cultures, which grew out of field work in the South Seas and in Africa.

—*Margaret Mead*

When one works with a living culture this wholeness is part of one's everyday experience. The people among whom one is living speak, walk, talk, sleep, pray, and die within a recognizable and related pattern. The infant one holds in one's arms shows by prefigurative tension in his muscles just how he expects to be carried, and there is an echo of his particular urgency in the pleading gestures of the sick and in the trembling touch of the dying. Living among a people whose skin color is gleaming copper, soft brown, or shining black, whose hair is straight and coarse as a horse's mane, or falls in waves, or curls so tight that it can be combed straight up in the air, it is very difficult both to attend to the ways a people embody the language they speak and the patterns they are living out and to remember that this language, which seems to be so appropriate to these lips, and these feelings may also occur half the world away—where all the externals are different—with as seeming entire appropriateness as one finds here. Watching a tall Sepik native, lime stick tasseled with records of the human heads he has taken, pounding the ground with the heavy end of a fallen palm leaf to scare away the ghosts, it is difficult to see this act, so perfectly integrated into a local ceremony, as "an element," unless one has also stood in a Balinese village and has seen the same pounding, in a setting so different, among a slender, exotic, peaceful, and ritualistic people of another race and with a quite different culture.

Many field workers who in the early twentieth century wrote the first monographs based on the study of living cultures were victims of this illusion of "fit." If they knew enough anthropology to realize that human cultures are human inventions, that they are learned anew by each generation, and that one people can borrow from another, not borrowing all but only a bit—a way of making a pot or of killing an enemy by magic, a form of courtship, or a method of cremating the dead—then the need to account for the coherence, the wholeness, of a culture became even more urgent.

Anthropologists dealt with this problem in different ways. Rivers, after making a vivid study of a single people, the Todas, accepted a totally historical viewpoint and ended his days treating discrete items of behavior as the residues of an earlier integration. Radcliffe-Brown, after having had an opportunity to work on one of the most isolated and integrated cultures in the world, that of the pygmies of the Andaman Islands, discounted all his experience of them as a living people—which would nevertheless sometimes peep out in conversation as he would describe how *they* peeped out, bright-eyed, from their tiny houses—and treated cultures, which afterward he never studied as wholes, as examples for the establishment of universally valid principles. Malinowski, repelled by his first field trip among the Mailu and captivated by the Trobrianders, pushed away all historical and areal considerations to concentrate on the way "elements" of culture were only meaningful within a functioning context. A generation later, Claude Lévi-Strauss, who was for a time entranced by the vivid detail of a living people, also turned to a search for universal principles which run like wires through the material, freezing people eternally into *tableaux vivants.* And those anthropologists who were less firmly grounded took refuge in theories of race or constitution to explain the patterned and consistent differences among peoples of different cultures.

But Ruth Benedict, piecing together bits from the old, sometimes vigorous, sometimes dull descriptions of Indians as long dead as the buffalo they once had hunted, or turning from the recitation of tales which had lost their functioning relevance in the Pueblo of Cochiti, faced no such problem. She never saw a whole primitive culture that was untroubled by boarding schools for the children, by missions and public health nurses, by Indian Service agents, traders, and sentimental or exiled white people. No living flesh-and-blood member of a coherent culture was present to obscure her vision or to make it too concrete, when, in the summer of 1927, she saw with a sense of revelation that it would be possible to explain the differences among the tribes of the Southwest or the Plains—both in what they had taken from one another and in what they had resisted—as one might explain the choices of an individual who, true to his own temperament, organized his life out of the myriad and often conflicting choices presented to him by a rich historical tradition. She had always been interested in Nietzsche, and his contrast between Apollonian and Dionysian seemed ready-made to her hand to describe the contrast between the Pima and the Zuñi. From Pima, she wrote to Boas in 1927, "These people have more in common with the Serrano than with the Pueblos. The contrast with the latter is *unbelievable.*"

During the following winter, in 1927-1928, I was writing *Social Organization of Manu'a,* happy in the freedom to write more technically, after my attempt to make the material on Samoan adolescence intelligible to educators in *Coming of Age in Samoa.* We spent hours discussing how a given temperamental approach to living could come so to dominate a culture that all who were born in it would become the willing or unwilling heirs to that view of the world. From the first Ruth Benedict resisted any idea of schematization in terms of a given number of temperaments—Jung's fourfold scheme, for instance. She saw the relationship between a culture, which was "personality writ large" and "time binding," and any individual, who might or might not fit in, as a way of so phrasing all deviation that the unfortunate could be pitied and the world seen as the loser because of gifts which could not be used. She wanted to leave the future open. No attempt to understand human cultures as limited by a given number of temperaments, and so with limited temperamental contrasts, ever pleased her.

Into discussions there came echoes of Koffka's *The Growth of the Mind,* which I had read and lent to Sapir in 1925, and of conversations between Sapir and Goldenweiser at the Toronto meetings in 1924, when Sapir had been stimulated by Jung and also by Seligman's recent article, "Anthropology and Psychology: A Study of Some Points of Contact," in which he discussed the possibility that certain recognizable pathologies, associated with Jung's types, were given more scope in one culture than in another.

Also into our discussions came my field plans for the next year's work in the Admiralty Islands, where I wanted to test whether one would find among primitive children the kind of thinking that Freud had identified as characteristic of children, neurotics, and primitives, and that Piaget, taking a clue from Levy-Bruhl's discussion of prelogicality, had also identified as primitive. These latter considerations I had hammered out in discussion with Reo Fortune who, before he had begun work in anthropology, had worked on Freud's and Rivers' theories of dreams. Working with Ruth Benedict, I supplied the psychological materials and the concrete experience of participation in a living culture and the way children experienced it, and she tested and retested her emerging theory against her knowledge of the Indians of the Southwest and of the literature on American Indian religion.

Historically, the first written application of her conceptualization was in my chapter on "Dominant Cultural Attitudes," in *Social Organization of Manu'a,* written in the winter of 1927-1928, before she wrote her own first formulation in **"Psychological Types in the Cultures of the Southwest."** . . .

The whole position is quite clear. I wrote:

> By this emphasis upon conformity to the all important social structure, I do not mean here the attempt of a society to make all those within it conform to all its ways of thought and behavior. The phenomenon of social pressure and its absolute determination in shaping the individuals within its bounds has been remarked too often to need laboring here. I mean to stress rather the particular implication in the lives of individuals of a particular kind of social pattern. As the Winnebago culture forced its children to blacken their faces and fast for a blessing, goaded them into a search for special experience often beyond any natural inclination in the individual child, so the Samoan emphasis upon social blessedness within an elaborate, impersonal structure influences every aspect of the Samoans' lives.

The chapter on "The Girl in Conflict" in *Coming of Age in Samoa* had been written in the autumn of 1926, and was already an organized part of our discussions before Ruth Benedict's summer with the Pima in 1927. That chapter began with a question which Ruth Benedict had taught me to ask:

> Were there no conflicts, no temperaments which deviated so markedly from the normal that clash was inevitable? Was the diffused affection and the diffused authority of the large families, the ease of moving from one family to another, the knowledge of sex and the freedom to experiment a sufficient guarantee to all Samoan girls of a perfect adjustment?

In the chapter, I discussed the cases of those deviants of whom this was not true.

Coming of Age in Samoa was published in the summer of 1928, close to the time of the Congress at which Ruth Benedict read her paper on **"Psychological Types in the Cultures of the Southwest."** *Social Organization of Manu'a* was not published until 1930. The extent to which my work had been shaped by her preoccupations and both of us had been shaped by Sapir's interests was so little remarked then or later that Ernst Kris could say to me, in 1946, that he thought Ruth Benedict's work showed signs of coming around to my point of view! David Mandelbaum's Introduction to the *Selected Writings of Edward Sapir in Language, Culture, and Personality* contains only one reference to Ruth Benedict: "Ruth Benedict has written [in her obituary of Sapir] that the position in Chicago was one he was uniquely qualified to adorn." In the posthumous volume in his honor, *Language, Culture and Personality, Essays in Memory of Edward Sapir,* three of the people who had profited most from his speculations about personality and culture—Ruth Benedict, John Dollard, and I—are not among the contributors.

Instead, posterity has been treated to reconstructions which give misleading impressions. So, for instance, Victor Barnauw, who had been her student, reconstructed in a long obituary article, which is frequently percipient but in which he ignored both written and living sources of information, the origins of the idea of ***Patterns of Culture***.

> Willingly Anne Singleton slipped on the rough hair shirt of discipline, took upon herself the exacting Boas regimen of hard work, read endlessly, endured the discomforts of ethnological field work, and finally emerged as "Dr. Benedict." But it is a measure of her individuality that Ruth Benedict never became a mere rubber stamp of the old man's thinking. In fact, her work represents a marked contrast to his. Boas had long ago rejected the "deep" intuitive plunges of German scholarship and philosophy; but in these same dubious sources Ruth Benedict now found inspiration. Under her master's somewhat jaundiced eye she turned to Nietzsche, Spengler and Dilthey, whose ideas she somehow blended with the Boas tradition of intensive field work in a particular area. From this unexpected amalgam she managed to fashion her famous ***Patterns of Culture***.

And there is Melville Herskovits' comment in his book on Boas:

> Broader uses of psychological concepts, such as those which attempted to assign entire societies to particular categories of mental set, as in the book ***Patterns of Culture*** by his student and colleague Ruth Benedict, seemed to him to raise methodological questions that had not been faced. Though for personal reasons he consented to write a brief preface for the work, he devoted several paragraphs to a critical discussion of the problem in his chapter on methods of research in the textbook he edited, especially pointed because he takes as his example the Northwest Coast Indians, who had been cited as an extreme case by Benedict. Indicating that "the leading motive of their life is the limitless pursuit of gaining social prestige and of holding on to what has been gained, and the intense feeling of inferiority and shame if even a part of the prestige is lost," he adds, "these tendencies are so striking that the amiable qualities that appear in intimate family life are easily overlooked."

The actual facts are that the theoretical part of the work—the usefulness of viewing the integration of a culture within an area in the light of the way individuals with specific temperaments integrated items from within their cultural heritage—was worked out with reference neither to Spengler nor to Dilthey. Nietzsche had been an old favorite of hers. Boas had approved the early manifestations of the theory. When he read *Coming of Age in Samoa,* which was written under his direct supervision, he made only one objection: "You haven't made clear the distinction between romantic and passionate love." He read Ruth Benedict's paper, **"Configurations of Culture in North America,"** written in 1932, and discussed it with her on the trip which they took to the Southwest together, and she went over with him every detail of the Kwakiutl material in hour-long discussions, which she explicitly acknowledges:

> For the Northwest Coast of America I have used not only Professor Franz Boas' text publications and detailed compilations of Kwakiutl life, but his still unpublished material and his penetrating comment upon his experience on the Northwest Coast extending over forty years.

And in the Introduction Boas writes:

> As the author points out, not every culture is characterized by a dominant character, but it seems probable that the more intimate our knowledge of the cultural drives that actuate the behavior of the individual, the more we shall find that certain controls of emotion, certain ideals of conduct, prevail that account for what seem to us as abnormal attitudes when viewed from the standpoint of our civilization. The relativity of what is considered social or asocial, normal or abnormal, is seen in a new light.

As for Dilthey, far from battling for her individuality against Boas' disapproval of Dilthey, it was Boas who insisted that she must discuss him, not out of sympathy for Dilthey's ideas but out of the special standards of scholarship which required mention of those who had used comparable ideas irrespective of whether or not one's own ideas derived from them.

From the fresh excitement of the 1927 summer in Pima, when she saw the basic contrast between the Pueblos and the other Indian cultures of North America "as the contrast that is named and described by Nietzsche in his studies of Greek tragedy," was a six year road, in the course of which she published two articles on the subject, both of which dealt with American Indian material. Only in 1932 did she decide that in the book it would be necessary to add a third culture—one which had been studied by a field worker whom she knew well and on which she could trust the material—to set beside Zuñi, where she had her own field work as a guide and a corrective, and the Kwakiutl, where she could test each smallest interpretation against Boas' detailed memory. She chose Dobu. The history of her interest in Dobu and of her choice of this culture is contained in a series of letters exchanged with Reo Fortune.

But between what seemed so obvious to me, writing in 1927—namely, that a culture shapes the lives of those who live within it—and the views of the literate world of 1934, when ***Patterns of Culture*** was published, there was a great gap. Her publishers in their choice of publicity materials stressed not what she regarded as its major contribution but rather what we had come to think of as obvious. Through a long and spirited correspondence with Ferris Greenslet of Houghton Mifflin, beginning with a request for a blurb, my writing of the blurb and her revision of it, and the publisher's choices from it, to her rebellious rewriting of the circular for the general reader, she fought for a clear statement of what she felt she had contributed that was new by writing this book. In the copy which she herself prepared for the publisher, she wrote: "In a straightforward style, the author demonstrates how the manners and morals of these tribes, and our own as well, are not piecemeal items of behavior, but consistent ways of life. They are not racial, nor the necessary consequence of human nature, but have grown up historically in the life history of the community."

Robert B. Downs (essay date 1971)

SOURCE: "Society versus the Individual: Ruth Benedict's *Patterns of Culture,* 1934," in *Famous American Books,* McGraw-Hill Book Company, 1971, pp. 290-97.

[*Downs is an American librarian and critic who has published a variety of works, including literary studies and several surveys examining books that have had a significant social influence. In the following essay, he discusses Benedict's approach to anthropology in* Patterns of Culture.]

For a serious and scholarly anthropological study to achieve sales in excess of a million copies was unheard of until the publication in 1934 of Ruth Benedict's ***Patterns of Culture***. In hardback and paperback editions this extraordinary work has made publishing history by reaching best-sellerdom in the English language and in numerous translations.

There may be significance in the fact, too, that Ruth Benedict's student and close friend Margaret Mead is also the author of several extraordinarily popular and successful studies of primitive societies. The two writers broke away from traditional approaches to anthropology and started new trends, which continue to dominate the field. Conceivably, the feminine viewpoint brought a warmth and understanding of human beings that was lacking in the dry, technical reports of their male confreres.

The older anthropologists were generally theorists who relied upon materials gathered by others—such as travelers' and missionaries' accounts. Attempts were made to reconstruct human history historically, using methods developed for the study of archaeology, linguistics, and biological evolution. Attention was centered on the diffusion of cultural traits, with the aim of tracing the spread of the human species, the history of inventions and technologies, etc. A leading early-twentieth-century anthropologist and Ruth Benedict's teacher, Franz Boas, emphasized exact descriptions. The case for the old anthropology is well stated in an introductory passage in ***Patterns of Culture***:

> Anthropological work has been overwhelmingly devoted to the analysis of culture traits, rather than to the study of cultures as articulated wholes. This has been due in great measure to the nature of earlier ethnological descriptions. The classical anthropologists did not write out of first-hand knowledge of primitive people. They were armchair students who had at their disposal the anecdotes of travelers and missionaries and the formal and schematic accounts of the early ethnologists. It was possible to trace from these details the distribution of the custom of knocking out teeth, or of divination by entrails, but it was not possible to see how these traits were embedded in different tribes in char-

> acteristic configurations that gave form and meaning to the procedures.

Nevertheless, Ruth Benedict did not reject the types of sources utilized by her predecessors. She found of value, for example, old eyewitness accounts of American Indians, such as those recorded in the *Jesuit Relations*. But the documentary sources were extensively and intensively complemented by field work among the Indians for first-hand observation of their cultures.

Attempts to study the customs of various cultures and then to draw overall deductions from them, for example, in mating or death practices, were compared by Mrs. Benedict to the building up of "a kind of mechanical Frankenstein's monster with a right eye from Fiji, a left from Europe, one leg from Tierra del Fuego, and one from Tahiti, and all the fingers and toes from still different regions. Such a figure corresponds to no reality in the past or present."

A definition of anthropology preferred by Ruth Benedict, and exemplified in ***Patterns of Culture***, as stated by the author, is "the study of human beings as creatures of society. It fastens its attention upon those physical characteristics and industrial techniques, those conventions and values, which distinguish one community from all others that belong to a different tradition." The premise is that every culture has individual features, that is, practices, beliefs, and institutions, which distinguish it from every other culture. A society must be viewed as a whole, in all its facets, and should not be judged in terms of isolated details. As a corollary, the individuals who go to make up a given society are molded by the culture into which they have been born. Man's life is lived according to the traditions of his group, and it is a rare individual who tries to break out of the mold.

The diversity of cultures is a paramount fact in the study of anthropology, and the range of differences is infinite. Further, cultural differences are only partially, if at all, explained by race, or by the accidents of geography, climate, or other features of the physical environment. The rate of change in a culture is far slower than in an individual member of a society. The latter, of course, is limited at best to a few score years, whereas a culture is "time binding," perhaps perpetuating itself for thousands of years.

For illustrative purposes, Ruth Benedict selected three radically different cultures. Two are American Indian and the other is that of a Melanesian people who live on the island of Dobu off the northern shore of Eastern New Guinea. Reasons for the decision to treat these three primitive civilizations in detail are thus stated by the author:

> A few cultures understood as coherent organizations of behaviour are more enlightening than many touched upon only at their high spots. The relation of motivations and purposes to the separate items of cultural behavior at birth, at death, at puberty, and at marriage can never be made clear by a comprehensive survey of the world. We must hold ourselves to the less ambitious task, the many-sided understanding of a few cultures.

Certainly, a worldwide search could scarcely have found three more diverse societies than those treated in depth in ***Patterns of Culture***. The first is the Pueblo Indians of the Southwest, one of the most widely known tribes of aborigines in Western civilization. Despite the fact that they live in mid-America and are much visited by outsiders, their culture is relatively unspoiled, and they continue to live after the old native fashion. The ancient dances of the gods are performed in their stone villages, life follows traditional routines, and anything taken from the white-man's civilization is adapted to their attitudes and requirements. The individual person is subordinated to the group. It is social values that count, and personalities must give way to the needs of the larger society.

Several Indian tribes lived in the Pueblos of the Southwest United States. ***Patterns of Culture*** concentrates principal attention on the Zuñi, who belong to the great western Pueblos. Pueblo culture, with a long homogeneous history behind it, is oddly a culture at wide variance with those surrounding it and indeed different from the rest of North America. The Zuñi are a ceremonious people, sober and inoffensive, their lives filled with cults of masked gods, healing, the sun, and sacred fetishes concerning war and the dead. "Probably most grown men among the western Pueblos," Mrs. Benedict observes, give to ritual "the greater part of their waking life," and the daily conversation of all the people in the Pueblo centers about it. The reason for the preoccupation is that Zuñi religious practices are believed to be supernaturally powerful.

The Zuñi place great reliance upon imitative magic. Their prayers are traditional formulas that ask for orderly life, pleasant days, and shelter from violence. Religious observances have one primary purpose: to bring rain and to increase fertility, both in the gardens and in the tribe. Given the culture's religious foundation, the priesthoods naturally stand on the highest level of sanctity. The heads of the major priesthoods make up the ruling body of the Zuñi, constituting a theocracy. The cult of the masked gods is popular; more than a hundred different masked gods exist in the Zuñi pantheon. The dances of the masked gods are conducted by a tribal society of all adult males, organized in six groups, each with its "kiva," or ceremonial chamber. When boys reach the proper age, they are initiated into a kiva.

Another great division of the Zuñi ceremonial structure is that of the medicine societies, whose supernatural patrons are the beast gods, chief of whom is the bear. The societies have amassed great stores of esoteric knowledge, imparted to the members, both men and women, throughout their lives. The Zuñi group war and hunting and clowning cults with the medicine societies.

Domestic affairs like marriage and divorce are casually arranged among the Zuñi. Marriages take place almost without courtship. Divorce is easy, though most marriages are permanent and peaceful. Economic wealth is comparatively unimportant, outweighed by membership in a clan with numerous ceremonial prerogatives.

In contrasting the Pueblo Indians with other North American Indians, Mrs. Benedict emphasizes a fundamental difference. The Indians of North America outside the Pueblos have what she characterizes as a "Dionysian" culture, the most conspicuous feature of which is the practice of obtaining supernatural power in a dream or vision, induced by hideous tortures, drugs, alcohol, fasting, or the frenzy of marathon dancing. The Pueblos, whose culture is described as "Apollonian," do not seek or tolerate any experiences outside of ordinary sensory sources. They "will have nothing to do with disruptive individual experiences of this type," notes Mrs. Benedict. "The love of moderation to which their civilization is committed has no place for them."

Individual authority is strictly subordinated among the Zuñi. Both in domestic and religious situations, the group is most important, and responsibility and power are always distributed. In their economic life, too, all activity is on a community basis: the planting, harvesting, and storing of crops; the building of houses; the herding of sheep, etc. Anger, marital jealousy, grief, and violent emotions of any kind are suppressed. Suicides are virtually unknown. The Zuñi priests and medicine men engage in supernatural practices, but not in malicious sorcery. Mrs. Benedict sums up the prevailing mores with the statement: "In the Pueblos, therefore, there is no courting of excess in any form, no tolerance of violence, no indulgence in the exercise of authority, or delight in any situation in which the individual stands alone."

The natives of Dobu Island provide a vivid contrast to the Zuñi. The Dobuans exist on rocky volcanic upcroppings with scanty pockets of soil. They are one of the most southerly of the peoples of northwestern Melanesia, and the population presses hard upon limited resources. Their barren environment is reflected in their reputations, for ***Patterns of Culture*** describes them as "the feared and distrusted savages of the islands surrounding them. . . . They are noted for their dangerousness. They are said to be magicians who have diabolic power and warriors who halt at no treachery." Until stopped by white men, they were cannibals. In short, the Dobuans are lawless and treacherous, and every man's hand is against every other man. All is suspicion, and a pleasant person is regarded as foolish, if not actually insane.

The Dobuan culture is classified as "Dionysian"; it includes the desire, in personal experience or in ritual, to attain a certain psychological state, to achieve excess. Such an emotion may be gained by drunkenness or working oneself into a state of frenzy.

The Dobuans function in groups of villages in a particular locality. Every grouping is a war unit and is on terms of permanent hostility with every other similar locality. There is also internecine warfare: "People with whom one associates daily are the witches and sorcerers who threaten one's affairs." It is believed that individuals within one's own locality "play havoc with one's harvest, they bring confusion upon one's economic exchanges, they cause disease and death." The only persons from whom one may expect any backing or for whom any affinity is felt are those in the mother's line. Within this line inheritance passes and cooperation exists.

Marriage is surrounded by elaborate customs. Husband and wife remain mutually antagonistic, and the illness or death of either is assumed to have been caused by evil sorcery on the part of the other. The jealousy, the suspicion, the fierce exclusiveness of ownership characteristic of all Dobu culture are strongly evident in Dobuan marriage. A sort of mania runs through the society, convincing the Dobuan that "all existence is cut-throat competition, and every advantage is gained at the expense of a defeated rival."

Religion among the Dobu is primarily concerned with magic:

> Yams cannot grow without incantations, sex desire does not arise without love magic, exchanges of valuables in economic transactions are magically brought about, no trees are protected from theft unless malevolent charms have been placed upon them, no wind blows unless it is magically called, no disease or death occurs without the machinations of sorcery or witchcraft.

In summary, Mrs. Benedict characterizes the Dobuan as dour, prudish, and passionate, consumed with jealousy, suspicion, and resentment, and certain that any prosperity he has achieved has been wrung from a hostile world. "Suspicion and cruelty are his trusted weapons in the strife and he gives no mercy, as he asks none."

For her treatment of a third primitive society, Mrs. Benedict turns again to America, but to a culture vastly different from the Pueblos: that of the Kwakiutl Indians of the Northwest Coast, a culture which fell into ruin during the latter part of the nineteenth century. The Kwakiutl lived on a narrow strip of Pacific seacoast from Alaska to Puget Sound. The economic basis of their society was fish, obtainable in great quantities with a minimum of effort. Practically all transportation, commerce, and intercommunication were by water, by seagoing canoes. Aside from fishing and hunting, the men's chief occupation was woodworking.

The tribes of the Northwest Coast were Dionysian in their culture, like most American Indians—except those of the Southwest Pueblos. In their religious ceremonies, the aim was to achieve states of ecstasy. Their dancers would work themselves into frenzies, during which they lost all self-control and were capable of doing irreparable harm, unless severely restrained. Among the Kwakiutl, one group, the Cannibal Society, whose members had a passion for human flesh, outranked all others. The Cannibal would even attack onlookers and bite flesh from their arms. But unlike the cannibals of Africa and Oceania, the Kwakiutl abhorred the actual eating of human flesh, and the Cannibal spat out or voided that which he took into his mouth. Many weird customs and ceremonies were associated with the cannibalistic rituals.

Extensive possessions were held by the tribes of the Northwest Coast: areas of the land and sea, fishing territories, such material things as houseposts, spoons, and heraldic crests, and such immaterial possessions as names, myths, songs, and special privileges. The women made great quantities of mats, baskets, and cedar-bark blankets, while the men accumulated canoes and the shells, or "dentalia," used for money.

Other striking features of the Kwakiutl culture included the acquisition of status by marriage; that is, a man transferred his privileges to his son-in-law. Further prerogatives and property were bestowed upon the son-in-law upon the birth of children. Both secular and religious organizations existed; that is, the tribes were organized in lineages, and there were also societies with supernatural powers—the Cannibals, the Bears, the Fools, etc. Behavior was dominated at every point by attempts to demonstrate the greatness of the individual and the inferiority of his rivals.

The culture of the Northwest Coast, Ruth Benedict observes, "is recognized as abnormal in our civilization," but "the megalomaniac paranoid trend is a definite danger in our society." In further defense of her detailed analyses of all three societies dealt with in ***Patterns of Culture***, the author asserts:

> It is one of the philosophical justifications for the study of primitive peoples that the facts of simpler cultures may make clear social facts that are otherwise baffling and not open to demonstration. . . . The whole problem of the formation of the individual's habit-patterns under the influence of traditional custom can best be understood at the present time through the study of simpler peoples.

Elvin Hatch (essay date 1973)

SOURCE: "From Irrationality to Utility in Cultural Integration: Ruth Benedict," in *Theories of Man and Culture,* Columbia University Press, 1973, pp. 75-91.

[*Hatch is an American anthropologist. In the following essay, he analyzes Benedict's view of the relationship between individuals and their culture.*]

Victor Barnouw, one of Benedict's graduate students at Columbia, describes the impression she made on him then. "Like most of Ruth Benedict's students, I looked up to her with a mixture of veneration and bewilderment." He speaks of her "silvery aura of prestige, dignity, and charm." This aura was partially due to her remoteness. She was hard of hearing, shy, and frequently melancholy, and consequently she tended to remain aloof from people. But she was also a remarkably generous person, for she gave freely of both her time and money to friends and students who were in need.

Benedict was born in New York City in 1887. Her father, a surgeon, died when she was two years old, leaving her mother to support the family as a teacher and librarian. Because of a scholarship, however, Ruth and her sister were able to attend Vassar, and they graduated together in 1909.

Ruth taught school for two years after graduation, and in 1914 married a biochemist at the Cornell Medical College.

Benedict was restless before her marriage, and she apparently hoped that her husband and new home would bring an end to her discontentment. But the life of a housewife turned out to be quite unsuitable for her. She engaged in a variety of diversionary activities, including rhythmic dancing and social work. She even tried writing, especially poetry, an interest which she retained throughout her life. In 1919—still searching for a meaningful preoccupation—she began attending lectures in anthropology at the New School for Social Research in New York City. Anthropology met a response in her, and in 1921 she went to Columbia University to study under Franz Boas. She earned her Ph.D. the following year.

Benedict began teaching at Columbia after receiving her Ph.D., and she was untiring in the assistance she gave Boas in running the department. She continued in this role until Boas' retirement in 1937. During the war she went to Washington to work in the Office of War Information, conducting research on such strategically important peoples as the Japanese and Thai. After the war she returned to Columbia where she continued her research on large, complex societies. She died in 1948, after an eventful summer of traveling and teaching in Europe.

Benedict's culture concept may be summarized under two main headings: her ideas about integration, and about the *sui generis* nature of culture.

CULTURAL INTEGRATION. Not only are Benedict's views about integration the best-known features of her thought, they are also the most important elements of her theory, since, to her, cultural integration is the master concept for the analysis of cultural phenomena. In Benedict's mind just as in Boas', integration is the principal "creative force" behind culture; although a culture is the chance accumulation of so many "disparate elements fortuitously assembled from all directions by diffusion," the constituent elements are modified to form "a more or less consistent pattern of thought and action." Her emphasis is on the term consistent. She cites the example of Gothic architecture, which began as "hardly more than a preference for altitude and light," but which "by the operation of some canon of taste" developed into "the unique and homogeneous art of the thirteenth century."

> What was at first no more than a slight bias in local forms and techniques expressed itself more and more forcibly, integrated itself in more and more definite standards, and eventuated in Gothic art.

Like Boas, Benedict thought that the creative force of integration is located in the individual mind, and that it consists in the selection, rejection, and modification of culture traits by individuals according to the subjective standards of their culture. She never went into detail about the way in which integration takes place, but she did mention two mechanisms. First, each culture has its "favorite" or "most cherished" customs, such as the potlatch of the Northwest Coast Indians or the religious ceremonies of the Zuni. The individual tends to focus his attention on these customs and to elaborate them, and consequently they become the dominant features of the culture. Second, she held that some people by temperament find their culture more congenial than others. Those who fit their culture best are the most successful and tend to become influential. As a result, they leave a stronger impression on their culture than other people, and they tend to incline it even farther in the direction in which it is moving.

Implicit in her discussion is a distinction between two levels at which the process of integration operates: the level of culture traits on one hand, and the level of emotional patterning on the other.

Considering first the level of traits, Benedict emphasized again and again that culture elements occur in limitless combinations. In one society a particular culture element, such as an art form, may be incorporated into the religious system, whereas in another society the same trait may be redefined as a valuable commodity and become part of the system of economic exchange. "The possibilities are endless and the adjustments are often bizarre."

In addition, there is an infinite number of possible emphases in a culture, since any trait or complex of traits can become a focal point and then be "elaborated past belief." For example, the Todas of India have singled out their buffalo herds and have made them the focus of their lives. Their religious ritual is essentially a dairy ritual, the dairymen are priests, and the sacred cowbell is the holy of holies. The Australian aborigines have elaborated the restrictions of exogamy in unparalleled fashion. The Kurnai of Australia have such rigid marriage rules that it is typically impossible for a young man to find an acceptable bride, and as a result he has to elope, risking death at the hands of the pursuing villagers. The Kurnai, according to Benedict, "have extended and complicated a particular aspect of behavior until it is a social liability."

An important feature of Benedict's views about integration is that no two cultures are ever alike. The mode of integration of a culture is fortuitous, the product of the almost arbitrary and limitless recombination, reinterpretation, and elaboration of traits.

The view that cultural integration is fortuitous was the direct outgrowth of diffusion studies. When a trait is followed from one society to another it is patently evident that the trait *does* enter into different combinations, assume different forms, and receive different emphases; and these changes seem to follow no pattern. Benedict's Ph.D. thesis, published in 1923, is exemplary. She set out to test various theories about the origin of religion, hoping to determine if there were "some fixed causality which is at work" behind religious beliefs. She focused on a trait which was found almost universally among North American Indians, the concept of the guardian spirit. Her problem was to determine which of its features were stable, and therefore necessary or causal. She concluded that nothing was stable in this complex; there was "no coalescence" or combination of traits "which we may regard as being other than fortuitous." Rather, she found a "fluid recombination" or "desultory association" of culture traits. Among the Thompson River Indians the guardian spirit complex was intimately associated with male puberty rites, whereas among the Kwakiutl the guardian spirit was a hereditary caste mark which was highly valued as a private possession. On the Great Plains the guardian spirit concept "developed along still different lines," for the Plains Indians imposed no limitation on the sex or age of the recipient of a guardian spirit, and the vision was obtained through isolation, fasting, and self-torture.

The diffusionist perspective which Benedict employed in this study was the immediate result of her training under Boas. Mead notes that Benedict began her graduate work at Columbia at a time when Boas was still having his students trace the diffusion of traits from culture to culture, "showing the changes which the trait or the complex of traits underwent."

The second level at which Benedict viewed cultural integration was that of emotion. The search for cross-cultural uniformities seemed fruitless to her, because in her view the conclusions of these studies would all be negative. Consequently, after completing her Ph.D. thesis she turned away from comparative studies and toward the problem of integration. She began to seek an abstract framework that would make sense of the general patterns which seemed to pervade each culture; she sought "some integrating principle" by which to explain the unity of culture which "she felt was there (Mead)." In the summer of 1927 the idea which she sought finally came to her, and she set forth her theory during the late twenties and early thirties. Consistent with her Boasian background, she did not locate the organizing principle behind culture in the phenomenal world of environmental, economic, or social structural factors, but at the level of subjective thought. She hit upon the idea that the differences between cultures can be explained like the differences between people: like an individual, each culture tends to have a distinct temperament. "Cultures from this point of view are individual psychology thrown large upon the screen, given gigantic proportions and a long time span." Benedict called this integrating principle the cultural ethos or configuration.

Perhaps the best examples of Benedict's configurationalism are her analyses of the Pueblo and Plains Indians. Benedict characterized the Pueblo configuration as Apollonian; it stressed moderation and cooperation, and gave little or no place to excess, frenzy, and individualism. For example, the religious rituals of the Pueblos were meticulously regulated and organized and allowed little expression of emotion. The leader in Pueblo society almost had to be coerced into serving, because he was reluctant to set himself above and apart from his fellow community members. Benedict characterized the ethos of the Plains Indians as Dionysian. The individualism and emotional frenzy which the Pueblos virtually eliminated were capitalized upon by the Plains cultures. For example, a dominant feature of Plains Indian religion was the vision quest, which entailed self-torture, fasting, and emotional frenzy. Warfare was highly developed on the Plains; it was pursued aggressively and violently, and exploits in war were a means of attaining personal glory.

The integrating principle which Benedict hit upon—the cultural configuration—is essentially an *emotional* pattern: it consists of an emotional bent or attitude which in time tends to pervade a culture. The distinctive feature of the Dionysian ethos of the Plains was not simply a unique organization of traits, or the dominance of certain culture elements or activities. It was an emotional tone: intemperate, excessive individualism. Similarly, the Apollonian ethos of the Pueblos was the attitude of moderation, non-demonstrativeness, and group-orientation. It might be said that in searching for an integrating principle below the level of culture traits, Benedict simply pulled together two threads of Boas' thought: first, his view that one of the primary creative forces of culture is the tendency toward consistency within the subjective sphere, and second, his view that custom is at bottom emotional. Benedict's configuration is an emotional consistency in culture.

Although Boas and others recognized the role of emotion in human behavior long before Benedict began working in anthropology, she is to be credited with carrying this insight a step farther by emphasizing the need for a systematic and thorough understanding of the emotional level of cultural life. She noted that Americans are likely to misunderstand the Pueblo snake dance if they fail to grasp the "emotional background" of the performance. To the American, the snake dance elicits a feeling of repulsion and horror, but for the Pueblo Indian "the whole procedure is upon the level of a dance with eagles or with kittens." Benedict argued that in the usual ethnographic monograph the "emotional background" of custom is not provided. She stated that ethnographic descriptions "must include much that older fieldwork ignored, and without the relevant fieldwork all our propositions are pure romancing."

A distinguishing feature of Benedict's view of cultural integration at the level of traits is that each culture has a different pattern of organization. The same is true at the level of emotion, for she held that each configuration is unique. It follows that anthropology cannot be a comparative science and that there is little possibility of developing a general body of theory that will apply to all peoples. For example, a political theory that would be applicable to the temperate and cooperative Pueblos would hardly apply to the excessively individualistic Plains Indians.

Some hold that Benedict's views about the incommensurability of cultures represent a dead-end in anthropology:

> The difficulty with the assumption of "incommensurability" is that, if it is taken literally, scientific work becomes impossible. If two objects or events are truly incommensurable, then no further statements can be made about them in the same universe of discourse (Aberle).

However, it would be a mistake to think that Benedict's scheme lacks explanatory power. The key to both anthropological explanation and the meaning of human affairs, in her view, is the concept of integration:

> for there is no axiom of cultural study which is more clearly established than the fact that a whole array of familial, political, economic and religious institutions mutually condition one another and conversely are unintelligible when considered in isolation.

In Benedict's view, explanation amounts to showing the context of each trait, or how it fits within the total integrational pattern.

Benedict implicitly distinguished between two levels of integration, and accordingly there are two different contexts within which a cultural item can be viewed. First is the level of traits. The ceremonial system of the Toda is intelligible by reference to the cultural focus on buffalo herds; outside that context such features as the holy cowbell and the dairymen's role as priests are without meaning. Similarly, the practice of elopement among the Kurnai makes sense only when viewed in relation to the cultural focus on marriage regulations.

An even more important context to Benedict was that of the cultural configuration, since, to her, integration at the level of traits is governed largely by the principles contained at the level of emotion: for example, because of the cultural ethos of the Pueblo Indians, it would have been virtually inconceivable for them to have elaborated the warfare complex the way the Plains Indians did; and the emphasis placed on warfare by the Plains cultures was quite consistent with their emotional theme.

The explanatory potential of Benedict's configuration concept is particularly evident when applied to problems of culture history. Living near the Pueblo Indians were a number of Dionysian peoples who employed alcohol and drugs extensively in their religious ritual. The intoxicants and drugs were used to achieve a religious experience or vision. However, "none of these alcohol and drug-induced excitations have gained currency among the Pueblos," because hallucinatory religious experiences were uncongenial to the Pueblo configuration. Moreover, the Pueblo religious functionaries practiced fasting in connection with their ritual performances. The fast was not used to induce visions as it was on the Plains and elsewhere, however, but was simply "a requirement for ceremonial cleanness." This culture trait—fasting—had been modified and brought into conformity with the ethos of Pueblo society.

Benedict's configuration concept is an explanatory device in a nonhistorical sense as well, for it supplies the meaning of human affairs. To view a trait within its configurational context is to see it in terms of its emotional and attitudinal matrix, and integrational analysis therefore amounts to a form of subjective understanding. Customs and behavior which seem absurd from the outside become quite reasonable once the emotional pattern behind them is grasped. As ridiculous and inhumane as Plains warfare and self-torture seems to a Western European, these institutions make sense from the perspective of the emotional theme of Plains culture.

The singularity of this configurational form of subjective understanding is thrown into relief when contrasted with [E. B.] Tylor's mode of analysis. To Tylor, societies at different levels of evolution exhibit different degrees of reason, but the same standard of rationality is applicable to the institutions of all peoples. Like Boas, Benedict was tacitly proposing that reason is subordinate and in a sense epiphenomenal to emotion, for reason is thoroughly distorted by emotional bias. What appears to an American as an irrational, paranoid approach to life is perfectly reasonable given the emotional slant of Dobuan culture. The same standard of rationality does not apply to all peoples, and in order to grasp the reasoning behind foreign institutions the emotional context must first be understood.

An important implication of Benedict's integrational approach is that it precludes the study of cultural institutions outside their larger context. In considering this issue it is again useful to distinguish between the two levels of integration implicit in her work, and to consider the level of traits first.

One of the primary assumptions of [A. R.] Radcliffe-Brown's approach is that social structure constitutes a system which can be studied and understood in terms of its internal principles. For example, he analyzed the structure of lineage systems by reference to such principles as unilineal descent and the equivalence of siblings. He also assumed that a cultural emphasis or de-emphasis on such features as art, puberty rites, and even economic activities is not important for his analysis, and if he brought the issue of cultural foci into his account he did so in order to explain them in terms of the social structure and not vice versa. To Radcliffe-Brown, understanding is achieved largely by reference to the principles of social structure.

Benedict's position was that each sector of culture has to be viewed in the context of the whole, for each is part of the larger system of integration and is subject to the principles which govern the whole. The Toda emphasized and elaborated a particular feature of their economic life, and the social structure had to be viewed in that context. Benedict would say that it was the focus on buffalo herds rather than the principles of social structure which explained the organization of Toda society.

To Benedict, integration at the level of emotion is even more basic than that at the level of traits, and she believed that the configurational context is essential for anthropological analysis:

> The significant sociological unit . . . is not the institution but the cultural configuration. The studies of the family, of primitive economics, or of moral ideas need to be broken up into studies that emphasize the different configurations that in instance after instance have dominated these traits.

The implications of this point of view for anthropological studies can be illustrated again by reference to Radcliffe-Brown's social structural framework. A number of anthropologists have attempted to show that the ease and frequency of divorce in society is a function of structural arrangements—in other words, that the principles of social structure explain differences in divorce patterns. In a society with strongly matrilineal lineages the jural rights in a woman are divided between the woman's matrilineal kin and her husband; consequently, the marital relationship is relatively unstable and divorce is comparatively easy and frequent. In strongly patrilineal societies the jural rights in a married woman are vested primarily in her affinal kin, particularly her husband, and as a result divorce tends to be infrequent and difficult. To Benedict, it is not the social structure which explains divorce patterns, but the cultural configuration. Divorce was frequent and easy in Pueblo society, but not primarily because the villages were organized on the basis of strongly matrilineal kin groups. Rather, the Pueblo configuration stressed nondemonstrativeness and village-wide cooperation. There was little emphasis on institutions such as marriage and divorce which were "matters for the individual to attend to." Nor was there much room in Pueblo culture for jealousy, or for an emotional attachment between husband and wife "that refuses to accept dismissal": this was a culture in which institutions "effectively minimize the appearance of a violent emotion like jealousy." In short, marriage was easily dissolved because of the Apollonian ethos.

Benedict's rejection of the possibility that institutions can be understood outside their integrational contexts recalls a point made earlier, that Benedict's approach denies the feasibility of comparative studies. To her, the pattern of integration of each culture is incommensurate. Anthropology can attempt to understand the features of specific cultures, but each cultural system has to be accounted for by a separate body of theory.

THE SUI GENERIS NATURE OF CULTURE. To Benedict, culture is to be understood in terms of its internal principles, and these are relatively autonomous from outside influences. The autonomy of culture emerges as an issue in her work in two separate contexts: in her views about the relationship between culture and the environment on one hand, and between culture and personality on the other.

Some anthropologists view culture in terms of its utilitarian functions, emphasizing its role in accommodating man to his natural habitat. According to this perspective the most important cultural processes are those involved in the relationship between culture and the environment. For example, culture change is seen largely as a result of the progressive adaptation of the total system to local circumstances. To Benedict, however, it is the *sui generis* principles of cultural integration which hold the key to cultural dynamics, and culture change is essentially the progressive unfolding and application of these principles. Technology and cultural adaptation are like puberty rites, warfare, or social structure: they are features which can be emphasized and elaborated in one culture but virtually ignored in the next:

> In one society technology is unbelievably slighted even in those aspects of life which seem necessary to insure survival; in another, equally simple, technological achievements are complex and fitted with admirable nicety to the situation.

If the relationship between culture and environment is important in a particular society, it is so essentially by chance.

Benedict went yet farther, for she implied that the relationship between culture and habitat is frequently whimsical or even fantastic. She stated that, in elaborating the features of his culture, man "has a passion for extremes." Economic pursuits need not be directed toward providing the necessities of life at all, but "toward piling up in lavish display many times the necessary food supply of the people and allowing it to rot ostentatiously for pride's sake." The first menstruation of a young girl may involve "the redistribution of practically all the property of a tribe." The Plains Indians who received supernatural power through visions believed they were bullet-proof, and they went into battle convinced of their invulnerability. Benedict writes that in his social institutions

> Man can get by with a mammoth load of useless lumber. . . . After all, man has a fairly wide margin of safety, and he will not be forced to the wall even with a pitiful handicap.

To Benedict, culture is hardly utilitarian in nature, designed for man's benefit. One of the things that anthropologists have made up their minds about, she wrote, is that "it is usually beside the point to argue the social usefulness of a custom." Indeed, in Benedict's view custom is frequently disadvantageous or impractical; in this sense it is irrational. Benedict's thought was very much like Boas' on this issue.

Benedict's view of the impracticality of custom is illustrated by her analysis of the potlatch of the Kwakiutl Indians. She interpreted the potlatch by reference to the cultural configuration of the Northwest Coast, which she characterized as megalomaniacal because of its emphasis on self-glorification and on the bettering and shaming of rivals. The chief who gave the potlatch strove both to demonstrate his superiority by distributing or destroying as much property as possible, and to shame those he had invited by the generosity of his gifts. Although the institution was understandable from the perspective of the cultural configuration, it was wasteful and costly from the practical point of view.

The distinctiveness of Benedict's interpretation of the potlatch is highlighted when it is compared with some of the later studies. One of these suggests that the institution should be understood as an adaptive mechanism, a response to variations and fluctuations in food supply. According to this analysis, not only were there differences in food productivity between localities, but in addition all localities suffered periods of relative scarcity. The potlatch functioned to redistribute food and thereby to equalize its availability. The Kwakiutl drive to achieve prestige was necessary to keep the system operating, for it provided the motivation to ensure that the people participated; but it was not the reason for the existence of the potlatch.

The second context in which the *sui generis* nature of culture emerged as an issue in Benedict's thought was in her conception of the relationship between culture and personality. She held that culture is virtually autonomous from natural processes of thought, because the latter are highly circumscribed, almost obliterated, by culture. Benedict noted that as detailed descriptions of different peoples accumulated, anthropologists began to question the earlier ideas about "human nature"; what had been thought of as natural inclinations or reactions came to be interpreted as culturally determined responses:

> In some societies adolescence was a period of rebellion, of stress and strain; in some societies it was a period of calm, a time when one especially enjoyed oneself. In some societies men were violent and quarrelsome; in some, no voice was raised above its wonted key and no man was known in all their memory to have struck another. The list of contrasts was endless, and the conclusion could not be avoided: a great deal of what had ordinarily been regarded as due to "human nature" was, instead, culturally determined.

Thought is so thoroughly determined that the individual willingly follows the dictates of custom even when they go directly against reason or his own practical interests. Culture can make the Kwakiutl chief ambitious enough to waste his energy, time, and wealth on the potlatch, and it can make the Plains Indian truly believe that a hallucination makes him invulnerable to bullets.

The reason culture has such a powerful hold on man is because of its emotional foundations. The individual acquires such a strong emotional commitment to his customs and beliefs that it is virtually impossible for him to question them, let alone reject them:

> Even given the freest scope by their institutions, men are never inventive enough to make more than minute changes. From the point of view of an outsider the most radical innovations in any culture amount to no more than a minor revision, and it is commonplace that prophets have been put to death for the difference between Tweedledum and Tweedledee.

If the emotional features of the mind are so thoroughly affected by culture, then it follows that different cultures produce fundamentally different types of personality. Not only did the Plains Indians and Pueblos differ in their customs, but the people themselves were different. The Plains warrior or vision seeker was not merely playing a Dionysian role: he *was* Dionysian, and his customs fit him like a glove. His personality had been so thoroughly molded and reworked by his culture that it could almost be said that he was a different species of animal from the gentle and unassuming Pueblo villager.

A corollary of Benedict's emphasis on culture as a determinant of the personality is her view that the mind is a *tabula rasa* at birth. Either the natural, pre-cultural features of the personality are all but nonexistent, or they are so malleable that they are obliterated once the process of socialization is complete. Mead states that the *tabula rasa* assumption was only a working hypothesis for field research, and that if there are intrinsic principles or features of the mind which are not culturally determined, they should be discovered by comparative research. I think Benedict would have agreed. In fact, however, the *tabula rasa* assumption was more than a working hypothesis in Benedict's work, for it had a major effect on her interpretation of data. Her analysis of the Pueblo Indians is illustrative.

Studies of Pueblo culture are numerous, and they have been classified by Bennett into two broad categories. The first he calls the organic theories, for they emphasize "the organic wholeness" of Pueblo life. This interpretation regards Pueblo culture as a highly integrated system, exhibiting a set of harmonious and consistent values which pervade nearly all aspects of life. The organic theory holds that the Pueblo personality is one "which features the virtues of gentleness, non-aggression, cooperation, modesty, tranquillity, and so on." Benedict's analysis is organic in this sense. The other interpretation Benedict calls the repression theory, according to which Pueblo society is "marked by considerable *covert* tension, suspicion, anxiety, hostility, fear, and ambition." The culture is repressive and coercive, and the individual reacts to it with suppressed hostility.

Benedict relates this difference in interpretation to differences in value orientations held by the investigators. Those who adhere to the organic theory, she feels, "show a preference for homogeneous preliterate culture," whereas those who hold the repression view have "a fairly clear bias in the direction of equalitarian democracy and nonneurotic, 'free' behavior." This controversy may be seen from another perspective as well. Benedict's organic interpretation assumes that the personality more or less passively accepts the shape that is given it by culture. It assumes that since Pueblo culture is Apollonian, the individual is as well. In brief, it assumes that culture is the primary determinant of the personality. On the other hand, the repression theory does not regard the personality as so completely determined or transformed by culture as Benedict believed; the individual, caught in a stifling and repressive milieu, reacts or fights back.

Sidney W. Mintz (essay date 1981)

SOURCE: "Ruth Benedict," in *Totems and Teachers: Perspectives on the History of Anthropology,* edited by Sydel Silverman, Columbia University Press, 1981, pp. 141-70.

[*Mintz is an American anthropologist who has written extensively on the cultures of Caribbean countries. In the following essay, he examines the way in which Benedict's anthropological writings reflected her personal character and concerns.*]

Ruth Benedict, whom Margaret Mead described as "one of the first women to attain major stature as a social scientist," came to anthropology relatively late in life, in comparison with her contemporaries. She discovered anthropology only after a long search, and after having sought fulfillment in many other pursuits, only one of which—writing poetry—seems to have provided her with deep satisfaction. Having discovered anthropology, she was to become one of its most distinguished and distinctive practitioners. It is because certain of her unusual and highly original contributions now appear to have been forgotten or ignored that I will offer here what is only a narrow view of her scholarship.

Benedict was born in 1887, the older of the two daughters of Dr. and Mrs. Frederick S. Fulton. Her father died while she was still a baby, and only a few weeks before the birth of her sister. The girls' mother did not remarry, and grieved her loss unremittingly. The emotional qualities of her widowhood lay very heavily on the children, as did, it appears, the economic constraints it imposed. Reading Benedict's own words, quoted at length in Mead's two books about her, one gets the impression of a saddened, often dreary childhood, wherein the moments of happiness came most freely when the little girl could play by herself, and enjoy her own fantasies. She was partially deaf, due to a childhood illness; and Mead gives the impression that most people (including her mother) preferred her more cheerful younger sister, Margery.

Benedict went to Vassar College, where she studied English literature. After graduation she taught school, somewhat desultorily. In 1913, when she was 26, she affianced herself to Stanley Benedict, who is described as a promising young biochemist. The ensuing years, when she lived in a Westchester suburb and worked at being a good housewife, must have been barren and bleak. Mead's citations from Benedict's letters and journal document her attempts to keep up her spirits and to accept her role as a dutiful wife. But she was not happy. At some point she learned that she could not have children, at least not without what Mead calls "a very problematic operation," for which her husband would not give his consent. Though she finished her long-planned essay on Mary Wollstonecraft—a portion of an important work on women she had conceived earlier—it was rejected for publication. Only in her poetry did she manage some early success. There, she concealed her own identity with pen names until well into her anthropological career; and though poetry remained important throughout her life as a form of expression and as a basis for strong bonds of friendship, it never became enough to fulfill her wholly.

It was in 1919 that Benedict happened upon anthropology; she took courses at the New School for Social Research with Alexander Goldenweiser and Elsie Clews Parsons, and was deeply affected by what she began to learn from these two radically different teachers. At that time she had been married for five years; and while neither she nor her husband appears to have been ready to confess failure, their marriage by this time was merely standing still. As Benedict's interest in anthropology grew, her husband's interest in her life seems to have declined the more. Much stimulated by what she was learning, Benedict became Boas' student; he accepted her on Parsons' urging. With Boas' blessing, she completed her doctorate at Columbia in three semesters.

From the publication of her dissertation in 1923 until Boas' retirement in 1936, Benedict remained at his side almost uninterruptedly. After his retirement, she continued to play a key role—though it was often obscured—both at Columbia and in the profession at large. Her work won her an international reputation, especially after the publication of ***Patterns of Culture***. But she was not elected president of the American Anthropological Association until 1947-48; and it was only in July, 1948, that Columbia saw fit to bestow upon her a full professorship, in a shamefully tardy attempt to make up for its previous treatment of a great scholar. At that time, Benedict had been teaching at Columbia for twenty-six years, the final twelve of them as an associate professor. She died two months later.

During her lifetime, Benedict's work was the subject of many reviews and evaluations. After her death, Mead wrote two important biographies of her—startlingly different in emphasis and interpretation, it seems to me—and others have also taken Benedict as their subject. In the accounts that have been written of her, much has been made of the enigmatic qualities of her character and of the contradictory forces that appears to have governed her—such as the conflict of marriage and motherhood versus a career, and of poetry versus anthropology. I should like to suggest that these contradictory forces are to a large extent played out, enacted as it were, in Benedict's scientific work: not that she "solved" any of her personal conflicts by becoming an anthropologist, so much as that the kind of anthropology she did actualized those conflicts. My feeling is that in Ruth Benedict, as in few others, a consistency of character, of calling, and of theoretical conception can be identified. That is, her anthropology was, in some basic way, her own self embodied.

I will mention three themes of her work to illustrate what I mean. First, the concern with coherence. This reverberates in Benedict's work; she was, from her first papers onward, very sensitive to what looked like coherence or consistency within a cultural system. It would be fair to hazard a guess that Benedict liked it when it all fell into place, that she got aesthetic satisfaction out of closure in her descriptions of culture. Second is the concern with a dominant strain as the expression of that coherence. This reveals itself particularly in ***Patterns of Culture***. In Boas' slightly evasive introduction to the book, he indicates his feeling, much as Benedict does herself, that some societies reveal a coherence and a dominant strain, and others do not. I think her work shows that Benedict found it aesthetically more satisfying, intellectually more gratifying, to deal with cultures that could be summed up in rather limited, dense terms. The adjectival renderings that typify her descriptions of the three major cultures in ***Patterns of Culture*** express this notion of a dominant trend. Finally, and most surprising in view of her training, was Benedict's repeated reversion to the notions of choice—that societies, or cultures, choose some particular direction out of the great arc of human variability, that there is choice for them much as there is choice for individuals.

I suggest, then, that the search for cultural harmony of parts in a single system, the preference for those systems that seemed to her to manifest some single dominant theme, and above all the idea that peoples choose their cultures, get only one, and then sometimes lose it irrevocably—remember her phrase about the cup which is fashioned and the cup being broken—that these views embody the conflicted personality of their inventor and the particular life circumstances in which she found herself. One had the feeling with Dr. Benedict that beauty and calm, and tolerance and humor, and life itself, had been very dearly bought. How was that communicated? I have not the slightest idea. But as with no one else I have known, I had the sense that Ruth Benedict was a person who all along had made choices, and that the notion of making choices was immensely important to her as an integral personality.

I wish to touch on two aspects of Benedict's work, before referring briefly to her personal influence on me. The first has to do with Benedict's contribution to an anthropology of the immediate, the relevant, and—lest it be forgotten—the political; the second relates to Benedict's contributions to an anthropology of modern life, particularly through her efforts to study national states and cultures.

"In the 1930's," writes Mead, "Ruth Benedict often chafed at the amount of energy Boas devoted to 'good works' and lamented the time lost to research and writing. But as the Nazi crisis deepened in Europe and World War II approached, she who had so vigorously rejected such good works was in the end drawn into them." Because of her espousal of cultural relativism, Benedict has sometimes been thought to have been politically uncommitted or neutral. This is a misreading, I believe, of her ideas; nor did her cultural relativism mean she was politically naive.

In Ruth Benedict, as in few others, a consistency of character, of calling, and of theoretical conception can be identified. That is, her anthropology was, in some basic way, her own self embodied.

—Sidney W. Mintz

In his paper "American Anthropologists and American Society," Eric Wolf has elegantly described American anthropology of the period during which Benedict's work had its early impact: the faith in human malleability, seen as nearly infinite; the educational process as an Aladdin's lamp of progress; democratic pluralism as the American way; and an unconcern with power and its nature. I think Wolf 's argument is illuminating, persuasive, and generally accurate. But I don't think Benedict was at all unaware of, or unconcerned with, the nature of power. Indeed, I think both Benedict and Boas were well aware of the problem power posed, and I am not even sure that they were really guilty of an overgenerous optimism about such power, even if they sometimes may have seemed actuated by such optimism. Anthropology at Columbia clearly suffered because Boas was outspoken and willing to take controversial stands—much more would have come his way had he kept his mouth shut—and his colleagues and students suffered with him. Long before Benedict became an anthropologist, Boas had managed to make himself highly unpopular in the United States, particularly in connection with his views on World War I. As a German and a Jew, he was already suspect; the stands he took on war, peace, spies, and nationalism only made him more so. His stress upon the equal potentialities of different races; upon culture as the distinctive attainment of the human species as a whole; upon the difficult social and psychological position of nonwhite people in the United States; and upon other politically sensitive issues earned him the enduring enmity or hostility of many of his professional contemporaries. To a varying degree, his students suffered because of his courageous outspokenness. Some imaginatively enlarged the distance that separated them from his views; others merely ignored the positions he took. Benedict seems to have paid little attention to Boas' public political stance until long after she received her degree. But she emphatically did not seek to disassociate herself from him.

During the years of World War II, Benedict became actively involved in the winning of the war itself; the intellectual achievements of her later years are intimately connected to the war experience. Beyond the meaning to her of personal involvement in a crucial test of American survival, however, in her work and perhaps for the first time, Benedict grasped fully the profound political implications of anthropology. Many of us are, I believe, familiar with the principal limitations of the cultural relativism and pluralism which Benedict espoused and believed in; perhaps we should be equally aware of the very positive aspects of these perspectives.

To begin, Benedict devoted a substantial portion of her intellectual energies from 1940 onward to fighting racial prejudice. Those of us old enough to remember what the treatment of racial minorities in this country was like at that time (even if we cannot be consoled by the present) ought to be able to see why the positions taken by people such as Boas and Benedict were absolutely essential to change. Yet it will not be enough simply to yea-say their work. Some of Benedict's views are worth citing at length these days—which is to say, the days of Ardrey, Jensen, Schockley, and Herrnstein, not to mention DeFunis, Bakke, and Weber:

> Those who hope for better minority relations need to consider equally, when they think out their strategy, the assets as well as the liabilities. The greatest asset we have in the United States is the public policy of the state. This is not to say that our Federal government, our states, our police forces, and our courts have been blameless; of course they have not. But as compared with the grass-roots discriminations and segregations current in the United States, public policy has been a brake, and not an incentive. This would not necessarily be remarkable in a country run, for example, by a benevolent dictator, but in a democracy where the people have a voice in selecting their legislators and their judges, it is something to ponder. The correspondence between popular prejudices and state action has been far from being one-to-one. In states where opinion polls and strong labor unions and powerful industries have been against hiring men without regard to color or creed or national origin, it has still been possible to get Fair Employment Acts passed. In cities where there is a quota for Jewish students in privately endowed colleges, there is no quota for Jews in the tax-supported city colleges. When New York State Negroes protest today that private medical colleges are willing to train such a bare minimum of Negro doctors that the supply is totally inadequate, they unquestioningly propose a state medical college to remedy the situation. In areas where there are restrictive covenants and "Jim Crow" city blocks, city and Federal housing authorities have been able to insist upon and administer housing projects which havc both Negro and white tenants. Even in this present postwar year [1947] when the record of civil liberties has been deteriorating, Chicago ruled against a "lily-white" policy in its new veterans' homes, and when a mob attacked the houses let to Negroes, the largest police force Chicago had ever called out was stationed to protect them. In Gary, Indiana, when white school children and their parents struck against allowing Negroes in the schools, the mayor broke the strike by use of the tenancy laws and upheld the city's policy on nonsegregation. On October 30, President Truman accepted as "a charter of human freedom in our times" a strong report on civil liberties for minorities written by the Civil Rights Committee which he had "created with a feeling of urgency," and which recommended laws to end segregation, poll tax and lynchings, the enactment of permanent Fair Employment Acts and of statutes to prohibit Federal or state financial assistance to public or private agencies "permitting discrimination and segregation based on race, color, creed, or national origin."
>
> This state policy is of the utmost importance in the United States. Of course it cannot be fully implemented in a democracy where there is so much free-floating racial and ethnic prejudice. But the fact that public authorities take such stands, often in the face of public sentiment, is a remarkable fact. For the great crises of racial and ethnic persecution have occurred in all countries precisely when the government gave the green light. From the pogroms of Czarist Russia to the mass murder of Jews in Hitler Germany, the constant precondition was a favorable state policy. The government in power was following a policy of eliminating the minority or was at least allowing matters to take their own course without intervention. The importance of whether the state is on the side of racism or is against it is just as true in matters of discriminatory behavior as it is in pogroms and violence. In a democracy or a dictatorship the state can use law and the police to defend the rights of minorities or to abuse them. When by Federal or city ordinance or by industrial negotiation umpired by the state, a new and less prejudiced situation has become a *fait accompli,* even those who protested most actively against it while it was under consideration tend to accept the arrangement and to become accustomed to it. Certainly in the United States it seems clear that more can be accomplished by these means toward ameliorating the job and housing discriminations than by any amount of work by good-will organizations.
>
> This is not to say that informal, private, and nonlegislative efforts to improve social relations and eliminate prejudice are therefore unimportant. In a democracy laws and court decisions must have the backing of interested citizens, or they become dead letters. The ultimate goals of all who work for better race and ethnic relations can never be achieved merely by enforcing laws, which can forbid only the most blatant and overt acts of discrimination. No fiat has ever made any man over so that he can respect the human dignity of a Negro or a Jew if he has lived all his life in a community which acted on premises of white supremacy and anti-Semitism.
>
> Any strategy for lessening our national shame of race and ethnic discrimination before the eyes of the rest of the world must therefore value interracial meetings of the women's auxiliaries of a Massachusetts town, and the We-Are-All-

> Americans pageants of a Middle Western city. But unless people who participate in such activities see to it that their efforts feed into a demand for Federal and state and city action they are guilty of bad tactics. For it is clear that the state can be used in America as an asset in their endeavours, and if they overlook this they are neglecting a major resource.
>
> Such workers have often been too idealistic to join hands with politicians who want minority votes, but it is by such means that measures are put through in a democracy such as ours. If the powers that be are not moved to act for the good of the total community, perhaps they can be prevailed upon to court a substantial group of voters. And these voters may be able to press for enforcement also, thereby gaining first hand experience in the business of acting as American citizens.

I find it nothing less than remarkable that Benedict should have called attention more than thirty years ago to the fact that the most important force for the elimination of institutionalized racism in America was the United States Government. Perhaps this is obvious; but if it is, we all must be either disposed to forget it or to bury it beneath our catalogue of complaints about that same government. Heaven protect us from the good-will organizations—and I emphatically include here the elite private universities of our fair land, with their eloquent defenders of privilege—whose vaunted struggle against racism appears ultimately to hinge on the pressure, however feeble, to which they are subjected by governmental bodies. What seems, after all, to rise above the pronunciamentos, the indignant denials, and the litanies about quality are the triumphs of the United States Army, the United States Post Office, and the State Department—of all things!—in providing minority citizens with a fair opportunity to perform and to excel.

In 1943, Benedict and Gene Weltfish published the pamphlet entitled ***The Races of Mankind***, a delightful item of popular education, to the fate of which an anecdote is attached. This pamphlet set forth a familiar position: it declared that races—insofar as one could speak of such categories in dealing with humankind—were equal in their potentialities. Mead writes that the pamphlet was denounced in Congress as subversive, "mainly because of a tactical error committed in the writing, in stating baldly that some Northern Negroes had scored higher in intelligence tests than had some Southern whites." In this instance, as in others, Benedict's view turns out to have been very militant for its time, and depressingly apposite today. Who among us has been more outspoken on the issue of racism than she; who has done as much to use his or her professional stature to impel our country toward social justice?

While I believe these materials exemplify Benedict's scientific and political posture in the postwar years, I am struck when I recall now, in the retrospect of three decades, some of the commonly held opinions of the time: that her views were retrograde, unscientific, even irrelevant. Such negative opinions had to do in part, I believe, with the "psychological" determinism she was thought to espouse, and with the lack of congruence between her theoretical positions and the evolutionary and materialist perspectives then in the process of rehabilitation at Columbia University. I am certainly as sure now as I was then that her critics, including some of my friends and classmates, were missing the point; though just as certainly I often found myself in disagreement with her views. No one sought to gainsay Benedict's position on race; but I suspect many persons thought that the belaboring of such views was superfluous. If so, then surely Benedict was right, and we who thought otherwise were wrong—not only was she right in what she thought, but also in her conviction that it had better be said, loudly, clearly, and repeatedly. She is, plainly, still right.

This brings me to another aspect of Benedict's scholarship to which I wish to refer: the studies of national cultures and national character for which she was famous. Her work in this regard is of special interest to me because I was both her student and Julian Steward's. Both of these scholars were interested in the anthropological analysis of large-scale, complex modern societies; their approaches were radically different. Steward's approach was very much in the ascendant in the mid-forties, Benedict's was not. With her death in 1948, research of the kind for which she had fought, and of which she herself was surely the most distinguished practitioner, went into a sort of eclipse. In spite of some work by Mead and others consistent with Benedict's approach, national character studies along the lines Benedict advocated have only grown rarer over the years.

The scientific promise of such research still needs to be evaluated. But my purpose here is rather to point to an aspect of the intellectual history of the time. Both Steward and Benedict were trained in the particularistic study of small-scale, non-Western societies, within some broad Boasian outlook. Though they took markedly different directions in their research, their interests overlapped, sometimes surprisingly. For instance, Steward's doctoral dissertation was on the ceremonial buffoon in native North America; while Benedict's paper on property rights in bilateral societies (1936) was published in the same year that Steward's paper on primitive bands appeared in the Kroeber Festschrift. Their interests intersected, in other words—perhaps even more, at times, than either of them recognized or acknowledged.

Who among us has been more outspoken on the issue of racism than Ruth Benedict; who has done as much to use his or her professional stature to impel our country toward social justice?

—*Sidney W. Mintz*

Both of these scholars moved from the study of small-scale societies toward the problems posed by big ones, at or about the same time—in the postwar years. Steward's view was ecological and stratificational, emphasizing the environment, the means and relations of production, the organization of institutions, and the role of class, among other features. Benedict's view was configurational, thematic, and value-oriented; differences in values and attitudes were expected to occur both within and between sectors of the same society, but underlying, generally shared understandings were also thought to typify the society at large.

This is not the place to attempt to evaluate or compare these two radically different approaches. But it does seem appropriate—particularly since they have often been seen as mutually exclusive theoretically—to stress that some scholars have benefited from both views, and that time has left the similarity of intentions of Benedict and Steward honestly revealed. Both wished to transfer interpretive procedures from small, relatively homogeneous societies to large, class-divided societies. Both believed such societies might be analyzable in terms of fundamental value orientations. Both were interested in the practical or policy implications of their findings. To note these similarities does not diminish in any way the very important differences, both methodological and theoretical, between the Steward and Benedict approaches—nor should it.

But neither should the differences obscure similarities of intent, or of their aspirations for the future of the profession. The critics of Benedict and the critics of Steward were usually of different sorts; but often they espoused a kind of anthropology equidistant from the work of both of these scholars. On the one hand, Steward was ostensibly not (or no longer) interested in the real subject matter of anthropology (which is to say, "primitives"); and his interests showed a discomfiting concern with what was happening in the real world. On the other, Benedict similarly had supposedly lost her interest in so-called primitive peoples, and had become attracted by real-life problems. Worse, she thought peoples had underlying values or orientations that might not be explainable either by class or by ecology—thus managing to be heretical in even more ways than Steward. Though Steward's students continued to work along the lines he had developed—and, of course, he survived Benedict by more than two decades—other anthropologies became the wave of the future in the 1960s and 1970s. Neither Benedictian configurationism nor Stewardian ecology would lead the way in those decades, when it was becoming clear to some that the New Ethnography would soon solve all important anthropological problems. Boas and Benedict were not the only optimists, it seems. Today, it may still be worth-while to touch anew on Benedict's approach to the study of national cultures.

In that work, Benedict revivified concepts she had developed in the study of technically simpler societies, and gave them new meanings: the idea of coherence within one culture; the presence of some dominant strain or theme as the expression of that coherence; and the relationship between cultural "givens" and the culturally constrained evolution of personality. Readers of ***The Chrysanthemum and the Sword*** are unanimous in the opinion that this is Benedict's crowning achievement in the study of national cultures. There have been innumerable criticisms; but in the light of the methods Benedict had to employ to write the book, few scholars would gainsay the penetrating originality of her analysis. In the years following the publication of that book, Benedict continued to work on national cultures, and provided many graduate students and colleagues with the opportunity to join her in the research.

A short presentation to the New York Academy of Sciences, made the same year as the publication of ***Chrysanthemum***, provides as clear a statement as any of her research aims at the time. In it, she discusses the problems posed by a plentitude of information ("Vast quantities of material are a handicap only when the crucial problems to be investigated are not formulated"); the lack of homogeneity in modern nations ("The conditions do not mean that investigation must be abandoned. The solution is to multiply the number of investigations"); and class differentiation ("The trained anthropologist . . . has to present both parties as actors in a patterned situation. He can see it as a kind of see-saw, and by studying the height of the fulcrum and the length of the board [in the study of classes, laws about property and land, general conditions of social security, and the like], he can show either that the group on the high end of the see-saw is necessarily very far up and the group on the low end very far down, or that they are more nearly balanced"). Most important, it seems to me now, was Benedict's insistence on the study of culture as a way to explain. This may seem obvious to a new generation of scholars; but it is historically interesting to observe how many decades it has taken some of us to discover that understanding class does not obviate the study of culture, and that culture is not reducible to class, when all is said and done.

Her view of the values of a culture as underlying its surface manifestations, resonating in different institutions and providing thematic unity to overt diversity, has been criticized and defended with equivalent zeal. It seems to me that nothing is likely to convince the skeptics; in my own case, I have always been uncertain how Benedict's hypotheses might be tested. But her attempts to distill the value essence of a social group by identifying some core of beliefs, then to show us how those beliefs serve as the mortar of the cultural edifice, impress me all the same with their daring and penetration. I have been unable to find any citation for a remark she once made in passing about the relations between conquering and conquered peoples in the history of European imperialism. She said that she thought the English had always done well with martial and bellicose subjects, like the Masai, the Sikhs, the Maori, the Gurkhas, etc., while the Dutch had always done well with submissive subjects—while neither had ruled wisely those of opposing temperaments. I recall being struck by the observation (without being certain either that it was true or that it could be tested). What impressed me was that it seemed like a way of summing up a very great deal swiftly and neatly—and that it touched on a very important issue, one I had never heard or read a scholar observe upon before. Benedict's unusual gift of providing highly original cameo accounts of this sort, as well as her extraordinary sense of humor—the sense of humor of a great lady—were revealed to me first in her classes, and again in the teacher-student conferences I was privileged to have with her. But perhaps I will be excused for mentioning how I came to be a student of Benedict's.

My first encounter with her in the fall of 1946 was part of my own search for a profession or occupation that would feel worth doing. One has the impression that similar searches have become popular again—or, at least, that they were for a while following the end of the Vietnam War. Like so many of my classmates, recently discharged from the armed forces, I was seeking with some bewilderment a career having "something to do with" the study of society. I cannot now remember who first suggested to me that I attend a lecture by Benedict; but I remember the lecture well. She was describing the organization of several societies by means of analogies, and I recall her employing "hourglass" and "siphon" designs to dramatize indigenous structures of power for the collection and distribution of valuables. She talked about the *kula* and about *potlatch*—new words for me. (It was a year or two later before the precise images came back to mind, this being when I first heard a lecture by Karl Polanyi.) Benedict stood before us, tall, spare, seeming rather distant, her voice startlingly low and slightly hoarse, plainly dressed, her silver hair short and severe, what I judged to be her shyness heightened by the contrast between the penetration of her ideas and the somewhat absent gaze with which she regarded us. I was astonished by her, and by her lecture. It simply had never occurred to me before that a total culture might be looked upon as if it were a work of art, something to be coolly contemplated, something utterly unique and distinctive, yet available to be studied, analyzed, understood. That any teacher at that time in my life could have impelled me to think of Keats—when I had not so much as looked at a poem in five years—was wonder enough for me. I decided to become an anthropologist because I heard Ruth Benedict give a lecture. And that is about as close to the truth of it as I can come.

Benedict first asked to see me after I had written a short paper for her, comparing the Passover *seder* as it had been observed by my grandfather, my parents, and my siblings. I remember clearly sitting nervously before her, while she explained that she had enjoyed the paper. I made an inane remark about having wanted to make the paper less literary, and more scientific. She smiled and said only: "Oh, I have no objection to good writing!" I was, of course, grateful and very flattered. In the course of the subsequent year-and-a-half, I attended courses given by Benedict, received her advice, and was employed by her in her Research in Contemporary Cultures project. One of the sturdiest memories I have of those times is of her complete evenhandedness with her male and female students, even though we returning male veterans were quite thoughtlessly shouldering out of the way our female contemporaries. While there was—as I remember it—an anti-female bias among many of my male classmates that extended itself to Benedict, it was not reciprocated. Throughout, I recall Benedict as serene, generous and courteous—more so, certainly, than she needed to be.

I have been asked several times whether I can specify how Benedict's anthropology affected my own work, and I have been at a loss to answer, mainly because I never tried seriously to think about it. I think I know the answer now, at least in one particular regard.

In 1948, when Benedict died, I was in Puerto Rico as a member of a graduate student group which, under Julian Steward's direction and John Murra's supervision, was at work on the project Steward had initiated there. I had studied with Benedict in the period 1946-48; but my interest in Steward's perspective and the chance to do fieldwork abroad had led me away from Benedict's research. By the time that I had returned from the field and wrote my dissertation, I had begun to do a kind of anthropology that was heavily historical, with particular emphasis on the economic history of the plantation system, and the evolution of forms of labor. That emphasis emerged when I studied the Puerto Rican south coast community I had chosen in early 1948; in subsequent years, I became a Caribbean specialist.

In the summer of 1953, I returned to Puerto Rico to start a new fieldwork project, this time entirely on my own. My aim then was to record a single life history, but that of a person from the community I thought I already knew fairly well. I did not realize at the time—though I certainly do, now—how much my interest and my theoretical aims had been influenced, partly by my undergraduate training in psychology, but considerably more by the training I had received from Benedict. In her sensitive analytic movement from cultural standard to individual response and back again, Benedict made us aware of the dominant place of culture in the profile of the individual; but she never portrayed culture—nor, I believe, conceived of it—as some impersonal monster, some bloodless computer, "encoding" us, or pouring us into rigid molds. Because I knew Taso, my chief informant, well, long before our work on the life history began; because I spoke his language comfortably (if not fluently); because I knew his family, friends and neighbors, their work, the place they lived, and a fair amount about its past—for these and other reasons, I hoped that the life history we prepared together would be of a piece with the study of the community that had preceded it. That, at least, was my aim. My search for congruence, though, was not a search for harmony. Benedict's work makes clear that while individuals are certainly "products" of their cultures, they cannot take on their characteristically distinctive identity, while growing up, without strain and suffering. The relationship between culture and individual, then, is neither straightforward nor simple, and Benedict's nuanced view of how cultures work, in and through persons, had surely affected me profoundly. But while I worked with Taso, I had only the dimmest notion of the ways my teacher, the person who had by her words decided me to try to become an anthropologist, had given shape to my ideas, and inspired me to try to test them, years after her passing.

One of Benedict's last published works was her presidential address to the American Anthropological Association, **"Anthropology and the Humanities."** She argues here that anthropology, more than any other of the so-called "social sciences," stands at the boundary between science and the humanities, deems this not only proper but necessary, calls her own view "heretical," and concludes:

". . . once anthropologists include the mind of man in their subject matter, the methods of science and the methods of the humanities complement each other. Any commitment to methods which exclude either approach is self-defeating." In this late paper, Benedict waxes particularly eloquent on the illumination provided by fieldwork. She points out that "the humanities . . . were an intense cross-cultural experience . . . their aims were often couched in the same phrases as those of modern anthropological investigation of an alien culture." She argues that "the mind of man . . . man's emotions, his rationalizations, his symbolic structures" are commonly included in American anthropology's definitions of culture—and that this inclusion makes of the humanities anthropology's greatest resource. Her plea is emphatically not an attack on science; though it is perhaps worth mentioning that her science was much damned by some colleagues in the final years of her career as being "no more than" art.

Rereading her presidential address recently, I thought back to the life history I had attempted to record and to fit within what I understood of the history of a community, a region and a class. "For more than a decade," Benedict had written:

> anthropologists have agreed upon the value of the life history. Some have said that it was the essential tool in the study of a culture. Many life histories have been collected—many more have been published. Very little, however, has been done even with those which are published, and field workers who collected them have most often merely extracted in their topical monographs bits about marriage or ceremonies or livelihood which they obtained in life histories. The nature of the life history material made this largely inevitable, for I think anyone who has read great numbers of these autobiographies, published and unpublished, will agree that from eighty to ninety-five per cent of most of them are straight ethnographic reporting of culture. It is a time-consuming and repetitious way of obtaining straight ethnography, and if that is all they are to be used for, any field worker knows how to obtain such data more economically. The unique value of life histories lies in that fraction of the material which shows what repercussions the experiences of a man's life—either shared or idiosyncratic—have upon him as a human being molded in that environment. Such information, as it were, tests out a culture by showing its workings in the life of a carrier of that culture; we can watch in an individual case, in Bradley's words, "*what is,* seeing that so it happened and must have happened."

Benedict makes her point again—what she calls "the common ground which is shared by the humanities and by anthropology as soon as it includes the mind and behavior of men in its definition of culture." "But if we are to make our collected life histories count in anthropological theory and understanding," she writes:

> we have only one recourse: we must be willing and able to study them according to the best tradition of the humanities. None of the social sciences, not even psychology, has adequate models for such studies. The humanities have. If we are to use life histories for more than items of topical ethnology, we shall have to be willing to do the kind of job on them which has traditionally been done by the great humanists.

But this important plea for anthropology's crossroads does not forget what anthropology itself has to offer. In a prophetic reference, Benedict tells us:

> Only with a knowledge of what the current ideas were about ghosts and their communications with their descendants can one judge what Shakespeare was saying in *Hamlet*; one can understand Hamlet's relations with his mother only with an acquaintance with what incest was in Elizabethan times, and what it meant to contract "an o'erhasty marriage" where "funeral baked meats did coldly furnish the marriage tables".

It seems to me that Benedict's insights here about the relation between culture and individual were lessons I had begun to learn from her at an earlier time, quite without realizing it. What Geertz has referred to as "Zola's maxim that character is culture seen through a temperament" is a maxim that was well understood by Benedict, and one she sought repeatedly to teach.

In the three decades since her death, Ruth Benedict and her work have been overshadowed to some extent by the enormous proliferation of anthropologies and anthropologists. I believe that what she offered us, however, is still fresh and penetrating, for those of us willing to contemplate it. That she gloried in diversity seems less and less quaint, in a world the sameness of which grows ever grayer. That she underlined our common humanity seems less and less academic, in a world still so unsure of what makes us human, or whether we are unique. That she wanted an anthropology of modern life made her a pioneer of our profession. That she wanted social justice for all Americans, without regard to gender or race, makes her as modern as our times.

Judith Schachter Modell (essay date 1983)

SOURCE: *"Patterns of Culture,"* in *Ruth Benedict: Patterns of a Life,* University of Pennsylvania Press, 1983, pp. 184-215.

[*Modell is an American anthropologist. In the following excerpt from her biography of Benedict she discusses the themes in* Patterns of Culture *in relation to Benedict's life and times.*]

In ***Patterns of Culture*** Ruth Benedict focused on a topic with personal ramifications and a professional legitimacy; self and society was not a new topic for her or her discipline. She went beyond the self-is-nothing-without-society theorem and, though readers did not always notice, beyond a mere equivalence of personality and culture. Ruth claimed that individuals needed society for their very individuality and that societies needed individualities in order to survive, adjust to crisis, and change.

Ruth also had a particular idea about how to present these

points. In proper anthropological fashion, her fieldwork experiences gave her a clue. She applied a Zuñi concept of "the ideal man" to her discussion of self and society and in the process substantiated her notion of "pattern."

Through their "ideal," Zuñi Indians perpetuated a standard of individual behavior. The standard reflected cultural values and became a vehicle for transmitting pattern from society to individuals. Ruth Benedict borrowed the idea to express connections between individual and culture without attributing cause or direction. She avoided Reo Fortune's occasional emphasis on institutional causes (overall, the two anthropologists agreed remarkably, perhaps with Margaret Mead's help). She also avoided an implication that individual (or personality) simply reflected culture, the person being only a blotter for cultural expectations.

"The ideal man in Zuñi is a person of dignity and affability who has never tried to lead, and who has never called forth comment from his neighbours." The Zuñi ideal man reiterated the culture pattern. The Dobuans, too, told of their ideal man, and Fortune wrote: "In other words the desirable man is he who has sought and gained the dangerous values unhurt by the black art of his rivals." And the Kwakiutl, never to be outdone, recreated an ideal man for future ethnographers: "You knew my father, and you know what he did with his property. He was reckless and did not care what he did. . . . He was a true chief among the Koskimo."

These are the protagonists of ***Patterns of Culture***. The three figures are not biographical subjects; rather, they represent personality types, embodying the "type" of the culture. Much as she relished her "heroes," Ruth in fact kept biography out of ethnography, in regard to persons if not to approach. She was not interested in particular personalities when she drafted ***Patterns of Culture*** and, with notable restraint, did not describe any of the people she met in the Pueblos. She wrote about the ideal person Nick and Flora recognized and, presumably, valued. Or maybe not Nick. According to Elsie Clews Parsons and other Southwest ethnographers, Nick embodied antithetical traits and was by no means the typical mild and unambitious Zuñi. Nick succeeded, thanks to visiting anthropologists and a last-minute rescue from the punishment due a witch, anyone who, like him, contradicted Zuñi prized virtues. Nick was exceptional. According to Ruth Benedict, usually the individual who most closely approximated the "ideal" succeeded in his or her setting. This congenial individual expressed in behavior and beliefs the dominant values of his culture. The congenial individual also won prestige and material rewards. Ruth added an important point: the accommodating and successful individual could effectively modify existing patterns. Here, however, she raised a problem and postponed discussion until her last two, nonethnographic chapters.

For Ruth Benedict individuality was a matter of expression, and the "ideal man" set boundaries for the expression of self in a society. Every culture provided channels for expression, in action and in gesture, channels that were both limiting and releasing. Ruth also included in her account the possibility of individuals for whom provided channels were not adequate or satisfactory or possible at all. The conventional forms of expression had to allow for the emotional as well as the intellectual impulses of human beings. Thus, Ruth returned to an old preoccupation, a fascination with the forces of irrationality in every society. That was her theme in "Animism" and in coincidental reviews of Lévy-Bruhl.

"The death of a near relative is the closest thrust that existence deals." Death tests the ability of a culture to handle profound individual emotions and to restore to a group its order. Ruth Benedict had picked a subject whose resonance to her life would not be noticed under the traditional attention given death customs in anthropology.

Death and mourning rituals dramatized the emotional content of an individual-culture link. Rituals, especially, highlighted the significance of conventionalized, formulaic expressions for individual grief. "Prayer in Zuñi is never an outpouring of the human heart. . . . And the prayers are never remarkable for their intensity. They are always mild and ceremonious in form." Ruth knew the value of structured expression for relieving agony; she also knew that individuals might be variously attuned to conventional patterns. Death, the supreme crisis for individual and society, was faced and handled uniquely by every person and every culture.

The Dobuan reacted to death with malice and vengeance. "Dobu in Dr. Fortune's words, 'cower under a death as under a whipping,' and look about immediately for a victim . . . the person to charge with one's fatal illness. On the Northwest Coast the Kwakiutl pitches his will against death: "Death was the paramount affront they recognized." The Zuñi individual hardly mourned and minimally acknowledged grief. The typical Zuñi accepted death calmly, expressed sadness only with others, resigned to that as to everything in life.

Ruth's conviction that individual "terrors" can be brought to bay within formal conventions and available traditions colored her middle three chapters. A reader remembers the Zuñi rhythmically scattering black cornmeal, the Dobuan locating and punishing the inevitable killer, and the Kwakiutl burning his house in arrogant protest against death. Through such vignettes the anthropologist reiterated but did not dissect the links between an individual and his culture. The artist in ***Patterns of Culture*** exploited the stylistic potential: Death comes near the end of each chapter.

Death provided a further lesson in the book. During her fieldwork Ruth Benedict asked the Zuñi about suicide and to her amazement found that no one recognized the idea. Even more startling, the Zuñi did not seem to require an idea of self-destruction: "They have no idea what it could be." (This point, among others, elicited severe criticism; anthropologists who objected to Ruth's approach stressed the violence in Zuñi life, toward oneself and others.) The Dobuan killed himself and the Kwakiutl did, each in characteristic fashion. In suicide, each carried out the themes of living. Absorbed by these contrasts, Ruth made a crucial suggestion: a culture pattern may entirely exclude certain attitudes and behaviors so that, not on the "segment," these do not even negatively affect individuals. Told of suicide, the Zuñi listened politely, then laughed.

There would always be in all cultures individuals unable to take the available channels: the suicide in Norwich (an act condemned by Ruth Fulton's grandparents and praised in books she read), the bitterly weeping Zuñi, the gently grieving Dobuan. And such individuals "have all the problems of the aberrant everywhere." There were always people who did not fit.

"Cultures in which these abnormals function at ease and with honor"

"Just as those are favoured whose congenial responses are closest to that behaviour which characterizes their society, so those are disoriented whose congenial responses fall in that arc of behaviour which is not capitalized by their culture. These abnormals are those who are not supported by the institutions of their civilizations." Ruth Benedict's phrases in the last chapter of ***Patterns of Culture*** have an intensity and poignancy revealing a more than disciplinary interest in her subject. Her protagonist in chapter 8 is the "disoriented" person whose "characteristic reactions are denied validity" and who faces a "chasm between them and the cultural pattern." She had long mulled over the problem of normal and abnormal, and she published an article nearly simultaneously with ***Patterns of Culture*, "Anthropology and the Abnormal."**

The last two chapters of ***Patterns of Culture*** focus on the individual in society. In her conclusions, Ruth not only completed the logic of the previous six chapters but introduced ideas and approaches central to her subsequent work and to the work of anthropologists from 1934 to the present. In these chapters, too, she revealed the grounds of her commitment to ethnographic inquiry. She asked how far an individual might depart from expected standards of behavior and of temperament without being ostracized, tortured, driven insane. In answering the question, Ruth Benedict embarked on a comparative evaluation of cultures in terms of permitted variations.

Ruth Benedict accommodated her "social engineering" to the ideas of John Dewey, to progressivism, and to a liberal-humanism that recalled Matthew Arnold and the nineteenth century. Social engineering, in her view, operated through the individual and through the individual's enlightened attitudes toward himself and—inseparably—toward his society.

—Judith Schachter Modell

She phrased the dilemma as one of creativity versus congeniality. Her book illustrated the dynamic quality of individual encounters with culture, the constant "creating" necessary to cultural survival. The self, Ruth knew, strained against conventions while depending on these for making sense of experience. The challenge was to accept convention yet fully realize self-integrity. "But no anthropologist with a background of experience of other cultures has ever believed that individuals were automatons, mechanically carrying out the decrees of their civilization." Being congenial, she said, did not mean conforming into self-obliterating passivity. Individuals do not drown in "an overpowering ocean" of custom, although every action, every decision, every intimate mood is colored by custom. A culture, she said, can be intricately patterned without submerging the component individualities. In a more venturesome vein, Ruth Benedict hinted that the intricately patterned culture might show the greatest tolerance for diversity.

The "passionately thought," not very disguised message of the book was that in other places, in other times, being congenial had other meanings. This was the hinge of a multiple-stranded argument. Ruth wrote her book and the article to controvert assumptions of "natural" human behavior, universal "personality types," and permanency of customs. In the process she showed how branding a "type" unnatural could lead to madness, neurosis, irreconcilable conflict.

Sexual and religious experiences were her prime examples for the varying definitions of normal and abnormal from society to society. One can speculate on the private impulses behind these publicly expedient choices. Sex and sexual behavior were popular topics in the 1920s, and Ruth never denied her desire for a wide audience.

> When the homosexual response is regarded as a perversion, however, the invert is immediately exposed to all the conflicts to which aberrants are always exposed. His guilt, his sense of inadequacy, his failures, are consequences of the disrepute which social tradition visits upon him, and few people can achieve a satisfactory life unsupported by the standards of their society. The adjustments that society demands of them would strain any man's vitality.

Society, not biology, produces the "aberrant" individual, frail and "useless to society." Ruth's version of culture-over-nature went with another point: culture can be changed.

Religious trance was her other example. "Trance is a similar [to homosexuality] abnormality in our society." Like the homosexual, according to Ruth Benedict the religious mystic had been branded "abnormal" and *therefore* became "neurotic and psychotic." With religion, she had chosen another biographically weighted subject to bolster her case for an enlightened, sensitive, and respectful social psychiatry.

For the moment, however (and this shifted over the next ten years), Ruth concerned herself less with cross-cultural psychiatry than with the intolerance of "abnormal" and marginal individuals which she detected in American society.

"He is an arid and suspicious fellow"

The force of custom (i.e., culture) had a positive side.

Throughout ***Patterns of Culture***, Ruth Benedict attempted to persuade readers of the possibilities and the mechanisms for changing the conditions under which they lived. Customs, she argued, are historical, arbitrary, and controllable. Her efforts had a personal motivation: "I can't swallow the solution in Plato's Republic," she had written more than ten years earlier. And the translation of mysticism into the approved channel of poetry no longer satisfied her. Anne Singleton expressed "visions" for a while; by 1930 the woman and writer reached for a wider audience, a more public statement. Ruth Benedict spoke about diverse societies to her own complex, and she thought constricted, society.

Exactly because of the personal motive and because Ruth was a persistently private person, she couched her pleas for change under the general rubric of "social engineering." The concept, if controversial, also struck a familiar chord for professional and lay readers of the time.

Ruth Benedict accommodated her "social engineering" to the ideas of John Dewey, to progressivism, and to a liberal-humanism that recalled Matthew Arnold and the nineteenth century. Social engineering, in her view, operated through the individual and through the individual's enlightened attitudes toward himself and—inseparably—toward his society. A teacher all her life, Ruth knew how attitudes should be changed. Offered the "right kind" of information, an individual would naturally take it upon himself or herself to alter a perspective, to expand horizons and rearrange circumstances. In ***Patterns of Culture*** Ruth presented the "right" information in ethnographic portraits that were unmistakable reflections of her own society. Experience convinced her that knowing self was a result of continuing contrast and comparison.

Ruth Benedict chose the Dobuan and Kwakiutl cultures because, she told Mead, she could talk to their ethnographers. She also chose the two cultures because each echoed American society in a particular way. That echo constituted another aspect of her comparative approach; differences cannot be so great as to make unrecognizable the alternative ways of meeting basic human needs.

[In her novel *The Waves*] Virginia Woolf composed a central persona from the reflections of six other characters; their voices created the "arid and suspicious fellow," Percival. Ruth similarly drew American culture from the images and reflections of three other cultures. She described the Dobuans so they sounded like American Puritans: stingy, prudish, suspicious—in a word, paranoiac. The Kwakiutl, in many ways the most vivid figure in ***Patterns of Culture***, resembled a side of American character that Ruth Benedict inclined toward while acknowledging her own stronger puritanical streak. The ebullient Kwakiutl stood for a spirit of greed, accumulation, confidence, encompassing ego—the megalomaniac trend in American society and the foundation of American "free enterprise." Like Walt Whitman, whose ebullient and greedy poetry Ruth admired, the Kwakiutl risked his pride to embrace experience, and Ruth envied the "ecstasy." She wrote of Whitman's "unwavering, ringing belief that the ME . . . is of untold worth and importance."

The Zuñi represented a potential, a goal for the culture built on the schizophrenic traits of puritanism and expansiveness. Ruth perceived in Pueblo life an ideal, a reference for America's future. She did not envision Utopia in the Pueblos; she emphasized traits out of which her contemporaries might create a better way at home. Nor did she recreate a portrait of herself in "The Pueblos of New Mexico" (really "The Zuñis of New Mexico"). Ruth admired the Pueblo design and did not hesitate to convey her admiration. But she did not read into the Pueblos her own "ideal virtues"; rather, she stressed in Pueblo life examples for careful melioration in American society.

The portraits resulting from the author's determination to open her readers' eyes onto themselves might be (often are) called one-dimensional. The portraits are not "flat." Ruth Benedict vividly and emphatically presented each unique type and, as vividly, an unmistakable contrast. She summarized her intentions for Houghton Mifflin:

> She has chosen three strongly contrasting primitive cultures, and described them in all their customs, from the way they plant their yams, or divorce their husbands, or go headhunting at death, as well-knit and internally consistent attitudes toward life. The details of their behavior have great intrinsic interest because of their striking character.

She expected, too, that her readers ordinarily saw the world in such sharp characterizations. Ruth was not far off; through a parade of epic figures from Puritan divines and witch-burners, through Paul Bunyan and Jesse James, to the Babbits of her own century, Americans realized their culture values in personality types. Ruth brought to her discipline a common-sense perception, and articulation, of culture pattern through individual type.

She chose the Dobu, Kwakiutl, and Zuñi cultures carefully, and equally carefully a vocabulary that would be immediately evocative—as recognizable as Paul Bunyan and Lewis Babbitt. Nietzsche's words bordered on the esoteric, but Ruth found his phrasings overwhelmingly persuasive. "The basic contrast between the Pueblos and the other cultures of North America is the contrast that is named and described by Nietzsche in his studies of Greek tragedy," she wrote, and happily included several quotations. She knew his contrast "on her pulses" as well as intellectually.

One December 3, probably 1930 (a diarist remembers the year), Ruth Benedict wrote:

> By the time I was eight I knew what Dionysian experience was, I had had to take account of fury, an experience that swept over me from somewhere outside my control—as I figured [?]—, lifted me like a tornado and dropped me limp at the end. But I'd also got also [sic] by that time my great response to this violence, and it was disgust. After a periodic scene I was likely to vomit. . . .

And she went on, in an extraordinarily Dionysian vein.

Disgust at excessive gestures and uncontrolled responses turned Ruth toward the Apollonian—the remembered calm of her dead father's face. She herself rarely achieved a "true" Apollonian attitude; she insisted upon the "moderation and measure" in Zuñi society almost in compensation. Zuñi culture did "objectify" a version of Ruth's dream, an order of life she admired. But she did not make up the Zuñi or imagine the relentless regularity and controlled ceremonialism. Before and since, visitors to the Pueblo have described these qualities, and if Ruth focused on ritualized expressions because of resonance to her private perceptions she also did so out of professional ambitiousness. Competing with colleagues, she wanted her book to achieve a unique standing.

The material available on Pueblo Indians when Ruth wrote seemed either so full of detail or so narrowly analytic as to obscure any sense of what these people were truly like. Ruth recreated the personality of Pueblo culture, an identifiable and integral entity that was perfectly distinct from her own culture and objectively distinct from her private values.

In many ways, in fact, the Dionysian more than the Apollonian "mirrored" the author. Dionysian objectified Ruth's wishes and suggested a strongly compelling motive of her life and her career. The Dionysian appeared mainly in poetry and in journals, and then insistently. "There is only one problem in life: that fire upon our flesh shall burn as a knife that cuts to the bone, and joy strip us like a naked blade."

The non-Nietzschean terms, paranoiac and megalomaniac, are farther from Ruth's private mode of interpretation. She expected her readers to recognize the popularized Freudian terms and from these form a lasting impression of Dobuan and Kwakiutl cultures. Ruth Benedict presented her protagonists so they would stick in her readers' minds. "People need to be told in words of two syllables what contrasting cultures mean," she told Reo Fortune. By "need" she referred to her ameliorative aim; with eyes opened to diverse constructs of life, people would engineer, reconstruct, the design of their own lives.

If Ruth thought her readers needed two-syllable words and graphic descriptions, she also had faith that these readers would become "the culture-conscious," the aware and self-critical individuals she trusted to change American society and (perhaps) the world.

"Men are never inventive enough to make more than minute changes"

Ruth Benedict wrote for an America over the "zesty" optimism of the 1920s and ready for the suspicious, stingy, tight-belted atmosphere of a depressed economy. Given the impending economic crisis, her Zuñi example takes on special meaning, an alternative to Dobuan malicious possessiveness and to Kwakiutl "conspicuous consumption." Zuñi culture also offered an alternative to the Marxism embraced by several friends and colleagues.

In the chapter titled "The Pueblos of New Mexico" the anthropologist made a statement about social policy, grounded in a liberal-progressive humanism. Ruth counted on individuals to move from envisioning to engineering alternatives. In her book the Zuñi are a persuasive alternative, a lesson in cooperativeness and harmony of interests that is hard to resist. But Ruth did not impose her lesson. From teaching she knew that a chosen lesson was a lasting one; she only tried to make the choice inevitable. With the Zuñi she described a culture of proportion and fairness where no one starved and no one was judged by property or power. She also described a culture sure of itself and well-enough integrated to avoid being destroyed by a dominant white culture.

"The Pueblos of New Mexico" bore a substantial burden. The chapter demonstrated the rightness of aspects of Zuñi culture and presented a set of images that would make agreement with the author powerfully "logical." But chapter 4 was one version of a many-sided argument, directed to a range of readers. Ruth Benedict did write a pedagogical anthropology; she thought of her discipline in terms of an audience to be instructed—the individuals "in the street" who, startled into awareness, worked toward an improved society. "Where else could any trait come from except from the behaviour of a man or a woman or a child?"

This belief in the power of every human being to recreate, repeatedly, the terms of existence underlay Ruth's humanism and her anthropological approach. Her faith in individualized and revisionary change prompted her support of New Deal policies and a hope that Franklin Roosevelt would prove congenial to American culture, spokesman for "dominant motives," and therefore an effective innovator. But she postponed discussion of these and other political issues until after her book was safely published and out, in bookstores all over the country. "Even Macy in this city does not have the book in stock, as every person I know who ordered one has waited ten days to have the order filled."

Ruth Benedict had constructed, implicitly, another heroic personage: the informed, creative individual who, understanding patterns, successfully altered surroundings. In the face of leaders like Hitler and Mussolini—men who seemed "congenial" to their cultures and times—Ruth even more strenuously counted on "common people" and "sanely directed change." Books like hers *had* to sell, and she made no effort to hide from friends and editors her intense desire that ***Patterns of Culture*** sell and sell widely. Her concern led to discussions of title, jacket color, and price, as well as to several revisions of publicity blurbs. At Houghton Mifflin, Ferris Greenslet patiently answered urgent and irritable letters.

The title took considerable time and thought, Ruth not knowing that the phrase she settled on would be ineradicably associated with her name. She did not pick "patterns" right away. "I've turned over titles and titles. I want the title of the book to clearly indicate that my competence is in anthropology, nothing else. That is, I don't want any psychologizing title. I shall suggest 'Primitive Peoples: An Introduction to Cultural Types.' " This August 1932 version nearly implied an equivalence: the isomorphism of "peoples" and "cultural types" Ruth tried to avoid in the text of the book. The links between "peoples" and "types" are part of the book and are implied finally by "patterns."

The early version may well have sounded pompous and pedantic. Ruth insisted upon the accessibility of her material, a priority as strong as that she be thought competent in anthropology; she had to keep both professional and popular audiences in mind.

> I have turned over in my mind some fifty titles for the book, and I find I have the strongest possible preference for a title as exact as possible under the circumstances. . . . Would you consider "Patterns of Culture"? "Patterns" has been used in the sense I have in mind and it is besides a pleasant English word.

Years earlier the "crowd" at Columbia had talked about "patterns." A small group of Boas students discussed patterns of behavior, of personality, of everyday interactions—an array of arrangements and habits both inter- and intrapersonal that reflected and confirmed the dominant values of culture. The word "pattern" stood for the ordering of a culture and the patterning in individual lives. Ruth and her friends added the "patterning" of words, in poetry and (with less enthusiasm by Ruth) in language itself: the creating of a coherent and comprehensible statement. They added process to stasis, and Ruth's word referred not just to "shape" but to "shaping."

Ruth considered several words more or less synonymous with pattern, especially "integrity" and "configuration"—or if not synonymous at least filling out the connotations of "pattern." For her book, it seems clear from letters, pattern had the special attraction of being a commonsense word with a strong link to poetry and art. Unlike the "configuration" of her 1932 article, pattern evoked responses that, she hoped, would carry without laboring a complex argument. Common-sense understandings of the word do clarify the anthropological meaning and to some extent relieved Ruth from having precisely to define her word. (Others later took up and all-too-thoroughly disputed the definitional issue.)

She meant by "pattern" what most people mean, a formal arrangement based on a theme or tendency. Theme can be considered interchangeable with propensity and motive; the Apollonian motive is a theme of Pueblo culture. Around a theme, pieces fall into place over time. The existing pattern determines the quality and structure of internal elements and, as well, the incorporation of new traits. Grammar and vocabulary come to mind, but Ruth Benedict preferred to relate her word to psychology and poetry. "A culture, like an individual, is a more or less consistent pattern of thought and action. Within each culture there come into being characteristic purposes not necessarily shared by other types of society." These frequently quoted sentences might be rephrased: the integrity of a culture and of an individual lies in the "unfolding" of pattern according to dominant tendencies, over time and uniquely—Ruth did not slight the biographical and historical past tense of a present constellation.

Patterning referred to culture and to personality at once. This way Ruth suggested a mutually creative connection and a similarity in type between culture and person. She did not explain the connection in ***Patterns of Culture***, except to say that individual character and actions followed culture patterns, and that the individual with more awareness of patterning could change himself and his surroundings. Ruth Benedict dealt in implications and assumptions; personal patterns reiterated culture patterns in content (what they were) and in form (how they came about and worked). Pattern also recalled Ruth's claim that individual personalities fit cultural types while retaining an idiosyncratic response, the distinctiveness of component pieces without which there could be no pattern. Again common sense illuminates the anthropological point.

Most broadly, Ruth Benedict talked about an aesthetic dimension in human life. She talked about the yearnings for order and the satisfactions in a coherent and selective presentation. She had appreciated the comprehensibility and strengths of a well-constructed statement. She applied similar standards to a person (who did not chafe against cultural expectations yet maintained self-integrity), to a poem (which used traditional forms to express innovative perceptions), and to a culture. Underlying all these judgments was Ruth's belief in the importance of making sense of existence and arranging—often wonderfully—the natural and supernatural forces that impinged upon any "living."

Poetic references were not accidental. In 1934 Reo Fortune, prompted by Margaret Mead, asked Ruth whether she had borrowed "patterns" from Amy Lowell's poem of that name. "I walk down the patterned garden path / In my stiff brocaded gown. / With my powdered hair and jewelled fan, / I too am a rare pattern. . . . " In her lines, Lowell conveyed a message about boundaries and taming and the end of desire that Ruth must have understood personally, whatever she thought critically. Edward Sapir disliked the poem: " 'Patterns' is piffle, like much of Amy's work," he told Robert Lowie in 1917. Ruth undoubtedly knew Amy Lowell's poetry. Whether she considered "Patterns" to be "piffle" is not known, nor is her answer to Fortune's question. One can only guess at her memories when she chose "pattern" for the book. Aesthetic connotations did influence her decision, whatever their source.

The aesthetic introduced an ethical dimension. Ruth consistently and self-consciously used the word "integrity"; she implied in pattern a kind of "truthfulness" of being, honesty in a sound arrangement. For Ruth the scattered and haphazard culture seemed not "neurotic" (as critics said) but literally of less integrity (one remembers Sapir's "genuine and spurious"). She drew this insight from her experiences—her dislike of the "random"—and in subsequent years refined notions of "soundness" in person, in culture, and in relationships between the two. She retained, as well, the cross-cultural perspective of chapter 8, making untenable any absolute definition of the "well-integrated" personality and any fixed definition of the ideal environment for personal development. (The consequences of varying cultural tolerances for diversity became a major focus of her later writings.)

"Pattern," then, had not been lightly chosen. The word contained a wealth of meanings, some outlined and some merely hinted at in the 1934 book. Ruth apparently liked the encompassing and connotative quality of the word.

Supplementing the common-sense and the poetic references, the word also referred to her ongoing self-interpretations. "It is curious to see how the basic patterns of our life hold from babyhood to decrepitude." Ruth eventually settled on "pattern" with a feeling of satisfaction; she kept the word for her 1946 book on Japanese culture.

The title stood out nicely on the turquoise-blue jacket, a color achieved after some negotiation. "The color of the back-strip paster I should much prefer in some more saturated color," she wrote to "My dear Mr. Greenslet" in June 1934; "this seems too light a turquoise, and difficult to read the printing on it in the bookcase. I am clipping onto this letter a slip of paper that seems to be more nearly the right tone." She wanted a bright Southwestern turquoise. She had other demands. The spelling should be British, not American. . . . , the price should be as low as possible. . . . And she asked about distribution. "I have received another letter from California saying that my books are not available there. This letter is from a person very used to purchasing books in Southern California. . . . " The publicity should be precise: she was an anthropologist, a present, "not *former*" (her emphasis), editor of the *Journal of American Folk-Lore,* "Mrs." not "Miss" Benedict. When asked, however, to write a brief biographical sketch, she withdrew. "Be a darling and do this for me," she scrawled across a letter from Greenslet and sent it to Margaret Mead.

Mead may have done the favor. She did publicize the book, in conversations, reviews, and comments. Her reviews acknowledged the dual audience Ruth projected. Mead praised ***Patterns of Culture*** for contributing to anthropological theory and method as well as for determining the contours of everyday thought. Acutely, Margaret Mead recognized that readers of ***Patterns of Culture*** would make "culture a household word," and use the concept in their daily conversations. These were the "Macy shoppers," the ordinary men and women who, according to Ruth Benedict, created a culture. Other anthropologists wrote favorable reviews—and Boas a guardedly pleased, short introduction. Some colleagues dismissed the book entirely, as poetry not social science. Few, even those most positive about the book, tried to do what Mead did not merge the "poetic," imaginative content with the anthropological argument of the book. Kroeber came the closest, since he like Mead understood the "impressions" not as fluff but as essential to the logic of ***Patterns of Culture***. He praised the book, in a remarkably apt if awkward phrase, for its "quality of distinctive, almost passionately felt, balanced thinking precisely expressed."

Lively debate about the book lasted for well over ten years. Ruth's colleagues seemed unable to let go of ***Patterns of Culture***, picking at its thesis, doubting the accuracy of ethnographic accounts, questioning the woman's method and her role in anthropological thought, and probably above all envying the style and success of the book. One of the most popular anthropology books of the twentieth century, Ruth's ***Patterns of Culture*** inspired more than small twinges of envy and rivalry. Readers throughout the world remember the Zuñi, the Dobu Islander, the Kwakiutl Indian, if not the revision of the "functional approach" or the argument about cross-cultural psychiatry. Readers remember the distinct contrasts and the vivid possibilities for arranging human life, if not a "comparative method" or the meaning of "typology" in Ruth Benedict's book. Finally, too, readers of ***Patterns of Culture*** must recognize that an existing state of affairs is neither permanent nor perfect nor inevitable.

Patterns of Culture established an intellectual attitude and conveyed an optimism about the ability of individuals to change their lives—a lesson from the author's life and badly needed in the 1930s. Ruth Benedict transmitted a powerful principle through the concrete data of her cross-cultural examples. The book, perhaps, conveyed more optimism than the author felt.

Clifford Geertz (essay date 1988)

SOURCE: "Us/Not-Us: Benedict's Travels," in *Works and Lives: The Anthropologist as Author,* Stanford University Press, 1988, pp. 102-28.

[*Geertz is an American anthropologist whose numerous works focus on the cultures of Indonesian countries and reflect a method of study that combines various disciplines—including history, philosophy, psychology, and literary criticism—to analyze cultural structures and phenomena. Describing himself as an "interpretive social scientist," he is considered one of the most important figures in contemporary anthropology. In the following essay, Geertz examines Benedict's prose style, beginning with a passage from her essay "The Uses of Cannibalism."*]

> We have done scant justice to the reasonableness of cannibalism. There are in fact so many and such excellent motives possible to it that mankind has never been able to fit all of them into one universal scheme, and has accordingly contrived various diverse and contradictory systems the better to display its virtues.
>
> The present decade, indeed, is likely to appreciate to an unusual degree the advantages that attach to cannibalism so soon as the matter may be presented. We have already had recourse to many quaint primitive customs our fathers believed outmoded by the progress of mankind. We have watched the dependence of great nations upon the old device of the pogrom. We have seen the rise of demagogues, and even in those countries we consider lost in a morally dangerous idealism we have watched death dealt out to those who harbor the mildest private opinions. Even in our own country we have come to the point of shooting in the back that familiar harmless annoyance, the strike picketer. It is strange that we have overlooked cannibalism.
>
> Mankind has for many thousands of years conducted experiments in the eating of human flesh, and has not found it wanting. Especially it has been proved to foster the feeling of solidarity within the group and of antipathy toward the alien, providing an incomparable means of gratifying with deep emotion the hatred of one's

enemy. Indeed, all the noblest emotions have been found not only compatible with it, but reinforced by its practice. It would appear that we have rediscovered that specific and sovereign remedy for which we have long perceived statesmen to be groping. . . .

It is necessary first to place beyond doubt the high moral sentiments with which the custom has been allied. It has been unfortunate that in our solicitude lest heroism, endurance, and self-control should perish from a world so largely devoted to commerce and the pursuit of wealth, we should have overlooked the matter of cannibalism. Certain valiant tribes of the Great Lakes and the prairies long ago made use of it to this purpose. It was to them their supreme gesture of homage to human excellence. It is told by old travelers that of three enemies whose death made the occasion for such a celebration of their valor, two were eaten with honor, while the one remaining was passed over untouched. For at death, this one had marked himself a coward, and cried out under torture. . . .

This is of course not the only excellent ethical use to which cannibalism has been put among the peoples of the world. There are tribes to whom it is an expression of tenderness to the most nearly related dead so as to dispose of their discarded bodies—a supreme cherishing of those for whom there can be no other remaining act of tenderness. . . .

Cannibalism has proved also to be extraordinarily well qualified to provide the excitement of an ultimate aggression. This has proved recently to be by no means the frivolous subject that it may appear. Indeed we have been confronted by the problem on such a large scale that, in the interests of progress, it is difficult not to press the matter. Without the infantile ostentations and unfortunate appeals to the hatred of one's fellow being which characterize our Black Shirts and our Red Shirts, the Indians of Vancouver Island found a heightened excitation, disciplined in endless ritual and taboo, in a ceremonial show of cannibalism. . . . When it was time for [an aristocrat] to become a member of [a secret] society, he retired to the forests or the graveyard, and it was said that the spirits had taken him. Here an almost mummified corpse was prepared and smoked, and at the appointed time, in the midst of great excitement, the noble youth returned to the village with the Spirit of the Cannibal upon him. A member of the society carried the corpse before him, while with violent rhythms and trembling of his tense body, he rendered in dance his seeking for human flesh. He was held by his neck-ring that he might not attack the people, and he uttered a terrible reiterated cannibal cry. But when he had bitten the corpse, the ecstasy left him, and he was "tamed." . . .

It is obvious that nothing could be more harmless to the community; one useless body per year satisfactorily satisfied the craving for violence which we have clumsily supplied in modern times in the form of oaths, blood-and-thunder, and vows to undertake the death of industrious households. . . .

All these uses of cannibalism are, however, of small moment in comparison [to] . . . its service in the cause of patriotism. Nothing, we are well aware, will so hold in check the hostile elements of a nation as a common purpose of revenge. This may be raised to a high degree of utility by various well-known phrases and figures of oratory which picture our determination to "drink the blood of our enemies." It has however been held essential that we pursue this end by the death, in great numbers and with distressing tortures, of young men in sound health and vigor. Nothing could show more lamentably our ignorance of previous human experiments. It is this aspect of cannibalism that has appealed most widely to the human species; it has enabled them to derive the most intense emotional satisfaction from the death, even the accidental death, of one solitary enemy, allowing them to taste revenge in a thoroughgoing and convincing manner, ministering to their faith in his extirpation, root and branch, body and soul. . . .

The Maoris of New Zealand [for example] before the feast, took from their enemies the exquisitely tattooed heads which were their incomparable pride, and setting them on posts about them, taunted them after this fashion:

"You thought to flee, ha? But my power overtook you.
You were cooked; you were made food for my mouth.
Where is your father? He is cooked.
Where is your brother? He is eaten.
Where is your wife? There she sits, a wife for me!"

No one who is familiar with the breakdown of emotional satisfaction in warfare as it is recorded in postwar literature of our time can fail to see in all this a hopeful device for the reestablishment of an emotional complex which shows every sign of disintegration among us. It is obvious that something must be done, and no suggestion seems more hopeful than this drawn from the Maoris of New Zealand.

The serviceability of cannibalism is therefore well established. In view of the fact that ends now so widely sought in modern war and its aftermaths can thus be attained by the comparatively innocent method of cannibalism, is it not desirable that we consider seriously the possibility of substituting the one for the other before we become involved in another national propaganda? Our well-proved methods of publicity give us a new assurance in the adoption even of unfamiliar programs; where we might at one time well have doubted the possibility of popularizing a practice so unused, we can now venture more boldly. While there is yet time, shall we not choose deliberately between war and cannibalism?

This modest proposal, written about 1925 when Ruth Benedict was, though nearing 40, at the very beginning of her career, and published only out of her *Nachlass* by (who else?) Margaret Mead more than a quarter of a century later, displays the defining characteristics of virtually all her prose: passion, distance, directness, and a relentlessness so complete as to very nearly match that of the giant who is here her model. She did not have Swift's wit, nor the furor of his hatred, and, her cases before her, she did not need his inventiveness. But she had his fixity of purpose and its severity as well.

This vein of iron in Benedict's work, the determined candor of her style, has not, I think, always been sufficiently appreciated. In part, this is perhaps because she was a woman, and women, even professional women, have not been thought inclined to the mordant (though the example of that other Vassarite, Mary McCarthy, might have worked against such an idea). In part it is perhaps a result of the fact that she wrote a fair amount of rather soft-focus lyric poetry and tended to begin and end her works with onward and upward sermons somewhat discontinuous with what the body of the work actually conveyed. And perhaps most of all it has been a result of a conflation of her with the larger-than-life Mead—her student, friend, colleague, and in the end custodian ("proprietor" might be a better term) of her reputation—from whom she could hardly be, on the page, more unlike. But whatever the reason, Benedict's temper, as both her followers and her critics for the most part conceive it—intuitive, gauzy, sanguine, and romantic—is at odds with that displayed in her texts.

The connection with Swift, and beyond him with that highly special mode of social critique of which he is in English the acknowledged master, rests on more than this particular piece of self-conscious impersonation, which may have been written as much to blow off steam as anything else. It rests on Benedict's use, over and over again, from the beginning of her career to its end, and virtually to the exclusion of any other, of the rhetorical strategy upon which that mode of critique centrally depends: the juxtaposition of the all-too-familiar and the wildly exotic in such a way that they change places. In her work as in Swift's (and that of others who have worked in this tradition—Montesquieu, Veblen, Erving Goffman, and a fair number of novelists), the culturally at hand is made odd and arbitrary, the culturally distant, logical and straightforward. Our own forms of life become strange customs of a strange people: those in some far-off land, real or imagined, become expectable behavior given the circumstances. There confounds Here. The Not-us (or Not-U.S.) unnerves the Us.

This strategy of portraying the alien as the familiar with the signs changed is most often referred to as satire. But the term is at once too broad and too narrow. Too broad, because there are other sorts of literary mockery—Martial's, Molière's and James Thurber's. Too narrow, because neither derision nor extravagant humor is necessarily involved. Every so often there is a sardonic remark, very dry and very quiet—"[Zuni] folktales always relate of good men their unwillingness to take office—though they always take it." "Why voluntarily hang yourself from hooks or concentrate on your navel, or never spend your capital?" But the pervading tone in Benedict's works is one of high seriousness and no ridicule at all. Her style is indeed comedic, in the sense that its purpose is the subversion of human pretension, and its attitude is worldly; but it is so in a deadly earnest way. Her ironies are all sincere.

The intrinsically humorous effects that arise from conjoining the beliefs and practices of one's most immediate readers to those of African witches and Indian medicine men (or, as our excerpt shows, of cannibals) are indeed very great; so great that Benedict's success in suppressing them in the works that made her famous, ***Patterns of Culture*** and ***The Chrysanthemum and the Sword***, both of which are organized from beginning to end in a look-unto-ourselves-as-we-would-look-unto-others manner, is the foundation of her achievement as an author-writer "founder of discursivity." "Self-nativising," to invent a general term for this sort of thing, produces cultural horselaughter so naturally and so easily, and has been so consistently thus used, from "Des cannibales," *Lettres persanes,* and *Candide* to *The Mikado, The Theory of the Leisure Class,* and *Henderson the Rain King* (to say nothing of intramural japes like Horace Miner's "Body Ritual Among the Nacirema," or Thomas Gladwin's "Latency and the Equine Subconscious"), that it seems built into the very thing itself. To get it out so as to change parody into portraiture, social sarcasm into moral pleading, as Benedict did, is to work very much against the tropological grain.

It is also to perfect a genre, edificatory ethnography, anthropology designed to improve, that is normally botched either by moral posturing (as in *The Mountain People* [by C. Turnbull]), by exaggerated self-consciousness (as in *New Lives for Old* [by Margaret Mead]), or by ideological *parti pris* (as in *The Moral Basis of a Backward Society* [by E. Banfield]). The reality of Zuni equanimity or Japanese shamefacedness aside, issues by now pretty well moot, this is a remarkable accomplishment. But what is even more remarkable, it is an accomplishment that arises not out of field work, of which Benedict did little and that indifferent, nor out of systematic theorizing, in which she was scarcely interested. It arises almost entirely out of the development of a powerful expository style at once spare, assured, lapidary, and above all resolute: definite views, definitely expressed. "[A] wood-cut page from an old 15th century Book of Hours," she wrote in her journal, perhaps sometime in the 1920's, "with its honest limitation to the nature of the wood it worked in, can give us a quality of pleasure which the superfluous craftsmanship of [the late nineteenth, early twentieth century white-line wood engraver] Timothy Cole can never touch. And a dozen lines of an etching by Rembrandt, each line bitten visibly into the metal, conjures up a joy and a sense of finality that the whole 19th century does not communicate."

So with words.

So indeed, when words, like wood and metal, are there to begin with. Benedict's style, as she herself as a professional anthropologist, was born adult. It was already in being, more or less in perfected form, in the early specialized studies through which she earned her, once it began, extraordinarily rapid entry to the discipline—and to the institutional center of it, Columbia's commanding heights, at that. The later works, upon which her wider reputation rests, the first published at 47, the second at 59, two years before her death, simply deploy it on a larger scale in a grander manner.

It had, of course, a kind of prehistory in her college writing, in some abortive fragments of feminist biography quickly abandoned when she turned to anthropology, and (though the nature of its relevance is normally misconceived) in her poetry. But as ethnography, her style was invariant from beginning to end: incised lines, bitten with finality.

From 1922:

> The Indians of the Plains share with the tribes to the east and west an inordinate pursuit of the vision. Even certain highly formalized conceptions relating to it are found on the Atlantic Coast and on the Pacific. Thus, in spite of all diversity of local rulings, the approach to the vision was, or might always be, through isolation and self-mortification. More formally still, the vision, over immense territories, ran by a formula according to which some animal or bird or voice appeared to the suppliant and talked with him, describing the power he bestowed on him, and giving him songs, mementoes, taboos, and perhaps involved ceremonial procedure. Henceforth for this individual this thing that had thus spoken with him at this time became his "guardian spirit."

From 1934:

> The Zuni are a ceremonious people, a people who value sobriety and inoffensiveness above all other virtues. Their interest is centered upon the rich and complex ceremonial life. Their cults of the masked gods, of healing, of the sun, of the sacred fetishes, of war, of the dead, are formal and established bodies of ritual with priestly officials and calendric observances. No field of activity competes with ritual for foremost place in their attention.

From 1946:

> Any attempt to understand the Japanese must begin with their version of what it means to "take one's proper station." Their reliance upon order and hierarchy and our faith in freedom and equality are poles apart and it is hard for us to give hierarchy its just due as a possible social mechanism. Japan's confidence in hierarchy is basic in her whole notion of man's relation to the State and it is only by describing some of their national institutions like the family, the State, religious and economic life that it is possible for us to understand their view of life.

Whatever this sort of writing is, it is all of a piece: the same thing said and resaid until it seems either as undeniable as the laws of motion or as cooked up as a lawyer's brief; only the examples change. This hedgehog air of hers of being a truth-teller with only one truth to tell, but that one fundamental—the Plains Indians are ecstatic, the Zuni are ceremonious, the Japanese are hierarchical (and we are, always, otherwise)—is what so divides Benedict's professional readers into those who regard her work as magisterial and those who find it monomaniac. It is also what brought her such an enormous popular audience. Unlike Mead, who achieved a somewhat similar result with a loose-limbed, improvisational style, saying seventeen things at once and marvelously adaptable to the passing thought, white-line curlicuing if ever there was such, Benedict found herself a public by sticking determinedly to the point.

The work in which this unlikely meeting of an aesthetic mind, rather at odds with the world around it, and a pragmatic mass audience, casting about for useful knowledge, first occurred is, of course, ***Patterns of Culture***. Brief, vivid, and superbly organized, the book, which has sold nearly two million copies in more than two dozen languages, clearly struck a chord, rang a bell, and sent a message. The right text at the right time.

The literary form of the work is at once so simple, so compact, and so sharply outlined, that it has proved more or less impossible even for those most maddened by it ever to forget it. A conjunction of a triadic descriptive scheme (three wildly contrasting tribal cultures), a dichotomous conceptual typology (two drastically opposed sorts of human temperament), and a unitary governing metaphor (alternative life-ways selected from a universal "arc" of available possibilities), its composition could hardly be more elementary, its structure more overt. Like *Travels into Several Remote Nations of the World* (though that was in four parts, and had Proportion for a metaphor), it stays in the mind.

Benedict's Houyhnhnms, Brobdingnagians, and Yahoos—the Zuni, the Kwakiutl, and the Dobu—provide a frame for her text that is not so much narrational (plotted tales imposing an explanatory logic on a train of events) as presentational (thematic set-pieces imposing a moral coloration on a system of practices). ***Patterns of Culture*** was not written to be cited. No one goes to it, and I doubt anyone ever much did, despite the overheated "Is it really so?" debates which arose around it, to settle factual issues about Pueblo, Northwest Coast, or Melanesian social life. (Two of her three cases were, of course, unconnected with any field research of hers. And even in the one with respect to which she did have some firsthand knowledge, she was not, given the highly circumscribed nature of her Zuni work, herself an important source of the material she reviewed.) Benedict trafficked, not only here but just about everywhere in her work, not in description (there is virtually nothing, folktales aside, of which she is the primary recorder) but in a distinctive sort of redescription: the sort that startles. Her real-life Luggnaggs and Lilliputs are, like the fictional ones, primarily meant to disconcert.

And so they surely do, either because they reproach us as the Zuni do (Why can we not be thus cooperative?), caricature us as the Kwakiutl do (Is not gaining status by setting fire to slaves but conspicuous waste writ conspicuously large?), or accuse us as the Dobu do (Do we not, too, half believe that "the good man, the successful man, is he who has cheated another of his place"?). The whole enterprise, three chapters absolutely crammed with detailed material of the most curious sort—Zuni passage rites, Kwakiutl chants, Dobu residence arrangements—has the air, the same one that remorseless descriptions of Blefuscu judicial procedures or Laputian linguistics have, of being concerned with something else, and somewhere else, rather closer to home. The whole thing is done with a progression of pointed contrasts in which the constant opposing term, the one that is pointed at, is—a reminding allusion now and then aside—eloquently absent. Not mere allegory, deep meanings secreted within Aesopean fables, but negative-space writing. What is there, bold and definite, constructs what isn't: our cannibal face.

Around this dominant trope—extravagant otherness as self-critique, we have met the Not-us and they are not-Us—are gathered, in the five short thesis-driving chapters that bracket the three long ethnographic ones, the more obvious and more mechanical Apollonian/Dionysian and arc-of-selection images. They are supposed, these clanking metaphors, to make the point fully explicit. But it is one of the ironies that haunt Benedict's work, along with the misassimilation of it to that of Mead and the misconception of it as documentational, that they have served in the event mainly to obscure it. Sometimes, less *is* more. Trying too hard to be clear, as someone who had been a poet ought to have known, can dim an argument best left oblique.

Benedict's Apollonian/Dionysian contrast—"[He who] keeps the middle of the road, stays within the known map" vs. "[He who] seeks to . . . escape from the bounds imposed on him by his five senses, to break through into another order of experience"—is taken, of course, though not with much else, from Nietzsche's *The Birth of Tragedy*. The arc-of-selection metaphor is taken, also with not much else, from phonology—"In cultural life as it is in speech, selection [from the inventory of physically available possibilities] is the prime necessity"—and capsulated in the famous Digger Indian proverb that serves as epigraph to the book: "In the beginning God gave to every people a cup of clay and from this cup they drank their life." Between them, these two figures, the one of temperamental extremes, radically incommensurable, the other of a range of choices, mutually exclusive, are designed to rescue the ethnographic material from its radical particularity; to make what is singular in its description general in its implications. Science through poetry—the study of "primitive civilizations" is to be the foundation for an analysis of culture as exact as biology:

> The understanding we need of our own cultural processes can most economically be arrived at by a détour. When the historical relations of human beings and their immediate forbears in the animal kingdom were too involved to use in establishing the fact of biological evolution, Darwin made use instead of the structure of beetles, and the process, which in the complex physical organization of the human is confused, in the simpler material was transparent in its cogency. It is the same in the study of cultural mechanisms. We need all the enlightenment we can obtain from the study of thought and behavior as it is organized in the less complicated groups.

This sorting out of beetles (a surprising image for a scholar so humanistically oriented to choose) leads however not to a narrativist representation of cultural variation of the sort one would expect from an anthropological Darwin, a historical story with a scientific plot, but to an attempt to construct a catalog of genres, cultural kinds appropriately named. Benedict is not really after "processes" or "mechanisms" (nor—some generalized remarks, more hortatory than analytical, about "integration" and "abnormality" aside—does she offer any); rather she seeks, once again, ways of making difference tell. The problem is that, in promising otherwise, she seems to have insured herself of being understood as testing out a theory when what she really was doing (and knew that she was doing) was pressing home a critique: "The recognition of cultural relativity," the famous—or infamous—last paragraph of the book runs,

> carries with it its own values. . . . It challenges customary opinions and causes those who have been bred to them acute discomfort. It rouses pessimism because it throws old formulae into confusion. . . . [But as] soon as the new opinion is embraced as customary belief, it will be another trusted bulwark of the good life. We shall arrive then at a more realistic social faith, accepting as grounds of hope and as new bases for tolerance the coexisting and equally valid patterns of life which mankind has created for itself from the raw materials of existence.

That someone so intent to disturb should so represent herself as engaged in constructing a *table raisonnée* of human possibilities is mainly to be accounted for by the intellectual environment in which she worked, but to which, coming late and with a metaphorical turn of mind, she never quite properly belonged. Between the wars, the conception of anthropology as uniquely positioned to find out the essentials of social life that are disguised or covered over in complex, modern societies reached perhaps its greatest peak, though it of course existed before in Durkheim (*"les formes élémentaires"*) and has hung on after in Lévi-Strauss (*"les structures élémentaires"*). Franz Boas, Paul Radin, Robert Lowie, Margaret Mead, and Edward Sapir in the United States, Bronislaw Malinowski, A. R. Radcliffe-Brown, A. C. Haddon, and C. C. Seligman in Britain all shared it and the image of primitive societies as "natural laboratories," anthropology's Galapagos, that went with it. But it fits ill with the view of such societies as funhouse mirrorings—this one elongated, that one squashed, the other twisted—of our own that was at the imaginative center of Benedict's sensibility.

The attempt to be (or anyway to look like) a "real scientist," as that beatifical state was then conceived, is what led to the two-bucket typology, the curveless arc, and to that disastrous final sentence about "equally valid patterns of life," which, as Elgin Williams pointed out years ago, contradicts everything that is conveyed by the substance of the book. In time, she at least half realized this and pulled herself free of methodological conceits she did not believe to produce (one unfortunate—and again, unfortunately memorable—chapter aside) the book most surely her own, and, though it has sold "only" 350,000 copies, the most certainly lasting: ***The Chrysanthemum and the Sword***.

The great originality of Benedict's book *The Chrysanthemum and the Sword* (which had its genesis, of course, in her intelligence and propaganda work during the war) and the basis of its force, a force even its severest critics have felt, lies in the fact that she does not seek to unriddle Japan and the Japanese by moderating this sense of an oddly made world populated by oddly wired people, but by accentuating it.

—Clifford Geertz

The Western Imagination, to the degree one can talk intelligibly about such a vast and elusive entity at all, has tended to construct rather different representations for itself of the otherness of others as it has come into practical contact with one or another sort of them. Africa, the Heart of Darkness: tom-toms, witchcraft, unspeakable rites. Asia, the Decaying Mansion: effete brahmins, corrupt mandarins, dissolute emirs. Aboriginal Australia, Oceania, and in part the Americas, Humanity *degré zéro:* ur-kinship, ur-religion, ur-science, and the origins of incest. But Japan, about the last such elsewhere located, or anyway penetrated, has been for us more absolutely otherwise. It has been the Impossible Object. An enormous something, trim, intricate, and madly busy, that, like an Escher drawing, fails to compute. From *Madama Butterfly* and *Kokoro* to *Pacific Overtures* and *L'Empire des signes,* the country (the only real place, save of course for England, that appears as more than a reference point in *Gulliver's Travels*) has looked not just distant but off the map: "a funny place." "The Japanese," Benedict's book opens, "[are] the most alien enemy the United States [has] ever fought"—a challenge not just to our power, but to our powers of comprehension. "Conventions of war which Western nations had come to accept as a fact of human nature obviously did not exist for the Japanese. [This] made the war in the Pacific more than a series of landings on island beaches, more than an unsurpassed problem of logistics. It made it a major problem in the nature of the enemy. We had to understand their behavior in order to cope with it."

The great originality of Benedict's book (which had its genesis, of course, in her intelligence and propaganda work during the war) and the basis of its force, a force even its severest critics have felt, lies in the fact that she does not seek to unriddle Japan and the Japanese by moderating this sense of an oddly made world populated by oddly wired people, but by accentuating it. The habit of contrasting an "as-we-know" us with an "imagine-that" them is here carried to climax; as though American Indians and Melanesians had been but warm-ups for the *really* different. And what is more, the contrasting is now explicit and particular, not, as in ***Patterns of Culture***, implied and general—specific this-es set against specific thats. I had thought to count the number of such "in America"/"in Japan" tropes in ***The Chrysanthemum and the Sword***, but soon gave it up as a tiresome task leading to an unscalable number. But the drumbeat of them resounds, instance upon instance, through the whole of the book.

On sleeping:

> Sleeping is . . . one of the most accomplished arts of the Japanese. They sleep with complete relaxation . . . under circumstances we regard as sheer impossibilities. This has surprised many Western students of the Japanese. Americans make insomnia almost a synonym for psychic tenseness, and according to our standards there are high tensions in the Japanese character. . . . Americans are used to rating sleeping as something one does to keep up one's strength and the first thought of most of us when we wake up in the morning is to calculate how many hours we slept that night. The length of our slumbers tells us how much energy and efficiency we will have that day. The Japanese sleep for other reasons.

On eating:

> According to Japanese ideas, involuntary deprivation of food is an especially good test of how 'hardened' one is. . . . [Being] without food is a chance to demonstrate that one can 'take it.' . . . [One's] strength is raised by one's victory of the spirit, not lowered by the lack of calories and vitamins. The Japanese do not recognize the one-to-one correspondence which Americans postulate between body nourishment and body strength.

On sex and marriage:

> They fence off one province which belongs to the wife from another which belongs to erotic pleasure. Both provinces are equally open and above board. The two are not divided from each other as in American life by the fact that one is what a man admits to the public and the other is surreptitious. . . . The Japanese set up no ideal, as we do in the United States, which pictures love and marriage as one and the same thing.

On masculinity:

> [Homosexuality falls] among those 'human feelings' about which moralistic attitudes are inappropriate. It must be kept in its proper place and not interfere with carrying on the family. Therefore the danger of a man . . . 'becoming' a homosexual, as the Western phrase has it, is hardly conceived. . . . The Japanese are especially shocked at adult passive homosexuals in the United States. Adult men in Japan would seek out boy partners, for adults consider the passive rôle to be beneath their dignity. The Japanese draw their own lines as to what a man can do and retain his self-respect, but they are not the ones we draw.

On drinking:

> The Japanese consider our American total abstinence pledges as one of the strange vagaries of the Occident. . . . Drinking *sake* is a pleasure no man in his right mind would deny himself. But alcohol belongs among the minor relaxations and no man in his right mind, either, would become obsessed by it. According to their way of thinking one does not fear to 'become' a drunkard any more than one fears to 'become' a homosexual, and it is true that the compulsive drunkard is not a social problem in Japan.

On Good and Evil:

> To American ears such doctrines [that no evil is inherent in man's soul; that virtue does not consist in fighting evil] seem to lead to a philosophy of self-indulgence and licence. The Japanese, however . . . define the task of life as fulfilling one's obligations. They fully accept the fact that repaying [moral debts] means sacrificing one's personal desires and pleasures. The idea that the pursuit of happiness is a serious goal of life is to them an amazing and immoral doctrine.

And on happy endings:

> [The] 'happy ending' is . . . rare in their novels and plays. American popular audiences crave solutions. They want to believe that people live happily ever after. They want to know that people are rewarded for their virtue. . . . Japanese popular audiences sit dissolved in tears watching the hero come to his tragic end and the lovely heroine slain because of a turn of the wheel of fortune. Such plots are the high points of an evening's entertainment. They are what people go to see. . . . Their modern war films are in the same tradition. Americans who see these movies often say that they are the best pacifist propaganda they ever saw. This is a characteristic American reaction because the movies are wholly concerned with the sacrifice and suffering of war. . . . Their curtain scenes are not victory or even banzai charges. They are overnight halts in some featureless Chinese town deep in the mud. Or they show maimed, halt and blind representatives of three generations of a Japanese family, survivors of three wars. . . . The stirring background of Anglo-American 'Cavalcade' movies is all absent. . . . Not even the purposes for which the war was fought are mentioned. It is enough for the Japanese audience that all the people on the screen have repaid [their moral debt to the Emperor] with everything that was in them, and these movies therefore in Japan were propaganda of the militarists. Their sponsors knew that Japanese audiences were not stirred by them to pacifism.

The empirical validity of these various assertions, taken from a mere ten pages, not unrepresentative, in the middle of the book, aside (and some of them do sound more like reports from a society supposed than from one surveyed), the unrelenting piling up of them, the one hardly dispatched before the next appears, is what give Benedict's argument its extraordinary energy. She persuades, to the degree she does persuade—significantly so, in fact, even among the Japanese, who seem to find themselves as puzzling as does everyone else—by the sheer force of iteration. The Us/Not-us motif is pursued through an enormous range of wildly assorted materials derived from wildly assorted sources (legends, movies, interviews with Japanese expatriates and prisoners of war, scholarly works, newspaper accounts, radio broadcasts, "antiquarian papers," novels, speeches in the Diet, military intelligence reports) with the sort of single-mindedness that compels either general belief or an equally general skepticism. Prevented, and not only by the war, but by deafness and disinclination, from "being there" literally, Benedict rests her authority on being there imaginatively—moving locus to locus across the Impossible Object, and confronting on every page what she herself calls "the ever-present question: What is 'wrong with this picture?' "

But, as one can see even from this short sequence of quotations, moving from examples in which "they" sound the odd case to ones in which "we" do, a disconcerting twist appears in the course of this forced march through cultural difference; an unexpected swerve that sets the campaign a bit off course. It comes in the fact that, as she proceeds through everything from Japanese incredulity that an American admiral should be awarded a medal for rescuing crippled warships to American incredulity that the Japanese can see fulfillment in suicide, Japan comes to look, somehow, less and less erratic and arbitrary while the United States comes to look, somehow, more and more so. There is, in fact, nothing "wrong with the picture," just with those who look at it upside down; and the enemy who at the beginning of the book is the most alien we have ever fought is, by the end of it, the most reasonable we have ever conquered. Japanese newspapers pronounce defeat as "all to the good for the ultimate salvation of Japan." Japanese politicians happily govern the country under MacArthur's umbrella-parasol. And the Emperor, urged by the General's advisors to disavow divinity, complains he is not really regarded as a god but does so anyway because foreigners seem to think that he is and it should be good for the country's image.

This peculiar passage from perversity to pragmatism on the Asian hand and from levelheadedness to provinciality on the American, rigidity and flexibility passing one another somewhere in mid-Pacific, is the real story ***The Chrysanthemum and the Sword*** has to tell, though again it tells it more in the form of an examples-and-morals homily than in that of a directionally plotted tale. What started out as a familiar sort of attempt to unriddle oriental mysteries ends up, only too successfully, as a deconstruction, *avant la lettre,* of occidental clarities. At the close, it is, as it was in ***Patterns of Culture***, us that we wonder about. On what, pray tell, do our certainties rest? Not much, apparently, save that they're ours.

So, again, and here more powerfully because more confidently (if, in ***Patterns of Culture*** she writes like a lawyer pleading a case, in ***The Chrysanthemum and the Sword*** she writes like a judge deciding one), Benedict dismantles American exceptionalism by confronting it with that—even more exceptional—of a spectacularized other. But again, too, the fact that that is what she in fact is doing, intends to be doing, and in the event gets pretty well done, is somewhat obscured, to the point that it is frequently not seen at all. And it is the same interpretive misstep, similarly encouraged by Benedict herself, her own best misreader, that causes all the trouble: the misassimilation of her work to the intellectual environment immediately surrounding it.

Benedict's courage, extraordinary when you think about it, in writing about the Japanese as she did, a few years after Pearl Harbor, the Bataan Death March, Guadalcanal, and a thousand Hollywood movies populated with myopic sadists lisping hatred, has been at least occasionally remarked; but the subversive effect of her doing so on her American readers' received views about which way is forward and which direction is up (something even riskier) has not. Although undergraduates, not yet appropriately instructed as to what one is not allowed to look for in an anthropological monograph, sometimes sense the book's satirical edge, and are disturbed by it, the common conception of the work has been that it amounts to a psycho-political how-to-handle-the-Japanese training manual, conceptually a bit flighty, empirically a bit weak, morally a bit dubious. What is surely one of the most acid ethnographies ever written—"[The Japanese] play up suicide as the Americans play up crime, and they have the same vicarious enjoyment of it"—and the most bleakly mocking—"[A Japanese's moral debts] are [his] constant shadow, like a New York farmer's worry about his mortgage or a Wall Street financier's as he watches the market climb when he has sold short"—is seen as a brief for a science and sensibility, can-do optimism.

That was certainly the context, intellectual and political (or, as this was wartime and just after, intellectual-political), within which the book was written. Now it was not the natural laboratory, *"formes élémentaires,"* behold-the-beetle image of what anthropology had "to contribute" that Benedict felt was necessary in order to raise her work above the level of mere *belles lettres* into something more scientifically respectable. Rather, now it was "national character," "policy science," and "culture at a distance." And the people around her now were not just the inevitable Margaret Mead, herself turned toward larger canvases and more strategic goals, but a whole phalanx of psychological warriors, propaganda analysts, intelligence experts, and program planners. Scholars in uniform.

The story of this particular phase in American social science (and it was a phase; by the late 1950's it was over, anyway in anthropology, killed by too much promising of elephants and bringing forth of mice) has yet to be written in a detached and analytical way. There are only anecdotes, puffs, and war-horse reminiscences. But the fact that Benedict was not altogether at home with its style, its purposes, and its cast of mind, what she herself might have called its temper, is clear. Here, too, what she says when she is talking about her subject and what she says when she is talking about why she is talking about her subject don't quite comport.

Because ***The Chrysanthemum and the Sword***, like ***Patterns of Culture***, only really gets started about fifty pages in and is essentially over about fifty from its close (Benedict's works, like most Moralities, seem naturally to climax at their center) this two-mindedness appears most obviously again in the opening and closing sections of the book. The first chapter, "Assignment: Japan," a drum roll, and the last, "The Japanese Since VJ-Day," a briefing paper, place the work with the appropriate breathlessness in the Science-in-the-Nation's-Service frame that the times seemed to call for: "Whether the issue [facing the U.S. Government] was military or diplomatic, . . . every insight was important." But it is in the penultimate chapter, "The Child Learns," that the intellectual style of the Foreign Morale Analysis Division of the Office of War Information and its Navy-sponsored civilian successor, Columbia University Research in Contemporary Cultures, most fatally invades Benedict's crisscross world. The apostrophes to the anthropology of leaflets and high policy have faded with the excitements that gave rise to them; but, like the pages on relativism in ***Patterns of Culture***, those on shame, guilt, swaddling, and teasing in ***The Chrysanthemum and the Sword*** have had only too much staying power.

Whatever the reasons this shy, courtly, rather depressive, rather disdainful, and anything but right-minded woman may have had for wanting to surround an aesthetic view of human behavior with the trappings of an activist social science (a sense of being out of step, a desire to connect, a will to believe, a Christian idealism even anthropology couldn't cure), they are lost in the mists of her personal life. That she was not altogether comfortable in doing so can be seen, however, in the sudden shift in the child-raising chapter from a confident descriptive idiom to a much less confident causal one. In the compact, close-focus middle chapters on Japanese conceptions of hierarchy, moral indebtedness, "the circle of feelings," and self-discipline, everything is a matter of a point in a pattern, the placing of some practice or perception or belief or value in a context such that it makes sense; or anyway, Japanese sense. In "The Child Learns," the longest and most rambling chapter in the book, the project turns to a search for *mechanisms,* for specific socialization practices that will induce, as heat induces boiling or infection scarring, psychological dispositions that can account for why it is that the Japanese "cannot stand ridicule," dislike unpruned gardens, put mirrors in their shrines, and regard their gods as benevolent. A discourse on forms becomes, confusedly, one on levers.

The levers involved are, of course, familiar, not to say notorious—heavy diapers, taunting mothers, peer group tyranny. But what is interesting is that they are, in a book otherwise so intellectually self-reliant as to seem hermetic, for the most part not hers. The swaddling business, which is passed over rather hurriedly as a matter of fact, comes of course from Geoffrey Gorer, the English enthusiast Mead brought into the Columbia and Washington circle after Bateson's withdrawal from it, and whom Benedict almost eloquently omits from her generous "Acknowledgements," though she does, rather coolly, cite him as having "also emphasized the role of Japanese toilet training." The teasing business (the child alternately abandoned and embraced), of which much more is made, comes from Bateson and Mead's 1942 monograph on Bali, where it is the pervading theme.

And the peer group business comes again from a wartime report of Gorer's, this time at least briefly quoted.

The externality to Benedict's book of these borrowed devices, awkwardly introduced and clumsily applied, can be seen in the progression of the chapter itself, as it moves uneasily past them to return, almost with a sigh of relief, to portraiture—cherry blossoms, tea ceremonies, the lacquered lives of Japanese men—toward its conclusion. But perhaps the most telling picture of the tension comes again from Margaret Mead. In her book on Benedict and her writings, which is mainly an attempt, a decade after Benedict's death, to incorporate the older woman's persona into her own—making a predecessor look like a successor with a vengeance—Mead describes, in an exasperated and even resentful tone, unique in a book otherwise hagiographic, why it was ***The Chrysanthemum and the Sword*** achieved the acceptance it did:

> Ruth Benedict herself was completely converted to the usefulness for the safety of the world, of the methods she had used. Certain other expositions of these same methods had antagonized readers because they had so bared their methods of deriving the insights that they reverberated uncomfortably in the minds of the readers. Her own lack of dependence upon psychoanalytic methods—which, in this case, meant a lack of dependence upon the zones of the body, which never made any sense to her—made the book palatable to readers who had resisted, as they now praised, the insights about the Japanese emperor originally developed by Geoffrey Gorer in 1942. Furthermore, her basic skepticism about American culture, which she shared with most liberals of her generation, made it possible for liberals to accept her sympathetic understanding of the virtues of Japanese culture without feeling forced to take a similarly sympathetic attitude toward their own culture, and this removed a stumbling block which stood in the way of anthropologists who did not feel this skepticism so strongly. It was the kind of book that colonels could mention to generals and captains to admirals without fear of producing an explosion against "jargon," the kind of book it would be safe to put in the hands of congressmen alert to resist the "schemes of long-haired intellectuals." The points were made so gracefully, so cogently, that the book disarmed almost all possible enemies except for those who leaned heavily to the Left and those who, through many years, had formed very clear and usually imperfect notions of their own Japanese experiences—the sort of people we used, in another context, to call "old China hands."

With anthropological authoring, as with other things, then, it all depends on the company you keep. Having decided what sort of discourse community she and thus Benedict, her John-the-Baptist, should belong to, Mead labors so desperately to keep her from escaping it because she seems to sense, and to sense that others sense, how insecurely Benedict rests there, how very less than complete that "conversion" to save-the-world anthropology in fact was, and how easily the image of ethnography for admirals slips away when one looks at what is there upon the page. Taking Benedict out of that community is, like putting her in, thus an interpretive act, and, if I may say so before someone else does, a contentious one with ambitions of its own.

To say one should read Benedict not with the likes of Gorer, Mead, Alexander Leighton, or Lawrence Frank at the back of one's mind, but with Swift, Montesquieu, Veblen, and W.S. Gilbert, is to urge a particular understanding of what it is she is saying. ***The Chrysanthemum and the Sword*** is no more a prettied up science-without-tears policy tract than *Travels Into Several Remote Nations of the World, In Four Parts, By Lemuel Gulliver, First a Surgeon and Then a Captain of Several Ships* is a children's book. Benedict, who actually hardly went anywhere either, also wrote, as Swift said that he did, "to vex the world rather than divert it." It would be rather a pity were the world not to notice it.

Margaret M. Caffrey (essay date 1989)

SOURCE: "Patterns of Culture: Between America and Anthropology," in *Ruth Benedict: Stranger in This Land,* University of Texas Press, 1989, pp. 206-40.

[*Caffrey is an American anthropologist. In the following excerpt from her biography of Benedict, she assesses the impact that* Patterns of Culture *exerted on anthropology as a developing field of study.*]

Patterns of Culture had a multiple impact on American thought. It acted as a signal of and a catalyst for the final acceptance of a profound paradigm change in the social sciences and in American society and set in place the new twentieth-century paradigm or world view which had been taking shape up to that time. In clear, compelling language Benedict drew together the scattered new ideas, filtered them through her own thinking and experience, and articulated a coherent social philosophy, a new set of axioms people could use to give direction to their lives and thoughts. In writing a book about configurations among primitive peoples, Benedict was covertly giving her readers a new underlying configuration for American culture based on the new values and beliefs. As a cornerstone of the new configuration, for the general educated public at large and for the other social sciences as well the book culminated the decade-long debate over biology versus culture. At the beginning of the decade biology was firmly entrenched as the primary motivator of humanity. Biological determinism allowed no leeway for change. One could not change one's gender, or the effects of one's hormones, or one's genes. Social change seemed possible only through rigorous, often cruel, weeding out of the "unfit." Benedict's demonstration of the overwhelming role of culture in creating three different lifestyles, those of the Zuñi, the Dobu, and the Kwakiutl, provided the final important evidence for replacing biology with culture as the major causal factor in human life. But she did not, like Kroeber, rule out the role of biology altogether in a strict cultural determinism. Instead she spoke of "the small scope of biologically transmitted behaviour, and the enormous role of the cultural process." Culture, unlike biology, carried within it the potential for and openness toward individual and social change. For culture, though largely unconscious, was human-made and could be modified to suit social demands once the forces of culture were made conscious. Culture seemed the key to a better, more desirable future world. The force of Benedict's argument was helped by the excessive ideas of the eugenics movement in the United States by 1934 and the bigoted policies abroad based on supposed racial and biological differences, especially the inferiority and superiority of certain peoples.

As a second important element of the new world view, for the general educated public at large ***Patterns*** both parodied the values of Victorian America and affirmed the end of that era's influence by replacing its absolute, universal standards with cultural relativity. Both Dobu and Kwakiutl were cultures that honored the worst excesses of the Victorian robber-baron mind-set. Dobu gave a central place to theft, cheating, and treachery toward others as ways to succeed in life. The Kwakiutl stressed self-glorification, arrogance, and the consequent humiliation of others. Like Victorian America, Dobu stressed excessive prudery and fostered sexual jealousy and suspicion. Among the Kwakiutl, marriage was a business proposition, as Charlotte Perkins Gilman insisted it had been for many nineteenth-century women. These were cultures Americans could only perceive as paranoid and megalomaniac, Benedict wrote, yet her readers could see the parallels with American society. The absolute standards of Victorian America had fostered the worst excesses of American society, her writing implied. They led to extreme selfishness, as in Dobu, or to the excesses of consumer culture, as among the Kwakiutl. In their place she offered the standard of cultural relativity. Each culture developed its own different goals and standards out of a universal pool of possibilities. There could therefore be no "right" or "wrong" standards, she wrote, thus affirming ethical relativity as well. For most people relativity had meant uncertainty, the potential for chaos. But Benedict made cultural relativity a positive quality, one consistent in important ways with the old goals and values of American society. "Much profit and enjoyment," she wrote, could come from "relations with peoples of different standards" once Americans understood and respected other cultures' mores. She framed the differences in terms of a great arc of possible human interests from which each culture selected those to emphasize, just as language picked a finite number of sounds from an almost unlimited set of possibilities, or individuals developed their own personalities from the potentials available to them. "The possible human institutions and motives are legion," she wrote, and "wisdom consists in a greatly increased tolerance toward their divergencies." This idea of tolerance and acceptance of others lay close to Jesus' command to "Love one another," and in line with the American acceptance of different peoples to its shores. She emphasized that with cultural relativity there could still be standards and order, not necessarily chaos.

To those struggling for a Modern perception of the world, Benedict's greatest contribution to the new world view was her answer to the great problem of Chaos—not an acceptance merely of social dissonance, or the negation of dissonance in a fixed, ordered, and artificial system, but the coexistence of Chaos and Order, as in the paintings of the Cubists, or Modern poetry. Hers was not a closed system. "It would be absurd to cut every culture down to the Procrustean bed of some catchword characterization," she said. She called nothing more unfortunate "than an effort to characterize all cultures as exponents of a limited number of fixed and selected types." She accepted the existence of dissonance. Not all cultures achieved a "balanced and rhythmic pattern." Some scattered; for them "lack of integration" seemed as characteristic as extreme integration did for others. But even in these cases she suggested an underlying order; dissonance due to a culture's bordering between two or more strong cultures; historical factors such as movement into a different culture's area or the influence of a newly migrated tribe on cultures in an area. Even in the most "disoriented" cultures, she wrote, one could follow "accommodations that tend to rule out disharmonious elements and establish selected elements more securely." Or, she suggested, the possibility existed that the description of the culture was disoriented, not the culture itself. Or "the nature of the integration may be merely outside our experience and difficult to perceive." Sustaining her acceptance of chaos was the belief that there existed underlying order, that within dissonance lay patterns which, if we were only acute enough to perceive them, could reorder our perspective of reality and create a new view of the universe, take people a step beyond the place where they were at that time and place. "Cultures," she wrote, "are more than the sum of their traits." They possess "new potentialities," a new level of complexity not present in their elements, and the same elements in other combinations behave differently. She, more clearly than any of her contemporaries, managed to reconcile the philosophical opposites of her day, and gave her readers a base from which to launch their own elaborations of the new paradigm. She suggested the possibility of a philosophy of the coexistence of Chaos and Order in the integration of seeming cultural dissonance.

To those struggling for a Modern perception of the world, Benedict's greatest contribution to the new world view was her answer to the great problem of Chaos—not an acceptance merely of social dissonance, or the negation of dissonance in a fixed, ordered, and artificial system, but the coexistence of Chaos and Order, as in the paintings of the Cubists, or Modern poetry.

—Margaret M. Caffrey

Next, for the social sciences and society in general, she dealt with the question of the individual in society. She condemned the nineteenth-century view and advocated a new view of the relationship between the individual and society. They were not antagonists, she wrote, as a misleading "nineteenth-century dualism" proclaimed. Because of this old idea of the conflict of the individual and society, "emphasis upon cultural behaviour" was often interpreted as denial of individual autonomy. What should be stressed, she wrote, was the pattern of "mutual reinforcement" between the two. This idea of individualism, an "unselfish" individualism, formed part of the new twentieth-century American paradigm. To the question of whether individuals changed society or were locked in step with it, she answered that again there was no dualism. Influence flowed both ways. Most people were influenced by culture but had no trouble fitting into it. But some individuals temperamentally were not in tune with their culture and therefore could not accept its standards and goals. She made no judgment of rightness or wrongness. She only described these people as different and implied that they could stop blaming themselves for their inability to fit into society.

As a corollary to the new paradigm she affirmed the relativity of normality, making a clear statement against homophobia in American society. Western culture tended "to regard even a mild homosexual as an abnormal," she wrote. The clinical picture of homosexuality stressed neuroses and psychoses arising from it and the "inadequate functioning of the invert." But looking at other cultures showed that homosexuals had functioned well and even been especially acclaimed, as in Plato's *Republic*. When homosexuality was regarded as perversion, she wrote, the person involved became exposed to conflicts. "His guilt, his sense of inadequacy, his failures" thus were actually the result of "the disrepute which social tradition visits upon him." She added, "Few people can achieve a satisfactory life unsupported by the standards of the society." She suggested that other means of dealing with misfits' alienation from society existed beyond "insisting that they adopt the modes that are alien to them." On one hand, the misfits could objectively learn more about their own preferences and how to live with and deal with their "deviation from the type." Learning how much their troubles were due to lack of social support, they could educate themselves to accept their difference, and achieve "a more independent and less tortured" existence. Second, education of society to tolerance needed to go hand in hand with individual self-education. In making these assertions concerning homosexuality, however, she was careful to use other examples of deviation with it, such as trance, and insisted on having her name on the cover page as *Mrs.* Ruth Benedict, even though she and Stanley had been separated for four years. Thus she brought to bear on what she had to say not only the authority of science and academia, but also her covert authority in American life as a married woman.

Benedict's philosophy in ***Patterns of Culture***, besides the other purposes it fulfilled, remained true to a feminist vision. In stressing the importance of culture and the relativity of cultural practices, Benedict laid the base for a reevaluation of relationships between men and women. If masculine and feminine were perceived as biological, then women could not escape the weakness and inferiority inherent in being female. But if masculinity and femininity were cultural, that is, learned behavior, then women's weaknesses were not inherent, but culturally learned, and could be changed. In the examples that she used of relationships between the sexes among primitive peoples she suggested alternative possible ways for men and women to relate to each other. The implied message was that American ways were not set in concrete—they should be questioned and if necessary changed. The Zuñi, for example, were a matrilineal culture in which women owned and inherited all properties and their husbands worked for them, a radical departure from typical United States male-oriented practices. Benedict talked of the ease of divorce among the Zuñi, the implication being that divorce did not have to be the traumatic experience it was in American society. She wrote of the Dobu, who lived one year with the wife's clan, where she dominated the household, and the next year with the husband's clan, where he dominated. She described the Kwakiutl, with whom inheritance was also matrilineal, but went to the husband of a daughter, and women were bartered like property among men to gain status and power. In choosing these and other examples, Benedict wanted her readers to stop and think about their own culture in contrast and give themselves permission, through the alternate possibilities of anthropology, to free themselves from their own conventional or stereotyped ways of thinking about men and women and to search for new ones.

Patterns of Culture did not initiate the trend but it confirmed anthropology as a source of moral authority in American life, superseding natural history. When one needed the aid of a pithy example to make a point, one would turn not to the insect or mammal worlds as at the turn of the century, but to the case of a "primitive society," and what happened in such societies became intimately linked to the happenings of American life.

The book had a "wave effect" in American culture. The first wave washed over a comparatively small group of people: leaders in the social sciences and among the general educated public who had been groping toward the expression of the new twentieth-century paradigm and for whom ***Patterns*** acted as a centering device to bring its elements together. Through these people the ideas of ***Patterns*** became the guiding principles for a new perspective of the world which became the underlying beliefs of the intellectual community. The second wave began in 1946, when ***Patterns*** was published as a twenty-five-cent paperback, and when it became "one of the first true anthropological best-sellers in this country." With this ***Patterns*** moved out of the intellectual community and into the consciousness of the mass reading public. In this way Benedict's ideas truly became "common coin" in the American psyche.

Among her colleagues, Benedict's approach was daring and novel. It took great courage to reintroduce subjectivity as a working tool for anthropologists, since they had spent the first twenty years of the century discrediting it. To the "scientifically minded" it seemed like the introduction of potential chaos into anthropology, with a resulting threat to soundness. But it was a subjective approach based on the verifiable facts of a culture's way of life, a subjectivity that gave promise of actually working to make cultures comprehensible. Some anthropologists saw ***Patterns*** as a step toward making their discipline a truly predictive science. If one can have a basic idea of *why* people act the way they do, as the configuration approach seemed to promise, one can then predict with a fair measure of success which programs they would accept or how they as a people would react to an issue—a necessary preliminary to workable social engineering. ***Patterns*** became a catalyst of the Culture and Personality movement in anthropology. But within the discipline the book marked a clear split for the rest of the decade and beyond between what Kroeber, writing in 1934, called "scientific" and "historical" anthropologists.

For Ruth Benedict personally, ***Patterns of Culture*** represented a summation of the meaning of her life to that point. But it also marked a path into the future: for America, for anthropology, and for herself.

For Ruth Benedict personally, *Patterns of Culture* represented a summation of the meaning of her life to that point. But it also marked a path into the future: for America, for anthropology, and for herself.

—*Margaret M. Caffrey*

By the mid-1930's Culture and Personality (C&P) studies had become a legitimate field of interest, bolstered by the support of the Social Science Research Council Committee on Personality and Culture and the National Research Council Committee on Culture and Personality, chaired by Edward Sapir. C&P studies had begun institutionally with Sapir's seminar on Culture and Personality at Yale in the fall of 1931, when he first introduced psychoanalytic ideas to anthropology students in an integrated way with the help of psychiatrist Harry Stack Sullivan, who commuted once a week from New York to participate. A showcase seminar in 1932-1933 sponsored by Rockefeller Foundation money generated through the interest of Lawrence Frank gave Sapir the opportunity to conduct his Culture and Personality class for a group of scholars chosen from various European countries. It provided a convincing display of the ability of C&P research to attract big money and tackle serious problems which influenced later SSRC [Social Science Research Council] and NRC [National Research Council] acceptance.

But the earliest signal event in the emergence of the Culture and Personality movement was the presentation of Ruth Benedict's **"Psychological Types in the Cultures of the Southwest"** in 1928. **"Psychological Types"** and later **"Configurations of Culture in North America"** were the first papers to use psychological ideas to make anthropological sense in a major way. Previous writers had floundered trying to integrate a basically individual-oriented, biologically rooted psychology with group-oriented, culturally rooted anthropology. Benedict's idea of culture as "personality writ large" pointed a direction anthropologists could follow, a theoretical approach that reached its greatest development in ***Patterns of Culture***. But ***Patterns of Culture***, after its initial favorable reception, precipitated to the surface a debate that had been latent through the 1920's on what kind of discipline anthropology was and should be. This identity struggle appeared in three different ways: a debate over whether anthropology should consider itself as primarily "historical" or "scientific"; a debate over whether a functional or a structural approach was more important; and, within C&P itself, the question of which was more important—the individual or the culture in which he or she was enmeshed.

During the first quarter of the twentieth century, anthropology in America had developed under Boas to consider itself a "historical science." By this anthropologists meant that they saw their discipline as a "science plus." Science was foremost. Anthropology's roots were in the biological sciences, and physical anthropology was definitely an experimental science in which hypotheses could be proposed and validated in mathematical terms. Ethnology had become scientific through its meticulous and scrupulous collection of masses of raw data and its attention to observable phenomena and to what they revealed rather than to the creation of largely unfounded generalizations common to the nineteenth-century "unscientific" anthropologists. Ethnology had attained scientific objectivity by refraining from direct value judgments on various cultures and from indirect value judgments through the comparison of cultures, both weaknesses of the nineteenth-century anthropologists. In the study of diffusion and the possibility of convergence anthropologists examined processes which held possibilities of explanation and prediction. In the analysis of cultural phenomena into their component parts, anthropologists hoped to be able to discover basic regularities or "laws" of culture as physics and chemistry had done in the inorganic world. The "plus" consisted of two principles concerning space and time taken from history to help the new scientists deal with the unstable human phenomena of their discipline. The first was an insistence that phenomena could not be torn out of their context and used to "prove" positions, as had been done by the nineteenth-century anthropologists. Information always had to be dealt with in context. The second was respect for phenomena as the end result of a sequence of events through time and the necessity of understanding as much of that sequence as was discoverable, by doing as much historical reconstruction as possible. As a result of this approach, Boas and his students were termed, somewhat misleadingly, the "historical school" of anthropology, or the users of a "historical approach."

With the declaration of independence from biological science in the early 1920's and the focus on the ambiguous concept of culture as the material of their discipline, ethnologists set themselves on a collision course with their own standards. To deal with "culture," if it were not to be seen as an endless array of haphazard items, meant opening the Pandora's box of interpretation, comparison, weighing values, all the heresies of the nineteenth century that anthropologists had learned to distrust. For a time this conflict was obscured by the necessity of defining culture and its component parts. But by the late 1920's rumblings had begun within the discipline. By that time it was also becoming apparent that historical reconstruction which relied on the study of diffusion had played itself out and convergence had proved an intellectual dead end. Anthropologists had come to feel the need for some kind of integrative approach to make culture coalesce, to deal with culture as a whole. There was a sense of identity crisis: where do we go from here as a discipline?

With ***Patterns of Culture*** the identity crisis came out into the open. In responding to the book anthropologists also revealed the way they identified themselves and their discipline and the struggle between various points of view concerning new hopes and old fears. ***Patterns of Culture*** taught the potential of integrative studies in anthropology. But it also served to reinforce the threat that with them anthropology would lose its status as a science and would fall back into the speculative philosophical realm of the nineteenth-century anthropologists it had spent the last quarter of a century totally discounting. To those who saw the potential, ***Patterns of Culture*** was an inspiration. They discounted its faults as endemic to any pioneer work, took Benedict's ideas as a direction in which to search for answers, and tried to go on from there. To those who saw mainly the threat, Benedict's work was "unscientific," too subjective, too vague, too interpretive. To an extreme fringe of this second group Benedict seemed a "delusionist" with obsessive investment in her idea, distorting or manipulating facts to support her stance.

The configuration theory of ***Patterns of Culture*** was extremely influential in anthropology. It established the principle that it was legitimate to deal with culture wholes and gave a working model for doing so, from which others could establish their own working models. For many anthropologists, as Morris Opler later wrote, Benedict's work was "liberating" and a "refreshing influence" on American anthropology. Moreover, while it was a step into the future it retained ties with anthropology as a "historical science." Franz Boas had written in his introduction to her book, "The interest in these socio-psychological problems is not in any way opposed to the historical approach." Boas had the reputation of quickly popping intellectual bubbles and withering practitioners of fragile speculative thinking with a glance. His approval gave assurance that there was substance to Benedict's work and added to the confidence of those who used Benedict's ideas to kindle their own.

Within anthropology, some spent time clarifying the configuration concept and making it more precise. Ralph Linton, for example, in *The Study of Man* (1936) broke down culture patterns into three types: universals, specialties, and alternatives. Universals were common to all adult members of a culture. Specialties meant traits or habits shared by a group within a culture but not by the whole culture. Alternatives were those ways used by individuals within a culture which gave different paths for achieving the same ends. John Gillin at the University of Utah wrote an article called "The Configuration Problem in Culture" (1936), defining configurations more clearly as to their properties, types, how they changed, the relations of configurations and their parts, why anthropology needed them, and possible directions of major configurational research.

One major focus of research, directly inspired by Benedict's section on the Zuñi in ***Patterns of Culture***, was the delineation and analysis of "ideal" and "real" patterns: cultural ideals versus actual behavior within a culture. The paradox of Zuñi was that although knowledgeable observers besides Benedict agreed that as a culture it stressed order, restraint, and communal over individual effort, as a society it was rife with factionalism, and acts of disorder by individuals were not unknown. Columbia graduate student Irving Goldman wrote about the Zuñi for *Cooperation and Competition among Primitive Peoples* (1937), edited by Margaret Mead, that "in spite of the formal phrasings of cooperation, nonaggressiveness, and affability, the Zuñi are in the opinion of a number of field workers a rather 'mean people,' " holding grudges and sharp personal animosities "that under the influence of white contact seem to have flowered into full-blown factionalism," especially between Catholics and Protestants, pro-whites and anti-whites. The Zuñi, he wrote, cooperated in all formal and ceremonial situations and did not use violence, except in the few cases of women's quarrels noted by Benedict. But they had "no love for their fellowmen" and were ready "to defame anyone on the least pretext." In short, he wrote, there was discord between the ideals which the Zuñi had laid out for themselves and the way they put those ideals into practice. "Beneath the surface of a cultural norm of benignity and of affability there appears to lie some restless irritability," he wrote. "It is difficult to account for it."

The pro-***Patterns*** group in anthropology explained the Zuñi paradox by deciding that Benedict's depiction was that of the ideal pattern of Zuñi life, often violated in actual practice, but setting goals, attitudes, and directions for Zuñi culture to follow. The study of ideal versus real patterns became an important one in anthropology. Clyde Kluckhohn, a pro-Patternist, called Benedict's picture of Zuñi that of her old informants of the pueblo, who told her of the ideal rather than the reality. Kluckhohn elaborated on ideal versus reality in "Patterning as Exemplified in Navaho Culture" (1941), in which he defined "ideal patterns" as those that show what people do and say when they completely conform to cultural standards: in other words, the "musts" and "shoulds" of a culture. Other patterns, "behavior patterns," came from observation of how people actually behaved. Usually, he wrote, there was a difference between the ideal and the behavior patterns. He also suggested five categories of ideal patterns: the compulsory, in which a culture allowed only one way to meet a situation; the preferred, in which out of several possible ways, one was most acceptable; the typical, in which out of several proper ways of behaving one was most usual; the alternative pattern, in which several behaviors were equally acceptable; and the restricted, in which behavior was acceptable only for some members or groups of society, not society as a whole. He proposed that "pattern" be used to talk about overt culture and "configuration" to talk about covert culture in an attempt to clarify terms. In "Covert Culture and Administrative Problems" (1943),

Kluckhohn elaborated on the ideas of "covert" and "overt" culture, which he attributed to Ralph Linton, another way of approaching ideal versus reality. Earlier C. S. Ford, in "Society, Culture, and the Human Organism" (1939), defined culture as a set of rules and beliefs that touched on but were not necessarily the same as actual behavior. George Peter Murdock, in "The Cross-Cultural Survey" (1941), also distinguished between ideal patterns and the behavior of people in a society. He considered real behavior irrelevant to a study of culture. Thus Benedict's work led cultural anthropologists to wrestle with the ideas of real behavior and ideal behavior, and the weight to assign to each.

A second direction that opened to the pro-Patternists was the idea of multi-characterization of culture. Benedict had concentrated on cultures with one dominant integration and had agreed in ***Patterns*** that most cultures did not have this degree of integration. In a search for ways to deal with more loosely integrated cultures, several anthropologists turned to a multi-causal framework. Morris Opler developed the idea of "themes" in cultures, the presence of several dominant elements interweaving within a culture, both reinforcing and blocking each other in varying degrees. John Gillin formulated the idea of "objectives" as cultural integrators in "Cultural Adjustment" (1944), each objective in turn made up of smaller components such as "trends" or "orientations" within the culture. Clyde Kluckhohn and Dorothea Leighton, in *The Navaho* (1946), used the idea of nine "basic convictions" or "premises" underlying Navaho life. The premises essentially set out a standard of behavior, explained how it worked in related situations, and included alternatives for satisfying the standard.

But the approach that attracted the most attention and gave the movement its name was the study of personality in and of culture. This ranged from James Woodard's rather crude but interesting attempt to explain cultural structure directly in terms of personality structure based on Benedict's idea of culture as "personality writ large," to psychoanalyst Abram Kardiner's very sophisticated formulation of "basic personality structure" in each culture, a concept his anthropological colleague Cora Du Bois later modified to "modal personality." Margaret Mead, writing in 1935 in *Sex and Temperament in Three Primitive Societies,* said her work took Benedict's "approved" personalities one step farther, making hers a study of "approved personalities of each sex." Anthropologists and psychologists together explored culture and personality, searching for "ideal" personalities or later "typical" personalities within cultures, those who conformed more or less to the ideals and standards of their cultures. Benedict had described the "ideal man" of Zuñi, the Plains, Kwakiutl, and Dobu cultures. Following studies attempted to put her ideas on a more scientific foundation.

The conflict point within the profession came at the Zuñi paradox. While both the enthusiastic and the unenthusiastic could accept the idea of real and ideal patterns and of configurations, the latter group balked at Benedict's Apollonian-Dionysian contrast. Many anthropologists had not been comfortable with it from its inception in **"Psychological Types."** The idea itself was a literary one, deliberately so on Benedict's part in an attempt to neutralize the terminology. As she wrote to Mead about Boas' response to psychoanalytic ideas, "I think Boas would accept all of it but the terminology—but that kills it." However, the idea backfired. To many the Apollonian-Dionysian contrast marked the epitome of the nonscientific method which they were determined to minimize in their discipline. Kroeber made their fears vivid in his article "History and Science in Anthropology" (1935) and subsequent articles on the same theme. The article suggested that anthropology was no longer a "historical *science,*" and that the discipline now faced a choice between an identity as "scientific" or "historical" anthropology. By "historical" he did not mean especially concerned with time, but with "a basic and integrative intellectual attitude" imported from history, just as objective analysis had been imported from science. Kroeber's use of the word *historical* was misleading because what he wanted to convey was the idea of an integrated holistic approach rather than scientific analysis into parts. He identified the work of Benedict and Mead, and to a lesser extent Fortune and Bunzel, as deriving from this historical side of anthropology. Critical of the "painstaking analysis and non-selective objectivity of the 'scientific' approach," this group, as did researchers in history, selected elements needed to build up a picture, omitted those not needed, or "slurred" them "with intentional subjectivity." This subjectivity caused a conflict with the "scientific" group, but Kroeber wrote that this was "no longer a defect as soon as its [their work's] essentially historical nature" was accepted.

Kroeber saw the subjective quality of Benedict's and her colleagues' work not as a flaw, but as an acceptable result of a different quality of interpretation. As he had explained in his review of ***Patterns of Culture***, the approach, that of finding the "genius" of a culture, could not be "measured or demonstrated." It lay outside the present narrow boundaries of science, which did not admit the validity of a "subjective empirical approach." Estimating the relative importance of a pattern in a culture had to be done "primarily by feeling," and validity depended on "the fit of the pattern parts" and on not leaving a significant part of the culture out of the picture. "Those who will," he wrote, "may quarrel with the approach as 'unscientific.' " But then they also had to quarrel with historian Jacob Burckhardt's *Renaissance,* Lord Bryce's *American Commonwealth,* or anthropologist Robert Redfield's *Tepoztlan,* all acknowledged and respected, though nonscientific, works of cultural insight, conveying essential truths about their subjects in "historical" style. Kroeber supported Benedict. He found her ideas "original, suggestive, and stimulating." Unfortunately, he wrote, the 1930's decade was a time "which rates science high and history low."

Anthropology was not the only social science experiencing this crisis of approach. In psychology in 1938 well-respected Harvard psychologist Henry A. Murray wrote of two movements in psychology, which he labeled the "peripheralists" and the "centralists," terms that more accurately describe what was also going on in anthropology than Kroeber's split into "history" and "science." The peripheralists equated to those in Kroeber's science category. They were objectivists, desiring to concentrate on the observable and measurable facts, the external data. When they did speculate they used limited conceptual schemes found useful in analyzing parts, not wholes. The culture area in anthropology was that type of scheme. The psychological objectivists saw the concept of personality as their counterparts in anthropology saw culture, as only the "sum total or product of interacting elements rather than a unity," something to analyze into parts.

The centralists, whom Kroeber would have identified under the term *history,* and with whom Ruth Benedict stood, were "attracted to subjective facts" and chiefly concerned with the "governing processes" of the brain (or culture). They found these processes by "listening to the form and content" of the personality (of culture). They used subjective terminology. They were "conceptualists," trying to observe behavior accurately but merging interpretation with perception, referring overt actions to underlying impulses which they conceptualized as there. They were "totalists," seeing the personality (or culture) as a "complex unity, of which each function is merely a partially distinguished integral." They were open to the use of empathic intuition; as "dynamicists" they ascribed action to inner forces rather than external ones. The centralists, unlike the peripheralists, felt "no compulsion to count and measure." Murray defended the need for centralists in psychology as Kroeber defended the need for "historians" in anthropology. In its present stage, Murray said, the study of persons needed people with broad views, who perceived "the interplay of general forces." Psychology in its then fluid state needed people with intuition, for "In the wake of intuition comes investigation directed at crucial problems rather than mere unenlightened fact collecting." Murray's analysis did not threaten his colleagues. But when Kroeber argued for a similar recognition in anthropology his terms were too full of negative connotations for anthropologists to accept.

Boas' response was to deny that such a dichotomy existed. Benedict and others who agreed with her approach, such as Kroeber, saw themselves as scientists, but of necessity forging a new definition and philosophy of science, a more realistic, flexible tool than the rigid ideal of "true" science borrowed erroneously from the physical sciences. Kroeber himself spent the 1930's trying to derive such a philosophy of science. But Kroeber had raised the spectre for other more sensitive readers that anthropology would no longer be accounted scientific in an intellectual milieu where, as Kroeber put it in a later paper, science had become "the god of innumerable laymen" with a "totalitarian realm" claimed for it, where even anthropologists made a "fetish" of science.

Moreover, the values of history were values that anthropologists had learned to discard, to avoid, to view as shoddy work. The "historical approach" was "subjective," the catch-all word in anthropology for worthless work. It depended on the view of the observer rather than the reality of the event or object observed. The historian received recognition for his or her ability at perceiving relations and building "convincing bridges" across gaps in knowledge. The historian was honored most especially for skill in interpretation: for reading between the lines, selecting elements to highlight, omitting or downplaying elements deemed unimportant, giving elements perspective—all scientifically damning practices. Historians did not "prove," as scientists tried to. They "inferred" more likely or less likely "probabilities of fact, of relation, of significance." The historian weighed possibilities, then selected and combined them into the most coherent whole or pattern. This was the method of conceptual integration, wrote Kroeber. If anthropologists were to follow Ruth Benedict's lead, this is how they would end up as a discipline. For many anthropologists this nonscientific projection was hard to stomach.

Benedict had first used the Apollonian/Dionysian comparison in 1928. In the nine years between 1928 and the publication of two major articles on the subject in 1937, the only one to attack it was Paul Radin, and his was an isolated case. Radin was of the first generation of Boas' students. Like the others his family had emigrated to America from Europe. He was an expert on the Winnebago and knew other American Indian tribes as well. But he had a love-hate relationship with academic life and for many years went from one temporary position to another. In 1926 he spent the winter in New York. He gave an informal class to Columbia graduate students and Benedict got to know him. Her diary from that year contains several references to him. She enjoyed him, but their views were not compatible. "Lunch with Radin—," she wrote, "much anthropological divergence." Radin was a Jungian, but paradoxically he believed in the basic historicity of mythology. Like Parsons and Kroeber but to a greater extreme, he saw historical reconstruction, or the piecing together of the historical backgrounds of cultures, as the major way of understanding cultural processes in the present. In quick succession he wrote two books—*Social Anthropology* (1932), which defended historical reconstruction, and *The Method and Theory of Ethnology: An Essay in Criticism* (1933), in which he severely criticized Boasian anthropologists for moving away from it. Benedict's ideas presented an approach to culture that threatened to replace historical reconstruction, which was already under attack, as the chief approach of the discipline. In *The Method and Theory of Ethnology* Radin wrote critically of her "Configurations" article. He talked of her "revolt" against the quantitative method, writing that "her whole temperament is that of a culture historian" even though she protested against historical reconstructions as "naïve and *simpliste.*" He accused her of "dogmatically" including and excluding things "in an unjustifiable and arbitrary manner," and added that since "unpalatable facts" might disturb the "desired harmony," Benedict "not only flies in the face of these facts; she calmly leaves them out." Apart from this, Radin thought it doubtful that "distilled syntheses" like Benedict's were ever really applicable to culture. They were fascinating but of extremely problematical value. They might hold for individuals but not for a specific culture or a culture area. Radin's attack on Benedict was minor compared to that on Boas and others in American anthropology. Kroeber wrote to Boas that Radin made him and Wissler feel like "the two thieves crucified by the side of the True Cross." It was generally recognized at the time that Radin was upholding his own rather extreme point of view in his books.

But after 1935 and the writing of Kroeber's "History and Science" article, the Apollonian-Dionysian configurations of Zuñi and the Plains became a primary focus of anthropological debate. Only Reo Fortune had been to Dobu, and there was no way to either prove or disprove his work. Nobody dared challenge Benedict's Kwakiutl interpretation in the face of Boas' approval. But Zuñi and the Plains lent themselves to an attack. Disproving the Apollonian-Dionysian contrast became the key symbolic activity for disproving or disparaging the historical approach and reaffirming the primacy of science in anthropology.

It took a few years for a serious attack to get going. The objectivists had the problem that Benedict's account of Zuñi was not just based on her own experience there and her own known expertise in Zuñi mythology but also upon the best data available at the time. Even Robert Lowie, a natural skeptic of holistic interpretations, remarked that Benedict's account of Zuñi was "so satisfactory" because it rested on "most ample documentation by herself and other observers." Later investigators also seemingly found corroboration for an Apollonian world view in the Pueblos among the Hopi. It was not until 1937 that two articles appeared, one a direct attack, the other more circumspect, yet seen as more damaging to Benedict's position. This latter was "Zuñi: Some Observations and Queries," written by a young Chinese anthropologist, Li An-che. The article was not a critique of Benedict per se. Li An-che wrote the article with the help of both Ruth Benedict and Ruth Bunzel. He intended to make the article a study of how observations about Zuñi by prior observers, even those aware of the problem, had been colored by unconscious and implicit expectations from Western society which he, being Chinese, could see around. He perceived himself as questioning "official view[s], native or otherwise," in favor of the realities of Zuñi culture. He singled out not only Benedict and Bunzel but also Kroeber for specific criticism and criticized the work of "almost all the students of Zuñi culture" and "the universal idea of the students of the area," adding that observers were "easily led astray by their own background." Of those points of Benedict's and Bunzel's he took exception to, their emphasis on the lack of personal elements in Zuñi religion, the idea of leadership in Zuñi, and the discipline of children, he stressed that they were "oversimplified" and "misleading" because of a "basic fallacy"—reasoning within "the logical implications of one's own culture." He saw research in Zuñi in general as unbalanced due to an unconscious Western point of view.

In Western society, he wrote, prayers as a fixed formula and as a spontaneous outpouring of the heart were antithetical, so Benedict and Bunzel had seen the formulaic religion of the Zuñi as impersonal and detached. But he himself had felt an intensity in the formulaic prayers of the Zuñi. Concerning leadership, he wrote that at least since white contact there had been struggles for individual leadership within Zuñi, stirring up strife between groups. But he also saw Benedict as caught in the Western idea that lack of personal competitiveness implied lack of desire to lead. He saw traditional Zuñi ambition as based in religious knowledge, not personal magnetism or ego. He also challenged the idea held by all Zuñi researchers and used by Benedict, that Zuñi parents did not discipline children. Here again, he wrote, reiterating his main point, it was not the observation that was at fault but "an interpretation based on an incomplete recognition of the factors involved." His own interpretation suggested that verbal discipline of children came from all adults, not just parents, and that adults instilled mental or religious fears in children to make them behave well, as effective as the fear of a spanking. Besides these points, he also challenged Kroeber's "Western" approach to marriage. Thus it was not facts Li An-che challenged in his article but the interpretation put upon the facts by Benedict and others. He did not call it unjustifiable and arbitrary as Radin had, merely uninformed and restricted by Western perceptions. Li An-che spent one summer season in Zuñi before writing his article. In part he was influenced by his own Chinese perspective. But his article provided the first specific ammunition for the view that the interpretation in ***Patterns of Culture*** was flawed.

The direct attack on the Apollonian-Dionysian contrast occurred when Bernard Aginsky, a graduate of the Columbia Anthropology Department now teaching at New York University, presented a paper before the annual joint American Anthropological Association-American Folk-Lore Society meeting at New Haven, Connecticut, in December 1937, called "Psychopathic Trends in Culture." As Aginsky understood it, Benedict had set up the Apollonian-Dionysian duality to apply to all North America, calling every tribe outside the Pueblos Dionysian. His purpose was to show that the Pomo Indians of California had both Dionysian and Apollonian traits, plus what he called an "Anxiety" pattern, and thus refute the idea that the Pomo were Dionysian, as they would be classified under Benedict's system as he understood it. This paper is the only one to which Benedict replied in print. In her **"Reply to Dr. Aginsky,"** published in the same issue of *Character and Personality* in which the article afterwards appeared, she stated that Aginsky's idea of her Apollonian-Dionysian contrast as "polarities of behavior . . . whereby cultures can be understood in toto" was totally wrong, "completely alien to my own theoretical position." She added that she had "constantly opposed any 'typing' of cultures into which any newly studied culture would have to be arbitrarily fitted." To call her Apollonian-Dionysian contrast such a system was an egregious misreading of her book. The system she espoused was an open and not a closed one. She also charged that he had used *Apollonian* with quite a different meaning than she had, shaping the word to his argument.

Lowie discussed Li An-che's criticisms of Benedict's work in his *History of Ethnological Theory* (1938). Typical of those troubled by the subjective implications of Benedict's work, he gave "qualified approval" to her configuration approach, agreeing that "cultural *leitmotifs*" existed and should be studied. But he attacked the Apollonian-Dionysian contrast. He argued that in that contrast Benedict had oversimplified a real antithesis. He compared her to a physicist finding out about electricity by looking it up in a dictionary rather than observing the actual phenomena involved. He thought Li An-che had shown that Benedict's emphases threw the picture "out of focus," rather than making it more precise. He argued that Benedict's use of terms like "trance," "frenzy," and "orgy" without giving them "precise and accepted" meanings "largely vitiates Benedict's interesting contrast of non-Pueblo and Pueblo cultures of North America." He argued that so-called Dionysian peoples conformed to that pattern "only to a moderate degree." The Crow, a people he had extensively studied, rarely talked of supernormal phenomena in terms of ecstasy, he wrote. This from the man who in 1922 had written a fictionalized account of a Crow warrior's life that was totally Dionysian. To counteract the idea of the ecstatic vision he cited from an article by Radin, "Ojibwa and Ottawa Puberty Dreams," the nonecstatic, carefully orchestrated case of an Ojibwa boy of seven who after fasting under the eye of his elders acquired "the sort of guardian spirit his instructors permit him to accept." If Lowie had looked he would have discovered that Benedict had talked about this type of vision and where it fit into the Dionysian scheme in ***Patterns***.

Elsie Clews Parsons' *Pueblo Indian Religion* came out in 1939. It was the most complete study of the Pueblos to date and is still a comprehensive master source of data. Parsons did not agree with the psychological approach to culture and therefore the book was not a resounding affirmation of ***Patterns of Culture***. Although she was against Benedict's subjective approach, her own scientific objectivity led her to confirm Benedict's information on several disputed points: the disinclination to drink; the almost unheard-of-quality of suicide and, in Zuñi, the point that it was so foreign to them that it caused laughter; that murder was almost as rare as suicide; that whipping in Pueblo families was infrequent, marginal behavior; whipping as a voluntary public rite of cleansing certain times of the year or in certain ceremonies; the fact of the boys getting to whip the katcinas at the end of their second initiation. At the one whipping rite where Parsons was present, only perfunctory whipping went on and it was a cleansing rite. She confirmed the idea of Zuñi as an orderly society where leaders had to be men of peace, a cooperative society where individuality was frowned upon. She affirmed that the scalp ritual was to cleanse the slayer, not celebrate victory.

But she tried through historical reconstruction to undermine Benedict's position by showing that social aggression had once existed in Zuñi. She suggested war, the threat of war, or internal feuds as bases for Pueblo migrations in early history. She also suggested that kiva groups originated as organizations of war brothers, an idea that provoked a sharp response from Benedict in her review that it would "hardly survive marshalled argumentation." Parsons also suggested that Pueblo children, while not punished into conformity, were frightened into it. She saw punishment as a factor in Pueblo whipping of adults, though not a major factor. All in all, Parsons supplied information that both sides could use to uphold or damn the Apollonian idea, but, if anything, the book tended to confirm Benedict's picture of Zuñi.

The controversy heated up still more in the 1940's. Laura Thompson and Alice Josephs' book, *The Hopi Way* (1944), offered major support to the Apollonian idea, as did Thompson's article, "Logico-Aesthetic Integration in Hopi Culture" (1945). But the objectivists intuitively felt that where there was factionalism and personal animosity there must be aggression in the culture. Benedict had stressed the nonviolence of Zuñi culture. Evidence of violence, aggression, or even a tendency to excess within the Pueblos would shatter the Apollonian idea once and for all. Dissenting research focused on such issues as discipline of children, lack of suicide, and the use of alcohol in Pueblo culture.

Li An-che had raised the question of how children were socialized in Zuñi. Esther Schiff Goldfrank examined this question in 1945 in "Socialization, Personality and the Structure of Pueblo Society (with Particular Reference to Hopi and Zuñi)," which she considered a major attack on Benedict's position on the disciplining of children and the Apollonian view. Though she agreed with Benedict that parents were very lenient, she disagreed with Benedict's statement that ceremonial whippings were so light they did not raise welts. She gave several graphic examples of severe whippings from Hopi, but her one explicit reference from Zuñi revealed that boys were whipped in layers of blankets, taken off one by one after each ceremonial whipping so that only the last touched the skin itself. Where she was most successful in undermining the Apollonian idea was in her point that contrary to Benedict's and Thompson's ideas, Zuñi and Hopi children were not gradually fitted into their cultural patterns, but forcibly coerced. She gave a plausible account of fears instilled into children so that they would behave correctly, positing that these fears led to the molding of children into cooperative adults. But even when attacking the Apollonian idea Goldfrank did it within the Culture and Personality approach, accepting Benedict's idea of the Zuñi configurational pattern, questioning only the supposedly Apollonian means by which Zuñis achieved cooperation. Anthropologist John W. Bennett, trying to explain the difference between Goldfrank's approach and that of Thompson and Benedict, said that Goldfrank's "critical realism" contrasted sharply with the "impressionistic, evocative" approach of Thompson and Benedict. Goldfrank was more the "literal-minded scientist," while Thompson was more subjective. This work followed an article written by Dorothy Eggan, "The General Problem of Hopi Adjustment" (1943), which argued that Hopi Indians in spite of loving infancies developed into adults exhibiting a high degree of anxiety, not Apollonian calm. Earlier, *Sun Chief: The Autobiography of a Hopi Indian* (1942) vividly described Sun Chief 's brutal whippings during his initiation ceremonies and the fearsomeness of the scare katcinas. However, the book was criticized in 1945 because it was unclear whether Sun Chief was a misfit or representative of Hopi in general and because only one-fifth of the original data had been used and there was no indication as to the effect of the condensing and editing on the final version.

On the issue of alcohol Benedict had written that unlike the situation with other Indians, alcohol was neither an "administrative problem" nor an "inescapable issue" among the Pueblos, that as a culture drunkenness was "repulsive" to them, in line with their Apollonian bent. The results of inquiry about alcohol were mixed. Studies done in the 1940's showed that some Zuñis did drink, especially around the time of a major festival, the Shalako. But it also seemed clear that there were strong social attitudes against drinking and that drunkenness was not the social problem it was for many American Indian tribes. Concerning Benedict's statement that suicide was almost outside the Pueblo world view, a totally foreign idea, a statement backed up by both Ruth Bunzel and Elsie Clews Parsons, the two anthropologists who had spent the most time in the Pueblos and knew the people best, former Columbia graduate student E. Adamson Hoebel used the principle of the negative instance against her, discovering three cases of suicide committed in Zuñi after 1939 by which he tried to cast doubt on Benedict's information. Hoebel was one of the most active in the 1940's in discounting the Apollonian-Dionysian idea. In *The Cheyenne Way* (1941) he showed that the supposedly Dionysian Cheyenne had what he considered many Apollonian features, such as the restrained behavior expected of chiefs and the low amount of aggressive behavior between members of the tribe. In *Man in the Primitive World,* (1949), he argued that the Western Pueblos, Hopi and Zuñi, differed from the Central and Eastern Pueblos; that all could not be considered Apollonian.

The war against the Apollonian-Dionysian contrast went on long after Benedict's death. In a 1954 article Hoebel cited the criticisms by Eggan (1943), Goldfrank (1945), Li An-che (1937), and Bennett (1946), saying exaggeratedly that they "only begin to indicate the extent of the artistic and poetic idealization of Pueblo culture that Benedict presented." He was forced to add however that it was a paradox that with her "highly questionable techniques of observation" she contributed "theory and methodological devices of such great import and lasting value." Even Kluckhohn by the mid-1950's agreed that Benedict's work had to be "qualified in many respects and modified or reexpressed in others if justice is to be done to the variety of behavioral fact" and the Zuñi ideal pattern. Victor Barnouw in 1963 cited "a tendency to overstatement and to ignore inconvenient inconsistent data." By the late 1950's anthropology had successfully relegated the Apollonian-Dionysian idea to the dust heap. In his revised edition of *Man in the Primitive World* (1958), Hoebel deleted the material about the suicides and that about the differences between the Western and Eastern pueblos. He also succinctly summed up the general anthropological position by then about ***Patterns of Culture***. He called it the "classic formulation of the idea of cultural configuration in relation to ideal personality types." He called it "persuasively written in fine literary style," but added, "it should not be taken as a reliable ethnography of the cultures discussed, although its major theme is acceptable."

It seems clear in retrospect that people saw in Benedict's work what they need to fortify their own version of anthropological reality—and also that the Apollonian-Dionysian contrast became a symbol of the underlying value struggle between what was perceived as science versus non-science as the framework of the discipline, with "true" science eventually winning out. Those who opposed the contrast most vehemently were those who believed in the necessity of anthropology being identified as a science in the traditional sense. Each side brought a different set of facts and interpretations to the argument, and on both sides the facts were true; only the viewpoint of the observer differed, and the observers divided at the boundary between a rigid definition of "science" and a flexible definition of science that was interpreted as "non-science." The evidence itself was ambiguous and could be read both ways. If the issue had just been that of the character of the Zuñi people, as it ostensibly seemed, the arguments against Benedict's work should have totally discredited it as a shoddy piece of field work and it should have been forgotten. But again and again in the following decades anthropologists discredited Benedict's cultural description but ended by accepting the premises on which that description was built.

According to their varying lights, both sides were "right." Accepting the values reinforced by the scientific side meant admitting that Benedict's work *was* subjective, literary, overstated, and oversimplified, and thus scientifically damned. From the history-minded side these same qualities became positive values and Benedict's work reinterpreted as integrative, clear writing that established a deeper level of insight into cultures than had been achieved before. This value difference probably accounts for the bafflement and ambiguity of response in the writing of some anthropologists in the 1950's and 1960's, who, after criticizing the description of Zuñi in ***Patterns*** as useless, still could not discard Benedict's insight into the heart of Zuñi life.

It seems clear that Ruth Benedict did not deliberately leave out information in an arbitrary and unjustified manner. She worked with the best available data of her time, relying on the field work of Ruth Bunzel, who had learned the Zuñi language and spent several years returning to Zuñi to study the culture. This information she supplemented with the work of Elsie Clews Parsons and others, bolstered by her own experience at Zuñi. "Benedict's description of Zuñi has found favor with the best judges," wrote Lowie in 1938. She built her theory on data, not airy speculation. That she selected and highlighted certain information is clear, but only in the humanistic tradition that allowed and encouraged such highlighting if it led to a clearer truth. Those who attacked her were excessive in upholding the rigid "scientific" tradition. She did downplay the tension and factionalism in Zuñi life. She did not omit them. She wrote of culturally sanctioned violence by women, where wives blackened the eyes of rivals and sisters broke furniture or took something from the other's house after quarreling. She spoke of critical village gossip as commonplace; of the war priests, war societies, and scalp ceremonies; of whipping as a common act in Zuñi, although as a "blessing and a cure," not as self-torture or torture. She wrote of witchcraft as an "anxiety complex" among the Zuñi, of people suspecting one another. She gave the example of one famous case of a man among the Zuñi whom she knew who got drunk, boasted he could not be killed (the sign of a witch), and was tortured by being hung up from the rafters by his thumbs for witchcraft, with the result that his shoulders were crippled for life.

She did not try to hide or repress information potentially damaging to her view of Zuñi. Writing to political scientist Harold Lasswell in 1935, she said that judging from her experience in Zuñi there was something "deep-seated in pueblo ethos" that allowed stresses to build up until they released disastrously. "Zuñi is intact," she wrote, "but its history could always be written in terms of factionalisms," and splits in Hopi were "just the logical extension of the usual pueblo situation." Again she wrote in ***Zuñi Mythology*** (1935), "Grudges are cherished in Zuñi. They are usually the rather generalized expression of slights and resentments in a small community." When graduate student Irving Goldman wrote about the Zuñi in *Cooperation and Competition* (1937), he did so after a number of conversations and discussions with Benedict and Ruth Bunzel. He made a number of revisions in the text at their suggestion. What he wrote about the Zuñi therefore had their stamp of approval. What he wrote suggests that Benedict and Bunzel were then working on answers to the problem of Zuñi factionalism. The paper suggests that Benedict first saw factionalism as a result of white contact and not integral to the Zuñi configuration. Moreover, she was dealing in ***Patterns*** with the "normal" person of Zuñi society, the approved person the society encouraged everyone to be. Gossip and bickering were not a part of the approved way to live although they were prevalent in reality. They existed outside of the Zuñi ideal.

We perceive this now as a limited idea, but then the configuration approach was a pioneering concept that Benedict felt it necessary to make clear above all else. Like all new ideas it took time for it to unfold in all its ramifications. There were some things Benedict just could not see at the beginning that later became clearer. By 1935 she had begun to see the gossip and factionalism as part of the configuration. By then she was working on the difference between sin and shame and how they act in a society. Goldman's paper suggests she saw a connection between the gossip and defamation in Zuñi and the culture's chief social sanction of shame, which made both public criticism and sensitivity to such criticism necessary. By 1935 she had also begun to see certain facets of Zuñi life as counterbalances and safety valves that helped preserve the amiability of Zuñi social life. Her book ***Zuñi Mythology*** pointed to mythology as an outlet for vicarious violence and wish fulfillment not allowed by actual Zuñi life that served to defuse actual violence in the society. She wrote to Elsie Clews Parsons in 1937, "Zuñi daily life is full of cherished grudges but no violence; the mythology allows the violent expression of them."

Aside from her reply to Bernard Aginsky's article, Benedict stayed out of the controversy surrounding her work. In a 1936 letter she wrote, "I haven't any claims to describing a culture in one word." Where there was a word available "to point up a discussion," such as Apollonian or Dionysian, she used it. "But," she wrote, "I don't attach any more meaning to it than a historian does to 'feudal' when he has to use that." In her effort "not to be technical" and her "dislike for the passive voice," she wrote, "I often omitted much that seemed to be obvious." If she had realized how her intentions would be misunderstood, she would have "left the clumsy sentences in." In a 1941 letter she called the Apollonian-Dionysian contrast between Plains and Pueblo "as important as the feudal non-feudal contrast is between Europe in the 13th Century and such a trade center as Florence." But the categories were neither universal nor necessarily transferable to other cultures or other times.

She gave her answer to the profession in her outgoing speech as President of the AAA in 1947, and that answer was a vision of an anthropology in which science and "history" did not fight each other, but melded together to create a more complete, complex picture of the life of humankind. She affirmed anthropology as a science but added that anthropology "handicaps itself in method and insight by neglecting the work of the great humanists." The humanist tradition had much to offer discriminating anthropologists, she stated, because humanists had a head start in studying "emotion, ethics, rational insight and purpose," which had become the subjects which with modern anthropologists were wrestling. They could "analyze cultural attitudes and behavior more cogently," she wrote, if they knew George Santayana's *Three Philosophical Poets,* Arthur Lovejoy's *Great Chain of Being,* or Shakespearian criticism. In *Three Philosophical Poets* Santayana studied the contrasting cultures of Lucretius, Dante, and Goethe as characterized by the "cosmic parables" they wove in their work. From both Santayana and Shakespearian criticism, Benedict wrote, she learned "habits of mind which at length made me an anthropologist." She learned from the criticism written in different eras how human thoughts were culturally conditioned. She learned from the standards of good criticism to take into account "whatever is said and done," discarding nothing relevant, to try to "understand the interrelations of discrete bits," to surrender oneself to the data and use all the insights one was capable of. Criticism, she wrote, taught the importance of contextual knowledge of facts, and studies of imagery taught techniques for studying "symbolisms and free associations which fall into patterns and show processes congenial to the human mind in different cultures." The humanities alone, however, provided only partial answers to human questions, as did the sciences alone. "Any commitment to methods which exclude either approach is self-defeating." The anthropologist should not be afraid to belabor the obvious or to be "subjective." For, she concluded, "The anthropologist can use both approaches."

Richard Handler (essay date 1990)

SOURCE: "Ruth Benedict and the Modernist Sensibility," in *Modernist Anthropology: From Fieldwork to Text,* edited by Marc Manganaro, Princeton University Press, 1990, pp. 163-80.

[*In the following essay, Handler considers Benedict's anthropological writings as representative of a "modernist sensibility."*]

In recent works, Michael Levenson (1984) and Kathryne

Lindberg (1987) have charted the tension within literary modernism between the quest for self-expression and the desire to recover a viable tradition. Both critics, in strikingly different ways, have presented the dialogue and debate between Ezra Pound and T. S. Eliot (among others) as emblematic of the larger opposition of individuality and tradition, or deconstructive originality and cultural constraint. In my work on the literary endeavors of Boasian anthropologists, I have examined a similar tension in the development of a culture theory that could accommodate both cultural holism and human individuality. Using Levenson and Lindberg to reexamine an essay in which I compare the literary and anthropological writings of Edward Sapir to those of Ruth Benedict, I might now offer the following formula: Pound is to Eliot as Sapir is to Benedict. Put less cryptically, the contrast between Pound's iconoclasm and Eliot's Catholicism is similar to that between Sapir's emphasis on the individual and Benedict's championing of culture. Sapir focused on the individual as a crucial locus of cultural action, and refused to reify culture, whereas Benedict emphasized cultural integration and the determination of individuals by culture.

This theoretical opposition between individual and culture can be located in the work of separate scholars (Sapir versus Benedict), but it can also be traced as a tension in the writings of either one of them. The present paper examines the *interaction* of the quests for individuality and tradition in the writings of Ruth Benedict. Although her developed theoretical position within anthropology places her among the champions of culture, I argue that her personal quest for self-expression led her to that position. Linked to this biographical argument is a structural argument, for I suggest that self-expression and cultural holism require each other in any formulation of the modernist sensibility.

My analysis begins with an examination of Benedict's journals, diaries and letters of the years 1912 to 1934, edited and published by Margaret Mead (1959) and exhaustively reviewed in two recent biographies of Benedict (Modell, 1983; Caffrey, 1989). Benedict's writings document a long period of personal struggle. Graduated from Vassar in 1909 with a major in English literature, Benedict traveled extensively in Europe, worked as a teacher and social worker, married and then watched her childless marriage disintegrate, tried her hand at writing both prose and poetry, and found her way to anthropology. Beginning her studies at the New School for Social Research in 1919, Benedict earned her Ph.D. from Columbia University in 1922. Her early years in anthropology were marked by continuing self-doubt, but she seems to have crossed a threshold to professional maturity during summer field trips among Pueblo Indians in 1924 and 1925. The 1934 publication of her first book, ***Patterns of Culture***, can be taken to mark the end, and fulfillment, of Benedict's quest for personality and achievement.

In Benedict's journals and diaries, we find the almost obsessive concern with self-realization and self-expression that is a hallmark of modernism. I take as characteristic of twentieth-century thought (of which modernism is one variety) the emergence of a fully secularized individualism. In this ethos, still prevalent today, one's highest duty is self-realization or the fullest possible development of one's personality. True to its Puritan origins, the modern personality proves its existence through work; or, phrased slightly differently, one expresses oneself through one's achievements. In the literary and scientific circles to which Benedict was drawn, work and self-expression meant the production of aesthetic objects, whether poems or scientific studies. The self—"hard," inviolable, unique, authentic—observed the world, experienced the world, mastered the world, proved itself as a locus of ultimate reality against the world. And from its observations and experiences, the self constructed intricate, original, beautifully patterned expressions. The successful products of self-expression could then be consumed by other, lesser selves—the vast public—who were also engaged in the business of self-realization, but vicariously, via contact with the productions of artists whose lives had been deemed 'authentic' [Lionel Trilling, 1971].

The second moment of my argument charts Benedict's progress toward a mature anthropological—and personal—vision, as represented in ***Patterns of Culture***. Benedict's private writings do not reveal a personality convinced of its own realization. Such self-assurance would come only with the publication of her first book in 1934, the last year in which Benedict published a poem. To trace Benedict's scholarly development, I focus on three articles that precede ***Patterns of Culture***. The first (**"A Brief Sketch of Serrano Culture"**) is a derivative piece representing Boasian anthropology as Benedict had learned it but before she had contributed to reshaping it. The latter two (**"Psychological Types in the Cultures of the Southwest"** and **"Configurations of Culture in North America"**) are preliminary versions of portions of ***Patterns of Culture***. A third moment of my analysis relates the authorial persona of her greatest works, ***Patterns of Culture*** and ***The Chrysanthemum and the Sword***, to the modernist quest for personality and tradition, and to the transcendence of both.

EXPERIENCE WITHOUT PATTERN

In a diary entry for December 1915, Benedict describes what she calls the "passionate blank despair" she felt when, as a freshman at Vassar in the winter of 1906, she puzzled over the purpose of life. In that mood, she read the conclusion to Walter Pater's *The Renaissance:*

> And then came Pater. Every instant of that late afternoon is vivid to me. I even know that I had to creep to the windowseat to catch the last dim light in that bare tower room of my Freshman days. The book fell shut in my hands at the end, and it was as if my soul had been given back to me. . . .
>
> Afterwards, I disbelieved. I had much in me to contradict Pater; my early religion which tried so hard to make me a moral being, my pity for others that almost made me an efficient one. But I was not run into either mould. And it is Pater's message that comes back to me as the cry of my deepest necessity: "to burn with this hard gem-like flame"—to gain from experience "this fruit of a quickened, multiplied consciousness," to summon "the services of philosophy[,] of reli-

> gion, of culture as well, to startle us into a sharp and eager observation."

Benedict's attraction to Pater epitomizes an enduring theme in her private writings: the desire to live intensely, to "have experiences" of an outer reality that prove to oneself the reality of one's personality. As she put it in another journal entry: "Anything to live! To have done with this numbness that will not let me feel." The passage concerning Pater, in which she recalls an apparently intense experience of communion with an intensity that matches the initial experience, suggests how early and how profoundly Benedict was committed to—or ensnared by—the modernist sensibility. The desire for experience, as formulated by Pater, leads in two contradictory directions: toward egoism or the cult of personality, and toward a reaction to the meaninglessness or incoherence of a reality defined solely in terms of fragmented personal experiences. In Levenson's genealogy of modernism, mid-Victorians such as Matthew Arnold attempted to ground Christian belief in personal experience instead of dogmatic assertion. But after Arnold, Pater "recognized . . . that to redefine traditional values as phases of the self was to weaken traditional sanctions. . . . [S]ubjectivity was a double-edged sword. In the hands of Pater, it was used not only to cut away the metaphysical, but also the traditionally moral, the traditionally religious, the objective and the permanent."

The follower of Pater, then, was left alone with the self. Benedict wanted to "realize" or develop that self, but she craved also a source of stability or order beyond the self. On the one hand, her private writings are replete with admonishments to believe in her own personality:

> I have been reading Walt Whitman, and Jeffries' *Story of My Heart*. They are alike in their superb enthusiasm for life[,] . . . their unwavering, ringing belief that the *Me* within them is of untold worth and importance. I read in wonder and admiration—in painful humility. Does this sense of personal worth, this enthusiasm for one's own personality, belong only to great self-expressive souls? or to a mature period of life I have not yet attained?

On the other hand, Benedict describes herself as unfulfilled by episodical epiphanies unconnected to larger patterns of significance: "The trouble is not that we are never happy—it is that happiness is so episodical. . . . I cannot see what holds it all together."

Benedict knew, however, what could *not* hold it all together: conventional culture. In 1912 she described her "real *me*" as hidden behind the "mask" she had donned in choosing the role of school-teacher. Later she described as "distractions" the customary rituals, such as funerals and weddings, that anthropology would teach her to examine more respectfully: "All our ceremonies, our observances, are for the weak who are cowards before the bare thrust of feeling." And elsewhere she spoke with mild contempt of the conformity of the masses, "lost and astray unless the tune has been set for them, . . . the spring of their own personalities touched from the outside."

Benedict was also dissatisfied with nonconventional answers to her existential dilemmas, even those formulated by the great creative personalities of history:

> The trouble with life isn't that there is no answer, it's that there are so many answers. There's the answer of Christ and of Buddha, of Thomas à Kempis and of Elbert Hubbard, of Browning, Keats and of Spinoza, of Thoreau and of Walt Whitman, of Kant and of Theodore Roosevelt. By turns their answers fit my needs. And yet, because I am I and not any one of them, they can none of them be completely mine.

Here an "answer," a believable and believed-in moral system, seems of less moment than the need of the personality to appropriate such an answer as "mine." As Benedict's meditation continued, she admitted that moral questions are never solved. "What we call 'answers' are, rather, attitudes taken by different temperaments toward certain characteristic problems—even the interrogation may be an 'answer'." The phrasing is egocentric ("attitudes," "temperaments") and relativistic—a striking prefigurement of the position developed later in ***Patterns of Culture***, where authentic cultures are portrayed not as "answers" but as existential attitudes in terms of which both answers and questions are constructed.

Benedict sought in biography to see life whole, to discover her own personal integrity by constructing storied, hence coherent, accounts of women whose lives had been judged by their contemporaries to be out of control. But the biographer could not achieve a satisfactory distance from her subjects: their lives and problems seemed too much her own.

—Richard Handler

In addition to the quest for personality and the rejection of convention—quintessentially modernist themes—Benedict's private writings reveal a painfully explicit consciousness of the dilemmas that the task of self-realization posed for women. She wavered between a belief that woman's "instinctive" vocation is domestic, and a reluctance to sacrifice apparently masculine aspirations to the domestic role. "[N]ature lays a compelling and very distressing hand upon woman," she wrote shortly after her marriage in 1914 to Stanley Benedict. Women might deny "that the one gift in our treasure house is love." However, their quests for fulfillment—"in social work, in laboratories, in schools," with marriage considered merely "a possible factor in our lives"—would end in failure. At other times, however, Benedict sensed that the sacrifice of self and self-development to domestic duties could not but lead to frustration, bitterness, and waste. After a year of marriage she felt that she needed a career or mission beyond her marriage: "it is wisdom in motherhood as in wifehood to have one's own individual world of effort and creation." Later she wrote that woman's sacrifice of self to family was both socially wasteful and psychologically harmful. Whatever natural differences there might be between the sexes—another question to be settled by anthropological inquiry!—both men and women had to face up to the "responsibility for achievement of a four-square personality." Yet disparities in culturally constructed gender roles (as we would say today) made the pursuit of self-development more problematic for women than for men: "The issue . . . is fine free living in the spirit world of socialized spiritual values—for men as for women. But owing to artificial actual conditions their problems are strikingly different." Small wonder that the first anthropology course in which Benedict enrolled was "Sex in Ethnology," taught by Elsie Clews Parsons.

As Benedict struggled to find her way, she sensed that fulfillment was most readily accessible to her in literary endeavor. As a child she had received familial encouragement for her writing, and later, she could record in her journal that "my best, my thing 'that in all my years I tend to do' is surely writing." "I long to prove myself by writing," she wrote in 1917, but her problem was to find an appropriate voice and genre. Her first major effort was biography, as she planned a book charting the lives of three famous women. She wrote at least six drafts of an essay on Mary Wollstonecraft, but was unable to finish the project after it was rejected for publication in 1919. As Modell has suggested, Benedict sought in biography to see life whole, to discover her own personal integrity by constructing storied, hence coherent, accounts of women whose lives had been judged by their contemporaries to be out of control. But the biographer could not achieve a satisfactory distance from her subjects: their lives and problems seemed too much her own. We can say the same thing of Benedict's poetry, which she wrote on and off for years: in her poems she could not achieve the "hard," polished self that she desired. Rather, her poems tended to express an unhappy and fragmented self, at times almost hysterically out of control.

Benedict's search for a literary voice is linked to still another recurrent theme in her private writings, summarized by what she called "detachment." Coupled antithetically to her desire to experience the world with the intensity that Pater advocated is her fear of that intensity. "I dread intense awareness," she wrote in her diary in 1923, on the day that she completed the writing of her doctoral thesis. Yet, having admitted the fear, she went on to express fear of its opposite: "And then it seems to me terrible that life is passing, that my program is to fill the twenty-four hours each day with obliviousness." By contrast, "detachment" seems to have represented a transcendence of both fears:

> I divide the riches of the mind into two kingdoms: the kingdom of knowledge, where the reason gives understanding, and the kingdom of wisdom, where detachment gives understanding. This detachment is the life of the spirit, and its fruit is wisdom. That would cover it fairly well—the life of the artist and the life of the mystic. Its essence is its immediacy—without the distractions of belief or anxiety. It has no dogmas, it has no duties. It is a final synthesis of knowledge, and it is also a laying aside of knowledge.

Here Benedict envisions an almost utopian solution to the modernist quest. It couples Pater's immediacy to a coherence of perspective that transcends the purely personal. Moreover, transpersonal coherence is not bought at the expense of personal integrity. There will be, Benedict tells us, no "distractions of belief or anxiety," no "dogmas" or "duties." It is almost as if she sought the vision, the voice, the perspective of a god, or of an omniscient narrator.

Drawing together these fragments of Benedict's private writings, we find a neat model of the modernist sensibility. Benedict sought to realize an authentic personality in an individually chosen career or lifework. Although tempted by conventional roles, including domestic duties and female professions, she found herself unable to settle for them. Coupled with her quest for self-realization was the desire to discover an authentic moral order, but such an order had to be acceptable to her personality and temperament. Thus, writing, through which one might create order in a fragmented world, came to represent a solution to her. Anthropology would give her the institutional framework within which to forge an alternative genre.

MASTERING PATTERN

When Ruth Benedict came to anthropology, the Boasian school was beginning a transition from the study of the distribution of isolated culture "traits" to the study of cultural wholes and the processes whereby traits are assembled to form such wholes. Boas had spent several decades attacking nineteenth-century evolutionary anthropology. He argued that evolutionary schemes of universal history were based upon ethnocentric and unreliable categories, and demonstrated their improbability when confronted with empirical studies of the diffusion and distribution of culture traits. But the ethnographic research that permitted Boas and his students to trace the empirical (as opposed to speculative) origins of culture traits raised new questions. How did such traits come to be amalgamated into living cultures, and what was the nature of the integrative force that held amalgamated traits together? To the latter question, Ruth Benedict's work would provide an important answer.

Like many of Boas's students, Benedict wrote a library dissertation treating not culture wholes but the diffusion of culture traits. (It was entitled ***The Concept of the Guardian Spirit in North America***.) The summer before she completed her dissertation, she traveled to Southern California to do "salvage ethnography" on an apparently disappearing Amerindian group, the Serrano. It is unclear whether Benedict lived among the Serrano for any length of time, or stayed mainly with her mother and sister in Los Angeles. Her work consisted in interviewing aging informants about past customs. In any case, not until her trip to Zuni in the summer of 1924 did Benedict experience what she considered to be her professional initiation, doing fieldwork in a living culture. She returned to the Pueblos the next summer, and made further field trips to the Southwest in 1927 and 1931.

According to Margaret Mead, "Anthropology made the first 'sense' that any ordered approach to life had ever made to Ruth Benedict." She arrived at Columbia at a time when "Boas was still interested in diffusion and in having his students laboriously trace a trait or a theme from culture to culture." Benedict's dissertation on the guardian spirit was just such a tracing, but apparently the work of poring over the technical literature on Amerindian culture did not discourage her: "A good day at relationship [that is, kinship] systems—not Mohave however," is a typical diary entry from 1923. Her field trips to the Pueblos seem to have marked a personal turning point for Benedict. Writing to Mead in 1925 from the Peña Blanca Pueblo, she described her newly won confidence: "three years ago it [a month's isolation] would have been enough to fill me with terror. I was always afraid of depressions getting too much for me. . . . But that's ancient history now."

"A Brief Sketch of Serrano Culture" was Benedict's first publication based on her own field materials (she had already published her dissertation and an article based on it). Modell points out that Serrano was a culture about which Benedict "had trouble writing . . . partly because data were scant and partly because she did not see a design in the disparate remaining elements of Serrano culture." The article is organized in terms of standard ethnological categories, with major sections on "Social Organization," "Ceremonial Observances," "Shamanism," and "Material Culture." Benedict announces at the outset that she will do little more than report "information . . . [that] is almost entirely exoteric," for "a great deal of the old meaning . . . is undoubtedly lost." From her perspective, the Serrano, like the anthropologist herself, faced the dilemma of a meaningless existence: "It is largely by guesswork that they can give the meaning of any of the ceremonial songs; and any religious connotation in such practices as rock-painting, for instance, is now unknown." However, it is equally possible that the anthropologist's quest for authenticity generated questions that informants could not answer, and thus led Benedict to perceive their situation as meaningless.

Benedict's Serrano article is little more than a listing of traits. Significantly, items that Benedict would bring together in later publications as elements of an internally meaningful ceremonial complex are here reported under different headings. . . . Also significant is the absence in this early work of holistic comparisons, for the placing of whole cultures side by side would become a cornerstone of her later narrative and epistemological method. By contrast, in the Serrano essay, cross-cultural comparison is confined to traits, as it typically is in the work of both evolutionists and diffusionists. For example, Benedict points out that Serrano joking relationships seem congruent with a form of moiety organization well known in the literature, but that kinship terms and joking status do not coincide as they should in the standard moiety system. Benedict's discussion here demonstrates deference to the authority of a technical jargon, but it lacks conviction. The article ends, abruptly and almost surrealistically, with a section on food. Describing Serrano methods for harvesting and preparing mesquite, nuts, and deer, Benedict tells us in the final sentence of the essay that "[t]he bones were pounded in mortars while fresh, and eaten in a sort of paste."

In the four years between the Serrano article and the first of the papers that resulted from the Pueblo field trips, Benedict reformulated Boasian anthropology into her own approach, in which, as Modell puts it, "culture wholeness became her disciplinary idea." As suggested, other American anthropologists were moving in the direction that Benedict took. Particularly important was a well-known essay by her close colleague Sapir, entitled "Culture, Genuine and Spurious," one of the first statements in American anthropology concerning what Benedict would call cultural integration. Benedict was also influenced by Jung and by the Gestalt psychologists, as well as by her reading of German philosophers of history such as Spengler and Dilthey. In 1928 she presented a paper on **"Psychological Types in the Cultures of the Southwest"** and in 1932 published **"Configurations of Culture in North America."** These papers, and a third on **"Anthropology and the Abnormal,"** published in 1934, together contain most of the central arguments of ***Patterns of Culture***.

Benedict's key idea was that cultures are configured or integrated around one or a few dominant drives, themes, or patterns. The obverse of the ongoing diffusion of culture traits is the absorption of borrowed traits into a preexistent culture whole. Benedict argued (in almost unavoidably personifying terms) that each culture selects from material available to be borrowed, as well as from the creative productions of its own members, and reinterprets the materials it chooses to incorporate. Such selection and reinterpretation are to be accounted for by the existence of a "fundamental psychological set" or "configuration" that can be taken to characterize and permeate the culture as a whole.

The 1928 paper on **"Psychological Types"** confines itself to these points, exemplified in a contrast Benedict draws between the Pueblos and other Native American cultures of the Southwest. She begins where the diffusionists leave off, pointing out that the most striking feature of Pueblo culture—its ceremonialism—hardly distinguishes it from other Native American cultures, since most of them also show "high ritualistic development." The difference, according to Benedict, lies in the spirit of Pueblo ceremonialism: the two groups of cultures differ in their "fundamental psychological sets," which she labels with terms taken from Nietzsche: "Apollonian" and "Dionysian." The Apollonian Pueblos share with their neighbors such religious and ceremonial traits as hallucinogenics, fasting, and the vision quest. However, the Pueblos have purged from these traits all traces of Dionysian ecstasy. Whereas diffusionists were content to plot the distribution of traits and trait complexes, Benedict sought to portray whole cultures by interpreting the inner spirit that knits traits together into a way of life that is meaningful and coherent to those who live it. As she concludes, "It is not only that the understanding of this psychological set is necessary for a descriptive statement of this culture; without it the cultural dynamics of this region are unintelligible."

A more sophisticated version of these arguments is found

in the 1932 essay on North American culture configurations. There, Benedict draws on the interpretive philosophies of history of Dilthey and Spengler in order to develop her notion of a culture's psychological set. She does not abandon psychologistic concepts, but enlarges her notion of culture so that her arguments can no longer be dismissed as psychological reductionism. Moreover, Benedict's comparative hermeneutics of culture is now developed in stunning fashion, setting up a paradoxical resolution to the modernist quest for holism.

Benedict begins by reviewing the "anecdotal" status of most of the ethnological data compiled in the past. These data, she claims, have been presented as "detached objects" with no attention to "their setting or function in the culture from which they came." She then praises Boas's field studies and Malinowski's functionalism as representative of a new anthropology that has begun to study cultures in holistic fashion. But Malinowski's functionalism is inadequate, she argues, because once it has shown that "each trait functions in the total cultural complex," it stops—without considering "in what sort of a whole these traits are functioning." In other words, analysis of a functioning whole differs from that of a meaningful whole, a distinction basic to Boasian anthropology, the roots of which lay deep in German historicism. As Sapir puts it, in his essay on genuine culture, "A magical ritual, for instance, which, when considered psychologically, seems to liberate and give form to powerful emotional aesthetic elements of our nature, is nearly always put in harness to some humdrum utilitarian end—the catching of rabbits or the curing of disease." Not only is the "emotional aesthetic" meaning of culture different from its function, it is, for Sapir and Benedict, more basic. Boas, Sapir, and Benedict all argue that humans rationalize—or invent reasons to justify—those aspects of their culture of which they become conscious. But they remain unconscious of the formal patterns (as in the grammar of one's language) that provide the ultimate ordering in culture. Thus Benedict takes care to distinguish the configurational order that she is trying to describe from the functional order of Malinowski:

> The order that is achieved is not merely the reflection of the fact that each trait has a pragmatic function that it performs—which is much like a great discovery in physiology that the normal eye sees and the normally muscled hand grasps, or . . . the discovery that nothing exists in human life that mankind has not espoused and rationalized. The order is due rather to the circumstance that in these societies a principle has been set up according to which the assembled cultural material is made over into consistent patterns in accordance with certain inner necessities that have developed within the group.

Benedict's phrasing continues to be evocative and imprecise—"principle," "consistent patterns," "inner necessities." However, her ensuing discussion, drawing on Dilthey and Spengler, makes it clear that culture has become for her a question of the meaning of life, as such meanings are constructed or patterned for the members of each culture. Disparate traits, assembled into a culture from heterogeneous sources, can be understood only in terms of the particular meaningful configuration of that culture; they take their meaning from their place in the pattern, not from their origins or function:

> Traits objectively similar and genetically allied may be utilized in different configurations. . . . The relevant facts are the emotional background against which the act takes place in the two cultures. It will illustrate this if we imagine the Pueblo snake dance in the setting of our own society. Among the Western Pueblo, at least, repulsion is hardly felt for the snake. . . . When we identify ourselves with them we are emotionally poles apart, though we put ourselves meticulously into the pattern of their behavior.

Although Benedict speaks here of emotional attitudes, the issue is, more broadly, one of cultural interpretation. In her example, we are asked to imagine ourselves in the place of the snake dancers. Without an understanding of the meaning of the snake in Pueblo culture, we will impose our own, Western understanding on the ethnographic material, and thus misinterpret the dance, however meticulously we note its external details. Sapir makes a similar argument in a 1927 essay on "The Unconscious Patterning of Behavior in Society," an essay that Benedict must have known. Sapir, like Benedict, concocts a thought "experiment." He asks the reader to imagine "making a painstaking report of the actions of a group of natives engaged in some form of activity, say religious, to which he has not the cultural key." A "skillful writer," Sapir suggests, will get the external details right, but his account of the significance of the activity to the natives "will be guilty of all manner of distortion. . . . It becomes actually possible to interpret as base what is inspired by the noblest and even holiest of motives, and to see altruism or beauty where nothing of the kind is either felt or intended." Sapir goes on to speculate about how it is that natives can regularly reproduce in their behavior cultural patterns of which they have no conscious awareness. By contrast, Benedict's discovery of cultural patterning leads her to issue a programmatic call to her colleagues to reorient field research in order to document the patterns of particular cultures. For her, the anthropologist's ability to master pattern was never in doubt. It was the anthropologist's business to stand aside and describe in objective terms the cultural patterns that make life meaningful for the peoples under study.

Yet Benedict's interpretive method is fundamentally comparative and hermeneutic. It thus implies the impossibility of objective descriptions of individual cultures—or, more precisely, of descriptions constructed by an observer occupying neutral ground. In the **"Configurations"** article, as in ***Patterns of Culture*** and ***The Chrysanthemum and the Sword***, cultures are never described in isolation. Rather, their characteristic configurations or patterns are delineated by way of contrast with the patterns of other cultures. Thus, a Benedictian description of a culture depends as much upon which culture the observer/writer chooses as the relevant point of comparison as it does upon the "facts" of the culture in question. As we have seen, the essay on **"Psychological Types"** is largely taken up with elaborating on the distinction between the Apollonian

Pueblos and their Dionysian neighbors. A similar method is developed to a high art in **"Configurations."** There Benedict rehearses again the Apollonian/Dionysian distinction. However, not content to stop there, she introduces other, crosscutting contrasts:

> In the face of the evident opposition of these two . . . types of behavior it is at first sight somewhat bizarre to group them together over against another type in contrast to which they are at one. It is true nevertheless. In their different contexts, the Southwest and the Plains [her example of Dionysian cultures] are alike in not capitalizing ideas of pollution and dread. . . . In contrast with the non-Pueblo Southwest, for instance, these two are alike in realistically directing their behavior toward the loss-situation instead of romantically elaborating the danger situation.

Benedict goes on to elaborate this realist-romantic distinction in a long review of attitudes toward the dead. She is now working with three cultural configurations: Apollonian realists (Pueblo), Dionysian realists (Plains), and Dionysian romantics (non-Pueblo Southwest). However, each discrete type comes into being, as it were, only by way of a contrast deliberately elaborated by the anthropologist. In other words, Pueblo and Plains, distinguished by the Apollonian/Dionysian contrast, turn out to be similar, as realists, when opposed to other cultures that can be characterized as romantics. Finally, Benedict introduces a fourth configuration, that of the "megalomaniacal" Northwest coast cultures. These peoples, too, are Dionysian, but their institutionalization of the "pursuit of personal aggrandizement" represents a new crosscutting of the Dionysian temperament. This yields a configuration that can be contrasted as significantly to the Dionysian realists of the Plains as to the Apollonian Pueblos.

At this point it is worth noting that the cultural configurations that serve as the apparently holistic units in Benedict's comparisons are themselves synthetic, built by the anthropologist from multiple ethnographic sources. Consider, for example, the following sketch of a Dionysian-romantic ritual:

> Years ago in the government warfare against the Apache the inexorable purification ceremonies of the Pima almost canceled their usefulness to the United States troops as allies. Their loyalty and bravery were undoubted, but upon the killing of an enemy each slayer must retire for twenty days of ceremonial purification. He selected a ceremonial father who cared for him and performed the rites. This father had himself taken life and been through the purification ceremonies. He sequestered the slayer in the bush in a small pit where he remained fasting for sixteen days. . . . Among the Papago the father feeds him on the end of a long pole. His wife must observe similar taboos in her own house . . . etc.

The footnotes to this passage list four sources, including Benedict's field notes, from which the account is constructed. From the mass of details afforded by the sources, she begins with one that emphasizes the practical consequences of an interpretive contrast. The ethnographer, Frank Russell, had noted that "The bravery of the Pimas was praised by all army officers . . . but Captain Bourke and others have complained of their unreliability, due solely to their rigid observance of this religious law." Just as Americans might read the Western horror of snakes into the Pueblo snake dance, and thus misunderstand it, so American army officers had mistranslated Piman religiosity as "unreliability." It is with this maximal contrast that Benedict chooses to begin her portrait of the rituals.

As Benedict's account develops, she individualizes general information, bringing readers closer to the authentic existence of the natives: "the Pima" (plural) becomes two people acting out a particular ritual: "He selected a ceremonial father. . . . This father had himself taken life. . . . " As the narration takes us through the by now personalized ritual, a "culture trait" from elsewhere is injected: a custom of the Papago that is strikingly illustrative of the Dionysian-romantic horror that Benedict wishes to stress. Note that the narration returns without explicit transition from the Papago father to the Piman wife. To be sure, the Papago were "closely related" to the Pima. Moreover, the implicit epistemology of Benedict's comparative method justifies her lumping together similar or related groups in order to contrast them, as a holistic culture configuration, to other peoples grouped together as representative of an opposing configuration. Yet the synthetic nature of her culture configurations is belied by much of the rhetoric and organization of ***Patterns of Culture***, the first book in which she spoke to the public in the coherent voice of a scientist and professional writer.

THE ANTHROPOLOGIST AS MODERNIST PERSONA

Ruth Benedict's most widely known work, read by several generations of American college students, presents her theory of culture illustrated with three apparently neatly bounded, holistic cultures. It is this image of a world of discrete cultures that undergraduates most easily retain. However, a close reading of ***Patterns of Culture*** will show that Benedict's comparative hermeneutic is vigorously at work even in a book whose core consists of three separate chapters devoted to three unproblematically separate cultures. This is obvious in chapter four, on "The Pueblos of New Mexico," which is an expanded version of the 1930 and 1932 articles, continuing the presentation of the Pueblos in terms of the Apollonian/Dionysian contrast. Her contrastive method is also apparent in the final two chapters, devoted to the problem of the individual and society. There, Benedict becomes a subtle but pointed critic of American culture, discussing American aggressiveness and competition in the comparative light of Pueblo sobriety and Northwest Coast megalomania. In other words, her own culture became an important contrastive focus in her work. Indeed, her final book, the ***Chrysanthemum and the Sword***, is more than a study of "Patterns of Japanese Culture," as its subtitle proclaims. Beyond that, it is a sustained contrast between American individualism and Japanese hierarchy in which almost every assertion about Japan is brought home by means of contrastive material on American culture.

But to return to ***Patterns of Culture***: the comparative aspects of the narrative notwithstanding, the book can easily be read as a description of three distinct cultures. The sixth chapter, "The Northwest Coast of America," elaborates the discussion begun in the 1932 article. However, the mediating configurations of that essay—Dionysian realists and romantics—have been eliminated, as has the argument about crosscutting configurational dimensions. The sixth chapter thus presents the Pueblos' Dionysian opposite, but it does so in such a way that the hermeneutic construction of a contrast is hidden, and cultural differences are made to seem *solely* a function of "objective" differences in two "on-the-ground" cultures. Moreover, chapter five, based on Reo Fortune's Melanesian material from Dobu, presents an example drawn from the opposite side of the globe, in place of the mediating North American examples used earlier. Thus is the geographical and configurational gradualism of the **"Configurations"** article replaced by three apparently well-separated and starkly contrasted culture wholes.

In *Patterns of Culture* Benedict discovered the authentic, holistic cultures that she sought and from which the modern world excluded her as a participant.

—Richard Handler

An individualizing vision, then, prevails in ***Patterns of Culture***, despite the hermeneutic twist implicit in Benedict's comparative method. The holistic culture sought by alienated modernists is there discovered in portraits of three "collective individuals," to use Louis Dumont's term. That term is peculiarly apt, given Benedict's characterization of cultures as "individual psychology thrown large upon the screen, given gigantic proportions and a long time span." Indeed, I would argue that modern social theory (dating from at least the eighteenth century) swings back and forth between reified conceptions of the individual (as in utilitarianism) and reified conceptions of society and culture (as in most twentieth-century sociology and anthropology). The modernists' quest for what Sapir called "genuine culture" was motivated in part by their perception that an atomistic, rationalistic science had destroyed tradition. But the modernist's genuine culture cannot, in the final analysis, be discovered by a social science that constructs cultural wholes on individualistic principles. Indeed, embodied in governmental policies, modernist social science paradoxically leads away from holism to the routinization of all aspects of social life, bureaucratically fragmented and administered.

These remarks on the individualistic premises implicit in the theory of cultural integration return us to Benedict's notion of detachment. In ***Patterns of Culture*** Benedict discovered the authentic, holistic cultures that she sought and from which the modern world excluded her as a participant. The Apollonian, anti-individualistic Pueblos are described with an almost utopian longing, for in them, apparently, the surrender of individuality to society is not even problematic. Here there is no question of conventional ceremonies repressing individual feelings (recall Benedict's rejection of funerals and weddings in her own society). But even in cultures that demanded that individuals assert themselves, as on the Northwest coast, the thorough determination of individual personality by cultural configuration meant that individuals were unself-conscious in their individualism. Sapir, in his essay on genuine culture, writes of cultural authenticity in terms of sincerity, but Benedict objects to the argument: "It seems to me that cultures may be built solidly and harmoniously upon fantasies, fear-constructs, or inferiority complexes and indulge to the limit in hypocrisy and pretensions." Her rejection of sincerity perhaps reflects the search for that intense yet detached cultural participation that she described in her journal. Sincerity implies self-consciousness, and Benedict sought worlds in which meaningfulness and participation could exist without such an awareness. The Northwest Coast potlatcher could pursue megalomaniacal successes unhindered by modernist self-doubt.

Detachment was also to be found in the persona of the scientist. As an anthropologist-narrator, Benedict wrote into being the holistic, genuine cultures that no longer existed in the modernist's world. At the same time, she preserved her own individuality, controlling and inviolate as a narrative voice. It seems clear that the voice of the scientist and the genre of scientific writing worked for Benedict: through them she achieved the "hard" personality that she desired but could not achieve as a writer of poetry and biography. In her anthropological writing she did not eliminate all reference to herself, to the "I." But that "I" was now a scientist, a cultural anthropologist working within an established community of scholars possessed of their own techniques and discourse. For example, in the first chapter of ***The Chrysanthemum and the Sword***, the authorial voice identifies itself in a variety of terms, shifting among them gracefully and apparently unproblematically. "In June, 1944, I was assigned to the study of Japan. . . . As a cultural anthropologist . . . I had confidence in certain techniques and postulates which could be used. . . . The anthropologist has good proof in his experience that even bizarre behavior does not prevent one's understanding it. . . . The student who is trying to uncover the assumptions upon which Japan builds its way of life has a far harder task than statistical validation." Thus, in spite of the book's hermeneutic method—Japan and America are each interpreted in terms of what the other is not—the narrative is presided over by an apparently objective persona. Indeed, that persona is more than objective: it is detached, its existence grounded either in its own individuality, or in the universal comprehension of science.

Ruth Benedict's conquest of a voice and a personality as she moved through biography and poetry to anthropology might be summarily described in the words of James Joyce's young artist:

> The personality of the artist, at first a cry or a cadence or a mood and then a fluid and lambent narrative, finally refines itself out of existence, impersonalises itself, so to speak. . . . The art-

> ist, like the God of the creation, remains within or behind or beyond or above his handiwork, invisible, refined out of existence, indifferent, paring his fingernails.

This is a famous passage, one "indelible in the memory of readers of a certain age," as Lionel Trilling puts it. Ruth Benedict was of that modernist age, and in her anthropological writing she achieved the integral personality that she and so many of her contemporaries sought. The achievement of integrity depended upon writing about—or writing into existence—cultures that could be seen to be whole, holistic, and authentic. That postcolonial, postmodern anthropology has produced a spate of biographies, histories, and literary-critical analyses of our ancestors testifies, perhaps, to an inauthenticity that we perceive in ourselves, and that we try to escape by writing the storied lives of others.

FURTHER READING

Biography

Mead, Margaret. *Ruth Benedict*. New York and London: Columbia University Press, 1974, 180 p.

Biography that draws extensively on Benedict's letters and private journals.

Ruth Fulton Benedict: A Memorial. New York: Viking Fund, 1949, 47 p.

Memorial tributes to Benedict, including contributions by Margaret Mead, Alfred Koeber, Erik Erikson, and Robert Lynd.

Criticism

Bennett, John W. "Echoes: Reactions to American Anthropology." *American Anthropologist* 55, No. 3 (August 1953): 404-11.

Discusses reactions to *The Chrysanthemum and the Sword* among Japanese scholars.

Briscoe, Virginia Wolf. "Ruth Benedict: Anthropological Folklorist." *Journal of American Folklore* 92, No. 366 (October-December 1979): 445-76.

Examines Benedict's contribution to folklore as a scholarly discipline.

Kardiner, Abram, and Preble, Edward. "Ruth Benedict: Science and Poetry." In their *They Studied Man*, pp. 204-14. Cleveland and New York: The World Publishing Co., 1961.

Overview of Benedict's major works.

Reuter, E. B. Review of *Race: Science and Politics*. *The American Journal of Sociology* XLVI (1940-41): 619-22.

Somewhat negative view of Benedict's study of race relations. Reuter finds the book lacking in "developmental process."

George M. Cohan

1878-1942

(Full name George Michael Cohan) American stage performer, playwright, songwriter, director, and producer.

INTRODUCTION

Cohan was a dominant force in shaping American musical theater in the early part of the century through a successful Broadway career that produced some of the biggest songs hits of the time. Known for his patriotic themes and sentimentality, his works embodied the attitudes of a country flexing its muscles as an emerging world power.

Biographical Information

Cohan was born in Providence, Rhode Island, the third child born to the vaudevillians Jeremiah and Helen Cohan, who with their daughter Josephine (the first child died in infancy), traveled from town to town as "The Four Cohans." After making his debut in his father's arms, the young Cohan, precocious, ambitious and confident, eventually took over the troupe. He began writing many of its skits and managed its business affairs, despite receiving little formal education. His first Broadway productions, *The Governor's Son* and *Running for Office,* were dismal failures but Cohan persevered and his third play, *Little Johnny Jones,* was a rousing success. Cohan went on to write 40 plays and more than 500 songs.

Major Works

Cohan's style was to create uncomplicated stories about easily identifiable characters that appealed to a broad audience. From his vaudeville training, he understood how to jerk a tear and elicit a laugh through mawkishness and a prankish manner. His unabashed appeals to American patriotism can be seen in the titles of some of his more popular songs and plays, including *The Yankee Prince,* "Yankee Doodle Boy," "I'm a Yankee Doodle Dandy," "It's a Grand Old Flag," and "Over There." While critics descried his works as unsophisticated and trivial, his work was wildly popular with audiences around the country for most of Cohan's career.

PRINCIPAL WORKS

The Governor's Son (drama) 1901
Running for Office (drama) 1903
Little Johnny Jones (drama) 1904
Forty-five Minutes from Broadway (drama) 1906
George Washington, Jr. (drama) 1906
The Talk of the Town (drama) 1907
Fifty Miles from Boston (drama) 1908
The Yankee Prince (drama) 1908
The Man Who Owns Broadway (drama) 1909
Get Rich Quick, Wallingford (drama) 1910
The Little Millionaire (drama) 1911
Broadway Jones (drama) 1913
Seven Keys to Baldpate (drama) 1913
Hello Broadway (drama) 1914
The Royal Vagabond (drama) 1919
The Song and Dance Man (drama) 1923
The Merry Malones (drama) 1927

CRITICISM

Arthur Ruhl (essay date 1906-1933)

SOURCE: "A Minor Poet of Broadway: George M. Cohan," in *The American Theater as Seen By Its Critics,* edited by Montrose J. Moses and John Mason Brown, W. W. Norton & Company, Inc., 1934, pp. 187-91.

[*In the following excerpts, which are from reviews that were published between 1906 and 1933 in various publications, Ruhl surveys the progress of Cohan's musicals as well as his performance in Eugene O'Neill's* Ah, Wilderness!]

If New York had a Montmartre and Mr. George Cohan were a Frenchman, one can almost imagine him wearing baggy clothes and a Windsor tie, and stalking up and down between the tables of his *café chantant* of an evening, singing his songs of Broadway. People would take him seriously, admire his lyrics because they were so "instinct" with the spirit of a certain curious fringe of society, and words and music would doubtless be published in limited de-luxe editions for circulation among the literati.

Mr. Cohan is a talented young man. He can dance in a way to charm wild beasts from their dens and make them sit up and wonder; he expresses the feelings of a certain metropolitan type as does no one else, and he not only sings and acts his pieces, but also writes their words and music. People who would naturally derive no pleasure from that conglomeration of noise and cheapness of which his musical plays superficially consist are often baffled to explain the odd fascination of Mr. Cohan's personal work. It seems to consist very much in the sincerity and artistic conviction with which he does the precise thing that you yourself probably would try not to do. He neither attempts to impersonate the gentleman in the narrower sense of the word, nor, on the other hand, to hide his own personality behind some such broad character part as the traditional Bowery tough boy. Instead he assumes the cheap sophistication of the blasé racing tout or book-maker, sings through his nose practically on one note, wears clothes that just miss being the real thing—in short, pitches everything in the key of slangy cynicism and cheapness characteristic of that curious half-world which foregathers at Forty-second Street and the shady side of Broadway. So clever a person could doubtless assume a superficial refinement for stage purpose if he wanted to. Mr. Cohan apparently doesn't; apparently he has carefully worked out a "method" aimed at sublimated cheapness, and got away with it.

In ***Forty-Five Minutes from Broadway,*** a curiously uneven conglomeration of "musical comedy," puns, and melodrama, ostensibly designed as a vehicle for the familiar humor of Miss Fay Templeton, Mr. Cohan has created in Kid Burns a character rather broader than he himself impersonates, but typical of his point of view. The Kid is "secretary" to a young millionaire who has just taken a house at New Rochelle, and through him the spectator views that suburb—not as it is, probably, but as it might appear in the day-dream of some good-humored bookmaker or wire-tapper lounging of a summer afternoon in the shade of the Metropole. As the Kid sings:

> Only forty-five minutes from Broadway. Think of the changes it brings,
>
> For the short time it takes, what a difference it makes in the ways of the people and things.

His droll amazement at the ease with which he can "get a laugh" with the stalest line—"all the old stuff goes here"—his genuine desperation at the inability of the suburbanites to understand his nimble slang—"You've gotta talk baby-talk to these guys—all they can understand is pantomime"—these and similar observations are given such sincerity and earnestness, such an almost pathetic appeal, by the quiet-voiced, lazily good-humored, plaintive Kid that for the moment the homesickness of this parasite of the town, as he thinks of himself, "standin' at the corner of Forty-second Street, smokin' a fi'-cent Cremo cigar, an' waitin' for the next race to come in," seems important. His principal song, with the lullaby-like refrain coming at the end of each verse—"only forty-five minutes from Broadway"—and Mr. Victor Moore's singing of it, are perfect of their kind. The emotion which makes the lights of Broadway the sun of one's existence, and its fatuous and premeditated gayety the music of one's soul, is not a heroic one, but to a certain corner of the world it is exceedingly real. And in Kid Burns Mr. Moore and Mr. Cohan unite in very entertainingly expressing it. . . .

January, 1906.

Mr. Cohan keeps developing. He not only sings of Broadway, but he is getting to be a sort of song-bird and prophet of that frank materialism characteristic of a certain side of New York, and, indeed, of America. It is for this reason that his ***Get-Rich-Quick Wallingford,*** which he has arranged from stories written by Mr. George Randolph Chester for one of the magazines, is a much more genuine expression of his audience's notions of fun than anything a Falstaff might do, and for them, at least, a more satisfying form of art. . . .

There is a certain special pleasure to be derived from any spontaneous art. Shakespeare's audiences liked to eat and drink, so they were amused at a sort of Gargantuan eater and drinker. Mr. Cohan's audiences like to make money, and it is natural that they should be amused by a man who makes it with absurd easiness and a light heart.

December, 1908.

In ***Broadway Jones,*** Mr. Cohan discards songs, chorus girls, and his own dances, and offers himself as a regular actor. One can easily imagine a stranger to America, inspecting us for the first time, finding this the freshest and most characteristic exhibit of our theatres. Polite comedy, such as Mr. Drew presents, timely melodrama, like *Within the Law,* musical plays—all these things are but imitations or duplications of things done just as well or better abroad. ***Broadway Jones,*** though but a flower of the Broadway asphalt, is wholly of the soil. . . .

Without Mr. Cohan's childlike cocksureness, without his clothes and his walk and his hat tipped over one eye and his way of talking through his nose, this unregenerate child of Broadway would lose half his charm. Mr. Cohan's more or less consciously elaborated surface "cheapness" actually makes his characters more likable by taking them into the region of caricature where ordinary judgments are disarmed. The black patent-leather shoes with tan tops and the nasal monotone have a relation to reality similar to that of the action of the play—express a similar taste and trust. The surface is farcical, but through the heightened light we see more clearly the genuine feeling beneath—the poetry, so to speak, of this quaint cheapness and vulgarity. Again, Mr. Cohan becomes its voice. The theatre, the play, and the principal part are his, and he does not rely, as far as I can recall, on a word of spoken slang. We may be writing about Mr. Cohan's "third period" or "later manner" before he gets through.

February, 1910.

Folks have complained of late, and I think with justice, that the Guild was a bit too inclined to express the acrid criticisms and complaints of a not very representative or significant minority. And Mr. O'Neill's plays have not infrequently been marred by a humorless overaccent, which, in the case of a dramatist less gifted and forceful, would have been described as sophomoric. But in *Ah, Wilderness!* we have the Guild, being as "American" as the most orthodox could ask, without in the least sacrificing its quality, while Mr. O'Neill, also without being any the less himself, writes as humorously and understandingly of a perfectly normal American father, mother, son and the latter's adolescent flounderings with the world and his first love as if he were a contemporary of George Ade and John McCutcheon and had been brought up in Indiana!

On top of all this we have Mr. Cohan, once a Minor Poet of Broadway, in the limited and parochial sense of the latter word, with a brown derby cocked over one eye, a nasal accent, and blindness and contempt for everything forty-five minutes away from Times Square, now, not suddenly, to be sure, but more urbanely and authoritatively than ever before, taking the part of what might be described as not merely the American, in the fullest sense of the word, but almost the "universal" father.

From *The New York Herald-Tribune,* October 15, 1933.

Current Opinion **(essay date 1914)**

SOURCE: "Is George M. Cohan to Be Regarded as a Joke or a Genius?" in *Current Opinion,* Vol. LVI, No. 3, March, 1914, pp. 192-93.

[*In the following essay, the critic appraises the popular appeal of Cohan's works.*]

Why not write a history of the drama from Shakespeare to George M. Cohan? a witty man recently asked in a tone of raillery. "Yes, why not?" remarks Joseph Bernard Rethy in the *International.* The world is beginning to take Cohan seriously as a playwright. Once upon a time, as Peter Clark MacFarlane maintains in *McClure's,* Broadway unhesitatingly would have pronounced Cohan a joke. Today many people are questioning whether he is not a genius. When we remember that George Cohan did not see the inside of a schoolroom after he was eight years old, nor often enough before to remember now how to set a stage for one; that he has never looked a private tutor in the eye; that since his childish days when he made his first début upon a donkey in a Wild West parade he has been lammed about from corner to corner of the country in the itinerant show business; and that, in spite of all, he is what he is, we agree that his career does exhibit elements explainable upon no other hypothesis than a superendowment of birthday gifts.

Cohan came up from Fourteenth Street ten years ago with ***Little Johnny Jones*** with bells and the thump of the big brass drum. But Broadway refused to be diverted. While the folks in front were looking him over, he was, in turn, looking them over. He noticed what made them laugh and what made them grave. After two short weeks, Cohan took his play to the one-night stands, where, each midnight, after the performance, he sat down to rewrite it, and on each morrow tried the new version on the next town. In a fortnight he came back and took Broadway by storm. He had found its funny-bones and was tickling them all at once.

> Successful innocence, reciprocated love, impugned honor, triumphant vindication—old, old, *old!*—were the elements of the story. But there was an accident in the play—its appeal to patriotic sentiments: American jockey winning English money—loving American maiden—English guile plotting ruin of American lover and incidentally breaking heart of American girl.
>
> The dramatic value of this set of sentiments was a great surprise to Cohan, but its lesson was not lost. It led him to create situations in which national feeling was aroused to the highest pitch, when at the proper moment he rushed the flag upon the stage and stood beneath it singing, cheering, waving, with such an unctuous, infectious enthusiasm that his audiences invariably joined in the chorus and were often swept to their feet, drowning the stage with cheers.
>
> And, never missing a cue from an audience, George met this very evident desire for debauches of patriotic enthusiasm by designing flag songs and flag ballets and flag choruses, and indeed whole flag plays—***George Washington. Jr., The American Idea,*** and ***The Yankee Prince***—in all of which, no matter what else happened, George or somebody else was there waving the flag.
>
> Cohan appeared deliberately to capitalize patriotism. He made it bring him dollars. He alluded to himself as the Yankee Doodle Boy, and it began to be humorously remarked that the whole Cohan family was eating off the American flag.

Immediately thereafter, Cohan's biographer goes on to say, the young playwright's self-confidence slipped upon a banana peel. He wrote a straight, non-musical farce called ***Popularity,*** which entirely failed to live up to its name.

> This failure, however, may have been one of the best things that happened to Cohan, for the trouble with the piece was in danger of becoming the trouble with Cohan. In ***Popularity*** the hero was an impossible upstart, of whom the public would have none. Cohan heroes had all been of this smart-Aleck type. Cohan himself, with his sudden riches, his loud clothes and his cocksureness of bearing, gave evidence of developing an ego as overweening as that of his hero.
>
> He seemed to lack refinement. True, he pleased his down stairs audience as well as his gallery; but his down stairs audience had an up stairs heart in it. The people who laughed with Cohan were not quite the same people who were pleased by John Drew or moved by Mrs. Fiske or delighted by Maude Adams.
>
> No doubt Cohan saw all this. Perhaps the failure of ***Popularity*** helped him to see it more clearly. Perhaps it struck in and tutored somewhat those personal tastes which, according to his critics, stood sadly in need of schooling.
>
> Anyway, from about this time forward his clothes became less noisy, his manner of life less ostentatious, and his performances showed here and there eliminations that marked an awakening sense of those eternal fitnesses which are the essence of good taste.

Cohan rewrote ***Popularity,*** sandwiched it with songs, studded the stage with chorus girls, stuck Raymond Hitchcock in the center, and called it ***The Man Who Owns Broadway***. This time the piece scored an uproarious success. Then came ***Get-Rich-Quick Wallingford***.

> ***Wallingford*** as a series of sketches presented pitfalls. It involved difficulties of selection and construction, it required niceties of adjustment to keep this pungent creation of George Randolph Chester's entertaining without becoming insufferable. It went upon the boards as straight, well-constructed satire. It was neither a work of creative genius nor a jumble of showman's tricks, but mere intelligent application of the principles of stage technique and an intimate

> knowledge of the public tastes. And it was not to be carried by Cohan's stage presence—he was not in the cast.

Get-Rich-Quick Wallingford and ***Broadway Jones*** were followed by ***Seven Keys to Baldpate***. With this latest play in mind, the writer goes on to say, we are forced to conclude that behind the mask of the farceur and under the spots of the harlequin, Mr. Cohan has been hiding something we did not see, harboring designs of which we were not aware, and nurturing ambitions which are worthy of our high respect. If we look, with Mr. MacFarlane, into Cohan's past, we find that his life, with its obscure beginning in music-halls, has never been entirely without the hint of a worthy future.

Herman J. Mankiewicz (essay date 1925)

SOURCE: "George M. Cohan on the Dusty Road to Broadway," in *New York Times Book Review*, April 19, 1925, p. 11.

[*In the following review, Mankiewicz unfavorably appraises Cohan's autobiography.*]

It was in the Summer of 1924 that travelers returning from Atlantic City kept bringing to sentimental Broadway the happy tidings that George M. Cohan was writing the story of his life. And great and natural was the rejoicing, for here was an author who had but to tell freely of the things he himself had lived and seen to re-create that exciting glorious era in which the new American theatre really has its fundamental roots.

Twenty years on Broadway—from the beginnings of the century into its third decade! Here, surely, would be the background of a handful of eager, ruthless, tireless, selfish, visionary young men who had carried the American theatre great distances on the surface of a new civilization. Here, beyond doubt, would be the story of how the American theatre had changed in twenty years from a small, imitative, inbreeding actors' tribune to a stage in which there would be room for the dreams and ideas of all, to a stage international and yet passionately American.

The years it took to get there—the years in which the Four Cohans toured tirelessly through the nation's wind-swept halls, ever on the march that was to find its triumphant goal in the George M. Cohan Theatre at Forty-second Street and Broadway, of course, for it could never have been built anywhere else. The years it took to get there—entwined so closely with the rise of an obscure backroom entertainment to the vaudeville that is today one of the leading amusement factors of the country; surely there would be a picture of those days and those struggles.

And now comes the long-awaited book, although those who have been eager for it have already read it in serial form in *Liberty*. It is unqualifiedly a disappointment.

Mr. Cohan has written a book that could easily have been written by any of ten thousand hack writers equipped with a memorandum of the important dates in Cohan's acting and producing life and the instruction that the legend of the Cohan ego was to be preserved throughout. Save for one or two inconsequential anecdotes, there is nothing in the book that could not be had from a reading of newspaper files and the exercise of a not necessarily lively imagination.

If it is obvious, then, that there is very little in the book, it is equally obvious that there is a good deal out of the book. Thus, after a few pages of incidental introduction, the actors' strike of 1919 is disposed of in 200 words, centred around the statement that "it isn't up to me to write the real story of the actors' strike of 1919." The minor point that the writing of a book about George M. Cohan's twenty years on Broadway might reasonably be expected to involve the real story of the Cohan attitude in the actors' strike of 1919 is handsomely ignored.

About 75 per cent. of Mr. Cohan's book is devoted to his surface survey of the years it took to reach Broadway, and easily 75 per cent. of this account is devoted to a good-natured if obvious exposition of the great belief in himself entertained by the young George.

Mr. Cohan, in his book, keeps alive the fiction of himself as a young man battling his way to the top through the forces of dislike and prejudice unleashed as well by his rivals as by the critics of the country. The circumstance that he was one of the famous men of the nation's theatre before he was 25 and the subject of long and laudatory articles before ever Gilbert Seldes let us know that there was a popular theatre he happily ignores.

The criticism, of course, has been of Mr. Cohan's account of his years and not of the way in which he has spent them. For his has been a strenuous and romantic career, and the appraisal of him as actor, playwright and producer, even from the pens of determinedly unfriendly critics, must be such as to put him at the very top of the American theatre.

There are those, of course, who will always remember him confusedly as the young man who sat on a suitcase, in a yellow light, with a derby over his ears, and thanked everybody and said something through his nose about rather being a lobster than being a wise guy. The more profound and the fairer, however, carry with them the realization that this is the man who wrote ***Seven Keys to Baldpate*** and the Cohan revues, and it is these unfortunates who ever and again moan wistfully and wonder when the man is going to get down to the work he can and should do.

Among the few interesting contributions Mr. Cohan, in his book, makes to the general stock of knowledge about his activities is the story of how the "Cohan style" of eccentric dancing came to be born.

> I had always done a dance in our four-act, to the tune of "Comin' Thro' the Rye," he writes. "I'd always claimed that the dance was all right but that the music killed it, so I asked the orchestra leader one morning if he could substitute some other tune for 'Comin' Thro' the Rye.' "
>
> "What kind of a dance is it?" he asked.
>
> "An old-fashioned essence," I replied.
>
> When we got to the spot in the act for the dance at the matinee that afternoon, I gave the leader

the cue and the orchestra started up the music (the new arrangement he had brought from his home). It was the weirdest melody I had ever heard, and the drummer accompanied the tune with a tomtom effect, characteristic of the American Indian. I tried my best to get into the dance, but my sense of rhythm was keen enough to make me immediately realize that the thing broke time and also that the piece did not carry an even number of bars. The melody continued, but instead of dancing I stood dead still in the centre of the stage, trying to figure out just why I couldn't do my essence steps to the music. It suddenly dawned on me that, instead of its being in six-eight time, to which I'd always done this particular dance, the thing they were playing was in two-four time.

A sudden idea came to me—naturally I had to think very fast. Why not try some buck steps? I'd always used two-four melodies for bucking. No sooner thought of than done. I was into my old "Lively Bootblack" routine before I knew it, but without the spread of the jig sand; and, besides, I was in a comedy "make-up." The tempo was very slow, so, in order to make the steps fit, I had to drag them out more or less, and so exaggerated the thing by leaping from one side of the stage to the other, instead of sticking to the centre.

The melody suggested comedy, so I made every move as eccentrically as I could. I did a jump with the "scissors-grinder" step, and threw my head back at the same time. It got a scream of laughter. I repeated this a moment later and got a second big laugh. Every time I threw my head back my hair (which I wore exceptionally long at the time) would fly up and then down over my face, and I'd brush it away and do another throw back and up and down the hair would go again. I faked a couple of funny walks to fit in the spots where I had to eliminate certain steps on account of the slow tempo, and each of the walks got hearty laughs and rounds of applause. I finished with an eccentric walking step, throwing my head back with the hair flying all over my face, and made an exit with the end of the strain instead of ending with the old-fashioned "break."

The dance was a sensational hit. Lucy Daly (now Mrs. Hap Ward) of the famous Daly family of dancers came running back stage after the act and went into ecstacies over the thing.

"That's the greatest eccentric dance ever done on any stage," she declared. It was a golden opinion, coming from her.

For twenty solid years I did this same dance to the same music, and this was the stunt which eventually not only revolutionized American buck dancing, but also set the "hoofers" to doing away with jig sand and letting their hair grow long enough to fall over their eyes.

The "Cohan style" they used to call it. But little did they guess that the thing was nothing more or less than an accident, brought about by an orchestra playing a two-four melody instead of a six-eight.

It is not necessary to recount the Cohan career here. Those people to whom the name of Cohan means anything at all are not unacquainted with the fact that he was one of the Four Cohans; that he wrote ***Little Johnny Jones*** and ***The Yankee Prince*** and such: ***Get-Rich-Quick Wallingford*** and ***Broadway Jones*** and such; ***The Song and Dance Man*** and such; ***Little Nelly Kelly*** and **"Mary"** and such; and the Cohan revues ***Seven Keys to Baldpate***. And **"Over There."** Although some grumblers in the A. E. F. were always wondering why the promised visit of Mr. Cohan in one of the entertainment units didn't materialize.

However, Mr. Cohan has had an amazing career, and there is every reason to believe that he will some day write his story over again, earnestly and intelligently that time. For does he not close the present volume with these words:

> With these few remarks, I now wish to announce my immediate and permanent retirement from the literary world.

John Mason Brown (essay date 1933)

SOURCE: "Mr. Cohan in *Ah, Wilderness!*" in *Two on the Aisle: Ten Years of American Theatre in Performance*, W. W. Norton & Company, Inc., 1938, 235-36.

[*In the following excerpt, originally published in 1933, Brown reviews Cohan's performance in Eugene O'Neill's* Ah, Wilderness!]

As the small-town editor in *Ah, Wilderness!* George M. Cohan gives the kind of performance about which, were his name Gregory Mussorgsky Cohansky and Mr. Cohan a member of the Moscow Art Theatre, Oliver M. Sayler would undoubtedly be writing polysyllabic books. The learned weeklies and highfalutin' monthlies would soon be devoting pages to it in which such fancy words as "rhythm," "pattern," and "antiphonal radiance" would be printed in even fancier type. Having been a simple Yankee Doodle Dandy, a flag-waver and a Song-and-Dance man, and being an actor who is even now appearing in a domestic drama which begins on the Fourth of July, Mr. Cohan may have to content himself with simpler and more enthusiastic adjectives. But praise he has already won in abundance, and cannot fail to win because of this most brilliant of his characterizations.

As is his wont, Mr. Cohan uses no make-up. A pair of spectacles slipped from time to time before his eyes is his only external aid to characterization. He is himself—his old, jaunty self, a little more stooped than formerly and draped in the short coats of an outmoded fashion. His eyes are full of their old mischief and given to occasional winks which are irresistible. His head still sways from side to side. And he meanders about the stage with that astonishing dancer's ease which has always been his.

He is his regulation self—with a difference. Mr. O'Neill's script has found its way into his heart even as Mr. Cohan aids in making it find its way into the hearts of all who see it. He acts with a new depth; with a mellow poignancy born of the play he is adorning.

He is one of our veteran performers, yet he has none of the older actor's tricks. He is a star (even at the Guild) who does not have to take on the cheap prerogatives of stardom. He dominates the stage and conquers his audience by playing down, by dodging all the easy vocal devices for pathos or for humor by means of which lesser performers of his generation would have faked the part—and ruined it. He shares his first entrance and takes positions which give the stage to others. By his very refusal to steal the show the stage becomes his. He dominates it with a generosity which never gets in the way of the real meaning of Mr. O'Neill's play. His pauses, his understatement and his relaxation are in themselves eloquent lessons in the art of acting.

George M. Cohan (essay date 1939)

SOURCE: "I Like Small-Town Audiences," in *The Rotarian,* Vol. LV, No. 3, September, 1939, pp. 10-13, 59-60.

[*In the following essay, Cohan reminisces about the early days of his career and the joys of playing before small-town audiences.*]

The boys who write the blurbs about George M. Cohan for the newspapers have me all wrong. They have given the public the idea that I and all my family have always been "big towners," and that we had been born and bred and fed on Broadway. The most that Broadway can claim of one or of all the four Cohans are the feathers that "the road" stuck in our caps.

We were all four small-town folks, when you get right down to it. Boston was really a small town when it gave Jerry Cohan, my father, to the world. Providence, Rhode Island, was what the profession affectionately called a "tank town" when Helen Cohan, nee Costigan, was born there. It wasn't much more than that one morning—now 61 years ago—when the whole town was shooting off fireworks, not to celebrate the blessed event of my birth, but because it was the Fourth of July. And it was in the Boston Museum—and not on Broadway—that many years later, as The Four Cohans, we launched into "big time."

Finally, it was neither the Big City nor the Windy City that first gave us the big hand and the inspiration that led up to it. It was the small towns of America, from New England to the Pacific Coast. We spent most of our early professional days solely in their company. On the "road." And by the "road" I mean the whole of a show-hungry America, outside of four or five big towns.

But the "road," our "road," is gone. For one reason because today it costs as much to move the scenery and the "props" of a show from stage to sidewalk as it once did to make the whole trip from New York to Chicago. There is no question of audiences. They are still there, as hungry as ever. Psychologically they had not changed a whit a couple of years ago when I did 25 weeks of one-night stands with *Ah, Wilderness!* that I'm still tingling over.

What I'm really trying to say is that the small-town audience has been an important factor in the education of the player and in the growth of the American theater. There was no time for the education of the children of factors' families, and no law to compel it, in those days. It was mainly a school of hard knocks and what you could learn from the study of other men—of audiences, in our case.

In the profession they called us "the travelling Cohans" because we spent nearly all our time on the road. After all these years I don't suppose there's a single American city—"small town" they could be rightly called on looking back—that I haven't played at some time or other. I could draw you a diagram of Main Street and a working plan of the opera house in the majority of cases. I can do this so readily perhaps because the memories are so deep, and are of things and experiences that gave the build up of my career as player and playwright. That's why I shall always love the very smell of the road. In many cases the smell came from those old narrow gauges, like the one that took us to Carbondale, Pennsylvania. I'll never forget that one because it carried us to our first "electrified" theater, over which we were greatly excited and not a little awed. That was back in 1890.

Even in the days that followed, the Edison lights often used to go out in the middle of a show and we had to fall back on the old reliable gas or even coal oil lighting. "The show must go on!" has been the battle cry of the theater, and we never failed our audience.

We were driven by another slogan, too: "The family must go on!" I think I must have crept out on the stage one night from my cradle in the wings and got a laugh and after that I was written in the show! It was something like that. Anyway, the small-town audiences, we discovered, like the real thing, the human touch. Their response is immediate and straight from the individual heart. They don't wait till the dramatic critic in the morning paper tells them what they should think of the show, the way city audiences have got in the habit of doing. That is why I have always tried out gags and songs and plays on the people "in the country," because they represent the people *of* the country.

Here's an example of what I mean. One of the most popular of many hundred songs I wrote was **"The Grand Old Flag."** When I composed it, however, I called it "The Grand Old Rag." I'll tell you why. I went to a soldiers' home and talked with the veterans and they affectionately spoke of the flag as "the grand old rag" and in a way that brought tears to my eyes. But nobody but they could use the term without seeming disrespect for the national banner, as I learned by singing it to a couple of road audiences. They were right, and I changed the title.

Our road setup in those earliest days was both simple and homespun. But because we were all simple and homespun together, they enthusiastically accepted us. My father sold the tickets, and, if sales were slow, he would give a ballyhoo on the sidewalk that he had learned in minstrel and medicine-show days. My mother collected the tickets at the door. Josephine, my sister, was the usherette. I was usually sent up to the corner of Main Street with handbills. Tickets sold at 25 and 50 cents for adults, 15 cents for children. Father blarneyed all the mothers by pinching the cheeks of their children and calling them all "the little darlin's!"—although he would have liked to charge them $1 admission because they were always disturbing the show. We were ever looking for a "$200 house." It would have taken all the worry out of the rest of a season. Sometimes we actually did find it by catching up with a county fair or a rural convention. Stack that up alongside my recent show, *I'd Rather Be Right,* where the boys in the "front office" began to grouse about poor business and talk of closing if we didn't gross $28,000!

That's the difference. It's all a business proposition today. It has to be. That's taken the old time fun out of it, when there was always something personal between us players and the small town audiences, yet with a whole lot of respect for each other at that. I remember that my father had a way of winking over the footlights at the heads of families in the audience as though to say. "This is confidential now, all that I'm sayin' to yez—between your family, God bless 'em!, and mine!" And it went over big in every place he did it.

The show itself was always of the same general character in those earliest days. Dancing, minstrelsy, and a sketch. That's when my sister first did her "Skirt Dance," which afterward became a famous headliner. This was followed by an ensemble minstrel number with songs, dances, and wisecracks. Then came the sketch. The last act consisted of individual dance "specials," the finale bringing out all four Cohans in a buck-and-wing "hoe-down" for the curtain. Then I jumped down in the crowd and sold our photographs at 10 cents each.

From the time I was 5 the family had me scraping tunes on an old fiddle we had picked up in a second-hand shop in Peoria, Illinois, billing me as "Tricks and Tunes, by Master Georgie, the Youngest Virtuoso." It brought out a knack laboring to be born in me, of picking tunes out of the air. They seemed to get the audience, making them either laugh or cry. And that's the essence of the whole show business: make 'em laugh or cry—no matter how! That was one of the most valuable lessons the road taught me, away back in my short-pants' day, and I've never ceased to be grateful for it. It was one of the most trying parts I ever played, however, due to the fact that the folks had dug up out of the "property" trunk a velveteen Little Lord Fauntleroy suit with a lace collar. After nearly every show I had to teach several small boys of the audience that I wasn't the kind of a sissie at whom they had been sticking out their tongues.

We prospered, and our company went out enlarged to six and became known as "The Cohan Mirthmakers." We put on our version of *The Exploits of Daniel Boone,* in addition to a variety bill. We took on a regular "advance man," who went ahead, hired a hall, an opera house, a tent, or whatever he could get. He billed the town and plastered it with "paper" enough to keep us out of any trouble that might arise. We carried another "extra," at $6 a week and board, as "baggage smasher." He took care of the theatrical trunks in which we carried the whole show—costumes, scenery, and properties.

In those barnstorming days we had no scripts, not even cues. You had to be a "natural" to get across. My father would assemble the company for first rehearsal, step out before us, clear his throat, and become very Irish. "And what could you do for your country, sir?" he would ask one of the newcomers. "An Irish comedian? So you think that, do you? Now, here's the idea of the show, I'll have you know," he would continue. And it was just a free-for-all. Give and take. A battle of wits. The lines were changed frequently, retaining only those that got a laugh or brought tears to the eyes of the audience.

But the Cohans soon learned that they had lost contact with the audience that had given them their inspiration. We thought at first that the audiences were slipping. But it was really our "augmented company" not making good. In that way, and it never fails, the smallest town is the biggest critic. Its judgment is as true as blue. Producers generally have come to recognize this fact and open productions somewhere "out of town." After 100 nights on Broadway I often wish I could take the show out on the road just to tone it up. You've simply got to be up on your toes during a one-night stand, for instance. Small-town audiences take a player for what he really is and what he is worth on that important occasion. Audiences may be more polite in the city, but they are not nearly so honest as their out-of-town cousin theater-goers.

A case in point was the group of small boys—especially the bad boys—who came to see our version of *Peck's Bad Boy,* all varnished up with vaudeville, with which vehicle we recaptured our intimate theater audiences again. Master Georgie, now at the advanced age of 18, stole the show with his impudent playing of the stellar rôle of the Bad Boy. Old folks roared, but small boys resented the portrayal, throwing things at me on the stage and wanting to fight me off stage. Our whole company got all steamed up when we played Madison, Wisconsin. For George W. Peck, Governor of the State and author of *Peck's Bad Boy,* was in the audience. We all expected to be decorated—or something. Instead the old boy went to sleep on us! He didn't even come backstage. It was the first, and only time I can remember that all or any part of any audience did not give us a square deal. I got my revenge in truly Peck's Bad Boy style, when later that evening my father and I recognized Governor Peck at the bar. I got a large pickle from the free-lunch counter and slipped it down his expensive full-dress shirt front under his vest, and hurried out to the train.

The time came when I added song writing to my career. Those were great days in Tin Pan Alley. Nobody ever had to worry about $1,000 royalty checks then . If you wrote a smash hit, the publisher would clap you on the back and maybe press a $10 bill in your hand. This was just about 25 years before the day that a certain Tin Pan Alley song publisher handed me a check—made out to the Doughboys' Welfare, I think it was, for they had been responsible for it—for $25,000 for a song called **"Over There!"** I had jotted it down on the back of an envelope on hearing a bugle call and the sound of thousands of marching feet on their way "over there" on my way down to the theater one morning.

What I am leading up to is that all this song and music writing gave me an idea that changed our lives—mine at least. I would rewrite the Cohan shows with music in the up-to-date vaudeville style that I had picked up in Tin Pan Alley. Even though we were still small-timers, yet non-Broadway audiences were growing up rapidly with the rest of the country, and we had to grow up with them. We went out on the bills as "The Four Cohans," and got out first break in big time "variety" in 1897. That year we got all the way across the United States to California for the first time, although I made it at least ten times during the next dozen years. It was still a long, long way to Tony Pastor's Theater, and Broadway was the shining goal. I'm not trying to be condescending to the road when I say that we made the grade in time, largely due to hard work and the human psychology lessons that small-town audiences had taught us. Perhaps the greatest difference between the road and the world audience of Broadway lay in that on the road there was an intensely personal affection for the actor and an honest feeling of awe for him that was a thing apart from the mere admiration of talent.

I used to remark, in those bright young days of 23 Summers, that the 20th Century was properly and officially opened with my first attempt at a play called ***The Governor's Son*** at the Savoy Theater on Broadway! "Look out for success, my son," I used to say before I knew what it really was. "There's always a gag in it!" It seemed to come true, because a year later the four Cohans broke up for the first time since I was born, and I went out on the road alone, with my second self-made show, ***Little Johnny Jones***. It was hard. I was always glancing in the wings for the "old man," or my mother, or Josie to come out and join me in my song and dance. There was that certain intimacy and friendliness, however, in the long-familiar audiences that both kept me up and pepped me up. Sentimental? I hope so. My gags and my lines were all back-yard stuff, because I had learned to figure out that everybody's got a back yard where he lives with his heart and sentiment. I saw to it that Little Johnny Jones was no stranger here. I had long since learned, too, that the whole country had a yen for the great American Baghdad and its Main Street, which I brought to the surface of every audience when I sang **"Give My Regards to Broadway!"** I don't think the so called sophisticated city ever quite got out of "I'm a Yankee Doodle Dandy," which I sang waving the flag, what its country cousins did. Some years later Abe Erlanger, who understood the Broadway audience better than that of the broad highway, said that I couldn't write a play without a flag in it. I took up his challenge and wrote three flagless plays in a row—***The Tavern***, ***The Miracle Man***, and ***The Seven Keys to Baldpate***.

The Four Cohans were reunited just once more, in ***The Yankee Prince,*** which I wrote with my heart in it because I knew it was our last appearance as a one family show. Every theater on the road seemed to turn out with houses crowded with old friends, as though they were saying "Hello!" and "Good-by!" to the Jerry Cohans and their kids. All the way from coast to coast we played with our eyes filled with Irish tears.

My shirt-sleeve, corned-beef-and-cabbage days in the theater were over. Fifteen years of from soup to nuts as a Broadway producer and partner of Sam Harris followed. Oh, no, I didn't stop trouping. If anything, I think I trouped farther and harder than ever before. We would play Broadway and then go out on the long road. They tell me that I've written and played in a couple of score of plays, a few of them collaborations. I've played in a couple that other people wrote. Funny thing about *Ah, Wilderness!* and the role I played in it. I seemed to know the part by heart. I had seen and met that country editor and *father* a hundred times over the footlights. I had always wanted to play him! Looking back, I've had nothing but fun out of it all. I guess that is because I put so much hard work into it. That's another thing I learned on the road: that you'll get a long way in the theater with plenty of hard work and a little honest hokum.

Finally, let me say that although I've always been "onto" Broadway, I never got into Broadway life myself. I've been to just one night club—years ago. I travel a pretty straight line between the theater and home. A homebody? Perhaps. I've always been that way, when I could be long enough in one place to have a home. Lonely? Not so long as I have a few cronies of many years' standing. They all show up perhaps once a week. Maybe we talk. Maybe we don't. That's friendship. True, I live in an apartment, but it's opposite the broad green acres of the Park. Once every day I walk round the Reservoir with a piece of grass between my teeth, and play with the squirrels.

In a small town everybody would know me and that I was 61 years old on the Fourth of July. But here in the "big town" nobody knows—or cares.

Walter Kerr (essay date 1940)

SOURCE: "Musical Biography," in *Theatre Arts,* Vol. XXIV, No. 7, July, 1940, pp. 517-19.

[*In the following excerpt, Kerr describes the production of a musical comedy based on Cohan's career.*]

George M. Cohan ordered a dish of pistachio ice cream, lit a cigarette, and shifted his chair nearer the window that looked out on Central Park. "A musical show at the University, is that it?"

"Yes, Mr. Cohan. A musical biography. We've got an idea that your career would make an exciting evening in the theatre."

"Nothing exciting about it. Just ups and downs, and a lot of things to wise up on. I don't see where you'll get enough material to make a play. But if you want to try it, kid, go right ahead. I'll call Jerry Vogel in the morning and you can get the music from him."

Go right ahead! As casually as that we gained the right to tell, on the stage at Catholic University, what is probably the most colorful story in modern "show business". And with the ingratiating right-sided smile that accompanied George Cohan's injunction, the show called ***Yankee Doodle Boy*** was turned from wishful thinking into ten weeks of writing, revising, designing, rehearsing and final gratification.

What has "musical biography" to do with a University theatre, you ask? What place, in a season that ranges from Marlowe's *Faustus* to Molière's *Miser,* has the "show business" which produced ***Forty-Five Minutes from Broadway*** and ***Broadway Jones***? To our way of thinking, a big one. Musical comedy is a valid theatrical form, in certain ways more genuinely "of the theatre" than many others; it is a living tradition. Too often the trained staffs of college producing units, doing the necessary and expert job of sustaining and revitalizing other traditions, dismiss this valuable property, relegating it to the extracurricular sphere and the social campus.

But to us ***Yankee Doodle Boy*** was too big for that. One of the functions of the tributary theatre—one of the services it can render a developing culture—lies in the recording and keeping alive of genuine Americana within its own boundaries. George M. Cohan has not only contributed to a consciously national theatre in this country, but has created large slices of it himself. He is no mere song-and-dance man, in spite of his own protestations to the contrary; rather, as the citation read him by the University says, he brought a fresh concept of native types to our theatre when such self-assertion was woefully needed.

When Mr. Cohan forecast difficulties in making a show of his career, he was right; but in the wrong direction. There was far too much material. Spanning fifty-odd years of writing, composing, dancing, acting and producing, in the conventional two-and-one-half hours of performance, was a problem. And to this professional history we added two introductory scenes: one allegedly from the first year of our hero's life, and the other noting briefly his first and practically only respite from the theatre when, at the age of seven, he developed an aversion for schooling and a passion for baseball.

This matter of continuity was especially difficult. The first and second acts divided themselves rather too sharply into different stories. The first act was a dramatic "natural" with a sound predicate of character. Cohan tells this story best, with a mellow and sly self-deprecation, in the 1925 autobiography, ***Twenty Years on Broadway***—the story of an offensively aggressive adolescent who nearly ruins his family's chances for success before he is jolted into an awareness of his own shortcomings. It became, quite easily, a study in family fortunes, affections and minor dissensions—those of the Four Cohans—and provided far more narrative body than is given to most writers of musical comedy books. It was almost a play in itself, with a complete action and resolution.

The second act was another matter. A success story is exciting in the theatre, but when you multiply it thirty or forty times a five-minute montage will exhaust its interest values. And by the time the central figure had become an independent producer, the family story was over. Our devices for sustaining some kind of unity other than that of the principal character were not brilliant, but they sufficed. And for a final, nostalgic link with the earlier story, we seized upon the fact that the star had taken *Ah, Wilderness!* for a one-night stand to his home town, and played another scene on the baseball lot (now a filling station) of Act One. We had to change home towns to do it, but then, so did Cohan.

The edited script still called for more than twenty settings; the show had to move fast, and the stage of the University theatre is small. As a result, designer Ralph Brown adopted the wing-and-drop settings of the period in which ***Yankee Doodle Boy*** began, reinforced these by flat set pieces which could be mounted and stacked swiftly, applied a slight stylization with his brush that paralleled the formality of musical comedy technique and complemented the "billboard" or "poster" motif which had been set directorially.

As a further frank emphasis on the theatricality of the materials, the brick walls of the University theatre were reproduced in vividly colored distortion as theatre walls in the backstage scenes and, to tie the two together and retain a backstage atmosphere over such scenes as were played elsewhere, a false proscenium and leg drops in wing positions repeated the brick pattern. Thus the principal figures, whether in hotel rooms, Central Park, or lavish offices never escaped the brick-wall boundaries of their professional lives, which helped to unify the extensive action.

The music was a great help, if not our complete salvation. It was all Cohan—twenty-three of his best-known songs—and had an indestructible unity of its own. If one national weekly reported that the music "was worked into the script cleverly and strictly as part of the swift-moving story," the compliment is Cohan's, and not ours. Written as sure-fire "show music" in the first place, it still stages itself, constantly suggesting narrative treatment, and bursting with opportunities for business and production devices. With a single exception, every scene of the show had at least one song, and the opening spot of the second act—a panoramic arrangement of the star's first major hits on Broadway—had four. When you have a score that includes nearly two dozen items with the zest and melody of **"Grand Old Flag," "Guess I'll have to Telegraph My Baby," "Harrigan," "So Long Mary,"** and **"Give My Regards to Broadway,"** the battle is more than half over. Incidentally, we reintroduced Mr. Cohan to at least one song he professes to have forgotten completely.

The principals were fortunate in being able to meet Mr. Cohan and discuss their roles during the early rehearsal period. He executed dance steps, sang and chatted with them on every subject but himself—the one topic on which he is maddeningly, albeit charmingly, reticent. Aside from the autobiography, we were on our own as to research. George M. was not stacking any cards in his own favor.

For the third performance at Catholic University, the original Yankee Doodle Boy flew to Washington from New York and sat in a theatre so jammed that an offer of twenty dollars for a seat went unheeded before curtain time. For him, he said, it was a thrilling evening.

Oscar Hammerstein II (essay date 1957)

SOURCE: "Tribute to Yankee Doodle Dandy," in *The New York Times Magazine,* May 5, 1957, pp. 14, 72, 78.

[*In the following essay, Hammerstein remembers Cohan as a writer and performer who personified popular American values and ideals of the time.*]

I was not one of George M. Cohan's close friends. I was just one of many Americans to whom he devoted his theatrical talents for nearly all of the sixty-four years of his life. An account of his impact on me should serve as a fair symbol of what he meant to millions of other theatregoers, thousands of other theatre workers.

To my friends, at school, George Cohan was "slick." Higher praise had we for no one. That was the word of the day. There is always one word which means "best." "Slick" has since been supplanted at various times by "keen," "hot," "cool," "terrific," "the most." In those early days of Cohan's stardom (*circa* 1905), "slick" was the adjective for him. He had to share it with lots of other people. The Yale football team was "slick," and so were some of our local school athletes.

The word seemed, however, to be especially suited to Cohan because, in addition to fitting him in its current slang sense, it was true of him in a dictionary sense. He was a smooth article on the stage, a polished performer, and the parts he wrote for himself demanded that he portray young men of poise, authority and quick wit. ***Little Johnny Jones*** was slick, and ***George Washington Junior*** was slick. So was ***The Governor's Son***. Here was the kind of young American we all hoped to be when we grew a few years older. His trousers had a razor-edge crease. His shoes were not only snugly fitting buttoned shoes, but they had gray cloth tops. A cane was one of the constant props he used on the stage, and how slickly he used it! His top hats, straw hats and derbies (gray or brown) were worn at a slickly tilted angle. When he sang songs he sang them out of the side of his mouth. This habit, accompanied by a kind of droop of the eyelids, made him seem so sophisticated, so casual, so above it all! He danced in a slight crouch and had a trick of letting his head wag loosely on his neck with a kind of jaded relaxation. He never tried any steps that were difficult for him. He used only steps which he could perform with such consummate ease that, as you watched him, you felt almost as if you were doing the dancing yourself. As I describe him, I miss him.

Never was a plant more indigenous to a particular part of the earth than was George M. Cohan to the United States of his day. The whole nation was confident of its superiority, its moral virtue, its happy isolation from the intrigues of the "old countries" from which many of our fathers and grandfathers had migrated. In those days some of our misguided millionaires married off their daughters to members of noble families on the Continent. The noblemen were happy to become suddenly rich and the girls and their families were proud to annex titles, but good, true-hearted Americans like George M. Cohan disapproved of wasting a young, pure, sweet American rose on the European marriage marts. Here is a song he wrote on the subject:

I'm to marry a nobleman
For the sake of the family.

Quite a dutiful girl am I,
Going to marry an earl, am I!

There are fellows in Yankeeland,
But the will of the family
Rules, you know,
And so
I'll marry a noble, marry a noble,
marry a nobleman.

I am aware of memory's tendency to create symmetry out of the disorder of history, and yet I cling to a persistent impression that, just as I was turning from childhood to youth, my country was going through a similar change, and George Cohan, at precisely this time, was graduating from the first phase of his precocious success and becoming a truly important figure in the American theatre. He joined with Sam Harris to form the most successful producing partnership of their era. Their company presented not only shows that starred George Cohan, but plays that were written by him for other stars (***The Man Who Owns Broadway,*** starring Raymond Hitchcock; ***Forty-five Minutes From Broadway,*** starring Fay Templeton and Victor Moore). They also produced plays and musical shows of other authorship and acquired control of several theatres.

As for our country in those days, it was most certainly emerging from carefree adolescence into a more sober maturity. The picturesque Teddy Roosevelt was supplanted by the more conventional and conservative William Howard Taft, and we were on our way to the serious-minded and responsible Woodrow Wilson.

As his country went, so went the Yankee Doodle Dandy who was born on the Fourth of July. Librettist, song-and-dance man, stage director, choreographer, Cohan now turned to the more serious theatre. He wrote his first play without music, ***Broadway Jones***. I recall that it was a definite success, but I can't remember any part of the story. What I do remember vividly was Cohan's performance as the star. I believe he was one of the best actors I have ever seen on the stage.

I would ascribe his success partly to an extraordinary talent for listening to other characters. He would "listen" so eloquently that you would be more likely to be watching him than the actor who was speaking. After the other actor had spoken Cohan would "carefully consider" his answer before delivering it. He would look at the other actor. He would turn away and then look back at him, and then, by the time he spoke his own line, one had a feeling that he had thought it all out and made it up right there on the stage. He was not an actor reciting a line written by an author. He was a person thinking of the answers and inventing the dialogue as he went along.

Cohan's transition from ***Little Johnny Jones*** to ***Broadway Jones*** may have constituted an entrance into a more adult theatre, but I don't think he became overimpressed with the change. It would have been impossible for him ever to have fallen victim to the temptation to be arty. The temptation was never there. He believed that it took all kinds of plays to *make* a theatre world. One kind of play was no better than another. All that mattered was whether a play was a good one of its kind.

He was a practical man, an instinctive showman, a man

who knew the theatre and understood its people. One of the most often told stories about him is his line to his partner, Sam Harris, after they had both had a violent disagreement with a certain actor. As the latter left their office, Cohan said: "Sam, don't ever hire that fellow again—unless we need him."

Another line I like was hid answer to Otto Harbach's question: "George, why do you give so many Irish titles to your shows—***Little Nelly Kelly, The O'Brien Girl***"? Cohan said: "It brings the Irish into the theatre. The Jews come anyway."

The first World War came in the summer of 1914, and the bright days of America's childhood became clouded. From our safe little nursery we could hear the violent sounds of our grownup relatives fighting. Our first reaction was to stay away and let them destroy one another if they wanted to. My history professor at Columbia addressed our class very solemnly and expressed the hope that the United States would never be foolish enough to be drawn into any European war. He went further and urged that if ever this happened, we as individuals would refuse to enlist. His was a 100 percent pacifist attitude.

But during the first term of Woodrow Wilson, in 1915, the Lusitania was sunk by a German submarine, and in the next two years everything changed, including my history professor. America got hopping mad. In 1917, into the war we went. The lighthearted boy among nations became a grim man, his chin thrust out, his gun in his hand, determined to put an end to this thing. And George M. Cohan, the typical American, typically neutral before, now became typically serious and purposeful. His former superficial flag-waving gave way to patriotism of a deeper and more passionate kind. He wrote America's war song, a song that was an accurate expression of the nation's mood.

"Over There" was an American's vague term for some place in Europe where the fighting was going on. That's where our troops were going. "Send the word" said the song, "that the Yanks are coming." Tell the Germans, whom we are going to fight, and the British and the French on whose side we feel we belong—"we're coming over, we're coming over, and we won't come back till it's over, over there."

This last line was not only an example of good songwriting, it was a timely stroke of international diplomacy. It was important to say we were coming over to aid our allies, but even more important to tell them that we were not coming over with any token aid or on any temporary basis. We did not intend to leave the job half done. We would not come back till it was "over, over there."

I don't believe Cohan had ever studied international diplomacy. I don't believe that he had analyzed the world situation and then attempted to compose words and music that were calculated shrewdly to help that situation. I think he wrote merely what he felt like saying at the moment, what he sensed in his heart that all Americans were feeling.

Of all literary forms, a song is perhaps the most difficult to write because the writer is not permitted to use the subtle shading available to a novelist or editorial writer. He has a limited time in which to say what he has to say, a small frame within which to paint his picture. Further, a song is heard, not read. Therefore, it had better be simple and clear or it is worth nothing at all. When you say, "Give my regards to Broadway, remember me to Herald Square," you may not have written great poetry, but you have expressed very briefly and vividly the longing of a lonely man in a foreign land. He is missing his friends and wants to return to them as soon as possible.

The essential values of simplicity, clarity and entertainment were present in all Cohan's songs. **"Over There," "It's a Grand Old Flag," "Give My Regards to Broadway"** were popular, not only in their day, but continue as lasting symbols of the time in which they were written, of the men and women who heard them and sang them. This one energetic American picked up the thoughts and feelings of his countrymen and put them into verse.

This is the function of the songwriter, the balladeer, the poet. He does not tell his countrymen or the world what they should think. He senses what they are thinking and, possessing a craftsmanship which they do not, he expresses their thoughts as they would, if they could. The French Revolution was not the result of the exhortation of Rouget de Lisle's "Marseillaise." The "Marseillaise" was the result of a spirit of revolution already shaking France. De Lisle expressed the spirit for Frenchmen, just as Cohan expressed America's thoughts and feelings in a later struggle.

Cohan received a Congressional medal for writing **"Over There"** and **"A Grand Old Flag."** It was a well-deserved and popular award. The songs were the specific reason for the honor he received in the White House, but behind the songs which had served America was a man whose whole career had served America, and most particularly a spot in America called Broadway. He was an original. He had many imitators, no equals. He belonged to this country, no other. He belonged to his own time, no other. He gave us his talents, his energy, and in a peculiar way he presented us with his personality, planted an image of himself in our hearts.

When I was told that there was talk of building a statue to commemorate George M. Cohan, I started immediately to wonder why it had not been done before. And then I tried to think of how many statues of American actors, playwrights or song writers I had seen in the parks or streets of American cities. I could think of none. Perhaps there are a few. I hope so. Here, at any rate, is a man who deserves quite obviously to be so honored. New York is the right city to have a statue of George M. Cohan, and the Broadway which he served so well is the right place in that city to harbor the statue.

David Ewen (essay date 1958)

SOURCE: "George M. Cohan," in *Complete Book of the American Musical Theater,* Henry Holt and Company, 1958, pp. 53-60.

[*In the following excerpt, Ewen chronicles Cohan's rise from vaudeville to Broadway producer and actor.*]

The son of veteran vaudevillians, George Michael Cohan was born in Providence, Rhode Island, on July 3, 1878. He was only an infant when he made his first stage appearance, carried on as a human prop for his father's vaudeville sketch. When he was nine, George made a more official stage bow, billed as "Master Georgie" in a sketch starring his parents in Haverstraw, New York. In 1888 the act was further extended to include still another Cohan, George's sister, Josephine. "The Four Cohans" soon became headliners across the country, and as time passed it was George Michael who was its spark plug. He was not only the principal performer, but also business manager and the writer of most of the songs and dialogue. By the time the century closed, the act boasted still a fifth Cohan in the person of the singing comedienne, Ethel Levey, who became George M. Cohan's wife in the summer of 1899.

In 1901 Cohan expanded one of his vaudeville sketches into a full-length musical comedy, ***The Governor's Son,*** produced at the Savoy Theatre in New York on February 25, 1901, starring the five Cohans. Cohan's debut on the musical-comedy stage was not particularly auspicious, since the play lasted only thirty-two performances. In 1903 Cohan made a second attempt at expanding a vaudeville sketch into a Broadway musical comedy, and once again met failure.

Then in 1904 Cohan entered into a producing partnership with Sam H. Harris. Their first venture was a completely new George M. Cohan musical, ***Little Johnny Jones***. As was often to be his practice in the future, Cohan not only helped produce the play and wrote book, lyrics, and music, but he also starred in it. At first ***Little Johnny Jones*** did not do well in New York, since the critics were hostile, but after a successful out-of-town tour, it returned to New York to establish itself as a hit.

For the next decade the firm of Cohan and Harris—and sometimes other producers—put on musicals by Cohan in which he often starred. Generally they were the cream of the season's crop. In 1906 there were ***Forty-Five Minutes from Broadway*** and ***George Washington, Jr.,*** two of Cohan's best musicals. After that came ***The Talk of the Town*** (1907), ***The Yankee Princess*** (1908), ***The Man Who Owns Broadway*** (1910), ***The Little Millionaire*** (1911), and ***Hello Broadway*** (1914).

Everything about Cohan was personalized. He injected a new note of brashness and informality into the American stage. As a performer he wore a straw hat or a derby slightly cocked over one eye, and in his hand he held a bamboo cane. He sang out of the corner of his mouth with a peculiar nasal twang; he danced with a unique halting kangaroo step. He had his own way of gesturing—with an eloquent forefinger. The way he strutted up and down the stage—often with an American flag draped around him—was singularly Cohanesque; so was the way he could create a bond between himself and his audiences with informal, at times slangy, salutations or little speeches or homey monologues.

As a writer of musical-comedy texts and songs he also introduced a fresh, new manner. The plays, like their author, were jaunty, swiftly paced, vivacious. As Heywood Broun once wrote, Cohan became "a symbol of brash violence in theatrical entertainment, a disciple of perpetual motion." Cohan was not equally gifted in all the departments in which he functioned. He himself once confessed his limitations by saying: "As a composer I could never find use for over four or five notes in any musical number . . . and as a playwright, most of my plays have been presented in two acts for the simple reason that I couldn't think of an idea for the third act." He also once remarked, "I can write better plays than any living dancer, and dance better than any living playwright." He had his limitations, and for all his bravado and self-assurance he recognized them. But he knew the theater and his audience, and he was a superb showman. He might frequently be "a vulgar, cheap, blatant, ill-mannered, flashily dressed, insolent smart Alec," as James S. Metcalf described him in Life magazine at the time, but he did succeed in bringing into the musical theater a new exuberance, a healthy vitality, a contagious excitement.

Up to 1919 Cohan continued to dominate the Broadway theater as producer, writer, composer, and actor. Several of his nonmusical plays were also outstanding hits, particularly ***Get-Rich-Quick Wallingford*** (1910), ***Broadway Jones*** (1912), and ***Seven Keys to Baldpate*** (1913). In 1917 he wrote the song destined to become one of America's foremost war hymns, **"Over There,"** inspired by America's entry into World War I. By 1919 he was at the height of his fame and power—one of the richest and most influential figures in the American theater.

But in 1920 he began to lose interest in the theater. One reason was his bitterness in losing a major battle with the Actors Equity Association, which in 1919 had called a strike to compel theater managers to recognize it as a bargaining representative for its members. Cohan lined up against Equity and expected all his actor-friends to do likewise. Their alliance with Equity appeared to him as personal betrayal. The complete victory of Actors Equity represented a personal defeat to Cohan, and he became a tired and bitter man. He withdrew his membership from both the Friars and Lambs Clubs; he refused to speak any longer to many who had been his lifelong friends; he dissolved the prosperous firm of Cohan and Harris.

Everything about Cohan was personalized. He injected a new note of brashness and informality into the American stage.

—David Ewen

But he did not withdraw completely from the stage, though at one point he threatened to do so. He continued writing and appearing in plays, both musicals and nonmusicals. Two nonmusicals were minor successes: ***The Tavern*** (1920) and ***The Song and Dance Man*** (1923). Most of the others were failures. "I guess people don't understand me no more," he remarked, "and I don't understand them."

What Cohan was suffering from was not merely the aftermath of his defeat by Equity, with its shattering blow to his ego. No less poignant to him was his discovery that the theater had been moving so rapidly forward that it was leaving him behind. Both on the musical and the nonmusical stage there had emerged writers with creative imagination, subtlety of wit, technical mastery, and inventiveness of ideas. Their best work was mature, slick, sophisticated. Cohan's plays and Cohan's songs—compared to theirs—seemed old-fashioned, and many of the audiences no longer responded to them. An unhappy episode in Hollywood in 1932, where Cohan went to star in the Rodgers and Hart screen musical *The Phantom President* and where he was continually ignored and slighted, accentuated for him his loss of caste in the theater.

Yet he was not forgotten, nor was he a man without honors. In the 1930's he was starred in two Broadway plays: Eugene O'Neill's homespun American comedy, *Ah, Wilderness!,* and the Rodgers and Hart musical satire, *I'd Rather Be Right,* in which he was cast as President Franklin D. Roosevelt. Both performances were acclaimed, and there were even some to consider him one of the foremost actors of the American stage. In May, 1940, by a special act of Congress, he received from President Roosevelt a special gold medal. And in 1942 his rich career in the theater was brilliantly dramatized on the screen in *Yankee Doodle Dandy,* with James Cagney playing Cohan.

Cohan was gradually recovering from an abdominal operation in 1942 when he insisted that his nurse allow him to tour Broadway in a taxi. Accompanied by the nurse, he cruised around Union Square, then up to Times Square and through its side streets. He stopped off for a few minutes at the Hollywood Theatre to catch a scene from *Yankee Doodle Dandy.* It was almost as if he were reviewing for the last time the highlights of his career.

A few months later—on October 5, 1942—he died. "A beloved figure is lost to our national life," wired President Roosevelt. Mayor La Guardia said: "He put the symbols of American life into American music." And Gene Buck hailed him as "the greatest single figure the American theater has produced."

> 1904 ***LITTLE JOHNNY JONES,*** a musical comedy, with book, lyrics, and music by George M. Cohan. Produced by Sam H. Harris at the Liberty Theatre on November 7. Staged by George M. Cohan. Cast included George M. Cohan, Ethel Levey, Jerry and Helen Cohan, and Donald Brian (52 performances).

During a visit to England seeing the sights, Cohan decided he must write a musical comedy using two locales that had impressed him. One was the pier at Southampton; the other, the court of Cecil Hotel in London. Back in America, he heard about Tod Sloan, an American jockey who had ridden in the Derby for the King of England in 1903. Cohan put two and one together and in short order came up with his first original musical comedy, ***Little Johnny Jones***.

Johnny Jones (George M. Cohan) comes to London to ride in the Derby. There he meets and antagonizes Anthony Anstey (Jerry Cohan), an American gambler who has made a fortune running Chinese gambling houses in San Francisco. When Johnny loses the Derby race, he is pursued to Southampton by angry mobs who accuse him of being crooked and having thrown the race. A detective who poses throughout the play as a drunkard and who is merely called "The Unknown," proves Johnny's innocence at the same time that he uncovers Anstey's role in destroying Johnny's reputation and his iniquitous activities in San Francisco's Chinatown. Now fully cleared, Johnny is able to win back the love of his estranged sweetheart, Goldie Gates (Ethel Levey).

Johnny Jones was Cohan's first starring vehicle, and he rose to the occasion by underplaying his part and by abandoning many of the little tricks and the absurd costume that up to now had been his trademark. With his first breezy entrance song, **"Yankee Doodle Boy,"** the "new Cohan" won the hearts of his audience completely; and he solidified that affection with his equally vivacious rendition of another Cohan classic, **"Give My Regards to Broadway,"** and his delivery of a sentimental sermon in verse, **"Life's a Funny Proposition After All."** Of the remaining numbers in the Cohan score the best were **"Good-Bye, Flo,"** sung by Ethel Levey, and an amusing ditty presented by six coachmen, **"Op in My 'Ansom."**

> 1906 ***FORTY-FIVE MINUTES FROM BROADWAY,*** a musical comedy with book, lyrics, and music by George M. Cohan. Produced by Klaw and Erlanger at the New Amsterdam Theatre on January 1. Cast included Fay Templeton, Victor Moore, and Donald Brian (90 performances).

The setting is New Rochelle, a New York suburb "forty-five minutes from Broadway." A local miserly millionaire has died and no will has been found. It had been assumed that his wealth would go to his housemaid, Mary Jane Jenkins (Fay Templeton), but due to the absence of a will the fortune passes to the dead man's only living relative, Tom Bennett (Donald Brian). Tom arrives in New Rochelle to claim his legacy, accompanied by his showgirl sweetheart, Flora Dora Dean (Lois Ewell), her nagging mother, Mrs. David Dean (Julia Ralph), and his secretary Kid Burns, former loafer and horse player (Victor Moore). Because of Kid Burns' bad manners and outspoken behavior, Tom gets into a fight with his sweetheart and her mother at a party at the Castleon mansion. Meanwhile, Kid Burns falls in love with the housemaid, Mary Jane. In an old suit of clothes Kid Burns finds the dead man's will in which the fortune goes to Mary Jane. When Kid Burns refuses to marry an heiress, Mary Jane destroys the document.

On the morning of the première of ***Forty-Five Minutes from Broadway,*** the New Rochelle Chamber of Commerce called an emergency session to pass several resolutions regarding this musical: (1) to institute a boycott; (2) to send out press releases denouncing the play as libelous to their community and its inhabitants. The Chamber of Commerce objected particularly to the title song which said that the town did not have a single café and which spoke of the males as having "whiskers like hay." After the show opened, the commotion in New Rochelle died down as the town came to realize that the play was succeeding in making New Rochelle famous.

Most of the critics did not like Cohan's new musical. The editor of Theatre reflected the prevailing opinion when he called it "rubbish" and added, "Mr. Cohan had little art" and intended only "to catch the unthinking crowd." But like ***Little Johnny Jones,*** the new musical, despite a comparatively short Broadway run, was a triumph on its road tour and returned to Broadway as a major success.

For Fay Templeton, the starring female role marked her first appearance in a so-called "clean play"—for twenty years before this she had been a burlesque star. She was a hit; and so was Victor Moore in the first of his many Broadway triumphs as a comedian, after many years in vaudeville and stock companies.

The best songs from the score are still remembered, including the title song, **"Mary's a Grand Old Name,"** and **"So Long, Mary."**

> 1906 ***GEORGE WASHINGTON, JR.,*** a musical comedy with book, lyrics, and music by George M. Cohan. Produced by Sam H. Harris at the Herald Square Theatre on February 12. Staged by George M. Cohan. Cast included the Four Cohans and Ethel Levey (81 performances).

Described as "an American play," ***George Washington, Jr.,*** had for its central theme the rivalry of two Senators in Washington, D.C.: James Belgrave (Jerry J. Cohan) from Rhode Island, and William Hopkins (Eugene O'Rourke) from the South. When Senator Hopkins makes a determined effort to expose corruption in the Senate, Belgrave decides to go off to England to buy his way into British society by inducing his son, George (George M. Cohan) to marry Lord Rothburt's daughter. But George is in love with Senator Hopkins' lovely niece, Dolly Johnson (Ethel Levey). Disgusted by his father's Anglophile tendencies, young George becomes a super-patriot and assumes the name of the first President of the United States. As it turns out, the lord and his "daughter" are frauds, hired by Senator Hopkins to get the goods on his rival. This fact is uncovered by young George, who sets his father wise. Senator Belgrave now becomes an intense patriot. Since Senator Hopkins is in love with Belgrave's widowed sister, he is ready to forget his hostility and at the same time give his blessings to George and Dolly.

The pace of the play is so swift, the dialogue so amusing, and the songs so effective that the editor of Theatre—who had recently referred to ***Forty-Five Minutes from Broadway*** as "rubbish"—said that there was "plenty that is genuinely and legitimately diverting" and called the play "mighty good entertainment."

The outstanding song in ***George Washington, Jr.,*** is **"You're a Grand Old Flag,"** in which Cohan institutes a routine for which he became famous and which he would repeat in many later plays—draping an American flag around his body and running up and down the stage singing the praises of flag and country. Strange to recall, a scandal followed the first performance of this song in the play. The idea for the song first occurred to Cohan when a G.A.R. veteran told him he had been a colorbearer during Pickett's charge at Gettysburg; pointing to the American flag, the old man said, "she's a grand old rag." In writing his song Cohan kept the expression "grand old rag." One day after opening night, several patriotic societies arose to denounce Cohan for insulting the American flag by referring to it as a rag. (Cohan insisted that this protest had been instigated by a New York drama critic who had been denied seats for his show.) When Cohan changed "rag" to "flag" all was forgiven, and the furor died down.

Two other songs became popular in 1906: Dolly Johnson's **"I Was Born in Virginia"** and **"You Can Have Broadway."** A high spot of the production was Cohan's delivery of some homey philosophy in a versemonologue entitled **"If Washington Should Come to Life."**

> 1911 ***THE LITTLE MILLIONAIRE,*** a musical comedy with book, lyrics, and music by George M. Cohan. Produced by Cohan and Harris at the Cohan Theatre on September 25, 1911. Staged by George M. Cohan. Cast included George M. Cohan, Jerry Cohan, Helen Cohan, and Lila Rhodes (192 performances).

The late Mrs. Spooner has left a will specifying that her fortune can be shared by her husband and son only if they get married. Since Robert Spooner, the son (George M. Cohan) loves Goldie Gray (Lila Rhodes) the demands of the will present no problem to him. However his friend Bill Costigan (Tom Lewis) is sure that Goldie is interested only in Robert's fortune, and does everything he can to break up the love affair. In this he is unsuccessful, since Goldie loves Robert for himself alone. To fulfill the requirements of the will, the father—Henry Spooner (Jerry Cohan)—courts and wins Goldie's aunt, Mrs. Prescott (Helen Cohan).

A pattern already established by Cohan in his musicals was here rigidly followed. The play was filled with sentimental recitations, topical songs and ballads, flag numbers, and eccentric dances. One of the leading song hits was a comedy number, **"We Do All the Dirty Work"**; other popular musical items included **"Oh, You Wonderful Girl," "Musical Moon,"** and **"Barnum Had the Right Idea."**

> 1914 ***HELLO BROADWAY,*** a musical comedy with book, lyrics, and music by George M. Cohan. Produced by Cohan and Harris at the Astor Theatre on December 25. Cast included George M. Cohan, William Collier, Louise Dresser, and Lawrence Wheat (123 performances).

Cohan described ***Hello Broadway*** as "a crazy quilt patched and threaded together." It was a burlesque in the style of those made famous by Weber and Fields in which Cohan plays the part of George Babbitt, the millionaire son of a Jersey City soap manufacturer, who returns to America from China in the company of his friend, Bill Shaverham (William Collier). The plot, however, was incidental to its satirical trimmings. Many of the current plays were burlesqued broadly. Cohan did a take-off of Leo Dietrichstein; Louise Dresser, of Mrs. Patrick Campbell as she had appeared in Shaw's *Pygmalion*; William Collier, of Pauline Frederick. Cohan's best songs were **"I Wanted to Come to Broadway," "That Old-Fashioned Cakewalk,"** and for one of his famous flag routines, **"My Flag."**

Stanley Green (essay date 1960)

SOURCE: "George M. Cohan," in *The World of Musical Comedy,* Grosset & Dunlap, 1960, pp. 24-35.

[*In the following excerpt, Green recounts the highlights of Cohan's career.*]

Victor Herbert and George M. Cohan were the two most important creative figures of the American musical stage during the first decade of the twentieth century. Apart from this, and the coincidence that both were of Irish descent, each man epitomized an entirely disparate form of musical theatre. Herbert, the thoroughly trained musician, sought to perpetuate the traditions of the Viennese operetta; Cohan, the untrained song-and-dance man, tried to break away from anything that suggested the Old World. For Herbert, the Broadway stage was something of a step downward from the elevated world of opera and the concert hall; for Cohan, it was a definite step upward from the world of vaudeville of which he had been a part since birth. Herbert felt that the music and the orchestrations and the singers were the most important elements, but Cohan, who created most of his tunes from four chords he could play on only the black keys of a piano, believed that the essential ingredient of a musical show was "Speed! Speed! And lots of it! That's the idea of the thing. Perpetual motion!"

In a larger sense, both men were symbols of the changes taking place in the age in which they lived. The portly, elegant, mustachioed Victor Herbert was a genuine Victorian figure whose carriage-trade entertainments kept alive the spirit of an earlier day which many people were reluctant to give up, whereas the brash, fast-talking George M. Cohan spoke and sang directly to a new world and to a new century. "Never was a plant more indigenous to a particular part of the earth than was George M. Cohan to the United States of his day," Oscar Hammerstein II once wrote in the New York *Times*. "The whole nation was confident of its superiority, its moral virtue, its happy isolation from the intrigues of the 'old country,' from which many of our fathers and grandfathers had migrated."

While these attitudes shone through most of Cohan's works, the character he himself usually portrayed was not a loud-mouthed braggart. Compared to the exaggerated antics of some of the comedians for whom Victor Herbert wrote—Frank Daniels (with his trick eyebrows), Francis Wilson, Montgomery and Stone—Cohan's characterizations were models of subtlety, frequently in contrast to the razzle-dazzle of his own entertainments. Strutting, prancing, talking a song out of the corner of his mouth in a deep nasal twang, he was the personification of the debonair man of affairs with whom audiences were happy to identify themselves.

As Cohan was the star-composer-lyricist-librettist-director-producer of most of his shows, the public image of the man was taken from his stage roles. And Cohan was delighted to encourage the impression that he was indeed the living incarnation of George Washington, Jr., The Yankee Doodle Boy, The Yankee Prince, The Little Millionaire, The Man Who Owns Broadway, and The Song and Dance Man. Conversely; many of Cohan's stage characters were based on actual people he had met or read about. In ***The Governor's Son*** and ***Running for Office,*** Cohan depicted Tammany politicians he became acquainted with at the chowder outings of Big Tim Sullivan, one of the local bosses. For his first hit, ***Little Johnny Jones,*** he modeled the title part to fit Tod Sloan, a famous American jockey, and for the other main character, "The Unknown," he took as his inspiration the personality of Big Tom Foley, a former New York sheriff. Kid Burns of ***Forty-Five Minutes from Broadway*** was copied directly from an ex-prizefighter whose name was really Kid Burns.

In his song, **"The Yankee Doodle Boy,"** Cohan said that he was "born on the Fourth of July." This started a myth that has persisted down to today. Actually, it was on the third of July, 1878, (verified by Ward Morehouse, Cohan's biographer), that George Michael Cohan was born in Providence, Rhode Island. His parents, Jeremiah (known as "Jerry") and Helen (known as "Nellie") were vaudeville performers; Georgie first appeared in front of the footlights as an infant, when he was carried on stage during a scene in one of his father's skits, *The Two Dans.* At eight, he played the violin in the pit orchestra; the following year he spoke his first lines on the stage. He later starred in *Peck's Bad Boy,* a part for which the pugnacious youth was exceptionally well qualified. Soon he began to write material for his family's act, The Four Cohans, which consisted of himself, his parents, and his sister Josephine.

The naïve, patriotic sentimentality of *Little Johnny Jones,* combined with its headlong pace, caught the spirit of a country just beginning to emerge as a world power.

—Stanley Green

Cohan's first song was published when he was sixteen. It was called **"Why Did Nellie Leave Her Home?"** (the girl was named after his mother), but the pleasures of its publication were greatly lessened when the young composer discovered that another writer, Walter Ford, had been called in to rewrite the lyrics. From then on, however, he wrote all of his own music and words. Some of his early successes were **"Hot Tamale Alley"** (a favorite of vaudeville star, May Irwin), **"Venus, My Shining Love,"** and **"I Guess I'll Have to Telegraph My Baby"** ("I need the money bad, 'deed I do").

As a vaudeville act, The Four Cohans had become one of

the nation's leading attractions by the turn of the century. In addition to writing all their material, George was also the business manager. He was able to demand the unusually high sum of $1,000 per week for the act in addition to specifying billing, routes, and lengths of engagements. But the uncertainties and discomforts of trouping all over the country made Cohan long for the prestige of appearing on Broadway, not as part of a variety program, but in his own musical comedy. To gain this end, he made a deal with Louis Behman of the Hyde and Behman vaudeville circuit, to have The Four Cohans tour for one season, after which they would star in a musical comedy on Broadway to be produced by Behman. Cohan had already written his Broadway script, based on his own vaudeville sketch, ***The Governor's Son***. So it was that the Four Cohans (with the addition of George's new wife, Ethel Levey) toured the country, and the following season, on February 25, 1901, New Yorkers saw the first musical written and directed by George M. Cohan.

The Governor's Son had a less-than-brilliant debut. The company, unaccustomed to a New York first-night audience, showed signs of nervousness. The pacing lacked spirit and spark. To make things worse, Cohan sprained his ankle in the first scene and had to limp through the rest of the performance. In spite of the discouraging critical verdict, the twenty-two-year-old author would not accept defeat. He closed the show after a month and took it on the road for a profitable tour. The following year, Cohan tried Broadway again with ***Running for Office,*** another expanded vaudeville sketch. Again he found New York audiences cool to his efforts.

This show also did well on the road, but it meant little to Cohan; Broadway, as he said, was "the only bell I wanted to ring." So determined was he to win recognition in the legitimate theatre that he formed a partnership in order to have some one to handle the business end while he devoted his time to improving his writing. Through a mutual friend, he met Sam H. Harris, a one-time manager of boxer Terry McGovern, who had had some experience producing melodramas on the Bowery with Al Woods and Paddy Sullivan. After a Sunday ride on a ferryboat, Cohan and Harris shook hands on a business partnership that was to last for fifteen years. (They were also related through marriage. Following his divorce from Ethel Levey in 1907, Cohan married Agnes Nolan, a dancer; two years later, Harris married her sister, Alice.)

Cohan's first Broadway success came in 1904; ***Little Johnny Jones*** followed the pattern of his first two musicals by opening to generally unfavorable reviews and an apathetic public. The company beat a fast retreat to the road. With Harris now taking care of the business details, however, Cohan could do considerable rewriting while the show was touring. When he bravely brought it back to New York the same season, it suddenly caught on and ran for a respectable three and a half months.

The naïve, patriotic sentimentality of ***Little Johnny Jones,*** combined with its headlong pace, caught the spirit of a country just beginning to emerge as a world power. Cohan's story of an American jockey wrongly accused of throwing a race in England served as a perfect vehicle for him to project his magnetic personality and to express such honest, direct emotions as the exultant **"Yankee Doodle Boy"** and **"Give My Regards to Broadway."** The tunes were meant to be whistled; the lyrics came from the heart. New York, as well as the entire country, soon responded to the electricity of George M. Cohan.

Everything that Cohan had written before 1906 had featured only himself, his family, and the American flag. It was, therefore, an irresistible challenge when producer A. L. (Abraham Lincoln) Erlanger approached him with the idea of writing a vehicle for Fay Templeton, a popular singer and comedienne who had won fame at the Weber and Fields Music Hall. "Think you could write a play without a flag?" Erlanger asked Cohan. Cohan's reply was typically flippant: "I could write a play without anything but a pencil."

Cohan and his pencil created ***Forty-Five Minutes from Broadway,*** an even bigger hit than ***Little Johnny Jones***. Opening on January 1, 1906 (one week after Victor Herbert's *Mlle. Modiste*), it was a well-constructed amalgam of melodrama and songs, among which were **"Mary's a Grand Old Name"** and **"So Long, Mary."** The title number, an amusing piece extolling the virtues of country life in New Rochelle, called the natives "Reubens" and noted their "whiskers like hay." These aspersions caused the local Chamber of Commerce to issue a proclamation urging the townspeople to boycott the show, thus giving Cohan some gratuitous publicity. Although Miss Templeton was the star, a young actor named Victor Moore, who had never appeared in a musical comedy before, gave an equally impressive performance as the "square-sporting man," Kid Burns. (When ***Forty-Five Minutes from Broadway*** was revived in 1912, Cohan himself took the part.)

With ***George Washington, Jr.,*** Cohan returned to his family and the flag. In spite of its preposterous story which dealt with a rich young man so incensed over his father's Anglomania that he adopted the name of the father of his country, the show succeeded chiefly because of the great appeal of Cohan and his songs. "I was born in Virgin-YUH! That's the state sure to win YUH!," sang Ethel Levey to the second balcony. With his head cocked to one side, Cohan delivered the irresistible **"You're a Grand Old Flag."** (Ironically, the song was originally called "You're a Grand Old Rag," but the protests of patriotic organizations forced the Yankee Doodle Boy to substitute "flag" for the affectionate term "rag.")

The originality and freshness soon ran out of George M. Cohan's musicals, even though they still found a wide audience. In 1907, Cohan offered a revised version of ***Running for Office*** called ***The Honeymooners,*** and he wrote ***The Talk of New York*** so that Victor Moore might again portray the popular character of Kid Burns. (The song hits were **"When We Are M-A-Double R-I-E-D"** and **"When a Fellow's on the Level with a Girl That's on the Square."**) ***Fifty Miles from Boston*** in 1908 (in which **"Harrigan"** was first sung) merely put the familiar Cohan characters into a new New Rochelle setting—this time North Brookfield, Massachusetts, where the author spent his summers.

Josie Cohan, who had left the act before ***Little Johnny Jones,*** was reunited with her family for ***The Yankee Prince*** in 1908, an occasion that inspired the star to bill himself as "George M. Cohan and his Royal Family." The customary chauvinism of Cohan's plots was here expanded to include a firm stand against the then-current practice of rich American families marrying off their daughters to titled foreigners. Cohan's feelings on the subject were expressed in the song, **"I'm to Marry a Nobleman"** ("Quite a dutiful girl am I, Going to marry an earl am I"). Two and one-half years later Jerry and Nellie Cohan made their final appearances on the stage. This was in George's ***The Little Millionaire***.

The trend toward revues accelerated in the mid-1910's. In an attempt to keep up with the change, Cohan presented ***Hello, Broadway!,*** "A Musical Crazy Quilt Patched and Threaded Together with Words and Music and Staged by George M. Cohan." There were also two editions of ***The Cohan Revue***. Irving Berlin contributed half the score to the second one, which was described by its baseball-loving author as "A Hit and Run Play Batted out by George M. Cohan." These shows presented broad travesties on current theatrical attractions very much in the spirit of the old Weber and Fields burlesques. They always had at least one character who visited various places and entertainments to give them some semblance of a theme. In ***Hello, Broadway!,*** for example, Cohan (co-starring with William Collier) played "George Babbit, the Millionaire Kid," whose tour of New York took him to see such attractions as Louise Dresser as "Patsy Pygmalion, a Flower Girl" in a lampoon of the latest Bernard Shaw comedy, and Peggy Wood impersonating Elsie Ferguson in the dramatic play, *Outcast*. Miss Wood recalls that she was also in the finale, "draped in a costume of white satin decorated with red beads embroidered in stripes, a blue bodice with silver stars, and a spiked crown. I leave it to you what I was as."

Even though younger musical talents, such as Jerome Kern and Irving Berlin, were soon surpassing Cohan in the freshness, skill, and variety of their work, Cohan continued to be active in all phases of the theatre. Yet his most famous World War I song, **"Over There,"** had nothing to do with show business. Skillfully built on the repetition of three bugle call notes and catchy enough to be whistled even after being heard but once, the song became the most popular musical expression of the war. Cohan later wrote a sequel to it which enjoyed a brief vogue. It was called **"When You Come Back, and You Will Come Back"** ("There's a whole world waiting for you").

One of Cohan's great skills was that of play doctor. In 1919, when an old-fashioned cloak-and-dagger operetta called ***The Royal Vagabond*** was floundering during its out-of-town tryout, Cohan rewrote and restaged it, and turned it into a hit as a "Cohanized Opera Comique." During the run of this show, the famous strike of Actors' Equity was called to compel producers to recognize the recently formed union. Even though Cohan was both an actor and a producer, his loyalties were entirely on the side of management, and he did everything he could to crush the eventually victorious union. For the rest of his career, Cohan steadfastly refused to join Equity and always had to receive special permission to perform.

The irony of this dispute is that throughout the rest of his life Cohan won far greater fame as an actor than as a writer or producer. Indeed, his two most distinguished performances, Nat Miller in Eugene O'Neill's *Ah, Wilderness!* (1934), and President Roosevelt in *I'd Rather Be Right* (1937), were in plays written and produced by others. Although Cohan had already presented two musicals not written by himself (*Mary* and *The O'Brien Girl,* both by Louis Hirsch, Otto Harbach, and Frank Mandel), his impersonation of F.D.R. was his only appearance in a musical created by other talents. It was no secret that while he was happy to be reunited with the producer, Sam Harris, he felt uncomfortable singing the songs Rodgers and Hart had written for him.

George M. Cohan died on November 4, 1942, at the age of sixty-four. As a creative force in the molding of the American musical theatre, however, his influence had ended many years before. His entire appeal as a writer was based on his youthful verve, his breeziness, and his popular flag waving. No matter what he wrote during his later life (his last musical, ***Billie,*** was produced in 1928), Cohan never progressed beyond the simple entertainments he had created early in the first decade of the century.

Victor Herbert and George M. Cohan were separate and distinct, yet typical, products of their time. They set the pattern for the two different kinds of musicals that were to flourish in the Twenties, the romantic operettas and the fast-moving musical comedies. Even today, we still see their influence at work. *My Fair Lady* may display a dramatic and musical cohesion undreamed of by Herbert, but it does follow in the stunningly theatrical tradition that he represented. And surely, the pace of a George Abbott show or the atmosphere and characters in *The Music Man* prove the lasting appeal of the kind of theatre that first burst upon the scene in the dynamic, sentimental, corny musicals created by George M. Cohan.

Brooks Atkinson (essay date 1970)

SOURCE: "For the Family and Its Tired Businessman," in *Broadway,* revised edition, Macmillan Publishing Co., 1970, pp. 97-121.

[*In the following essay, Atkinson traces Cohan's rise in the American theater and subsequent decline after the Actors' Equity strike in 1919.*]

In 1901, Broadway had no idea of what was going to happen to it when it ignored a comedy called ***The Governor's Son***. But George M. Cohan did. Twenty-two years old at the time, he knew what was going to happen to Broadway. He was going to overwhelm it.

The next season, Broadway rejected his second play, ***Running for Office,*** and it did not have much enthusiasm for his third, ***Little Johnny Jones,*** when it opened in 1904. But Cohan refused to accept a third failure as final. Taking ***Little Johnny Jones*** on tour with his mother, father, and sister in the cast, he rewrote it extensively, and brought it back to Broadway. On the return engagement, he got what he always knew he deserved: he got success. His story of an American jockey unjustly accused of dishonesty in England proved to be acceptable, since it was essentially jingoistic, and since two of Cohan's songs suited New York audiences completely—**"I'm a Yankee Doodle Dandy,"** and **"Give My Regards to Broadway,"** in which he took the liberty of writing like an established Broadway celebrity. He was twenty-six years old. For the last four years, Broadway had been brushing him off. But in 1905, he gave his regards to Broadway as if he were one of its most familiar inhabitants:

Give my regards to Broadway,
  Remember me to Herald Square,
Tell all the gang at 42nd Street
  That I will soon be there.
Whisper of how I'm yearning
  To mingle with the old-time throng,
Give my regards to old Broadway
  And say that I'll be there ere long.

The lyrics expressed a sentiment that may have been presumptuous in 1905. But in the immediate years that followed, he fitted them. He became the king of Broadway. Broadway was his favorite subject—in ***Hello, Broadway!, Broadway Jones, Forty-five Minutes from Broadway,*** and ***The Man Who Owns Broadway***. He had a profound influence on the popular theater for the next fourteen or fifteen years.

Since he wrote comedies, musical shows, and songs, and since he staged them and acted in many of them, it is impossible to classify him neatly. He was a virtuoso theater man. His combination of facility and energy suited the contemporary taste. His shameless flag-waving, his sentimentality, his electricity, his rhythm, his noisiness, his brash personality were the essence of show business. In 1955, Oscar Hammerstein II accounted for Cohan's immense popular success by observing: "A song writer's genius, or rather Cohan's genius, was to say simply what everybody was subconsciously feeling." Cohan's songs, both words and music, were sublimations of the mood of their day. They said what millions of people would have said if they had had Cohan's talent.

George Michael Cohan was born on July 4, 1878 (skeptics maintain that the birthday was actually July 3), in Providence, Rhode Island, into a family of vaudeville performers. He had very little formal schooling and no life outside the theater. He was abnormally bright, ingenious, energetic, and self-confident, and spectacular success was not his hope so much as his obsession. "I'm a freak figure in the theatrical game," he remarked when people started to inquire into the mystery of his success. He was a freak only because his instincts for show business were uncannily shrewd. Ten years after his first show was staged on Broadway, he built a large theater on Broadway between 42nd and 43rd Streets, with his name over the canopy. It was decorated with American flags and other symbols of his career. No one ever made it so big so rapidly. There may have been something significant in the fact that he opened his own theater with his own adaptation of ***Get Rich Quick, Wallingford***.

Onstage his personality could not be ignored. He rolled his eyes and dropped his eyelids with a confidential grimace that seemed to be directed at individual members of the audience; he sang through his nose, carried a jaunty cane, wore his hat on the side of his head, and danced exuberantly. Since he was a short man, he avoided standing near taller people and wore thick heel lifts that added about an inch to his stature. But no one was likely to notice details because he was overpoweringly loud and busy. He invented a type of musical show in which everybody talked at the top of his voice, everybody sang full out and danced ferociously. Once Cohan established his style, he adhered to it. H. T. Parker of the *Boston Evening Transcript* said that Cohan impersonated himself.

He could write as fast as he could dance. Working at night, after the rest of Broadway had gone to bed, he was able to write 140 pages or so at one sitting, afterwards reducing the 140 to about 45, or one full act. If he could not get the seclusion he needed at home or in a hotel, he would take a drawing-room in a Pullman car en route to any city far enough away to give him the time he needed. He wrote his songs after he had written the books for his musical plays. Instead of writing the music, he whistled the air to someone who transcribed it. Between 1905 and 1912, he wrote twelve musical shows, in addition to some straight plays. He could write to order easily. When Fay Templeton, a well-loved singing actress, was on his payroll but doing nothing, he wrote ***Forty-five Minutes from Broadway*** for her (and also for Victor Moore, who was in the cast). Two of the songs for that show became classics, and still are: **"Mary Is a Grand Old Name"** and **"So Long, Mary."**

He said he wrote for Joe Blatz—his stereotype for an average audience. Joe Blatz, Cohan said, had the "two-dollar heart." "What the fifteen-year-old, clean-faced, fresh-minded, full-of-life American boy or girl likes, the average American audiences will like," he believed. Joe Blatz, according to Cohan, liked clean plays with a dash of melodrama, fast dancing, and easy, lilting tunes. Cohan was contemptuous of the academic discussion of "audience psychology." He said he "would rather make one man laugh than one thousand cry." He did exactly that in about fifty comedies and musical productions. The level of his personal taste is indicated by the fact that he thought George Ade's *The College Widow* was the greatest play he had ever seen.

When he was still in his thirties, he was both rich and generous. He was idolized as not only the cleverest but the most charitable star in the profession, and he was a frequent guest of honor at testimonial dinners. In 1912, he led off the campaign for the Titanic Fund by giving $500 for the survivors of the Titanic sea disaster. He gave an elderly actor $10,000 to pay his expenses in a nursing home, with a promise of more money if needed. At one banquet the toast to him consisted of a song:

If every person you have helped
  Should drink a toast to thee
In one small glass of wine tonight
  Why, no more wine there'd be.

Although he was charitable, he was not generous-minded. A kind of shallow egotism made him a difficult companion, and his brash temperament could be abrasive. "There's one thing I can say about you, George," Gus Williams, a comedian, once declared. "You have convinced me that capital punishment is absolutely necessary." Cohan's career on Broadway began to deteriorate in 1919, when he took the side of the managers and theater owners against the actors in the Actor's Equity strike, which was one of the fundamental events in Broadway history. Although he had begun as an actor and often continued to be an actor and although he belonged to a family of actors, he opposed the strike of actors, not passively but actively. He organized Actors' Fidelity in opposition. He issued defiant statements. "Every dollar I have, and I have a few, is on the table in this fight against the actors who have been misled," he said. "The actors have overlooked one important thing, and that is me." When the managers and theater owners surrendered and signed the Equity contract, Cohan remained unreconciled. He said he would never sign an Equity contract, and he never did. He continued to produce plays and musicals, and occasionally he appeared himself, but only because Actors' Equity was more magnanimous than he was. It gave him a special dispensation.

The rest of Cohan's career was less triumphant. In 1920, with his coproducer, the obliging Sam Harris, he produced a burlesque melodrama, ***The Tavern,*** which delighted the public, and ***The Song-and-Dance Man,*** two years later. In 1933, he had a new and happy experience. For the first time, he played in a drama written by someone else and produced by someone else—Eugene O'Neill's *Ah, Wilderness!,* produced by the Theater Guild. As the puzzled parent of a disorderly adolescent boy, he gave a soft, winning, and memorable performance unlike anything he had done on his own. In 1937, he humorously impersonated Franklin Delano Roosevelt in a musical cartoon, *I'd Rather Be Right,* written by George S. Kaufman and Moss Hart, with a score by Richard Rodgers and Lorenz Hart.

Cohan's success in a new style of theater confirmed the authenticity of his stage talent. Although the style had changed, he was still a first-rate actor. In 1939, President Roosevelt, whom Cohan had caricatured the year before, gave him a Congressional Medal in recognition of the national value of two of his war songs—**"Over There"** and **"It's a Grand Old Flag."** Cohan died on November 5, 1942; the funeral at St. Patrick's Cathedral acknowledged his eminence as a citizen of Broadway. The mark he had made on the theater was thus impressively commemorated. Seventeen years later, a statue was erected to him at Broadway and 46th Street, after a campaign initiated and conducted by Oscar Hammerstein II. Cohan is the only theater man who has been honored by a statue on Broadway.

FURTHER READING

Autobiography

Cohan, George M. *Twenty Years on Broadway.* New York and London: Harper & Brothers, 1924, 264 p.

Traces Cohan's career from his start in his family's vaudeville troupe to his role as influential Broadway producer, writer, actor and librettist.

Cohan, George M. and Nathan, George J. "The Mechanics of Emotion." *McClure's,* Vol. XLII, No. 1 (November 1913): 69-77.

Enumerates technical methods to manipulate an audience's emotions, elicit laughter and create suspense.

Criticism

Dale, Alan. "The Real George M. Cohan." *Cosmopolitan* (March 1913): 547-549.

An interview with Cohan reveals a self-effacing modesty and a preference for writing over performing.

Francis, Robert. "American All the Way." In *The American Legion Leader,* selected by Victor Lasky, pp. 65-70. New York: Hawthorn Books, 1953.

Discusses the theme of patriotism in Cohan's plays and performances, appraising it as a genuine expression of sincerity that met with disdain from critics and support from theatergoers.

Morehouse, Ward. *George M. Cohan, Prince of the American Theater.* Philadelphia and New York: J.B. Lipincott, 1943, pp. 120-137.

Draws upon anecdotes from many of Cohan's associates to portray him as a loyal and generous man with a darker side that alienated many.

Ormsbee, Helen. *Backstage with Actors.* New York: Thomas Y. Crowell, 1938, pp. 230-265.

Profiles Cohan as a sensitive, prolific genius with a soothing, avuncular style.

Sara Jeannette Duncan

1861-1922

(Also wrote under the pseudonyms Cecil V. Cotes and Jane Wintergreen) Canadian novelist, short story writer, travel writer, and journalist.

INTRODUCTION

A respected journalist and fiction writer, Duncan is best known for her novels of Canadian, British, and Anglo-Indian society at the turn of the century. In her works, which range from stories drawn from her experience as a resident of India to novels satirical of British and American society, Duncan wrote with a journalistic attention to detail and dramatized such themes as the effects of British imperialism on colonial culture and the clash of idealism, imagination, and talent with tradition and conformity.

Biographical Information

Duncan was born in 1861 in Brantford, Ontario. Her father, Charles Duncan, was a Scottish-born merchant, while her mother, Jane Bell, was of a Protestant family in Ulster. Educated in Brantford, and later at the Toronto Normal School, Duncan gave up teaching in favor of pursuing her childhood dream of becoming a writer. One of the first professional women journalists in Canada, she worked for a time at the local Brantford newspaper and as a freelance correspondent for the *Toronto Globe* and *The Week*. In 1886, she took a full-time position at the *Washington Post*, followed by one at the *Montreal Star* in 1887. The next year, Duncan, along with her colleague Lily Lewis, embarked on a year-long trip around the world. Duncan recounted their visits to western Canada, Japan, India, Egypt, and England in a series of travel sketches for the *Star*, which she later collected and fictionalized in her first novel, *A Social Departure: How Orthodocia and I Went Round the World by Ourselves.* In Calcutta Duncan met Everard Cotes, an English museum official and journalist, and the two married in 1890. She spent the next twenty-five years living in India with Cotes, first in Calcutta and later in Simla. Meanwhile, she followed her first novel with the publication of two more light-hearted works, *An American Girl in London* and *Two Girls on a Barge*. Having shifted the focus of her writing from journalism to fiction, Duncan produced twenty-two works in all, including a series of Anglo-Indian novels, beginning with *The Simple Adventurcs of a Memsahib* and ending with *The Burnt Offering*. Duncan lived in England the last few years of her life and wrote several plays and adaptations of her novels, none of which met with any commercial or critical success. She died in England in 1922.

Major Works

Duncan's works generally fall into one of three categories: early pieces of journalism, comic novels of manners, and works dealing with more serious social themes. In her journalism, Duncan set out many of the major issues that she later explored in her fiction, including the nature of Canadian nationality identity, Canada's position as part of the British Empire and the larger questions of imperialism, and the role of women in modern society. Several of these topics appear in two of her earliest novels, *An American Girl in London* and *The Simple Adventures of a Memsahib*, both of which portray an innocent young woman living in a foreign land. In the former, Mamie Wick records her impressions of a stuffy and highly class-conscious Britain in the 1890s. The latter describes the exploits of an English woman who marries into Anglo-Indian society. Although accentuated by touches of pathos and melodrama, these works are humorous and light in contrast to the novels Duncan produced in the middle of her career. In *The Imperialist*—Duncan's only novel set in Canada—Lorne Murchison, a young lawyer, fails in his attempt to gain a parliamentary seat when his idealistic imperialism clashes with the practical politics of Elgin, his hometown and Duncan's fictionalized portrait of Brantford, Ontario. Like *The Imperialist, Cousin Cinderella* confronts the issue of Canadian identity as it follows Graham and Mary Trent, two vital Canadians placed within the contexts of a stultified English society. In *The Burnt Offering*, Duncan returned to the theme of imperialism as the misguided benevolence of Vulcan Mills, an easily manipulated British member of parliament, triggers a terrorist uprising in early twentieth-century India.

Critical Reception

Although Duncan's novels and journalism were popular in her day, her writings fell into relative obscurity after her death. Not until the 1960s—in conjunction with an increased interest in feminism and Canadian nationalism—did scholars turn their attention to her works. *The Imperialist*, for example, was the topic of much discussion at the time of its first printing, and since its republication in 1961 it has rekindled scholarly interest and continues to generate the majority of Duncan criticism. Despite a renewed interest in Duncan, however, critics have generally considered her works to be artistically flawed. Many have disapproved of the journalistic mode of her novels, calling them superficial or insubstantial, or have attacked her works for their overtly didactic and often condescending tone. Other commentators have found Duncan's writing uneven and self-contradictory. In contrast, many scholars have praised her careful observations of her contemporaries in Canadian, English, American, and Indian society, and have lauded the sophistication of her ironic narrative style. *The Imperialist* and *Cousin Cinderella*, both among her greatest achievements, are considered classics of Canadian literature.

PRINCIPAL WORKS

A Social Departure: How Orthodocia and I Went Round the World by Ourselves (novel) 1890
An American Girl in London (novel) 1891
Two Girls on a Barge [as Cecil V. Cotes] (novel) 1891
The Simple Adventures of a Memsahib (novel) 1893
A Daughter of Today (novel) 1894
The Story of Sonny Sahib (novel) 1894
Vernon's Aunt: Being the Oriental Experiences of Miss Lavinia Moffat (novel) 1894
His Honour, and a Lady (novel) 1896
Hilda: A Story of Calcutta (novel) 1898; also published as *The Path of a Star*, 1899
A Voyage of Consolation (novel) 1898
On the Other Side of the Latch (memoir) 1901; also published as *The Crow's Nest*, 1901
Those Delightful Americans (novel) 1902
The Pool in the Desert (short stories) 1903
The Imperialist (novel) 1904
Set in Authority (novel) 1906
Cousin Cinderella (novel) 1908; also published as *A Canadian Girl in London*, 1908
Two in a Flat [as Jane Wintergreen] (memoir) 1908
The Burnt Offering (novel) 1909
The Consort (novel) 1912
His Royal Happiness (novel) 1914
Title Clear (novel) 1922
The Gold Cure (novel) 1924
Selected Journalism (journalism) 1978

CRITICISM

Alfred G. Bailey (essay date 1973)

SOURCE: "The Historical Setting of Sara Duncan's *The Imperialist,*" in *Journal of Canadian Fiction,* Vol. II, No. 3, Summer, 1973, pp. 205-210.

[*In the following essay, Bailey describes the historical and political contexts of Duncan's novel* The Imperialist.]

Sara Jeannette Duncan's ***The Imperialist*** was less a tract for the times than a recreation of the scenes and people of her native place, affectionately conceived, but at the same time in a spirit of detachment and irony, rare in a Canadian writer of her day. At the date at which it was written, almost certainly in 1902 or 1903, more probably the latter, she had not lived for some years in the small western Ontario city of Brantford to which the student of her work must go in search of some of those formative influences that shaped both her and her novel. A knowledge of the historical background, from which she drew, is essential to a proper appreciation of the work, a statement which is particularly relevant because of the special social and political content upon which its milieu and action are based. Undoubtedly, however, there are some factors that will continue to elude those who may do so, partly because she wrote of the place as it continued to be present in her mind long after she had left it, after she had lived in India for some years, and because the theme suggested by the title had not yet begun, to any extent, to trouble Canadians, or British people anywhere, in the days of her girlhood. While imperialism was in many respects a consequence of the state of international anarchy in which the great powers found themselves in the early years of the twentieth century, there is no reason to suppose that the people of her native place, which she calls "Elgin" in her story, would have come to differ in outlook, in any essential way during the intervening time.

Readers old enough to remember the early years of the present century may well experience a pleasurable nostalgia on taking up this volume. In countless small towns of that period the milkman's cart was known to move fitfully over the unpaved streets, and the ice man, an equally familiar figure, went his rounds delivering large cakes of ice to each household, unconscious of the invention of electrical refrigeration that was to render him obsolete before the century was far advanced. The motor car, with all its attendant evils, had not yet come to disturb the quiet of the streets. Although Sara Duncan's Brantford was still, in her school days, a place of eight or nine thousand, it was busy enough, and from where Alexander Graham Bell lived, on Tutelo Heights overlooking the Grand River, it seemed a place of church steeples and factory chimneys, symbols not incompatible in the minds of many of the inhabitants. The well-to-do class to which she belonged lived in their own areas, largely removed from those to whom she refers in ***The Imperialist*** as the smut-faced, who did not appear in the streets with their jangling dinner pails until 6 p.m. on their way home from their ten-hour day. A few years later a native noted the preponderance, in the better residential areas, of white brick houses set in wide streets, bordered by gardens of hollyhocks, sweet peas, and morning glories, fronting on yards filled with apple, plum, and pear trees. There were no noteworthy public buildings and few historic associations, apart from those on the lands of the neighbouring Six Nations Indians, yet the place possessed a charm and a character of its own, deriving from many sources. Already it was a distributing centre for one of the richest agricultural areas in Canada. This and other facts of an economic and technological nature are important to note; Sara Duncan did not grow up in an isolated and static environment. The production of timber and wheat, that had engrossed the efforts of so large a part of the Upper Canadian population, in the earlier years of that province, were by the third quarter of the century becoming elements in a more complex amalgam characterized increasingly by secondary industry. Producers of castings, iron-ware, of all sorts of leather goods, clothing, and, indeed, a great variety of factory products, had begun in company with the like-minded elsewhere to seek a measure of protection from the competition, in the domestic market, of the more mature industrial establishments of the mother country and the United States.

It was clear that the Galt tariff of 1858 and later, more definitely, Macdonald's National Policy, were straws in the wind. One effect of all this was to instill in sections of the population a sense of independent status within the Empire. There were also those who had come to believe the severence of the imperial tie to be inevitable, and annexation to the United States a likely consequence. As the depression of the seventies and eighties deepened, an increasingly vocal group, including the powerful advocate, Goldwin Smith, looked forward to commercial union or unrestricted reciprocity with the Republic. Earlier Smith had aligned himself with the men of the Canada First movement, William Alexander Foster, a young Toronto barrister, George T. Denison, scion of a famous military family, and their associates. Some members of this group leaned towards what afterwards became known as dominion status, while others such as Denison, became advocates of a British Empire that would be closely knit by federal institutions, and in which the dominions would have equal representation and status with the Mother Country. Denison's imperialism was quite incompatible with Goldwin Smith's support for closer union with the United States, and the accusation of treason which he leveled at Smith was the occasion for a violent quarrel between the two men and their respective allies, which later, in fictional form, was reflected in the streets and school yards of Elgin. "If you would not serve . . . the greatness of Britain," wrote Sara Duncan in ***The Imperialist,*** "you were held to favour going over to the United States; there was no middle course. It became a personal matter in the ward schools, and small boys pursued small boys with hateful cries of 'Annexationist'!"

Although the pursuit of that middle course, which would have led to an independent Canada, in association with the Mother Country, was never altogether abandoned, its viability was increasingly doubted as the boyant hopes of the Confederation years gave way to disillusionment concerning Canada's prospects of survival, let alone prosperity. The impact of the United States on western Ontario, in particular, was augmented by such undertakings as the construction of the Grand River canal linking Brantford with Lake Erie, the purpose of which was to provide an outlet for the food-stuffs and manufactures of the area. While it was undertaken by the two erstwhile Yankees, W. H. Merritt and Absolom Slade, in order to supplement the Welland Canal and render Canada's waterways competitive with those of the United States, it served to open up the Brantford area, on its completion in 1849, to diverse American influences. The wheat barges that crowded the canal were compelled to make way for the two passenger steamers, *Red Jacket* and *Queen,* on their regular trips between Brantford and Buffalo, with the bands playing and their decks crowded with sightseers; and with the building of the Brantford and Buffalo Railway which within a very few years, superceded the canal, contacts across the international border became intensified.

It was therefore not to be wondered at that even the accents of the inhabitants of Elgin were borrowed, with local modifications, "from the other side of the line", except among those families whose social aspirations prompted them to adopt what they hoped would pass for upper-class English. It was perhaps not so much to the point to note that the rocker was American, that the hammock, in which "the Imperialist's" sister reposed, came from New York, or that Canadian feet were remarkably adaptable to American shoes, as that "the Imperialist's" father, John Murchison, was a regular reader of the pink evening paper published in Buffalo as well as of a well-known Toronto daily. Sara Duncan herself, like the characters in her novel, was exposed to, and on the whole encouraged, the flow of ideas from across the border. New attitudes were revealed through the importation of American fiction which increased rapidly after 1875; partly as a result of the enterprise of Canadians living in the United States who undertook the publication of cheap editions of popular works. Soon established American houses were producing the so-called 10-cent libraries, a commodity on which Sara Jeannette Duncan is said to have spent the whole of her prize of ten dollars won while a pupil in the Brantford Collegiate school. In later years she ventured to generalize from her own experience when she remarked that "of the numbers of English and American contemporary writers familiar to the present generation, the latter would be found to preponderate in almost anybody's experience." Chief among the writers who influenced her most in her own development as a novelist were William Dean Howells and Henry James to whom the task of the novelist was to picture ordinary life objectively and accurately, and thus heighten the quality of living. As she herself put it, in writing in the Week, June 9, 1887, "The novel of today may be written to show the cumulative action of a passion, to work out an ethical problem of everyday occurrence, to give body and form to a sensation of the finest or the coarsest kind, for almost any reason which can be shown to have a connection with the course of human life, and the development of human character."

Long before she attained to the degree of sophistication to which the passage quoted above so clearly testifies, she had been moulded by other influences than those emanating from the American Republic; or perhaps it would be more accurate to say that she was a product in great part of a social environment characterized by the convergence and intersection of several dominant influences of which the American was one, although perhaps not the least. Improvements in communication not only accelerated a northward flow from the United States, they also involved Canadian centres of population in networks of railway lines, connecting them with the seaports and thus bringing what had been relatively remote parts of the Dominion into closer rapport with the United Kingdom; but also what was perhaps of more immediate significance, serving to accelerate a movement of population from one part of Canada to another, with the result that a sense of community and of common interests emerged in a way that would not otherwise have been possible. A sense of national distinctiveness gradually overcame the effects of isolation, dispersion and depression, a sense that was not strong but nevertheless was stubborn and persistent. For all the common origins of Americans and Canadians, both ethnic and institutional, they were divided by the gulf created by the American Revolution which the one had achieved and the other repudiated. Even in western Ontario which extended like a wedge into American territory, and which in many ways reflected the consequences of the fact, almost unnoticed the shaping forces of a self-identity were present to a degree. That middle ground between Americanism and colonialism, of which Sara Jeannette Duncan despaired, she elsewhere suggested as a possible factor, however recessive, in the character of the population of her fictional city of Elgin. "The cautious blood and far sight of the early settlers, who had much to reckon with," she observed in ***The Imperialist,*** "were still preponderant social characteristics of the town they cleared the site for." The pioneer stock was not watered down by more recent immigrants, according to Professor Johnson, the historian of Brantford, for they brought with them from the British Isles "many of the good old well-tried customs amidst which they passed their happy days of childhood." On the whole it was a sober and enterprising stock to which families such as the Cockshutts and Penmans belonged. It was such men who built the Massey-Harris industrial empire, who fostered the growth of the busy little city on the banks of the Grand River. It was a typical Canadian city and, although it was more given to the development of manufacturing than many, one could find much of what it was, and what it stood for, duplicated in many parts of the country. If Canadians did not know quite what they were, they at least knew they were neither Americans nor old-country British, even when they persisted in referring to England or Scotland as "home", which some of them continued to do long after having departed from the British Isles, even, at times, to a second generation.

In a later novel Sara Duncan sought to establish a Canadian identity, but she recognized that her Canadian visitors to England would invariably be taken for Americans, and would on frequent occasions be compelled to resort to anxious protests to the contrary. The strange thing was that, having gone over there as to their spiritual home, they found to their surprise that they were "colonials no longer", that "home" was not in England's green and pleasant land, but in the little Ontario town and countryside from which they had started out to discover what was, it seemed, not to be found there. The emergence of something home-grown among the welter of traits evidently to be found in "Brantford-cum-Elgin" was undoubtedly one important source of her keen perception of, and sensitivity to, the distinctions in manner, custom, speech, and outlook between Americans, Canadians, and old-country British which, with variations, provided the setting and the theme for some of her most important novels. Taking her cue also, no doubt, from Henry James, she produced ***The American Girl in London*** (1892), ***Those Delightful Americans*** (1902), a novel based on the reverse situation; ***Cousin Cinderella: the Canadian Girl in London*** (1908), and ***The Imperialist*** (1904) which, while belonging to this group, differs from the others in embodying a recreation of a particular place with a vividness and with a density of imagery that only first-hand experience of a prolonged and fundamental kind could have provided. It is this characteristic which tempts the reader to identify the novel almost completely with its background, almost to regard it as a document upon which the social historian might legitimately draw for his own purpose, while at the same time not losing sight of its essential nature as a work of fiction of outstanding merit.

While ***The Imperialist*** undoubtedly does, in many respects, provide the key to the origins and nature of its own substance it can be found to be a source, only in part, of the explication of its author's having become the novelist that she was. A factory town in late-nineteenth century Ontario might be expected to produce enterpreneurs, as it did, as well as technologists, and even scientists, but may seem, in spite of all that has been said, an unpromising seed-bed for literature. Much may be attributed to the mingling of external influences, as indicated; but one would expect to be able to detect the presence of a catalyst the identity of which has not been determined. Perhaps a not altogether different set of factors produced Sara Jeannette Duncan's contemporary, the Anglo-Mohawk poetess, Pauline Johnson, since they seem to have attended the same school at about the same time. Robert Kennedy Duncan, unrelated to Sara, diverged from the norm of existence in Brantford by achieving some distinction in science; and his brother, Norman, after a career in journalism which took him, as correspondent for Harpers, to various countries of the near and far east, ended up as a writer of such popular works of fiction as the Billy Topsail adventure stories for boys, as well as *Dr. Luke of the Labrador,* published in the same year as ***The Imperialist,*** and *The Cruise of the Shining Light* (1907). It seems worth mentioning in passing that Adelaide Hunter Hoodless, a Brant country native, founded the first Women's Institute there, the nucleus of what came to be a world-wide movement. Books were accessible in the library of the Mechanic's Institute, destroyed by fire when Sara was seventeen, but certain enlightened individuals overcame the fears of spouses that their wives might become novel-readers, or worse, and founded a civic library in 1884 to replace the one lost. Clearly the area was not entirely devoid of cultural resources nor of their expectable consequences.

Moreover, one cannot help suspecting that the, in a sense, accidental arrival in Brantford of the Bell family may have contributed something, more than has been suggested, to Sara Duncan's intellectual development and literary tastes. Although she was only nine years old at the time that the man who was to invent the telephone took up residence with his parents on Tutelo-Heights, it is said that she became a frequent visitor to the Bell homestead, and there mingled with the members of a family who had always, up to that time, lived in an academic atmosphere with individuals of broad culture and like interests. It may seem of almost equal significance to note that she was known to be a visitor on occasion, to the country home of the Honorable George Brown, now retired from politics, but still a power behind the Liberal party and the Toronto *Globe* in which she was before very long to launch a women's page under the name of Garth Grafton, after a short stint at school teaching for which she trained at the Toronto Normal School.

That excursion into journalism which was destined to widen Sara Duncan's horizons far beyond what was customary, or even possible, for most young women of her day, seemed to develop her sense of the human comedy and gave her an opportunity for that objective appraisal of political motives and events that stood her in good stead as a member of the staff of the Toronto *Globe,* as correspondent of the *Washington Post,* and in 1888 as political reporter at Ottawa for the Montreal *Star*. Her many-sided experience in these roles enabled her to write, in ***The Imperialist,*** with some authority on public affairs without destroying her capacity to portray not only the surface but also the essential nature of the institutions of her native place, not least that of the churches. It would be difficult to find in any Canadian novel a more effective treatment of religion, which is here seen as one of the primary formative influences of the community in which she was reared and, one would guess, of herself. It can be surmised that a sober and regulatory spirit had gained ground since 1833, a year in which a visiting clergyman had found Brantford "a veritable Sodom" without a place of worship, and from which reports of wickedness came to him, while visiting the neighbourhood, as roars of distant thunder, conjuring up images of unspeakable debauchery. No doubt conditions steadily improved as the century advanced, although the temperance people never succeeded entirely in flushing out those dens of iniquity, the grog shops, and Mrs. Murchison, the mother of "the Imperialist", when her son, Lorne, became a candidate in a federal by-election, thought it a little short of scandalous to go on Sunday to talk politics in a hotel, ". . . a place of which the smell about the door was enough to knock you down even on a weekday." Although the church had stood in vain against such places, it held a close rein on the behaviour of the families of the well-to-do and respectable classes, as Sara Duncan wrote of Dr. Drummond the Presbyterian minister, who was as proud of the Murchison children as their own parents could possibly be, "regarding himself in a much higher degree responsible for the formation of their characters and the promise of their talents." In her observation on the role of the churches it is possible to see an additional influence, and perhaps a fundamental one, on her own character and intellectual development. "It was the normal thing", she wrote, "the thing which formed the backbone of life, sustaining to the serious, impressive to the light, indispensible to the rest, and the thing that was more than any of these, which you can only know when you stand in the churches among the congregations. Within its prescribed limitations it was for many the intellectual exercise, for more the emotional life, and for all the unfailing distraction of the week. The repressed magnetic excitement in gatherings of familiar faces, fellow-beings bound by the same convention to the same kind of behaviour, is precious in communities where the human interest is still thin and sparse."

She testified on more than one occasion to the belief that "Elgin" was an example of such a community as she had in mind. "The arts conspire to be absent;", she wrote: "letters resided at the nearest university city; science was imported as required, in practical improvements. There was nothing, indeed, to interfere with Elgin's attention to the immediate, the vital, the municipal . . . " Even Toronto was soon seen as "that faintly exhilarating provincial capital." Early in her journalistic career she seemed rapidly to transcend her origins as can be surmized from her Arnoldian attack on the mores of the middle class which dominated Ontario, that " 'one great camp of the Philistines', whose intellectual diet was made up of 'politics and vituperation, temperance and vituperation, religion and vituperation.' " Nevertheless, that very religion, as it had affected her, may have contributed something to her occasional recourse to philosophical and historical speculation, concerning the causes of the intellectual backwardness which she felt to be all around her in the Canada of her day. Whistler had said that art happens, but why, she asked, did it happen so seldom in Canada? Sometimes the causes of her country's plight seemed to be cosmic in their scope and unalterable in their incidence. They were sometimes explained as the result of an economic dispensation of an overruling Providence. The conclusion, she wrote, was usually that "owing to the obscure operation of some natural law" literature was not indigenous to Canada. She knew that genius was often regarded as "a strange and beautiful flower of the ego," irreducible to a scientific nomenclature springing up unpredictably in all climates and conditions, defying, so she felt, all the wisdom of the botanists of civilization.

Had she continued to remain in Canada she might have revised this pessimistic pronouncement. Not long after her voyage around the world in 1889, described in her first novel, ***A Social Departure, How Orthodocia and I Went Around the World by Ourselves,*** her marriage to Everard Cotes, journalist and museum curator, eventuated in her spending the remainder of her life largely in Anglo-India, with the result that she was not able to witness at first hand what amounted to a minor flowering, in the work of the Canadian poets, during the last decade of the nineteenth century. Furthermore the *via media*—between annexation to the United States, and a condition of prolonged colonial debasement—for which Sir John Macdonald had striven throughout his entire political life, was to become at last within reach of the beleagured Dominion. Professor Creighton has drawn attention to the crucial fact that the growth of secondary industry in the United States had begun to outrun domestic agricultural production which was thus increasingly absorbed within that country. Thus freed from American competition a huge overseas market in the British Isles, and on the continent, became available to the rapidly expanding wheat economy of the Canadian prairie. The fear of absorption into the United States was quickly dispelled; and at the same time Canadian manufacturers became assured of an enlarged market in their own country which enabled them to regard, with some measure of equanimity, the steep upward revision of the tariff with which the Americans continued to foster their secondary industries in the decades following the Civil War. It was not only as sources of provisions that many in Britain had begun to cherish the colonies and particularly the dominions. The view held by the Little Englanders, earlier in the century, that the overseas possessions were a costly and unwanted responsibility had given way to a new spirit marked by the founding of the Colonial Institute in 1869, and such as had animated Disraeli in his Crystal Palace speech of 1872.

The new outlook was to be found enshrined in the writings of James Anthony Fronde and J. R. Seeley, especially the latter's influential work, *The Expansion of England,* published in 1883. The Imperial Federation League, founded in the Motherland in 1884, drew an immediate and enthusiastic response from Canada, especially among those sections of the population that had fallen, in greater or lesser degree, under the influence of the Canada First Movement, which was not so much defunct as transformed by the changed circumstances of the time. It was however the altered position of the Mother Country in relation to other powers, more than the importunities of the colonies and dominions, that caused men to reflect upon the question of the value of the outer empire, and gave rise to new doctrines. Earlier protection of dependencies by tariffs had come to seem an impediment to the realization of industrial world dominance by Britain. With her advanced industrial structure she could undersell the products of almost all other countries in a free and open market, unencumbered by tariff walls. In return for a ready acceptance of her manufactured goods, Britain would allow the flow of their primary products into the markets of the empire. The application of the doctrine of Free Trade, especially in the 1840's, had thus fostered a species of economic imperialism on the part of Great Britain, which ensured to her a favourable balance of trade, and thus made a great part of the world, economically speaking, colonial to her. All this was now changing as such countries as Germany and the United States began to overtake Britain as industrial nations, and to resort to tariffs to protect their own somewhat less developed manufactures from competition by British goods in their own domestic markets. International rivalry thus began to become acute. An intensification of competition for the control of colonial areas ensued, not only for the raw materials to be drawn from them, or because they provided markets for the products of the metropolitan states. To these purposes which were, if anything, more important than ever, was the added demand for the exclusive control of backward areas as fields for profitable investment of the great accumulations of finance capital to be found in the hands of entrepreneurs of the industrial states. Germany in particular affected to find the British control of much of the colonial world intolerable; and the Kaizer, disregarding the advice of Bismark, embarked upon a programme of naval expansion with a view to challenging the might of the Royal Navy, a policy that culminated in the greatest naval battle of world history, on the gray seas of Jutland in 1916. A truculent spirit began to vitiate the relations of the states, the cost of maintaining far-flung communications with Dominions and dependencies forced Britain to consider that the daughter nations should be asked to bear a part of the burden of imperial defense in which they all had a stake. If this aim were to succeed it became evident to those concerned that coordinate measures would be necessary, such as intra-imperial trade preferences, and, more spectacularly, a federation of the dominions with the Mother Country in a mutually advantageous relationship. Joseph Chamberlain, in speaking in Toronto in December, 1887, at the time of the first Colonial Conference, referred to Canada and Britain as branches of one family, and voiced the hope that the Canadian federation of 1867 "might be the lamp to light our path to the confederation of the British Empire." When however, Sir Charles Tupper, the Canadian High Commissioner in London took up the cry in 1889, he was forced by Sir John Macdonald to make a public retraction, which, when British public men learned the attitude of the Canadian government, struck a body blow at the movement, and the League was dissolved in 1893.

Sir John might declare, "A British subject I was born, a British subject I will die," but his National Policy was based four-square on the protection of Canadian secondary industries. When Lorne Murchison the young Elgin lawyer of Sara Duncan's novel, returned from a trade mission to England, aglow with the spirit of the new imperialism, and as Liberal candidate in a by-election, sought to interject the issue into his campaign, his chief opponents were the manufacturers of his native city. They remained unmoved by his vision of England "down the future" as "the heart of the Empire, the conscience of the world, and the Mecca of the race." While no flag but the Union Jack would ever fly over Canada in the opinion of Octavius Milburn, "his ideal of life was to be found in a practical, go-ahead, self-governing colony, far enough from England actually to be disabused of her inherited anachronisms and make your own tariff, near enough politically to keep your securities up by virtue of her protection . . . He was born, one might say, in the manufacturing interest . . . " He "was of those who were building up the country, with sufficient protection he was prepared to go on doing it long and loyally; . . . " In a sumptuous biographical dictionary entitled *Canadians of Today,* sold by subscription "he was described as the 'Father of the Elgin Boiler.' " Even Lorne's father, while he was willing to admit the validity of "common interest" with the Mother Country, was categorical on other heads: "common taxation, no, for defence or any other purpose. The colonies will never send money to be squandered by the London War Office. We'll defend ourselves, as soon as we can manage it, and buy our own guns and our own cruisers." But, rejoined his interlocutor, "let 'em understand they'll be welcome to the use of it, but quite in a family way—no sort of compulsion." Thus was succinctly stated what soon came to be Sir Wilfred Laurier's naval policy. Already he had talked vaguely in favour of imperial federation, and, with a stroke of genius, devised in 1897 the imperial preference which pleased many Anglo-Canadians, far and wide, throughout the Dominion. He managed also to generate a wave of imperial sentiment by his skillful adoption of a formula for Canada's participation in the South African War, thus reducing French Canada's opposition to a possible minimum. It might therefore seem strange that the Colonial Conference of 1902 rejected the proposal for imperial federation out of hand, and it is therefore necessary to examine a situation that may appear at first glance paradoxical.

The fact was that at the very time, one may guess, that Sara Jeannette Duncan was writing her novel, she would have been aware that such countries as Australia and Canada had moved so far along the road to a discrete nationalism, as to have rendered extremely unlikely a change of direction in such a way as to secure the adoption of a programme for effecting the political unification of the Empire. Furthermore the Free Trade dogma was too tenaciously held in Britain to permit of the realization of an imperial zollverein, in spite of Joseph Chamberlain's resignation from the British cabinet in 1903 in order to pursue that goal with increased vigour and single-mindedness. He could not expect to be sustained in his endeavours by the Liberal Party which, after healing the breach in its ranks caused by differences of South African War policy, went on to victory in 1906 on a platform of domestic social reform. It was therefore realistic, and in accord with the trend of the times, especially in the years 1902 and 1903, for Sara Duncan to conclude her novel with the defeat of the "imperialist" Lorne Murchison and the frustration of all his hopes for the realization of what had been the aims of the old Imperial Federation League and the less prestigious British Empire League that followed it.

That is not, however, by any means the whole story. The resolution of the paradox, if such indeed it was, to which we have referred in a previous paragraph, had been successfully attempted by the Governor-General, Lord Elgin, back in the 1840's, when he urged upon the home government that the loyalty of the colonists could never be ensured through the use of coercive political instruments. At a time when there seemed a danger of a reenactment of the Rebellions that had taken place in 1837, he had the wisdom to see that by giving the colonists freedom to govern themselves they would voluntarily stand by the Mother Country, whereas to force them to bow in subjection could end only in disaster. It appeared to many at the turn of the twentieth century that to don the harness of imperial federation would mean a return to the state of colonial subservience that had existed to a degree before the granting of responsible government to the provinces in 1847-1849, although this is far from what was intended by such famous protagonists of imperial unity as George R. Parkin and George Munro Grant. The former had resigned from his position as headmaster of the Fredericton Collegiate School in the eighties to become the chief publicist of the Imperial Federation League. To both him and Grant, the principal of Queens University, imperial preferences and political arrangements to effect the unity of the Empire were simply means to a supreme end which was essentially religious. "Three hundred millions of mankind," Parkin wrote, "who do not share British blood, of various races in various climes, acknowledge British sway, and look to it for guidance and protection; their hopes of civilization and social elevation depend upon the justice with which it is exercised, while anarchy awaits them should that role be removed?" "We have a mission on earth" said Grant in the Jubilee year of 1897, "as truly as ancient Israel had". "Our mission was to make this world the home of freedom, of justice, and of peace, and to serve these ends the British Empire was the highest secular instrument the world had ever known". In a more homely and domestic way "The Imperialist's" mother, Mrs. Murchison, was conscious of the spirit necessary to the justification of imperial power. As Sara Duncan had it, "Lorne came after Advena, at a period of a naive fashion of christening the young sons of Canada in the name of their Governor-General. It was a simple way of attesting a loyal spirit, but with Mrs. Murchison more particular motives operated. The Marquis of Lorne was not only the deputy of the throne, he was the son-in-law of a good woman, of whom Mrs. Murchison thought more and often said it, for being the woman she was than for being twenty times a Queen; and he had made a metrical translation of the psalms, several of which were included in the revised psalter for the use of the Presbyterian Church in Canada, from which the whole of Knox Church sang in the praise of God every Sunday."

One could easily be brought to believe that Mrs. Murchison's son, Lorne, would not have found these sentiments, quoted above, in any way repugnant, and even that they might in fact constitute one source of the eloquent pronouncements so characteristic of him throughout his political campaign. The passionate idealism by which he was moved, and through the expression of which he clearly held his fellow citizens in awe, was worthy of Parkin and Grant in their most exalted moments of advocacy. As a reporter for the press Sara Jeannette Duncan may have heard some of the public addresses of these men, and it is possible that she should have modelled the Murchison oration upon them. If she originated it herself in the form in which it is found in her novel one can only suppose that, while her reason and experience led her to conclude that it was the embodiment of an impossible ideal, it was one to which her own heart was not altogether a stranger.

Carole Gerson (essay date 1975)

SOURCE: "Duncan's Web," in *Canadian Literature,* No. 63, Winter, 1975, pp. 73-80.

[*In the following essay, Gerson argues that* The Imperialist *accesses "the universal concerns of literature" by examining the nature of political and moral idealism and exhibiting a complex pattern of perception and point of view.*]

While the overt subject of ***The Imperialist*** is indeed imperialism, the novel's deeper structural unity derives from its focus on idealism and its internal patterning of perceptions and points of view. Sara Jeannette Duncan uses Canada not only to provide the history of the imperialist movement, but also to supply a foil for the old world, so that in the interaction between old world and new world experiences and personalities she can scrutinize subtleties of idealism and levels of vision. Hence her concern is not narrative for the sake of narrative but the effect of event on the formation of vision; as she herself says of Lorne Murchison's trip to England, "what he absorbed and took back with him is, after all, what we have to do with; his actual adventures are of no great importance." In the context of turn-of-the-century Canadian fiction, marked as it was by a strong emphasis on "actual adventures", Duncan's ability to work into the fabric of her narrative the abstract problem of the levels, limitations and horizons of vision distinguishes ***The Imperialist*** from the story-telling of Gilbert Parker, Norman Duncan and Ralph Connor. Much of her distinction may be due to her long absence from Canada, which may have helped to expand her artistic vision and give her greater detachment and a more universal frame of reference than her Canadian contemporaries. This detached perspective, combined with her personal knowledge of Canada and her dexterous manipulation of characters and ideas, renders ***The Imperialist*** one of the most carefully structured and unduly neglected Canadian novels.

The skill of Duncan's structural technique lies in her meticulous interweaving of narrative threads so that all events and characters implicitly comment upon one another, and through the various attitudes manifested by various characters the "figure in the carpet" slowly and surely emerges. Within this scheme of levels of vision the highest focal point—the horizon—is idealism, political in the case of Lorne Murchison, moral in the case of Hugh Finlay. Just outside central focus sit the two characters who function on the lesser plane of self-interest, Alfred Hesketh and Dora Milburn. And the substantial background to the whole is provided by Elgin, Ontario, recognized by John Murchison to be "a fair sample of our rising manufacturing towns," and by his son Lorne to be a microcosm of eastern Canadian society: "Elgin market square . . . was the biography of Fox County, and, in little, the history of the whole province."

Elgin's vision focuses on "the immediate, the vital, the municipal." Anchored in common-sense pragmatism, the town distrusts imaginative eccentricity. In Elgin religious fervour "was not beautiful, or dramatic, or self-immolating; it was reasonable"; and young daydreaming Advena Murchison learns that "No one could dream with impunity in Elgin, except in bed." As the microcosmic example of the level-headed, business-minded Canadian community, Elgin supplies the formal testing-ground for Lorne's idealism and judges less by principle than by economic practicability. When Lorne accepts the Liberal nomination in a federal by-election and makes imperialism the keynote of his platform, the whole country looks to Elgin to indicate the national reaction to the Idea and sees in Elgin a mirror of itself.

The town's solid, practical personality manifests itself in Mrs. Murchison and, on a more sophisticated level, in Dr. Drummond. "The central figure . . . with her family radiating from her," Mrs. Murchison contains the stability of everyday reality: she knows that the crises of ordinary living are whether Abby's baby has the whooping cough and what to serve the minister for tea. On her own level of apprehension she sees through the ideal of England when Lorne returns with his clothes "ingrained with London smut," and she implicitly understands the emotional realities that Advena and Finlay try so hard to idealize away because, in her common-sense world, no young man and young woman can see so much of one another without falling in love. Dr. Drummond, the Scottish Presbyterian minister, exemplifies a similar intuitive grasp of ordinary life. While his limitations are those of any man who moves "with precision along formal and implicit lines" and whose study is lined "with standard religious philosophy, standard poets, standard fiction, all that was standard and nothing that was not," his fundamental knowledge of human behaviour enables him to confront Finlay's misguided idealism and to inform him that he and Advena are "a pair of born lunatics" for their determination to sacrifice love to principle.

While Elgin, Mrs. Murchison and Dr. Drummond represent the primary level of vision—namely common sense and practical conduct—there runs in them a deep vein of old loyalties and half-hidden emotional ties waiting to be tapped by Lorne's more penetrating imagination. For all its spirit of North American enterprise, Elgin, "this little outpost of Empire," maintains its umbilical ties in its annual lively celebration of the Queen's Birthday; the importance of this event to the Murchison children fills Duncan's opening chapter. Dr. Drummond and John Murchison emigrated from Scotland together and transferred their concerns entirely to the new world, yet "obscure in the heart of each of them ran the undercurrent of the old allegiance." Allegiance to tradition inspired Mrs. Murchison to name her first two daughters after their grandmothers, Lorne after the Marquis de Lorne (Governor-general of Canada from 1878 to 1883) whose mother-in-law was Queen Victoria, and two sons after Canadian Liberal party leaders. In addition, Lorne Murchison grows up in the old Plummer place, a home distinguished by the "attractiveness of the large ideas upon which it had been built and designed." This atmosphere of "large ideas," Elgin's lingering "sentiment of affection for the reigning house," and Lorne's early manifestation of "that active sympathy with the disabilities of his fellow-beings which stamped him later so intelligent a meliorist" are all absorbed into his earnest personality and into the making of his idealistic imperialism. In her careful plotting of Lorne's background Duncan weaves an intricate fabric of colonial affections which requires only Lorne's personality to tailor it into the imperialist banner.

But even more important than the content of Lorne's idealism is his idealism itself, as ***The Imperialist*** focuses squarely upon the personality of the idealist. For Duncan, idealism results more from temperament than from philosophy. Hence her two principal idealists, Lorne Murchison and Hugh Finlay, are described in remarkably similar terms although the actual forms of their idealism differ greatly.

Hugh Finlay, the young Presbyterian minister from Dumfriesshire, and Lorne Murchison, the young Canadian lawyer, are two examples of the same "type": sincere, open, at times almost simple, and noticeably different from everyone else in intensity and visionary focus. Both inhabit a dimension beyond the ordinary, both appeal to others by their strength of personality, and Duncan describes both in terms of expanded horizons. Lorne's face is "lighted by a certain simplicity of soul that pleased even when it was not understood"; he is "frank and open, with horizons and intentions; you could see them in his face." Similarly Finlay is "a passionate romantic . . . with a shock of black hair and deep dreams in his eyes . . . a type . . . of the simple motive and the noble intention, the detached point of view and the somewhat indifferent attitude to material things." Like Lorne, he has "horizons, lifted lines beyond the common vision, and an eye rapt and a heart intrepid." Circumstance and place of birth rather than temperament direct Lorne's idealism towards political theory, and Finlay's towards personal sacrifice and the upholding of old moral allegiances. While the story of Lorne's political career has nothing to do with the story of Finlay's romantic involvements, the parallel plots complement one another as the new world idealist finds his moral inspiration in the old world, and the old world idealist looks to the new world for "elbow-room" yet cannot shake off his old world ties.

Lorne's incipient idealism finds its focus when he is invited to be secretary to a deputation from the United Chambers of Commerce of Canada shortly to wait upon the British government "to press for the encouragement of improved communications within the Empire." For Lorne the Empire immediately becomes "the whole case"; Canada has stuck with and must continue to stick with England for "the moral advantage." Once in England, Lorne alone is not disillusioned by "the unready conception of things, the political concentration on parish affairs, the cumbrous social machinery . . . the problems of sluggish overpopulation" which depress the other members of his delegation. Instead he colours all with his idealism, and sees "England down the future the heart of the Empire, the conscience of the world, and the Mecca of the race" if only the colonies will come to her economic aid.

Once Lorne's idealistic temperament attaches itself to imperialism, enthusiasm rather than reason determines the course of his career. On his return to Canada his gift for transmitting his earnestness becomes the source of his political attractiveness: "at the late fall fairs and in the lonely country schoolhouses his talk had been so trenchant, so vivid and pictorial, that the gathered farmers listened with open mouths, like children, pathetically used with life, to a grown-up fairy tale." That imperialism is little more than a "grown-up fairy tale" is implied by the outcome of Lorne's career. His growing feeling that he rides "upon the crest of a wave of history," and that he is the instrument of "an intention, a great purpose in the endless construction and re-construction of the world" severs him from the pragmatic reality of Elgin. Once the Idea takes possession of him he proves incapable of following the advice of the Liberals to subdue his imperialism which is becoming increasingly suspect in the business community. As a result he barely wins the election, and when irregularities are charged by both sides and the seat is to be recontested, the Liberals ask him to withdraw. Lorne's idealistic vision—his overly expanded horizons which cause him to lose touch with the primary, common-sense vision of his community—makes him a unique figure in the canon of Canadian hero-victims: he wins the election, but he loses the seat.

Into her pattern of levels of vision Duncan works an Elgin-level idealist who, by juxtaposition, accentuates Lorne's loftier idealism. Elmore Crow, Lorne's former schoolmate, goes out west only to discover that from a common-sense point of view normality is best: "you've got to get up just as early in the mornings out there as y'do anywhere, far's I've noticed. An' it's a lonesome life. Now I *am* back, I don't know but little old Ontario's good enough for me." Having "wore out his Winnipeg clothes and his big ideas," Crow returns to the family farm and makes himself useful.

But like Lorne, Finlay and Advena live far above the plane of useful reality. The lovers are saved from the adverse consequences of their idealism only by the *deus ex machina* intervention of Dr. Drummond. The two meet after Advena has already loved Finlay from afar, and much of Finlay's bungling stems from his inexperience with women and his inability to perceive Advena's love until things have already progressed to a point of deep emotional commitment. Artistically, perhaps the finest passage of the book is the scene of their first real encounter which sets the subsequent direction of their relationship. Late on an April afternoon—the time of year is the transition into spring, and the time of day the transition into evening—Finlay overtakes Advena on his way home. They walk in silence together, and Advena feels that the event is "pregnant, auspicious"—like the time of day and the time of year, the brink of something. When they turn a corner and the sunset suddenly bursts upon them, Finlay, the recent emigrant from the old world, marvels that "it's something to be in a country where the sun still goes down with a thought of the primaeval." Advena, born and raised in Canada, prefers "the sophistication of chimney-pots" and longs "to see a sunset in London, with the fog breaking over Westminster." After some witty exchange they go their separate ways. Finlay's road lies "to the north, which was still snowbound," while Advena's is into the "yellow west, with the odd sweet illusion that a summer day was dawning."

In the paradoxes worked into this scene Duncan maps the lovers' course. For all his admiration of the "primaeval," Finlay remains morally and intellectually "snowbound" by convention. By birth a northern man (from Dumfriesshire), his northern route to his home in the new world concretely expresses his old world vision, which is embodied in his intractible resolve to honour an engagement of convenience to a distant cousin made before his departure for Canada. In contrast, Advena's new world vision and western direction signify her greater consciousness of passion and emotional freedom, and her capacity to see that Finlay's "dim perception of his own case was grotesque." While she glances intellectually towards chimney-pots and Westminster, and does try to support Finlay's conventionalism and his marriage to Christie Cameron, it is her passion that finally shatters their idealistic self-renunciation. So long as they maintain their idealism—their intellectual refinement which allows them the illusion that theirs is a "friendship of spirit"—the course of their relationship runs northerly, towards frozen passion and ice-bound convention. But when Advena meets Finlay in a thunderstorm and passionately declares "We aren't to bear it", and Dr. Drummond conveniently decides to marry Christie himself, the lovers turn abruptly towards the yellow west and the frontier of emotional freedom.

In Duncan's pattern of levels of vision Lorne and Finlay are two versions of the same thing: two sides of the woven carpet, to return to Henry James's metaphor. While Lorne's idealism is directed outward, towards an impossible "union of the Anglo-Saxon nations of the world," Finlay's is entirely personal, designed to avoid "the sacrifice of all that I hold most valuable in myself." Just as Lorne expatiates on the moral advantages of imperialism without working out the concrete economic details, so Finlay expatiates on the freedom of the new world without perceiving his imprisonment by the conventions of the old world. As idealists, they are removed from the primary, common-sense vision of Elgin; but because they are idealists, their motivation is well-intentioned: Lorne wishes to save the Empire, Finlay to save his principles.

Duncan adds another dimension to her pattern of levels of vision with the self-centredness of Alfred Hesketh and

Dora Milburn. As with everything else, Lorne's apprehension of Hesketh, an independently wealthy, apparently benevolent young Englishman whom he meets in London, is coloured by his idealism: "Hesketh stood, to him, a product of that best which he was so occupied in admiring and pursuing. . . . There is no doubt that his manners were good, and his ideas unimpeachable in the letter; the young Canadian read the rest into him and loved him for what he might have been." Hesketh is sufficiently inspired by Lorne's infectious idealism to come to Elgin, but once he arrives Lorne realizes that Hesketh is a useless twit. "I certainly liked him better, over there," he confesses to Advena, "but then he was a part of it. . . . Over here you seem to see round him somehow." Lorne's doubts about Hesketh's place in Canada are borne out when Hesketh, campaigning for Lorne, succeeds only in alienating his audience by his condescension and snobbery. Like Finlay, Hesketh carries all his old world attitudes to the new world; he fails even to perceive the gap between his class-conscious Englishness and middle-class Elgin's egalitarianism and pragmatism. Hence he admires the affectedly English Milburns as "the most typically Canadian family" for "Miss Milburn will compare with any English girl." But unlike Finlay, Hesketh lacks principles. While his ostensible purpose in coming to Elgin is to help Lorne spread the gospel of imperialism under the aegis of the Liberal party, he finds it easily convenient to swing his allegiance to the Conservatives—Mr. Milburn's party—when he becomes involved with Dora, and to develop a consuming interest in Milburn's traction engines. Hesketh completes his betrayal of Lorne when he announces his engagement to Dora, to whom Lorne had already given a ring. But in Duncan's scheme Dora and Hesketh belong together, for by their self-importance they hold themselves aloof from Elgin society, and by their lack of principle and their selfish motivation they operate on a level far beneath the high-mindedness of the idealists.

Lorne's romanticized vision of Dora prevents him from perceiving the selfishness underlying her coyness and her continual evasion of a definite promise. Not at all the goddess of Lorne's conception, Dora presents "a dull surface to the more delicate vibration of things," and to her one of the most significant ramifications of Lorne's trip to England is that she will lose her escort to the regatta. She cannot stand to see propriety disturbed—"When she was five years old and her kitten broke its leg, she had given it to a servant to drown"—and Lorne's enthusiasm disturbs propriety. She also cannot stand to be ignored, and when she feels at times that "Between politics and boilers . . . the world held a second place for her," she graciously accepts the attentions of Alfred Hesketh. While Elgin views the world from the level of common sense, and Lorne and Finlay see things through their exalted idealism, Hesketh's and Dora's level of vision is limited to self-interest.

Even after her pattern became clear, Duncan's personal attitude toward her characters remains strangely vague. The first-person voice which frequently enters the narrative is probably Duncan herself, but even this voice remains so detached that apart from overt disapproval of the self-centred characters it refuses to commit itself to more than a distant, ironic sense of sympathy with both the common-sense community and the idealists. If there is a character who represents the author's point of view it would have to be Advena, who straddles the common-sense and the idealistic worlds, and who views Elgin and her brother with detached sympathy. Advena appears to abandon the solid reality of her parents' world when she supports Finlay's marriage to Christie, but her common-sense roots finally assert themselves. When she passionately declares to Finlay that she can no longer maintain their ideal she feels that all is lost: "Before she had preferred an ideal to the desire of her heart; now it lay about her; her strenuous heart had pulled it down to foolish ruin." But the ruin of the ideal is "foolish" to Advena only initially; Duncan makes it clear that it is the ideal itself that is foolish—the fabrication of two people "too much encumbered with ideas to move simply, quickly on the impulse of passion." Lorne destroys his political career because his idealism is too passionate; Finlay and Advena nearly ruin their lives because their idealism is too intellectual. If Duncan intended any message beyond her exploration of the different levels of vision at which different people operate, it could be the Renaissance ideal of temperance—the balance of passion and reason which produces concrete human achievement.

The Imperialist has unfortunately suffered the neglect accorded to much literature based on a topical political situation. What in 1904 the *Canadian Magazine* found "opportune" the modern reader now finds obscure, since Duncan assumes her readers' familiarity with the imperialist movement. Like Marvell's *Painter* satires, ***The Imperialist*** requires some annotation and explanation. But once made accessible, the book reveals itself to be one of the most sophisticated and penetrating Canadian novels written before World War I. Sara Jeannette Duncan's scheme of levels of vision, her ability to work ideas into the structure of her narrative, and her detached sympathy for both her idealists and her common-sense characters raise ***The Imperialist*** above the local and the historical into the universal concerns of literature.

S. Nagarajan (essay date 1975)

SOURCE: "The Anglo-Indian Novels of Sara Jeannette Duncan," in *Journal of Canadian Fiction,* Vol. III, No. 4, 1975, pp. 74-84.

[*In the following essay, Nagarajan discusses Duncan's* Set in Authority *and* The Burnt Offering *as representative of her Anglo-Indian novels.*]

The work of the Canadian novelist, Sara Jeannette Duncan is not generally known outside her own country, and even in Canada, all but one of the nearly two dozen books she wrote are out of print. Many of these novels deal with the life of the British in India—Anglo-Indian fiction, we may call these novels, after Bhupal Singh—and Canadian readers, unless they have a special interest, are not naturally drawn to them. (Significantly, the novel that has been reprinted, ***The Imperialist,*** has a Canadian setting.) But that reason does not explain why historians of Anglo-Indian fiction also tend to overlook her. It is true she is a minor writer compared to Kipling or Forster, but that may be *too* drastic a criterion to invoke since it would extinguish the historical consideration of *all* Anglo-Indian fiction. Miss Duncan's work deserves our notice because we can see in it how some of the major features, issues and personalities of British Indian society and politics at the turn of the century appeared to an intelligent contemporary writer who was in a sense an outsider. Her work can also help in bringing home to us the 'feel' of the period and its diversity, especially the diversity in the attitudes and relationships of the British and the Indians amongst themselves and toward each other. She writes unevenly and is unsuccessful on the whole in presenting a coherent vision of Anglo-India, but at times, she could also write extremely competently, with great humour and sympathy.

She came to her career as a novelist of Anglo-India with some advantages. She was an unorthodox person for her times. She had worked for some time as Parliamentary correspondent of the Montreal *Star* at Ottawa. She could appreciate the clash of interests and personalities in political life and the surprising ways in which the public life and the private life mesh with each other. She could sense, without always making sense of, the nationalism that lay just beyond the horizon of what appeared to many of her abler contemporaries in official life as mere agitation against authority. She had travelled widely, accompanied only by a girl of her own age. The book which described her travels was rightly called ***A Social Departure: How Orthodocia and I Went Round the World by Ourselves*** (1890). She dedicated the book to Mrs. Grundy 'as a slight tribute to the omnipotence of her opinion and a humble mark of profoundest esteem.' Thus, when in 1892 she married an Englishman, Everard Charles Cotes, and came out to live in Calcutta, the then Imperial capital where her husband was the Curator of the Museum (later he became the Managing Director of the Indian News Agency), she was, one may say, in a more favourable position than most women of her class to see what was going on around her and comment upon it. In her earliest book on Anglo-India, ***The Simple Adventures of a Memsahib*** (1893) she described very amusingly how a simple, fresh and innocent English girl who came out to India with all kinds of plans and good intentions for the improvement of the heathen was gradually metamorphosed into a *memsahib* whose 'tissues are made of a substance somewhat resembling cork.' "She is growing dull to India, too, which is about as sad a thing as any. She sees no more the supple savagery of the Pathan in the market-place, the bowed reverence of the Mussulman praying in the sunset, the early morning mists lifting among the domes and palms of the city. She has acquired for the Aryan inhabitant a certain strong irritation, and she believes him to be nasty in all his ways. This will sum up her impressions of India as completely years hence as it does today. She is a memsahib like another. . . . I hope she may not stay twenty-two years." In later years Miss Duncan came to see with greater sympathy and pity the tragedy of these Anglo-Indian women—boredom, alienation from their environment and physical exhaustion often ending in sudden death.

Between 1893 and 1905 she wrote five other novels on Anglo-India, but for the introductory purpose of this article, I have selected two novels, ***Set in Authority*** (1906) and ***The Burnt Offering*** (1909). In order to appreciate them, however, a little historical background is necessary.

After the Rising of 1857, especially during the 70's and 80's a perceptible change came over the attitudes and the mutual relationships of the British and the Indians—as some of the 'natives' were now beginning to think of themselves. Trust and confidence gave place to suspicion and suppressed hostility, aggravated by the Englishman's barely concealed scorn for the 'native.' Social intercourse between the two races was replaced with a purely formal, official contact. Better means of communication between India and England—the telegraph and the Suez Canal, for example—made it unnecessary for the large majority of Englishmen to look upon the country as their home for the best part of their working lives. There were also more Europeans in the country, and an exclusive European society of sorts was now possible; a small, claustrophobic, inbred society, though, rigid in its taboos and resembling an army of occupation that has been ordered not to fraternize with the local population. A feeling of restless, impatient doubt about why they were in the country grew up in place of the earlier affectionate curiosity about the country and the sense of an imperial mission—to lead one-sixth of the human race toward nationhood and self-government. Many British officials and Liberal statesmen deplored and fought against their tendencies but with only indifferent success. At the same time the effects of the English education that the Indians had been receiving for some decades were also beginning to be felt. The Indians wished to graduate from admiration for the democratic thought and institutions to their masters to their practical adoption for themselves. They were encouraged in these aspirations by the tenour of the Queen's Proclamation of 1858 and the frequent pronouncements by leading British statesmen, notably of the Liberal Party. The birth of this aspiration at first delighted the Englishmen who saw in it the fulfilment of their plan and their responsibility. But for the majority of the British in India, the side from the notion of imperial trusteeship to that of a chosen race lording it over the lesser breeds proved irresistible. When they met educated Indians who expressed the new aspiration, they were at first, puzzled and incredulous; later, they became sullen and angry or sarcastic and insulting. The Indians were told that they were not fit as yet, wouldn't be for a long while, either for self-administration or even for a share in the administration at the higher levels. They were told that the reform of Indian society was the prior task and responsibility that they should undertake; Mill *On the Subjection of Women* and not Mill *On Liberty* was what they should be learning from. While some Indians were persuaded, others felt that a society which had not been confronted with the challenge of self-government calling for decisive choices of goals and methods, would not transform itself with any sense of urgency or necessity. Many of the measures of the Government during the last two or three decades of the century strengthened the feeling among educated Indians that their country was to be ruled to promote British interests, sometimes the interests of the Conservative Party, and that they were to be victims of racial discrimination in their own country. The notorious Anglo-Indian agitation over the Ilbert Bill strengthened this feeling. It was also suspected—not without justification—that British policy in India encouraged centrifugal tendencies, retarding the progress of the country toward nationhood. Thus the fears to the Muslims of the Hindu majority over whom they had ruled for centuries were sought to be allayed by measures that in fact institutionalised those fears. Parties that acquiesced in the *status quo* were encouraged. (Their identity, economic, social or religious, differed from region to region; nor was it always an internally consistent identity.) Indians who offered constructive criticism were regarded as a seditious, loud-mouthed urban minority of no consequence. It was contended that the vast majority of the country, the tillers of the soil, did not care about these political matters and were solidly behind the Government. (This was true enough, but it did not remain so for long—thanks to Gandhi who swung the balance away from the Government.) But the fact was inescapable—not many tried to escape it—that a gulf had opened up between ruler and ruled, between British and Indian.

That fact received its topographical expression and won its symbolic status in Anglo-Indian fiction in the division of towns where both Indians and Europeans lived into a native area and a European cantonment. The town of Pilaghur, the capital of the Province of Ghoom, in ***Set in Authority*** is so divided:

> Reflecting, we must call Pilaghur two capitals. There is the Pilaghur which the ladies of the station think of, and which figures—it has a cathedral—in diocesan reports. It has a parade-ground as well as a Cathedral and a station-club where are tennis-courts and the English illustrated papers, and public gardens set with palms and poinsettias where the band plays twice a week in the evenings after polo. Two or three roads lie fairly parallel in Pilaghur, and two or three lie more or less across, broad empty roads named after Indian administrators, bordered with tamarinds and acacias. There are certainly lamp-posts and infrequent in the distance, a bright, red letter-box; but the absence of everything else gives a queer, quiet, theatrical look to the highways. . . . The sun-suffused roads run up into rubbly banks on either side, and these are crowned with grey-green cactuses, many-armed and dusty. Behind them, indeterminately far in, indeterminately far apart, are houses, thick-looking low houses. They stand in the sun as a child might draw them on a very simple plan and rather crooked, with inexplicable excrescences, made too as a child might perhaps make them, chiefly of mud and colour-washed. . . . They are all of one substance . . . cream-coloured, but some are pink and some are yellow; there are even blue ones. I cannot conceive why they do not give Pilaghur a more cheerful appearance than it has. Perhaps it is because they stand, behind their cactus hedges and their hibiscus bushes, so remote from one another; they insist upon their approaches, they *will* have their atmosphere, and do not justify either. Or perhaps Pilaghur is depressed because, it has properly speaking, no shops. In one bungalow, standing in a roomy acre of its own, with three crooked sago palms in a far corner and nothing else, a photographer does business, but does so little that his two terriers bark furiously at any customer. In another, the small discoloured pink one by the tank, Miss Da Costa, from a well-known Calcutta firm, is understood to make very nice blouses; and I could show you where to find Mrs. Burbage, spoken of lamentably as an officer's widow. . . . But all this is hidden away . . . The eye rests comforted on a small sign, the sign of Ali Bux, General Stores Dealer. . . . Ali Bux seems to be permitted rather than encouraged or relied upon; we miss the backbone of life. From a point in mid-air, far enough up, this Pilaghur would have the vagueness of a family-wash, spread out in the manner of the country, to dry upon the ground.
>
> The other Pilaghur crowds upon the skirts of this—a thick embroidery. Far out it spreads imperceptibly into a mustard-fields; but here below Dalhousie Gardens, and all along to the old Mosque of Akbar it falls close packed to the river; and beyond the reservoir it lives; with indifference round the upright stone finger of an old conquest that still points to history the way of the Moghuls. Out there the multitudinous mud-huts are like an eruption of the baked and liver-coloured earth, low and featureless; but in the narrow ways of the crowded city by the river the houses jostle each other to express themselves. The upper storeys crane over the lower ones, and all resent their neighbours. They have indeed something to say with their carved balconies of wood and even of stone, with the dark-stained arches, pointed and scalloped, of their shop-fronts, their gods in effigy, their climbing, crumbling ochres and magentas. They have the stamp of the racial, the inevitable, the desperately in earnest, which is the grim sign of cities; there is no sign of vagueness, nothing superimposed, in Pilaghur-by-the-river. Never is there room for the tide of life that beats through it, chaffering and calling, ox-carts pushing, water-carriers trotting, vendors hawking, monkeys thieving, and Ganeshi Lal who wires a price to London for half the seed-crops of Ghoom. . . . Ganeshi sits on the floor, he wears a gold-embroidered velvet cap, and the scalloped window frames him to the waist. There are hundreds of such pictures. . . . The Oriental gutter runs along the side, the Oriental donkey sniffs at the garbage; there is an all-pervasive Oriental clamour and an all-pervasive Oriental smell. The city by the river trenches hardly anywhere on the station beyond; only the Brass Bazaar in one place strays across. You have to drive through it to get to the railway station. Pariahs dash out at bicycles, there are one or two haunting lepers, and cholera usually begins there; but it has a pictorial twist and a little white temple under an old banyan tree which the ladies of the station always praise and generally sketch. And there is no other way of getting to the railway station. These are Pilaghur.

It was not only in her 'natural descriptions' that Miss Duncan could achieve, when she was writing at her best, a symbolic meaning, an 'objective correlative,' but in her characterizations also. One instance must suffice, again from ***Set In Authority***. This is the contrast between Ruth Pearce, and extremely capable and dedicated surgeon, and her rather ignorant *ayah*. Miss Duncan is able to convey through the broken English of this *ayah* the unmistakable contrast between vitality and mere energy.

Resolute attempts were made by many British administrators to bridge what Lord Curzon described as the "chasm of racialism" in Anglo-Indian relations; he warned that racialism would 'split the Empire asunder.' Admitting Indians to European Clubs was not possible. "According to English standards a man is not 'clubbable' if he thought you were unfit to associate with his womenkind and if he lived half his life in a *milieu* from which he claimed rigidly to exclude you." *Ad hoc* 'bridge-parties' (to use E. M. Forster's term) were tried as a substitute. In ***Set In Authority*** Sir Ahmed Hossein is posted to Pilaghur as District and Sessions Judge. The European community discusses whether he should be socially recognized. " 'Is there a Lady Hossein?' asks the General's wife. 'If there is one and Sir Ahmed lets her go out to dinner, we will ask them and dine with them. But if he keeps her behind the *purdah,* I am neither to invite them to our house, nor will the General let me set foot in theirs—Judge or no Judge." A party is however held, and Sir Ahmed is invited; Lady Hossein, it mercifully transpires, is away in her village. At the party, writes the novelist, "in every eye he saw the barrier of race forbidding natural motions." Eventually he is elected to the exclusive Pilaghur Club, all the military members voting for him because he has passed a very light sentence on a soldier found guilty of the murder of an Indian. Whether he had let him off lightly because he wanted to win the favour of the English community or because although a Muslim he hated taking life, even the life of a scorpion,—'the twentieth century permits such religious eclecticism,' he says—or because he felt that racial feelings, already bad, would become worse if a heavy sentence were imposed, are points that are deliberately left vague in the novel.

There is an even more interesting example of a 'bridge party' in ***The Burnt Offering***. It is arranged by the wife of a senior British official. The Rani Janaki who has been educated at Oxford and who is the daughter of a judge of the Calcutta High Court explains the party to Joan Mills, a Girton graduate who is visiting India with her father, a Radical M.P.:

> "I do not know why, but suddenly they decided they would know us. The ladies of Calcutta, the *burramems*. They found they had a duty not only to those who go about like me, but to all the little ladies who keep *purdah*. It was very kind. They consulted some of us, and we agreed to join and persuade our friends. You will see."
> "It doesn't sound *real* ", said Joan.
>
> "It was very kind."
>
> The Anglo-Indian ladies moved about with painstaking friendliness; and now and then, in response to an invitation, one or two of the Indian ones would rise and follow them obediently in the direction of the refreshments. The Indian faces were all polite, and smiled responsively, but they spoke little English. Topics were plainly difficult to find, and the air was full of pauses.
>
> "Not an Englishwoman in the room understands Bengali," said Janaki, "and their Hindustani—poor dear ladies—it is of the kitchen"
>
> "There seems to be very little in common", Joan ventured.
>
> "What can they have in common?" said Janaki, "the ladies of the zenana and the ladies of the gymkhana? But, yes, there is one thing. That is politics. Every Bengali woman in this room is in her way a politician. But, naturally, they will not speak of that."
>
> "*Naturally?*" exclaimed Joan. "Is any one afraid to talk politics, under the British flag?"
>
> "We will say that they are shy", said Janaki. "But wait . . . "
>
> (And on being invited to sing, one of the Bengali ladies sings a patriotic song.)
>
> "They are all families of the Moderates, those ladies."
>
> "Even the one who sang?" asked Joan.
>
> "Oh yes. She has several relatives in the Civil Service. Their husbands and fathers are Moderates—but they sing. I too am a Moderate, and I do not even sing. I think," she added in a lower tone—and Joan could not see her face for a fold of her *sari,* "that I have lost my voice."

Joan Mills asks Mrs. Foley, the wife of the Standing Counsel to the Government, whether the Viceroy's band ever plays Indian music. "Oh no, our instruments aren't adapted to it." "It is what I am beginning very strongly to think. Whatever our instruments produce in India, it isn't music."

Racial discrimination and estrangement showed itself in several ways. I shall, however, refer only to those aspects of it that are taken up prominently by Miss Duncan. First, there was the question of the entry of Indians to the Covenanted Services, of which the most prestigious, the most powerful and the best-paid too, was the I.C.S. (the Indian Civil Service). Recruitment to this Service was done by means of a competitive examination held in England, and the age-limits were low. In effect this meant that very few Indians could get in. Curzon held the view that the I.C.S. should be for the most part in the hands of Englishmen; they were uniquely qualified for it by heredity, upbringing, integrity, vigour of character and knowledge of the principles of administration. His view was shared by several British administrators. In 1887 out of about a 1700 superior posts (with a salary of Rs. 800/—p.m. or more) only 77 were held by Indians; in 1903, of about 32003 posts, only 85 were held by Indians. In 1906 the Viceroy, Lord Minto frankly stated that it was impossible to appoint an Indian to a Governorship since the Services would not tolerate it. Questions of race and colour always came up in the appointment of Indians to superior posts. When it was proposed that an Indian should be appointed to the Viceroy's Council as part of the Morley-Minto Reforms of

1909, the King felt that the step "was fraught with the greatest danger for the Indian Empire." When Minto eventually chose S. P. Sinha (later Lord Sinha of Raipur who, as Under Secretary of State for India, piloted the Montagu-Chelmsford—Reforms in the House of Lords soon after the First World War) in preference to Asutosh Mukherjee, the Vice-Chancellor of the Calcutta University, an argument in favour of Sinha, was that Sinha was comparatively white whereas Mukherjee was 'black as my hat' and the opposition in the official world "would not be regardless of mere shades of colour." A great deal of mental energy was expended by both Morley and Minto on the problem of how to give representation to an Indian on the Viceroy's Executive Council in the most innocuous way. Morley told Minto truly enough that what the educated classes in India wanted a million times beyond political reform was access to the higher administrative posts. (a) The problem was aggravated by the fact that the educational system was churning out hundreds of Arts graduates who were utterly dependent upon the Government for employment. (b) Failing to find it, they turned against the Government. One reason that the Government put out for not employing Indians in the I.C.S. was that the Punjabi would not tolerate a Bengali as Head of the District (Kipling!) and the Muslims would feel insecure in an administration whose officers were predominantly Hindu.

This question is taken up by Miss Duncan in several novels. In ***The Simple Adventures,*** Mr. Sayter, a senior I.C.S. officer tells a visiting Radical M.P. who wishes to champion the cause of the 'natives':

> You will of course endeavour to extend the employment of baboos in the higher branches of the Covenanted Service—the judicial and administrative. They come much cheaper, and their feelings are very deeply hurt at being overlooked in favour of the alien Englishmen. You could get an excellent baboo for any purpose on earth for thirty rupees a month. . . a nice, fat, wholesome baboo who could write a beautiful hand—probably a graduate of the Calcutta University. (Mr. Sayter refers in the conversation to 'the extraordinary aptitude of the Bengali for the retention of printed matter.')

Since Mr. Sayter is presented as a character worthy of the reader's approval, his views are apparently offered for serious acceptance. In ***Set in Authority*** a constrast is drawn between Sir Ahmed Hossein and the English Chief Commissioner of the province in their official attitudes and approaches. The Government of India suggests to the Chief Commissioner that he should prefer an appeal in the Calcutta High Court against the lenient sentence awarded to the English soldier. The Viceroy is bitterly opposed to racial discrimination and wants to show that British justice is impartial. The Chief Commissioner agrees that the sentence was light but opposes the suggestion till the Viceroy personally orders him to appeal. The Commissioner feels that the appeal would be interpreted by the Anglo-Indian community as an act of interference with the judiciary and racial tensions would increase. He is neither subservient to the Viceroy nor disobedient. The High Court sentences the soldier to capital punishment. However, the soldier contrives, with the connivance of the English warders of the gaol, to commit suicide by swallowing an overdose of opium. After his death evidence comes to light that the case against him had been concocted by the Muslim *munshi* of the town with the help of the corrupt local Police to settle an old Mutiny score against the soldier's regiment. Again the Commissioner refuses to give publicity to the new evidence on the ground that the peace of the Empire would be disturbed and the position of the King-Emperor's Representative would be embarrassed. It is important to preserve the Viceroy's image because he is the "shadow of the King, but the substance of kingship is curiously and pathetically his, and his sovereignty is most real with those who again represent him. In lonely places which the Viceroy's foot never presses and his eye never sees, man of his own race find in his person the authority for the purpose of their whole lives. He is the judge of all they do and the symbol by which they do it. . . . He stands for the idea, the scheme and the intention to which they are all pledged. . . . The Viceroy may be a simple fellow, but his effigy is a wonderful accretion." This attitude of the Chief Commissioner contrasts with that of Sir Ahmed Hossein who sinks into despondency and even contemplates suicide when he learns that the Viceroy is displeased with him. He has had an Oxford education; he refers to Shakespeare and Blake as 'our poets'; and when he applies for leave to go to England, it is 'home leave' for him, but the essential traits of an English administrator have eluded him.

This conviction that Indians do not make good administrators and that they have a long way to go is also expressed by John Game, the Government Home Secretary in ***The Burnt Offering***. Game is represented as a very decent person and indeed one of the best of the British bureaucrats, altogether free from racialism. He is asked whether the disqualification that had been recently announced of an Indian from the I.C.S. for his failure to pass the riding-test (rather as Sri Aurobindo was) was justified. "Are many Englishmen disqualified for the same reason," asks Joan Mills. Game justifies what has been done on the ground that much of the work of a District Officer is done on horseback, and Englishmen naturally know how to ride. "As all Englishmen are naturally able to govern," is the sarcastic comment of Joan. "Precisely," Game retorts, ignoring the sarcasm. He concedes that an I.C.S. officer is 'put on the rails' and the Service is 'an iron system.' But it also offers great opportunity for service, and seen in that light, 'the job is too high for the best of us.' He admits that the British administration is guilty of lapses and failures—'We are only a Government, not god Almighty'—but these judgements of fitness and achievement are after all relative. Game's view was widely shared by both Conservative and Liberal statesmen of England, and Indian leaders also did not, on the whole, seriously disagree that England had an imperial mission to fulfil—service and the education of the native. The Indians argued that the fulfilment called for the increasing participation in the legislative and executive functions of Government. Democracy is a game that is learnt only by playing it. The Indians began to agitate when they felt that no serious attempt was being made to fulfil the promises. In its early phase the aim of the agitation was to remind the British of the responsibility they owed to India. In its later phase its aim was to convince the British that they had no option in the matter, that India could not be ruled without the consent of the Indians, a consent that was strictly time-bound. Gandhi's achievement consisted in teaching the Indians how to express this consent, or lack of it, in ways that suited their character and temperament and the circumstances of time and place. However before Gandhi appeared on the scene, there was a brief phrase of terrorist agitation, chiefly in Bengal, in the first decade of the century. The agitation failed of course—as it deserved to—but it had several ambiguous features which are very skilfully recaptured by Miss Duncan in ***The Burnt Offering***. (The title itself reflects this ambiguity.)

The novel opens very effectively with a scene in which a young Bengali youth, educated at Cambridge and Paris, is most insolently refused admission to a first class carriage on a railway train by a couple of European planters, a class that was notorious for its racial arrogance.

> "You can't get in here, Baboo. There isn't room."
>
> The train was standing in the little pink station of Pubni, on its way to Calcutta. A lean old man with water in a goat-skin slaked the platform with a flourishing jet from his fingers, and the afternoon suns slanted on the purple bougainvilliers over the gate-posts of the station-master's garden. It was a warm, gentle, still halting-place; between the grunts of the pausing engine a bee buzzed audibly in the bougain-villiers; and a crow in a pipal across the lines seemed to deliver himself for the whole district.
>
> "How many persons are in this carriage, sir?"
>
> "Never mind about that, Baboo. There isn't room for you."
>
> The young man spoke good-naturedly enough, but he definitely barred the entrance with the lower half of a leg in flannel trousers, and a foot in a brown leather boot. He had not taken the trouble to shut the door.
>
> The person addressed as "Baboo," who wore neat European clothes and a small white and gold twisted head-dress, nevertheless ventured to step upon the footboard and look into the carriage, which contained a good deal of dusty luggage and one other younger gentleman, stretched upon the opposite seat and reading the *Planters' Gazette.*
>
> "I must insist upon coming in here," he said; "you are but two passengers."
>
> "No, you don't," said the owner of the brown leather boot; but the roll-up of the new-comer was already being pushed by a coolie under the barrier leg. This awoke the young man on the seat opposite to sudden and expressive wrath. He raised himself threateningly on one elbow.
>
> "Get out of this," he exclaimed, "or damn it, I'll hoof you out."
>
> All the world might hear, if the world had not been fortunately absent. One person did, a tall English girl who seemed to be the only other passenger. She was walking up and down the platform sending her long shadow in front of her, and she heard. She paused for an instant, startled; then she simply stopped and listened. The approaching water-carrier waited with difference until she should resume her walk, gave it up and ran on, shedding his cascades in a semicircle before her. With her hands thrust into the pockets of her dust-cloak she made a casual but attentive spectator.
>
> The coolie pushed the roll-up further in, and followed it with a bag.
>
> "Excuse me," said Bepin Behari Dey, making an attempt to pass the defensive leg, "I have a first-class ticket and I claim accommodation."
>
> "Oh, get out, Baboo," said the youth at the door, "and don't give trouble. No admittance here, don't you see? Can't have you spitting about here."
>
> "Ticket or no ticket, you can jolly well travel somewhere else," announced he who was lying down, and sprang up to enforce his words. "Here—out you go."
>
> The Indian could not be said to be in, but his luggage, sped by a couple of vigorous kicks, went out for him, alighting not far from the feet of the girl looking on, who came, with interest, a step nearer.
>
> "Sir, I do not expectorate."
>
> "Oh yes, you do, Baboo. You expectorate all right. Anyhow"—and the door finished the sentence with a bang.
>
> The young native certainly showed self-control. There was cloud in his glance, but no lightning. He looked more determined to enforce his point than indignant at his repulse. The resentment and dislike in the fact he turned upon the occupants of the carriage seemed rather a settled and habitual thing than any outcome of his present treatment.
>
> "I will send for the station-master," he said.
>
> "By all means," returned the second defender of the carriage. "Here he comes, Hi, there—Station-master! Here's this Baboo making a most infernal disturbance trying to shove himself into this carriage. Just run him in somewhere else, will you?"
>
> The station-master, a fat Eurasian, a good deal darker than the Bengali looked at him with the expression of a gentleman who could sympathise with the grievance of his fellows, and waited in irritated official tolerance for what an inferior might have to say.
>
> Bepin produced his ticket.
>
> "It is first-class," he said, "and I think the only other first-class is a ladies' compartment."
>
> The station-master took the ticket, examined it, frowned upon it, and handed it back.

"What is the use of getting in where you know objection will be taken?" he said in the clicking, doubling talk of the mixed race. "Further on there is a second-class carriage which you can have entirely to yourself. You can be private there."

"If I wished to be private I was at liberty to reserve a carriage," protested the Bengali. The arbiter looked as if nothing in the world would make him responsible.

"Well, you had better get in somewhere," he said. "She is going now. I cannot stop the train for disputes amongst passengers," and turned upon an indifferent heel.

Appeal to authority having failed him, and the carriage door being now definitely shut in his face the young man stepped back upon the platform, and the hovering coolie again seized his luggage. When Joan Mills spoke to him he gave her a violent look, as if some further indignity was to be expected from her. But that was not her intention.

"The other first-class carriage is not reserved for ladies," she told him. "My father is with me, and there is plenty of room. Will you not come in there?"

Her voice trembled with anger, but it was equally characteristic of her that she did not take her hands out of her pockets.

"Thank you, I am obliged to you; but I do not wish to intrude in your carriage."

"It is not our carriage, and you will be very welcome," said Miss Mills, casting, as she spoke, a glance upon the victorious occupants of the compartment in which they might have read a measure of contempt for her race as excusable as it was extravagant.

"Then I will come."

The girl led the way, Bepin following with the laden coolie. . . .

"Father," said the girl, as she and Bepin entered the carriage, and the train moved out, "I have told this gentleman there is plenty of room in here. . . . "

"I was only thinking—How monstrous!" said the girl. "This gentleman," she said to her father, "was refused admittance to their carriage in the most brutal manner, by a couple of Europeans just now. We had heard such things happened, but we could hardly believe it," she added.

Her father took his pipe from his lips, which composed themselves sternly. He opened them to say, "I thought as much."

Bepin, to hide his embarrassment, laughed. All sorts of things were hidden in the laugh which, on the outside deprecated, made nothing of the incident.

"Oh," he said, "that is very common. European gentlemen in India do not like travelling with the people of the country. We are not always able to assert our rights."

"European gentlemen!" breathed Joan. "And these are the people who govern you—these are your civil administrators!"

"No. The officials do not speak in that way to Indians. Those were common men, what we call chotasahibs—mill assistants, I think."

"I wish I knew for certain." Plainly, she would have preferred to be right.

"If you do—if you think it worth while," said the girl with quick tact, "you may count upon me as a witness. I saw the whole thing."

"It should not be allowed to pass," urged her father.

Bepin looked contemptuous. "Oh, I can complain," he said, "but what is the use? That would not prevent the same thing happening again. Besides, it is a small matter. I am not hurt."

"Then," said Joan, "you must be a philosopher."

"Yes—I hope. But I am not so good a philosopher as my father was. He is dead now, but for years he always travelled third-class, and he was not a poor man."

"Why did he do that?" asked Joan.

Bepin laughed again. "It was a fancy of his, since one day he was travelling in a first-class carriage and two young officers got in, with very wet and muddy boots, at a small station where they had been shooting the jheels. They were very angry finding my father in the carriage, and told him to get out. He refused to get out, so when the train started they ordered him to pull off their boots. He refused this also, but they stood over him and compelled him to do it, and being an old man he dared not resist. So after that he travelled third-class rather, with the coolies."

Joan's eyes blazed.

"In your own country!" she exclaimed. "How can you bear it!"

"I think you are strangers," young Dey replied, always with the laugh which defended him from sympathy. "Only strangers would ask that. We have no alternative."

"Yes," said the elderly man, "we are strangers. But we have come to learn, and we are learning," he added, "very fast."

Joan's father is Vulcan Mills, Radical M.P. for Further Angus who is visiting India to see things for himself. He was probably modelled after Keir Hardie who visited India for a few months in 1907 and wrote a series of letters on India in *The Labour Leader* which he later collected into the book, *India, Impressions and Suggestions* (1909). He made a sympathetic and intelligent assessment of the Indian scene, and offered a number of sensible suggestions to improve the administration and bring it closer to the people, and the climate of progressive opinion. He particularly noted that the 'colour line was being more rigidly drawn every year' and gave several instances of it.

> When I entered the train at Madras, there were two Indian gentlemen in the compartment. One of them rose as I entered, and said, "Shall we move to another compartment, Sir?" I stared at the man, and asked whether he had paid his fare. "Oh, yes," he replied; "but English gentlemen don't as a rule like to travel with natives". Now I knew that in parts of America the colour line was strictly drawn, but I was not prepared for this kind of thing in India. Here, be it remembered, is a people who have inherited a civilization which was old as the West had begun to emerge from savagery. Those who travel first or second-class are mostly men with a University education, and speak English fluently. Some of them are wealthy, and many of them are of ancient lineage and noble descent. And yet, travelling on a Government railway in their own country, they are treated by the governing white caste much as they themselves treat the poor outcast pariahs.

Nearer to the episode in the novel is another instance that Hardie gives of a Muslim gentleman, of handsome, refined appearance, descended of an illustrious family, educated at Cambridge (as Dey in the novel is) and called to the Bar. On his return from England, he entered a first-class carriage in which two Englishmen were travelling. He was at once ordered out—the compartment was not reserved—'and in the end, for his own comfort, was forced to go out to escape the studied insults of his travelling companions.' Hardie declared that 'one way to break down the colour line was to raise the official status of the people. So long would they be looked down upon by their rulers. . . . In this, as so much else, self-government is the solvent to which we must look for dissolving a difficulty rapidly becoming unbearable.' He quoted Mill's dictum that such a thing as the government of one people by another did not and could not exist. Hardie's utterances and contracts with Indian leaders gave much offence to the Government of India, and he was seriously misrepresented and caricatured in the London Press also. The Viceroy Cyord Minto wrote to Morle the Secretary of State, that the modern House of Commons was 'absolutely incapable of understanding Indian humanity' and constituted 'the greatest danger to the continuance' of British rule in India.

Miss Duncan's portrait of Keir Hardie as Vulcan Mills, Socialist M.P. for Further Angus, is not unsympathetic, though eventually she deports him from India just as he is about to address a meeting in Calcutta in defiance of the Act for Prevention of Seditious Meetings.

> Vulcan Mills is described as 'the romance of the British proletariat. . . . He stood for their actual and private emotions, he was their larger heart, and with a tongue that did not stumble, he celebrated that which they desired to believe. . . . He never faltered in the ideals he had, as it were, undertaken on their behalf, and as his social proposals were still very far from serious consideration or practical test by the Commonwealth, he could hold them up with every happy advantage. He sat earnestly at Westminster with his feet upon the floor—and his policy in the clouds; and every time he spoke, the millennium came nearer in the eyes of Further Angus. Pending its realization he did spade work on committees upon labour-questions which was generally admitted to be useful. . . . He was a man singularly without personal ambition in politics. He tramped after his ideal wherever he saw it, tramped after it in the same old heavy boots. . . . He belonged emphatically to the earlier emergence of the socialistic idea before it had learned the necessity of compromise or the value of business methods, when the voice in the wilderness carried all before it, and organization was as irrelevant as quadratics.'
>
> The Standing Counsel to the Government who thinks Vulcan Mills rather a nuisance admits that 'he has heart and eloquence of a sort, and he's quite honest. The people like him too because he's never climbed on their shoulders into a silk hat and a frock coat.'

(A reference probably to Keir Hardie's famous cap.) When Mills meets his Indian friends, he tells them—after rebuking one of them for calling his fellow-Indians 'natives'—that 'the people must govern themselves. That is the proclamation of the twentieth century. Not in England, not in America only, but in every cursed Dependency and emasculated Crown Colony on the fact of the earth.' He urges them to 'agitate, agitate. It is my first word to you, and I foresee it will be my last. Agitate every way you know. We—your brothers—in England—are oppressed by class-domination there just as you are here, but we have found that we can shake it by agitation.' Miss Duncan perceived that the leaders of the terrorist movement did not believe in the Western type of secular democracy. Swami Yadava, the Hindi *sanyasin* in the novel wants the British to stay on though he knows that 'they as a people have little affection for us as a people,' because as champions of the *status quo,* they will help to keep the old social order intact with the Brahmin at the top. And they will do the job much less expensively than, for instance, the Japanese (whose stock had gone up in India after the Russo-Japanese war) or the Americans in similar circumstances. When Swami Yadava speaks to Mills of the danger of new wine in old bottles, Mills retorts: 'Let the bottles burst. The people will drink the new wine, and it will hearten them for great deeds. . . . Excuse me, Swami Yadava, you are a priest, and there never was a priest yet who did not find sacerdotal domination was easier in political coma.' For the leaders of the terrorist movement their activity constituted a 'burnt offering' to God, or rather, to 'the Mother.' When Aurobindo retired to Pondicherry he had not giving up politics for religion; he had never given up religion. In the novel, the guru of the terrorists is Ganendra Thakore, ostensibly the editor of a newspaper, *The Lamp of Youth,* and the director of a school (*Anushilansamithi*) for physical and cultural education. (The young man involved in the railway train incident quoted earlier, B. B. Dey, is a member of the gang but Mills is unaware of these affiliations.) Ganendra thinks that the Western model of government is unsuited to the genius of the country. 'But give us back our Mother, and we shall not trouble about the fashion of her dress, he says to Mills, and in order, no doubt, to bring home to him how keenly the deprivation of freedom was being felt, asks Mills whether he had ever been forcibly separated from his mother. To which, Mills replies, with breezy unsentimentality, 'I never had one,' and repeats, 'No mother and no gods.' Joan Mills also fails to comprehend this language of the heart. (Curzon, it will be recalled, also could not understand this language and refused to attach any importance to the Bengali agitation against the Partition of Bengal.) When Swami Yadava rather loftily tells Vulcan Mills that Indians have another kind of freedom than representative institutions, Mills gives him 'a glance of half-contemptuous pity,' and retorts: "There is no other kind. And you in India must rouse yourselves to feel that. It is what I preach to my friends here day and night."

Vulcan Mills of course simplifies the issues but Miss Duncan shows how dangerous it is to mix politics and religion. More boys wish to join the school of Ganendra Thakore so that they may study the Gita and hate the English. "Already we hate them—but not truly. . . . the holy Gita strengthens the heart. . . . We are religious and wish to be made ready to die for our sacred mother." The High Court judge, Sir Kristodas Mukherjee who sentences Ganendra for sedition, tells him before pronouncing judgement:

> The fact remains, and you have made it abundantly clear to me this afternoon, that the religious emotion, however pure, can furnish no sound basis for political life. These things stand aside one from the other; and from the bottom of my heart I adjure you, and all others like you, who believe that they need only fan a desire to turn it into fact, to understand and believe that this is not possible, and to turn their souls from crime in whatever disguise it may present itself. . . . You have held out the arm of the priest to point the way to violence and crime. That this has been a source of true spiritual satisfaction to you many will doubt, and that spiritual satisfaction should make a feather's weight against the gravity of your misdeeds all will deny.

Gandhi attempted, with some success, to show that instead of defiling religion with politics, politics could be purified with religion. In politics the end is all important; but religion teaches that means are as important as ends. It is to the credit of Miss Duncan that writing at a period when terrorism had brought Indian religion as a whole under suspicion, she was able to perceive that at least in its original intention the religious inspiration of the terrorist movement was noble. That perception is presented in a fairly sophisticated dialectical way. There is Swami Yadava who is presented in his conversations with Mukherjee and his daughter—he is their *guru*—and with John Game as a man of some spirituality. (Like Swami Vivekananda he is widely travelled and has American disciples also.) But he is an obscurantist in politics, and a police informer to boot. The character of Sir Kristodas Mukherjee is more ambivalent. (His christian name is a tactful combining of Krishna and Christ.) At the end of the novel we see him renouncing his knighthood and retiring to the Himalayas. But his earlier reformist beliefs and practices are unambiguously ridiculed. He had started off as an extremely orthodox Brahmin, bathing in the Ganges everyday and spending several hours in worshipping the *Sivalinga*. After the K.C.I.E. (Knight Commander of the Order of the Indian Empire) had been conferred on him, he had the Ganges water brought to his bath-room and shifted the *Sivalinga* to an upper shelf in the library 'where it was flanked by Spencer on one side and Mill on the other.' "He presently dined with Englishmen, soon smoked their cheroots, and finally drank their champagne." He gave out that he had liberalized his views, and even published a book on the future of caste which, says the novelist, was too philosophic to be progressive. He was even prepared to arrange a second marriage for his daughter who had been widowed in early life. He sent her to Oxford, but recalled her when her letters became somewhat critical of the *Raj*.

But this satire is altogether absent from the portrait that Miss Duncan presents of Ganendra Thakore at his trial. He justifies his conduct in a speech which, as Sir Kristodas Mukherjee acknowledges, has a strangely moving power. It deserves to be quoted since Miss Duncan never wrote anything finer:

> "My Lord Judge," said Ganendra Thakore slowly, "I, Ganendra Thakore, accused in this case, have no wish to defend myself from the charges brought against me, in the ordinary sense of the term. The charges as they stand must remain, and I may venture to hope will ever remain, associated with my name." Sir Kristodas looked up sharply; but there was in the prisoner's bearing no arrogance. His head was bent, his hands clasped behind his back. One would have said, a man realizing himself at the most serious moment of his life. The judge uttered no rebuke.
>
> "Personally I would prefer that this case should go down to history undefended, either by me or by any one on my behalf. But there are other considerations, and therefore I speak, no not for myself, but for my offence. I am not a lawyer, and I have small experience of Courts of Justice. I do not know how far I will be heard in urging the moral sanction, the moral justification, of the offence I have committed, and how far I must plead extenuation only."
>
> "You had better confine yourself to extenuating circumstances," said the Judge.
>
> Ganendra lifted his head.
>
> "Then, my Lord," he said in a stronger voice, with careful self-control, "shall hope to show extenuation so great, pollution so wide, that it will reach beyond this Court to the legislators of this country. So it may be that my offence, having been committed, shall disappear; and if such result comes of it I shall think myself happy, my Lord Judge.
>
> "I am accused of inciting to hatred and disaffection; but I submit that these harsh words do not truly describe the new emotion which is begin-

ning to thrill the hearts of my countrymen. A new emotion they have, and through it they are finding a kind of life for their souls. It may be a feverish life. I do not ask you to believe that it is yet very sane or well-regulated. But I do ask a hearing when I maintain that it is the only one they have; and that before they found it they were dead. I know that before I found it I was dead. I ate and drank complacently, in agreement with the world as it had produced me; but I did not know my own spirit. In my fortieth year came the misfortune which awakened me, my Lord, to what your law calls hatred and disaffection; and while I cannot even yet bless that misfortune, there is no moment of the life of the soul into which it ushered me that I would exchange for all the forty dead years that went before.". . .

"My Lord Judge, I was raised from the dead. Is it a thing incredible to your Lordship? I stand before you not in my corruptible body, but in my incorruptible body. I, who am permitted by the clemency of this Court to address you, have consciously and gloriously partaken of the Divine essence. I have spoken with the Lord of the Herds, and in part the vision of Arjuna has been mine." . . .

"I came into this estate by the way of what your law calls hatred and disaffection. Not hatred of any person or disaffection to any potentate, but hatred and disaffection toward the political conditions which were numbing the manhood, and silencing the voice, and destroying the traditions of my own great and ancient people. I placed this estate against the fat prosperity of a few rich men, against the disturbing of our immemorial peace with a few more railroads, against all the other economic blessings which we are so often bidden to count. I placed against it the Pax Britannica. And I chose the word of the Lord.

"Having found my own soul I looked, my Lord, with the eyes of my soul, for the soul of the Mother, I saw it dumb and dying in the souls of her sons. The Troubler of Men spoke to me and gave me a message. Then I saw and knew why my own soul had been shown to me; and from that moment to this I have never ceased to deliver the message—this message. The men of my race must come out of political bondage; they must tear themselves at any sacrifice from ignoble dependence upon an alien power, from the poor comfort and security that we are asked to value above our birthright—in order that they may enter into the first condition under which they can realise and proclaim to the world the Divinity that from the beginning has loved this land above all others.

"I say the first of the conditions. For God is *mukta*—free. He is *buddha*—enlightened. He is *suddha*—pure. Those who would be clothed with His mission must be all three, but freedom comes first. And India claims His mission to the world—India, whose God is older than light or thought, whose inspiration gave the West a religion which it dares to retail to us at second-hand India is the guru of the nations. Let others invent their luxuries, build their ships, forge their great instruments of war. The mission of India is to proclaim and to prove the union of God and man, the supreme, universal, and eternal necessity of knowledge. India holds the torch of the spirit, and would hold it high. This is the mission of Nationalism, miscalled hatred and disaffection, for the sake of which I am accused before you to-day.

"Hatred and disaffection? Not to any person or to any potentate. Were Bhishma and Drona, men meet for honour, my Lord, fought with disaffection of the field of the Kurus? Had the blind King hate from Pritha's son? Was not the fight made at the bidding of a voice which said, 'If thou wilt not wage this lawful battle, then wilt thou fail in thine own Law and thine honour?' And was that voice other than the voice which the Nationalists of this country hear today?

Sir Kristodas, listening sat forward, with his elbow on the desk, his hand now shading his eyes. The spectators listened too, a little perhaps, as if to a poet or a performance, but closely, intently. . . .

"I believe," summed up Ganendra, "that the law takes cognisance of what it describes as good and bad intention. I do not hope to establish my intention in the eye of the law—but I know, I *know,* that I have established it in the eye of God."

Sir Kristodas sentences him to ten years in a penal colony, but says in the course of his summing-up, "It may be that it would be wiser for the Government which rules and must continue to rule this land and better for us if they would try to understand our people more by the light of those old books from which you have quoted." Ganendra dies in prison before he is removed to the penal colony—which seems to have been Miss Duncan's way of tempering law with justice. Miss Duncan was no doubt in the final reckoning a writer of 'imperialist' novels, but she felt the appeal of India and the claims of Indian nationalism. The Viceroy in the novel concludes his Convocation Address to the Calcutta University with the nationalist cry, *Bande Mataram* (Obeisance to the Mother). The novelist describes the cry as 'the watchword of the nascent nation, unloved by authority, dear to the people, and as they caught it from the Viceroy, his audience laughed and sobbed together and would have carried him out like a Krishna image at the Festival of Vishnu, the Preserver of Men.' Joan Mills wants to marry Dey (rejecting Game, the Home Secretary of the Government) and settle in India to work for India's 'awakening.' Her former life in England of committees and campaigning for women's rights seems to her, in comparison, like the beating of a nursery drum. She tells Mrs. Foley: 'It is all tawdry and feverish, full of expediency and vulgarity. I love the larger peace and the deeper dream of India.' Miss Duncan is again very successful in capturing that larger peace in her description of the landscape:

The band ceased, and the curious, soft silence spread about them that falls with every evening about Calcutta. Now and then a horse shifted

> restlessly with a clink of harness, or a crow, settling on his branch for the night, cawed a raucous protest against intrusion; but there was hardly any other sound. A hawker of buttonhole bouquests offered his basket from carriage to carriage. The scent of his tuberoses and jasmine wandered through the still air, and his voice sounded timid and tentative in the quiet. The palms of the gardens stood theatrically in the electric light which burnished and importance of the policeman who moved about regulating the ranks of the carriages. Further out in one direction, the circle showed a dim funnel or two, and died away in another toward the jewelled expanse of the Maidan. Within stood saliently the white marble figure of a British admiral who once brought his blue jackets and their cutlasses up the river, and now seemed to contemplate, not without criticism, the scene he had helped to save for his country.

Joan sees her dedication to India as a duty. "How else can one so completely devote one's self to these unhappy browbeaten people whose heart is spurned by the heel of our race? How can one do anything short of identifying one's self with them? And how little it is, how little, after all the arrogance, the misunderstanding, the contempt. In the whole world is there love enough to blot it out?" Her father, the Radical M.P., 'saw the dedication of his future activities to the cause of India somewhat less simply than his daughter did' but the essential validity of Joan Mills's approach to the Indian problem—India's freedom and India's relations with England—derives its attestation from the opening scene of the novel that I have quoted above. Dey shoots himself after an unsuccessful attempt on the life of the Viceroy, but even after his death, Joan wants to stay on in India. "What does it matter," she says when she hears of his suicide, "what does it matter a little disorder—a life here and a life there—so long as a principle shines out brighter and clearer than before?"

That the principle does indeed become a little clearer and brighter than before is what makes these novels of Miss Duncan worth our attention—in spite of the fact that their overall 'philosophy' does not have the courage to assimilate their own experience. In her dreams Miss Duncan saw an India that Anglo-India did not seem very often. But the pity was that she could not remember her dreams when she woke up to drive in her *tikka-gharry* to Pilaghur Cantonment. *Tikka-gharry* and Pilaghur Cantonment have gone, with Dey, into the shadows, but the dreams remain.

Frank Birbalsingh (essay date 1977)

SOURCE: "Sara Jeannette Duncan's Indian Fiction," in *World Literature Written in English,* Vol. 16, No. 1, April, 1977, pp. 71-81.

[*In the following essay, Birbalsingh examines Duncan's fiction, commenting on the flaws he finds therein: superficiality, anticlimax, and contradiction.*]

Sara Jeannette Duncan was born in 1861 in Brantford, Ontario, Canada. By 1889, when she first visited India, she had already established a reputation, both in Canada and the United States, as an articulate journalist and a versatile publicist of topical issues. In India she met Charles Everard Coates, an Anglo-Indian whom she married in 1891. She then lived in India, almost continuously, for more than twenty years. Of the nineteen works of fiction which she completed, before her death in London in 1922, nine deal with her Indian experience.

Miss Duncan's first Indian work, ***The Simple Adventures of a Memsahib*** (1893) records the experiences of an English girl, Helen Frances Peachey, who leaves home to marry an Anglo-Indian clerk in Calcutta. If the record of Helen's new experiences appears monotonous, the monotony is relieved by an ironic tone which prevails in the contrast between the heroine's own culture and the exotic customs of Anglo-Indians. The tone throughout is genial, without malice, but it lacks seriousness. Thc author seems less concerned with analysing the actual—psychological and intellectual—effect of India upon her heroine than with providing factual information about routine, everyday, aspects of Anglo-Indian society.

Vernon's Aunt, Miss Duncan's third Indian work, parallels ***Memsahib*** both in its vivid record of Anglo-Indian customs and in its prevailing humour which, again, is sustained by the ironic contrast between the heroine's English culture and the exotic manners of Anglo-Indians. The novel, however, is notable for its description of a love affair—at any rate, an attempted one—between Miss Moffat and Abdul Karim Bux, a middle-aged, half-educated Moslem clerk who works under Vernon Hawkins. Bux is the only one who takes his advances to Miss Moffat seriously, and the one-sided affair is doomcd from the start. When he first conducts Miss Moffat from the railway station to meet her nephew, he warns her not to disclose their (as he believes) spontaneous intimacy to Hawkins:

> Mr. Ockinis—I do not know—Mr. Ockinis may not like that I find favour with Miss Eemuffitty. I think Mr. Ockinis may be jealous that I have touch the heart of his so intelligent ant! I think it will be better madam does not say she has isspoken to me.

His speech alone proves that his romantic feelings for an English memsahib are preposterous; and when, in the end, these feelings lead him to commit irregularities in his job, Bux is lucky to get away with mere blows and a reprimand from Hawkins. Serious implications of the love affair—the psychological conflicts of interracial marriage, or the moral aspects of sexual union between a member of the ruling caste and one of the ruled—are not considered.

As ***Memsahib*** and ***Vernon's Aunt*** show, Miss Duncan's books provide an authentic and closely-observed, if superficial record of Anglo-Indian society in the closing decades of the nineteenth century. In some books, where the social portrait is not the chief objective, Miss Duncan uses it as a background for stories of adventure, or intrigue and romance. ***The Story of Sonny Sahib*** (1894) for example, is a Kiplingesque story of an English boy who is cared for by Indians during the Indian mutiny. The boy is finally "rescued" by English troops, but nobly refuses to divulge military secrets of his Indian benefactors. ***The Pool in the Desert*** (1903), a volume of four long stories, also illustrates the author's skill in constructing fluent and vivid romantic narratives. At the same time, the unlikely complications, sudden convenient coincidences, and pointless anticlimax in these narratives confirm the general impression of Miss Duncan's Indian books as being less concerned with serious, artistic criteria than with light, good-humoured melodrama.

But the humour and melodramatic interests of those books so far mentioned do not completely obscure a serious theme which shows itself more openly in the author's remaining Indian novels. Hints of the theme are given in ***Memsahib*** and ***Vernon's Aunt*** where some English characters show awareness of British moral responsibility to people in less developed or less powerful societies. This awareness of "the mother country's duty to the heathen masses who look to her for light and guidance" partly inspires nineteenth-century Imperialism, which forms the main theme of Miss Duncan's most ambitious writing about India. Miss Duncan's view of Imperialism was strongly influenced by her Canadian experience; for by the 1890's, Canadians were among the foremost supporters of a proposed Federation of the British Empire aimed at furthering the cause of Imperialism. The proposal was for a more egalitarian and pragmatic regrouping of British Colonies and Dominions in order to promote the social, cultural, political, and economic welfare of all members of the Federation: Britain would provide cultural prestige and political stability; the white Dominions would open their vast natural resources to economic investment; and the ensuing prosperity and security would better enable Britain and the Dominions to bear "the great Imperial sacrifice" of moral upliftment in the black colonies of Africa, Asia, the Caribbean, and the Pacific. From a Canadian point of view, too, such a Federation had the not inconsiderable virtue of helping to stave off the threat of possible political annexation or economic absorption by the United States.

So far as her Indian fiction is concerned, Miss Duncan's fullest treatment of Imperialism appears in three novels—***His Honour and a Lady*** (1896), ***Set in Authority*** (1906), and ***Burnt Offering*** (1909). The action in all three novels takes place during the last quarter of the last century. The action of ***His Honour and a Lady*** centres on the conflict between John Church who is Governor of Bengal, and Lewis Ancram who is his Chief Secretary. The conflict between the two men derives from their different approaches to Imperialism. Church's approach is religiously inspired, though undesirable:

> He [Church] believes this earth was created to give him an atmosphere to do his duty in; and he does it with the invincible courage of short-sightedness combined with the notion that the ultimate court of appeal for eighty million Bengalis should be his precious Methodist conscience.

Church's commitment to Indian "progress" makes him favour higher education for Indians. Ancram however, who pays lip service to Church's policies while treacherously aiding his opponents, believes that higher education will be harmful to Indians within the existing colonial conditions:

> When we have helped these people [Indians] to shatter all their notions of reverence and submission and self-abnegation and piety, and given them, for such ideals as their fathers had, the scepticism of the West, I don't know that we shall have accomplished much to our credit.

In Ancram's view, higher education encourages economic dislocation and creates "a starveling class that find nothing to do but swell mass meetings on the Maidan and talk sedition." His approach to Imperialism, as the author explicitly states, is more paternalistic than Church's. The conflict between the two men is partially reconciled by Church's death; but it reappears when Ancram becomes Governor and wishes to marry Church's widow Judith. Then Judith accidentally discovers Ancram's former treachery to her dead husband and rejects his suit.

Lord Thane, the principal character of ***Set in Authority*** is modelled on Lord Ripon who was Viceroy of India from 1880 to 1884. Like his historical prototype, Lord Thane attempts to reform Anglo-Indian administration to bring it more in line with his own idealistic views of Imperialism. His attempts focus on the trial of a British soldier, Morgan, who is accused of kicking an Indian servant to death. Lord Thane insists not only that Morgan should be tried for the alleged offence, but that he should be tried by an Indian judge. The first half of the novel sets the scene for a presumably gripping climax as Morgan is condemned to be hanged by Justice Sir Ahmed Hoosein. Morgan's fellow soldiers protest vehemently against the verdict, and as his execution approaches, are close to virtual mutiny. The Anglo-Indian community as a whole, in sympathy with the soldiers, send a letter of protest to Queen Victoria. Anarchy seems near. But Lord Thane resolutely stands by his Imperialistic ideals of justice, and refuses to intervene. Then, on the eve of his expected execution, Morgan commits suicide by swallowing opium. Soon after, Lord Thane is recalled to England in premature retirement, and public hysteria subsides.

Burnt Offering, the last of Miss Duncan's Indian works, describes the visit of a British Member of Parliament to India. The MP, Vulcan Mills, is accompanied by his daughter Joan, who is strongly influenced by her father's radical, political views. Both of them are outraged by what they perceive to be abuses of Anglo-Indian officialdom. They quickly throw in their lot with a revolutionary Indian group that is led by Ganendra Thakore whose adopted son, Bepin Behari Dey, is one of the most active members of the group. Prolonged political association leads Dey to fall in love with Joan Mills and propose marriage. Meanwhile, Joan receives a second proposal from John Game, Secretary to the Government of India in the Home Department. But she accepts Dey. Then the promise of another tense climax is unfulfilled: Thakore is given a summary conviction; Mills is transported from India with peremptory haste; and Dey is arrested. Dey is later released on bail, whereupon he tries to shoot the Viceroy, misses, and wounds Game instead; he then commits suicide. Joan returns to England.

The characters of ***Burnt Offering*** are as disembodied as those of ***His Honour and a Lady*** and ***Set in Authority***. Its action is equally undramatic, and its plot just as perfunctory; for the obvious tension implicit in subjects such as sedition, revolution, attempted assassination, interracial marriage, is again substantially diluted by pervasive reportage. Altogether these three novels reveal much information about social attitudes, political grievances, and popular opinions in late Victorian India; but they give no consistent personal reactions, or definite individual responses to these attitudes, grievances, and opinions. On the whole the information they provide is so generalized that it is just as readily available in nonfictional forms such as letters, journals, travel narratives, newspaper articles, or polemical treatises. Consequently they are less interesting as works of fiction than as documents of social history or polemical exposition. Consequently too, Miss Duncan's role as a novelist must be taken essentially as that of a publicist: one who dramatises public issues in an impersonal, generalized way, by stressing the importance of their ideological implications, while largely neglecting the psychological implications and human interest normally generated by such issues.

Miss Duncan's role as a publicist works effectively in "non-serious" books such as ***Memsahib*** and ***Vernon's Aunt*** which are, frankly, dramatised social documents. Since these novels do not study a coherent theme, their varied assortment of social or historical information, garnished with wit and good humour, can prove extremely palatable, even if their intrinsic artistic value is no more than modest. But where a coherent theme—Imperialism—is involved, for example, in the three novels just discussed, or in ***The Imperialist*** which deals with Imperialism in Canada, the author's exclusive role as a publicist is artistically damaging. Miss Duncan's main theme is brilliantly described in these four novels, usually by portraying its more striking aspects in conflict with each other. But since this conflict is not also represented, convincingly, in psychological terms, its resolution seems less the inevitable result of plausible motives than of the author's arbitrary will in contriving any smooth or convenient dénouement. Nor is this contrivance just psychologically implausible: in dramatic terms, it is often anticlimactic, and in terms of thematic significance, sometimes self-contradictory and confusing. It is the general feeling of uncertainty and confusion, emphasized by the contrived dénouement in these four novels, that damages their sense of conviction, their coherence, and ultimately, their artistic worth.

Judith Church's rejection of Ancram at the end of ***His Honour and a Lady*** serves no discernible purpose beyond providing a faintly salacious flavour to a smoothly melodramatic conclusion which, so far as the theme is concerned, lacks coherence or significance. The end of ***Set in Authority*** too, is either incoherent or self-contradictory. The main action in the novel is designed to win sympathy for the hero's political views, by consistently implying that Indians are victims of an oppressive Anglo-Indian administration. After Morgan's (anti)climactic suicide, however, it is discovered that the Indian witness whose evidence secured his conviction bore a grudge against British soldiers. While this discovery no doubt contributes an extra melodramatic flourish, it also contradicts the preceding action by inducing sympathy for Anglo-Indian "villians" and casting suspicion on their Indian "victims." Similarly, in ***Burnt Offering,*** Dey's suicide is not strictly demanded by the need of the plot to demonstrate the failure of the revolutionary movement: this need is already amply satisfied by Thakore's conviction, Mills's deportation, and Dey's own arrest. Dey's death is another of the author's belated flourishes, which does not serve a thematic function but promotes a sensational dénouement. His death may also be a racist ploy to prevent Dey's marriage to Joan Mills, at all costs. At any rate, it illustrates Miss Duncan's expert use of slick, literary techniques presumably to satisfy popular taste. While these techniques do not obstruct the principal aim in these novels, which is to publicize topical issues, they infringe strictly artistic criteria such as thematic coherence, dramatic consistency, and psychological plausibility.

The Imperialist contains probably the best examples of the artistic weaknesses that are being discussed here. The novel is set in Canada at the turn of century, and describes the political views of Lorne Murchison, a Liberal Party candidate who is an ardent and committed Imperialist. The author devotes most of her novel to Murchison as he expounds his political, economic, and social arguments in favour of Imperialism. The extreme passion and intensity of Murchison's arguments clearly imply the author's own sympathy for Murchison's views. But in the end, Murchison is eased out of his candidacy, which he tamely accepts, although it means the frustration of his Imperialistic hopes. The pattern here is the same as in the three Indian novels dealing with Imperialism. Like Lord Thane, Murchison's tame reaction to defeat is psychologically implausible because, like the Viceroy, he is presented throughout the action as passionate, zealous, and resolute. His quiet departure from political life, like Lord Thane's silent return to England, is simply out of character. As in the Indian novels too, there are elements of anticlimax and self-contradiction in ***The Imperialist***. Murchison's defeat, like Morgan's suicide or Dey's death, is abrupt, presented without explanation or without the tragic sense due to such an ostensibly climactic event. It also contradicts the novel's previously implied avowal of Imperialism. If ***The Imperialist*** is more memorable than its Indian counterparts, it is not for intrinsic artistic reasons; for the presentation of its main theme is confusing and its human interest is implausible or negligible. ***The Imperialist*** is remembered because it effectively displays public issues of Miss Duncan's homeland which she knew best and felt most deeply about. Her authoritative knowledge and undoubted technical skill combine, in this novel, to produce perhaps the best description that exists in fiction of Canadian provincial attitudes at the turn of the century.

Her provincial Canadian background influences Miss Duncan's mixed artistic achievement in so far as it fails to provide a stable literary and cultural tradition upon which she can draw. At the start of her writing career, Canada was still a "colonial nation": a self-governing state which felt it could retain political independence, while maintaining existing (colonial) cultural ties with Great Britain. This need for divided loyalty—both to Canada and Great Britain—created an ambivalent outlook which is evident in Canadian politics, culture, and literature at the end of the nineteenth century. Stephen Leacock, the most distinguished Canadian writer of Miss Duncan's generation, exploits his peculiar national outlook with good artistic effect. In many other Canadian writers, however, Leacock's double-edged irony is replaced by contradiction and incoherence. E. J. Pratt, for example, is constantly troubled by a profound sense of ambivalence that flaws some of his major poems, for example, "The Truant" which seems to advocate both atheism and orthodox Christianity. Miss Duncan's self-contradiction can therefore be attributed, to some extent at least, to profoundly ambivalent cultural conditions, which not only promoted her faith in Imperialism, but encouraged her to apply this faith, rashly and indiscriminately, to a people of alien culture and ancient civilization. When applied to India, her (Canadian-based) Imperialism seems self-righteous and sentimental because, like the views of some of her English characters, it derives from vague, generalized feelings rather than from specific, personal experience and real knowledge of individual Indians within their local environment. This is why Miss Duncan has difficulty in reconciling her (theoretical) commitment to Imperialism with the (practical) abuses which she observed in India. But, as biographical evidence proves, she held steadfastly to her faith in Imperialism, despite the evidence of her eyes. Hence the febrile vacillation in her novels, between praise and dissatisfaction toward Imperialism.

Technically, Miss Duncan's writing is influenced by Victorian novelists who may not always be precisely identified. Her fluent diction and racy dialogue may owe something to Thackeray; but these features are as standard in novels of the period as her mechanically well-designed, chronologically-based plots. Her fondness for unlikely complications, superficial intrigue and insignificant sensational flourishes may be more directly traceable to lesser Victorian novelists who indulged in intrigue and melodrama at the expense of psychological insight and realistic detail. There may also be a trace of Henry James's belief in human intelligence as the real theatre of personal conflicts and dilemmas. James successfully insinuates the tensions and conflicts of his characters into intellectual relationships which are elaborately analysed, often at inordinate length, to produce action that seems over-refined and rarefied. This is paralleled in Miss Duncan's novels by the general paucity of dramatic action and a corresponding excess of lengthy discussion, commentary, and debate. But if her fiction does acquire a certain Jamesian perfunctoriness, it does not acquire the penetrating psychological examination and intricate moral analysis which make Henry James a classic novelist.

When all possible ideological, cultural, and technical influences are considered, however, Miss Duncan's fiction must, finally, be viewed in the perspective of the literature of the British Empire produced by authors as varied as Henty, Kipling, Conrad, and in our own time, Somerset Maugham, John Masters, and Mazo de la Roche. The most important of these writers—Conrad, Kipling, Cary, Forster, Orwell—generally analyses the exact consequences of colonial rule for both coloniser and colonised, although their political views may vary greatly. Kipling, for example, gives an informed analysis of the effect of British rule in India, incorporating both its ideological and psychological implications. It is true that in stories such as "The Head of the District" and "Lispeth," his own ideological stance is warped—too subjectively in favour of Imperialism. But despite such jingoistic bias, Kipling's stories generally provide realistic action in which the reader can share, and on which he can pass judgement. The stories of the less important writers of the British Empire generally provide unrealistic action in which the Imperial setting is largely an exotic location for romantic adventure and intrigue. In such stories, the interests and preoccupations of the characters are mainly personal or idiosyncratic, remote from the actual conditions and practical problems of their local, colonial environment. Miss Duncan is best placed among this second category of writers, whose work is less notable for its rendering of actual human experience than for its description of fresh subjects, strange customs, and exotic scenery.

More exactly, Miss Duncan can be placed in the specific category of Anglo-Indian writers such as Sir George T. Chesney, Sir Henry S. Cunningham, and particularly Mrs. Flora Annie Steel who was, according to an earlier commentator [E. F. Oaten in *A Sketchbook of Anglo-Indian Literature,* 1908], "perhaps the greatest novelist, in the strictest sense of the word, of whom Anglo-Indian literature can boast." After giving an outline of the history of Anglo-Indian literature, from the letters and travel narratives of its beginnings, to the more sophisticated forms achieved by the 1890's when Miss Duncan was writing, the same commentator concludes that, although its forms had changed, the basic substance of Anglo-Indian literature remained "the light and shade" of Anglo-Indian life:

> Those Anglo-Indian writers who attempted fiction can be said to have achieved their principal, if modest aim, that of giving a more or less faithful picture of native or Anglo-Indian life in a form more attractive than the hackneyed "Letters" or volume of travels which were such a marked feature of the early literature.

This helps us to understand why Miss Duncan's Indian fiction is exclusively preoccupied with material which lends itself to expression, just as readily, in nonfictional forms: she was partly following the fashion of the historical literary situation in which she found herself. The best that can be said of her Indian fiction, as a whole, is that it gives as vivid and authentic a portrait of general customs and public attitudes as can be seen in such Anglo-Indian "classics" as Chesney's *The Dilemma* (1876), and Mrs. Steel's *On the Face of the Waters* (1896).

The best writing of Miss Duncan's career is her professional journalism for North American newspapers such as the *Globe,* the Washington *Post,* and the Montreal *Star.* This early work, done before she went to India, is distinguished for its lucid commentary and fluent exposition, which make even her more pungent views, for example her feminist ones, appear congenial and convincing. Her best novels—they are more accurately described as social sketches rather than novels—employ the structure of a travelogue, as in ***Memsahib*** and ***Vernon's Aunt***. The effec-

Her provincial Canadian background influences Miss Duncan's mixed artistic achievement in so far as it fails to provide a stable literary and cultural tradition upon which she can draw.

—Frank Birbalsingh

tiveness of this structure is seen in ***On the Other Side of the Latch*** (1901), the most successful of the author's Indian works, which simply consists of the random thoughts and occasional observations of the wife of an Anglo-Indian official during a summer spent in Simla, the North Indian hill station. It is as if, freed from the encumbrance of a plot in which incidents must convey significance within a comprehensive pattern, Miss Duncan is able to express her most sincerely-felt thoughts, most convincingly. Nor does she lay any claim to seriousness. Her literary interests were, frankly, superficial, topical, domestic, as her narrator hints:

> I have not yet formed a precise opinion as to the function of the commonplace in matter intended for publication. But surely no one should scorn domestic details, which make our universal background and mainstay of our existence. Theories and abstractions serve to adorn it and to give us a notion of ourselves; but we keep them mostly for lectures and sermons, the monthly reviews, the original young man who comes to tea. All would be glad to shine at odd times, but the most luminous demonstration may very probably be based upon a hatred of tinned salmon and a preference for cotton sheets.

It is no accident that her best novels, ***An American Girl in London*** (1891) and ***Cousin Cinderella*** (1908), if not exactly concerned with "a hatred for tinned salmon and a preference for cotton sheets," are preoccupied with similarly commonplace subjects—broad social practices and general cultural differences—which are most effectively treated by means of commentary and exposition, the publicist's skills at which Miss Duncan is most adept.

Clara Thomas (essay date 1977)

SOURCE: "Canadian Social Mythologies in Sara Jeannette Duncan's *The Imperialist,*" in *Journal of Canadian Studies,* Vol. 12, No. 2, Spring, 1977, pp. 38-49.

[*In the following essay, Thomas analyzes* The Imperialist *in terms of two mythologies common in Canadian literature, those of the small town and the "hero and nation-builder."*]

Sara Jeannette Duncan had been living away from Canada for thirteen years when she wrote ***The Imperialist***. During that time she had travelled widely, stopping in India to work as a journalist in Calcutta, and there marrying Everard Cotes, curator of the British museum. In 1902, from Simla, she wrote to John Willison, editor of the *Globe* in Toronto:

> I have taken it upon myself to write a Canadian novel with a *Political motif,* and I am rather anxious that none of you shall be ashamed of it. I feel a little helpess so far from my material and I write to ask if you will very kindly send me a little. I want a week's issue of the *Globe,* preferably numbers dealing editorially with the question of *Imperial Federation* and I want, if they are to be had in pamphlet form, *all Sir W. Laurier's speeches* on the subject, or any of the others that may be useful. It is asking a good deal of a busy man to look up this sort of thing, I know, but I trust your interest in the results will excuse me. I am trying very hard to make it my best book, and the ground is practically unbroken. . . .

The Imperialist was published in 1904. Its "political motif " is contained in the story of Lorne Murchison, a rising young lawyer and politician of Elgin. Lorne's idealistic commitment to the dream of Empire federation obscures for him the realities of Ontario party politics and he loses his candidacy after a burst of imperialist oratory that dismays his leaders and alienates the solid farmer voters of Fox County. Parallel to this "politics of politics" theme, Duncan set a "politics of love" motif, concerning the love of Lorne for Dora Milburn, a superficial, self-centred flirt, and of his sister Advena for Hugh Finlay, a Scotch Presbyterian minister and immigrant to Elgin, and a man of ideals and ethics as lofty on a personal as are Lorne's on an international scale.

Providing both background and dynamic for these plotlines is the town of Elgin, the commercial centre of Fox County. From Simla Duncan looked back at the Ontario town as she remembered it. Elgin certainly has some of the lineaments of Brantford, her home town, and the Murchison family may well have their roots in Duncan's own family. But her creation of town and people transcends particularity to move into the area of social mythology, those beliefs and legends which cohere in the history of a place and a people to establish what Northrop Frye [in *The Secular Scripture,* 1976] calls "the area of serious belief. . . . essentially a statement of a desire to attach oneself to, or live in or among, a specific kind of community." The basic fabric of ***The Imperialist*** is an interweaving of two of our powerful and pervasive mythologies—"the Small Town," and "The Hero and Nation-Builder (Scotch)."

Duncan's distance and detachment from Canada must certainly have given point and wit to ***The Imperialist***'s best passages. Likewise its best and one of its few external and climatic descriptions may well have originated in a cooling memory of Ontario from a Simla veranda in the hills, with the Indian plains shimmering in a heat-haze below.

> They slipped out presently into a crisp white winter night. The snow was banked on both sides of the street. Spreading garden fir trees huddled together weighted down with it; ragged icicles hung from the eaves or lay in long broken

> fingers on the trodden paths. The snow snapped and tore under their feet; there was a glorious moon that observed every tattered weed sticking up through the whiteness and etched it with its shadow. The town lay under the moon almost dramatic, almost mysterious, so withdrawn it was out of the cold, so turned in upon its own soul, the fireplace. It might have stood, in the snow and the silence, for a shell and a symbol of the humanity within, for angels or other strangers to mark with curiosity. Mr. and Mrs. Murchison were neither angels nor strangers; they looked at it and saw that the Peterson place was still standing empty, and that old Mr. Fisher had finished his new porch before zero weather came to stop him.

The duality that passage expresses, between the town, "almost dramatic, almost mysterious," and Mr. and Mrs. Murchison, "neither angels nor strangers," but eminently reasonable and practical townspeople, contains the duality of Sara Duncan's point of view as well. Her picture of Elgin is, on balance, warm with remembered affection and romantic with its potential to individuals for challenge and growth. Her narrator's voice, however, moves easily and often into the ironic range, interrupting the action of the novel to instruct the reader on Elgin's past and present, its social hierarchy, opportunities and constraints. She constantly and successfully invites us to a double-focus vision of Elgin, sometimes pointing out areas of positive value and potential that its people are not aware of, at other times deflating individual or corporate areas of pretension or meagreness of spirit. Her narrator's voice, all-wise and insistently instructive, is sometimes condescending to her reader and sometimes, also, to the town and the people of Elgin.

With a precision of detail that often seems documentary, and that can even be mistaken for totality of detail, Duncan records a town in southern Ontario in the last quarter of the nineteenth century. Her detail is, of course, highly selective, but for all that she takes great trouble to show us how complex, not how simple, a society her town represents. Her straight focus shows us Elgain as the kind of town that hard-working, gradually prospering and God-fearing Protestant Canadians liked to think they lived in and were building. The corporate personality of a small town became very strong, as scores of works in our literature attest, and it was strong precisely because the controlling townspeople were disposed to believe in and perpetuate the kind of structure that Duncan particularizes so minutely. Her ironic focus is a corrective to the idealized, or sentimentalized, vision of the small town, but the two views together do not subtract from the quality of the picture. They add detail, depth, movement and the possibilities of laughter to it.

The town of Elgin is no simple static setting for the action of ***The Imperialist,*** but a dynamic element in the action, established from the beginning of the book when Duncan set up its time continuum and establishes its past. She may have been conscious, as Henry James was, of difficulties in writing the romance of a new land where the monuments of the past, its glamorous ruins, were not readily visible and available to the writer (James on Hawthorne). Certainly in India the sense of layer upon layer of history could hardly have failed to touch and modify her imagination. In any case she makes it clear from the very beginning that Elgin is no frontier town perched in a new continent at the beginning of its history. Elgin already has its own past, partly known through its institutions, and partly mysterious. Old Mother Beggarlegs, the gingerbread woman of the introduction, is a living relic of the past and a piece of its folklore. She presides "like a venerable stooping hawk, over a stall in the covered part of the Elgin market-place, where she sold gingerbread horses and large round gingerbread cookies, and brown sticky squares of what was known in all circles in Elgin as taffy." Magic stories were told about her, that she was a witch, coming with the dawn and vanishing with the night:

> She belonged to the group of odd characters, rarer now than they used to be, etched upon the vague consciousness of a small town in a way mysterious and uncanny; some said that Mother Beggarlegs was connected with the aristocracy and some that she had been "let off" being hanged.

In her presence and in her functions, Mother Beggarlegs' influence is benign. For the children, who will bring the future to Elgin, she conjures up a glamorous and scarifying past, stretching their imaginations beyond the town's boundaries, as her gingerbread and taffy are provisions outside the boundary of their mothers' kitchens.

Neither the history of Elgin as a matter of dates and records, nor its topographical and geographical locations concern Duncan very much, though she gives us a short, concrete outline. It is a manufacturing town in southern Ontario on the Grand Trunk Railway. It is the centre of an agricultural district and the Moneida Indian Reservation is within its periphery. The town has a "right" and a "wrong side of the tracks," the wrong being the East Ward where streets of small houses have sprung up, and the Methodists (Wesleyans) are a challenge to Presbyterian strength. Elements of its social history, however, are introduced repeatedly. Five pages of what she calls "an analysis of social principles of Elgin, an adventure of some difficulty," are inserted to introduce a dancing party. This long passage incorporates a short history of the social leaders of the town, "who took upon themselves for Fox County, by the King's pleasure, the administration of justice, the practice of medicine and of the law, and the performances of the charges of the Church of England a long time ago." The decline of these people she calls "a sorry tale of disintegration with the cheerful sequel of rebuilding, leading to a little unavoidable confusion as the edifice went up . . . we are here at the making of a nation." Realities, traditions, prejudices and achievements of the past are all shown as active elements of the present: racial attitudes—Mrs. Murchison's "you can never trust an Indian . . . I thought they were all gone long ago;" religious segregation—" 'Wesleyan are they?' a lady of Knox Church would remark of the newly arrived, in whom her interest was suggested, 'then let the Wesleyans look after them' "; and the historically based lines of party adherence—

> They're all Tories together, of course, the

> Ormistons . . . 'Old Ormiston's father,' contributed the Editor of the Express, 'had a Crown grant of the whole of Moneida Reservation at one time. Government actually bought it back from him to settle the Indians there. He was a well-known Family Compact man, and fought tooth and nail for the Clergy Reserves in 'fifty.'

The passage evoking the dignity of Mrs. Crow, a work-worn farm wife, is one of the finest vignettes in our literature;

> She was waiting for them on the parlour sofa when Crow brought them in out of the nipping early dark of December, Elmore staying behind in the yard with the horses. She sat on the sofa in her best black dress with the bead trimming on the neck and sleeves, a good deal pushed up and wrinkled across the bosom, which had done all that would ever be required of it when it gave Elmore and Abe their start in life. Her wiry hands were crossed in her lap in the moment of waiting: you could tell by the look of them that they were not often crossed there. They were strenuous hands; the whole worn figure was strenuous, and the narrow set mouth, and the eyes which had looked after so many matters for so long, and even the way the hair was drawn back into a knot in a fashion that would have given a phrenologist his opportunity. It was a different Mrs. Crow from the one that sat in the midst of her poultry and garden-stuff in Elgin market square; but it was even more the same Mrs. Crow, the sum of a certain measure of opportunity and service, an imperial figure in her bead trimming, if the truth were known.

The movement of past into present and its dynamic for action in the future is recapitulated and climaxed in Duncan's description of an Elgin market-place and Lorne Murchison's recognition of belonging, responsibility, and opportunity: "Elgin market square, indeed, was the biography of Fox County and, in little, the history of the whole province . . . It was the deep root of the race in the land, twisted and unlovely, but holding the promise of all." As Lorne looked at the market scene, "the sense of kinship surged in his heart; these were his people, this his lot as well as theirs." Lorne's recognition involves his commitment to his place and people; it also contains a sudden revelation of his own opportunity: "What leapt in his veins till he could have laughed aloud was the splendid conviction of resource."

> At that moment his country came subjectively into his inheritance as it comes into the inheritance of every man who can take it, by deed of imagination and energy and love. He held this microcosm of it, as one might say, in his hand and looked at it ardently; then he took his way across the road.

Dynamic energy, able to effect the forward movement of progress, is especially personalized in Lorne, the hero. But the sense of a social order already in the process of change from dreams of privilege for a few to reality of opportunity for the many is first established in the book through Lorne's father John Murchison, and Duncan's description of the Murchison family home.

> The house was a dignified old affair, built of wood and painted white, with wide green verandahs compassing the four sides of it, as they often did in days when the builder had only to turn his hand to the forest. It stood on the very edge of the town; wheat-fields in the summer billowed up to its fences, and corn-stacks in the autumn camped around it like a besieging army. The plank sidewalk finished there; after that you took the road, or, if you were so inclined, the river, into which you could throw a stone from the orchard of the Plummer place. The house stood roomily and shadily in ornamental grounds, with a lawn in front of it and a shrubbery at each side, an orchard behind, and a vegetable garden, the whole intersected by winding gravel walks, of which Mrs. Murchison was wont to say that a man might do nothing but weed them and have his hands full. In the middle of the lawn was a fountain, an empty basin with a plaster Triton, most difficult to keep looking respectable and pathetic in his frayed air of exile from some garden of Italy sloping to the sea. There was also a barn with stabling, a loft, and big carriage doors opening on a lane to the street.

The house had been built by "one of those gentle folk at reduced income who wander out to the colonies with a nebulous view to economy and occupation to perish of the readjustment." Mrs. Murchison never tired of calling it too big to "overtake," but was nontheless proud of it. It satisfied and sustained her husband, John, who had emigrated poor, but with the Scotchman's sense of opportunity and vigour, and who had built himself up a successful hardware business.

> He seized the place with a sense of opportunity leaping sharp and conscious out of early years in the grey 'wynds' of a northern Scottish town; and its personality sustained him, very privately, but nonetheless effectively, through the worry and expense of it for years. He would take his pipe and walk silently for long together about the untidy shrubberies in the evening, for the acute pleasure of seeing the big horse chestnuts in flower; and he never opened the hall door without a feeling of gratification in its weight as it swung under his hand. Insofar as he could, he supplemented the idiosyncracies he found. The drawing-room walls, though mostly bare in their old-fashioned French paper—lavender and gilt, a grape-vine pattern—held a few good engravings; the library was reduced to contain a single bookcase, but it was filled with English classics. John Murchison had been made a careful man, not by nature, by the discipline of circumstances; but he would buy books. He bought them between long periods of abstinence, during which he would scout the expenditure of an unnecessary dollar, coming home with a parcel under his arm for which he vouchsafed no explanation, and which would disclose itself to be Lockhart, or Sterne, or Borrow, or Defoe.

The house is unique among houses in Elgin and it is a very real symbol of John Murchison's place in his own concept of Canada, and even more so, of his idea of the future progress of his family in Canada. The house is a fitting shelter for his family, a setting for their growth and a launching-point for their future. By so far had John Murchison come from his origin in Scotland to become a leading citizen of Elgin, by so much the farther did he have every reason to believe that his children would progress in prosperity and in influence from Elgin, their centre, to all Canada beyond.

All six of the Murchison children had grown up in the house and, "whatever the place represented to their parents, it was pure joy to them. It offered a margin and a mystery to life." Both outside and in, the house gave them room to grow in body and in imagination.

> And they had all achieved it—all six. They had grown up sturdily, emerging into sobriety and decorum by much the same degrees as the old house, under John Murchison's improving fortunes, grew cared for and presentable. The new roof went on, slate replacing shingles, the year Abby put her hair up; the bathroom was contemporary with Oliver's leaving school; the electric light was actually turned on for the first time in honour of Lorne's return from Toronto, a barrister and solicitor; several rooms had been done up for Abby's wedding.

Prudence and thrift, added to natural ability and taste, have assured John Murchison's steady progress in business prosperity. His children are first generation Scotch-Canadian—they are to become the agents for Canada's future growth. The old colonial order, represented by those who built the house, has crumbled. The present pretension, time-serving and prejudice of such neocolonialists as the Englishman, Octavius Milburn, "the father of the Elgin boiler," are clearly to be vanquished by the rising generation. Hesketh, the young emigrant Englishman, set up as a foil to Lorne Murchison, is shown up to be quite ridiculously unaware of the temper of the past and the present of Canada—and by Canadians' standards, a snob to boot. But, in a cautionary lesson to Canadians, Duncan also shows him to be adaptive. He does not have to learn the hard lessons Lorne must learn in order to temper his idealism to the realities of Fox County, or Canada.

There is nothing subtle about the racial aspect of Duncan's social mythology. In Canada she shows the Scotch and their offspring to be builders, men to usher in the future; the English are reactionary, cautious, conservative and ridiculously class-ridden in a society which sees itself as classless. In effect, Duncan polarizes the two racial strains to the point of substituting her own élite establishment, Scotch and Presbyterian, for the old colonial élitism of British and Anglican. Duncan's élitism, however, is always based on the ideals of moral probity and industry, buttressed and enhanced by education and given dynamic by the assurance she shares with Lorne, her hero—"the splendid conviction of resource" in the land of Canada. Her own distance from home and her observation of the British Raj in India may well have fostered pride in her own people and prejudice against English colonialism. Nevertheless, her attitudes are far from idiosyncratic. A social mythology surrounding the Scotch in Canada had been evolving before his time and is potent still.

As the home is the centre and support of the Murchison family, so is the family the central institution of the town of Elgin. It is buttressed on the one hand by the Presbyterian church and on the other by John Murchison's successful hardware business. Home, business, church—in a series of introductory scenes, Duncan establishes their importance and shows us their interactions. In the prologue, we see the young Murchison family in the home, with the mother very much ruler in her territory and the father worried about business, his territory. Chapter II has moved on in time by a decade: "We've seen changes, Mr. Murchison. Aye, we've seen changes," is Dr. Drummond, the Presbuterian minister's opening remark as he stands with John Murchison in the door of the hardware store, now established for thirty years. Next, we are shown an expanded view of the grown family and the home; then Dr. Drummond preaching a sermon; and finally, the scene-setting for the book's action climaxes with the ritual visit of Dr. Drummond to the Murchison's for supper—this last perhaps the best description in Canadian fiction of good food and a company occasion.

> The chicken salad gleamed at one end of the table and the scalloped oysters smoked delicious at the other. Lorne had charge of the cold tongue and Advena was entrusted with the pickled pears. The rest of the family were expected to think about the tea biscuits and the cake, for Lobelia had never yet had a successor that was any hand with company. Mrs. Murchison had enough to do to pour out the tea. It was a table to do anybody credit, with its glossy damask and the old-fashioned silver and best china that Mrs. Murchison had brought as a bride to her housekeeping—for, thank goodness, her mother had known what was what in such matters—a generous attractive table that you took some satisfaction in looking at. Mrs. Murchison came of a family of noted housekeepers; where she got her charm I don't know. Six-o'clock tea, and that the last meal in the day, was the rule in Elgin, and a good enough rule for Mrs. Murchison, who had no patience with the innovation of a late dinner recently adopted by some people who could keep neither their servants nor their digestions in consequence.

On the whole, business takes precedence over the church among the central institutions of Elgin. The town had begun as the centre of trade for the farmers of Fox County. It had grown and prospered, but any ostentation along Main Street's business premises was suspect, "and it was felt that Bofield—he was dry goods, too—in putting in an elevator was just a little unnecessarily in advance of the times."

> Main Street was really, therefore, not a fair index; nobody in Elgin would have admitted it. Its appearance and demeanour would never have suggested that it was now the chief artery of a thriving manufacturing town, with a collegiate institute, eleven churches, two newspapers, and an asylum for the deaf and dumb, to say nothing of a fire department unsurpassed for organization and achievement in the Province of Ontario. Only at twelve noon it might be partly realized, when the prolonged "toots" of seven

> factory whistles at once let off, so to speak, the hour. Elgin liked the demonstration; it was held to be cheerful and unmistakable, an indication of "go-ahead" proclivities which spoke for itself. It occurred while yet Dr. Drummond and Mr. Murchison stood together in the store door.

The religion that Duncan writes of centres in the church as an institution and it is a religion of ethics and social decorum before personal passion or "emotional lift." She describes it, certainly knowingly, in business terms.

> In Elgin religious fervour was not beautiful, or dramatic, or self-immolating; it was reasonable. You were perhaps your own first creditor; after that your debt was to your Maker. You discharged this obligation in a spirit of sturdy equity: if the children didn't go to Sunday school you knew the reason why. The habit of church attendance was not only a basis of respectability, but practically the only one: a person who was "never known to put his head inside a church door" could not be more severely reprobated, by Mrs. Murchison at all events. It was the normal thing, the thing which formed the backbone of life, sustaining to the serious, impressive to the light, indispensable to the rest, and the thing that was more than any of these, which you can only know when you stand in the churches among the congregations. Within its prescribed limitations it was for many the intellectual exercise, for more the emotional lift, and for all the unfailing distraction of the week.

The law, the press and education are the other institutional components of Elgin, peripheral but very necessary to the central three. Early in the book the law, through the skill of Lorne Murchison, brings to justice the outsiders, Miss Belton and her accomplice, in their conspiracy to rob the bank and let the blame fall on Squire Ormiston's son. Lorne, then, comes to his candidacy for the Liberals through his reputation as a brilliant young lawyer. At the end of the book the law is called in to determine the legality of the election returns and finally Lorne is established as a figure of influence and future growth in Elgin through his acceptance of a partnership in Cruickshank's law firm.

Education provides the basic means for progress and advancement in Elgin. Duncan's ironic voice as she describes Lorne Murchison, Elmer Crow and the "potential melting pot" of the Collegiate Institute makes clear the gap between the rhetoric of education in a "classless" society and its realities. She first engages in the kind of Ontario educational rhetoric that has been familiar since Ryerson's day and is familiar still.

> [Lorne] and Elmore Crow, who walked beside him, had gone through the lower forms of the Elgin Collegiate Institute together, that really "public" kind of school which has so much to do with reassorting the classes of a new country. The Collegiate Institute took in raw material and turned out teachers, more teachers than anything. The teachers taught, chiefly in rural districts where they could save money, and with the money they saved changed themselves into doctors, Fellows of the University, mining engineers. The Collegiate Institute was a potential melting-pot: you went in as your simple opportunities had made you; how you shaped coming out depended upon what was hidden in the core of you. You could not in any case be the same as your father before you; education in a new country is too powerful a stimulant for that, working upon material too plastic and too hypothetical; it is not yet a normal force, with an operation to be reckoned on with confidence. It is indeed the touchstone for character in a new people, for character acquired as apart from that inherited; it sometimes reveals surprises.

She then deflates her rhetoric by particularizing the cases of Lorne and Elmer.

> Neither Lorne Murchison nor Elmore Crow illustrates this point very nearly. Lorne would have gone into the law in any case, since his father was able to send him, and Elmore would inevitably have gone back to the crops since he was early defeated by any other possibility. Nevertheless, as they walk together in my mind along the Elgin market square, the Elgin Collegiate Institute rises infallibly behind them, a directing influence and a responsible parent.

When she talks of the avid party press of Elgin, the Grit *Express* and the Tory *Mercury,* Duncan's ironic tone is at its broadest. She was a working member of the press herself for several years; she undoubtedly knew her types, the editors of small town papers, and as she shows their shrewdness, conceit, cunning, buffoonery and above all, party competition, her irony is very close to Leacock's in *Sunshine Sketches* (published in 1913, nine years later than ***The Imperialist***).

> Of course, it was most of all the opportunity of Mr. Horace Williams, of the *Elgin Express,* and of Rawlins, who held all the cards in their hands, and played them, it must be said, admirably, reducing the *Mercury* to all sorts of futile expedients to score, which the *Express* would invariably explode with a guffaw of contradiction the following day. It was to the *Express* that the Toronto reporters came for details and local colour; and Mr. Williams gave them just as much as he thought they ought to have and no more. It was the *Express* that managed, while elaborately abstaining from improper comment upon a matter *sub judice,* to feed and support the general conviction of young Ormiston's innocence, and thereby win for itself, though a "Grit" paper, wide reading in that hotbed of Toryism, Moneida Reservation, while the Conservative *Mercury,* with its reckless sympathy for an old party name, made itself criminally liable by reviewing cases of hard dealing by the bank among the farmers, and only escaped prosecution by the amplest retraction and the most contrite apology.

The institutions and the people of Elgin are bound together into a community with a well-developed social hierarchy which Duncan makes very explicit as she describes the Milburn's dancing-party. Here too are antecedents of Leacock's humour, particularly of his Peter Pupkin, the bank-clerk. In Elgin, she says, "the young men were more desirable than the young women; they forged ahead, carrying the family fortunes, and the 'nicest' of them were the young men in the banks."

What Duncan omits in her picture of Elgin is, of course, at least as interesting as what she includes, because only by sensing areas of omission can we really appreciate the social mythologies which she records. There are no poor in her book—there are townfolk and countryfolk, represented by the Crows, but one would certainly not presume to call the Crows "poor." The Indians on the reservation hardly count as people to the citizens of Elgin and they only become visible, so to speak, when their votes become important in an election. Outside of Mother Beggarlegs, and she is described as an exotic, there are none of any community's pathetic outsiders, the so-called "shiftless" failures, or even of its wage-earning working men and their families. The name of the game pictured by Elgin and its society, is "Opportunity and Progress," and its keywords are work, education and protestant ethics.

Among the novel's major characters, the one misfit to everything Elgin represents, is Advena Murchison, the oldest of the family. Mrs. Murchison is shown often ironically, but on the whole affectionately, to be the very epitome of the mother-housewife and her managerial role in the affairs of the family is given full weight. Daughter Abby has followed her mother's path, marrying well and early and swiftly becoming housewife and mother herself. Advena is, and always has been, "different," the despair of her mother as far as aptitude for housewifery is concerned. She only becomes the object of her mother's grudging pride when she is completely removed from the domestic sphere, a teacher in the Collegiate Institute. Advena, like Sara Duncan herself, is one of the first generation of women in Canada to be educated for a career beyond the home. In the novel's structure, she is a parallel for her brother Lorne: her idealism equals his; her intelligence equals his—but her opportunities and her future, by comparison, are circumscribed. Her romance with Hugh Finlay culminates in marriage, but only through the determined manipulation of Dr. Drummond. She and Finlay are to take up mission work in White Water, Alberta—there, the reader need not be told, Advena will certainly have to learn and practice the housewife's skills that she has resisted; there, also, the poetic conversations which she and Finlay have will be singularly incongruous. There is a kind of void surrounding Duncan's portrait of Advena—her characterization and her destiny do not seem falsely contrived, but all too real. She has had many sisters in Canadian fiction and in life, women who were trained and talented beyond the scope that their destined role as wives and mothers could possibly bring them. Duncan herself, after a short time as teacher, got away from the Elgins of Ontario and finally from Canada. Stella, the youngest of the Murchisons, is already a young lady of independent thought, action and speech, "well-equipped for society," and possessed of two qualities which are likely to take her far—"the quality of being able to suggest that she was quite as good as anybody without saying so, and the even more important quality of not being any better." Stella, in fact, has many of the book's best ironic lines. But Advena is an outsider in Elgin, as she will be an outsider in White Water, and the necessity Duncan felt to write in her romance did not exclude a residue of sadness in its telling. For Advena, unlike Lorne, there can be no "splendid conviction of resource" and unlimited opportunity.

Politics is described by Duncan as one of the "controlling interests" in Elgin (the other being religion), and politics is the activating force in ***The Imperialist***'s central plot. People are as known and marked by their party as by their church affiliations and a shift from one allegiance to another, as when Squire Ormiston moves from Tory to Grit during Lorne's campaign, is a serious business, providing great comment—and great satisfaction for the local Liberal leaders. Politics is, in fact, Elgin's "Great Game," a serious game, and taken very seriously. Beyond that, however, and most important, politics and the right of male suffrage bring excitement, colour, novelty, individual importance and, above all, the thrill of contest, to the sober citizens of Elgin and Fox County around it.

What Duncan omits in her picture of Elgin is, of course, at least as interesting as what she includes, because only by sensing areas of omission can we really appreciate the social mythologies which she records.

—Clara Thomas

The "political motif" that Duncan wrote of to John Willison, is the theme of Imperialism as it is espoused and voiced by Lorne, the Liberal candidate. Even before going to England as secretary to lawyer Cruickshank and his Trade Commission, Lorne's unusual abilities and the range of his vision made him a likely proponent of a dream that encompassed both the elevation of his own country's destiny and the ultimate federation of the Empire. In England Lorne's sense of Canada's unique opportunities was confirmed and he also became a proselytizer of Imperialism, strongly affected by Wallingham's (Chamberlain) abounding imperial rhetoric. Throughout the book, Duncan repeatedly prepares the reader for his eventual disappointment, but Lorne himself is too caught up in the dream to recognize its adversary—indifference, not antagonism. Lorne's climactic speech profounds the Empire idea first as a mission in itself and then, in phrases that seem totally contemporary, as a bulwark against the encroachments of the United States.

> If we would preserve ourselves as a nation, it has become our business, not only to reject American overtures in favour of the overtures of our own great England, but to keenly watch and actively resist American influence, as it already threatens us through the common channels of life and energy. We often say that we fear no invasion from the south, but the armies of the south have already crossed the border. American enterprise, American capital, is taking rapid possession of our mines and our water power,

> our oil areas and our timber limits. In today's *Dominion,* one paper alone, you may read of charters granted to five industrial concerns with headquarters in the United States. The trades unions of the two countries are already international. American settlers are pouring into the wheat-belt of the Northwest, and when the Dominion of Canada has paid the hundred million dollars she has just voted for a railway to open up the great lone northern lands between Quebec and the Pacific, it will be the American farmer and the American capitalist who will reap the benefit.

Lorne's audience applauds him well, but the party leaders present are dismayed and the Cabinet Minister speaking after him, the Hon. Mr. Tellier, gives a speech practical and factual in every detail, from the Government's successful railway policy to the imminence of a new Drill Hall for Elgin.

> It was a telling speech, with the chink of hard cash in every sentence, a kind of audit by a chartered accountant of the Liberal books of South Fox, showing good sound reason why the Liberal candidate should be returned on Thursday, if only to keep the balance right.

The responsibility for ousting Lorne Murchison from the candidacy falls on the Liberal party men of Elgin, not on the voters who elect him by a majority of seventy. When the results are contested and a new election called, Bingham and Williams ask Lorne to step down.

> 'The popular idea seems to be,' said Mr. Farquharson judicially, 'that you would not hesitate to put Canada to some material loss, or at least to postpone her development in various important directions, for the sake of the imperial connection.'
>
> 'Wasn't that,' Lorne asked him, 'what, six months ago, you were all prepared to do?'
>
> 'Oh, no,' said Bingham, with the air of repudiating for everybody concerned. 'Not for a cent. We were willing at one time to work it for what it was worth, but it never was worth that, and if you'd had a little more experience, Murchison, you'd have realized it'.

Like Leacock, Duncan exposes the restricted vision, the corruption and the petty pork-barrel aspects of party politics. "Dash these heart-to-heart talks," says one of the men, after Lorne has left, "it's the only thing to do, but why the devil didn't he want something out of it? I had the Registrarship in my inside pocket."

Throughout the book, Duncan has described Imperialism as a noble, but losing dream. In neither Canada nor England does it have the appeal to counteract the sheerly practical, short-term concerns of voters, and in Canada the party-men will not throw their weight in the direction of England at the expense of their precarious triangular balance between England and the United States.

Duncan's final concern, however, is not with her "political motif," but with Lorne as Hero and Builder. He is not crushed and he has learned—"Another time he would find more strength and show more cunning; he would not disdain the tools of diplomacy and desirability, he would dream no more of short cuts in great political departures." He resists the offer of a friend, of a law partnership in Milwaukee, and after a short time in the west comes back to Elgin to be a partner in Cruickshank's law firm. Cruickshank has recognized Lorne's quality and so, by implication, will Elgin—and Canada.

The Canadian mythology of the Scotch was based, of course, on a solid ground of fact—on the numbers of Scotch who were prominent in the exploring and settling of the country, in its fur trade and later, on every level of government and financial enterprise; on the Presbyterian church, the Established Church of Scotland and so a prime and powerful institution to its people; and above all, on the pride of race and clan among the Scotch, a pride that distance from the homeland enhanced and fostered. What Carl Berger says [in *Sense of Power,* 1970] of the Loyalist is also true of the Scotch tradition: "[It] began, as did all myths of national origins, with the assertion that the founders of British Canada were God's chosen people." The vastly popular novels of Sir Walter Scott, their heroes and their elevation of the common people were certainly a force in the propagation of the mythology. Philippe Aubert de Gaspé, for instance, acknowledges Scott's influence in the text of *Les Anciens Canadiens* (1863), and his work celebrates the two races, Scotch and French Canadian.

The work of Carlyle, his philosophy of Heroes and his doctrine of work certainly played its part as well. In his instructions for the teaching of History in Ontario schools, Ryerson made a special point of the use of Biography—by the time Duncan wrote her novel, three generations of students were undoubtedly familiar with the Carlylean Hero and the Carlylean work ethic which dovetailed so neatly with the actual necessities and opportunities of an expanding nation. In *Novels of Empire* (1949), Suzanne Howe did not deal with Canadian works—she did, however, deal with the influence of Carlyle on the novelists of British India, and her words apply equally to Duncan's ***The Imperialist*** and to all the novels of Ralph Connor.

The abundant lore of the Scotch in Canada began to cohere into a consciously promulgated mythology in the last quarter of the nineteenth century, as did the Loyalist tradition, and like the Loyalist tradition, its rise was in part defensive. According to census figures, from 1850 on the Scotch were always outnumbered by the Irish and the Presbyterians by both Anglicans and Methodists. The pressure to be differentiated from Americans played its part in Scotch, as in Loyalist, myth-building, and individuals of influence, most notably George Munro Grant, were powers in its promulgation.

The social mythology of the Small Town is also based on a groundwork of historical fact—on a time when Canada was predominantly rural, and towns like Elgin were important centres of their agricultural districts, purveyors, for their areas, of education, religion and culture, as well as of the necessities of trade. The hey-day of the small town, in Ontario at least, was over by 1900, but for long after we were largely an urban people, Canadians liked to think of themselves as farm, not city-centred and of the town as a centre of society and commerce. Our writers have followed our fantasies—even now, we have relatively few urban novels—and they have also recognized in the small town setting a manageable microcosm of our society as a whole.

Among our novelists, Duncan and Connor have given us the "classic" statements of the Scotch Hero and Builder mythology; Duncan and Leacock of the Small Town; all of these between 1901 and 1913. Lorne Murchison and his father John, for together they make the complete hero, are unique in Duncan's dozen-odd novels. By contrast, Connor rewrote the Scotch-Canadian hero in different guises and situations in virtually every one of his thirty-odd novels. In portraying their towns, Duncan and Leacock overlap enough in their selection of detail about persons or events so that each provides a check on the validity of the other. There is one massive difference between the towns, however—the captains and the kings have departed from Mariposa; Leacock's narrator is one of them. He remembers Mariposa from his arm-chair in the Mausoleum Club, but the city, and the Mausoleum Club, are where the real business of the country is done. The episodes begin, rise and fall and, essentially, nothing in Mariposa changes. The town stagnates. On the contrary, Elgin's influence reaches outside of itself and its young are very much designated to be capably in charge of a progressive future in Canada. Mariposa and its people are broadly and briefly drawn; Duncan's portrayal of Elgin and its people is replete with detail. She tells us much more than she shows us in action and a certain slowness of pace and density of fabric are the consequence. That fabric, however, is alive with remembered detail and enlivened by remembered colloquial speech, a source for nineteenth-century Canadianism that has not yet been explored.

There is no other social mythology so pervasive in our literature as that of Scotch—and perhaps that is true of our histories as well. Certainly the Laurentian thesis implies a great band of Heroes and Builders and certainly the Scotch are paramount among them. Among our major novelists, Hugh MacLennan and Margaret Laurence have both built on and revised our mythology of the Scotch. In characters such as Neil Macrae and Alan Ainslie, in the restricted Cape Breton community of *Each Man's Son,* and in the essays, *Scotchman's Return,* MacLennan has examined the burdens as well as the triumphs of the Scotch-Canadian heritage. Margaret Laurence has worked with both the Small Town and the Scotch mythologies in all of her Canadian works. Like MacLennan she rejects superficial complacencies: Jason Currie, of *The Stone Angel,* is a builder indeed, but he has turned towards power, pride and the death of natural feeling—he is a "fledgling pharaoh in an uncouth land." The town of Manawaka symbolizes constraint far more than opportunity for its young. But her devotion to the old heroic myth of the Scotch is also evident in *The Diviners,* in Christie Logan's tales of Piper Gunn and the coming of the Sutherlanders to Manitoba. Both MacLennan and Laurence have written of a double Canadian heritage, however: French Canada has been prominent in MacLennan's work ever since *Two Solitudes;* and Christie Logan's tales share their mythic place in *The Diviners* with the Métis tales of Jules Tonnerre.

The Small Town mythology works towards the integration of individuals into a closely-knit community. For all Duncan's irony, Elgin is "The Good Place"; and for all Laurence's exposure of Manawaka's limitations and constraints, all her characters carry Manawaka with them always, and finally accept that they do so. The Scotch mythology moves towards the separation of the individual from the group, towards an identification that is at once élite and egalitarian, based on privations and hardships overcome or, at the very least, endured with pride in the endurance. It is a Canadian mythic and secular doctrine of the elect and it retains its strength—or gains strength—in times of high Canadian nationalism such as our own.

Thomas E. Tausky (essay date 1980)

SOURCE: "Sara Jeannette Duncan as a Novelist," in *Sara Jeannette Duncan: Novelist of Empire,* P. D. Meany Publishers, 1980, pp. 73-90.

[*In the following excerpt, Tausky discusses narrative technique and similarities of plot and theme in Duncan's novels.*]

[Sara Jeannette Duncan] began reviewing fiction at a time when the controversy between the proponents of realism and of romance was at its height. Her own attitude . . . was to avoid what she took to be extreme positions on either side. It is not surprising to discover, therefore, that elements of realism and romance co-exist, sometimes happily, sometimes uneasily, in her novels.

Realists, a distinguished critic [M. H. Abrams, in *A Glossary of Literary Terms,* 1957] has said, choose to write about "people without exceptional endowments, who live through ordinary experiences of childhood, adolescence, love, marriage, parenthood and infidelity." Sara herself scornfully referred to such subjects as "cabbages, vegetable or human," but seventeen years later we find her making literary produce of the Elgin market:

> Bags of potatoes leaned against the sidewalk, apples brimmed in bushel measures, ducks dropped their twisted necks over the cart wheels. . . . On the fourth side of the square loads of hay and cordwood demanded the master mind, but small matters of fruits, vegetables and poultry submitted to feminine judgment. The men "unhitched," and went away on their own business; it was the wives you accosted, as they sat in the middle, with their knees drawn up and their skirts tucked close, vigilant in rusty bonnets, if you wished to buy. . . . There was a little difficulty always about getting things home; only very ordinary people carried their own marketing . . . it did not consort with elegance to "traipse" home with anything that looked inconvenient or had legs sticking out of it.

In its careful observation of undramatic life, the passage is a fine example of pure realism. Yet in the same novel, one can easily find a passage saturated with romance conventions:

> He bent his head and lowered his umbrella and lost sight of her as they approached, she with the storm behind her, driven with hardly more resistance than the last year's blackened leaves that blew with her, he assailed by it and making the best way he could. Certainly the wind was taking her part and his, when in another moment her skirt whipped against him and he saw her face glimmer out. A mere wreck of lines and shadows it seemed in the livid light, with suddenly perceiving eyes and lips that cried his name. . . . Pitifully, the storm blew her into his arms, a tossed and straying thing that could not speak for sobs; pitifully and with a rough incoherent sound he gathered and held her in that refuge.

Though these storm-crossed lovers (Hugh Finaly and Advena Murchison) are elsewhere described in less exalted terms, here they are forced to play heroic melodrama, while Nature is conscripted to act a moody supporting part. Romance is, of course, a respectable fictional form with a much longer history than realism, but in Sara Jeannette Duncan's hands the sentiments are cloying and the rhetoric over-blown. She is generally at her best as a realist writer and at her worst as a writer of romance. There are many passages of realism throughout her fiction as good as the ones I have quoted, and many equally embarrassing passages of romance.

There are two characteristic kinds of romance in Sara Jeannette Duncan's work: delight in the charms of the English aristocracy or the American rich; and scenes of anguished and passionate, but inarticulate, love. A definition relevant to Sara's brand of realism is found in an American critic's account of the novel of manners [James W. Tuttleton, in *The Novel of Manner in America,* 1972]:

> We may define a novel of manners as a novel in which the closeness of manners and character is of itself interesting enough to justify an examination of their relationship. By a novel of manners I mean a novel in which the manners, social customs, folkways, conventions, traditions and mores of a given social group at a given time and place play a dominant role in the lives of fictional characters, exert control over their thought and behavior, and constitute a determinant upon the actions in which they are engaged, and in which these manners and customs are detailed realistically—with, in fact, a premium upon the exactness of their representation.

These characteristics are evident in Sara Jeannette Duncan's account of the Elgin market. In the passage already quoted, the market scene is certainly described accurately and minutely. Miss Duncan then goes on to analyze the "closeness of manners and character" evident in the market ritual. Generations of sober frugality had produced a distinctive regional character:

> It was a scene of activity but not of excitement, or in any sense of joy. . . . Life on an Elgin market day was a serious presentment even when the sun shone. . . . It was not misery, it was even a difficult kind of prosperity, but the margin was small and the struggle plain. Plain too, it was that here was no enterprise of yesterday, no fresh broken ground of dramatic promise, but a narrow inheritance of the opportunity to live which generations had grasped before. There were bones in the village grave-yards of Fox County to father all these sharp features; Elgin market square, indeed, was the biography of Fox County, and, in little, the history of the whole Province. . . .

A novelist interested in the influence of manners upon character is more likely to be a literary sociologist than a psychologist. Some writers are both, or move from one interest to the other; Sara Jeannette Duncan's best work, however, is achieved when she confines herself to the novel of manners. Her understanding of human nature is impressive when she is concerned with social roles: Anglo-Indian bureaucrats, small-town Canadian politicians and English country gentry are all convincing when called upon to express the attitudes and emotions that the environmental influences shaping their characters dictate. They acquire a sudden awkwardness when Sara tries to look deeper into their souls, into the more individual recesses untouched by social forces.

F. Scott Fitzgerald once said that he wanted "to recapture the exact feel of a moment in time and space." The best passages in Sara Jeannette Duncan's work, the passages that mark her as a clever observer of manners, realize that ambition. For example, the reader is made to understand the pretentiousness of a prominent Elgin family, and to sympathize with the discomfiture of their first guest:

> No one would have supposed, from the way the family disposed itself in the drawing room, that Miss Filkin had only just finished making the claret cup, or that Dora had been cutting sandwiches till the last minute. . . . It was impossible to imagine a group more disengaged from the absurd fuss that precedes a party among some classes of people; indeed, when Mr. Lorne Murchison arrived . . . they looked almost surprised to see him. . . .
>
> To be the very first and solitary arrival is nowhere esteemed the happiest fortune, but in Elgin a kind of ridiculous humiliation attached to it, a greed for the entertainment, a painful unsophistication. A young man of Elgin would walk up and down in the snow for a quarter of an hour with the thermometer at zero to escape the ignominy of it; Lorne Murchison would have so walked.

Even more impressive is the account of one-upsmanship at a Calcutta dinner party when the Viceroy is mentioned. One of the guests inquires about the roses on the table:

> Mrs. Daye pitched her voice with a gentle definiteness that made what she was saying interesting all round the table—"they came from the Viceroy's place at Barrackpore. Lady Emily sent them to me; so sweet of her, I thought! I always think it particularly kind when people in that position trouble themselves about one; they must have so *many* demands upon their time."
>
> The effect could not have been better. Everybody

> looked at the roses with an interest that might almost be described as respectful; and Mrs. Delaine, whose husband was Captain Delaine of the Durham Rifles, said that she would have known them for Their Excellencies' roses anywhere—they always did the table with that kind for the Thursday dinners at Government House—she had never known them to use any other.
>
> Mrs. St. George, whose husband was the Presidency Magistrate, found this interesting. "Do they really?" she exclaimed. "I've often wondered what those big Thursday affairs were like. Fancy—we've been in Calcutta through three cold weathers now, and have never been asked to anything but little private dinners at Government House—not more than eight or ten, you know!"

The two passages I have just quoted have in common the fact that they satirize various forms of snobbery. Hostility to snobbery is not a fixed value in Sara Jeannette Duncan's fiction, however, for the simple reason that Sara herself was a terrible snob. Indians (North American and Asian), working class people, servants, tradesmen, and even *nouveaux riches* and impoverished Italian aristocrats are constantly dismissed or patronized in her work because of their inferior social status. Sara's real objection to the Milburn family and to the Daye dinner guests is not that they are snobs, but that they are very stupid snobs without any distinction of their own. Their stupidity manifests itself in an inability to engage in, or even imagine, any departure from strictly conventional behaviour. The background of Miss Duncan's novels is always filled with such characters, and they seem to dominate the societies under scrutiny.

A characteristic Sara Jeannette Duncan plot seems to involve an effort on the part of imaginative, unconventional characters to realize their talents or desires in the face of pressures exerted by the conformists. In Miss Duncan's first three books, the struggle is uncomplicated and results in a clear victory for the adventurous heroines. They are obviously justified in their decisions to go round the world (***A Social Departure***), or to bring American informality to England (***An American Girl in London***) or to go on an unchaperoned barge trip (***Two Girls on a Barge***). Young women of sound moral character should be absolutely free to pursue their decorous inclinations. Sara's confidence in her principle gives these books much of their spirit and charm, though the principle itself is hardly profound.

But what if a young girl's efforts at self-realization lead her to more dubious moral realms? Elfrida Bell, the heroine of Sara's first serious novel, decides that to become an artist she must go to the Latin Quarter of Paris, and we all know what those bohemians are like. In actual fact, Sara does not seem to know, but she hints darkly, and eventually Elfrida's quest ends in suicide. A later heroine is an actress in a seedy Calcutta company; she gains more of her creator's sympathy, but there are also occasional hints of moral disapproval. Both of these characters, as well as Sara Jeannette Duncan's other heroines, are presented largely in terms of their relationship to society, rather than in terms of deeply examined personal sensibilities. They react against the norms of society, but their rebellion is presented as the adoption of an alternative set of "manners," and involves an acute awareness of the norms they have chosen to abandon.

Sara Jeannette Duncan's heroines are not all artists; some are just intelligent and/or sensitive women who want more out of a life than a conventional marriage with a conventional, bureaucratic bore. They are frequently put in the position of being tempted by opportunities for extramarital affairs. Sara does not, however, allow her characters to go beyond temptation. One rejects a potential lover because of his political misconduct; a second is unable to persuade a priest to abandon his vows of celibacy; a third limits herself to platonic self-restraint. Sara no doubt was restrained herself by the fiction-writing conventions of her time; only the most daring novelists wrote about adultery, and they were abused for it. My own intuition is, however, that Sara's personal convictions were chiefly responsible for the limits she placed on her fiction.

F. Scott Fitzgerald once said that he wanted "to recapture the exact feel of a moment in time and space." The best passages in Sara Jeannette Duncan's work, the passages that mark her as a clever observer of manners, realize that ambition.

—Thomas E. Tausky

Whatever his own moral convictions, the reader of Sara Jeannette Duncan's novels is often left in some confusion. Both the individualistic heroine and the society against which she reacts seem to be condemned.

The explanation may be found in Sara's character, a mixture . . . of daring and conservatism. Like her early heroines, she longed for freedom and adventure, and was determined enough to make her dreams into reality. Yet from first to last she never abandoned the conservative values she probably absorbed in her youth. She loved the monarchy and was deeply suspicious of democracy. She never questioned the worth of free enterprise, of standards of taste in literature and in life, and of British political institutions. Her values, in short, were often closer to those of the conventional people she mocked than to the values of the more extreme rebels they rejected. In her final Indian novel, ***The Burnt Offering,*** Sara's sympathies became so closely identified with the British interest, then being severely challenged by Indian agitation, that she glamorized the officials and heaped ridicule upon her last nonconformist, a British girl who dared to contemplate marriage with a Hindu.

Recent critics have observed that the uncertainties arising out of the transition from Victorian to modern consciousness made a major impact on both the form and the substance of the late Victorian and turn of the century novel.

Writers such as Henry James, E. M. Forster and Joseph Conrad perceived and dramatized the inherent confusion in minds which had abandoned old values without finding adequate substitutes. Sara Jeannette Duncan was certainly aware of ethical changes; in her early journalism she wrote a great deal, if not very precisely, about the modern spirit and in her novels she sometimes explicitly comments on such developments. But I cannot feel that Sara Jeannette Duncan really understood the drift towards a modern consciousness. In some, though not all, respects, she embodied it, but she was too divided in her loyalties to be able to present it effectively in her work.

The value of Sara Jeannette Duncan's fiction is sometimes, but not always, undercut by her failures of comprehension. When her heroines are too extreme for her own taste, her satire becomes aimless, since it is simultaneously directed at both liberal and conservative attitudes, and the only moral standard is the author's consciousness of her own rectitude. But when the heroine is imaginative and relatively emancipated without being radical or immoral, Sara has a standard of character which makes her satire of conventionality effective. The result may not be a revelation of human nature or the contemporary situation, but it can be a clearly structured, ethically coherent, sharply observed and entertaining fiction.

Most of Sara Jeannette Duncan's books have points of interest, but only five, in my judgment, can be termed successful and whole novels: ***An American Girl in London***; ***The Simple Adventures of a Memsahib***; ***His Honour, and a Lady***; ***The Imperialist***; and ***Cousin Cinderella***. In each case one of the principal women characters (Mamie Wick, Mrs. Perth Macintyre, Rhoda Daye, Advena Murchison and Mary Trent respectively) resists or at least scorns conventional behaviour without venturing into radicalism. Each of these characters is given a distinctive personality, but each, in her own way, is superior in imagination to her environment, and conscious of her superiority. In each case, the plot, the dialogue and the narrator's comments all serve to reinforce the reader's consciousness of the qualitative distinction between the heroine and her uncomprehending milieu.

The novels may have a similarity of theme and outlook, but they display considerable variety in fictional technique. Sara did not seriously emulate the technical innovations of Henry James, though in certain novels she tries to be equally obscure. She was content (as were writers like E. M. Forster or Arnold Bennett) to remain within the formal conventions of the nineteenth century novel. Within those limits, however, she worked with several writing styles and narrative techniques.

Of the five novels I have just listed, three are first person narratives, and two are told in the third person. Of Sara Jeannette Duncan's total output, nine books are in the first person and eleven in the third. This apparently even balance conceals a pronounced switch in preference from first person to third; her first four books, and six of her first eight, were written in the first person, but of the nine novels written after 1903, only one (***Cousin Cinderella***) is in the first person.

It did not take Sara Jeannette Duncan long to master the art of revealing character through first person narration. As we have seen, the narrator of ***A Social Departure*** is not especially well defined, but the clever characterization of Mamie Wick, the narrator of ***An American Girl in London,*** is largely responsible for that novel's charm. ***The Simple Adventures of a Memsahib*** represents another advance, in that Mrs. Perth Macintyre is a much more subtle and enigmatic character than Mamie Wick. Mary Trent of ***Cousin Cinderella*** is also a brilliantly successful characterization.

Sara Jeannette Duncan's efforts to achieve an equally satisfying style of impersonal narration were not always so fortunate. ***A Daughter of To-Day,*** the first attempt at third person narration, is, not surprisingly, as awkward in its way as ***A Social Departure***. After a relatively slight challenge in the juvenile ***Story of Sonny Sahib,*** Miss Duncan revealed a technical assurance in her next major novel, ***His Honour, and a Lady,*** that she never subsequently surpassed or perhaps even repeated. This novel, from which the account of the Dayes' dinner party was taken, evokes the official world of Calcutta masterfully without resorting to the lengthy authorial commentary of some of the later works. In the dinner party scene, for example, Mrs. Daye is caught gazing at her prospective son-in-law, Lewis Ancram:

> His eyes were certainly blue and expressive when he allowed them to be, his hostess thought, and he had the straight, thin, well-indicated nose which she liked, and a sensitive mouth for a man. His work as part of the great intelligent managing machine of the Government of India overimpressed itself upon the stamp of scholarship Oxford had left on his face, which had the pallor of Bengal, with fatigued lines about the eyes, lines that suggested to Mr. Ancram's friends the constant reproach of overexertion. . . . It was ridiculous, Mrs. Daye thought, that with so agreeable a manner he should still convey the impression that one's interest in the Vedic Books was not of the least importance. It must be that she was over-sensitive. But she would be piqued notwithstanding. Pique, when one is plump and knows how to hold oneself, is more effective than almost any other attitude.

In the space of a few sentences, Sara Jeannette Duncan provides Mrs. Daye's thoughts about Ancram (twice), his friends' view of Ancram, Mrs. Daye's image of herself, and, finally, the narrator's less flattering view of Mrs. Daye. In a later scene, Sara shows that she can be equally skilful in presenting a sustained succession of one character's thoughts. Ancram is seen rationalizing his decision to break off the engagement with Rhoda Daye:

> Nothing could be more obvious than that the girl did not care for him; and, granting this, was he morally at liberty, from the girl's own point of view, to degrade her by a marriage which was, on her side, one of pure ambition? If her affections had been involved in the remotest degree—but he shrugged his shoulders at the idea of Rhoda Daye's affections. He wished to Heaven, like any schoolboy, that she would fall in love

> with somebody else, but she was too damned clever to fall in love with anybody. The thing would require a little finessing; the rupture must come from her.

The first rank of Sara Jeannette Duncan's fiction includes only one other novel written in the third person, ***The Imperialist***. Here again, she can enter persuasively into a character's thoughts if she chooses. Perhaps aided by memories of her own mother, she gives a vigorous and colloquial impression of Mrs. Murchison's despair about her house:

> The originating Plummer, Mrs. Murchison often said, must have been a person of large ideas, and she hoped he had the money to live up to them. . . . It was trying enough for a person with the instinct of order to find herself surrounded by out-of-door circumstances which she simply could not control, but Mrs. Murchison often declared that she could put up with the grounds if it had stopped there. It did not stop there. Though I was compelled to introduce Mrs. Murchison in the kitchen, she had a drawing-room in which she might have received the Lieutenant-Governor, with French windows and a cut-glass chandelier, and a library with an Italian marble mantelpiece. . . . She had far too much, as she declared, for any one pair of hands and a growing family, and if the ceiling was not dropping in the drawing-room, the cornice was cracked in the library, or the gas was leaking in the dining-room, or the verandah wanted re-flooring if anyone coming to the house was not to put his foot through it; and as to the barn, if it was dropping to pieces it would just have to drop.

The virtues and limitations of Mrs. Murchison's practical wisdom are very effectively captured in this passage, but on the whole such passages are far less frequent than in ***His Honour, and a Lady***. Much more often, Sara Jeannette Duncan chooses to communicate information through an impersonal and omniscient narrator. We could find out about Elgin's religious temper through the musings of one of the novel's two ministers, but instead the narrator tells us what to think:

> In wholesome fear of mistake, one would hesitate to put church matters either before or after politics among the preoccupations of Elgin. It would be safer and more indisputable to say that nothing compared with religion but politics, and nothing compared with politics but religion. In offering this proposition also we must think of our dimensions. There is a religious fervour in Oxford, in Mecca, in Benares, and the sign for these ideas is the same; we have to apply ourselves to the interpretation. In Elgin, religious fervour was not beautiful, or dramatic, or self-immolating; it was reasonable.

Few modern novelists would guide the reader in so direct and forceful a manner. It is, however, the method of most of the great eighteenth and nineteenth century English novelists, and should not be condemned out of hand. The real question is not whether the method is right or wrong, but whether Sara Jeannette Duncan uses it to good purpose.

William Dean Howells is always a useful source of comparison with Sara Jeannette Duncan, since we know Sara admired his work. In Howells' first major novel of American life, *A Modern Instance,* there is a comparable passage about the place of religion in a small Maine town:

> Religion there had largely ceased to be a fact of spiritual experience, and the visible church flourished on condition of providing for the social needs of the community. It was practically held that the salvation of one's soul must not be made too depressing, or the young people would have nothing to do with it. Professors of the sternest creeds temporized with sinners, and did what might be done to win them to heaven by helping them to have a good time here. The church embraced and included the world.

The generalization is different, but the air of patronising detachment is very similar. If one of each novel's main objects is to convince the reader that the author thoroughly understands Elgin, or Equity, Maine, then the omniscient style of narration can be justified as the appropriate medium for that particular message.

The technical challenge for the novelist using this method is that he must persuade the reader of his qualifications for assuming so imperious a role. To be taken as authoritative, he must write authoritatively. It is in her execution, rather than in her choice of method, that Sara Jeannette Duncan sometimes fails to impress, in ***The Imperialist*** and elsewhere. Her remarks about religion may be as wise as Howells's views, but they are not nearly as effective stylistically. The Howells passage is smoothly written, and smoothly integrated with the story: a few sentences later, Howells says, "But Bartley Hubbard [the central character] liked the religious situation well enough" and moves from some character analysis back into the plot. The Sara Jeannette Duncan passage occurs about halfway through an entire chapter of generalizations, and in reading it one is deterred from accepting its content wholeheartedly by doubts about its manner. Is "more indisputable" a suitable expression? The third sentence is awkward and the fourth obscure—what does the part after the semicolon mean? Also, one suspects that the religious fervour of Oxford, Mecca and Benares is similar only if an author is trying to make a rhetorical point.

None of these criticisms is significant in itself. It is important, though, that the reader's confidence not be undermined by doubts about grammar, fluency, rhetoric and the validity of generalizations. To be fair, it must be added that in ***The Imperialist,*** Sara Jeannette Duncan inspires confidence more often than not. In some other works, the inadequacy of the narrator is a basic fault of the novel.

Several of the works I have in mind immediately precede ***The Imperialist***. Between 1899 and 1903, Sara published four books. One of them, ***Those Delightful Americans,*** is narrated by a provincial Englishwoman and captures a particular manner of speaking and thinking very effectively. The other three, all of them potentially of considerable interest, are disfigured by stylistic experimentation. Sara always attempted to achieve originality of manner, but in this period a very precious style is combined with strained and unsuccessful efforts at psychological subtlety.

The difference between good and bad Sara Jeannette Duncan prose can be easily demonstrated. In a passage from one of her better books, ***An American Girl in London,*** the heroine goes in search of lodgings:

> One of the drawing-rooms was "draped" in a way that was quite painfully aesthetic, considering the paucity of the draperies. The flower-pots were draped, and the lamps; there were draperies round the piano-legs, and round the clock; and where there were not draperies there were bows, all of the same scanty description. The only thing that had not made an effort to clothe itself in the room was the poker, and by contrast it looked very nude. There were some Japanese ideas around the room, principally a paper umbrella; and a big painted palm-leaf fan from India made an incident in one corner. . . . [The landlady] came into the room in a way that expressed reduced circumstances and a protest against being obliged to do it. I feel that the particular variety of smile she gave me with her "Good morning!"—although it was after 4 P.M.—was one she kept for the use of boarders only, and her whole manner was an interrogation.

The interview goes on for another two pages. The incident in itself is a very trivial one, but Sara has brought it to life. We see the absurd pretentiousness of the room and the pathetic gentility of the landlady; the narrator is wittily superior to the scene without being snobbish herself. Sara's success with a light subject is all the more evident when we consider her later efforts to grapple with a much more substantial matter. In the title story of ***The Pool in the Desert,*** the narrator discusses the social consequences in British India of a scandalous divorce:

> Mrs. Harbottle was only twenty-seven then and Robert a major, but he had brought her to India out of an episode too color-flushed to tone with English hedges; their marriage had come, in short, of his divorce, and as too natural a consequence. In India it is well known that the eye becomes accustomed to primitive pigments and high lights; the esthetic consideration, if nothing else, demanded Robert's exchange. He was lucky to get a [Punjab] regiment, and the Twelfth were lucky to get him; we were all lucky, I thought, to get Judy. It was an opinion, of course, a great deal challenged, even in Rawul Pindi, where it was thought, especially in the beginning, that acquiescence was the most the Harbottles could hope for. That is not enough in India; cordiality is the common right. I could not have Judy preserving her atmosphere at our tea-parties and gymkhanas. Not that there were two minds among us about "the case"; it was a preposterous case, sentimentally undignified, from some points of view deplorable. I chose to reserve my point of view, from which I saw it, on Judy's behalf, merely quixotic, preferring on Robert's just to close my eyes.

One dimly suspects that the narrator is suggesting that she herself is more sensitive and broad-minded than her Anglo-Indian compatriots, but any interest in characterization is shattered by the effort required to make any sense whatever out of the passage. Contemporary reviewers claimed to sniff the influence of Henry James in Sara Jeannette Duncan's work of this period. Perhaps they were right, but the effect of indirection in her case was to obscure motivation and thought processes, rather than to illuminate them, as James does.

It might be suggested that the two passages just quoted merely prove that Sara Jeannette Duncan was at her best in light comedy and could not handle more serious emotions. There is an element of truth in this view, in that Sara's treatment of serious personal relationships is often unsatisfactory. But three of the five novels I have found to be her best (***The Simple Adventures of a Memsahib, His Honour, and a Lady*** and ***Cousin Cinderella***) all have a pronounced streak of melancholy. The central characters' relationships with others are not always successfully described, but the sadness of their isolation is convincingly realised. In a passage superficially about the comforts of domesticity, the narrator of ***Cousin Cinderella*** reveals her provincial uncertainty in the metropolis:

> All this time the flat was our constant joy, the basis and background for the whole pageant, solidly our own for retreat and reflection, always invitingly there. It made a kind of stronghold for us, against feeling too much as London wanted us, wanted everybody to feel—I mean impressed and intoxicated and carried away . . . with rapture to let her play upon us any tune she liked. The flat stood for us, just for Graham and me . . . it was somehow good for our self-respect to drive from marble halls and talk it over in front of Miss Game's twelve remaining mantel ornaments, when Graham had made up the fire in the grate. And if it was a retreat when London was too alluring, it was also a refuge when she set us at naught, and made us more or less conscious of lapses and blunders and country manners.

This passage has the clarity of the quotation from ***An American Girl in London,*** as well as the emotional subtlety Sara Jeannette Duncan was trying so desperately to achieve in the passage from **"The Pool in the Desert."** The writing is not simple, but it draws attention to the character of the narrator, rather than to itself. There is a smooth progression, in emotional and logical terms, from one statement to the next, rather than a breathless succession of stops and starts.

Having learned to become a skilful and subtle writer, Sara Jeannette Duncan did not practise her mature art for long. The four novels written from 1904 to 1909, from ***The Imperialist*** through ***Set in Authority*** and ***Cousin Cinderella*** to ***The Burnt Offering,*** are all serious, thoughtful, substantial works. Then, after a weak attempt at a political novel (***The Consort,*** 1912), Sara turned to writing the light fiction of her early career. It is easier to repeat conventions than to recapture their spirit, however, and these last books are joyless productions.

Sara's last significant novel was published thirteen years

before her death. As she was only sixty when she died, we can hardly blame senility for her decline. Nor did she become less conscientious: the manuscripts of plays written in her last period show that she worked doggedly at revising them.

There are three speculative explanations one can offer to account for the barrenness of this period. Perhaps, to begin with a simple possibility, Sara Jeannette Duncan was just artistically tired after seventeen books; not tired enough to give up going through the motions, but too tired to produce effective results. It is also possible that she drew unfortunate conclusions about the critical reception of her work. Of the four ambitious novels just mentioned, only one (***Set in Authority***) was much praised; ***The Imperialist*** was very sharply attacked, ***Cousin Cinderella*** was judged worthy of lukewarm approval, and ***The Burnt Offering*** does not seem to have been widely reviewed. Sara might well have looked back fondly to the dazzling success of her first two books, and resolved to emulate their style.

In her later years Sara Jeannette Duncan developed a passionate interest in the theatre, and it seems likely that this new interest affected her ambitions as a novelist. In addition to writing several independent plays, she produced adaptations of all three of her last novels; their energetic plots, and the virtual abandonment of narration in favour of dialogue, suggest that the theatre might have been her objective right from the start. Sadly enough, if indeed she worried about her success as a novelist, she eventually had much more reason to be depressed about her failures as a dramatist.

We have been forced to acknowledge that in Sara Jeannette Duncan's fictional bushel, not all the apples are first grade. Some are too small, and many have imperfections. But some are very good. . . .

George Woodcock (essay date 1983)

SOURCE: "The Changing Masks of Empire: Notes on Some Novels by Sara Jeannette Duncan," in *The Yearbook of English Studies,* Vol. 13, 1983, pp. 210-27.

[*In the following essay, Woodcock traces Duncan's development as a novelist.*]

Sara Jeannette Duncan is a better and more interesting writer than the caprices of posthumous reputation have allowed. For almost forty years of her relatively short life she was an industrious and capable journalist (writing for Canadian, American, and eventually Indian papers) and she wrote twenty books which appeared in her lifetime or shortly afterwards. Most of them were published in both London and New York, and some in Toronto as well. From the beginning of her career they were on the whole well received, and in the latter part of her career she generally gained the respect that is accorded a writer of acknowledged standing. Like other Canadian writers of her time she was probably more highly regarded abroad, where in any case she spent half her life, than in her native Canada.

The fate of posthumous oblivion after a life of success is not uncommon among writers, but rarely so complete as it has been in the case of Sara Duncan. She wrote six novels about India, where the last thirty years of her life were mostly spent, yet her name is not even mentioned in any of the recent studies of Anglo-Indian writing (such as Allen J. Greenberger's *The British Image of India* (1960) and Belinda Parry's *Delusions and Discoveries; Studies on India in the British Imagination* (1962)), though her novels of British life in India are better written than those of such contemporaries as Maud Diver and Flora Annie Steele, to whom considerable attention has recently been paid, and more interesting for the light they throw on the social life and the political motivations of the imperialists.

There is in fact only one book by Sara Jeannette Duncan, ***The Imperialist,*** that is now at all well known, and this owes its revived reputation to the attempt on the part of Canadian scholars and critics to create a past for the national literature which, as a recognizable tradition, is a comparatively recent one with few native roots. ***The Imperialist*** is a bright, perceptive, and somewhat nostalgic novel about Canadian political life in a small Ontario town, which Duncan wrote more than a decade after she left Canada to become a *chota memsahib* in Calcutta. Reprinted in 1961 as a paperback in the New Canadian Library, it has been fairly widely read since then, and is now recognized as one of the few mature and sophisticated novels to be written by a Canadian before the Great War.

In a more general way, Sara Jeannette Duncan has undergone a rehabilitation among literary historians who recognize her importance as one of the first dedicated professional woman writers to begin their careers in Canada. But, apart from ***The Imperialist*** and a brief selection of her newspaper writings, none of her work has been reprinted, and only during the 1970s have serious critical studies of her books (other than ***The Imperialist***) begun to appear in Canadian journals, culminating in the publication of the sole book-length study of her writings, Thomas E. Tausky's sound and comprehensive *Sara Jeannette Duncan: Novelist of Empire* (1978). So far as I have been able to discover, this recent small surge of interest in Sara Jeannette Duncan has been limited to Canada; it has not spread to Britain or the United States, where her books were most widely published and read during her lifetime, or to India, where she lived half her life and about which she wrote some of her best books.

The reasons for the neglect from which Sara Jeannette Duncan's reputation has only recently begun to emerge are closely connected with the character and even the virtues of her writing, and especially with the political vision with which her best-known works were associated. She was a remarkably good journalist in a style that became dated because its sometimes rather frenetic brilliance was a manifestation of the self-consciousness which their role in a world dominated by men imposed on young women writers seeking a career in the press (sometimes it also imposed on them masculine pretences, for there was a time when Sara Jeannette wrote under the *nom de plume* of 'Garth Grafton'). She was also a novelist always tempted towards the didactic, which sometimes imposes a fatal topicality. She was particularly interested in the movement for imperial federation that rose and foundered about the turn of the century and was especially associated with Joseph Chamberlain in England and with the remnants of the Canada First movement in Canada.

Though the influence of George Eliot is certainly visible in a book like ***The Imperialist,*** Sara Jeannette Duncan's literary inclinations were shown already in an early article she wrote on a visit to New Orleans in 1885, when she remarked that 'literary taste is high in New Orleans. On the table in your boarding-house you will find Turgenev, Hawthorne, Arnold, James, where at home you would be greeted by such celebrities as Mary Jane Holmes, Mrs Braddon, or the Duchess' (***Selected Journalism***). She was to see herself always in the sophisticated company of the Turgenevs and the Jameses and outside the sentimental conventions of Victorian women's writing, though she was not lacking in her own kind of romanticism. And though her stress on realism made her sympathetic to Turgenev, it was to be largely in the United States that she found her literary models. In her generally clear-sighted way she recognized the reason for this inclination even before she took to writing books, when in 1888 she contributed a piece on **'American Influence on Canadian Thought'** to Goldwin Smith's magazine, *The Week:*

> The lack of moneyed leisure is not the only condition of life common to Americans and Canadians. If it were, American literature would be as impotent, at any price, to change the character of Canadian literature as it is to effect a literary revolution in England. But, like the Americans, we have a certain untrammelled consciousness of new conditions and their opportunities, in art as well as in society, in commerce, in government. Like them, having a brief past as a people, we concentrate the larger share of thought, energy, and purpose upon our future. We have their volatile character, as we would have had without contact with them; volatility springs in a new country as naturally as weeds. We have greatly their likings and their dislikings, their ideas and their opinions. In short, we have not escaped, as it was impossible we should escape, the superior influence of a people overwhelming in numbers, prosperous in business, and aggressive in political and social faith, the natural conditions of whose life we share, and with whom we are brought every day into closer contact. (***Selected Journalism***)

Appearing in the journal which Goldwin Smith, a former imperial federationist, was now using to put forward his pleas for commercial union with the United States, this passage reads more like an argument for the inevitability of American annexation than Sara Jeannette Duncan perhaps intended. For politically her loyalties always inclined towards the Empire, the British connexion, and when she did leave Canada for good it was not to emigrate to the United States, along the road taken by so many Canadian writers from Major John Richardson onward, but to find her place in one of the poles of Empire, the city of Calcutta, which before the building of New Delhi was the capital of the Viceroys of India. Yet she felt always the distinction between Britain and parts of the empire that had developed their own style of life, and an earlier piece in *The Week,* **'Our Latent Loyalty',** set out some of the reasons why, sharing so much with the Americans, Canadians had loyalties that lay elsewhere.

> Sentiment is difficult of analysis, and the sentiment of the flag of the most difficult sort. We owe more to Britain than we are ever likely to pay; gratitude may be detected in it. We love our Queen: for the span of a long lifetime she has been to us the embodiment of all the tender virtues of a woman, all the noble graces of a queen. Thousands of her subjects in Canada were born in her kingdom; and nothing is more contagious than the loyalty they colonized with. Rideau Hall is an isolated fact in our social life. It has, and can have, no translatable meaning as a centre for the very irregular circumference it should dominate. Such old-world practices as obtain there we rather rejoice to see, feeling again in their dignity the bond of connection with the most dignified of commonwealths, and in their great incongruity, assurance that they can never become indigenous. We are glad to know that Her Majesty's representative is comfortable in Ottawa, and can be made so in his own way; and for esteeming his presence there or here an honour, with the history he bids us share, the traditions he commits to our keeping, and the flag he points our love and loyalty to, we cannot think of apologizing. (***Selected Journalism***)

Such a passage helps to explain why, like the Canada Firsters who also embraced imperialism, Sara Jeannette Duncan rejected the idea of Canada as a colonial dependency, since she shared with them the vision of equal peoples accepting a realm of common interest based on past connexions even if by now, as she also remarked, the ancient symbols of the loyalties involved might have become 'alien to our social system'.

Her sense of the complexities inherent not only in political loyalties but also in the relations between people from different cultures (even cultures using the same language) drew Sara Jeannette Duncan especially towards William Dean Howells and Henry James, the American writers for whom she expressed the greatest admiration. It is Howells with whom she shows the nearest affinity as a writer, for whenever she seems to be emulating James's complexities of manner her prose tends to lose the lucidity and springiness that are its most attractive qualities. Like Howells, she was always a novelist of manners, so that when we read books like ***The Imperialist*** and ***His Honour, and a Lady,*** we get the same sense of the living texture of everyday life, of the average as a setting for the exceptional, as Howells evoked, while, like Howells, Duncan used her experience of travel to illuminate the worlds she knew (Canadian, English, American, Anglo-Indian) by introducing into them sensitive and perceptive travellers from other cultures.

Particularly when she was a journalist training herself to be an author, Duncan thought and wrote interestingly about the nature of literature, which she once called 'the noblest product of civilization', and particularly about the modern trends in which she felt herself involved. **'Outworn Literary Methods'** was one of the articles she wrote for *The Week* in 1887. She touched on the 'literature of travel', in which she was already engaged as a journalist, and on fiction, upon which she intended shortly to embark. Of travel literature she remarked that the modern writer had abandoned Ruskinian descriptiveness and Baedeker-like historicism, 'and writes graphically instead of the humanity about him, its tricks of speech, its manner of breaking bread, its ideals, aims, superstitions' (***Selected Journalism***). On fiction she writes with a kind of half-baked libertarianism (let us remember that she was still only 25!) which nevertheless seems to embody a recognition of what Howells and his American contemporaries meant when they proclaimed their dedication to 'fidelity to experience and probability of motive'.

> To the casual observer little order or method seems to prevail in the set of circumstances taken apparently at random from anybody's experience, and cut off at both ends to suit the capacity of the cover. But in this respect appearances are deceitful. The novel of today may be written to show the culminative action of a passion, to work out an ethical problem of everyday occurrence, to give body and form to a sensation of the finest or of the coarsest kind, for almost any reason which can be shown to have a connection with the course of human life, and the development of human character. Motives of this sort are not confined to any given school or its leaders, but affect the mass of modern novel writers very generally, and inspire all whose work rises above the purpose of charming the idle hour of that bored belle in her boudoir whose taste used to be so exclusively catered to by the small people in fiction. The old rules by which any habitual novel reader could prophesy truly at the third chapter how the story would 'come out' are disregarded, the well-worn incidents discarded, the *sine qua non* audaciously done without. Fiction has become a law unto itself, and its field has broadened with the assumption. (***Selected Journalism***)

As a journalist, Sara Jeannette Duncan had already learnt that 'she must have some unworn incident, some fiber of novelty or current interest to give value to her work' in the eyes of editors and the reading public, and her newspaper pieces contain many vignettes that still evoke vividly how ordinary Canadians lived a hundred years or so ago. When she went into fiction it was by way of travel journalism, for her first book, ***A Social Departure*** (published in 1890), was a collection of travel dispatches written for the *Montreal Star* during a world journey, streamlined into a narrative and given a fictional form in which the interest is concentrated on the ways in which two young women of different backgrounds travelling together (the Canadian narrator and her archly-named English companion Orthodocia) experience their mildly exotic adventures in Japan and India and the Middle East. There is a triple movement in the book, embodied in the varying responses of the two travellers to strange settings, and the way in which they affect each other. On this level the claims of fiction are somewhat shallowly fulfilled, and a frame is provided for the bright but rarely more than superficial observations of unfamiliar societies and their strange life styles. From this pattern Sara Jeannette Duncan never entirely escaped. She always tended to be the victim of her own verbal cleverness, and to imagine that when she had brought people into amusing confrontation in settings that emphasized their peculiarities of character she had written a novel. Such charming fictions of manner and setting, which fail in her own requirement of 'the development of human character', punctuate her career.

The first of her Indian books, ***The Simple Adventures of a Memsahib*** (1893), is an early example. A young man in trade in Calcutta, and therefore without expectation of ever becoming a *burra sahib,* sends for his fiancée from England, they are married, set up house in Calcutta, and young Mrs Browne goes through all the exotic and often exasperating experiences of establishing a household and finding her level as a *chota memsahib* (little lady, as against *burra memsahib,* great lady) in the highly stratified Anglo-Indian society. An ironic touch is given to the narrative, since it is told by an older woman, Mrs Perth McIntyre, who had gone through the same experiences as Mrs Browne, and who watches the way in which the young woman's eager response to an unfamiliar way of life has been destroyed by the communal pressure to conformity; for the English in India, conformity was self-defence. The novel ends on a note of quiet pathos.

> It was a very little splash that submerged Mrs Browne in Anglo-India, and there is no longer a ripple to tell about it. I don't know that life has contracted much for her. I doubt if it was ever intended to hold more than young Browne and the baby—but it has changed. Affairs that are not young Browne's or the baby's touch her very little. Her world is the personal world of Anglo-India, and outside of it, except in affection for Canbury, I believe she does not think at all. She is growing dull in India, too, which is about as sad a thing as any. She sees no more the supple savagery of the Pathan in the market-place, the bowed reverence of the Mussulman praying in the sunset, the early morning mists lifting among the domes and palms of the city. She has acquired for the Aryan inhabitant a certain strong irritation, and she believes him to be nasty in all his ways. This will sum up her impressions of India as completely years hence as it does today. She is a memsahib like another. . . . I hope she may not stay twenty-two years. Anglo-Indian tissues, material and spiritual, are apt to turn in twenty-two years to a substance somewhat resembling chalk. And I hope she will not remember so many dead faces as I do when she goes away—dead faces and palm fronds grey with the powder of the wayside, and clamorous voices of the bazar crying, 'Here iz! memsahib! Here iz!' . . . So let us go our several ways. This is a dusty world. We drop down the river with the tide to-night. We shall not see the red tulip blossoms of the silk cottons fall again.

The Simple Adventures of a Memsahib carries the process of fictionalization a step farther than ***A Social Departure***. It is no longer through the eyes of two real people turned into characters, but through those of invented characters, that we are looking at and otherwise experiencing a strange world, but still the author is mainly engaged in writing graphically of the humanity about her, 'its tricks of speech, its manner of breaking bread, its ideals, aims, superstitions'. And we can reasonably take it that ***The Simple Adventures*** is Sara Jeannette Duncan's way of telling us something of how she adjusted to a strange life when in 1891 she went out to marry Everard Charles Cotes, the curator of the Indian Museum who shortly afterwards went into journalism and became the editor of the *Indian Daily News*. Certainly neither of the Brownes emerges as a strongly delineated personality, and (except for a visiting and meddling British politician portrayed with acerbic dislike) the remaining characters are all shallow types of Anglo-India rather than people with interesting inner lives. Nor, indeed, do we have much access to the inner life even of Mrs Browne, the central figure of the novel, and this is not entirely because her experiences are told from the outside, by the observant Mrs Perth McIntyre. It is because she is so neutral as a person, so much the experiencing membrane, that she never takes on shape in our minds as a woman whose feelings are deep and real or whose relation to her world is much more than an excuse for the author to record her own impressions of India and its English expatriate community as she first saw them.

This temptation to present a world in which the manners are more important than the men and women who practise them trapped Sara Duncan recurrently into writing bright and insubstantial novels of the same kind as ***The Simple Adventures of a Memsahib,*** which introduce an unfamiliar society to those who do not know it, and give its inhabitants a new view of themselves, by using observant, experiencing stranger's as principal characters. We are still surprisingly near to ***A Social Departure*** and the boundary where journalism merges into fiction even in some of the novels of Sara Jeannette Duncan's mature period, such as ***Those Delightful Americans,*** published in 1902 (nine years after ***The Simple Adventures***). A young Englishman and his wife (the narrator) go to New York to settle some business affairs affecting his family, and are offered splendid hospitality by an American lawyer involved in the corporation the Englishman is visiting. They are passed on to the household of one of the bigger financial magnates, a man who has risen from poverty and still retains many of the simplicities of his former existence. The life of the American leisured classes, their business methods, their eating practices and their courting habits, and especially the characteristics of the American Girl, are entertainingly and informatively displayed. The visitors' business is safely concluded, and the rather placidly-flowing plot is given what little complication it assumes by two American courtships which take on a twist more worthy of a West End comedy than a serious novel, when the couples shuffle themselves at the end of the novel and the American Girls, in their magnificent independence, pick the men neither the narrator nor the readers had expected them to choose.

The preoccupations of the novelist who wrote ***Those Delightful Americans*** were in many ways similar to those of the young journalist who had written perceptively and wittily of the Creole belles of New Orleans in the 1880s. One of Sara Duncan's most persistent literary personae was the sophisticated essayist who from the beginning had moved on the frontiers of fiction, spicing her facts with fancy when she was producing reportage, and stuffing her fiction with *faits divers* when she was writing her lighter novels. This inclination she shared with many Canadian novelists who have also been remarkably good essayists and whose fiction has retained not only the elegance and informativeness of the essay but also its tendency towards the opinionated and the didactic. Stephen Leacock, Hugh MacLennan, Robertson Davies, and Hugh Hood are representative examples of the Canadian writers who have not ceased to be essayists by turning to fiction; Sara Jeannette Duncan was their ancestress.

For even when she did move into more substantial fiction, into novels where the characters were well developed and the action became tense with conflict, it was under the influence of the didactic impulse of politics. At her best, in ***The Imperialist,*** or in her more impressive works on India, like ***His Honour, and a Lady*** and especially ***The Burnt Offering,*** Sara Duncan became one of the few Canadians who have written genuine political fiction to which, as Thomas E. Tausky has pointed out, Irving Howe's classic definition [in *Politics and the Novel,* 1957] clearly applies when he differentiates the political from the social novel, defining it as 'the kind in which the idea of society, as distinct from the mere unquestioned workings of society, has penetrated the consciousnesses of the characters in all of its profoundly problematic aspects, so that there is to be observed in their behaviour, and they are themselves often aware of, some coherent political loyalty or ideological identification'.

Early in her career as a journalist Sara Duncan wanted to become involved in political writing, and in March 1888 she gained her first opportunity when she was appointed parliamentary correspondent in Ottawa for the *Montreal Star*. It was a brief assignment, for in the last summer she was already in Brantford preparing for her departure in September on the world tour that led to her first book, ***A Social Departure***. The columns she wrote suggest that she was more interested in the pageant and the personalities of Canadian government than in the issues at stake during the brief session she reported, for her dispatches are strong on description of parliamentary events and weak in analysis of policies, which may well explain why the *Star* was so happy to send her on the world tour where her descriptive powers would be more appropriately used.

However, her interest in politics remained, and was put to journalistic use when she began in the middle 1890s to write editorials for the *Indian Daily News*. It surfaced in the first Indian novel, ***The Simple Adventures of a Memsahib,*** where she introduced, in the person of Jonas Batcham M.P., her first sketch of the gullible travelling politician who visits India and acquires a superficial knowledge of the situation there which leads him to make misleading accusations regarding the administration of the local officials. On a very simple level, the attitude towards the Raj that Sara Duncan maintained in the thirty years of her connexion with India was already established in this early book. She looked with a satiric eye on the social pretensions and the snobbish distinctions within the

Calcutta Anglo-Indian community. She disliked the Bengali 'baboos' who had received a partial education in the English manner and belonged to neither the new western nor the traditional Indian culture. She looked on Indian princes as material for comedy, and when she did portray an Indian character convincingly and in depth he usually turned out to be something of a villain. An example is the Indian nationalist, Ganendra Thakore, in ***The Burnt Offering,*** who was based on an actual nationalist leader, Bal Gandhadur Tilak, a pious Hindu advocate of the use of extreme and violent means to rid India of British domination. Sara Duncan had clearly studied Tilak's record and his character very carefully, for Ganedra Thakore is a thoroughly believable Indian leader of the Tilak kind without being a literal portrait; he is also diabolically convincing in his pietistic evil. Almost everything that Sara Duncan wrote of India spoke well of those Anglo-Indian idealists who saw themselves taking up the White Man's Burden and offering the Indians, despite their ungrateful opposition, the way to a more healthy and industrious life by which, in the long rather than the short run, they would be prepared to take their places within the Empire as equals. Sara Duncan's Indian politics were nearer to those of Lord Curzon than to those of the regular Indian establishment, and this means, of course, that they were more consciously Imperialist in the ideal sense than most India hands allowed themselves to be in practice.

His Honour, and a Lady (1896), published three years after ***The Simple Adventures of a Memsahib,*** shows a considerable advance in Sara Duncan's understanding of the moral ambience of the Raj. Reading this and her other Indian novels we have to remember the special position, almost ideal for ironic observation, which she held in Anglo-Indian society. As wife of the curator of the Indian Museum she did not belong to the commercial strata of Anglo-Indian society, yet her husband was not one of the all-powerful members of the Indian Civil Service. Leaving the museum to become a newspaper editor, he (and Sara) remained somewhere between the commercials and the civilians, so that they never became *burra sahibs* yet had fairly free access to almost every Indian presence, whether in Calcutta or in the hot-weather capital of Simla. This mobility, combined with the special access to political issues conferred by her newspaper work, allowed Sara Duncan to write with irony on Anglo-Indian social relationships at the same time as she seriously considered the political issues that faced the rulers of India and the moral struggles out of which their decisions and their subsequent actions arose.

His Honour, and a Lady shows admirably the dual aspects of Duncan's Indian novels. The title is more weightily ambiguous than most critics have realized. To begin, it refers to one of the leading figures, John Church, who as the novel opens is receiving the news that he has been picked out from his remote District Commissionership to become acting Lieutenant-Governor of Bengal; he will be referred to as His Honour. By the time the book ends, Church has lost his post in a political storm and has died of cholera, and his secret enemy Lewis Ancram has been appointed Lieutenant Governor and become His Honour. The Lady with whom both their Honours are involved is Church's wife Judith, who married him, a man more than twice her age, because it meant an escape from spinsterhood in a grey English industrial town to the romantic possibilities of life in India. Judith does not love John, but she immensely respects his devotion and his idealism, and when she falls in love with Ancram, and he with her, she cannot sacrifice her marriage. Partly, we see, she is moved by fear of the unknown, of the consequences in the Victorian world of adultery or (even worse) of divorce, but she is also influenced by her deep loyalty to the man whose struggle to use his power for the good of Indians she entirely admires.

Church's great plan, on which he risks his position and his reputation, is to change education in Bengal, superseding Macaulay's system of English liberal-style education (which by the end of the nineteenth century had produced a host of unemployable and discontented graduates in arts and law), with a system more orientated towards technical training, which would benefit the sons of peasants rather than the sons of landowners and moneylenders educated under the existing system. Ancram, who is Chief Secretary to the Bengal Government, pretends to admire Church and to support his proposal, but in fact despises him as a politician and intrigues with Bengali nationalists who seize on the educational issue to fan opposition to the regime; Ancram is the real author of the article in a Bengal paper which has most influence in Britain, forcing the Secretary of State to demand Church's resignation. Fortuitously (perhaps too fortuitously) Church is already sick from the cholera of which he is to die when the news is communicated to him by the Viceroy.

What makes Ancram interesting as a character is the division between his love for Judith Church and his hatred for John Church. His lack of true passion is shown by the fact that he does not hate Church emotionally as a rival in Judith's love, but intellectually as an administrator whose reforms, whatever their merits, are not in accordance with what he regards as the experience of imperial rule. Nevertheless, when Church dies, Ancram hopes he will not only gain his position as Lieutenant Governor but also win his wife. But Judith learns at the last minute how Ancram betrayed Church with his anonymous article, and she declines to marry him. And here the title takes on one of its secondary meanings. For this 'Lady' there is only one 'His Honour'; Ancram's title is shown to be specious as we realize that Sara Duncan is writing not merely about the honorific aspects of office, but also about the honour involved in political morality. John Church is an honourable man because he carries out, to the point of risking and accepting death, the obligations of his office, and refuses to bow to political expediencies when he is devising a new system which he believes will be to the ultimate benefit of the people he rules as a surrogate monarch. Ancram is a man without honour, since he allows expediency to make him an ally of those who are seeking to frustrate, by their specious visions of independence, the positive efforts of the British rulers.

This battle of political ideals and personal honour take place against the background of an expatriate society projected partly through the eyes of the narrator and partly through the shrewd observation of the second important woman in the novel, Rhoda Daye, an independent-minded young person with a witty tongue who is engaged to Ancram but jilts him because she recognizes his hollowness; there is a great deal in Rhoda, one feels, of her creator. In portraying the meretricious Anglo-Indian social life Sara Duncan's talents as a novelist of manners are well deployed, and the 'composite dinner party' given by Mrs Daye, Rhoda's mother and the wife of a Commisariat Colonel, shows admirably how she could balance sharp dialogue and analytical narrative.

> Mrs Daye always gave composite dinner parties, and this was one of them. 'If you ask nobody but military people to meet each other', she was in the habit of saying, 'you hear nothing but the price of chargers and the prospects of the Staff Corps. If you make your list up of civilians, the conversation consists of abuse of their official superiors and the infamous conduct of the Secretary of State about the rupee'. On this occasion Mrs Daye had reason to anticipate that the price of chargers would be varied by the grievances of the Civil Service, and that a touring Member of Parliament would participate in the discussion who knew nothing about either; and she felt that her blend would be successful. She could give herself up to the somewhat fearful enjoyment she experienced in Mr Ancram's society. Mrs Daye was convinced that nobody appreciated Mr Ancram more subtly than she did. She saw a great deal of jealousy of him in Calcutta society, whereas she was wont to declare that, for her part, she found nothing extraordinary in the way he had got in—a man of his brains, you know! And if Calcutta resented this imputation upon its brains in ever so slight a degree, Mrs Daye saw therein more jealousy of the fact that her family circle was about to receive him. When it had once opened for that purpose and closed again, Mrs Daye hoped vaguely that she would be sustained in the new and exacting duty of living up to Mr Ancram.
>
> '*Please* look at Rhoda', she begged, in a conversational buzz that her blend had induced.
>
> Mr Ancram looked, deliberately, but with appreciation. 'She seems to be sufficiently entertained', he said.
>
> 'Oh, she is! She's got a globe-trotter. Haven't you found out that Rhoda simply loves globe-trotters? She declares that she renews her youth in them.'
>
> 'Her first impressions, I suppose she means?'
>
> 'Oh, as to what she *means*—'
>
> Mrs Daye broke off irresolutely, and thoughtfully conveyed a minute piece of roll to her lips. The minute piece of roll was Mr Ancram's opportunity to complete Mrs Daye's suggestion of a certain interesting ambiguity in her daughter, but he did not take it. He continued to look attentively at Miss Daye, who appeared, as he said, to be sufficiently entertained, under circumstances that seemed to him inadequate. Her traveller was talking emphatically, with gestures of elderly dogmatism, and she was deferentially listening, an amusement behind her eyes with which the Chief Secretary to the Government of Bengal was not altogether unfamiliar. He had seen it there before, on occasions when there was apparently nothing to explain it.
>
> 'It would be satisfactory to see her eating her dinner', he remarked, with what Mrs Daye felt to be too slight a degree of solicitude. She was obliged to remind herself that at thirty-seven a man was apt to take these things more as matters of fact, especially—and there was a double comfort in this reflection—a man already well up in the Secretariat and known to be ambitious. 'Is it possible', Mr Ancram went on, somewhat absently, 'that these are Calcutta roses? You must have a very clever gardener.'
>
> 'No'—and Mrs Daye pitched her voice with a gentle definiteness that made what she was saying interesting all round the table—'they came from the Viceroy's place at Barrackpore. Lady Emily sent them to me: so sweet of her, I thought! I always think it particularly kind when people in that position trouble themselves about one; they must have so *many* demands upon their time.'
>
> The effect could not have been better. Everybody looked at the roses with an interest that might have been described as respectful; and Mrs Delaine, whose husband was Captain Delaine of the Durham Rifles, said that she would have known them for Their Excellencies' roses anywhere—they always did not table with that kind for the Thursday dinners at Government House—she had never known them to use any other.
>
> Mrs St George, whose husband was the Presidency Magistrate, found this interesting. 'Do they really?' she exclaimed. 'I've often wondered what those big Thursday affairs were like. Fancy—we've been in Calcutta through three cold weathers now, and have never been asked to anything but little private dinners at Government House—not more than eight or ten, you know!'
>
> 'Don't you prefer that?' asked Mrs Delaine, taking her quenching with noble equanimity.

Sara Jeannette Duncan did not become so preoccupied with Anglo-Indian society or with the politics of the Raj that she easily forgot her Canadian Links, and in an article (**'Imperial Sentiment in Canada'**) published in the *Indian Daily News* in the same year as ***His Honour, and a Lady*** appeared she sketched a theme that eight years later would be fictionally fleshed out in her only completely Canadian novel, ***The Imperialist***. In this piece she made clear that her own sympathies were with Joseph Chamberlain and his idea of a 'practical Federation of the British Empire based on a mutual system of preferential tariffs': an idea that would be kept alive into the 1930s by a Canadian expatriate politician operating from Britain, Lord Beaverbrook. Sara Duncan castigated Sir John Macdonald for paying lip service to Canada's British links, while his National Policy 'was conceived and carried out in plain opposition to British interest as a whole, and many of its tariff provisions were directly aimed at British manufactures'. And she was encouraged by a statement of the newly elected Liberal Premier, Laurier, that 'he and his Liberals looked with favour upon designs for Imperial Federation based on a preferential tariff for the goods of British Columbia and her colonies'. She was gratified that Joseph Chamberlain 'should find the first sincere welcome to his scheme for Imperial Federation offered by the Liberals of Canada, with whose economic principles it accords, and who are proud to claim a part in the greatness it prefigures' (***Selected Journalism***). Sara Duncan was expecting too much from Laurier, for Canada at no time committed herself to the cause of Imperial Federation. Eight years later, in ***The Imperialist,*** she used this Liberal betrayal, as it seemed to her, for her basic situation.

The Imperialist is not, any more than the other novels by Sara Duncan that I am discussing, entirely a political novel. The aborting of Lorne Murchison's parliamentary career through the conflict between ideals and practical politics in the Ontario town of Elgin is only one of the novel's leading strains, and though the fiasco of young Murchinson's election campaign provides the most visibly dramatic action, his sister Advena's finally-successful efforts to achieve a marriage of true minds with the preacher, Hugh Finlay, is almost as important in balancing the structure and heightening the emotional tension of the novel. The contrast between the intellectual Advena's steadfastness in love and the fickleness of the shallow-minded Dora Milburn, who jilts Lorne for a visiting English snob, parallels the contrast between Lorne's steadfastness to his imperial ideal once he had adopted it and the calculating expediency of the Liberal-party hacks who veer immediately they see the vote endangered by idealist politics and who eventually desert Lorne when a re-electrion is ordered and they feel they need a more cynical candidate.

The Imperialist is as much a social as a political novel, and a great deal of its lasting appeal in Canada lies in the nostalgic vividness with which Sara Duncan recreates, in the small town of Elgin, the Brantford in which she spent her childhood and her youth. A great deal of the local colour that she shared with Howells enters the passages of urban description in which she sets the scene for her political drama. It is there with a special felicity in the opening passage of the book where the bizarre figure of the half-mad gingerbread-seller, 'old Mother Beggarlegs', introduces the celebration in loyal Elgin of the Queen's Birthday, and it appears in a more solid way, giving a sense of the devotion of Elgin people to the immediate advantages of life, in the passage describing the market square where Lorne's legal office is situated.

> During four days in the week the market square was empty. Odds and ends of straw and paper blew about it; an occasional pedestrian crossed it diagonally for the short cut to the post-office; the town hall rose in the middle, and defied you to take your mind off the ugliness of municipal institutions. On the other days it was a scene of activity. Farmers' wagons, with the shafts turned in, were ranged round three sides of it; on a big day they would form into parallel lines and cut the square into sections as well. The produce of all Fox County filled the wagons, varying agreeably as the year went round. Bags of potatoes leaned against the sidewalk, apples brimmed in bushel measures, ducks dropped their twisted necks over the cart wheels; the town hall, in this play of colour, stood redeemed. The produce was mostly left to the women to sell. On the fourth side of the square loads of hay and cordwood demanded the master mind, but small matter of fruit, vegetables, and poultry submitted to feminine judgment. The men 'unhitched', and went away on their own business; it was the wives you accosted as they sat in the middle, with their knees drawn up and their skirts tucked close, vigilant in rusty bonnets, if you wished to buy. Among them circulated the housewives of Elgin, pricing and comparing, and acquiring; you could see it all from Dr Simmons's window, sitting in his chair that screwed up and down. There was a little difficulty always about getting things home; only very ordinary people carried their own marketing. Trifling articles, like eggs or radishes, might be smuggled into a brown wicker basket with covers, but it did not consort with elegance to 'trapes' home with anything that looked inconvenient or had legs sticking out of it. So that arrangements of mutual obligation had to be made: the good woman from whom Mrs Jones had bought her tomatoes would take charge of the spring chickens Mrs Jones had bought from another good woman just as soon as not, and deliver them to Mrs Jones's residence, as under any circumstances she was 'going round that way'.

This is not mere stage scenery, for the mixture of formality and calculation shown in the market behaviour of Elgin housewives is extended into the whole of the little town's society as it is laid out before us, dominated by the materialism of its factory interests yet led also by more tenuous considerations of class and convention that derive from a history different from that of the Americans. It is of course the tendency for material self-interest to compete with wider and more nebulous loyalties that Lorne Murchison has to fight in his effort to win election on the basis of a policy that, by dismantling Sir John Macdonald's tariff barriers to let British manufactures in, might harm the profits of Elgin factory-owners and the wages of Elgin workers. The full bitterness of Lorne's situation emerges when we realize that it is material self-interest on the lowest level, the eagerness of a few men to earn bribes which the political 'boys' offer them, that puts Lorne's marginal electoral victory in jeopardy. And this leads to the situation in which the rival political machines agree to a 'saw-off' that will halt investigations of corruption on both sides provided the judges order a new election. It is when the party bosses send for him that Lorne finally understands how ideals are used in practical politics, being adopted and discarded as expediency dictates.

> They had delegated what Horace Williams called 'the job' to Mr Farquharson, and he was actually struggling with the preliminaries of it, when Bingham, uncomfortable under the curi-

ous quietude of the young fellow's attention, burst out with the whole thing.

> 'The fact is, Murchison, you can't poll the vote. There's no man in the Riding we'd be better pleased to send to the House; but we've got to win this election, and we can't win it with you.'
>
> 'You think you can't?' said Lorne.
>
> 'You see, old man', Horace Williams put in, 'you didn't get rid of that save-the-Empire-or-die scheme of yours soon enough. People got to think you meant something by it.'
>
> 'I shall never get rid of it', Lorne returned simply, and the others looked at one another.
>
> 'The popular idea seems to be', said Mr Farquharson judicially, 'that you would not hesitate to put Canada to some material loss, or at least to postpone her development in various important directions, for the sake of the imperial connection.'
>
> 'Wasn't that', Lorne asked him, 'what, six months ago, you were all prepared to do?'
>
> 'Oh, no', said Bingham, with the air of repudiating for everybody concerned. 'Not for a cent. We were willing at one time to work it for what it was worth, but it never was worth all that, and if you'd had a little more experience, Murchison, you'd have realized it'.
>
> 'That's right, Lorne', contributed Horace Williams. 'Experience—that's all you want. You've got everything else, and a darned sight more. We'll get you there, all in good time. But this time—'
>
> 'You want me to step down and out', said Lorne.

And after a little more conversation he agrees, and leaves the other men, 'and they stood together in a moment's silence, three practical politicians who had delivered themselves from a dangerous network involving higher things'.

One ends ***The Imperialist*** with more than a suspicion that Sara Duncan is sceptical of the ability of democratic politics ever to rise above the level of expediency and self-interest, and this attitude is developed further in the second political novel about India which I am here discussing, ***The Burnt Offering***. If ***His Honour, and a Lady*** is about how practical politics destroys honour, and ***The Imperialist*** is about how it erodes ideals, ***The Burnt Offering*** is really about how ideals applied without sufficient knowledge of a situation can be as destructive as the most cynical of manipulative policies; in fact mistaken ideals and political manipulation, in Sara Duncan's view, seem to work together and feed each other.

The Burnt Offering draws its life from the political ferment that arose when India was released in 1905 from the glacial bureaucratic peace of Lord Curzon's viceroyalty. In 1906 a Liberal government came to power in Westminster, intent on introducing reforms that would hasten India on the road towards constitutional government. The Anglo-Indian community, led by the Viceroy, Lord Minto, was sceptical of the practicality of John Morley's reforms, which in the Indian Councils Act of 1909 introduced the elective principle into the selection of legislative councils; justification seemed to be given to this caution by the fact that between 1907 and 1910 the Bengali and Mahratta terrorists became powerful in the Indian independence movement and, under Bal Ganghadur Tilak, challenged the moderates led by Gopal Krishna Gokhale, Gandhi's predecessor. Tilak was imprisoned for sedition in 1908, and a rash of terrorist attempts followed, including one on Minto's life. The British replied by restricting freedom of speech, press, and meeting and by other stringent emergency measures.

Sara Duncan was in India throughout this turbulent period, and recognized the opportunities it offered for a powerful political novel. ***The Burnt Offering,*** which appeared in 1909, while the terrorist campaign was in progress and the British were buttressing their regime by strong police action, was therefore extremely topical, and its very topicality in 1909 is one of the reasons why it is historically so interesting in thc 1980s. It gives a vivid sense of the ambience in which both the English and the educated Indians lived in Calcutta, which was still the capital of India as well as of Bengal, and if Sara Duncan has taken the liberties with the actual pattern of events that fiction demands she still evokes, both vividly and authentically, the political forces then at work in India.

Indian characters are more numerous in ***The Burnt Offering*** than in any of Sara Duncan's earlier novels, and their variety suggests how closely she had observed the types with which an enquiring Anglo-Indian was likely to come into contact. The common people other than servants (coolies, policemen, peasants, cabbies) are seen from the outside, portrayed as a genre painter might do, with a quick stroke that sets them in the mind's eye: 'Lower down a steamer had been coaling, and along the footpath on the riverside trooped some scores of blackened coolies, each in his rag of loin-cloth, chattering and gesticulating as they pressed on to the shelter and the meal that stood for their share of life.' The coolies are seen not without compassion, but with no sense of how, given the nature of Indian life, their lot can be changed.

The change in Indians who have been in contact with Europeans are evident. Ganendra Thakore longs to return to the old ways of Brahminical India, but to that end willingly condones forms of violence that require weapons and explosives imported from Britain and in one instance disguised as Brand's Essence, which as an extract of beef is of course repugnant to all good Hindus. In the case of Bepin Behair Dey, the young son of a family belonging to the reformed sect of Brahmo Samaj, his education in Oxford, London, and Paris had turned him into a nationalist extremist willing to sacrifice himself in an act of terrorism. Sir Kristodas Mukerji, the pious Brahmin judge, is torn between his lawyer's sense of the fairness of British administration and his traditionalist's longing that, fair or not, the rule of the aliens shall come to an end.

It is Sir Kristodas who sentences Thakore for sedition (he gives him ten years while Tilak got only six), and then resigns his judgeship and his Order of the Indian Empire to become a pilgrim wandering through the sacred places of India with his daughter, the Rani Janaki, who has eaten of western culture and found it a dusty Dead Sea Fruit, and the Swami Yadava, who combines the role of a *sanyasin* with that of a spy for the British police. Yadava is the least authentic of all the characters who populate the book, whether Indian or British, and this is perhaps because he is so obviously derived from the Tibetan lama who played a similar double role in Kipling's *Kim,* while the other Indian characters are clearly related to, though not directly modelled on, the real Indians whom Sara Duncan encountered either socially or as a journalist.

The catalytic figures in the novel are the two English people who come from outside the Anglo-Indian world: Vulcan Mills and his daughter Joan. Vulcan Mills is the most developed example of one of Sara Duncan's recurrent types, the globe-trotting British M.P. who is sketched out in the unpleasant Jonas Batcham, M.P. of ***The Simple Adventures of a Memsahib*** and appears fleetingly as a boring dinner guest in ***His Honour, and a Lady***. For Vulcan Mills, Sara Duncan took as her model the Scottish labour leader, Keir Hardie, who made a trip to India in 1907, travelled around with open eye, and in his book, *India: Impressions and Suggestions,* was predictably critical of British methods, which he regarded as authoritarian but unstatesmanlike. A little sympathy and conciliation, he felt, would achieve more than a great deal of oppression, and he believed that the extension of the Indian participation in governmental affairs should be carried on with a view to eventual Dominion status. His book was moderate, sensible, and perceptive, and it was obvious that Hardie was nobody's fool.

Vulcan Mills, on the other hand, is represented as pompous, vain, and easily misled, and his daughter Joan as an ecstatic enthusiast of the most gullible kind. Such figures Sara Duncan evidently felt necessary to stress the central message of her book; that India's problems must be solved by those who know the country and have brought it forward into the nineteenth century, and that benevolent intruders from outside who do not realize the complexity of the situation are likely to play into the hands of forces which, under the cloak of patriotism, will turn India back towards its dark ages. Ganendra Thakore feeds Vulcan's sense of the total injustice of the Raj, and flatters him with suggestions of how his influence in Britain may change the situation. But Vulcan in his turn challenges Thakore to greater extremities, and eggs him on to make the speech that will lead to his imprisonment. The imprisonment in turn provokes Thakore to give the secret sign that will trigger Dey's self-destructive attempt on the Viceroy's life, so that Mills, who sees himself as a man of peace, unknowingly precipitates a sequence of deadly violence.

In ***The Burnt Offering*** the moderate Congress adherents of G. K. Gokhale never appear. Doubtless this was because Calcutta, where Sara Duncan lived, was the centre of terrorist action at the time she was writing the novel. At the same time the stress on Thakore and his fellow conspirators makes for a more dramatic book than the intrusion of moderate nationalism would have allowed, and if Sara Duncan disturbs political actuality by this choice she also enhances the fictional intensity, as Conrad did in his departure from the true history of anarchism in *The Secret Agent,* which Sara Duncan may well have read, since it appeared in 1907 and she had already expressed her admiration for Conrad's work in a review of *An Outcast of the Islands* which she wrote in 1896.

Thus the internal dynamics of the novel led Sara Duncan to make Vulcan Mills very different from Keir Hardie in real life, just as they led her to violate the sentimental conventions of her time by showing how love as well as idealism are mangled by political realities, so that there is no neat pattern of happy amorous conclusions, as in ***Those Delightful Americans***. The lovers, each in his or her own way, are destroyed by the situation in which they are trapped. John Game, a high official, falls in love with Joan Mills, which means the disappointment and eventual withdrawal from the world of the Rani Janaki, who loves him. Joan, however, falls for the blandishments of Dey, and agrees to marry him (which Thakore thinks will be a great gain for the nationalist cause), but before their wedding can take place he has shot himself after his failed assassination attempt. The only victim of the attempt, apart from a pariah dog, is John Game, who is thrown from the Viceroy's carriage and dies, not from the explosion, but agonizingly from tetanus; Calcutta mud has got into his blood through his grazed skin. And Joan, who thinks to serve Dey's memory by remaining in India and working for the cause, is forced to leave by his female relatives, whom events have scared back into conservatism, and who no longer want the daughter of Vulcan Mills among them.

The Burnt Offering shows a far deeper understanding of the undercurrents of Indian life than Sara Duncan's first book on the country, ***The Simple Adventures of a Memsahib,*** and it is more sophisticated and more critical in its portrayal of Anglo-Indian society than ***His Honour, and a Lady***. Duncan's awareness of the divisions between political ideals and political realities is as certain as it was in ***The Imperialist,*** which in my view rivals ***The Burnt Offering*** as her best novel. And if, in the end, I consider ***The Burnt Offering*** the better, if not the more plausible book, it is because Sara Duncan has not been afraid to shake off verisimilitude when she found it necessary to give dramatic or grotesque form to the shape of political violence, whether in the mind or in the streets. She showed her understanding of Stendhal's maxim: 'Politics in a work of literature is like a pistol-shot in the middle of a concert, something loud and vulgar, and yet a thing to which it is not possible to refuse one's attention.'

Peter Allen (essay date 1984)

SOURCE: "Narrative Uncertainty in Duncan's *The Imperialist,*" in *Studies in Canadian Literature,* Vol. 9, No. 1, 1984, pp. 41-60.

[*In the following essay, Allen attributes many of the ambiguities in* The Imperialist *to Duncan's own uncertainty about the Imperial Question and Canada's future.*]

In recent years a number of Australian films have won acclaim in Canada, as elsewhere, for their sympathetic and realistic depiction of colonial life in the years before World War I. The common theme of such films as *The Getting of Wisdom, My Brilliant Career, Picnic at Hanging Rock* and *Breaker Morant* is the process of maturation from colony to nation: they are preoccupied with Australia's ambivalent relation to British social traditions and Britain itself. These are notable examples of successful regional art—works that command an international audience for a subject that might have been of merely local interest.

English-speaking Canadians may well be jealous. There are so few films in English that give a vivid sense of Canadian life and almost none of our evolution from a colonial past. The Australians' success is not only a sad commentary on our film industry but reveals a curious gap in our cultural records. Leacock's *Sunshine Sketches of a Little Town* should never be ignored if one is looking for insight into English-Canadian life in the period after the pioneers and before World War I, but Leacock's perspective is of course neither serious nor realistic. In this context, a much less well-known work of fiction, Sara Jeannette Duncan's ***The Imperialist,*** appears as the remarkable achievement it is. Unlike the Australian filmmakers, Duncan did not have the benefit of historical hindsight. ***The Imperialist*** was published in 1904 and for the most part deals with the contemporary scene. In subject-matter and perspective, however, it is very similar to Leacock's *Sunshine Sketches*. Her theme is the ambiguity of Canadian identity and especially the mixture of excitement and scepticism or apathy with which we viewed our role in the British Empire. She vividly depicts that period of relative calm before the eruption of the modern age, a time in which British attitudes and customs were being slowly but unmistakably altered by the demands of a new country, and the Mother Country's political and cultural dominance was coming increasingly into question.

Like the Australians, Duncan sought to interest an international audience in a local issue, but unlike them her degree of success was very moderate. In the last twenty years, however, her novel has become a standard text in Canadian studies. Publication in the New Canadian Library paperback series has helped make it a standard offering in university courses, and a good deal of useful critical commentary has accumulated around it. With the spread of Canadian studies to other countries it may be hoped that Duncan will eventually earn the wider readership she deserves. In any case it seems likely that ***The Imperialist*** will be increasingly recognized as an unusual and accomplished testimony to an important stage in the development of our nation.

Whatever its historical significance and artistic merit, ***The Imperialist*** is not likely to win wide popularity, mainly because of the very considerable difficulties it presents its readers. Duncan's narrative voice is the chief puzzle. Although her subject is a provincial way of life, she herself as narrator is notably cosmopolitan, sophisticated, witty, complex, altogether hard to catch and hold. The problem is partly a matter of tone: she alternates between an ironic and an objective mode of reporting, and we cannot always be sure how to take her. It is partly a matter of style: she has a penchant for clever obliquity that makes her a consistently demanding writer and occasionally a very obscure one. It is partly a matter of narrative method: she moves unpredictably and abruptly from one topic to another, sometimes with the explicit suggestion that her novel-writing is a spontaneous affair, a little uncertain and not entirely under her control. An affection or simply the truth? The question is not easy to answer, though the narrator's cultivated sensibility and considerable intellectual self-confidence may make us suspect that we are in the hands of someone who knows what she is about, even when we don't.

Careful readers will discover that ***The Imperialist*** is tightly, indeed elaborately, organized, a fact that has been clearly established by its modern critics. But the published criticism, valuable as it is, has only begun to explain the curious mixture of artistic control and the apparent lack of it that we find in this novel. Several critical problems present themselves. The general tendency of the novel is well understood, but the detail of the pattern deserves more thorough treatment. A consideration of the way her central themes affect her treatment of minor characters and individual scenes will show something of the painstaking care with which she works. The inconsistencies in her narrative method become the more striking. Of these, the most obvious is the disparity in treatment between the main and sub-plots. Her conclusion presents yet another problem. Finally, there is the general question of how far her narrative uncertainty constitutes an artistic flaw.

. . . . .

Duncan begins her novel in Elgin's market square, which is central to the town both literally and metaphorically. She repeatedly returns to this setting, always to suggest that it represents the unchanging fact of the practical, commercial spirit that rules the community. Her hero's misunderstanding of the market and its people is of a piece with his misunderstanding in general. In chapter nine, having become a young lawyer, Lorne Murchison looks out over the market from the passageway to his office and dreams about its importance and his own. He feels an affinity with the people of the market, as indeed he should, considering that he is the privileged eldest son of a man who has struggled with great effort to a high place in the commercial world. He recognizes the market people as the foundation of the world he has inherited and is filled with a sense of his own power and purpose. But he and the narrator see the market in different terms. She stresses the harshness of the struggle it represents. It is a grim, joyless process, a "twisted and unlovely" tradition, "no fresh broken ground of dramatic promise, but a narrow inheritance of the opportunity to live which generations has grasped before." Lorne overlooks the "sharp features" of the market and sees it in terms of its promise. He is seized with tenderness "for the farmers of Fox County" or rather for "the idea they presented" to him.

The narrator is not suggesting that Lorne is wrong in thinking Elgin has a promising future, at least commercially. She consistently presents Canada as a thriving, expanding and very North American enterprise, a place of new opportunities that subtly converts the British immigrant into someone who thinks in new and wider terms. Nor is Lorne wrong to think well of his own future. But he does not understand how far his world and he himself are controlled by the tradition of single-minded commercialism that the market represents. As his father later says, he takes too much for granted that other people are like himself. He fails to recognize the limitations of their minds, the dogged resistance to attempted amelioration with which he will be met.

In this particular scene Lorne's failure of understanding is dramatized by his confrontation with Elmore Crow and his mother. Elmore is a cautionary parallel to Lorne himself. Having been Lorne's fellow-student at the Collegiate Institute—a notable avenue to social advancement in a new country—he dreamed of making a new start out West, only to find that the frontier is governed by the same principles as Elgin itself. Now that he has returned he has become even more a victim of economic necessity. Since his father is old and his brother Abe is to become a dentist, Elmore must take over the family farm. He tries to ignore his mother's existence—"If you had been 'to the Collegiate,' relatives among the carts selling squashes were embarrassing." But she and the life she represents are inescapable. She may be a "frail-looking old woman," but she shows no signs of weakness whatsoever. She treats Elmore as though he were a child. She is shrewd, suspicious, a sharp businesswoman, impatient of "big ideas" and utterly unimpressed by Lorne's claims to be treated as an unusual individual. If you don't buy Mrs. Crow's rhubarb at her price, you can do without rhubarb altogether.

Mrs. Crow is a pretty close parallel to Mother Beggarlegs, with whom Duncan began the novel. These characters represent the base fact of Lorne's community and one he is never able to deal with effectively. Like the farmers of Fox County, Mother Beggarlegs is a traditional, indeed ancient, institution. Her antecedents are mysterious, and she is the subject of speculation, especially by Lorne, who see her as a kind of dramatic possibility. The idea is typical: from the first pages of the novel we are led to think of Lorne's world as one that may inspire great ideas in children and other imaginative types but ultimately defeats them. Mother Beggarlegs' gingerbread comes without gilt, and no other is for sale in Elgin, a place where the only safe dreams are the ones you have in bed.

Mrs. Crow and Mother Beggarlegs are two of the many characters who personify the intractability of society in general. Like the punctilious Peter Macfarlane, most people are quite unvarying in their social routine. Lorne is perpetually disconcerted by this fact. In England he dreams of getting to know the working classes by talking to bus conductors but gets no further than he did with Mother Beggarlegs and Mrs. Crow. The little he does learn is not comforting. "There was the driver of a bus I used to ride on pretty often," he tells his family, "and if he felt like talking, he'd always begin, 'As I was a-saying of yesterday—' Well, that's the general idea—to repeat what they were a-saying' of yesterday; and it doesn't matter two cents that the rest of the world has changed the subject." As a result the imperial scheme makes headway slowly. Wallingham is able to convert some people in the upper reaches of society, but there is a problem with "the resistance of the base," and Lorne admits that at present the promoters of the scheme are "fiddling at a superstructure without a foundation."

With the federal by-election Lorne has a chance to put his fine new ideas before the people themselves. Once again he encounters Mrs. Crow, as much an inescapable fact in the political process as she was in the market, since the two are in fact different aspects of the same ruling principle. Perfectly set in her ways, the very picture of the social type she represents, she waits for the Liberal politicians in her parlour:

> She sat on the sofa in her best black dress with the bead trimming on the neck and sleeves, a good deal pushed up and wrinkled across the bosom, which had done all that would ever be required of it when it gave Elmore and Abe their start in life. Her wiry hands were crossed in her lap in the moment of waiting: you could tell by the look of them that they were not often crossed there. They were strenuous hands; the whole worn figure was strenuous, and the narrow set mouth, and the eyes which had looked after so many matters for so long, and even the way the hair was drawn back into a knot in a fashion that would have given a phrenologist his opportunity. It was a different Mrs. Crow from the one that sat in the midst of her poultry and gardens-tuff in the Elgin market square; but it was even more the same Mrs. Crow, the sum of a certain measure of opportunity and service, an imperial figure in her bead trimming, if the truth were known.

A key word here is "imperial." The title of the novel is of course ironic as well as literal. Lorne, the bearer of the imperial ideal, is presented as a kind of Canadian prince, receiving the admiration and acknowledgement of all as he passes through the market square. Ultimately, however, he is governed by the people he would lead. The emphasis on Mrs. Crow's limitations as a nurturing parent is also significant and typical of the novel as a whole. Like Mother Beggarlegs and the Mother Country she is certainly not going to take Lorne to her bosom. She may have given Elmore and Abe their start in life, but they, and anyone else like them, had better look after themselves now.

It is not simply that Lorne and his fellow-idealists are defeated by the lower orders, though they present the reality with which the idealist must contend in its starkest and most unmistakable form. Though Dr. Drummond is sympathetically portrayed, he is no less fixed and certain in his ways than Peter Macfarlane. His study is lined with "standard religious philosophy, standard poets, standard fiction, all that was standard, and nothing that was not." He is a "beneficent despot," and Knox Church is his "dominion." It is he who controls the action of the sub-plot, confronting Hugh Finlay with the inescapable fact of his love for Advena and, when Hugh will not be governed by him, marrying Christie Cameron himself. As a figure of authority he is very like John Murchison: both are kindly, thoughtful, dignified, imaginative but educated by the "discipline of circumstances," preoccupied by the world of practical necessity and as perfectly inflexible in their own spheres as are Mother Beggarlegs and Mrs. Crow in theirs. John Murchison is an excellent parent, but he cannot give his children money for their Victoria Day celebrations when he doesn't have it. If Mrs. Murchison is more forthcoming on this occasion she is no less resolute and unchanging in her views in general. As the sub-plot is controlled by Dr. Drummond, so the main plot is controlled by Henry Cruickshank. It is he who gives Lorne the chance to go to England, suggests his name for the Liberal nomination, and resolves his final dilemma by offering him a law partnership in Toronto. Like Dr. Drummond, Cruickshank is especially welcome in the Murchison home and bears some resemblance to John Murchison in character and social status. Thus Lorne and Advena grow up in a tightly-knit, stable social group that is closely supervised by a few highly respected and powerful elders. The newspaper editor Horace Williams takes not just his social announcements but his editorials virtually from Dr. Drummond's dictation, and public opinion tends to follow their lead respectfully. In short, the dominance of parents and parental figures is a major theme of the novel (which is dedicated, incidentally, to Duncan's father, the supposed original of John Murchison). Through her imagery the theme is extended to Britain and Canada. For Lorne the imperial idea means that "the old folks" in Britain will come to accept the leadership of "the sons and daughters." The immediate response is that "England isn't superannuated yet." We Canadians are "not so grown up but what grandma's got to march in front," Horace Williams later remarks.

To note the universality of this theme is not to deny the importance of the distinctions Duncan is careful to make among the various social groups she portrays and among the individuals within these groups. One of the strengths of the novel is the precision of her social analysis. Although the same principles are shown to prevail in Britain as in Canada, British and Canadian attitudes are carefully distinguished. Her main characters are drawn from Elgin's "polite society," which is set off both from the factory workers of the town and from the farming community. As children, Lorne and Advena attended the lacrosse match on the twenty-fourth of May when they could afford the admission, unlike "the young Flannigans and Finnigans, who absolutely couldn't" but went anyway. Within polite society there are marked contrasts between Dr. Drummond and Hugh Finlay or between the Murchison and Milburn families; within the Murchison family, between Advena and her sisters or between Lorne and his brothers. Even here there are differences: Lorne's brothers seem interchangable, but Stella seems likely to become a more intelligent conformist than her sister Abby.

Differences in imaginative capacity are especially important. This is not a matter of social class: Elmore Crow is as capable of "big ideas" as is Lorne. The members of the Murchison family are "all imaginative," though in varying degrees, and are regarded as slightly odd by the townspeople, whose attention (says the narrator sardonically) is typically restricted to "the immediate, the vital, the municipal." The Murchisons live at the very edge of town in the old Plummer Place, an unusually spacious house that is "in Elgin, but not of it" and that had been built by an earlier settler with "large ideas." Henry Cruickshank, who becomes Lorne's mentor, is characterized as having "lofty but abortive views." His opposite is Octavius Milburn, the "representative man," who is incapable of imagining anything beyond the narrowest practical necessities. Lorne characteristically imputes his own imaginative sympathy to others and tends to assume that older people will all be as benevolent as those who dominate the little world he was raised in. He hopes that Milburn imagines him to be a suitable prospective son-in-law, when in fact Milburn is holding the garden gate open for him merely because it is more convenient than closing it. Once again Lorne is making his appeal to the wrong sort of parental figure. In a pleasant twist on this pervasive theme, Milburn is the "Father of the Elgin Boiler" and of Dora Milburn, two products that have in common a certain hard, commercial quality. Lorne will be no more successful with the Milburns than he was with Mrs. Crow and Mother Beggarlegs or than Advena will be when she utters "her ideal to [the] unsympathetic ears" of the visiting Scotchwomen. She had "brought her pig, as her father would have said, to the wrong market."

The elaborately particular social world that Duncan depicts thus appears to be the scene of a perpetual conflict between a romantic world of imagination and controlling world of hard fact. From the first pages the world of children is associated with imagination, romantic dreams, the transmutation of the ordinary into the miraculous, the dramatic, the splendid. Against this tendency there is the steady pull of mundane or market-place reality, bringing the imagination back to earth, containing and disciplining it. This is the pre-existing or parental world, into which the imaginative mind is born and to which (in this novel) it must ultimately accommodate itself. Not that the imagination is invariably subordinate: Lorne's legal career is launched when his imaginative sympathy for Walter Ormiston allows him to penetrate Florence Belton's hard, businesslike dignity and to score in the face of "probability, expectation, fact." Nor are the townspeople in general without imaginative qualities, if of a somewhat opportunistic sort. Following his courtroom success, they see Lorne as a promising young fellow. But they desert him when he fails to deliver in the only terms they can really understand, just as his fellow Liberals are not willing to sacrifice their short-term interests for the sake of the imperial connection, though they were willing to "work it for what it was worth." Having been defeated by the business community's distaste for the idea, they turn to the second-rate Carter as "the admitted fact." Similarly, the Canadian delegation to Britain is forced to accept the fact of British apathy and misunderstanding. Hugh Finlay must accept that the fact of his relationship with Advena "is beyond mending" and that the "whole fabric of circumstance was between them." The Murchison parents "acknowledge their helplessness before the advancing event" of Christie Cameron's arrival. She appears as "the material necessity, the fact in the case," Advena finds it impossible to deny the fact of her physical passion, but it takes the hardheaded Dr. Drummond to strike the bargain that will set the lovers free.

In a characteristic passage Duncan begins with the everyday occasion of a Murchison family outgoing to church, sketches in a winter's night in Elgin and concludes by contrasting what an imaginative mind might have made of the scene and what the Murchison parents actually did make of it:

> Mr. and Mrs. Murchison, Alec, Stella, and Advena made up the family party; Oliver, for reasons of his own, would attend the River Avenue Methodist Church that evening. They slipped out presently into a crisp white winter night. The snow was banked on both sides of the street. Spreading garden fir trees huddled together weighted down with it; ragged icicles hung from the leaves or lay in long broken fingers on the trodden path. The snow snapped and tore under their feet; there was a glorious moon that observed every tattered weed sticking up through the whiteness, and etched it with its shadow. The town lay under the moon almost dramatic, almost mysterious, so withdrawn it was out of the cold, so turned in upon its own soul of the fireplace. It might have stood, in the snow and the silence, for a shell and a symbol of the humanity within, for angels or other strangers to mark with curiosity. Mr. and Mrs. Murchison were neither angels nor strangers: they looked at it and saw that the Peterson place was still standing empty, and that old Mr. Fisher hadn't finished his new porch before zero weather came to stop him.

This passage is very like the novel as a whole. It is factual, precise and vivid. We are made aware both of the scene and of the narrator's literary sensibility. The key issue is the restraint placed on the human imagination by the social world she depicts. An angel or stranger might have found the scene dramatic, mysterious, symbolic, but their long years in Elgin have taught Mr. and Mrs. Murchison to restrict their vision to the ordinary. The idea of a limiting world is subtly reinforced by the detail of Mr. Fisher's failure to build the porch he had planned. Yet the general impression left by the scene is one of romantic potential. Mr. and Mrs. Murchison may not be able to appreciate it, but the narrator does, and she keeps alive the hope that the young people of the novel (who are closer to being angels and strangers) will somehow make more of this world than their elders have.

This sort of teasing possibility pervades the novel and makes for persistent difficulties of interpretation. What precisely is the relationship of her idealistic young people to the parental world that surrounds them? Will they transform it, be defeated by it, merge into it? Duncan admired W. D. Howells, and in part ***The Imperialist*** proceeds by arousing and then undermining the reader's romantic expectations, as in *The Rise of Silas Lapham*. But only in part. Catherine Sheldrick Ross points out [in *Studies in Canadian Literature* IV, No. 1 (1979)] a major problem. The spinsterish Advena, with her nose in a book, is clearly a realistic foil to Dora Milburn, in whom Duncan parodies the appearance and manners of the conventional fictional heroine. Thus Lorne's love affair with Dora is treated in an ironic, anti-romantic way and comes to an appropriate conclusion. But "Advena is in fact involved in a plot with exactly the same structure as that which used to propel the old-time heroine from 'an auspicious beginning, through harrowing vicissitudes, to a blissful close'." The disparity between the main and sub-plot is the most obvious example of Duncan's inconsistency. But even here it is no simple matter to explain why we are led to feel that an inconsistency exists.

. . . . .

The Imperialist is as elaborately constructed in terms of scene and plot as it is in theme and character. The scene in which Lorne is introduced to Mrs. Crow is a case in point. The situation will recur when Lorne introduces Hesketh to his father, but with the important difference that it is the person being introduced, and not the introducer, who is embarrassed. The scene with Mrs. Crow begins with Lorne looking out across the market and finding it good. At the end of the novel, after hearing he has been dumped by the Liberals, he is again in "the companionship of Main Street" but finds the view not nearly so encouraging. At this point he encounters Hesketh, who caps his revelations with a line that Lorne himself had used in an earlier scene: "is this a time to be thinking of chucking the Empire?"

The correspondence among other scenes is equally striking and especially her careful paralleling of scenes from the two plots. As Lorne and his parents confer with their visitors, Drummond and Cruickshank, in the drawing room, Advena confers with hers, Hugh, in the library. The two parties meet at the front door, and we understand that the affairs of both Murchison children are prospering. Lorne returns with discouraging news from England, and in the next chapter (xviii) discouraging news from Scotland arrives for Hugh. When he tells Advena about his engagement, she understands what is really happening, but he does not. In the next chapter (xix), Lorne tries to become engaged to Dora; again the woman is the one who understands. Their secret engagement is both a parallel and a contrast to Hugh's, and both are ended by surprising marriages.

The correspondence of the two plots in theme and characterization is even more obvious. Lorne and Advena are alike in character, unlike in sex and hence in social destiny. The family expects much of Lorne, little of Advena, and would rather prefer that she conformed to the town's conventions for young women. Lorne's professional position makes him as prominent as Advena's makes her obscure. His prospects for advancement are excellent, hers are nil. It may seem a little odd that she sees a sunset as "a hateful reminder . . . of how arbitrary every condition of life is," but social frustration has been the main fact of her life. Hugh Finlay is perhaps too neatly paralleled to her as a sensitive soul who has been cooped up in a harshly unimaginative world of practical necessity and small-mindedness, but in fact he too is a realistically portrayed character—a "great gawk of a fellow," as Mrs. Murchison says, with a flair for his profession that resembles Lorne's but even less understanding of life outside it. He is of course both paralleled and contrasted to the plausible Alfred Hesketh, another recent immigrant who eventually forsakes his old-world attitudes for the fresh prospects afforded by the new.

The disparity in treatment between the main and sub-plots

is thus not a matter of structure, characterization or the handling of theme. The main problem is of course the implausibility of the conclusion. Duncan works hard to make the conclusion seem realistic and in keeping with the novel as a whole, but the reader is unlikely to be convinced, largely because a shift in her narrative perspective has already been announced by a shift in her use of language.

Although Lorne is her hero, her view of him is sufficiently dispassionate to be in keeping with her generally ironic and realistic tone. We are aware of his faults and are certainly not asked to identify uncritically with him. Her view of Hugh is less consistently objective. "He was a passionate romantic," we are told, with "deep dreams in his eyes." "His face bore a confusion of ideals; he had the brow of a Covenanter and the mouth of Adonais." Advena is fascinated by this mouth, which she takes to be evidence of his genius. The narrator ironically accepts her view, considering the "difficulty of providing anything else," but then adds, "he had something, the subtle Celt; he had horizons, lifted lines beyond the common vision, and an eye rapt and a heart intrepid." The final phrase destroys the illusion of ironic and realistic commentary. She seems momentarily to have adopted Advena's overheated perspective, and this impression is sustained throughout the scene that follows, that of their first conversation. This is a meeting of souls, marked by much highflown and rather unlikely dialogue. The scene could only be saved for the cause of realism if the narrator made fun of her overly serious characters a little, as she will later do in describing their tryst at the Murchison home. But in this case all irony is forsaken, and the scene ends with Advena going on "into the chilly yellow west, with the odd sweet illusion that a summer day was dawning." This uncritically romantic tone recurs in describing Advena's growing love for Hugh: "she walked beside him closer than he knew. She had her woman's prescience and trusted it. Her own heart, all sweetly alive, counselled her to patience." All sweetly alive? Warned by this sort of language that we are not to take the subject of Advena's love ironically, we can only read the climactic scene between the lovers as unrestrained melodrama:

> Pitifully the storm blew her into his arms, a tossed and straying thing that could not speak for sobs; pitifully and with a rough incoherent sound he gathered and held her in that refuge . . . Yet she was there, in his arms, as she had never been before; her plight but made her in a manner sweeter . . . It was the moment of their great experience of one another; never again, in whatever crisis, could either know so deep, so wonderful a fathoming of the other soul.

If we compare this with the climactic scene between Dorothea and Will in chapter eighty-three of *Middlemarch,* we will see the difference between subordinating melodramatic elements to the general design of the novel and failing to do so. What seems to have happened is that Duncan's intense sympathy for Advena's dilemma has subverted her narrative technique and created an unnecessary gap between the main and sub-plots. Though her deviations from the general tone of sophisticated social comedy are infrequent, they constitute a serious flaw, for they all concern Advena and serve to isolate her story from the main concerns of the novel.

. . . . .

Even if we resolutely ignore such slips in narrative tone, the conclusion of ***The Imperialist*** is perplexing. The Milburn family seems to be central to the puzzle. Clara Thomas [in *Journal of Canadian Studies* XII, No. 2 (1977)] points to the racial element in Duncan's thought and suggests that the "pretension, time-serving and prejudice of such neo-colonialists as the Englishman, Octavius Milburn . . . are clearly to be vanquished by the rising generation" of Scotch-Canadians represented by the young Murchisons. For Thomas Tausky [in *Sara Jeannette Duncan: Novelist of Empire,* 1980] the novel is more ambiguous: "she seems to have the Murchisons and the Milburns in mind as two alternative directions for the evolution of a more advanced culture," and her conclusion is highly uncertain. Yet another possibility is that these families represent two contending social principles, neither of which can entirely prevail over the other.

There is no doubt that Duncan portrays a society in the process of change. She strongly emphasizes the passing of the seasons and the years, the rise to social dominance of such men as John Murchison and Dr. Drummond, the emergence of a new generation in the young people of the novel. In a characteristic passage the Murchison parents sit on their verandah talking over the development of their children's lives. Now that the Murchisons have "overstamped the Plummers" in the town's consciousness, their home is known as the Murchison Place. The horse chestnut blooms as it had done for thirty years; the "growing authority of his family" has led John Murchison to forsake shirtsleeves for more formal dress; the coming of Abby's babies has led Mrs. Murchison to take out her old patterns for children's clothes. Such gradual developments are presented as part of a larger historical pattern that will determine Canada's future. "[W]e are here at the making of a nation," Duncan remarks at one point.

It is also true that in treating this historical pattern she reveals strong racial sympathies. She likes the Scotch and views Indians with contempt. The Murchisons, who certainly have her sympathy, are represented as part of a general movement that has supplanted the Anglican colonial gentry. But she presents this change as political and social rather than simply racial, as a move from the Tory centre to the Liberal provinces. The Anglican gentry were succeeded in political office by "young Liberals" and their "grandsons married the daughters of well-to-do persons who came from the north of Ireland, the east of Scotland, and the Lord knows where." Octavius Milburn is not actually an Englishman but a nationalistic and highly conservative Canadian, one who "was born, one might say, in the manufacturing interest, and inherited the complacent and Conservative political views of a tenderly nourished industry." His wife and his wife's sister ape the manners of the British upper class and have taught his daughter Dora to speak with an English accent. The family is Anglican as well as Conservative and has links through the local rector with an English family, the Chafes, whose social and political position much resembles theirs. Thus the Milburns seem related to the tradition of British colonialism, and Duncan plainly views them with distaste. But again the reason may be political. Wallingham and Williams are not Scottish names, but their owners are liberals and are sympathetically treated. Squire Ormiston is even more clearly a remant of a bygone era and is certainly of English descent, but he is not viewed negatively, perhaps because he does not pose a present threat to the liberal interest. Indeed the good old fellow turns out to be a whig, deep down. Duncan's racial prejudices are undeniable, but her political prejudices are even stronger. One reason that the Milburns are treated as the villains of the novel is that they represent the continuing force of conservative opinion in Canadian society.

Will the Milburns be supplanted by the Murchisons? No doubt Duncan hopes so, but her novel does not give much hope of it. Octavius and Dora Milburn are especially notable as being more clear-sighted in their views of what is going on in society than the characters whom we are expected to like, and at the end of the novel there is no sign that their powers are on the wane. Octavius Milburn has no illusions at all about the likely fate of the imperial ideals. His daughter is equally realistic. In her own drawing-room "she was very much aware of herself, of the situation, and of her value in it, a setting for herself she saw it, and saw it truly." She has a calculating eye for Lorne's chances. Like the town in general, she begins by taking up with him as a very likely opportunity and ends by discarding him as not really to the purpose. When Lorne rhapsodizes about the English ("they're rich with character and strong with conduct and hoary with ideals") Dora merely replies, "I don't believe they are a bit better than we are." Of course she is right, as the career of Alfred Hesketh will show. Lorne discovers that narrow-minded materialism prevails as much in England as at home, and the idealistic Wallingham is ultimately helpless against it.

Catherine Sheldrick Ross says that Advena "is marked out by name and character as the heroine of the future." But the novel concludes with Dora still ascendant over conventional society in Elgin while Advena and Hugh Finlay, having been set free by the grace of Dr. Drummond, are to bring their combined idealism to bear on life at the White Water Mission Station in Alberta. Why should we expect two such impractical dreamers to make more of life out West than Elmore Crow did? If the mission is to the Indians, we know too well what Duncan thinks of them. The ending of the main plot presents a similar problem. Duncan suggests that Lorne and Henry Cruickshank will sustain each other against the onset of cynicism and will continue to struggle for a better Canada. Why should we expect them to be any more successful in the future than they have been in the past?

A modern reading of the novel is necessarily affected by the fact that we know the outcome of the imperial question. Octavius Milburn's skeptical predictions have proved to be the simple truth. It seems that Duncan has dramatized her fears for the future of Canadian society in the figures of the Milburns, her hopes in the Murchisons. In her final paragraph Cruickshank's offer of a partnership to Lorne is compared with the British government's moves towards imperial federation. Is it too soon for these to be accepted by Canada, she asks, or is it too late?

The Milburn faction have won in the short run, but will they win in the long? Duncan tries to leave the issue open, but even to her contemporary readers it might well have seemed that the future of the social world she depicts is more likely to lie with Stella Murchison, who knows how to appear no better than other people, than it does with idealists such as Lorne and Advena. Our final image is of Lorne going "forth to his share in the task among those by whose hand and direction the pattern and the colours [of destiny] will be made." This is intended to assert his significance, but it also suggests his submergence in the crowd. Just as Lorne was "an atom in the surge of London" and just as Canadians are "atomic creatures building the reef of the future," so Lorne is powerless to do more than lend his hand to the building of a nation that is ruled, for the most part, by narrowminded practicality. The Milburns represent a basic conservatism to which society, however liberal-minded it may appear, is always likely to revert. In fact Duncan's liberals are ultimately contained by conservatism. The Liberal party will take up with Lorne when he seems the coming thing, but will desert him just as surely as Dora does when the going gets rough. The Milburns are unattractive figures because they present in its purest form the values that actually prevail in society, without the sympathetic qualities that offset these same values in such figures as Dr. Drummond and John Murchison, and without the excuse of economic necessity that explains such lives as Mrs. Crow's.

As Thomas Tausky remarks, the action of ***The Imperialist*** "inspires pessimism," yet the work as a whole is not pessimistic. Rather it presents social life as a constant battle in which the human imagination must always be curbed and disciplined by circumstances but in which the heroic quality of life comes from the continued assertion of human ideals in the fact of their continued defeat. Certainly human beings without ideals are an unattractive spectacle, as Duncan presents them. Yet idealism itself is ambiguously presented. Is her hero Lorne Murchison, as she says, or his father? John Murchison and Henry Cruickshank seem to represent the best that society has to offer. Perhaps Lorne's role is to become like them and in his turn to offer fatherly guidance for the idealistic impulse in others. Duncan does not tell us, and evidently she was not sure. She plainly believed in the progressive amelioration of society by liberal principles. Her experience of life and particularly of Canadian life had taught her that this process was at best an arduous and painful one, perhaps even futile. Yet she was not prepared to see the submergence of liberal principles as simply an unhappy ending.

Claude Bissell invites a comparison of Duncan and George Eliot, and the idea is a useful one. The detached yet sympathetic analysis of a provincial community, the insistent theme of social determinism, the use of contrasting yet matched or paired characters (and especially the use of a pair of idealists one male and one female, as central figures in separate plots)—in all these ways we may be reminded of *Middlemarch*. The correspondence in imagery is sometimes striking, as in Lorne's being "fast tied in the cobwebs of the common prescription." Dora is very like Rosamund Vincy in her selfishness, her shallow materialism and her conventional beauty. But the pattern of causality in *Middlemarch* seems so complex and far-reaching that no one can grasp it, and certainly not Rosamund. Duncan is concerned with a simpler and more limited pattern, one that so acute and hard-headed a person as Dora has no trouble understanding. This quality of understanding also means that Dora cannot bring about so tragically destructive an outcome as Lydgate's eventual fate. Dora finds the right mate in Hesketh, and Lorne at least does not find the wrong one in her. Furthermore, such tragic potential as Duncan's material possesses is nullified by the intervention of kindly parental figures. The impossibly idealistic Finlay is saved from disaster by Dr. Drummond, just as Henry Cruickshank saves Lorne from the unhappy fate of trying to become an American. The reader is led to identify with her idealistic young people but at the same time led to understand that there will always be someone around who knows how the world really works and can save the idealists from themselves. Duncan's allegiances are divided: she wants the idealists to win but regards it as simply part of the social comedy when they do not, very likely because she has an underlying faith in the world of John Murchison and her own father. The result is a curious mixture: the social realism she had learned from George Eliot and others gives way ultimately—and yet not entirely—to the conventions of popular romantic comedy.

. . . . .

Duncan's narrative uncertainty is not always a weakness. It can be an amusing affectation, as when she finds herself launched on "an analysis of social principles in Elgin" despite her desire to get herself and her characters to the Milburns' party. But it is not simply an affectation, for the novel has a distinctly improvisational cast. A single final example will show how this quality contributes to its general character.

In describing Lorne's first meeting with Elmore Crow the narrator permits herself an aside on the subject of the Collegiate Institute's importance in the life of Elgin. Evidently thinking of her British readers, she identifies the Institute as "that really 'public' kind of school which has so much to do with reassorting the classes of a new country." She then develops this theme at a little length:

> The Collegiate Institute took in raw material and turned out teachers, more teachers than anything. The teachers taught, chiefly in rural districts where they could save money, and with the money they saved changed themselves into doctors, Fellows of the University, mining engineers. The Collegiate Institute was a potential melting-pot: you went in as your simple opportunities had made you; how you shaped coming out depended upon what was hidden in the core of you. You could not in any case be the same as your father before you; education in a new country is too powerful a stimulant for that, working upon material too plastic and too hypothetical; it is not yet a normal force, with an operation to be reckoned on with confidence. It is indeed the touchstone for character in a new people, for character acquired as part from that inherited; it sometimes reveals surprises.

At this point in the paragraph she turns abruptly back to the subject at hand:

> Neither Lorne Murchison nor Elmore Crow illustrates this point very nearly. Lorne would have gone into the law in any case, since his father was able to send him, and Elmore would inevitably gone back to the crops since he was early defeated by any other possibility. Nevertheless, as they walk together in my mind along the Elgin market square, the Elgin Collegiate Institute rises infallibly behind them, a directing influence and a responsible parent.

Clara Thomas suggests that in the first part of this paragraph Duncan was being ironic. This is a charitable view, but it seems just as likely that she was carried away for the moment by her nationalistic sympathies, then remembered that her characters did not fit her thesis and simply said so, rather than revising the paragraph. She is concerned to present Canada as a young and developing nation, and so she falls into rather conventional North American rhetoric about educational opportunities in the new world. But she has already made it clear that class distinction remains all-important in Elgin, however much the traditional barriers may have shifted, and the scene she is depicting turns on this fact. Her apparent confusion on the point derives from her ambivalence about the traditional or parental world. In part, the dead hand of tradition lies on Elgin's hopes; in part, Elgin is moving towards a brighter future. Thus the market is described with notable ambiguity as containing Canada's heart—"the enduring heart of the new country already old in acquiescence . . . the deep root of the race in the land, twisted and unlovely, but holding the promise of all." Canada is new but old, crippled but flourishing, dominated by the past but the country of the future. In any case, the Collegiate Institute is clearly "a directing influence and a responsible parent." But what kind of parent? One that restricts its children or sets them free? Duncan knows it is the first: much of what happens at the Institute is an extension of the social principles that separate a Lorne Murchison from an Elmore Crow. In fact, Elmore *will* be what his father was before him, and if Lorne will not, it is because of his father's social position. Yet she trusts it is somehow the second. After all, Elmore's brother will become a dentist. Because of the Collegiate Institute? No doubt, but also because "the old folks are backin' him."

The confusion revealed in this passage is fundamental to the novel. Duncan's uncertainty about the Collegiate Institute is of a piece with her uncertainty about the imperial question and her uncertainty about Canada itself. The result is not simply a flawed novel. Much of the work's complexity and richness derives from her not having been able to decide. She has dramatized her hopes and fears and at the same time has been seemingly compelled simply to tell the truth as far as she knew it. The unevenness and difficulty of the novel are part of its interest and ultimately reveal an imaginative mind grappling with the most perplexing and compelling of all questions to Canadians, that of their own uncertain nature. Will Canada become a major power through her association with the British Empire? Duncan sympathized with the youthful excitement and idealism that accompanied this idea but guessed shrewdly at the forces that would in time make it irrelevant. Will Canada's Lornes and Advenas transform the parental world as they inherit it? The question is left open, though the disparity in Duncan's treatment of her hero and heroine shows her unacknowledged disbelief in the likelihood of much improvement in the unconventional woman's lot. In both her certainty and uncertainty, in her realism and occasional lapses from it, Duncan is an eloquent and important witness to the ambiguity of our developing national identity in the years before World War I.

Misao Dean (essay date 1985)

SOURCE: "The Process of Definition: Nationality in Sara Jeannette Duncan's Early International Novels," in *Journal of Canadian Studies,* Vol. 20, No. 2, Summer, 1985, pp. 132-49.

[*In the following essay, Dean argues that Duncan's early international novels articulate a theme of Canadian nationalism that reconciles the extremes of freedom and tradition as represented by the United States and Britain respectively.*]

Since Confederation, Canadians have often attempted to define what Canada *is* by first discussing what it is *not.* A process of negative definition has been forced upon Canada by history and geography; the ever present threat of assimilation into the British or American Empires has prompted defensive attacks on both Britain and the United States with the aim of preserving Canadian independence. Canadian imperialists such as George Parkin, G. M. Grant, and George Taylor Denison engaged in a critique of Britain and the United States as a first step toward defining a unique Canadian nationality. Sara Jeannette Duncan's first four international novels, ***An American Girl in London*** (1891), ***A Voyage of Consolation*** (1898), ***A Daughter of Today*** (1894), and ***Those Delightful Americans*** (1902) provide a similar critique for, it would seem, a similar purpose.

The major points of Duncan's critique are clear in the novels. In her view, American society conducts itself on the false assumption that total personal freedom and equality are a natural basis for stable society. For Duncan unrestrained freedom leads away from social stability to social atomization, egoism, selfishness and amorality. In contrast, she sees British society as based upon the force of tradition. Britain's citizens are dominated by the forms and conventions of a highly structured, class-conscious society which no longer understands the ideal principles behind the forms. Britain, therefore, is afraid of change, is enervated and morally bankrupt.

Duncan develops her critique of the United States and Britain by means of subtle fictional techniques which have not been analysed fully by critics. As a result there does not yet seem to be sufficient recognition either of Duncan's literary skill or the purpose to which she uses it in her first four international novels. ***An American Girl in London, Those Delightful Americans,*** and ***A Voyage of Consolation*** employ first-person narration by a young British or American woman; in them, Duncan uses irony to undercut the moral position from which the narrator judges the nation she visits. The ironic narrator satirizes the people she meets, but she is in turn satirized to an equal extent. Duncan's criticisms of her American narrator, however, have not been clearly seen: Thomas Tausky states [in *Sara Jeannette Duncan: Novelist of Empire,* 1980] that "on balance, Sara Jeannette Duncan is considerably less sympathetic to English manners than she is to North American culture." Duncan does indeed admire the energy of her American characters, but she does so much as Thomas Chandler Haliburton admires his Sam Slick; in both cases admiration is balanced by a demonstration of the destructive elements of a personality shaped by the United States.

A Daughter of Today is similarly a source of confusion concerning Duncan's technique. The novel is a complex portrait of a talented young woman, told from the detached viewpoint of a third person narrator who remains unidentified. Aside from the central problem of nationality, several major themes are touched upon: sex and its influence upon art, the distinctions between popular and serious art, the morality of sexual behaviour, and the possibility of friendship between women. But when critical attention is focussed upon the problem of nationality in the novel, the point of view assumes specific cultural direction: as in the other early international novels, Duncan judges from the viewpoint of a Canadian and finds the two other cultures wanting.

Duncan expresses the Canadian viewpoint in the novel which deals centrally with Canadian nationality, ***Cousin Cinderella.*** In this work, as well as in her journalism, Duncan presents her view that Canada is a philosophical middle path between the extremes of freedom and tradition represented respectively by the United States and England, capable of judging the two and bringing their respective strengths into harmony. Canadian nationality is the implied norm from which she judges Britain and the United States. In her approach, Duncan agrees with the views of many of her imperialist contemporaries. Canadian imperialists were centrally concerned, according to Carl Berger [in *The Sense of Power,* 1970], with criticism of the political thought and reality of Britain and the United States; moreover, such criticism was not "primarily a fretful, sterile and rootless phenomenon." Duncan's imperialist contemporaries attempted to define Canada as "stable, ordered and destined to become a great imperial power" by examining and criticizing the negative aspects of Britain and the United States.

Canadian criticism of the United States centred on its Constitution. Many Canadians felt that equality, unrestrained freedom and individualism were not legitimately ruling forces in human nature, and thus were not a stable base for a community. This view held that political corruption in the United States government during the 1870s and 1880s, the accompanying violent labour/management confrontations, and the social evils resulting from industrialization and rapid urbanization were a direct result of the inferior United States Constitution. Berger sums up the Canadian attitude:

> [Americans] could not have social organization because they espoused an unworkable theory of society. Rejecting the binding force of convention and the legacies of the past, possessing no secure anchor in human nature, lacking a sense of social obligation and bereft of all principle except money-making, American society stood as a living proof . . . that men cannot adopt a constitution any more than they can adopt a father.

Canadian imperialists considered the British Constitution superior to all others. The British mix of representative democracy and aristocracy, and of written and unwritten laws seemed to combine the best elements of government in a flexible way. In the Canadian view, however, British practice was not consistent with that fundamental political flexibility. Canadians emphatically criticized the "rigid class structure of England" and avowed, in contrast, that "Canadians did not need any antique code or musty rules from a Herald's office to tell them what to respect." They objected to the free trade policy of the British government which emphasized industrialization and resulted in "the gross slums and wretched poverty of industrial England which brutalised the poor and destroyed for them all the higher spiritual elements of life." Canadians saw the refusal of the British government to take Canadian advice on colonial trade policy and the Canadian fisheries and Alaska boundary disputes as further evidence of British shortsightedness and obtuseness.

For Duncan, as for other Canadians of her time, the social forces of freedom and tradition had to be in balance if there was to be an ideal society. The balance had been disturbed in the English-speaking community by the American Revolution. Britain was cut off from her educated, democratic citizens and from a source of wealth and economic energy, and so became stagnant and conventional. The United States, cut off from the stabilizing effect of British tradition, deteriorated into an individualistic society obsessed with money-making, having scant regard for the poor and no conception of social justice. Canada received the salutary influences of British tradition and American freedom, and discovered that these principles were not essentially in opposition; rather, for Canadians they became the complementary principles necessary in an ideal society. In Duncan's novels, evolving Canada is that ideal society which reconciles freedom and tradition.

Duncan's assessment of British, American and Canadian nationalities surfaces first in her journalism. In her columns for *The Week*, she interpreted Canadian literary culture as a complex synthesis of elements from both British and American sources. She was wary of American cultural influence, which came across the border in a deluge of books, newspapers and magazines. She worried that American influence would stifle original method and content in Canadian writing:

> It is not the taste or the literary culture implied in the fact, but the fact itself which is pertinent to our argument. Once Canadian minds are thoroughly impregnated with American matter, American methods, in their own work, will not be hard to trace.

Duncan does not argue that American taste is defective. Most critics acknowledge her admiration for the work of Henry James and W. D. Howells. But she does argue strongly that the Canadian way is not the American way. She is equally hostile to the British presence in Canadian literary endeavour, and draws a sharp line between the previous generation of colonial writers and the current generation of Canadian-born authors. Of the previous generation, she writes:

> Their ideals were British, their methods were British, their markets were chiefly British, and they are mostly gathered to their British fathers, leaving the work to descendants, whose present, and not whose past, country is the actual, potential fact in their national life. There is a wide difference, though comparatively few years span it, between a colonial and a Canadian. . . .

Duncan rejects the United States and Britain as determining forces in Canadian culture, choosing to see both as formative influences. "There is no use endeavouring to disguise our complexity," she writes, for Canadians are not "a simple unit with a single purpose." She remarks that "candour compels us to admit the ramifications that history and geography have conspired to bring about in us," and goes on to explain, for the benefit of our southern neighbours, that we are not ashamed of our British heritage. Canadians choose to maintain the British connection while rejoicing in their freedom, with the confidence that English ways "can never become indigenous."

In Duncan's novels, an American spirit of freedom and a British respect for tradition are united in Canadian society and Canadian individuals. For Duncan, Canadian society satisfies the two important needs in political man: the need for self-government, and the need to look up to an ideal example. With these two important principles firmly embedded, the nation has the capacity to move to material prosperity without giving up the humanistic goals of charity, political stability, and universal education.

G. M. Grant and George Parkin, two of Canada's most important imperialist thinkers and Duncan's contemporaries, agree that the distinguishing element of Canada is the reconciliation and harmonizing of the republican and monarchial tendencies. "In many ways Canada holds a curious middle position in political thought between Great Britain and the United States," Parkin writes in *The Great Dominion*. "In framing her system, Canada took many hints from the United States." However, "in the practical work of government the United States might well take lessons from Canada," he adds, citing political corruption, partisan organization of the Civil Service, and regional marriage laws as instances of the contemporary failure of United States republican government. He praises Canada's adoption of the American federal system, "in harmony with British institutions," expressing the hope that federalism will become a model for the Empire.

Grant believes that good government "consists in the union of two truths that are contrary but not contradictory." He criticizes the United States because it is based only on his first truth,

> That the people are the ultimate fountain of all power. . . . In consequence, all appeals are made to that which is lowest in our nature, for such appeals are made to the greatest number and are most likely to be immediately successful. The character of public men and the national character deteriorate. Neither elevation of sentiment, nor refinement of manners is cultivated. Still more fatal consequences, the very ark of the nation is carried periodically into heady fights; for the time being, the citizen has no country; he has only his party, and the unity of the country is constantly imperilled.

According to Grant [in *Ocean to Ocean,* 1925], the will of the people must be countered by a second truth, "That Government is of God, and should be strong, stable and above the people. . . . " These two truths are perfectly balanced in the British Constitution, he states, and for that reason are balanced in Canadian government.

Canadian imperialists felt that Canada's reconciliation of freedom and tradition gave the nation an international role. For Grant, Canada's duty is to "make this world the home of freedom, of justice and of peace" by forming a living link between the powerful and often belligerent countries, Britain and the United States, as an initial step toward the spiritual unification of all peoples. Both Grant and George Parkin subscribed to the "popular creed of Idealism" of their time that has been analysed by Terry Cook [in *Journal of Canadian Studies* X, No. 3 (1975)]. The creed held that human beings are not merely material creatures, but aspects of a unified, ideal spirit which is akin to God and which opposes "materialism, secularism and anarchic individualism." For Duncan, Canada stood forth as the first nation to approximate the realization of idealist aims by reconciling material prosperity with Christian social and spiritual values. Canada could thus contribute to the spiritual unity of mankind by promoting peaceful cooperation among nations through the mechanism of the Empire. It could show other nations the way to spiritual self-improvement by reconciling the forces of freedom and tradition.

Duncan's first four international novels reflect this Canadian judgement of the United States and Britain. Duncan shows the ease with which Americans give up their supposed democratic views and adopt a system of entrenched privilege when it flatters their own egos. Americans lack a sense of social obligation in Duncan's novels and promote individualism in its place. In ***A Daughter of Today*** the two poles of freedom and tradition are represented as United States' egoism faces strict and artificial standards in British society. Britain is dominated by contrived formulas which stifle intuition and make communication difficult. The author invites the reader, by her exposure of the characteristics of the two nations, to reject both, and embrace the implied Canadian alternative which she eventually dramatizes in ***Cousin Cinderella***.

. . . . .

An American Girl in London is the story of Mamie Wick, an American heiress who goes to London hoping to gain an understanding of British culture. She is recognized as a typical American girl by Lady Torquillin and her nephew, Charles Mafferton, who is seeking an American heiress to marry. Mafferton arranges for Mamie to visit most of the tourist attractions of London and escorts her through London society. After her presentation at court, Mamie is forced to leave Britain because of the scandal created when she refuses Mafferton's offer of marriage.

An incomplete reading of Mamie's character has caused misinterpretation of Duncan's purpose in writing the novel. Thomas Tausky interprets Mamie as a literary derivative of W. D. Howells' Kitty Ellison in *A Chance Acquaintance* and sums up the correspondences he finds:

> Both are innocent, in the sense of having a limited experience of life, yet shrewd and observant. Both seek out an older civilization (in Kitty's case Quebec, in Mamie's case London) and they react in similar ways, rejecting what they take to be snobbishness and arrogance but feeling attracted to the romance inherent in charming traditions. Both record their impressions in an engaging, flippant style.

There is no doubt that Mamie resembles Kitty, and that the novel is influenced by Howells. But Kitty is an idealization of American womanhood, while Mamie is a parody of it. The snobbishness Kitty reacts against is the snobbishness of a Bostonian man who woos her; and her rejection of his life is an affirmation of her American self-image. Mamie parodies the American self-image, revelling in British elitism while insisting that her "democratic principles are just the same as ever." She voices Duncan's own criticism of British society, but her egoism, cultural blindness and acceptance of the rigid British class system are self-condemning and permit Duncan to make a strong criticism of the roots of action in United States society.

In Duncan's novels, an American spirit of freedom and a British respect for tradition are united in Canadian society and Canadian individuals. For Duncan, Canadian society satisfies the two important needs in political man: the need for self-government, and the need to look up to an ideal example.

—Misao Dean

Mamie arrives in London with the conviction that the British mix of political equality and elitism is inferior to American equality, but she leaves with that conviction shaken. While riding on the top of a double decker bus, she begins to enjoy looking down on others, and "to understand the agreeableness of class distinctions." She admits that Americans find the elitism of British society very attractive, even though she discovers that American ideals of equality are not universally applicable, as she thought they were, but seem confined only to her little bit of the United States: "Americans coming over here with all their social theories in their trunks, so to speak . . . very seldom seem to find a use for them in England." She discovers that her own standards, which she believes are based on freedom, the most true and important fact of human existence, are not fully shared by mankind. Instead, she begins to see that the pageantry of the monarchy and the elevation of the aristocracy in England "encourages sentiment, and is valuable on that account."

Mamie's acceptance of British elitism is based not only on her observation of the workings of society, but on a trait which Duncan implies is culturally acquired: egoism. Mamie was raised in a nation founded on the "good-as-you feeling carried into politics"; in England she discovers that she can be set on a level with people who seem much higher than her friends in the United States. She appreciates the class structure because it places her on its highest pinnacle. Mamie's presentation at court is the most striking example of the way her egoism affects her principles. The elaborate and strictly regulated preparation of a gown and hairstyle suitable for the occasion give her an exalted sense of self-importance. She describes her appearance as she steps into the carriage that will take her to the palace: "I was wearing, as well as a beautiful sweeping gown, a lofty and complete set of monarchical prejudices . . . I was too much fascinated by my outward self." Mamie is enchanted by the effect which monarchical pageantry has on her own person; she is made to feel important and elegant. When she finally is called forward to curtsy to the Queen, her adoption of England is complete: "*Did*n't you believe in queens, Miss Mamie Wick, at that moment? I'm very much afraid you did."

Duncan does not criticize Mamie for giving up her democratic principles. She implies that Mamie's conversion to monarchy is a predictable phenomenon, one which is overwhelmingly appropriate given the experience of a presentation at court. Mamie is quite rightly overwhelmed by the ideal represented by the monarch. In comparison, American presidents "didn't look like anything." Her continued defense of equality is, thus, in complete conflict with her actions and points out the essential contradiction Duncan senses in American social identity.

Mamie's relationship with Charlie Mafferton is the initial clue to the fact that Mamie's pronouncements are not always to be taken seriously. Despite numerous hints in the text which communicate to the reader that Charlie Mafferton considers he is almost engaged to Mamie, she seems to consider his special attentions as simply hospitality. Mafferton takes pains to explain his family situation to Mamie, and his aunt, Lady Torquillin, arranges for Mamie to live with her. Mafferton escorts Mamie to various tourist attractions and engages in the sort of bantering conversation which would seem to be reserved for acknowledged lovers. Mafferton's family expresses great interest in meeting her, and in fact Mamie realizes Mafferton's intention only when she is introduced to his father. Until then she believed her position as an American entitled her to such special treatment.

Mamie's misinterpretation of Mafferton is based, in part, on the fact that in the United States his attentions would not have seemed remarkable. Mamie repeatedly compares him to Mr. Winterhazel, a young American man who corresponds with her and escorts her in the evenings without benefit of a chaperone. Mamie simply assumes that, like Winterhazel, Mafferton has no intentions of proposing marriage and simply enjoys her company. Mamie's misinterpretation of Mafferton is based on her assumption that American standards of social conduct are universal.

Duncan's criticism of Mamie is transferable to the United States as a whole because Mamie is intended to represent the typical product of American society. Her family rose from obscurity by fulfilling the American dream of making a business fortune. Her father, who manufactures baking powder, remarks that "it is to baking powder that we owe everything," pointing out that honest, Christian charity and hard work are not necessary in the United States—the rising effect of baking powder alone is responsible for his success. Mamie presents herself from the outset of the novel as a typical American girl attempting to set right a few popular misconceptions: "It has occurred to me that, since so much is to be said about the American Girl, it might be permissible for her to say some of it herself." Lady Torquillin confirms that she is everything the British expect of an American girl: "This is an independent American young lady—the very person I went especially to the United States to see. . . . " Other aspects of Mamie's background which make her typical of fictional American girls of the period include her father's intention to run for the American Senate, and Mamie's instinctive, practical business sense.

The Preface to the American edition denies that Mamie is a typical American girl. Supposedly written by Mamie, it states that "while it is unreasonable to apologize for being only one kind of American girl, I do not pretend to represent the ideas of any more." However, the Preface was included in the New York edition only, and may have been added by an editor. Perhaps Duncan's publisher was attempting to forestall critical condemnation in the United States with a clear and strategic statement. However, the rest of the novel gives sufficient evidence to warrant presentation of Mamie as representative of the United States and to transfer Duncan's criticisms of Mamie to the country as a whole.

Mamie's judgements of British society closely resemble those of Duncan's Canadian contemporaries. She finds a great deal of poverty in London, and is repelled by the tired conventions which seem to govern individual lives. She is introduced to London by a newspaper column of want-ads which disclose its large number of financially embarrassed or poverty stricken citizens:

> 'A young subaltern, of excellent family, in unfortunate circumstances, implores the loan of a hundred pounds to save him from ruin. Address, care of his solicitors.'
>
> We have nothing like this in America. It was a revelation to me—a most private and intimate revelation of a social body that I had always been told no outsider could look into without the very best introductions. Of course, there was the

> veil of . . . the solicitors' address, but that was as thin and easily torn as the "Morning Post," and much more transparent, showing all the struggling mass, with its hands outstretched, on the other side.

The creeping poverty of the British upper classes is brought home more forcibly to Mamie when she encounters Lady Bandobust, an impoverished aristocrat who is in the business of arranging marriages between commercial money and old families. She tells Mamie that entry into almost any level of British society can be had for money.

The inflexibility of British society is represented by Charles Mafferton. His stodgy manner constantly frustrates Mamie's desires for new experiences: "It took very little acquaintance with Mr. Mafferton to know that, if he had never seen it done, he would never do it." Mafferton clings to his preconceptions concerning Americans (mostly gained from reading American novels) and refuses to modify those ideas even when faced with an actual American. Mamie is dismayed by his British inability to recognize a joke which focusses on his own shortcomings: "You are never in the least amused at yourselves," she tells him.

The Bangley Coffin family illustrates the British tendency to live according to social convention. The parents and the two Misses Bangley Coffin invite Mamie to accompany then to Ascot, where they are unable to secure lunch in socially acceptable surroundings and reluctantly allow themselves to be taken to a restaurant. Mamie is frustrated by the fact that they would beg for an invitation to an Ascot box rather than simply buy their own lunch, even though the cost is unimportant. Mamie finds the Misses Bangley Coffin completely dominated by their mother, and she feels that their individual personalities are lost behind their fantastic "Ascot frocks." She remarks that their entire lives are governed by unwritten rules and conventions:

> The Bangley Coffins were all form. Form, for them, regulated existence. It was the all-compelling law of the spheres, the test of all human action and desire. 'Good form' was the ultimate expression of their respect, 'bad form' their final declaration of contempt. Perhaps I should misjudge the Bangley Coffins if I said form was their conscience, and I don't want to misjudge them—they were very pleasant to me. But I don't think they would have cared to risk their eternal salvation upon any religious tenets that were not entirely *comme il faut*. . . .

The Bangley Coffins are not only stifled by rules; they are immoral in the sense that they allow fashion to dictate such important matters as their religious principles. Duncan shows her judgement of such persons by giving them a name which comically suggests physical death, the lid banging on a coffin.

Duncan continues to explore American and British personality in ***A Voyage of Consolation,*** the sequel to ***An American Girl in London***. The focus of the irony shifts from Mamie to her father, Senator Joshua P. Wick, who tends to judge everything by standards governed by "the perfection of enlightenment found in Chicago." Senator Wick believes that all men are equal, but his manner and his social position contradict that belief. Accustomed to servants who resent their position and who make him feel less like the privileged wealthy man he knows himself to be, he is surprised and offended by the servility of the lower classes in England. A servant who acts like one makes him feel guilty:

> He said he was glad to leave England, it was demoralizing to live there; you lost your sense of the dignity of labour, and in the course of time were bound to degenerate into a swell. He expressed a good deal of sympathy with the aristocracy on this account, concentrating his indignation upon those who, as it were, made aristocrats out of innocent human beings against their will.

Mamie's British "relation," Mrs. Portheris, her daughter Isabel, and Mr. Mafferton reappear exhibiting the same stuffy conventionality which is the dominant British trait in ***An American Girl***. Europeans who appear in the novel are slickly polite and well versed in all the arts necessary for removing money from American pockets. Neither the British nor the Europeans are very sympathetically portrayed.

In ***An American Girl in London*** and ***A Voyage of Consolation,*** Duncan characterizes Americans as egotistical and naturally inclined toward rigid class distinctions, the British as ruled by convention and artificial standards of morality. Excessive personal freedom is the weakness of American personality, while inflexible adherence to tradition enslaves British personality. The novel implies a standard of judgement which is a mean between the two—the possibilities of Canadian nationality.

A Daughter of Today explores the serious moral consequences that result from the emphasis on individual freedom in the United States. Elfrida Bell, the heroine, is an undisciplined, self-confessed egoist who recognizes none of the conventions of society. Encouraged as a child to think of herself as an artist, and to think of art as the expression of individual personality, her self-image has grown to dwarf her legitimate artistic talent. The egalitarianism of the United States is evident in Elfrida's feeling that she is equal to the best artists of her day, and thus superior to her contemporaries.

Elfrida goes to France to study painting, but when she meets with obstacles in Paris she gives up visual art for a career in journalism in London. While in London she socializes with her artist friend John Kendall, and accepts as her literary mentor the cold and distant Janet Cardiff. Kendall and Cardiff are alternatively attracted and repelled by their unconventional friend, but tend to excuse her on the grounds of her national background rather than to confront her with their criticisms. Elfrida is personally destroyed when she encounters a reflection of her amorality and egoism in a portrait of herself by John Kendall. Her response is to commit suicide.

Elfrida's egoism begins with childish vanity, but grows into a conception of artistic personality. While in Paris she takes to wearing a remarkable cloak which is very becoming: it "suited her so extremely well that artistic considerations compelled her to wear it occasionally, I fear, when other people would have found it uncomfortably warm." Elfrida's extravagance in dress is, for her, an artistic tent. In the United States, her artistic impulses had the function of "tacit exhibition of her superiority to Sparta [her hometown]," rather than the creation of any serious work. She tells John Kendall, "my egotism is like a little flame within me. All the best things feed it, and it is so clear that I can see everything in its light." All of Elfrida's ideas and judgements are formed in relation to the enhancement of her own ego.

Elfrida's subordination of moral principle to the satisfaction of her ego results in false judgements about sexual morality. She can accept her friend Nadie's liaison with a fellow art student because she feels that an artist should have liaisons. Elfrida judges her friend Golightly Ticke to be "of the elect" (despite his dependence on the favours of a popular actress) simply because he maintains the same posture of artistic suffering which she exalts. Elfrida's own relationship with Lawrence Cardiff, in which she calculatingly tantalizes him with favours but refuses to make a commitment either sexually or in terms of a conventional marriage, is immoral because insensitive on her part and violently painful to Cardiff. In each of these cases, Elfrida's assessment of herself as free from convention and uniquely superior to others is her governing principle.

Elfrida's art suffers from her egoism. In Paris, her teacher Lucien remarks that her work is inferior to Nadie's because she cannot subordinate her femininity and her ideas to the demands of the subject material. Her rejected journalism consists of personal impressions and idiosyncratic theories which suffer from her lack of moral judgement and position. Her editor explains that "their public wouldn't stand *unions libres* when not served up with moral purpose—that no artistic apology for them would do." Her work is not "designed to please the public of the magazines—in England," Lawrence Cardiff remarks, arguing that England is afraid and ashamed of the American freedom which characterizes Elfrida's journalistic style. Elfrida's British friends emphasize her American origin in order to explain her character and help ease her failures. John Kendall explains his compromising behaviour with Elfrida by saying that she is "from America." Janet Cardiff begins to introduce Elfrida to George Jasper as her American friend, but quickly corrects herself by saying "my very great friend." Kendall and Janet are not sympathetically portrayed; in a sense they manipulate Elfrida's reputation to protect their own. But clearly Americanness is a determining factor in their view of her and, consequently, in the reader's view.

Elfrida offers her work to the British public but does not realize that Britain is a closed, conventional society. Ashamed of her American background, she believes success in England is superior to success at home. Lawrence Cardiff's remark implies that while Elfrida will never "please the public" in England, her methods and attitudes might be perfectly acceptable to an American audience. Her great mistake is her assumption that Britain is somehow superior to the United States; Duncan shows through the characters of Kendall and Janet Cardiff that it is not.

John Kendall and Janet Cardiff are destroyed by their Britishness just as Elfrida is destroyed by her Americanness. Like Elfrida, Janet and Kendall have real artistic talent, but neither of them can create art without the inspiration that characterizes Elfrida's freedom. Their art is formed upon a structure of control which is arid and lacks intuition and emotional force. Janet is almost ashamed of the impropriety, as she sees it, of her creativity:

> As for [her] own artistic susceptibility. . . . She breathed it, one might say, only occasionally, and with a kind of delicious shame. She was incapable of sharing her caught-up felicity there with anyone, but it was indispensable that she should see it sometimes in the eyes of others less contained, less conscious. . . . Her own nature was practical and managing in its ordinary aspect, and she had a degree of tact that was always interfering with her love of honesty.

Janet is too dominated by the forms of social intercourse to be a complete artist in herself; she needs the refreshing influence of Elfrida, who reflects Janet's artistic sensibility without threatening her essential "managing" nature. For John Kendall, art is the imposition of controls on the uncontrolled freedom represented by the American girl, and Kendall feels as he paints "a silent, brooding triumph in his manipulation, in his control." Neither Janet nor Kendall recognizes that each needs Elfrida and the freedom she represents in order to become whole. When she is destroyed, their own artistic talent is also destroyed, and they settle into a mediocre middle age.

The only true art in the novel—Kendall's portrait and Janet Cardiff's novel—is created through a conjunction of freedom and convention. The tragedy of the novel is that no character recognizes the essential connectedness between the two seemingly exclusive tendencies. Cardiff and Kendall impose their moral judgement on Elfrida without realizing how they need her; Elfrida rejects their conventionalism and follows her own path without realizing how much she needs a measure of their tact and control. Ironically, after her death Elfrida's sensationalist novel is published successfully by the same firm which handled Janet Cardiff's novel. The moral seems to be that British conventionality is suitable for a British audience, and American freedom for an American one, but that to create great art a mix of the two is necessary.

Duncan thus repeats her serious criticism of British and American personality through her characterization of Kendall, Janet Cardiff, and Elfrida Bell. Moreover, she adds a dimension by employing the language of aesthetics. She shows that the wholeness necessary to produce art of merit requires that the fragmentary personalities interact and influence one another. Kendall reveals Elfrida Bell to herself in his best painting. But she destroys it instead of facing the revelation; and she destroys herself rather than face the disciplines she would have to learn in order to be whole. For their parts, Kendall and Janet Cardiff are moved by the liberating influence Elfrida has upon them. When she is withdrawn they shrivel as artists and as people. The condition of the three characters is examined by the third person narrator who reveals all that the reader must see to know life and to judge the actions of the characters. The narrator is, of course, Sara Jeannette Duncan and she provides the normative point of view, the argument for a reconciliation of qualities that makes wholeness—and indeed greatness—possible.

Those Delightful Americans reverses the formula of Duncan's international novels by employing an ironic narrator from Britain who observes and judges the United States. The tone of the novel is light, the dialogue witty, and the plot, in general, mere entertainment; like ***An American Girl in London, Those Delightful Americans*** is primarily a popular work written to appeal to an audience with few artistic pretentions. Yet a vein of serious comment underlies the obviously popular appeal of the novel, and the surface irony should not blind the reader to the subtext of social criticism. The veil of irony is often a protective garment for the writer who belongs to a marginalized group, and Duncan was marginalized both as colonial and as woman.

The protagonist, Carrie Kemball, is a young British woman who travels to New York with her husband and is hosted by his business acquaintances, both in town and at a summer home outside the city. Carrie is dismayed to discover a new aristocracy in the United States which lacks a sense of social obligation to the poor and politically disenfranchised majority. But Carrie undercuts the strength of her observations by revealing herself to be narrow and governed by social convention.

The Ham family, the Kemball's hosts in the United States, shows the deterioration of American egalitarianism and its replacement with an aristocracy of wealth. The elder Hams grew up in stable New England, surrounded by neighbours they had known from childhood, on an economic level with their friends. The new emphasis on social freedom and the corresponding focus on money-making elevated the Hams above their friends. Carrie discusses the changed life of the Hams:

> ". . . I expect she talked Emerson and Thoreau to Mr. Ham when he was paying her attention—very likely they used to repeat the Psalm of Life together. And now—"
>
> "And now?"
>
> "Now he listens to her worries with the servants and she looks at his beans."

The glorious future of the United States, symbolized by the names of Emerson and Thoreau, has been defeated by the principle of money-making. The Hams' peace of mind is destroyed, and all that remains of Thoreau's dream of peaceful co-existence with nature is Mr. Hams' lonely patch of beans. The second generation of Americans, represented by Violet Ham and her friends Verona and Val, accept their privileged status and make no attempt to bring their own lives in line with egalitarian principles. They have no sense of social obligation, nor do they consider offering help to those below them. Carrie feels guilty when she dines with Val and Verona at an elegant hotel, "enjoying grapes in June and fresh asparagus in December," and is shocked by the fact that her hosts do not: "there we were, every mouthful exposed in the highest light, and there was the shifting, staring multitude outside in the dark, and not one of the 500 diners apparently wished to have it otherwise." Val Ingham confirms that the idea of democractic equality is dead in the United States, referring repeatedly to the difference between "the masses" and "the better class of Americans."

Carrie shows her own moral stance when she seems relieved and almost fascinated by American amorality. Dominated for so long by dusty conventions which have little relation to reality, Carrie sees the United States as an escape: "I hope it does not reflect on one's loyalty, but I had a tremendous feeling of escape for the time being from what one was expected to do into a wide and wonderful region where one could do exactly as one pleased." Carrie's long devotion to tradition has destroyed her independent sense of right and wrong; instead, she only sees the opposition between doing "what one pleases" and doing "what one is expected to do." There is no possibility in her mind that the two could be synonymous, or that morally right action could be separate from both.

Carrie is convinced that she has an open mind, and that the United States deserves a fair consideration from the British. However, she proves herself narrow-minded and arrogant when she meets Mrs. Adams, the wife of her husband's business associate in the United States. Mrs. Adams, Carrie states incredulously, "seemed to think that, because the people of the States thought a thing right and proper, it was right and proper—I mean, just as right and proper as any opposite habit that might prevail in England." Carrie has difficulty grasping that her own standards are not universal, and that any habit which differs from British convention could possibly be "right and proper."

In ***Those Delightful Americans,*** Duncan continues to criticize the United States and Britain from a detached viewpoint in harmony with the ideas of her Canadian contemporaries. The United States is almost proud of the excess of its moral deterioration, and its new ruling class is indifferent to the social obligations imposed by wealth. The British characters, Carrie and Kaye Kemball, return home with their British conventionality intact, and with little understanding of the driving forces which separate their nation from the United States. Both countries seem determined to continue their blunder downwards from the ideal.

. . . . .

For Duncan, as for other Canadians of her time, the process of defining Canada begins with the definition and criticism of Canada's two greatest influences, Britain and the United States. Canada emerges as a *via media,* a middle path between the extreme of freedom and tradition those nations represent. Of course, the idea of reconciling freedom and tradition in an ideal society is not original with Duncan; she was greatly influenced by Matthew Arnold, whose *Culture and Anarchy* seems to have provided a vocabulary for Duncan's discussion of Philistinism and Culture in *The Week.* But Duncan locates the possibility of an ideal social order in Canada—in the farmers of ***The Imperialist*** (1904), who represent the "development between" Britain and the U.S.; in Arthur Youghall of ***His Royal Happiness*** (1914), who politically reconciles Britain and the United States; and in Mary Trent, who discovers Canadian identity in ***Cousin Cinderella***.

Ironically, Mary Trent discovers her own country while on a visit to London, England in company with her brother Graham. Up until that time Mary has experienced life as a child, daughter and sister; in England she takes upon herself the role of observer while Graham becomes involved in social and political issues. Like Canada, Duncan seems to suggest, Mary has ordinarily felt herself to have little identity beyond that given her by parental association and material wealth, and so she has been content to be directed by others. But in London Mary's view of herself and her country changes. She is invited to become a naturalized Briton by allowing herself to be moulded by British social standards. She watches her brother change under the influence of London, and discovers that he loses more than he gains when he forsakes his Canadian nationality. Mary discovers her Canadian identity together with her personal role in life; she fulfills both when she marries Lord Peter Doleford, the Prince Charming of the novel.

While Mary comes to understand her nationality through inaction, Graham Trent is crippled by his ability to act. His actions almost bring about the loss of his identity, and stimulate Mary to a recognition of her own. Graham feels a "mission to bring the morality of the 'true north strong and free' . . . as well as its practical benefits, in terms of natural and financial resources, to the preservation of Britain." He feels himself to be the bearer of something infinitely precious and important to the history of the world, and becomes bitter and sarcastic when rebuffed. He attempts to find the appropriate method of bringing his wealth to the aid of Britain, and explores the alternatives of collecting antiques, salvaging manuscripts, and contributing to research. He eventually determines to save the ancestral home of the Pavisay family from the auction block by marrying the daughter, Lady Barbara. In doing so, Graham discovers that he must give up his distinctive Canadian identity and become an English Country Gentleman. Graham attempts to be absorbed by Britain, but he finds the task difficult. His decision to bury himself in British identity is not in keeping with his Canadian sense of independence and makes him unhappy. His ability to take the lead, to act, prevents him from seeing that he is not taking the appropriate path, and Mary remarks that "it is not wonderful that you have trouble with your heart."

From Graham's experience, Mary learns that Canada partakes of freedom and independence as well as British tradition. Graham cannot be happy in a union which subjugates his birthright of Canadian freedom to the authority of convention. Mary discovers, moreover, that her Canadian nationality gives her a distinctive understanding of the balance between tradition and freedom, as well as a responsibility to help other nations of the Empire. Her union with Peter Doleford, based upon love and equality, represents the fulfillment of both her personal and national identity.

Mary Trent discovers her own autonomy and her Canadian identity in two moments of extraordinary clarity. The first takes place when she is riding in Mrs. Jarvis' electric car, and realizes that she is being offered an active role in the trans-Atlantic dream. Mrs. Jarvis has a son, Billy Milliken, whom she would like to settle in life; Mary and her money seem to be the ideal anchor for the empty-headed Billy. Mary realizes that she has something London wants, or perhaps needs; she loses her awe of London, and gains a sense of independence:

> It is the kind of thing one is ashamed to write, but I must confess that I drew from Mrs. Jarvis at this moment the definite thrill of a new perception, something captivating and delicious. Suddenly, without Graham, without anybody, moving through the lovely, thronged, wet, lamplit London streets in Mrs. Jarvis's electric brougham, I felt myself realised—realised in London, not only by the person who happened to be near me, but in a vague, delightful, potential sense, by London. Realised, not a bit for what I was—that wouldn't, I am afraid, have carried me very far—nor exactly for what I represented, but for something else, for what I might, under favourable circumstances, be made to represent.

Mary's moment of self-discovery is not egotistical—she does not feel that her essential essence has been recognized and rewarded—but that her independence has been given to her. Her dowry allows her to dictate the terms of a marriage, and the "solicitation" of London makes her realize that she, like Canada, can use her wealth to a purpose. Her mere existence, as a woman with a dowry, gives her the power to act, as it gives Canada the basis for power in international affairs.

Mary also realizes that she can have London, if she wants it. As a colonial, she has no history, as a girl from the manufacturing north would have a history; she can be part of the aristocracy if she chooses. Mary states that she is accepted for "what I might, under favourable circumstances, be made to represent": "I was only a possibility, a raw product, to be melted or hammered or woven into London, by my leave." Mary understands that she needs only give leave in order to be accepted as part of the new aristocracy, one of the "geographical anomalies" who become Canadian Lords and MPs. From her new perspective, Mary feels it is possible to know a "divine disdain of London" and senses that she has the power to make a choice, once and for all, whether or not she wants to become more than just a colonial, whether she wants to become a Briton. When Billy Milliken finally proposes, Mary refuses to marry him. By then she has discovered both that she does not want to be a Briton and what makes her own nationality unique.

Mary begins to understand what Canada is when she contemplates her brother's decision to marry Barbara Pavisay. Mrs. Jarvis introduces the key idea when she dismisses Canada as an element of Graham's character which is a minimal influence and easily erased:

> "Colonial he certainly is, but only to the extent of a few mannerisms, which he would soon lose.

> Try to think of him as a country gentleman in England, and he's quite in the picture, isn't he?"

Mary begins to wonder if Canadian nationality is simply a few mannerisms, and she concludes that it is more. She discovers that Graham would give up more than he would gain by adopting the manners and the standards of judgment which characterize his British counterparts. She experiences her second moment of clear understanding when she watches Graham walking along the railway platform at Lady Lippington's departure for Canada:

> He, Graham, was more free than they, more free of a thousand things—traditions and conventions and responsibilities, privileges and commandments, interests and bores, advantages and disadvantages and fearful indispensable sign-manuals. That was the great thing that was published in him as he went swinging up and down the platform with the other man; and surely it was something as precious in its way, I reasoned, as any opportunity or any possession, something which gave even Pavis Court one aspect of a mess of pottage.

Graham's birthright of freedom is just as important as his birthright of tradition, and Mary realizes that she, too, has not only the power to act autonomously, but that she has a heritage of values to guide her actions. Her nationality is built on the balance between freedom and tradition, on a revitalized British ideal, the median point between the present excesses of American immoral adaptability and British insensitivity and commercialism.

Mary's discovery of her own identity does not shut her off from her community, but rather underlines her responsibility to it, and in this Mary demonstrates Duncan's idealization of Canadian identity. Mary discovers herself in the context of the ties of family, of society, and of nation; she has no desire, indeed no need, to free herself from the rules and responsibilities imposed by those ties. Duncan shows that the essential difference between Canadians and their British and American counterparts is the ability of Canadians to express themselves as individuals within the structure of society. Evelyn Dicey, the American, is indifferent to that structure; Barbara Pavisay, her opposite, will never know herself as an individual. But Mary can reconcile her personal goal of marriage to the man she loves with the community will to save Pavis Court and to strengthen the bond of filial love between Canada and Britain.

Duncan's initial project in her fiction, the definition and criticism of Britain and the United States, is thus clearly related to her attempt to articulate Canadian nationality. The early rejection of the possibilities offered by Britain and the United States in the early international novels implies the context of a third standard, Canada, and this context radically informs all her work. For Duncan, Canada continues to strive toward the ideal, offering a basis for social reform in the balance of freedom and tradition which is her unique heritage.

Elizabeth Morton (essay date 1986)

SOURCE: "Religion in Elgin: A Re-evaluation of the Subplot of *The Imperialist* by Sara Jeannette Duncan," in *Studies in Canadian Literature,* Vol. 2, No. 1, 1986, pp. 99-107.

[*In the following essay, Morton examines the romantic subplot of* The Imperialist *in terms of opposing religious concepts that parallel those of the political struggle in the novel's main plot.*]

Lack of unity in the plot of ***The Imperialist*** has generally been explained in terms of character and theme—either the theme of idealism or the theme of love. Carole Gerson has pointed out [in *Canadian Literature* No. 63 (1975)]: "While the overt subject of ***The Imperialist*** is indeed imperialism, the novel's deeper structural unity derives from its focus on idealism." And Clara Thomas has suggested [in *Journal of Canadian Studies* 12, No. 2 (1977)]:

> Parallel to this "politics of politics" theme, Duncan set a "politics of love" motif, concerning the love of Lorne for Dora Milburn, a superficial self-centered flirt, and of his sister Advena for Hugh Finlay, a Scotch Presbyterian minister and immigrant to Elgin and a man of ideals and ethics as lofty on a personal level as are Lorne's on an international scale.

While both love and idealism are important elements of the structure of ***The Imperialist,*** there is a third way in which the two plots are united in the portrait of Elgin. The political burden of the main plot is complemented by a discussion of the other preoccupation in Elgin—religion.

The infusion of love and idealism into the subplot clouds the religious perspective, but the purpose of the subplot is nevertheless to provide a view of religion in Elgin, just as the main plot gives Duncan's understanding of politics in South Fox. If the religious theme is kept in mind, the complexity of the social vision embodied in the novel becomes evident, and the parallels between Lorne and Advena are seen to be not fortuitous, but, rather, Duncan's exploration of the way in which the idealist responds to a world epitomized by Mr. Milburn's "averages, balances, the safe level." Both Lorne and Advena have a tendency to adopt extreme positions, and the dynamics of the novel involve a resolution of these extremes in favour of a balance between idealism and pragmatism.

Evidence of the importance of religion in Elgin and a justification of the designation of religion as the primary theme of the subplot are found in Chapter VII, where the narrator states: "The town of Elgin thus knew two controlling interests—the interest of politics and the interest of religion," and she elaborates:

> In wholesome fear of mistake, one would hesitate to put church matters either before or after politics among the preoccupations of Elgin. It would be safer and more indisputable to say that nothing compared with religion but politics, and nothing compared with politics but religion.

Given this understanding of Elgin's social dynamics, it seems unlikely that Duncan would not include a treatment of religion as a corollary to the discussion of politics included in the main plot. Just as politics is filtered through the idealism of Lorne and the practical manoeuvering of Bingham and Williams, so religion is filtered through the idealism of Advena and Finlay and the balancing pragmatism of Dr. Drummond.

A distinction must be made between religion as social institution and religion as embodiment of emotional faith, for it is as an institution that the church is apprehended in Elgin. The narrator reveals how important the social function of the church is and how the average inhabitant of Elgin relates to the church:

> In Elgin religious fervour was not beautiful, or dramatic, or self-immolating; it was reasonable. . . . The habit of church attendance was not only a basis of respectability, but practically the only one: a person who was "never known to put his head inside a church door" could not be more severely reprobated, by Mrs Murchison at all events. It was the normal thing, the thing which formed the backbone of life, sustaining to the serious, impressive to the light, indispensable to the rest, and the thing that was more than any of these, which you can only know when you stand in the churches among the congregations. Within its prescribed limitation it was for many the intellectual exercise, for more the emotional lift, and for all the unfailing distraction of the week.

Church membership is largely responsible for one's sense of identity and feeling of community: members look after their own, and Dr. Drummond sets the example by buying within the congregation at Murchison's. Furthermore, courting is carried on through church attendance, a custom which accounts for the absence of young men from evening services, although, ironically, it is the wife who worships with the husband. The social functions of religion demonstrate the way in which the demands of society dictate matters of faith; in a similar manner Dr. Drummond's pastoral visit to the Murchisons is treated by Mrs. Murchison as a social rather than a religious occasion. People in Elgin tend to be reticent about their faith and beliefs, and the conversation over tea centres instead on the Ormiston case. As the narrator explains,

> It is not given to all of us to receive or to extend the communion of the saints: Mr and Mrs Murchison were indubitably of the elect, but he was singularly close-mouthed about it, and she had an extraordinary way of seeing the humorous side—altogether it was paralysing, and the conversation would wonderfully soon slip around to some robust secular subject, public or domestic.

Dr. Drummond himself epitomizes some of the more worldly preoccupations of the church and its members in his annual anniversary sermons, where he reviews the number of members, and in the conflict with East Elgin, where only the certain defection of Presbyterians to the nearby Methodist chapel produces reform. The intertwining of secular interests and religion is most evident in the concern over politics in the sermon and is also reflected in Dr. Drummond's regular prayer for the Royal Family, the General Assembly of the Church of Scotland, and the British Prime Minister. If the Murchisons are reserved about the spiritual aspects of their religion, they nevertheless represent all that Dr. Drummond expects from his congregation, for he recognizes in Mr. Murchison one of the "future elders and office-bearers of the congregation, a man who would be punctual with his pew rent, sage in his judgements, and whose views upon church attendance would be extended to his family."

The family's disappointment at the loss of Abby to the Episcopalians and Mrs. Murchison's own code regarding church attendance are demonstrated in the following exchange with Abby:

> "Well, what I want to know is," said Mrs Murchison, "whether you are coming to the church you were born and brought up in, Abby, or not, tonight? There's the first bell."
>
> "I'm not going to any church," said Abby. "I went this morning. I'm going home to my baby."
>
> "Your father and mother," said Mrs Murchison, "can go twice a day, and be none the worse for it."

One gets a clear sense of Mrs. Murchison's talents and accomplishments as a homemaker and of her adherence to the outward forms of her religion, but the exact nature of her faith and belief is not open to inspection, and in this respect she seems to be representative of Elgin's approach to religion.

It is therefore clear why Advena and, to some extent, Finlay seem out of place in this society and within this religious framework. Duncan makes it clear from the beginning that Advena and her brother Lorne are imaginative and idealistic: their response to the Independent Order of Foresters in the Victoria Day parade is emotional and symbolic, reflecting the questioning attitude Lorne will later assume toward politics and the way in which Advena will regard religious matters. Based on an emotional commitment similar to a vision or a communion in which "his country came subjectively into his possession," Lorne finds an outlet for his idealism and becomes a prophet for a new Canada at the centre of a revitalized Empire.

Advena, however, has no such opportunities or encouragement, and her excursions into the outside world extend as far as "taking the university course for women at Toronto, and afterward teaching the English branches to the junior forms in the Collegiate Institute." According to her mother, Advena had never demonstrated the talents appropriate for a girl, and, as a result, she functions in society as an exile, by withdrawing from the circles in which she cannot be useful. The litany of her failures—unable to make her bed properly, always with a book in her hand, pouring cupfuls of soap suds to see the foam rise while washing dishes, wanting her mother to adopt a papoose, refusing to take piano lessons, reading novels, canoeing at six o'clock in the morning and walking "in the rain of windy October twilights"—is epitomized in the condemnation that no man had ever come to court her.

Advena's adoption of a philosophical attitude is justified by Mrs. Murchison's opinion of the value and opportunities of a single woman like Advena: " 'I don't deny the girl's talented in her own way, but it's no way to marry on. She'd much better make up her mind just to be a happy, independent old maid; any woman might do worse. And take no responsibilities.' " This assumption that the single woman can barely justify her existence leads Advena to withdraw from the society in which she, unlike Lorne, can take no active part, and she embraces a stoic asceticism. Her retreat from the physical world into the realm she has always occupied as a dreamer is appropriate, because within its limitations her intellectual capabilities, unsuited to a wife and mother (according to Elgin's definition), are validated, and her differences from Abby, Stella, and Dora Milburn become positive rather than negative ones.

The narrator describes Elgin as a centre in which "The arts conspired to be absent; letters resided at the nearest university; science was imported as required, in practical improvements"—a small town partaking somewhat "of the ferocious, of the inflexible, of the unintelligent." In this kind of atmosphere, it is not surprising that Advena has no legitimate role, except as a teacher. But, sending "up her little curl of reflection in a safe place," she continues her reading and becomes a devotee of Browning.

Her reading of Browning's most obscure work, *Sordello,* a work considered by the Victorians to be badly written and incomprehensible, indicates the degree to which Advena lives outside the standard intellectual pursuits of Elgin and reveals her interests in writers who were also questioning those things "go-ahead" Elgin takes for granted. Her "queer satisfactions and enthusiasms" also include philosophy and Eastern religion—Buddhism, Yoga, and Plato. It is significant that these philosophies preach the rejection of earthly considerations and physical desire as a means of release from suffering, and it is just this religious model which Advena espouses in her life.

The only individual in Elgin who shares Advena's concerns is the new Presbyterian minister, Finlay, who is described as being a "passionate romantic," "with deep dreams in his eyes," "a man with horizons, lifted lines beyond the common vision, and an eye rapt and a heart intrepid," whom Mrs. Murchison dismisses as " 'A great gawk of a fellow, with eyes that always look as if he were in the middle of next week!' ". He, too, is isolated in Elgin, as Mrs. Murchison derisively comments: " 'He may be able to talk to Advena, but he's no hand at general conversation; I know he finds precious little to say to me. . . . He comes here because, being human, he's got to open his mouth some time or other, I suppose.' "

A brief consideration of Mrs. Murchison's own character and enthusiasms will reveal why Finlay finds little in common with her, and why she finds Advena's talents so useless. She has little patience with her own husband's intellectual pursuits, and no use for books whatsoever: "Mrs Murchison kept a discouraging eye upon such purchases. . . . Mrs Murchison was surrounded indeed by more of 'that sort of thing' than she could find use or excuse for." Her dismissal of Plato and of philosophy reveals her lack of sophistication and narrow horizons: " 'Besides, if I know anything about Plato he was a Greek heathen, and no writer for a Presbyterian minister to go lending around. I'd Plato him to the rightabout if it was me.' " While Mr. Murchison demurs from this criticism, one nevertheless feels that Mrs. Murchison represents the inflexible and unintelligent character of Elgin.

Dr. Drummond, on the other hand, is a figure who, like Mr. Murchison, balances the sentimental and the practical, the imaginative and the prosaic, and both Dr. Drummond and Mr. Murchison function as father-figures in the subplot and main plot respectively. Mr. Murchison's own approach can be seen in discussions with Lorne concerning imperialism: "While the practical half of John Murchison was characteristically alive to the difficulties involved, the sentimental half of him was ready at any time to give out cautious sparks of sympathy with the splendor of Wallingham's scheme." Dr. Drummond assumes a fatherly role when he attempts to dissuade Finlay from honouring his engagement to Christie Cameron, and the narrator notes that Dr. Drummond considered that he was just as responsible as the parents of his congregation for the outcome of their children.

The traditional religious doctrines preached by Dr. Drummond do not reflect the spiritual questioning of Advena and Finlay, just as his library consists, instead, of "standard religious philosophy, standard poets, standard fiction, all that was standard, and nothing that was not." Secure of his position in Elgin, Dr. Drummond is equally secure in his faith and in his place in the church: "Religious doctrine was to him a thing for ever accomplished, to be accepted or rejected as a whole. He taught eternal punishment and retribution, reconciling both with Divine love and mercy." The balancing of opposites so important to him is also evident in his own philosophy: "He was a progressive by his business instinct, in everything but theology, where perhaps his business instinct also operated the other way, in favour of the sure thing."

Dr. Drummond is, therefore, very disturbed by Finlay's misguided idealism and sense of honour regarding Christie Cameron, for Dr. Drummond is progressive in rejecting old world notions of honour, and conservative in proposing that Finlay marry Advena, whose feelings for him and character are a known commodity and therefore a "sure thing." But Finlay rejects Dr. Drummond's advice because he " 'will not be a man who has jilted a woman,' " ironically foreshadowing Christie's jilting of him in favour of Dr. Drummond.

Advena's response to the problem of Finlay's engagement reflects her absorption of the philosophies of renunciation, and she finds in her dilemma the ultimate opportunity to put those teachings into effect. Her idealism becomes fanatically cerebral, as she realizes that the only relationship open to her and Finlay is what Finlay describes as a " 'friendship of ideas,' " and beyond that, " 'a friendship of spirit'." The extremes to which Advena goes set her apart from Elgin and place her in the context of the fervour associated with Oxford, Mecca, and Benares; she has ceased to be reasonable and Presbyterian in the fashion of Dr. Drummond, and has become like a member of the Oxford Movement, a Muslim, or a Hindu. However, this response corresponds to her way of dealing with Elgin's lack of recognition of her talents.

The narrator states that Advena and Finlay "had abandoned the natural demands of their state," but it is Advena, rather than Finlay, who conceives of this ideal and who, apparently, derives the most satisfaction from it. Advena's conscious self-sacrifice is therefore part of a larger context apart from Finlay, for she has been forced to sacrifice many of her talents, since there was no use for them in Elgin, and has, as a result, become virtually useless in Elgin society. Thus Advena's urge for self-sacrifice is linked with her overwhelming desire to be useful in a practical way.

One reads Advena's statements—" 'If I could be of any use I should be very glad to go over them with you,' " " 'I should have liked so much to be of use,' " and " 'I would like to help you in every little way I can' "—made during the brief husband-and-wife tableau in the study in the context of her need to be a useful sacrifice. The narrator emphasizes the corollary nature of this yearning when she states that Advena is "privately all unwilling to give up her martyrdom" and is preoccupied with "the aesthetic ecstasy of self-torture."

Advena dramatizes her vision of the ascetic ideal in her discussion with Finlay. She says, " 'I look forward to the time when this—other feeling of ours will become just an idea, as it is now just an emotion, at which we should try to smile. It is the attitude of the gods'." Moving from Plato to the Yogi's renunciation of the body, she hypothesizes, " 'I look forward to the time . . . when the best that I can give you or you can give me will ride upon a glance,' " and she expresses her fear that the world ultimately sullies all relationships: " 'Isn't there something that appeals to you . . . in the thought of just leaving it, all unsaid, a dear and tender projection upon the future that faded—a lovely thing we turned away from, until it was no longer there?' " Finlay's answer, however, has already been given in his musing, " 'I used to feel more drawn to the ascetic achievement and its rewards . . . than I do now.' "

The theme of usefulness combined with conscious self-sacrifice is continued in Advena's ill-advised visit to Mrs. Kilbannon and Christie Cameron. Once again, Advena

> was there simply to offer himself up, and the impulse of sacrifice seldom considers whether or not it may be understood. . . . to do the normal, natural thing at keen personal cost was to sound that depth, or rise to that height of the spirit where pain sustains. We know of Advena that she was prone to this sort of exaltation.

She repeats to Christie her desire to be useful: " 'And I want you to let me help you about your house, and in every way possible. I am sure I can be of use'." The only things that save Advena from becoming pathetic are her sense of humour and her recognition, at last, that her self-sacrifice is out of all proportion to the situation.

After her discovery that Christie Cameron's affections "might have been in any one of her portmanteaux," Advena gives up her ideal: "now it lay about her; her strenuous heart had pulled it down to foolish ruin." Both she and Finlay have renounced their ideal relationship, but only Advena has been purged of the pride that is at the source of their dilemma; it remains for Dr. Drummond and Christie Cameron to complete the process for Finlay. Dr. Drummond's function in the subplot is to restore the balance between emotion and reason, and he achieves this through his pragmatic solution to Finlay's dilemma regarding Christie Cameron. A pragmatic approach is necessary because Advena and Finlay veer between extremes of the cerebral and emotional, and Dr. Drummond is able to see that their situation requires an infusion of typical Elgin reasonableness.

Living in intellectual and emotional isolation in Elgin, Advena is unable to reconcile her imaginative perspective of the world, which led to her asceticism, with her need to fulfill a useful role, which Elgin defines solely in terms of limited, gender-oriented concepts. The subplot therefore involves the purging of Advena's religious asceticism to allow her to reconcile her intellectual and emotional needs with the role of wife, so that she can become, in the eyes of Elgin, and perhaps in her own eyes, useful.

While the subplot reads like a love story whose purpose is to provide a foil for Lorne's romance with Dora Milburn and a counterpoint to Lorne's emotional idealism, its true function can be seen in the interplay of opposing religious concepts—that of the reasonable, secure, socially-oriented institution exemplified by Dr. Drummond and Mr. and Mrs. Murchison, and the idealistic asceticism espoused by Advena and Finlay. The Liberal party of South Fox rejects Lorne's idealistic dream of Empire in favour of a realist who recognizes the importance of the "chink of hard cash" in Elgin politics, and, in a similar fashion, Dr. Drummond uses his influence to show Advena and Finlay that their proposed self-sacrifice is not only futile but also ridiculous in the religious atmosphere of Elgin, noted for its denial of the "beautiful, or dramatic, or self-immolating." Just as Lorne returns to the eminently safe and reasonable world of law with Cruikshank, so Advena escapes the "dramatic end" prophesied by Elgin, and she and Finlay learn to function within the reasonable religious limitations of Presbyterian Elgin, having found in each other the ideal Elgin could not provide.

Ajay Heble (essay date 1991)

SOURCE: " 'This Little Outpost of Empire': Sara Jeannette Duncan and the Decolonization of Canada," in *Journal of Commonwealth Literature,* Vol. XXVI, No. 1, 1991, pp. 215-28.

[*In the following essay, Heble, through an analysis of narrative technique in* The Imperialist, *maintains that Duncan was committed to the same imperial idea in the novel as in her journalism.*]

> Imperialism means . . . the realization of a Greater Canada . . . I . . . am an Imperialist because I will not be a Colonial.
>
> —Stephen Leacock

There is a two-cent stamp issued by this country for Christmas 1898 which bears the following inscription:

"We hold a vaster empire than has been." The stamp displays a map of the world, with North and South America prominently located in the centre of the picture. All British possessions are marked in red, and Canada, the reddest spot on the entire map, is given the distinct privilege of being topped by a crown. Perhaps what is most striking about this stamp is its use of the term "we"—a term which suggests a community of involvement, invokes a shared history, and acknowledges, anticipates, and ultimately authorizes our participation and complicity in the process of imperialist expansion and domination. The stamp reflects the prevailing sentiment of the time, that of the English-Canadian majority, and is useful because, among other things, it provides us with a possible explanation as to why Canada and Canadian literature tend to be excluded from so many important studies of empire. The almost non-existent status accorded to Canada in these studies may, at some level, be the result of the widespread impression, which our stamp and its inscription certainly do nothing to mitigate, that Canada had been part of the *dominating* group rather than the oppressed and *dominated* one. What this impression refuses to admit, in short, is that Canada was, and to a certain extent still remains, a colony. The conflict between our colonial "victim status" and our desire to be a vital part of the Empire, to rally round the British flag in times of need, played an especially important role in the Canadian way of life during the period between 1884 and 1914. It is this conflict which is dramatized in Sara Jeannette Duncan's ***The Imperialist***.

Published in 1904, ***The Imperialist*** was written well after Sara Jeannette Duncan had left Canada to take up residence in Calcutta. Though she wrote several novels about Anglo-India, none of these have, until recently, received much critical attention. This neglect of her work is particularly disturbing because some of Duncan's writing about India is indeed quite perceptive and compelling. In ***The Burnt Offering,*** for example—a novel published in 1909—Duncan is already responding to the rise of Indian nationalism by registering an ironic, critical attitude towards the role of the British in India. Her novel anticipates what E. M. Forster would do fifteen years later in *A Passage to India*. Forster's text is strikingly reminiscent of ***The Burnt Offering,*** and though we do not know whether he had read any of Duncan's Anglo-Indian fiction, the fact that the two writers were acquainted with one another has been documented in Forster's letters.

Much commentary on Duncan's Canadian novel, ***The Imperialist,*** tends to praise the author for her realistic presentation of life in a small Ontario town at the turn of the century. Claude Bissell, in his "Introduction" to the New Canadian Library edition of ***The Imperialist,*** insists that "Duncan is not making a statement, or parading her own convictions . . . which ultimately ran counter to the logic of her fictional creation." Bissell commends Duncan for her ability to remain critically detached from the events and issues which she describes in her novel, especially since in "real life" she was an ardent imperialist. We know about Sara Jeannette Duncan's convictions in "real life" because she was a journalist as well as a writer of prose fiction, and, in the columns she wrote, no attempt was made to disguise her loyalty to the imperial cause in Canada. Why, then, should Duncan write a novel which, as most critics would have it, ran counter to the feelings which she so vehemently expressed in her non-fictional writing? Or *is* this what Sara Jeannette Duncan was doing in ***The Imperialis*?** Despite Bissell's contention that Duncan is not parading her own convictions, despite the attempt of another critic, Francis Zichy [in *English Studies in Canada* 10, No. 3 (1984)], to maintain that Duncan, through Lorne Murchison's celebrated speech in praise of loyalty to Britain, is "calling into question the very tradition being invoked," I would like to suggest that Sara Jeannette Duncan is as committed to the "imperial idea" in her novel as she is in her journalism. One of the ways that Duncan reveals her true bias, in ***The Imperialist,*** is through her manipulation of narrative technique. More specifically, as we shall see in a moment, the *way* Duncan writes ***The Imperialist*** cannot finally be separated from the novel's political content.

In order to recognize the political implications of Duncan's narrative technique, I would like first, before turning to the novel itself, to situate the term "imperialism" more precisely within the context of late 19th century Canadian history. During this time, the growth of military power among European nations, and a sense of economic insecurity in England, prompted calls for a more tightly-knit British empire. In 1895, Joseph Chamberlain was appointed to the Colonial Office. Chamberlain, who finds a fictional counterpart in Duncan's Wallingham, was one of the principal spokesmen for the cause of Imperial Federation, a cause which, it was believed, would help offset Britain's relative decline in power.

Canada, meanwhile, was experiencing serious doubts about its own future. Though we had legally achieved our nationhood in 1867, cultural and economic subordination to external powers prevailed, as, in many respects, it still does. Canada, as is well known, has undergone three stages in its history of colonization. From 1534 to 1760, the first stage, we were a French colony. In 1760, with the establishment of English rule we became *British* Canada. Now, well over one hundred years after Confederation, we are, as many Canadians will testify, an economic colony of the United States.

As Britain, then, was turning to its colonies for support, Canada, during the late nineteenth century, was beset by an overriding sense that things were simply not working out. As Berger notes [in *The Sense of Power,* 1970], "the cumulative impact of the long depression, the failure of Macdonald's National Policy to generate prosperity and economic integration, and the cultural crisis that followed the execution of Louis Riel, produced a widespread feeling of pessimism about Canada's future." To add to this feeling of pessimism, Canadians, at the time, displayed a general lack of confidence in the possibility of ever being able to create an indigenous culture. This lack of confidence prevails, to a certain extent, even today and it is perhaps not surprising that Northrop Frye has maintained [in *The Bush Garden: Essays on the Canadian Imagination,* 1971] that Canada is "practically the only country left in the world which is a pure colony, colonial in psychology as well as in mercantile economics."

It is clear that our status as a colony, whether legal or psychological, has had and continues to have a profound bearing on the role of Canadian culture. Much nineteenth and early twentieth century Canadian literature, for instance, tended to be derivative. Writers often found it highly inviting to imitate British authors in terms of both style and content. Canadians, we begin to recognize, maintained their colonial attitude, partly *by choice*. As William Toye explains in *A Book of Canada*. "They [Canadians] were not, and *did not want to be,* wholly independent. The cultural standards and interests they developed had little to do with Canada." The question which so many critics of Canadian studies are left to ponder, even today, is whether an indigenous culture can *ever* be created in a society whose roots are in colonialism.

It is not to my purposes here to provide a direct response to this question; instead what I aim to reveal is the extent to which the cultural dilemma precipitated by Canada's colonial status was responsible for the attitude exemplified by the stamp with which I began this essay, the attitude which is foregrounded in and sanctioned by Sara Jeannette Duncan's ***The Imperialist***.

The mood of pessimism which infected Canada years after it had officially become a nation, then, was both a political and a cultural phenomenon. It was a phenomenon which, when combined with the relative decline of power in Britain, would predispose both nations to seek Imperial Federation. But there is yet one more "overlapping experience"—to borrow Edward Said's phrase—which needs to be mentioned here. In 1891, Goldwin Smith published his highly provocative *Canada and the Canadian Question*. In this work, Smith urged that the only solution to Canada's problems was that of continental unity. Smith's plea for unrestricted reciprocity, for the elimination of tariff barriers between Canada and the United States, produced a curious effect. Far from convincing Canadians to incorporate themselves into the American Union, it provided the impetus for a strengthened campaign of Imperial Federation. The very threat of annexation with the United States gave rise to the feeling that Canada's only hope for national survival was intimately connected with the future of the British Empire. The desire for Canadians to maintain and strengthen their connection with this Empire, thus, was not simply a matter of coming to the aid of Britain in times of need. Nor was it *only* the result of our own sense of cultural and economic failure. The growing strength of the imperial cause in Canada must *also* be attributed to the feeling, shared by much of the English Canadian population, that Canada's attachment to Britain would better enable Canadians to defend themselves against the United States. Canadian imperialism, then, which was a response to a series of interconnected and intertwining experiences—cultural, political and economic—taking place at roughly the same period of time in Britain, the United States *and* Canada, grew out of a desire for defending and preserving Canada's status as a nation.

The central proponents of imperialism in Canada—George R. Parkin, George M. Grant, and George T. Denison—all believed that Canada could achieve full status as a nation only by holding onto its connection with Britain. The "imperial idea," then, was irrevocably bound up with Canada's national development. As Carl Berger has convincingly demonstrated, "Imperialism was one form of Canadian nationalism." Far from being concerned with the acquisition and exploitation of foreign territories, Canadians who embraced the "imperial idea" saw it as a necessary prerequisite for the self-preservation of their nation. While there were those who still stood opposed to imperialism on the grounds that it was absolutely incompatible with Canada's national interests, a vigorous attempt was made, by its supporters, to promote imperialism as the only means by which Canada would shed its colonial status.

This is precisely the attitude which Sara Jeannette Duncan attempts to promote in ***The Imperialist***. The goal which Lorne Murchison, the imperialist of the title espouses, is explicitly linked with nationalism. Lorne "believed himself," Duncan writes, "at the bar for the life of a nation." That Duncan herself believes this is made apparent when she intrudes—and I will return to the question of authorial intrusion in a moment—into her narrative and tells us "we are here at the making of a nation." Imperialism, then, for both Lorne and for Sara Jeannette Duncan, means precisely what it meant for Parkin, Grant and Denison—a form of Canadian nationalism. Lorne makes the connection between the imperial idea and nationalism most evident in his speech given in the opera-house to the electors of South Fox:

> The imperial idea is far-sighted. England has outlived her own body. Apart from her heart and her history, England is an area where certain trades are carried on—still carried on. In the scrolls of the future, it is already written that the centre of the Empire must shift—and where, if not to Canada.

Though I will return to this quotation a little later, I would like here to point out that its prediction for Canada's future testifies to the nature of Lorne's appeal. The argument is clearly a nationalistic one and it smacks of nothing so much as Duncan's own article, **"Imperial Sentiment in Canada,"** where she too sees Imperial Federation as prefiguring Canada's greatness.

Other aspects of Lorne's opera-house speech reinforce the notion that Canadian imperialism was the result of the conditions which we have been considering:

> "The question that underlies this decision for Canada is that of the whole stamp and character of her future existence. Is that stamp and character to be impressed by the American Republic effacing"—he smiled a little—"the old Queen's head and the new King's oath? Or is to be our own stamp and character, acquired in the rugged discipline of our colonial youth, and developed in the national usage of the British Empire?"
>
> ". . . the alternative before Canada is not a mere choice of markets: we are confronted with a much graver issue. In this matter of dealing with our neighbour our very existence is involved. If we would preserve ourselves as a nation, it has become our business, not only to reject Ameri-

> can overtures in favour of the overtures of our own great England, but to keenly watch and actively resist American influence, as it already threatens us through the common channels of life and energy."

Imperial Federation, then, was construed to be for the political advantage of Canada; it was a step necessary for our self- preservation. But its impact, as Lorne demonstrates, went far beyond the political realm. Part of what imperialism meant was a deeply felt devotion to the British heritage. "Belief in England," writes Duncan, "was in the blood, it would not yield to the temporary distortion of facts in the newspapers." Before Lorne goes to England, he tells Dora Milburn, the woman with whom he has fallen in love, that Canada has derived a "moral advantage" from its connection with Britain:

> But I'll see England, Dora; I'll feel England, eat and drink and sleep and live in England, for a little while. Isn't the very name great? I'll be a better man for going, till I die. We're all right out here, but we're young and thin and weedy. They didn't grow so fast in England, to begin with, and now they're rich with character and strong with conduct and hoary with ideals. I've been reading up on the history of our political relations with England. It's astonishing what we've stuck to her through, but you can't help seeing why—it's for the moral advantage. Way down at the bottom, that's what it is. We have the sense to want all we can get of that sort of thing. They've developed the finest human product there is, the cleanest, the most disinterested, and we want to keep up the relationship—it's important.

The novel abounds in such speeches in praise of England; what I want to bring to our attention is the explicit shift in focus which takes place once Lorne Murchison, in his official capacity as secretary to the Cruickshank deputation, has returned from his trip to England. This shift is important because it signals a crucial stage in the process of Canada's decolonization. Before Lorne sets out for Britain, he sees his fellow Canadians as "young and thin and weedy." His hometown of Elgin, which operates as a microcosm for all Canada and which Duncan refers to early in the text as "this little outpost of empire," is teeming with inhabitants who are more English than the English themselves. Elgin's attitude, or the attitude of a number of its inhabitants, towards the Mother Country, is delineated with precision through Duncan's presentation of two passages which occur early in the novel. The first of these is Duncan's description of the enthusiasm with which Canadians celebrate the Queen's Birthday. "Here," Duncan writes, "it was a real holiday, that woke you with bells and cannon." This is the kind of enthusiasm, Duncan insists, which, in England, is only reserved for a "Bank holiday." The second passage which announces the extent to which a loyalty to Britain dominated everyday life in Canada is a passage in which Duncan explains how the Murchison children came to receive their names:

> Lorne came after Advena, at the period of a naive fashion of christening the young sons of Canada in the name of her Governor-General. It was a simple way of attesting a loyal spirit, but with Mrs Murchison more particular motives operated. The Marquis of Lorne was not only the deputy of the throne, he was the son-in-law of a good woman, of whom Mrs Murchison thought more, and often said it, for being the women she was than for being twenty times a Queen; and he had made a metrical translation of the Psalms, several of which were included in the revised psalter for the use of the Presbyterian Church in Canada, from which the whole of Knox Church sang to the praise of God every Sunday. These were circumstances that weighed with Mrs Murchison, and she called her son after the Royal representative, feeling that she was doing well for him in a sense well beyond the mere bestowal of a distinguished and a euphonious name, though that, as she would have willingly acknowledged, was "well enough in its place."

Both of these passages alert us to the fact that Elgin, when the novel begins, is steeped in the rudiments of a colonial tradition. The slavish imitation of British customs, to which these examples testify, goes hand in hand with Lorne's insistence on the superiority of the British race. Lorne, while still abroad, insists that England is "the heart of the Empire, the conscience of the world, and the Mecca of the race."

Once Lorne returns to Canada, however, he demonstrates a significant change in attitude. Duncan, as if signalling the importance of this turning-point in her novel, prepares us for this change by *telling* us that "what [Lorne] absorbed and took back with him is, after all, what we have to do with; his actual adventures are of no great importance." It is here that I wish to return to Lorne's opera-house speech. While abroad Lorne has become aware of England's "unready conception of things," its "political concentration upon parish affairs," its "cumbrous social machinery," and its "problems of sluggish overpopulation." When he returns to his homeland, these observations lead him to the conclusion that England has "outlived her own body." Lorne becomes conscious of the advantages which Britain's decline could have for his own nation and he accordingly posits a future with Canada as "the centre of the Empire." No longer a "little outpost" teeming with "young and thin and weedy" inhabitants, Canada, "in the scrolls of the future," abandons its colonial position of dependency and becomes a full-fledged nation. This shift in focus from Britain as "the heart of the Empire" to Canada as "the centre of the Empire" is accompanied by a change in the rhetoric of imperialism. Not content to concern himself simply with the rhetoric of self-preservation, Lorne now feels compelled to introduce, if only by implication, the notion of power into the discourse of Canadian imperialism.

Lorne's attempt to centralize Canada's position within the imperial scheme—by ascribing to his nation a future greatness—should remind us of the considerations with which I began this essay. The sentiment reflected in Canada's stamp of Christmas 1898 is very much the same sentiment which Lorne Murchison expresses in his opera-house speech when he envisions Canada as the centre of the Empire. In our stamp, we will recall, Canada occupies a central position in terms of both its prominent location on the map and its striking inscription. The "we" of this inscription testifies to the extent to which Canada felt great pride in its participation in the Empire. It is like the "we" which Duncan herself uses when she makes what seems to be an implicit comment on Canada's participation in the Boer War:

> Indifferent, apathetic, self-centred—until whenever, down the wind, across the Atlantic, came the faint far music of the call to arms. Then the old dog of war that has his kennel in every man rose and shook himself, and presently there would be a baying! The sense of kinship, lying too deep for the touch of ordinary circumstance, quickened to that; and in a moment "we" were fighting, "we" had lost or won.

Here, Duncan seems to imply that our loyalty to Britain is ultimately more important for Canada than it is for the Mother Country. It is our participation in the Empire, she tells us, which will relieve us of our indifference, apathy and self-centredness. By coming to the aid of Britain, by helping fight wars for the Mother Country, we experience the sense of power which accompanies the enactment of our imperial duties and we move one step closer to an affirmation of our own national identity. Duncan, in other words, legitimizes our involvement in overseas wars by suggesting that such involvement is for our own good. Her employment of the pronoun "we," like the use made of it in our stamp's motto, is indicative not only of the pride which many Canadians took in belonging to the Empire, but also of the pride which they felt in being at its very centre: " 'we' were fighting, 'we' had lost or won."

Sara Jeannette Duncan contributes to this process of centralization by the very way she writes her novel. The point-of-view employed by Duncan in ***The Imperialist*** is a curious one. Much of the novel is presented from a third-person omniscient perspective. Frequently, however, Duncan will intrude into her narrative, usually with the use of a first-person narrator. This narrator, it should be noted, does not present herself as a character in the fiction; rather she is Duncan herself, the writer of this particular history. Duncan's strategy is a peculiar one and, I think, one which deserves some consideration. She is clearly comfortable with the conventions of a third-person narration and she likes the fact that it allows her to see into the minds of her characters. Most of ***The Imperialist*** is written from this perspective presumably because Duncan wants to be able to transcend the limitations of a first-person point-of-view: she wants her characters to be knowable, and she, the narrator, wants the privilege of knowing and seeing all.

But, as I suggested above, Duncan also wants to present herself as the real-life author that she is, as someone who holds her own opinions and judgements—in short, as the writer of this history. She is all too willing, when she finds it convenient, to enter into the text and offer her own views on what she has just been describing. Consider, for instance, the following passage in which Duncan makes explicit her own positive attitude towards her protagonist:

> The characteristics of him I have tried to convey were grafted on an excellent fund of common sense. He was well aware of the proportions of things; he had no despair of the Idea, nor would he despair should the Idea etherealize and fly away.

By using the first-person here, and in other passages in the novel, Duncan endeavours to validate the discourse of imperialism through the authority of her own self-presence. To put it another way, Duncan intrudes into the text and formally acknowledges her protagonist's "excellent" characteristics precisely in order to guide her reader's attitude toward Lorne and toward the imperial ideal which Lorne represents.

Duncan's authorial intrusions, in telling us how we should look upon her characters, remind us of the extent to which part of the "author-function"—if I may borrow Michel Foucault's term—is to restrict and limit meaning. That Duncan's first-person remarks serve this purpose is quite evident. As one critic of her work [Joseph M. Zezulka in *Beginnings,* edited by John Moss, 1980] has correctly pointed out, "Duncan's style emphasizes telling rather than showing, and . . . [her] bemused and frequently astringent intrusions are clearly intended to guide the reader's response to Elgin society." By *telling* us what to think through an appeal to her own authority, Duncan is attempting to limit our range of personal response.

But Duncan is not content with this. A world of only restricted meanings and first-person judgements is not perfectly compatible with her urge for narrative omniscience. When Lorne goes to Britain, for instance, Duncan wants to be able to tell us what he "absorbed" while he was there. Because she is not a character in the fiction, she cannot, in realistic terms, go abroad with him—though she would undoubtedly like to do so. If the novel were being written strictly in the first-person, Duncan would here be faced with a structural and epistemological problem: the inability of the individual perceiving mind to know about what went on when the Other was not in its presence. Duncan, of course, never encounters this problem because she maintains a third-person omniscient narration which, by its very convention, allows her to know what Lorne "absorbed" in Britain without our ever having to deal with the question of whether or not she, Duncan, was present. The privileged position of omniscience allows Duncan to create a syntax where there would otherwise be only gaps and fissures. My point here—and this is why an analysis of Duncan's narrative strategy is so important for my discussion of Canada's position within the Empire—is that Duncan's account of Elgin's, and by implication Canada's, history depends on and is determined by the imagination. And the novel, as we shall see in a moment, makes an explicit connection between the imagination and imperialism.

But first, let me be more precise about what I mean here. In the omniscient sections of the narrative, which comprise, as I said earlier, most of ***The Imperialist,*** the whole problem of the first-person narrator, this "I" who appears every now and again, is essentially forgotten. We accept the conventions of the third-person narration so completely that we forget—except when Duncan sees fit to remind us—that the author of this history is, in fact, an "I" who has been positing herself as the centre of authority. What becomes evident, then, is that Sara Jeannette Duncan wants the best of both perspectives. She wants her status as a real-life author to count for something because of the authority that goes along with it; but she also, as we have seen, wants to have the totality of vision which accompanies omniscience. By combining the two points-of-view, Duncan enables herself to enjoy and exhibit power on both levels. The first-person point-of-view puts her at the centre of the text as its real-life writer—a writer with the power to guide and manipulate the response of her readers. The third-person perspective bestows upon her the power of the imagination—the power to recount events at which she need not have been present. That Duncan herself is aware of this power is made strikingly evident at one point in the novel. I am referring here to a passage in which Lorne has just encountered an ex-schoolmate named Elmore Crow. Suddenly, Sara Jeannette Duncan, in the first-person, admits that this entire episode is the result of her own invention:

> Nevertheless, *as they walk together in my mind* along the Elgin market square, the Elgin Collegiate Institute rises infallibly behind them, a directing influence and a responsible parent. (emphasis added)

Duncan's capacity to imagine, to recount an event which takes place solely in her mind, links her explicitly with Lorne Murchison, Elgin's central proponent of imperialism. Lorne, we are told, is "gifted with the power of imagination and energy and love." Lorne, as Thomas Tausky reminds us in his analysis of Duncan's novel, has the ability to "conjure up an *imaginative* vision of Canada's future destiny." [In *Sara Jeannette Duncan: Novelist of Empire,* 1980], Tausky observes, quite correctly I believe, that an explicit connection between imperialism and the imagination is made by the novel. That Duncan, herself gifted with the power of the imagination, favours imperialism for Canada is suggested by the fact that "the line dividing the proponents from the opponents of imperialism also divides the imaginative characters from the unimaginative." Unlike Lorne, who is concerned with the future destiny of his nation, the characters who stand opposed to imperialism are shallow and self-centred. They are, as Dora Milburn so aptly illustrates, leftovers of a colonial tradition. The imitation of British manners which we see in the Milburns—Dora "had been taught to speak, like Mrs Milburn, with what was known as an 'English accent' "—attests to what Tausky calls their "unthinking conformity." There is very little doubt about where Duncan's sympathies rest.

Sara Jeannette Duncan, then, in ***The Imperialist,*** is herself implicated in two specific acts of creation which depend on and are determined by the power of imaginative vision. These two acts of creation, the creation of a novel and the creation of a nation, are linked in such a manner that Duncan's very method of writing becomes a reflection of the way she would like to see her country governed. By combining third-person omniscient narrative with first-person authorial commentary, she alerts us to the sense of power and influence which she exhibits in her own writing. It is precisely this sense of power and influence which Duncan wishes Canada to attain through its participation in the imperial scheme. Although Lorne Murchison, Elgin's proponent of the imperial idea, fails in both his short-term political career and his affair with Dora Milburn, Sara Jeannette Duncan, in her own way, succeeds in her attempt to promote Canadian imperialism. She succeeds because her novel operates not only as a depiction, but also as a representation of an important stage in the process of Canada's decolonization. ***The Imperialist*** represents that stage—the stage of power and centralization, the stage so incisively registered in the stamp which inaugurated this whole discussion—by enacting it through Duncan's very mode of presentation. Duncan, to put it another way, translates Lorne's idealistic conception of imperialism into the practical realm of her own writing. That she should do this, of course, comes as no surprise. The decolonization of Canada is, after all, a cultural process as much as it is a political one.

Misao Dean (essay date 1991)

SOURCE: "A Different Point of View: The Colonial Perspective in Sara Jeannette Duncan's Novels" and "A 'Colonial Edition'," in *A Different Point of View: Sara Jeannette Duncan,* McGill-Queen's University Press, 1991, pp. 3-18, 154-58.

[*In the following excerpt, Dean examines Duncan's political and philosophical outlook as reflected in her novels.*]

What makes Canadian writing Canadian? This question has interested readers and writers at least since the Confederation period, when Archibald Lampman suggested that our cold climate would not only produce a distinctive, striving spirit in literature but a whole new race. Attempts to identify a "tradition" in Canadian literature have often been frustrated by the facts of our colonial heritage: Canadian writers seldom took works by other Canadians as models, and the work of those who did was often judged to be inferior to the work of those who consciously emulated foreign models. Attempts to identify a paradigm or theme common to all Canadian creative writing have been hampered by the limitations of their own methodology; such approaches have often led to superficial readings that merely demonstrate how certain works may be "plugged in" to a model.

Many Canadian writers themselves confronted the question of the "Canadianness" of Canadian writing; Sara Jeannette Duncan was one of them. Born in Brantford, Canada West, in 1861, she grew up in a booming industrial centre that was, paradoxically, at the far edge of English-speaking intellectual life. She was two generations away from the Rebellion of 1837, when citizens from the Brantford area had formed a significant part of the homespun crew that scattered across Yonge Street, confusedly attending at "the making of a nation." She was one generation away from those august gentlemen in decent broadcloth who made Confederation; that event, and the nationalist literary and political flowering it inspired, provided the context for her own work. Her novels and journalism address themselves to the "difference" that her sex and ex-centric nationality allowed her to feel, to the question of what it means to be a colonial, to the colonial point of view.

"Point of view" was an important concept for late nineteenth-century novelists; Henry James, in his novels and his prefaces, argues that the choice of a point of view from which to tell the story is an important technical consideration that actually determines the story itself. With his famous analogy of the "House of Fiction" he suggests that the process of writing is like looking out a window onto the world; the choice of window limits what exactly the novelist sees, and to some extent how the novelist interprets truth. As modern ideas of subjectivity and scientific research developed (from about the 1880s onwards), scholars began to explore comparative religious studies, social engineering, and the "higher criticism," and to question long-accepted ideas. English-speaking readers came to accept that while truth exists, it is not always something that can be agreed upon; it depends upon your point of view.

Applying ideas drawn from James and other modern writers to her Canadian experience, Sara Jeannette Duncan envisaged a collective colonial point of view, created by the colonials' experience of living in, and of commitment to, life on the margins of Empire. Suspicion of British and American imperialist assumptions and respect for colonial independence were her Canadian inheritance; born at the height of the British Empire, Duncan herself had witnessed many examples of inflexible British administration as well as the first flowering of American militaristic belligerence. Duncan's marriage in 1891 to Everard Cotes, an Anglo-Indian civil servant, and her subsequent experience of life in Calcutta and Simla had shown her the connections between her Canadian experience and that of other colonials, and had confirmed her view that the colonial point of view on international affairs, while often overlooked by centrist legislators, usually offered the most practical solutions to local problems. Yet as a professional journalist (for *The Week,* the *Montreal Star,* and *The Globe,* among other newspapers), and later as a novelist, Duncan also saw herself as part of a monologic idealist tradition of literature in English that included Matthew Arnold and Thomas Carlyle. A vigorous and witty controversialist, she made no bones about her commitment to the future of the Empire and her personal identification with British history and British mission. Like many of her contemporaries, she saw the Empire as a bulwark against the destructive social effects of materialist capitalism; an effective check on U.S. militarism; and a preserve for the ideals of justice, disinterested debate, altruism, and community which were threatened by the conditions of modern life. Her work speaks to the contradiction, as common among Canadians of her day as of ours, between commitment to the ideals of our European heritage and suspicion of its imperialist motives, to the difference that is the Canadian point of view.

Duncan's view of her position as a Canadian was intimately related to her view of her role as a woman. The nationalism of the 1880s that fostered Duncan's understanding of the colonial point of view coincided with the first organized feminist movement, in favour of women's suffrage (a coincidence that has been repeated in more recent history with the revival of both feminism and nationalism in the 1960s and 1970s). Duncan's early declaration in favour of women's suffrage, like her belief in the legitimacy of Canada, again placed her on the margins of centrist ideology. As a woman, created and defined as "other" by malestream ideology, Duncan was aware that social, political, and literary conventions imposed artificial limitations on women, just as British colonial stereotypes placed artificial limits on Canadians. Moreover, her comments on the role of the heroine in the modern novel clarify her view that to write as a colonial in an international context is to write in a feminine voice. Her fellow Canadians consistently characterized their country as feminine; "Miss Canada" appeared in political cartoons and popular patriotic poetry next to England's "Mrs Britannia" and "John Bull," and the American "Cousin Jonathan" and "Uncle Sam." Canada's lack of legal power in diplomatic affairs, its creation of cultural identity through relationship with "family members"—the U.S. and England—and its emphasis on the mediating role in international politics characterize it as feminine.

The voice of colonial India, Duncan's adult home, was also feminine: popularly conceived of as the "bride of the Anglo-Saxon race," India was traditionally the passive field upon which the potent imperialist exercised his racial superiority. But here again Duncan's allegiances did not follow the imperial norm: her race identified her with the imperialist, yet her colonial orientation and her idealism made her sympathetic to the Indian movement for independence and to what she perceived as the contemplative, religious "oriental mind."

Like her nationalism, Duncan's feminism was also ambivalent: despite her allegiance to the colonial feminine, she was married and committed to living within patriarchal society. In her writing, she joined in the discourse of power and submission that was the essence of popular romantic fiction. As a woman and a colonial, she was [in the words of Rachel Blau DuPlessis in *Writing Beyond the Ending,* 1985] "neither wholly 'subcultural' nor, certainly, wholly maincultural, but negotiate[d] difference and sameness, marginality and inclusion in a constant dialogue." In the overt political content and in the narrative strategies of her novels, Duncan presents a view from the margin of Anglo-American ideology, writing against the developing aesthetic and ideological traditions of imperialist patriarchy while fully implicated in them.

In *A Room of One's Own,* Virginia Woolf characterized the "double consciousness" of living both inside and outside British culture as typical of women, yet her description also captures the emotional relationship of the Canadian of British descent to England. Like Woolf, Duncan and her colonial characters confronted a civilization that assumed their loyalty without offering a significant return, that demanded their sacrifice without acknowledging their interests. Like Woolf, Duncan may have been "surprised by a sudden splitting off of consciousness, say in walking down Whitehall, when from being the natural inheritor of that civilisation, she becomes, on the contrary, outside of it, alien and critical." The double consciousness of being female and Canadian yet middle class and British, an inheritor of British civilization yet alien from it, made Duncan "(ambiguously) nonhegemonic"—non-hegemonic by virtue of her opposition to the dominant culture, but only ambiguously so, because by definition no one can be outside hegemony. Duncan could not be a whole-hearted nationalist because she was an imperialist, could not be an unqualified feminist because she finally accepted patriarchally imposed definitions of the female. Like most colonials, she struggled to integrate what she knew by virtue of her colonial experience with what she accepted of the discourse that defined her as object.

Duncan's view of her position as a Canadian was intimately related to her view of her role as a woman. The nationalism of the 1880s that fostered Duncan's understanding of the colonial point of view coincided with the first organized feminist movement, in favour of women's suffrage.

—Misao Dean

Duncan's subtle opposition to the status quo of British and American intellectual life in itself constituted her art as political, for both writer and reader. Although Duncan did not commit herself to a political program, much less to a specific political party, her insistence that the colonial point of view must be respected in international affairs as well as in sexual politics often offends modern readers trained to view such commitment as "rhetoric." Nevertheless, modern critics of Duncan's work have generally resisted the view that her novels primarily address political issues. The reason for this resistance may lie partly in the prevailing definition of the political novel. In his critical biography of Duncan, *Novelist of Empire,* Thomas Tausky adopts a definition of the political novel that follows the liberal distinction between form and content by focusing on the perceived political affiliation of the characters. Tausky points out that only one of Duncan's novels clearly fits his definition, although by slightly loosening his criteria he discusses three novels in his chapter on Duncan's politics. But even the wider framework excludes ***His Royal Happiness,*** despite its clear criticism of American democracy and its idealization of Canada. Nor can it include ***The Simple Adventures of a Memsahib,*** which challenges the patriarchal emphasis on heterosexual romantic love as the fulfilment of a woman's life. In *Redney,* her book on Duncan, Marian Fowler assumes a similar distinction between art and politics: she interprets Duncan's preoccupation with political themes in ***The Consort*** as a sign of her personal frustration and waning creative powers. Fowler opposes genuine motivation, which she identifies with passion, to politics: "Redney is using politics instead of passion to whip the muse . . . now she merely shuffles through the old ritual dance." Fowler's use of the novels as evidence of personal dissatisfaction bordering on neurosis allows her to downplay the political content of Duncan's work to the point that she sees the focus of ***The Imperialist*** as simple nostalgia, "a long, lyrical love letter, addressed to Redney's family, to her home town, to her country."

A more useful perspective on Duncan's novels is gained by placing them in the context of late-nineteenth-century English fiction by women. Many late-nineteenth-century women took to the novel as a platform for the dissemination of ideas about society, since almost all other intellectual occupations were closed to them. For the female intellectual or reformer, the novel was a natural medium for ideas. [According to Vineta Colby in *The Singular Anomaly: Women Novelists of the Nineteenth Century,* 1970], "as she and her contemporaries were fully aware, the novel was a medium for the expression of ideas about the society in which man lives. The vital issues of the day . . . were also the issues of much of the fiction of her age . . . No serious intellectual or practical issue, from the place of God in the universe to the effects on society of the development of cotton-weaving machines, eluded the nineteenth-century novelist . . . [she] had a sense of mission, a categorical imperative to observe, to write, and to influence readers." Like her contemporaries in Britain and the U.S., Duncan saw no contradiction between art and ideology, and unabashedly saw her art as that of "dramatizing" an effective "leading idea," as a medium for intellectual debate.

Moreover, in her novels, both the form and the content constitute political statement. Like those feminist writers who "write against the tradition," Duncan deliberately and self-consciously challenged the expected conventions of the romance novel in order to express her sense of the artificial limitations that the romance script imposes upon women in both narrative and society. Such challenges to convention (in both the aesthetic and the social senses of the word) announce her refusal to fit in to predetermined social and political categories. Such challenges to narrative conventions (and, by implication, social and ideological ones) are more readily found in authors who are doubly marginalized—by both their gender and their ethnic or national allegiances—and are [according to DuPlessis] "practices available to those groups—nations, subcultures, races, emergent social practices (gays?)—which wish to criticize, to differentiate from, to overturn the dominant forms of knowing and understanding." The doubly marginalized narrator, made aware of "outsiderness" because both female and Canadian, is still joined to the ideological centre by her class, her education, and her race; "in marginalised dialogue with the orders she may also affirm." Duncan worked from within the system by continuing to acknowledge the traditional norm as norm, yet asserting a different point of view.

The identification of Duncan as a doubly marginalized writer presupposes her allegiance to her sex and her nationality, but the idea that Duncan was consciously Canadian and a self-aware woman has traditionally been problematic for critics of her work. Duncan was born in Canada and began her career as a journalist contributing to the Toronto *Globe,* the *Washington Post,* the *Montreal Star,* and *The Week.* Her first book, ***A Social Departure,*** is a semifictional account of her trip around the world with fellow journalist Lily Lewis. Many of the foreign reviewers did not even notice that the narrator of the book was a Canadian; Duncan allowed Canada to fade into the background as her fictionalized persona left the CPR for a ship that took her to Japan, Southeast Asia, and India. Of the nineteen signed books that follow ***A Social Departure,*** sixteen make only token references to Canada, concentrating instead on life in London, New York, and Calcutta. Duncan's early years seem, at first glance, to have had very little impact upon her work.

The general critical response to Duncan's work has been governed by the fact of her international career. In 1893, Lampman was the first to congratulate "Miss Sara Jeannette Duncan" on having escaped the "small prospect of advancement" in her native country in favour of the greener fields of Europe. (Lampman seems to have been unaware that Duncan had actually gone to India, a questionable career move.) Claude Bissell places her firmly in the "cosmopolitan" tradition in his introduction to ***The Imperialist,*** and Lionel Stevenson remarks in *Appraisals of Canadian Literature* that Duncan "does not set out to interpret Canada either to her own inhabitants or to outsiders." For these critics, the exclusion of most of Duncan's work from consideration as Canadian is based on a definition that prescribes a Canadian setting or significant Canadian characters. Tausky follows that definition when he remarks that "students of Canadian literature have little cause to love" Everard Cotes, the Anglo-Indian civil servant who married Duncan and introduced her to India and England; in his view, if Duncan had remained in Canada her work might have been "100% Canadian content," and so automatically of interest.

Judged by the criteria of setting or national identification of the characters, the works of Henry James would have scant claim to a place in American literature, and Joseph Conrad would arguably be undeserving of British notice. The cases for considering James as American and Conrad as British are based on viewpoint, literary influence, and philosophical background. If Canadian writing were considered similarly, as part of a canon of writing interesting in itself, to Canadians if to no one else, Duncan's work should not be included or excluded on the grounds of setting or character alone. Duncan's attitude to Canada, her sense of the rightness of Canadian habits and customs, her willingness to see Canadian personality as the norm or even the ideal, and the relation of her ideas to those of major Canadian thinkers are the real indicators of whether Duncan is a Canadian writer. Canadian criticism has perhaps suffered from the same marginality that Duncan revealed in her explorations of point of view; as part of a colonized minority ourselves, Canadian critics have only recently seen the possibility and the value of relating Duncan's work to that of her contemporaries in ways which suggest that it was part of a developing intellectual tradition.

Duncan's technique of employing a detached, ironic narrator further confuses attempts to identify her national allegiance. The narrator of ***The Imperialist*** (the only novel set in Canada) speaks in a superior and almost scientifically detached voice. This prompted Northrop Frye to quote a passage from the novel [in *The Bush Garden: Essays on the Canadian Imagination,* 1971] as a classic example of the author who refuses to advocate any position or to ally herself with any tradition: "Here is a voice of genuine detachment, sympathetic but not defensive either of the group or of herself, concerned primarily to understand and to make the reader see." While for Frye ironic detachment from nationality is a sign of a mature writer, for other critics Duncan's irony is merely confusing. Michael Peterman remarks that Duncan's seeming lack of national orientation has in effect excluded her from consideration by American, British, or Canadian critics: "Much of the instability of her reputation today grows out of the fact that, because of her flexibility and cosmopolitan ease, she seemed in her time a homeless writer, one who could write trenchantly of India's political difficulties, of life in Parisian garrets, of social comedy in London and New York, but one who never clearly identified herself with a national literary tradition . . . the 'delightful' manner in which she made use of the international theme, had the effect of de-nationalising her."

Moreover, because modernism privileges cynical irony as a mode of seeing the real, for many critics Duncan's irony seems to be merely objective realism. The realism she drew from writers such as William Dean Howells and James thus contributes to the impression that her work is detached from, rather than politically engaged with, the issues of colony and empire. (Some critics have also implied that her interest in work of Howells and James made her fiction more American than Canadian). But Duncan's attitudes to realism and irony must be placed in the context of the intellectual dualism of the real and the ideal and the accompanying oppositions of democracy and authority, realism and romance, that dogged the nineteenth-century intellectual. Duncan, like many colonial writers, used irony as a technique to disguise her critique of the ideology of the centre. She relied on the reader to decipher the "parallax," the point of view from which her ironic statements would make sense, turning away from the chaotic implications of "romantic irony" towards the ultimate meaning that idealist philosophy seemed to promise. Duncan's irony is not de-nationalizing, nor is it simply objective realism (though it may seem so to a modern reader), and confusion about these elements disappears when her ironic technique and her theory of realism are closely examined.

As A. B. McKillop, Leslie Armour, and Elizabeth Trott have argued, the characteristically Canadian response to the dualism of the ideal and the real was to try to reconcile the two. Duncan reconciled the perceived opposition of the real and the ideal through the popular version of idealism, derived from Carlyle and Arnold, which eventually came to dominate Canadian intellectual life and which persisted in Canada long after the rest of the English-speaking world had gone on to modernist materialism. Canadian intellectuals saw the material world as an embodiment of transcendent values whose significance could be brought out in realist fiction through careful selection of detail. While Duncan admired the realism of the Americans Howells and James, her own aim was quite different from what she saw as theirs: Duncan felt that Howells glorified life for the sake of its material commonplaces, while she went beyond the commonplace to show the representative significance of realistic details.

The idealism that underlies Duncan's novelistic method also provides a focus for addressing social issues such as the independence of the colonies, the institution of democratic government, universal education, and female suffrage. The version of idealism that became known through Carlyle's writings is essentially a framework that makes sense out of the chaotic revolutions of the nineteenth century: such change is not to be feared but rather welcomed as part of a general movement toward a predetermined and definitively good end. Social change is to be undertaken, with the ultimate ends of justice, peace, and equality in view, by changing institutions within a seemingly stable framework. British idealism, however, tended to focus on abstract ends rather than means, and so "turned right" with the more conservative politics of Carlyle and F. H. Bradley, while Canadian idealism remained essentially a reformist philosophy which held that the real and the ideal existed equally. The struggle to make the real conform to the ideal through the secularization of religious thought gave thinkers such as G. M. Grant, Agnes Maule Machar, and John Watson the inspiration to propose ameliorations of the materialist capitalism that they confronted. [According to McKillop, the] "reorientation of the Canadian academic community towards idealism," which took place at the end of the nineteenth century and the beginning of the twentieth, quickly became a popular reorientation as well, as thinkers such as Machar, Watson, and Paxton Young became influential through their numerous publications and involvement in the training of Presbyterian clergy and the formation of the United Church.

The legitimacy of the individual which the reconciliation of realism and idealism suggested to Canadians provided a philosophical basis for Canadian autonomy within the wider community suggested by the Imperial Union movement. Imperial union, based on the idealist conception of diverse physical manifestations of a universal truth, would allow for a peaceful federation of contending nationalities and a wider union of the human race, but would still allow for the individuality of the various member countries. For Canadians such as Duncan, a united empire would reconcile the two important needs of political man: the need for self-government and the need to look up to an ideal example. With these two principles firmly in view, individual nations could move to material prosperity witout giving up the human goals of charity, political stability, and universal education. Duncan applied the standard she derived from her Canadian experience and from the Canadian view of empire in her descriptions of the social and physical conditions of the U.S. Canada, England, and India, and attempted to show how the fullest development of individuality could be achieved through recognition of the highest good.

Duncan's interest in and support of the Imperial Federation movement is another factor that lends support to the idea that she thought of herself as a particularly Canadian citizen of Empire. Robert Grant Haliburton calls the United Empire Loyalists the first imperial federationists, on the grounds that they suffered and died for the ideal of the unity of the race even while they were betrayed by British policy. Carl Berger suspects that the claim that Canadians originated imperial federation was a myth, created by the nationalist stream of the Imperial Federation movement to increase their sense of moral superiority to both Britain and the U.S. on the other hand, George Parkin, one of the most influential Canadian imperialists, stated categorically that "Imperial Federation is of Colonial—not of English—origin." (One is tempted to add that, as the most famous spokesman for the movement, he should know.)

The "popular idealist" philosophy so influential in Canadian conceptions of a united empire also suggested a rationalization for the movement towards self development for women. The ideal of womanhood, including her "moral superiority" to men and her ability to create and maintain peaceful relations among family members, was traditionally embodied in the role of homemaker and bearer of children. Duncan, however, influenced by the "maternal feminists" (who advocated the extension of women's maternal role into social policy) and the ideology of the "new woman," portrayed the ideal as embodied in a new generation of women pursuing their best impulses in a felt vocation for higher education and professions. The ideal remained the same, but its embodiment changed.

While Duncan's idealism and her support for the federation of the British Empire suggest her agreement with her contemporaries on the composition of the Canadian point of view, the particular form in which she represented the eventual union of the Empire shows the influence of her feminism. She rejected the idea that male-dominated systems of trade and government are sufficient to create peaceful relations between the countries of the Empire, and used the metaphors of family alliances between parent and child, husband and wife, to illustrate the bonds of "sentiment" which must exist between nations in order to promote peace and prosperity. The male characters in Duncan's books attempt to unite the Empire using the tools of trade and diplomacy, but the female characters actually unite the Empire with the tangible ties of marriage and children. Women traditionally have a special duty in the family to promote affection and understanding among the members, and this duty becomes a public one as women fulfill a special role in the Empire, creating the affectionate ties that are the most important part of diplomatic alliances and bind countries to support each others' interests.

The preservation of affectionate ties between races, classes, and nations, as between individuals, is the moral constant in Duncan's portrayal of political rivalries, one that recent feminist scholarship has identified as constitutive of feminine psychology as created in the nuclear family. Nancy Chodorow's description of the daughter's creation of identity through relationship with others, rather than through separation and independence, suggestively recalls Duncan's portrayal of a kind of colonial self-government that unites the values of independence from and connection to England. Carol Gilligan's corollary research into women's moral decisions suggests that women consistently choose to maintain relationships rather than to pursue abstract concepts of good and evil. Duncan's characterization of the nations of the Empire as "one race" who cannot and must not be separated by abstractions "of so little consequence as a form of government" similarly seems to connect to Gilligan's ideas about characteristically feminine traits as produced in the nuclear family. Thus Duncan's ideas about women, about the Empire, and about nationhood seem to reflect her feminism and her femininity.

Duncan often used the metaphor of marriage to symbolize alliances between countries, but she also portrayed actual international marriages that gave women power as intercultural interpreters and bearers of family wealth. Creating India as "the bride of the Anglo-Saxon race" was a cliché of orientalist discourse, but Duncan wrote against the stereotype by showing that the alliance with British law would bring the Eastern bride not protected passivity but independence, education, and relief from abuse. The Canadian bride, such as Advena Murchison in ***The Imperialist*** or Mary Trent in ***Cousin Cinderella,*** gains power through her ability to bestow the dowry that represents her nation: wealth, a field for action, and the possibility of a new social harmony. The American bride in Duncan's later books brings the healing of the schism between Britain and the U.S. and the possibility of fruitful alliance in time of war. In Duncan's books, as the narrator states in ***The Simple Adventures of a Memsahib,*** "Feminine connections . . . [are] the only sort which are really binding" between nations.

Duncan's political views were often those of a small-c conservative, but her belief in social reform and women's suffrage and her attacks on colonialism and entrenched privilege belie a simple identification with any one party. George Lukacs points out [in *The Historical Novel,* 1962] that movements that oppose bourgeois democracy on the basis of a communitarian ideal often blur party lines: "The opposition movements . . . always run the danger of swinging over from a left to a right-wing criticism of bourgeois democracy, i.e. from dissatisfaction with *bourgeois* democracy to opposition to *democracy in general.* If one, for instance, follows the careers of . . . important writers like Bernard Shaw, one sees . . . zigzag movements of this kind from one extreme to the other." During Duncan's lifetime, political lines in Britain and Canada were extremely fluid. Both Benjamin Disraeli and Joseph Chamberlain began their careers as Radicals and ended as Tories; Disraeli and Herbert Henry Asquith both considered forming governments of efficiency or reconciliation that would do away with party lines. Carlyle's ideas were variously associated with the right and the left, and the Fabians flirted with eugenics and fascism as well as with democratic socialism. In Canada, the Canada First movement began by opposing all party divisions as inefficient and petty; it ended by forming its own party. The Liberal Party of Canada seesawed between support for commercial union and imperial federation. Duncan is often called a conservative, but during her lifetime she remained friends with John Willison, editor of a Liberal paper. She admired and quoted John Stuart Mill and Arnold; she upheld the free market system but also supported relief payments to the poor. The political philosophy she espoused eventually became the basis of the CCF.

Duncan's political stance might more constructively be defined within that elusive (and largely extinct) Canadian ideology, red toryism. The red tory believes in a natural social hierarchy similar to the one described in ***The Imperialist*** and the maintenance of that hierarchy in a flexible way in the interests of preserving order. The red tory also believes, generally, in progress and social reform, but with the limit that man is probably not perfectable. Increases in personal freedom are not necessarily progressive (as Duncan maintained when she argued that the aim of the movement for women's rights is not freedom in itself); progress, for the red tory, consists in restraining the more vicious human traits to prevent the victimization of the weak—in practical terms, state legislation to restrain capitalism. The red tory thus shares with the socialist a belief in the necessity of state intervention based on a collectivist view of the social good, the view that Pamela Pargeter comes to when she campaigns on behalf of the Labour Party in ***The Consort***. In Canada, red tories and their socialist allies have historically been the basis of the nationalist movement; red tory nationalists have generally fought modern liberal capitalism (the descendant of Mill's utilitarianism), and so have fought Canada's incorporation into the U.S. economic empire.

Red toryism, or "tory radicalism," has been a major factor in the intellectual history of Canada. Gad Horowitz accounts for the differences between Canadian and us culture by the "touch of toryism" that survived the homogenizing influence of North American liberalism. He believes that the dominant liberal ideology in Canada is "considerably mitigated by a tory presence initially and a socialist presence subsequently." He agrees that the two are fundamentally connected by a "corporate-organic-collectivist" view of society, which is the result of the "non-Liberal British elements" that have entered "into English-Canadian society *together* with American liberal elements at the foundations." Of course it would be an exaggeration to claim self-conscious political radicalism for nineteenth-century Canadian conservatives. But certainly the "pink toryism" that Robin Mathews claims for Susanna Moodie was the ideology of a significant minority. Like Duncan, Moodie "supported meritocracy. She moved toward the breakdown of class as it was defined in Europe. She rejected individualism and—in a not fully articulated way—capitalist exploitation." Like Moodie, Duncan may be called a pink tory: "pro-British in culture, pro-Canadian in aspirations for the future, socially committed to community and responsibility and, therefore, fearful of individualist, republican 'democracy.' "

The pink tory was often an imperialist. Support for the strengthening of ties between the self-governing nations of the British Empire was one strategy for combatting materialism and deterioration of social bonds. The Empire was supposed to be held together by ideals that transcended the profit motive, and to be motivated by the desire to do good works by bringing the benefit of British civilization to the "lesser breeds without the law." While acknowledging that the Empire was originally an instrument for money-making, Canadian imperialists saw the future of the Empire in the preservation of the ideals embodied in British history. G.M. Grant declared that the mission of man was "to think great thoughts, to do great things, to promote great ideals," and to overcome "the vulgar and insolent materialism of thought and life, which is eating into the heart of our people." To this end, Canadian imperialists took Carlyle's suggestion to 'work thou in well-doing,' infusing the concept of secular work with religious enthusiasm. Support for the Empire seemed to provide the ideals and the opportunity for work (in the governing of dependencies and the building of new nations), as well as an economic mechanism for resisting the dominating influence of the quintessential materialists, the Americans.

The pink tory, if she was a woman, was also often a suffragist, for the majority of the members of the Canadian suffrage movement were politically conservative reformers, not revolutionaries. The radical call for the vote, which was founded in the belief in the essential equality of women, was rejected by the majority of the maternal feminist suffragists. They called for the vote as a first step toward necessary social reforms, such as temperance laws, legislation to give mothers equal custody of their children, and welfare and unemployment relief, that would "clean house" for the nation.

One of the earliest women journalists to call for the ballot (in her *Globe* columns of 1885), Duncan agreed that most women would prefer to marry and have children, and she consistently depicted female characters in her novels who are "formed" for marriage. Yet she argued for the goal of women's financial and moral independence from men and for freedom of choice for women who felt the drive toward higher education and professions. Asserting that women had grown strong enough to bear the responsibility of the ballot, she demanded that they be treated as adults, with both the duties and responsibilities of citizens. She argued that women are as individual as men in their aptitudes and capabilities, and that their different callings and vocations must be respected. Chafing against the artificial legal strictures placed on women made her aware of the literary restrictions: those which created the passive heroine, the love story, the flirt, and always, always, a marriage at the end. Her ability to question stereotypes in life broadened to include a questioning of much received opinion. . . .

In all her work, Duncan wrote from a different point of view, one that consciously differed from the received wisdom of the imperial centre yet included it as norm; she wrote as a colonial both committed to and different from the empire that created her.

. . . . .

The novels of Sara Jeannette Duncan question and challenge the view from the centre of Empire. They present a critique of the totalizing systems of materialism, bourgeois democracy, imperialism, and patriarchy by delineating the colonial point of view—the view from the margin, both part of and outside the central ideology. That point of view is informed by the idealism that many Canadian intellectuals saw as an antidote to the increasingly materialist view of both fiction and politics current in the U.S. and Britain, and by the feminist advocacy that resisted the colonizing ideology of the patriarchal centre by expanding limited definitions of woman and of femininity.

Duncan's political views had their genesis in the idealism expressed by British and Canadian political and social writers of the last half of the nineteenth century. Matthew Arnold and, through him, Thomas Carlyle were the most important for Duncan. Through them and their Canadian interpreters, Duncan saw traditional society in Canada, England, the U.S., and India as threatened by the new values of materialism, scepticism, and political anarchy; in opposition to those values she saw idealism, heroism, and Arnoldian culture. While she depicts the forces of materialism as strong, her novels always imply the constant evolution of society towards the end predicted by Carlyle, when all humanity will see justice and the face of God.

The most important basic belief conveyed to Duncan through her reading was a kind of popular idealism that pervaded Canadian intellectual life in the late nineteenth century. This popular version of the idealism of Carlyle and Arnold included a belief in transcendent and immutable values (which may or may not be identified with a christian God). These values might be approximated in human life by those with the gift of divining them (Carlyle's heroes) or through study of British history and its evolution towards the ideal. These values denied the claims of materialistic science to ultimate knowledge, kept alive the religious impulse through study of literature and religious traditions, and made fully human life (of whatever race or culture) the ultimate test of all technological innovation.

In Canada, idealism was the major philosophical tradition touching all levels of intellectual life in the last few decades of the nineteenth century. Carlylean ideas dominated education at all levels; Arnold's works must have been familiar to educated readers of *The Week,* as Duncan could use his terms "philistines" and "culture" in her columns with no accompanying explanation. In addition, John Watson arrived in Canada in 1872, and his views dominated Canadian academic philosophy by the mid-1880s. His interpretation of Kantian idealism influenced Duncan's Presbyterian church and was the focus of debate in magazines such as *The Canadian Monthly and National Review.* Duncan's journalism and novels show the influence of all these streams of thought. Moreover, she shared the major idea common to Canadian idealists: support for a continued link between Canada and England as a bulwark against the rampant materialism and anarchic democracy that seemed to threaten from the south.

The idealism of Duncan's novels is distinctly unfashionable today. It is responsible, some say, for the repeated claim in the mid-twentieth century that Canada is still a "Victorian" society, out of step with the intellectual and artistic world; the part played by idealism in the justification of imperialist war and the arms race has made idealism and its trappings objects of well-earned revulsion. Yet Duncan's work implies that to abandon mutually agreed upon definitions of justice, truth, and compassion, to abandon the possibility of community, is to leave us open to the grossest violations of elementary human freedoms; the struggle for justice can be waged only by communities united by those common abstractions. While we may deplore Duncan's elitism, her racism, and her class consciousness, we may applaud and subscribe to her vision of a community united in its attempt to realize "justice and freedom and that sort of thing" in real life, through negotiation, affection, and sensitivity to other cultures.

The critique of democracy, and especially republican democracy, that is evident in Duncan's work comes directly from her idealism. Duncan depicts human beings as a complex of self-interest and self-transcendence; personal selfishness and common good constantly war in the characters she depicts. In her novels, simply giving the vote to more people does not necessarily ensure better government, because government is to be judged by a higher standard, not by the advantages it awards to interest groups. The issue of democracy is directly connected to social reform. The increasing triumph of materialist capitalism, which treats human beings as commodities, over traditional aristocratic responsibility for the poor made social reform a necessity for Britain; yet, in ***The Consort,*** giving the poor the vote, through which they could exact "revenge" upon the rich, seems to do little to ameliorate their problems. For Duncan, a meritocracy (which Carlyle defends in *Past and Present*) drawn from an independent, educated population is the solution that the colonies of Canada and Australia offer the British working poor.

The depiction of nationality in the novels is inevitably connected with Duncan's belief in the essential unity of English-speaking peoples, which she characterizes as the "Anglo-Saxon race." Although Canada, the United States, Britain, and India are unique nationalities formed by different histories and different physical and social conditions, they are linked by the common ideals of their British heritage and by ties of familial "sentiment." While the novels look forward to a re-unification of England and her colonies and former colonies, unique nationalities are not devalued in a drive for uniformity; the personal initiative of Americans, the traditions of Britons, the flexibility of Canadians, and the contemplative nationalism of Indians—all are legitimate points of view from which a prospective union would draw strength.

Canada is idealized in the novels for its ability to meld respect for British ideals with a unique North American belief in personal freedom. In ***The Imperialist,*** the citizens of Elgin, Ontario, are able to follow their "man of vision" toward an ideal future; while Lorne Murchison is defeated by corruption and self-interest, the ideal he represents persists in the history of the nation. This persistence of the British ideal in Canadian culture is even clearer in Mary Trent of ***Cousin Cinderella*** and Arthur Youghall of ***His Royal Happiness;*** both characters find their personal freedom and their vocation in helping to revitalize Britain's own sense of mission and strengthen her ties to the colonies.

The burgeoning nationalism of the "Canada First" era in Canadian political life, like the nationalism of the 1960s and 1970s, ran parallel to the beginnings of feminist organization and feminist action. While Duncan would not have called herself a feminist, her work disputed patriarchally imposed definitions of women's role and advocated importing the "feminine" values of affection, sentiment, negotiation, and connection into political life. She challenges the limited roles allowed to women by both social and literary convention in ***A Social Departure*** and, in her early journalism, encourages women to discard useless feminine weakness and to cultivate firmness of purpose. She redefines the traditional sentimental heroine in ***Vernon's Aunt, The Simple Adventures of a Memsahib,*** **"A Mother in India,"** and other works, creating a protagonist who moves beyond the conventional narrative of love story and happy ending. She argues for giving women a role in political life through the ballot, as well as demonstrating in ***Cousin Cinderella, The Consort,*** and ***The Burnt Offering*** how women can participate in inter-cultural debates and, through marriage, choose to be actors in public life.

Duncan's novels show the relationship between countries to be a familial one, in which the feminine virtues of negotiation, connection, and affection are the most important in maintaining peace and harmony. In ***The Burnt Offering,*** India asks for "affection" from her British rulers; the enthusiasm of Lorne Murchison's "heart" favours closer ties within the Empire. Women themselves had a part to play in the international politics of empire: Helen Browne, Rani Janaki, Mary Trent, and other Duncan heroines offer a tangible way to promote love and sympathy among the countries of the Empire when they marry. In the idealist sense, these heroines find both personal identity and an important way to serve the best interest of the community in the fulfillment of their love.

Indian nationality is a melding of British and Indian elements in Duncan's novels. Duncan accepted the common justifications for the British rule of force in India: the good of the people, the benefits of education, and democratic reforms. Her Indian novels depict the future of India as a marriage between the best of India and England, formed through affection and compatible gifts. The novels focus on the workings of the Imperial Idea of social reform: they contrast the gradual reforms of "culture," based on knowledge of the social situation and on general flexibility of mind as well as acquaintance with ideals, to the "Morrison's Pill" approach of attempting to enforce compliance with a single idea. The novels reveal Western education, dominated by science and scepticism, as a mixed blessing for a culture already closer to its God than the British.

The Indian novels also depict racial difference. Duncan's fictional method of creating "types," as well as the discourse of racism and orientalism, lead to her depiction of Indians as incapable of self-government. While she often displays her cultural ethnocentricity and regularly makes use of the negative stereotypes of Indians, she refuses to accept such stereotypes as final; her definitions of "others" are always open to redefinition and to possible alliance.

Duncan's novels are, finally, "colonial editions," which reproduce the aesthetic and political controversies common to the English-speaking world of her time from a Canadian and a female point of view. Her rejection of materialism in art and in its political forms of republican democracy, individualism, and the rule of "selfishness" reflects the general dominance of idealism in Canadian philosophy and literature long after the materialism and "psychologism" of modernism dominated elsewhere in the English-speaking world. She locates the centre of that materialism in the United States, which she depicts as losing its commitment to ideals in the War of Independence; her Americans provide a link between the cautionary tales of Thomas Chandler Haliburton and the plutocrats of Stephen Leacock. Duncan's Britons are less benign than Leacock's "Remarkable Uncle," because they retain enough power over Canadian foreign affairs for their ignorance to be threatening; yet, like the community-building Britons of John Richardson and Susanna Moodie, Duncan's Britons retain their status as inheritors of British values and still remain open to the influence of ideals. Canadians, as inheritors of both North American freedom and the cultural products of British evolution, are Duncan's ideal people. Common sense to the contrary, Canadians have responded to Lorne Murchison's call to community with other Canadians and within the Empire by reaffirming the country's "dominion status" and continuing to see the Commonwealth as an important forum for negotiation and for the achievement of social justice.

Jennifer Lawn (essay date 1992)

SOURCE: *"The Simple Adventures of a Memsahib* and the Prisonhouse of Language," in *Canadian Literature,* No. 132, Spring, 1992, pp. 16-30.

[*In the following essay, Lawn explores the linguistic complexities of* The Simple Adventures of a Memsahib.]

> "Here, you see, sir, all the chairs," stated the little baboo, waving his hand. "I must tell you, sir, that some are off teak and some off shisham wood. Thee shisham are the superior."
>
> "You mean, baboo," said young Browne, seriously, "that the shisham are the less inferior. That's a better way of putting it, baboo."
>
> "Perhaps so, sir. Yessir, doubtless you are right, sir. The less inferior—the more grammatical!"

This exchange between George Browne and a furniture-selling "baboo" in Sara Jeannette Duncan's novel ***The Simple Adventures of a Memsahib*** introduces the premise of this paper, that the normative, systematic principles of language provide a model for other social practices. The extract illustrates several systems: that of cross-cultural interaction implied in the forms of address ("sir" and "baboo"); the specific sub-language of bartering; and even the correct "grammar" of wood types. Within a few brief words, categories of status, buying power, and quality are established. I propose to explore the workings of such social "languages" in ***Simple Adventures,*** particularly in relation to issues of power raised by the colonial setting of Duncan's text.

The concept of "cultural grammar" is a sociological extension of the linguistic principles developed by the early structuralist theorists Ferdinand de Saussure, Edward Sapir, and Benjamin Whorf. Saussure first articulated the theory of language as a self-enclosed system, with language use being determined by convention rather than by any natural relationship between sign and referent. Members of a speech community are, however, "naturalized" to their native tongue and speak it unconsciously, forgetting its arbitrary nature. Saussure distinguished *langue,* the the sum of all linguistic rules, from *parole,* the individual utterance enabled by *langue. Langue* is always present yet never knowable in its entirety, and although it changes through time, it remains beyond the modifying power of any one individual.

Sapir and Whorf are, of course, best known for their "Sapir-Whorf hypothesis," the concept that "the structure of a human being's language influences the manner in which he understands reality and behaves with respect to it." In consequence, language itself is the product of a social contract, for we "organize [nature] into concepts, and ascribe significances as we do, largely because we are parties to an agreement to organize it this way—an agreement that holds throughout our speech community." Furthermore, if a language articulates an entire cultural universe, then "translation can literally involve the erasure of a shared mode of functioning in the world, and . . . the loss of a language can mean the destruction of an entire cosmos."

Subsequent critical discussion has differentiated a "strong" and a "weak" form of the Sapir-Whorf hypothesis, labelled, respectively, "linguistic determinism" and "linguistic relativity." The former espouses the idea that

> every language is a vast pattern-system, different from others, in which are culturally ordained the forms and categories by which the personality not only communicates, but also analyses nature, notices or neglects types of relationship and phenomena, channels his reasoning, and builds the house of his consciousness.

Whorf 's sometimes vague writings also embraced the concept of linguistic relativity, which holds that the structures of language influence cognition and thought processes to a certain extent, without determining them entirely. In either form, the hypothesis views language as a social institution of extraordinary power, circumscribing potentiality by providing some terms, and not others, for describing the world. Sapir's observation that "human beings do not live in the objective world alone . . . but are very much at the mercy of [language]" has found more extreme expression in post-structuralist theory. J. Hillis Miller, for example, asserts that "language is not an instrument or tool in man's hands, a submissive means of thinking. Language rather thinks man and his 'world'."

The anthropologist Claude Lévi-Strauss applied the Saussurean linguistic model to cultural phenomena, such as kinship relations, myths, and even cooking practices. In the cross-cultural context provided by anthropology, the customs of one culture become denaturalized against the background of another, just as in ***Simple Adventures*** the institutions of the colonizing British system appear alien in the territory of India. Duncan's text thus foregrounds or "defamiliarizes" cultural systems at various levels. At the broadest level, the novel opposes West and East. Within western culture, there occurs a split between English and Anglo-Indian. Further subdivisions emerge: "Calcutta" has its own class system or "tagography," its own rules of fashion, interior decoration, housing location, visiting etiquette, religious habits, recreational pastimes. Viewed from this angle, ***Simple Adventures*** traces the ways in which one "gradually [comes] within the operation of custom." The agency of this clause is significant: it is custom which "operates" upon the individual. "Calcutta" itself, referring not to the geographical location but rather to the complex Anglo-Indian social network in that city, is personified as a woman whose decree is absolute:

> Calcutta, in social matters, is a law unto herself, inscrutable, unevadable. She asks no opinion and permits no suggestion. She proclaims that it shall be thus, thus it is, and however odd and inconvenient the custom may be, it lies within the province of no woman—the men need not be thought of—to change it, or even to discover by what historic whim it came to be.

Calcutta thus acts as a *langue* which "speaks" its inhabitants. Those wilful or alienated individuals who do not conform are "ungrammatical," stepping outside the categories imposed by society.

Dealing with whole species more than with individuals, ***Simple Adventures*** celebrates "the great British average." The narrator, Mrs. Perth Macintyre, refers on several occasions to the ordinariness of the Brownes. She warns the reader "under no circumstances to expect anything extraordinary from Helen," and declares that George is "undoubtedly . . . very like other young men in Calcutta." Altogether, "they were not remarkable people, these Brownes." The characters' typicality focuses the reader's attention on the mechanism of the various systems which operate upon them; the text is a primer in cultural linguistics, a whimsical guide-book illustrating the subject-verb-object of Anglo-Indian society.

The customs associated with marriage provide a good example of a cultural system. The "syntax" of conventional western marriage consists of intimate acquaintance, engagement, and wedding. Any rearrangement of these elements—as in India, where engagement may precede acquaintance—is deemed unorthodox, "ungrammatical" in a British context. Likewise, any omission of one or more of the elements is socially distressing: hence Mrs. Perth Macintyre's defensiveness and embarrassment that her niece has failed to become engaged, despite innumerable opportunities for acquaintance. The marriage "sentence" also has a paradigmatic aspect: just as the subject of a linguistic sentence must be a noun phrase, the acquaintance must take place between a man and a woman. Since *langue* rather than *parole* takes precedence in ***Simple Adventures,*** it is not strictly important as to which individual is chosen from the axis of selection. The narrator comments, "I will go so far as to say that if Helen had not been there—if she had spent the summer with an aunt in Hampshire, as was at one time contemplated—one of the other Misses Peachey might have inspired this chronicle." It is ungrammatical for "intimate acquaintance" to take place between a married woman and an unattached man: hence Helen's concern, "in the interests of the normal and the orthodox," to encourage engagement between Jimmy Forbes and Josephine Lovitt and so break up a relation (between Jenny Lovitt and Jimmy) that was "too delicately adjusted to come under any commonly recognized description."

The marriage sentence of George and Helen proceeds perfectly grammatically, despite the slight blip of an unusual adverbial: the wedding takes place in India rather than England, but nonetheless Canbury sends hearty wishes for the future Brownes "as if they had behaved properly in every respect." Helen and George, being natives of British culture, regard the whole marriage process as entirely natural. They fall in love "according to approved analytical methods," having "arrived at a point where they considered themselves indispensable to each other in the most natural, simple, and unimpeded manner."

The Brownes naturally view their case of marriage as special, and Mrs. Perth Macintyre would risk a "good deal" of criticism from Helen to suggest otherwise. No doubt George, too, would be offended were he informed that his decision to marry was prompted, not by love, but by auspicious material prospects and the biological urge to mate. The narrator, however, implies the influence of such pragmatic and socially unmentionable factors by likening marriage to the wholly unromantic system of trade. On board ship Helen felt "that she ought properly to be in an air-tight box in the hold, corded and labelled and expected to give no further trouble. She realized, at moments, that she was being 'shipped' to young Browne." Sexual slang frequently identifies women as goods; even in the nineteenth century Anglo-Indian women who returned Home without husbands or fiancés were known as "Returned Empties." Although the issue invites feminist analysis, men are also stamped and priced in the Anglo-Indian marriage market: " 'Three hundred a year dead or alive' " was at one time "distinctly the most important quotation in the matrimonial market for India."

Simple Adventures similarly dehumanizes many other social groups. For example, the Government treats functionaries of Empire as goods, as George cynically notes:

> The valuation of society is done by Government. Most people arrive here invoiced at so much, the amount usually rises as they stay, but they're always kept carefully ticketed and published, and Calcutta accepts or rejects them, religiously and gratefully, at their market rates.

Other less striking examples occur. Pellington, Scott & Co. deal in "rice and coolies chiefly." The narrator metonymically describes the women of the Viceregal Drawing-Room as "shimmering trains" or "grey bengaline and gold embroidery and a cream crêpe de Chine and pearls." Batcham is a "large red globe-trotter," suggesting a breed of dog; other animal images occur, such as the likeness of both the Indian bearers and Mrs. Macdonald's "men-friends" to flies. Thus systems—including that of the animal world—"cross-infect" each other, and deflating analogies defamiliarize cultural givens.

. . . . .

> The English are a sensitive people, and yet when they go to foreign countries there is a strange lack of awareness about them.
>
> —Jawaharlal Nehru

Post-colonial texts, according to the authors of *The Empire Writes Back,* are necessarily cross-cultural because they "negotiate a gap between 'worlds'." Ashcroft, Griffiths, and Tiffin establish a model in which post-colonial culture—defined widely as "all the culture affected by the imperial process from the moment of colonization to the present day"—"writes back" against the imperial centre by replacing metropolitan "English" with local "english." This "remoulding" of language proceeds through "abrogation" and "appropriation," defined thus:

> Abrogation is a refusal of the categories of the imperial culture, its aesthetic, its illusory standard of normative or 'correct' usage, and its assumption of a traditional and fixed meaning 'inscribed' in the words. . . . Appropriation is the process by which the language is taken and made to 'bear the burden' of one's own cultural experience.

Although Ashcroft *et alia* do not specifically address the Sapir-Whorf hypothesis, they do reject the "essentialist" idea that "words somehow embody the culture from which they derive." They reason that the essentialist view prevents any possibility of the changes in linguistic practice which have occurred in post-colonial literatures. Yet it is precisely the case that language use, if it embodies culture, will alter in accordance with cultural change; all language systems contain rules for such change, such as compounding, metaphoric extension, or new morphemic combinations. The authors go on to espouse the view that untranslated words in post-colonial texts "have an important function in inscribing difference." They argue that language variance is metonymic of cultural difference: thus social, creating a "space," a "psychological abyss" between cultures. This insight does not disprove the idea that "words embody culture."

An application of the model proposed in *The Empire Writes Back* illuminates several aspects of ***Simple Adventures***. For example, Ashcroft *et alia* oppose the glossing of non-English words, for it implies a simple, one-to-one transference of meaning and negates the culturally-specific resonances of a word. It also "gives the translated word, and thus the 'receptor' culture, the higher status." The reductive nature of glossing is apparent in Duncan's text. To translate "Raj" as "government," for example, obliterates any connotations of domination or cultural imposition. Furthermore, the term "government" will evoke different images according to the nationality of the reader: Whitehall, Parliament Hill, and the White House vary markedly from each other, and all are inappropriate as equivalents of the Raj.

Duncan's novel resists the classification, established in *The Empire Writes Back,* between "colonial" and "metropolitan" texts. ***Simple Adventures*** is written by a Canadian but set in India, focusing upon British citizens in temporary exile. The orientation of the text—the ethnicity of both the author and the projected audience—influences how we "situate" the work in a post-colonial context. Canada is a minority, "marginal" culture in relation to Britain, but a representative of the metropolitan culture in relation to India. Thus the occurrence of Hindustani words in ***Simple Adventures*** will have a different "message," for example, than the use of Parsi terms in the short stories of Rohinton Mistry.

Duncan's Anglo-Indians pepper their conversation with Hindustani terms. We may immediately dispense with the possibility that they do so to avoid the ethnographic pitfall of representing one culture in the language of another and thus "creat[ing] the reality of the Other in the guise of describing it." According to Mrs. Perth Macintyre, the memsahib has no concern for accuracy: "she gathers together her own vocabulary, gathers it from the east and the west, and the north and the south, from Bengal and Bombay, from Madras and the Punjab, a preposition from Persia, a conjunction from Cashmere, a noun from the Nilgherries." Helen, the neophyte memsahib, eventually discovers that it is more "desirable" to speak like a memsahib than a native.

Hindustani, being the "tongue in which orders are given in Calcutta," aids domestic and state administration in ***Simple Adventures***. British administrators assert power by learning only those terms absolutely necessary for maintaining control—and learning them badly, at that. Even gentle Helen complains that she "[hasn't] the Hindustani to be disagreeable in." Language misuse thus becomes a figure for cultural imposition. The authoritative colonizing power may pronounce decrees which have no correspondence to established native custom; similarly, in Mrs. Perth Macintyre's depiction the memsahib

> makes her own rules, and all the natives she knows are governed by them—nothing from a grammatical point of view could be more satisfactory than that. Her constructions in the language are such as she pleases to place upon it; thus it is impossible that she should make mistakes.

The memsahib narcissistically congratulates herself when her order is obeyed: "the usually admirable result is misleading to the memsahib, who naturally ascribes it to the grace and force and clearness of her directions. Whereas it is really the discernment of Kali Bagh that is to be commended." The Indians have thus accommodated far more than have the Anglo-Indians. Even the mallie has a perfect understanding with English flowers, which is "remarkable, for they spoke a different language."

As for the sahib, he is "pleased to use much the same forms of speech as are common to the memsahib." The "heathen mind" may manipulate, but it is the sahib, with his power of dismissal, who has the last word: "He has subdued their language, as it were, to such uses as he thinks fit to put it, and if they do not choose to acquire it in this form, so much the more inconvenient for them. He can always get another kitmutgar." Thus the sahib learns only the familiar forms of address, for he has no intention of speaking to a native as an equal. He has a "vague theory that one ought not to say *tum* to a Rajah, but he doesn't want to talk to Rajahs—he didn't come out for *that*." To wield authority, the colonizing power must never meet the colonized culture halfway; it is "the essence of the imperialist vision" that one world-view, one language—English—should reign supreme.

Despite George's warning to his wife, it is not true that "Anglo-India sanctions Hindustani for grim convenience only, declining to be amused by it in any way whatever." Drawing-room conversation "scintillates" with Hindustanisms, and the narrator does not doubt that the native language even "creeps into the parlance of Her Excellency." Such terms not only provide local colour for the novel, but also indicate that the Anglo-Indians themselves seek to "inscribe difference" against the metropolitan centre. They have developed a distinct lifestyle which resists some of the Mother Country's norms. After all, there are no sanctions against Sunday tennis in Calcutta. Furthermore, the use of Hindustani gives Anglo-Indians a measure of identification with the new territory they inhabit: not a desire for "indigenization," for they will forget the language when they "sail away from the Apollo Bunder," but rather an indication of partial adaptation, the illusion of success in "translating" from one culture to another.

The Anglo-Indian abuse of Hindustani exposes the profound irony of the opening sentence of chapter twenty, with its mock formality: "for the furtherance of a good understanding between the sahibs and the Aryans who obey them and minister unto them, the Raj has ordained language examinations." ***Simple Adventures*** in fact opposes the view implicit in linguistic relativism, that learning another language enables conciliation between alien world-views. Batcham, a broad target for satire in the text, believes that language provides the only barrier to intercultural rapport: " 'It's the terrible disadvantage of not knowing the language!' responded Mr. Batcham, in a tone which suggested that the language ought to be supplied to Members of Parliament." Mrs. Perth Macintyre's delicate comment on the collusion between Mr. Banerjee and Ambica Nath Mitter parodies Batcham's simplistic view: "Considering how discreetly Mr. Banerjee explained [Batcham's difficulty], the sympathetic perception shown by Ambica Nath Mitter was extraordinary. It might possibly be explained by the fact that they both spoke Hindustani." In fact, Banerjee and Mitter "speak the same language" in more than one sense, both being tuned to the same profit-making wavelength.

Despite many such laughable misunderstandings in ***Simple Adventures,*** the text does not suggest that translation between cultural systems is altogether impossible. Helen herself masters a new "language" in the course of her memsahib apprenticeship. She learns the techniques of bartering and commanding, becomes an initiate into the secrets of "social astronomy," and even discovers the hierarchy of recreational pursuits ("tennis was certainly going out—everybody went in for golf now—links all over the place"). By the end of the novel Helen speaks memsahibese as if to the manner born, naturalized to the language so that she no longer notices its absurdities. She has even acquired the accompanying body language, having "fallen into a way of crossing her knees in a low chair that would horrify her Aunt Plovtree, and a whole set of little feminine Anglo-Indian poses have come to her naturally." If anything, Helen has "acclimatised too soon." As a result "she is growing dull to India":

> She sees no more the supple savagery of the Pathan in the market-place, the bowed reverence of the Mussulman praying in the sunset, the early morning mists lifting among the domes and palms of the city. She has acquired for the Aryan inhabitant a certain strong irritation, and she believes him to be nasty in all his ways . . . She is a memsahib like another.

Helen's fortunes demonstrate that it is reasonably easy to transfer from one cultural system ("gentlewoman") to another parallel system still founded on a British world-view ("memsahib"). ***Simple Adventures*** is less sanguine about the possibilities of successfully transplanting British institutions into the soil of a wholly different culture. The wedding cake "certainly had not carried well: it was a travelled wreck." The abortive effort to recreate the snug, homely atmosphere of a log fire with the kerosene stove illustrates "the foolishness of a sahib who tried to plant his hearth-stone in India." Mrs. Week's attempts to transfer a set of religious beliefs reap no fruits other than the tentative questions, " '*eggi bat,* would the memsahib please to tell them why she put those shiny black hooks in her hair?' ". These images present ludicrous aspects of the imperial endeavour itself.

Even within British culture, broadly defined, the class system inhibits social interaction. In chapter fourteen, geographical boundaries map out both cultural and social division. Like linguistic relations, social demarcations are arbitrary, but those caught within the hierarchy regard them as "natural" and do not question them. [In *Orientalism,* 1979], Edward Said notes the alienation which results:

> this universal practice of designating in one's mind a familiar space which is "ours" and an unfamiliar space beyond "ours" which is "theirs" is a way of making geographical distinctions that *can be* entirely arbitrary. I use the word "arbitrary" here because imaginative geography of the "our land—barbarian land" variety does not require that the barbarians acknowledge the distinction. It is enough for "us" to set up these boundaries in our own minds; "they" become "they" accordingly, and both their territory and their mentality are designated as different from "ours."

A window separates Helen from her bustee neighbours: through it East and West may gaze at each other but never touch. The Brownes regard their boisterous, casual jockey neighbours even more wistfully. Because the members of the jockey household are white, their social estrangement seems less necessary: "[jockeys] belonged to the class Calcutta knows collectively, as a sub-social element, that nevertheless has its indeterminate value, being white, or nearly so, as a rule."

Mrs. Perth Macintyre smiles at the type of the arrogant Royal Engineer: "we may even share his pardonable incredulity as to whether before his advent India was at all." From a structuralist viewpoint, however, the Royal Engineer is not far off the mark. A major factor inhibiting any meaningful encounter between systems is the necessity to understand new experiences in terms of pre-existing categories. India is particularly prone to such preconceptions, as Sayter notes: "India is the only country in the world where people can be properly applied to for their impressions before they leave the ship." Mrs. Peachey is captive within such a cultural "prisonhouse." She dimly realises "it was not likely that a little Bengali could be baited with a Bath bun," but nonetheless allows herself to "picture Helen leading in gentle triumph a train of Rajahs to the bosom of the Church—a train of nice Rajahs, clean and savoury." Batcham is the object of more severe criticism, in his self-serving determination to see only what he wishes to see:

> It was interesting to watch Mr. Batcham in the process of forming an opinion of Anglo-Indian society; that is, of making his observations match the rags and tags of ideas about us which he had gathered together from various popular sources before coming out.

A more subtle illustration of the way in which established epistemological frameworks determine what is "culturally marked" occurs on the Brownes' honeymoon, in which they could "wander for miles in any direction over a country that seemed as empty as if it had just been made." The Brownes, with their English cultural blinkers, presumably regard cities, monuments, and neatly fenced farms as signs of an "established" country. Yet this criticism is by no means limited to the Anglo-Indians. We inevitably approach any text, whether literary or otherwise, with a mixture of knowledge, expectations, and preconceptions, just as Helen and other characters approach the "text" of India. India is necessarily "always-already-read" in Fredric Jameson's sense:

> We never really confront a text immediately, in all its freshness as a thing-itself. Rather, texts come before us as the always-already-read; we apprehend them through sedimented layers of previous interpretations, or—if the text is brand-new—through the sedimented reading habits and categories developed by those inherited interpretive traditions.

. . . . .

> How little more than illustrations the men and women have been, as one looks back, pictures in a magic lantern, shadows on a wall!
>
> —***Simple Adventures***

Systems have many sinister aspects. They can, for example, become mere impersonal mechanisms and subsume the individual completely. Indeed, Lord Cromer, England's representative in occupied Egypt from 1882 to 1907, imagined the apparatus of colonialism in such terms. Said comments:

> Cromer envisions a seat of power in the West, and radiating out from it towards the East a great embracing machine, sustaining the central authority yet commanded by it. What the machine's branches feed into it in the East—human material, material wealth, knowledge, what have you—is processed by the machine, then converted into more power.

The same image of machinery is not obsolete today, for it turns up without evident irony in Geoffrey Moorhouse's recent history, *India Britannica* (1983). It also occurs in ***Simple Adventures,*** referring specifically to the central imperial authority:

> We tell our superior officers, until at last the Queen Empress herself is told; and the Queen-Empress is quite as incapable of further procedure as Mrs. Browne; indeed, much more so, for she is compelled to listen to the voice of her parliamentary wrangling- machine upon the matter, which obeys the turning of a handle, and is a very fine piece of mechanism indeed, but not absolutely reliable when it delivers ready-made opinions upon Aryan problems.

This passage reduces human agency, so that even the Queen Empress herself must bow to a system which, like *langue,* is beyond modification by any one individual. Duncan never allows the novel's tone to darken, however. She has Mrs. Perth Macintyre step back from such overt political criticism by identifying it as mere hearsay, a second-hand report of a casual comment ("At least I am quite sure that is my husband's idea, and I have often heard young Browne say the same thing").

The danger of this mechanistic view is the very same feature which makes it so seductive for the bureaucrat: the fact that critics of any "wrangling machine" are unable to attribute blame for poor decisions to any one person. Incidents in ***Simple Adventures,*** however, suggest that canons of taste—both linguistic and cultural—do not emerge in such an inscrutable, impersonal manner. Members of a dominant group, or even particularly influential individuals such as Her Excellency, have the power of legitimation and redefinition. Returning to the passage which opened this paper, for example, it is young Browne who "corrects" the baboo's language usage. The term "baboo" itself is not neutral, for the former term of respect was "often used with a slight savour of disparagement" among Anglo-Indians [according to Henry Yule and A.C. Burnell in *Hobson-Jobson: A Glossary of Colloquial Anglo-Indian Words and Phrases,* 1968].

Systems create hierarchies. The Anglo-Indians elaborately codified their own "social astronomy" in the Warrant of Precedence, "which was designed as an infallible guide to hierarchy in India, indispensable to the proper arrangement of [a] ceremony, conference or even of a mere dinner party." Even ostensibly "innocent" systems, such as modes of transport in Calcutta, are expressions of "power cultural," which establishes "orthodoxies and canons of taste, texts, values." To borrow the terminology of one of Janet Frame's characters, such norms can be "tippykill": typicality can "kill" the rebellious or marginalized individual who does not match any pre-fabricated mold. Duncan, however, depicts very few characters who stand opposed to social custom. The text is, after all, a prose version of the comedy of manners, in which serious emotional and interpersonal conflicts would jar. Mrs. Perth Macintyre does touch upon the way in which systems create "insiders" and "outsiders," but with a characteristic wry humour that excludes pathos. For example, in describing the Viceregal Reception she includes the detail of the "Mohammedan lady of enormous proportions" in crimson satin, who incites polite derisive convulsions from the inner circle, the ladies of the Private Entrée. On board ship, even Miss Stitch, M.D., scorns the "foreign" woman who is "about four annas in the rupee." And in a thoughtful mode, the narrator remarks upon the "cramping" alienation which Helen experiences in her own neighbourhood: "I mention the local isolation of these young people because it is typical of Calcutta, where nobody by any chance ever leans over anybody else's garden gate."

Systematic categorisation tends to be restrictive and reductive. Again, the issue appears in ***Simple Adventures*** with a deft, humorous touch. The limitations of Mrs. Toote's trenchant distinction between the frivolous and the unfrivolous become manifest with the next visitors: "Helen wondered in vain to which of Mrs. Toote's two social orders [the Wodenhamers] belonged." Duncan thus smiles at social practices which, even today, continue to oppress whole peoples. Said asks, "Can one divide human reality, as indeed human reality seems to be genuinely divided, into clearly different cultures, histories, traditions, societies, even races, and survive the consequences humanly?" Om Juneja, in a curt and damning review of Duncan's oeuvre [in *Ambivalence: Studies in Canadian Literature,* 1990], writes, "India in her fiction is an exotic commodity meant for the consumption of white masters. Sara Jeannette Duncan is a typical Anglo-Indian novelist who reinforces the stereotypes of a Memsahib." Juneja fails to note that stereotypes are the very stuff of the comic mode and that ***Simple Adventures*** abounds with "fixed" characters, both Indian and Anglo-Indian. By the end of the novel even Helen's character becomes calcified: "this will sum up her impressions of India as completely years hence as it does to-day."

Yet comedy as much as any other genre must confront the constraining effects of stereotyping, particularly in a cross-cultural context. ***Simple Adventures*** does raise the question as to whether it is possible to escape restrictive categorisation, to stand outside one's native culture to the extent that it seems a "foreign language." In this respect linguistic determinism is self-contradictory for, as [Robert H. Robins notes in *Universalism versus Relativism in Language and Thought,* edited by Rik Pinxten, 1976], "if we [were] unable to organize our thinking beyond the limits set by our native language, we could [never] become aware of these limits." Robins thus rejects linguistic determinism in favour of relativism:

> Adopting a physical metaphor, it would seem best to liken language not to a tramline nor to an open road, as far as thought and categorization are concerned, but to sets of grooves or ruts, along which it is easier and more natural to direct one's thinking, but which with some effort can be overcome.

The minds of most of the Anglo-Indians in ***Simple Adventures*** are firmly "grooved." Their cultural awareness is dismal. Mrs. Macdonald, for example, fails to realise that Hindustani sounds like English precisely because certain items did not exist in India until the advent of the colonisers ("It's awfully funny, how like English the language is in some words?"). A knowledge of one's own culture requires awareness of how social institutions *might otherwise be organised.* Anglo-Indian society, however, "inclined to be intellectually limp," discourages inquisitive intellectual probing. Mrs. Macdonald assures Helen that she is "going the wrong way about it" in studying a Hindustani grammar to learn the language. Helen learns (the Anglo-Indian variety of) Hindustani by immersion, in the same way that she acquired her native language, and thus loses the comparative "objectivity" gained in a systematic approach. Once she has graduated to memsahibship, Helen "takes the easiest word and the shortest cut," thereby following "the groove along which it is easier and more natural to direct one's thinking."

The Brownes initially think themselves above the petty social-laddering of Anglo-India. As the acerbic Mrs. Perth Macintyre warns, however, this "tranquil" state is merely temporary, and the Brownes will lose their objectivity once they assimilate ("It is charming, this indifference, while it lasts, but it is not intended to endure".) Sayter, like Mrs. Perth Macintyre, maintains a wry, ironic distance from Anglo-Indian culture, yet even his cynicism is a form of Anglo-Indian pose, available to those with sufficient social status. Sayter mocks, but does not fundamentally challenge, the foibles of Calcutta.

Mrs. Perth Macintyre credits herself with a superior, ironic stance, as one who still has "eyes to see," claiming greater powers of observation than her fellow characters. Describing the scene in the Viceregal Drawing-Room, for example, she writes, "I have no doubt one wouldn't observe this to the same extent if one were amongst them." The reader, however, must assess her reliability as a narrator. In some cases an additional layer of irony operates, in which the implied author and the reader snicker together behind Mrs. Perth Macintyre's back. For example, in the opening of chapter twenty-eight the joke is clearly on Mrs. Perth Macintyre, who sidles around the touchy issue of her niece's lingering state of singleness. The worthy narrator herself claims absolute fidelity to the facts of the fictional world. "It will be my fault if you find [Helen] dull," she writes, "I shall be in that case no faithful historian, but a traducer." Conscientiously she cites her sources, explaining, for example, how she came to know the story of Mr. Batcham, Ambica Nath Mitter, and the six rupees. In the world of ***Simple Adventures*** however, any character's claim to truth is dubious. The reader doubts the accuracy of the gossip "coming straight from Jimmy Forbes"; servants' recommendations all have a "horrible mendacity";

Chua's law suit is a farce, with both parties bribing the witness; and the evidence which Batcham collects in pursuit of Truth is anything other than "unbiassed in every particular." Mrs. Perth Macintyre herself does not escape from the snobbishness which she attributes to her fellow memsahibs. She spurns the Private Entrée ("everybody knows we wouldn't take it now"), but lets it slip that she is acquainted with the Viceregal couple: "can it be that circumstances—chiefly viceregal dinners—have thrown us more together?"

The uncertainty surrounding evidence within the fictional world also obtains in the broader textual system of reader, implied author, and narrator. The extensive use of free indirect discourse in ***Simple Adventures*** creates difficulties for the reader in ascribing value judgments to either the "unreliable" sources of character and narrator, or the "reliable" source of the implied author, who provides the yardstick for the text's norms. The following description of the *dâk wallah,* for example, reveals "orientalist" proclivities but leaves doubt as to whether they stem from Mrs. Perth Macintyre, the Brownes, or Duncan herself: "On he went, jingling faint and fainter, bearing the news of the mountains down into the valleys, a pleasant primitive figure of the pleasant primitive East." The sentiment is not far removed from the narrator's sardonic comment that the travelling public in India sees only "an idyllic existence which runs sweetly among them to the tinkle of the peg and the salaams of a loyal and affectionate subject race." The implied author similarly teeters between self-undermining parody and alliance with suspiciously orientalist views in respect of the travel narrative convention. Mrs. Perth Macintyre scorns travel journals and their creators yet ***Simple Adventures*** itself contains four chapters of travel narrative, not including Helen's sea voyage. Such ambivalent, finely-balanced irony, typical of Duncan's narrators, has prompted contradictory responses even within the bounds of authorial reading. On the one hand, Juneja accuses Duncan of complicity with the colonial power; on the other, [in *A Different Point of View: Sara Jeannette Duncan,* 1991] Misao Dean regards narratorial irony as a subversive strategy enabling Duncan to "covertly criticize the assumptions of the ideological centre without betraying her own or her reader's allegiance to them." The latter view is far more alive to the wry subtleties of ***Simple Adventures***.

Irony even pervades the title of the novel. Helen's "adventures" are scarcely "simple," for they raise profound questions about the operation of society. East and West alike are beleaguered by systems, and all minds, not only that of the baboo, "run in grooves." Duncan herself maintains a discomforting ironic poise by refusing to "take sides" with or against her characters, so that ***Simple Adventures*** only rarely employs full-blown satire, which demands a clear moral standard on the part of the implied author. The machinery of systems will, above all, continue to grind, as each generation passes its traditions to the next. The narrator's last gesture for Helen is to donate her drawing-room furniture, and the novel closes as Mrs. Perth Macintyre's "sentence" as a memsahib reaches its term.

FURTHER READING

Biography

Fowler, Marian. *Redney: A Life of Sara Jeannette Duncan.* Toronto: Anansi, 1983, 333 p.

Critical biography of Duncan.

Criticism

Bissell, Claude. Introduction to *The Imperialist,* by Sara Jeannette Duncan, pp. v-ix. Toronto: McClelland and Stewart Limited, 1971.

Discusses *The Imperialist* as a novel of social criticism and of the "conflict between manners and morals . . . and the promptings of the human heart and mind."

Cloutier, Pierre. "The First Exile." *Canadian Literature* 59 (Winter 1974): 30-37.

Examines *A Daughter of Today* as the first Canadian novel concerned with "the development of a young, sensitive, artistic imagination exiled abroad."

Dean, Misao. "Duncan's Representative Men." *Canadian Literature,* No. 98 (Autumn 1983): 117-19.

Explores Duncan's ironic use of "representative men," such as Octavius Milburn in *The Imperialist,* to critique the sort of leaders produced by American society.

———. "The Paintbrush and the Scalpel: Sara Jeannette Duncan Representing India." *Canadian Literature,* No. 132 (Spring 1992): 82-93.

Argues that Duncan sought both "to gain artistic 'impressions,' as defined by the aesthetic movement, and to analyse 'material,' using the techniques of scientific realism" in her Indian novels.

———. "The Struggle for the Ideal: Political Change in Sara Jeannette Duncan's Novels." *The Literary Criterion* XIX, Nos. 3-4 (1984): 93-104.

Investigates Duncan's theme of "the shift in political power from the aristocracy to the majority" in *The Imperialist* and *The Burnt Offering.*

Smith, Marion. "Period Pieces." *Canadian Literature,* No. 10 (Autumn 1961): 72-7.

Review of *The Imperialist* and two other Canadian novels republished in 1961.

Additional coverage of Duncan's life and works is contained in the following source published by Gale Research: *Dictionary of Literary Biography,* Vol. 92.

Nikolai Gumilev

1886-1921

(Born Nikolai Stephanovich Gumilev) Russian poet, critic, and dramatist.

INTRODUCTION

A Russian poet and literary theorist, Gumilev was a founder and an influential proponent of Acmeism, a literary movement emphasizing clarity of expression, vivid imagery based in concrete experience, and respect for the structure and precision of traditional literary craftsmanship. His poetry, unique in Russian literature for its lavish descriptions of life in foreign lands, reflects a high regard for courageous adventurers and an interest in the ethnology of other cultures. Gumilev's literary and critical writings influenced the development of modern Russian poetry in spite of their repression in the Soviet Union from the time of his execution in 1921 until the mid-1980s.

Biographical Information

The son of a navy doctor, Gumilev was raised in St. Petersburg and attended Tsarskoe Selo Lyceum, where he came under the influence of the noted poet Innokenty Annensky and began seriously writing verse. While at the lyceum, Gumilev also met Anna Akhmatova, another aspiring poet who later became his wife. In 1905 he published his first collection of poems, *Put konkvistadorov.* Gumilev's early verse was written in the Symbolist style, but he soon became disillusioned with the lack of clarity of Symbolist verse and developed his own poetic style, which he called Acmeism. In 1911 he founded a group called the Poets' Guild in order to promote and disseminate the principles of Acmeism, rapidly becoming one of the most prominent Russian poets. Gumilev fought in Prussia and Poland and served on the staff of the Russian Expeditionary Corps in Paris during World War I. In 1918 he returned to Russia and began providing large-scale translations of foreign literature, including Samuel Coleridge's *Rime of the Ancient Mariner,* for Maxim Gorky's publishing firm. Divorced from Akhmatova in 1918, Gumilev remarried in 1919, and remained active as a poet, lecturer, translator, and editor until his execution in 1921 for alleged participation in an anti-Soviet conspiracy.

Major Works

Gumilev's first books of poetry, including *Put konkvistadorov, Romanticheskie tsvety,* and *Zhemchuga,* reflect his early Symbolist orientation and exhibit a wide range of themes, including American exoticism, classical mythology, and European Christianity. *Chuzhoe nebo* has been called the most Acmeist of Gumilev's work; this volume marked his break with the Symbolist school. In later volumes such as *Kostyor, Shatyor,* and *Ognennyi stolp*—the last two of which are considered by many critics to contain his finest poetry—Gumilev exhibits a neo-classical treatment of such themes as death, reincarnation, and the convergence of mysticism and earthly concerns. Gumilev's dramatic works, written predominantly in verse, reflect a wide range of subject matter. Of his three early one-act dramas, only *Acteon,* which retells the mythological story of Acteon and Diana, is considered by critics and scholars to rank among Gumilev's best work. Later verse dramas include *Ditya Allakha,* notable for its use of Eastern verse forms, and *Gondla,* a piece set in ninth-century Iceland. Gumilev's most extensive dramatic work, *Otravlennaya tunika* (*The Poisoned Tunic*), is a classical tragedy in five acts set in sixth-century Byzantium. A fragment of yet another verse drama, presumed to be based on the Fenian cycle of Irish legends and believed to have been written between 1918 and 1921, surfaced in the Central State Archive of Literature and Art in Moscow after Gumilev's death.

Critical Reception

Although his poetry has been well received, Gumilev is

not considered one of the best Acmeist poets. Rather, he is valued as a literary theorist whose essays on the creation and translation of poetry were, despite their official obscurity, influential in the development of both Soviet and dissident writers. His essays, many of which appeared in the literary journal *Apollon* between 1909 and 1916, are considered to be among his most valuable contributions to early twentieth-century Russian literature.

PRINCIPAL WORKS

Put konkvistadorov (poetry) 1905
Romanticheskie tsvety (poetry) 1908
Zhemchuga (poetry) 1910
Chuzhoe nebo (poetry) 1912
Acteon (drama) 1913
Kolchan (poetry) 1916
Ditya Allakha (drama) 1917
Gondla (drama) 1917
Kostyor (poetry) 1918
Ognennyi stolp (poetry) 1921
Shatyor (poetry) 1921
Ten ot palmy (essays) 1921
K sinei zvezde (poetry) 1923
Pisma o russkoy poezii (essays) 1923
The Abinger Garland (poetry) 1945
**Otravlennaya tunika* [*The Poisoned Tunic*] (drama) 1952
Sobranie sochinenii. 4 vols. (poetry) 1962-68
Selected Works of Nikolai S. Gumilev (poetry, short stories, drama, essays) 1972
On Russian Poetry (essays) 1977

*This work was completed in 1918.

CRITICISM

Nikolai Gumilev (essay date 1919)

SOURCE: "On Translations of Poetry," in *Nikolai Gumilev on Russian Poetry,* edited and translated by David Lapeza, Ardis, 1976, pp. 34-8.

[*In the following essay, Gumilev demonstrates the Acmeist emphasis on formalism and precision in literary structure in his outline of nine criteria for the proper translation of poetry.*]

There are three methods for translating verse: by the first, the translator uses whatever meter and combination of rhymes happen to come into his head, his own vocabulary, often alien to the author, and at his personal discretion now lengthens, now shortens the original; clearly, such translation can only be called amateurish.

By the second method, the translator acts, for the most part, in the same way, but introduces a theoretical justification for his act; he assures us that if the poet being translated had written in Russian, he would have written in just that way. This method was very widespread in the eighteenth century. Pope in England, Kostrov in our country translated Homer that way and enjoyed extraordinary success. The nineteenth century rejected this method, but traces of it remain in our own day. Even now some still think that it is possible to substitute one meter for another, for example, pentameter for hexameter, forego rhyme, introduce new images and so forth. The spirit preserved is supposed to justify everything. However, a poet worthy of the name uses precisely the form as the only means of expressing the spirit. I shall try to outline now how this is done.

The first thing that attracts the reader's attention and, in all probability, the most important, if often unconscious, basis for the creation of a poem is its idea or, more exactly, its image, since a poet thinks in images. The number of images is limited, evoked by life, and the poet is rarely their creator. Only in his relationship to them is his personality revealed. For example, the Persian poets thought of the rose as a living being, the medieval poets as a symbol of love and beauty; Pushkin's rose is a beautiful flower on its stem, Maikov's rose is always a decoration, an accessory; in Vyacheslav Ivanov the rose assumes mystical value, etc. Naturally, in all these cases both the choice of words and their combinations are essentially different. Within the bounds of the same relationship there are thousands of nuances: thus, the comments of Byron's Corsair stand out against the background of the author's psychologically flowery description of him in their laconism and technical choice of expressions. In his gloss to "The Raven," Edgar Allan Poe speaks of an undercurrent theme, scarcely outlined, and for that very reason producing an especially powerful impression. If someone translating that same "Raven" were to transmit with greater care the external plot of the movements of the bird, and with less—the poet's longing for his dead beloved, he would have violated the author's conception and failed to complete the task he had taken upon himself.

Immediately after the choice of image, the poet is confronted with the question of its development and proportions. Both determine the choice of the number of lines and stanzas. In this the translator is obliged to blindly follow the author. It is impossible to shorten or lengthen a poem without at the same time changing its tone, even if the quantity of images is retained. Both laconism and amorphousness of image are determined by the conception, and each extra or missing line changes its degree of tension.

As for stanzas, each of them creates a particular train of thought, unlike the others. Thus, the sonnet, stating some proposition in the first quatrain, reveals its antithesis in the second, outlines their interaction in the first tercet and in the second tercet gives it an unexpected resolution, condensed in the last line, often even in the last word, for which reason it is called the key of the sonnet. The Shakespearian sonnet, with quatrains unconnected by rhyme, is supple, flexible, but devoid of sufficient strength; the Italian sonnet, with only feminine rhymes, is powerfully lyrical and stately, but of little use for narrative or description, for which the usual form is perfectly suited. In the ghazal, the same word, sometimes the same expression repeated at the end of every line (the Europeans incorrectly break it into two lines) creates an impression of gaudy ornament or incantation. The octave, extensive and spacious like no other form, is suitable for calm and unhurried narration. Even such simple stanzas as the quatrain and the couplet have their peculiarities which the poet takes into account, if only unconsciously. Moreover, for any sort of serious acquaintance with a poet it is essential to know what stanzas he preferred and how he used them. For that reason exact retention of the stanza is the duty of the translator.

In the realm of style, the translator should really master the author's poetics in regard to this question. Each poet has his own vocabulary, often supported by theoretical considerations. Wordsworth, for example, insists upon using colloquial language. Hugo—upon employing words in their direct senses. Hérédia—upon their precision. Verlaine, on the contrary, upon their simplicity and casualness, etc. One should also elucidate—and this is especially important—the character of the translated poet's similes. Thus, Byron compares a concrete image with an abstract one (a famous example is Lermontov—"The air as pure and fresh as a child's kiss"), Shakespeare—an abstract with a concrete image (an example in Pushkin—"A sharp-clawed beast, gnawing at the heart, is conscience"), Hérédia—a concrete with concrete ("Like a flock of falcons flown down from their native cliffs . . . the warriors and captains bid Palos farewell"); Coleridge draws the image of a simile from among the images of a given play ("and each soul sang, like that arrow of mine"); in Edgar Allan Poe the simile moves into development of image, etc. In poetry there are often parallelisms, complete, inverted, shortened repetitions, exact indications of time or place, quotations interspersed in the stanza, and other devices with special hypnotizing effects upon the reader. It is advisable to preserve them carefully, sacrificing less essential things. Besides, many poets have paid great attention to the semantic meaning of rhyme. Théodore de Banville even maintained that rhyme words, as the dominant ones, arise first in the consciousness of the poet and form the poem's skeleton: for this reason it is desirable that at least one of a pair of rhymed words correspond to the word at line-end in the original.

It is necessary to warn the majority of translators with regard to the use of such particles as "already," "only," "just," "you know," "won't it?" etc. These all possess a powerful expressiveness and usually double the verb's effective power. One can avoid them, choosing among synonymous but non-homologous words, of which there are many in Russian, for example: "road—way," "Lord—God," "Love—passion," etc., or resorting to contractions, like "wind," "dreaming," "song," etc.

Slavonicisms or archaisms are permissible, but with great caution, only in the translation of old poets, who predate the Lake School and Romanticism, or of stylists like William Morris in England or Jean Moréas in France.

Finally, there remains the acoustical side of verse: it is hardest of all for the translator to transmit. Russian syllabic verse is still too little developed to reconstruct French rhythms; English verse allows an arbitrary mixture of masculine and feminine rhyme, which is not characteristic of Russian. It is necessary to resort to relative transmission: to translate syllabic verse in iambs (sometimes trochees), to introduce regular alternation of rhymes into English verse, resorting here, where possible, to masculine rhymes only, as more characteristic of the language. Nevertheless, it is essential that this relative transmission be strictly adhered to, because it was not created by chance and, for the most part, really gives an adequate impression of the original.

Each meter has its own feeling, its own peculiarities and purposes: the iamb, as if going down stairs (the accented syllable being lower in pitch than the unaccented), is free, clear, firm and beautifully transmits human speech, the tension of the human will. The trochee, rising, winged, is always agitated and now anxious, now moved, now amused; its sphere is song. The dactyl, leaning on the first accented syllable and swinging the two unaccented ones as a palm tree does its top, is powerful, stately, speaks of the elements at rest, of the deeds of gods and heroes. The anapest, its opposite, is impetuous, fitful, it is the elements in action, the tension of inhuman passion. And the amphibrach, their synthesis, lulling and transparent, speaks of the peace of an existence divinely light and wise. Different measures in these meters also differ in their characteristics: thus, iambic tetrameter is most often used for lyric narration, pentameter—for epic or dramatic narration, hexameter—for discourse, etc. Poets often struggle with these characteristics of form, demand other possibilities of them and at times succeed in this. However, such a struggle always affects the image, and for that reason, it is essential to preserve its traces in the translation, strictly observing the meters and the measure of the original.

The question of rhyme has been of great interest to poets: Voltaire demanded acoustical rhyme, Théodore de Banville—visual; Byron readily rhymed proper names and used compound rhyme, the Parnassians—rich rhyme; Verlaine, on the contrary, used suppressed rhyme; the Symbolists often resort to assonance. The translator should determine the character of his author's rhyme and follow it.

Also extremely important is the question of the run-over of a sentence from one line to another, the so-called *enjambement*. Classical poets like Corneille and Racine did not permit this; the Romantics brought it into general use; the modernists have developed it to the extreme. In this too, the translator should consider the views of the author.

From all that has been said, clearly, the translator of a poet must be a poet himself and, besides that, a careful investigator and perceptive critic, who, selecting what is most characteristic for each author, allows himself to sacrifice the rest when necessary. And he must forget his own personality, thinking only of the personality of the author. Ideally, translations should not be signed.

One wishing to advance the technique of translation can go even farther: for example, maintain the rhymes of the original, render syllabic verse as such in Russian, find words for rendering characteristic modes of speech (British military language in Kipling, Laforgue's Parisian jargon, Mallarmé's syntax, etc.).

Of course, for the ordinary translator this is by no means obligatory.

Let me repeat briefly what it is obligatory to observe: 1) the number of lines, 2) the meter and measure, 3) the alternation of rhyme, 4) the nature of the *enjambement*, 5) the nature of the rhyme, 6) the nature of the vocabulary, 7) the type of similes, 8) special devices, 9) changes in tone.

These are the translator's nine commandments: since there is one less than those of Moses, I hope that they will be better observed.

Marc Slonim (essay date 1953)

SOURCE: "After the Symbolists," in *Modern Russian Literature: From Chekhov to the Present,* Oxford University Press, 1953, pp. 211-33.

[*Slonim was a Russian-born American critic who wrote extensively on Russian literature. In the following excerpt, he discusses Gumilev's development as a poet and his influence, citing his recurrent themes of strength, combativeness, and heroism as those most often reflected in later Soviet literature.*]

The Acmeist group, founded by Gumilev in 1912, and succeeded by his Guild of Poets, included a great many people of diverse literary aspirations. They had no other unity save that of negation: they all rejected what they considered the aberrations of Symbolism, but they differed vastly in their personalities, the character of their work, and their contributions to literature. The leader of Acmeism, Nicholas Gumilev (1886-1921), was the son of a naval physician; he studied under Annensky in the *gymnasia* of Czarskoe Selo, at the University of St. Petersburg, and at the Sorbonne. In 1910 he married Anna Gorenko, who became famous under the pen name of Anna Akhmatova; they separated during World War I and were divorced in 1918. Gumilev traveled widely in Africa, the Near East, and Europe. In 1914 he volunteered for the army, went to the front as an officer, and was awarded the Cross of St. George for bravery. After the Revolution he boasted of his monarchical sympathies, became involved in the Tagantsev affair, an anti-Soviet conspiracy, and was executed by a Communist firing squad in August 1921.

In his short and adventurous life Gumilev displayed the same zest for action, the same romantic sense of heroic effort that he had glorified in his virile and dynamic poems. From his first book, ***The Path of the Conquistadors*** (1905), through subsequent collections (***Romantic Flowers,*** 1908, ***Pearls,*** 1910, ***Alien Skies,*** 1911, ***The Quiver,*** 1916, ***The Campfire,*** 1918), to his last volumes of verse (***The Tent,*** 1920, ***The Pillar of Fire,*** 1921, and ***To the Blue Star,*** published posthumously), he maintained an amazing consistency of direction. A disciple of the Symbolists, and particularly of Briussov, who taught him the clangorous sonority of full rhymes and the mastery of his chill poetics, Gumilev became scornful of the lyrical softness, vagueness, and femininity of the Decadents and mystics. 'Thought is movement,' he has stated, 'and poets should use verbs and not adjectives.' He gave the expressive line priority over the musical one and wanted to 'restore the forthright, direct, full, and exact meaning of words.' 'To name means to create, and poets must find virgin appelations.' This statement was directed against Mallarmé's dictum that the artist ought to suggest while the reader ought to guess, since 'to name means to destroy two-thirds of the enjoyment.' Gumilev rejected the obscurity and the morbid 'mystery' of the Symbolists. His poetic credo called for clarity, concreteness, and plasticity. Descriptive and realistic imagery regains its place in his work; it goes hand in hand with a somewhat Nietzschean streak of 'virile individualism' and attachment to earthy sensations.

This poet, who celebrated the fullness of being, struggle, motion, fulfilment, loved the poetic forte. Most of his poems are in a major key, and he uses striking and often brutal images and resounding rhymes. The richness of his vocabulary and the abundance of his metaphors are, however, toned down by the severity of his highly polished rhythms. 'Be calm, my Muse: like bronze thy voice shall ring—that is the only way to sing.'

Heroism and exoticism colored most of Gumilev's poems during the first stage of his development. He admired pioneers, conquistadors, gallant soldiers, and bold mariners. His heroes are the adventurers, the lusty captains of the seven seas—the names of Columbus, Vasco de Gama, La Pérouse, and Cortez often appear in his poems. These men knew that 'a blind nothing is better than a golden yesterday'; they rejected the fusty routine of security, and each spring the Muse of Distant Travels pushed them toward new endeavors.

Gumilev's collections of African verse, in which some Soviet critics found a 'reflection of colonial imperialism,' revealed the same romantic predilection for the heroic—but this time with an exotic background of fierce combats, savage natives, and East African landscapes (these are to be found for the most part in ***Quiver***). In the forest and deserts of the Dark Continent he found not only proud fighters who die superbly, such as his Dahomean warlord, but also a violence of colors, a power, and a spontaneous and magnificent outburst of the life instinct. He confided to his friends what a genuine relief all this was after the sophistications of a Viacheslav Ivanov and the twilight of St. Petersburg.

It is quite possible that Gumilev's idealization of strength, combativeness, and virility was a means of overcoming his own sensitivity and shyness: the intrepid conquistador was not the real Gumilev, but his romantic superego, what he wished and attempted to be. Moreover, there was often a mixture of genuine feelings and of braggadocio in Gumilev's gestures, and even in his literary activity. This poet who introduced Kiplingesque overtones into his work was basically a product of those very aesthetic, Symbolist, and individualistic milieus against which he fought so successfully in his poems and articles. Although heroic and soldierly motifs never disappeared from his poetry, he struck new chords about 1915, when Acmeism was at its apogee. Next to stressing man's stoic acceptance of his fate, Gumilev glorified romantic visions of love and hidden religious aspirations. He addressed to his beloved lyrical songs of a troubadour and assured her that 'the flutter of her eyelashes was more delectable than an angel's trumpetings.' At the same time he revealed a somewhat mystical bent, spoke of the Sun of the Spirit, and indulged in surrealistic dreams in which all the limitations of time and space were abolished and psychic experience foretold his own death in a prophetic illumination (**'The Last Trolley,'** one of his most impressive poems of those years). Toward the end of his life the romantic and idealistic trends of this anti-Symbolist became extremely obvious; he spoke of the fourth dimension and predicted the expansion of man's perception: 'Under the scalpel of nature and art our spirit screams, our flesh is racked in giving birth to the organ of a sixth sense.' Yet even the most daring poems of this new trend of his were firm in structure, verbally precise, and perfectly intelligible: Gumilev remained faithful to the Acmeist aesthetics. Although the last book Gumilev read in prison was the *Iliad,* he was scarcely a lover of the classics, preferring Renaissance and romantic writers; one of his best translations is that of Coleridge's *The Rime of the Ancient Mariner.*

The semi-epical form of Gumilev's ballads, the descriptive quality of his poems (including brilliant pictures of European lands and towns), and the severely beautiful mold of his verse had a strong influence on his contemporaries. He was respected as a Poet Warrior who lived his poetry and applied his code of military honor and the Nietzschean Superman morality to daily routine, and was greatly admired as a master of prosody—an assured and impeccable craftsman. This rare combination of personal and professional attributes made him an ideal person for literary leadership. He was not the genius some *émigré* critics, deeply impressed by his tragic fate, had attempted to prove him, but he was an excellent poet and he occupied an important place in pre-Revolutionary letters. He enjoyed his position and was quite conscious of his role of having initiated a vast poetic movement; he opposed the accepted canons of Symbolism not only with new themes and moods, but also with a new, vigorous, and expressive style. The concreteness of his approach, his masculine 'anti-eloquent' attitude, his technical mastery all had a stimulating effect. The Guild of Poets became, under his leadership, a training school for dozens of prominent literati, and many contemporaries learned a great deal from Gumilev.

Although his name is omitted from Communist textbooks and his works are seldom quoted by Soviet critics without a conformist addition of derogatory qualifications, the truth is that the impact of this 'Decadent counter-revolutionary' is evident in many Soviet poets, from Tikhonov to Bagritsky. The praise of heroism and vitality that has become almost a commonplace in post-Revolutionary letters can be traced directly to Gumilev's poetic tradition. The Acmeists and their leader fought against Symbolism in order to prepare for the advent of a more concrete, sober, and strong poetry inspired by this earth and not by any illuminations from beyond. In this they are predecessors of trends that Soviet critics have erroneously declared to be the exclusive features of Communist art. It is somewhat paradoxical, however, that a monarchist executed as a counter-revolutionary plotter should be one of the formal teachers of proletarian poetry. No wonder Moscow critics obstinately refuse to admit any such degrading lineage, and interpret Acmeism as 'a new phase of Symbolism,' claiming that the mysticism and exoticism of the latter are fully maintained in the poetry of Akhmatova and Gumilev, and that Gumilev also expresses his hatred of the proletarian Revolution. 'Acmeism is the fullest and most consistent expression of Imperialism in Russian literature'—this statement and others like it have become clichés of Soviet criticism.

Vyacheslav Zavalishin (essay date 1958)

SOURCE: "The Acmeists: Nikolai Gumilyov (1886-1921)," in *Early Soviet Writers,* Frederick A. Praeger Publishers, 1958, pp. 42-6.

[*In the following excerpt, Zavalishin discusses the recurring theme of monarchism in Gumilev's poetry, which may have led to his execution in 1921 for counter-revolutionary activity.*]

After Gumilyov's execution in Soviet Russia in 1921, Georgi Ivanov, one of his followers, paid him the following tribute:

> Why is it that he traveled to Africa, went to war as a volunteer, took part in a conspiracy, and demonstratively, with a sweeping gesture, made a sign of the cross in front of every church he passed in Soviet Petrograd, and told the examining official to his face that he was a monarchist, instead of attempting to exonerate and save himself?
>
> His close friends know that there was nothing of the warrior or the adventurer in Gumilyov. In Africa he was hot and bored, as a soldier he was painfully miserable, and he had very little faith in the conspiracy for which he perished. His attitude to all these matters was that of a typical Chekhov intellectual. He really loved and was interested in only one thing in the world—poetry. But he was firmly convinced that only that man has the right to call himself a poet who will endeavor to be first in any human undertaking and who, more deeply aware than others of human weakness, selfishness, mediocrity and fear of death, will strive afresh each day to overcome the old Adam in himself.
>
> And so this naturally timid, gentle, sickly, bookish man commanded himself to become a big game hunter, a soldier—and as such he was twice awarded the Order of St. George—and a conspirator who risked his life to re-establish the monarchy. What he did with his life, he also did with his poetry. A dreamy, melancholy lyricist, he stifled his lyrical strain and changed the pitch of his not overly strong but remarkably clear voice in an endeavor to return to poetry its former majesty and direct effect on men's souls, to be a ringing dagger, and to set men's hearts afire. . . . He sacrificed himself to his ideal of unflinching strength of will, high human integrity and conquest of the fear of death.

Originally a disciple of Bryusov, to whom the architectonics of verse was an end in itself, Gumilyov strove for virtuosity merely as a means of expressing thought and "the will principle." He studied at the Sorbonne and translated Théophile Gautier, but his early poetry—***The Way of the Conquistadors*** (1905) and ***Romantic Flowers*** (1908)—is reminiscent rather of Edgar Allan Poe and Rider Haggard.

Pearls (1910) is an excursion of a romantic dreamer into the epoch of the discovery and conquest of new territories, in which the exotic past comes suddenly alive with a flapping of ships' sails, cracking of pistols and muskets, and whistling of arrows.

The Quiver (1916), which contains Gumilyov's war poems (he had enlisted in a cavalry regiment in 1914), voices his belief in the righteousness of Russia's cause and in the duty of every Russian to fight in her defense.

I shout, and my voice is savage,
Like brass on brass—and free;
A vessel of living thought,
I cannot cease to be.
Like thunderous hammer blows,
Like tides that never rest,
The golden heart of Russia
Is beating in my breast.

In battle the poet is sustained by a deep religious feeling:

Our cause is great and blessed,
In pride our banner flies,
And shining winged seraphim
Behind each warrior rises.

. . . . .

Here a white-faced soldier kisses
His fallen comrade on the lips,
There a priest in tattered robes
Chants a psalm, beatified.

. . . . .

Give him strength, oh Lord, on earth below,
Give him victory in war's alarms
Who can say unto the conquered foe:
"Let me clasp you in a brother's arms!"

Gumilyov has been accused of giving expression to tsarist Russia's imperialist aspirations in his narrative poem ***Mik*** (1918) and in ***The Tent*** (1921), both of which were based on his travels in Africa before World War I (his last trip, in 1913, had been made as chief of an expedition organized by the Academy of Sciences).

The Soviet writer A. Volkov, in his *Poetry of Russian Imperialism* (1935), treated Gumilyov as a disciple of Kipling, that "bulldog of His Britannic Majesty," and asserted that Gumilyov undertook his journey to Africa with a view to impressing the colonial experience of British imperialists into the service of their Russian counterparts. To be sure, Gumilyov at one time looked upon Abyssinia as a logical area for the extension of Russian rule. He was incapable of remaining a passive observer of the collapse of the Russian state, and had mourned the downfall of the monarchy even before its occurrence:

Burdensome, burdensome, shameful—
To live, having lost our king.
("Agamemnon's Warrior")

Years of disaster followed
The end of the kingly race,
As freedom, that will-o'-the-wisp,
Led us a merry chase.

(Gondla)

In the belief that the stability of the British throne was in part the result of Great Britain's colonial policy, Gumilyov desired to see that policy in operation in Africa. The observations which he expressed symbolically in ***Mik,*** however, are far from bearing out the opinions on racial superiority ascribed to him.

Just as Lermontov had admired the conquered Caucasian mountain tribes for their courage, heroism and sense of honor, Gumilyov admires the same qualities in the Africans. And in ***Mik,*** although the young French boy, symbol of "white supremacy," is at first made king of the beasts of the forest, it is the native slave boy Mik, son of a defeated Abyssinian chieftain, who finally returns to civilization as a triumphant prince, having given himself to the forest forces which Louis had deserted and which had finally killed him.

Gumilyov found that Russian imperialism was more merciful and humane than British, but that Great Britain too was progressing toward friendly treatment of the conquered. He also saw Great Britain beginning to overcome a defect which threatened the Russian state as well—the sharp cleavage between the government and the intellectuals on the one hand and the people on the other. The antiquated Russian monarchy, he concluded, could maintain itself only in a union with the Russia of the peasants.

Gumilyov's political views were set forth not in the conventional medium of political articles, but in his poems, and before the revolution little attention was paid to that side of him; in 1921, however, he was shot for counterrevolutionary activities.

In time, the flowering of Gumilyov's talent coincided with the revolution, and the volume entitled ***Pillar of Fire*** (1921) contains some of the best poems he ever wrote. Their common denominator is hatred of the revolution, which coerced people into surrender of the individual will principle and turned them into a mob blindly obeying the organizers.

The mood is surrealist:

Look, there's a vegetable store,
Its sign in letters dripping red;
Those are not pumpkins on the floor—
Each object is a human head.
The blank-faced executioner
Chopped off my head as well, you know.
It lay with all the others there
In staring-eyed and grinning show.

The presentiment of death, which gave a bitter tang to his early ***Romantic Flowers*** but which disappeared from Gumilyov's poetry for a long time, is strong in ***Pillar of Fire,*** as in his other poems of the revolution.

In **"The Worker"** the poet foretold his own death at the hands of those schooled to destruction by the new leaders:

He stands before his flaming forge,
An aging man of middle height.
His eyes have a submissive look
From blinking at the reddish light.
His comrades are asleep in bed.
He wakes alone, he will not rest,
Intent on fashioning the lead
That will fly homing to my breast.

In a collection of poems published posthumously, in Petrograd, ***To the Blue Star*** (1923), Gumilyov once more returned to his delicate lyricism.

His prose has not received the recognition it deserves. It has had an undoubted influence on Soviet literature, in particular on the work of Tikhonov and Grin in his later period. Gumilyov's last stories were published after his execution in the book entitled ***Shade from a Palm,*** 1922.

Despite his hostility to the new regime, Gumilyov served as associate in Gorki's publishing firm World Literature, for which he made several brilliant translations, notably of Coleridge's *Rime of the Ancient Mariner* and of the Babylonian legend of Gilgamesh (from a French translation). He also issued some of his own work and several collective volumes under the imprint of the Poets' Guild [*Tsekh poetov*], the name adopted by the Acmeist group in 1912. For a time he taught younger writers although, unlike Blok, who wanted to bring the semi-literates in Red Army helmets into the stream of Russian culture, Gumilyov desired to protect that culture from the onslaught of the Bolsheviks. The disagreements between the two poets after the Revolution arose largely from their difference of opinion on that score.

Renato Poggioli (essay date 1960)

SOURCE: "The Neoparnassians," in *The Poets of Russia: 1890-1930,* Harvard University Press, 1960, pp. 212-37.

[*Poggioli was an Italian-born American critic and translator. Much of his critical writing is concerned with Russian literature, including* The Poets of Russia: 1890-1930 *(1960), which is one of the most important examinations of this literary era. In the following excerpt, he discusses Gumilev's treatment of such themes as war, danger, and adventure with what he terms "vigorous and virile Romanticism."*]

The emergence of Gumilev was for Russian poetry an event not too different in kind (although far less in degree) from the earlier appearance in England of Kipling, and in Italy of the martial and patriotic D'Annunzio. Gumilev's sudden rise on the horizon of Russian poetry was viewed at first as a novel miracle, as a wonder of youth. Gumilev came to the fore in the shape of a new David, a gay rogue who relied on his arm and eye no less than on his God, and the weary spirit of the giant, Russian Symbolism, seemed to collapse under the shot from his sling. Gumilev was aware of the novelty, or rather, of the timeliness of his message. He felt that he had come to restore to manliness and health a poetry which had degenerated into the vices opposed to those two virtues. Thus, in the poem entitled **"My Readers"** he prided himself for sparing them from all those morbid, effete, and mystical impressions which the poetry of his elders tried to achieve: "I do not offend them with neurasthenia," said the poet, "I do not humble them with a soft heart, nor do I bore them with complex symbols about the shell of a sucked-out egg."

The Decadents had viewed poetry as if it were a descent into the underworld of the senses; the Symbolists, as an ascent toward the heaven of the soul. Gumilev refused to explore both the forest of symbols and the cave of our dreams, since the path going through them may lead to what is either too base or too lofty for the heart and the mind of man. He rejected the temptation to wander into the ghostly realms of the metaphysical and the occult, and ventured instead into the material and physical world. His quest was not for Eden or Hell, but for a remote oasis or a lonely island, an unbeaten desert or a virgin continent. What spurred him was not the external urge of literary exoticism, but a romantic and passionate nostalgia for the venturesome discovery of new worlds. The frequence in his poetry of Southern and Eastern landscapes may remind us of the Parnassian predilection for the same distant countries and faraway seas. Yet one must not forget that for the Parnassians those landscapes were hardly more than ornamental frames or decorative backgrounds, while in Gumilev's poetry they are direct illustrations of his states of mind. This may serve as a further proof that, all appearances to the contrary, Gumilev's conception of poetry is hardly Parnassian in the real sense of the term. The Russian poet cannot accept the Parnassians' detachment and indifference, as well as their outright denial of any sense of order in the universe beyond the sphere of art. It is against both Parnassian nihilism and Symbolistic mysticism that Gumilev proclaimed, in strongly moral accents, that "religion and poetry are but opposite sides of the same coin." For the Parnassians poetry is but the triumph of a lucid eye and a firm hand on a brute and blind matter, and such a triumph is possible only when no subjective concern affects the artist, at least while he is shaping his object. This is the doctrine of poetic impersonality, which the French Symbolists had inherited from the Parnassians, and were later to impose on many of their followers outside of France. The doctrine, as we well know, had little effect on the Russian disciples of French Symbolism, except on Brjusov, and Gumilev reacted perhaps against the only one among his elders whom he respected as a master when he restated the Romantic belief that "poetry is for man one of the means by which to express his personality." It is to poetry, not less than to religion, that Gumilev assigns the task of educating mankind, or, as he says, of "raising man to the level of a higher type."

Gumilev also took a middle position toward some of the main poetic issues of his time, protesting equally against the Parnassian tendency to treat the word as a mere object and the Symbolist one to treat it almost as pure spirit, and choosing to treat it as if it were a living thing: "poetry, as a living organism, has its anatomy and its physiology; and it is primarily in word combinations that we see what one might call its flesh." He viewed the word also as an instrument of action, through which man makes, or remakes, the world. Once, said he in the poem **"The Word,"** men used words to stop the sun, or to lay a city in ruins. For primitive man, even numbers were endowed with the magic power of words. But modern man has mechanized and materialized both numbers and words, and the latter lie now like dead bees in the empty hive of modern life.

It is with words which are both complex and simple that Gumilev sings his main themes, war, danger, and adventure. He celebrates a free life in a wild world, and praises among men only those with whom one can share a common undertaking or the same risk. It is in such men, "strong, wicked, and happy, loyal to this planet," that he sees his ideal readers. Like them, Gumilev respects the body, which he deifies. In his poem **"Memory,"** as a matter of fact, he reverses the doctrine of reincarnation by assigning a series of different souls to a single physical being. It is perhaps this ability to understand in all its complexity the problem of personality that enables this imperialist to understand and admire the "lesser breeds." Gumilev feels himself the friend and the equal of any native, of a decrepit beggar in Beirut or of an old Ethiopian outlaw. An uncanny feeling of the ties between physical and psychic forces allows him to describe animals, especially wild beasts, in a light of poetic and natural innocence, avoiding at once the pitfalls of sentimental idealization or emblematic stylization, as can be seen in many pieces, especially in the lovely poem **"The Giraffe."**

Conscious of being born a leader, Gumilev knows that he has the right to excel and to command: he considers his own poetry as an example of courage, as a lesson in self-discipline. In **"My Readers"** he defines his own poetic task as that of teaching all his peers "not to dread, and to do what must be done." In brief, Gumilev's ethos is a martial one, and rests on the warrior's acceptance of fate and death. There is no better proof of this than the poem **"The Worker,"** written during the war, describing a little, old, German workingman in the act of shaping the bullet destined to pierce the poet's heart. The poem remains prophetic, although we know that that bullet was molded, or at least fired, by Russian hands. Later the poet dared to face again the vision of his own death in **"The Derailed Streetcar,"** the nightmarish poem he composed shortly before the end of his life.

Gumilev's early work perhaps lacks the visionary power which distinguishes such poems as these. Born too late in a world too old, the youthful poet had felt too much the anguish of living in a shrunken space: and this is why he had tried to find not only escape, but also self-realization, in the faraway corners of this all-too-narrow planet of ours. Yet it would be a mistake to define the early Gumilev as merely "the poet of geography," as the critic Julij Ajkhenval'd did, with the intent of praising him. In reality, even the early Gumilev searched not so much for new lands as for the tree of life; and that tree spreads its roots in depth, not in width. This is why he changed from a geographer and an explorer into an ethnographer and an archaeologist. Perhaps what he sought was to be found in the caves of prehistory, rather than in the broad expanse of a geographical world. Hence the importance of a poem such as **"The Stellar Fright,"** which evokes the terror felt by primitive man at the vision of the star-filled sky. This sense of awe before the sacred mystery of nature is perhaps one of the most vital strains of Gumilev's inspiration. It is from that sense that the poet derives his belief that man's destiny is ultimate defeat, and that his duty is to accept that destiny readily, with heroic resignation and silent stoicism. In this Gumilev recalls Vigny, from whom he drew the epigraph for one of his books. Such an attitude is obviously Romantic: yet Gumilev's is a vigorous and virile Romanticism, impatient of all sentimental vagueness and moral perplexity. What he called Acmeism was but a projection of the literary side of his personality, which he expressed, at its best and most directly, in the book which he prepared for publication just before his death. The muse which dictated that book was life rather than literature: and this is why the figure of its author seems still to stand and shine before our eyes like "the pillar of fire" of its title.

Sam Driver (essay date 1969)

SOURCE: "Nikolaj Gumilev's Early Dramatic Works," in *Slavic and East-European Journal,* Vol. 13, No. 1, Spring, 1969, pp. 326-47.

[*In the following excerpt, Driver focuses on Gumilev's dramatic works, discussing his early influences and the autobiographical themes of his plays.*]

Of the major poets who began their careers as Acmeists, Nikolaj Gumilev remains relatively obscure. In recent years, works by and critical studies of Axmatova and Mandel'štam have been published both in the Soviet Union and abroad. Gumilev, who gave organization and primary impetus to the Acmeist movement, has for the most part been studied only by a small but dedicated group of émigré scholars. It is paradoxical that Gumilev's general reputation rests not so much on his poetry as on his role as a theoretician for Acmeism—yet poetic theory was probably the weakest of his varied and not inconsiderable literary talents.

If political reality has precluded publication of scholarly works on Gumilev's poetry in the Soviet Union, a major obstacle to study in the West has been the difficulty of access to materials. Both problems seem now on the way to at least partial solution: the *Biblioteka poèta* series has projected a volume which is to include Gumilev's works, and in the United States Gleb Struve and Boris Filippov have edited a four-volume collection.

The third volume contains a number of short dramas in verse which have been practically inaccessible since their original publication. These plays, together with the two longer and more familiar ones, make up a curious body of material—and, at first glance, a quite heterogeneous one. They range from farce to tragedy, from theatrical experiment to the well-made classical play, from the superficial and almost frivolous to the serious artistic effort, and from quite facile verse to a remarkable technical virtuosity.

The three earliest plays (about 1912-1913) are one-act verse dramas. ***Igra*** (***The Cardgame***) is no more than a brief dramatic scene, a semi-serious and rather puzzling little piece in which the hero is essentially the lyric *persona* of Gumilev's early poems of adventure and exoticism: poet, prince, and warrior. The setting is a Parisian gaming house at the time of the Restoration. ***Don Žuan v Egipte*** (***Don Juan in Egypt***) is a partly facetious and altogether unusual reworking of the theme; the time is the present and the setting is an ancient temple on the Nile. Neither work ranks among Gumilev's best efforts; they are perhaps not far removed from the bizarre little plays which Gumilev wrote simply for amusement and which were enacted by the poet and his friends. In contrast, ***Acteon*** is a superb treatment of the classical myth of Acteon and Diana; from the technical point of view alone, this verse drama is a small masterpiece.

The second group of plays (1916-1918) are considerably longer. ***Ditja Allaxa*** (***A Child of Allah***), subtitled *arabskaja skazka,* is set in the fairy-tale world of the Arabian Nights; it was intended for the puppet theater. Less successful, perhaps, than the tightly structured ***Acteon,*** it is interesting for its experimentation in genre, in exotic Eastern verse forms. ***Gondla*** is labeled *dramatiçeskaja poèma.* Its exoticism is of an altogether different order: The play is set in ninth-century Iceland and draws on the tradition of the Celtic and Icelandic sagas. Only the last play, ***Otravlennaja tunika*** (***The Poisoned Tunic***) is a play in the usual sense—a classical tragedy in five acts. Its setting is the Byzantine court of Justinian and Theodora.

Gumilev's dramatic works are dissimilar in form, in intent, and in color, but, unexpectedly, there emerge from these widely disparate works a number of common features, particularly in character types and basic action, which give a certain unity and serve as a means of interpreting the plays. ***The Cardgame*** and ***Don Juan,*** if taken alone, would be somewhat enigmatic, and even ***Acteon,*** read merely as a reworking of the myth, would lose a dimension Gumilev intended for it. Similarly, there is much in the later plays which would be difficult to interpret without the pattern which the early plays help establish. What Brjusov observed about the imaginary world of Gumilev's poetry can be applied equally to his plays:

> [Gumilev's poetry] lives in an imagined and almost transparent world. It is somehow alien to contemporary life, it creates countries for itself and populates them with beings created by itself: people, beasts, demons. In these countries—one may say, in these worlds—phenomena are not subject to the usual laws of nature, but to new ones, which the poet commanded into being. The people in those worlds live and act not according to ordinary psychology, but according to strange, inexplicable caprices, suggested by the author-prompter.

If the common features in the plays provide an orientation in these strange "worlds," they also link the major dramatic characters with the person of Gumilev's lyric poems, and with the poet's own problematic personality.

There is reason to believe that the relationship between the character of the playwright and the characters in the plays is a closer one than is usually the case. It is not unheard of that a playwright should incorporate in his characters facets of his own personality. Puškin, for example, criticized Byron for doing precisely this in his tragedies: "When [Byron] began to compose his tragedy, he assigned to each of the characters one of the composite parts of [his own] gloomy and powerful personality, and thus divided his own majestic person into shallow and insignificant characters." Gumilev's characters are also oddly one-sided, and it is possible that they were created in a similar manner.

There is no intention here, of course, to suggest a complete identification of the author with a character or characters; such a suggestion would be quite as misleading as accepting the lyrical person of Gumilev's poems as the poet's own person. Gumilev's critics have tended to make this identification—notably Julij Ajxenval'd, whose impressionistic essay on Gumilev is the source of many of the critical clichés still current. It is possible, nevertheless, to investigate the relationship between author and characters without suggesting any complete congruence. Two facts indicate that such an investigation is at least warranted: (1) the hero of each play is cast in the role of poet; (2) Gumilev was intensely concerned in his theoretical works about the nature of the poet, and in his personal life, about the role which he as a poet should play.

The only intensive study yet published on any of Gumilev's dramatic works ["An Unpublished Tragedy by Nikolaj Gumilev," *ASEER* III (1949)] maintains that Gumilev intended two opposing figures in ***The Poisoned Tunic*** to represent contradictory facets of his own nature. The author, Mary Kriger, bases her contention on some highly interesting schematic notes which Gumilev used in creating his *dramatis personae* and organizing their interaction in the plot. There are a great many details, categories, and cross references, but, unfortunately, the outline is far too schematic for complete and positive interpretation. At least one thing, however, is clear: Gumilev's primary concern was character types, and their juxtapositions and confrontations.

It seems quite likely, as Kriger asserts, that Gumilev gave to one figure, Imr, the character to which he aspired, and which was at least in part his own: the vital poet-warrior, the idealized person of many of Gumilev's early lyric poems. Following the character's name, there is a parenthetical note in the outline: *subjectifs.* A list of characteristics for Imr is given. After the name of the opposing figure, the "King of Trebizond," there is the designation *objectifs.* Kriger argues convincingly that the parenthetical designations indicate Gumilev's subjective view of himself (i.e., the idealized view), and the "objective" assessment: reasoning rather than inspired, introspective and retiring rather than outgoing and adventuresome, physically unattractive and unfortunate in love.

The drama turns on the rivalry of the two men for the hand of Zoë, the beautiful daughter of Justinian. Imr is the poet-prince-warrior; he seeks the alliance of Justinian in order to lead a military force to regain his rightful throne. Imr and Zoë fall in love. Her betrothed, the King of Trebizond, is not a handsome man nor an inspired one, but he is brave and just. He is in a position of power, and is favored by Justinian, but he lacks the divine spark of poetry.

Theodora's machinations bring Imr to death through the poisoned tunic of the title and drive the King to throw himself from a parapet of St. Sophia. At the end, there is an unexpected development: innocent, thirteen-year-old Zoë is shown to be no less guilty than Theodora; she is tainted with the blood of the Imperial Byzantine house. The accumulated sins of generations course through her veins. This odd development is nowhere earlier motivated in the play, but it is surprisingly convincing in artistic terms—largely due to the force of the poetry in Theodora's lines.

Kriger's surmise with regard to the opposition Imr/King of Trebizond is supported in some measure by the fact that comparable oppositions occur, *mutatis mutandis,* in all the preceding plays, and that these oppositions stand in a curious relationship to Gumilev's own character.

The minimal statement of the play's action is sufficient to serve as a reference point in considering the dramatic development in the earlier works. The obvious disparities notwithstanding, it appears that the plays contain variations on the same basic situations and more or less the same character types, disguised according to the exotic settings.

The central constant—the hero as poet—is of varying importance to the action. In ***The Child of Allah*** and ***Gondla,*** it is central to the plot. In ***The Poisoned Tunic,*** it is not really germane to the action, although it is the key to Zoë's love for Imr. The fact of hero as poet is not part of the Acteon myth (although Gumilev incorporates it entirely successfully). In ***The Cardgame,*** the suggestion of hero as poet seems entirely unmotivated, and in ***Don Juan,*** the hero's eloquence is in contradiction to the tradition.

To be sure, Gumilev's interest in defining the poet's nature and function was scarcely unique in his time. The Symbolists had raised the poet to an exalted plane, had given him priestly knowledge and princely rank. Brjusov could speak, like the Pope, *urbi et orbi;* Bal'mont could compare himself to the sun; Annenskij complained that Blok invited God to tea on Fridays, Fontanka 83. The idea of the poet-priest, a leader of men and a superior being with access to special knowledge, was an idea which did not wane as quickly as some others in the post-Symbolist period. The Futurists adopted a similarly exaggerated stance, and if the other Acmeists followed Annenskij in rejecting the Symbolists' high claims for the poet, Gumilev appeared unwilling to do so.

There seems to have been much more, however, to Gumilev's idea of the poet than merely sharing a common convention or continuing a somewhat outmoded fashion. According to his contemporaries, Gumilev was compelled, contrary to his basic nature, to enact in life the role he assigned the poet in theory. Georgij Ivanov felt that this kind of role-playing resulted in a serious personality conflict.

Gumilev's fondness for role-playing in life is noted in quite different contexts. One may recall in this connection Gumilev's pastime, mentioned above, of composing facetious playlets to be acted out by himself and his friends. One of the original actors remembers that Gumilev also assigned "characters," to which he and his friends would conform in ordinary daily life. It is probable that this kind of role-playing, as well as the occasional dramatic pieces, led Gumilev to his more serious attempts with dramatic form.

Gumilev was not especially interested in the theater as such. In the Introduction to the volume of Gumilev's plays, Setchkarev quoted the sometimes light-minded but often intuitively perceptive poet Mixail Kuzmin, who was at one time quite close to Gumilev. Kuzmin observed that Gumilev did not like the theater and did not understand it. Why then the choice of the dramatic form for Gumilev's major efforts? Certainly, the fondness for role-playing is of clear significance here, but part of the answer lies also in the word "form." Gumilev loved formal experimentation, and ***A Child of Allah*** is a kind of tour de force in this regard. It is a verse drama which combines elements of the Eastern tale and the Russian *skazka,* and includes exotic formal verse patterns such as the pantum and the gazella. Its characters are stylized, as is suitable for the puppet theater.

Strangely enough, the characters in the other plays are scarcely less stylized than those in ***A Child of Allah***. The characters are set; they are neither developed nor probed. They are almost scrupulously one-sided; many are not even given names. Identification is by other means, usually by some generalized type: the Old Royalist and the Count in ***The Cardgame;*** in ***A Child of Allah,*** there are a *pēri* (a figure from Eastern folklore), a youth, a Bedouin, a calif, a cawdi, etc., all nameless. In ***Don Juan,*** the millionaire pork butcher from Chicago is named Mr. Poker, but his name is not used; in the stage directions, he and his daughter are referred to as *amerikanec* and *amerikanka*. The figures are symbolic rather than dramatic personages in the usual sense.

If there is conflict in the plays, it is typically between characters rather than within them. In the two cases where inner conflict may be said to exist, Gumilev treats the characters in a most unusual way. In ***Gondla,*** the heroine (Lera by day, Laik by night) has two separate personalities; each is discreet from the other, and the conflict seems less an internal struggle than between two different people. Zoë in ***The Poisoned Tunic*** is shown to have a contradictory side to her nature only in the final scene; she herself is entirely unaware of it throughout the play.

It is clear that the usual requirements of the theater are not followed in Gumilev's dramatic works, and that they were not a matter of principal concern. Rather, there is experimentation with the dramatic form in poetry on one hand, and on the other, the creation of a number of peculiarly onesided dramatic characters who appear in various guises, but who act consistently in what is effectively the same basic action. Because of the schematic plot, symbolic characters, and often obscure motivations, the plays are somewhat mystifying; working from the plays alone, it is difficult to determine Gumilev's intent with any positiveness. The very repetition of plot and characters, however, along with numerous parallels in Gumilev's lyric poems, suggests that he was dealing with a matter of deep and abiding personal concern. If this matter is not immediately evident from the material of the plays themselves, biographical information may help to clarify it.

Gumilev's biography is far from complete, and much of the material is of doubtful validity. In a private correspondence before her death, Anna Axmatova wrote that all the extant sources were "completely unreliable"; she specified the principal ones by name, and observed that some of the memoirists were "simply liars." Although Axmatova was given to sweeping statements of this sort, much of the information does seem questionable. Unfortunately, it is impossible to determine exactly what is valid and what is not. From the jumble of biographical materials, however, one thing is clear: the impression, right or wrong, which contemporaries received of Gumilev's character is directly related to certain of the types in the plays.

There seem to be as many differing assessments of Gumilev's personality as there were people who wrote about him. Contradictory as they are, none apparently is altogether incorrect.

Gumilev's portrayal of himself in childhood is a sensitive and melancholy youth, without companions and wanting none. In the school years at Carskoe Selo, Gumilev was reserved and aloof; "haughty" is Axmatova's word. Yet a resident of Carskoe Selo remembered Gumilev as a young scapegrace, "a fop and a tireless Don Juan," who threw himself enthusiastically into student escapades. Such contradictions are characteristic also as concerns Gumilev's relationship to politics while a student. At sixteen, Gumilev was engaged in radical political activity, yet only two years later, when the events of 1905 erupted and the entire *gimnazija* was in turmoil, Gumilev remained detached and uninvolved.

Such inconsistencies in behavior continued throughout Gumilev's life. After 1918, Gumilev lectured and led seminars in poetry; as a teacher he was serious, formal, even a little pompous—but Xodasevič remembers seeing Gumilev in a heap of students, wrestling in a free-for-all in the corridor of the *Dom Iskusstv*. The very number of the reports of Gumilev's often bizarre behavior suggests less that the observers were at fault than that the vagaries of Gumilev's own character were indeed accurately reported. It is apparent that Gumilev was by turns morosely taciturn and amiably gregarious; he seems to have vacillated between a cold aloofness and a seemingly compulsive periodic *engagement*.

After graduation from the *gimnazija* Gumilev went to Paris in 1908 to study at the Sorbonne. In Paris that year, he sat for a portrait by the painter Farmakovskij. It shows a refined and almost effete young elegant with sensitive hands, and nails as long as Puškin's. The figure in the portrait is far removed from the "conquistador," and a most unlikely candidate for a long and arduous journey, not without danger and hardship, into the Sudan and Abyssinia. Nevertheless, this is precisely what Gumilev did. His early-developed taste for the exotic was reason enough for the trip, but it appears that there was also a certain amount of role-playing involved. In part, the excursions were an enactment of Gumilev's earlier poems of adventure, and in part they were in imitation of the French poets. Brjusov, whose protégé Gumilev had been, was much influenced by Hérédia's literary exoticism and heroism and had translated some of Hérédia's poems. Gumilev's ***Path of the Conquistadors*** is strongly reminiscent of Hérédia, while the enacted escape to Africa must certainly have been inspired by Rimbaud.

Whatever Gumilev's motivations for such an undertaking, they are in any case surely more complex than simple love of adventure and exotic tastes. To understand Gumilev, as Ajxenval'd has done, as the "last of the conquistadors, a poet-warrior, a poet-cuirassier, with the soul of a Viking" is simply naive, an injustice to a sensitive and highly complex personality. Ajxenval'd's characterization is, however, true in part. There is no doubt that Gumilev was unusually brave in the face of physical danger; he even seems to have lacked the ordinary sense of it.

Typically, he chose the most dangerous military service, the cavalry (he was the only prominent literary figure to elect front-line duty). He saw action almost immediately, was twice commended for bravery, and was given a battlefield commission. Although he was transferred in 1917 to administrative sinecures in London and Paris, he tried desperately to be sent to the Mesopotamian Front. After the outbreak of the October Revolution, he returned as quickly as possible to Petersburg, which was by then in the hands of the Bolsheviks. There, he made inflammatory statements and openly mocked the regime. It seems quite possible and even likely that in 1921 Gumilev was involved as charged in a counter-revolutionary plot. He was arrested, and was executed on 4 August 1921.

This is the man whom Georgij Ivanov, a poet and a close friend of Gumilev, described as "a naturally timid, gentle, sickly, and bookish man." According to Ivanov, Gumilev drove himself by force of will to become in fact the idealized poet-warrior of his poetry. Ivanov saw in Gumilev an inordinate pride which prompted an ambition to lead, a desire for fame, a desire "to be first in every human endeavor."

It is difficult even to speculate on the subconscious motivations for such a fierce pride and driving ambition. Nikolaj Ocup, who knew Gumilev well only after 1918, makes one tentative suggestion: a psychological complex something like the Byronic clubfoot. Ocup notes that Gumilev was morbidly sensitive about his appearance, especially about what he considered to be an abnormally elongated skull (in Ocup's words, it was "as though squeezed by an accoucher's forceps").

There is little to support Ocup's theory beyond his own close acquaintance with Gumilev, but it is at least not incompatible with what is known of Gumilev's actions, and some psychological complex of this order must have been at the source for Gumilev's often puzzling behavior. His over-weening pride and his coldly superior air in society could well have been compensatory, and, indeed, the foppishness in dress and calculated Don Juanry only another kind of compensation. The deeply lyrical poem "Don Juan" suggests the utter superficiality of the amorous pursuits, while on a deeper level, there is longing and profound self-dissatisfaction.

If the Don Juan mask is removed in the lyric poem, the Don Juan of the play is the idealized figure. Setchkarev writes, "The figure of Don Juan, of the strong, brave and passionate warrior, was indisputably close to Gumilev." Ocup, in an entirely different context, hazards a direct connection: "Considering himself deformed, he tried the harder to pass for a Don Juan; he swaggered, he exaggerated."

Unlike the Don Juan of the play, the hero of ***Gondla*** is not idealized. He is a poet and prince, but the antithesis of the brave warrior. He is weak, reticent, and gentle. He is ugly and scorned, mocked and ridiculed—and he is a hunchback. Ocup gives this interpretation to Gondla's deformity:

> [***Gondla***] is a profoundly autobiographical piece, as I have noted already in speaking about the childhood of Gumilev. Being ugly, Gumilev found in a cycle of Celtic legends the figure for his long, concealed suffering: a hunchback, but one who was a marvelous singer of songs, a faithful man and good—and so the hero-poet must have felt himself in the most secret places of his soul, the hero-poet who was vain and almost overbearing, but only in outward appearance, and only with those unlike him.

Such speculations are at least possible, if only because they are not contradicted by either the biographical material or by what may be deduced from Gumilev's literary works. They remain, however, only speculations.

Much less speculative than the exact nature of the subconscious motivations is the evidence of their results. It seems clear that there was in Gumilev a certain tendency to paranoia; his friends recognized in him two more or less distinct personalities, and Gumilev was himself conscious of the duality. He even employed it as a device in one of the plays and in a number of lyric poems.

Of those who left biographical materials on Gumilev, Sergej Makovskij probably knew him best. The two young men were collaborators on *Apollon* and neighbors at Carskoe Selo. Makovskij felt that the positive postures of the poet-warrior "self" were peripheral in Gumilev's character. Much closer to the center, he found an inexpressible sadness and a hopeless pessimism, connected with a profound self-disillusionment. Periodically, Gumilev shrugged off his despair and mounted a search for a "mystical union with the Muse," bound up in part with the search for a perfect human love.

Makovskij's idea scarcely conforms to the usual image of Gumilev, either as an individual or as an Acmeist poet, but it probably comes closest to the underlying spirit of Gumilev's mature lyric poems.

Makovskij avoids psychologisms, nor are they needed. If his intuition is correct, an inescapable pattern is set. Fed on the Symbolists' exalted notions of the poet, familiar with Nietzsche, and driven by a fierce pride of his own, Gumilev set impossibly high goals for himself; failure resulted in self-dissatisfaction, pessimism, and a despair which is often, in the lyric poems, almost as deep as Annenskij's. It is not surprising that suicide is a pervasive motif in Gumilev's works, nor that he should have presentiments of an early death. Escape is one of the strongest themes in Gumilev's lyrics: escape from society and its values, escape from his own position and reputation, escape even from close family ties and personal attachments—escape to some distant land to search for the ideal of which Makovskij speaks.

There is an almost Romantic quality to Gumilev's pessimism and disillusionment with self: on the one hand, a longing for an unattainable ideal, and, on the other, a kind of Romantic fatalism, the searching for his fate, the tempting of fate.

Earl Sampson (essay date 1971)

SOURCE: "In the Middle of the Journey of Life: Gumilev's *Pillar of Fire*," in *Russian Literature Triquarterly*, No. 1, Fall, 1971, pp. 283-96.

[*In the following essay, Sampson characterizes* Pillar of Fire *as the volume most representative of Gumilev's poetic skill.*]

Artistic careers may be divided into two main types: those which sometime during the artist's active life reach a peak, after which the artist does not develop further, but either declines or maintains more or less the level of that peak; and those which are or seem to be interrupted by the artist's death, i.e. those in which the artist's last creations are his best, and give promise of still greater potential achievement. Examples of the first type might be Turgenev and Tolstoy, Gogol and Goncharov, Bryusov and Bely; of the second: Pushkin, Lermontov, Dostoevsky, Chekhov, and the subject of this article, Nikolai Gumilev, who was executed in 1921, at the age of thirty-five, when his literary career just seemed to be reaching its apogee.

Gumilev was by no means a precocious poet like Pushkin and Lermontov. Although he began writing poetry fairly early (he first published at the age of sixteen, and his first collection of poetry appeared when he was nineteen), his development was slow, almost painfully slow. That first collection—***The Path of Conquistadors (Put' konkvistadorov,*** 1905)—is definitely, irritatingly adolescent. Gumilev himself later regretted having published it, and when he began reissuing his earlier collections after his return to Russia in 1918, he chose not to republish ***The Path***. While the next two collections show maturation and development, the progress was by no means rapid. But if his development was slow, it was constant; he never halted on any plateaus, but constantly sought new themes and new means of expression, and this process was still under way at his death.

Gumilev's last collection of verse, ***Pillar of Fire (Ognennyi stolp),*** appeared shortly after his death; he had prepared it for publication himself before his arrest. The critics generally agree that it is his best and most significant work, and it is mainly on the strength of this book, and also to some extent on the strength of ***The Pyre (Koster,*** 1918) and other verse of his last period (1917-21) that he is recognized as a major poet (or nearly, or potentially a major poet, depending on the critic). But despite this general critical recognition, Gumilev's later poetry has not yet, I believe, received its due share of attention. He is most commonly referred to, and thought of, as the "poet-warrior," the poet of battle and conquest, of exploration, sea-faring, big-game hunting, in general of exploits of physical bravery. Gumilev assiduously cultivated a public image as a hero, a fearless hunter, explorer and soldier, and this image perhaps more than any other factor has contributed to the inordinate emphasis that has been placed on that part of his poetry which fits the image. I say "inordinate emphasis" because, while this part of his work, his "hero poetry," includes some fine poems, it does not on the whole constitute the best part of his work. The themes of physical bravery are characteristic mainly of his middle period (*ca.* 1912-1916) and to some extent of his early period, but are almost absent from his last and most mature period. And even in the middle period, when the hero poetry is most prominent, many of the best poems do not fit into that category—for example, **"Ballade," "The Pilgrim" ("Palomnik")**, and "I believed, I thought" from ***Foreign Skies (Chuzhoe nebo);*** and **"In Memory of Annensky," "Rain," "Evening,"** and **"The Invalid"** (***"Bol'noi"***) from ***The Quiver (Kolchan)***. Thus the general public image of Gumilev's poetry has not been based on his best work, but on the generally weaker portion of the poetry of a time when he had not yet reached full artistic maturity.

To properly appreciate Gumilev one must look past the anthology pieces about sea-captains and soldiers to the more complex poetry of his last period. I would like to discuss ***Pillar of Fire*** as a representative sample of that poetry, and to indicate some of its characteristic features. But first I would like to give a brief outline of Gumilev's development as a lyric poet in order to provide a framework for understanding the place within his total *oeuvre* that this last book occupies.

The period of Gumilev's apprenticeship in poetry, approximately 1900-1910, i.e., from the rise of his serious interest in poetry through the publication of his third collection, ***Pearls (Zhemchuga),*** coincides rather closely with the flowering of Russian Symbolism, so it is not surprising that his early work is strongly influenced by Symbolism. This is especially true of ***The Path of Conquistadors,*** which is highly derivative, with notes reminiscent of most of the leading Russian Symbolists, as well as Western "Decadent" trends, especially Nietzscheanism.

In the next two books, ***Romantic Flowers (Romanticheskie tsvety,*** 1908) and ***Pearls*** (1910), Gumilev's growth as a poet, both technically and in terms of content, is gradual but clearly noticeable. These two books are far less imitative than the first, without yet being clearly original, and as late as the publication of ***Pearls,*** Gumilev still considered himself a student of one of the Russian Symbolists: the book carried the inscription: "Dedicated to my teacher Valery Bryusov" (Bryusov's influence, only one among several in the first book, becomes dominant in the next two.)

It is only in his fourth book, ***Foreign Skies*** (1912), that Gumilev definitely emerges from the ranks of followers of Symbolism to appear not only as an individual, independent poet with his own themes and techniques, but as an antagonist of Symbolism. The year 1912 was also the year of the formation of the Acmeist school, and ***Foreign Skies*** is the one book of Gumilev's *oeuvre* that most fully exemplifies the tenets of Acmeism, as outlined by Gumilev and his co-founder, Sergei Gorodetsky, in their manifestos. Gumilev saw his new school as the successor to Symbolism and as a reaction, or a corrective, to some of the excesses of Symbolism: its mystical-religious tendencies; its stress on the musical qualities of verse, as opposed to pictorial qualities; its subordination of all elements of poetic technique to the symbol, that is, its striving to invest every possible element of the poem with a symbolic significance; and the resultant preference for the abstract, vague and suggestive over the concrete and precise. Acmeism's opposing principles, then, were: to avoid an overweening concern with mysticism, to prefer this world to other, unknown ones; and to portray the reality of *this* world in plastic, concrete and precise images, with a more rational use of words than was true of Symbolism.

These are some of the chief traits distinguishing the Gumilev of ***Foreign Skies*** from the earlier Gumilev. The contrast is not absolute, of course, but there is an amazingly sharp difference between the overall impression created by ***Foreign Skies*** and that created by ***Pearls,*** published only two years earlier.

I referred above to Gumilev's middle period as the years 1912-1916, that is, from ***Foreign Skies*** to his next book, ***The Quiver***. This could also be labelled his "Acmeistic" period: the Acmeistic character of ***Foreign Skies*** is still present in most of the poetry of ***The Quiver***. At the same time, however, a new note may be distinguished in ***The Quiver,*** and it is to a great extent to this new note, anticipatory of the trends of Gumilev's further development, that the collection owes its interest and significance.

The novelty consists in large part of a more directly personal element than had been typical of the earlier Gumilev, a strain of true lyricism breaking through the mask of Parnassian impersonality that he had so laboriously fashioned for himself. This is the essential quality, but other elements of the change that his poetry began to undergo with ***The Quiver*** can be isolated, including a growing religious note; repeated allusions to a transcendental reality; and an increasing use of fantasy. On the basis of these traits, at least two critics [Gleb Struve and Vissarion Saianov] have designated the later development of Gumilev as a return to Symbolism. Such a formula is accurate enough, and useful enough in indicating the general direction of that development, so long as it is not interpreted too narrowly, and in particular as long as it is not taken to imply any sort of regression to an earlier stage, either in Gumilev's own work, or in the development of Russian poetry in general. For one thing, while Gumilev in his late poetry may be said to have transcended Acmeism, he cannot be said to have abandoned entirely the technical and formal achievements of his more Acmeistic work: the clarity, precision, concreteness and plasticity of imagery and diction. For another, those traits of the later poetry suggestive of Symbolism take on quite a different appearance from analogous traits in his early poetry. This difference is partly due to the superior craftsmanship of the later verse, but perhaps more to the tremendous difference in creative personality between early and late Gumilev, a difference expressive of the spiritual Odyssey that the poet had undergone in the intervening years. It would be no great exaggeration to speak not just of a difference in creative personality between the early and late Gumilev, but of the virtual absence of a personality in the early poetry versus a clearly apprehensible (if not yet quite clearly defined) personality in the late verse. Perhaps the most telling criticism that can be levelled against his early work is that it is superficial and impersonal—impersonal in the sense of *bezlichnyi* ("lacking in distinctive personality"), more than in the sense of detached, objective. Most of it has the atmosphere of a series of exercises on given themes or in given poetic manners, created, as it were, without any participation of the poet's individual psyche. The cold surface brilliance to which this poetry aspires (and which much of it attains) is due primarily to the example of the French Parnassians, both direct and through the medium of Bryusov; its superficiality may also be laid in part at Bryusov's door—the Bryusov who wrote, *"I vsem bogam ia posviashchaiu stikh"* ("And I dedicate a verse to every god") and *"Byt' mozhet, vse v zhizni lish' sluchai / Dlia iarkopevuchikh stikhov"* ("Perhaps everything in life is but a pretext / For brightly-singing verses")—but is primarily traceable, it must be admitted, to Gumilev's own artistic and spiritual immaturity.

It is only in ***Foreign Skies*** that a definite, individualized poetic personality emerges from Gumilev's verse. However, the personality that we descry in ***Foreign Skies*** and in much of ***The Quiver*** reflects not so much the "real" Gumilev as the public image that he had created for himself, the poet-warrior image. And it is only in the poetry of his last period that he appears without his mask—or to use a more appropriate metaphor, his armor—and to allow his poetry to express his real inner being, with all its complexities and contradictions.

I spoke earlier of the increasing use of fantasy as one of the traits distinguishing Gumilev's late poetry from that of his middle period—one of the most striking characteristics of ***Pillar of Fire*** is the prominence of the fantastic element. Gumilev's poetry, to be sure, was never completely free of fantasy, even in his most Acmeistic and thus most realistic book ***Foreign Skies*** (e.g. "I am certainly ill . . ." or "From a serpent's lair"), but fantasy is most prevalent at the two extremes of his career: ***The Path of Conquistadors*** and ***Pillar of Fire***. However, the general contrast I have drawn between his early and late work applies specifically to his use of fantasy: the fantastic element of ***Pillar of Fire*** is very different from that of ***The Path***. It is more original, personal and individual, in contrast to the conventional, "bookish", highly abstract fantasy of the early poetry; and it is much more varied, ranging from the completely personal nightmare of **"The Streetcar Gone Astray,"** through the original metaphysics of **"Soul and Body"** and the "created legend" of **"Stellar Horror,"** original in substance but conventional in narrative manner, to poems like **"The Forest," "The Ring,"** and **"The Bird-Maiden,"** which makes extensive use of common folklore motifs but are nonetheless original in their treatment and, beneath the surface, expressive of Gumilev's individual psyche.

Gumilev's late poetry owes much of its interest to its lyricism, that is, to the extent to which it expresses the poet's personality, his insights and experience. This lyricism finds a variety of forms of expression in ***Pillar of Fire:*** at times it is relatively simple and direct, as in **"Memory"** or **"My Readers";** at other times it is highly complex and indirect, as in **"The Streetcar Gone Astray"** or **"The Bird-Maiden."**

A discussion of ***Pillar of Fire*** may begin very appropriately with the poem **"Memory,"** for it is this piece, with its form of a sort of retrospective spiritual diary, that introduces most of the major themes of the book: the poet's own life-experience; religion and metaphysics; and poetry. The only major theme of the book that does not appear here is that of love.

In **"Memory"** Gumilev takes us through several stages of his life: three or four past stages (Gumilev himself is uncertain of the number, as we shall see), the present stage, and a future stage. The idea of a poetic summation and evaluation of one's past life is of course not new; Pushkin, for example, took it up several times ("Reminiscence," "Again I have visited," etc.). However, Gumilev formulates the theme with a touch of originality by means of the concept of "changing souls," that is, of several different "souls" (personalities) inhabiting in turn the same body, to which he contrasts the snake's habit of shedding its skin ("Only snakes shed their skins . . . We change our souls, not our bodies."). These phrases recur at the beginning and end, giving the poem a circular construction: they comprise the first and last lines of the opening quatrain, the last two lines of the closing one.

The first "soul" to inhabit Gumilev's body was the lonely dreamer of his childhood. This section (stanzas 3 and 4) echoes the earlier poems **"Autumn"** and **"Childhood,"** from ***The Pyre*** ("shaggy and red, my dog, who is dearer to me than even my own brother . . ."; and "As a child, I loved large / Meadows that smelled of honey, / Copses, dry grasses . . ."). The obvious interpretation of the phrase ". . . a wizard-child, / Who would stop the rain with a word" (that the child lived in a world of the imagination) finds its confirmation in a passage from Irina Odoevtseva's memoirs: " 'My childhood was strangely magical,' he told me. 'I really was a wizard-child. I lived in a world that I created myself, not understanding yet that it was the world of poetry'." " 'In the evenings I would lock my door, stand in front of the mirror and hypnotize myself into becoming handsome. I firmly believed that I would change my appearance by strength of will'."

The second soul, that of the poet (stanzas 5 and 6), is the one, strangely, that appeals least to the present Gumilev, while his favorite is the third, the hunter-explorer (stanzas 7 and 8). This personality is obviously closely related to the one who volunteered for combat in World War One (stanzas 9 and 10), and Gumilev himself is not sure whether they are separate stages ("Was it he, or another one / Who exchanged his joyous freedom / For the sacred, long-awaited battle"). What is significant here is not the similarity between these two souls, but the possibility of their separation, for while in one sense his military service was only an extension of the desire for adventure and challenge that took him to Africa, in another sense the war seems to have been a significant landmark in his spiritual growth, as indicated by the greater psychological complexity and philosophical depth of his post-war poetry. This is expressed in the poem by the sudden shift from the war stanzas to an unmediated expression of the major concern of the "present" Gumilev—his sense of a religious mission (stanzas 11 and 12). The image in stanza 11 of the building of a temple as a metaphor for a spiritual feat had appeared earlier in Gumilev: in **"The Middle Ages"** (***The Quiver***) and in the first version of that natural companion-piece to **"Memory," "Five-foot lambs."** In both the earlier poems the source of the metaphor in Masonic imagery is made explicit. Incidentally, the parallel between **"Memory"** and the first version of **"Five-foot lambs"** suggests the possibility that the turning point in Gumilev's inner development may not have been the war itself, but some other experience of those years, perhaps the failure of his relationship with Akhmatova. The first seven stanzas of **"Five-foot lambs,"** treating the poet's last trip to Africa and his break with Akhmatova, are the same in both versions. In the first version (published in ***Apollo*** in 1913), these seven stanzas were followed by five more expressing the poet's renunciation of sensual love and his dedication to the building of the temple. In the second version (published in ***The Quiver***), these five stanzas are replaced by seven entirely different ones, devoted to Gumilev's perception of his war experience. Thus, at least in the history of this poem, the idea of a religious mission pre-dated the war. Probably it would be most accurate to see Gumilev's crisis neither in the war alone nor in the break with Akhmatova alone, but in a whole series of experiences, including these two as well as the Revolution and his unhappy love affair in Paris in 1917.

The completion of the religious mission will bring about the final, future stage, which is one of entry into a transcendent reality, as indicated by the apocalyptic tone and the allusions to Revelation (Professor Struve, by the way, has pointed out the similarity in wording of one of these allusions—to the new Jerusalem—to Blake's lines, "I will not cease from Mental Fight, / Nor shall my sword sleep in my hand / Till we have built Jerusalem / In England's green and pleasant land"). The poem then closes with the repetition of the formula from the first stanza. However, at its second appearance, the formula takes on a new resonance: it now serves to emphasize the finality of the final stage, for once the soul has been confronted by the Christ of the Apocalypse, no further change is possible ("I shall cry out . . . But will anyone help / To save my soul from death? / Only snakes . . .").

Space does not allow a discussion here of the nature and content of the religious mission that Gumilev mentions in **"Memory,"** and his other poetry offers precious little towards such a discussion. But independent of its nature, its very existence is significant: we can see Gumilev here seeking still another field for heroic exploits. In speaking of the first soul, the child, he had said, "Memory, Memory, you won't find the sign, / You'll not convince the world that that was I." Yet there is a "sign," a link between all stages: the Superman impulse, the desire for experience and achievement beyond the reach of ordinary human beings. The child is a "wizard-child"; the poet "wanted to become a god and a tsar"; the explorer is envied by the clouds, and the waters sing to him: and the "builder" is going to bring about the Millenium.

"The Streetcar Gone Astray," like **"Memory,"** is a poem that looks at the poet's past and into his future. But aside from this thematic similarity, the poems are very different. **"Memory"** is relatively simple and straightforward in its revelation of the poet's inner world. The expression is metaphorical, but the images are uncomplicated, logical in themselves and in their relation to one another. The composition is logical too, moving chronologically through the stages of the poet's life. **"The Streetcar Gone Astray"** is quite another matter: the images are more obscure and puzzling, the composition involuted; it displays a continual shifting and interplay of temporal (and spatial) planes, which has led various commentators to call the poem "surrealistic." That term also conveys the dream-like atmosphere of the poem: **"The Streetcar"** is one of those nightmare visions that recur throughout Gumilev's poetry, but with increasing frequency, vividness, force, and I would say, psychological reality, in his last period. The most noteworthy nightmare poems leading up to **"The Streetcar"** are **"The Bird"** and **"The Invalid"** (***The Quiver***), **"Norwegian Mountains"** and **"Stockholm"** (***The Pyre***), and **"The Forest"** from ***Pillar of Fire***. But the terms "dream" and "nightmare" mean more in regard to this poem than the quality of individual images and the apparent disorder in their interrelationships; they imply also the poem's roots in the irrational, subconscious levels of the poet's mind, its nature as a poetic vision, not just a transcription of conscious experience into metrical and metaphorical speech. The very nature of the imagery in this poem differs from that in **"Memory."** Take for instance the central organizing images of the two poems: the "changing of souls" in the one, and the streetcar in the other. The former is definitely a cerebral image; it is a metaphor and no more than that, and the poet, like a good Acmeist, has it under his conscious control, not allowing it to overstep its bounds, but using it to help him organize his perception of reality. In **"The Streetcar,"** on the other hand, the metaphor has control of the poet, as it were, leading his consciousness at will; metaphor and reality become inextricably intertwined; this can happen because the reality of the poem is not the reality of the everyday rational consciousness, but a deeper inner reality.

The difference in atmosphere between the two poems is emphasized by the difference in meter. **"Memory"** is written in regular syllabo-tonic verse (trochaic pentameter); **"The Streetcar"** is in a four-stress *dol'nik* line on a dactylic base (i.e. with a zero anacrusis), a form of *dol'nik* unusual for Gumilev. The greater rhythmical freedom and variety of the *dol'nik,* as compared to syllabo-tonic verse, is in harmony with the atmosphere of the poem.

Despite its apparent lack of logic and order, the composition of the poem has its own logic, the key to which is found in the third stanza: "It went astray in the abyss of time" (cf. **"Stockholm"**: ". . . I was lost forever / In the blind corridors of space and time"). The streetcar has jumped the tracks of chronological time, and is free to cross at will between past, present and future. First it carries the poet into his past, and crosses in rapid succession the three rivers that have been an important part of that past—the Neva, the Nile, and the Seine (the juxtaposition of temporal planes automatically involves juxtaposition of spatial planes as well, since different moments of the past are associated with different locations). At this point, the poet realizes that he has left the normal space-time continuum, and thus other levels of reality are open to him (". . . the station where one can buy a ticket to the India of the Spirit"). After a brief foray into the future, where the poet sees himself beheaded, he is carried into another part of the past, and here (stanzas 9-11) the temporal relationships become even more involved. In stanza 11, the poet has been carried outside his personal past to a time before his birth (the phrases "powdered queue" and "to present myself to the Empress" and the archaism *svetlitsa* suggest the eighteenth century); perhaps to the past of an ancestor, or an earlier incarnation—the idea of memory of a former existence or of a racial past occurs several times in Gumilev, e.g. the sonnet "I am certainly ill . . ." (***Foreign Skies***), **"Stockholm"** and **"Pre-Memory"** (***The Pyre***) and **"Olga"** (***Pillar of Fire***). It is unclear, and the ambiguity is no doubt deliberate, whether the Mashenka of this episode is intended to have any relationship to the poet's "real" past ("real" in the context of the poem); her reappearance in the last stanza implies that she does. Some of Gumilev's associates have "identified" her as Maria Kuzmina-Karavaeva, a cousin with whom Gumilev was in love several years earlier and who had died in 1912, but Odoevtseva's account denies her any literal biographical significance: "Mashenka on that first morning [after the poem's creation—E.S.] was called Katenka. Katenka turned into Mashenka only several days later, in honor of *The Captain's Daughter* . . . " Whether or not we accept Odoevtseva's explanation of the choice of the name, I think we understand the poem better if we do not try to associate Mashenka with anyone in Gumilev's biography—she is not any individual woman, but an image of the ideal love that Gumilev had sought throughout his life and poetry.

This excursion into the past is followed by a rather obscure metaphysical insight ("Now I understand . . . "—stanza 12), which in turn seems to bring the poet back to the present place and time ("And suddenly a sweet, familiar wind . . . "—stanzas 13 and 14). But the temporal planes are still not completely sorted out, for the poet is going to attend a service for the health of the dead Mashenka and a requiem mass for himself. The details of the scene to which the poet returns after his excursion through time are a masterly combination of concrete precision and symbolic significance, and as such may serve as an archetypical example of the tendencies of the mature Gumilev's art. These details are chosen so as to define quite precisely the physical perspective: approaching the Bronze Horseman (Falconet's equestrian statue of Peter the Great) from the left, as one faces it, a vantage from which the dominant details would be the Tsar's outstretched right hand and his horse's raised front hooves, with the dome of the Cathedral of St. Isaac against the sky in the background. At the same time, they indicate the poet's return to his two major extrapersonal concerns in the present, the fate of Russia and the fate of Orthodoxy; these are followed immediately by his two main personal concerns: his ideal love and his own fate (second half of stanza 14). The last stanza ends the poem on a note of searing emotional pain.

I have analyzed these two poems at some length because they seem to me to be central to the collection and to a complete image of the mature Gumilev, in terms of both poetic technique and content. **"Memory"** exemplifies the essentially Acmeistic technique of the bulk of Gumilev's earlier work, while using that technique to express ideological concerns somewhat at variance with the conventional image of Gumilev the Acmeist; **"The Streetcar"** exemplifies the more complex, denser style toward which he seemed to be moving. The two together embrace all of the major themes of the book: the poet's own life experience, including his past adventures and his future fate; religion and metaphysics; poetry; and love. There are certainly other poems in the collection of equal or nearly equal significance, but space does not permit a discussion of all of them. I would just like to mention that the theme of poetry occupies a much more significant place in the book as a whole than it does in these two poems; it is the central theme of such important poems as **"The Word," "Persian Miniature"** (a poem that bears some similarity to Yeats' "Sailing to Byzantium"), **"Sixth Sense," "The Artisan's Prayer,"** and **"My Readers"**; and it is a subsidiary theme in several others (**"The Forest," "With the Gypsies,"** and **"The Bird-Maiden"**).

A discussion of the versification of ***Pillar of Fire*** could also be of interest. Alongside the poems written in conventional syllabo-tonic verse, there are examples of several other verse forms in the book, some of them more or less experimental. The book includes no examples of the form of *dol'nik* most characteristic of Gumilev, the three-stress *dol'nik* on an anapestic base, but one does find: one of his few four-stress *dol'niki* (**"The Streetcar"**); a poem in "free" *dol'niki,* i.e. one in which all the lines fit the *dol'nik* pattern, but the number of stresses varies irregularly (**"The Bird-Maiden"**); a poem with regular alternation between *dol'nik* and conventional amphibrachic lines (**"The Ring"**); and two in a form transitional between *dol'nik* and accentual verse, the form that Gasparov labels *taktovik* (**"Olga"** and **"With the Gypsies"**). Finally, there is the only example in Gumilev (not counting a couple of humorous pieces) of free verse (**"My Readers"**).

Pillar of Fire was not Gumilev's first idea for a title for this collection; he had previously considered another title, a fact which lends particular interest to the question of the meaning of the title: why did he decide on this title, what significance did he attach to it? It is not derived directly from the title or text of any of the poems in the book, but with its obvious Biblical associations it seems to me to be related to the religious mission of **"Memory"**: the poet's task was to lead his people out of the wilderness, to build for them a new Jerusalem. We may probably assume, in the light of Gumilev's political position, that the wilderness involved political and cultural as well as religious implications, but the latter are, I think, predominant. It may well be, by the way, that Gumilev had in mind not only the well-known pillar of fire passage from Exodus, but also the verse from Revelation: "And I saw another mighty angel . . . clothed with a cloud: and a rainbow was upon his head, and his face was as it were the sun, and his feet as pillars of fire" (10:1). This chapter is about the seventh angel, the one who gave the prophet the little book to eat, and told him, "Thou must prophesy again before many peoples, and nations, and tongues, and kings" (10:11), much as Pushkin's prophet was sent out to "Burn with the Word the hearts of people."

Sergei Makovsky offers another explanation of the title, but it does not seem very convincing. He derives it from Gumilev's lines, "And henceforth I burn in the fire / Which rises up to heaven out of hell" (*"I otnyne ia goriu v ogne, / Vstavshem do nebes iz preispodnei"*). The lines are from the 1917 poem **"Love,"** one of the cycle of poems devoted to Gumilev's unhappy love affair in Paris; the cycle was published posthumously (1923) under the title ***To a Blue Star (K sinei zvezde)***. The fire here is clearly a symbol of love, in spite of the quasi-religious imagery; the quoted lines are preceded by "Can you really not burn / With the secret flame [*plamenem*] you know so well, / If you could appear to me / As the blinding lightning of the Lord . . . " But if Gumilev had intended the title of his last book to imply the fire of love, I doubt that he would have chosen a phrase with such strong religious overtones. Fire imagery is very prominent throughout Gumilev's poetry (*ogon', plamia,* and their derivatives, in metaphorical and sometimes literal meanings, are among his favorite words), but the love poems of ***Pillar of Fire*** do not use fire imagery at all, whereas fire images do occur in metaphysical contexts: "My heart will be burned by a flame / Until the day when the bright walls / Of the new Jerusalem rise . . . " (**"Memory"**); ". . . like a rosy flame, / The Word floated in the heights" (**"The Word"**); ". . . until the fiery Apocalypse" (**"Soul and Body"**). The lines that Makovsky cites may, on the other hand, be related to another of Gumilev's titles—***The Pyre:*** he included several of the poems of the ***Blue Star*** cycle in that collection, and fire as an image of love does occur in them.

The other title that Gumilev had considered for his last book was *In the Middle of the Journey of Life (Po seredine stranstviia zemnogo)*, a translation of the first line of the *Divine Comedy: Nel mezzo del camin di nostra vita*. That title has a dual significance, both ironic and tragic: when he considered it, Gumilev was not in the middle of his life's journey, but very nearly at its end; on the other hand, the poetry of ***Pillar of Fire*** tells us that he was in the midst of his creative development, that he still had new creative paths to follow, had fate so decreed.

Sidney Monas (essay date 1972)

SOURCE: An introduction to *Selected Works of Nikolai S. Gumilev,* edited and translated by Burton Raffel and Alla Burago, State University of New York Press, 1972, pp. 3-26.

[*In the following excerpt, Monas places Gumilev and his works in the context of early twentieth-century Russian literary culture.*]

Gumilev lived in a world of obstacles. At home, as a child, he had an older brother and a morose father to rival him for the attention of a young mother and a pretty girl cousin. Later, there were the Symbolists; and, above all, Alexander Blok. Conscious of his own homeliness and awkwardness, he was a performer, a surmounter, an overreacher. He cultivated the matter-of-fact ease of the tightrope walker and the assurance of the trapeze artist: the difficult and dangerous act carried through with unflappable *sang-froid*. Those who knew him well write nevertheless of his freshness of spirit and his childlike good nature, his utter lack of hatred or malice and his spontaneous enthusiasm and indefatigable energy as a teacher. It was a formidable pose in which he clothed himself, and it became a kind of second nature.

He was proud of difficulties overcome. The Symbolists groaned and suffered the difficulties of the literary life; before departing for Africa or the battlefield, Gumilev wrestled with the devices of poems, spread the works out on the table and put them back together again. His was a grimier, sweatier angel, he implied, and he was proud of it.

Having translated Theophile Gautier's "L'Art," Gumilev set himself in a chiseled, white-marble, Parnassian stance: balance, precision, clarity, craftsmanship, tradition, restraint. It required a Greek name, and he gave it one. *Akmê*: the peak, the ripening, the perfection. He called the "movement" Acmeism.

Like Anglo-American Imagism, which it much resembles, Acmeism grew out of and at the same time opposed *fin de siècle Romanticism*. During the period between 1909 and 1913, a decadent Symbolism gave rise to two modernist movements, which, without it, could scarcely have existed, but which nevertheless deeply criticized and severely undermined Symbolist themes, attitudes, and atmospheres: Acmeism and Futurism.

In their antagonistic relationship, Acmeism seemed to take the conservative, Futurism the radical position. Acmeism emphasized tradition and craftsmanship, clarity, balance, and understatement. Futurism, with Mayakovsky and Khlebnikov as its greatest representatives, studied provocation, Bohemian rebelliousness, innovation, and hyperbole. Gumilev called the Futurists hyenas in the track of the Symbolist lion. Vladimir Markov, a gifted critic, but very partial to Futurism, has recently written that if Gumilev had not had the bad luck to have been shot in the cellars of the Cheka, there would have been no need to invent Socialist Realism.

Both Futurists and Acmeists, however, emphasized poetry as a craft, a thing made. Both saw it as a movement from the irrational to the rational: a bringing to consciousness. Both emphasized technique and a pragmatic, matter-of-fact, craftsmanly approach. The Formalist critics, who defined a work of art as "the sum of its devices," and who prided themselves both on their scientific approach to literature and their pragmatic approach to particular texts, although they have been traditionally associated with the Futurists, welcomed both Futurists and Acmeists as kindred spirits.

Much of Gumilev's work, however, justifies Markov's suspicions. As another acute critic, George Ivask, has recently pointed out, many of his poems seem to lack a dimension. They work out too well, all too explicitly, their intended meaning. Gumilev's insistence on and pride in "a firm, manly attitude," comes dangerously close to what we tend to see as a boy scout attitude, gotten up in somewhat supercrackly rhetoric. When we read of angel-wings hovering over soldiers on the battlefield, we tend to wince. He glorified:

> Explorers, discoverers,
> not frightened by hurricanes,
> at home with whirlpools and sandbars,
> Their hearts not stuffed with the dust
> of forgotten manuscripts, but steeped in sea-salt,
> setting a course with bold strokes
> on a torn map, starting some daring voyage.

The White armies are said to have memorized his poems and recited them in battle. The emigration, after his death, regarded him as a martyr. Although his poems have not been published in the USSR and his name, at least since the late 1920s, has rarely appeared in print there, he is nevertheless a favorite among Soviet youth, and in the current revival of Russian nationalism, or neo-Slavophilism as it is sometimes called, a movement which contains some quite loyal party members, his poetry plays a conspicuous role. He himself had boasted of the non-literary nature of his readers:

> . . . strong, vicious, gay,
> killers of elephants, killers of people,
> dead in deserts,
> frozen at the edge of eternal ice—
> as it should be, on this
> strong, gay, vicious planet—
> and they carry my poems in their saddlebags.

Again, it is among those who understand true difficulty, not those contaminated by too-long exposure to "dusty manuscripts," that he wishes to be respected. He has been one of them himself.

I mean no disrespect to the dignity of the elemental in poetry or prose, but this particular posture of Gumilev's seems to me, as in Kipling, to hover close to the juvenile.

Alexander Blok was six years Gumilev's senior. While too great a poet to fit easily into any school, he belonged for a time to the Symbolists and many of his attitudes were characteristically Symbolist and characteristically those that Gumilev set himself to oppose. Of course, one must bear in mind that Gumilev rather liked slogans and banners and programs, while Blok tended to view them with distaste.

On the subject of literary translation—an interest both shared—Blok emphasized the importance of recreating the "atmosphere" of a poem. Gumilev, fond of prescriptions, listed nine characteristics and devices that must be transposed "unchanged." Ironically, Gumilev's most eloquent translation, the Babylonian epic, *Gilgamesh,* violates almost everything he lists as "obligatory."

For Blok, inspiration sometimes meant a kind of possession by the muse. During one of those extraordinary encounters in the House of Art during the time of the Civil War, Gumilev argued that in Blok's famous poem about the Revolution, "The Twelve," the figure of Christ at the end seemed out of place, false and distasteful. Blok replied morosely that he, too, disliked it; but what could he do? In that way the poem had come to him.

Blok's muse was obscure and uttered things sometimes incomprehensible to him. Gumilev's, on the other hand, spoke a language mutually understood, and he took it down.

For the Dionysian Blok, poetry was a dangerous descent into chaos in a quest for rebirth into the realm of the unconscious life of the instincts. Culture itself he called "the music by which the world grows." For the Apollonian Gumilev definiteness, clarity of line, sustenance of will were the virtues; one must not let go.

Blok was a Populist and believed in the masses. Gumilev, in praising Valery Briusov, a Symbolist, but the closest of all the Symbolists to Acmeism and a man Gumilev regarded as one of his masters, compared him to Peter the Great. Not by chance was Gumilev a monarchist.

Against Symbolism, Gumilev brought two major charges: that its emphasis on metaphor tended to produce a private and at the same time liturgical, a self-isolated language in which "like bees in a deserted hive / the dead words rot and stink" and that their quest for ultimate mystery involved the Symbolists in a whoring after strange gods, the theosophy and anthroposophy of Andrei Biely or the magic and Manicheism of Fyodor Sologub. For the Symbolists everything was something it wasn't. Every phenomenon, Gumilev insisted, had a right to exist (in poetry as in life) as and for itself. Or, in that so familiar phrase of Gertrude Stein's, "A rose is a rose is a rose." . . .

Acmeism was sometimes called Adamism by Gumilev and his disciples. Thus, a kind of alpha and omega: a primal beginning and a final ripeness. Adam was the first poet, the name-giver, and as one who worshipped the living word it was natural for Gumilev to identify with Adam. And also with the primal and the primitive in general; with Africa; with its energy; and the setting it provided for the bringing into a fullness of being the "basic" human impulses—poetry, battle, kingly rule, erotic passion. And the contention of impulses, each wrought to its uttermost—poet and warrior, priest and king, body and soul; the primitive drama, and possibly also the primal scene.

Gumilev identifies himself with Adam both before and after the fall. In a number of his early poems there are traces of infatuation with "my friend Lucifer," a haunting diabolism and a sense of doom: "Lucifer my friend gave me five horses." They are the five senses. In a much later poem, Gumilev details the painful formation of a **"Sixth Sense."** In the early ballad quoted above, he quite explicitly names that sense:

And laughing, mocking, contemptuous,
Lucifer threw open the gates of darkness: for me.
And he gave me a sixth horse,
and the horse was named Despair.

Despair, martyrdom, suicide, these are themes in Gumilev that appear almost inevitably in connection with a shadowy female presence, a "moon-girl," or a "bird-girl"; often there is a flame or a "pillar of fire," always there is a sense of haunting unattainability, erotic frustration: "and there I saw a girl, and her face was sad." Perhaps like Pushkin's Tsarskoe Selo statue she contemplates her "shattered urn." Perhaps another name for the shattered urn is incest, the prerogative (or fate) of aristocracy.

In Gumilev's play, ***Gondla,*** the incest theme becomes very explicit. The play is set in Iceland of the eighth century. The hero, Gondla, is a poet, the son of an Irish skald, doomed to martyrdom in pagan Iceland. Unlike the hero of ***The Poisoned Tunic,*** also a poet but beautiful and powerful in body, Gondla is a hunchback and ineffectual against the Icelandic warriors. Yet his soul has as its proper emblem the swan, and he is a Christian, as opposed to his Icelandic antagonists, who are people of the wolf, and pagans. Gondla falls in love with and marries his half sister in whom the swan and the wolf contend. For the Christian Gondla, incestuous love becomes the very fabric of his doom. In the end, he dies a martyr's death. On the basis of his death, a new civilization is founded.

In his neoclassical drama, ***The Poisoned Tunic,*** Gumilev's playwrighting suggests the symmetry of the art of mosaic. The action is set in sixth-century Byzantium. There is much about the play that is adolescent in taste and tone; except for the craftsmanship and the characterization of Zoe, it is reminiscent, say, of James Elroy Flecker's *Hassan* or the overblown poetic dramas of Edmond Rostand. Yet the craftsmanship—the "difficulty"—seems not altogether misapplied.

There are two Adams—both noble and eloquent: one, the king of Trapezond; the other, the pagan Arab poet, Imru-al-Kaish. Both are corrupted and destroyed by the city, symbolized by Theodora, the universal whore. Both fall in love with Theodora's stepdaughter, Zoe, so desirable in her innocence amidst the corrupt city as to be inevitably destructive. Overtly there is no question of incest, and even Zoe's age (she is thirteen) is referred to the customs of time and place. Yet Imru has sworn a warrior's vow to remain chaste until the accomplishment of his mission; and Zoe has been officially betrothed to the king of Trapezond, who is inspired at first also by a kind of paternal attitude towards Imru. Zoe's seduction by Imru impels Trapezond to suicide and results in the agonized death of Imru in a poisoned tunic prepared by Justinian. The vows broken are not without analogy to the incest taboo. In the end, the seemingly innocent Zoe, like her whorish stepmother, is completely identified with the city of her birth and she is compared in her impact on men to the tunic. (Curiously enough, the play was a product of Gumilev's Parisian love of 1917 with "Elena D.," to whom the poems of ***The Dark-Blue Star*** were written.)

Behind the figure of Eve there flickers the "moon-girl," Lilith, who haunts every love. Whether she tokens the lost innocence of the garden or a more drastic "fall" is far from clear.

What I took from the serpent's nest,
the serpent's nest in Kiev,
was a witch, not a wife.

In an earlier poem to Akhmatova (who was once sketched in her long-necked grace by Modigliani), Gumilev uses as an analogue for his wife's mysterious and ambiguous beauty the silent, ineffable movements of a giraffe:

. . . far, far away, near Lake Chad
a delicate giraffe grazes up and down.

One of Gumilev's late poems is called **"Bird-Girl."** Written in a ballad form congenial to Gumilev, it has a distinctly Symbolist, indeed even Maeterlinckian, setting—the never-never land of Celtic mists and myths, where the Arthurian romances, and most particularly the tales of Merlin (son of a forest-virgin and the devil himself) and Vivien (the wellspring of life) and the crystal cave, have their origin. Yet it is too explicit to be a Symbolist poem. Indeed, the explicitness of the sexual encounter between the shepherd and the bird-girl brings the poem to the edge of the absurd. Nevertheless, at that far edge of taste and credibility, the absurd blends with a vision of horror and solitude that is genuinely haunting.

The "happy shepherd" piping his affirmation of life is confronted by the beautiful but melancholy bird-girl in the never-never land of Broseliana. Everything about her hints at tormented complexities,

. . . a flame-red
bird with a tiny girl's head.

It sang, then stopped, then sang,
then stopped, like a baby crying in its sleep.
Its lazy black eyes reminded him
of Indian slaves.

She bewails her solitude:

"Nowhere on the green earth,
nowhere, is there another

"Like me. . . . "

And she seems almost to reproach the shepherd for his normalcy:

"You're young. You'll marry,
you'll father children,"

while she promises to haunt even his descendants with the vision of her suffering beauty:

"and then the Bird-girl
will be remembered. . . . "

She prophesies that she will give birth to a son, cursed with her own loneliness, and unable to relieve her solitude,

". . . for I
must die for him to be born.

. . . . .

"He'll fly here, there,
he'll sit in these elms,

he'll call to his mate,
and his mate will be dead."

But the bird-girl dies immediately after her encounter with the shepherd—her death is part of the encounter—and no son is born. Except, of course, that the shepherd becomes her son as well as her mate. In taking him as her lover, she makes him also her heir:

The shepherd pipes funeral songs
over her body.

Twilight.
Gray mist.
He drives his flock home,
away from Broseliana.

The poems about destiny and fate in the last two volumes of Gumilev's poetry, ***Bonfire*** and ***Pillar of Fire,*** display a depth and a resonance beyond his earlier poems. **"The Muzhik"** is a poem about Rasputin; at the same time it is a vision of the half-pagan Russian peasants marching from the damp, dark places of the primitive Russian forests against the fragile cross hung over Saint Isaac's and the Kazan Cathedral in Petrograd to overwhelm the rudiments of urban civilization, to claim back their own. **"A Workman"** is a curious poem of praise to the artisan who will forge the bullet that will kill Gumilev:

. . . And this was done by the small
old man in the faded grey blouse.

The worker, who is calm and submissive to fate as Gumilev is, performs his job, stubbornly acts out his anonymous role in the fated event that is to be Gumilev's death. In **"Primal Memories"** Gumilev speaks out against the teeming energy of Africa, and in favor of the quiescence of India, the calm and detachment of oriental philosophy, which also intimates an analogue with his approaching death:

And when will I finally end
this dream, and be myself—
a humble Indian dozing
in the sacred twilight, along some quiet river?

The greatest of these poems is called **"The Lost Tram."** The scene is immediately set in an urban landscape, an unfamiliar street in Petrograd, through which sound ominous rumblings:

. . . crows
croaking, then the sound of a lute
and thunder crawling slow
from a distance. . . .

If Lermontov, whom Gumilev seems so much to resemble, describes his cosmic destiny as setting out alone along a highroad, Gumilev describes his as leaping on a tram from an unfamiliar street to an unknown destination: cheap, modern transportation; democratic (anybody can ride; everybody does), convenient (it goes right by; you just have to jump on) and commonplace—yet, powerful, ineluctable, and mysterious:

. . . a trail
of fire streaking like sunrays.

Rushing like a storm with dark wings. . . .

The oncoming tram and the oncoming storm are analogous.

Although on rails, "the tram blundered and was lost." The passenger repeats the recurrent nightmare of all those who have used the public transport of a large metropolitan city: the conductor doesn't hear, the doors won't open, the crowd refuses to give way; he is caught. The tram takes him from Petersburg to all the places of his life, and back to Petersburg. He is haunted by the brief glimpse of a blind beggar in Beirut. The beggar is dead and gone. As in a death-wish dream, the appearance of a person known to be dead presages the dreamer's own wished-for death. The beggar has "knowing eyes."

The tram is lost in time as well as space. Fragments of the past, present, future flash by. . . .

If Blok's "The Twelve" was the poem of the Revolution, Gumilev's **"Lost Tram"** becomes the poem of Saint Petersburg, Imperial City and monument to civilization. Ironically, the one image in the poem that seems forced is that likening Saint Isaac's dome to "God's true hand," for the opulent and oppressive Imperial spirit is elegantly embodied in the gold and marble of Nicholas's cathedral—Nicholas I, the persecutor of Pushkin—and by the cathedral itself one is reminded rather of "Religion hid in War," as in Blake's "Milton," than of peace and understanding.

Gumilev once wrote that the essence of a poem was "sensuality repressed." So Freud wrote of civilization. The tram is now an archaic vehicle, and Petersburg is Leningrad; but somehow Gumilev's poem, like the discontent of our civilization, hovers in the air like a cry.

Ewa M. Thompson (essay date 1975)

SOURCE: "Some Structural Patterns in the Poetry of Nikolaj Gumilev," in *Die Welt der Slaven,* Vol. 19-20, 1974-75, pp. 337-48.

[*In the following essay, Thompson identifies a range of symbols and ideas that appear in opposite pairs throughout Gumilev's poetry.*]

Gumilëv is a notoriously unknown poet. He was the spiritus movens of the *Poets' Guild,* an amorphous literary group from which Acmeism originated: therefore, all textbooks of Russian literature pay him lip service and a canon of his poems appears in the anthologies of Russian verse. So far, however, his poetry has not been assimilated by those interested in Russian literature either in the West or in his native country. Interpretations of Gumilëv's writings have been fragmentary. With one exception, I do not know of any study of this poet that would consider in a more than an introductory manner the totality of his poetic output. The exception is E. Demjanjuk's "The Literary Development of Gumilëv" presented at a language conference at Melbourne in 1964. The author of this study divided the work of Gumilëv into three periods: metaphysical, adventure-oriented and religious, and supplemented this with a certain amount of analysis. These categories, however, as well as the evidence presented, seem to me too general and too remote from the specific features of poetry to really say much about the poems in question. Other essays on Gumilëv include the Introduction (by Sidney Monas) to his *Selected Works* in the English translation, a number of articles in the *Collected Works* in Russian (*Sobranie sochinenij v chetyrëx tomax,* edited by Gleb Struve), Poggioli's essay in his well known book *The Poets of Russia,* and several articles in literary journals.

These introductions usually share two remarks. The first is a consensus on Gumilëv's theoretical interest in craftsmanship. Lectures and discussions which he initiated in St. Petersburg and which lead from the *Poets' Guild* (1911-1914, reactivated in 1918) to the outline of a *Poetics* left by him among his papers, testify to his concern with theoretical problems of poetic expression. The second point of agreement is Gumilëv's preoccupation with the heroic, the pose of a conquistador which he adopts with great persistency in many of his poems. Statements concerning this characteristic of Gumilëv usually contain a certain amount of condescension: in our day and age, the market for the consciously heroic attitudes seems to be rather small. Critics are apt to be embarrassed by what they perceive as a boy scout attitude. Sidney Monas writes: "I mean no disrespect to the dignity of the elemental in poetry or prose, but this particular posture of Gumilëv seems to me, as in Kipling, to hover close to the juvenile." The charge of a juvenile pose goes hand in hand with another charge: that of a lack of depth, dragging the point home in too obvious a manner, transforming Kuz'min's "beautiful clarity" into excessive clarity. Vladimir Markov goes so far as to compare Gumilëv's verse to that fathered by socialist realism, on the account that in both cases the poems deal with the righteous and desired experience rather than with the real one. On the other hand, some Russian emigré critics treat these poetic attitudes as worthy of esteem. Demjanjuk praises them as part of Gumilëv's genuine religious preoccupation—a rare thing in his day and time. "Glory to you, o hero!" (Slava tebe, geroj!)—this last line from Irina Odoevceva's poem about Gumilëv summarizes this kind of evaluation. Thus, while Gumilëv's interest in the "brave discoverers of the new lands" (otkryvateli novyx zemel') has been noted by every commentator of his poetry, its appraisals range from contemptuous disapproval to deep admiration.

The problem of alleged or real immaturity of Gumilëv is a convenient point from which to start a holistic interpretation of this poet. It seems to me that his heroic pose can be identified with the juvenile or the immature only if it is considered in separation from other, no less persistent, elements of his verse. Taken as part of a larger design, it ceases to solicit either positive or negative evaluation. The question is then changed from "Is it praiseworthy or not to write about the longing to become a conquistador" to "What is the design of Gumilëv's poetry, and is it carried out in an artistically convincing manner."

My contention is that Gumilëv's poetry oscillates within a certain range of symbols and ideas which tend to appear in opposite pairs, as series of antonyms. Gumilëv is fascinated by such concepts and counter-concepts as victory-defeat, flight-conquest, good-evil, strength-weakness, man-woman, activity-passivity, attraction-repulsion. The second important characteristic of Gumilëv's poetry is the recurrence in it of the elements of the prodigal son parable. The story of the prodigal son as told in St. Luke's *Gospel,* involves the initial desire to leave the well beaten paths of the parental way of living, the period of conquest and joy and disorder, then disappointment, a new vision of the self and of the world and, finally, the element of return. Gumilëv's poetry, when seen as a whole, embodies this particular sequence of qualities. This does not mean that each of his poems contains some kind of *abcdef* sequence, the symbols *abcdef* representing the elements of the prodigal son parable. Occasionally, one can see them so neatly presented; in most cases, individual poems take up only one, or two of these elements instead of all of them. Chronology of the sequence is seldom preserved either. In the main, the sequence *abcdef* is formed in our minds. It transcends the diachronic habits of mind. Individual poems can be schematized as *a, b, c, abc, bdf, fa,* etc. What is important is not to treat Gumilëv's poetry as a collection of separate pieces dealing with various aspects of life, a medley of isolated outcries, but to see it as an *oeuvre* in which individual poems echo one another and throw light on one another. Such synchronic reading yields substantial artistic rewards and I propose it here instead of the customary diachronic one, which leads to a simplified view of this poet.

In regard to the set of qualities which recur in Gumilëv's verse, one more point should be mentioned. Within the sphere of influence of Christian civilization, the prodigal son parable is the most obvious and familiar frame of reference; within a broader cultural sphere, the reference can be extended to what Mircea Eliade has called the myth of the eternal return. In the book under this title Eliade gathered substantial evidence as to the recurrence in various civilizations of a story, or stories, symbolically presenting the severing of man's fellowship with the godhead, the period of orgiastic chaos following the severance and, finally, the stage of epiphany, the return to God, reestablishment of the "sacred time" in which man and the world become part of the sacred timelessness.

In its entirety, the myth of the eternal return contains the idea of cyclicity. The idea of the New Year, for instance, common to all human societies and constituting a part of the myth of the eternal return, implies that the creation of the world is reproduced each year. Eliade points out, however, that this myth is seldom preserved as a unified whole. Various societies preserve various fragments or elements of it. Thus, even though cyclicity is missing from the prodigal son parable, there are enough common points between it and the myth of the eternal return to justify the association of the two. This association puts Gumilëv's poetry into a perspective far surpassing the one hitherto adopted.

I shall start my analysis with the poem **"The Prodigal Son" ("Bludnyj syn")** from the ***Foreign Skies* (*Chuzhoe nebo*)** collection. This poem can serve as an example of both structural features mentioned earlier: the prodigal son, or the myth of the eternal return, thematics and the binary opposition-oriented pattern of thinking.

The beginning of the poem expresses the dream of flight,

the desire to leave the safety and dullness of well known ways and to discover a new and more active mode of living. The flight, however, is to the sea, with all the ambiguities of water imagery inevitably present: the unconscious, the feminine, purification. The surface speaker is masculine, straightforward and self-assured; the water imagery represents the opposite qualities. Thus, the beginning of the poem can be seen as a manifestation of the author's fascination with the opposite qualities. The warrior thirsting for danger, adventure and joy of conquest, is the facade behind which one perceives a thirst for more subtle layers of human psyche, as well as for the softness and security of the feminine—a flight to the womb, to use psychological terminology.

Part Two of the poem expresses the enjoyment of the newly gained freedom, the continuing lust for battle, and proud rejection of the old rituals. The surface persona does not change. Then in Part Three the desire and joy coming out of the fulfillment of the desire, are replaced by disappointment with the new ways, destruction of the dream and, eventually, ripeness for new perception which comes in Part Four.

When the speaker reaches the point of seeing anew the world and his situation in it, the desire to return to what he had previously rejected is born in him. As in the parable, he abandons the mode of being which brought him disappointment and returns to his father's house. Soon after the quality of return is introduced, however, the plot of the poem takes an unexpected turn: instead of the father welcoming the son back, the bride steps forth to greet the newcomer. The female image which appears at the end of the poem is, like the water imagery, characteristic of Gumilëv's preoccupation with the opposites and constitutes a departure from the original parable in St. Luke's *Gospel*. In this poem, the return which Gumilëv's supermasculine poetic persona accomplishes, involves the feminine principle.

"The Prodigal Son" is the poem which best introduces the general pattern of Gumilëv's poetry and the sequence of qualities which appear in the parable of the prodigal son, as well as in the myth of the eternal return: desire, conquest, joy, disappointment, new perception, and return. As mentioned earlier, poems in which all of these qualities appear in chronological order are rare, and one would get nowhere trying to establish this order. Instead, I shall attempt to point out how and in what circumstances these qualities become the foci of individual poems, what imagery expresses them and how does Gumilëv's preoccupation with the opposites merge with the dominant thematic element of individual poems.

The first two qualities that set the tone of the prodigal son parable are the desire to act and joy stemming from activity and conquest. Gumilëv has written a great number of poems which celebrate these two themes. In such poems, the initial situation involves a Wagnerian hero (usually a male) who is longing for a contest. The best known characters encountered in such poems are sea captains or conquistadors: e.g., the title of his first volume of poems, ***The Conquistadors' Road*** (***Put' konkvistadorov***), the title of a poetic cycle **"The Captains" ("Kapitany")**, or the cycle devoted to Odysseus. There are, however, many other embodiments of this persona, and they range from animals and birds traditionally associated with royalty (such as eagles or lions) to inanimate entities with whose powerfulness and assumed energy the speaker identifies (such as the African continent). The agents in such poems can be kings, tsars, Zarathustras, princes of fire, prophets, gods, ancient heroes, the primeval Adam, fierce and reckless hunters. Such Wagnerian heroes go to battle; they encounter the danger they were longing for. The battle also appears in various disguises: it can take the form of travel into unknown lands, bold flights into cosmic space, gambling, vengeance, realization of one's freedom. The only necessary ingredient here is some kind of struggle. The full sequence of qualities in such poems will be, then, struggle-victory-joy. The final victory is usually of a different kind than that envisaged at the beginning: there occurs a shift from the bold initial dream to the possibilities of its realization. Nevertheless, it is still a victory; in the tone of such poems, joy still prevails. It can be added that poems ending in a victorious note usually consist of five to seven four-line stanzas. The final shift—from the intended to the available victory—usually comes in the last two lines.

An interesting example of Gumilëv's resourcefulness in concretizing this pattern is the poem **"The Eagle" ("Orël")**. The eagle enjoys his flight toward the "mighty throne" (prestol sil) and his escape from a confining situation. It turns out, however, that permanent victory in the skies is impossible: the eagle cannot reach the throne, he cannot endure the grandeur of cosmic space and dies, "suffocating from bliss" (umer, zadoxnuvshis' ot blazhenstva). Live he cannot; but, at the same time, he is no longer subject to gravitation forces: the tremendous effort of the flight liberated him from them. He therefore cruises in cosmic space like the planets; he becomes their equal. He could not reach "the mighty throne" but nevertheless succeeded in liberating himself from earthly bondage. Greatness and the satisfaction of victory, Gumilëv conveys in poems of this type, are not always a matter of total and complete success.

A similar development occurs in **"Choice" ("Vybor")** where the stoic speaker foresees the failure of human strivings but asserts that the final victory lies in man's right "to choose the manner of his own death" (nesravenennoe pravo / Samomu vybirat' svoju smert'). In **"To the Girl" ("Devushke")** the positive statements are crammed into the last stanza, while the first three stanzas define the pattern by contrast. They describe a heroine whose way of life is the exact opposite of that of the speaker. She is always reasonable and never takes a trip without first sketching her route on the map. The "reckless hunter" (bezumnyj oxotnik) realizes the folly of aiming his arrows at the sun but nevertheless finds satisfaction and delight in the very fact of doing it, regardless of the results. In **"The Slave's Song" ("Nevol'nich'ja")**, the slave who thinks of murdering his master asserts his satisfaction with the final turn of affairs: he is by no means reconciled to his situation as a slave but he is willing to "displace" his feeling of victory from the situation in which he would be free to one in which he murders his master in order to become free. In **"Five Bulls" ("Pjat' bykov")**, the laborer who saw his neighbor poison his livestock, enjoys feasting on the last bull while he watches the neighbor's death in flames. Satisfaction coming from vengeance constitutes a replacement of the satisfaction which he would have felt if his hopes of material well being had been satisfied. In **"The Cross" ("Krest")**, the desperate gambler stakes his golden cross at the gambling table. He has long lost the hope of conventional victory (winning the money), but he now hopes to overcome his bad luck by his final and extraordinary feat. His victory here consists not in an actual monetary winning but in making a tremendous effort to win and, by means of that, regaining his self-respect.

"The Barbarians" ("Varvary") is an example of an even more complex way to embody the pattern of struggle-conquest-joy. Here the contest takes place between the oncoming victorious armies of northern barbarians, and the beautiful queen and temptress of southern lands. She offers her body to the victors knowing that their yielding to the temptation will reverse the roles: she will triumph over them, and they will become her slaves. The conquerors win their final and decisive victory by turning away from her. They conquer the temptation by turning their backs on it and setting out, in a grandiose way, for their own country.

Let us now look at the group of poems singled out as representing disappointment. In the prodigal son parable, there occurs a moment when the son begins to perceive how the world has fooled him, how full of undreamt-of dangers it is and how easy it is for any personal design to collapse. Similarly, a number of Gumilëv's poems deal with the themes of death, humiliation, hardship, ill luck, total personal catastrophe.

In **"The Blinding Light" ("Oslepitel'noe")** the discovery of disappointment is celebrated. The speaker views his previous attitudes of the "discoverer of the new lands" with melancholy and despair. He has come to understand that Eldorado cannot be discovered, that the most magnificent efforts of sea conquerors lead to nothing. The only thing left for him is "to drop onto the armchair / Keep the light away from his face with his hands / And cry for Levant" (Ja telo v kreslo uronju / Ja svet rukami zaslonju / I budu plakat' o Levante). **"The One in Rags" ("Oborvanec")** mourns the absolute unavailability of the dream woman. **"The Old Maid" ("Staraja deva")** does the opposite: it mourns the unavailability of the dream man. The atmosphere of hopelessness pervades both poems. The spinster sees herself as a young princess admired by all, and in the next moment she notices the humdrum appearance of her living room and the tired objects which seem to have been permanently placed there. The hobo remembers "for the hundredth time" the glance a rich lady gave him while entering a first-class train carriage; since then, he stubbornly walks along the railway tracks. Total disaster and gloom permeate **"Flowers do not live at My Place" ("U menja ne zhivut cvety")**. The speaker confesses his absolute inability to be happy or enthusiastic about anything. For a moment, he seems to like flowers, but this lasts a moment only: the flowers wither in the flower vase just as they do in his soul. His mental state reflects upon all living things that come into contact with him: not only flowers, but also birds die swiftly in his dwelling. The silent rows of books—bought from a used book dealer whose store was "next to an accursed cemetery"—stand still like eight rows of teeth: the witnesses—and perhaps the causes—of the state of hopelessness he is in. **"The One Who Has Lost" ("Oderzhimyj")** presents a character who is shamefully and overwhelmingly defeated by the "monstrous grief" (chudovishchnoe gore) which descends upon him in the darkness of the night. Gloomy vengeance is celebrated in **"Stone" ("Kamen' ")** where a big stone is seen as an agent of death and destruction. Intimations of death appear in **"The Animal Trainer" ("Ukrotitel' zverej")**, **"The Poisoned One" ("Otravlennyj")**, **"The Bird" ("Ptica")**, **"Death" ("Smert' ")**. "Only death is true", declares the speaker in the **"Second Canzonette"**: everything, including love, is sentenced to "merciless disappearance".

As was the case with the theme of desire and joy, resignation and gloom sometimes appear in strikingly unexpected disguises. For instance, **"The Founders" ("Osnovateli")** underlines the primacy of death and does it at such an unlikely moment as the time of founding the city. Upon the establishing of Rome, Remus's first concern is to have the burial vaults close to his own mansion, i.e., to the center of the city. Another example: in **"Childhood" ("Detstvo")** there appears an unexpected remembrance of the child's feelings: "And I trusted that I would die" (I ja veril, chto ja umru). The tone of the poem is set by the boy's belief in death that finally makes all things equal.

Analyzing the poems in which the second of the grand themes of Gumilëv appears, I have noticed that they display a much more diverse and chaotic structure than the poems about joy. Unlike the joy poems, they do not present a well defined type of hero and a uniform way of bringing this hero to a defeat.

The third set of qualities which constitute the essence of the prodigal son parable and the myth of the eternal return, consists of the new vision, new serenity and the return itself—in other words, of some kind of the "regeneration of life". A number of poems belonging here stress the epiphanic aspect of regeneration. This happens in **"The Sixth Sense" ("Shestoe chuvstvo")**. The poem deals with the painful effort of growing up and becoming worthy of the new vision. Man's life leading to the epiphany is compared here to the strange and painful feeling of a prehistorical creature "howling in helplessness" while it felt the moment approach when the wings would grow on it. Similarly, **"The Sun of the Spirit" ("Solnce duxa")** celebrates the awakening of the spirit while the body "not understanding anything, / Follows it blindly" (telo, nichego ne ponimaja, / Slepo povinujetsja emu). In **"The Eternal" ("Vechnoe")**, the speaker blesses "the road from the worm to the sun" (Dorogu k solncu ot chervja) and looks forward to the day of epiphany (O den', kogda ja budu zrjachim / I stranno znajushchim, speshi!). In **"Contemporaneousness" ("Sovremennost" ')**, the finishing of the Iliad is associated with the ending day and the new time beginning. In some poems, the qualities of disappointment and death precede the new vision. In **"Invitation to a Voyage" ("Priglashenie v puteshestvie")**, the voyage leads to the moment of death treated as an apogee of life—unlike in Baudelaire's poem under the same title. In **"Childhood"**, the boy's intimation of death is paired with the new vision: "And behind the farthest skies / I shall suddenly understand it all" (I za dal'nimi nebesami / Dogadajus' vdrug obo vsëm).

The change in the characteristics of the speaker is a frequent feature of the "return and new vision" poems. From conquistador he changes into a pilgrim, or a wanderer, or a bitterly experienced man. The poem **"Pilgrim" ("Palomink")** describes the very act of pilgrimage. In **"The Blinding Light"** even the old sea voyages are seen as pilgrimages toward a new understanding. "I sailed, the humble pilgrim . . . " (Ja plyl, pokornyj piligrim . . .) In **"Rhodos"**, the remnants of a medieval order of knights attract the attention of the speaker. **"The Turkestan Generals" ("Turkestanskie generaly")** was inspired by Russia's conquest of Turkestan in the middle of the nineteenth century. The poem itself, however, deals with later times and expresses the longing after the sun of Turkestan, the desire to return there, rather than actual battles. **"The Lost Streetcar" ("Zabludivshijsja tramvaj")** is a presentation of the poetic speaker's wanderings which end with the return to Russia and to St. Petersburg. While the cinema technique makes this poem different from the typical poems of Gumilëv, its essential thematic feature (voyage and return) attaches it to the major body of Gumilëv's verse.

Peacefulness and relief of a pilgrimage and return are put to focus in many poems. In **"Eternity" ("Vechnost' ")**, the assurance and relief of **"We have come" ("My prishli")** distinguishes itself sharply from the insecure eagerness of the conquistador poems. **"Return" ("Vozvrashchenie")** describes a pilgrimage to China, the ultimate aim of which is Buddhist serenity and holiness. **"Ancient Memory" ("Prapamjat' ")** consists of a meditation on the monotony of "the raging flame, the trumpets sounding, the red horses rushing forward" and contrasts this with the joy of the opposite kind of existence: "When shall I finally awaken and become again a simple Hindu, dozing at the creek during a holy evening?" In **"The Church of the Gospels" ("Evangelicheskaja cerkov' ")**, Christian symbolism of return prevails: "This is the way in which a son returns to his father". (Tak mozhet syn vojti k otcu). And one of the last lines Gumilëv ever wrote reads: "I often think of my old age, / Of wisdom and of peace". (Ja chasto dumaju o starosti mojej, / O mudrosti i o pokoje.)

Such is the basic thematic pattern which, in smaller or larger fragments, consistently appears in Gumilëv's poetry. It has been my contention that in its essential features, this pattern is identical with that which appears in the prodigal son parable and in the myth of the eternal return.

The second structural feature of Gumilëv's poetry is the fascination with the opposites, the urge not to let an idea or an image alone until its antonym is also introduced and explored. The sequence of qualities in the prodigal son parable can in itself be seen as consisting of several sets of antonyms. The triumphal tone of the conquistador contrasts sharply with the desperate voice of the "disappointment" poems: joy and desire for struggle on the one hand, gloom and inertia on the other. In addition, the return poems express the opposite of the departure for conquest which the conquistador poems celebrated.

Side by side with the oppositions implicit in the prodigal son parable, Gumilëv's verse display other, related sets. Perhaps the most prominent among them are the juxtapositions male versus female, and the "black" heroine versus the "white" heroine. The masculine persona of Gumilëv's poems is both attracted and repulsed by the set of qualities that have been traditionally associated with femininity. (Gumilëv would get poor marks from the women's liberationists today.) It has been mentioned that the prodigal son cycle of poems contains an element not appearing in the original version of the parable: it is the hero's sister, then the bride, and only then the father, that greet him upon his return. Poems such as **"Rhodos"** and **"To the Girl"** express the fascination with the archetype of the feminine. In the first of these, the speaker is attracted to it: the woman is "the heavenly bride" symbolizing peace, serenity and security. In the second, the balanced state of mind of the serene girl is challenged by the "reckless hunter" who opts for the opposite qualities. The "reckless hunter" represents masculine vigor while the girl stands for cautious level-headedness and the restraining power of the feminine. The conflict between the masculine and the feminine, the simultaneous attraction and repulsion toward the white heroine, are expressed in the poem **"The Two Adams"**: while one of them longs for permanence of a relationship with an idealized woman, the other ridicules such feelings and opts for adventure and fight.

The persistence of water imagery is another example of the omnipresence of the feminine archetype and of the ambiguous attitude adopted toward it. I cannot think of any poet who would so stubbornly return to the ocean and the lake and the ship and the sea voyage. Gumilëv's speaker sees them in dreams and in his conscious memory, he uses them as bases of metaphors, events and situations. Among the multiple suggestions which water imagery brings about, the feminine principle looms large. Thus Gumilëv's preoccupation with the super-masculine conquistadors and sea captains is only one aspect of the water imagery connotations: the other is the feminine.

Gumilëv's archetype of the feminine, in turn, splits into the pair of opposites which can be called the black and the white heroine. Those poetic references to the feminine which were discussed above, were all references to the white heroine, one that is "the lightest, the tenderest, the dearest" (see the poem **"The South"**). On many occasions, however, the feminine principle is presented as destructive and hateful, overwhelming and victorious. This happens, for instance, in the poem **"At the Fireside" ("U kamina")**, where the tired wanderer confronts a woman "with evil and triumphant eyes." He had hoped for empathy and selflessness on the part of the listener, and encountered a hostile and self-contained force. In **"To the Cruel One" ("Zhestokoj")**, the speaker expresses anger and envy at the encounter with a lesbian. In **"The Animal Trainer" ("Ukrotitel' zverej")**, the woman appears as a destructive force, the mistress of a wild animal that will finally destroy the speaker. In poems of this type, the dominant element is fear of the feminine. This fear contrasts sharply with the self-assurance of the conquistador poems and with the longing for, and idealization of, the feminine principle in the "white" heroine poems. To use the language of psychology, in Gumilëv's verse one observes an alternation of the flight to the womb and the fear of castration. A frivolous remark suggests itself here: what a beautiful topic for the women's liberation movement's analyses of male writers!

In some poems, the idea of joining the opposites is brought in. The dissolution of conflict between the opposing forces is presented mainly in regard to the male-female archetype. In such poems, Gumilëv seems to follow the idea of Vladimir Solov'ëv about the myth of the androgyne as representing a perfect human being. **"The Androgyne" ("Androgin")** presents a new being which arises out of selfless union of the male and the female. Perfection is its mark, and it reenters the condition of closeness to the godhead immediately after its birth (in this respect, **"The Androgyne"** belongs to the "return" poems). In this poem, in fact, godhead itself is an androgyne. In **"The Woods" ("Les"),** one of the best poems of Gumilëv, a fantastic and uncanny forest is the décor in which the male and the female unconscious meet—and merge. "Maybe this forest represents your soul, maybe it represents mine," muses the speaker at the end. "And maybe, we shall both enter it when we die."

These examples of Gumilëv's preoccupation with the opposites by no means exhaust his inventiveness in the matter. They do show, however, his predilection for contrasts rather than gradual passing from one quality to another. Gumilëv resembles those keyboard composers who, before the modern piano was invented, would change the amplitude of sounds in a piece of music not by means of crescendos and diminuendos but by sudden changes of register, unexpected jumps from piano to forte to fortissimo, and then back to pianissimo. This technique is still used in composing for those keyboard instruments which, like organ, are unable to produce crescendos and diminuendos. In the same manner, Gumilëv avoids gradations on every level, preferring to it sudden changes of mood and theme.

An awareness of these two structural patterns: fondness for binary oppositions and the sequence of qualities present in the prodigal son parable and in the myth of the eternal return, leads to the conclusion that Gumilëv is by no means a poet of one tune only, a sort of military rhymer who learned to write verse by studying a rhetoric manual. In its own way, his poetry participates in verbalizing one of the essential mythic structures that humanity has produced. He has based this thematic pattern on a principle that is basically very simple but seldom used to such an extent: that of binary opposition. By means of these characteristics he wins a place in Russian poetry that is unmistakably his own.

N. Elaine Rusinko (essay date 1977)

SOURCE: "The Theme of War in the Works of Gumilev," in *Slavic and East-European Journal,* Vol. 21, No. 2, Summer, 1977, pp. 204-13.

[*In the following excerpt, Rusinko characterizes Gumilev's war poems as abstract, heroic and "rhetorical," and compares them to his wartime prose sketches, which she considers more realistic.*]

Gumilev's poems on the theme of war have been both praised and condemned, but he is generally acknowledged as the outstanding Russian soldier-poet of the Great War. His treatment of this theme, along with his exotic adventure poems, is largely responsible for his subsequent position in the history of Russian poetry as the stereotyped "poet-warrior." Actually, Gumilev's war poems are not numerous. In all, there are only ten poems dealing with the war as the central theme, and it appears peripherally in but a few more. Other poets of the time, notably Sergej Gorodeckij and Georgij Ivanov, produced more war poetry, and patriotism is more pronounced in the works of Blok and Belyj than it is in Gumilev's. However, it is Gumilev's name which is most often associated with the Russian poetic experience of the First World War.

One of the reasons for this inevitable association is that Gumilev was the only major Russian poet to see actual service in the Imperial Army. Although he had a medical exemption, Gumilev volunteered for service just one month after Russia entered the war. The immediacy of his intention is indicated by a poem dated the day after Russia's declaration of war, where he writes, "Zovet menja golos vojny" ("The voice of war calls me"). He entered the guards regiment of Her Majesty's Uhlans and was assigned to Her Majesty's squadron.

In addition to poetry, Gumilev wrote a series of prose sketches entitled **"Zapiski kavalerista" ("Notes of a Cavalryman")** for the Petersburg newspaper *Birževye vedomosti.* The style of the sketches has been referred to as "simple realism," and it has been contrasted with the eloquent rhetoric of the war poems. However, Gumilev's conscious artistry is as prominent in the seemingly straightforward sketches as it is in the eloquent poetry, and the distinction is primarily one of perspective and narrative persona.

Gumilev's war poems are usually exalted and rhetorical in tone. He treats the "poetic" aspects of the situation (honor, courage, sacrifice) with little concern for objective reality. Dmitrij Karenin comments, "In Gumilev's verses, dubious deeds are vested in exaggeratedly bright, but unconvincing, garments," and he adds that if Gumilev actually believed in these bright trappings of the war, he was unusual in his idealism. The question is not one of sincerity, however, but of a conscious choice of artistic style. The war offered Gumilev an opportunity to exercise his rhetorical power, and he did this consciously. In a poetic critique of "modern times" from the collection ***Kolçan,*** he wrote, "Pobeda, slava, podvig—blednye / Slova, zaterjannye nyne". ("Victory, glory, exploit—pale / Words, now lost"). As Ejxenbaum noted in a review of the collection, in his war poems Gumilev rediscovers these "lost" words and employs them lavishly.

The rhetorical exuberance of Gumilev's style is clear in

one of the most famous of his war poems, **"Solnce duxa"** (**"The Sun of the Spirit"**), which begins, "Kak mogli my prežde žit' v pokoe / I ne ždat' ni radosti ni bed." ("How could we have previously lived in peace / Expecting neither joy nor misfortune.") The poem praises the warriors who are inspired and uplifted by the "sun of the spirit." The idea expressed here is typical of the patriotic fervor generated by the situation, and there is no doubt but that the feeling was genuine. However, Gumilev does not speak as an individual moved by the intensity of emotion, but as an orator attempting to inspire a general audience with noble zeal. His point of view is the rhetorical "we" and his tone is forceful and declamatory. The poetic figures are those of oratory—rhetorical questions and exclamation ("Kak mogli my" ["How could we"]); repetition (of the titular phrase "solnce duxa"); contrast of body and spirit; parallelism ("v dikoj prelesti . . . v tixom tainstve" ["in wild charm . . . in quiet mystery"]); epithets ("ognezarnoj boj" ["fire-lightning battle"], "rokoçuşçaja truba pobed" ["the resounding trumpet of victory"]); and lofty diction ("dreva duxa" ["the tree of the spirit"]). Ejxenbaum notes that Gumilev does not know the measure of his words: "One must be more cautious with such words. They are too solemn and full of meaning in themselves. They clang like bells, drowning out the inner voice of the soul."

To be sure, exaggeration is inevitable in this kind of poetry, and the standards for its judgment are necessarily different from those of reflective, personal lyric poetry. It is questionable, for example, whether Gumilev intended to express the "inner voice of the soul" in this poem. And Ejxenbaum is correct in noting the absence of a subjective poetic voice—the orientation is clearly rhetorical. However, it is by no means certain that **"Solnce duxa"** succeeds even as rhetoric, if by that term is implied poetry which persuades, inspires, and moves to action. Gumilev exploits the rhetorical tropes in this poem to the detriment of structure and development. The poem has no informing consciousness or focus (the "sun of the spirit" is not developed sufficiently to unify the thoughts), and there is no clear line of development. In an extensive review of ***Kolçan,*** M. Tumpovskaja described this effect: "The words do not flow in an orderly procession, but break loose . . . in a brilliant and powerful throng." The effect is a glorification of war and an effusion of emotional fervor, but not an impelling or effectual exhortation. . . .

Ejxenbaum calls the poems on the theme of war "psalms" and characterizes Gumilev's perception of the war as a "misterija duxa." It has often been noted that Gumilev reacted to the war spiritually and expressed this emotion in his poems by means of the frequent Christian motifs. Struve, for example, comments that Gumilev combines the military and Christian traditions and sees war as "a valuable spiritual experience." In commending Gumilev's war poems for their counterpoint of lofty and simple vocabulary, Struve counters Ejxenbaum's criticism and agrees with Žirmunskij, who approves Gumilev's attraction to the "rhetorical splendor of eloquent words." In Gumilev's poems on the war, Žirmunskij sees a union of the "individual life force at its extreme intensity" with the "super-individual force" (nadindividual'naja sila), wherein the individual achieves "eternal, mystical heights." This approach would lead to an interpretation of **"Solnce duxa"** and **"Vojna"** as a "metaphysical" vision of war.

But although Gumilev could possibly have undergone a spiritual renewal in his war experience, it would seem that this speculation does not deserve special emphasis. There is a general proliferation of religious imagery in Gumilev's poetry of this period, and in any case the Christian element is a basic feature of the Russian patriotic-literary tradition. It is likely that the spiritual tone of these poems is as much a conscious artistic choice on his part as it is an expression of personal sentiment. In his Acmeist manifesto of 1912, Gumilev had rejected the supernatural as a subject of poetry and insisted that the elements of "the other world" have value in poetry only as artistic devices. It is in this sense that he utilizes the seraphim and "the sun of the spirit" in the war poems. To be sure, the patriotic mood of the early days of the war was imbued with a sense of Holy Russia and the sanctity of the war effort. Gumilev certainly shared this patriotic-religious temperament and added the overlay of artistic tradition to give it a fitting expression. But to identify Gumilev as the "Holy Warrior" on this basis would be unjustified. The same religious imagery, idealization of death, and praise of valor and honor appear as well in his adventure poems, as, for example, in **"Otkrytie Ameriki"** (**"The Discovery of America"**). In **"Snova more"** (**"Again the Sea"**), a poem which invokes the persona's love of travel and adventure, the image of "the sun of the spirit" appears with no spiritual or patriotic overtones. **"Afrikanskaja noç' "** (**"African night"**) deals with the theme of war in the same religious and rhetorical spirit as the poems cited here, but the war in question is a jungle war of white colonializers against the natives, rather than the patriotic Great War. N. Uljanov aptly notes that for Gumilev war is not holy because it has a noble goal, but simply because it is a valuable experience in itself, and he comments, "Under the Christian covering, there appears the religion of a Viking."

In fact, whatever the patriotic spirituality of the poems might seem to indicate, it is probable that Gumilev's basic approach to the war did not differ significantly from his approach to African safaris. The persona of the sketches, who is a modest cavalryman rather than an eloquent orator, constantly underplays the "veliçavoe delo" and regards it as a game or adventure. He compares the battle to hunting: "Only when hunting great beasts, leopards, buffalo, have I experienced the same sensation—when anxiety for oneself suddenly gives way to the fear of losing a magnificient prey." He faces danger in a casual manner: "It was rather dangerous, somewhat complicated, but for all that, extremely fascinating." And he enjoys the excitement of the "game" of war, comparing it to "hide and seek." Obviously, this is as much a conscious posture as the exuberant rhetoric, and in this sense Soviet critics are not incorrect in seeing Gumilev's approach to the war as an extension of his romantic fantasies.

"Nastuplenie" (**"The Attack,"**) presents a romantic conception of war that is not unlike Gumilev's expressions of bravado in the adventure poems. The persona of this poem, the "bearer of a great idea" (*nositel' mysli velikoj*), is quite different from that of **"Solnce duxa,"** whose "we" was generalized and rhetorical. Here the situation is particularized—the "we" is a group of soldiers about to enter combat, and later it is narrowed to an individual participant in the attack. The situation is seen from this soldier's point of view, and his peculiar perspective stresses the validity of the experience. The reader perceives the religious-patriotic feelings of the persona ("Zolotoe serdce Rossii / Merno b'etsja v grudi moej" ["The golden heart of Russia / Deliberately beats in my breast"]) along with his sensations ("Nado mnoju rvutsja šrapneli, / Ptic bystrej vzletajut klinki" ["Above me shrapnel howls, / Fragments start faster than birds"]). And because of the authority established by the consistent point of view and the seeming simultaneity of the action, they acquire credibility. Despite the grandiose vocabulary, hyperbolic imagery, and extreme sentiments, there is a genuine intensity of feeling in **"Nastuplenie."** The rhetoric is motivated and integrated and, most importantly, controlled by the presence of a definite lyrical persona. The poem thus succeeds to a greater extent than the more general and diffuse emotional philosophizing of **"Solnce duxa,"** for example. And it comes closer to what might be expected from a poet who saw front-line action.

In contrast to most of the war poetry, Gumilev's sketches, **"Zapiski kavalerista,"** are quite consciously the work of a front-line cavalryman. In his poetry, Gumilev exploits traditionally "poetic" topics—honor, courage, sacrifice. The poetry is highly abstract, with little relation to the objective realities of the experience. In the sketches, the subject matter is closer to reality—hunger, fatigue, discomfort—apparently "realistic" topics not suited for idealistic poetry.

However, the matter of selection is but the superficial level of the distinction. Given a single author and an identical body of source material, divergence implies a differentiation in viewpoint, that is, a distinction of personae. The difference between the two genre treatments is a consequence of varying perspectives. The persona of the sketches is still a propagandist, still the romantic adventure. But while the poetic persona was an orator whose purpose was to impress and inspire, the persona of the sketches is a writer-journalist whose purpose is to report, more or less honestly, the facts of experience. While the immediate impression left by the journalistic style is one of simplicity, closer examination reveals it to be a studied simplicity. The impression of straightforward, unpretentious narration is deceptive. On the contrary, Gumilev makes a conscious artistic effort to achieve this effect.

One of the literary devices Gumilev uses to achieve a sense of forthright, subjective narration is irony. The cavalryman expresses seemingly "honest" emotions which, by their modesty, create the impression of realism. For example, the narrator is apparently candid about acknowledging feelings of fatigue, discomfort, and even fear—feelings that would be inconceivable for the poetic persona. He admits his desire to maneuver himself into a position in headquarters so as not to be sent out into the cold, reproaches himself with cowardice, and admits to feelings of fear: "I felt that kind of fear which can be conquered only by an effort of will." Of course, he does conquer fear, and he is sent out into the cold, and he follows orders, or there would be no point to the story. Therefore, what seems at first to be honest realism is in fact another conscious artistic posture, disguised by the unpretentious manner of narration. The posture here, in contrast to the heroic persona of the poems, is sympathetic and within the sphere of ordinary human experience, so it is scarcely conspicuous as a pose, and thus the reader is led to believe that he is witnessing the author's direct and unadorned personal reflections.

It is interesting to compare Gumilev's prose with his theoretical precepts, as indicated in his review of Kuzmin's prose from 1910: "The distinctive characteristics of M. Kuzmin's prose are the definition of the plot, its smooth development, and a particular modesty of thought. . . . He simply and clearly, and thus, perfectly, narrates about this and that. Before you is not a painter, not an actor, but a writer." Gumilev's theoretical demands in prose are not unlike the Acmeist precepts he set forth for poetry. He demands clarity, objectivity, and modesty (*celomudrie*), and for the most part, his prose on the theme of war achieves these goals to a greater extent than does his war poetry.

In the same review, Gumilev wrote: "In order to charm the reader, to capture and master him, one must relate the uninteresting in an interesting manner. . . . What can be less interesting than the everyday events of another's life?" Gumilev is a good story-teller. His sketches move at a brisk pace and the plot unravels smoothly with humor and suspense. Scenes and events are depicted in clear, precise language in a logical manner: "Toward lunch time, a rumor reached us that five men of our squadron had been taken prisoner. Toward evening, I already saw one of these prisoners, the rest were sleeping in the hayloft. Here's what happened. There were six of them in the outpost. Two were standing guard, four were sitting in the hut. . . . " And the narrator proceeds in this laconic manner to recount the events. Again, however, the straightforward style is deceptive. Gumilev's technique of sustaining interest is to produce a burst of insight, emotion, or sympathy in the sudden realization of the contrast between the significant content and its understated style. As in his best poems, he eschews exposition and explanation, presenting a visual tableau which speaks for itself:

> Patrols converged from all directions, squadrons came in from their positions. The early arrivals were cooking potatoes and brewing tea. But there was no opportunity to take advantage of this, because we were formed into a column and led out to the road. Night fell, quiet, blue, frosty. The fluttering snow glimmered. The stars seemed to be shining through glass. We were ordered to stop and wait for further instructions. And for five hours we stood on the road.

His verbal economy is notable, and his personal "modesty" is emphasized by his stylistic understatement. After a carefully detailed account of a midnight reconnaissance mission, Gumilev concludes: "All the same, the intelligence we gathered proved to be useful, they thanked us, and for that night I received the Cross of St. George." Of course, by understating his romantic bravado the persona is in effect emphasizing it, and a heroic pose emerges subtly from the unassuming prose style.

The irony inherent in Gumilev's contrast of noble content with simple expression becomes more obvious when the contrast is reversed, when the style is more lofty than the idea expressed. An example is his hyperbolic description of a moment spent with a hot glass of tea in the security of a peasant hut as the happiest moment of his life, or in his mock-rhetorical paean to comfort and "low, stuffy huts," which might almost be a self-parody on the style of the patriotic poems.

There are other departures from the general denotative mode, and the persona occasionally displays a more serious and philosophical temperament:

> That day our squadron was the leading squadron of the column and our platoon was the vanguard. I hadn't slept all night, but the excitement of the attack was so great that I felt completely vigorous. I think that at the dawn of mankind people lived by their nerves in the same way, created much and died early. It is difficult to believe that a man who dines every day and sleeps every night can contribute anything to the treasurehouse of the culture of the spirit. Only fasting and vigil, even if they are involuntary, awaken in men special, heretofore slumbering forces.

The ideas here are similar to those expressed in the poem **"Nastuplenie,"** but the style is more subdued. In other ways as well, the personae overlap. Many familiar metaphors and motifs reappear: "Bullets buzzed like big, dangerous insects"; "It was an experienced, renowned regiment, which went into battle as if to ordinary field work." There are many passages, particularly in the nature descriptions, which indicate the poet's sensitive perception of the world, and perhaps, in its attention to detail, an "Acmeist" perception. Gumilev intersperses humorous anecdotes in his sketches, usually at the Germans' expense. And there are occasional vignettes which recall the visual poetic style of Acmeism:

> I especially remember a grave old gentleman, sitting at the open window of a big manor house. He was smoking a cigar, but his brows were knit, his fingers nervously tugged at his gray moustache, and sorrowful astonishment was read in his eyes. The soldiers passing by looked at him shyly and shared their impressions in a whisper: "A stern gentleman, probably a general . . . and deadly, no doubt, when he curses". . . .

Throughout the sketches, there can be felt the presence of the poet, which imbues them with genuine artistry, but it is tempered by the predominance of the cavalryman-journalist, creating the impression of ingenuous and unadorned directness.

The contrast between the poetry and the prose sketches on the war theme is, to repeat, not as clear-cut as it might seem on first impression. The personae take different approaches, but the aim is essentially the same—the patriotic glorification of war and the soldierly mystique. The poet speaks as self-appointed orator, the "bearer of a great idea," whose appeal is philosophical and intellectual. By contrast, the author of the sketches is a cavalryman, a participant in the action whose insight is limited to his own observations and experiences. His goal is to relay to his readers the experience of war as perceived by the cavalryman in its midst. (The fact that this particular cavalryman is also a poet necessarily modifies the perception somewhat, but allows for its expression, and the autobiographical veracity contributes to its credibility.)

In the sketches, Gumilev achieves the standard of prose he demanded in his theoretical statements—modesty of thought (*celomudrie mysli*). However, this "modesty" is not the result of naive subjectivity. On the contrary, the poet's conscious play with personae is a feature of his developing artistic style and represents a more mature and discerning approach to his basic romanticism. Similarly, to emphasize the poet's spiritual approach to the war in his poetry is to stress speculative biographical and ideological content over artistic features, an approach which has persisted in Gumilev scholarship despite its generally recognized inadequacy. Despite his romantic temperament and adventurous spirit, Gumilev is first and foremost a conscious artist, constantly aware of the formal conventions of literary tradition that shape and discipline his personal emotions. Like his love poems, his literature on the theme of war is best understood not as the direct expression of personal sentiments, but as the distilled experience of a poet, molded by literary tradition.

FURTHER READING

Criticism

Graham, Sheelagh Duffin. "N. S. Gumilev and Irish Legend: An Unpublished Fragment from 'The Beauty of Morni.' " In *Irish Slavonic Studies* No. 5, 1984, pp. 167-80.

Discusses Gumilev's works based on Irish originals and presents a translation of the only known portion of an Irish-themed verse drama believed to have been written by Gumilev between 1918 and 1921.

Matlaw, Ralph E. "Gumilev, Rimbaud, and Africa: Acmeism and the Exotic." *Proceedings of the Sixth Congress of the International Comparative Literature Association,* Stuttgart: Kunst und Wissen, 1975, pp. 653-59.

Discusses the style of Gumilev's African poems.

Nilsson, Nils Ake. "The Dead Bees: Notes on a Poem by Nikolaj Gumilev." In *Orbis Scriptus,* edited by Dmitrij Tschiževskij. Munich: Wilhelm Fink Verlag, 1966, pp. 573-80.

Commentary on "The Word" ("Slovo"), one of Gumilev's best-known poems.

Rusinko, Elaine. "Gumilev in London: An Unknown Interview." *Russian Literature Triquarterly,* No. 16, 1979, pp. 73-85.

Traces Gumilev's association with British literary figures including G. K. Chesterton, Aldous Huxley, and C. R. W. Nevinson, as interpreted through letters, journals, and a 1917 interview with C. E. Bechhofer, published in *The New Age,* XXI, 9 (June 28, 1917).

———. "*K Sinej Zvezde:* Gumilev's Love Poems." *Russian Language Journal* XXXI, No. 109 (Spring 1977): 155-66.
Analysis of a series of love poems Gumilev wrote in late 1917.

Hagiwara Sakutarō

1886-1942

Japanese poet, critic, and essayist.

INTRODUCTION

Hagiwara Sakutarō is considered by many critics to be the father of modern Japanese poetry. He was among the first poets to break away from the traditional, strictly metered forms of Japanese poetry–tanka and haiku. He also established a new aesthetic in Japanese poetry in which he attained a sustained poetic lyricism by using colloquial Japanese speech in free verse poems. Hagiwara was deeply influenced by European nihilistic philosophies, and his poems, which often center on existential anxiety, are pervaded by melancholy and nostalgia.

Biographical Information

Hagiwara was born into a middle-class family in the provincial town of Maebashi, where his father was a successful physician. While in middle school, he took a keen interest in literature and began submitting traditional tanka poems to the literary magazine *Bunko.* He later withdrew from school due to poor health, and he made sporadic attempts to earn his high school degree into his twenties. At home, Hagiwara devoted himself to poetry and the study of Japanese and European literature. He also had an aptitude for music, and he studied the mandolin and guitar. By 1910, Hagiwara had become a regular contributor to several poetry journals. He spent several years living a somewhat Bohemian life, drifting between his hometown and Tokyo. During this time he explored his interest in Western philosophy and literature, and for a brief period he attended Christian churches. His lifestyle drew criticism from the Maebashi bourgeoisie, and his poetry includes many spiteful remarks about his native community. In 1916, he cofounded the magazine *Kanjō* with Murō Saisei, an author whose poems he greatly admired. The magazine featured a new style of modern Japanese poetry that was distinct from the highly intellectual poems that other magazines of the day were publishing. The following year Hagiwara published his first poetry collection, *Tsuki ni hoeru.* The collection, which introduced Hagiwara's extraordinary talent for using colloquial speech in a free verse style, gained wide critical acclaim and established his reputation as a significant new voice in Japanese poetry. He followed this success with several more volumes of poetry, criticism, and poetic theory. Despite his solid literary reputation, Hagiwara relied on his family for financial support throughout his life. In 1919, Hagiwara married Uedo Ineko, with whom he had two daughters. The marriage ended in divorce in 1929. His second marriage, to Ōya Mitsuko in 1938, lasted only eighteen months. Much of Hagiwara's poetry conveys the isolation and loneliness that he felt, and his later works, particularly the poems in his 1934 collection *Hyōtō,* are characterized by an increasingly despondent and nostalgic tone. He taught at the University of Meiji in Tokyo from 1934 until the year of his death. He died in 1942.

Major Works

Hagiwara's first poetry collection, *Tsuki ni hoeru,* had a wide and immediate impact on the Japanese literary community. Although the collection contains some traditional tanka, many of the poems are written in a colloquial vernacular in a loose, unmetered form. Hagiwara's success at elevating common Japanese speech to a poetic form was unprecedented. In this volume, commentators noted, Hagiwara essentially created a new aesthetic in modern Japanese poetry. In the preface to the work Hagiwara wrote, "Before this collection not a single poem had been written in colloquial language of this style, and before this collection the animation in the poetry one senses today did not exist." Critics also note that the poems in this collection were among the first in modern Japanese poetry to address questions of existential anxiety. In the title piece, "Howling at the Moon," Hagiwara likened the desperate psychological state of humanity to a lonely dog plaintively wailing at the moon. Throughout the collection, in poems such as "A Hanging in Heaven" and "An Ailing Face at the Bottom of the Earth," Hagiwara created characters who are ridden with despair. Hagiwara's second collection of poems, *Aoneko,* achieved even greater critical acclaim than his first. The poems in this volume reveal Hagiwara's personal interest in the nihilistic philosophy of Arthur Schopenhauer and the pessimistic ideology of Buddhism. The collection centers on abstract, metaphysical themes in which characters are nostalgic for times and places that they have never experienced. Hagiwara published a second "definitive" edition of the volume in 1936, in which he included the poem "The Corpse of a Blue Cat." The piece is a sad and nostalgic love poem in which time and memory are displaced. In it, the speaker says, "We have no past, no future, / And have faded away from the things of reality." Hagiwara's last major collection of poetry, *Hyōtō* (1934), received mixed critical reviews. In this volume, Hagiwara abandoned his innovative use of colloquial Japanese and returned to writing in a more formal language in metered verse. The poems in the volume are set in a more realistic context, and they convey an overwhelming sense of despair and bitterness. In the autobiographical poem "Returning to My Parents' Home," for example, Hagiwara recounted the anger and rejection that he felt after his first wife left him. In addition to his poetry, Hagiwara was widely respected for his volumes on poetic theory. His most noted work, *Shi no genri* (1928), laid out his conception of what he contended should be the principal aims of poetry. In aphoristic statements Hagiwara asserted that poetry should strive to convey transcendental themes and be critical of reality.

PRINCIPAL WORKS

Tsuki ni hoeru [*Howling at the Moon*] (poems) 1917
Aoneko [*The Blue Cat*] (poems) 1923
Junjō Shōkyoku Shū [*Short Songs of Pure Feelings*] (poems) 1925
Shi no genri [*Principles of Poetry*] (criticism) 1928
Hyōtō [*The Ice Land*] (poems) 1934
Nekomachi [*The Cat Town*] (prose) 1935
Kyōshū no shijin Yosa Buson [*Yosa Buson: The Poet of Nostalgia*] (criticism) 1936
Face at the Bottom of the World, and Other Poems (poems) 1969

CRITICISM

Graeme Wilson (essay date 1969)

SOURCE: An introduction to *Face at the Bottom of the World, and Other Poems* by Hagiwara Sakutarō, translated by Graeme Wilson, Charles E. Tuttle Company, 1969, pp. 11-32.

[*In the following excerpt, Wilson discusses Hagiwara's contributions to modern Japanese poetry, noting the influences of European philosophy on his works and his success at integrating western and Japanese poetic styles.*]

Hagiwara began writing during that critical period in the history of Japanese literature when western influences, almost overwhelming in the Meiji Era (1868-1912), were at last being so successfully assimilated as to permit the regrowth of that essentially Japanese spirit which characterized the succeeding Taisho Era (1912-26). By 1910 the seeds dropped from foreign flowers, not all of them *Fleurs du Mal,* into the loam of Japanese consciousness were coming up like cryptomeria. *Wakon yōsai,* that Meiji slogan stressing the need to meld "western learning and the Japanese spirit", was still a living inspiration; and Hagiwara, working in full awareness thereof, achieved universality.

It is still sometimes said that the artist's function is to hold a mirror up to nature. The time when that remark was true, if ever such a time there was, is now long past. The photographers have taken over; the photographers who implement the lawyers' pettifogging mania for reasonable facsimiles. The artist's function is (and has, I fancy, always been) to hold up mirrors that transmit not the photographers' literal reality but the artist's individual, even his cracked, perception of the universe. His function in the world is, I believe, to create unreasonable facsimiles thereof. For artists, especially lyric poets such as Hagiwara, are not concerned with truths verifiable by photographs, by the due processes of the law, or by the disciplines of formal logic. They have those reasons reason does not know. Hagiwara was once asked to explain the meaning of an early poem. He replied by asking if his questioner considered beautiful the nightingale's song. On receiving the inevitable affirmative, he then asked what that bird-song meant. . . . For Hagiwara holds no mirror, cracked or commonplace, up to nature: mirrors need light. Instead, he turns a radar onto nature's hitherto unpenetrated darknesses, feeling out shapes invisible. The resultant images, shining, golden or greeny-silver, often indeed distorted, may, to a photographer's eye, seem odd; but they are authentic versions, visions even, of the truth. For Hagiwara was a native of that strange world where Dylan Thomas' question ("Isn't life a terrible thing, thank God") really needs no answer. And of that world his poems are a terrible, but a beautiful, reporting.

Hagiwara's earliest truly modern poems, of which the first examples appeared in magazines during 1913, show traces of the influence of Baudelaire and the French Symbolists. He has, in fact, been called "the Japanese Baudelaire" but, though there are obvious resemblances in their attitudes, Hagiwara's poetry (as distinct from his prose) contains none of the intellectualism of his predecessor. Similarly, those poems in which he shows most resemblance to Rimbaud are in the lighter lyrical field; and it is interesting to compare Hagiwara's **"Elegant Appetite"** with Rimbaud's *Au Cabaret Vert,* the latter the poem in which Ezra Pound considers Rimbaud's real originality to be found. Though Hagiwara's work rings with a certain natural pessimism and despair (themselves reflections of ill health, ill nerves and plain ill-luck), its tone was deepened by study of Nietzsche, Bergson and Schopenhauer. Not only his first book but also his middle-period poetry (notably the poems in **"To Dream of a Butterfly"** of 1923 and **"Blue Cat"** of the same year) exhibit that pure but desperate lyricism which German critics have called "the Keats' sickness". These poems do not argue: they sing. They are, in Japanese, songs of those very nightingales which, in T. S. Eliot's poem,

> Sang within the bloody wood
> When Agamemnon cried aloud
> And let their liquid siftings fall
> To stain the stiff dishonoured shroud.

As Hagiwara aged, his poetry began to lose its lyrical purity and, though it never sank to the level of logical argument, it did begin to organize its imagery into a sort of argument by visual analogy. At the same time he reverted to a more frequent use of the classical Japanese literary vocabulary (a vocabulary or, to be more precise, a syllabary derived from the Chinese), and his poems so acquired a clanging rather than a singing quality. These stylistic changes, of which **"Late Autumn"** is a good example, have been praised as marking Hagiwara's development, albeit belatedly, towards a more masculine manner. Such may indeed have been the poet's own intention, but I share Miyoshi's view that the change was a retrogression. I would not go so far as to echo that comment ("Even the powerful bow weakens in the end") which so annoyed Hagiwara, but there can be no doubt that his later poetry contains intellectual elements which adulterate, if they do not actually sour, his earlier pure lyricism. His prose writings demonstrate his reasoned (and, I think, rightly reasoned) antipathy to the styles of political poetry which, almost world wide, characterized the schools of the 1930s; but so far as these poets were poets and not political theorists or would-be politicians, Hagiwara shared their ever-deepening sense of anger, sadness and despair. Some of his later poems such as **"Useless Book"** and **"What I Don't Have Is Everything"** are almost querulous. He became eventually so bankrupt of all hope that, in Auden's terrifying words (which might well have been his own), he moved towards the ultimate silence of death

Saying Alas
To less and less.

. . . . .

The reasons for Hagiwara's importance in the history of modern Japanese literature (and, indeed, in the whole history of Japanese literature) may be summarized under the following six headings: his use of novel forms, his use of novel language, his escape from the bonds of traditional metric rhythms, his entirely personal music, his astonishing personal vision, and his unprecedented achievement of sustained lyricism.

The earliest collection of Japanese poetry (the *Manyōshū* of 759) consists largely of *tanka,* but it also contains many poems in the longer forms of the *chōka* and *sedōka*. However, by the time that Ki no Tsurayuki wrote his catalytic Preface to the *Kokinshū* (the First Imperial Anthology of 905), the Japanese poetic tradition had already begun to crystallize into a tradition of pure lyricism. "Poetry", wrote Tsurayuki, "has its seeds in man's heart"; and this view of poetry as lyricism necessitating no breadth of learning in the lyricist has remained the main strand of the Japanese poetic tradition. Such a tradition demands precisely that intensity of feeling which is always most tellingly expressed in short forms; and for this reason the *chōka* and *sedōka* withered away. Though at various times in the subsequent development of Japanese poetry, poets struggled for the freedom of such other longer forms as the *imayō, kouta, dodoitsu* and *jōruri,* the five-line *tanka* remained the normal mode of expression. Some measure of freedom appeared to be offered by the development of linked verse (*renga*) in which often different poets would compose successive three-line and two-line groups: but, in the event, this breaking of the *tanka* into a three-line upper hemistich (*kami no ku*) of 5:7:5 syllables and a two-line lower hemistich (*shimo no ku*) of 7:7 syllables merely resulted in a yet greater compression of Japanese poetic form. For the upper hemistich embarked on an independent development to become that flower of Edo poetry, now shriveled to a tourist's gaud, the three-line *haiku*. Thus, at the time when contact was reestablished with the outside world in 1868, the main tradition of Japanese poetry was rigidly confined within the narrow courses of the *tanka* and the *haiku*. The notion of poetry as a vehicle for intellectual thought, the concept of the poetry of social protest, the didactic element in Chinese poetry; all these had perished with Yamanoue no Okura (660-733) from the Japanese tradition.

The first result in the poetic field of the Meiji reopening of windows on the west was the appearance in 1882 of *Shintaishi* (*New Style Poetry*), a collection of translations of early nineteenth century English poems edited by three Professors (significantly of philosophy, botany and sociology) at the University of Tokyo. The Preface sharply attacked the cramping brevity of traditional forms ("How can a consecutive thought be expressed in such tight forms?"); and three further collections (Shimazaki Tōson's *Seedlings* in 1887, Mori Ōgai's *Semblances* in 1889 and Ueda Bin's *Sound of the Tide* in 1905) pursued the same line of attack but broadened the scope of European impact to include French, German and Italian influences. Nevertheless, the main stream of Japanese poetry continued to flow in the form of *tanka* (notably in the work of Yosano Akiko) and Hagiwara himself wrote hundreds of early poems in that form; the first five appeared in his school magazine in 1902 and the last group (influenced by Kitahara's work in that mode) in 1913. Thus, when in 1913 Hagiwara began to write poems in all manner of irregular and typically "modern" forms, he was by no means the first to abandon traditional Japanese practice, but he was undoubtedly the first Japanese poet successfully to exploit the innovations of form derived from western examples for the expression of traditional Japanese lyricism. It is perhaps worth noting here that Hagiwara did not at any time follow western example into those striking departures from the Japanese lyric tradition which, picking up the didactic tradition where Okura had left it in the eighth century, eventually developed into modern Japanese proletarian poetry and those contemporary schools which, though named after Eliot's early lyrics, in fact derive from his later (and very un-Japanese) "thinking poetry".

Similarly, though Buson (1716-83) had tentatively experimented with the use of the spoken colloquial language (*kōgotai*), it was not until the Shintaishi movement was very well developed that any serious attempt was made to break away from the literary language derived from Chinese models (*bungotai*) in which *tanka* and *haiku* were traditionally written. The three Tokyo Professors expressed in their Preface "regret that poetry has not hitherto been written in the colloquial language", but the language used to express the subsequent flow of imitations of European poets did little to assuage that sorrow. It was almost certainly Murō Saisei who first fully realized that the future of Japanese poetry lay in the use of *kōgotai* but, especially after Murō turned to the writing of novels, it was left for Hagiwara to exploit that realization and so to become the true father of modern Japanese poetry. Hagiwara exploited the rich resources of the colloquial right down to the darker levels of the vernacular; his claim that "all new poetic styles issued from this book" (***Barking at the Moon***) is, I think, a fair one.

Though the *Manyōshū* contained poems with lines of a notably irregular syllable-count, all subsequent Japanese poetry was constructed from patterns of lines of five and seven syllables; the so-called seven-five metric rhythm (*shichi go chō*). The words of the Japanese language are so built up from unaccented syllables all ending in vowels that rhyme has never been used in its poetry. In parenthesis, one might here remark that one of the further peculiarities of Hagiwara's earliest "modern" poems is that some of them do, in fact, appear to rhyme. However, this basic structure of the language has resulted in a prosody very closely linked to syllable-count, and long experience has confirmed the tradition that the *shichi go chō* is the rhythm most natural to the language. None of the poets of the Shintaishi movement, despite their attacks on traditional form and traditional language, made any attempt to break away from this traditional metric rhythm. The first real efforts in that direction were made by Kawaji Ryūkō in his volume of poems *Hakidame* (*Rubbish Heap*) published in 1908. But again, though Hagiwara was not the pioneer, he was the first Japanese poet since Manyō times successfully to exploit rhythms other than the *shichi go chō*.

It may well be that Hagiwara's success in that exploitation of Ryūkō's pioneering work was a reflection of his almost professional knowledge of music. He was, lifelong, obsessed by music. As early as 1908 he brought home a violin for the school holidays. In 1910 he wrote to one of his class-mates that "I have three possibilities: as a merchant, through medical school or suicide by pistol", but only his somewhat childish (he was then twenty-four) love of dramatizing his feelings of being misunderstood could have led him to omit the very real possibility that he would become a musician. In 1911 he spent some four months learning the mandolin under an Italian teacher, and made his usual ineffective efforts, this time to prepare for the entrance examination to the Ueno Music School. In 1912 he was studying the guitar in Tokyo, and as late as 1914 he was actually teaching the mandolin in a small western-style music-school then recently established in Maebashi. He organized, conducted and played publicly in musical groups. He published criticism both of western music and of the decline of the *samisen,* and in later life even some minor compositions of his own. Though Beethoven was his favorite composer and though Japanese critics have emphasized the symphonic structure of his middle-period poetry (notably that in ***Blue Cat***), his poems reveal an essentially melodic interest. In this connection it is perhaps worth suggesting that the poetry of Hagiwara and the poetry of Frederico Garcia Lorca (his almost exact Spanish contemporary) merit comparative study. It has been acutely remarked that, whereas Lorca was obsessed with the terror of envisaged horrors, Hagiwara was transfixed in lasting horror of terrors long arrived. The two poets shared an absorption in greenness ("Here", wrote Hagiwara, "is a little flute whose music is pure green"; "Green, how I love you, green", wrote Lorca). They shared a feeling for loneliness, for rivered landscapes, moonlight and horizons bounded by the barking of dogs. But, above all, they shared a passion for music, for the melodies in struck strings. Though there are, of course, great differences between them (the differences, basically, between the guitar and the mandolin), their high-strung similarities remain. There is no evidence that Hagiwara was aware even of Lorca's existence, and his introduction of an almost western melodic line to Japanese poetry is an entirely original contribution. But it is so real a contribution that some of his poems (notably **"Dice of Pure Silver"**), if they are ever successfully to be translated out of Japanese, will probably have to go into music.

Hagiwara's most astonishing originality lies, however, in his unique vision of the world. He had, highly developed, the poet's one essential gift: to see first what all can see once it has been shown to them. "Truth", said John Donne, "is a mountain: who would know Truth, about it and about must go". Hagiwara saw that mountain from his own strange belvedere, and his poems remain like arrow-slits in some cold and lonely siege-tower commanding their singular view of the truth. Some have said that his viewpoint was so restricted as to present a topsy-turvy truth, the universe *in camera oscura:* others, that he stood so close to Donne's great mountain that inevitably he stood in shadow. But there seems no dispute that, whatever aspect of the truth he saw, none had quite so clearly studied it before him. It is, I think, irrelevant that Hagiwara revealed so dark a beauty.

> Who, grown, can look in a true mirror
> And have no horror?

Hagiwara saw everything (not, perhaps, everyone) afresh, as if new-made, as if in vision. Indeed, I deduce he must have had constant access to that admittedly lowest level of mystical experience, the Vision of Dame Kind. How rarely are his poems concerned with relations other than relations with things (a characteristic of that Vision); and how frequently he uses not only the word "things", but the visionary's key-word "shining". I know no other poet, except perhaps Rimbaud in *Les Illuminations,* so simultaneously lucent and obscure. It is as though Hagiwara knew that the sun, that symbol of Japan, rises as much to cast shadow as to give light. Having abandoned not only traditional forms, traditional language and traditional rhythms but also what little residue of thought lay in the associated traditional stock of ideas, he is sometimes criticized for lack of intellectual content, for failing to react positively to the western revivification of the old Chinese didactic tradition and, in particular, for an uncritical acceptance of the Pathetic Fallacy. But lyric poets are not concerned to maintain logical or philosophical consistencies, and lyricists of Hagiwara's animistic sympathies might well not think that Fallacy fallacious. Though he is buried in the cemetery attached to the Buddhist Shōjun Temple in Maebashi, he seems never to have adopted any specific religion or philosophy, but to have remained a humanistic (or, rather, an animistic) free-thinker all his life. It is, however, relevant to mention, since it explains the otherwise curious frequency of Christian imagery in his poems, that, as a young man, he was much influenced by that cousin, Hagiwara Eiji, a convinced Christian, to whom ***Barking at the Moon*** is dedicated.

Finally, though Hagiwara stands squarely in the mainstream of the Japanese lyric tradition and though one strand of his poetic ancestry can be traced back through Bashō to that chill and bitter figure, the one-time master-archer of the late twelfth century, Priest Saigyō, he can also claim a place in the main continental European tradition running down through Baudelaire and the Symbolists to the Imagists and their successors. For the element in Hagiwara's work which is utterly unprecedented in the Japanese poetic tradition is the sheer staying-power of his lyric inspiration, the unexampled length of poem throughout which he was able to sustain an intensity of feeling which, before he wrote, had only been achieved in poems brief as *tanka*. More than for all his other innovations, Hagiwara's chief claim to greatness lies in his unparalleled sustention of lyric intensity. The peculiarly piercing quality of his poetry has been compared to that of a babe newborn into our terrible world. But Hagiwara cried for a lifetime, and in poems that will last as long as the Japanese language.

. . . . .

Contemporary Japanese poets and critics, while acknowledging Hagiwara's primacy, still tend to regard his work as a dead-end. This is, essentially, the criticism made of such slight and minor poets as A. E. Housman; but it seems to me unjustified in respect of Hagiwara. It is argued that the startling originality of his themes and imagery is no more than a direct reflection of the poet's persistent physical ill-health and of his spiritual and intellectual neurasthenia. His poetry's consequent aura of irremediable *malaise,* this argument continues, inevitably appeals to our own distempered times but it disqualifies Hagiwara from a major place in any healthy tradition. Though it can with perfect cogency be answered that all lyric poetry reflects some kind of serious disorder in the lyricist, even an admission of Hagiwara's quintessential sickness seems to me irrelevant to the reasons for the continuing importance of his work. I do not suggest that there would be any merit in contemporary imitation of his individual style, diction, imagery or themes; but I do very strongly suggest that Hagiwara's poetry is almost the only example in modern Japanese literature of the successful integration of the Japanese and western poetic traditions. His poetry is a living synthesis of alien elements, and poets working in either tradition would do well to study the means of his achievement: for Hagiwara has shown that the traditionally compressed Japanese intensity of lyric feeling can be perfectly expressed in the forms and at lengths derived from the western tradition, that the heart of Priest Saigyō can beat in the breast of Lorca. The scientists and surgeons, still baffled by problems of "rejection", struggle along fifty years behind him.

It took Japanese poets some fifty years to absorb the shock of the Meiji admission of western influences, and it may well take another fifty years for the shock sustained in 1945 to be similarly absorbed. The comparative worthlessness, *sub specie aeternitatis,* of the early Meiji imitations of European poets at least suggests the probable worthlessness of contemporary Japanese imitations of the current poetic vogue-styles, themselves not improbably worthless, of the west. There is, of course, no necessary reason why an obsession with the resources of typography, with the re-structuring of established syntax and the theories of Yves Bonnefoy, with Olson's Projective Verse, with Concrete Poetry and with the Intentionalist and Affective Fallacies should result in worthless Japanese poetry; but, in practice, worthlessness appears to result. "Tradition", said Eliot, "is a matter of much wider significance [than novelty]. It cannot be inherited and, if you want it, you must obtain it by great labour. It involves, in the first place, that historical sense nearly indispensable to anyone who would continue a poet beyond his twenty-fifth year. The historical sense compels a man to write not merely with his own generation in his bones, but with a feeling that the whole literature of his own country composes a simultaneous order". In precisely those terms Hagiwara, by enormous labor, established himself in the Japanese tradition. Only those who, like him, can refine and develop the poetic tradition of their own country can hope to become great poets in the future of Japan. Shinoda Hajime has recently expressed the seminal thought that perhaps the similarities between Hagiwara and Eliot reflect their common derivation of essential elements in their work from the main continental European tradition; and, if that thought be accepted, the work of Hagiwara holds lessons not only for Japanese poets of the future but for the future poets of the world. Only time will tell; though I dare in Auden's words to think that "Time will say nothing but I told you so". These matters affect only consideration of Hagiwara's status as a major poet of the world. That he is a major poet of Japan and a poet of as-yet-undetermined world-status cannot, I believe, seriously be challenged. His phenomenal perceptiveness, his lyric hypersensitivity, his remorseless wringing of the nervous system of the soul are unique. And, if in the long run of our tears he does eventually fail to achieve major world-status, it will only be because those very characteristics which give him such laser-sharp penetration necessarily narrow the breadth of his vision. For his, indeed, is the heart-break at the heart of things.

Charles Dunn (essay date 1970)

SOURCE: A review of *Face at the Bottom of the World, and Other Poems,* in *Pacific Affairs,* Vol. XLIII, No. 3, Fall 1970, pp. 481-82.

[*In the following review, Dunn offers a favorable review of Hagiwara's* Face at the Bottom of the World, and Other Poems.]

This book includes forty poems by Hagiwara (1886-1942), in an English version by Graeme Wilson, who also provides a short but enthusiastic introduction. I think it is true to say that Hagiwara's poems were characterized by a freshness of thought, and a clarity of description, in which language not greatly differing from the ordinary was used to write about things that were blinding by original, and sometimes shocking, at the time. The English versions appeal to me very much as poetical utterances (though I suspect that readers in their twenties might find them rather artificial), with some very telling collocations, and some fine effects of rhyme and alliteration, but they seem to go much further in the direction of poetic language than does Hagiwara. Are they the same poems as the Japanese originals? I doubt it very much, and if anyone were bold enough to translate them back into Japanese, they would, I wager, be very different from what Hagiwara wrote. Graeme Wilson disarms criticism by likening what he has done to what Fitzgerald did for Omar Khayyam. I think that this little book is very worth-while. Some paintings by York Wilson are included.

The Times Literary Supplement **(essay date 1971)**

SOURCE: "Transmutations of a Westernizer," in *The Times Literary Supplement,* No. 3618, July 2, 1971, p. 755.

[*In the following review, the critic asserts that translator Graeme Wilson's use of traditionally western images distorts the meaning of the poems in Hagiwara's* Face at the Bottom of the World, and Other Poems.]

Owing to some remarkable resemblances in tone and imagery Hagiwara Sakutarō has had the misfortune of being dubbed "the Japanese Baudelaire". In much the same way Chikamatsu Monzaemon became "Japan's Shakespeare" and Osaka (of all places) "the Venice of Japan". Such pairings compel invidious comparisons and are invariably unfair to the supposed Japanese counterparts. Chikamatsu and Hagiwara are major writers, but the juxtapositions with Shakespeare and Baudelaire serve only to point up their shortcomings.

Hagiwara Sakutarō (1886-1942), who has also been described as "the father of modern Japanese poetry", is undoubtedly the most important of all the Western-style poets since the Meiji Restoration. His work is hypersensitive, introspective, and often deeply affecting. The title-poem, one of the most successful of Graeme Wilson's ingenious versions, suggests his writing at its best:

Face at the bottom of the world:
A sick, a lonely face,
One invalided out
Of every inner place;
Yet, slowly there uncurled.
Green in the gloom the grasses sprout.

And, as rat's nest stirs,
Its million tangled hairs
One queasy quivering,
Thinnest of winterers,
The bamboo shoot prepares
Its green grope to the spring.

Sad in the ailing earth,
Tongue-tender with dispair,
Green moves through grief 's grimace;
And, sick and lonely, there
In the gloom of the under world,
At the bottom of the world, a face.

With recurrent images of disease, pain, and decay Hagiwara evokes a nightmare world populated with slithering earthworms, disgusting sea animals, and putrefying corpses: "Around the area of the dead white stomach / Something unimaginable flows."

The poems are virtually devoid of live people, except for the overwhelming person of the writer himself who spares no self-pity in describing the constant assaults on his sensibility. The verse is often powerful, but it is marred by a certain monotony of tone, a plangent hypersensitivity, and a total absence of intellectual backing. In traditional Japanese verse of the tanka and haiku variety these would be minor blemishes at the worst; in a Western form of poetry they became serious defects.

On the title-page the poems are described as having been "translated"; but in his introduction Mr Wilson defines them, more accurately, as "transmutations", and explains that they

> are translations only in the sense that Fitzgerald's *Rubaiyat* is a translation of the work of Omar Khayyam. I have not regarded the literal words in Hagiwara's texts as of prime or even secondary importance. Instead, I have sought first to convey the feel and intent of his work, the meaning of the feelings behind the vocabulary. . . .

The trouble with this approach is that we can never tell whether it is Mr Wilson's poetry we are reading or Hagiwara's. It is only a scholarpoet with the overwhelming linguistic command of an Arthur Waley who can permit himself to take such liberties with the text; and at times even Waley went too far.

The use of rhyme, which is of course entirely absent from the Japanese, sometimes forces Mr Wilson into strange convolutions and archaisms ("quietude innate", for instance, to rhyme with "man's animal estate"); but far more damaging in a book that purports to represent the work of a major Japanese poet is Mr Wilson's proclivity to add images and ideas that have not the remotest equivalent in the original text. Two examples will suffice. **"Green Flute"** (**"Midoriiro no Fue"**) ends in Japanese with the following simple sentence: *"Isso konna kanashii bokei no naka de, watakushi wa shinde shimaitai no desu. Ojosan"*. (Literally, "Girl, I should prefer to die in such sad evening twilight".) As transmuted by Mr Wilson this becomes:

Girl, I could easily
In such a placc concerning
Grief and the end of day,
Grief and the night returning,
To death's menagerie
Stagger away.

The final stanzas of **"In the Bar at Night"** are:

Even when drunk
And the glass ringing
Like a tolled bell,
The ghost so summoncd
From that rum world
Will tell you nothing,
Proves infidel.

Even when drunk . . .
O doomed Madonna,
Suffer us stare
At the dark green wall
In the bar at night;
For the hole is there.

"Infidel", "doomed Madonna"—strange words indeed for even the most Westernized of Japanese poets! But before the unwary reader jumps to any conclusions about alien influences on Hagiwara's thinking, it should be pointed out that "doomed Madonna" corresponds in the original text to the standard Japanese word for "ghost" (*yōkai*), while "proves infidel" corresponds to nothing at all ("rum", incidentally is Mr Wilson's rendering of the ordinary Japanese word *iyō,* "strange").

It is all very well to say that such alterations convey "the feel and intent of [Hagiwara's] work"; but unless Mr Wilson enjoys some form of direct communication with the spirit of the departed poet, by what possible licence can he insert a phrase like "O doomed Madonna", with all its complex implications for the Western reader when nothing even remotely similar exists in the Japanese text? Mr Wilson's outstanding poetic gifts could be used far better in creating his own verse than in inventing ideas and images for other writers.

F. D. Reeve (essay date 1971)

SOURCE: *Face at the Bottom of the World, and Other Poems,* in *Poetry,* CXVIII, No. 4, July 1971, pp. 234-38.

[*In the following review, Reeve offers a positive assessment of Hagiwara's* Face at the Bottom of the World, and Other Poems *and praises Graeme Wilson's translations of the poems in the collection.*]

Having no Japanese and not trusting Amy Lowell's *What's o'Clock?* or other Imagist imitations of Japanese style, such as Richard Aldington's:

One frosty night when the guns were still
I leaned against the trench
Making for myself hokku
Of the moon and flowers and of the snow

I hesitantly admire Graeme Wilson's translations of forty poems by Hagiwara Sakutarō. Although Hagiwara (1886-1942) was a sort of skeptical humanist who knew Baudelaire's work and who led a loose, drunken if not raunchy life, he seems to have overcome both the insipidity of early 20th-century Japanese culture and a prevailing subservience to Western models. With him I admire

The sleeping earth; and how therein
The simple creatures now begin
Building the house of your repentance.

My hesitation is caused only by what seems to be Mr. Wilson's excellence. In his introduction he says that he sought to report the tonal wholeness of Hagiwara's verse, that he could not and would not be literal. But his English versions are so readable that they tease us into wanting to know Japanese, that we might follow subtle shifts of view linked by the *kakekotoba,* evanescent suggestiveness, connections established by homonyms, by the "cutting word," by syllabic movement—linguistic features and prosodic devices to which we have no access in our Western languages. Only with difficulty and never with certainty can we grasp that—though not how—Hagiwara introduced colloquial speech into an aristocratic poetic tradition and, after long practice in *tanka* and other accepted patterns, worked out longer, larger, more open forms. Knowing that in Japanese rhyme is incidental and that Hagiwara passionately and relentlessly peered into himself, we cannot be sure, in **"Sad Moonlit Night,"** to what extent the ending is introspective or derivative (Hagiwara's) or to what extent it is rationalized and rhymed (Mr. Wilson's):

On the rotting wharf that pilfering cur,
Pale yapping waif of a wharfinger,
Barks at the moon:
The lonely at the lonelier.

O listen hard. By the wharf 's stone wall
Where in the dark the water curls
To lap at land's ramshackledom,
There gloomy voices rise and fall,
Gloomy voices of yellow girls
Singing, singing of kingdoms come.

Why must I hear such singing; why
Must I be so ware of the world gone wry;
And why, pale dog,
Unhappy dog, am I always I?

The fault is my ignorance. I doubt that even as generous and imaginative a translator as Mr. Wilson can get more than a third of the double-and-triple-meaning Japanese words into my syntaxed head, although sometimes, as in **"Death of an Alcoholic,"** I find it hard to believe that anything has been left out:

The grass is sharp as shattered glass
And everything is shining
With radium's eerie light.

Landscape of despair,
Landscape with the moon declining.

Ah, in such a lonely place
The whitish murderer's hanging face
Laughs like a shimmer in the grass.

When Graeme Wilson has completed his project of translating all of Hagiwara's work, the darkness may be lifted a little from us all.

Graeme Wilson (essay date 1972)

SOURCE: "Some Longer Poems of Hagiwara Sakutarō," in *Japan Quarterly,* Vol. 19, No. 2, 1972, pp. 170-81.

[*In the following essay, Wilson assesses critical appraisals of Hagiwara's works.*]

The last few years have seen a steady enhancement, both within Japan and outside Japan, of the reputation of Hagiwara Sakutarō as the best poet there to have emerged during the last hundred years. His outstanding quality has, of course long been recognized by his more perceptive fellow-countrymen. "He was," wrote Miyoshi Tatsuji, "the greatest poet on earth. Such a poet could hardly be found in an hundred years." But that recognition has often been qualified by a basic feeling, however variously expressed, that he really went too far; that his neurasthenic vision of reality was less a poetic analysis or exposure of extreme states of human feeling than a deliberate harrying by a skilled poet of the human nervous system. There will always be many in any human group, even among the Japanese (whose refusal to compromise in matters of emotional conviction is more generally relentless than among other groupings of mankind), who prefer the moderate approach. But the unrelenting heart is a major item in the working equipment of a poet: for, as another man of total conviction once remarked, staking his life (which he lost) on his convictions, "less than thorough will not do it." Nevertheless, perhaps because Hagiwara's extremism seems markedly less extreme in these days of unbridled self-expression, there are multiple current evidences of his widening reputation. "Hagiwara," said Akutagawa

Ryūnosuke some 30 years ago, "is the test-tube in which the gods on high seek to create poems; but he will without doubt have greater influence on the poets of tomorrow than on the poets of today." The growth of Hagiwara's reputation can be deduced not only from the appearance of scholarly critical articles in specialized cultural magazines but even from brief notes in the literary columns of daily newspapers. It is not just that new editions of his poetry continue to appear and to sell. In April 1971 Shibuya Kunitada published his excellent *Hagiwara Sakutarō Ron* (Essays on Hagiwara) and as recently as November 1971 a collection of some 50 poems in manuscript, most of them written nearly 60 years ago, was published by the poet's elder daughter, Hagiwara Yōko. An indicator of his popular appeal was the successful run last year of Kikuta Kazuo's biographical play, *Yogishano Hito* (Man on the Night Train).

Outside Japan, at least until about five years ago, the general tendency was to regard (even to dismiss) Hagiwara as probably the best modern Japanese exponent of nineteenth century Western poetic concepts, especially those deriving from Baudelaire and the French Symbolists. With the notable exception of Mikolaj Melanowicz of the University of Warsaw, there was no readiness whatever to consider him a poet of world importance and some reluctance even to accept him as anything more than a Taishō poet of moderate achievement. Indeed, one of the editors of the 1964 Penguin *Japanese Verse* (in which Hagiwara is represented by a single poem, while some dozen other modern poets no better than Tsuboi Shigeji have four or five) went so far as to tell me that Hagiwara was a sort of MacNiece being mis-presented in translation as an Auden. Generally speaking, American authorities on modern Japanese literature have shown themselves both better informed and more perceptive in their judgments. But even they were disposed to denigrate Hagiwara's work for its lack of such intellectual content as can be found in (and is alleged to improve) the poetry of T.S. Eliot. This criticism takes inadequate account of the fact that all Japanese poetry, from the death of Yamanoue no Okura in 733 to the rise of the Proletarian School in this century, is characterized by its rejection of intellection as a proper subject for poetry. Such Western critics can, of course, perfectly fairly reply that their criticism does indeed apply to all Japanese poetry: but if that criticism is valid at all, and I don't believe that it is, it must also then be applied to much excellent European poetry, notably that of the Symbolists and their successors. A recent article in the *Times Literary Supplement* pointed out that such Shakespearian lyrics as *Who is Sylvia* are not normally considered failures by reason of their lack of intellectual content and that, correspondingly, the undeniable intellection of Shakespeare's *Phoenix and the Turtle* does not save it from failure as a poem. I seem to recall having read that Dégas, having shown some of his poems to Mallarmé and been told that they were no good, somewhat plaintively replied that they still seem to him to contain some good ideas. "Poems," said Mallarmé with deadly finality, "are written with words, not ideas." Mallarmé's message seems at last to have got through to Hagiwara's American critics, for one notes that their most recent acknowledgments of his pre-eminence omit the earlier reservations. Nevertheless, this general pattern of criticism survives in the context of a not wholly fair stigmatization of Hagiwara as "the Japanese Baudelaire." Thus Denis Enright, while acknowledging that it is easy to see why Hagiwara should have been so dubbed, asserts that Baudelaire will never be known as the French Hagiwara because Baudelaire's poetry does include that intense intellection, reflecting his quarrel with god, which makes his work a supremely important analysis of the human condition at levels never reached by Hagiwara. Quite apart from the fact that this line of criticism begs fundamental questions as to the true nature of the human condition, it seems relevant to point out that, while the French are scarcely renowned for speed in recognition of the merits of other cultures, the leading French anthologist of modern Japanese poetry, Steinilber Oberlin, is on record as saying that "Hagiwara is a natural flower that bloomed in the garden of Baudelaire; while Baudelaire is an artificial flower that has grown in the hot-house of Hagiwara." Though it is broadly true, as Professor Enright pointed out in his *World of Dew,* that the Japanese have no consciousness of being damned (which T.S. Eliot apparently considered man's greatest glory), Hagiwara was in fact haunted all his life by a most curiously Western consciousness of sin. "There is nobody in modern Japan," wrote Itō Sei who knew the poet intimately, "who grasped as certainly as Hagiwara the consciousness of sin."

Another Western critic has recently delivered himself of the view that Hagiwara was ignorant of the complex implications for Western readers that are contained in such words as "infidel" and "doomed Madonna." No reason was offered for this view, though the critic went on curiously to suggest that anyone believing Hagiwara was not thus ignorant must be claiming direct communication with the spirit of the departed poet. One need not take too seriously a critic who not only keeps up the irrelevant howl that Hagiwara's poetry shows a "total absence of intellectual backing" but even, when Hagiwara's most obvious claim to notice is his introduction of an entirely new melody and music to Japanese poetry, complains that his work is "marred by a certain monotony of tone." Nevertheless, even the most ill-informed and unscholarly critic in this field ought to know that there is ample evidence for the depth and breadth of Hagiwara's understanding of precisely such Western religious concepts. On the testimony of his friend and fellow-townsman, the well-known Japanese expert in the field, the poet and critic Itō Shinkichi, Hagiwara was peculiarly deep-versed in the Bible. One lacks space to itemize the relevant prose and the many poems (such as *Good Friday*), to identify the Christian priests and missionaries (notably those connected with St. Matthew's Church in Maebashi) with whom the poet associated or to document the intensity of his relationship with his cousin Eiji, who was a proselytizing Christian: but the truth is sufficiently indicated by the fact that, of the two poets with whom during the key-period of his poetic life he was intimately associated in the running of the *Ningyō Shisha* (1914), *Takujō-funsui* (1915) and *Kanjō* (1916-19), Yamamura Bochō was an ordained Minister of the Anglican Church while Murō Saisei was a student of the Sacred College at Tabata. All three went regularly to church (primarily for the music, but missionaries are trained to gild their wares), and Hagiwara was still attending Sunday School in 1917 when he was 30. It seems particularly relevant in this context to point out that the declared objective of *Takujō-funsui* was not just the study of poetry; but the "study of poetry, religion and music."

Perhaps because there is a general, and generally sensible, recognition in the West that Westerners cannot really understand the East, there is a compensatory Western inclination to assume that it must follow that Easterners cannot understand the West. The fact that Japanese intellectuals since the Meiji Restoration of 1868 have, almost without exception, in their maturity rejected those Western concepts which so obsessed their youth has fostered a Western assumption that their youthful fascination by the West was superficial, a sort of calf-love, a depthless infatuation with the unknown and the unknowable. And that the eventual rejection was a consequently equally superficial decision. But it is at least worth pondering whether that rejection might not, in fact, be based on genuine comprehension of the West. It is undoubtedly true that some part of the initial fascination was shallow; that Hagiwara did not mean it when he wrote to Kitahara Hakushū in September 1917 saying that the type of woman he would wish to marry was "Charlie Chaplin's Mabel," poor Mabel Normand, "with her diamond face and pointed chin"; that he was merely going further than most in matters of dress when he walked about Maebashi in self-designed clothes derived from Beardsley drawings and became a registered subscriber to *Vogue*. But ***Return to Japan,*** his book of March 1938, contained the mature judgment of a man who for more than forty years had steeped himself in Western culture; and had found it wanting.

Another manifestation of this Western proclivity to doubt the reality of Japanese understanding of the West may be suspected in the comment of Professor Donald Keene that Hagiwara's poetry was "the fruit of other men's long years of translation". Examination of books surviving from Hagiwara's library would seem to support the implication that his knowledge of Western literature was derived from such translations as Ueda Bin's *Kaichōon* (Sound of the Tide) of 1905 and Nagai Kafū's *Sangoshū* (Coral Collection) of 1913; but there is significant evidence that he could read and perhaps even write at least English and German. His **"Reminiscences of My Primary School Days"** (1893-1900) states that that *Alice in Wonderland* and her adventures in the mirror-world were his favorite fairy tales. I have not been able to establish the date of the first translation of these books into Japanese but, though there were three references to them in *Jogaku Zasshi* (The Girl's Magazine) during 1889, the books themselves were still not available in translation by 1896. One wonders how Hagiwara acquired his passion for these books if he could not read English. In 1907, aged nearly 21, he began a year's study of English Literature at Kumamoto High School; and in 1908, when he launched out upon a two-year course in German Law at the Sixth Higher School at Okayama, his marks for English were 75 per cent, for German Language 75 per cent, for German Grammar 89 per cent and for German Conversation 88 per cent. His essay on **"The Characteristics of Japanese Poetry"** in ***Shi no Genri*** (***The Principles of Poetry***) of 1935 contains specific comment on sound in German poetry and refers to his own efforts to reproduce such sounds in the group of poems entitled "Nostalgia for One's Native Place". Finally, the reproductions of his manuscripts recently published by his daughter show handwritten scribbles in both English and German. It would, I think be imprudent to assume that this highly intelligent man, who was so long engaged in study of Western culture (the musical-box of his babyhood played *God Save the Queen* and his baby-books were in English), could not read at least English and German. And it would seem unlikely that a poet so deeply interested in Baudelaire and the French Symbolists, the author of a poem beginning "Would that I might go to France", was totally ignorant of French.

The foregoing picture of a fundamentally serious man, the writer of some of the most excruciating poems in the world, is confirmed by the fact that his first wife, Ueda Ineko, eventually left him largely because she found life with her intellectual husband insupportably boring. But there is ample evidence to show that Ineko was very much a "flapper" and that her mindless exuberance totally erased Hagiwara's earlier feelings, born from his fruitless love-affair with Elena, that women are gentle and delicate things. "Woman," he wrote in ***Kyomō no Seigi*** (***False Justice***) of 1929, "is a strong machine which cannot be broken even by a violent hand. Women are all primitive and very simple mechanisms, while men are delicate engines with a complicated system. But people think the opposite." Nevertheless, he was not a dull man. Indeed his friends testify that he could be extremely amusing, and Nishiwaki Junzaburō (whose sense of humor was perhaps made slightly odd by reason of long residence in England) even found some of his poems funny. He was a devotee of the early silent film comedies and it was not purely the facial resemblance, those knowing eyes and that sad long mouth, which led his cronies to give him the nickname "Keaton". I deduce that the initial K, used in the poem ***Group of Three Persons*** associated with this article, refers to that nickname; and it would seem likely that the initials Y and U refer to Yamamura and Murō. However, one suspects that his true nature was indeed tragic, and that his comic abilities, his musicianship and even his conjuring tricks were all masks that failed to shield a heart wide-open to catastrophe. The Chinese used to pay large sums of money for rocks dredged up from the depths of lakes because those objects were held to embody *Wei,* a concept of the horror and danger of the utterly incomprehensible. One feels that Hagiwara was continuously conscious of *Wei,* not only in things but in every human being that he met; even in himself. May Swenson, that brilliant American critic and still-undervalued poet, once pointed out that, though that late Symbolist poet Yeats went a long way toward the truth in defining poetry as "the thinking of the body", poetry does also seem to draw upon further and still-nameless "extra-senses" within man's apperceptive system. She then quoted Stendhal's comparison of man with a fly which, born in a summer's morning and dead by its afternoon, can have no understanding of the night. Hagiwara was a poet hideously endowed with those "extra-senses" and, though he died comparatively young, aged 55 in May 1942, he knew, none better, night. His poems give off what Garcia Lorca rightly considered the mark of all great works of art, *sonidos negros:* black, unfathomable sounds; echos of truths beyond the reach of reason.

Makoto Ueda (essay date 1983)

SOURCE: "Hagiwara Sakutaro," in *Modern Japanese Poets and the Nature of Literature,* Stanford University Press, 1983, pp. 137-83.

[*In the following excerpt, Ueda discusses the conception of poetry that Hagiwara put forth in his* Principles of Poetry *and analyzes his works within that critical framework.*]

Hagiwara Sakutarō (1886-1942) is generally considered the most original of the poets who helped perfect the art of free-style poetry in modern Japan. Shi existed before him: Shiki, Akiko, and Takuboku, along with many other poets, tried their hands at that new verse form. But in two respects Sakutarō's contribution outweighs that of anyone else. First, his consummate skill with words demonstrated that modern spoken Japanese could be used for verse writing in an artistically satisfying way. Takuboku and some others had made use of the vernacular in their works, but their diction was little different from that of everyday speech. With Sakutarō, modern Japanese became a poetic language for the first time. Second, he was the first Japanese poet to write successful poems about the existential despair of a modern intellectual. Born into a wealthy physician's family, he never experienced the financial struggles Takuboku confronted. Yet his extraordinary sensitivity and resulting personal conflicts led him to harbor grave misgivings about the meaning of human existence, eventually driving him to a helpless sense of loneliness, melancholy, and despair. Modern pessimism, rooted in Nietzsche and Schopenhauer, blossomed in Japan in the poetry of Hagiwara Sakutarō.

Sakutarō's three major books of poetry, ***Howling at the Moon*** (1917), ***The Blue Cat*** (1923), and ***The Ice Land*** (1934), had an immense impact on the Japanese poetic scene. He was equally known to his contemporaries as a literary theorist through many books of essays and aphorisms that promulgated his idea of poetry. The pivotal work among his theoretical writings, ***Principles of Poetry,*** took ten hard years to write: it is difficult to think of any other major Japanese poet who would have spent so long writing a book on literary theory. Sakutarō was also an indefatigable debater who never shied away from literary controversies, as well as a perceptive reader who put forward imaginative interpretations of classical tanka and haiku. Consequently, one who studies his poetic has to cope with a massive amount of material. In the following pages, I shall be able only to touch on the highlights of his concept of poetry.

. . . . .

A poem is a poem less on account of its form than on account of a certain spirit it embodies: this is one of the basic ideas Sakutarō took great pains to explain to amateur poets who sought guidance from him. He felt a need to emphasize the truism because much contemporary poetry, as he saw it, was distinguished from prose only by its syllabic patterns. Therefore, in his ***Principles of Poetry*** he chose to expound the inner spirit of poetry at length before answering questions on poetic form. What identifies poetry as poetry, he kept insisting, is ultimately *shiseishin,* a poetic spirit that can manifest itself in a variety of other forms, albeit to a lesser degree. He recognized that spirit not only in such other literary genres as the novel and drama but also in ethics, religion, and even natural science. According to him, the Christian Bible and the Confucian *Analects,* Plato's philosophy and Lao-tzu's ethics, all contain shiseishin and thereby move the hearts of those who read them. However, he found the purest manifestation of shiseishin in poetry, especially in lyric poetry. He stressed that without it poetry would lose its raison d'être.

To find out what that all-important poetic spirit is like, one can do no better than to read Sakutarō's aphorisms, collectively entitled "Characteristics of Shiseishin." There are eight in all:

1. Poetry soars *above reality*. Hence shiseishin is essentially romantic.

2. Poetry seeks ideals. Hence shiseishin is essentially subjective.

3. Poetry corrects language. Hence shiseishin is essentially rhetorical in intent.

4. Poetry demands form. Hence shiseishin is essentially normative.

5. Poetry ranks beauty higher than truth. Hence shiseishin is essentially aesthetic.

6. Poetry criticizes reality. Hence shiseishin is essentially pedagogic.

7. Poetry dreams of a transcendental world. Hence shiseishin is essentially metaphysical.

8. Poetry demands the noble and the rate. Hence shiseishin is essentially aristocratic (antidemocratic).

These aphorisms point to the core of Sakutarō's thoughts about the nature of poetry. In the following pages they will be examined in the light of his other writings, beginning with the statements that concern the relationship between poetry and reality.

The first of the aphorisms is that "poetry soars *above reality.*" (Sakutarō italicized the last two words for emphasis.) The point is related to the sixth aphorism, which states that poetry criticizes reality. In both instances the word "reality" refers to ordinary physical reality, the routine existence of an average person in the everyday world. The first question to be asked, then, is what Sakutarō thought prompted a poet to flee reality. Does any element of physical reality repel shiseishin?

Unlike Takuboku, Sakutarō seems to have found the main cause of the poet's flight not in the contemporary social order but in the poetic temperament. In his opinion, it is because he has a poetic temperament that the poet finds falsehood, corruption, and ugliness in the physical world and feels an urge to abandon it for the world of Ideas. "Such a poetic temperament is entirely due to fate," Sakutarō said. "It is an inborn disposition, a heaven-given nature, which is not humanly changeable. A poet is born, not made; his fate has been sealed from the outset."

How Sakutarō came to hold such a deterministic view of his own character is a question difficult to answer. In his early teens he seems already to have been a confirmed pessimist. He once recalled how as a middle-school student he used to listen to his classmates tell their dreams of becoming statesmen, scholars, or military officers, while he alone was not able to hold any rosy hopes for the future. Of course, youthful disillusionment has not been uncommon in any century or in any country, but young Sakutarō's was not a passing phase, and his disillusion was directed at the very fact of his own existence.

Such existential despair soon found an outlet in verse writing. A look at one of Sakutarō's poems from ***Howling at the Moon*** will help define the nature of his feelings:

"Dangerous Walk"

When spring arrived
I had rubber soles attached to my new shoes
so that no footstep would be audible
however rough a sidewalk I might walk on.
I am carrying plenty of breakables,
a dangerous venture in the extreme.
Now it is time to begin my walk.
Be still, every one of you.
Be still, please!
I am worried, so very worried.
No matter what may happen
don't look at my misshapen feet.
There is no way out for me.
Like a sick balloonist
I keep tottering, staggering,
forever in this exasperating place.

The poem presents the image of a person in a grave predicament who places the blame on himself rather than on society or the people around him. He feels that he is crippled, and he is extremely self-conscious. His body is a cracked receptacle carrying many breakable things; it is fragile enough to shatter at the faintest sound of a footstep. He is like a balloonist in his wish to leave the earth, yet he is sick. All he can do is totter about, his body emaciated and his mind exasperated, in a place that has no exit.

Howling at the Moon is filled with poems portraying this kind of person, a man plagued with shiseishin. **"An Ailing Face at the Bottom of the Earth"** depicts a sick man whose ghostly face looms in the subterranean darkness. **"Hanging in Heaven"** presents a suicide who tearfully hangs himself from a heavenly pine tree. **"An Alcoholic's Death"** describes a murdered alcoholic whose body is rotting. In other poems the man possessed by shiseishin has been transformed into an animal or a plant. In **"Dawn,"** for example, he appears as a deformed dog howling at the moon, and in **"Rotting Clam"** he is transformed into a clam whose insides have begun to decompose. His pained consciousness is metamorphosed into a delicate stem of grass in **"The Stem of Grass,"** into a dying chrysanthemum in **"Chrysanthemum Turning Sour,"** and into wintry bamboo plants in two poems entitled **"Bamboos."** Images and metaphors differ, but common to all these poems is the poet's agonized awareness that something essential and vital within his being is deformed, ailing, or decomposing. Although the word "sin" is used in some poems, the root of evil is more physiological than religious or moral. There is something seriously wrong with the poet's basic life-force, the hidden energy that should keep his roots alive.

When Sakutarō said poetry criticizes reality and soars above it, he meant that poetry gives expression to the inner life of a man who, because of his acute awareness of a spiritual ailment, is forever at odds with normal human existence and feels an urge to flee it if at all possible. The actual world looks superficial and false to him because it is insensitive to his need. It often does not understand that for a man with a poetic temperament living in itself is painful.

The next question to be answered concerns the destination of the poet's flight. A poet soars above reality, but to where? The second of Sakutarō's aphorisms answers that question, but only in a very general way: "Poetry seeks ideals." One of Sakutarō's most direct statements about the nature of these ideals appears in ***Principles of Poetry***. After observing that all poets have been idealistic seekers, he wrote, "In my opinion, what they sought was some Platonic Idea, which they could never hope to attain in actual life. They had been gripped by a nostalgia for the eternal homeland of their souls—for an existence projected by their longing." The remark contains two key words that Sakutarō used time and again throughout his essays: "Ideas" and "nostalgia." The former, which he borrowed directly from the Greek, had Platonic overtones, as in this quotation. Sakutarō used it to refer to a higher order of existence, of which the physical world is but a shadow. There is, he believed, an archetypal world beyond this one, to which people with shiseishin long to soar. That longing is "nostalgia," for the Platonic world of Ideas is the ultimate homeland of the human soul. According to him, an ordinary person longs for his physical home; a poet, for his metaphysical home.

Despite this dualistic world view, Sakutarō stressed that poets seek Ideas not with the intellect but through emotion and sensation. To make the concept clearer, he proposed using the Chinese character *meng* ("dream"), with a pronunciation "idea" written beside it. A philosopher constructs a world of Ideas through discursive reason, but a poet dreams it as objects that are tangible, although they transcend physical reality. Hence the seventh of Sakutarō's aphorisms, "Poetry dreams of a transcendental world." The poet's yearning for a higher order of reality must be rooted deep in the unconscious, since his loathing of human existence is physiological; it is an instinctive impulse. "This is probably akin to the instinctive way in which certain creatures are attracted to light," Sakutarō speculated. "It is *eros,* the longing of a human soul instinctively flying toward a certain being." He once gave form to this longing in a short poem:

"Moonlit Night"

Flapping large heavy wings
what feeble hearts they have!
On a night when the moon is as bright as a gaselier
watch the swarm of white creatures flowing.

Watch their calm direction.
Watch the suffocating emotion those creatures have.
On a night when the moon is like a bright gaselier
what a doleful flight of moths!

Through the images of the moths, the light, and the moon, this poem presents the soul possessed by shiseishin drawn upward by instinctive attraction. The moths must be drawn to an earthly light, but the only "gaselier" that appears in the poem is a description of the moon. Thus the poet not only recognizes in the moths an image for himself, but by seeing the moon as like a lamp, he places himself in the same relation to it as the moths are to the lesser light. He notes its surface similarity in size, shape, and brightness, but the fact that he makes the comparison reveals a deeper similarity, this time between himself and the moths—like them, he feels an instinctive attraction to light.

In an essay written many years later and entitled **"The Moon and Shiseishin,"** Sakutarō identified a physical instinct as the source of the moon's attractiveness. Referring to the habits of certain fish and insects that are instinctively drawn to light, he remarked, "All those creatures perhaps sense their existential homeland, the very origin of their lives, when they see a beautifully burning light. The phenomenon belongs to the primeval mystery of life shared by all creatures." Such arts as poetry and music, he believed, probe into that mystery through the artist's preempirical memories. In another essay written about the same time, he wrote: "In poet's consciousness there reside a priori memories handed down from the ancestors through millions of years. In those memories they find themselves to be cave dwellers, or shellfish eaters, or apes, or (going back further) birds or beasts or reptiles."

It is unlikely that Sakutarō knew about Jung when he wrote **"Moonlit Night,"** but these later essays outline a concept close to Jung's idea of the unconscious. However, unlike Jung, for whom the collective unconscious contained archetypal forms that organize human behavior, Sakutarō saw the "collective unconscious" primarily as a reservoir of subtle and complex sensations, sensations that at their deepest level are at the boundaries not only of human consciousness, but also of human being—they phase off into an empathy for the evolutionary origins of our consciousness in other forms of life. For him, a poet's nostalgia arises from his contact with these sensations; their attraction for him may resemble the numinous quality Jung ascribed to symbols that externalize the archetype. Through attention to these deep-seated sensations, the poet hopes to reach the source of his being.

A number of poems dealing with the sensation of preempirical memory are collected in ***The Blue Cat***. In a number of them, the sensations provide a basis for emphatic identification with animals, and the poem is written through the eyes of a horse, a cat, a bat, a cock, or a crab. In a particularly fine example, Sakutarō instead imagines his way back to Adam, who as the first man is the very boundary between human and nonhuman being, the point at which human consciousness becomes itself:

"Most Primitive Emotion"

Deep in a jungle
gigantic rubber trees grow
like ghostly elephants' ears.
Shadowy figures crawl on the marsh,
one on the heels of another: ferns, reptiles,
snakes, lizards, newts, frogs, salamanders, and so on.

During his melancholy longing at midday
what did Adam recollect?
Primeval emotion is like a cloud,
like infinitely sweet love.
It floats on the other side of memory
far beyond my reach.

Being the first man, Adam has no personal recollections as subsequent mortals know them. Instead he has only the urge to remember, sparked by a vague sense of something beyond his reach, some primal and prior being he cannot quite touch. Because he cannot identify those forms below consciousness, they are "like a cloud." May they be the sensations of that vaguely evolutionary line of shadowy figures crawling "one on the heels of another"? Adam himself cannot know; he can only feel an unaccountably sweet, ineffable nostalgia, the tantalizing, fascinating attraction of something we almost remember but cannot quite touch.

At other times, the metaphysical homeland Sakutarō glimpsed developed itself quite differently. However, the visions he presents in the following two poems are linked to that of **"Most Primitive Emotion"** by the feeling that infuses them, an emotion Sakutarō termed "romantic nostalgia" in commenting on the first:

"Skyscape"

Run, softly creaking wagon,
along the faintly glimmering sea
and far away from the flowing wheat.
Run, softly creaking wagon.
Through a skyscape luminous with fish and birds
and through buildings windowed blue,
run, softly creaking wagon.

"Elegant Appetite"

Walking through a pine grove,
I saw a cheery-looking café.
Too far from the city streets
for anyone to come and visit:
there the café was, hidden in the grove of memories and
dreams.
A maiden, lovingly bashful,
brought me a special dish as refreshing as dawn.
Casually I picked up a fork
and ate omelet, fried food, and such.
A white cloud floated in the sky,
and I had a very elegant appetite.

The worlds of these poems are displaced, not in evolutionary time, but through dreamlike images. The setting continually reminds us of its distance from practical reality: the wagon is a vehicle nonexistent in Japan, and the cafe is "hidden in the grove of memories and dreams." Moreover, Sakutarō uses figurative language that emphasizes the ideational nature of these places by combining disjunctive things rather than similar ones—employing synaesthesia in "softly creaking wagon" and illogical conjunctions in "a skyscape luminous with fish and birds" and "a special dish as refreshing as dawn." The connections that unite these images are the emotive processes of the mind itself, not resemblances noted in the physical world. It is thus, perhaps, that they flee external reality as perceived and approach another, more congenial homeland of the soul.

Interestingly enough, in all three poems things Western join the objects of dream and of projected preempirical memory. The poet found himself to be Adam rather than any hero in Japanese mythology; he rode in a Western wagon rather than in a Japanese oxcart; and he used a fork rather than chopsticks to satisfy his elegant appetite. How could Sakutarō's nostalgia be directed toward Europe? Two possible answers can be given. First, Sakutarō's nostalgia seems to exist at the boundaries of the ordinary consciousness centered on everyday life, so it feeds on the unfamiliarity of dream or of distance in space or time. The West, being remote, thus provided an apt focus for poetic energy. In this respect Sakutarō admired what he called the "childlike romanticism" of his Meiji forefathers, who had an insatiable passion for Western civilization. In his nostalgia, he may have longed to share with them that pure passion. Second, Sakutarō probably wanted his world of Ideas to be a synthesis of both East and West. For him, preempirical memory must have encompassed all of Western, as well as Eastern, history.

To sum up, then, in Sakutarō's view a poet is an existentially deformed man who dreams of returning to a complete self existing on another level of reality. The spirit of poetry, shiseishin, must therefore be subjective and idealistic; it must be "romantic" in that sense. The poet aims to achieve and present a vision, either a painful vision based on his own crippled existence or a sweet vision based on his longing, his subtle attunement to deeper impulses and sensations neglected in a normal life. Either way, the vision does not and should not present physical reality as it is. "The difference between photography and painting," Sakutarō once said, "is that the former contains all reality and no falsehood, whereas the latter presents reality by depicting falsehood. Of course, literature is painting and not photography."

Sakutarō once categorized romantic poets in two groups by examining whether they were more concerned with search or with defiance. He called the first type of poets "adventurers," for they sought adventure in an unknown land. Sakutarō thought many French poets belonged to this category, citing Baudelaire, Rimbaud, Valéry, and Cocteau, as well as Poe. He called the second type of poets "sentimentalists"; these were misfits who because they sought lofty ideals always were angered by the world in which they actually lived. His examples included Goethe, Heine, Verlaine, Dehmel, Rilke, Nietzsche, and Novalis, and he observed that this type was more common in Germany.

Sakutarō himself appears to have changed from the first type of poet into the second as he grew older. When he wrote the poems collected in ***Howling at the Moon*** and ***The Blue Cat,*** he was largely an adventurer who sought every opportunity to roam in a visionary land. But in his last book of verse, ***The Ice Land,*** he was more of a sentimentalist angry with the actual world. Describing his frame of mind at the time, he wrote, "I was angered by everything. I never stopped feeling like shouting at the top of my voice." That suppressed shouting found its way into his poetry, as in this example from ***The Ice Land,*** composed when Sakutarō's wife left him and their two young children:

"Returning to My Parents' Home"

In the winter of 1929 I was separated from my wife and
went back to my native town with my two children.

The train pushes forth against a gale
toward my native town.
Awakening from sleep, all alone by the window,
I hear the steam whistle scream in the dark
and see flames brighten the plain.
Have the Kōzuke mountains come within our sight?
In the pale light of the night train
the motherless children sob in their sleep.
Furtively, all measures my gloom.
What homeland am I heading for,
this refugee from the capital?
My past leads to the valley of solitude,
and my future to the shore of despair.
How gravelike this life is!
With my strength long gone,
I am too weary to live out the melancholy days.
How can I return to my native town
and stand alone by the Toné River again?
The train pushes forth across the wilderness
toward the desolate shore of Nature's will—
only to intensify my rage.

This poem is considerably different from the ones cited earlier. The sentiments it contains are more directly related to the actual situation, that of a man deserted by his wife, and they are expressed through more realistic images, including two actual places. Inevitably, there is a degree of fictionalization, yet here the poet definitely lives in the same sphere as the man on the street. [The critic adds in a footnote: "Sakutarō and his two daughters returned to his native town by train in July 1929. In the poem he changed the season to winter."] He despairs of that life, but he is there.

Japanese critics have long argued about which type of poetry is of higher value. Those who favor ***Howling at the Moon*** and ***The Blue Cat*** have charged that the poems in ***The Ice Land*** are limited in their visualization of basic human existence, and that they represent a marked decline in Sakutarō's imaginative power. On the other hand, critics who prefer his later poetry have replied that Sakutarō was an escapist in his early works and that only in ***The Ice Land*** did he face reality with total honesty. It is impossible to determine which of the two appraisals is correct, for the judgment is ultimately personal and depends on whether one sees reality in the daily existence of an average man or in a transcendental sphere of which this life is only a shadow.

In terms of Sakutarō's own poetic, however, the poems in ***Howling at the Moon*** and ***The Blue Cat*** seem closer to the ideal. As we have seen, he felt that poetry should soar above reality, trying to present a visionary world by "metaphysical" means—that is, by using metaphors and symbols that distance or distort the objects within the poem, dissolving their ties with reality as it is ordinarily perceived. He did say that poetry should criticize reality, but he added that the criticism should be done in a "pedagogic" way; negative criticism alone would not suffice. Elsewhere in his writings he observed that the criticism of contemporary society belongs more to the realm of prose than to that of poetry. He implied this, for instance, in a brief aphoristic passage called **"Poetry and Prose"**:

> Life consists of two kinds of time: nighttime and daytime, dream and reality, subconscious life and conscious life. Hence literature is divided into two categories, too. Poetry deals with images floating in a dream at night; prose, with conscious perceptions of reality in the daytime. In its own dreamlike manner, which ignores reason or grammar formulated by common sense, poetry gives expression to the essence of the poet's self, which appears and disappears in the twilight zone of consciousness. Ideally speaking, a person can attain complete self-expression only when he works in both types of literature (poetry and prose), the one articulating his subconscious being and the other his conscious life.

The poems in ***The Ice Land*** seem to embody conscious perceptions of reality rather than images floating in a dream. **"Returning to My Parents' Home,"** for example, presents the poet's acute awareness of the sad situation facing him at the time. The autobiographical notes he added to it and to some other poems in the same volume embed his poetic material in a flow of prosaic circumstance like that depicted in a novel, a diary, or an autobiographical essay—one could even imagine these poems being written in prose. Such explanations indicate a move away from the pure, dreamlike poetry he advocated; no such notes appear in ***Howling at the Moon*** or ***The Blue Cat***.

After the publication of ***The Ice Land,*** Sakutarō wrote essays, aphorisms, and prose poems, but almost no poetry in verse. According to him, poetry was to soar above reality, and in his later years he had lost his wings. **"At the Zoo,"** one of the poems in ***The Ice Land,*** ends with these lines:

> Now as autumn nightfall approaches
> the wind rages over the deserted road,
> yet I cannot soar away like a bird
> across the endless expanse of solitude.

. . . . .

Sakutarō's ***Principles of Poetry,*** comprehensive though it is, says little about the process through which a poem comes into being. Apparently he had planned to treat the question, for he scribbled notes about it at some length in a notebook he used in preparing the book. These jottings even have a title, "Two Types of Creative Psyche," which suggests that he intended to make them into a chapter of the book. The title refers to a classification of artists into two general types: inspirational artists, like Mozart and Poe, who create their works through lightning flashes of inspiration, and laborious artists, like Rodin, who produce art through long, sustained effort. The chapter was never written, however, and Sakutarō stopped just when he seemed ready to enter a serious discussion of the creative mind. When hints on the subject are gathered together from among his other writings, they suggest that he thought of the creative process in three stages: inspiration, expression, and correction. They indicate, moreover, that he may have been unable to write systematically about the creative process because in his own case a crucial part of both inspiration and expression took place in the subconscious mind. He himself did not fully know how he wrote a poem.

Sakutarō repeatedly wrote about the unpredictable way in which creative inspiration is born. In his experience, inspiration would occur without forewarning, in a way he himself could not explain. It was like "a spark that flares up and dies in an instant," or was "something mysteriously vague and itchy billowing up from within the mind." At one time he was inclined to explain it as "divine inspiration"; at another he preferred to relate it to "physiological anomaly." The passage that comes closest to describing it appears in a notebook dated in or around 1914, at the beginning of the fertile period that produced ***Howling at the Moon***. Using physiological metaphors, there he vividly traced the way a poem took root in his mind:

> Some while ago a strange, unidentifiable light was conceived within me. It has slowly begun to move about. But because the walls are thick, it cannot break through. That is agonizing in the extreme—the suffocating pain before childbirth. Every day I scribble incomprehensible things on a piece of paper. Finally it looks as if the Sentimental Nirvana were approaching. The heaven and the earth are so radiant they dazzle my eyes. The September sun is covered with thick clouds. There is a halo around everything I see. What joy! What excruciating pain! I can't breathe. This is too much!

In an article called **"How to Write Poetry,"** Sakutarō once speculated about possible means of inducing such inspiration. His main suggestion echoes the physiological emphasis in the passage just quoted; it was to bring about "physiological anomaly" in one way or another, so that the normal pattern of thinking would be drastically changed. He referred, half in jest, to various experimenters in the past who tried to attain inspiration by taking opium, fasting, or shaking their heads to the frenzied rhythm of delirational music. The most practical method, he wryly commented, was to utterly exhaust the body by excessive drinking, debauchery, lack of sleep, or some other act detrimental to one's health. At the conclusion of the article, however, he stated that of course he himself had never written a poem by such means. In his opinion, true poetic inspiration visits, not a poet who takes opium for its sake, but a poet who has to take opium because he cannot stand reality otherwise. Opium, alcohol, and sleeplessness are at most catalysts. "A poem should naturally seep up from the bottom of the poet's soul," said Sakutarō. "It should be neither devised by intellect nor aroused by opium or any other artificial means." To quote another of his articles, the ideal poet, temperamentally unfit for the world, is "a romantic in the broad sense of the word, a man who by his inborn nature possesses his own subjective Ideas."

According to Sakutarō, poetic inspiration also has an aesthetic, and hence impractical, component: what a poet conceives through inspiration is not an ordinary sensation directly related to practical affairs. Sakutarō once called such ordinary sensations jikkan, inviting protests from those accustomed to the definition of the term given by Yosano Akiko and her associates. In defense he clarified his terminology, saying that in his usage jikkan was a feeling restricted by practical concerns, whereas its opposite, *bikan* ("aesthetic feeling"), aspired to transcend the utilitarian sphere.

After it is conceived by inspiration, a poetic sentiment needs to be given verbal expression. Sakutarō once gave the name "liquefaction" to this phase of the creative process. "Verse writing," he said, "is an art by which the poet, using rhythm, liquefies the subject or material he has acquired through experience." He continued, "In liquefaction, all matter loses the forms it had when it was solid. It is for this reason that poetic expressions have vague, mysterious beauty: all actual experience has been transformed into images. A literary work that still retains raw experience in its solid form cannot be called poetry." He was implying that poetic expression is the ordinary process of verbalization plus two additional factors. First, a sentiment or experience conceived in the poet's mind must be transformed into "images." Second, it must be accompanied by rhythm. If a work lacks these two elements, it is a prose piece instead of a poem.

Sakutarō's term "images" (he used the English word in the quotation cited above) must refer to symbols—that is, to images that imaginatively expand beyond their exact denotation. Otherwise they could not have "vague, mysterious beauty." Why the poet must use images in this expanded sense is explained in ***Principles of Poetry,*** where Sakutarō distinguishes between two types of artistic expression. One is "description," an attempt to delineate the external form of an object; this method is employed more often by painters, novelists, and writers of realistic drama. The other method, often used by poets, musicians, and opera-writers, is *jōshō,* a word Sakutarō coined by joining the two words *jō* ("emotion") and *shō* ("image"). Even when poets and musicians depict an external object in their work, their depiction is so subjective, he felt, that the outlines of the object become blurred. The object is transformed into an image that produces vague, mysterious beauty; solid matter is "liquefied."

Sakutarō attributed the necessity of rhythm in poetic expression to the intensity of the sentiment to be expressed. "When a man's sentiment is heightened," he said, "his language forgets its expository function; his words automatically become a kind of exclamation. It is for this reason that the language of poetry has musical tones and rhythms, and allows no prosaic description." To support his point, he cited primitive poetry and children's songs. Poems of all races at the dawn of civilization, he pointed out, had clearly recognizable rhythms, and so do the songs that today's children spontaneously sing at play. He did not know exactly why heightened language should be rhythmical, but he speculated that this might be due to man's "aesthetic instinct."

According to Sakutarō, every intensified sentiment contains a rhythm in itself, and a poem resulting from the sentiment should approximate that rhythm. As will be discussed in more detail later, this is the basis of his defense of free verse.

When expression is completed, there follows the third phase of the creative process, "correction." Either rhythm or imagery can be corrected. "As soon as you finish writing a line, read it aloud and see if it sounds pleasant to your ear," Sakutarō advised beginning poets. "Next," he added, "be wary of a word's connotative function." Every correction, of course, should be made so that the initial inspiration is approximated more closely.

Sakutarō advised that a good deal of caution be used when undertaking correction long after the original composition of a poem. In an article entitled **"On Revising One's Own Poems,"** he argued that a poem can be reworked and improved long after its initial writing only when the poet's shiseishin remains the same throughout the intervening time. He felt that too often a poet changes temperamentally as he grows older; he then attempts to improve his earlier work and ends up changing it for the worse. As examples of such unfortunate reworking, Sakutarō cited several poets he otherwise admired, including Yosano Akiko, who later detested and tried to revise the tanka of her youth. He felt that the only major poet in contemporary Japan who was discreet in this respect was Shimazaki Tōson.

How did Sakutarō himself write poems? To answer the question, we shall trace his creative process in two specific instances. The first resulted in the poem **"The Corpse of a Cat"**; the second, in **"Howling Dog."**

"The Corpse of a Cat" was first published in a magazine in 1924, during a period that Sakutarō later recalled as "the most depressing rainy season of my life." A man well over thirty with no job, he had been living a miserable life at his parents' home. Marital problems intensified his depression, for by the arrangement of his parents he had married a woman he hardly knew. According to his own description of his life with her, no love, understanding, or delicate sentiment was communicated between them; they were merely male and female, connected by sensual desire, living together under the feudalistic family system. To make the situation worse, children were born to them. Sakutarō was mentally too exhausted to take any positive action; he would simply lie sprawled on a sofa, dreaming of his dead sweetheart. In his vision the dead woman, dressed in pink, roamed a graveyard on spring nights. He dreamed of his body dissolving to nothing, whereupon his soul would go out to embrace her tearfully by the graves. The vision eventually crystallized into a poem:

"The Corpse of a Cat"
In a spongy landscape
it is big and swollen, soaking wet.
No living creature is around
except a strangely sad waterwheel crying.
In the hazy shade of a willow
I see my sweet love waiting.
A thin shawl wrapping her body
and a lovely, vaporous garment trailing behind,
she wanders silent as a ghost.
Oh, Ura! Lonely woman!
"Darling, you are always late."
Possessing neither a past nor a future,
we have disappeared from *things real*. . . .
Ura!
In this odd landscape
please bury the corpse of the muddy cat.

[The critic adds in a footnote that "ura" is a "Japanese word meaning 'seacoast.' "] Sakutarō left a later comment on the poem, in which he explained in detail several of its images:

> Ura was my Ligeia. And the whole of my family life was "The Fall of the House of Usher." Possessing neither a past nor a future, it had disappeared from "things real"; it was an unlucky, cursed, nihilistic existence—an existence like that of the House of Usher. That unlucky, ugly existence is symbolized in the corpse of a muddy cat. "Ura! Don't touch it with your hand!" So I always cried out in my dream, trembling with an instinctive fear.

The note reveals the stages of inspiration and expression in Sakutarō's creative process. He was inspired by a dream, or a series of dreams, during a time when he felt he could not bear his daily life. Through shiseishin, both his life and his longing were imaginatively removed from "things real" into a distorted and heightened realm, conceived in terms of exotic Western analogues. There, in the course of expression the poetic spirit "liquefied" the material of actual experience. The forms of longing condensed into the single figure "Ura," whose name suggests both the beauty and the loneliness of a remote seacoast. She was originally a young woman whom Sakutarō admired, but she was dead, purified by memory and transformed into a symbol of ideal love. [The critic adds in a footnote: "The woman's name was Baba Naka: Sakutarō nicknamed her Elena. She died in 1917 at the age of 27."] The opposite forms, the repugnant experiences of his married life, took shape in the image of the dead and muddy cat, projected into the visionary landscape. In the poem's final wish, Sakutarō beseeches the image of desire to bury that of reality and to free him from its burden.

At the stage of correction, Sakutarō made only one significant change in the poem. When he republished it in 1928, 1929, 1936, and 1939, he made almost no internal revisions (except for minor changes in punctuation and spacing), but in the 1936 version he added a subtitle, "To a Woman Called Ula." This meant that the name of the woman, which appears twice in the body of the poem, has to be read "Ula" also, even though the Japanese language has no liquid consonant "l." After making the revision, Sakutarō emphasized the importance of this aural effect. As he explained, "The poem's motif is embodied mainly in the sound of the name 'Ula.' A reader who is sensitive enough to the sound to catch its musical sentiment will be able to grasp the poem's main theme clearly. A reader whose sensitivity falls short of that will not be able to understand the general meaning of the poem." The motif is "a musical image of nostalgia like a wind coming from a desolate graveyard." *Ura* ("Seacoast") already evokes a sense of beauty and loneliness; the sound "Ula" may create such a "musical image" because the substitution of the consonant "l," which does not exist in Japanese, makes the name sound even more otherworldly to Japanese ears. "Ula" may also evoke associations of Ulalume and the nocturnal world of Poe's poetry to which Sakutarō referred in his note. In any event, Sakutarō must have been absolutely certain that "Ula" was better than "Ura," because he was extremely cautious about revising a poem after a considerable length of time, and twelve years had elapsed between the first publication of the poem and the addition of the subtitle.

Sakutarō was, of course, less cautious about revision while he was still in the process of composing a poem. Probably he made more than one draft before he initially published **"The Corpse of a Cat"** in 1924, although the drafts have not been preserved. Our next example, **"Howling Dog,"** focuses on revisions he made during the initial process of composition.

We do not know what specifically motivated Sakutarō to write this poem. Its origins apparently date back to 1914, when he was an especially ardent admirer of Nietzsche, so the image of a howling dog may have originated in a similar image in *Thus Spake Zarathustra*. At any rate, a vision of a dog came to him one day in late 1914, and he tried to record it in his notebook:

On a moonlit night
a dog
runs round a willow tree.
The dog has sensed something.
His soul glows luminously
like fluorescent light.

Soon after writing this down, he went about transforming it into a better poem. His notebook shows that he changed a number of words until he settled on this second draft:

"Dog"

On a moonlit night
a dog runs round { a willow tree. / a tombstone in the graveyard. }
The dog howls at the distant center of this globe.
He has sensed his master's safe hidden deep in the impenetrable earth,

a safe filled with nephrites and noctilucent stones.
The howling dog has a soul that glows white, its heart radiating fluorescence through the body.
The pale dog struggles to dig the hard surface of the earth
with his forepaws,

a dog who has clearly sensed something that
faintly stirs in
the far, far netherworld.
The dog, wailing and sick, struggles to dig up
something he
has sighted on a moonlit night.

This is quite a substantial elaboration on the initial image of a dog running around a willow tree. The flash of inspiration being over, Sakutarō seems to have begun to grope for the meaning of the insight, using intellect as well as emotion. In the main, he appears to have tried to see what it was that the dog in his initial inspiration had sensed, and subsequently he introduced a safe loaded with nephrites and other luminous stones. This and similar elaborations transform the impressionistic poem of the first draft into the metaphysical poem of the second.

The poem went through further extensive revisions. It was first published in the February 1915 issue of the magazine *Poetry* in the following form:

"Howling Dog"

On a moonlit night, a dog runs round a tombstone in the
graveyard,
The dog howls at the distant center of this globe.
For he has sensed his master's safe hidden deep
in the im-
penetrable earth, a safe he knows is filled with
nephrites
and noctilucent stones.
The howling dog has a soul that glows white, his
heart ra-
diating fluorescence through the body.
This pale dog struggles to dig the hard surface
of the earth
with his forepaws, for he has sensed something that faintly
stirs in the far, far netherworld.
The howling dog, wailing and sick, struggles to
dig up some-
thing he has clearly sighted in the graveyard
on a moonlit
night.

The howls are poetry.
You, a loyal, sensitive, and yet utterly lonesome
dog! You
keep howling, until you are shot by your cal-
lous neighbor
or until you starve to death, telling of mystery
to your
last breath.
The howling dog is the poet on a pale moonlit
night.

Here the willow tree is completely gone. Apparently Sakutarō decided to write another poem centering on that image; entitled **"About a Willow Tree,"** it was published in the same issue of *Poetry* as was **"Howling Dog."** A more significant change is the addition of another stanza, in which Sakutarō identifies the dog as a poet and the dog's howl as poetry. It is as if he had a firmer grasp of the import of his initial inspiration. The identification clarifies considerably the meaning of the poem, but at the same time it limits that meaning, too.

Revisions were not as extensive in the fourth version of the poem, but they were no less significant:

"Howling Dog"

On a moonlit night, a dog roams the graveyard.
The dog howls at the distant center of this globe.
For he has sensed a safe hidden deep in the impenetrable
earth,
a safe he knows is filled with nephrites and noctilucent
stones.
The howling dog has a soul that whitely glows
and radiates
fluorescence from his heart.
This pale dog struggles to dig the hard surface
of the earth
with his forepaws,
for he has sensed something that faintly stirs in
the far, far
netherworld.
The howling dog, grieving and frenzied, struggles to dig up
something he has clearly sighted in the graveyard on a
sorrowful moonlit night.

The howling dog is man.
You, a loyal, sensitive, yet utterly lonesome dog!
You keep howling until you are shot by a neigh-
bor who has
a sick child.
The howling dog is man on a pale moonlit night.

Sakutarō decided to change "the poet" to "man." This significantly broadens the implications of the poem, which then portrays the plight not just of the poet but of all men possessed by shiseishin. Sakutarō was satisfied with this version and did not revise the poem any more in subsequent publications, except for slight changes in punctuation.

The process by which **"Howling Dog"** developed reveals the passivity of the poet in the initial stage of verse writing, as well as his positive efforts in subsequent stages. A subconscious flash of insight occurs, and he himself does not understand its full meaning at the time. He can only jot down the vision. As he contemplates it, he gradually comes to understand its significance. The vision, intuitively perceived, is now studied in his mind, both intellectually and emotionally. Expression helps the study, for words clarify thoughts. Through many drafts, in a conscious, deliberate effort, the poet then carries out the process of fully understanding his thought as he transforms it into words.

Sakutarō eloquently summed up this process in a letter he wrote to a friend in March 1917, shortly after the publication of ***Howling at the Moon:***

> I am practically blind to my own poem at the time of its creation. I do not know what I am singing about. The thoughts or emotions I harbor in my mind, or what I am trying to write, all are beyond my comprehension. I simply pick up a rhythm flowing at the bottom of my heart and follow it automatically. At the time of creating a poem, therefore, I am half-conscious, merely an automated machine. Even after com-

> pleting the poem, I am often unable to grasp the core of thought or emotion embodied in it. Hence, I feel I am not entitled to talk about my poem immediately after its composition. But, strangely enough, as time passes (say, a few months or a year) I come to clearly understand the core of the poem's thought without effort on my part.

. . . . .

Sakutarō was more deeply concerned with the issues of literary criticism than were most other contemporary poets. He wrote many articles both expounding his idea of poetry and explicating poems written by other poets, and he published two books of practical criticism, ***Masterpieces of Tanka on Love*** and ***Yosa Buson: A Poet of Nostalgia,*** which offered his interpretations of selected tanka and haiku. Although he never published a similar book on shi, his critical comments on free-style poems frequently appeared in literary magazines. He was a regular columnist for several magazines at one time or another, and when asked also lectured on such topics as "The Appreciation and Interpretation of Poetry."

Sakutarō was one of the first Japanese critics to recognize multiple levels of meaning in a poem and to conceive positive significance in a meaning not consciously intended by the poet. This was so because he was aware of the poet's passivity in the initial stage of the creative process. "In all cases the best interpreter of a poem is not the poet but the reader," he conceded. "The poet is like a sleepwalker; he is not cognizant of what he has written." The main responsibility for interpretation lies not with the poet but with the reader. Of course, readers' literary sensibilities differ, allowing for widely different interpretations of the same poem. Sakutarō once compared this variation to two people listening to the same piano piece by Chopin: one listener might hear in the music the patter of rain, whereas another might associate it with a series of gunshots. Sakutarō's conclusion about reading poetry was that there was no right or wrong interpretation, that there were merely "shallow" and "profound" ones.

The principal question, then, is what makes an interpretation shallow or profound. Sakutarō mentioned three criteria: a correct understanding of vocabulary, empathy, and a grasp of the poetic sentiment. As for the first, each word has a history of usage in literature, and the profundity of an interpretation depends upon the extent to which the reader is aware of that history as well as upon the degree of appropriateness with which he identifies a specific use in a given poem. The second and third criteria also seem to refer to an understanding of what is appropriate in a given poem: an interpretation is profound, Sakutarō implies, in proportion to the degree to which it empathizes with the poetic sentiment embodied in the poem. But what is meant by "poetic sentiment"? The original Japanese word is *shijō, shi* meaning "poem" and *jō* meaning "sentiment," "emotion," or "heart." Shijō comes close to the meaning of shiseishin except that it refers to a sentiment particularized in the context of a given poem. In other words, shiseishin is the spirit of poetry; shijō, the spirit of a specific poem. Sakutarō suggests that an interpretation is profound when it is based on a reader's empathy with shijō, and thus with the shiseishin lying beneath. When the reader fails to empathize, his reading will be superficial.

Because shiseishin is critical of reality and longs for a transcendental world, the poetic sentiment manifest in an individual poem tends to be idealistic in its implications, too. A critic wishing to come up with a profound interpretation of a poem will need to empathize with that idealistic mood. In the following two instances, Sakutarō the critic operates on that principle.

The first example centers on a haiku by Buson:

> When we join our palms
> together and scoop it, how
> muddy the water grows!

Premodern annotators gave a didactic interpretation to the poem. In their view, this haiku teaches that an act that is blameless when done by one man may become complicated or even corrupt ("muddy") when he is joined by others. Sakutarō would not want to say this interpretation was wrong, but he had a totally different one. As he saw it, the haiku embodied Buson's nostalgia for childhood: the aging poet fondly remembered a bygone day in spring when he and a little girl played together by a stream. Clearly Sakutarō's reading is based on empathy with Buson's heart, which he believed often yearned for the idyllic, innocent world of his happy childhood.

The next instance is also a haiku, this one by Chiyo (1703–75):

> The piercing wind:
> in the screen, there still remain
> holes poked by a finger.

Sakutarō referred to two extant readings of the poem. According to the first explication, the haiku concerns the sorrow of poverty: the poet is too poor to have her sliding screens repaired, and consequently the cold wind comes in through the holes. In contrast, the second interpretation sees the poet as mourning over her lost child. The child, once so vivacious and mischievous, is dead and gone, leaving only the holes he made in the screens with his fingers. Sakutarō sided with the second interpretation, empathizing with the mother who longed for a nonexistent being. To him, the first reading seemed superficial because that empathy was lacking.

Sakutarō used the principle of empathy as the main criterion throughout both his critical commentaries and his books of practical criticism. Two examples from ***Masterpieces of Tanka on Love*** demonstrate how it applies to tanka. The first is an anonymous poem included in *The Collection of Ancient and Modern Poems*:

> When evening comes
> I gaze at the banner-shaped clouds
> and think of things
> as my heart yearns for a woman
> living in the distant sky.

Of this tanka, Sakutarō wrote, "Evening clouds, shaped like banners, hang in the sky over the distant horizon. His beloved lives in the place where the doleful sun sinks, across far-off mountains and cities that loom as if in a dreamland. His love is a piece of music: it is a nostalgic melody played to the lonely evening sky. A person in love is a philosopher whose soul calls to an ideal existence, an Idea that lies at the end of space and time." The originality of this explication appears when it is compared to the usual interpretation, which takes the woman to be a noble lady who far outranks the poet. In his reading, Sakutarō made a real woman into an ideal one.

Sakutarō gave an even more imaginative interpretation to a group of tanka on the sea included in *The Collection of Ten Thousand Leaves*. Although they are not love poems, he was so attracted to them that he decided to include them in his book. Here is one of the seven poems he cited:

> As I stand and gaze
> from the shore of Sahika
> in Kii Province,
> lights on the fishermen's boats
> flicker amid the waves.

The poem is little more than a fragment from a traveler's diary. At a certain coastal town one evening, the traveler went out to the shore and watched the lights of fishing boats on the sea; the scene was so beautiful he wrote a tanka. But Sakutarō, commenting on this and six other undistinguished tanka on the sea, observed:

> Sea poems in ***The Collection of Ten Thousand Leaves*** all create a mysteriously solemn music, sounding like a boundless ocean that lies in the distance. They lead us to a vague feeling of nostalgia, the kind we feel when we put a seashell to our ear and hear the sound of the ocean. In my opinion, those ancient people expressed such nostalgia in their poems on the sea because they had inherited memories from their ancestors who migrated from the continent across the sea. The nostalgia stemmed from their recollections of the distant homeland they had never seen.

This is an ingenious interpretation. At work is Sakutarō's idea that true poetic nostalgia reaches after sensations at the bounds of consciousness, sensations sparked by the underlying forms of archetypal Ideas or by the inchoate stirrings of inherited memory.

As a critic, Sakutarō awarded high acclaim to poems that he thought showed ample nostalgia. For that reason he considered Buson the greatest of all haiku poets, although he respected Bashō, too. Among classical tanka poets, he especially favored Priest Saigyō (1118-90) and Princess Shikishi (?-1201). At the other end of the scale, he disliked the haiku of Shiki and his followers, since he thought they did nothing but copy physical reality. And he did not like poetry written by novelists, such as Ihara Saikaku (1642-93) and Ozaki Kōyō (1867-1903), because again he thought they were more concerned with actual rather than transcendental reality. He praised Takuboku for his "wanderer's nostalgia," but condemned other contemporary tanka poets for having lost true shiseishin. Possibly the most brutal attack in Sakutarō's critical writings is directed at *One Hundred Best Tanka of the Shōwa Period,* a widely publicized collection of 31-syllable poems by leading contemporary poets. "Their signboards say '*Shasei-ism*' and 'Empathic Observation of Reality,' sounding as if they were following some profound poetic principles," he wrote. "But in practice they are no different from a modish photographer who, showing off his expensive Leica, takes many pictures of an unimpressive landscape and boasts of his photographic skill."

In retaliation, Sakutarō was attacked by other critics and scholars, to whom his critical comments seemed highly idiosyncratic. His book on Buson was especially controversial, because Buson had never before been considered "a poet of nostalgia." An example will illustrate the nature of the controversy:

> White plum blossoms . . .
> Who was it? Since olden days,
> outside the fence.

In his book on Buson, Sakutarō took the plum blossoms to symbolize a lover. According to him, as a sensitive young boy Buson felt as though a maiden, beautiful and pure as white blossoms, were standing outside his fence, and that feeling still remained in his memory after a great many years. "On a spring day," Sakutarō wrote, "he felt nostalgia for a spiritual homeland existing somewhere in the universe, and he longed for the eternal soulmate he had never seen."

In his review of the book, the haiku poet Itō Gessō (1899-1946) declared that Sakutarō had completely misread the poem. In Gessō's reading, Buson was simply looking at white plum blossoms and wondering who had built the fence near the tree. Buson felt uncomfortable about the tree's being *outside* the fence, and that uneasiness became the motive for writing the haiku. Reading Gessō's interpretation, Sakutarō was astounded. When he responded to the review in an essay entitled **"On Interpreting Haiku,"** he did not insist on the superiority of his own reading, but he clearly had little sympathy with Gessō's interpretation.

Which interpretation is more valid? Sakutarō's identification of plum blossoms with an adolescent lover is imaginative and poetic, but there is simply too little internal evidence to support it. If Buson intended the poem to mean what Sakutarō said, he would have included some small hint to indicate that the blossoms stood for a maiden. Gessō's interpretation, on the other hand, seems too prosaic. It makes Buson into an amateur gardener who is curious about the position of the fence in relation to the tree. An explication that is at once poetic and faithful to the wording of the poem might take the haiku as expressing Buson's curiosity about the origin of the plum tree. Gazing at the beautifully blossoming tree, Buson wondered who had planted it outside the fence. He probably thought the tree had grown there by itself, for the owner of the house would have planted it *inside* the fence. In any event, while at the scene Buson must have mused on his own past—his home, his boyhood, and perhaps his adolescent love—for white plum blossoms, one of the most familiar flowers for Japanese children, lead one to recollect one's childhood. To that extent, Sakutarō had a point.

Thus although Sakutarō advocated empathizing with the sentiment of a poem, too often he sought nostalgia, the poetic spirit of longing for an ideal world, in any poem on which he commented. Intent on finding that spirit, he at times stretched the meaning of a word or phrase, or read too much into a poem. Yet if a poem was by an idealistic poet, Sakutarō's imaginative insight reached deep into its core. More through empathy than through analysis, he grasped the aspiration lurking almost imperceptibly in the poem. Controversial as it was, his book on Buson helped awaken Japanese scholars, who had been inclined to rely too much on historical and biographical criticism.

In the final analysis, for Sakutarō the beauty of poetry is equivalent to the beauty of nostalgia. One of his most haunting statements of that belief, fundamental to both his own verse writing and his criticism of others' work, is an aphorism entitled **"Beauty."** "Beauty does not own a body," he wrote. "It is for this reason that every beautiful thing—a piece of music, a poem, a landscape—is as sad as romantic love. Beauty is nostalgia for a body it does not own."

. . . . .

Foremost among the hints about Sakutarō's idea of poetic form included in the previous discussion is the aphorism "Poetry demands form. Hence shiseishin is essentially normative." By seeking a form beyond the raw material of experience and feeling, the medium of poetry echoes the poet's spiritual search, inspired by shiseishin, for a homeland of the soul beyond the flux of life in the everyday world. Like a Platonic Idea, form could be conceived as an ideal shape, a norm that the poet discovers underlying its contingent manifestation in the things that actually surround him. However, in his writings on poetic form Sakutarō takes another course. He concentrates not on the shaping power of poetry but on rhythm, the element that dissolves discreet objects and words in the flow of sound and feeling that constitutes the whole. His idea of form, like his critical emphasis, is thus governed by nostalgia—not by an attempt to define and communicate metaphysical truth, but by an urge to sing out the yearning that impels the poet to seek sensuous experience of that truth in vision and waking dream.

Sakutarō's concept of rhythm is a complex and sometimes confusing one. He used the term many times in his critical writings, not always in the same sense. His most coherent statement on the topic is an article entitled **"On Rhythm,"** in which he attempted to clarify the concept for others, as well as for himself. There he distinguished between two kinds of rhythm, one in a narrow and the other in a broad sense. According to his definition, rhythm in the narrow sense is "a flow of melodies," a temporal movement of sounds that produces an intended emotional effect. It is the prime formative element of music. Applied to language, it designates a regulated flow of accents, beats, and other phonetic elements. As for rhythm in the broad sense, Sakutarō termed it variously "emotive rhythm," "metaphysical rhythm," and "shapeless rhythm." This rhythm resides in all things beautiful—whether painting or sculpture or scenic landscapes—and stirs the spectator's mind to soar toward the higher world. It does not have to be aural; it can be an arrangement of colors, forms, or any other sensory stimulants that produce an aesthetic response. When used in reference to language, it denotes a flow of verbal nuances. To simplify terminology, I will call the former "auditory rhythm" and the latter "emotive rhythm" in the following pages. Sakutarō concluded that much of the confusion in the current use of the word "rhythm" was caused by an inability to distinguish between the two.

In Sakutarō's opinion, a syllabic pattern did not constitute a rhythm in the narrow sense. Thus the Japanese language, which has no accentual stress, must be considered lacking in auditory rhythm; if auditory rhythm is a prerequisite of verse, then Japanese can be a vehicle for prose but not for verse. This logic led Sakutarō to conclude that all Japanese poetry had been written in a rhythmless language—prose. As he said, "Japanese poetry is totally different from the poetry of other countries. . . . In Japan, there is no such thing as verse in the true sense of the term."

Sakutarō felt that past Japanese poets, because their language lacked auditory rhythm, were forced to explore and to utilize emotive rhythm. According to him, the rhythm in tanka and haiku is largely of this type. "Frankly, I must say," he once wrote, "that of the total emotional impact of a Japanese poem, 70 percent is derived from nuance and 30 percent from rhythm." By "rhythm" he meant auditory rhythm: he thought that in classical Japanese poetry 70 percent of the rhythm was emotive, and only 30 percent auditory. Among the examples he offered to demonstrate his point was the following:

Inazuma ga
tōku no sora de
hikatteru

Lightning
in the distant sky
flashes.

Sakutarō rightly observed that this is neither haiku nor poetry, even though it has the 5-7-5 pattern. As far as he was concerned, it was a plain prose sentence. In order to make it into a haiku, he suggested the following change:

Inazuma ya
tōku no sora no
usuakari

Lightning:
in the distant sky,
a faint flash.

The main difference, he explained, was the particle *ya,* which creates a caesura. The verbal flow temporarily stops at the end of the first line, making it possible for the following words to rise to an emotional height and refresh the mood. Sakutarō stressed that the effect is attained psychologically, not through any aural quality.

This example illustrates Sakutarō's point conveniently, but it is not a good haiku, as he knew. His favorite examples were poems by Bashō and Princess Shikishi. Here are two of them, the first a haiku by Bashō:

Araumi ya
Sado ni yokotau
amanogawa

The wild sea:

extending over Sado Isle,
the River of Heaven.

Sakutarō remarked, "The sublime effect created by this poem does not come from its auditory rhythm. Aurally it is a monstrous-sounding poem, consisting of all even-toned words. Nevertheless it has an extraordinary appeal because in it the reader tastes the nuances of such words as *araumi ya* ('the wild sea') and *yokotau* ('extending'). To put it another way, here verbal nuance has been substituted for rhythm, serving the same function." He probably was referring to the artful sequence and interplay of the delicate shades of meaning implied in the individual words that constitute the poem. The word *araumi,* for instance, does not mean just a sea that has become wild because of a storm; it implies a sea that has been wild for eons because of its geographic location. The nuance complements the sense of permanence evoked by the images of Sado Island and the Milky Way. *Yokotau,* literally "horizontally lying," makes one think of a long bridge extending from the seashore to the distant island and beyond. It is as if the heart of the poet standing on the shore went out to an infinite distance where the sky and the sea merged.

The second example is a tanka by Princess Shikishi:

Show me the way,
Wind, through the eightfold waves
of this markless sea.
My rowboat is astray, not
knowing which way you blow.

This is a love poem, the wind symbolizing a man whose feelings toward the poetess are painfully ambivalent. Sakutarō, as usual, found nostalgia in the poem—in a woman desperately attracted to a lover who lived far beyond the ocean. He felt that the nostalgia was presented entirely through the music of words, and analyzed that music: "The music played here is not the kind that is heard through the ear. It is complex music that emerges through a combination of meanings embodied in different semantic units. After all, music in poetry is nothing other than a symphony unifying all elements of the language (tones, moods, associations, colors, thoughts, and so on)." The parenthetical comment reveals the nonauditory linguistic elements that Sakutarō felt constituted emotive rhythm.

Despite his emphasis on emotive rhythm, Sakutarō did not completely rule out auditory rhythm in Japanese poetry. Having been interested in music since childhood, he sometimes went out of his way to seek musical qualities in Japanese poems. In articles such as **"Rhythm in Tanka"** and **"Musical Qualities in Bashō's Haiku,"** he attempted to show how auditory rhythm helps to enhance the poetic effects of certain tanka and haiku. ***Masterpieces of Tanka on Love, Yosa Buson: A Poet of Nostalgia,*** and other critical works on classical Japanese poetry also are distinguished by attention to such qualities as rhyme, alliteration, and repetition of consonants or vowels—qualities that many traditional critics ignore. Sakutarō sometimes romanized a tanka or haiku to show more clearly what he thought was a deliberate arrangement of vowels and consonants. Some of his discoveries were quite original and represent definite contributions to Japanese literary scholarship.

Sakutarō believed that tanka had more potential for auditory rhythm than did haiku. With characteristic hyperbole he once asserted, "The difference between tanka and haiku can be compared to the contrast between the Dionysian and the Apollonian in poetry. Whereas shiseishin in tanka is sentimental and passionate and makes one feel a flaming fire, haiku has observant, wisdom-filled eyes that gaze at its subject calmly and discover what lies in the depths of nature." The perception of this difference led him to conclude, "Tanka and haiku, therefore, differ from each other as music and painting or romanticism and realism differ." Tanka is more lyrical and melodious, whereas haiku tends to be imagistic and to create visual comparisons or contrasts. Haiku is at its best when it tries to catch a momentary insight into the mystery of nature; tanka takes advantage of its greater length to vent the poet's overflowing emotion.

It is no wonder that Sakutarō, who yearned for auditory rhythm in poetry, chose to write tanka rather than haiku in his youth. Nevertheless, he stopped writing tanka and devoted his creative energy to free verse. In the end he gave up attempts to write in the traditional verse forms altogether. He had many reasons for doing so.

One was his increasingly skeptical attitude toward syllabic pattern as a device for creating rhythm. He came to feel that the 17- or 31-syllable form was only a superficial outer shell and that the true form resided in the inner emotive rhythm of the poem. If the syllabic pattern had little to do with the rhythm of the poem, it might as well be abandoned. Sakutarō demonstrated that the true rhythm of tanka or haiku was created not through syllabic pattern but through an arrangement of other linguistic factors. As we have seen, he observed that rhythm is created by the particle *ya* in the haiku

Inazuma ya
tōku no sora no
usuakari

Lightning:
in the distant sky,
a faint flash.

He then wrote two free-verse lines that he thought were rhythmically better than the haiku:

Inazuma su
sora no tōki ni mie

Sora no tōki ni hikari
inazuma su

Lightning flashes—
in the distant sky.

Flashing far in the sky,
Lightning.

Sakutarō indicated that in these lines *su* and the *ri* in *hikari* create caesuras. These words spotlight the inner rhythm of the lines, obscured in the haiku by the outer rhythm of 5-7-5. Consequently, for Sakutarō the free-verse lines (although otherwise not markedly superior)

created "clearer impressions" than did the haiku. Some of that clarity may have derived from the lines' fresh and modern sound, their freedom from traditional values.

Another reason for Sakutarō's rejection of tanka and haiku was the fixed lengths of these forms. The fact that they do not allow a poet to write a long poem disturbed him. Pondering why the Japanese had written almost no long poems, he found the answer in the nature of the language: syllabic patterns, the prime auditory element in Japanese poetry, would be too monotonous in a long poem. Tanka, in his view, was the longest possible verse form in Japanese that could effectively avoid monotony. "Try adding to tanka one more 5-7 line," he challenged. "Tension will be gone, and the reader will find the rhythm monotonous and dull." It would be the same, he continued, if a poet used a 6-4 or an 8-4 pattern. The only solution would be to mix 7-5, 6-4, 8-5, and other syllabic patterns in a single poem, which would be the same as writing a poem in prose. Thus he arrived at a paradoxical conclusion: "In Japanese, the more prosaic the language is, the closer it approaches verse." Free verse, written in a mixture of various syllabic patterns—that is, in prose—seemed freer from monotony and hence more poetically rhythmical than tanka and haiku.

A more extrinsic social factor made Sakutarō lean toward free verse, too. He was keenly aware of the rapid Westernization taking place in all phases of Japanese life, and he found tanka and haiku incapable of adequately serving the emotional needs of a twentieth-century Japanese. He explained, "Whether or not we like the West, the fact remains that Japan is being Westernized today. We have been educated at Western-style schools where Western science, Western music, and other such subjects are taught. The books we read are all Western thoughts translated into Japanese. . . . Naturally our tastes and sentiments are becoming Westernized. That is a fact of life in contemporary Japan." In his opinion, the Westernization of Japanese poetry was socially inevitable. And, unlike Shiki, he felt tanka and haiku were too much a part of the Japanese cultural tradition to be Westernized. Undoubtedly referring to Shiki and his followers, he remarked, "Some may insist that from tanka and haiku we can inherit just verse forms and replace the traditional content with the sentiments of our new age. In all the arts, however, form reflects content. If today's poetic sentiments are not traditional ones, which they are not, there must necessarily be a new form to express them." By "a new form" he meant shi. A verse form invented for translating European poems into Japanese, shi was the form most suitable for articulating the Westernized sentiments of a modern Japanese poet. Without it, Sakutarō thought, the vital sentiments of modern Japanese life could not be expressed.

Sakutarō was disturbed by the comments of foreign visitors who did not seem to understand that fact. Once he was irritated at a lecture given by Georges Bonneau, an eminent French specialist on Japan, who praised classical Japanese poetry highly and criticized recent Japanese efforts to emulate Western poetry. He likened Bonneau's remark to a comment by Jean Cocteau, who wondered why the Japanese came to substitute Western-style clothes for their beautiful kimonos in modern times. In Sakutarō's view, these foreigners did not understand the realities of contemporary Japanese life. "They are tourists," he said. "They are not residents of today's Japan."

The final and possibly the most important factor that contributed to Sakutarō's choice of free verse over tanka and haiku as his main poetic medium was the nature of his nostalgic impulse. He felt classical verse forms were too much a part of traditional Japan to allow a poet to soar toward the far-off land of his heart's desire. Sakutarō was attracted to Western-style shi, not only because the West represented the future of Japan, but also because Western poetry reflected a more dynamic culture. He explained:

> The literary writings that we call poetry derive their basic spirit from "struggles with routine life." Poe and Baudelaire are obvious cases, but the spirit of all Western poetry lies in a hatred of "the routine" and in a longing for unrealistic Ideas and dreams. All poets are symbolists or transcendentalists or surrealists or romanticists or some other "-ists"; that is to say, they are all believers in some doctrine that rejects routine daily life. In contrast, all tanka and haiku derive their spirit from "conformity to routine life." Haiku in particular finds its subject matter in the familiar things of everyday life, such as an insect singing in the garden and the sound of water boiling in a teakettle. Such poeticizing of ordinary life presumes enjoyment of daily routine; underneath it lies an optimistic view of life native to Orientals. It is no wonder that in an age of anxiety like ours such a poetry of elegant beauty and leisurely pleasure has begun to bore readers.

Sakutarō was expressing a feeling shared by many progressively minded Japanese poets of his day. A poet who wrote haiku or tanka automatically placed his work against the background of the classical tradition—at least, that was how readers treated it. One may recall Akiko's plea that her tanka not be read in the light of the classical tradition; she had reason for her complaint. Sakutarō, feeling as she did, wanted to place his poetry outside the classical tradition altogether. In free verse, his nostalgic impulse could be expressed without being constrained by the practice of previous poets.

Yet the choice of free verse for his medium posed a serious challenge. Shi was still an experimental form, with a number of problems yet to be solved. The biggest of these was language. Sakutarō did not want to use classical Japanese, since he felt its expressive capacity was limited to the sentiments of premodern Japan. Modern spoken Japanese, on the other hand, was largely a practical language lacking in artistic maturity. Because it had not been used in literature for long, it had not developed a capacity to express complex psychological reality or delicate shades of meaning. Sakutarō said he even had difficulty finding a proper word for the personal pronoun "you" when writing a love poem in modern Japanese. Adding to the problem was the paucity of auditory rhythm, a deficiency that was greater in the modern language. Classical Japanese poets, knowing the weakness, did their best to improve the language and had succeeded to a degree, but no one had even made the attempt for modern Japanese, which was not yet half a century old. In terms of aural effects, classical Japanese was more resilient, more sonorous, simpler, and crisper, whereas its modern descendant seemed prosaic, slack, heavy, and pedestrian in comparison. Yet most twentieth-century poets were not even aware of the risk involved in using modern Japanese. The result was depressing. "I have read hundreds of free-verse poems written by today's poets," Sakutarō observed, "but I have yet to meet a poem that creates a rhythm so beautiful as to entice me to recite it aloud."

Sakutarō did recognize a small number of poets who were painfully conscious of the problem and trying to find a solution. Some of them were writers of what he termed "impressionistic prose"; they saw no possibility of creating auditory rhythm in modern Japanese and had abandoned any effort to do so in their free verse. Like haiku poets of the past, they turned their attention to creating imagistic, associational, and nonauditory poetry: their poems were to be seen, not to be read aloud. Other poets tried to find another route to a solution. Although well aware of the auditory poverty of modern Japanese, they still tried to make its musical qualities work in their poetry. The actual works of poetry by this second group were quite experimental and were not as successful as those written by the first.

In his own work, Sakutarō synthesized the efforts of both groups. In his first volume of poetry, he was primarily a member of the first one. "Most of my poems collected in ***Howling at the Moon*** have no charm from the viewpoint of rhythmical beauty," he himself observed. In the poems collected in ***The Blue Cat,*** on the other hand, he attempted to incorporate rhythmical charm as well. As we have seen, he thought 70 percent of the rhythm in Japanese was nonauditory and 30 percent auditory; he wanted to make the best of that 30 percent. In an essay appended to the first edition of ***The Blue Cat,*** he explained the rhythm of his free verse: "I make a comprehensive use of all the attributes of words—tone, tempo, nuance, mood, idea—as well as auditory rhythm. I try to create a symphony with words." In other words, he tried to synthesize auditory and emotive rhythms to enhance the total effect of a poem. He succeeded in that effort to a remarkable degree.

How Sakutarō did so can best be seen through actual examples, such as this poem from ***The Blue Cat***:

"Littoral Zone"

I have strayed into a littoral zone
where horses and camels roam in the lonely sunlight.
There is neither a market
nor any other place to sell my blanket.
Without a single store
lonely tents line up on the sand.
How could I pass at such an hour!
Like dreadful weapons of the natives
curses hang all over.

The scenery grows dim and dark
as a weird gale whirls the sand.
I don't see any signboard,
and even if I could trade, that wouldn't help me much.
I would rather be a tired, lazy man
lying face up on the white sand.
Then I would go and seek a passionate love affair
with a dark-skinned girl.

As he tells us in his explication, Sakutarō wanted to write a "heart-rending lyric that incites nostalgia." He tried to do so through the music of words. "For that one purpose," he explained, "I used words as pliantly and as lyrically as possible, like the steel spring of a musical clock automatically unwinding." He deliberately repeated negative conjunctives, such as "neither" (*naishi*), "not able to" (*dekiwashinai*), and "without" (*naku*), which he thought had lazy, weary tones. He also made frequent use of tentative verb forms, such as "would go" (*ikō*), "would do" (*shiyō*), and "would be" (*iyō*) because he thought these words aurally created a feeling of indecisiveness, inaction, and ennui. He was fond of such words as "then" (*sōshite*), "like" (*yōni*), and "is there not?" (*aru de wa naika*), as they seemed to sound soft and lyrical to the ear. These sound effects were employed to create an auditory rhythm that resulted in a nostalgic mood. When that rhythm was combined with the image of a desolate littoral zone, there emerged an emotive rhythm appropriate to the meaning of the poem.

In effect, in **"Littoral Zone"** and other pieces in ***The Blue Cat*** Sakutarō added musical qualities to otherwise imagist poems. Other poets had written similar poems, but seldom had they paid such deliberate attention to the aural values of the modern Japanese words they used. Fortunately for Sakutarō, the slack, pedestrian, and "dull" rhythm of spoken Japanese matched the mood of ennui he wanted to create in the poems of ***The Blue Cat***. He consciously looked for such words as *naishi* and *yōni* and used them so that not only their connotations but also their aural effects contributed to the impact of the poem. In this respect he was daringly experimental and, when successful, brilliantly original. Below are two more examples of how he expanded the poetic potential of modern spoken Japanese.

One is his use of the word "like" (*yōni*), a word that frequently appears in ***The Blue Cat***. In ordinary speech it is a connective indicating a simile. Sakutarō felt the word sounded mysteriously soft and ambiguous, and he exploited that nuance poetically. For instance, in one of his poems he wanted to say:

A quail, flapping its wings,
flits over the tall wild roses.
Likewise my heart
wanders over the grassy wilderness.

He was able to cut the length of the section in half by a special use of *yōni*:

Watakushi wa uzura no yōni habataki nagara
sōshite take no takai noibara no ue o tobimawatta.
Flapping my wings like a quail
I flit over the tall wild roses.

The Japanese syntax is looser than the English, so that in the original there is more ambiguity as to who, the poet or the bird, is flitting over the moor. The conjunctive *yōni,* in bridging the two possible levels of meaning, blurs the borderline between the subjective and the objective, which is precisely what Sakutarō wanted. No one before him had used the modern Japanese word in this way.

An even more striking feature of Sakutarō's poetic language is onomatopoeia, which he used often in ***The Blue Cat*** as a way of bringing more aural elements into poetry. Fearing the intrusion of conventional associations, he consistently avoided using traditional Japanese onomatopoetic words, but invented new ones more appropriate to the moods of his poems. In a poem entitled **"Cats,"** for instance, he had two felines meow *owaa* and *ogyaa*; the uncanny babylike meowing enhances the sick, weary, yet somehow erotic atmosphere of a spring night. In another poem, **"Clock,"** he described the tolling of a clock in a dream, which he wanted to sound mysterious and dreamy, as if coming from an infinite distance. The result was the coinage *jibo-an-jan*. Similar inventions include *bumu bumu* for a fly's buzz, *tefu tefu* for a butterfly's flutter, *doobon doobon* for the firing of a cannon, *nowoaaru towoaaru yawaa* for a dog's bark, and *zushiri batari dotari batari* for the footsteps of marching soldiers. His personal favorite was *Too-Te-Cūr Too-Ru-Mour* [The critic adds in a footnote:"This is Sakutarō's own romanization. The standard romanization would be *towotekuu toworumou*"] for a rooster's crow, which appears in one of the finest poems in ***The Blue Cat***:

"Rooster"

Near daybreak
a rooster crows outside the houses.
That long, quivering cry—
it is Mother calling from the lonely countryside.
Too-Te-Cūr Too-Ru-Mour Too-Ru-Mour.

In the morning's cold bed
my soul flaps its wings.
A peek through the storm door's crack:
the outside is beginning to brighten.
Yet, near daybreak
a sorrow slips into my bed.
Over the hazy treetops
it is the rooster calling from the distant countryside.
Too-Te-Cūr Too-Ru-Mour Too-Ru-Mour.

My love!
My love!
In the shade of cold screens at twilight
I sense the faint scent of a chrysanthemum,
like the scent of an ailing soul,
the faint scent of a white chrysanthemum decay-
ing.
My love!
My love!

Near daybreak
my heart wanders in the shade of a graveyard.
Oh, someone is calling me! How exasperating!
I can't stand this pale pink air.
Love!
Mother!
Come at once and turn off the light.
I hear the roar of a typhoon far out at the corner
of the
earth.
Too-Te-Cūr Too-Ru-Mour Too-Ru-Mour.

Sakutarō explained that in this poem he tried to put into words a mixture of frustration, sorrow, gloom, and other "sour" sentiments that many modern men feel as they lie awake in bed in the twilight of dawn. His aim being what it was, he felt the ordinary Japanese cock-crow, *kokekokkō,* would not fit the poem. To his ear, the repetition of the consonant "k" sounded too strong. He wanted the crow to sound more "quiet, doleful, distant, and suggestive." To produce that effect he chose to rely on "t" and eventually came up with *Too-Te-Cūr Too-Ru-Mour.*

Through Sakutarō's efforts, the language of Japanese poetry became auditory to an unprecedented degree. More than anyone else, he was aware of the limitations of modern spoken Japanese as a poetic language, yet he managed to use its aural effects most skillfully. In that respect the poems collected in ***The Blue Cat*** provide examples of the ultimate poetic potential of spoken Japanese.

Yet Sakutarō had to resort to classical Japanese when he began writing the poems for ***The Ice Land***. He did not like doing so; indeed, he called the move a "shameful retreat." But he felt he had no alternative, because in ***The Ice Land*** he wanted to vent intense anger and hatred, and the rhythm of modern Japanese was too lax and weak for the purpose. In his previous volumes of poetry he wanted to articulate boredom and gloom, for which spoken Japanese provided an apt vehicle. Now needing to express intense anger, he had to return to classical Japanese, which sounds more sonorous and resolute, crisp and strong. He also liked the Chinese flavor of classical Japanese, with its many assimilated and contracted sounds.

Sakutarō's use of classical Japanese in ***The Ice Land*** was quite successful; as noted before, some critics consider it to be his best book of poetry. Still, to his last days Sakutarō seems to have been unhappy about the question of poetic language. His essay on the language of ***The Ice Land,*** written six years before his death, ends on a sad note: "After desperate attempts to discover a new language for Japanese poetry, I ended up returning to the age-old literary language. In doing so I abandoned my cultural mission as a poet. I have aged. May new poets emerge and open a new road, a road I failed to build in my time!"

. . . . .

Although much of his own poetry consists of lyrics that sing out personal feelings and visions with no reference to current social or political issues, Sakutarō's thoughts on the use of poetry are distinguished by a strong belief in its social function. It was not that he did not recognize the personal usefulness of poetry: in the preface to ***Howling at the Moon*** he compared poetry to a young maiden's consoling hand, and such comments on the pleasures of verse writing are scattered throughout his work. But there is no doubt that he wanted to see the prime function of poetry in the much wider context of human history and civilization. That social function forms the major theme of a collection of essays entitled ***The Poet's Mission***.

What is the poet's mission? In brief, Sakutarō's answer in his essays was that a poet serves society as a "journalist."

He explained, "A journalist's prime mission lies not merely in reporting news but in enlightening contemporaries with his pen, scrutinizing new cultural trends and taking leadership as a 'guide of the public.' Likewise, a poet's mission goes beyond being a mere versifier. Poets in the correct sense of the word are those who set the trend of the times through their criticism of contemporary civilization. 'Poet' and 'journalist,' in the words' most basic senses, are synonymous." In his view, Goethe, Byron, and Victor Hugo were journalists who heralded the intellectual current of their time, Romanticism, whereas the Parnassians helped to guide their age toward naturalism. In modern Japan, he considered Akiko and Takuboku to be two outstanding examples of true journalists. Akiko's romantic tanka, he felt, suggested the future direction of the spirit of the age, whereas Takuboku's poetry gave full expression to the despair and the revolutionary spirit of contemporary young men who were born too late to live under the old morality and too soon to establish a new one. Unfortunately, journalism had fallen into the hands of profit-seeking publishers in Sakutarō's own time, and poets were driven into hiding by commercial journalists. "Japanese poets are unfortunate," he observed. "But even more unfortunate are those men of letters who are being led not by poets but by businessmen."

Sakutarō thought a poet could be a true leader of contemporary society because he believed poetry deeply affected the human mind. "Politics changes social institutions, and art changes human sentiments," he once said. "But social institutions are founded on human sentiments. Hence politics is a means for attaining the end of art, and not vice versa." Social and natural sciences affect the human psyche, too, but Sakutarō placed poetry above them. "As a rule, man's thought processes follow certain phases," he explained. "At first a vague vision emerges, then a more concrete idea follows, and finally a theoretical vindication is devised. The vague vision in the first phase is poetry, and the vindication in the last phase is science." He made the same point elsewhere in ***The Poet's Mission***. "A poet intuitively feels truth," he said. "Whereas a philosopher *thinks,* a poet *feels.* And in all cases *feeling* precedes *thinking.*" One is reminded of how Sakutarō, in writing a poem, first conceived a vision and then went on to elaborate it consciously.

The idea that feeling precedes thinking led Sakutarō to make another set of rankings. He felt a poet was more a forerunner of new culture than was an essayist or a novelist because poetry depended more on feeling. "If I compare culture to a mountain," he said, "poetry is located at its very summit, essays and criticism are perched halfway to the top, and prose fiction lies at its foot, adjacent to the plain where the general public resides. In the name 'PEN Club,' the order is poet-essayist-novelist, too." Despite the joke about PEN, he was serious about his list. In his view, a novelist can never be as purely subjective as a poet because he must mingle with the general public and depict the realities of contemporary society. A poet is different because, as Sakutarō said in his aphorism, "Poetry demands the noble and the rare. Hence shiseishin is essentially aristocratic (antidemocratic)." In his opinion, haiku and tanka are more like prose fiction in this respect; he thought these two traditional verse forms represented "conformity to routine life." In spite of Akiko's and Takuboku's innovations, many modern tanka and haiku derived their inspiration from traditional Japanese sentiments, taking their material from the familiar things of daily life. To Sakutarō, the poets who wrote these poems seemed to be leading the public back to premodern Japan, not toward the new, Westernized Japan of the future. They were people of feeling rather than thought, but their feelings were behind, not ahead of, the present age.

Ultimately, Sakutarō saw the use of poetry in its prophetic capacity. A poet can become a prophet because he is by nature a dreamer who, with his shiseishin, always tries to soar ahead of his age and civilization. Sakutarō wrote, "The best artist is also the best teacher of the public. The best teacher always has within him the most fervent longing for ideal beauty; he is by nature a poet. . . . By definition, a poet is a romantic, a man who has dreams. For that reason he is a pacesetter of culture and a leader of the public." Here is his syllogism: to be a good teacher one must be a prophet; a poet is by nature a prophet; therefore a poet is a good teacher.

Sakutarō's conception of the use of poetry contains a paradox, however. He used poetry's idealistic nature as grounds for claiming that it can be the best means of edifying the masses, but idealism often alienates the masses, as he indicated when he said shiseishin was antidemocratic. How can poetry be a pacesetter of culture when the general reading public is alienated from it? Sakutarō tended to blame the commercialism of his time for the diminished role of poetry in society. Writing well before the age of television, he predicted that the public would be increasingly attracted to visual communications media, neglecting the more painstaking method of reading. "What will become of literature in the future?" he asked. "In all likelihood literature will not die out. But from now on it will no longer enjoy the kind of prevalence and popularity it has had in the past. Literary works will retreat to a quiet room in the library where books on science and other scholarly subjects are shelved, and they will be sought only by a small group of select readers." Sakutarō fervently believed in the edifying power of poetry, but he also knew that in actuality the public would not take advantage of it. Thus his concept of the social usefulness of poetry turned into a dream, into wishful thinking not firmly grounded in social reality. He was a dreamer even in his conception of the use of poetry.

Donald Keene (essay date 1984)

SOURCE: "The Taishō Period (1912-1926)," in *Dawn to the West, Japanese Literature of the Modern Era: Poetry, Drama, Criticism,* Vol. 25, Holt, Rinehart and Winston, 1984, pp. 255-91.

[*In the following excerpt, Keene discusses the emotional characteristics of Hagiwara's poetry and his innovative use of colloquial language.*]

Hagiwara is by common consent the chief figure of modern Japanese poetry. He is not an easy poet, and the exact interpretations of many works elude the exegesis of even his most devoted admirers, but his work both commands the respect of other poets and critics and is popular with the general public. The novelist and poet Fukunaga Takehiko gave a representative evaluation: "Hagiwara Sakutarō is the outstanding writer of Japanese modern poetry; it is a recognized fact that his works constitute the most beautiful crystallizations of the Japanese language."

Hagiwara was born in Maebashi, an unremarkable city famous chiefly for its gusty winds. He is known as a poet of nostalgia, and a number of moving poems are recollections of Maebashi; but these are essentially references to his own past, rather than affectionate descriptions of buildings or landscapes. Although imposing mountains are visible from Maebashi, and the nearby countryside was still beautiful in Hagiwara's youth, he frequently expressed his lack of interest in the country and his love of the crowds and excitement of a big city. Eventually he moved to Tokyo, but his early collections were composed in Maebashi, where he lived in comfortable circumstances as the chief literary light of a provincial town.

Hagiwara first began to submit his poetry to *Myōjō, Bunko,* and other Tokyo magazines while he was still in middle school. Poetry absorbed him so completely that he neglected his studies; he did not graduate from middle school until he was twenty and kept up his spasmodic attempts to finish high school until he was twenty-five; he was apparently under no pressure from his family to earn a living. Hagiwara also studied the mandolin and the guitar, even intending at one time to become a professional musician. So far little suggested he would develop into the great Japanese poet of the twentieth century.

In 1913 Hagiwara published some tanka in the magazine *Zamboa* (*Pomelo*), then being edited by Kitahara Hakushū. An infatuation with Hakushū's poetry colored his early work, and this association with *Zamboa* marked the beginning of his serious work as a poet. Twenty-seven was unusually late for a start; most Meiji poets produced all of their important work before they were thirty. But Hagiwara seems to have been in no hurry to impress the literary world. In 1914, having reconciled himself to living in Maebashi, he built a study in the corner of his parents' garden, furnished entirely in Western style. There he drank black tea, still an exotic beverage in Maebashi, played the mandolin, and read European literature. He began to attend Christian churches and visit the houses of foreign missionaries, enjoying this approximation of life abroad. It was about this time that he wrote the poem **"Ryojō" (Going Away)**. It begins:

> I think I would like to go to France,
> But France is so very far away;
> At least I will try to take a trip of my own choosing,
> Wearing a new suit of clothes.

In June 1914 he and the two poets Murō Saisei and Yamamura Bochō formed the Ningyo Shisha (Mermaid Poetry Society), which had as its avowed purpose the study of poetry, religion, and music. Hagiwara's interest in Christianity lingered on a few years longer. One night in April 1916 he experienced a kind of religious ecstasy, the source no doubt of the distinctly religious tone in part of his first collection, ***Tsuki ni hoeru (Howling at the Moon),*** published in February 1917. Words like *tsumi* (sin), *inoru* (to pray) and *zange* (confession) dot the first half of the collection, as in the well-known poem **"Tenjō Ishi" ("A Hanging in Heaven,"** 1914):

> Tōyo ni hikaru matsu no ha ni,
> Zange no namida shitatarite,
> Tōyo no sora ni shimo shiroki,
> Tenjō no matsu ni kubi wo kake.
> Tenjō no matsu wo kouru yori,
> Inoreru sama ni tsurusarenu.

> Onto pine-needles glittering in the distant night
> Drip the tears of his confession;
> White in the sky of the distant night
> The pine of heaven where he hangs.
> For having loved the pine of heaven
> He has been strung up in a posture of prayer.

This difficult poem has been analyzed [by Tanazawa Eichi in *Taishōki no Bungei Hyōron*] in these terms: "What is meant by the 'pine of heaven' where a man is hung? Obviously it does not refer to a tree. The 'pine of heaven' stands for the sacred, for God, for purity, and so on. It is a place of confession, designated in visionary terms. When the poet speaks of being 'strung up in the posture of prayer,' this metaphor expresses the intensity of his confession; while in this posture his confession is completed by death." Hagiwara wrote on a picture of the Crucifixion he owned at the time the words "A Hanging in Heaven."

The poem is certainly not typical of Hagiwara's early poetry as a whole, but it displays one important characteristic: apart from its religiosity, it is striking because of the obscurity of expression, which arouses not a sense of bewilderment or irritation but of mystery and depth, similar to the effect of yūgen in the classical tradition. Although Hagiwara is celebrated as the first master of the free-verse, colloquial poem, this work (like many others in ***Howling at the Moon***) was in the classical language and in regular meter, each line consisting of seven plus five syllables.

A few months later Hagiwara wrote the short poem **"Kaeru no Shi" ("Death of a Frog,"** 1914), also included in ***Howling at the Moon:***

> Kaeru ga korosareta,
> Kodomo ga maruku natte te wo ageta,
> Minna issho ni,
> Kawayurashii,
> Chidarake no te wo ageta,
> Tsuki ga deta,
> Oka no ue ni hito ga tatte iru.
> Bōshi no shita ni kao ga aru.

> A frog was killed.
> The children, forming a circle, raised their hands;
> All together
> They raised their adorable,
> Blood-smeared hands.
> The moon came out.
> Someone is standing on the hill.
> Under his hat is a face.

This poem is in the colloquial, and the meter is free, confirming Hagiwara's self-assertive claim: "Before this collection not a single poem had been written in colloquial language of this style, and before this collection the animation in the world of poetry one senses today did not exist. All the new styles of poetry sprang from this source. All the rhythms of the lyric poetry of our time were engendered here. In other words, because of this collection a new epoch was created."

The fact that the language of this poem is simple—common words drawn from daily speech—does not mean that the meaning is obvious. The last line startles not by unusual imagery but by the flat statement of a seemingly irrelevant fact: of course there was a face under the man's hat, but why mention it? Is this the face of an adult watching the children at their cruel sport? Or of the poet himself, as a child detachedly observing his companions? The ambiguity compounds the basic unreality: Did the children really lift their blood-smeared little hands in the moonlight? The poem is an enigma that somehow strikes the heart, fulfilling the definition of poetic expression Hagiwara gave in the preface to the collection:

> The object of poetic expression is not merely to evoke an atmosphere for its own sake. Nor is it to describe illusions for their sake. Nor, for that matter, is it to propagandize or make deductions about any particular variety of thought. The true function of poetry is, rather, to scrutinize the essential nature of the emotions vibrating in a man's heart and to disclose these emotions to the full through poetic expression. Poetry is a capturing of the nerves of the emotions. It is a living, functioning psychology.

Later in the preface he wrote:

> What I hope for from readers of my poetry is that they will perceive through their senses not the ideas expressed on the surface nor the "circumstances," but the feelings that are the internal core itself. I have expressed my "grief," "joy," "loneliness," "fear," and other complicated and particular emotions difficult to express in words or sentences through the rhythm of my poetry. But rhythm is not an explanation; it is a communion of mind with mind. Only with the man who can without words sense that rhythm can I converse, taking his hand in mine.

Despite the difficulties involved in interpreting Hagiwara's poems, the reader never receives an impression of willful obscurity. His disciple Miyoshi Tatsuji, contrasting Hagiwara's ambiguities with those of Kitahara Hakushū, claimed that Hagiwara rejected the "mystification" of the late Symbolist poets, and treated by preference events and emotions associated with ordinary life. Miyoshi went so far as to suggest that Hagiwara, despite his reiterated dislike of the Naturalists, was actually influenced by their manner of expression; certainly some of his most affecting poems are direct to the point of Naturalism. **"Yogisha"** (**"Night Train,"** 1913), Hagiwara's first importnat poem, describes the break of day in the oppressive atmosphere of a night train, where the poet and another man's wife share passion and despair. But the more typical poems in ***Howling at the Moon*** go beyond direct personal experience to the realm of the vision, as in **"Take"** (**"Bamboo,"** 1915):

> On the shining ground bamboo grows,
> Green bamboo grows;
> Below the surface bamboo roots grow.
>
> Roots gradually tapering,
> From the root ends fine hair grows,
> Faintly smoldering fine hair grows.
> It faintly trembles.
>
> On the hard ground bamboo grows,
> On the ground, sharply, bamboo grows,
> Precipitously bamboo grows;
> The frozen knots piercingly cold,
> Under the blue sky bamboo grows,
> Bamboo, bamboo, bamboo grows.

The rhythm of the poem creates its atmosphere; obviously Hagiwara did not intend it as a realistic description of growing bamboo. The season is early spring, when the bamboo breaks the hard ground; but the poet's thoughts turn to the invisible roots extending fine hairs into the darkness of the soil. It has been suggested that these images are related to the poet's psychological state. A few years earlier he had written of "always stretching his hands toward the light" but of "falling instead, increasingly, into a dark abyss." The morbid sensitivity of his poetry is suggested by the fine hairs extending into subterranean depths. The poem not only expresses Hagiwara's feeling for bamboo but his own psychology.

Hagiwara's first poem in the colloquial, **"Satsujin Jiken"** (**"A Case of Murder,"** 1914), was of crucial importance in his development as a poet. Kawaji Ryūkō (1888-1959) had published some graphically realistic poems in the colloquial a few years earlier, and Kitahara Hakushū had also experimented with the colloquial, but Hagiwara was essentially correct when he boasted of being the first to employ this medium successfully. **"A Case of Murder"** opens with these lines:

> Tōi sora de pisutoru ga naru.
> Mata pisutoru ga naru.
> Aa watakushi no tantei wa hari no ishō wo kite,
> Koibito no mado kara shinobikomu,
> Yuka wa shōgyoku,
> Yubi to yubi no aida kara,
> Massao no chi ga nagarete iru,
> Kanashii onna no shitai no ue de,
> Tsumetai kirigirisu ga naite iru.
>
> In the distant sky a pistol resounds.
> Again the pistol resounds.
> And my detective, in his clothes of glass,
> Slips in through the lady's window.
> The floor is of crystal.
> From between her fingers
> Deathly pale blood flows,
> And on the unhappy woman's corpse
> A chilly grasshopper sings.

The colloquial is used to superb effect, its casual tone making the unbelievable "facts" related seem all the more extraordinary. The cold, glassy surface of the poem and the atmosphere of fantasy share much with other poems in the collection, but it also has the faintly humorous overtones of a silent film.

When ***Howling at the Moon*** was first published it fell under the ban of the censors because it contained two poems adjudged to be harmful to public morals. These poems, **"Airen" ("Love")** and **"Koi wo koi suru Hito" ("A Man Who Loves Love")**, are without question sensual, but hardly a danger to morals. **"Love"** concludes:

> Ah, I hug your breasts tightly to me;
> And you press with all your strength against my body.
> In this manner, in the middle of this deserted field,
> Let us play as snakes play.
> I will treat you with piercing tenderness, in my fashion,
> And smear your beautiful skin with juice from green leaves of
> grass.

In some poems Hagiwara experimented with the musical values of the colloquial and of onomatopoeia. In **"Kaeru yo" ("You, Frog!")** he twice gives the line:

> Gyo, gyo, gyo, gyo, to naku kaeru.
>
> "Gyo, gyo, gyo, gyo," cries the frog.

These sounds, to at least one Japanese commentator, conveyed an impression of "blank loneliness." Other examples of Hagiwara's use of onomatopoeia included dogs barking in the distance (*no-ooaru, to-ooaru, yawaa*), and roosters crowing *to-otekuu, to-orumou, to-orumou*. Hagiwara explained the latter:

> I have represented cockcrows heard in the distance from my bed at daybreak with the sounds *too-ru-mor, too-te-kur,* and have employed these sounds as the principal idea-words of the poem. Properly speaking, the crying of animals, the noise of turning machinery and the like are purely auditory; unlike words, they have no meaning of their own to put forth; they can therefore be interpreted as expressing anything one pleases, according to the subjective feelings of the listener. As a consequence, such sounds make excellent materials that provide a maximum freedom of use in the expression of poems centered around musical effects.

Years later (in 1933) Hagiwara recalled:

> Among the poems I wrote years ago there is one called **"Niwatori" ("Rooster")**. To tell the truth, this was an adaptation of Poe, and my representation of the rooster's crowing as *totekuu, mouruto* and so on was an attempt to produce a poetic effect similar on the whole to Poe's "Raven" by means of similar techniques of expression.

He analyzed "The Raven" in these terms:

> The expressive effect of Poe's unrhymed (*sic*) poem "The Raven" results from the repeated echoes of the gloomy, eerie sounds of such words as *nevermore* and *Leonore,* which sound like the wind blowing from some lonely, distant graveyard. Poe intentionally repeated these words, and made the feelings produced by their periodic repetition serve as the motifs of the entire poem. If these sounds were removed from "The Raven," nothing would remain; the poem would be no more than a meaningless arrangement of letters. Could any translator, no matter how gifted, transfer this effect to Japanese? This example makes it evident how impossible it is to translate poetry.

Hagiwara's fascination with Poe and his use of sound suggests his connection with Baudelaire, another great admirer of Poe.

Whether or not dogs barking in the distance actually sounded like *no-aaru, to-oaaru, yawaa* to Hagiwara, he used the transcription to superb effect in a poem suggesting a child's terror at hearing strange noises at night; *no-oaaru to-oaaru, yawaa* evoke the mystery of the dark far better than a mere *woof-woof.* Onomatopoeia is also at the heart of the short poem **"Neko" ("Cats")**:

> Makkuroke no neko ga nihiki,
> Nayamashii yoru no yane no ue de,
> Pin to tateta shippo no saki kara,
> Ito no yō na mikazuki ga kasunde iru.
> "Owaa, komban wa"
> "Owaa, komban wa"
> "Owaaa, koko no ie no shujin wa byōki desu"
>
> Two jet-black cats
> On a melancholy night roof:
> From the tips of their taut tails
> A threadlike crescent moon hangs hazily.
> "*Owaa,* good evening."
> "*Owaa,* good evening."
> "*Owaaa,* the master of this house is sick."

Hagiwara's interest in sound was not restricted to animal noises. Many poems deliberately employ repetitions of words and phrases in the interests of rhythm. **"Shun'ya" ("Spring Night,"** 1915) opens:

> Asari no yō na mono,
> Hamaguri no yō na mono,
> Mijinko no yō na
> mono. . . .
>
> Something like a mussel,
> Something like a clam,
> Something like a water-flea. . . .

Later in the poem these lines occur:

> Soyo soyo to shiomizu nagare,
> Ikimono no ue ni mizu nagare. . . .
>
> *Soyo-soyo* the salt water flows,
> Over living creatures the water flows. . . .

Such uses of sound create a peculiarly dreamlike atmosphere, evocative of a spring night. The words go beyond their conventional meanings to approach the realm of pure sound.

The insistence on sound, as opposed to verbal meaning, should not, of course, suggest that Hagiwara intended his poetry to be read as pure melody, nor that the poet is absent from his creations. The portrait of the poet dimly visible behind the early poems is of an acutely sensitive man with a masochistic sense of guilt. Although Hagiwara lost his interest in Christianity, he retained an awareness of original sin that continued to torment him. His long poem **"Sabishii Jinkaku" ("A Lonely Character,"** 1917), written while under the influence of Dostoevski, has been interpreted as a release from his guilt and inferiority complexes. Dostoevski certainly figured prominently in his thoughts. In the preface to ***Howling at the Moon*** he wrote:

> People, individually, are always, eternally, perpetually in terrible solitude. . . . Our faces, our skins are all different, one from the other, but as a matter of fact each human being shares traits with all the others. When this commonality is discovered among fellow human beings, "morality" and "love" among humankind are born. When this commonality is discovered between human beings and plants, "morality" and "love" in nature are born. And then we are never lonely again.

This was the "salvation through love" Hagiwara found through Dostoevski. He also explained his opposition to the "sensual mysticism of the school of Mallarmé and to the Symbolist poetry of that school" as a result of his contact with "the philosophy of Dostoevski."

Hagiwara's second collection, ***Aoneko*** (***The Blue Cat,*** 1923), was greeted with even greater enthusiasm than ***Howling at the Moon***. In 1934, when he published the "definitive edition" of ***The Blue Cat,*** he explained in the preface the circumstances of composition and the meaning of the title:

> Mr. Hinatsu Kōnosuke, in the second volume of his *History of Poetry in the Meiji and Taishō Eras,* has stated that my ***Blue Cat*** is merely an extension of ***Howling at the Moon*** and contains no changes or development, but as far as I am concerned, this collection was a *poésie* that sprang from totally different and separate origins. My maiden collection ***Howling at the Moon*** had a purely imagistic vision for its poetic domain, and its basic quality was a physiological terror, but ***The Blue Cat*** is quite different; the basic nature of its *poésie* arises entirely from pathos. There are no tears or pathos in ***Howling at the Moon***. . . .
>
> There is no collection of my poetry I think of with such nostalgia and sadness as ***The Blue Cat***. The images and the vision in its poems are magic-lantern pictures reflected on a retina of tears; though I wipe them away, these representations of grief keep returning again and again, like mist on a windowpane on a rainy day. ***The Blue Cat*** is not an Imagist collection. Together with my recently published ***The Iceland,*** it is for me a collection that sings of pure feelings. . . .
>
> I have frequently been asked about the meaning of the title of the book, ***The Blue Cat***. I intended by the word "blue" the English word: that is, I used it to embrace the meanings of "hopeless," "melancholy," and so on. . . . The meaning of the title is, in other words, "a melancholy-looking cat." Another meaning, also found in the title-poem **"The Blue Cat,"** was the result of imagining that the bluish-white sparks from electric lines reflected on the sky over a big city were a huge blue cat. This meaning conveyed the intense yearning I felt for the city while writing these poems in the country. In addition, I was infatuated with Schopenhauer when I compiled the collection, and a world-weary, passive ennui based on his philosophy of the negation of the will, together with the Hinayana Buddhistic pessimism of bliss through annihilation, inevitably lurked beneath the sentiments in the poems.

Fukunaga Takehiko characterized the differences between ***Howling at the Moon*** and ***The Blue Cat*** in other terms: "In ***Howling at the Moon*** he believed in what he could see with his eyes. The sick man's world really existed. But here he believed in what he could not see, and attempted to see conceptual objects beyond his life, to fix his fugitive emotions."

The Blue Cat is marked by the frequent use of the word *yūutsu* (melancholy or depression), and the collection has been termed "a confession of failure in life." The title poem is especially important. The first half describes his longing for the metropolis, its excitement, tall buildings, and beautiful women; the second half, in a more characteristic vein, suggests more elusively the nature of his fascination with Tokyo:

> Ah, the only thing that can sleep at night in this huge city
> Is the shadow of one blue cat,
> The shadow of a cat that tells the sad history of mankind,
> The blue shadow of the happiness we are ever seeking.
> That must be why, in quest of such a shadow,
> I have longed for Tokyo even on days of sleet;
> But huddled with cold against a back-street wall,
> This beggar who resembles a man—what is *he* dreaming of?

The last lines indicate the poet's awareness of the misery crouching in the streets of the city he longs for so passionately; but because the beggar is treated with irony rather than compassion, Hagiwara's lack of concern with social issues shocked the critics; even his disciple Miyoshi Tatsuji compared these lines to Bashō's equally "unfeeling" verse on seeing an abandoned child at Fuji River. Hagiwara was interested only in his inner feelings; the beggar was not so much a fellow human being in distress as a projection of his own uncertainties.

The Blue Cat contains poems that represent Hagiwara's most successful experiments with the modern Japanese language. **"Kuroi Fōkin" ("Black Harmonium,"** 1918) opens:

> Orugan wo o-hiki nasai onna no hito yo
>
> Play the organ, please, good woman!

Not only is there alliteration on words beginning with *o,* but this vowel occurs seven times out of the sixteen in the line. Of the twenty-eight lines in the entire poem, eleven begin with *o* and nine with *a,* the vowel with which *o* is associated in the quoted line. Apart from these effects of repetition, the distinctively colloquial rhythms produce effects that would have been impossible in classical Japanese. Hagiwara's use of alliteration and related consonants suggests at least indirect influence from the French Symbolists like Gustave Kahn, who in 1885 wrote, "Free verse, instead of being, as in old verse, lines of prose cut up into regular rimes, must be held together by the alliterations of vowels and related consonants."

When the "definitive edition" of ***The Blue Cat*** was published, Hagiwara added various poems composed after the original compilation in 1923. **"Neko no Shigai" ("The Corpse of a Cat")** was among these additional poems. It has been described as being "the apogee of the love poetry composed after the early works in ***The Blue Cat***." It concludes:

> We have no past, no future,
> And have faded away from the things of reality.
> Ula!
> Here, in this weird landscape
> Bury the corpse of the drowned cat!

In his notes to the poem Hagiwara wrote:

> This Ula is not a real woman, but a ghost-woman dressed in vaporous garments who breathes amid the images of a love poem. She is a lovable, melancholy woman smeared with the fresh blood of passion. This nostalgically remembered woman always reminds me of music. It is a music connected sadly and inconsolably to the past, present, and future, that breathes painfully in a calendar of eternal time.
>
> That is why the central theme of the poem is concentrated on the sound *Ula*. If the reader can sense the musicality of Ula by pronouncing the name, he can probably grasp quite clearly the main thought of the poem; if he fails to sense it, he probably will be unable to understand the meaning of the poem as a whole. To put it in different terms: *Ula* serves the same function with respect to the formal structure of the composition as *Nevermore* or *Leonore* to Poe's "Raven."

Hagiwara elsewhere compared the world evoked by this poem, which reflects his own life at the time of composition, to "The Fall of the House of Usher":

> My family life in every way resembled "The Fall of the House of Usher." There was no past, no future, and the portentous, accursed, empty present—a present appropriate to the House of Usher—had faded away from the "things of reality." This ominous, squalid situation was symbolized by the muddy corpse of the cat. Ula! Don't touch it! I was always, instinctively afraid.
> I shuddered, weeping in my dreams.

The poem has also been interpreted as Hagiwara's farewell to the poetic world he created in ***The Blue Cat:*** this is the corpse he intends to bury.

In 1925 Hagiwara moved definitively to Tokyo. In the same year he published the collection ***Junjō Shōkyoku Shū*** (***"Short Songs of Pure Feelings"***). The first half of this book consists of early poems antedating even ***Howling at the Moon,*** the second half of ten poems composed in 1924 describing scenes at Maebashi. The early poems include such famous works as **"Night Train,"** the later ones some of Hagiwara's masterpieces. Although, as we have seen, Hagiwara had a special place in his heart for ***The Blue Cat,*** there is something morbid about these poems, and the reader may turn with relief to the "pure feelings" of the later collection. A period of ten years separates the composition of the first and second halves of the book, but Hagiwara himself felt that unity was provided by their both being in the same style, poems written in plangent literary language.

Hagiwara did not state his reasons for returning to the classical language after ten years of brilliant colloquial poems. Undoubtedly the choice was dictated by the materials he used, remembered scenes more easily described in the classical language, with its own distant associations, than the aggressively contemporary modern language. When he published his last collection of poetry, ***Hyōtō*** (the cover bears the English title ***The Iceland***), in 1934 he stated that his use of the literary language was a "retreat" after years spent opposing it and perfecting free verse in the colloquial. "But," he went on, "when I wrote the poems in ***The Iceland,*** the literary language was for me an absolutely necessary poetic diction. In other words, it was impossible to express the emotions in that collection in any other language but the literary one." No doubt much the same reasons impelled Hagiwara to choose the literary language for his "poems of pure feeling." A well-known work in this series was the short **"Koide Shindō" ("New Koide Road,"** 1925):

> The new road opened here
> Goes no doubt straight to the city.
> I stand at a crossway of this new road,
> Uncertain of the lonely horizon around me.
> Dark, melancholy day.
> The sun is low over the roofs of the row of houses.
> The trees in the wood have been sparsely felled.
> How, how to change my thoughts?
> On this road I rebel against and will not travel
> The new trees have all been felled.

Compared to the poems in ***The Blue Cat,*** the meaning is clarity itself, though commentators have emphasized the obscurities. But even if fine points can be debated, there is no mistaking the poet's sense of desolation over the road that now rips through the forest he had loved.

Other poems in the sequence are dominated by the same mood, and sometimes the same turns of phrase recur. The finest poem, **"Ōwatari-bashi" ("Ōwatari Bridge")**, was praised by Miyoshi Tatsuji in these terms: "It is not only the jewel among Hagiwara Sakutarō's poems, but a masterpiece that occupies a prominent place among the countless poems written since shintaishi became free verse."

> The long bridge they've erected here
> No doubt goes from lonely Sōsha Village straight to Maebashi town.
> Crossing the bridge I sense desolation pass through me.
> Carts go by loaded with goods, men leading the horses.
> And restless, nagging bicycles.
> When I cross this long bridge

Twilight hunger stabs me.

Ahh—to be in your native place and not go home!
I've suffered to the full griefs that sting like salt.
I grow old in solitude.
How to describe the fierce anger today over bitter memories?
I will tear up my miserable writings
And throw every scrap into the onrushing Tone River.
I am famished as a wolf.
Again and again I clutch at the railing, grind my teeth,
But it does no good: something like tears spills out,
Flows down my cheeks, unstanched.
Ahh—how contemptible I have been all along!
Past me go carts loaded with goods, men leading the horses.
This day, when everything is cold, the sky darkens over the plain.

The self-hatred and nihilism that mark this poem reached even greater extremes of expression in Hagiwara's last collection of poetry, ***The Iceland,*** which consisted of poems composed between 1916 and 1933. These poems are not only in the classical language but have (for Hagiwara) an exceptionally high proportion of words of Chinese origin. Hagiwara characterized the poetry in ***The Iceland*** as "screams" (*zekkyō*) of anger, hatred, loneliness, denial, doubt, and all the other strong emotions he felt. Words of Chinese origin, with their sharper contours, were better suited to such expression than the softer Japanese words. The poems are otherwise marked by the strong influence of Nietzsche. The best-known work in the collection, **"Hyōhakusha no Uta" ("The Wanderer's Song")**, especially reveals the influence of *Also Sprach Zarathustra*. The poet sees himself as a lonely wanderer:

You, wanderer!
You come from the past and go by the future,
Pursuing your eternal nostalgia.

The poem concludes:

Ah, man of loneliness,
You climb the slope of the sad sunset
And wander over the precipice of will-lessness,
But you will not find a home anywhere.
Your home surely does not exist!

The value of this poem and, indeed, of the entire collection ***The Iceland*** has been much debated by Japanese poets and scholars. Hagiwara's outstanding disciple, Miyoshi Tatsuji, labeled the collection the work of a jejune and decadent period in Hagiwara's life. He found that it consisted of "odd repetitions and distasteful retrogressions" and that, for a collection by Hagiwara, the workmanship was extremely poor. His strictures were echoed by Naka Tarō, who believed that Hagiwara, having realized that the springs of his creative imagination had dried up, was forced to describe a commonplace world of which he himself probably felt ashamed. But ***The Iceland*** has also had its defenders, some because they welcomed the light it sheds on a particularly unhappy period of Hagiwara's life, others because they are convinced that this collection was the crowning masterpiece of his career.

The poems in ***The Iceland*** are almost without exception gloomy in tone, with frequent repetitions of such words as *sabishiki* (lonely), *yūshū* (melancholy), *kyomu* (nothingness), *kodoku* (solitude), and *uree* (grief). It is easy to imagine why certain critics have read these poems mainly as autobiographical documents describing Hagiwara's lonely life after separating from his wife. But they are certainly more than items of historical interest; the poems have a lean, stark beauty that is not the product of an exhausted mind but of a ripe and austere one.

During the years between the publication of ***The Iceland*** in 1934 and his death in 1942 Hagiwara composed almost no poetry. He wrote numerous works of poetical criticism including a famous essay on Buson, aphorisms, and brief studies of the nature of Japanese culture. The great esteem he enjoyed during his lifetime has never wavered since.

Tonio Kröger

Thomas Mann

The following entry presents criticism of Mann's novella *Tonio Kröger* (1903). For information on Mann's complete career, see *TCLC*, Volumes 2 and 8. For discussion of *Der Tod in Venedig* (*Death in Venice*), see *TCLC*, Volume 14; *Der Zauberberg* (*The Magic Mountain*), see *TCLC*, Volume 21; *Buddenbrooks*, see *TCLC*, Volume 35; and *Doktor Faustus* (*Doctor Faustus*), see *TCLC*, Volume 44.

INTRODUCTION

Tonio Kröger is Mann's semi-autobiographical story of a disillusioned writer who rediscovers his love for humanity. Produced early in Mann's career, the novella introduces several themes that Mann subsequently explored in such novels as *Buddenbrooks* and *Doctor Faustus*, including the nature of artistic self-consciousness and the role of the artist in society. *Tonio Kröger* examines these issues through a series of dichotomies, one of which is symbolized in the protagonist's name: *Tonio*, reminiscent of his artistic, southern, and aesthetic background; *Kröger*, of his bourgeois, northern, and social side. The reconciliation of these two poles is achieved in the story through Tonio's lyrical and sometimes sentimental reflection on the past. In this respect, *Tonio Kröger* differs from Mann's subsequent writings, while on a technical level it shares with his later works an extensive use of leitmotif, a device using an almost musical repetition of phrase or event to portray character and theme.

Plot and Major Characters

Tonio Kröger consists of three narrative sections. The first is set in Tonio's hometown on the Baltic Sea, which, though unnamed, resembles Mann's native Lübeck. This section includes two brief episodes from Tonio's childhood: the first, a walk through town with his friend Hans Hansen, and the second, a dancing class with Ingeborg Holm. Blue-eyed and blond-haired, Hans and Ingeborg are both objects of Tonio's youthful admiration and reminders of his isolation from the bourgeoisie, an estrangement that he analyzes in the central, reflective portion of the novella. In this middle section, Tonio, now a writer in his early thirties living in Munich, visits Lisabeta Ivanovna, a young painter. Their discussion of the artistic life and temperament ends in Tonio's decision to visit his ancestral homeland of Denmark in order to escape the sterility of his life in the south and to experience the ordinary joys that he had missed in his childhood. Of several incidents in Denmark, the most significant forms the final portion of the novella. In this final scene, which occurs several months after his arrival in the north, Tonio observes a couple dancing whom he imagines to be Hans Hansen and Ingeborg Holm. He does not approach them, however, and the story ends with Tonio composing a letter to Lisabeta, a confession to his fellow artist of his alienation surmounted at last by his love for humanity.

Major Themes

The thematic structure of *Tonio Kröger* relies largely on the struggle Tonio perceives between the life of the artist and that of the bourgeoisie. In the work, Mann explored the youthful disillusionment of Tonio by contrasting it with the happiness and blithe naivete of Hans Hansen and Ingeborg Holm. Tonio, characterized by a sensitive, artistic temperament, feels estranged from the contentment that these two enjoy. Creating a dichotomy between art and life, as well as intellect and nature, Mann explored the ramifications of this separation and portrayed Tonio—the writer and artist—as the agent of reconciliation between these facets of existence. Isolated from others, Tonio also faces the danger of an escape into sterile aestheticism, which promotes art as a refuge from actual living. He avoids this, however, by going to Denmark to experience life again. While there, he reaffirms his faith in humanity and love for life.

Critical Reception

Written in 1902, *Tonio Kröger* prefigures many of Mann's later works in terms of style and theme and serves as a structural model for the remainder of Mann's novels. It follows a modernist poetic in figuring the artist as excluded from ordinary society. It also contains many autobiographical elements common to Mann's writings on the nature of artistic self-consciousness and creation. The work differs, however, from his later novels in terms of its personal tone, which some have called excessively sentimental. Others see the work as his most lyrical, and Mann himself called the work a "prose ballad." Critics differ on this point but most acknowledge that the story has elicited a strong emotional response from readers. Detractors of the work note shallow characterization among its chief weaknesses, and some fault Mann's universalization of a particular type of artist, one isolated from society. Still, most critics have found in *Tonio Kröger* a compelling and well-wrought story of artistic discovery and consciousness.

CRITICISM

E. M. Wilkinson (essay date 1944)

SOURCE: "*Tonio Kröger*: An Interpretation," in *Thomas Mann: A Collection of Critical Essays,* edited by Henry Hatfield, Prentice-Hall, Inc., 1964, pp. 22-34.

[*In the following essay, originally published in 1944, Wilkinson analyzes theme and technique in* Tonio Kröger.]

I. Themes

Tonio Kröger occupies a central position in Thomas Mann's spiritual and artistic development. But a work of art must contain its own justification, and to appreciate the story there is no need to know anything of the author's physical or literary antecedents, nor to have read anything else he has written. Taken in and for itself, ***Tonio Kröger*** is many things—above all a tender study of youth, of its yearnings and sorrows and its soaring aspirations, of the incredible bitterness of its disillusion. Herein lies, perhaps, its widest appeal. But it is also the story of the growth of a man and artist into self-knowledge, while yet another major theme is an account of the process of artistic creation. Much of this process, its later stage of shaping and craftsmanship, lies outside our actual experience. Even these the poet may enable us to experience imaginatively, so that under his spell we embrace even the alien and unknown. But in one vital aspect of artistic creation, its early phase of "seeing" as distinct from "shaping," we share directly.

This, the aesthetic experience, is a special kind of awareness of the universe. It comes in those moments when we experience things and people, not in their bearing on our own needs and affairs, but for their own sake. They are then no longer simply particular people, things, or events. We see through their accidental bounds and discover immense vistas beyond. Such moments of profound recognition are often the moments of "idle tears" which well up "from the depths of some divine despair"; idle in the absence of personal-practical cause or end, tears not for sorrows but for Sorrow. "What business of yours is the king who weeps because he is lonely?" Tonio asks with tender irony. And Hans could but have answered "What indeed?" Yet this power to weep with the king implies knowledge of a kind that Hans will never have, "star pupil" though he be. For it is not the result of gifts or ability, but of an inner relation to events. Tonio converts [what T. S. Eliot, in *The Family Reunion,* called] the "continual impact of external event" into real experience, endows fortuitous happenings with pregnant meaning and reads the pattern out of life. For him the walnut tree and the fountain, his fiddle and the sea, are more than themselves. Into them he sees "contracted" the "immensities" of beauty and art. Above all he possesses a Hamlet-like clairvoyance about his own reactions to people. He despises his teachers for their rejection of his verse-making. Yet he cannot help seeing their point of view too, so that, "on the other hand," he himself feels this verse-making to be extravagant, and "to a certain extent" agrees with them. These qualifying phrases haunt him painfully early. He is poignantly aware of this complexity in his relations to his parents. The contrast between them is more than just a contrast between two individuals. It is evocative of deeper issues, a symbol of the dualism in his own nature. His relation to Hans is equally complex. Tonio knows well enough that it is a relation which can never bring fulfilment, a love in which all the longing and burning, all attempts at closeness and all torture at their frustration, will be on one side. But he knows far more than this. And it is just in this *more* that the quality of awareness emerges most clearly. For even at fourteen he senses the universality held within this personal experience. Anyone so aware of life as he, cannot help being open and vulnerable to literature too, where the art of the poet underlines the universal within the particular. But this again cuts him off from Hans, for whom bangs and explosions are associated with fireworks, but scarcely with thrills over *Don Carlos*!

In this story Thomas Mann dwells mainly on the pain which awareness brings, on the separating effect of this kind of knowledge. Its compensations are ignored. Yet they are very real, as Tonio must ultimately have known. The joy it brings outweighs the pain. And even though awareness may make the pangs of suffering sharper, it yet removes from it the destructive quality of blind sorrow. To be so involved that we can see nothing beyond ourselves, to be so completely sufferer that light is shut out, and we grope along in the darkness of almost animal pain, is a deadening experience. "*Dumpfheit,*" mere hollow existence, Goethe called such blind living, and preferred "a life eternally resonant," whether it brought him joy or sorrow.

This awareness, the power of being absorbed in something beyond oneself, of responding to the essential quality of a thing or event, the artist shares with others. But in him the mood is more intense and more permanent. The differentiation within the self is such that he more continuously perceives meanings which are hidden when we are absorbed in our own affairs. Of him it is especially true that "there is one man in us who acts and one who watches." Thomas Mann holds fast for us the very moment when this watching trembles on the brink of becoming literature, the transition from awareness to the communication of it through the medium of words. We can distinguish four phases in Tonio's love for Hans; not in time, for they may have happened in one single illumination, but in quality and depth of experience. First he loved Hans and suffered much on his account. That is a purely personal experience expressed in particular terms. Then he was so organized that he received such experiences consciously and recognized the hard fact that he who loves more must suffer more. That is a general human experience expressed in universal terms. But now—and this is the transition from "watching" to "shaping"—"he wrote them down inwardly," that is, the experience became formed, a kind of blueprint of a poem. Finally we get the hallmark of the artist, the pleasure in the experience, with all its bitter knowledge, for its own sake, without any thought of its practical value for his living: "to a certain extent he took pleasure in these experiences, without indeed adjusting his personal life to them nor gaining practical advantage from them."

Much of Tonio's delight in his beloved "fountain, walnut tree, his violin and, far away, the sea, the Baltic," is due to the music of their names, "names which can be included in verses, with good effect." It is the delight the poet takes in calling "the bright, unshadowed things he sees by name." When Lisaveta speaks of the "redeeming power of the word," she surely means that through his medium the artist's insight becomes manifestly fruitful. But again Tonio chooses to ignore the rewards and to dwell rather on the toll which the artist must pay for having surrendered to the power of his medium, a toll paid in sterility and isolation. Even as early as his love for Inge, Tonio realized that he must be in some sense remote from an experience in order to be able to "form" it into literature, remote, not in space or time, but in attitude. Later his joy in the world and the need for "distance" took such possession of him that he became merely an onlooker of himself and others. The roots of such an artist's loneliness lie deeper than is normally supposed. The restlessness which chafes at domesticity, the need to conserve his energy, these are only the more superficial aspects of the problem. His inner loneliness springs rather from his deep sense of failure as a human being. At some point in an experience words become more exciting to him than the experience itself. Even in an intimate relationship he fears he may be sidetracked by his artist's eye, his urge to form may suddenly "see" it, crying out to be shaped by his hand into a work of art. Tonio gives utterance to this sense of failure: "To see clearly, even through a cloud of tears and emotion, to recognize, notice, observe . . . even in moments when hands clasp each other, lips meet, when man's eyes are blinded by feeling."

Tonio has nothing but scorn for the dilettanti, those spare-time artists, who make the mistake of thinking they can pluck "one leaf, one single little leaf" from the laurel tree of art without paying for it with life itself. "The sterile branch" from Goethe's *Tasso* might serve as a motto to this whole conversation with Lisaveta. So humanly impotent does the artist seem to Tonio that he even questions his virility, and again a remark of Goethe's: "Every poem is, as it were, a kiss, which one bestows on the world; but children aren't born from mere kissing," might well complete the sentence he leaves unfinished: "We sing so beautifully that it's really moving. However. . . ." It is the serene finality of art, its contrast with the deadly earnestness of all actuality, which tortures Tonio, as it tortured Nietzsche when he spoke of the flame of genius, "from whose bright circle everything flees, because, lit by the flame, it seems so like a Dance of Death, so foolish, thin as a lath and vain."

Just because Tonio feels equally strongly the pull toward life, he carries within him the possibility of harmony. But Hans is represented as completely lacking in imagination, and we cannot help wondering whether this must always and inevitably be so. Will Tonio's language never be, in part at least, his language? Will he forever be saying resignedly to the Hansens of this world: "Do not trouble to read *Don Carlos*"? We know that it need not be so, that, though it seems likely that this Hans will remain all his life what he is, there is also Hans Castorp, who begins as one of the "innocent, unseeing ones," but ends by discovering that the germs of imagination, which are in all of us, must not be surrendered, must be tended and harnessed in the service of life. When Tonio stands lost in window-longing, unable to join in the dance, he needs some friendly hand to help him out of his lonely introspection. But even more do Hans and Inge need a push in the opposite direction, need jolting out of the confident assumption that they are the hub of the universe. For only a balance between these two ways of experiencing can bring maturity: doing and seeing, being one of the crowd and being an onlooker. The important thing is that life should not only be lived in and for itself, but that it should also be known.

Tonio does go a considerable way toward maturity. By bringing his problem into the light, he rids himself of much of the bitterness which had been accumulating while he pursued a way of life so alien to one side of his nature. This clearing away of the old is essential if new values are to be born: "Die and be born again!" The irony of his final remark: "That settles me!" symbolizes the destruction of a former self. Soon after this self-confession, he feels the need to go back to his beginnings. As in a dream, he revisits his childhood, passes in review figures which have become symbols, and re-estimates their value for him. Despite his apparent emancipation, the influence of his father had been at work underneath, as his dreams betray clearly enough, secretly sapping his energy and undermining his confidence in himself and his calling. When now, in his dream return, he sees the old house, symbol of the burgher's way of life, filled with books, children begotten of the spirit, what a revelation it must seem of the way he ought to go! What an indication that the "toughly persistent diligence" of the burgher can play its part just as effectively in his own realm of the spirit. The tenderness with which the whole incident is suffused is a sign that the bitterness has been eased and the tensions relaxed.

An artist cannot fence off his living from his creating.

They must run fluid one into the other. But he has also to learn not to let his entity as an artist be disturbed by the life he lets in. And he can only achieve this security if he accepts his art, if he believes in his mission of making life expressive for the inarticulate. Then he need not fear lest his art be shaken by rich, vital experience, nor lest his human relationships suffer because of the artist in him. Tonio comes to maturity when he accepts himself as an artist, an artist "from the very beginning, born and fated to be one," and repudiates that aestheticism which, through fear and insecurity, takes flight from the spring into the rarefied atmosphere of the coffeehouse! It remains eternally true that "What is to live in song immortal, Must be destroyed in mortal life"; but equally true that "one must first *be* something, if one is to create something." "To have died" is only one stage in the process of artistic creation; and for the artist to cut himself off from life altogether means going out into the waste land of pure form and art for art's sake.

As a man, too, he matures. The journey to self-knowledge has brought him the courage to face the isolation of personality, and he is now content to leave those he loves in their "otherness" without wishing to possess them. Out of the growing acceptance of himself, the longing for what he is not is eased, and he can watch with tender understanding their small intensities which are none of his intensity, and love them with the love which is extolled in the thirteenth chapter of St. Paul's First Epistle to the Corinthians.

II. Artistry

> The art of story-telling, that is quite simply the art of compelling people to listen, even if one disregards the content.

No analysis of the artistry by which Thomas Mann compels us to listen to his story can ever take the place of direct appreciation. Criticism is never a substitute for the aesthetic experience. After—and only after—we have been exposed to the direct impact of a work, analysis can perhaps help us to further deepened and enriched experience of it. But there remains always the task of synthesizing what has been analyzed, and this cannot be done by a simple process of adding parts. The whole is always greater than the sum of the parts, and different. Synthesis can only be achieved by surrendering again to the power of the story itself.

The architectonic outlines of this *novella* grow naturally out of the requirements of the story. Its mixture of epic and dramatic, the absence of connecting links, justify Thomas Mann's own description of it as a prose ballad. Two brief episodes give the essence of the youthful Tonio. There follows a short narrative passage leading to the central reflective part, where all that was implicit is made explicit. It is a commentary on those dramatic scenes which were directly presented to our imagination, but there is nothing artificial about it. It is natural that Tonio, caught at a turning point in his life, should render account to himself of all he has been and is becoming. This is the critical turning point of the *novella,* and it occurs simultaneously on three planes. In the outer world of space and time the turning point is marked by his decision to leave Munich. In the inner world of the spirit it is a moment of rebirth, marked by his wholehearted affirmation of life. And in the timeless world of form the ballad-style here gives way to long monologues of introspective reflection. The final part is again dramatic, but in a different way. In revisiting his past Tonio trails behind him the cloak of all that has happened in between. There is consequently a large measure of introspection to this second drama. Not only are the episodes of the first part fused into one experience, but the conversation with Lisaveta vibrates beneath. With the final admission that his deepest love is still for the "blond, the blue-eyed," the *novella* returns to its beginnings.

The perfect symmetry is achieved by the skilful weaving of the strands, backwards and forwards, so that the past fulfils the future as surely as the future fulfils the past. The Hans and Inge *motifs,* announced separately at first, are loosely intertwined as Tonio paces the streets of Lübeck. But in Denmark these strands are pulled taut and woven together with symbolic value. How subtle are the variations in this disturbingly familiar quadrille scene! There is no M. Knaak, but the directions are in French all the same and with "nasals"! The second confession to Lisaveta, this time in letter form, rounds off the whole. Nothing is lacking to complete the symmetry. Even the short epic transition leading to the scene with Lisaveta finds its echo. For, as Tonio lies in bed after his encounter with Hans and Inge in Denmark, his thoughts run back to those years of "rigidity, desolation, ice. . . . "

The two first episodes are brilliant illustrations of the choice of a "pregnant moment." Each, the walk and the dancing lesson, occupies at most an hour. How in so short a time does the author manage to convey a relationship so that we breathe its very essence? He does it by skilful choice of time and place, catching the relationship at flood tide and in a situation calculated to reveal all the pull and thrust of tensions. The books we like, the people we admire, the activities we pursue, are eminently revealing, and Thomas Mann makes full use of this fact. Hans loves horse-riding, and the contrast between his "books about horses, with snapshots" and Tonio's *Don Carlos* brings out strikingly the incompatibility of their natures. When Mann introduces Erwin Immerthal we experience directly the ease of Hansen's manner with his own kind, and his awkwardness with Tonio is thereby thrown into greater relief. In the Inge episode the contrasts are between the sheer physical delight in the dance and Tonio's escape into the imaginative world of *Immensee,* between Inge's admiration of M. Knaak and her scorn of Tonio's clumsiness. Despite the unmistakably different atmosphere of these two stages of adolescence, there is a marked parallelism which gives a satisfying sense of form.

Just as the symmetry grows naturally out of the requirements of the story, so too the ironic style is the ideal form for a hero who stands between two worlds and for a situation in which the artist admires and needs the burgher, and the burgher replies by arresting him! As long as spirit (*Geist*) and life remain unreconciled in Thomas Mann's work, they are treated with irony, "something in between, a neither-nor and both-and." Hence those qualifying phrases so akin to our English understatement and derived no doubt from that Low German parentage which we and he have in common. The style of a writer, he declares, is ultimately, if one listens closely enough, a sublimation of the dialect of his forefathers: "and I make no secret of the fact that . . . in its absence of passion and grandiloquence, in its proneness to mockery and pedantic thoroughness, my style is a typical Lübeck mode of speech." His dry humor often results from an aside which jerks the reader out of his absorption in the story, inviting him to study the character with detachment: "for he played the violin"; "for he often said. . . . " Understatement has the special virtue of arousing interest while leaving scope for the imagination to complete the picture. How effectively it is used here to convey that moment when some ordinary and familiar object or person is suddenly illumined by a new and unearthly light: "He had seen her a thousand times; on one evening however he saw her in a *certain* light, saw how she . . . laughing, threw her head to one side in a *certain* proud manner, in a *certain* manner raised her hand . . . to the back of her head . . . heard how she accented a word . . . in a *certain* way. . . . That evening, he took her image away with him." The repetition of "certain" implies far more than is actually said and sends our imagination in pursuit of what Tonio saw.

Ideas are but the raw material of art, and only by taking on body can mind become spirit. Thomas Mann, being first and foremost an artist, expresses his thoughts naturally in images. His are not the primordial, universal images we find in poetry. They are suggested by figures and events of his immediate surroundings: father and mother, the friends and loves of his youth, a criminal banker he has known, a lieutenant he has met, a prince in civilian clothes, a young businessman, an actor without a part. Everything is presented in sensuous form rather than in concepts: not sterility, but the laurel tree; not separateness, but the mark on his brow; not responsibility, but immaculate sober dress; not Bohemianism, but a ragged velvet jacket and a red silk waistcoat; not art versus life, but "fixative and the odor of spring," "the perilous knife-dance of art and life's sweet, banal waltz time." The names are symbolic, too. Why is Lisaveta a Russian except that she acts as confessor to Tonio's introspection in the manner of Turgenev? Or M. Knaak so typically Low German except to emphasize the spuriousness of his French pretensions? Why Magdalena, except that in some obscure way intimate associations had formed in the author's mind between this name, moral- or physical-falling, and those early Christians "with clumsy bodies and fine souls?" Or take the ring of Tonio's own name, upper-middle-class like the cuisine of his Lübeck home, and derived from *Krog,* which occurs so frequently in Low German place names, signifying an inn! How it contrasts with the exotic Tonio, clearly his mother's choice, so that the very title announces the theme of the story!

An image becomes a symbol when it is remembered for the sake of some special significance it had for us. It is then stripped of irrelevant and extraneous detail, and details from other images of similar significance are often superimposed on the first and become part of the symbol. The episode of the lieutenant was clearly an actual incident in Tonio's experience. But we know at once that it has more than anecdotal significance for him, because it is related to the other anecdotes he tells solely by the accident of its connection with his own problem. This is the only thread on which all these stories are strung. Sometimes we can trace the development of an episode into a symbol. At first the girl "who often fell down while dancing," is a real person, and we are told details about her; her surname, her father's profession, that she asked Tonio to dance and to show her his poems, even that she asked him to do so twice, a detail quite irrelevant for the meaning of the symbol. Of all this he remembers only the connection between physical clumsiness and love of poetry, and in the conversation with Lisaveta makes the generalisation: "people with clumsy bodies and subtle souls, people who are always falling down, so to speak." The actual experience has become symbol. Later this symbol is transmuted into art. Magdalena is brought to life again, but no longer as an individual person. There adhere to her traits derived from his other experiences of people with spirit. She has become the symbolic peg on which to hang such associations.

Nowhere is the poet's power "to ring up the curtain for us" more evident than when, in Tonio's dream return to his home, he conveys the bittersweet melancholy of the days that are no more. The problem here is to raise an idea from the level of a mere concept to that of an emotional experience. The idea to be conveyed is a familiar one. When we relive something in the memory, everything happens much more quickly. The whole experience is telescoped. We do not have to take Tonio's word for it that this is what happens now. We go through the experience itself. Tonio lives his early life again, but we relive the first part of the *novella.* We do this because memory permeates the language and sets it vibrant, because the words are similar enough to awaken in us the same reminiscent melancholy which stirs in him. Yet there is that slight difference which is always there when we revisit a familiar scene or dream about it. We, too, feel that quality of pastness which is inseparable from memory. Hans and Tonio watched the train go by and, with the trustful confidence of children, waved to the man perched up on the last coach. The grown man, less spontaneous and more circumspect, merely gazes after him. Without any comment, merely by means of this slight alteration, we feel the whole weight of the intervening years. Similar variation is used with twofold effect at the gate of Hansen's old house. No mention of sedateness or of the time that has passed, but the same weight of years comes across merely because he swings the gate with his hand instead of riding on it. And here we see very clearly the telescoping effect of recollection. It all happens more quickly, detail and dialogue fall away. And whereas the first time we had the simple statement: "their hands, when they shook them, had been made quite wet and rusty by the garden gate," now Tonio's mood of pensive reflection is conveyed by the addition of: "Then for a while he examined his hand, which was cold and rusty." This is enough, without any direct reference to his emotional state.

The trance-like quality of this return is suggested by the magic use of words connected with *sleep* and *dream,* by the hypnotic effect of "Where was he going?" thrice repeated at regular intervals to mark the stages in this progress between sleeping and waking, by the tenderness with which he perceives that the narrow-gabled streets have become poignantly small! How directly we share in his experience when it says: "He would have liked to have kept going for a long time. . . . But everything was so cramped and close together. Soon one was at one's destination"! We, too, are brought up sharply, because we have arrived sooner than we expected.

The same dream light shines on his experiences in Denmark. Now that Hans and Inge have become symbols, they have the strangeness of all dream figures. In masterly fashion the uniqueness, the personal immediacy of this experience is preserved, while at the same time it is lifted beyond the particular to the typical. That they are not the old Hans and Inge, but figures on to which he has projected all his own imaginative yearning, is brought out by the significant little phrase: "who was perhaps his sister." This is indeed the Inge Holm he—and we—knew, and this the same little Hans Hansen grown up; the same and yet different, for she is every Inge, and he is every Hans.

Mann is passionately concerned with the meaning of words, and the musical quality of his prose does not lie so much in their rhythmical arrangement, as in the repetition of certain phrases in different contexts, phrases which call up a whole world of associations as a snatch of song might do.

—E. M. Wilkinson

In a purely artistic sense, Thomas Mann suggests, it was probably its musical qualities which most endeared his "lyrical *novella*" to its readers. "Here for the first time I grasped the idea of epic prose composition as a thought-texture woven of different themes, as a musically related complex—and later, in ***The Magic Mountain,*** I made use of it to an even greater extent. It has been said of the latter work that it is an example of the 'novel as architecture of ideas'; if that be true the tendency towards such a conception of art goes back to ***Tonio Kröger***." When he speaks of a musical structure in his works he does not mean, like so many modern poets, that he is more concerned with the rhythmical arrangement of words than with their sense. The meaning of poetry is much more than that conveyed directly to the intelligence; far more is conveyed indirectly by the musical impression upon the sensibility. But, even so, this musical impression of poetry is never the same as that conveyed by music itself, for words have a meaning before they are rhythmically arranged in poetry. Thomas Mann is passionately concerned with the meaning of words, and the musical quality of his prose does not lie so much in their rhythmical arrangement, as in the repetition of certain phrases in different contexts, phrases which call up a whole world of associations as a snatch of song might do. This is the leitmotif technique which he adopted from Richard Wagner.

In ***Buddenbrooks*** the linguistic leitmotif was handled on an external and naturalistic basis. A descriptive phrase was attached to a character, a label, which usually called up some outward and accidental aspect of him rather than his essence. In ***Tonio Kröger*** the leitmotif is transferred from the outward to "the more lucent medium of the idea and the emotions, and thereby lifted from the mechanical into the musical sphere." From being a mere label each leitmotif now bears a strong emotional content arising from the central problem of the story, and they are woven into the texture with contrapuntal effect, each theme being pointed against another to express the fundamental opposition between art and life. Nowhere is this method used more skilfully or with greater effect than in the conversation with Lisaveta. Art and life run parallel throughout, both in theoretical formulation and in symbols ranging from one single word ("fixative" and "odor of spring") through phrases ("who are always falling down") to symbolic anecdotes (the lieutenant and the banker). First one voice announces the theme, then another takes it up. A contrasting theme is announced, and they are played off against each other as in a Bach fugue. Our delight is in tracing the emergence, the blending, the dividing and dying of the themes.

The reason for the effectiveness of the verbal leitmotif, when used in this way, is that we remember not only in images, but also emotionally. When a pregnant phrase is repeated, chords of remembrance are struck, which go on echoing in us long after the notes have died. Instead of recapturing only Tonio's remembrance of the past, we recall the whole emotional aura of our own original reaction to the phrase, a whole train of personal associations for which the author is not directly responsible.

Even when a leitmotif in Tonio is of a descriptive nature, it is nevertheless not used in the same way as in ***Buddenbrooks***. Tonio's father is first described by a phrase which is little more than a label giving the essence of the burgher. But the context in which it occurs endows it immediately with emotional quality, for we connect Herr Kröger's concern at his son's bad report with his formal correctness. The next time this motif appears, the descriptive element recedes (his blue eyes are omitted); the appearance of the father is becoming symbolic of one side of the conflict in Tonio's breast. People see his way of life as an outward sign of the decay of the family. "The tall, thoughtful gentleman," his father, dies—that is, one side of himself dies, or goes into abeyance. The third time the symbolic aspect entirely predominates: "perhaps it was his inheritance from his father—the tall, thoughtful, cleanly dressed man, with a wildflower in his buttonhole, which made him suffer so much down there." Is the variant "cleanly" introduced as a kind of contrast to his own feeling of being sullied through his adventures of the flesh? It is as if the same theme were given out by another instrument. The fourth time it is modulated into a minor key. Time, by removing all nonessentials, has brought mellowness. Tonio's understanding of his father is growing, although he has long been dead. With deepened insight he sees through the impassive mask and knows that behind the immaculate gravity there lies something of wistful melancholy: "the tall, correct, rather melancholy and pensive gentleman with a wildflower in his button-hole." Each time the father motif is repeated, it is pointed against that of the mother, for together they symbolize the theoretical formulation of the problem: life—spirit, burgher—artist, North—South. Finally, in the letter to Lisaveta they are no longer used merely as leitmotifs, to evoke associations. Tonio now analyzes the significance of these symbols, thus fusing thought and emotion, idea and image.

But most of the leitmotifs in ***Tonio Kröger*** are not descriptive at all. It is fascinating to trace the development of a motif such as "to give form and shape to something, and in serene aloofness to fashion a complete whole out of it," to note how its emotional connotation varies each time it appears. It is first repeated twice within a few lines, so that we know at once that symbolic value is attached to it. Then it is blended with "effective *pointe,*" thereby establishing the symbolic significance of this alternative motif for shaping and forming. Henceforward they can be used, either separately or together, to call up the same associations. When they are played off against life within Tonio himself, against his love for Inge, for the spring or the walnut tree, these symbols of craftsmanship fall in the scale of values. But when they are contrasted with life outside him, with the slightly ridiculous figure of the blunt policeman, they rise. For then the shaping impulse is not pulling against his own urge to life, and he can note with satisfaction the "effective *pointe*" he has made. Finally, with increasing harmony, a balance of values is achieved. The sea inspires him to poetry, but he is too much under the stress of emotion to shape it. Yet he accepts this knowledge without impatience, content to wait for the "serenity" which will surely alternate with intensity of living. "It was not complete, not formed and shaped and not serenely fashioned to something whole. His heart was alive. . . ." These simple, independent statements are free of all the fret, the pull and thrust, of the two dependent clauses in which the motif first made its appearance.

It is no accident that three great influences in Thomas Mann's life were Schopenhauer, Wagner and Nietzsche, all passionate lovers of music. It was the symphonic music of Schopenhauer's thought which appealed to his very depths, and of Nietzsche he wrote: "his language is itself music." His apprehension of things was aural rather than visual, and it is little wonder that he paid such enthusiastic tribute to Schiller's *Spontaneous and Sentimentive Poetry,* in which the distinction between musical and plastic poetry was first made. This accounts for the criticism so often levelled against his work, that there was no landscape in it. In his defence he urges firstly that his is an urban scenery, to be more precise, the characteristic Gothic setting of his native Lübeck, with its tall towers, pointed gables, arcades and fountains, its grey skies and the damp wind whistling down the narrow streets which wend their crooked way from the harbor to the market square. And then, much more important, the sea beyond, Travemünde, the town he knew from boyhood. "The sea is no landscape, it is the vivid experience of eternity, of nothingness and death, a metaphysical dream." It is the solace for all who have seen too deep into the complexity of things. Looking at it Tonio experiences "a deep forgetting, a free soaring above space and time," thereby anticipating Mann's absorption with the problem of time in ***The Magic Mountain***. The sea, its rhythms, its musical transcendence, vibrates in the language of all his books, even when there is no talk of it. And no German since Heine, whom he idolized in his youth, has written of it so that we not only hear its rush and roar, but feel the spray and the salt tang on our lips and crush the shells beneath our feet.

Thomas Mann speaks of certain lyric poems by Theodor Storm which, "however old one becomes . . . cause this tightening of the throat, this being seized by an implacably sweet and sad sense of life; it was for its sake that one was so devoted, at sixteen or seventeen, to this cadence." One can say the same of his own ***Tonio Kröger***. If we are young we experience this tightening of the throat because Tonio is part of all of us; as we grow older, because he is what we were and because, like him, we too have to come back to our beginnings and recognize that it could not have been otherwise, that it all had to happen thus. Like him we hope to be able to accept this knowledge.

> We shall not cease from exploration
> And the end of all our exploring
> Will be to arrive where we started
> And know the place for the first time.
> Through the unknown, remembered gate
> When the last of earth left to discover
> Is that which was the beginning.

Henry Hatfield (essay date 1952)

SOURCE: "Narcissus," in *Thomas Mann: An Introduction to His Fiction,* Peter Owen Ltd., 1952, pp. 52-63.

[*An American educator and critic, Hatfield is the author of numerous books on German literature and has served as editor of the* Germanic Review. *In the following excerpt, he discusses theme, structure, and style in* Tonio Kröger.]

Tonio Kröger is Mann's most lyrical story. As a direct *apologia,* it is warmer in tone than the earlier stories. Mann is closer to autobiography here than ever before, and sympathy with Tonio, and a pity approaching self-pity, are not restrained.

Tonio Kröger is a writer of great talents, though he finds production a slow, unrelenting torment. But it is primarily the basic condition of his existence from which he suffers: he is doubly isolated. He has escaped from the world of his paternal tradition, but he is no more at home among the Bohemians of Munich than he had been among the burghers, and the latter he had at least respected. Either to resolve his dilemma, or at least to find a means of making it bearable and fruitful, is the "problem" of Tonio's existence. He himself prefers to put it more grandiloquently, in terms of the eternal and irreconcilable conflict between "spirit" and "life."

In part, no doubt, Tonio is the victim of his own ideology. The "spirit" (including of course art and the intellect) is conceived of as dead, while "life" is utterly bourgeois and banal. Once one has escaped from the fascination of Mann's language, one realises that his great antithesis is after all only a very arbitrary one. But to Tonio this extreme dualism reveals the essence of the universe; it is small wonder that he finds his existence "a bit hard," as he says with studied understatement. If one accepts the assumption that "the artist" is necessarily and eternally cut off from all vitality and human warmth, then the masochistic analogies Tonio draws between the artist and the outcast or the eunuch are sound. "And if I, I all alone, had achieved the Nine Symphonies, *The World as Will and Idea* and the 'Last Judgment,' you would be eternally right in laughing at me," he exclaims (in thought) to a blonde young lady. Any "normal" person is superior to Beethoven, Schopenhauer, and Michelangelo—this is the "treason of the intellectuals" with a vengeance. Coming from Tonio, the sentiment is understandable, and it is a tribute to Mann's skill that one does not immediately realise its enormous absurdity. But even Tonio cannot really believe it.

To turn from these abstractions to the work itself: ***Tonio Kröger*** is clearly and symmetrically constructed. The first pages develop Tonio's sense of isolation and inferiority, largely by the vivid account of his unreciprocated feelings for Hans Hansen and Ingeborg Holm, the exemplars of the seductive beauty of normality. (They are blond, he is not; this note is heard again and again.) The growing consciousness of his gifts as a writer only cuts him off the more from the world of "life." He flees from this milieu, though he never completely rejects it psychologically; he is plagued by the sense of apostasy from the traditions of his father. Lisaveta Ivanovna, his confidante, makes him recognise his true position for the first time. He is a bourgeois after all, but a "lost burgher," a "Bohemian with a bad conscience." This insight, strategically placed in the centre of the novella, is its turning point. In search of further self-knowledge, Tonio returns to the North. After an ironic interlude in his native city he experiences, in Denmark, what Joyce would have called an epiphany. Hans Hansen and Ingeborg Holm return, not in person but as types; again he is overwhelmed by their beauty and unproblematic self-sufficiency. But by now he has come to accept his own position: it is precisely his frustrated love for the Nordic-normal-bourgeois which gives him the inner tension that makes him creative. Henceforth he will try neither to identify himself with the Bohemian nor to seduce the burgher into the realm of art. He will stand between, a sympathetic if ironic mediator. In a letter to Lisaveta which forms the ending of the story, he draws the balance of his existence:

> I gaze into an unborn and shadowy world, which needs to be given order and form; I see a throng of shadows of human figures, who beckon to me that I weave spells to redeem them: tragic and ridiculous figures, and those that are both at the same time—and to these last I am much devoted. But my deepest and most secret love belongs to the blond and blue-eyed, the clear, vital ones, the happy, lovable, and commonplace.
>
> Do not find fault with this love, Lisaveta; it is good and fruitful. There is a longing in it and melancholy envy and the least trace of scorn and a complete, chaste bliss.

These last lines of Tonio Kröger remind one of the magnificent ending of *A Portrait of the Artist as a Young Man*. Mann's lyrical novella occupies a place in his development similar to that of Joyce's pedagogical novel within his work. Both Tonio and Stephen Dedalus come to accept the role of the artist; each has a sense of mission; each gives a programmatic statement of his ambitions. Yet in Dedalus' words:

> Welcome, O life! I go to encounter for the millionth time the reality of experience and to forge in the smithy of my soul the uncreated conscience of my race.

there is a fanfare of trumpets, a determination which makes one aware of a certain softness and sentimentality in Mann's protagonist. Tonio, no doubt, would have found such youthful exuberance naive. In his most positive affirmation an elegiac note remains. The strength, the sense of activity of Joyce's passage lie beyond the grasp of Mann's gentler and somewhat narcissistic hero. In Gustave von Aschenbach he was to portray an artist of more heroic stamp.

In ***Tonio Kröger,*** Mann uses the leitmotif more abundantly and in a more "musical" manner than in any previous work. It has among others a structural function: the whole action is held together by the motifs which bind a late passage to an early one. For example, as a boy Tonio expresses his pride in his family and his middle-class conscience in the words: "We are no gypsies in a green wagon"; when it recurs later, the phrase draws the whole passage associated with it back into close contact with what has gone before; and the entire novella gains in solidity. The sense of recognition and reminiscence is such that Tonio almost literally relives his own past. Repetition is not limited to words and phrases; that Hans and Inge or the dancing of the quadrille "recur" is a natural extension.

Above all, the motifs seem to have been chosen to produce nostalgia and loneliness, almost as if they had been borrowed from lyrics by Heine or Storm. Thus the wildflower in his father's buttonhole, and the "old walnut tree," always linked with a fountain and the sea. The effect of melancholy isolation is increased by weaving in references to Hamlet (whom the Germans generally romanticise), to Schiller's *Don Carlos,* and to a poem of Storm's. Mann once implied that ***Tonio Kröger*** was the work most peculiarly his own, and its warm, personal, somehow youthful quality explains in part its vast popular appeal. It is, if the paradox is allowable, a sentimental masterpiece.

Frank Donald Hirschbach (essay date 1955)

SOURCE: "The Coming of the Stranger God," in *The Arrow and the Lyre: A Study of the Role of Love in the Works of Thomas Mann,* Martinus Nijhoff, 1955, pp. 1-32.

[*In the following excerpt, Hirschbach examines Mann's portrayal in* Tonio Kröger *of the role of the artist in society, particularly focusing on the protagonist's attempt to reconcile nature and the intellect.*]

Tonio Kröger combines almost all the ideas and trends of the young Mann; it is typical in every respect for both his thinking and technique during the years preceding the First World War. In spite of the many attempts to stamp this story as merely autobiographical the hero is not just Thomas Mann but rather a type, a symbol for many like him, among whom Mann may have counted himself. At the same time he is an ideal to which Mann may have inspired. Nor is Tonio the only "type" of the story. Such figures as Hans Hansen, Ingeborg Holm, Magdalena Vermehren, or Lisaweta Iwanowna are of an intentionally shadowy quality, and to give them more distinct characteristics or a greater role in the story would have detracted from their chief function, that of being typical. There are other "types" that are described by Tonio in his talk with Lisaweta: Adalbert, the novelist; the lieutenant, an occasional poet; the actor off stage; the prince in a crowd. Finally the author employs the leitmotif here in a manner which stresses certain characteristics in individuals which he considers typical of other individuals (there is, for instance, the case of Magdalena Vermehren, "the girl who always fell down," a motif which is later widened to include a whole audience of "people with awkward bodies and delicate souls, people who always fall down, as it were"). Thus, we can hardly go wrong if we consider Tonio's experiences in the field of love as somewhat typical for the artist.

Tonio Kröger has two erotic experiences in his youth. As a fourteen-year old boy he loves a boy of his age who is his complete opposite in every respect. As a sixteen-year old adolescent he falls in love with a girl in his dancing class who is equally different and who takes little notice of him. In both cases Tonio is disappointed and hurt through lack of understanding and love on the part of the person whom he loves. As in [other early stories by Mann], this youthful love affair (we can well regard Hans and Inge as a single object of Tonio's love) is of great significance, but it does not begin a process of disintegration or engender a permanent hate but rather has somewhat positive consequences.

In the great central chapter of the story Tonio takes account of his state of mind in this particular spring of his life, and he finds a basic split in his personality and artistic existence which for the time being he can only express through a description of its manifestations. He can tell Lisaweta that spring bothers him; that he anxiously searches his audiences in the vain hope that among those present there may be one of those "who do not need the spirit" and for whom his works are written; that he feels highly uncomfortable when a lieutenant, a man of the world, makes a fool of himself by reading mediocre poetry which he has written; that he both envies and detests Adalbert, the novelist, who can refrigerate his feelings in order to preserve them for later literary use. When Tonio travels "home", it is not only to rediscover the springs of his existence but to try and resolve this basic conflict. The "solution" comes to him not in his hometown but in a little Danish sea resort where on the occasion of a dance he sees two young people who remind him greatly of Hans Hansen and Ingeborg Holm. They are not, of course, the two companions of his youth, and only a careless reader could miss the several indications to the contrary. They are "types" again, and as such they aid Tonio to come to certain conclusions which do not only fit a specific case but become generally valid.

What is the solution at which Tonio has arrived, and which he expresses in his letter to Lisaweta? It becomes clear to him, first of all, that he is truly "ein Bürger", a bourgeois, an ordinary human being who has strayed so far from the ordinary path that he cannot find the road back even though he is still in sight of the path. And he is convinced now that it is useless for him to even try to get back to the highway on which most of his fellow humans travel, for he is one of those, "who must of necessity go astray because there is no right way for them."

Unlike some of his fellow artists Tonio cannot delight in being different; isolation is far from splendid to him. The decision to leave the group and join the fringe is fraught with perils of which he is fully aware. The acceptance of the spirit, of art involves a receptivity toward a sweet and rewarding disease which may well destroy the recipient. With Hamlet's fate in mind Tonio declares to Lisaweta that he still wishes to stand at the terrace at Kronberg, though he must know that "conscience does make cowards of us all, and thus the native hue of resolution is sicklied o'er by the pale cast of thought."

But the very fact that Tonio chooses the more perilous course in full knowledge of its potential consequences, coupled with the resolution, expressed in his letter, to create greater and better works, proves that his decision is not an egotistical one but one taken for the good of his artistry. And his artistry, in turn, is a mission to him rather than a selfish act of gratification.

If the struggle between *Natur* and *Geist,* nature and the intellect, the will and the idea would end in a complete triumph for either, it would be a catastrophe. Tonio recognizes this and is convinced that it is the artist's responsibility to reconcile the two through the medium of communication. To assume this responsibility he finds it necessary to be lonely, to stand on a high plane, to renounce certain contacts with the other world of light and love. But the loneliness must never be so complete, the plane never be so high that the artist loses sight of the other world completely. He must forever be within reach of the forbidden fruit.

The picture of the mature Tonio Kröger, pressing his face against the window of the ballroom in which his beloved are dancing but suppressing his desire to go in and join them, is symbolic then of the idea of positive renunciation which is the fruit of Tonio's Northern trip. He is a truly tragic hero because he realizes that his greatness stems from the very tension which makes him suffer and because he is willing to embrace suffering as a permanent sacrifice on the altar of service.

Erich Heller (essay date 1958)

SOURCE: "The Embarrassed Muse," in *The Ironic German: A Study of Thomas Mann,* Little, Brown and Company, 1958, pp. 68-115.

[Heller was a Bohemian-born English educator and critic who specialized in German literature. In the following excerpt, he examines theme and style in Tonio Kröger *within the context of a discussion of the modern conception of the artist.]*

Even before ***Buddenbrooks*** was accepted for publication Thomas Mann began ***Tonio Kröger***. As early as 29 December 1900, in a letter to his brother Heinrich, he mentions his plan for the 'elegiac *Novelle*' which six weeks later (13 February 1901) is tentatively given the title 'Literature'; and he adds in brackets: *'Illae lacrimae!'* In the same letter he says: 'When spring comes, I shall have survived a winter full of inward excitement. This very unliterary and unsophisticated experience has proved one thing to me: there is still something left in me which is not mere irony, something which is straight-forward, warm, and good. No, not everything in me has been distorted, corroded, laid waste by cursed literature. Literature is death, and I shall never understand how one can be enslaved by it without hating it bitterly.' The experience to which he refers is 'not a love affair, at least not in the ordinary sense, but a friendship which is—incredible though it seems to me—understood, reciprocated, rewarded, and yet assumes at times, particularly in hours of depression and solitude, too painful a character. . . . ' (There is little doubt that this friendship is the same that is mentioned in the autobiographical sketch of 1930: ' . . . a kind of resurrection of my feelings for that fair-haired schoolmate'—the Hans Hansen of ***Tonio Kröger***—'but much happier, thanks to far greater intellectual closeness.' Some forty years later, in ***Doctor Faustus,*** the memory of this early Munich experience obviously helped to form the relationship between Adrian Leverkühn and Rudi Schwerdtfeger.)

The main theme of ***Tonio Kröger*** was unmistakably engendered by the mood of that letter; for the rest, the *Novelle* is as close to ***Buddenbrooks*** as a fresh shoot to the original plant. Once more we are with a Hanno Buddenbrook who, having survived his music and typhoid fever, struggles with the 'curse' of literature, that ghost from the Flaubertian estate, which has haunted many an artistic dedication and turned writing into the enemy of the *'cœur simple',* the heart alive with innocent love and unchilled by irony. ***Tonio Kröger*** is the lyrically delicate vessel of a heavy freight and yet carries its burden with the accomplished sense of balance which is the gift of aesthetic mastery. Again, the plot is a plot of ideas, and the story itself is so slight it is hardly worth recounting. Tonio (for his mother comes from somewhere 'deep down on the map') Kröger (for his father is Consul Kröger, grain merchant in an old German city on the Baltic—Lübeck again) is a boy chosen, against his will, by the spirit of art. He is bad at his lessons, but good at reading, dreaming, and writing verse. The fountain and the old walnut tree in the garden, the yellow dunes and green waves of the Baltic Sea—these are the things he loves. But he also loves his schoolmate Hans Hansen, fair, blue-eyed, well-built, and 'ruthless', the very boy, it seems, in whom Thomas Buddenbrook yearned to live on after death. Will Tonio ever succeed in winning him over and make him feel, for instance, what he himself feels when reading Schiller's *Don Carlos,* the scene above all where the courtiers are speechless at the news that in his cabinet the King, the great, hard, and powerful King of Spain, weeps because the man he loved and trusted has deceived him? Or does Tonio even wish to succeed? Is it not just because Schiller and weeping kings mean nothing to Hans Hansen that he loves him so dearly? Just as a little later he loves fair, healthy, and stupid Ingeborg Holm, destined to remain unimpressed by his being a poet—and loves her not least because she will for ever laugh at his clumsiness, and would laugh even 'if he had produced all by himself the nine symphonies, *The World as Will and Idea,* and the Last Judgment'.

Tonio Kröger grows up to be a successful writer. Having learned early in life, as early as his love for Hans Hansen, that 'he who loves most is the most easily defeated and must suffer', and knowing also that warmth of feeling is not the temperature in which the written word prospers, he sets out to kill his heart in adventures of the flesh and excesses of intellectual detachment. And he works—'not like a man who works that he may live; but as one who is bent on living only in his work' because 'one must die to life in order to be entirely a creator'. Yet his conscience keeps protesting, for he is not, as we have heard already, 'a nihilist'. In Munich, where he now lives, his painter friend Lisaveta, at the end of a long conversation which holds the central place in the story, diagnoses his complaint in words which have become an examination platitude of modern German literature: 'You are a burgher who has lost his way.' Whereupon the burgher decides to have a holiday with the burghers: he goes to a place by the Baltic Sea, stopping on the way in his native town which he has not seen for thirteen years, and where his family mansion now houses a public library. He is in danger of being arrested in Lübeck: the police look for an imposter presumed to be *en route* for Denmark; and Tonio Kröger is strangely reluctant to clear up the misunderstanding: 'After all, were they not almost right, these guardians of civic order? In a sense he quite agreed with them', just as once upon a time he used inwardly to agree with his father's scolding him for his bad performances at school.

In Denmark, after some early autumn days spent on the beach and bemused by solitude, he finds Hans Hansen and Ingeborg Holm again, or rather their images re-embodied in two young members of a party which has come to his hotel for a night of dancing. Watching them at the dance—through a glass door, as befits this writer's vision of 'life'—Tonio Kröger is in a trance of memories and 'his heart is alive once more'. 'But what is it that lies between that past and this present, and has made him what he now is? A waste land, coldness, desolation; and ah, sensibility! And Art!' Next day Tonio writes, as he has promised, to Lisaveta:

> . . . a burgher who has strayed into art, a bohemian homesick for the tidy house of his childhood, an artist with a guilty conscience. . . . I stand between two worlds. I am at home in neither. . . . You artists call me a burgher, and the burghers try to arrest me. . . . For surely it is my burgher conscience which forces me to see in art . . . something profoundly ambiguous, suspect and dubious, and makes me fall in love . . . with the blond and blue-eyed . . . and

> commonplace. . . . If anything can turn a *littérateur* into a poet, then it is this burgher love of mine. . . .

This is all there is of a story in ***Tonio Kröger,*** a work which could hardly be called a *Novelle* if one insisted upon Goethe's definition of the genre as the narration of a spectacular event. It gently defies all rules worked out for this class of literature, very much in the manner of Chekhov's eluding the orthodox laws of drama. There is no 'event', and what occurs could not be less spectacular. Amazing is merely the literary charm which resolves in lyrical simplicity an exceedingly problematical state of mind, the lucid presentation through incident and reflection of a poetic mood intricately composed of thought and emotion. ***Tonio Kröger*** is more in the nature of an extended poem in prose; in a sense, it is even rhymed, with the repetition of certain motifs assuming the unifying function of rhyme.

The *leit-motif*—Thomas Mann's acknowledged debt to Richard Wagner—already played its part in the composition of ***Buddenbrooks,*** either in the form of the Homeric *epitheton ornans,* an unchanging attribute of a person's appearance, character, or manner of speech, or of identical words to describe significantly similar situations. In ***Tonio Kröger*** the same technique is used with even subtler effect. There is not only the rhythmical recurrence of images, sounds, configurations: the wild flower in Consul Kröger's button-hole, the peculiarly inclined attitude of Tonio's head and his habit of softly whistling when he is in a sad or pensive mood, the gypsies in their green wagon opposing with vagrant rootlessness the burgher's respectable domesticity—there is, in fact, all the ***Buddenbrooks***-proven strategy of the story-teller to make his medium Time yield a little to his vain desire to establish the whole story, like a picture or a sculpture, at every moment of its duration. But there are also innovations. For instance: at the beginning of the story the author describes the feelings which Hans Hansen's one gesture of affection inspires in the boy Tonio; and at the end the writer Tonio Kröger uses the very same words, as it were in his own right, to speak of that love of life which may still save his problematical literary existence. By so taking the words out of his author's mouth, Tonio seems to say: 'It is truly *my* story that has been told', just as the author, on his part, demonstrates in this manner that it is recognizably *his* world in which the story takes place. Such reassurance is badly needed where the loss of real existence—'dying to life'—is felt to be the condition of artistic creativeness. Thus the *leit-motif,* tidy symbol of a significantly ordered life, becomes for Thomas Mann the seal of possession secure beyond loss, as well as proof, valid beyond doubt and deprivation, of having mastered reality through knowing the secret of its organization. To make sure that the world makes sense despite all insinuations to the contrary, indeed to make it yield sense if it is unwilling to do so on its own, wholly to possess it on the strength of the created order of the work of art, and yet always to doubt the efficacy of this act of appropriation—it is this kind of creativeness, both possessive and melancholy, which Thomas Mann's style suggests. This style, passionate and pedantic, seeking real certainty through imaginative conquests and ironically bringing their value into question again, has its happiest moments when language, in its unavoidably onesided outspokenness, yet approaches the state of music and carries the echo of those complex harmonies in which the soul, possessed and possessing, is momentarily at rest. Essentially musical, the *leit-motif* is but the crystallization of an all-pervasive element in Thomas Mann's literary mind. In ***Tonio Kröger*** it conveys, more effectively than any explicit utterance, the foremost problem of the hero: how to defend his work, and indeed himself, against the encroachment of non-entity. And entity consists in meaningful organization, visibly vindicated by the *leit-motif.*

Does Tonio Kröger truly 'love life', the 'ordinary' and 'commonplace', and does he love it with a love which merits the name by which he calls it: *Bürgerliebe,* burgher love? He is, to judge by his story, manifestly deluded. As is proper for a tale the theme of which is a man's separation from ordinary human existence, no other being, apart from himself, comes to life in it. Hans Hansen is a mere creature of Tonio's youthful Eros, a blond and blue-eyed apparition invoked by an erotic craving the burghers would be anxious to disown. The same is true, within safer conventions, of Ingeborg Holm. Lisaveta, in her turn, is hardly more than his sister-confessor. And the rest of the story's population is made up of amusing caricatures of bourgeois society: Herr Knaak, the ludicrous dancing teacher and master of bourgeois ceremonies, or Herr Seehaase, the embarrassed hotel proprietor in Lübeck, or the Hamburg business man on the boat whose oceanic observations on the starry universe are sadly interrupted by the oceanic effects of a surfeit of lobster. Certainly, more lovable than these, in the story's own emotional climate, are the fountain and the walnut tree, undemanding instigators of lyrical feeling, and then again the sea, element of infinite fluidity—symbol, for Thomas Mann, of life blissfully halted at the stage of boundless potentiality and not yet subject to the rigorous restriction of finite forms, intimation of the inarticulate, immeasurable, infinite, and closest approximation within the material world to the eternal void and nothingness.

Is such the love of a burgher, or the love for the burgher's world? Clearly, what Thomas Mann calls 'burgher' is simply a name, suggested to him by his social origins, for a certain ethical attitude. It takes the form of a moral protest against all those practitioners of art who, at the beginning of this century, artistically and intellectually throve on the disintegration of their social *milieu,* mistaking libertinism for liberty, licentiousness for poetic licence, a disorderly soul for the mark of genius, and untrammelled self-expression for the prerequisite of artistic accomplishment. And it is his moral indictment of the artist's 'dwelling in possibility', as Emily Dickinson put it, an expression of the moral discomfort suffered in the inability or unwillingness to commit himself to a definite form of existence which, with the seriousness of an irrevocable choice, would cut off the free play of the imaginative, and reduce to a sadly lingering sense of loss the inexhaustible offerings of the 'fluid element'. Yet the refusal to make the confining choice, to forgo the continuous exploration of 'possibility', involves, so it seems to the moral consciousness of Tonio Kröger and his author, a far greater loss: the loss of 'real life', or, as Kierkegaard put it, the loss of 'existence'.

Tonio Kröger is deeply suspicious of the moral status of the mere aesthetic recorder; it is this suspicion which produces what Thomas Mann later called his 'amorous affirmation' of 'the unproblematical and innocent form of existence', of 'everything which is not spirit and art'. And in the *Novelle,* according to ***Meditations of a Non-Political Man,*** 'the name of life . . . was given, sentimentally enough, to the world of the burgher'. Had Thomas Mann known Kierkegaard at the time he would have discovered that Tonio Kröger lived not so much in a half-way house between burgher and artist as in that border-region between the aesthetic and the ethical state in which Kierkegaard saw the proper home of irony.

The sentimental vagueness of the concept 'burgher' in Thomas Mann's earlier writings is indeed most conspicuous. It seems an elusive but powerful organism capable of absorbing into its indefinitely expansive system a vast variety of incommensurable things: a measure of Christian piety and a measure of Will to Power, Goethe's doctrine of resignation and Nietzsche's dithyrambic excesses, Stifter's untempestuous ideal and Wagner's musical demon, Schopenhauer's will to saintliness and Bismarck's *Realpolitik*; it seems, in fact, an inexhaustibly magnetic 'And', an 'And in itself ', and thus perhaps truly deserving of the name of 'life'. But having eaten the fruits from a whole orchard of trees of knowledge, it certainly no longer has the blue eyes of innocence. 'A burgher gone astray'—if to be a burgher is to walk in such a maze, what else can one do but lose one's way? And Tonio Kröger may be right in reflecting that 'if he went wrong it was because for some people there is no such thing as a right way'. Yet as the right way is nevertheless in some obscurely commanding sense the way of the burgher, the way of the burgher can only mean that 'actuality of commitment' which is immune from the lures of the 'realm of possibility', and acknowledges the moral superiority of life actually lived over all forms of aesthetic reflection.

Tonio Kröger's burgher love, the artistic affection for everything that is not art, is a sentiment akin to that which leads to the *'trahison des clercs',* and Thomas Mann is right in saying that in his *Novelle* Nietzsche's philosophy of Life gains the upper hand over Schopenhauer's denial of it, tilting the scales of Will and Spirit, which stood ironically balanced in ***Buddenbrooks,*** in favour of Life. Yet in spite of this, Spirit does not entirely lose in status what Life seems to gain; on the contrary, Tonio Kröger submits to the 'curse' of literature as one accepting a mission. Going to Denmark, he too will 'stand on the platform of Elsinore where the spirit appeared to Hamlet, bringing misery and death to that poor and noble youth'. The spirit which had insidiously crept into the life of the Buddenbrooks, unsteadying, bewildering, corroding it, now seems to issue a clear if tragic commandment: die to 'life' for the sake of 'art'!

Blurred as the image of the burgher remains in ***Tonio Kröger,*** the sense of loss and sacrifice in the artist becomes poignantly clear. To Lisaveta it seems that Tonio is devoutly dedicated to his vocation. 'Don't talk about vocation,' he replies, 'literature is not a calling, it is a curse.' And this curse lies in the necessity to be almost

> something extra-human, inhuman, to cultivate a strange aloofness, indeed indifference towards human existence in order to be able, or even tempted, to play with it aesthetically, portray it in good taste and to good effect. The very gift of style, form and expression, is nothing but this cool and fastidious attitude towards human life; its very condition is impoverishment, a desperate lack of spontaneity. . . . The artist is finished as soon as he becomes a man and begins to feel. . . . I tell you I am often sick to death of having to represent what is human without myself having a share in it.

And Tonio goes still further in his denunciation of the artist's 'inhumanity': 'To see things clearly, if even through tears, to recognise, notice, observe, even at the very moment when hands are clinging and lips meeting, and the eye is blinded with feeling—it is infamous, indecent, outrageous. . . . ' And 'He is mistaken who believes he may pluck a single leaf from the laurel tree of art without paying for it with his life.'

. . . . .

Is Tonio Kröger's vision of life, art, and artists true? The very question is likely to stir up a nest of hornets buzzing with literary criticism. For is it at all a permissible question? Were it not, to speak with Horatio (and Tonio who quotes him), to consider too curiously, to consider so? The organization of the story, the subtle intertwining of motifs, the appropriateness of the idiom, the subjective coherence and plausibility of the hero's mind, be he right or mistaken—these are valid criteria of literary worth. True. Yet after all is said and done, there lingers curiosity concerning the nature of that which is organized, the sense in the intertwining, and what exactly it is to which the idiom is appropriate. In the case of ***Tonio Kröger*** these are, as it were, doubly literary considerations. For, firstly, its hero is a questioning mind, and the quality of his questions must determine not only the manner of their literary presentation but also the status of the literary work; and, secondly, the problem he raises is literature itself. And the sense of truth with which, and the level of truth on which, a writer creatively perceives this problem is a measure of his genius. Moreover, our understanding of ***Tonio Kröger,*** and of the position this obviously only semi-imaginary young writer holds in the real history of literature, may gain considerably if we realize that our reluctance to ask the question of truth would be due to our belief in the essential correctness of Tonio's diagnosis of literature and life. It is a diagnosis shared, consciously or not, by many a literary critic. For only if 'life' and 'letters' are preordained strangers, only then are questions arising from the business of 'living' out of place if applied to 'writing'. And certainly, if life has to 'die' so that 'literature' can live, then the critic paying attention to anything that is not 'strictly literary' merely busies himself with attending funerals.

There can be little doubt that ***Tonio Kröger*** expresses a subjective truth about the relationship of art and life, a truth so intensely felt that the prolonged argument in the middle of the *Novelle* is not only smoothly absorbed into the lyrical substance of the work, but is also reflected in its atmosphere and embodied in its incident. This would in itself suffice to carry conviction even if we did not know that the Tonio-experience was so compelling that it claimed a large share in almost all the future productions of Thomas Mann. 'A man of character has his typical experience which will recur again and again', said Nietzsche: and the typical experience of Thomas Mann is that which is the sole subject-matter of ***Tonio Kröger***. It is an experience so strong that Mann's last great works, ***Doctor Faustus*** and ***Felix Krull,*** are in the nature of an apotheosis, the one tragic, the other comic, of the Kröger-theme; and so typical that is insisted, in ***Lotte in Weimar,*** upon bending the incommensurable nature of Goethe's genius into some gestures of conformity with the Lübeck archetype. The immense literary fruitfulness of this subjective truth is, however, due to its coinciding with a vast and weighty historical truth, a coincidence which gives to Thomas Mann's achievement, however it will fare with the incalculable judges of eternal value, its singular historical importance. To see Thomas Mann's work in its historical perspective means to see not only more than it, but also more of it.

We have heard Tonio Kröger curse as 'infamous' and 'outrageous' his fate of having to cultivate a 'strange aloofness' from human existence, of having to see, observe, and represent life without vitally sharing in it. It is a fate which Schopenhauer blessed. The genius of art, he said, consists in the faculty of 'pure contemplation', in the power of the mind to conquer the Will and lose itself entirely in the vision of the object to be represented: 'Genius is perfect objectivity.' It is a person's ability

> to become immersed in seeing and observing, to recall the mind from that service for which it was originally meant: the service to the Will, that is, to lose sight of his own interest and volition, of all his own aims and purposes, and hence to disown for some time his whole personality and survive alone as a pure subject of knowledge, as a medium of lucid vision. . . .

It would be interesting and profitable to analyse this grand definition of genius, which ever since Schopenhauer has been used and varied incessantly by artists anxious to describe and justify the 'extraordinary' character of art and their own estrangement from the world. Once more we might ask what precisely it is that the 'pure contemplation' contemplates if it is not, in Schopenhauer's own terms, the spiritually so unrewarding Will objectified as World? For only because the World for him is Will can Schopenhauer proclaim that the original purpose of mind is to be the Will's servant, a thesis almost Marxian in its metaphysical subordination of the spirit to a kind of cosmic greed. However, be it enough here to say that this most radical separation of artistic vision from the 'real person', of aesthetic creativity from 'empirical living', is prompted by the suspicion that world and persons are in a sorry state indeed.

It is, perhaps, the state which Goethe, in a rare apocalyptic mood, prophesied as the 'Prosaic Age' when all poetry would cease, and which Hegel, so vigorously despised by Schopenhauer for turning metaphysics into historicism, declared a historical necessity that in his time had actually come to pass. 'The mode of prose', Hegel wrote, 'absorbs all the concepts of the mind, impressing them with its prosaic stamp', and so much so that 'art is, and will remain, a thing of the past'—unless it miraculously rises above the historical hour, creating in precariously intense isolation, and 'out of its own pure self', a supra-historical thing called 'absolute poetry'. If this diagnosis may be decried as dangerous historicism, it is yet true as a statement of what poets did feel: Schiller, for instance, when in a letter to Herder (4 November 1975) he wrote: 'This supremacy of prose in the whole of our condition is, I believe, so strong and definite that the poetic mind, rather than conquering it, would unavoidably be infected with it and perish. Therefore I know no salvation for the spirit of poetry than to withdraw from the real world, shun the dangerous coalition with reality, and aim at the strictest separation.' It is the classical formula of that which the English genius for understatement (so often merely the overstatement of the slightest touch of banality in a thought or an experience) has termed 'escapism'; the programme too for a poetical departure, as un-Schillerian as can be, which leads to the purest distillation of poetic essences, and defies—in Rimbaud, Mallarmé, Valéry—the slightest encroachment of prosaic reality. Theoretically and philosophically, the separation of poetry from the condition of reality is most strictly prepared by Schopenhauer's metaphysics of art, this fountain-head of a current of aesthetic speculation which is at its mightiest in the theory of French symbolism, is still powerful in the thought of Rilke, Valéry, and T. S. Eliot, and comes to stagnate in all the more whimsical absurdities of modern criticism.

Empirical reality, as conceived by Schopenhauer, is so thoroughly estranged from all true inspiration that *every* true inspiration must be sought in a region close to saintliness. And Schopenhauer does not hesitate sublimely to embarrass the artist by making him go to and fro between the world and the ultimate place of lonely distinction: in his creative moments the artist shares, according to the pessimistic philosophy, the vision of the saints, but without gaining their '*lasting* freedom from the Will'. 'Comforted only for a while', he returns to the world, suffering henceforward the pain of deprivation and the embarrassment of knowing better—a Platonic cave-dweller who for a moment stood in the light of the Ideas and lost to them the eyesight meant for finding his way in the darker sphere.

The history of nineteenth-century literature reverberates with the laments of poets and writers at the injuries their 'empirical persons' have received in the exercise of 'pure vision', just as, *vice versa,* the history of criticism abounds with diagnostic findings of wounds taken to be the real provocations of artistic practice. From Goethe's Tasso, who 'from his inmost being' released the thread of poetry and spun 'the delicious cocoon' in which to enclose himself 'as if in a coffin', through many a romantic agony, through Flaubert, Rimbaud, Ibsen, to Valéry, Rilke and indeed Thomas Mann, the feud between art and life has never ceased, demanding great sacrifices of 'real entity' and 'identical self'. 'The Sun, the Moon, the Sea and Men and Women who are creatures of impulse'—Schopenhauer would have said: creatures of Will—'have about them an unchanging attribute—the poet has none', writes Keats in the celebrated letter to Richard Woodhouse (27 October 1818) and goes on to confess the 'wretched thing' 'that not one word I ever utter can be taken for granted as an opinion growing out of my identical nature—how can it, when I have no nature?' Here a poet experiences dejectedly the 'extinction of personality' which for Schopenhauer is the seal of the glorious brotherhood between artist and saint. Once again we witness the amazingly speedy shift of values attached to the same situation, changing in the twinkling of an eye, an eye now angelic and now evil; and once again it is in Nietzsche, that epochal manipulator of contradictions, that we may watch the *volte-face*.

In *The Birth of Tragedy* it is, in youthful obedience to Schopenhauer, the saints and angels who are by the side of the artist: 'In so far as the subject is an artist, he is liberated from his individual will and, as it were, transformed into a mere medium through which the one and only real subject (the Will) is redeemed in pure appearance.' Yet, once again, the 'pure *appearance*' bodes ill for the stability of the redemption. And indeed, fourteen years later, in *Concerning the Origins of Morality,* the 'redeeming power' has passed into the hands of mocking demons who cynically seem to receive Keats's wretched confession and turn the 'medium of redemption' into 'manure':

> Certainly, one does well to separate artist and work, not taking *him* as seriously as one takes *it*. He is, after all, not more than a condition of his work, the womb, the soil, sometimes the mere manure, from which it grows. One must forget him if one wishes to enjoy his work. . . . Beware of the error . . . of mistaking him for that which he represents, imagines, and expresses. The truth is that if he were all this, he could not possibly represent, imagine, and express it. . . . The perfect artist is for ever and ever shut off from all 'reality'.

It might serve as a motto for ***Tonio Kröger***.

Among Thomas Mann's works, Tonio Kröger is only the idyllic prelude to the more violent encounters between the non-reality of the artist and the reality of life, tragically treated in *Death in Venice* and *Doctor Faustus,* and outrageously as high comedy in *Felix Krull.*

—Erich Heller

Without the slightest change in the philosophical basis of the argument, and with a mere injection of psychology, the Schopenhauerian vessel of the glorious vision has become precisely the 'wretched thing' of Keats. And how well Nietzsche understands Keats's complaint and Tonio Kröger's distress! 'I tell you I am often sick to death of having to represent what is human without having myself a share in it', we have heard Tonio say, and: 'What a fate! That is, if you have enough heart left, enough warmth of affections, to feel how frightful it is!' It might be by Keats; and as if commenting on both their outcries, Nietzsche continues: '. . . on the other hand, it is understandable that sometimes the artist should tire, to the point of desperation, of this eternal "non-reality" and falseness of his inner existence, and try to venture into the most forbidden territory—the real, try in fact to exist in earnest. How successfully? One may guess . . . ' But there is no need to guess. We know the outcome of the dangerous experiment from Goethe's *Torquato Tasso,* Grillparzer's *Sappho,* from the lives of Novalis, Hölderlin, Nietzsche himself, indeed from what amounts to a whole library of nineteenth-century literary biographies. And among Thomas Mann's works, ***Tonio Kröger*** is only the idyllic prelude to the more violent encounters between the non-reality of the artist and the reality of life, tragically treated in ***Death in Venice*** and ***Doctor Faustus,*** and outrageously as high comedy in ***Felix-Krull.***

Rilke's *'Anschaun, das nichts begehrt, des grossen Künstlers Anschaun',* his artist's contemplative gaze which desires nothing, Proust's exiling himself from the actuality of life within the insulated cell of memories and words, Valéry's Monsieur Teste with his frozen feelings and the mind's crystalline constructions, all this is prompted by the presumed insight, the Tonio-Kröger-insight, into the aesthetic uselessness of the immediacy of life, and more often than not by horribly bungling it.

This state of affairs, with all its refinements and sophisticated eccentricities, has not only the sanction of Nietzsche's psychology of art, but also of Schopenhauer's lofty metaphysics. Naturally, literary criticism had to adjust itself eventually to these persistent revelations of the poet's self-experience, their insistence on the essential 'otherness' of art and life. T. S. Eliot's essay 'Tradition and the Individual Talent' marks the moment of this critical awakening, and it is a little triumph of the *Zeitgeist* that some of its assertions read like the soberly Anglo-Saxon versions of philosophically and lyrically more exalted Germanisms. Thus Goethe's silkworm spinning himself to death for the sake of the 'delicious fabric' of poetry, and Schopenhauer's artist who 'disowns for some time his whole personality', become T. S. Eliot's 'continual surrender of himself as he is at the moment to something which is more valuable', namely to Schopenhauer's 'pure subject of knowledge, the medium of pure vision'. And when T. S. Eliot writes: 'The progress of an artist is a continual self-sacrifice, a continual extinction of personality', he means the same 'progress' which for Tonio Kröger lies in the discovery that he may only 'pluck a single leaf from the laurel tree of art by paying for it with his life'. And when Tonio Kröger says: 'It isn't so much a matter of the "redeeming power" of the "Word" as it is of storing your feelings on ice', he uses almost the same metaphor as Eliot [in *Selected Essays,* 1948]: 'The poet's mind is in fact a receptacle for seizing and storing up numberless feelings, phrases, images, which remain there until all the particles which can unite to form a new compound are present together.' Nor is there the slightest difference between Nietzsche's saying that the poet is a 'mere medium', 'mere soil', so that 'one must forget him if one wishes to enjoy his work', and Eliot's 'that the poet has not a "personality" to express, but a particular medium . . . in which impressions and experiences combine in peculiar and unexpected ways'.

The historical truth of Tonio Kröger's vision of life, art, and artists seems indisputable. Would it also have struck artists of other ages as true? It is hardly thinkable that the builders of Greek temples or medieval cathedrals were haunted by a sense of non-being, or that Homer, or Aeschylus, or Dante, felt that their poetic pursuits entailed a loss of personality. But even much later this manner of interpreting the nature of artistic creation might have met with nothing but blank incomprehension even in the highest ranks: from Bach, for instance, or Mozart. Certainly, there is no doubt that the creation of a work of art has always been something other than the 'artistic' expression of subjective feelings and experiences; no doubt whatever that the vision of the artist must reach beyond the field hemmed in by the wilful purposes of the self. Certainly, genius consists in the gift, rare at all times, to surrender freely to a command issuing from a truth beyond appearances. But only a complete reversal of the order and hierarchy determined by the spiritual tradition of Europe could suggest the name of non-reality and nothingness for that which is comprehended in the saintly vision, and which is equated by Schopenhauer and his followers so liberally with the aesthetic imagination. And what a perverted doctrine of the human person had to be accepted by the world before artists could feel that they ceased to be persons precisely at the point where the real person should begin: in the act of submitting to an objective vision!

This, then, is yet another theme in modern literature, as new and as revealing as that of the demonic boredom and the sickly Eros. It postulates the obscurest of transcendental realms: the *aesthetic* transcendence. For where exactly grows the straw with which the bricks are made for the aesthetic edifice? Where is the point of vision from which the artist's mind observes the world as if from outside or above? What is the nature of the medium into which the creator 'depersonalizes' himself? And if Heidegger, very much in keeping with the spirit of the prevalent aesthetic theory, says [in *Holzwege,* 1950] that 'the artist is, in relation to his work, an irrelevancy, hardly more than a passage . . . for the transit of the work'—whence and whither does the passage lead? It is neither irreverence nor idle curiosity which asks these questions, but an anxiety inspired by the 'transcendent' satanic company which a still more 'depersonalized' Tonio Kröger, in his final incarnation as the composer Doctor Faustus, will one day seek and find. Amid all this aesthetic pother the suspicion grows that there must have been a time when the artist shared the reality of his fellow-men, and was distinguished from them not so much by a unique vision and agony as simply by the power to give surpassing form and shape to the common intimations of meaning. For a world in which the makers of beautiful and meaningful things are barred from 'real' existence is indeed a strangely inhuman and deeply disquieting world—a world immune from that idea of creation which, beside much sorrow and darkness, also knows the reality of grace. The aesthetic transcendence is then, perhaps, nothing but an optical delusion enforced upon the eye by the dark prospect of a historical period, and caused by a pathological narrowing of the common vision—by an insidious deficiency in the concept of what is real. When the sea recedes, many a strange creature of the ocean is left behind on the sands, dazzled and dazzling outcasts from another medium. At high tide they are in their own and need not transcend quite as much.

Schopenhauer's genius of art, transcending all self-centred purposes and coming face to face with the Absolute, Goethe's poet engaged in the self-annihilating service to his demon, Keats's surrender of all individual identity, the young Nietzsche's redemption of the empirical world in the aesthetic phenomenon, Rilke's pure contemplation, T. S. Eliot's doctrine of the continual self-sacrifice of the artist's personality, Thomas Mann's artist who pays with his life for a leaf of the laurel tree—it all appears to be spoken in the idiom of religion, in the language of ' . . . but whosoever shall lose his life . . . ' It is therefore less surprising than may appear at first glance that from ***Tonio Kröger*** Thomas Mann turns to Fra Girolamo Savonarola, contrasting and yet linking in ***Fiorenza*** the spirit of art with the spirit of religion—or at least with what at the time, instructed by Nietzsche, he took to be religious genius. This play—or 'dialectical *Novelle*', as he once called it—is an illuminating failure. What it illumines is the utter precariousness of that extreme spiritualization of art in an age dispossessed of any concrete notion of the 'spirit'. Thomas Mann himself says in a letter to his brother (18 February 1905)—and more or less repeats in ***Meditations of a Non-Political Man***—that in ***Tonio Kröger*** he had gone too far 'in running into one the concepts of "spirit" and "art" '. ***Fiorenza*** was to show the 'hostile opposition' between them. But the opposition, alas, is not maintained. They come together again. Both end in Nietzschean psychology.

Lilian R. Furst (essay date 1961)

SOURCE: "Thomas Mann's *Tonio Kröger*: A Critical Reconsideration," in *Revue Des Langues Vivantes,* Vol. 27, 1961, pp. 232-40.

[*Furst is an Austrian-born American educator and critic who has written a number of studies on Romanticism. In the following essay, she suggests that reader sentiment has interfered with proper critical assessment of* Tonio Kröger.]

'Von allem, was ich schrieb, meinem Herzen am nächsten': this is how Thomas Mann described ***Tonio Kröger*** nearly thirty years after its publication. He added too, that this *Novelle* was 'noch immer von jungen Leuten geliebt'. The words which Mann used to describe the reaction to ***Tonio Kröger,*** 'meinem Herzen am nächsten' and 'geliebt', are highly significant, implying as they do not merely popularity, but a strong emotional response on the part of the reader, as well as an emotional involvement of the author. Another thirty years have now elapsed and today as yet the attraction of ***Tonio Kröger,*** particularly for the younger reader, is still as potent as ever. The nature of this attraction is not hard to analyse. ***Tonio Kröger*** is first and foremost a poignant tale of adolescence, of the acute problems confronting a sensitive youth as he grows up and learns to come to terms with himself and the world. Since these crises of self-knowledge, disillusionment and adjustment are common to us all, the reader instinctively tends to identify himself with Tonio Kröger, often perhaps without knowing it. Hence the special place of this story in our hearts.

But this tendency to identify ourselves with the hero is not without its dangers. Thus much of the critical writing about ***Tonio Kröger*** is coloured by an element of sentiment; sympathy for Tonio Kröger reverberates through it. For instance, critics nearly always refer to the hero by his Christian name (although Tonio Kröger himself was so embarrassed by this name, which seemed to him not only outlandish but really quite ridiculous). Yet surely it is an absolutely essential prerequisite of any fair evaluation, that the critic must have achieved a certain degree of detachment from the work under consideration. In the case of ***Tonio Kröger*** this critical detachment is all the more vital in that it denotes also something of the self-detachment of maturity. On the other hand, the reader who responds to ***Tonio Kröger*** with his heart alone is lacking in that detachment, and this predominantly emotional reaction can and does blind him to some aspects of the *Novelle.* Two or three concrete examples will illustrate the way in which an admixture of sentiment can interfere with, and distort our judgement.

In the opening sections of ***Tonio Kröger,*** the walk home from school with Hans and the dancing-class, Mann sketches with masterly economy and delicacy archetypal experiences in the adolescence of any sensitive youth. The acute awareness of isolation, of 'differentness', the longing to conform to the normal pattern, yet at the same time the nascent pride in individuality, the alternation of confidence and difference, the gawky self-consciousness: how familiar and how ably portrayed these complex and inarticulate states are! In Tonio Kröger's life, the problems of adolescence are crystallised in his successive encounters with Hans Hansen and Ingeborg Holm, who become the objects of his love and longing. Hans, the son of a wealthy, respected old family, has the good fortune to have been born not only handsome, but also with an uncomplicated disposition; he is the prototype of the healthy extrovert, whose feet are firmly planted on the ground and who will stride through life happily and light-heartedly without reflecting, guided simply by the dictates of instinct and feeling. His feminine counterpart is Inge, a pretty, gay young girl with laughing blue eyes and thick blond hair. These are 'die Blonden, Blauäugigen' on to whom Tonio Kröger, himself dark-haired and sad-eyed, fixes all his intense love and longing—'Zu sein wie du . . . ' Throughout the story Hans and Inge are seen through Tonio Kröger's eyes, with the prejudiced judgement of the lover. Never are we allowed to glimpse the objects of his love and longing as they really are; consequently a detached, sober view of their respective characters provides rather a shock: Are Hans and Inge not in reality banal, intolerably dull and smug, one-sided and complacent? Are they not in fact related to the objectionable Klöterjahn, who is the butt of so much ridicule in ***Tristan***? Hans, with his all-consuming passion for horses and horse-books, certainly has a one-track mind; how bored he is when Tonio Kröger tries to convey to him the pathos of the scene in *Don Carlos* where it is reported that the king had wept, and how relieved he is when Erwin Jimmerthal appears and the conversation reverts to topics more congenial to him, such as riding! How petty also is his ill-disguised shame of his friendship with a boy as strange as Tonio Kröger and his refusal to address him by his Christian name in the presence of others. Likewise, how insensitive and unperceptive Inge is both in her admiration for that vain fool, the dancing-master, and in her cruel laughter at Tonio Kröger's absurd, absent-minded mistakes. Our attention is never allowed to dwell on these aspects of Tonio Kröger's idols, so much so that it is only with difficulty that Hans and Inge can be seen in this sober light at all. While in ***Tristan*** the 'children of life' are subjected to a reducing irony, in ***Tonio Kröger,*** on the contrary, they are illuminated by an elevating idealisation. Yet the reader only too easily fails to realise the full extent of this idealisation because he is so deeply involved in the story that he unconsciously shares the viewpoint of Tonio Kröger. Thus a virtue of the *Novelle,* the emotional force with which it carries the reader along, can in certain circumstances turn into a danger, if the reader thereby loses his independent judgement.

This danger is not of such great consequence in Mann's oversimplified portrayal of Hans and Inge as in another instance: in his one-sided conception of the artist. At the opposite pole to the loved and lovable world of the simple 'children of life' lies the world of art and of 'Geist'. This is the realm of 'die Stolzen und die Kalten', of those who take refuge from the stirring spring air in the neutral, seasonless shelter of a café, of those who cultivate all that is extraordinary and outré in outward appearance as well as in attitude. Moreover, Thomas Mann discerns 'etwas tief Zweideutiges, tief Anrüchiges, tief Zweifelhaftes' in this world of art. It is a theme upon which he merely touches in ***Tonio Kröger,*** notably in the anecdote concerning the banker who began to write novels while serving a prison sentence, and in the attempted arrest of Tonio Kröger during his visit to his native city. This is, however, only one aspect of the artist's 'dubiousness' and later, in ***Der Tod in Venedig,*** Mann develops this notion more fully. The whole force of the antithesis between 'life' and 'art' is most trenchantly expressed in the image in which Mann contrasts 'des Lebens süsser, trivialer Dreitakt' with 'dem schweren, schweren und gefährlichen Messertanz der Kunst'.

That this conception of art and of the artist is decadent, has been said often enough; similarly, it is a commonplace that Mann's attitude to the artist is largely determined by his own bourgeois origins and heritage, so that the world of art appears to him profoundly dubious and suspect. He repeatedly portrays artists who are like himself: men of dualistic parentage, who stand between the two worlds, tortured by a feeling of guilt, a bad conscience about their artistic activities. But instead of recognising there isolated, unusual characters as freaks, Mann treats them as typical artists: a most dangerous procedure. Perhaps the crassest example of this distortion occurs in ***Der Tod in Venedig,*** where Mann accepts the case of Aschenbach as a prototype and generalises it to include *all* artists and art itself in his wholesale rejection. What he says may well be true of Aschenbach, one particular, peculiar, indeed pathological artist, who falls victim to a decadent type of beauty; but it does not follow that it therefore applies to all artists. Mann himself is dimly aware of the one-sidedness of his conception of art and of the artist; witness the words of Lisaweta Iwanowna who points to

> die reinigende, heiligende Wirkung der Literatur, die Zerstörung der Leidenschaften durch die Erkenntnis und das Wort, die Literatur als Weg zum Verstehen, zum Vergeben und zur Liebe, die erlösende Macht der Sprache, der literarische Geist als die edelste Erscheinung des Menschengeistes überhaupt, der Literat als vollkommener Mensch, als Heiliger.

Although Mann is able to formulate this 'other side of the medal', he never depicts artists who fulfil such a positive function. His artists remain 'Reflexionsmenschen', social misfits; it is the 'Schattenseiten des Künstlertums' which fill the foreground, to the total exclusion of other aspects. Lisaweta Iwanowna's wise words to Tonio Kröger can well be applied to Thomas Mann himself:

> Übrigens wissen Sie sehr wohl, dass Sie die Dinge ansehen, wie sie nicht notwendig angesehen zu werden brauchen. . . .

But does the reader also share this knowledge or is he not only too prone, under the spell of this poignant narrative, to overlook the fallacies of Mann's antithetical and oversimplified thinking and to accept his one-sided conception of the artist? Herein lies a grave danger.

The third and final example of the way in which emotional prejudice may prevent a realistic judgement of ***Tonio Kröger*** is as amenable to proof as is possible in literary criticism. To put it bluntly, the end of ***Tonio Kröger*** is not convincing. Or rather, it appears convincing at the first reading because the reader is personally too involved in the narrative to detach himself for a sober analysis; later, however, when that critical reconsideration does take place, the defects in the logic of the second part of the *Novelle* become plainly apparent. It is worth examining this point in some detail for it illustrates most clearly the dangers of a purely emotional response.

At the outset, in his adolescence, Tonio Kröger is bitterly conscious of his apartness; he has an exotic mother, an outlandish name and interests which diverge widely from those of his school-fellows. Like every sensitive adolescent, he suffers from his 'differentness'; he rebels against it and longs to be 'normal' and 'ordinary' like Hans Hansen and Erwin Jimmerthal (though already he feels the tiniest grain of contempt for their philistinism). Then, in the course of the *Novelle,* which spans several years of Tonio Kröger's life, his development is shown, a development along the path of growing awareness ('Erkenntnis' as he would call it) towards a reconciliation with himself and his position in the world. He gradually ceases to rebel and comes to accept what he now recognises as the inevitable. He no longer craves to be only like Hans and Inge and Erwin, for he has finally realised that he will reap nothing but frustration if he forces himself along channels totally alien to his personality. With his growing acceptance of himself and of his apartness, he loses his bitterness and gains a certain new serenity, as is revealed by the calm of his final letter to Lisaweta, which contrasts so sharply with the agitated outbursts in their long conversation earlier on. It is true that at the end Tonio Kröger still has something of his old 'Sehnsucht' and 'Liebe zum Leben' —'meine Bürgerliebe zum Menschlichen', which he admits quite candidly. But instead of allowing these feelings to split his personality, to embitter him and to undermine his allegiance to art, he now declares his intention of canalising these emotions into his creative activity. And he is convinced that it will be to the good of his art:

> Alle Wärme, alle Güte, aller Humor kommt aus ihr (i.e. aus der Liebe zum Menschlichen) und fast will mir scheinen, als sei sie jene Liebe selbst, von der geschrieben steht, dass einer mit Menschen- und Engelszungen reden könne und ohne sie doch nur ein tönendes Erz und eine klingende Schelle sei.

Through his acceptance of the inevitable Tonio Kröger is able to transform it; what had hitherto been the source of his misery now becomes his greatest asset. The antithesis between 'life' and 'art', between the 'Lebensmensch' and the 'Reflexionsmensch' has not been overcome, nor was it ever to be overcome by Thomas Mann. The artist remains isolated and apart, he will still be watching the dance, but he will no longer necessarily be unhappy in that apartness. The mood of Tonio Kröger's final letter is one of sober joy as he looks forward hopefully to the future ('Ich werde Besseres machen, Lisaweta—dies ist ein Versprechen') and reflects on the peculiar pleasure which he derives from his creative activity, the pleasure he had already felt in his youth whenever he had succeeded in formulating some complex emotion. Moreover, it is not only Tonio Kröger himself who derives joy from his art; for although Hans and Inge and Erwin remain indifferent to his writings, Magdalena Vermehren and the likes of her are certainly responsive, they being the people 'denen die Poesie eine sanfte Rache am Leben ist', a compensation and also a secret source of pleasure. As an artist, therefore, Tonio Kröger does give of himself; he gives to those who need art, and he is thereby released from his introspective narcissism. Tonio Kröger's final position is very similar to that of the prince Klaus Heinrich in ***Königliche Hoheit,*** in that both are apart from the common herd but no longer unhappy and, above all, both are giving of themselves. The difference is that whereas Klaus Heinrich's happiness is achieved by a touch of a magic wand, Tonio Kröger's is the more sober and potentially the more valuable solution to the problem of the artist for being firmly anchored in the real world.

The word 'potentially' was chosen deliberately, for ***Tonio Kröger*** does not fulfil its own promise. It is not entirely convincing, especially not the ending. The sceptic can legitimately ask whether Tonio Kröger will in fact really do as he promises in his final letter to Lisaweta since, like ***Königliche Hoheit,*** this *Novelle* too stops at the crucial point, on the brink of a happier future. The positive solution to Tonio Kröger's problems is only foreshadowed, not actually shown in operation. What we are left with is a vague promise which we have good reason to doubt, not only because the abstract hopes expressed in the last section remain theoretical, but also, indeed chiefly, because they are not adequately supported. We are asked to believe that a radical change has taken, or is taking place in Tonio Kröger—but what evidence can we find of this change other than his own contentions? The previous sections, those in which his visit to his native city and his stay in Denmark are depicted, certainly do not prepare for the change in him sufficiently. Some change and development is of course implied. He no longer wishes to convert Hans from his horse-books to *Don Carlos*:

> Hast du nun den *Don Carlos* gelesen, Hans Hansen, wie du es mir an eurer Gartenpforte versprachst? Tu's nicht! Ich verlange es nicht mehr von dir. Was geht dich der König an, der weint, weil er einsam ist? Du sollst deine hellen Augen nicht trüb und traumblöde machen vom Starren in Verse und Melancholie.

Tonio Kröger is still tortured by the old longing 'zu sein wie du!' but at the same time he is beginning to recognise and, what is more important, to accept the inevitability of his position. He cannot become like Hans, nor vice versa, he admits to himself, bitterly enough; consequently he must progress to a new 'Weltanschauung'—or so we conclude. A clearer example of Tonio Kröger's development is evident in his rejection of the attitude of Adalbert, the novelist of whom he speaks to Lisaweta. Adalbert had sought refuge from the disturbing spring air in the seasonless atmosphere of a café and when telling Lisaweta of this encounter, Tonio Kröger had added: 'vielleicht hätte ich mitgehen sollen'. Now on the contrary he rejects this flight from the living and with it the conception of a 'cold', 'dead' art with a contemptuous shrug of the shoulders:

> einmal, durch irgendeine Verknüpfung von Vorstellungen erinnerte er sich flüchtig eines fernen Bekannten, Adalberts, des Novellisten, der wusste, was er wollte, und sich ins Kaffeehaus begeben hatte, um der Frühlingsluft zu entgehen. Und er zuckte die Achseln über ihn. . . .

With what remarkable economy Thomas Mann succeeds in conveying the beginnings of a whole new 'Weltanschauung' in that one slight gesture. The leitmotif technique may be open to criticism on the grounds that it is irritatingly repetitive and mannered, but it does allow such strokes of artistic concentration. From this rejection of Adalbert's attitude it is but a short step to the demand for the interaction of art and life which Tonio Kröger will make at the end.

Nevertheless, in the sections under discussion, more emphasis is placed on the sameness of the situation and of Tonio Kröger's reactions than on the change in him. Firstly, several phrases occur which explicitly draw the parallel with the similar situation and reaction in the earlier part of the *Novelle*: 'Wie früher, ganz wie früher war es gewesen!' or 'Ja, wie damals war es' or again the frequent 'wie immer' which clearly underlines the permanence of Tonio Kröger's attitude. Moreover, many of the earlier happenings and leitmotifs are repeated in their original form: the quadrille is danced again and Tonio Kröger blushes in his hiding-place as he remembers his embarrassing mistake; counterparts to M. Knaak and Magdalena are introduced; the young couple whom Tonio Kröger takes for Hans and Inge, resemble their counterparts of the opening chapters in both dress and gesture; while in his native city Tonio Kröger sees his walnut-tree and experiences the same old painful melancholy; he walks along the very roads along which he had accompanied Hans from school, he swings the rusty gate again and all the time he feels the old longing. That he is less naively adolescent, more awake and aware, with a much deeper insight into the nature of art is revealed when he quotes for the second time the line 'Ich möchte schlafen, aber du musst tanzen', to which he now adds a far more penetrating commentary than that of which he had previously been capable. But this does not alter the fact that basically and substantially his 'Weltanschauung' appears to be the same as it had been. The repetition of situations similar to those at the beginning of the *Novelle* would have provided an excellent opportunity for showing the change in Tonio Kröger by recording the differences between his former and his present reactions; it is the simplest and most effective literary technique for revealing the development of a character. Thomas Mann, however, does no such thing; on the contrary, as the memories are recalled and the situations unfolded again, the stress is on the similarity, not the contrast to the earlier parallel happenings. Tonio Kröger's attitude and reactions are essentially the same as before, and from this it is not unfair to conclude that he himself has not in fact changed radically. Moreover, this supposition is confirmed by the concluding phrase of the *Novelle* in which the supposedly mature Tonio Kröger describes his love for the banal bourgeois in exactly the same words as had been used by the fourteen year old in the opening section:

> Sehnsucht ist darin und schwermütiger Neid und ein klein wenig Verachtung und eine ganze keusche Seligkeit.

The final section with its confident and grandiose hopes for the future comes as a great surprise. At first reading it seems acceptable enough because the reader is carried along by the high emotional charge of the story: he too feels that painful melancholy when Tonio Kröger returns to the scenes of his childhood and relives his youthful experiences, so that he is in no mood to stop, question and consider. Therein lies perhaps a great merit of the work, that it can hide its own defects, at least for a time. It is, however, only for a time since on closer consideration this ending is found to be unconvincing.

But why is it that the reader allows his rational judgement to be distorted by an emotional response to ***Tonio Kröger***? Surely the answer cannot lie solely in the poignant subject matter of the *Novelle*. There are other works which present the dilemmas of youth without, however, evoking a similar reaction. Thus, for instance, *Die Leiden des jungen Werther,* while generally read as an interesting literary and psychological document, does not issue that direct, essentially personal appeal, that invitation to self-identification with the hero in the same way as ***Tonio Kröger***. Nor does the difference lie in the mere fact that ***Tonio Kröger*** is in any sense more topical, more 'up-to-date' than *Werther*. It lies rather in literary technique. The whole narrative manner of ***Tonio Kröger*** is geared to evoke an emotional response. This is particularly true of Thomas Mann's use of the leitmotif in this *Novelle*. Whereas in his earlier works, in ***Buddenbrooks*** and ***Tristan,*** the leitmotif had been largely a vehicle of physical description, in ***Tonio Kröger*** it assumes also a moral connotation and, above all, a musical function. As Mann himself commented:

> Hier wohl zum ersten Mal wusste ich die Musik stil- und form-bildend in meine Produktion hineinwirken zu lassen. Die epische Prosakomposition war hier zum ersten Mal als ein geistiges Themengewebe, als musikalischer Beziehungskomplex verstanden.

The entire *Novelle* is built out of the counterpoint of the two antithetically conceived notions of 'life' and 'art'. In the first half of the story Mann creates the leitmotifs ('die Blonden und Blauäugigen', 'die Leute mit ungeschickten Körpern und feinen Seelen'; horse-books and *Don Carlos*) which subsequently form the fabric of the latter half of the work. It is the repetition of these lietmotifs which provokes an emotional, irrational response on the part of the reader. The repetition itself has an hypnotic effect, under the spell of which the critical faculties are easily lulled and blunted. Moreover, it creates a certain atmosphere of intimacy; on recognising the repeated leitmotifs, the reader feels not only at home within the narrative, but also in secret conspiracy with the author. And having experienced the sensation of 'déjà vu' in the recurrent leitmotifs, he extends it to Tonio Kröger's problems, which he then correlates to his own. So there arises that emotional involvement which leads in turn to a distorted judgement.

Yet even long after its weaknesses and one-sidedness have been recognised and rationally acknowledged, ***Tonio Kröger*** for better or for worse continues to hold a special place in our hearts. Perhaps it is to the good that 'le cœur a ses raisons que la raison ne connaît point'; for who would dare to judge a work of art by the rational standards of the intellect alone?

Ronald Gray (essay date 1965)

SOURCE: *"Tonio Kröger; Death in Venice,"* in *The German Tradition in Literature, 1871-1945,* Cambridge at the University Press, 1965, pp. 137-45.

[*Gray is an English educator and critic specializing in German literature. In the following excerpt, he maintains that* Tonio Kröger *dramatizes the artist's attempts to reconcile himself with society.*]

The structure of ***Tonio Kröger*** divides cleanly into three movements, the argument proceeding almost as though it were a syllogism. First, Tonio's childhood isolation and yearning for acceptance by the 'Bürger' is shown; then, as a young writer, he is seen discussing in Munich with his friend Lisaveta Ivanovna the relationships of the artist with society; lastly, he returns north to his home and makes the journey to Elsinore, where his reconciliation is realized. In the course of all this, a good deal of entertainment is provided: the teenagers' dancing-class, the orange-haired American boys who drink hot water, the Romantic vision of Tonio's former loves, his embarrassment in the public library are all vividly and sometimes amusingly drawn, in fact the whole story has a relaxed atmosphere which is certain to please. At the same time, however, it has the air of illustrating a point which can be stated in abstract terms. It attempts to be more than a series of vignettes and caricatures, and it is the total impression gained from it that must concern us here.

The incidents are meant to add towards this whole. The scene in which the Americans appear at Tonio's hotel table is more than an observed moment, it is included for a purpose:

> Dann waren nur noch drei grosse amerikanische Jünglinge mit ihrem Gouverneur oder Hauslehrer zugegen, der schweigend an seiner Brille rückte und tagüber mit ihnen Fussball spielte. Sie trugen ihr rotgelbes Haar in der Mitte gescheitelt und hatten lange, unbewegte Gesichter. 'Please, give me the wurst-things there!' sagte der eine. 'That's not wurst, that's schinken!' sagte ein anderer, und dies war alles, was sowohl sie als der Hauslehrer zur Unterhaltung beitrugen, denn sonst sassen sie still und tranken heisses Wasser.
>
> Tonio Kröger hätte sich keine andere Art von Tischgesellschaft gewünscht.
>
> Besides him the company consisted only of three tall American youths with their governor or tutor, who kept adjusting his glasses in unbroken silence. All day long he played football with his charges, who had narrow, taciturn faces and reddish-yellow hair parted in the middle. 'Please give me the *wurst*-things there', said one. 'That's not *wurst,* it's *schinken*', said the other, and this was the extent of their conversation and their tutor's, as the rest of the time they sat there dumb, drinking hot water.
>
> Tonio Kröger could have wished himself no other kind of table-companions.

Tonio is content with this comically dull society not because he finds it comic, but, more pretentiously, in connection with the 'Weltanschauung' he is beginning to formulate. At this point, we have heard him discuss his situation with Lisaveta, and have heard the strange defence he offers of a vaguely defined 'bürgerlich' life: briefly, it is this. For Tonio, humanity divides into two classes, the unreflective, healthy-minded enjoyers of life, among whom those with blue eyes and blond hair are supreme—there is a touch of racialism about his preference—and the critical, mistrusting destroyers whose perceptiveness fills them with a disgust so deep that they become either satanical ironists or helpless misfits. It is a fantastically exaggerated dichotomy: on the one hand, the Army lieutenant, a 'lord of creation' in Tonio's eyes, who demeans himself by reciting verses in public ('Ein Herr der Welt! Er hätte es doch wahrhaftig nicht nötig'); on the other hand the artist, a criminal, a eunuch, a charlatan, a fake, doomed to an onanistic excitation ('only the excitations and cold-blooded ecstasies of the artist's corrupted nervous system are artistic'). The Russian woman, Tonio's partner in the conversation, does, it is true, put in amused objections from time to time, but these are thrust aside with renewed outbursts of fanatical assertion: Tonio is allowed to win the last trick, his initial assumptions are allowed to remain unquestioned. 'Everyone knows that artists are "sensitive" and easily wounded, just as everybody knows that ordinary people with a good conscience and a well-founded confidence in themselves are not.' The 'Bürger' possesses this good conscience and well-founded self-assurance; that the artist does not is proof of his inferiority. Tonio's argument is as unreasonable as that.

There is a point at which the discussion goes deeper than these sweeping assertions, the point when Lisaveta advances a conception of literature as a 'guide to understanding, forgiveness and love' and of the writer as 'perfect man, a saint'. Tonio's reply, in which he sees such a conception as the basis of the Russian novel, is, however, as irrational and evasive as the rest of his comments. He sees the issue in a way which neither Dostoevsky nor Tolstoy could have recognized as their own. For him, the question is not whether human faults can be forgiven, or humanity loved despite awareness of its imperfection, but rather whether it is possible to feel a moral superiority in oneself: 'Not to let the sadness of the world unman you; to read, mark, learn, and take into account even the most torturing things and to be of perpetual good cheer, in the sublime consciousness of moral superiority over the horrible invention of existence—yes, thank you!' The concession in this 'yes, thank you!' (ja freilich!) indicates that this is how Tonio imagines the Russians to have felt: for him it is a matter of perceiving imperfection and yet continuing to pride himself on his distinctiveness, continuing to be in good spirits. The remainder of his reply then seeks to demonstrate that this, not love or forgiveness, is an impossibility. And, significantly enough, for such obliqueness and irrelevance in argument is typical of all Mann's work, Lisaveta fails to point out that her objection has been disregarded in a flood of words which, by the end of the paragraph, has become completely unintelligible.

The best understanding we can reach of Tonio's attitude, in which he does nevertheless achieve a sense of superiority, comes from a passage a little further on. Having asserted that renewed insights into human nature constantly destroy such peace of mind as he can attain, Tonio comes to his solution. It is, in short, that life continues despite all criticism that may be made of it: 'You see, the literary man does not understand that life may go on living, unashamed, even after it has been expressed and thereby done with. No matter how much it has been redeemed by becoming literature, it keeps right on sinning—for all action is sinning, viewed with the eyes of the Spirit'. That is to say, that although the literary writer may 'express' life and thereby have 'done with' it; although he may point out its faults and thereby (in a sense understandable only in a way peculiar to Mann's thought) 'redeem' it, life will go on 'sinning', for any action is certain to be sinful if regarded from that 'spiritual' position which the artist occupies. With this, Tonio expresses himself in a confusion difficult to unravel. The term 'Literat', or 'literary man', is obviously pejorative: writers in general, we are to understand, fail to realize how pointless their criticisms of life really are. 'Geist', on the other hand, is a term of approval: from the viewpoint of the 'Spirit', which presumably some writers adopt, the criticisms are valid. The validity, however, is limited to the sphere of 'Geist', and has no real relevance to life. Thus the criticisms of the artist can be both praiseworthy and damnable (we recall the expression 'godlike-diabolical' used in relation to Goethe) and yet have no consequences for living. 'Life' goes on unashamedly just as did the elder Johann Buddenbrook, or Hugo Weinschenk before he went to prison. It 'sins boldly', to recall Luther's phrase, but not in his sense, that it does so through faith in its redemption, but rather because the sinning is of no importance. It is on these terms that Tonio now goes on to declare that he loves life, not as Nietzsche did, but for the sake of 'the normal, respectable and lovable', 'a little friendship, devotion, familiar human happiness'. The fact that 'the respectable', presumably, is also sinful from the standpoint of the Spirit, that he cannot use these terms at all from the position he has just adopted, does not occur to Tonio, nor does his exclusion of more passionate ways of living seem to him to require any justification. The 'disgust with knowledge', and the capacity of Life to go on sinning despite criticism have nothing to do with this conclusion, which merely reasserts a few values that were, earlier, implicitly supposed to be undermined by the artist's perceptiveness.

This discussion—or rather, assertion, for Tonio's partner does nothing of any consequence to hold him to the point—is the core of the story. The incidents before and after it are presented in such a way as to seem illustrations and confirmations of Tonio's conclusion. At times they please, and may invite us to side with him: a benevolent approval is easily given to the American boys, to Ingeborg Holm and Hans Hansen, even to the tipsy Hamburg businessman who contemplates the stars in sentimental mood after a lobster supper. If that were all the story amounted to, if it were simply a somewhat sentimental, slightly comic description of people in more or less happy circumstances, there would be nothing to complain about, or it would be overdoing things to complain. But the discussion and the conclusion make the story more ambitious. Tonio seems to claim that he has overcome his 'disgust with his perceptions', yet the fact is, we see nothing in the story that might cause him disgust, still less anything that might cause him a disgust so deep that he despairs of living. For all that we see of them, these people simply are 'ordinary, decent citizens', learning to dance, enjoying themselves at a week-end hop, going about their business in a 'normal' way. We know nothing of their motives, nothing even of their circumstances for the most part; we never see below the surface or have a glimpse of their minds.

The 'artist', on the other hand, is cavalierly dismissed. Tonio prefers the simple wonder of the Hamburg businessman to the writings of some unnamed philosopher who also contemplated the stars, but we are not told the reasons for this preference. He concedes, when the hotel authorities take him for a criminal, that they may be in the right to do so, although not on the grounds they allege, and here the justification seems to be simply that they are 'men of the social order', while he is not. Towards the end, seeing the young Danish woman who reminds him of his first love Ingeborg, he demeans himself to the point of declaring that, had he achieved the works of Beethoven,

Schopenhauer and Michelangelo together, she would be entitled to laugh him out of court as she did in her childhood. This is mere self-abasement, the counterpart and justification of the self-assertion to come.

Yet it is on such a groundwork that Tonio reaches his final solution, communicated in his letter to Lisaveta:

> Ich bewundere die Stolzen und Kalten, die auf den Pfaden der grossen, der dämonischen Schönheit abenteuern und den 'Menschen' verachten—aber ich beneide sie nicht. Denn wenn irgend etwas imstande ist, aus einen Literaten einen Dichter zu machen, so ist es diese meine Liebe zum Menschlichen, Lebendigen und Gewöhnlichen. Alle Wärme, alle Güte, aller Humor kommt aus ihr, und fast will mir scheinen, als sei sie jene Liebe selbst, von der geschrieben steht, dass einer mit Menschen- und Engelszungen reden könne und ohne sie doch nur ein tönendes Erz und eine klingende Schelle sei.

> I admire those proud, cold beings who adventure upon the paths of great and daemonic beauty and despise 'mankind'; but I do not envy them. For if anything is capable of making a poet of a literary man, it is my *bourgeois* love of the human, the living and usual. It is the source of all warmth, goodness, and humour; I even almost think it is itself that love of which it stands written that one may speak with the tongues of men and of angels and yet having it not is as sounding brass and tinkling cymbals.

This contradicts what Tonio had said earlier: 'the artist is done for, the moment he becomes human and begins to feel at all', and it is not at all clear how Tonio passes from the one view to the other. So much is clear, that this is his reply to Lisaveta's objection on behalf of the Russian novelists, that he means this to be his own achievement of saintly love, embarrassing though it is to hear him claim it on his own behalf. Yet he cannot really mean the Pauline 'agapé' to which his words refer, for that was never understood to be restricted to a particular class, or to 'the ordinary' and 'the decent'. He has in mind something more akin to a Nietzschean definition of love, whereby love consists in not reflecting deeply about others, and the grounds for preferring this relationship with them are quite simply, as he himself confesses, that he has a 'fond weakness' for what is simple, loyal, pleasantly normal and decent. Indulging this weakness, if that is what it really amounts to (and what is weak about it, so far as it goes?), liking what is for the most part likable by definition, sounds a far cry from what Lisaveta described as 'the purifying and healing influence of letters'. So far as Tonio is concerned, the 'Bürger' remains stupid (one remembers how this word was used also of the first motif in Hanno's improvisation); he feels a certain contempt for him on this account, as well as a certain envy that the 'Bürger' should be 'in agreement with everybody'. But this contempt and envy are the twin effects of his desire to feel morally superior to the world he lives in. He swings from one to the other, as he swings from self-abasement to self-assertion, precisely because he misinterprets Lisaveta's words.

Tonio Kröger confusedly illustrates a confused argument. Being a story, it still remains interpretable as the intentional portrayal of such a confusion, and yet this view is unsatisfying. The reader is put to such pains, sorting out the evasions and the illogicalities, the story has so much the air of presenting a satisfactory solution (and has in fact been taken in that sense), that he can hardly feel the author has given him enough help in penetrating his meaning, supposing the author to have maintained some deeply ironical reservations. . . . What does emerge much more clearly from ***Tonio Kröger*** is Mann's concern to present the case for conformity with the Wilhelmine society of his day. The artist is suspect here because he is opposed to that society in which Army lieutenants generally were regarded as lords of creation, and in which liberal-minded citizens were expected to bow down to the 'men of the social order'—and if this could be justified in the name of established religion, so much the better. More than this, Mann gives a handle to anyone who needs his support in defence of the racial superiority of this society. Tonio, while avowing his affection for tragic and comic figures, confesses, 'But my deepest and secretest love belongs to the blond and blue-eyed, the fair and living, the happy, lovable and commonplace'. This is essentially nothing else than Thomas Buddenbrook's preference for the healthy boy of his vision, whose unreflective happiness drove the unhappy to despair. The boy's cruelty has gone, or at least is not explicitly mentioned; the triumphant egoist has become more clearly identified with the 'Bürger'; in other respects the ideal remains the same. We can, then, readily understand the comment of a contemporary newspaper critic who found in Mann 'perhaps the finest German prose-writer of today'. 'His manner', said this contributor to the *Rheinisch-Westfälische Zeitung,* 'is absolutely Germanic, or alternatively Nordic. No sign of that Gallic quality, from which our literature suffers so much harm, is to be found in him.' This was what Mann's readers expected, and this was what he gave them. 'What a victory there is here [in the story ***Tristan***] for vital living', the same critic continued; 'how matter-of-course it is, how cruelly it persuades us. Robust concreteness is Life, all else but poetic imaginings, dreams. And men of finer mettle are here but to suffer.' It was not exactly Mann's meaning; it left out of account his perfunctory pretence at a confrontation with moral issues, and his reaffirmation beyond 'disgust with knowledge'. But it was what the normal and decent, simple-hearted and loyal 'Bürger', prospering without scruples in the Empire Bismarck had founded, most wanted to hear. To such people ***Tonio Kröger*** offered no difficulties at all. To anyone who read it more subtly it still said essentially the same thing, for as always in Mann the end returns to the beginning. Even the conforming phrase with which Tonio concludes in his maturity repeats exactly the phrase used of him in his schooldays. He has done no more than reiterate his condition with awareness.

J. R. McWilliams (essay date 1966)

SOURCE: "Conflict and Compromise: Tonio Kröger's Paradox," in *Revue Des Langues Vivantes,* Vol. XXXII, No. 4, 1966, pp. 376-83.

[*In the following essay, McWilliams interprets Tonio Kröger's psychological motivations as an artist.*]

Central to the interpretation of Thomas Mann's ***Tonio Kröger*** is the concept of the "lost bourgeois", or, as Tonio describes himself: "ein Bürger, der sich in die Kunst verirrte, ein Bohemien mit Heimweh nach der guten Kinderstube, ein Künstler mit schlechtem Gewissen." Critics have taken Tonio's words at face value, disregarding to a great extent that he is primarily a character in a story rather than a spokesman of the author. Although Thomas Mann has called this story "mein Eigentliches", it is first and foremost a work of literature in which the hero speaks for himself. Tonio comes forth as a fallible human being, who, like all of us, utters words which do not always correspond with his innermost feelings. His ambiguous pronouncements and the extent to which he fails to back them up by deeds reveal a breach in his nature which demands careful investigation. Tonio uses words concerning his bourgeois origin obviously to protect himself against certain demands of life and to rationalize away his conflict with his art.

Tonio Kröger is little different from many of Thomas Mann's heroes who are burdened by a sense of guilt which inhibits them from total involvement in an active life. His sense of sin and doubt reach such proportions that he feels like a criminal indelibly branded by the mark on his brow. (A number of critics have equated this sign to that of a murderer: the mark of Cain.) As a result of his pitiless conscience he is preoccupied by death as the promising end to his guilty existence. Tonio thus turns to art, a refuge which enables him to escape the claims of life. In it he finds a substitute for emotions involving people. But because he is a genuine artist whose deepest feelings are linked to his art, he needs to take further precautions. He is acutely aware of the dangers of unrestricted feeling, and, consequently, he conceives of his art as essentially opposed to life, as a sphere from which his emotions must be banned before he can achieve aesthetic excellence. The cold breath of death should still every human sensation, for "das Gefühl, das warme herzliche Gefühl ist immer banal und unbrauchbar, und künstlerisch sind bloss die Gereiztheiten und kalten Ekstasen unseres verdorbenen, unseres artistischen Nervensystems . . . Es ist aus mit dem Künstler, sobald er Mensch wird und zu empfinden beginnt."

Therefore, the artist's work really exists outside of life. Tonio continues: "Was aber das 'Wort' betrifft, so handelt es sich da vielleicht weniger um eine Erlösung als um ein Kaltstellen und Aufs-Eis-Legen der Empfindung." Tonio leaves no doubt that art should be devoid of the human and the personal. Yet, the credo of "frigid art", of being emotionally dead for the sake of art is a contradiction in that it coincides in time with the hero's statement that he loves life. Tonio's claim of loving life lacks conviction, for one does not try to escape what one loves. He finds in the cold, controlled creativity of art a substitute for the threats and exigencies of life, for in choosing to place his energies in art rather than in life, he avoids the perils of human involvement. In longing for "die Blonden und die Blauäugigen", Tonio rationalizes a desire for active involvement in life while, at the same time, he compulsively maintains the repressive prohibition against the release of these very emotions. As a consequence he must dissemble whenever he claims he loves life. In reality it is a dubious love-affair, for his real inclinations are diametrically opposed to his avowal of passion. The element of doubt which accompanies his affirmation of this point is so strong that Tonio seems hard put to convince himself, much less his companion Lisaweta Iwanowna: "Ich bin am Ziel, Lisaweta. Hören Sie mich an. Ich liebe das Leben,—dies ist ein Geständnis. Nehmen Sie es und bewahren Sie es,—ich habe es noch keinem gemacht. Man hat gesagt, man hat es sogar geschrieben und drucken lassen, dass ich das Leben hasse oder fürchte oder verachte oder verabscheue. Ich habe dies gern gehört, es hat mir geschmeichelt; aber darum ist es nicht weniger falsch. Ich liebe das Leben . . . Sie lächeln, Lisaweta. . . . "

Lisaweta's smile does not seem very reassuring. And at the very end Tonio writes to Lisaweta: "Schelten Sie diese Liebe nicht, Lisaweta; sie ist gut und fruchtbar. Sehnsucht ist darin und schwermütiger Neid und ein klein wenig Verachtung und eine ganze keusche Seligkeit." He anticipates by "Schelten Sie" the disbelief his words will evoke in Lisaweta. "Neid" and "Verachtung", despite the manner in which they are modified, still contain overtones of resentment and aversion and are not calculated to convince Lisaweta or strengthen his case for an affirmation of life. The very fact that Tonio feels the need to endorse life categorically is perhaps the best proof that he seriously doubts its value. And since he cannot declare his love with unconditional enthusiasm or without qualification, we are forced to conclude that he is another one of Thomas Mann's ambivalent heroes who possesses more hostility against life than love for it, the consequence of which is a latent longing for death. This antipathy towards life, so typical of many of Mann's heroes, is only superficially canceled by Tonio's simple confession. In actuality the deathwish is too deeply ingrained in the artist crippled by guilt and unable to share in the spontaneous enjoyment of living, the artist whose inability to love breeds feelings of hatred. Also implied in Tonio's words is the underlying reason for his ambivalent attitude. In "keusche Seligkeit" we have a hint of the sexual, the primary source of Tonio's guilt. His ideal of chastity is inimical to a genuine love relationship, which demands physical contact and the investment of one's deepest feelings.

Tonio Kröger compares the artist to the papal *castrato*: "Ist der Künstler überhaupt ein Mann? Man frage 'das Weib' danach! Mir scheint, wir Künstler teilen alle ein wenig das Schicksal jener präparierten päpstlichen Sänger . . . Wir singen ganz rührend schön. Jedoch—." The artist finds it difficult to create in the spring of the year, when, Tonio is told by his artist friend, "es kribbelt Ihnen auf eine unanständige Weise im Blute und eine Menge von unzugehörigen Sensationen beunruhigt Sie. . . . " Spring is the time when life stirs; it represents the quickening of those urges which spell uneasiness and which threaten the necessary restrictions Tonio Kröger places on his instincts. He decries pathos and feelings, and with justice, for his are repressed so thoroughly as to become unmanageable if released.

The dire nature of these repressed impulses, criminal in a literal sense, is surmised by Tonio in his opinion of his poet-banker friend, who incidentally achieved his best creations while undergoing the penance of incarceration in a penal institution. Tonio cannot escape the suspicion that the source and essence of his friend's art has less to do with his life in prison than with the reason that brought him there.

Tonio knows that he cannot afford to give way even on a small scale to his dark desires, for it might easily lead to sexual debauchery and self-destruction as in the case of Gustav von Aschenbach in ***Der Tod in Venedig***. He aids the repression by his impeccable dress, highly reminiscent of Thomas Buddenbrook, and by his gentlemanly bearing. That he is quite capable of yielding to his urges comes out in the description of his stay in Italy: "Aber da sein Herz tot und ohne Liebe war, so geriet er in Abenteuer des Fleisches, stieg tief hinab in Wollust und heisse Schuld und litt unsäglich dabei." Indeed, his attitude toward the sexual is of a frantic and obsessive nature. The very intensity of his repressions calls forth all the more readily that which he fears. He is flung to and fro forever between two crass extremes: between icy intellect and scorching passion, and leads an exhausting life under the pressure of his conscience. Having thus compounded his guilt he once more embarks on as ascetic course, abhorring with a vengeance the Bohemian, despite his knowledge that he is to himself a Bohemian. In false protestation he states: "Ich bin doch kein Zigeuner im grünen Wagen." The emphatic tone is indispensable because basically Tonio is a gypsy and feels the need to deny it, out of fear of life as "verführerisch": desire and danger in one. To ward off this threat he finds it necessary to wear proper clothes and behave outwardly like a respectable person. Another target of his repressive outlook is the demonic sensuality of the Italian Renaissance as typified by Caesar Borgia: "Italian ist mir bis zur Verachtung gleichgültig! Das ist lange her, dass ich mir einbildete, dorthin zu gehören. Kunst, nicht wahr? Sammetblauer Himmel, heisser Wein und süsse Sinnlichkeit . . . Kurzum, ich mag das nicht. Ich verzichte. Die ganze *bellezza* macht mich nervös. Ich mag auch alle diese fürchterlich lebhaften Menschen dort unten mit dem schwarzen Tierblick nicht leiden. Diese Romanen haben kein Gewissen in den Augen."

Like Hanno Buddenbrook he too yearns for death: "Es gibt etwas, was ich Erkenntnisekel nenne, Lisaweta: der Zustand, in dem es dem Menschen genügt, eine Sache zu durchschauen, um sich bereits zum Sterben, angewidert (und durchaus nicht versöhnlich gestimmt) zu fühlen. . . . "

By using the lofty word *Erkenntnis* Tonio Kröger lends an air of respectability to all his groping, searching and resultant disillusionment. But in spite of this subterfuge he is numbed by the awareness of his guilty existence. He knows that behind his dignity and propriety is his own miserable state—"Komik und Elend." He realizes the painful truth, that he is unable to love, that he cannot compete without incurring remorse or increasing his inner travail: "Hellsehen noch durch den Tränenschleier des Gefühls hindurch, erkennen, merken, beobachten und das Beobachtete lächelnd beiseite legen müssen noch in Augenblicken, wo Hände sich umschlingen, Lippen sich finden, wo des Menschen Blick, erblindet von Empfindung, sich bricht. . . . " His paralyzing insight is brought home to him at that specific moment when two people commit themselves to passion.

Tonio's own words show that it is necessity which inspires his dictum of "frigid art." A contrived concept of deadness is employed by Tonio to shield himself from the horror of exposure. In this way he suffers chronically from a prevailing feeling of loneliness and of being cut off; but his suffering is not violent, as it might be if he confronted directly uncertainties of life. His gaze is consequently focused on the past, trying nostalgically to recover that period in which his heart once lived. The doctrine of "frigid art" takes on, therefore, a mantle of protection by becoming a rationalization that frees him from the lurking excesses of his inner drives, but it *also* becomes, paradoxically, the motivation to pursue his artistic calling.

In keeping with his artistic theory is his relation to Lisaweta Iwanowna. He is above reproach in his dealings with her, so much so that she chides him for his excessive propriety as well as for his faultless patrician *dehors*. She is a woman who is safe for him, one who will not cause him to become emotionally involved. In some respects she is a female counterpart to Tonio Kröger: artistic, reserved, proper, and completely intellectual. Her function in the story is not to live as a character but to perform dialectics, that is, to be an intellectual foil to Tonio's pedagogical opinions on art. As a spokesman Lisaweta helps tone down the stark realization that Tonio Kröger's beliefs rest on a shaky inner foundation. When she tells him that he is a burgher on the wrong path, she helps to dull his awareness about his inner conflict, for he has not strayed off the bourgeois path in becoming an artist. Actually, as an extremely successful author he gains the respect and envy of the bourgeois world. Tonio toils, indeed suffers, to produce masterpieces which give pleasure to his fellow citizens. But by defining his occupation as a guilty offense against middle-class society, he tries to shield himself from the sting of his conscience. His condition therefore goes deeper than the abstract concepts of "Bürgertum" and "frigid art" which are only a screen for an entirely inner personal conflict.

Tonio Kröger feels his art to be a consolation but at the same time a curse. In effect he is a man condemned by an inner voice to suffer in servitude: "Die Literatur ist überhaupt kein Beruf, sondern ein Fluch,—damit Sie's wissen. Wann beginnt er fühlbar zu werden, dieser Fluch? Früh, schrecklich früh. Zu einer Zeit, da man billig noch in Frieden und Eintracht mit Gott und der Welt leben sollte." And no matter how perfect the artist's clothing or dignity may be, he believes himself perpetually on exhibition. Tonio feels that he would hardly need to give a glance or speak a word before everyone knew that he was not a human being but something else: something queer, different, inimical. An episode on his trip north, when he is nearly arrested by a policeman in his home town, seems to prove Tonio's overwhelming complex of guilt. Interestingly, Tonio is, as Erich Heller points out, strangely reluctant to clear up the misunderstanding with the police. It is as if he wished to bargain for punishment in order to placate his conscience, that is, as if he derived masochistic pleasure from the incident.

Why does Tonio Kröger go north? Is it to rediscover the springs of his existence, as Frank Donald Hirschbach says? Perhaps Tonio travels north for this reason, but in another sense his trip can be attributed to an urge to revisit the scene of his original guilty experiences. Tonio is embarrassed by Lisaweta's shrewd guess that his real reason for the trip is to visit his home and not merely to spend his holidays in Denmark:

> "Wie fahren Sie, Tonio, wenn ich fragen darf? Welche Route nehmen Sie?"
>
> "Die übliche", sagte er achselzuckend und errötete deutlich.
>
> "Ja, ich berühre meine—meinen Ausgangspunkt, Lisaweta . . . "

The use of inflectional endings is revealing. Tonio substitutes "meinen" for "meine", and in doing so catches himself just in time to avoid saying "meine Heimat."

A moment later Lisaweta knowingly says: "Ich verspreche mir einen erlebnisvollen Brief von Ihrer Reise—nach Dänemark. . . . " In her hesitation there is a hint that Tonio's trip north is incidental to an inner aim which takes precedence over his conspicuously conflicting feelings. He does *not* seek out people or demonstrate affections. He acts as if he has completely forgotten his confession of love for life. Paradoxically, by his aloofness and even contempt for his fellow men, he takes no steps to lessen his "middle-class guilt." There is actually an element of displeasure in his stay in the North, as if to clinch the argument of "frigid art" that his heart must be dead. Indeed, it is surprising how little Tonio enjoys himself except for his isolated vigil at the sea: his yearning for the final absolution of death. The Danish coast fits his needs in the same way as the Travemünde beach episode did for Hanno Buddenbrook. Among his experiences in the North it is the mighty power of the sea which has the greatest effect on him and is aesthetically most impressive for him: "In ihm schwang sich ein Jauchzen auf, und ihm war, als sei es mächtig genug, um Sturm und Flut zu übertönen. Ein Sang an das Meer, begeistert von Liebe, tönte in ihm. Du meiner Jugend wilder Freund, so sind wir einmal noch vereint. . . . " Contrary to what he told Lisaweta, he does not concern himself with ordinary people, the representatives of life, but rather with the natural landscape, the magnificent sunrise, and the immensity of the expanse of the water. Only the powers of an impersonal nature succeed in stirring the deepest sources of his creative energies, despair, and passion.

Tonio Kröger is always the outsider on his journey into the world of the bourgeois; he continually observes and never takes part, unless people intrude on his self-imposed isolation. The verbs "lauschen" and "horchen", as in the early short story **"Der kleine Herr Friedemann,"** keynote his passivity. In fact, his inert behavior makes us wish to question his own severity in regard to his art. Tonio does not consciously distill his exuberant feelings for his art; he

Mann has drawn a complete portrait of the intellectual artist who, lacking a capacity for direct feeling, can not even endure the sensual in art but rather finds in his calling a cleansing effect and the destruction of passions.

—J. R. McWilliams

coldly subdues his emotions from painful necessity rather than from conscious intention.

Within the story itself Thomas Mann curiously invalidates his own thesis that feelings have no place in art. For no one who has read ***Tonio Kröger*** can fail to be moved by the emotional quality of this work. Thomas Mann has drawn a complete portrait of the intellectual artist who, lacking a capacity for direct feeling, can not even endure the sensual in art but rather finds in his calling a cleansing effect and the destruction of passions. Thus, although the intellectual Lisaweta episode with its didactic tendencies is the heart of the story, its appeal to us is meager by comparison to the actual expression of felt sorrow and the veritably passionate nostalgia in the scene of Tonio's childhood. "Damals lebte sein Herz." The warm emotional tones which characterize Tonio Kröger as a young boy and also his dream-like recollection later on of the same situations live in a real, aesthetic sense and are by no means banal and futile for artistic evaluation. In fact, it is the anguished undertone of self-pity and the sentimental yearning of the hero as well as the blurred and mysterious quality of the dream which give this novella its impact. It appeals poignantly to our own nostalgic attempts to escape into the past and to recapture the dream of youth. Tonio's ambivalence, plaintive and lyrical, touches a chord in all of us that echoes our own loneliness.

Benjamin Bennett (essay date 1976)

SOURCE: "Casting Out Nines: Structure, Parody and Myth in *Tonio Kröger*," in *Revue Des Langues Vivantes*, Vol. XLII, No. 2, 1976, pp. 126-46.

[*In the following essay, Bennett explores the ways in which* Tonio Kröger *parodies several other works of German literature concerned with the role and development of the artist in society.*]

I

One consequence of that leaning toward the autobiographical which Thomas Mann so frequently indulges, is that when he speaks of his own works he tends to concentrate more upon their spirit than upon their structure. The remarks about ***Tonio Kröger*** in the *Lebensabriss* of 1930, however, form somewhat of an exception to this rule: "Die epische Prosakomposition war hier zum erstenmal als ein geistiges Themengewebe, als musikalischer Beziehungskomplex verstanden, wie es später, in grösserem Masstabe, beim 'Zauberberg' geschah." But although Mann's emphasis in this case has led one or two critics at least to glance at the structure of ***Tonio Kröger,*** it does not seem to me that the very simplest and most obvious points have yet been made.

In particular, eight of the novella's nine chapters are arranged in pairs, Chinese-box fashion (i.e. 1-9, 2-8, 3-7, 4-6), with Chapter 5 serving as the pivot on which the whole is balanced. Or to express it differently, the story represents first a descent and then an ascent through the same four stages. Chapter 1 corresponds to Chapter 9 in that both deal generally with Tonio's ambivalent, melancholy love for the bourgeois, which love is characterized at the end of both chapters in exactly the same words. Chapters 2 and 8 both treat the dance of life, from which the poet is excluded. Chapter 3 describes Tonio's extravagant existence with its violent oscillations between the sensual and the intellectual, which is then refigured by the storm in Chapter 7, along with the symbols of tiger and polar bear. Chapters 4 and 6 both focus directly upon the problem of self-consciousness and self-definition; in Chapter 4 Tonio is "erledigt" by Lisaweta with the words "Sie sind ein Bürger," and in Chapter 6, though he had experienced a certain superior satisfaction at the hotel manager's inability "ihn hierarchisch und bürgerlich unterzubringen," still, at the end, by using his printer's proofs to legitimize himself, Tonio must admit in effect that his is a perfectly respectable bourgeois profession. Chapters 4 and 6 are the chapters where Tonio walks through a door and is confronted by a mirror to his true being, in Lisaweta's unfinished painting ("in meinem Kopf sieht es genau aus wie auf dieser Leinwand" and in the spectacle of men writing against a background of nothing but books ("Literatur") in what had been the home of his childhood. The self-complicating emptiness of self-consciousness, which had been revealed discursively in Tonio's speeches to Lisaweta, now appears in visual form:

> Das Geschoss war drei Stuben tief, deren Verbindungstüren offenstanden. Die Wände waren fast in ihrer ganzen Höhe mit gleichförmig gebundenen Büchern bedeckt, die auf dunklen Gestellen in langen Reihen standen. In jedem Zimmer sass hinter einer Art von Ladentisch ein dürftiger Mensch und schrieb.

These three men sitting one behind the other are clearly meant to remind us of the repeated image one sees when positioned between two mirrors, a phenomenon familiar to everyone who has ever sat in a barber-chair: hence the idea of Tonio's self-consciousness, as "ein dürftiger Mensch" among nothing but books, mirroring itself in endless hopelessness. And Chapter 5, finally, the central chapter, contains Tonio's decision to return to his "Ausgangspunkt," which he then in a sense does, by passing in reverse order through the stages represented by Chapters 1-4.

Not only is this structure clear in itself, but it also embodies an allusion to the completed first part of Novalis' *Heinrich von Ofterdingen,* which treats exactly the same theme, the development of a young poet, and is constructed on exactly the same pattern. Chapters 1 and 9 of *Ofterdingen* present the vision of universal salvation, first in the form of Heinrich's interrupted dream, then in the full development of Klingsohr's "Märchen." Chapters 2 and 8 both center on discussions of the nature of poetry, first by way of the merchants' vague admiration for this art, then in the form of Klingsohr's clear, craftsmanlike advice. Chapter 3 is the story of the young man who wins his princess by singing, which prefigures the betrothal of Heinrich and Mathilde in Chapter 7. Chapters 4 and 6 are the two festivities, first that of the Crusaders, at which Heinrich feels somewhat out of place, then his grandfather's in which he can participate wholeheartedly, and Zulima of course corresponds to Mathilde. And Chapter 5 is the descent into the earth, symbolically into the self, the beginning of Heinrich's more explicit self-consciousness and awareness of his fate (which is depicted in the Provençal book), thus the nadir and turning-point at which a more fully realized re-enactment of the novel's first four stages becomes possible.

But if ***Tonio Kröger*** and *Heinrich von Ofterdingen* are similar in structure and theme, the meaning of the two works is entirely different. Whereas self-consciousness is the very principle of Heinrich's development, equivalent in its increase to increasing self-realization—the better Heinrich *knows* himself, the more fully he *is* himself—self-consciousness for Tonio is a snare in which he becomes entangled (Chapters 1-4) and from which he must then extricate himself by a kind of half-deliberate regression (Chapters 6-9). Far from promoting self-development, self-consciousness in ***Tonio Kröger,*** especially as Tonio practices it in Chapter 4, is a mere aimless whirling upon itself of the intellect when it can seize no external object, and is thus symbolized later by the racing of the ship's propeller when it comes out of the water, which phenomenon, significantly, causes Tonio "arge Übelkeit." This implied criticism of Novalis' idea of the artist's development is made still clearer by a specific parallel between the pivotal Chapters 5: like Heinrich, who here reads his actual destiny in a book, though he does not yet understand it, Tonio in this chapter *imagines* himself able to read his destiny in *Hamlet,* intends to enact that destiny on location in Elsinore—and turns out to be completely mistaken, for he is not a tragic figure after all. The references to *Hamlet,* incidentally, also remind us of Goethe's *Meister,* and this, together with the parody of Novalis, perhaps supplies a key to Tonio's apology in Chapter 1: "ich möchte, weiss Gott, lieber Heinrich oder Wilhelm heissen." But Tonio is neither Wilhelm Meister, who renounces art, nor Heinrich von Ofterdingen, for whom artistic development is an unimpeded progress of self-discovery.

In its details the parody of Novalis is really quite bitter. There is a fairly clear relation in the Chapters 6 between Heinrich's arrival in Augsburg, where he is welcomed into a happy family, and Tonio's in Lübeck, where he is suspected of being a swindler; but the more specific object of parody here is the following passage from the introduction to Chapter 6 of *Ofterdingen*:

> Es sind die Dichter, diese seltenen Zugmenschen, die zuweilen durch unsere Wohnsitze wan-

> deln, und überall den alten ehrwürdigen Dienst der Menschheit und ihrer ersten Götter, der Gestirne, des Frühlings, der Liebe, des Glücks, der Fruchtbarkeit, der Gesundheit, und des Frohsinns erneuern; sie, die schon hier im Besitz der himmlischen Ruhe sind, und von keinen törichten Begierden umhergetrieben, nur den Duft der irdischen Früchte einatmen, ohne sie zu verzehren und dann unwiderruflich an die Unterwelt gekettet zu sein. Freie Gäste sind sie, deren goldener Fuss nur leise auftritt, und deren Gegenwart in allen unwillkürlich die Flügel ausbreitet.

Tonio Kröger—especially in Chapter 6 where Tonio the wanderer delicately sniffs the atmosphere of Lübeck—includes a parody of practically every word here, but most particularly of the idea that our "inner wings" open instinctively in the poet's presence, which is burlesqued in the more or less aggressive suspiciousness of the librarian, the hotel manager and the policeman. There may even be a more specific reference to Novalis, suggested via the idea of "Nasenflügel," when we are told that the policeman, upon hearing Tonio's name, "reckte sich auf und öffnete plötzlich seine Nasenlöcher, so weit er konnte." This, in reality, is the way our "wings" open when the poet introduces himself to us.

And in Chapter 7 the parody becomes, if anything, even bitterer, in that Heinrich, who has himself had poetic thoughts about "Der Chor der Gestirne" at the end of Chapter 6, is now made to take the rôle of the freshly scrubbed merchant from Hamburg. In particular, Klingsohr's advice to an overenthusiastic Heinrich in Chapter 7—"Begeisterung ohne Verstand ist unnütz und gefährlich, und der Dichter wird wenig Wunder tun können, wenn er selbst über Wunder erstaunt"—reflects exactly that idea of poetry upon which Tonio bases his conclusion about the young Hamburger: "Au . . . nein, der hat keine Literatur im Leibe!" It is true that some of Klingsohr's advice can be applied to Tonio himself: for example, "Glaubt nicht . . . dass ich das letztere ['jenes überfliessende Gefühl einer unbegreiflichen, überschwenglichen Herrlichkeit'] tadle; aber es muss von selbst kommen, und nicht gesucht werden. Seine sparsame Erscheinung ist wohltätig; öfterer wird sie ermüdend und schwächend." But in Chapter 7 of ***Tonio Kröger,*** Tonio, who in Lübeck had deliberately sought a rebirth of feeling, has already learned this lesson and is now about to experience an *unsought* enthusiasm ("es muss von selbst kommen") in the storm, whereas the position of the emotion-hunting amateur, Henrich's position in Chapter 7 of *Ofterdingen,* is occupied by the ridiculous young businessman.

II

We have not really accomplished anything, however, until we go further into the question of what this element of parody implies about the meaning of ***Tonio Kröger,*** and we can begin by noting that there is also a specific parallel between the Chapters 1 in Mann and Novalis. Heinrich's father, we recall, during his stay in Rome, had actually had a chance to achieve the blue flower but had failed to commit himself to that quest, and this idea is repeated in the figure of Tonio's father, a man "mit sinnenden blauen Augen" who always wears "eine Feldblume" and who has imported his wife from even further south. The point of this parallel is to suggest, as is also suggested by Hans's flash of interest in *Don Carlos,* by the figure of the lieutenant reading his poetry, and by the Romantic merchant on shipboard, that even in normal bourgeois life there is an inherent poetic tendency, a desire for salvation through the intellect. Tonio and Heinrich are both the realization of a repressed or confused tendency in their own fathers. The poet merely realizes a power which is latent in all men, or as Klingsohr says, "Es ist recht übel . . . dass die Poesie einen besondern Namen hat, und die Dichter eine besondere Zunft ausmachen. Es ist gar nichts Besonderes. Es ist die eigentümliche Handlungsweise des menschlichen Geistes. Dichtet und trachtet nicht jeder Mensch in jeder Minute?"

In ***Tonio Kröger,*** in fact, despite Tonio's attempt to understand art as a kind of crime against bourgeois order, there is a suggestion of direct *kinship* between the blond, blue-eyed ones and precisely those artists who are most fully committed to their art. "Iwanowna" is of course the patronymic derived from the Russian equivalent of "Johann" or "Hans," so that it means essentially "Hansen," and Lisaweta is thus a kind of sister to Tonio's childhood friend; and when we hear of the "aggressive style" in which Tonio's colleague Adalbert exclaims "Gott verdamme den Frühling!" we are inclined to recall Hans's "verwöhnte und selbstbewusste Art, seine Sympathien und Abneigungen kundzugeben." These touches, together with Tonio's use of his art as bourgeois self-legitimization in Lübeck, make clear that the basis for the parody of Novalis is a recognition that art, as practiced by those whom Tonio calls "ihr Anbeter der Schönheit," is nothing but bourgeois existence all over again. Tonio may be "ein verirrter Bürger," but Lisaweta, Adalbert and Heinrich von Ofterdingen are "Bürger" without even being "verirrt." They have all found a niche in society with which they are satisfied. The atmosphere in Lisaweta's studio may contain that "Konflikt und Gegensatz" which torments Tonio, but Lisaweta herself is not at all bothered by it; she divides her life, like her room, into two distinct compartments, and does not let one interfere with the other. Her art is not a problem to her, and it is precisely the feeling of art as a *problem* that makes Tonio consider himself unique in his "Künstlertum . . . so tief, so von Anbeginn und Schicksals wegen, dass keine Sehnsucht ihm süsser und empfindenswerter erscheint als die nach den Wonnen der Gewöhnlichkeit."

The idea of a close kinship between the fully committed artist and the simple burgher is developed by yet another parody woven into the novella's structure, the parody of yet another well-known nine-part work in German literature, Goethe's *Hermann und Dorothea.* This poem as a whole of course bears less relation to ***Tonio Kröger*** than *Ofterdingen* does, but the section-by-section parallels are obvious enough to make the parody unmistakeable. It is not entirely clear why Canto II of *Hermann und Dorothea* should be entitled "Terpsichore," but it is perfectly clear that this muse presides over Chapter 2 of ***Tonio Kröger,*** the dance-chapter, and Tonio's *faux pas* in dancing *mouli-*

net des dames corresponds to Hermann's at the neighbor's house when he asks about "Pamina" and "Tamino." Then Tonio's going forth into the world in Chapter 3 recalls the father's wish in Goethe, "es solle sich Hermann auf Reisen / Bald begeben," and when we hear that "Die alte Familie der Kröger war nach und nach in einen Zustand des Abbröckelns und der Zersetzung geraten," we think of the whole of the father's long speech about degenerate modern youth and Hermann in particular. But the most striking parody is Tonio's conversation with Lisaweta in Chapter 4, which corresponds to Hermann's conversation with his mother in Canto IV; both conversations arrive at exactly the same conclusion: that the young man in question has been Romanticizing his situation—Tonio in his self-image as doomed artist, Hermann in his as a soldier—and really ought to be content as "ein Bürger." And then, finally, at the end of Chapter 8, Tonio's assistance to the fallen Danish girl is a comic re-enactment of Hermann's catching of Dorothea at the end of Canto VIII, when she stumbles.

The pattern of parody in ***Tonio Kröger,*** then, is the following: Chapter 1, *Ofterdingen*; Chapters 2, 3, 4, *Hermann*; Chapters 5, 6, 7, *Ofterdingen*; Chapter 8, *Hermann*. The parody of Novalis is thus interwoven with that of Goethe, and the suggestion, clearly, is that the development of the quintessential artist, leading toward a metaphysical marriage by which the whole world is redeemed, is not basically different from the development of the quintessential bourgeois, which culminates in a thoroughly mundane marriage. In both cases the central character finds "the right way" to his destiny, and from the perspective of ***Tonio Kröger*** this is a bit of an oversimplification, "weil es für etliche einen richtigen Weg überhaupt nicht gibt." The parodies thus elaborate the idea of Tonio's position "zwischen zwei Welten," but with the added suggestion that these "two worlds" are not really different from one another.

III

There is, however, more to be said about this suggestion. We have already pointed out that despite Tonio's references to the blue-eyed ones "die den Geist nicht nötig haben," a number of incidents in the story clearly reflect the existence of an ingrained intellectual tendency or desire in precisely these people. The main incidents we have in mind, moreover, are three in number and serve by their disposition to mark off yet another manifestation of the story's structure, a division into three phases of three chapters each. The first phase is introduced in Chapter 1 by Hans's interest in Tonio and in *Don Carlos*; the second in Chapter 4 by the story of the lieutenant with his poetry; and the third in Chapter 7 by the star-struck Hamburger. There is, moreover, a clear progression from phase to phase. At first, in the case of Hans, Tonio encourages this inchoate bourgeois intellectuality, hoping thereby to establish a bond between himself and society at large. In the second phase, Tonio specifically rejects the idea of such encouragement ("man sollte nicht Leute, die viel lieber in Pferdebüchern mit Momentaufnahmen lesen, zur Poesie verführen wollen!" and had been mortally embarrassed at the lieutenant's making a spectacle of himself, for it now somehow gratifies him to think of art as a kind of shameful offense against life. But by the time Tonio encounters the young man on shipboard, he has clearly passed beyond this stage, since he is not embarrassed at all; he simply discounts the notion that such forced cosmological humility has anything to do with literature ("nein, der hat keine Literatur im Leibe!") and continues listening to the man's chatter "mit einem heimlichen und freundschaftlichen Gefühl."

By chapter 7, therefore, Tonio has achieved a new equilibrium; he no longer reacts emotionally, as he had earlier, to signs of an intellectual stirring in the bourgeois. And what this at least ought to mean, as we have already suggested in connection with the structural similarity and philosophical contrast to *Ofterdingen,* is that Tonio is now somehow managing to extricate himself from the confusions of self-consciousness. We shall begin to understand more fully how this works if we note that each of at least the first two phases in the novella (Chapters 1-3 and 4-6) focuses upon a specific *question*.

The question Tonio finds himself asking in Chapter 1 is the fundamental question of self-consciousness, "What am I?"—"Was aber ist mit mir, und wie wird dies alles ablaufen?" In reality, however, even at this early point, Tonio has already begun writing and so already knows, or at least suspects, that his destiny has to do with "[die] Macht des Geistes und Wortes, die lächelnd über dem unbewussten und stummen Leben thront." The attempt to draw Hans Hansen over to his side is merely an attempt to avoid, or at least postpone the uncomfortable consequences of this knowledge by establishing a direct link with human normality; and even as a child Tonio senses that this attempt is self-contradictory and futile, in the same way that later he knows there is no chance of Inge Holm's coming to him in the corridor. By Chapter 3, therefore, he at last seems to be facing the facts squarely, "Denn er war gross und klug geworden, hatte begriffen, was für eine Bewandtnis es mit ihm hatte."

But in the final analysis, even Tonio's commitment to literature is only another way of *avoiding* the question "What am I?"

> Er arbeitete nicht wie jemand, der arbeitet, um zu leben, sondern wie einer, der nichts will als arbeiten, weil er sich als lebendigen Menschen für nichts achtet, nur als Schaffender in Betracht zu kommen wünscht und im übrigen grau und unauffällig umhergeht, wie ein abgeschminkter Schauspieler, der nichts ist, solange er nichts darzustellen hat.

Tonio thus attempts to resolve the question of the self by the simple expedient of *eliminating* the self, which cannot possibly work. The idea "dass man gestorben sein muss, um ganz ein Schaffender zu sein" contains an obvious logical contradiction, and Chapter 4, accordingly, opens with the question "Störe ich?" The answer to this question is of course yes; Tonio's "ich" is still there, as a "disturbing" element in his calculations.

In Chapter 4, then, at the beginning of the story's second phase, Tonio formulates his still unanswered question more generally, "Aber *was ist* der Künstler?" And like the question in Chapter 1, this question is basically rhetorical, for Tonio thinks he already knows the answer. The artist, as opposed to the conventional, instinctive bourgeois, is that man who has committed himself wholly to the practice of intellectual consciousness and thus, by consequence, to a kind of self-destruction.

> Ist Ihnen das Herz zu voll, fühlen Sie sich von einem süssen oder erhabenen Erlebnis allzusehr ergriffen: nichts einfacher! Sie gehen zum Literaten, und alles wird in kürzester Frist geregelt sein. Er wird Ihnen Ihre Angelegenheit analysieren und formulieren, bei Namen nennen, aussprechen und zum Reden bringen, wird Ihnen das Ganze für alle Zeit erledigen und gleichgültig machen . . . Was ausgesprochen ist, so lautet sein Glaubensbekenntnis, ist erledigt. Ist die ganze Welt ausgesprochen, so ist sie erledigt, erlöst, abgetan . . .

Explicit, articulable consciousness is the death of experience, and if we cease to experience, do we not cease to exist? Can the artist, therefore, even be said to exist in the first place? "Ist der Künstler überhaupt ein Mann? Man frage 'das Weib' danach! Mir scheint, wir Künstler teilen alle ein wenig das Schicksal jener präparierten päpstlichen Sänger." Not only is the artist not "ein Mann," he is not even "ein Mensch": "Sie [you, the artist] werden kaum die Augen aufzuschlagen und ein Wort zu sprechen brauchen, und jedermann wird wissen, dass Sie kein Mensch sind, sondern irgend etwas Fremdes, Befremdendes, anderes."

This at least is what Tonio thinks, but it still does not answer his question because he himself after all still *does* exist. His own feeling refutes his definition of the artist as a mere intellectual, and it is for this reason that he decides to return to his native city, in the hope of penetrating beyond the domain of self-consciousness and rediscovering the true organic roots of his personal destiny. As we have already seen, however, he is unsuccessful in this. His search for his own origin is only a potentiation of self-consciousness, it is a self-consciousness now critically applied to self-consciousness itself, and this is revealed to Tonio when, on opening the door of his own house, he is confronted by that image of mirror-mirroring-mirror which we have discussed above. What Tonio learns here is that self-consciousness does in truth lead toward nonexistence, that when developed to a sufficient degree it becomes not art but rather a useless, hopeless and above all unproductive vortex of self-preoccupation comparable to the racing of a ship's propeller when it leaves the water. This lesson, combined with the enforced recognition (when he legitimizes himself to the policeman) that his own art is not a daredevil teetering on the brink of nonentity so much as a perfectly acceptable bourgeois pursuit, implies for Tonio the very simple but very important conclusion that *there is no such thing as the quintessential artist*. There is no such thing as an artist *totally* committed to the conscious analysis and articulation of all reality, for such a man would be, even in relation to himself, *nothing* but a mirror, which is impossible, and even if he managed somehow to exist, he would certainly not produce.

As a corollary to this proposition, moreover, it follows that Tonio's distinction between those who live and those who sacrifice life to art is not in reality nearly so strict as he had wanted it to be, and his recognition of this now makes him receptive to a truth which is expressed throughout the story via the thematic appearance of intellectual tendencies in otherwise normal people: the truth that *there is no such thing as the quintessential bourgeois*. Hence Tonio's reaction, or lack of it, to the sentiments of the young man on deck. Earlier, he had felt the lieutenant's poetry as a kind of personal attack and had concluded his relation of the incident by saying, with perfect illogic but with a serious if strained tragic pride, "Da stand er und büsste in grosser Verlegenheit den Irrtum, dass man ein Blättchen pflücken dürfe, ein einziges, vom Lorbeerbaume der Kunst, ohne mit seinem Leben dafür zu zahlen." But now, confronted with the melancholy speculations of his fellow-passenger, Tonio simply thinks, "nein, der hat keine Literatur im Leibe," and expresses thereby the recognition that what he is being regaled with is a perfectly normal manifestation of bourgeois existence, having no special relation to his own profession or self-esteem. The pure bliss of a bourgeois existence wholly contained within its narrow horizons simply never happens in reality, any more than does the pure, horizonless universality of an artistic existence. Hence the two interwoven parodies we have spoken of, for the works parodied represent things and states that do not really exist. In reality there is not a world of art opposed to a world of life. There is only one world, which includes all men with their various degrees and modes of self-consciousness, the world where Hans and Lisaweta are brother and sister, and although this is a world in which Tonio can feel rather more at ease than he had before, it is also a world in which the question of the nature and the rôle and the specific necessity of art seems further than ever from being answered.

IV

But this is not the only problem. For if Tonio, by the end of Chapter 6, has achieved emotional equilibrium with respect to his profession, then we must also ask why he goes through with his trip to Denmark anyway, and we can begin by discussing the irony in a passage we have already mentioned:

> Die Bürger sind dumm; ihr Anbeter der Schönheit aber, die ihr mich phlegmatisch und ohne Sehnsucht heisst, solltet bedenken, dass es ein Künstlertum gibt, so tief, so von Anbeginn und Schicksals wegen, dass keine Sehnsucht ihm süsser und empfindenswerter erscheint als die nach den Wonnen der Gewöhnlichkeit.

What kind of a "Sehnsucht" is it that one can judge according to how "empfindenswert" it is? Clearly there is an intellectual distance here between the writer and the experience he is describing; what this passage actually expresses is only a yearning *for* the yearning it speaks of, and this is precisely as it must be, for Tonio now knows perfectly well that the "ecstasies of being ordinary" simply do not exist in reality.

Tonio is thus in the situation of yearning for something he

knows does not exist, which is not essentially different from his situation in Chapter 1—where he had made no attempt "zu werden wie Hans Hansen"—except that now he appears to have maneuvered himself into it *deliberately*. This is the reason for the trip to Denmark. The advantage of Denmark is that its people are similar to those North Germans Tonio dreams of, except that they speak a different language, a language Tonio does not understand. In Chapter 2 the words "seine Sprache war nicht ihre Sprache" describe a situation in which Tonio involuntarily *finds* himself; but as applied more literally to Chapter 8 ("Denn ihre Sprache war nicht seine Sprache"), these words describe a situation Tonio deliberately *creates* for himself. The language barrier denies Tonio all intellectual contact with the Danes, thus all direct perception of that intellectual tendency which, even in the bourgeois, keeps perfect ordinariness from ever actually happening. In Denmark, therefore, Tonio can at least experience the *illusion* that those "ecstasies of being ordinary" do exist after all.

But what possible importance can Tonio attach to such a deliberate and necessarily fleeting self-delusion? We can approach this question by recognizing first that the novella embodies yet one further section-by-section parody of a nine-part work from earlier German literature, Hölderlin's elegy "Brod und Wein." In section 1 of this poem we hear:

> Aber das Saitenspiel tönt fern aus Gärten;
> vieleicht, dass
> Dort ein Liebendes spielt oder ein einsamer
> Mann
> Ferner Freunde gedenkt und der Jugendzeit;
> und die Brunnen
> Immerquillend und frisch rauschen an duftendem Beet.

This awakens all sorts of associations with ***Tonio Kröger,*** but especially with Chapter 1 where we are told of those times "wenn er [Tonio] mit seiner Geige (denn er spielte die Geige) in seinem Zimmer umherging und die Töne, so weich, wie er sie nur hervorzubringen vermochte, in das Plätschern des Springstrahls hinein erklingen liess, der drunten im Garten unter den Zweigen des alten Walnussbaumes tänzelnd emporstieg."

Then, in Chapter 2, we hear:

> Aber obgleich er [Tonio] genau wusste, dass die Liebe ihm viel Schmerz, Drangsal und Demütigung bringen müsse, dass sie überdies den Frieden zerstöre und das Herz mit Melodien überfülle, ohne dass man Ruhe fand, eine Sache rund zu formen und in Gelassenheit etwas Ganzes daraus zu schmieden, so nahm er sie doch mit Freuden auf, überliess sich ihr ganz und pflegte sie mit den Kräften seines Gemütes, denn er wusste, dass sie reich und lebendig mache, und er sehnte sich, reich und lebendig zu sein, statt in Gelassenheit etwas Ganzes zu schmieden. . . .

And this recalls the deliberate affirmation, in "Brod und Wein," section 2, of an irrational nocturnal existence as opposed to "der besonnene Tag." Indeed, the words "reich und lebendig" suggest a more specific echo of the idea that "[die Nacht] muss uns auch . . . vollern Pokal und kühneres Leben [gönnen]." And Tonio's departure southward in Chapter 3 then clearly corresponds to the departure for Greece in section 3 of the elegy: "Göttliches Feuer auch treibet, bei Tag und bei Nacht, / Aufzubrechen."

Chapters 4, 5 and 6 do not correspond in quite the same detail to Hölderlin, but their general movement is similar. In section 4 of "Brod und Wein" the initial mood of despair at the idea of a still physically existing Greece now emptied of its essential spirit ("wo die Gefässe, / Wo mit Nectar gefüllt, Göttern zu Lust der Gesang?") is transformed, by the mere shift from interrogative to declarative, into an ecstatic if still preterite vision of that spirit's greatness, in much the same way that the inherent nihilism in Tonio's intellectual attack on the intellect is transformed into its opposite ("Jedoch ich bin kein Nihilist") by the idea of a love for life; and Lisaweta's "answer," that Tonio is not really the solitary tragic hero he imagines himself but rather still in essence belongs to communal bourgeois existence, is a kind of reminder that "es ertrug keiner das Leben allein." Then, in Chapter 5, Tonio comes to the full recognition that "fast ward ihm Unheiliges heilig," that his pursuit of artistic existence in the form of extravagant intellectual adventures and complexities has been misguided, and it is for this reason that he now decides to face his destiny directly, as it were "zu schaun die Offenbaren," to bring to light the true source and nature of his artistic "Gabe" by returning to the city of his origin; it can even be said of him that "nun aber nennt er sein Liebstes," in that he speaks to Lisaweta of the name "'Ingeborg,' ein Harfenschlag makellossester Poesie." And now, accordingly, Tonio goes home, to a seaport, one of those "Städte . . . sie gehn über Gestaden empor," and just as these words in the elegy are the signal for a return to the despairing interrogatives of section 4, so Tonio, in the public library at Lübeck, discovers that he has not yet really progressed beyond the essentially nihilistic self-consciousness of his conversation with Lisaweta earlier. Or we think more specifically of the lines:

> Warum zeichnet, wie sonst, die Stirne des Mannes ein Gott nicht,
> Drükt den Stempel, wie sonst, nicht dem Getroffenen auf?

Tonio, we recall, has returned to Lübeck in order to re-experience the original meaning of "das Mal an seiner Stirn," and discovers instead that he does not really bear the mark of Cain after all, but that his art in fact serves as a bourgeois passport.

The closest parallels with Hölderlin, however, are those between the respective seventh parts. "Aber wenn wir da hinaufsehen," says the Hamburger, "so müssen wir doch erkennen und versdehen, dass wir im Grunde Gewürm sind, elendes Gewürm und nichts weiter," which is a burlesque exaggeration of the idea that the gods have departed, leaving us alone in immensity: "Zwar leben die Götter, / Aber über dem Haupt droben in anderer Welt . . . und scheinens wenig zu achten, / Ob wir leben." Then, the idea that "Nur zu Zeiten erträgt göttliche Fülle der Mensch," and that we who desire the gods' return must wait "Biss dass Helden genug in der ehernen Wiege gewachsen," is symbolized in Tonio's being able, unlike the young merchant, not only to endure but to rejoice in that divine elemental fury which now re-awakens and fills his heart; and the idea of a "brazen cradle" then corresponds to the rocking metal steamer on board which this rebirth takes place. Indeed, before the storm, when Tonio and that interlocutor with whom he has so little in common had decided to retire, Tonio had fulfilled almost literally the lines, "Indessen dünket mir öfters / Besser zu schlafen, wie so ohne Genossen zu seyn." And his Dionysian rebirth now reveals that Tonio, himself a "Dichter in dürftiger Zeit" and on a nocturnal voyage, is also comparable, like Hölderlin's poet, to "des Weingotts heilige Priester, / Welche von Lande zu Land zogen in heiliger Nacht."

The parody of "Brod und Wein," however, unlike the other two we have talked about, involves a wholly positive attitude toward its object. Both the elegy and the novella deal with the problem of the poet's isolation in an uncongenial world, the impossibility nowadays of "Freude, mit Geist," and in both works, though neither claims to solve this problem, the poet at least makes peace with his situation and achieves a viable idea of his immediate task. In fact, Hölderlin's consolation for the disorder of our world, that a messenger of the highest god still comes "unter die Schatten herab," is to an extent echoed in Tonio's formulation, "ich sehe in eih Gewimmel von Schatten menschlicher Gestalten, die mir winken, dass ich sie banne und erlöse." And the last line of the elegy, "Selbst der neidische, selbst Cerberus trinket und schläft," suggests the possibility that those shades, with their guard asleep, may now somehow be released from their shadowy realm, which is apparently also something like what Tonio has in mind.

But the most important feature, for our purposes, of this affirmative parody of Hölderlin, is what it suggests about Chapter 8 of ***Tonio Kröger***. Section 8 of the elegy deals with the gods' departure and their leaving behind of bread and wine as pledges of an eventual return:

> Nemlich, als vor einiger Zeit, uns dünket sie lange,
> Aufwärts stiegen sie all, welche das Leben beglükt,
>
> . . . . .
>
> Liess zum Zeichen, dass einst er da gewesen und wieder
> Käme, der himmlische Chor einige Gaaben zurük,
> Derer menschlich, wie sonst, wir uns zu freuen vermöchten.

And at least tentatively, we are fairly safe in concluding that Tonio, on his trip to Denmark, is seeking just such a sign, a pledge that will restore his confidence in "das Leben," at least as a meaningful ideal if not a real possibility. On the one hand, Tonio has been forced to recognize that "das Leben" in its pure form simply does not occur in reality, but on the other hand, the specific existence of art, or of the analytic, anti-vital intellect, logically implies at least the ideal existence of something that is its opposite—"Fixativ und Frühlingsarom, nicht wahr? Kunst und—ja, was ist das andere?" By going to Denmark, where the language barrier denies him any perception of intellect in the people he encounters, Tonio is deliberately staging for himself a situation in which he will be able to see, or at least *envision* "das Leben" in an entirely unsullied form, for without such a vision his "Kunst" has no validity either.

Or to return to another of the approaches we have initiated above: if the thematic question of the story's first phase (Chapters 1-3) is Tonio's "What am I?" and if the second phase (Chapters 4-6) is characterized by the question "What is the artist?" then it ought to be clear by now that the corresponding question in the third phase (Chapters 7-9) is, "What is man?" That the explicit statement of this question in Chapter 7 is made not by Tonio but rather by the young Hamburger, in his absurd comparison of man's meager achievements with the hugeness of the stars, does not reduce the importance of the question in the story's structure. The question "What am I?" arises from Tonio's wonder at his own unusually intense self-consciousness; the question "What is the artist?" arises from Tonio's idea of art as a unique excess of intellect; and accordingly, when at the beginning of the story's third phase Tonio has recognized that *all* men (not only himself and not only the artist) partake of intellect in essentially the same way, if in different degrees, then by analogy with the first two phases the question that *must* arise is the question, "What is man?"

And an answer to this question is suggested at the very end of the story:

> Ich schaue in eine ungeborene und schemenhafte Welt hinein, die geordnet und gebildet sein will, ich sehe in ein Gewimmel von Schatten menschlicher Gestalten, die mir winken, dass ich sie banne und erlöse: tragische und lächerliche und solche, die beides zugleich sind,—und diesen bin ich sehr zugetan.

Or in Hölderlin's words, "wir sind herzlos, Schatten." Intellect, which tends to destroy the emotional life of the heart, is an ineradicable quality not only of the artist but of all men, whence it follows that the whole of the human world has the tendency to become a realm of heartless wraiths. As Tonio himself has said earlier, "Das Reich der Kunst nimmt zu, und das der Gesundheit und Unschuld nimmt ab auf Erden." The difference is that Tonio's strict distinction between art and life has now been replaced by a less drastic distinction between "tragische und lächerliche [Gestalten]," between people who are tormented by the intellect and people who are made ridiculous by it, and this new form of the distinction reflects the recognition that it is simply impossible for a man to live *unaffected* by the intellect.

Thus, in view of what we have said above about the nihilistic tendency of self-consciousness, it now follows that not only Tonio himself (as in the first phase, where he concludes by attempting to eliminate his own person) and not only the artist (as in the second phase, where Tonio's artistic self-image is in the end revealed as nothing but mirror mirroring mirror) but *man in general* has an ingrained bent toward non-existence. It is because of his understanding of this truth that Tonio goes through with his trip to Denmark, for this truth in itself—the truth that human nature gravitates toward the void—is useless and potentially deadly; it leads nowhere but to despair ("so liesse sich ein Mensch denken, der . . . durch psychologische Hellsicht ganz einfach aufgerieben und zugrunde gerichtet würde," since thinking or reasoning about it merely plays into the hands of intellect. Therefore Tonio must create for himself, as Hölderlin does in "Brod und Wein," a *myth* of divinely fulfilled humanity and of the possibility of an eventual return of such humanity; therefore Tonio goes to Denmark and waits for the sign, the pledge which eventually appears in his vision of Hans and Inge reincarnate. It does not matter if this vision is merely an illusion created by Tonio's linguistic ignorance; the only question that matters, as also for Nietzsche, is whether the vision is *useful for life,* life as opposed to deadly despair; perhaps, as Nietzsche suggests, any idea that is useful for life *must* be an illusion. But it does not matter.

Of course, as we have already indicated in connection with his use of the word "empfindenswert," Tonio has an ironic perspective upon his submission to an illusion; he *knows* it is an illusion. But even this does not matter. He still does submit to the illusion, and the love he speaks of is strictly genuine: "Aber meine tiefste und verstohlenste Liebe gehört den Blonden und Blauäugigen, den hellen Lebendigen, den Glücklichen, Liebenswürdigen und Gewöhnlichen." This love is genuine for the simple reason that there is absolutely no alternative to it. The only conceivable alternative, for someone who understands what Tonio understands, would be sheer non-existence, utterly empty despair, and this is not really an alternative one could choose.

V

The real subject matter of ***Tonio Kröger,*** then, is the artist's creation of a *private myth* as protection against the despair which must follow from exposure to sheer truth, and this leaves us only with the question of why: of what use is such a myth to the artist? What does Tonio mean when he promises Lisaweta, "Ich werde Besseres machen"? And how does he propose to release those human "shades" he speaks of from their shadowiness? Given the recognition that all human existence is an intellectual teetering on the brink of nonentity, the artist's job is clearly to counteract this, somehow to endow mankind with more shape and substance; or as Mann says specifically in the ***Betrachtungen eines Unpolitischen,*** the "Dichter" is by nature a "Menschenbildner," as opposed to the "Literat" who merely passes judgment. But again, how shall Tonio Kröger's "Bürgerliebe zum Menschlichen, Lebendigen und Gewöhnlichen" transform *him* from a "Literat" into a "Dichter"?

I think there is only one possible answer to this, and that it is an obvious one. The poet's job, first of all, is to achieve existential stability for man by resolving into clear form that flux of human experience which, because of its ingrained intellectualness, gravitates toward the void; this is what is meant by the idea of rescuing human shades from their vague shadowiness. The trouble with this definition is that it does not seem at all different from the idea Tonio has criticized bitterly in Chapter 4: "Was aber das 'Wort' betrifft, so handelt es sich da vielleicht weniger um eine Erlösung als um ein Kaltstellen und Aufs-Eis-Legen der Empfindung?" Tonio, it seems, is simply going to go on doing what he has hated himself for doing before, and this raises the question of whether there is really any development in the story.

But there is a development. The difference between the poet and the man of letters ("Literat") lies not in *what* they do but in *how* they do it. Like charity for St. Paul ("jene Liebe selbst, von der geschrieben steht, dass einer mit Menschen- und Engelszungen reden könne und ohne sie doch nur ein tönendes Erz und eine klingende Schelle sei," the difference between the poet and the man of letters is an utterly vital but *invisible* difference. A poet is a writer who, while reducing human experience to verbal form, still always keeps in view, as his goal, that admittedly illusory but absolutely necessary vision of "das Leben" which Tonio has deliberately contrived for himself in Denmark. The man of letters operates on the assumption that humanity simply exists, as the object of his cognitive and pictorial endeavors, while the poet, on the other hand, in that his work is silently dedicated to an unrealized and perhaps ultimately unrealizable vision, knows constantly *that it is his responsibility to bring man into being,* that otherwise human existence, because of the contradictions inherent in self-conscious intellect, tends inexorably toward the void. Man for the "Literat" is an object; man for the "Dichter" is an unrealized ideal.

In actual practice, once again, this difference is infinitesimal. In practice the poet and the man of letters both do exactly the same thing; they resolve the flux of human experience into verbal form, and it is by no means certain that the reader will always be able to tell one from the other by their works. But once again, this does not matter. Onc of the things Mann has learned from Nietzsche is to regard the work of art as an act, not a fact, to regard art from the point of view of the creator, not the recipient, and from this point of view there is all the difference in the world. The "Literat" is passive (even the word is grammatically a passive participle); he *is* nothing but the object of his own consciousness, and so must always entangle himself in the sort of confusion Tonio experiences in Chapter 4. The "Dichter," on the other hand, is active (again, the form of the word suggests this). Even if he is a "Dichter in dürftiger Zeit," even if the world is set up in such a fashion that there is no "right way" for him, still he knows, "Aber das Irrsaal / Hilft, wie Schlummer und stark machet die Noth und die Nacht"; his work, from his own personal point of view, is an ethical activity that itself justifies his existence, an activity in the service of man, whether or not actual men appreciate it as such.

But surely we cannot conclude with the idea that poetry is poetry, as opposed to "literature," *only* by virtue of the poet's own subjective notion of what he is doing. Surely true poetry must enter into a specifically poetic relation with the *reader* as well. Or in particular, there must be a way for the reader at least to sense that the work is the product of a poetic mentality; otherwise the work is bound to affect him merely as "literature," as an intellectually detached "Kaltstellen" of human experience, thus ultimately nihilistic, rather than a self-affirmative human activity by which our existence is shaped and held fast.

And the key idea for understanding the relation of poetry to its reader is an idea we have already introduced, the idea of *myth,* which we must now go into a bit more deeply, especially in its Nietzschean sense. In the first place, a myth is not something one *believes* in objectively:

> Denn dies ist die Art, wie Religionen abzusterben pflegen: wenn nämlich die mythischen Voraussetzungen einer Religion unter den strengen, verstandesmässigen Augen eines rechtgläubigen Dogmatismus als eine fertige Summe von historischen Ereignissen systematisirt werden und man anfängt, ängstlich die Glaubwürdigkeit der Mythen zu vertheidigen.

The Greek did not believe in his gods, but rather he knew, in the very act of worshipping, that those gods represented an illusion—"Es ist ein Traum! Ich will ihn weiter träumen!"—just as Tonio knows full well that his Danish vision of "das Leben" is illusory. A myth is not an object of belief but rather a continuing mental activity, an artistic, illusion-creating activity, on the part of the celebrant. The utter horror of existence on the brink of the nameless void, says Nietzsche, that horror which the Greeks experienced more deeply than anyone else, "wurde von den Griechen durch jene künstlerische *Mittelwelt* der Olympier fortwährend von Neuem überwunden, jedenfalls verhüllt und dem Anblick entzogen." Especially important here are the words "fortwährend von Neuem"; a myth is not a fact that exists once and for all, but rather exists only by virtue of the continuing activity that brings it forth.

The importance of these considerations becomes clear as soon as we recognize that the myth with which *we* are presented, as readers, in ***Tonio Kröger,*** is not Tonio's own personal myth of the blond, blue-eyed ones. The vision experienced by Tonio, after all, depends precisely upon his exclusion from verbal intercourse, whereas we, as readers, are confronted with language and nothing but. Clearly, from the point of view of the reader, the central myth of ***Tonio Kröger*** is *the myth of the poet*—again, as in Hölderlin—and that we are in fact meant to approach this idea as a myth is made clear to us *by the analogy* with Tonio's vision of "das Leben." Just as Tonio knows perfectly well that his Danish vision is illusory, so also we, for our part, know that objectively speaking there is no difference whatever between "poetry" and "literature." What we learn from Tonio's insistence upon his "Bürgerliebe," however, is that we have an ethical duty to *insist* upon the differentness of poetry, regardless of what we "know" objectively. There must be such a thing as poetry; otherwise mankind is utterly abandoned to its intellectual penchant for nothingness. And to the extent, then, that we do carry out that ethical duty, to the extent that we realize the story as poetry by our insistence upon *taking* it as such, to precisely that extent ***Tonio Kröger*** *is* poetry in its own definition.

The deepest intention of the story, therefore, is not to explain or demonstrate an objective difference between poetry and literature, but rather to maneuver the reader into a position of understanding the absolute need for poetry, a position in which he has no choice but to affirm the poetic as opposed to the literary, whereupon such affirmation, as a continuing creative attitude, becomes poetry's existence. The brilliance of ***Tonio Kröger*** is thus contained less in what it does say than in what it does *not* say. Tonio's concluding letter does not in any concrete particular reflect an advance beyond his position in Chapter 4; his mood is more reconciled but his position is still the same. And the decisive event in Chapter 8 ("Dann aber kam einer [ein Tag], an welchem etwas geschah") derives its eventfulness entirely from Tonio's imagination, from the way he insists on seeing it. Considered objectively, therefore, the story is unconvincing; it does not convince us that either Tonio or we ourselves have really learned anything about the nature of poetry. But again, precisely this is the intention. What we are meant to learn is that poetry exists, as distinct from literature, only by virtue of our continuing insistence upon it, not as a demonstrable quality of this or that text, and a more convincing demonstration of the nature of poetry would only have clouded this truth. Hölderlin's Great Night of the World does not pass over automatically; it requires of us, rather, that spirit of thanksgiving (at least "einiger Dank"), that poetically affirmative attitude which sees even in the most common and trivial things, like bread and wine or Hans and Inge, not their superficial objective nature but rather symbols of unchanging humanity, of that higher human state which was and will be and at the same time always *is,* by virtue of our own visionary energy.

T. J. Reed (essay date 1988)

SOURCE: "Text and History: *Tonio Kröger* and the Politics of Four Decades," in *Publications of the English Goethe Society,* n.s., Vol. LVII, 1988, pp. 39-54.

[*In the following essay, Reed examines* Tonio Kröger *within the political and cultural contexts of early twentieth-century Germany.*]

No one who knew Ida Herz will have been surprised by her wish that we should 'spread the word and work of Thomas Mann'. From 1925 on, when she catalogued Thomas Mann's increasingly unmanageable library for him and became part of his entourage, he was the central experience of her life. Later, the value of his writings for her, and for many Germans like her, was intensified by the horrors of twentieth-century German history. As Nazism engulfed Germany and then Europe, Thomas Mann became for them a light in the darkness. His work was comfortingly sane: in a world of vicious distortion and brutal propaganda, it elaborated humane values with honesty and ironic moderation, and yet ultimately also with passionate commitment. His declared opposition to fascism, both before and after Hitler came to power, was a single-handed rehabilitation of the conservative cultural background he came from, which had always tended to let political matters go by default. Besides its sanity, Mann's work was comfortingly monumental: the massive novels and the interlocking essays were a world in themselves, and a spiritual rallying-point—after Mann's exile in 1933, an internationally visible one. So it is not surprising to find in the document that deprived Ida Herz of her German citizenship after she emigrated to England that one of the sources of outrage to the Nazis was the way she had gone on voicing her enthusiasm for the exiled writer Thomas Mann under the new order that had driven him into exile.

Miss Herz's phrase 'to spread the word' of Thomas Mann has distinct religious associations. Remembering the parable of the sower and the various kinds of ground on which the seed may fall, I take ***Tonio Kröger*** as my starting-point, so as to have at least some well-prepared ground.

It may seem a surprising notion to link the story with the politics of four decades. ***Tonio Kröger*** seems to have nothing to do with politics: it is about the sufferings of a sensitive literary soul over his exclusion from normal life. The question 'Who did Tonio Kröger vote for?' would seem even more irrelevant to this novella than the question 'How many children had Lady Macbeth?' to Shakespeare's play. Mann's text simply doesn't acknowledge that area—that kind—of reality. And in not doing so, it is true to its author's vision, and limitations of vision, at the time he wrote it: that is, in 1902, when political life in Germany was relatively inert and uninteresting to the great majority of writers, who were content to see it remain so.

***Tonio Kröger* offers us a structural model for understanding tensions, temptations, and resolutions that are found in [Mann's] subsequent career.**

—T.J. Reed

That in a sense is already a political fact, and there is a type of critical approach which would make something out of precisely what the work of literature excludes. Certainly the apolitical character of much German writing has had consequences both political and literary. But I am not going to argue from what *isn't* there in the story, but from what everyone knows *is* there, namely the problem and attitudes of the hero and their thinly-veiled autobiographical character; because these have a political potential which is realized later when the right circumstances (or perhaps one should say the wrong circumstances) arise. In other words, ***Tonio Kröger,*** which Thomas Mann once agreed contained the essential Thomas Mann, offers us a structural model for understanding tensions, temptations, and resolutions that are found in his subsequent career. What is more, these things prove to be not peculiar to him. They help us to see him as part of a larger pattern, so that in studying the individual case, even the single work, we are already looking at history.

The central theme of ***Tonio Kröger*** is usually said to be the opposition of 'Geist' and 'Leben'—that is of literary sensitivity and detachment on the one hand, and ordinary harmonious vitality on the other. Tonio Kröger certainly uses these ambitiously general terms himself in the conversation scene. But (as emerges from a careful reading of the story) it isn't simply a matter of Mind against Life, each element pitting itself without reservation against the other. For one thing, Life hardly seems to notice Mind—that is part of the trouble. And more importantly, Mind itself, as represented by Tonio Kröger, is inwardly divided, suffers from contradictory loyalties. The normality (as it seems to him) of socially integrated people, their naturalness and beauty—at least when they happen to be young and blonde and blue-eyed—are a reproach to what he does and always has instinctively done: to literary observation, analysis, and the recording of human behaviour. He suffers not just from being excluded from something he would like to have and enjoy, but from the fact that he accepts *it* is normal and *he* isn't. Far from being at daggers drawn with Life, he takes its side against himself, he suffers from an inferiority complex. It becomes the defining characteristic of 'Geist' as he embodies it that it tends to self-betrayal. Mann later describes this as 'irony'; but in practice it means that the status and value of literature and everything it stands for—reflection as against thoughtless action, breadth of human sympathy as against the uncritical will to power—is highly precarious.

Of course, the case for literature is put too. As a fated writer—and in various ways it is made clear that Tonio Kröger has only fulfilled a destiny that there were no two ways about—he knows what literature can do and has apparently given himself wholeheartedly to his profession:

> Er ergab sich ganz der Macht, die ihm als die erhabenste auf Erden erschien, zu deren Dienst er sich berufen fühlte, und die ihm Hoheit und Ehren versprach, der Macht des Geistes und Wortes, die lächelnd über dem unbewussten und stummen Leben thront.

No sign of an inferiority complex there, quite the reverse; and there are a number of contexts in which Mann and his characters express their irritation at that un-consciousness of Life, the 'unbewusster Typus' dominant in society, from the viewpoint of the superior knowledge and understanding that literature gives. Literature (as the passage just quoted goes on to say) penetrates the façade of pretentious phrases—'die grossen Wörter'—reveals men's souls, and opens up the realities of the world that lie beneath the surface.

But all this is surveyed in narrative retrospect as an earlier stage of Tonio Kröger's outwardly successful career; and by the time he comes to talk his problems over with Lisaweta Iwanowna in the central conversation-piece, it is unease and the price of success that dominate. Literature comes to seem almost a Faustian pact, giving him knowledge but making him pay for it inexorably. Knowledge, 'Erkenntnis', both the process and the results it produces, now make him sick ('Erkenntnisekel'). Yet the literary consciousness is a thing which, once acquired, can't easily be got rid of or switched off. Tonio Kröger's situation parallels the biblical Fall of Man—which was also a matter of 'Erkenntnis'—and is thus, of course, part of a notorious German tradition going back to Kleist and Schiller. Tonio Kröger is unable to return to the pre-conscious Garden of Eden, or a state of grace. He can only resolve (and this is the conclusion in his letter to Lisaweta that ends the novella) to moderate his critical consciousness with love, the bourgeois love for ordinary humanity which he compares to the Christian charity (in German, straightforwardly 'Liebe') of I Corinthians xiii. He also, significantly, hopes that a form of writing inspired by this love will somehow transform him from a mere 'Literat' into a 'Dichter'—that is, from a practising man of letters into a writer of recognized importance. The German word 'Dichter' is rich not just in aesthetic but in social meanings, ranging from 'not being a critical intellectual of the kind who probes into customs and assumptions in a disturbing way' to 'being a household word among those who have no interest in literature'. In a number of respects, then, for Tonio Kröger to become a recognized 'Dichter' would be very nearly a return to the fold after the exclusion which his literary career seemed necessarily to entail.

Other details from the conversation with Lisaweta point up the issues: the absolute requirement (so Tonio Kröger sees it at this stage of the story, in obedience to the modernist poetics of the turn of the century) that the writer should be 'etwas *Ausser*menschliches': the motif of exclusion. Then again, literature as a curse which is felt very early, at a time when you ought to be living 'in Frieden und Eintracht mit Gott und der Welt': the motif of a desired harmony with the world you live in. And the contrast too with 'den Gewöhnlichen, den Ordentlichen': the motif of ordinariness as the thing that is right and proper, confirmed in the now more emotional utterance that 'das Normale, Wohlanständige und Liebenswürdige ist das Reich unserer Sehnsucht', culminating in the lyrical paradoxes of 'das Leben in seiner verführerischen Banalität' and the 'Wonnen der Gewöhnlichkeit'. The images of a *kingdom,* and of the *joys* of ordinariness, stay close to the quasi-religious notion of a lost paradise or state of grace. And then, most alarming for Tonio Kröger, there is the realization that he is not just cut off from that kingdom, but is actually doing his bit to undermine it; and he tells himself, like some ecological protester against the acid rain of literature, that healthy innocent Life is losing ground, and art and its melancholy refinements are taking over more and more: why should one try to get innocent people who only like horses and books about horses (Hans Hansen of course becomes in his mind a symbol) to read high literature instead?

That echo of the first episode in the story is typical of Mann's delicate craftsmanship and the way he links the larger problem to his character's intimate experience. There is a great deal of abstract discussion in modern German fiction, quite a lot of it in Thomas Mann's other works, and rarely is it done so deftly as here and with such a marrying of general theme and enlivening detail. Everything is rooted in what Tonio Kröger (and behind him, his author) has gone through emotionally in order to reach this point intellectually. In biographical terms, we now know what private attachments made Thomas Mann present this picture of the writer as a sufferer from his art, as a man whose capacity for human feeling had survived the effects of his work, or had come alive again as he matured to new insights. And it has long been commonplace to read Tonio Kröger's discomforts with literature in the light of Mann's Lübeck background, the commercial patriciate, the decline of the family as narrated in ***Buddenbrooks,*** and the escape into art as a necessary stage in the progress of decadence. ***Tonio Kröger,*** then, seems rooted in a wholly private history.

But there is also a broader scene than the biographical, with pressures that were as real for the writer—the literary and cultural scene in Wilhelmine Germany which we can reconstruct very much as Thomas Mann saw it. 'The literary scene' is a difficult concept to use with precision, yet it is also indispensable, and it becomes the more indispensable as we get into the complexities of modern societies, with their multiple streams of opinion, ideals, fashions, fads and so on which are swirling about the (in this respect) anything but detached writer. He could hardly ignore them if he wanted to—among other things, they are his public and his market, and he will find himself willy-nilly responding to them in some way. We shall see that the conflict of 'Geist' and 'Leben' was not just limited to the private history and wistful conscience of Tonio Kröger.

To generalize first: Thomas Mann's lifetime had seen the rise of what was called (and self-consciously called itself) the Modern Movement, 'die literarische Moderne'. That vague phrase embraced more than one sub-style—Naturalism, Impressionism. But overall, contemporary serious literature was widely perceived as subversive of conventional values. It analysed and dissected, whether psychological or social phenomena. Sometimes, as in the social dramas of Naturalism—at the extreme, Gerhart Hauptmann's *Die Weber*—it was sharply critical, if only by implication. Such analysis and criticism were not always welcome, and by a strange transference they were sometimes themselves declared unhealthy and degenerate. Works of compassion that documented a social problem, like Hauptmann's *Hanneles Himmelfahrt* with its death of a poor child in a workhouse, were felt to *be* a social evil. A member of the Berlin court strayed into a performance of the play, and was so revolted that he had to resort to an expensive restaurant and a bottle of champagne in order to restore (as he said) a 'menschliche Stimmung'. The Kaiser himself was, of course, quick to give his view on these questions, as on all other matters. The greatest task of culture, he said, was the fostering of ideals. Analytical literature, clearly, could only undermine them.

But there were writers too who preached a literature of health and normality against the advanced modernity of specialized literary circles sitting in literary cafés in the big cities—the kind of cafés that the writer Adalbert in ***Tonio Kröger*** takes refuge in from the uncomfortable tingling in his blood that the spring has brought on. The *Heimatkunst* movement, a kind of 'back-to-the-land' group, spoke up for the clear air of the country and the provinces as against the corruption of the cities which were out of touch with what ordinary people thought and felt. A healthy affirmation of life, not analytical criticism, emotions rather than cerebrality—these were the terms of the confrontation. And there was more than a whiff of anti-intellectualism about some more way-out movements yet which preached vitalism and a nationalistic primitivism. If we discount this lunatic fringe, it is possible to hear echoes of such criticisms of modern literature and such demands for cultural regeneration and a healthier literature in the prickings of conscience and the attempted return to simpler feelings to which Tonio Kröger gives voice.

We can be the more sure that these impinged on Thomas Mann's thinking because a lot of detail about them is contained in a set of notes he built up during the early years of the century, out of which he tried in 1908-09 to make an authoritative non-fictional statement about the role of 'Geist' in culture. It was to be an essay entitled 'Geist und Kunst'.

Notice the terms of the title: no longer 'Geist' and 'Leben', but 'Geist' and 'Kunst'. The reader of ***Tonio Kröger*** would expect to find those two used interchangeably, certainly not occurring on opposite sides of an argument. But as Mann looks at the culture of the day, he sees that it has set its face against literature as an art too much dominated by 'Geist'—and yet that it values other kinds of art, visual art and music, especially Wagnerian opera. It only has time for literature if it somehow approximates to the condition of visual art, creating beauty and adornment rather than probing and analysing: in short, 'Dichtung' rather than 'Literatur'. These preferred forms of art, if not wholly devoid of 'Geist' (they can scarcely be produced without *any* operation of the mind) have no commitment to the assumed subversiveness of intellectuality. Rather than criticizing life, they offer a protective façade against the prying gaze. They hinder 'Erkenntnis'. (Nietzsche once said that nothing expressed such mortal hatred of 'Erkenntnis' as Wagner's music.) 'Kunst' in *this* sense can well be an agent more of 'Leben' than of 'Geist'; 'Geist' and 'Kunst' can be as much an opposition as 'Geist' and 'Leben' ever were.

Faced with this situation, Thomas Mann sets out, especially in what seem to be the earlier notes for his project, to defend and preach the values of a literature that enlarges understanding, undoes prejudice, improves society through analysis. He argues for literature as something especially needed in Germany; he notes that the word 'Literat'—the practitioner of 'Literatur'—is currently used as a term of abuse. He reflects that hostility to literature is a deeply German characteristic; he draws on his local experience of anti-literary feeling in Munich (where he had spent the whole of his writing career) and contrasts it with Berlin, where literary culture has some tradition, largely thanks to the Jewish element in the population.

There is a good deal more in this vein—the notes for 'Geist und Kunst' are extensive. But as they proceed, there is a perceptible veering away from the course that seemed set at the start. Doubt creeps in, and so—frankly—does a kind of self-interest, an attempt to read the cultural signs in order to adapt and keep on top:

> Das Interesse, das, au fond, die Generation beherrscht, zu der Hauptmann, Hofmannsthal und ich gehören, ist das Interesse am Pathologischen. Die Zwanzigjährigen sind weiter, Hauptmann sucht eifrig Anschluss. Jemand sollte zählen, wie oft im Griechischen Frühling 'gesund' vorkommt. Auch Hofmannsthal wird sich auf seine Art zu arrangieren suchen. Die Forderung der Zeit ist, alles, was irgend gesund ist in uns, zu kultivieren.

This is a somewhat cynical view of literary opportunism: of the three leading writers (one can say) of his generation, one is apparently busy adjusting to the demand for a renewed 'healthy' culture; another is expected to make his adjustments soon; and as for Thomas Mann himself, far from watching all this with a purist's critical eye, he merely recognizes that the 'requirement of the times' is to make the most of anything healthy that he too may have in him (which, for such a self-avowedly pathological author with pathological interests, is a problem). But then: does he really have an obligation to keep to the rigorous requirements of 'Geist'? Is culture—to which literature must ultimately belong—not perhaps also a matter of deeper, darker, more 'natural' forces than simply 'Geist'? That, at any rate, is what we find him asking himself, in a very tentative ruminating way (the tentative tone is important for what comes later):

> Der Geist ist zwar solidarisch und identisch mit der Kultur, sofern Kultur der Gegensatz von Natur ist. Aber das ist sie ja nur in einem gewissen Sinne, und es gilt hier, sich über die Begriffe der Kultur und der Zivilisation zu verständigen . . .

Yet he has been aware from the first that the things he criticizes are not just part of the culture about him but are in him too. In the act of criticizing them, he has been criticizing himself; and exposing them doesn't (he says) necessarily mean that he is denying or rejecting them. 'Damit, dass ich sie klarstelle, verneine ich sie noch nicht'. In fact, the sharp and polemical tone he has used on them may only mean that he is shouting down inner doubts—that is, doubts about the basis from which he polemicizes against them, doubts about whether his old, simple 'Geist' position is justifiable.

But then, *was* his old 'Geist' position ever really simple? We saw that in ***Tonio Kröger*** it already wasn't; and so the planned essay 'Geist und Kunst' is really a non-fictional replay of the issues of the early novella; the uncertainties of the fictional character's conscience are restated now as a much larger cultural dialectic, and with a distinct direction of change which draws Thomas Mann along with it. The principal difference, in the evolution we are watching, between the novella and the essay-project is that Mann was able to round off the story and finish it, by turning Tonio Kröger's unease into a positive creative principle, a promise for his poetic and perhaps social future; but the essay, having to work wholly in intellectual terms and not being able to end with a gesture towards the future, has no clear resolution. It duly never gets finished at all. Thomas Mann is unable to make up his mind because it is still as ever a divided mind, divided between the radical intellectuality of 'Geist' and the compromise that all 'Kunst' is tempted to enter into with 'life'. 'Geist und Kunst' is then passed, in ***Der Tod in Venedig,*** to Gustav von Aschenbach, who in the fiction has managed to finish the essay—with consequences that become clear in *his* fate.

You may feel that it is a bit much for a writer to go on being so indecisively poised for so long—but that is the nature of the beast. The ruminating, tentative tone that I drew attention to, like the emotional dividedness between Tonio Kröger's own values of 'Geist' and the infiltrating ones of 'Leben', may be very uncomfortable for the inner life, but in a sense it is also a *luxury of* the inner life. There may be pressures and tensions to respond to, but there is no deadline set for a final resolution: indeed, the absence of *final* resolutions makes it possible to produce a large body of work on a constant theme, with multiple variations.

But then comes a deadline that suddenly does resolve everything: the outbreak of war in 1914. For the last time in European history there was a massive enthusiasm for war in all the combatant countries, a kind of festive mood that overrode almost all criticism and carried even formerly cool and detached people away. Partly this can be explained politically, by the increased tensions and expectations of war as one international crisis followed another in the years before 1914; yet there is also evidence of a different kind of expectation, a feeling that war or revolution—some major cataclysm—was needed as a cure for the present state of civilization. 'If only there could be a war, I should be healthy again'—'Gäb es nur Krieg, gesund wäre ich'—reads an entry in the poet Georg Heym's diary in May 1907. The idea that war brings purification and regeneration may go back to the images of war we find in Nietzsche, whom practically every writer in the generations preceding 1914 read and was deeply affected by. At all events, Thomas Mann too experienced the war, when it came, as morally purifying and simplifying; above all, it resolved old conflicts and divisions. That was what was supposed to have happened in the outside world, in politics: the Kaiser, in a famous phrase, said he saw before him no longer parties, only Germans. The same was true of individuals' inner conflicts and divisions. There are any number of examples, from French and English as well as German and Austrian sources; but the first of Rilke's *Fünf Gesänge,* written in August 1914, puts things with ideal clarity. It describes a young man about to go off to fight, and sets the uncertainties of peace, when a pluralistic society surrounded him with many conflicting voices, against the simplifying effect of the one great necessity. The emergency of war, paradoxically, is something to rejoice at, because you can be sure what you must do, and anything else must seem, in comparison, merely arbitrary:

> ihm, der noch eben
> hundert Stimmen vernahm, unwissend, welche
> im Recht sei,
> wie erleichtert ihn jetzt der einige Ruf: denn *was*
> wäre nicht Willkür neben der frohen, neben der
> sicheren Not?

And the next phrase is: 'Endlich ein Gott'. A quasi-religious certainty has replaced the puzzling complexities of life with a simple duty.

Much the same is true of Thomas Mann. Instead of wavering any longer between alternative values, suddenly and dramatically he becomes a public spokesman for his country, adopts a nationalist, even a militarist position, defends Germany's right to march through neutral Belgium in execution of the Schlieffen plan. That brings him into head-on conflict with his brother, the writer Heinrich Mann, who was one of the few to speak out within Germany against German actions (indeed, his was one of the few voices raised in any of the belligerent countries against the war generally). Thomas's intervention was a shock not only to Heinrich Mann; even those who were not critics of German policy were surprised to see him play this public role. But the path we have been tracing shows the history and inner logic of that seemingly sudden change; and the 'Geist und Kunst' notes allow us to watch the change in preparation in precise detail.

What Thomas Mann did in his first wartime essay, ***Gedanken im Kriege,*** was to defend Germany against the line taken by Western propagandists, that the violation of Belgian neutrality and the atrocities committed by the army along the way proved Germany was not a civilized nation: the war was a fight between (Western) civilization and (German) barbarism. The German answer, not invented by Thomas Mann but exploited in his article, was to reject civilization as the ultimate value, and to claim for Germany something more profound and more precious. 'Civilization' was only a matter of rational arrangements in society, technical achievements, things that the human mind at its most superficial could achieve. There was a much higher value, and that was *culture*. 'Culture', great art, architecture, style in the forms of life, coherence in national ethos—history showed that these were entirely compatible with atrocities of all kinds which no merely 'civilized' country would countenance. So what price civilization? And what price peace too, which (Mann says) had not been a very desirable condition. It 'swarmed with the vermin of Mind' ('dem Ungeziefer des Geistes'), it stank with the 'corrosive substances of civilization'—by which he means of course not substances that corrode civilization, but civilization as itself a *source* of corrosion, destroying things of greater value. To all of this, he argues, there has now been a moral reaction, an end to moral laxity. The reaction was ready and waiting for just such an event; war consequently came as a purification and liberation.

The whole of the essay ***Gedanken im Kriege*** embodies this dubious 'purification'. Once again we can see the mechanism of change in precise stylistic and syntactical shifts in Mann's use of formulations we have met before. That tentative sentence from the 'Geist und Kunst' notes is taken over in substance, but the emphases are transformed:

> Zivilisation und Kultur sind nicht nur nicht ein und dasselbe, sondern sie sind Gegensätze, sie bilden eine der vielfältigen Erscheinungsformen des ewigen Weltgegensatzes und Widerspieles von Geist und Natur . . .

Autumn 1914 was no time for the earlier 'zwar' and 'aber', but for flat denial and firm assertion. What follows in both texts is a list of the things that history shows can be compatible with culture—oracles, magic, pederasty, human sacrifice, orgiastic cults, the Inquisition and so forth; and both texts contrast with these the values of mere civilization—reason, enlightenment, scepticism, subversion, and ultimately 'Geist' itself. Such things, already beginning to show up in a less favourable light in the later 'Geist und Kunst' notes, are now rejected altogether. 'Geist' itself is called 'civilian'—enough to damn it in time of war. The Germany that once seemed to need enlightening and civilizing through literature now appears as heroic precisely in its *un*literary innocence. Where the Western Entente has literature as its weapon in the struggle for world opinion, Germany is the 'unliterary land' (thus one of the chapter-headings early in the ***Betrachtungen eines Unpolitischen***). And Heinrich Mann, the champion of the Entente and critic of his own country, is pilloried as the 'Zivilisationsliterat'—two scorned concepts in one compound.

What had happened? For most observers, it was a shock that Thomas Mann, the detached, ironic intellectual writer had simplified all issues, simplified himself, and taken a stance which appeared to contradict everything he had once been devoted to. Yet Mann himself knew that the simplification wasn't that simple: that there had always been the element in him that doubted what he was doing as a writer, even while he did it; that hated observing even while he observed, that was sick of analysis even while he analysed, and that thought wistfully of living instead 'in Frieden und Eintracht mit Gott und der Welt'. Much of the wartime book of this 'Unpolitical Man' is taken up with explaining and justifying his apparent volte-face, admitting that he was implicated in all those 'enlightened', civilizing tendencies he now rejects, but saying that there was always another side. Yes of course, he says, I was part of the radical process of decadence and civilization-through-literature; but I also had contrary, conservative tendencies in me, even if I didn't then see them as political. And where does he see them now but in ***Tonio Kröger***?

> Nur dass ich von jeher, im Gegensatz zum radikalen Literaten, auch erhaltende Gegentendenzen in mir hegte und, ohne mich politisch selbst zu verstehen, frühzeitig zum Ausdruck brachte. Das machte der Begriff des Lebens, den ich von Nietzsche hatte, und mein Verhältnis zu diesem Begriff, das ironisch sein mochte, aber nicht ironischer war als mein Verhältnis zum 'Geist'. Dieser Begriff des Lebens bekommt nationale Aktualität ums Jahr 1900, als der Fruchtbarkeitssturz einsetzt. Er ist ein *konservativer* Begriff, und kaum ist der Verfallsroman fertig, als konservativer Gegenwille in Form von Ironie sich anmeldet, als diese Wörter 'Leben' und 'konservieren' in meiner Produktion eine Rolle zu spielen beginnen. Ich schrieb: 'Das Reich der Kunst nimmt zu, und das der Gesundheit und Unschuld nimmt ab auf Erden. Man sollte, was noch davon übrig ist, aufs sorgfältigste *konservieren,* und man sollte nicht Leute, die viel lieber in Pferdebüchern mit Momentaufnahmen lesen, zur Poesie verführen wollen! . . . Es ist widersinning, das *Leben* zu lieben und dennoch mit allen Künsten bestrebt zu sein, es auf seine Seite zu ziehen, es für die Finessen und Melancholien, den ganzen kranken Adel der Literatur zu gewinnen' ('Tonio Kröger'). Man sieht, ich wandte jene Begriffe und Wörter auf rein moralisch-geistige Dinge an, aber unbewusst war ganz ohne Zweifel dabei politischer Wille in mir lebendig, und noch einmal zeigt sich, dass man nicht den politischen Aktivisten und Manifestanten zu machen braucht, dass man ein 'Asthet' sein und dennoch mit dem Politischen tiefe Fühlung besitzen kann.

So Thomas Mann's own view matches and confirms the argument I have been putting forward: namely, that what seemed a private confession by a troubled writer had a political potential. But we needn't see it in every respect through his eyes. The question is, whether what the Thomas Mann of 1914-18 wanted to conserve—the simple, noble land attacked on all sides by literature and intellectuality—was the real Germany of the Kaiser and the generals that was fighting the real war. Was this Germany really the idyll of blonde hair and blue eyes that Tonio Kröger loved and wanted to protect from the undermining influence of such as himself ? And, beyond that, was Tonio Kröger's blonde-haired, blue-eyed society not already in 1902 itself a gross over-simplification, very little to do with human and social realities—in short, a myth?

The incongruity of equating those idealized figures and their innocence with social realities is brought out sharply by a chance wording in one of Karl Kraus's attacks on the conformist intellectuals of autumn 1914. The Austrian satirist, reviewing the warlike enthusiasms of Gerhart Hauptmann, Richard Dehmel, Hugo von Hofmannsthal and a whole train of dilettantes, is appalled by the mismatch between their high poetic mood and the paltry reality they have sold out to: 'Noch nie vorher hat es einen so stürmischen Anschluss an die Banalität gegeben'. For Tonio Kröger, 'banality' was a bewitching thing, a seductive ordinariness, 'die verführerische Banalität'. Karl Kraus undoes that paradoxical combination and restores the true nature of 'banality'. It is not a seductive, but (when you look at it soberly) a very unideal reality.

What gave banality its fascination and the myth of ordinariness its power was, of course, Tonio Kröger's and Thomas Mann's subjective sense of exclusion, self-doubt and guilt about what they were and did. These feelings are the things which I said at the outset were not peculiar to them among the writers of their day. A sense of their own abnormality, and of the decadence of literature, is a common thread in the painfully self-aware writing of many early twentieth-century figures—Rilke, Hofmannsthal, Kafka and others. Any road to regeneration was bound to look tempting, any invitation by circumstances to rejoin the 'normal' community must be compelling. A wholesale abandoning of literary detachment under the guise of a necessary new 'morality' was an obvious possibility. Literature was precarious. If we look at what literary intellectuals wrote in the opening months of the war as they swung into line with the jubilant majority, the motive often lies very plainly in the relief at being able, at last, to abandon their allegiance to mere literature and 'Geist' and come in from the cold. Heinrich Mann hit it exactly when he spoke of 'Orgien einer komplizierten Naivität, Ausbrüche einer tiefen und alten Widervernunft . . . '. The enthusiasm for war was an orgy of some primitive irrational religion, in which the sophisticated modern mind perversely chose to be absorbed into the collective.

My title promised the 'politics of four decades', and here we are only a decade-and-a-half on from ***Tonio Kröger,*** with not much time left. It may also seem that ***Tonio Kröger*** has sent us off down a road that doesn't lead to anything remotely like that clear-sighted opposition of Thomas Mann's to Nazism which meant so much to Ida Herz and her generation. How can we cover the remaining historical span, and also find out how Thomas Mann's politics changed from what we might call the conformism of cultural nostalgia into something more realistic and more rational?

In detail, we can't: his conversion after the war from a committed nationalist into a supporter of the Weimar Republic (which all good nationalists hated) and into a prophet warning against a yet more terrible orgy of nationalist irrationalism is a long story. But there *is* time to suggest the general shape of that development, and to show it is still understandable in the old ***Tonio Kröger*** terms. Under a thin disguise, the elements and responses we have been looking at remain at root unchanged. The quest for regeneration in German culture from the early years of the century reappears in the Nazi propaganda conception of a nation with restored health, throwing off the disintegrative ways of modern society and starting afresh: 'Deutschland erwache!' as the motto on Nazi banners read. The criticism of intellectual literature, and ultimately of intellect itself, as decadent recurs in the Nazi campaign against the 'asphalt literature' of the cities. The 'Heimatkunst' movement, reasserting the ways of the healthy provinces against the bloodless avant-grade, becomes the literature of blood and soil, 'Blut and Boden'. The witch-hunting of degenerate art, 'entartete Kunst', is a near neighbour. The vitalism of earlier decades leads into racial theory, which often links Jewishness with intellectuality as if they were two sides of the same coin. In sum, the pressures that helped to shape ***Tonio Kröger*** at the start of the century turn out to have had, just like Tonio Kröger's and Thomas Mann's responses to them, a political potential, and of a very unpleasant kind.

And there is one more thing that stays the same: these increasingly evil forms of banality continue to have a seductive power over writers who hanker after cultural regeneration and are still longing, as Tonio Kröger did, to be at one with an idealized collective—writers who include not just minor fellow-travellers and opportunists of the right, but a poet and essayist as sophisticated as Gottfried Benn. For him Nazism seemed a benign turning-point in history, the birth of a new evolutionary type of human being, not just a political but almost a transcendent phenomenon.

Benn's case is the measure of Thomas Mann's transformation. Mann had by now begun to look about him at the realities of his society and to react to what was actually going on in it. He was no longer to be taken in by myths and illusions about ideal types. Above all, the old doubts about the status and value of 'Geist' had been resolved in a new way: what the intelligent observer owed his community, especially in times of extremism, was not a secret worship of its vital energies and thoughtless actions, but a detached answer to the question: whether its actions were right. It was no longer the function of 'Geist' to indulge in the lyrical masochism of self-betrayal, no longer permissible to accept that 'Geist' was itself merely a decadent and inferior offshoot of 'Leben'. The critical mind had to have the courage of its own independence. In achieving that insight, Thomas Mann liberated himself from his oldest compulsions. It is the real ending to the story of Tonio Kröger.

Steven Millhauser (essay date 1994)

SOURCE: "Some Thoughts on *Tonio Kröger,*" in *Antaeus,* Nos. 73-4, Spring, 1994, pp. 199-223.

[*Millhauser is an American novelist and critic. In the following essay, he examines the structure and major themes of* Tonio Kröger.]

TIME

An immediately striking fact about ***Tonio Kröger*** (1903), Mann's second novella, is that it covers a large amount of time: some seventeen years. There is no law of fiction, no principle of imagination, that requires a short narrative to take place in a short span of time, but it remains true that the physical shortness of a story or novella invites concentrated effects. Mann's own practice in his four other major novellas is instructive. The action of ***Tristan*** (1903), his first novella, begins in January, reaches its climax in February, and ends in the spring. ***Death in Venice*** (1913) begins in the spring and ends in the summer; the past is briskly disposed of in the short second chapter, which serves as a summarizing flashback. ***Disorder and Early Sorrow*** (1926) takes place in one afternoon and evening. ***Mario and the Magician*** (1930) begins with an introductory movement that covers several summer weeks and continues with the long narration of the events of a single evening. The lengthy temporal span of ***Tonio Kröger*** sets it radically apart from these other novellas and immediately raises the question of structure. A fifty-page story that covers nearly twenty years and is arranged chronologically risks a dissipation of its effects, risks, that is, becoming scattered or diffuse; and a writer committed to such a scheme must continually strive to overcome the dispersive tendency of his narrative. What the writer needs is a method of binding together the various parts of his tale—a method that cuts across chronology, that serves to halt or defeat the relentless advance of fictional time. It is precisely as such a method that the technique of *repetition*—the famous technique of the leitmotif—finds its central justification.

LEITMOTIF

The deliberate repetition of phrases and sentences in widely separated portions of a narrative constitutes the device known as leitmotif. The device serves a number of purposes, such as simple emphasis: a repeated phrase, like any repeated element in a work of art, draws attention to itself—among the vast number of details that compose even a short work of literature, *this* one is thrust upon our awareness. But the deepest purpose of the leitmotif is that of uniting one part of a narrative to another. By the device of repetition, which Mann in his climax broadens to include an entire episode, the past is summoned into the present: as we read forward, we are also reading backward. At the moment of repetition, past and present become one, or rather are held in the mind separately but concurrently. For an instant, confluence abolishes chronology. Time is deceived, outwitted, overcome.

CHRONOLOGY

But let us look more closely at the chronological development of ***Tonio Kröger*** against which the technique of the leitmotif is used as a counter-weight. In doing so, it will be useful to keep in mind that the story is divided into nine parts or chapters; the divisions are numbered in the Fischer Verlag edition of Mann's collected works, but erroneously left unnumbered by H. T. Lowe-Porter in what is still the most widely read translation. The first chapter is a fully rendered scene in which fourteen-year-old Tonio is shown during a significant afternoon meeting with Hans Hansen, whom Tonio loves but who does not love him in return. In the second chapter, Tonio Kröger is sixteen years old; Hans Hansen has vanished from the action and has been replaced in Tonio's affections by pretty Ingeborg Holm, who does not return his love. The structure of the chapter differs from the structure of the first chapter in one important respect: although it contains another fully rendered scene, this time at Herr Knaak's dancing class, the chapter begins and ends with several paragraphs of temporal summary. We learn of Tonio's love for Ingeborg Holm, are led gradually and almost imperceptibly into the fully rendered scene, and are ushered out of the scene into unspecific time by means of the word "often" ("Often after that he stood thus, with burning cheeks in lonely corners . . . "). The short third chapter summarizes Tonio Kröger's life in Italy and covers what we feel to be a great many years. (Later we are told that he has been away from home for thirteen years, but we never learn how many of those years were spent in Italy and how many in Munich.) Chapter 4 takes place on a single spring day in Munich; it opens when Tonio Kröger is "slightly past thirty" and consists of a long conversation with Tonio's friend Lisabeta Ivanovna. Chapter 5 opens in the autumn of the same year and records Tonio Kröger's decision to travel to Denmark. From this point on, the narration is continuous. In chapter 6 he spends two days in his native town (the scene of the opening chapter); in chapter 7, which begins on the evening of the second day, he crosses to Denmark, where he arrives the next morning and spends three days; in chapter 8, "some days pass" in Denmark before he has a decisive experience; and the brief final chapter consists of a letter that he writes to his friend Lisabeta.

From this sketch of Mann's temporal scheme, a curious fact emerges. Whereas the action of the first five chapters covers some seventeen years, the action of the last four chapters covers roughly two weeks. The two uneven temporal divisions are nearly equal in reading time: the first five chapters span pages 77-106 of the Vintage International edition, and the last four chapters span pages 106-132. The scheme is this:

1/2 novella	chapters 1-5 (age 14-31)	about 17 years
1/2 novella	chapter 6: 2 days chapter 7: same night; 3 following days chapter 8: "some days" and "several days" chapter 9: the letter	about 2 weeks

The effect of such an arrangement is to throw the weight of the story onto the second half, when the story for the first time becomes continuous, without odd leaps of time in the white spaces between chapters; our attention is focused on a series of closely connected actions that swell to a climax in chapter 8. The temporal continuity of the second half has the effect of changing our experience of the first half: the early chapters settle into place as preparatory (the long speech of chapter 4 is a special case, which will be considered later). In fact it begins to seem as if the first half of the story exists solely in order to be summoned back in changed form in the second half. In short, although the temporal span of the novella is seventeen years, and although the order of events is chronologically straightforward, the actual temporal arrangement is in significant imbalance—an imbalance that works fruitfully against the incohesiveness of a drawn-out chronological scheme.

LEITMOTIF AND FLASHBACK

Leitmotif and flashback are both devices by which a work of art condemned to move forward in time can break the habit of progression and evoke, in the present, time past. But there is a crucial difference. The flashback, however vivid it may be, and however artfully it may be introduced into the flow of later time, always has the effect of introducing a pause in the narrative. The present comes to a heavy halt as the past replaces it. This is true of both major kinds of flashback: the summarizing flashback, used by Mann in the second chapter of ***Death in Venice*** and the second chapter of ***The Magic Mountain,*** and the scenic or dramatic flashback, used by Mann in chapter 4 of ***The Magic Mountain,*** when Hans Castorp is cast back to a vivid memory of Pribislav Hippe ("Quite suddenly he found himself in the far distant past . . . "). The interruptive quality of the flashback may find its justification in the annihilating power of memory, but the flashback is always accompanied by a certain creaking of machinery in its entrances and exits, while the poor reader stops short, coughs into his fist, and perhaps out of sheer kindness averts his eyes. The leitmotif, though no less a contrivance, is never interruptive. If the reader failed to notice the fact of repetition, the narrative would proceed without the chronological wrenchings required by flashbacks. But of course the leitmotif wishes to be noticed, and the result is curious: the reader experiences simultaneously the present and the past. In this respect the leitmotif is psychologically superior to the flashback, for, except in cases of hallucination or insanity, the uprushing of the past is always accompanied by a sense of the present. The summoning of the past is itself of interest, for the leitmotif, in evoking past instances of itself, will also summon forth past settings or situations or even entire scenes—a whole cluster of pasts.

In this way the past of the text is continually carried forward into the present. It remains true that the leitmotif is narrower in range than the flashback, because the leitmotif can never go outside the text itself. But in a text that covers a long span of time it is not necessary to seek a past outside the text, since the past evoked by flashback in a temporally concentrated narrative will in a temporally drawn-out narrative be represented directly as part of the unfolding temporal scheme. The flashback encourages effects of temporal concentration; its flaw is its interruptive nature, which undermines the very concentration that is being sought. The leitmotif is suited to narratives with a long time span; it is an attempt to overcome a diffuseness that it perhaps secretly encourages.

THE LAST SENTENCE

The last sentence of ***Tonio Kröger,*** in the Lowe-Porter translation, reads:

> There is longing in it, and a gentle envy; a touch of contempt and no little innocent bliss.

The sentence is very close to the final sentence of chapter I:

> His heart beat richly: longing was awake in it, and a gentle envy; a faint contempt, and no little innocent bliss.

We are unquestionably meant to connect the two passages, and the repetition brings about an interesting effect: a sentence that in the first instance applies to a particular person, Hans Hansen, has suddenly widened its meaning to include all the blond and blue-eyed, that is, all of everyday, healthy, unproblematic life. But Mann's German makes it clear that the relation between the two passages is even closer than the one indicated by Lowe-Porter. Mann's final sentence reads:

> Sehnsucht ist darin und schwermütiger Neid und ein klein wenig Verachtung und eine ganze keusche Seligkeit.

The last sentence of chapter I reads:

> Damals lebte sein Herze; Sehnsucht war darin und schwermütiger Neid und ein klein wenig Verachtung und eine ganze keusche Seligkeit.

The two German passages beginning with "Sehnsucht" are identical, with a single exception: the final sentence of the novella is in the present, whereas the final clause of chapter I is in the past (this identity is preserved in the recent translation by David Luke). The effect is disarming: as Erich Heller has said, Tonio Kröger here takes the words out of the author's mouth. In fact, it isn't easy to explain the precise effect of this apparent plagiarism of Mann by his own character. Mann probably intended us to feel that the mature Tonio Kröger has become fully conscious of an emotion that he recalls having had at the age of fourteen, and which only now is he able to express. But there remains the nagging sense that in this instance Tonio Kröger has quoted a sentence by Thomas Mann, as if at the moment the story ends the fictional author becomes the actual author.

GEOGRAPHY

As if to refuse geographical as well as temporal concision, the novella moves restlessly from place to place. It opens in Tonio Kröger's native northern town (unnamed, but clearly the Lübeck of Mann's youth), shifts to Italy in chapter 3, moves to Munich in chapter 4, returns to the native town in chapter 6, crosses the Baltic to Copenhagen in chapter 7, and ends in Aalsgaard, a resort on the Øresund in north Zealand. The motion from place to place is of course a sign of the hero's restlessness and dissatisfaction, but gradually a deeper pattern emerges: like smaller details in this intricately organized work, cities and countries themselves form a system of significant antitheses. The decisive opposition here is north and south: Tonio Kröger's native town lies in the north, he becomes an artist in the south (Italy), as a grown man he lives in southern Germany (Munich), and at a moment of spiritual crisis he travels to the far north (Denmark). The north/south scheme of the nine chapters is this:

> 1-2 North (Lübeck)
> 3-5 South (Italy and Munich)
> 6-9 North (Lübeck and Denmark)

The geographical structure reflects a division in the name of the protagonist of which he himself is conscious: Tonio (south) and Kröger (north). To put it another way, Tonio Kröger in his travels is entering opposed regions of himself, the Tonio region and the Kröger region. Travel in Mann is always a form of spiritual voyage; ***Death in Venice*** and the opening pages of ***The Magic Mountain*** are famous examples, but movement here is no less burdened with meaning. Geography keeps turning into psychology.

MUNICH

Unlike Tonio's native northern town, which is portrayed in careful and tender detail, Munich is little more than a word, an element in the geographical structure. Nevertheless, its role is crucial and complex. Although Munich is in south Germany, and is opposed in specific ways to the unnamed northern birthplace, it is at the same time opposed to Italy: Tonio Kröger dislikes Italy and chooses to live in Munich. Munich is in the south, which in Mann's scheme is always the place where art is possible, but it is not as far south as the Italian south. It is as if, by traveling to Italy, Tonio Kröger explores the deepest or most extreme region of the southern half of his divided nature, and then pulls back: in Munich he is still in the artistic south, but he is not all the way south. In this sense, Munich represents a middle place between south and north. It is the place in which Tonio Kröger is able to articulate his crisis, and it is also, significantly, the place to which he will return after his northern journey—there is never any question of actually living in the north, as the letter that ends the novella makes clear. If, then, the southernness of Munich is essential to the geographical and spiritual structure of the story, its function as a midpoint between the extremes of north and south is no less important. In this respect it is interesting to recall the use Mann makes of Munich in ***Death in Venice***. There, Munich represents not the south but the Germanic north, to which Venice is opposed: Aschenbach is making the classic voyage from northern Europe to the Mediterranean south.

But in a brilliant passage in chapter 4, where Mann describes Aschenbach's summer home in the mountains, Munich changes for an instant to the middle place between the sensuous, death-ridden Latin south and the stormy Teutonic north, now represented by Aschenbach's mountain home where violent storms extinguish the lights of the house at night, and ravens—birds associated with Friedrich Barbarossa asleep in the Kyffhäuser and with Odin—swing in the tops of fir trees. Munich remains a fluid place in Mann's imagination, attracting to itself opposite and even contradictory qualities that in turn depend on the precise use to which the city is put in a particular work.

DENMARK

If Italy is the far south, the south that is south of Munich, then Denmark is the far north: it is north of Tonio Kröger's native northern town, it is *north of north*. The decision to stage the climax of the novella in Denmark was a brilliant one. It must have seemed tempting to arrange the climactic dance in Tonio's childhood town and thereby to complete the circle perfectly, but to have done so would have been to commit the one esthetic crime for which there is no forgiveness: not sentimentality, but banality. A first-rate instinct warned Mann to take his story farther north. In a sense, he has it both ways: he has his hero return to his native town and visit his childhood home, but only as part of a longer journey, and the real return takes place in a country he has never visited before. By going north of north, the divided hero enters the deepest part of his Kröger nature: he passes beyond his childhood home into his spiritual home, he passes beyond nostalgia and its attendant ironies to a more intense place, where rebirth becomes possible.

But long before the climactic day in the hotel at Aalsgaard, the theme of return is clearly sounded. In Copenhagen, where Tonio Kröger studies the sights in the manner of a conventional tourist, he sees not exactly the Frauenkirch, or Thorwaldsen's statues, or the Tivoli, all of which are carefully named, but rather something else: he sees the familiar baroque gables of his native town, he sees the familiar names on the house doors, he sees nothing less than his childhood; and when he draws "deep, lingering draughts of moist sea air" it is as though he were entering, in a foreign place, a deeper layer of his own past. But even this is not enough for him, he longs to be farther north, close to the sea; and he takes a ship northward, along the coast of Zealand. At Aalsgaard he spends his mornings and afternoons on the beach, and, like Aschenbach in the lyrical-mythological fourth chapter of ***Death in Venice,*** he loses the sense of time: we hear of "some days" passing and then of "several days." And there is a nice touch: he likes to sit (Lowe-Porter unaccountably makes him stand) so that "he had before his eyes not the Swedish coast but the open horizon." That is, he is so far north on the island of Zealand that instead of looking only at the Øresund, the body of water separating Zealand from Sweden, he can look north to the broad waters of the Kattegat. It is as if, at the end of his northern journey, he wishes to take in as much sea as possible, to immerse himself utterly in the "wild friend" of his youth. The mornings and afternoons on the beach at Aalsgaard are themselves a return to the summer vacations of his childhood and boyhood, summoned briefly in chapter I, when he liked to sit dreaming on another beach, on the Baltic shore not far from his native home. It is in this carefully composed atmosphere of sand and sea, in a foreign hotel whose veranda leads directly down to the beach ("druch die Veranda wieder an Strand hinuntergehen"), that the climax of the story takes place—a climax that is above all a climax of memory.

HAMLET

When Tonio Kröger leaves Copenhangen and travels by ship northward along the coast of Zealand, he is said to be headed "towards Helsingør"; from the seaport of Helsingør he takes a carriage to Aalsgaard. The final scene therefore takes place in the vicinity of Helsingør; indeed, the guests who will later dance are specifically said to be tourists from Helsingør. When, in ***A Sketch of My Life,*** Mann speaks of his actual visit to Aalsgaard before the writing of ***Tonio Kröger,*** he notes that it was "near Helsingør." The emphasis on Helsingør is deliberate: Helsingør, Englished, is Elsinore, the site of Hamlet's castle. In chapter 5, when Tonio Kröger tells Lisabeta Ivanovna of his plan to travel north, he says that he wants to stand on the terrace at Kronborg (i.e., Kronborg Castle), where the ghost appeared to Hamlet. With his usual tact, Mann omits Hamlet's castle from his hero's itinerary, but it is no accident that the climactic scene takes place in the vicinity of Elsinore.

Mann has taken pains to sound the Hamlet theme throughout his composition. In the attack on art delivered to Lisabeta Ivanovna in chapter 4, Tonio Kröger speaks of being "sick of knowledge" and adds: "Such was the case of Hamlet the Dane, that typical literary man." Hamlet is a literary man because it was enough for him "to see through a thing in order to be sick to death of it"—a reading of Hamlet's nature that is not far from Nietzsche's bold formulation in the seventh chapter of *The Birth of Tragedy*: "Dionysiac man might be said to resemble Hamlet: both have looked deeply into the true nature of things, they have *understood* and are now loath to act." When Tonio Kröger voyages to Denmark, he is therefore embarking on a double voyage: a voyage to the spiritual center of his childhood, and a voyage to the realm of Hamlet, that is, the realm of bitter knowledge. His heart has died in Italy, in the carefree south; his heart's awakening takes place in the shadow of Elsinore. At the very end, when Tonio Kröger writes to Lisabeta Ivanovna that "if anything is capable of making a poet of a literary man, it is my bourgeois love of the human, the living and usual," he is asserting his separation from Hamlet, that typical literary man, just as earlier he had asserted his separation from Adalbert the novelist, that other literary man. Tonio Kröger remains part Hamlet, for he cannot unknow what he knows, but he is a Hamlet who tempers knowledgesickness with love. Hamlet is a fate that he flees. Hamlet is the *dark* side of the north, the side of the north that lies on the other side of blond and blue-eyed innocence. And is it possible that Tonio Kröger's father, that melancholy northern gentleman with his thoughtful blue eyes, has a touch of Hamlet in him? Is he a Hans Hansen with some bitter draft of northness in his being? Hamlet is the place where the stern, melancholy north coincides with the knowledge-heavy darkness of the south. Is it a wonder that Tonio Kröger is drawn to Hamlet's home?

HANS HANSEN'S CAP

In the seventh paragraph of chapter I Mann pauses, in the leisurely and scrupulous manner of a good nineteenth-century storyteller, to describe the clothes and features of Tonio Kröger and Hans Hansen. A reader new to the story is struck by the clear, swiftly established system of contrasts, which extends even to the hats of both boys: Hans Hansen is wearing "a Danish sailor cap with black ribbons" and Tonio Kröger is wearing a "round fur cap." Among the carefully, perhaps too carefully, arranged contrasts, we experience this one as particularly apt: Tonio's cap is less boyish that his friend's, darker, more formal, less lively. But for a reader familiar with the story—for a re-reader—Hans Hansen's cap takes on the kind of sudden, spacious significance that details in Mann often do: the Danish sailor cap seems to contain within itself the entire voyage to Denmark, the strong salt wind of the Baltic, the long mornings and afternoons on the beach in Zealand, the vision of the Danish Hans Hansen in the hotel at Aalsgaard, the Danish dance, the Hamlet theme, the ocean theme, the whole array of motifs associated with the far north; and one seems to see, in this minor detail sketched in with a naturalist's light but careful touch, the long, inescapable shadow cast backward by the story's future.

SECONDARY ARTISTS

Sometimes in a story about an artist Mann will insert a minor character who is also an artist of sorts and whose role is to form an ironic commentary on the central artist. In ***Death in Venice*** the secondary artist is the barber who dyes Aschenbach's hair black and colors his cheeks and lips; Mann calls him an "artist in cosmetic." The barber-artist is a parody of Aschenbach. Instead of plumbing the depths of souls, he attends only to appearances; his sole interest is deception and illusion. Since the genuine artist also has what Nietzsche calls a will to illusion, the comic barber has a touch of the sinister: he is that aspect of art which is indifferent to everything except illusion. He is Aschenbach stripped of belief. It is no accident that Aschenbach succumbs to him only after his obscene, shattering dream.

In ***Tonio Kröger*** the secondary artist is Herr Knaak, the dancing master from Hamburg who instructs the sons and daughters of leading families. Herr Knaak is an artist of dance, of social grace, and despite his grotesquerie he is no less self-assured in the practice of his public art than Tonio Kröger is of his private art. The resemblance between them is driven home by Herr Knaak's dark eyes, for the story emphasizes a distinction between blue, bourgeois eyes and dark, artistic eyes. But there is another resemblance as well. Herr Knaak's full name is François Knaak; the violent, comic contrast between the smoothflowing French syllables of the first name and the harsh German gutturals of the last name echoes the division in Tonio Kröger's name. The art of which Herr Knaak is a master is significant: dancing is a social art, and it is fitting that Tonio Kröger should dance badly.

FRAULEIN KROGER

During the quadrille conducted by Herr Knaak, a small mishap occurs. Herr Knaak announces the *moulinet des dames,* a division of the dance for women only; Tonio Kröger, brooding over Ingeborg Holm and the poetry of Storm, dreamily joins the girls. Knaak assumes a ballet pose "conventionally expressive of horror" and cries:

> Stop! Stop! Kröger among the ladies! *En arrière,* Fräulein Kröger, step back, *fi donc!*

Everyone laughs; the episode is soon forgotten. Fifteen years later Tonio Kröger delivers an attack on art to a painter friend in Munich. In a burst of bitterness he asks:

> Is an artist a male, anyhow? Ask the females! It seems to me we artists are all of us something like those unsexed papal singers . . . we sing like angels; but—

The outburst grows out of his angry and frustrated sense that the artist stands apart from life, observing it coldly, but the nature of the outburst remains startling and extreme. Is it possible to imagine Stephen Dedalus asking such a question?—to say nothing of Paul Morel. Tonio Kröger's scornful questioning of the artist's masculinity is not peculiar to his character, for in several stories of the same period Mann presents satirical portraits of artists whose masculinity is dubious. In **"The Infant Prodigy,"** published in the same year as ***Tonio Kröger,*** the child prodigy wears a silk bow in his hair and greets the crowd with a shy, charming gesture, "like a little girl"; in ***Tristan,*** written in 1902 and published in the same collection as ***Tonio Kröger*** (***Tristan. Sechs Novellen***, 1903), Detlev Spinell, the grotesque writer who lives in a sanatorium because he likes its Empire furnishings, is in his early thirties, like Tonio Kröger, and has a face "without a vestige of a beard. Not that it was shaven—you would have told; it was soft, smooth, boyish, with at most downy hair here and there." Mann in his own way can be as self-punishing as Kafka; this is the bourgeois in him, sneering at the artist. It is perhaps also a man raging at his own uncertain or undefined sexuality, for Mann much later confessed in a diary entry to what he called his "sexual inversion." But is it also more than that? May it not be the artist's own savage recoil against art, his protest against the price exacted by the harsh, monastic discipline of art? If the practice of art is by necessity solitary and austere, if beauty itself, in Baudelaire's phrase, has a heart of snow ("La Beauté"), is there not something in the very nature of art that is inimical to life? Stephen Dedalus's discovery of his vocation as artist is at the same time a welcoming of life, represented by the birdlike girl in the stream. Mann's view of art is always more ambiguous than Joyce's, at once more doubting and more probing. For Mann, art is always on the verge of moving in either of two directions: that of the sickly, the decadent, the precious, the unhealthy; or that of the criminal, the forbidden, the demonic. It is precisely his bourgeois distrust of art that leads Mann down dark paths of insight; it is his conservative temperament that drives him to his most radical questionings.

ART AND LIFE (1)

In the dialectic of the story, art and life are in opposition. The meaning of the antithesis seems to me clear enough, but it is worth considering for a moment what it means for an artist to feel that he is in any sense opposed to life. After all, the artist is alive, he is part of life. For him to feel opposed to life is for him to experience himself as a contradiction—to experience himself, that is, as a *problem*. And it is only when the artist experiences himself as a problem that there arises a literature with an artist as a central figure. Artists as human beings are of little interest to Renaissance dramatists; an occasional artist appears as a minor character, like the sycophantic Poet and Painter in *Timon of Athens,* and when an artist very infrequently appears as a protagonist it is always satirically (witness Ben Jonson's attack on Marston and Dekker in *The Poetaster* and Dekker's counterattack in *Satiromastix,* or Buckingham's brutal attack on Dryden in *The Rehearsal*). The artist as a serious figure first becomes interesting to the European imagination in the late eighteenth and early nineteenth centuries—precisely at a time when artists begin to experience themselves as problematical. German Romantic literature is filled with disturbed artist figures, of whom E. T. A. Hoffman's crazed composer is only the most famous; and it is significant in this respect that one of the earliest treatments of an artist is Goethe's *Torquato Tasso* (1790), a play that explicitly presents the artist as a problem. In this sense ***Tonio Kröger*** is directly in the line of German Romanticism. Like ***Death in Venice*** ten years later, it is German Romanticism carried into the twentieth century, but made sharper and drier and more rigorous—it is Romanticism that has passed through the discipline of Flaubert and Chekhov.

But there is a further consideration. A writer such as Mann, producing an early-twentieth-century work of art in which the artist is presented as a problem, is writing for a largely bourgeois audience that is ready and indeed eager to read about the problem of the artist. In the second chapter of ***Death in Venice*** Mann writes: "Men do not know why they award fame to one work of art rather than another. Without being in the faintest connoisseurs, they think to justify the warmth of their commendations by discovering in it a hundred virtues, whereas the real ground of their applause is inexplicable—it is sympathy." The fame of ***Tonio Kröger*** in its own time suggests that the problem of the artist was not the peculiar obsession of a particular writer but the expression of a malaise in the society for which he wrote. Looked at in one way, the problem of the artist, at least as formulated by Mann, is also the problem of the burgher: the real problem is the relation between the two. Is it possible that Mann was wrong, and that the artist is not the only one with a bad conscience? Is is possible that at a certain moment of history, the burgher also has a bad conscience—that he longs, not for the bliss of the commonplace, but for the uncommon, the exotic, the morally dubious, in short, for the artist?

ART AND LIFE (2)

The antithesis is not original with Mann, although he plays with it and extends its range in ways that are entirely his own. The most immediate and likely precedent is Ibsen's *When We Dead Awaken* (1899), in which art, in the person of the sculptor Rubek, is presented as a betrayer or destroyer of life. Mann was an early and lifelong admirer of Ibsen. He used four lines of verse by Ibsen as the motto for the ***Tristan*** volume, which contained ***Tonio Kröger***—lines that insist on a distinction between living and writing—and when, in a bravura passage in the essay ***Sufferings and Greatness of Richard Wagner,*** Mann compares Wagner with Ibsen, those two "northern wizards," those "crafty old weavers of spells," he says of *When We Dead Awaken* that it is "the awesome whispered confession of the production-man bemoaning his late, too late declaration of love of life." But even apart from Ibsen, European literature in the last quarter of the nineteenth century provided innumerable pairings of life and art (or the imagination)—usually to the disadvantage of life. A well-known example is Villier de l'Isle Adam's symbolist drama *Axel* (1890), with its notorious line: "Living? Our servants can do that for us"; while in England the witty disparagement of life in relation to art became for Wilde a fashionable habit. But even these late-nineteenth-century dichotomies are only a specialized development of a much broader debate waged in Europe since the Renaissance, in which the active terms were Art and Nature and which had its roots in the classical world (see *Nature and Art in Renaissance Literature* by Edward Tayler for countless classical, medieval, and Renaissance examples). What is new, late in the nineteenth century, is not the antithesis itself but the sense that art and life have become hostile to each other, that they have no connection, that an abyss separates them. It is precisely this sense of separation that Tonio Kröger experiences and attempts to overcome. Detlev Spinell experiences an identical separation and glories in it—it is as if Mann would distinguish the genuine artist from the decadent by the degree of his refusal to succumb to the feeling that life and art are hopelessly separated. But even for Tonio Kröger the gulf remains: art continues to be experienced as a *deviation* from life. In this sense, is he really so different from Adalbert the novelist?

ADALBERT THE NOVELIST

"God damn the spring!" says Adalbert the novelist—and goes into the "neutral territory" of a cafe to work. The difference between Tonio Kröger and Adalbert the novelist is that Tonio Kröger doesn't follow him into the cafe. His decision *to be disturbed,* which is also a decision not to work, is a judgment passed on Adalbert the novelist: the cafe becomes an evasion rather than a solution. With a witty speech and a shrug of his spiritual shoulders, Adalbert the novelist dismisses the crisis that torments Tonio Kröger, dismisses the very possibility of crisis. We all know him, Adalbert the novelist: nothing can stem the tide of his copious and mediocre prose.

But are we really so certain we know him, Adalbert the novelist? May there not be another way of looking at him, a way that releases him from caricature? If we shift our standpoint ever so slightly, if for a moment we remove our sympathy from Tonio Kröger and cast a skeptical eye on his assumptions, it becomes possible to think of Adalbert the novelist as someone akin to Lisabeta Ivanovna: the artist who goes about his business without fuss or melodrama, the artist who refuses the invitation to suffer. For looked at in a certain way, doesn't Tonio Kröger's judgment of Adalbert the novelist amount to disdain for his failure to be tormented? It is the hatred of the romantic for the craftsman—and the banning of the craftsman from the brotherhood of artist-saints whose motto is loneliness and whose sign is suffering.

IDLENESS AND INDUSTRY (1)

As a schoolboy, Tonio Kröger is no Stephen Dedalus: he is absent-minded in class and receives poor grades. His school idleness is specifically connected with his habit of brooding over his intuitions and writing poems. Hans Hansen, who prefers horse books to *Don Carlos,* is described as a "capital scholar" ("ein vortrefflicher Schüler"—an excellent student). Hans Hansen, that is to say, is the industrious student who always gets good grades. He is in no sense an intellectual, but neither is he stupid or slow; rather, he is the diligent, obedient, and proper son of a prominent businessman (his father owns a big lumberyard), and his diligence and good grades are part of his middle-class nature. Tonio's idleness is precisely a sign of apartness, of class betrayal—for he too is the son of a prominent businessman (a grain merchant, like the Buddenbrooks) and is said to live in the finest house in town. But he flees the fine house for Italy, where he learns to be an artist. And it is then that his name—"that good middle-class name with the exotic twist to it"—becomes a synonym for, among other things, "persistent industry." It is very interesting: the indolent schoolboy now works "not like a man who works that he may live; but as one who is bent on doing nothing but work." Idle as a student, he is industrious as an artist: it's as if, having cast off a bourgeois calling, he assumes almost ferociously all the bourgeois virtues, turned, however, in the opposite direction—the direction of art. Tonio Kröger is never more middle-class than when he is going against the grain of the middle class; only in the act of disloyalty can he permit himself to display his loyalty.

IDLENESS AND INDUSTRY (2)

But the relation between idleness and industry does not stop at the contrast between schoolwork and art, adolescence and maturity. Industry is the opposite of idleness, but it is also a cure for idleness; in this sense, the industry of the artist is a continual overcoming of a tendency toward indolence and dream that is also part of the artist's nature. The mature Mann recognized this truth in ***A Sketch of My Life*** in a passage describing his love of the carefree summer vacations at Travemünde on the Baltic: the idyllic life at the seashore "encouraged my native tendency to idleness and dreams—corrected much later and with difficulty." One suspects that native tendencies are stubborn and that correction does not imply eradication. Indeed, one might argue that idleness and dreams are as essential to the creation of art as industry itself. But idleness and dreams, which are anathema to the burgher, are no less disturbing to the disciplined artist, since they threaten his way of life even as they nourish it. The theme of the seductiveness of relaxation, of the temptation of idleness, sounds throughout Mann's mature work, most movingly in ***The Magic Mountain*** and ***Death in Venice***; and his early stories are filled with idle, dilettantish characters whom he sometimes treats with a savagery that suggests a secret fear.

ANTITHESIS

Tonio/Kröger, art/life, south/north, mother/father, artist/burgher, idleness/industry, dark eyes/blue eyes, dreamy eyes/keen eyes, idle and uneven walk/elastic, rhythmic tread, *Don Carlos*/horse books, exotic /commonplace, fixative/the breath of spring, the perilous knifedance of art/life's lulling, trivial waltz-rhythm—the antitheses are so abundant and alluring that one begins to long for an escape from the habit of opposition, which desires to account for every detail by drawing it into a system that is both wide-ranging and constrictive. The deep attraction of antithesis is the prevention of randomness and irresponsible profusion; its danger is the exclusion of the mysterious, the unaccountable, the inexplicable.

EYES

Eye color, like hair color, has long been the occasion of significant contrast in fiction, usually serving as the outward sign of an inward difference. In the literature of north European countries, such as England, Germany, and France, blue or grey eyes are the standard against which dark eyes are measured and in contrast to which dark eyes are felt to be disturbing, exotic, passionate, foreign, vital, evil, or even ugly; hence, for example, the repeated attention given by Sidney to Stella's dark eyes, an attention carried over by Shakespeare to dark-eyed ladies such as Rosaline in *Love's Labour's Lost* and the dark lady of the sonnets. By the nineteenth century, contrasts between blue and dark eyes have become a novelistic cliché: consider blue-eyed Rowena and dark-eyed Rebecca in *Ivanhoe,* blue-eyed Alice and dark-eyed Cora in *The Last of the Mohicans,* the blue-eyed Lintons and the dark-eyed Earnshaws in *Wuthering Heights*. But it is not until ***Tonio Kröger,*** at the beginning of the next century, that a work of literature raises eye color to a central place in the symbolic structure.

The crucial contrast is that between dark eyes (artist eyes) and blue eyes (burgher eyes), but Mann complicates the antithesis in ways that prevent it from remaining merely mechanical. Tonio Kröger's eyes are dreamy as well as dark; they stand in contrast to Hans Hansen's blue eyes, which are both "keen" and "clear." But the simple opposition is complicated by the first statement of the father-leitmotif: "A tall, fastidiously dressed man, with thoughtful blue eyes, and always a wild flower in his buttonhole." The eyes of the father are blue, but thoughtful; there is a touch of introspection and melancholy in these eyes (the father is called "slightly melancholy" in the last appearance of the leitmotif) that is not present in Hans Hansen's eyes and that corresponds to something in Tonio himself—the father here betrays a kinship to Thomas Buddenbrook, the grain merchant who reads Schopenhauer. Ingeborg Holm's *laughing* blue eyes are merely another version of Hans Hansen's eyes, but there are four additional pairs of dark eyes, all of which belong to artists or artist-types.

There are first of all the eyes of Tonio Kröger's piano-playing mother, eyes that are never mentioned but that we infer are dark, for she has black hair and is from "the south"; since she is characterized by blitheness and moral indifference, we imagine her eyes as having less depth than her son's eyes. François Knaak, the artist of dance, has "beautiful brown eyes" that "did not plumb the depths of things to the place where life becomes complex and melancholy"; his eyes, like his art, are superficial. But immediately a secondary antithesis is established between the depthless dark eyes of Herr Knaak and the thoughtful blue eyes of Herr Kröger, almost as if Mann wished to insist that the initial contrast between dark and blue should not be taken literally, but only symbolically. Among the dancers in Herr Knaak's class is Magdalena Vermehren, who has "great, dark, brilliant eyes, so serious and adoring"; she is interested in Tonio's verses, she is *artistic,* but she is also clumsy—she falls down in the dance. Her brilliant, dark, serious eyes are the eyes not of an artist but of an artist-adorer: the adult Tonio Kröger cruelly describes her as the kind of person for whom poetry serves as a mild revenge on life. The friend to whom he offers this description is Lisabeta Ivanovna, a painter, who also has dark eyes: "little bright black eyes." She is a genuine artist, who works even as she listens to the opening of Tonio Kröger's tirade against art ("I will just finish this little place—work out this little effect"), but she is an artist for whom art is not a problem: in this respect she stands midway between Herr Knaak and Tonio Kröger. Thus without ever losing the central opposition between dark eyes and blue eyes, Mann manages to cover a wide and almost contradictory range, extending all the way to thoughtful blue and superficial dark.

FURTHER THOUGHTS ON STRUCTURE: THE FOURTH CHAPTER

The temporal and geographical schemes that I have suggested for ***Tonio Kröger*** overlap in certain respects but are by no means identical; and neither fully accounts for the elusive and perhaps not finally explicable experience that we call the *structure* of a work of fiction. If we try once again to fathom the plan of the novella, with the sense that something has remained unaccounted for, we may be struck by the peculiar nature of the fourth chapter, which stands out from the other chapters almost in the manner of an essay inserted into a dramatic tale. Almost: for the chapter isn't an essay, and the story into which it is inserted is not notably dramatic. But the fourth chapter does have the effect of standing out from the surrounding material, of stopping the flow of narrative, of presenting itself as an exception, even as an obstacle. In this sense the novella breaks into three parts: the first three chapters, which recount Tonio Kröger's youth; the essayistic fourth chapter; and the last five chapters, which recount his northern voyage and deliberately recapitulate elements of the first three chapters.

Mann confessed to having had great difficulty with the fourth chapter. For months the story wouldn't budge; he was unable to write a word. His decision to write what he calls, in ***A Sketch of My Life,*** the "lyric-essayistic middle part" ("das lyrisch-essayistische Mittlestück"—Lowe-Porter translates the concise phrase as "the middle part, lyric and prose essay in one"), was a bold one, but the chapter nevertheless remains a problem. In it the central conflict of the story is brought to precise articulation, and the effect can seem to be a deliberate abandonment of drama, a flirtation with esthetic collapse. Mann is aware of the dangers and, having gone out of his way to violate the conventional dramatic development of his story, makes every effort to draw the chapter back into the realm of the dramatic. His main technique for doing so is to have Tonio Kröger allude obliquely to experiences that are familiar to us from earlier chapters. When he speaks of people who are always falling down in the dance, we remember Magdalena Vermehren and the dancing lesson; when he says that one ought not to tempt people to read poetry who would rather read books about the instantaneous photography of horses, we are invited to recall not only a particular moment in chapter I but the entire incident concerning *Don Carlos* and Hans Hansen's betrayal, indeed the entire chapter in all its meanings as they radiate out from the image of horse books. In addition to drawing on earlier moments of drama, Mann repeatedly attempts to overcome the essayistic tendency of the chapter by reminding us of the speech's occasion. That occasion is nothing less than a crisis in the hero's spiritual life: things have reached such a pass that, unlike Adalbert the novelist, who seeks out the neutral territory of a cafe when confronted with the distractions of spring, Tonio Kröger can no longer work. We are urged to experience the speech as the long revelation of a problem—as part of the plot. It is the tormented though orderly outpouring of a man in deep spiritual trouble; and the orderly, logical nature of the outburst is entirely in keeping with Tonio Kröger's character. But if so much is granted, it nevertheless remains true that the chapter radically refuses to behave like other chapters. It tends to sit like a lump in the middle of the story—even if it is a lump that the story can digest. Despite its air of redeeming boldness, the chapter cannot entirely evade the suspicion that important material has simply failed to be incorporated dramatically in the story.

THE TREATMENT OF PASSING TIME

How shall a work of fiction, with its continual urge toward particularization as it attempts to create and sustain the illusion of a world, handle the passing of time? Events in the fictional world that are presented as the temporal equivalent of events in the reader's world invite specification—invite, that is, the careful and abundant accumulation of significant detail. But what of the passing of days, of weeks, of entire years? Here, by the very nature of the case, accumulation is discouraged. One method of overcoming the hampering effects of swiftly passing fictional time is to arrange the material of the fiction so as to permit the greatest number of detailed scenes, which are then joined by brisk passages that report the passing of time. This is essentially the method of ***Tonio Kröger,*** although it would be a mistake to think of it as the only one. It would be a mistake, in particular, to think of the passages in ***Tonio Kröger*** in which days or years pass as efficient, workmanlike segments that exist solely to convey information before permitting the real story to continue. There are passages of this kind, but there are also episodes of passing time that are meant to be experienced in their own right—are meant to have a flavor distinct from the flavor of a fully rendered scene.

Two such passages are the opening movement of chapter 8, in which Tonio Kröger passes "some days" and then "several" more days at Aalsgaard before arriving at the particular day on which the climactic dance takes place, and all of chapter 3, which recounts his Italian years. A difference between the passages immediately presents itself—a difference that may partially be explained as the difference between treating the passing of days on the one hand and years on the other, but that is not exhausted by this first and rather too easy explanation. For it is important to notice that the Danish passage, which covers an unknown number of days in six paragraphs, is characterized by an abundance of precise and evocative details. The sea that Tonio Kröger watches in the long mornings and afternoons sometimes lay "idle and smooth, in stripes of blue and russet and bottle-green." The jellyfish lying on the sunny beach are captured in a single memorable detail: "the jellyfish lay steaming." In an inspired simile, the sound of the surf is a noise "like boards collapsing at a distance." The guests in the dining room, who play no part in the story, are as sharply seen as minor characters in Dickens: an old fish dealer from Copenhagen "kept putting his beringed first finger to one nostril, and snorting violently to get a passage of air through the other." There is, very deliberately, no *scene* in these six paragraphs, for the experience being described is *habitual*: it is important that we lose the sense of precise moments in order to bathe in an atmosphere, to gain a sense of significantly repeated sights and gestures and sounds. But the absence of a close-up scene does not mean the loss of precise detail: it is merely that the detail comes at us in a different manner.

The effect of the ten paragraphs of the Italian chapter is distinctly different. Here there is a sudden and striking loss of detail:

> He lived in large cities and in the south, promising himself a luxuriant ripening of his art by southern suns. . . .
>
> he fell into adventures of the flesh, descended into the depths of lust and searing sin. . . .
>
> And then, with knowledge, its torments and its arrogance, came solitude. . . .

It isn't that large, general statements are impermissible in a work of literature; it is, rather, that large, general statements need to grow out of sharply rendered details, require a precise habitat. Such details as in fact are present in the Italian chapter are all details of leitmotif, which connect Tonio Kröger to his past. But Italy itself remains strikingly unrendered; it is an abstract space in which certain mental events take place. My point is that the failure to *render* Italy cannot be explained away as a necessary consequence of treating a large span of time; the absence of a specific scene, as the Denmark passage shows, does not require the absence of the kind of precise detail we usually associate with a specific scene. Mann, who completed the story at the still youthful age of twenty-seven, has simply made an error here: he has treated the passing of time as if it were independent of *things*. His sentences in this section retain a firm thematic relation to the novella—there is never any loss of structural clarity—but they tend to sound curiously abstract, rhetorical, disconnected from the stuff of experience, and this at the very moment when they are making large assertions about experience. The cause of the failure may be psychological—Mann's inability to speak of his Italian years, or of sexuality—but the result is technical: an absence of detail, a vacuity.

IMMENSEE

Sixteen-year-old Tonio Kröger stands brooding in the corridor outside the room where Ingeborg Holm is dancing and thinks, "So lovely and laughing as you are one can only be if one does not read *Immensee* and never tries to write things like it." That *Immensee* was a cherished book of his own adolescence is confirmed by Mann in his affectionate essay on Theodor Storm, whom he names as one of the two "spiritual fathers" of ***Tonio Kröger***—the other being Turgenev.

Did Mann have *Immensee* in mind when composing ***Tonio Kröger***? In *Immensee* he would have found an arrangement of nine short chapters, often separated by large gaps of time; a chapter of childhood love; a broad time span, ranging from an experience of the protagonist at ten years old to his experiences as a young man of unstated age, who appears to be in his middle or late twenties (as well as a hoary frame-device that shows him in old age); the theme of unrequited love; an emphasis on love-sorrow, loneliness, and nostalgia. Above all, he might have received a hint for his own recapitulative scheme, for in the penultimate chapter Reinhard has two experiences that repeat moments in earlier chapters: he watches Elisabeth sitting in the shade of an overhanging branch and has the sense that it has all happened before, while the reader recalls a similar moment when Reinhard watched her seated in the shade of a tree when he was seventeen; and he sees a beggar girl who looks at him wildly and sings a song he remembers being sung by a gypsy girl in his university days. The similarities between the novellas are real but slight, and should not be exaggerated; perhaps what connects them most closely is what is most questionable in ***Tonio Kröger***: a certain heaviness of feeling, a tendency toward the lyricism of sorrow, toward the dubious pleasures of nostalgia.

BIOGRAPHY

Mann completed ***Tonio Kröger*** in December 1902—it appeared in the February 1903 issue of the *Neue Deutsche Rundschau,* and again in the volume of stories called ***Tristan*** that appeared later in the same year—but precisely when he began it is unclear. The first evidence of actual composition occurs in a letter to Heinrich Mann of 8 January 1901, in which he complains that what he is writing is too long for *Simplicissimus,* the journal in which several of his earlier stories had appeared. A month later he complains to Heinrich that the artist theme has so thrust itself forward that the long-planned story ought to be called "Literature." But in this same letter he reports that he is at work on ***Tristan,*** which he calls a burlesque and which he appears to have completed in the spring of 1901. A question immediately presents itself: was it only by creating the satiric and even cruel portrait of the artist found in ***Tristan*** that Mann was able to release himself into ***Tonio Kröger***? Was it only by mocking the pretensions and affectations of the artist that he could feel free to treat the artist seriously in a work of fiction? Detlev Spinell is a decadent Tonio Kröger, a Tonio Kröger corrupted by preciousness; his sinister kinship is suggested by the fact that he shares not only Tonio Kröger's age but his habit of holding his head to one side (a trait later given to Hans Castorp when he listens to music). In any case, the release, if it was one, was by no means immediate, for Mann later complains to a friend that he has made no progress on ***Tonio Kröger*** during the entire winter (the winter of 1901-1902); only in the spring of 1902 does he report that he is at work, but the work is torment: he speaks of doubts, hesitations, dissatisfaction. He is still at work when the proofs of the five other stories of the ***Tristan*** collection arrive in October, and he finishes only in mid-December.

But even this checkered history of composition, extending over nearly two years, is only part of the story. In ***A Sketch of My Life*** (1930), Mann claims that he conceived the idea for ***Tonio Kröger*** while still working on ***Buddenbrooks***: "I spent a two weeks' holiday in that excursion via Lübeck to Denmark which is described in the tale; and the impressions of my visit to Aalsgaard am Sund, near Helsingör, were the nucleus round which the elements of the allusive little composition shot together." Just when the elements shot together is by no means clear, for in an address called ***Lübeck als geistige Lebensform,*** delivered on the occasion of Lübeck's 700th anniversary in 1926, he says somewhat enigmatically that ***Tonio Kröger*** was "unconsciously sketched" at Aalsgaard ("der ***Tonio Kröger*** unbewusst entworfen wurde"), the "unconsciously" suggesting that the story had not yet even been imagined. The trip to Lübeck and Aalsgaard took place in September 1899 (***Buddenbrooks*** was completed in July 1900, a month after his twenty-fifth birthday), and the timing of the trip is worth noting. In *Thomas Mann: The Making of an Artist,* Richard Winston points out that, in the writing of ***Buddenbrooks,*** Mann had arrived at the death of Senator Buddenbrook's mother and the sale of the house, and suggests that Mann might have wanted to pay a visit to his old house in order to set the scene. But Hans Rudolf Vaget in his *Kommentar zu sämtlichen Erzählungen* (*Commentary on the Complete Stories*) makes what seems to me a more pregnant suggestion: "TM stand vor der Aufgabe, die Jugend Hanno Buddenbrooks zu gestalten und verspurte wohl das Bedürfnis, seine Erinnerungen aufzufrischen und noch einmal seinen 'Ausgangspunkt' zu berühren." ("TM faced the task of shaping the youth of Hanno Buddenbrook, and probably felt the need to refresh his memories and touch his 'point of origin' again.") That is, Mann was about to plunge into a detailed evocation of a childhood very much like his own. The composition of ***Tonio Kröger*** therefore attaches itself spiritually to the last movement of ***Buddenbrooks,*** and it surrounds, so to speak, the composition of ***Tristan***. To put it another way, it has its origin in the sickly artist-figure of Hanno Buddenbrook, and surrounds the decadent artist-figure of Detlev Spinell, who writes with excruciating slowness and who lives in a sanatorium because he likes the decor. It is as if ***Tonio Kröger*** represents an overcoming of both Hanno Buddenbrook and Detlev Spinell—as if Tonio's bad conscience is a knowledge of the disease and decadence that might have been his own, had Mann not lavished them on other characters instead.

EVALUATION

The harshest thing one can say about ***Tonio Kröger*** is that it is not ***Death in Venice***. Exactly what it is, however, has proved more difficult to say. Far more than ***Death in Venice,*** it carries with it the distinct and somewhat faded flavor of its time, without begging the indulgence accorded to the mere period piece. The oppositions have a disturbing clarity that make them seem more suitable to comedy, and history has complicated our response to the blond and blue-eyed Hans Hansens of the North in a way that interferes seriously with Mann's intellectual scheme. The image of the lonely artist at odds with the world takes its place more clearly than ever as part of the history of European Romanticism, but the attempted resolution lacks the fine daring and bravado of romantic rebellion. The energy of narrative is in a significant degree recollective, and does not always resist the perilous enticements of nostalgia.

It must nevertheless also be said that the problem which the story painstakingly examines—the problem of the artist in his relation to the world, which is also the problem of the artist in relation to his art—is one that has not only not vanished in the twentieth century but has increased in urgency even as the conditions of the problem have changed. The artist in exile, the artist at odds with the state—those quintessential artists of the century—may put the problem differently, but the choices they make are forms of spiritual allegiance that are kin to the crucial antitheses of ***Tonio Kröger***. In a bitter attack on literature called "A Poet Between East and West," Czeslaw Milosz, who even manages to sound like Mann when he calls poetry "morally suspect," says that he now accepts a dark premise of ***Tonio Kröger*** (the unhealthy origin of art) that he had rejected in his youth. But the issue of relevance is itself highly equivocal, since a work of art may be vital in ways bearing little relation to the questions it may seem to raise. Formally, the recapitulative method of ***Tonio Kröger*** remains impressive: the final chapters draw on earlier chapters in a precise, subtle, and exhaustive way that is unprecedented in the history of fiction. The story is bold in its extensive use of a device, the leitmotif, that goes against the grain of narrative cause and effect and introduces a different principle of organization, and it is no less bold in its use of a large essayistic chapter that knowingly takes the risk of violating the forward movement of the story. And in a work that in many ways looks back to the nineteenth century, Mann strikes a peculiarly modern note by treating art itself, that holy of holies, as problematic. From the very beginning, Mann's fascination as a writer lay in his peculiar combination of the cautious and the daring, the conservative and the destructive—a combination that separates him, for example, from his near-contemporary, Kafka, who was all daring and destruction—and the tension of that division in his temperament gave rise to ***Tonio Kröger,*** which Kafka is known to have admired, as well as to later and darker works. For it must never be forgotten that ***Tonio Kröger*** is a youthful story, written by a young man of twenty-six and twenty-seven, who, it is true, had already written ***Buddenbrooks***—a young man, in short, whose youthfulness is itself complex and problematic, with its fruitful mixture of indolence and almost soldierly discipline, of pessimism and ambition, its habit of questioning the whole enterprise of art while practicing that art with unalterable devotion.

FURTHER READING

Bibliography

Jonas, Klaus W. "*Tonio Kröger* (1903)." In *Fifty Years of Mann Studies: A Bibliography of Criticism*, pp. 131-32. Minneapolis: University of Minnesota Press, 1955.

Brief bibliography of essays on *Tonio Kröger* from the first half of the twentieth century.

Criticism

Apter, T. E. "The Romantic Dilemma." In *Thomas Mann: The Devil's Advocate*, pp. 13-37. London: Macmillan Press Ltd., 1978.

Includes a discussion of the opposition between life and imagination as dramatized in *Tonio Kröger*.

Berendsohn, Walter E. "The World of Yesterday." In *Thomas Mann: Artist and Partisan in Troubled Times*, translated by George C. Buck, pp. 8-60. University: University of Alabama Press, 1973.

Draws biographical parallels between *Tonio Kröger* and Mann's life, and focuses on Mann's attempt within the story to highlight "the contrast between literary art and the naive life."

Brennan, Joseph Gerard. "The Artist's Isolation in a Bourgeois World." In *Thomas Mann's World*, pp. 3-36. New York: Russell & Russell, Inc., 1962.

Explores the theme of isolation in *Tonio Kröger* and other works by Mann.

Eddy, Beverley Driver. "Teaching *Tonio Kröger* as Literature about Literature." In *Approaches to Teaching Mann's 'Death in Venice' and Other Short Fiction*, edited by Jeffrey B. Berlin, pp. 119-25. New York: Modern Language Association of America, 1992.

Takes a biographical approach to understanding and teaching *Tonio Kröger*.

Feuerlicht, Ignace. "Stories." In *Thomas Mann*, pp. 108-49. New York: Twayne Publishers, Inc., 1968.

Presents an overview of *Tonio Kröger* in a section entitled "Loves of an Outsider."

Neubauer, John. "Identity by Metaphors: *A Portrait of the Artist* and *Tonio Kröger*." In *Neverending Stories: Toward a Critical Narratology*, edited by Ann Fehn, Ingeborg Hoesterey, and Maria Tatar, pp. 124-37. Princeton: Princeton University Press, 1992.

Compares the narrative strategies used in *Tonio Kröger* and James Joyce's *A Portrait of the Artist as a Young Man*.

O'Neill, Patrick. "Dance and Counterdance: A Note on *Tonio Kröger*." *German Life and Letters* XXIX, No. 3 (April 1976): 291-95.

Discusses dance as the symbolic and thematic touchstone to *Tonio Kröger*.

Springer, Mary Doyle. "The Maturing of Tonio Kröger and Some Others." In *Forms of the Modern Novella*, pp. 148-57. Chicago: University of Chicago Press, 1975.

Examines *Tonio Kröger* as a "novella of learning and maturing," while focusing on the work's structure and stylistic devices.

Swales, M. W. "Punctuation and the Narrative Mode: Some Remarks on *Tonio Kröger*." *Forum for Modern Language Studies* VI, No. 3 (July 1970): 235-42.

Analyzes the liberal use of ellipses in *Tonio Kröger*, and argues that this structural device serves an integral thematic purpose in the work.

Von Gronicka, André. "The Mediator." In *Thomas Mann: Profile and Perspectives*, pp. 113-34. New York: Random House, 1970.

Discusses the "tension between [Mann's] bourgeois heritage and his artistic temperament," especially as it is borne out in *Tonio Kröger*.

Ward, Mark G. "More Than 'Stammesverwandtschaft'? On Tonio Kröger's Reading of *Immensee*." *German Life and Letters* XXXVI, No. 4 (July 1983): 301-16.

Traces thematic parallels between *Tonio Kröger* and Theodor Storm's *Immensee*.

Additional coverage of Mann's life and career is contained in the following sources published by Gale Research: *Contemporary Authors*, Vols. 104, 128; *Dictionary of Literary Biography*, Vol. 66; *DISCovering Authors*; *Major 20th Century Writers*; *Short Story Criticism*, Vol. 5; *Twentieth-Century Literary Criticism*, Vols. 2, 8, 14, 21, 35, 44; and *World Literature Criticism*.

Leo Perutz

1882-1957

(Full name Leopold Perutz) Austrian novelist, short story and novella writer, and dramatist.

INTRODUCTION

Although Perutz's writings include short stories, novellas, and at least one published play, the international reputation he enjoyed during the 1920s and 1930s stemmed primarily from his novels, which include suspense-filled psychological dramas and meticulously constructed historical tales set in Europe during periods of political and cultural conflict. Forced into exile when Hitler came to power in Austria, Perutz published to a diminished audience following World War II, yet he remained convinced that his fiction would become widely read once again. Recent decades have proven him right: since the late 1950s, a growing number of Perutz's works have been translated and reissued to critical and popular acclaim.

Biographical Information

Perutz was born in 1882 to wealthy Jewish parents in Prague, when the city was part of the Austro-Hungarian Empire. When his father's business was destroyed by fire in 1889, the family emigrated to Vienna, Austria, where Perutz and a group of fellow students at the Erzherzog Rainer-Real-Gymnasium launched a literary club called the "Freilicht" (Free Light), which served as a forum for the reading and discussion of their writings. This early affinity for literature notwithstanding, Perutz studied mathematics before becoming a respected insurance actuary. In 1915 he published his first novel, *Die dritte Kugel.* Later that year, Perutz enlisted in the army. A chest wound cut short his active duty in 1916, and he served out his assignment writing war reports from the military press headquarters in Vienna. Perutz wrote prolifically during the next two decades, producing more than a dozen novels. Newspapers vied for the right to serialize his stories and novellas, and many of his works were translated into foreign languages. In 1938, upon Hitler's annexation of Austria to Germany, Perutz fled with other Jews to Tel Aviv, Palestine. The difficulties of writing in exile and his isolation from German-language readers severely affected Perutz's literary output and reduced his reading audience. He struggled to produce two more novels, only one of which was published during his lifetime. In 1957, while visiting friends in Austria, Perutz died of a heart attack; his final novel was published posthumously in 1959.

Major Works

Perutz's reputation as a writer of tightly constructed narratives placed in historical settings was established with the publication of his first novel. Set during the sixteenth-century Schmalkadic War and imbued with elements of the fantastic, *Die dritte Kugel* was enthusiastically received. His second novel, *Zwischen neun und neun* (*From Nine to Nine)*—a tension-filled psychological thriller—appeared in 1918 and was as successful as his first. Two years later Perutz published *Der Marques de Bolibar* (*The Marquis de Bolibar*), a historical novel that traces a Spanish nobleman's commitment to restore his family's honor during the Napoleonic Wars. Over the next three decades, Perutz's published work included a dozen novels, a collection of novellas, and a play. His 1934 novel, *St. Petri-Schnee* (*The Virgin's Brand;* also translated as *St. Peter's Snow),* has been described as a reflection of Hitler's rise to power in its portrayal of a man's ability to influence others in his single-minded pursuit of victory. Perutz's novels uniformly feature retrospective narration by a character whose involvement in the story is deliberately left ambiguous. Other elements characteristic of his work include historically accurate accounts of political intrigue and military maneuvers, insightful psychological depictions of fictional and historical figures, and a recurring treatment of time as both a subjective and an objective reality. Perutz's frequent suggestion that supernatural phenomena can determine the destiny of his characters intensifies the sense of irresolvable uncertainty present in his narratives.

Critical Reception

Some critics minimize Perutz's accomplishments as a novelist, asserting that his literary reputation ensues from his least intellectual fiction—the commercially popular adventure tales he published during the 1920s. Others, including Argentinian writer Jorge Luis Borges, laud Perutz's compositional style. The Austrian novelist Robert Musil, in recognition of Perutz's detailed and historically accurate narratives, credited him with developing a new genre that Musil termed "journalistic fiction." Friedrich Torberg, who once characterized Perutz's literary style as the "possible result of an illicit union of Franz Kafka with Agatha Christie," is among the critics who commend Perutz's ability to sustain narrative tension while enriching his fiction with both psychological insight and macabre mysticism. Perutz himself contributed to the apparent lack of serious critical attention given his fiction by claiming that his stories were not meant to be studied, but simply read and enjoyed. A resurgence of scholarly attention to Perutz's fiction during the 1950s and 1960s led to the reprinting, in 1975, of a large body of his work. In subsequent decades, selected novels have been issued in new translations in response to public and academic interest in Perutz and his works.

PRINCIPAL WORKS

Die dritte Kugel (novel) 1915
Zwischen neun und neun [*From Nine to Nine*] (novel) 1918
Das Gasthaus zur Kartätsche: Eine Geschichte aus dem alten Österreich (novella) 1920
Der Marques de Bolibar [*The Marquis de Bolibar*] (novel) 1920
Die Geburt des Antichrist (novella) 1921
Der Meister des Jüngsten Tages [*The Master of the Day of Judgment*] (novel) 1923
Turlupin (novel) 1924
Der Kosak und die Nachtigall [with Paul Frank] (novel) 1927
Wohin rollst du, Äpfelchen . . . [with Paul Frank] [*Where Will You Fall?*; also translated as *Little Apple*] (novel) 1928
Flammen auf San Domingo: Roman nach Victor Hugo's "Bug-Jargal" (novel) 1929
Die Reise nach Preßburg: Schauspiel in 3 Atken (9 Bildern) mit einem Vor- und einem Nachspiel (drama) 1930
Herr, erbarme Dich meiner! (novellas) 1930
St. Petri-Schnee [*The Virgin's Brand*; also translated as *Saint Peter's Snow*] (novel) 1934
Der schwedische Reiter (novel) 1936
Nachts unter der steinernen Brücke: Ein Roman aus dem alten Prag [*By Night Under the Stone Bridge*] (novel) 1953
Der Judas des Leonardo [*Leonardo's Judas*] (novel) 1959

CRITICISM

The New York Times Book Review **(essay date 1926)**

SOURCE: "A German Mystery," in *The New York Times Book Review,* August 8, 1926, pp. 9, 12, 16.

[*In the following review, the critic characterizes* From Nine to Nine *as an excellent mystery, but suggests that the tale is too sophisticated to achieve popular success.*]

The blurb that proves to be an understatement is a rare one, indeed. But such a distinction would seem to be achieved by ***From Nine to Nine***; it is really better than the publishers, perspicuous though they are of its merits, lead you to suppose. It is, as they say, something new under the sun—at least to Americans who are forced to maintain the same literary diet year after year. Why could no such thing as ***From Nine to Nine*** any more than *The Cabinet of Dr. Caligari* in the movies, come out of America? We have writers of mystery stories who show as much ingenuity as Herr Perutz does. We have writers who show as much imagination, perhaps. We have a few whose books are even more exciting. But this book shows a versatility, an artistic level, which American mystery stories lack; it combines a fascinating story with striking characterization, keen knowledge of human nature and piquant humor. It represents much art spent upon a little thing. A man who has Herr Perutz's gifts, some people are likely to say, should do something more significant than carve the curious cherrystone of imagination and ingenuity which he calls ***From Nine to Nine***. We are rather glad he did. He wrote something mentally refreshing, physically exciting, and artistically sound.

From Nine to Nine is in essence a mystery story with two splendid shocks for the reader—one toward the middle of the book and another at the end. The first of these revelations does nothing to dull the interest of the book, for whereas its secret absorbed the reader by mystifying him until it was explained, its knowledge absorbs him equally because it still remains a secret to the characters in the book and he can watch it mystifying them.

The student, Stanislaus Demba, who causes the mystery, is a real, an almost unforgettable, creation. For the first half of the book the reader does not know what to make of him. As the blurb says, he is starving yet will not eat, he craves money yet refuses to take it by honorable means, he loves yet cannot act. He moves from one scene to another in a long black cape with his hands concealed beneath it. He tells one person that he has no arms, yet when in pity she leaves a few heller for him on a park bench, he sticks out two skinny fingers and picks them up. A professor finds him ravenous for food one minute, yet giving his sandwiches to a dog the next. He frightens a girl who reaches beneath his cape and feels the cold touch of steel—a revolver, she supposes! It is a very pretty mystery, indeed.

Then, toward the middle of the book, the secret of the mystery is revealed—Demba is handcuffed! That is why his hands are hidden, that is why Sonia Hartman touched cold steel, that is why two outstretched fingers grabbed the heller. He has been arrested for selling a book that belongs to the public library, and he has escaped.

Marvelous to relate, the interest of the book mounts rather than falls when this secret becomes known, otherwise we should not be so inconsiderate as to reveal it. Demba wants to go away with Sonia Hartman and needs 200 kronen. The record of his attempts to get them without using his hands, with only the reader aware that he is handcuffed, is one of the most delightful pieces of pure narrative that have come our way in a long time. It is a mixture of humor and pathos, of superb ingenuity on Demba's part, an ingenuity always frustrated in the end by a small miscalculation or accident. And all the time Demba is dancing on the brink of a precipice, for he realizes that if once his handcuffs are noticed it will be all up with him! This skating over thin ice provides a thoroughly exciting undercurrent to the record of Demba's attempts to get the money.

The story moves on to a climax in a Viennese café, where excitement and humor run over, and simultaneously human nature is portrayed with considerable neatness. The dénouement which follows this climax comes as the second shock in Herr Perutz's splendidly contrived story, and though it is not completely satisfying or even necessary, it carries the story to its final conclusion with a swift and surprising effect.

It is doubtful whether ***From Nine to Nine*** will become a popular success. It is too sophisticated. It cares too much for other things than mystery to have a thoroughly popular appeal. Herr Perutz has not catered to the taste which demands a murder or an abduction in every chapter. He has woven a story out of nothing more blood-curdling or solid than a handcuffed man. To carry such a story through with the success he has achieved demands less an amplitude of material than a knowledge of art. It demands, too, versatility.

The Times Literary Supplement (essay date 1926)

SOURCE: A review of *The Marquis de Bolibar,* in *The Times Literary Supplement,* No. 1284, September 9, 1926, p. 594.

[*In the following excerpt, the critic questions Perutz's handling of magic in* The Marquis de Bolibar *while offering a generally favorable review of the novel.*]

The Marquis De Bolibar by Leo Perutz has considerable distinction; at its weakest one is conscious that there is a superior and original mind behind it. The plot is good enough, the characterization excellent, the air of a memoir well simulated. Where it fails is in the treatment of the magical events upon which the story mainly hinges. These are sometimes trivial and sometimes clumsy, and the fashion in which the tone changes from the ironical to the rhetorical when they are dealt with is unsatisfactory. It is, nevertheless, a novel quite out of the ordinary.

Its theme is an imaginary episode of the Peninsular War, the destruction by Spanish irregulars of two regiments of the Rhenish Confederation in the French service; and it is supposed to be an abridgment of the papers of Edward von Jochberg, the sole survivor. Jochberg tells us how the officers of one of these regiments, the Nassau Dragoons, brought the disaster upon themselves, almost of set purpose, in the grip of fate and of two guilty secrets shared by them: that they had all been lovers of the Colonel's dead wife, the beautiful Françoise-Marie, and that they had killed the Marquis de Bolibar because he had discovered the fact. As Bolibar was a spy, whom they would in any case have executed, as they were all soldiers of fortune far from squeamish in moral affairs, it does not appear why the second should have troubled them. Here the magic makes its appearance, in a form which it would be unfair—to readers as well as writer—to reveal. It is also represented in the figure of Captain de Salignac, the Wandering Jew in person, who is quite unnecessary to the plot save in so far as he brings ill-luck on those with whom he is associated. These blemishes apart, it is an excellent romance, high-coloured and swift in action, but at the same time intelligent. . . .

L. P. Hartley (essay date 1926)

SOURCE: A review of *The Marquis de Bolibar,* in *The Saturday Review,* London, Vol. 142, No. 3698, September 11, 1926, pp. 292-93.

[*In the following excerpt, Hartley offers a generally enthusiastic appraisal of* The Marquis de Bolivar.]

Romantic, heroic, symbolic, fantastic, obscure, occult—epithets that fit some aspect of ***The Marquis de Bolibar,*** suggest themselves readily enough. But it is much less easy to catch the author's whole intention and condense it in a word. Here is what purports to be an incident in the Peninsular War. The preface, a monument of Teutonic thoroughness, short but solid, introduces us to the memoirs of Edward von Jochberg who was, at the time of the capture of La Bisbal, a lieutenant in a Hessian regiment serving under Napoleon. Our interest, we must own, slumbered through Mr. Leo Perutz's well-worn device to awaken it: we learned that neither Dr. Hermann Schwartze, nor F. Krause, nor H. Leistikow, nor Fischer of Tübingen, could offer an explanation of the mysterious destruction of the two regiments, but we were not impressed. We did not feel curious to know the gallant von Jochberg's secret.

But after reading a few pages we were consumed with curiosity, avid to learn. It is true, perhaps, that the best part of the book comes first; it never quite recaptures the excitement of the scene by the camp-fire when the Marquis de Bolibar hears of his nephew's perfidy:

> "Is he dead?" asked the Marquis. He stood erect without moving, but his shadow danced madly as the flames leapt up, so that it looked as if it were not the old man, but his shadow, that was waiting with such anxiety for the Tanner's news.
>
> "Many nations fight in the French Armies," said the Tanner, shrugging his shoulders, "Germans and Dutchmen, Neapolitans and Poles. So why, I ask you, shouldn't a Spaniard occasionally take service with the French?"
>
> "Is he dead?" cried the Marquis. . . .

The scene is wonderfully conceived, the melodrama preserved from staginess by imagination and emotion. These qualities persist throughout the story, enhancing immeasurably the effect of its unforeseen and incredible developments. We are sorry that the Wandering Jew had to be called in to explain one character away; we regret Captain de Salignac's prayer and one or two instances when medieval mythology usurps the stage. Explanations of the supernatural are always tedious, even when they take the form of an appeal from a vague to a formulated superstition. And there are signs, portents and coincidences, altogether too many finger-posts and milestones leading to Hell, the descent to which, as we know, is easy and discernible without prompting or the aid of concrete signs. There are evidences of the prevalent Teutonic tendency towards huge cloudy symbols, which do not necessarily carry with them a high romance. But in spite of lapses into the manner of great opera, ***The Marquis de Bolibar*** preserves an altogether unusual measure of enchantment. The characters, especially Captain Brockendorf, are well drawn; but Mr. Perutz's chief power lies, as we have said, in presenting marvellous events without any diminution of emotional effect. Understatement, the refuge of most writers when they reach their strong scenes, he disdains; not a curse, not a groan, not a sigh, not a tear, does he willingly leave out. His book is like a child's story written for the grown-up, romantic yet mature, always absorbed in the present yet always looking ahead. It would make an admirable film, so remarkable is its pictorial quality, but its strangeness is at least as much a matter of the mind as of the mind's eye. The book makes an assault on the imagination, and no one who reads it will soon forget the four officers inflamed with jealous longing for their colonel's mistress, or the death and reincarnation of the Marquis of Bolibar.

L. P. Hartley (essay date 1927)

SOURCE: A review of *From Nine to Nine,* in *The Saturday Review,* London, Vol. 143, No. 3727, April 2, 1927, pp. 527-28.

[*In the following excerpt, Hartley reviews* From Nine to Nine *and suggests that readers who enjoyed* The Marquis of Bolivar *may be disappointed by the comparative plot and character limitation of this harsh psychological drama.*]

Imagine a nightmare beset by two kinds of misery—first, the misery of having to do a thing against time, and secondly, of being always thwarted when success is in sight—and you have the theme of ***From Nine to Nine***. Stanislaus Demba wanted some money to take him and the girl he loved for a trip abroad. He needed it at once, because otherwise a rival, the detested Weiner, would take her instead. He might have got the money by one of several ways, but he began with the most obvious and the most unfortunate. He tried to sell a book that belonged or had belonged to a library; and the antiquarian, seeing the label, telephoned to the police, who arrested Demba on the spot—and handcuffed him. At the cost of a long heavy fall from a window he got clean away; but beneath the spreading cloak his hands remained handcuffed. He dared not show them to anyone except his sweetheart. She tried a file, she took a wax impression of the lock, but all was in vain. It was only safe for Demba to take something up and put it in his pocket when he was absolutely alone. He could have had the money several times over; he could have eaten as many square meals as he liked, if only he could have shown the world his wrists. But that would have meant arrest and possibly imprisonment, whereas he had to do everything in the twelve hours between nine and nine.

Those who read ***The Marquis of Bolibar*** will turn eagerly to Mr. Perutz's most lately translated book. They may be a little disappointed. The imagination which burned so smokily and strongly in the earlier book shows itself here too, but in servitude, manacled, like poor Demba, by the exigencies of the plot. The author has to account for twelve hours of Demba's life; and, since the story has no real development and ends with a catastrophe, he is compelled to multiply incidents, all more or less of the same character and illustrating the same idea. Ingenious as the incidents are, and brilliantly told, they do not stand on their own feet. They are variations in the theme of Demba's anxiety and helplessness, and the more they change the more, essentially, they are the same thing. Ever and again symbolism lifts its head and receives from Mr. Perutz a gentle pat of acknowledgment; Demba's predicament shows how hard it is to get money "without lifting a hand." His final conclusions about life seem to be that rest is better than freedom. But Mr. Perutz pursues symbolism only so far as it serves his turn, just as, when it suits him, he applies to the novel the technique of the cinema. His originality, which is so delightful, springs naturally out of the satisfaction of his creative caprice: he is one of the few contemporary novelists who seems always to write to please himself. He is very modern; at times he seems to set more store by the effect than by the cause; and yet his work is never merely a procession of warning shapes and shadows dire. He tries to alarm the mind as well as the emotions. ***From Nine to Nine*** is a *tour de force,* with the *tour de force*'s immediate appeal to the aesthetic sense, but it is also more than that, it interprets life, harshly and bitterly, but at least effectively.

Francis Lloyd (essay date 1930)

SOURCE: A review of *The Master of the Day of Judgment,* in *The London Mercury,* Vol. XXI, No. 123, January, 1930, pp. 272-73.

[*In the following excerpt, Lloyd reviews* The Master of the Day of Judgment, *asserting that the quality of the English translation preserves the tone, style, and atmosphere of Perutz's carefully crafted prose.*]

We are grateful for the translation that allows us to read the ***Master of the Day of Judgment***: and we are particularly grateful to Mr. Hedrig Singer who has so well converted the original German of Herr Leo Perutz that it is possible for us to feel the force of atmosphere so powerfully. The obliquities of translation scarcely intrude themselves. For an atmosphere of real growing tension and horror it would be hard to find many equals in similar books of recent years. The use of the graphic present, which so often sounds unreal in a translation from the German, here is carefully controlled to heighten the vividness of the presentation. A haze of supernatural horrors clouds the book with increasing density, and the explanation which might easily, in the hands of a less distinguished writer, fall into the banal and commonplace, here takes on the correct tone of unearthly reality. It is decidedly not a book for the bedside: the strings of naked pagan fear are so well played on that an uncomfortable chill sensation must be left on even the midday reader. Those who like sensation will certainly not be disappointed. We all know the contrasts of the real and unreal which are so striking and forcible when the mind is in a hypersensitive state, and we must applaud the art which handles these delicate sensations, so that we are never oppressed, but feel a heightened absorption in the mind which is their focus. Too much has been made of this kind of technique in modern German literature and cinematograph films: the insignificant movements of other people and things that bore down into the memory when the mind has been unhinged by a terrific shock are so easy for an author to invent, but so hard to make significant and impressive. Herr Perutz has done this difficult feat with consummate art. The rapid stream of the plot is never impeded by its excursions through the caverns of mental psychology. It is a book not easy to forget.

Rose C. Feld (essay date 1930)

SOURCE: "A Macabre Tale of Murder in Vienna," in *The New York Times Book Review,* April 20, 1930, p. 7.

[*In the following review, Feld lauds the storytelling technique Perutz employs in* The Master of the Day of Judgment.]

Leo Perutz, author of ***The Master of the Day of Judgment,*** was born in Prague and later emigrated to Vienna. According to Dr. Fritz Wittels, who has written an illuminating introduction to the book, the literature of Perutz is saturated with the "curiously somber and mysterious character" of this strangely fascinating metropolis of present-day Czechoslovakia built by Germans in the midst of a Slav population. Tales of adventure and horror, he says, breed there and recall the fact that Gustav Meyrink's *Golem* had its action laid in the medieval Ghetto of Prague. It is an extremely interesting foreword and prepares the mind of the reader for the compelling tale of mystery which follows. Prague, as a matter of fact, does not figure in this story at all. The scene is laid in Vienna and the peculiar influence that controls the lives of the people of the book reaches out from the Florence of the days of the Medicis.

The story is told in the first person by Baron von Yosch, Austrian cavalry officer, who, out of a clear sky, is accused of the murder of Eugene Bischoff, a famous actor. The scene is typically Viennese. Von Yosch, at the invitation of Dr. von Gorsky, rather unwillingly accepts an invitation to go the Villa Bischoff for an evening of chamber music. Dina Bischoff, before her marriage to the actor, had been von Yosch's mistress, and the latter, although accepting his new status, still loves her. While they are playing a Brahms trio they are interrupted by a newcomer, Engineer Waldemar Solgrub, a friend of the Bischoffs. When the music ends Bischoff, who, it is known, is worried about his failing art as a creator of new rôles, tells his guests a weird story of two suicides that recently occurred in Vienna, one that of an art student, the second that of a naval officer, brother of the first. In each instance the decision to meet death seemed instantaneous; each suicide was strangely preceded by the smoking of a cigarette.

To change the macabre trend of the evening's conversation, Bischoff is asked to give a rendition of his new rôle at the theatre, that of Richard III. After much talk he consents, but asks to be excused while he goes to the Summer house to prepare for the recital. Shortly after two shots ring out and Bischoff is found dead, a smoking revolver in his hand. Shortly after Felix, Dina's brother, accuses von Yosch of murder, pointing out that the latter's pipe, still glowing, was found near the body.

Solgrub is certain it was suicide and asks for time to solve the mystery. His investigations lead him to a similar case of attempted suicide that took place the day after Bischoff's death, that of a young art student whom the actor had befriended. She, too, was found with a smoking cigarette. Convinced that some horrid monster has controlled the destinies of all the people who sought death so strangely, Solgrub continues the search until he discovers the source of evil. At this point the story goes back to a short tale of horror and alchemy in Florence. It explains the mystery of the "Master" of the day of judgment, but not until Solgrub, too, has succumbed to the spell of death.

Perutz tells his tale in a flowing, worldly manner that gives the very flavor of life in Vienna in the old days, cultured, mocking, gay. The book makes interesting reading both for its story and the fine technique of its telling.

The Times Literary Supplement (essay date 1934)

SOURCE: A review of *The Virgin's Brand,* in *The Times Literary Supplement,* No. 1698, August 16, 1934, p. 564.

[*In the following essay, the critic describes* The Virgin's Brand *as a mirror of Europe's troubled political milieu in the mid-1930s.*]

The publishers describe ***The Virgin's Brand*** . . . as "a story of great dramatic tension, of adventure and mystery and withal a love story of moving intensity." Up to a point this is a just description (except that the love story, however moving and intense, is a somewhat irrelevant intrusion presumably introduced as a sop to public demand). The author, whose reputation on the Continent is considerable, is a very capable story-teller, with a gift for making the strange events he narrates sound probable and for creating the atmosphere of terror, mystery and suspense appropriate to these events. We miss the whole point of the fantasy, however, unless we understand it as a portrayal, disturbing to our complacency and sense of security, of the forces of destruction latent in European society to-day.

Baron von Malchin, the central figure in the drama, which takes place in a remote country district in Westphalia, believes that two things are necessary for European recovery—first, the restoration of the authoritative monarchical system of government as it existed during the Middle Ages; and secondly, the revival of the religious enthusiasm of the Middle Ages. He gathers around him a number of aspirants to European thrones, including an alleged descendant of the Tudors and an alleged descendant of Emperors of the Holy Roman Empire. But how to create the religious enthusiasm which will lift them to their rightful seats and keep them there? His researches lead him to the discovery that religious ecstasy can be artificially induced by a drug secreted in corn which is attacked by a disease which was well known in the Middle Ages and called the Virgin's Brand. Having succeeded in manufacturing the drug in his laboratory, he administers it to the peasants in the district. The results are startling. The expected religious revival occurs; but instead of singing hymns to the Virgin and agitating for a restoration of their rightful kings the peasants fervently sing the "Internationale," form themselves into a revolutionary committee and march upon the Baron's domain armed with knives, flails and scythes.

The story is narrated in the first person by a young doctor recovering in hospital after an accident; and the author skillfully inter-weaves the suggestion that he dreams it all while lying under an anaesthetic with the counter-suggestion that the events are actual and that he was taken to hospital wounded by one of the revolting peasants. . . .

Claudio G. Segrè (essay date 1989)

SOURCE: "Revenge Before Love," in *The New York Times Book Review,* September 10, 1989, p. 37.

[*In the following review, Segrè suggests that the characters, plot, and setting of* Leonardo's Judas *constitute prime operatic material.*]

Attention, opera composers and librettists: [***Leonardo's Judas***] may provide wonderful material. Consider the premise of this last work by the Czechoslovak novelist, mathematician and classical scholar Leo Perutz. . . . : Leonardo—*the* Leonardo, of course—is having trouble completing *The Last Supper.* He can't find a suitable model for Judas, a contemporary face that will convey the mystery and anguish of the betrayal.

Enter Joachim Behaim, a proud German merchant who has sworn to recover a debt from a usurer named Boccetta. While conniving against Boccetta, Behaim falls hopelessly in love—with Boccetta's daughter Niccola. And in observing Behaim's decision to sacrifice love for vengeance, Leonardo finds the inspiration to complete his masterpiece.

Reminds you of Kafka? Hardly, though the publisher claims that Perutz has "sometimes been compared" to his brooding countryman. Rather, in Eric Mosbacher's smooth translation from the German, the charm of ***Leonardo's Judas*** lies in its color, its old-fashioned melodrama and morality. Real characters mix with imaginary ones on Perutz's historical sets. And those sets themselves seem made for opera: the ducal court in Milan; the rustic inn where Behaim carouses with artists and craftsmen; the wretched hovel that is Boccetta's home; the churches and inns where the lovers tryst; the hospital where the mysterious poet Mancino dies and the denouement takes place.

But although this scenery is beguiling, I had some trouble with the novel's ironies and its twists of plot. I don't quite believe, for example, that Mancino climbed in the window of Boccetta's house to return the money that Niccola, out of love for Behaim, stole from her father. Or that Behaim turned away from his true love so easily. Or that Niccola would really say she would never have loved Behaim "if I had known he had Judas's face." But in an opera, I'd believe—and I might even cry a little.

Amy Clyde (essay date 1990)

SOURCE: A review of *By Night Under the Stone Bridge,* in *The New York Times Book Review,* May 27, 1990, p. 16.

[*In the following review, Clyde praises* By Night Under a Stone Bridge *as imaginative and pleasant to read.*]

In Prague at the end of the 16th century, the court of the mad Emperor Rudolf II bulges with flatterers, opportunists and spies, while the city itself swarms with pestilence, destitution and crime. Corrupt from top to bottom, the remains of the Holy Roman Empire teeter on the verge of economic and moral collapse. But in this charming fable by Leo Perutz, . . . moments of connection, both earthly and surreal, draw the community together. Rudolf won't choose a bride because he's fallen irretrievably in love with a completely unsuitable woman—Esther, the beautiful wife of a ghetto merchant named Meisl, a man "so rich that he spreads sugar on his honey." To keep the peace, the Great Rabbi casts a spell enabling the lovers to tryst every night in their dreams. To detail the plot any further would be to destroy the pleasure of the tale, which unfolds in a suggestive, fragmentary way. Suffice it to say that ***By Night Under the Stone Bridge*** is full of surprising characters, including jesters, talking dogs and aristocrats in disguise. Likewise, the story line takes many bizarre, mannerist turns; it's punctuated by such staples of myth and fantasy as curses, prophecies and visitors from the world of the spirits. The result, which has been richly translated from the German by Eric Mosbacher, is a tantalizing blend of the occult and the laughable, of chaos and divine order. Some of Perutz's revelations shed light on the age of the Reformation, and much of what he depicts is eternal.

Dwight Garner (essay date 1992)

SOURCE: A review of *Little Apple,* in *VLS,* No. 106, June, 1992, p. 6.

[*In the following essay, Garner discusses characteristic themes and stylistic traits of Perutz's fiction and reviews* Little Apple.]

"Every writer," Jorge Luis Borges wrote, "creates his own precursors." Small wonder that Borges, who had not yet composed his *ficciones* when the Prague-born novelist Leo Perutz published the bulk of his eleven novels in the late 1920s and early '30s, was charmed by Perutz's work. Perutz so knowingly inventoried the characteristics that streak Borges's prose—the metaphysical dream logic, the attention to senseless truths, a penchant for the fantastic—that Perutz could almost have concocted the Argentinian master as an antecedent.

Happily for the thousands of readers who gobbled down his popular fictions as they were serialized in German-language newspapers, Perutz had a gift for terse, breathless narrative. His novels rush you over the river and through the woods on a political, moral, or romantic quest. In ***Saint Peter's Snow*** (1933), an immaculately crafted political fable banned by the Nazis, neither the suspense nor the bizarre Dr. Caligari atmosphere snaps until the final pages. (Even then we're left adrift in shadows and fog.) In ***The Marquis of Bolibar*** (1920), one of Borges's favorites, a mysterious prayer uttered by a dying officer sends a young soldier into a hallucinogenic, self-destructive free fall. These dark sagas move at a brisk clip; there's little wasted motion. This is what you'd get if you mixed Kafka with a hypercerebral Graham Greene.

Little Apple . . . is an elaborate and thoroughly perverse revenge fantasy. When Vittorin, a young Austrian officer, is released from a Russian POW camp near the end of

World War I, he can't stomach his "old, uneventful, well-ordered way of life" in Vienna. "Back to the dreary daily grind? Back to the typewriter? Up at seven every morning to brew the breakfast coffee on a gas ring?" To the dismay of his friends, family, employer, and girlfriend, Vittorin insists on returning to revolution-torn Russia so he can bring retribution on a POW camp commander who treated him shabbily. The camp commander, a fairly innocuous fellow, is for Vittorin nothing less than "the evil personification of a degenerate age . . . the medium through which Vittorin hated everything sordid that met his eye—all the crooks, currency speculators and human predators that had shared out the world between them."

Perutz charts Vittorin's doomed, phantasmagorical manhunt, which makes up much of ***Little Apple***'s narrative arc, with a steady hand. Absurdity is perched atop absurdity as Vittorin blindly pursues his goal, causing the wrongful deaths of dozens of men, including a political leader who might have saved Russia from the Bolsheviks. (I lost track of the body count early on.) Vittorin also forfeits opportunities in Vienna for great love and an outsized fortune, and at the book's close the ghosts of his now-vanished youth are paraded in front of his bloodshot eyes.

As compelling as Perutz's prose can be, occasionally his clipped, headlong style seems dated. There are more than a few sentences like these: "Vittorin straightened up. Determination flooded through him." Perutz also has an annoying habit of advancing matters by posing a flurry of questions. ("Was Emperger implying that he wouldn't return to Russia under any circumstances? What if the choice fell on him? Was there some ulterior motive behind his remark? Was he . . . " etc.) And because he's far more interested in ideas and rudely twisted fates—there's rarely a simile to be found—he elects not to fully pencil in his characters. Precise descriptions of what they wear, or eat, or look like, and all such too human clutter, are generally struck from his books. This is a loss only because Perutz now and then displays a real affinity for evocative detail:

> Vittorin made all kinds of discoveries: that a man could live on cheese rinds and rotten fruit when work was scarce; that trains existed for travellers other than those with tickets; that in certain humble hostelries a piece of bread and a glass of wine could be purchased with cigarette-ends gleaned from the pavements by day.

A sad, subtly orchestrated eroticism, which translator John Brownjohn maintains admirably in his English version of ***Little Apple,*** is the one sweetener Perutz consistently allows himself. In ***Saint Peter's Snow,*** a frustrated love provides a wistful counterweight to the book's political machinations. In ***Little Apple,*** Vittorin's post-POW-camp fortunes crash precipitously when he rejects his Viennese girlfriend, a woman who cries, sweetly, "because of the dismal autumn weather, or because her boss had shouted at her during the day, or because her mother wouldn't allow her to keep a canary, or simply because life was so sad and wonderful and short."

This small, uncanny novel takes its title from a Russian marching song that asks, "Where are you rolling, little apple?" Perutz's answer: Away from reason, away from love, away from any place that feels like home.

FURTHER READING

Criticism

Adler, Jeremy. "Voices in a Metaphysical Madhouse." *The Times Literary Supplement* (October 7-13, 1988): 1121.

Brief discussion of *Wohin rollst Du, Äpfelchen.* Adler lauds Perutz's simultaneous treatment of "local concerns" and "greater European ones" in the novel.

Durrant, Digby. "Odd Men Out." *London Magazine* 29, Nos. 9-10 (December-January 1989/1990): 134-37.

Asserts that *By Night Under the Stone Bridge* is a surprising and engaging tale.

Finkelstein, Barbara. Review of *Little Apple. The New York Times Book Review* (April 26, 1992): 18.

Characterizes the novel as a successful "travels-in-hell Baedeker of revolutionary Russia."

Grube, G. M. A. Review of *Where Will You Fall? The Canadian Forum* XL, No. 129 (June 1931): 350-51.

Praises Perutz's creation of "splendidly alive" characters in *Where Will You Fall?*

Review of *The Master of the Day of Judgment. The Times Literary Supplement* (January 30, 1930): 72.

Brief review that praises Perutz for infusing his old-fashioned horror story with contemporary psychological analysis.

Vansittart, Peter. "Multiple Divisions." *London Magazine* 29, No. 182 (April-May 1989): 151-54.

Admires Perutz's depiction of artist Leonardo da Vinci in *Leonardo's Judas* and praises the "grimly realistic war scenes" and "dimension of mystery" in *The Marquis de Bolibar.*

Additional coverage of Perutz's life and works is contained in the following sources published by Gale Research: *Contemporary Authors,* Vol. 147; and *Dictionary of Literary Biography,* Vol. 81.

Twentieth-Century Literary Criticism

Cumulative Indexes
Volumes 1-60

How to Use This Index

The main references

Calvino, Italo
1923-1985.....CLC 5, 8, 11, 22, 33, 39, 73; SSC 3

list all author entries in the following Gale Literary Criticism series:

BLC = *Black Literature Criticism*
CLC = *Contemporary Literary Criticism*
CLR = *Children's Literature Review*
CMLC = *Classical and Medieval Literature Criticism*
DA = *DISCovering Authors*
DC = *Drama Criticism*
HLC = *Hispanic Literature Criticism*
LC = *Literature Criticism from 1400 to 1800*
NCLC = *Nineteenth-Century Literature Criticism*
PC = *Poetry Criticism*
SSC = *Short Story Criticism*
TCLC = *Twentieth-Century Literary Criticism*
WLC = *World Literature Criticism, 1500 to the Present*

The cross-references

See also CANR 23; CA 85-88; obituary CA 116

list all author entries in the following Gale biographical and literary sources:

AAYA = *Authors & Artists for Young Adults*
AITN = *Authors in the News*
BEST = *Bestsellers*
BW = *Black Writers*
CA = *Contemporary Authors*
CAAS = *Contemporary Authors Autobiography Series*
CABS = *Contemporary Authors Bibliographical Series*
CANR = *Contemporary Authors New Revision Series*
CAP = *Contemporary Authors Permanent Series*
CDALB = *Concise Dictionary of American Literary Biography*
CDBLB = *Concise Dictionary of British Literary Biography*
DLB = *Dictionary of Literary Biography*
DLBD = *Dictionary of Literary Biography Documentary Series*
DLBY = *Dictionary of Literary Biography Yearbook*
HW = *Hispanic Writers*
JRDA = *Junior DISCovering Authors*
MAICYA = *Major Authors and Illustrators for Children and Young Adults*
MTCW = *Major 20th-Century Writers*
NNAL = *Native North American Literature*
SAAS = *Something about the Author Autobiography Series*
SATA = *Something about the Author*
YABC = *Yesterday's Authors of Books for Children*

Literary Criticism Series Cumulative Author Index

Anthony, John
See Ciardi, John (Anthony)

Anthony, Peter
See Shaffer, Anthony (Joshua); Shaffer, Peter (Levin)

Anthony, Piers 1934- . . . . **CLC 35**
See also AAYA 11; CA 21-24R; CANR 28; DLB 8; MTCW

Antoine, Marc
See Proust, (Valentin-Louis-George-Eugene-) Marcel

Antoninus, Brother
See Everson, William (Oliver)

Antonioni, Michelangelo 1912- . . . . . **CLC 20**
See also CA 73-76; CANR 45

Antschel, Paul 1920-1970
See Celan, Paul
See also CA 85-88; CANR 33; MTCW

Anwar, Chairil 1922-1949 . . . . **TCLC 22**
See also CA 121

Apollinaire, Guillaume . . **TCLC 3, 8, 51; PC 7**
See also Kostrowitzki, Wilhelm Apollinaris de

Appelfeld, Aharon 1932- . . . . **CLC 23, 47**
See also CA 112; 133

Apple, Max (Isaac) 1941-. . . . . **CLC 9, 33**
See also CA 81-84; CANR 19; DLB 130

Appleman, Philip (Dean) 1926- . . . . . **CLC 51**
See also CA 13-16R; CAAS 18; CANR 6, 29

Appleton, Lawrence
See Lovecraft, H(oward) P(hillips)

Apteryx
See Eliot, T(homas) S(tearns)

Apuleius, (Lucius Madaurensis)
125(?)-175(?) . . . . **CMLC 1**

Aquin, Hubert 1929-1977. . . . . **CLC 15**
See also CA 105; DLB 53

Aragon, Louis 1897-1982 . . . . **CLC 3, 22**
See also CA 69-72; 108; CANR 28; DLB 72; MTCW

Arany, Janos 1817-1882. . . . . **NCLC 34**

Arbuthnot, John 1667-1735 . . . . **LC 1**
See also DLB 101

Archer, Herbert Winslow
See Mencken, H(enry) L(ouis)

Archer, Jeffrey (Howard) 1940- . . . . **CLC 28**
See also BEST 89:3; CA 77-80; CANR 22

Archer, Jules 1915- . . . . **CLC 12**
See also CA 9-12R; CANR 6; SAAS 5; SATA 4

Archer, Lee
See Ellison, Harlan (Jay)

Arden, John 1930- . . . . **CLC 6, 13, 15**
See also CA 13-16R; CAAS 4; CANR 31; DLB 13; MTCW

Arenas, Reinaldo
1943-1990 . . . . **CLC 41; HLC**
See also CA 124; 128; 133; DLB 145; HW

Arendt, Hannah 1906-1975 . . . . **CLC 66**
See also CA 17-20R; 61-64; CANR 26; MTCW

Aretino, Pietro 1492-1556 . . . . **LC 12**

Arghezi, Tudor. **CLC 80**
See also Theodorescu, Ion N.

Arguedas, Jose Maria
1911-1969 . . . . **CLC 10, 18**
See also CA 89-92; DLB 113; HW

Argueta, Manlio 1936- . . . . **CLC 31**
See also CA 131; DLB 145; HW

Ariosto, Ludovico 1474-1533. . . . . **LC 6**

Aristides
See Epstein, Joseph

Aristophanes
450B.C.-385B.C. . . . **CMLC 4; DA; DC 2**

Arlt, Roberto (Godofredo Christophersen)
1900-1942 . . . . **TCLC 29; HLC**
See also CA 123; 131; HW

Armah, Ayi Kwei 1939- . . . . **CLC 5, 33; BLC**
See also BW 1; CA 61-64; CANR 21; DLB 117; MTCW

Armatrading, Joan 1950- . . . . **CLC 17**
See also CA 114

Arnette, Robert
See Silverberg, Robert

Arnim, Achim von (Ludwig Joachim von Arnim) 1781-1831 . . . . **NCLC 5**
See also DLB 90

Arnim, Bettina von 1785-1859. . . . **NCLC 38**
See also DLB 90

Arnold, Matthew
1822-1888 . . . . . **NCLC 6, 29; DA; PC 5; WLC**
See also A. E.
See also CDBLB 1832-1890; DLB 32, 57

Arnold, Thomas 1795-1842 . . . . . . **NCLC 18**
See also DLB 55

Arnow, Harriette (Louisa) Simpson
1908-1986 . . . . **CLC 2, 7, 18**
See also CA 9-12R; 118; CANR 14; DLB 6; MTCW; SATA 42; SATA-Obit 47

Arp, Hans
See Arp, Jean

Arp, Jean 1887-1966. . . . . **CLC 5**
See also CA 81-84; 25-28R; CANR 42

Arrabal
See Arrabal, Fernando

Arrabal, Fernando 1932- . . . **CLC 2, 9, 18, 58**
See also CA 9-12R; CANR 15

Arrick, Fran. . . . . **CLC 30**
See also Gaberman, Judie Angell

Artaud, Antonin 1896-1948 . . . . . **TCLC 3, 36**
See also CA 104

Arthur, Ruth M(abel) 1905-1979. . . . **CLC 12**
See also CA 9-12R; 85-88; CANR 4; SATA 7, 26

Artsybashev, Mikhail (Petrovich)
1878-1927 . . . . **TCLC 31**

Arundel, Honor (Morfydd)
1919-1973 . . . . **CLC 17**
See also CA 21-22; 41-44R; CAP 2; CLR 35; SATA 4; SATA-Obit 24

Asch, Sholem 1880-1957 . . . . **TCLC 3**
See also CA 105

Ash, Shalom
See Asch, Sholem

Ashbery, John (Lawrence)
1927- . . . . . . **CLC 2, 3, 4, 6, 9, 13, 15, 25, 41, 77**
See also CA 5-8R; CANR 9, 37; DLB 5; DLBY 81; MTCW

Ashdown, Clifford
See Freeman, R(ichard) Austin

Ashe, Gordon
See Creasey, John

Ashton-Warner, Sylvia (Constance)
1908-1984 . . . . **CLC 19**
See also CA 69-72; 112; CANR 29; MTCW

Asimov, Isaac
1920-1992 . . . . . . **CLC 1, 3, 9, 19, 26, 76**
See also AAYA 13; BEST 90:2; CA 1-4R; 137; CANR 2, 19, 36; CLR 12; DLB 8; DLBY 92; JRDA; MAICYA; MTCW; SATA 1, 26, 74

Astley, Thea (Beatrice May)
1925- . . . . **CLC 41**
See also CA 65-68; CANR 11, 43

Aston, James
See White, T(erence) H(anbury)

Asturias, Miguel Angel
1899-1974 . . . . **CLC 3, 8, 13; HLC**
See also CA 25-28; 49-52; CANR 32; CAP 2; DLB 113; HW; MTCW

Atares, Carlos Saura
See Saura (Atares), Carlos

Atheling, William
See Pound, Ezra (Weston Loomis)

Atheling, William, Jr.
See Blish, James (Benjamin)

Atherton, Gertrude (Franklin Horn)
1857-1948 . . . . **TCLC 2**
See also CA 104; DLB 9, 78

Atherton, Lucius
See Masters, Edgar Lee

Atkins, Jack
See Harris, Mark

Atticus
See Fleming, Ian (Lancaster)

Atwood, Margaret (Eleanor)
1939- . . . . . **CLC 2, 3, 4, 8, 13, 15, 25, 44, 84; DA; PC 8; SSC 2; WLC**
See also AAYA 12; BEST 89:2; CA 49-52; CANR 3, 24, 33; DLB 53; MTCW; SATA 50

Aubigny, Pierre d'
See Mencken, H(enry) L(ouis)

Aubin, Penelope 1685-1731(?) . . . . **LC 9**
See also DLB 39

Auchincloss, Louis (Stanton)
1917- . . . . **CLC 4, 6, 9, 18, 45**
See also CA 1-4R; CANR 6, 29; DLB 2; DLBY 80; MTCW

Auden, W(ystan) H(ugh)
1907-1973 . . . . . . **CLC 1, 2, 3, 4, 6, 9, 11, 14, 43; DA; PC 1; WLC**
See also CA 9-12R; 45-48; CANR 5; CDBLB 1914-1945; DLB 10, 20; MTCW

Audiberti, Jacques 1900-1965 . . . . . . **CLC 38**
See also CA 25-28R

Audubon, John James
1785-1851 . . . . **NCLC 47**

Auel, Jean M(arie) 1936- .... **CLC 31**
See also AAYA 7; BEST 90:4; CA 103; CANR 21

Auerbach, Erich 1892-1957 .... **TCLC 43**
See also CA 118

Augier, Emile 1820-1889 .... **NCLC 31**

August, John
See De Voto, Bernard (Augustine)

Augustine, St. 354-430 .... **CMLC 6**

Aurelius
See Bourne, Randolph S(illiman)

Austen, Jane
1775-1817 ..... **NCLC 1, 13, 19, 33, 51; DA; WLC**
See also CDBLB 1789-1832; DLB 116

Auster, Paul 1947- .... **CLC 47**
See also CA 69-72; CANR 23

Austin, Frank
See Faust, Frederick (Schiller)

Austin, Mary (Hunter)
1868-1934 .... **TCLC 25**
See also CA 109; DLB 9, 78

Autran Dourado, Waldomiro
See Dourado, (Waldomiro Freitas) Autran

Averroes 1126-1198 .... **CMLC 7**
See also DLB 115

Avison, Margaret 1918- .... **CLC 2, 4**
See also CA 17-20R; DLB 53; MTCW

Axton, David
See Koontz, Dean R(ay)

Ayckbourn, Alan
1939- .... **CLC 5, 8, 18, 33, 74**
See also CA 21-24R; CANR 31; DLB 13; MTCW

Aydy, Catherine
See Tennant, Emma (Christina)

Ayme, Marcel (Andre) 1902-1967 ... **CLC 11**
See also CA 89-92; CLR 25; DLB 72

Ayrton, Michael 1921-1975 .... **CLC 7**
See also CA 5-8R; 61-64; CANR 9, 21

Azorin .... **CLC 11**
See also Martinez Ruiz, Jose

Azuela, Mariano
1873-1952 .... **TCLC 3; HLC**
See also CA 104; 131; HW; MTCW

Baastad, Babbis Friis
See Friis-Baastad, Babbis Ellinor

Bab
See Gilbert, W(illiam) S(chwenck)

Babbis, Eleanor
See Friis-Baastad, Babbis Ellinor

Babel, Isaak (Emmanuilovich)
1894-1941(?) ...... **TCLC 2, 13; SSC 16**
See also CA 104

Babits, Mihaly 1883-1941 .... **TCLC 14**
See also CA 114

Babur 1483-1530 .... **LC 18**

Bacchelli, Riccardo 1891-1985 ..... **CLC 19**
See also CA 29-32R; 117

Bach, Richard (David) 1936- .... **CLC 14**
See also AITN 1; BEST 89:2; CA 9-12R; CANR 18; MTCW; SATA 13

Bachman, Richard
See King, Stephen (Edwin)

Bachmann, Ingeborg 1926-1973 ..... **CLC 69**
See also CA 93-96; 45-48; DLB 85

Bacon, Francis 1561-1626 .... **LC 18**
See also CDBLB Before 1660; DLB 151

Bacon, Roger 1214(?)-1292 ...... **CMLC 14**
See also DLB 115

Bacovia, George .... **TCLC 24**
See also Vasiliu, Gheorghe

Badanes, Jerome 1937- .... **CLC 59**

Bagehot, Walter 1826-1877 ...... **NCLC 10**
See also DLB 55

Bagnold, Enid 1889-1981 .... **CLC 25**
See also CA 5-8R; 103; CANR 5, 40; DLB 13; MAICYA; SATA 1, 25

Bagritsky, Eduard 1895-1934 ..... **TCLC 60**

Bagrjana, Elisaveta
See Belcheva, Elisaveta

Bagryana, Elisaveta .... **CLC 10**
See also Belcheva, Elisaveta
See also DLB 147

Bailey, Paul 1937- .... **CLC 45**
See also CA 21-24R; CANR 16; DLB 14

Baillie, Joanna 1762-1851 .... **NCLC 2**
See also DLB 93

Bainbridge, Beryl (Margaret)
1933- .... **CLC 4, 5, 8, 10, 14, 18, 22, 62**
See also CA 21-24R; CANR 24; DLB 14; MTCW

Baker, Elliott 1922- .... **CLC 8**
See also CA 45-48; CANR 2

Baker, Nicholson 1957- .... **CLC 61**
See also CA 135

Baker, Ray Stannard 1870-1946 ... **TCLC 47**
See also CA 118

Baker, Russell (Wayne) 1925- ...... **CLC 31**
See also BEST 89:4; CA 57-60; CANR 11, 41; MTCW

Bakhtin, M.
See Bakhtin, Mikhail Mikhailovich

Bakhtin, M. M.
See Bakhtin, Mikhail Mikhailovich

Bakhtin, Mikhail
See Bakhtin, Mikhail Mikhailovich

Bakhtin, Mikhail Mikhailovich
1895-1975 .... **CLC 83**
See also CA 128; 113

Bakshi, Ralph 1938(?)- .... **CLC 26**
See also CA 112; 138

Bakunin, Mikhail (Alexandrovich)
1814-1876 .... **NCLC 25**

Baldwin, James (Arthur)
1924-1987 ...... **CLC 1, 2, 3, 4, 5, 8, 13, 15, 17, 42, 50, 67; BLC; DA; DC 1; SSC 10; WLC**
See also AAYA 4; BW 1; CA 1-4R; 124; CABS 1; CANR 3, 24; CDALB 1941-1968; DLB 2, 7, 33; DLBY 87; MTCW; SATA 9; SATA-Obit 54

Ballard, J(ames) G(raham)
1930- .... **CLC 3, 6, 14, 36; SSC 1**
See also AAYA 3; CA 5-8R; CANR 15, 39; DLB 14; MTCW

Balmont, Konstantin (Dmitriyevich)
1867-1943 .... **TCLC 11**
See also CA 109

Balzac, Honore de
1799-1850 .... **NCLC 5, 35; DA; SSC 5; WLC**
See also DLB 119

Bambara, Toni Cade
1939- .... **CLC 19, 88; BLC; DA**
See also AAYA 5; BW 2; CA 29-32R; CANR 24; DLB 38; MTCW

Bamdad, A.
See Shamlu, Ahmad

Banat, D. R.
See Bradbury, Ray (Douglas)

Bancroft, Laura
See Baum, L(yman) Frank

Banim, John 1798-1842 .... **NCLC 13**
See also DLB 116

Banim, Michael 1796-1874 ...... **NCLC 13**

Banks, Iain
See Banks, Iain M(enzies)

Banks, Iain M(enzies) 1954- .... **CLC 34**
See also CA 123; 128

Banks, Lynne Reid .... **CLC 23**
See also Reid Banks, Lynne
See also AAYA 6

Banks, Russell 1940- .... **CLC 37, 72**
See also CA 65-68; CAAS 15; CANR 19; DLB 130

Banville, John 1945- .... **CLC 46**
See also CA 117; 128; DLB 14

Banville, Theodore (Faullain) de
1832-1891 .... **NCLC 9**

Baraka, Amiri
1934- .... **CLC 1, 2, 3, 5, 10, 14, 33; BLC; DA; PC 4**
See also Jones, LeRoi
See also BW 2; CA 21-24R; CABS 3; CANR 27, 38; CDALB 1941-1968; DLB 5, 7, 16, 38; DLBD 8; MTCW

Barbauld, Anna Laetitia
1743-1825 .... **NCLC 50**

Barbellion, W. N. P. .... **TCLC 24**
See also Cummings, Bruce F(rederick)

Barbera, Jack (Vincent) 1945- ...... **CLC 44**
See also CA 110; CANR 45

Barbey d'Aurevilly, Jules Amedee
1808-1889 .... **NCLC 1; SSC 17**
See also DLB 119

Barbusse, Henri 1873-1935 .... **TCLC 5**
See also CA 105; DLB 65

Barclay, Bill
See Moorcock, Michael (John)

Barclay, William Ewert
See Moorcock, Michael (John)

Barea, Arturo 1897-1957 .... **TCLC 14**
See also CA 111

Barfoot, Joan 1946- .... **CLC 18**
See also CA 105

Berrigan, Edmund Joseph Michael, Jr. 1934-1983
See Berrigan, Ted
See also CA 61-64; 110; CANR 14

Berrigan, Ted . . . . **CLC 37**
See also Berrigan, Edmund Joseph Michael, Jr.
See also DLB 5

Berry, Charles Edward Anderson 1931-
See Berry, Chuck
See also CA 115

Berry, Chuck . . . . **CLC 17**
See also Berry, Charles Edward Anderson

Berry, Jonas
See Ashbery, John (Lawrence)

Berry, Wendell (Erdman)
1934- . . . . **CLC 4, 6, 8, 27, 46**
See also AITN 1; CA 73-76; DLB 5, 6

Berryman, John
1914-1972 . . . . . . **CLC 1, 2, 3, 4, 6, 8, 10, 13, 25, 62**
See also CA 13-16; 33-36R; CABS 2; CANR 35; CAP 1; CDALB 1941-1968; DLB 48; MTCW

Bertolucci, Bernardo 1940- . . . . **CLC 16**
See also CA 106

Bertrand, Aloysius 1807-1841 . . . . **NCLC 31**

Bertran de Born c. 1140-1215 . . . . . **CMLC 5**

Besant, Annie (Wood) 1847-1933 . . . **TCLC 9**
See also CA 105

Bessie, Alvah 1904-1985. . . . . **CLC 23**
See also CA 5-8R; 116; CANR 2; DLB 26

Bethlen, T. D.
See Silverberg, Robert

Beti, Mongo. . . . . **CLC 27; BLC**
See also Biyidi, Alexandre

Betjeman, John
1906-1984 . . . . **CLC 2, 6, 10, 34, 43**
See also CA 9-12R; 112; CANR 33; CDBLB 1945-1960; DLB 20; DLBY 84; MTCW

Bettelheim, Bruno 1903-1990 . . . . . . **CLC 79**
See also CA 81-84; 131; CANR 23; MTCW

Betti, Ugo 1892-1953 . . . . **TCLC 5**
See also CA 104

Betts, Doris (Waugh) 1932- . . . . **CLC 3, 6, 28**
See also CA 13-16R; CANR 9; DLBY 82

Bevan, Alistair
See Roberts, Keith (John Kingston)

Bialik, Chaim Nachman
1873-1934 . . . . **TCLC 25**

Bickerstaff, Isaac
See Swift, Jonathan

Bidart, Frank 1939- . . . . **CLC 33**
See also CA 140

Bienek, Horst 1930-. . . . . **CLC 7, 11**
See also CA 73-76; DLB 75

Bierce, Ambrose (Gwinett)
1842-1914(?) . . . . **TCLC 1, 7, 44; DA; SSC 9; WLC**
See also CA 104; 139; CDALB 1865-1917; DLB 11, 12, 23, 71, 74

Billings, Josh
See Shaw, Henry Wheeler

Billington, (Lady) Rachel (Mary)
1942- . . . . **CLC 43**
See also AITN 2; CA 33-36R; CANR 44

Binyon, T(imothy) J(ohn) 1936- . . . . **CLC 34**
See also CA 111; CANR 28

Bioy Casares, Adolfo
1914- . . . **CLC 4, 8, 13, 88; HLC; SSC 17**
See also CA 29-32R; CANR 19, 43; DLB 113; HW; MTCW

Bird, Cordwainer
See Ellison, Harlan (Jay)

Bird, Robert Montgomery
1806-1854 . . . . **NCLC 1**

Birney, (Alfred) Earle
1904- . . . . **CLC 1, 4, 6, 11**
See also CA 1-4R; CANR 5, 20; DLB 88; MTCW

Bishop, Elizabeth
1911-1979 . . . . . . **CLC 1, 4, 9, 13, 15, 32; DA; PC 3**
See also CA 5-8R; 89-92; CABS 2; CANR 26; CDALB 1968-1988; DLB 5; MTCW; SATA-Obit 24

Bishop, John 1935-. . . . . **CLC 10**
See also CA 105

Bissett, Bill 1939-. . . . . **CLC 18**
See also CA 69-72; CAAS 19; CANR 15; DLB 53; MTCW

Bitov, Andrei (Georgievich) 1937-. . . **CLC 57**
See also CA 142

Biyidi, Alexandre 1932-
See Beti, Mongo
See also BW 1; CA 114; 124; MTCW

Bjarme, Brynjolf
See Ibsen, Henrik (Johan)

Bjornson, Bjornstjerne (Martinius)
1832-1910 . . . . **TCLC 7, 37**
See also CA 104

Black, Robert
See Holdstock, Robert P.

Blackburn, Paul 1926-1971 . . . . . . **CLC 9, 43**
See also CA 81-84; 33-36R; CANR 34; DLB 16; DLBY 81

Black Elk 1863-1950 . . . . **TCLC 33**
See also CA 144; NNAL

Black Hobart
See Sanders, (James) Ed(ward)

Blacklin, Malcolm
See Chambers, Aidan

Blackmore, R(ichard) D(oddridge)
1825-1900 . . . . **TCLC 27**
See also CA 120; DLB 18

Blackmur, R(ichard) P(almer)
1904-1965 . . . . **CLC 2, 24**
See also CA 11-12; 25-28R; CAP 1; DLB 63

Black Tarantula, The
See Acker, Kathy

Blackwood, Algernon (Henry)
1869-1951 . . . . **TCLC 5**
See also CA 105; DLB 153

Blackwood, Caroline 1931- . . . . **CLC 6, 9**
See also CA 85-88; CANR 32; DLB 14; MTCW

Blade, Alexander
See Hamilton, Edmond; Silverberg, Robert

Blaga, Lucian 1895-1961 . . . . **CLC 75**

Blair, Eric (Arthur) 1903-1950
See Orwell, George
See also CA 104; 132; DA; MTCW; SATA 29

Blais, Marie-Claire
1939- . . . . **CLC 2, 4, 6, 13, 22**
See also CA 21-24R; CAAS 4; CANR 38; DLB 53; MTCW

Blaise, Clark 1940-. . . . . **CLC 29**
See also AITN 2; CA 53-56; CAAS 3; CANR 5; DLB 53

Blake, Nicholas
See Day Lewis, C(ecil)
See also DLB 77

Blake, William
1757-1827 . . . . **NCLC 13, 37; DA; PC 12; WLC**
See also CDBLB 1789-1832; DLB 93; MAICYA; SATA 30

Blasco Ibanez, Vicente
1867-1928 . . . . **TCLC 12**
See also CA 110; 131; HW; MTCW

Blatty, William Peter 1928-. . . . . **CLC 2**
See also CA 5-8R; CANR 9

Bleeck, Oliver
See Thomas, Ross (Elmore)

Blessing, Lee 1949-. . . . . **CLC 54**

Blish, James (Benjamin)
1921-1975 . . . . **CLC 14**
See also CA 1-4R; 57-60; CANR 3; DLB 8; MTCW; SATA 66

Bliss, Reginald
See Wells, H(erbert) G(eorge)

Blixen, Karen (Christentze Dinesen)
1885-1962
See Dinesen, Isak
See also CA 25-28; CANR 22; CAP 2; MTCW; SATA 44

Bloch, Robert (Albert) 1917-1994 . . . **CLC 33**
See also CA 5-8R; 146; CAAS 20; CANR 5; DLB 44; SATA 12

Blok, Alexander (Alexandrovich)
1880-1921 . . . . **TCLC 5**
See also CA 104

Blom, Jan
See Breytenbach, Breyten

Bloom, Harold 1930- . . . . **CLC 24**
See also CA 13-16R; CANR 39; DLB 67

Bloomfield, Aurelius
See Bourne, Randolph S(illiman)

Blount, Roy (Alton), Jr. 1941- . . . . . **CLC 38**
See also CA 53-56; CANR 10, 28; MTCW

Bloy, Leon 1846-1917. . . . . **TCLC 22**
See also CA 121; DLB 123

Blume, Judy (Sussman) 1938- . . . **CLC 12, 30**
See also AAYA 3; CA 29-32R; CANR 13, 37; CLR 2, 15; DLB 52; JRDA; MAICYA; MTCW; SATA 2, 31, 79

Blunden, Edmund (Charles)
1896-1974 . . . . **CLC 2, 56**
See also CA 17-18; 45-48; CAP 2; DLB 20, 100; MTCW

Bly, Robert (Elwood) 1926- .... **CLC 1, 2, 5, 10, 15, 38**
See also CA 5-8R; CANR 41; DLB 5; MTCW

Boas, Franz 1858-1942........... **TCLC 56**
See also CA 115

Bobette
See Simenon, Georges (Jacques Christian)

Boccaccio, Giovanni 1313-1375 .... **CMLC 13; SSC 10**

Bochco, Steven 1943-............. **CLC 35**
See also AAYA 11; CA 124; 138

Bodenheim, Maxwell 1892-1954 ... **TCLC 44**
See also CA 110; DLB 9, 45

Bodker, Cecil 1927- .... **CLC 21**
See also CA 73-76; CANR 13, 44; CLR 23; MAICYA; SATA 14

Boell, Heinrich (Theodor) 1917-1985 .... **CLC 2, 3, 6, 9, 11, 15, 27, 32, 72; DA; WLC**
See also CA 21-24R; 116; CANR 24; DLB 69; DLBY 85; MTCW

Boerne, Alfred
See Doeblin, Alfred

Boethius 480(?)-524(?) .... **CMLC 15**
See also DLB 115

Bogan, Louise 1897-1970 .... **CLC 4, 39, 46; PC 12**
See also CA 73-76; 25-28R; CANR 33; DLB 45; MTCW

Bogarde, Dirk .... **CLC 19**
See also Van Den Bogarde, Derek Jules Gaspard Ulric Niven
See also DLB 14

Bogosian, Eric 1953- .... **CLC 45**
See also CA 138

Bograd, Larry 1953-.............. **CLC 35**
See also CA 93-96; SATA 33

Boiardo, Matteo Maria 1441-1494 .... **LC 6**

Boileau-Despreaux, Nicolas 1636-1711 .... **LC 3**

Boland, Eavan (Aisling) 1944-... **CLC 40, 67**
See also CA 143; DLB 40

Bolt, Lee
See Faust, Frederick (Schiller)

Bolt, Robert (Oxton) 1924-1995 .... **CLC 14**
See also CA 17-20R; 147; CANR 35; DLB 13; MTCW

Bombet, Louis-Alexandre-Cesar
See Stendhal

Bomkauf
See Kaufman, Bob (Garnell)

Bonaventura.................... NCLC 35
See also DLB 90

Bond, Edward 1934-....... **CLC 4, 6, 13, 23**
See also CA 25-28R; CANR 38; DLB 13; MTCW

Bonham, Frank 1914-1989......... **CLC 12**
See also AAYA 1; CA 9-12R; CANR 4, 36; JRDA; MAICYA; SAAS 3; SATA 1, 49; SATA-Obit 62

Bonnefoy, Yves 1923-........ **CLC 9, 15, 58**
See also CA 85-88; CANR 33; MTCW

Bontemps, Arna(ud Wendell) 1902-1973 .... **CLC 1, 18; BLC**
See also BW 1; CA 1-4R; 41-44R; CANR 4, 35; CLR 6; DLB 48, 51; JRDA; MAICYA; MTCW; SATA 2, 44; SATA-Obit 24

Booth, Martin 1944-.............. **CLC 13**
See also CA 93-96; CAAS 2

Booth, Philip 1925-.............. **CLC 23**
See also CA 5-8R; CANR 5; DLBY 82

Booth, Wayne C(layson) 1921- ..... **CLC 24**
See also CA 1-4R; CAAS 5; CANR 3, 43; DLB 67

Borchert, Wolfgang 1921-1947 ..... **TCLC 5**
See also CA 104; DLB 69, 124

Borel, Petrus 1809-1859......... **NCLC 41**

Borges, Jorge Luis 1899-1986 ... **CLC 1, 2, 3, 4, 6, 8, 9, 10, 13, 19, 44, 48, 83; DA; HLC; SSC 4; WLC**
See also CA 21-24R; CANR 19, 33; DLB 113; DLBY 86; HW; MTCW

Borowski, Tadeusz 1922-1951 ...... **TCLC 9**
See also CA 106

Borrow, George (Henry) 1803-1881 .... **NCLC 9**
See also DLB 21, 55

Bosman, Herman Charles 1905-1951 .... **TCLC 49**

Bosschere, Jean de 1878(?)-1953... **TCLC 19**
See also CA 115

Boswell, James 1740-1795 .... **LC 4; DA; WLC**
See also CDBLB 1660-1789; DLB 104, 142

Bottoms, David 1949-............. **CLC 53**
See also CA 105; CANR 22; DLB 120; DLBY 83

Boucicault, Dion 1820-1890...... **NCLC 41**

Boucolon, Maryse 1937-
See Conde, Maryse
See also CA 110; CANR 30

Bourget, Paul (Charles Joseph) 1852-1935 .... **TCLC 12**
See also CA 107; DLB 123

Bourjaily, Vance (Nye) 1922- .... **CLC 8, 62**
See also CA 1-4R; CAAS 1; CANR 2; DLB 2, 143

Bourne, Randolph S(illiman) 1886-1918 .... **TCLC 16**
See also CA 117; DLB 63

Bova, Ben(jamin William) 1932-.... **CLC 45**
See also CA 5-8R; CAAS 18; CANR 11; CLR 3; DLBY 81; MAICYA; MTCW; SATA 6, 68

Bowen, Elizabeth (Dorothea Cole) 1899-1973 ...... **CLC 1, 3, 6, 11, 15, 22; SSC 3**
See also CA 17-18; 41-44R; CANR 35; CAP 2; CDBLB 1945-1960; DLB 15; MTCW

Bowering, George 1935-........ **CLC 15, 47**
See also CA 21-24R; CAAS 16; CANR 10; DLB 53

Bowering, Marilyn R(uthe) 1949-... **CLC 32**
See also CA 101

Bowers, Edgar 1924- .... **CLC 9**
See also CA 5-8R; CANR 24; DLB 5

Bowie, David .... CLC 17
See also Jones, David Robert

Bowles, Jane (Sydney) 1917-1973 .... **CLC 3, 68**
See also CA 19-20; 41-44R; CAP 2

Bowles, Paul (Frederick) 1910- .... **CLC 1, 2, 19, 53; SSC 3**
See also CA 1-4R; CAAS 1; CANR 1, 19; DLB 5, 6; MTCW

Box, Edgar
See Vidal, Gore

Boyd, Nancy
See Millay, Edna St. Vincent

Boyd, William 1952-........ **CLC 28, 53, 70**
See also CA 114; 120

Boyle, Kay 1902-1992 ..... **CLC 1, 5, 19, 58; SSC 5**
See also CA 13-16R; 140; CAAS 1; CANR 29; DLB 4, 9, 48, 86; DLBY 93; MTCW

Boyle, Mark
See Kienzle, William X(avier)

Boyle, Patrick 1905-1982.......... **CLC 19**
See also CA 127

Boyle, T. C.
See Boyle, T(homas) Coraghessan

Boyle, T(homas) Coraghessan 1948- .... **CLC 36, 55; SSC 16**
See also BEST 90:4; CA 120; CANR 44; DLBY 86

Boz
See Dickens, Charles (John Huffam)

Brackenridge, Hugh Henry 1748-1816 .... **NCLC 7**
See also DLB 11, 37

Bradbury, Edward P.
See Moorcock, Michael (John)

Bradbury, Malcolm (Stanley) 1932- .... **CLC 32, 61**
See also CA 1-4R; CANR 1, 33; DLB 14; MTCW

Bradbury, Ray (Douglas) 1920- ... **CLC 1, 3, 10, 15, 42; DA; WLC**
See also AITN 1, 2; CA 1-4R; CANR 2, 30; CDALB 1968-1988; DLB 2, 8; MTCW; SATA 11, 64

Bradford, Gamaliel 1863-1932..... **TCLC 36**
See also DLB 17

Bradley, David (Henry, Jr.) 1950- .... **CLC 23; BLC**
See also BW 1; CA 104; CANR 26; DLB 33

Bradley, John Ed(mund, Jr.) 1958- .... **CLC 55**
See also CA 139

Bradley, Marion Zimmer 1930-..... **CLC 30**
See also AAYA 9; CA 57-60; CAAS 10; CANR 7, 31; DLB 8; MTCW

Bradstreet, Anne 1612(?)-1672 ...... **LC 4, 30; DA; PC 10**
See also CDALB 1640-1865; DLB 24

Brady, Joan 1939- .... **CLC 86**
See also CA 141

Bragg, Melvyn 1939- . . . . **CLC 10**
See also BEST 89:3; CA 57-60; CANR 10, 48; DLB 14

Braine, John (Gerard) 1922-1986 . . . . **CLC 1, 3, 41**
See also CA 1-4R; 120; CANR 1, 33; CDBLB 1945-1960; DLB 15; DLBY 86; MTCW

Brammer, William 1930(?)-1978 . . . . **CLC 31**
See also CA 77-80

Brancati, Vitaliano 1907-1954 . . . . . **TCLC 12**
See also CA 109

Brancato, Robin F(idler) 1936- . . . . . **CLC 35**
See also AAYA 9; CA 69-72; CANR 11, 45; CLR 32; JRDA; SAAS 9; SATA 23

Brand, Max
See Faust, Frederick (Schiller)

Brand, Millen 1906-1980 . . . . **CLC 7**
See also CA 21-24R; 97-100

Branden, Barbara . . . . **CLC 44**

Brandes, Georg (Morris Cohen) 1842-1927 . . . . **TCLC 10**
See also CA 105

Brandys, Kazimierz 1916- . . . . **CLC 62**

Branley, Franklyn M(ansfield) 1915- . . . . **CLC 21**
See also CA 33-36R; CANR 14, 39; CLR 13; MAICYA; SAAS 16; SATA 4, 68

Brathwaite, Edward Kamau 1930- . . . **CLC 11**
See also BW 2; CA 25-28R; CANR 11, 26, 47; DLB 125

Brautigan, Richard (Gary) 1935-1984 . . . . **CLC 1, 3, 5, 9, 12, 34, 42**
See also CA 53-56; 113; CANR 34; DLB 2, 5; DLBY 80, 84; MTCW; SATA 56

Braverman, Kate 1950- . . . . **CLC 67**
See also CA 89-92

Brecht, Bertolt 1898-1956 . . . . . . **TCLC 1, 6, 13, 35; DA; DC 3; WLC**
See also CA 104; 133; DLB 56, 124; MTCW

Brecht, Eugen Berthold Friedrich
See Brecht, Bertolt

Bremer, Fredrika 1801-1865 . . . . . **NCLC 11**

Brennan, Christopher John 1870-1932 . . . . **TCLC 17**
See also CA 117

Brennan, Maeve 1917- . . . . **CLC 5**
See also CA 81-84

Brentano, Clemens (Maria) 1778-1842 . . . . **NCLC 1**
See also DLB 90

Brent of Bin Bin
See Franklin, (Stella Maraia Sarah) Miles

Brenton, Howard 1942- . . . . **CLC 31**
See also CA 69-72; CANR 33; DLB 13; MTCW

Breslin, James 1930-
See Breslin, Jimmy
See also CA 73-76; CANR 31; MTCW

Breslin, Jimmy . . . . **CLC 4, 43**
See also Breslin, James
See also AITN 1

Bresson, Robert 1901- . . . . **CLC 16**
See also CA 110

Breton, Andre 1896-1966 . . . **CLC 2, 9, 15, 54**
See also CA 19-20; 25-28R; CANR 40; CAP 2; DLB 65; MTCW

Breytenbach, Breyten 1939(?)- . . **CLC 23, 37**
See also CA 113; 129

Bridgers, Sue Ellen 1942- . . . . **CLC 26**
See also AAYA 8; CA 65-68; CANR 11, 36; CLR 18; DLB 52; JRDA; MAICYA; SAAS 1; SATA 22

Bridges, Robert (Seymour) 1844-1930 . . . . **TCLC 1**
See also CA 104; CDBLB 1890-1914; DLB 19, 98

Bridie, James . . . . **TCLC 3**
See also Mavor, Osborne Henry
See also DLB 10

Brin, David 1950- . . . . **CLC 34**
See also CA 102; CANR 24; SATA 65

Brink, Andre (Philippus) 1935- . . . . **CLC 18, 36**
See also CA 104; CANR 39; MTCW

Brinsmead, H(esba) F(ay) 1922- . . . . **CLC 21**
See also CA 21-24R; CANR 10; MAICYA; SAAS 5; SATA 18, 78

Brittain, Vera (Mary) 1893(?)-1970 . . . . **CLC 23**
See also CA 13-16; 25-28R; CAP 1; MTCW

Broch, Hermann 1886-1951 . . . . **TCLC 20**
See also CA 117; DLB 85, 124

Brock, Rose
See Hansen, Joseph

Brodkey, Harold 1930- . . . . **CLC 56**
See also CA 111; DLB 130

Brodsky, Iosif Alexandrovich 1940-
See Brodsky, Joseph
See also AITN 1; CA 41-44R; CANR 37; MTCW

Brodsky, Joseph . . **CLC 4, 6, 13, 36, 50; PC 9**
See also Brodsky, Iosif Alexandrovich

Brodsky, Michael Mark 1948- . . . . . **CLC 19**
See also CA 102; CANR 18, 41

Bromell, Henry 1947- . . . . **CLC 5**
See also CA 53-56; CANR 9

Bromfield, Louis (Brucker) 1896-1956 . . . . **TCLC 11**
See also CA 107; DLB 4, 9, 86

Broner, E(sther) M(asserman) 1930- . . . . **CLC 19**
See also CA 17-20R; CANR 8, 25; DLB 28

Bronk, William 1918- . . . . **CLC 10**
See also CA 89-92; CANR 23

Bronstein, Lev Davidovich
See Trotsky, Leon

Bronte, Anne 1820-1849 . . . . **NCLC 4**
See also DLB 21

Bronte, Charlotte 1816-1855 . . . **NCLC 3, 8, 33; DA; WLC**
See also CDBLB 1832-1890; DLB 21

Bronte, (Jane) Emily 1818-1848 . . . . **NCLC 16, 35; DA; PC 8; WLC**
See also CDBLB 1832-1890; DLB 21, 32

Brooke, Frances 1724-1789 . . . . **LC 6**
See also DLB 39, 99

Brooke, Henry 1703(?)-1783 . . . . **LC 1**
See also DLB 39

Brooke, Rupert (Chawner) 1887-1915 . . . . **TCLC 2, 7; DA; WLC**
See also CA 104; 132; CDBLB 1914-1945; DLB 19; MTCW

Brooke-Haven, P.
See Wodehouse, P(elham) G(renville)

Brooke-Rose, Christine 1926- . . . . . . **CLC 40**
See also CA 13-16R; DLB 14

Brookner, Anita 1928- . . . . . . **CLC 32, 34, 51**
See also CA 114; 120; CANR 37; DLBY 87; MTCW

Brooks, Cleanth 1906-1994 . . . . . **CLC 24, 86**
See also CA 17-20R; 145; CANR 33, 35; DLB 63; DLBY 94; MTCW

Brooks, George
See Baum, L(yman) Frank

Brooks, Gwendolyn 1917- . . . . . . **CLC 1, 2, 4, 5, 15, 49; BLC; DA; PC 7; WLC**
See also AITN 1; BW 2; CA 1-4R; CANR 1, 27; CDALB 1941-1968; CLR 27; DLB 5, 76; MTCW; SATA 6

Brooks, Mel . . . . **CLC 12**
See also Kaminsky, Melvin
See also AAYA 13; DLB 26

Brooks, Peter 1938- . . . . **CLC 34**
See also CA 45-48; CANR 1

Brooks, Van Wyck 1886-1963 . . . . . . **CLC 29**
See also CA 1-4R; CANR 6; DLB 45, 63, 103

Brophy, Brigid (Antonia) 1929- . . . . **CLC 6, 11, 29**
See also CA 5-8R; CAAS 4; CANR 25; DLB 14; MTCW

Brosman, Catharine Savage 1934- . . . . **CLC 9**
See also CA 61-64; CANR 21, 46

Brother Antoninus
See Everson, William (Oliver)

Broughton, T(homas) Alan 1936- . . . **CLC 19**
See also CA 45-48; CANR 2, 23, 48

Broumas, Olga 1949- . . . . **CLC 10, 73**
See also CA 85-88; CANR 20

Brown, Charles Brockden 1771-1810 . . . . **NCLC 22**
See also CDALB 1640-1865; DLB 37, 59, 73

Brown, Christy 1932-1981 . . . . **CLC 63**
See also CA 105; 104; DLB 14

Brown, Claude 1937- . . . . **CLC 30; BLC**
See also AAYA 7; BW 1; CA 73-76

Brown, Dee (Alexander) 1908- . . **CLC 18, 47**
See also CA 13-16R; CAAS 6; CANR 11, 45; DLBY 80; MTCW; SATA 5

Brown, George
See Wertmueller, Lina

Brown, George Douglas 1869-1902 . . . . **TCLC 28**

Brown, George Mackay 1921- . . . . **CLC 5, 48**
See also CA 21-24R; CAAS 6; CANR 12, 37; DLB 14, 27, 139; MTCW; SATA 35

Brown, (William) Larry 1951- . . . . . . **CLC 73**
See also CA 130; 134

Brown, Moses
See Barrett, William (Christopher)

Brown, Rita Mae 1944- . . . . . **CLC 18, 43, 79**
See also CA 45-48; CANR 2, 11, 35; MTCW

Brown, Roderick (Langmere) Haig-
See Haig-Brown, Roderick (Langmere)

Brown, Rosellen 1939- . . . . **CLC 32**
See also CA 77-80; CAAS 10; CANR 14, 44

Brown, Sterling Allen
1901-1989 . . . . **CLC 1, 23, 59; BLC**
See also BW 1; CA 85-88; 127; CANR 26; DLB 48, 51, 63; MTCW

Brown, Will
See Ainsworth, William Harrison

Brown, William Wells
1813-1884 . . . . **NCLC 2; BLC; DC 1**
See also DLB 3, 50

Browne, (Clyde) Jackson 1948(?)- . . . **CLC 21**
See also CA 120

Browning, Elizabeth Barrett
1806-1861 . . . . . **NCLC 1, 16; DA; PC 6; WLC**
See also CDBLB 1832-1890; DLB 32

Browning, Robert
1812-1889 . . . . **NCLC 19; DA; PC 2**
See also CDBLB 1832-1890; DLB 32; YABC 1

Browning, Tod 1882-1962 . . . . **CLC 16**
See also CA 141; 117

Brownson, Orestes (Augustus)
1803-1876 . . . . **NCLC 50**

Bruccoli, Matthew J(oseph) 1931- . . **CLC 34**
See also CA 9-12R; CANR 7; DLB 103

Bruce, Lenny . . . . **CLC 21**
See also Schneider, Leonard Alfred

Bruin, John
See Brutus, Dennis

Brulard, Henri
See Stendhal

Brulls, Christian
See Simenon, Georges (Jacques Christian)

Brunner, John (Kilian Houston)
1934- . . . . **CLC 8, 10**
See also CA 1-4R; CAAS 8; CANR 2, 37; MTCW

Bruno, Giordano 1548-1600 . . . . **LC 27**

Brutus, Dennis 1924- . . . . **CLC 43; BLC**
See also BW 2; CA 49-52; CAAS 14; CANR 2, 27, 42; DLB 117

Bryan, C(ourtlandt) D(ixon) B(arnes)
1936- . . . . **CLC 29**
See also CA 73-76; CANR 13

Bryan, Michael
See Moore, Brian

Bryant, William Cullen
1794-1878 . . . . **NCLC 6, 46; DA**
See also CDALB 1640-1865; DLB 3, 43, 59

Bryusov, Valery Yakovlevich
1873-1924 . . . . **TCLC 10**
See also CA 107

Buchan, John 1875-1940 . . . . **TCLC 41**
See also CA 108; 145; DLB 34, 70; YABC 2

Buchanan, George 1506-1582 . . . . **LC 4**

Buchheim, Lothar-Guenther 1918- . . . **CLC 6**
See also CA 85-88

Buchner, (Karl) Georg
1813-1837 . . . . **NCLC 26**

Buchwald, Art(hur) 1925- . . . . **CLC 33**
See also AITN 1; CA 5-8R; CANR 21; MTCW; SATA 10

Buck, Pearl S(ydenstricker)
1892-1973 . . . . **CLC 7, 11, 18; DA**
See also AITN 1; CA 1-4R; 41-44R; CANR 1, 34; DLB 9, 102; MTCW; SATA 1, 25

Buckler, Ernest 1908-1984 . . . . **CLC 13**
See also CA 11-12; 114; CAP 1; DLB 68; SATA 47

Buckley, Vincent (Thomas)
1925-1988 . . . . **CLC 57**
See also CA 101

Buckley, William F(rank), Jr.
1925- . . . . **CLC 7, 18, 37**
See also AITN 1; CA 1-4R; CANR 1, 24; DLB 137; DLBY 80; MTCW

Buechner, (Carl) Frederick
1926- . . . . **CLC 2, 4, 6, 9**
See also CA 13-16R; CANR 11, 39; DLBY 80; MTCW

Buell, John (Edward) 1927- . . . . **CLC 10**
See also CA 1-4R; DLB 53

Buero Vallejo, Antonio 1916- . . . **CLC 15, 46**
See also CA 106; CANR 24; HW; MTCW

Bufalino, Gesualdo 1920(?)- . . . . **CLC 74**

Bugayev, Boris Nikolayevich 1880-1934
See Bely, Andrey
See also CA 104

Bukowski, Charles
1920-1994 . . . . **CLC 2, 5, 9, 41, 82**
See also CA 17-20R; 144; CANR 40; DLB 5, 130; MTCW

Bulgakov, Mikhail (Afanas'evich)
1891-1940 . . . . **TCLC 2, 16; SSC 18**
See also CA 105

Bulgya, Alexander Alexandrovich
1901-1956 . . . . **TCLC 53**
See also Fadeyev, Alexander
See also CA 117

Bullins, Ed 1935- . . . . **CLC 1, 5, 7; BLC**
See also BW 2; CA 49-52; CAAS 16; CANR 24, 46; DLB 7, 38; MTCW

Bulwer-Lytton, Edward (George Earle Lytton)
1803-1873 . . . . **NCLC 1, 45**
See also DLB 21

Bunin, Ivan Alexeyevich
1870-1953 . . . . **TCLC 6; SSC 5**
See also CA 104

Bunting, Basil 1900-1985 . . . . **CLC 10, 39, 47**
See also CA 53-56; 115; CANR 7; DLB 20

Bunuel, Luis 1900-1983 . . **CLC 16, 80; HLC**
See also CA 101; 110; CANR 32; HW

Bunyan, John 1628-1688 . . **LC 4; DA; WLC**
See also CDBLB 1660-1789; DLB 39

Burckhardt, Jacob (Christoph)
1818-1897 . . . . **NCLC 49**

Burford, Eleanor
See Hibbert, Eleanor Alice Burford

Burgess, Anthony
. **CLC 1, 2, 4, 5, 8, 10, 13, 15, 22, 40, 62, 81**
See also Wilson, John (Anthony) Burgess
See also AITN 1; CDBLB 1960 to Present; DLB 14

Burke, Edmund
1729(?)-1797 . . . . **LC 7; DA; WLC**
See also DLB 104

Burke, Kenneth (Duva)
1897-1993 . . . . **CLC 2, 24**
See also CA 5-8R; 143; CANR 39; DLB 45, 63; MTCW

Burke, Leda
See Garnett, David

Burke, Ralph
See Silverberg, Robert

Burney, Fanny 1752-1840 . . . . **NCLC 12**
See also DLB 39

Burns, Robert 1759-1796 . . . . **PC 6**
See also CDBLB 1789-1832; DA; DLB 109; WLC

Burns, Tex
See L'Amour, Louis (Dearborn)

Burnshaw, Stanley 1906- . . . . . **CLC 3, 13, 44**
See also CA 9-12R; DLB 48

Burr, Anne 1937- . . . . **CLC 6**
See also CA 25-28R

Burroughs, Edgar Rice
1875-1950 . . . . **TCLC 2, 32**
See also AAYA 11; CA 104; 132; DLB 8; MTCW; SATA 41

Burroughs, William S(eward)
1914- . . . . **CLC 1, 2, 5, 15, 22, 42, 75; DA; WLC**
See also AITN 2; CA 9-12R; CANR 20; DLB 2, 8, 16, 152; DLBY 81; MTCW

Burton, Richard F. 1821-1890 . . . . **NCLC 42**
See also DLB 55

Busch, Frederick 1941- . . . **CLC 7, 10, 18, 47**
See also CA 33-36R; CAAS 1; CANR 45; DLB 6

Bush, Ronald 1946- . . . . **CLC 34**
See also CA 136

Bustos, F(rancisco)
See Borges, Jorge Luis

Bustos Domecq, H(onorio)
See Bioy Casares, Adolfo; Borges, Jorge Luis

Butler, Octavia E(stelle) 1947- . . . . . **CLC 38**
See also BW 2; CA 73-76; CANR 12, 24, 38; DLB 33; MTCW

Butler, Robert Olen (Jr.) 1945- . . . . . **CLC 81**
See also CA 112

Butler, Samuel 1612-1680 . . . . **LC 16**
See also DLB 101, 126

Butler, Samuel
1835-1902 . . . . . . **TCLC 1, 33; DA; WLC**
See also CA 143; CDBLB 1890-1914; DLB 18, 57

Butler, Walter C.
See Faust, Frederick (Schiller)

Butor, Michel (Marie Francois) 1926- . . . . **CLC 1, 3, 8, 11, 15**
See also CA 9-12R; CANR 33; DLB 83; MTCW

Buzo, Alexander (John) 1944-. . . . . . **CLC 61**
See also CA 97-100; CANR 17, 39

Buzzati, Dino 1906-1972 . . . . **CLC 36**
See also CA 33-36R

Byars, Betsy (Cromer) 1928-. . . . . . . **CLC 35**
See also CA 33-36R; CANR 18, 36; CLR 1, 16; DLB 52; JRDA; MAICYA; MTCW; SAAS 1; SATA 4, 46, 80

Byatt, A(ntonia) S(usan Drabble) 1936- . . . . **CLC 19, 65**
See also CA 13-16R; CANR 13, 33; DLB 14; MTCW

Byrne, David 1952-. . . . . **CLC 26**
See also CA 127

Byrne, John Keyes 1926-
See Leonard, Hugh
See also CA 102

Byron, George Gordon (Noel) 1788-1824 . . . . . . **NCLC 2, 12; DA; WLC**
See also CDBLB 1789-1832; DLB 96, 110

C. 3. 3.
See Wilde, Oscar (Fingal O'Flahertie Wills)

Caballero, Fernan 1796-1877. . . . . **NCLC 10**

Cabell, James Branch 1879-1958 . . . **TCLC 6**
See also CA 105; DLB 9, 78

Cable, George Washington 1844-1925 . . . . **TCLC 4; SSC 4**
See also CA 104; DLB 12, 74

Cabral de Melo Neto, Joao 1920-. . . **CLC 76**

Cabrera Infante, G(uillermo) 1929- . . . . **CLC 5, 25, 45; HLC**
See also CA 85-88; CANR 29; DLB 113; HW; MTCW

Cade, Toni
See Bambara, Toni Cade

Cadmus and Harmonia
See Buchan, John

Caedmon fl. 658-680. . . . . **CMLC 7**
See also DLB 146

Caeiro, Alberto
See Pessoa, Fernando (Antonio Nogueira)

Cage, John (Milton, Jr.) 1912- . . . . . **CLC 41**
See also CA 13-16R; CANR 9

Cain, G.
See Cabrera Infante, G(uillermo)

Cain, Guillermo
See Cabrera Infante, G(uillermo)

Cain, James M(allahan) 1892-1977 . . . . **CLC 3, 11, 28**
See also AITN 1; CA 17-20R; 73-76; CANR 8, 34; MTCW

Caine, Mark
See Raphael, Frederic (Michael)

Calasso, Roberto 1941- . . . . **CLC 81**
See also CA 143

Calderon de la Barca, Pedro 1600-1681 . . . . **LC 23; DC 3**

Caldwell, Erskine (Preston) 1903-1987 . . . . **CLC 1, 8, 14, 50, 60; SSC 19**
See also AITN 1; CA 1-4R; 121; CAAS 1; CANR 2, 33; DLB 9, 86; MTCW

Caldwell, (Janet Miriam) Taylor (Holland) 1900-1985 . . . . **CLC 2, 28, 39**
See also CA 5-8R; 116; CANR 5

Calhoun, John Caldwell 1782-1850 . . . . **NCLC 15**
See also DLB 3

Calisher, Hortense 1911- . . . . **CLC 2, 4, 8, 38; SSC 15**
See also CA 1-4R; CANR 1, 22; DLB 2; MTCW

Callaghan, Morley Edward 1903-1990 . . . . **CLC 3, 14, 41, 65**
See also CA 9-12R; 132; CANR 33; DLB 68; MTCW

Calvino, Italo 1923-1985 . . . . . **CLC 5, 8, 11, 22, 33, 39, 73; SSC 3**
See also CA 85-88; 116; CANR 23; MTCW

Cameron, Carey 1952- . . . . **CLC 59**
See also CA 135

Cameron, Peter 1959-. . . . . **CLC 44**
See also CA 125

Campana, Dino 1885-1932. . . . . **TCLC 20**
See also CA 117; DLB 114

Campbell, John W(ood, Jr.) 1910-1971 . . . . **CLC 32**
See also CA 21-22; 29-32R; CANR 34; CAP 2; DLB 8; MTCW

Campbell, Joseph 1904-1987 . . . . **CLC 69**
See also AAYA 3; BEST 89:2; CA 1-4R; 124; CANR 3, 28; MTCW

Campbell, Maria 1940-. . . . . **CLC 85**
See also CA 102; NNAL

Campbell, (John) Ramsey 1946- . . . . **CLC 42; SSC 19**
See also CA 57-60; CANR 7

Campbell, (Ignatius) Roy (Dunnachie) 1901-1957 . . . . **TCLC 5**
See also CA 104; DLB 20

Campbell, Thomas 1777-1844 . . . . **NCLC 19**
See also DLB 93; 144

Campbell, Wilfred. . . . . **TCLC 9**
See also Campbell, William

Campbell, William 1858(?)-1918
See Campbell, Wilfred
See also CA 106; DLB 92

Campos, Alvaro de
See Pessoa, Fernando (Antonio Nogueira)

Camus, Albert 1913-1960 . . . . **CLC 1, 2, 4, 9, 11, 14, 32, 63, 69; DA; DC 2; SSC 9; WLC**
See also CA 89-92; DLB 72; MTCW

Canby, Vincent 1924-. . . . . **CLC 13**
See also CA 81-84

Cancale
See Desnos, Robert

Canetti, Elias 1905-1994 . . . . **CLC 3, 14, 25, 75, 86**
See also CA 21-24R; 146; CANR 23; DLB 85, 124; MTCW

Canin, Ethan 1960-. . . . . **CLC 55**
See also CA 131; 135

Cannon, Curt
See Hunter, Evan

Cape, Judith
See Page, P(atricia) K(athleen)

Capek, Karel 1890-1938 . . . . . **TCLC 6, 37; DA; DC 1; WLC**
See also CA 104; 140

Capote, Truman 1924-1984 . . . . . . **CLC 1, 3, 8, 13, 19, 34, 38, 58; DA; SSC 2; WLC**
See also CA 5-8R; 113; CANR 18; CDALB 1941-1968; DLB 2; DLBY 80, 84; MTCW

Capra, Frank 1897-1991. . . . . **CLC 16**
See also CA 61-64; 135

Caputo, Philip 1941-. . . . . **CLC 32**
See also CA 73-76; CANR 40

Card, Orson Scott 1951- . . . . **CLC 44, 47, 50**
See also AAYA 11; CA 102; CANR 27, 47; MTCW

Cardenal (Martinez), Ernesto 1925- . . . . **CLC 31; HLC**
See also CA 49-52; CANR 2, 32; HW; MTCW

Carducci, Giosue 1835-1907. . . . . . . **TCLC 32**

Carew, Thomas 1595(?)-1640. . . . . **LC 13**
See also DLB 126

Carey, Ernestine Gilbreth 1908- . . . . **CLC 17**
See also CA 5-8R; SATA 2

Carey, Peter 1943- . . . . **CLC 40, 55**
See also CA 123; 127; MTCW

Carleton, William 1794-1869. . . . . . **NCLC 3**

Carlisle, Henry (Coffin) 1926-. . . . . . **CLC 33**
See also CA 13-16R; CANR 15

Carlsen, Chris
See Holdstock, Robert P.

Carlson, Ron(ald F.) 1947-. . . . . **CLC 54**
See also CA 105; CANR 27

Carlyle, Thomas 1795-1881 . . **NCLC 22; DA**
See also CDBLB 1789-1832; DLB 55; 144

Carman, (William) Bliss 1861-1929 . . . . **TCLC 7**
See also CA 104; DLB 92

Carnegie, Dale 1888-1955 . . . . **TCLC 53**

Carossa, Hans 1878-1956. . . . . **TCLC 48**
See also DLB 66

Carpenter, Don(ald Richard) 1931- . . . . **CLC 41**
See also CA 45-48; CANR 1

Carpentier (y Valmont), Alejo 1904-1980 . . . . **CLC 8, 11, 38; HLC**
See also CA 65-68; 97-100; CANR 11; DLB 113; HW

Carr, Caleb 1955(?)-. . . . . **CLC 86**
See also CA 147

Carr, Emily 1871-1945. . . . . **TCLC 32**
See also DLB 68

Carr, John Dickson 1906-1977 . . . . . . **CLC 3**
See also CA 49-52; 69-72; CANR 3, 33; MTCW

Carr, Philippa
See Hibbert, Eleanor Alice Burford

Carr, Virginia Spencer 1929- .... **CLC 34**
See also CA 61-64; DLB 111

Carrere, Emmanuel 1957- .... **CLC 89**

Carrier, Roch 1937- .... **CLC 13, 78**
See also CA 130; DLB 53

Carroll, James P. 1943(?)- .... **CLC 38**
See also CA 81-84

Carroll, Jim 1951- .... **CLC 35**
See also CA 45-48; CANR 42

Carroll, Lewis .... **NCLC 2; WLC**
See also Dodgson, Charles Lutwidge
See also CDBLB 1832-1890; CLR 2, 18; DLB 18; JRDA

Carroll, Paul Vincent 1900-1968.... **CLC 10**
See also CA 9-12R; 25-28R; DLB 10

Carruth, Hayden
1921- ...... **CLC 4, 7, 10, 18, 84; PC 10**
See also CA 9-12R; CANR 4, 38; DLB 5; MTCW; SATA 47

Carson, Rachel Louise 1907-1964... **CLC 71**
See also CA 77-80; CANR 35; MTCW; SATA 23

Carter, Angela (Olive)
1940-1992 ...... **CLC 5, 41, 76; SSC 13**
See also CA 53-56; 136; CANR 12, 36; DLB 14; MTCW; SATA 66; SATA-Obit 70

Carter, Nick
See Smith, Martin Cruz

Carver, Raymond
1938-1988 ... **CLC 22, 36, 53, 55; SSC 8**
See also CA 33-36R; 126; CANR 17, 34; DLB 130; DLBY 84, 88; MTCW

CARY, ELIZABETH 1585-1639 .... **LC 30**

Cary, (Arthur) Joyce (Lunel)
1888-1957 .... **TCLC 1, 29**
See also CA 104; CDBLB 1914-1945; DLB 15, 100

Casanova de Seingalt, Giovanni Jacopo
1725-1798 .... **LC 13**

Casares, Adolfo Bioy
See Bioy Casares, Adolfo

Casely-Hayford, J(oseph) E(phraim)
1866-1930 .... **TCLC 24; BLC**
See also BW 2; CA 123

Casey, John (Dudley) 1939-........ **CLC 59**
See also BEST 90:2; CA 69-72; CANR 23

Casey, Michael 1947-.............. **CLC 2**
See also CA 65-68; DLB 5

Casey, Patrick
See Thurman, Wallace (Henry)

Casey, Warren (Peter) 1935-1988 ... **CLC 12**
See also CA 101; 127

Casona, Alejandro .... **CLC 49**
See also Alvarez, Alejandro Rodriguez

Cassavetes, John 1929-1989........ **CLC 20**
See also CA 85-88; 127

Cassill, R(onald) V(erlin) 1919-... **CLC 4, 23**
See also CA 9-12R; CAAS 1; CANR 7, 45; DLB 6

Cassity, (Allen) Turner 1929- .... **CLC 6, 42**
See also CA 17-20R; CAAS 8; CANR 11; DLB 105

Castaneda, Carlos 1931(?)-......... **CLC 12**
See also CA 25-28R; CANR 32; HW; MTCW

Castedo, Elena 1937- .... **CLC 65**
See also CA 132

Castedo-Ellerman, Elena
See Castedo, Elena

Castellanos, Rosario
1925-1974 .... **CLC 66; HLC**
See also CA 131; 53-56; DLB 113; HW

Castelvetro, Lodovico 1505-1571..... **LC 12**

Castiglione, Baldassare 1478-1529 ... **LC 12**

Castle, Robert
See Hamilton, Edmond

Castro, Guillen de 1569-1631........ **LC 19**

Castro, Rosalia de 1837-1885 ..... **NCLC 3**

Cather, Willa
See Cather, Willa Sibert

Cather, Willa Sibert
1873-1947 .... **TCLC 1, 11, 31; DA; SSC 2; WLC**
See also CA 104; 128; CDALB 1865-1917; DLB 9, 54, 78; DLBD 1; MTCW; SATA 30

Catton, (Charles) Bruce
1899-1978 .... **CLC 35**
See also AITN 1; CA 5-8R; 81-84; CANR 7; DLB 17; SATA 2; SATA-Obit 24

Cauldwell, Frank
See King, Francis (Henry)

Caunitz, William J. 1933- .... **CLC 34**
See also BEST 89:3; CA 125; 130

Causley, Charles (Stanley) 1917-..... **CLC 7**
See also CA 9-12R; CANR 5, 35; CLR 30; DLB 27; MTCW; SATA 3, 66

Caute, David 1936-............... **CLC 29**
See also CA 1-4R; CAAS 4; CANR 1, 33; DLB 14

Cavafy, C(onstantine) P(eter)...... **TCLC 2, 7**
See also Kavafis, Konstantinos Petrou

Cavallo, Evelyn
See Spark, Muriel (Sarah)

Cavanna, Betty .... **CLC 12**
See also Harrison, Elizabeth Cavanna
See also JRDA; MAICYA; SAAS 4; SATA 1, 30

Cavendish, Margaret Lucas
1623-1673 .... **LC 30**
See also DLB 131

Caxton, William 1421(?)-1491(?)..... **LC 17**

Cayrol, Jean 1911-............... **CLC 11**
See also CA 89-92; DLB 83

Cela, Camilo Jose
1916- .... **CLC 4, 13, 59; HLC**
See also BEST 90:2; CA 21-24R; CAAS 10; CANR 21, 32; DLBY 89; HW; MTCW

Celan, Paul ...... **CLC 10, 19, 53, 82; PC 10**
See also Antschel, Paul
See also DLB 69

Celine, Louis-Ferdinand
.... **CLC 1, 3, 4, 7, 9, 15, 47**
See also Destouches, Louis-Ferdinand
See also DLB 72

Cellini, Benvenuto 1500-1571 .... **LC 7**

Cendrars, Blaise .... **CLC 18**
See also Sauser-Hall, Frederic

Cernuda (y Bidon), Luis
1902-1963 .... **CLC 54**
See also CA 131; 89-92; DLB 134; HW

Cervantes (Saavedra), Miguel de
1547-1616 ...... **LC 6, 23; DA; SSC 12; WLC**

Cesaire, Aime (Fernand)
1913- .... **CLC 19, 32; BLC**
See also BW 2; CA 65-68; CANR 24, 43; MTCW

Chabon, Michael 1965(?)- .... **CLC 55**
See also CA 139

Chabrol, Claude 1930- .... **CLC 16**
See also CA 110

Challans, Mary 1905-1983
See Renault, Mary
See also CA 81-84; 111; SATA 23; SATA-Obit 36

Challis, George
See Faust, Frederick (Schiller)

Chambers, Aidan 1934- .... **CLC 35**
See also CA 25-28R; CANR 12, 31; JRDA; MAICYA; SAAS 12; SATA 1, 69

Chambers, James 1948-
See Cliff, Jimmy
See also CA 124

Chambers, Jessie
See Lawrence, D(avid) H(erbert Richards)

Chambers, Robert W. 1865-1933... **TCLC 41**

Chandler, Raymond (Thornton)
1888-1959 .... **TCLC 1, 7**
See also CA 104; 129; CDALB 1929-1941; DLBD 6; MTCW

Chang, Jung 1952- .... **CLC 71**
See also CA 142

Channing, William Ellery
1780-1842 .... **NCLC 17**
See also DLB 1, 59

Chaplin, Charles Spencer
1889-1977 .... **CLC 16**
See also Chaplin, Charlie
See also CA 81-84; 73-76

Chaplin, Charlie
See Chaplin, Charles Spencer
See also DLB 44

Chapman, George 1559(?)-1634...... **LC 22**
See also DLB 62, 121

Chapman, Graham 1941-1989 ...... **CLC 21**
See also Monty Python
See also CA 116; 129; CANR 35

Chapman, John Jay 1862-1933 ..... **TCLC 7**
See also CA 104

Chapman, Walker
See Silverberg, Robert

Chappell, Fred (Davis) 1936-.... **CLC 40, 78**
See also CA 5-8R; CAAS 4; CANR 8, 33; DLB 6, 105

Author Index

Clark, John Pepper 1935- . . . . **CLC 38; BLC; DC 5**
See also Clark, J. P.
See also BW 1; CA 65-68; CANR 16

Clark, M. R.
See Clark, Mavis Thorpe

Clark, Mavis Thorpe 1909- . . . . **CLC 12**
See also CA 57-60; CANR 8, 37; CLR 30; MAICYA; SAAS 5; SATA 8, 74

Clark, Walter Van Tilburg 1909-1971 . . . . **CLC 28**
See also CA 9-12R; 33-36R; DLB 9; SATA 8

Clarke, Arthur C(harles) 1917- . . . . . . **CLC 1, 4, 13, 18, 35; SSC 3**
See also AAYA 4; CA 1-4R; CANR 2, 28; JRDA; MAICYA; MTCW; SATA 13, 70

Clarke, Austin 1896-1974. . . . . **CLC 6, 9**
See also CA 29-32; 49-52; CAP 2; DLB 10, 20

Clarke, Austin C(hesterfield) 1934- . . . . **CLC 8, 53; BLC**
See also BW 1; CA 25-28R; CAAS 16; CANR 14, 32; DLB 53, 125

Clarke, Gillian 1937- . . . . **CLC 61**
See also CA 106; DLB 40

Clarke, Marcus (Andrew Hislop) 1846-1881 . . . . **NCLC 19**

Clarke, Shirley 1925- . . . . **CLC 16**

Clash, The
See Headon, (Nicky) Topper; Jones, Mick; Simonon, Paul; Strummer, Joe

Claudel, Paul (Louis Charles Marie) 1868-1955 . . . . **TCLC 2, 10**
See also CA 104

Clavell, James (duMaresq) 1925-1994 . . . . **CLC 6, 25, 87**
See also CA 25-28R; 146; CANR 26, 48; MTCW

Cleaver, (Leroy) Eldridge 1935- . . . . **CLC 30; BLC**
See also BW 1; CA 21-24R; CANR 16

Cleese, John (Marwood) 1939- . . . . . **CLC 21**
See also Monty Python
See also CA 112; 116; CANR 35; MTCW

Cleishbotham, Jebediah
See Scott, Walter

Cleland, John 1710-1789 . . . . **LC 2**
See also DLB 39

Clemens, Samuel Langhorne 1835-1910
See Twain, Mark
See also CA 104; 135; CDALB 1865-1917; DA; DLB 11, 12, 23, 64, 74; JRDA; MAICYA; YABC 2

Cleophil
See Congreve, William

Clerihew, E.
See Bentley, E(dmund) C(lerihew)

Clerk, N. W.
See Lewis, C(live) S(taples)

Cliff, Jimmy. . . . . **CLC 21**
See also Chambers, James

Clifton, (Thelma) Lucille 1936- . . . . **CLC 19, 66; BLC**
See also BW 2; CA 49-52; CANR 2, 24, 42; CLR 5; DLB 5, 41; MAICYA; MTCW; SATA 20, 69

Clinton, Dirk
See Silverberg, Robert

Clough, Arthur Hugh 1819-1861. . **NCLC 27**
See also DLB 32

Clutha, Janet Paterson Frame 1924-
See Frame, Janet
See also CA 1-4R; CANR 2, 36; MTCW

Clyne, Terence
See Blatty, William Peter

Cobalt, Martin
See Mayne, William (James Carter)

Cobbett, William 1763-1835 . . . . . **NCLC 49**
See also DLB 43, 107

Coburn, D(onald) L(ee) 1938- . . . . . . **CLC 10**
See also CA 89-92

Cocteau, Jean (Maurice Eugene Clement) 1889-1963 . . . . **CLC 1, 8, 15, 16, 43; DA; WLC**
See also CA 25-28; CANR 40; CAP 2; DLB 65; MTCW

Codrescu, Andrei 1946- . . . . **CLC 46**
See also CA 33-36R; CAAS 19; CANR 13, 34

Coe, Max
See Bourne, Randolph S(illiman)

Coe, Tucker
See Westlake, Donald E(dwin)

Coetzee, J(ohn) M(ichael) 1940- . . . . **CLC 23, 33, 66**
See also CA 77-80; CANR 41; MTCW

Coffey, Brian
See Koontz, Dean R(ay)

Cohan, George M. 1878-1942 . . . . . **TCLC 60**

Cohen, Arthur A(llen) 1928-1986 . . . . **CLC 7, 31**
See also CA 1-4R; 120; CANR 1, 17, 42; DLB 28

Cohen, Leonard (Norman) 1934- . . . . **CLC 3, 38**
See also CA 21-24R; CANR 14; DLB 53; MTCW

Cohen, Matt 1942- . . . . **CLC 19**
See also CA 61-64; CAAS 18; CANR 40; DLB 53

Cohen-Solal, Annie 19(?)- . . . . **CLC 50**

Colegate, Isabel 1931- . . . . **CLC 36**
See also CA 17-20R; CANR 8, 22; DLB 14; MTCW

Coleman, Emmett
See Reed, Ishmael

Coleridge, Samuel Taylor 1772-1834 . . **NCLC 9; DA; PC 11; WLC**
See also CDBLB 1789-1832; DLB 93, 107

Coleridge, Sara 1802-1852. . . . . . . **NCLC 31**

Coles, Don 1928- . . . . **CLC 46**
See also CA 115; CANR 38

Colette, (Sidonie-Gabrielle) 1873-1954 . . . . . . **TCLC 1, 5, 16; SSC 10**
See also CA 104; 131; DLB 65; MTCW

Collett, (Jacobine) Camilla (Wergeland) 1813-1895 . . . . **NCLC 22**

Collier, Christopher 1930- . . . . **CLC 30**
See also AAYA 13; CA 33-36R; CANR 13, 33; JRDA; MAICYA; SATA 16, 70

Collier, James L(incoln) 1928- . . . . . **CLC 30**
See also AAYA 13; CA 9-12R; CANR 4, 33; CLR 3; JRDA; MAICYA; SATA 8, 70

Collier, Jeremy 1650-1726. . . . . **LC 6**

Collier, John 1901-1980. . . . . **SSC**
See also CA 65-68; 97-100; CANR 10; DLB 77

Collins, Hunt
See Hunter, Evan

Collins, Linda 1931- . . . . **CLC 44**
See also CA 125

Collins, (William) Wilkie 1824-1889 . . . . **NCLC 1, 18**
See also CDBLB 1832-1890; DLB 18, 70

Collins, William 1721-1759 . . . . **LC 4**
See also DLB 109

Colman, George
See Glassco, John

Colt, Winchester Remington
See Hubbard, L(afayette) Ron(ald)

Colter, Cyrus 1910- . . . . **CLC 58**
See also BW 1; CA 65-68; CANR 10; DLB 33

Colton, James
See Hansen, Joseph

Colum, Padraic 1881-1972. . . . . **CLC 28**
See also CA 73-76; 33-36R; CANR 35; CLR 36; MAICYA; MTCW; SATA 15

Colvin, James
See Moorcock, Michael (John)

Colwin, Laurie (E.) 1944-1992 . . . . **CLC 5, 13, 23, 84**
See also CA 89-92; 139; CANR 20, 46; DLBY 80; MTCW

Comfort, Alex(ander) 1920- . . . . **CLC 7**
See also CA 1-4R; CANR 1, 45

Comfort, Montgomery
See Campbell, (John) Ramsey

Compton-Burnett, I(vy) 1884(?)-1969 . . . . . . **CLC 1, 3, 10, 15, 34**
See also CA 1-4R; 25-28R; CANR 4; DLB 36; MTCW

Comstock, Anthony 1844-1915 . . . . **TCLC 13**
See also CA 110

Conan Doyle, Arthur
See Doyle, Arthur Conan

Conde, Maryse 1937- . . . . **CLC 52**
See also Boucolon, Maryse
See also BW 2

Condillac, Etienne Bonnot de 1714-1780 . . . . **LC 26**

Condon, Richard (Thomas) 1915- . . . . **CLC 4, 6, 8, 10, 45**
See also BEST 90:3; CA 1-4R; CAAS 1; CANR 2, 23; MTCW

Congreve, William 1670-1729 . . . **LC 5, 21; DA; DC 2; WLC**
See also CDBLB 1660-1789; DLB 39, 84

Connell, Evan S(helby), Jr. 1924- .... **CLC 4, 6, 45**
See also AAYA 7; CA 1-4R; CAAS 2; CANR 2, 39; DLB 2; DLBY 81; MTCW

Connelly, Marc(us Cook) 1890-1980 .... **CLC 7**
See also CA 85-88; 102; CANR 30; DLB 7; DLBY 80; SATA-Obit 25

Connor, Ralph .... **TCLC 31**
See also Gordon, Charles William
See also DLB 92

Conrad, Joseph 1857-1924 .... **TCLC 1, 6, 13, 25, 43, 57; DA; SSC 9; WLC**
See also CA 104; 131; CDBLB 1890-1914; DLB 10, 34, 98; MTCW; SATA 27

Conrad, Robert Arnold
See Hart, Moss

Conroy, Pat 1945- .... **CLC 30, 74**
See also AAYA 8; AITN 1; CA 85-88; CANR 24; DLB 6; MTCW

Constant (de Rebecque), (Henri) Benjamin 1767-1830 .... **NCLC 6**
See also DLB 119

Conybeare, Charles Augustus
See Eliot, T(homas) S(tearns)

Cook, Michael 1933- .... **CLC 58**
See also CA 93-96; DLB 53

Cook, Robin 1940- .... **CLC 14**
See also BEST 90:2; CA 108; 111; CANR 41

Cook, Roy
See Silverberg, Robert

Cooke, Elizabeth 1948- .... **CLC 55**
See also CA 129

Cooke, John Esten 1830-1886 ..... **NCLC 5**
See also DLB 3

Cooke, John Estes
See Baum, L(yman) Frank

Cooke, M. E.
See Creasey, John

Cooke, Margaret
See Creasey, John

Cooney, Ray .... **CLC 62**

Cooper, Douglas 1960- .... **CLC 86**

Cooper, Henry St. John
See Creasey, John

Cooper, J. California .... **CLC 56**
See also AAYA 12; BW 1; CA 125

Cooper, James Fenimore 1789-1851 .... **NCLC 1, 27**
See also CDALB 1640-1865; DLB 3; SATA 19

Coover, Robert (Lowell) 1932- .. **CLC 3, 7, 15, 32, 46, 87; SSC 15**
See also CA 45-48; CANR 3, 37; DLB 2; DLBY 81; MTCW

Copeland, Stewart (Armstrong) 1952- .... **CLC 26**

Coppard, A(lfred) E(dgar) 1878-1957 .... **TCLC 5**
See also CA 114; YABC 1

Coppee, Francois 1842-1908 ...... **TCLC 25**

Coppola, Francis Ford 1939- .... **CLC 16**
See also CA 77-80; CANR 40; DLB 44

Corbiere, Tristan 1845-1875 ..... **NCLC 43**

Corcoran, Barbara 1911- .... **CLC 17**
See also AAYA 14; CA 21-24R; CAAS 2; CANR 11, 28, 48; DLB 52; JRDA; SAAS 20; SATA 3, 77

Cordelier, Maurice
See Giraudoux, (Hippolyte) Jean

Corelli, Marie 1855-1924 .... **TCLC 51**
See also Mackay, Mary
See also DLB 34

Corman, Cid .... **CLC 9**
See also Corman, Sidney
See also CAAS 2; DLB 5

Corman, Sidney 1924-
See Corman, Cid
See also CA 85-88; CANR 44

Cormier, Robert (Edmund) 1925- .... **CLC 12, 30; DA**
See also AAYA 3; CA 1-4R; CANR 5, 23; CDALB 1968-1988; CLR 12; DLB 52; JRDA; MAICYA; MTCW; SATA 10, 45

Corn, Alfred (DeWitt III) 1943- .... **CLC 33**
See also CA 104; CANR 44; DLB 120; DLBY 80

Corneille, Pierre 1606-1684 .... **LC 28**

Cornwell, David (John Moore) 1931- .... **CLC 9, 15**
See also le Carre, John
See also CA 5-8R; CANR 13, 33; MTCW

Corso, (Nunzio) Gregory 1930- ... **CLC 1, 11**
See also CA 5-8R; CANR 41; DLB 5, 16; MTCW

Cortazar, Julio 1914-1984 ...... **CLC 2, 3, 5, 10, 13, 15, 33, 34; HLC; SSC 7**
See also CA 21-24R; CANR 12, 32; DLB 113; HW; MTCW

Corwin, Cecil
See Kornbluth, C(yril) M.

Cosic, Dobrica 1921- .... **CLC 14**
See also CA 122; 138

Costain, Thomas B(ertram) 1885-1965 .... **CLC 30**
See also CA 5-8R; 25-28R; DLB 9

Costantini, Humberto 1924(?)-1987 .... **CLC 49**
See also CA 131; 122; HW

Costello, Elvis 1955- .... **CLC 21**

Cotter, Joseph Seamon Sr. 1861-1949 .... **TCLC 28; BLC**
See also BW 1; CA 124; DLB 50

Couch, Arthur Thomas Quiller
See Quiller-Couch, Arthur Thomas

Coulton, James
See Hansen, Joseph

Couperus, Louis (Marie Anne) 1863-1923 .... **TCLC 15**
See also CA 115

Coupland, Douglas 1961- .... **CLC 85**
See also CA 142

Court, Wesli
See Turco, Lewis (Putnam)

Courtenay, Bryce 1933- .... **CLC 59**
See also CA 138

Courtney, Robert
See Ellison, Harlan (Jay)

Cousteau, Jacques-Yves 1910- ...... **CLC 30**
See also CA 65-68; CANR 15; MTCW; SATA 38

Coward, Noel (Peirce) 1899-1973 .... **CLC 1, 9, 29, 51**
See also AITN 1; CA 17-18; 41-44R; CANR 35; CAP 2; CDBLB 1914-1945; DLB 10; MTCW

Cowley, Malcolm 1898-1989 .... **CLC 39**
See also CA 5-8R; 128; CANR 3; DLB 4, 48; DLBY 81, 89; MTCW

Cowper, William 1731-1800 .... **NCLC 8**
See also DLB 104, 109

Cox, William Trevor 1928- ... **CLC 9, 14, 71**
See also Trevor, William
See also CA 9-12R; CANR 4, 37; DLB 14; MTCW

Coyne, P. J.
See Masters, Hilary

Cozzens, James Gould 1903-1978 .... **CLC 1, 4, 11**
See also CA 9-12R; 81-84; CANR 19; CDALB 1941-1968; DLB 9; DLBD 2; DLBY 84; MTCW

Crabbe, George 1754-1832 .... **NCLC 26**
See also DLB 93

Craig, A. A.
See Anderson, Poul (William)

Craik, Dinah Maria (Mulock) 1826-1887 .... **NCLC 38**
See also DLB 35; MAICYA; SATA 34

Cram, Ralph Adams 1863-1942 .... **TCLC 45**

Crane, (Harold) Hart 1899-1932 .... **TCLC 2, 5; DA; PC 3; WLC**
See also CA 104; 127; CDALB 1917-1929; DLB 4, 48; MTCW

Crane, R(onald) S(almon) 1886-1967 .... **CLC 27**
See also CA 85-88; DLB 63

Crane, Stephen (Townley) 1871-1900 .... **TCLC 11, 17, 32; DA; SSC 7; WLC**
See also CA 109; 140; CDALB 1865-1917; DLB 12, 54, 78; YABC 2

Crase, Douglas 1944- .... **CLC 58**
See also CA 106

Crashaw, Richard 1612(?)-1649 ...... **LC 24**
See also DLB 126

Craven, Margaret 1901-1980 .... **CLC 17**
See also CA 103

Crawford, F(rancis) Marion 1854-1909 .... **TCLC 10**
See also CA 107; DLB 71

Crawford, Isabella Valancy 1850-1887 .... **NCLC 12**
See also DLB 92

Crayon, Geoffrey
See Irving, Washington

Creasey, John 1908-1973 .... **CLC 11**
See also CA 5-8R; 41-44R; CANR 8; DLB 77; MTCW

Crebillon, Claude Prosper Jolyot de (fils) 1707-1777 .... **LC 28**

Credo
See Creasey, John

Creeley, Robert (White) 1926- ..... **CLC 1, 2, 4, 8, 11, 15, 36, 78**
See also CA 1-4R; CAAS 10; CANR 23, 43; DLB 5, 16; MTCW

Crews, Harry (Eugene) 1935- .... **CLC 6, 23, 49**
See also AITN 1; CA 25-28R; CANR 20; DLB 6, 143; MTCW

Crichton, (John) Michael 1942- .... **CLC 2, 6, 54**
See also AAYA 10; AITN 2; CA 25-28R; CANR 13, 40; DLBY 81; JRDA; MTCW; SATA 9

Crispin, Edmund .... **CLC 22**
See also Montgomery, (Robert) Bruce
See also DLB 87

Cristofer, Michael 1945(?)- .... **CLC 28**
See also CA 110; DLB 7

Croce, Benedetto 1866-1952 ...... **TCLC 37**
See also CA 120

Crockett, David 1786-1836 .... **NCLC 8**
See also DLB 3, 11

Crockett, Davy
See Crockett, David

Crofts, Freeman Wills 1879-1957 .... **TCLC 55**
See also CA 115; DLB 77

Croker, John Wilson 1780-1857 .. **NCLC 10**
See also DLB 110

Crommelynck, Fernand 1885-1970 .. **CLC 75**
See also CA 89-92

Cronin, A(rchibald) J(oseph) 1896-1981 .... **CLC 32**
See also CA 1-4R; 102; CANR 5; SATA 47; SATA-Obit 25

Cross, Amanda
See Heilbrun, Carolyn G(old)

Crothers, Rachel 1878(?)-1958..... **TCLC 19**
See also CA 113; DLB 7

Croves, Hal
See Traven, B.

Crowfield, Christopher
See Stowe, Harriet (Elizabeth) Beecher

Crowley, Aleister.................. **TCLC 7**
See also Crowley, Edward Alexander

Crowley, Edward Alexander 1875-1947
See Crowley, Aleister
See also CA 104

Crowley, John 1942-.............. **CLC 57**
See also CA 61-64; CANR 43; DLBY 82; SATA 65

Crud
See Crumb, R(obert)

Crumarums
See Crumb, R(obert)

Crumb, R(obert) 1943-............ **CLC 17**
See also CA 106

Crumbum
See Crumb, R(obert)

Crumski
See Crumb, R(obert)

Crum the Bum
See Crumb, R(obert)

Crunk
See Crumb, R(obert)

Crustt
See Crumb, R(obert)

Cryer, Gretchen (Kiger) 1935-...... **CLC 21**
See also CA 114; 123

Csath, Geza 1887-1919........... **TCLC 13**
See also CA 111

Cudlip, David 1933-.............. **CLC 34**

Cullen, Countee 1903-1946 ...... **TCLC 4, 37; BLC; DA**
See also BW 1; CA 108; 124; CDALB 1917-1929; DLB 4, 48, 51; MTCW; SATA 18

Cum, R.
See Crumb, R(obert)

Cummings, Bruce F(rederick) 1889-1919
See Barbellion, W. N. P.
See also CA 123

Cummings, E(dward) E(stlin) 1894-1962 ...... **CLC 1, 3, 8, 12, 15, 68; DA; PC 5; WLC 2**
See also CA 73-76; CANR 31; CDALB 1929-1941; DLB 4, 48; MTCW

Cunha, Euclides (Rodrigues Pimenta) da 1866-1909 .... **TCLC 24**
See also CA 123

Cunningham, E. V.
See Fast, Howard (Melvin)

Cunningham, J(ames) V(incent) 1911-1985 .... **CLC 3, 31**
See also CA 1-4R; 115; CANR 1; DLB 5

Cunningham, Julia (Woolfolk) 1916- .... **CLC 12**
See also CA 9-12R; CANR 4, 19, 36; JRDA; MAICYA; SAAS 2; SATA 1, 26

Cunningham, Michael 1952- .... **CLC 34**
See also CA 136

Cunninghame Graham, R(obert) B(ontine) 1852-1936 .... **TCLC 19**
See also Graham, R(obert) B(ontine) Cunninghame
See also CA 119; DLB 98

Currie, Ellen 19(?)-............... **CLC 44**

Curtin, Philip
See Lowndes, Marie Adelaide (Belloc)

Curtis, Price
See Ellison, Harlan (Jay)

Cutrate, Joe
See Spiegelman, Art

Czaczkes, Shmuel Yosef
See Agnon, S(hmuel) Y(osef Halevi)

Dabrowska, Maria (Szumska) 1889-1965 .... **CLC 15**
See also CA 106

Dabydeen, David 1955- .... **CLC 34**
See also BW 1; CA 125

Dacey, Philip 1939- .... **CLC 51**
See also CA 37-40R; CAAS 17; CANR 14, 32; DLB 105

Dagerman, Stig (Halvard) 1923-1954 .... **TCLC 17**
See also CA 117

Dahl, Roald 1916-1990..... **CLC 1, 6, 18, 79**
See also CA 1-4R; 133; CANR 6, 32, 37; CLR 1, 7; DLB 139; JRDA; MAICYA; MTCW; SATA 1, 26, 73; SATA-Obit 65

Dahlberg, Edward 1900-1977... **CLC 1, 7, 14**
See also CA 9-12R; 69-72; CANR 31; DLB 48; MTCW

Dale, Colin...................... **TCLC 18**
See also Lawrence, T(homas) E(dward)

Dale, George E.
See Asimov, Isaac

Daly, Elizabeth 1878-1967......... **CLC 52**
See also CA 23-24; 25-28R; CAP 2

Daly, Maureen 1921-............. **CLC 17**
See also AAYA 5; CANR 37; JRDA; MAICYA; SAAS 1; SATA 2

Damas, Leon-Gontran 1912-1978 ... **CLC 84**
See also BW 1; CA 125; 73-76

Daniel, Samuel 1562(?)-1619........ **LC 24**
See also DLB 62

Daniels, Brett
See Adler, Renata

Dannay, Frederic 1905-1982 .... **CLC 11**
See also Queen, Ellery
See also CA 1-4R; 107; CANR 1, 39; DLB 137; MTCW

D'Annunzio, Gabriele 1863-1938 .... **TCLC 6, 40**
See also CA 104

d'Antibes, Germain
See Simenon, Georges (Jacques Christian)

Danvers, Dennis 1947-............ **CLC 70**

Danziger, Paula 1944-............ **CLC 21**
See also AAYA 4; CA 112; 115; CANR 37; CLR 20; JRDA; MAICYA; SATA 36, 63; SATA-Brief 30

Da Ponte, Lorenzo 1749-1838.... **NCLC 50**

Dario, Ruben 1867-1916 .... **TCLC 4; HLC**
See also CA 131; HW; MTCW

Darley, George 1795-1846........ **NCLC 2**
See also DLB 96

Daryush, Elizabeth 1887-1977.... **CLC 6, 19**
See also CA 49-52; CANR 3; DLB 20

Daudet, (Louis Marie) Alphonse 1840-1897 .... **NCLC 1**
See also DLB 123

Daumal, Rene 1908-1944......... **TCLC 14**
See also CA 114

Davenport, Guy (Mattison, Jr.) 1927- .... **CLC 6, 14, 38; SSC 16**
See also CA 33-36R; CANR 23; DLB 130

Davidson, Avram 1923-
See Queen, Ellery
See also CA 101; CANR 26; DLB 8

Davidson, Donald (Grady) 1893-1968 .... **CLC 2, 13, 19**
See also CA 5-8R; 25-28R; CANR 4; DLB 45

Davidson, Hugh
See Hamilton, Edmond

Davidson, John 1857-1909 .... **TCLC 24**
See also CA 118; DLB 19

Davidson, Sara 1943- .... **CLC 9**
See also CA 81-84; CANR 44

Davie, Donald (Alfred)
1922- .... **CLC 5, 8, 10, 31**
See also CA 1-4R; CAAS 3; CANR 1, 44; DLB 27; MTCW

Davies, Ray(mond Douglas) 1944- .. **CLC 21**
See also CA 116; 146

Davies, Rhys 1903-1978 .... **CLC 23**
See also CA 9-12R; 81-84; CANR 4; DLB 139

Davies, (William) Robertson
1913- ..... **CLC 2, 7, 13, 25, 42, 75; DA; WLC**
See also BEST 89:2; CA 33-36R; CANR 17, 42; DLB 68; MTCW

Davies, W(illiam) H(enry)
1871-1940 .... **TCLC 5**
See also CA 104; DLB 19

Davies, Walter C.
See Kornbluth, C(yril) M.

Davis, Angela (Yvonne) 1944- ...... **CLC 77**
See also BW 2; CA 57-60; CANR 10

Davis, B. Lynch
See Bioy Casares, Adolfo; Borges, Jorge Luis

Davis, Gordon
See Hunt, E(verette) Howard, (Jr.)

Davis, Harold Lenoir 1896-1960 .... **CLC 49**
See also CA 89-92; DLB 9

Davis, Rebecca (Blaine) Harding
1831-1910 .... **TCLC 6**
See also CA 104; DLB 74

Davis, Richard Harding
1864-1916 .... **TCLC 24**
See also CA 114; DLB 12, 23, 78, 79

Davison, Frank Dalby 1893-1970 ... **CLC 15**
See also CA 116

Davison, Lawrence H.
See Lawrence, D(avid) H(erbert Richards)

Davison, Peter (Hubert) 1928- ..... **CLC 28**
See also CA 9-12R; CAAS 4; CANR 3, 43; DLB 5

Davys, Mary 1674-1732 .... **LC 1**
See also DLB 39

Dawson, Fielding 1930- .... **CLC 6**
See also CA 85-88; DLB 130

Dawson, Peter
See Faust, Frederick (Schiller)

Day, Clarence (Shepard, Jr.)
1874-1935 .... **TCLC 25**
See also CA 108; DLB 11

Day, Thomas 1748-1789 .... **LC 1**
See also DLB 39; YABC 1

Day Lewis, C(ecil)
1904-1972 .... **CLC 1, 6, 10; PC 11**
See also Blake, Nicholas
See also CA 13-16; 33-36R; CANR 34; CAP 1; DLB 15, 20; MTCW

Dazai, Osamu .... **TCLC 11**
See also Tsushima, Shuji

de Andrade, Carlos Drummond
See Drummond de Andrade, Carlos

Deane, Norman
See Creasey, John

de Beauvoir, Simone (Lucie Ernestine Marie Bertrand)
See Beauvoir, Simone (Lucie Ernestine Marie Bertrand) de

de Brissac, Malcolm
See Dickinson, Peter (Malcolm)

de Chardin, Pierre Teilhard
See Teilhard de Chardin, (Marie Joseph) Pierre

Dee, John 1527-1608 .... **LC 20**

Deer, Sandra 1940- .... **CLC 45**

De Ferrari, Gabriella 1941- .... **CLC 65**
See also CA 146

Defoe, Daniel
1660(?)-1731 .... **LC 1; DA; WLC**
See also CDBLB 1660-1789; DLB 39, 95, 101; JRDA; MAICYA; SATA 22

de Gourmont, Remy
See Gourmont, Remy de

de Hartog, Jan 1914- .... **CLC 19**
See also CA 1-4R; CANR 1

de Hostos, E. M.
See Hostos (y Bonilla), Eugenio Maria de

de Hostos, Eugenio M.
See Hostos (y Bonilla), Eugenio Maria de

Deighton, Len .... **CLC 4, 7, 22, 46**
See also Deighton, Leonard Cyril
See also AAYA 6; BEST 89:2; CDBLB 1960 to Present; DLB 87

Deighton, Leonard Cyril 1929-
See Deighton, Len
See also CA 9-12R; CANR 19, 33; MTCW

Dekker, Thomas 1572(?)-1632 .... **LC 22**
See also CDBLB Before 1660; DLB 62

de la Mare, Walter (John)
1873-1956 .. **TCLC 4, 53; SSC 14; WLC**
See also CDBLB 1914-1945; CLR 23; DLB 19, 153; SATA 16

Delaney, Franey
See O'Hara, John (Henry)

Delaney, Shelagh 1939- .... **CLC 29**
See also CA 17-20R; CANR 30; CDBLB 1960 to Present; DLB 13; MTCW

Delany, Mary (Granville Pendarves)
1700-1788 .... **LC 12**

Delany, Samuel R(ay, Jr.)
1942- .... **CLC 8, 14, 38; BLC**
See also BW 2; CA 81-84; CANR 27, 43; DLB 8, 33; MTCW

De La Ramee, (Marie) Louise 1839-1908
See Ouida
See also SATA 20

de la Roche, Mazo 1879-1961 ...... **CLC 14**
See also CA 85-88; CANR 30; DLB 68; SATA 64

Delbanco, Nicholas (Franklin)
1942- .... **CLC 6, 13**
See also CA 17-20R; CAAS 2; CANR 29; DLB 6

del Castillo, Michel 1933- .... **CLC 38**
See also CA 109

Deledda, Grazia (Cosima)
1875(?)-1936 .... **TCLC 23**
See also CA 123

Delibes, Miguel .... **CLC 8, 18**
See also Delibes Setien, Miguel

Delibes Setien, Miguel 1920-
See Delibes, Miguel
See also CA 45-48; CANR 1, 32; HW; MTCW

DeLillo, Don
1936- ..... **CLC 8, 10, 13, 27, 39, 54, 76**
See also BEST 89:1; CA 81-84; CANR 21; DLB 6; MTCW

de Lisser, H. G.
See De Lisser, Herbert George
See also DLB 117

De Lisser, Herbert George
1878-1944 .... **TCLC 12**
See also de Lisser, H. G.
See also BW 2; CA 109

Deloria, Vine (Victor), Jr. 1933- .... **CLC 21**
See also CA 53-56; CANR 5, 20, 48; MTCW; NNAL; SATA 21

Del Vecchio, John M(ichael)
1947- .... **CLC 29**
See also CA 110; DLBD 9

de Man, Paul (Adolph Michel)
1919-1983 .... **CLC 55**
See also CA 128; 111; DLB 67; MTCW

De Marinis, Rick 1934- .... **CLC 54**
See also CA 57-60; CANR 9, 25

Demby, William 1922- .... **CLC 53; BLC**
See also BW 1; CA 81-84; DLB 33

Demijohn, Thom
See Disch, Thomas M(ichael)

de Montherlant, Henry (Milon)
See Montherlant, Henry (Milon) de

Demosthenes 384B.C.-322B.C. ... **CMLC 13**

de Natale, Francine
See Malzberg, Barry N(athaniel)

Denby, Edwin (Orr) 1903-1983 ..... **CLC 48**
See also CA 138; 110

Denis, Julio
See Cortazar, Julio

Denmark, Harrison
See Zelazny, Roger (Joseph)

Dennis, John 1658-1734 .... **LC 11**
See also DLB 101

Dennis, Nigel (Forbes) 1912-1989 .... **CLC 8**
See also CA 25-28R; 129; DLB 13, 15; MTCW

De Palma, Brian (Russell) 1940- .... **CLC 20**
See also CA 109

De Quincey, Thomas 1785-1859 ... **NCLC 4**
See also CDBLB 1789-1832; DLB 110; 144

Deren, Eleanora 1908(?)-1961
See Deren, Maya
See also CA 111

Dorn, Edward (Merton) 1929- . . . **CLC 10, 18**
See also CA 93-96; CANR 42; DLB 5

Dorsan, Luc
See Simenon, Georges (Jacques Christian)

Dorsange, Jean
See Simenon, Georges (Jacques Christian)

Dos Passos, John (Roderigo)
1896-1970 . . . . . . **CLC 1, 4, 8, 11, 15, 25, 34, 82; DA; WLC**
See also CA 1-4R; 29-32R; CANR 3; CDALB 1929-1941; DLB 4, 9; DLBD 1; MTCW

Dossage, Jean
See Simenon, Georges (Jacques Christian)

Dostoevsky, Fedor Mikhailovich
1821-1881 . . . . . . **NCLC 2, 7, 21, 33, 43; DA; SSC 2; WLC**

Doughty, Charles M(ontagu)
1843-1926 . . . . **TCLC 27**
See also CA 115; DLB 19, 57

Douglas, Ellen . . . . **CLC 73**
See also Haxton, Josephine Ayres; Williamson, Ellen Douglas

Douglas, Gavin 1475(?)-1522 . . . . **LC 20**

Douglas, Keith 1920-1944 . . . . **TCLC 40**
See also DLB 27

Douglas, Leonard
See Bradbury, Ray (Douglas)

Douglas, Michael
See Crichton, (John) Michael

Douglass, Frederick
1817(?)-1895 . . . . **NCLC 7; BLC; DA; WLC**
See also CDALB 1640-1865; DLB 1, 43, 50, 79; SATA 29

Dourado, (Waldomiro Freitas) Autran
1926- . . . . **CLC 23, 60**
See also CA 25-28R; CANR 34

Dourado, Waldomiro Autran
See Dourado, (Waldomiro Freitas) Autran

Dove, Rita (Frances)
1952- . . . . **CLC 50, 81; PC 6**
See also BW 2; CA 109; CAAS 19; CANR 27, 42; DLB 120

Dowell, Coleman 1925-1985 . . . . **CLC 60**
See also CA 25-28R; 117; CANR 10; DLB 130

Dowson, Ernest Christopher
1867-1900 . . . . **TCLC 4**
See also CA 105; DLB 19, 135

Doyle, A. Conan
See Doyle, Arthur Conan

Doyle, Arthur Conan
1859-1930 . . . . **TCLC 7; DA; SSC 12; WLC**
See also AAYA 14; CA 104; 122; CDBLB 1890-1914; DLB 18, 70; MTCW; SATA 24

Doyle, Conan
See Doyle, Arthur Conan

Doyle, John
See Graves, Robert (von Ranke)

Doyle, Roddy 1958(?)- . . . . **CLC 81**
See also AAYA 14; CA 143

Doyle, Sir A. Conan
See Doyle, Arthur Conan

Doyle, Sir Arthur Conan
See Doyle, Arthur Conan

Dr. A
See Asimov, Isaac; Silverstein, Alvin

Drabble, Margaret
1939- . . . . **CLC 2, 3, 5, 8, 10, 22, 53**
See also CA 13-16R; CANR 18, 35; CDBLB 1960 to Present; DLB 14; MTCW; SATA 48

Drapier, M. B.
See Swift, Jonathan

Drayham, James
See Mencken, H(enry) L(ouis)

Drayton, Michael 1563-1631 . . . . **LC 8**

Dreadstone, Carl
See Campbell, (John) Ramsey

Dreiser, Theodore (Herman Albert)
1871-1945 . . . . **TCLC 10, 18, 35; DA; WLC**
See also CA 106; 132; CDALB 1865-1917; DLB 9, 12, 102, 137; DLBD 1; MTCW

Drexler, Rosalyn 1926- . . . . **CLC 2, 6**
See also CA 81-84

Dreyer, Carl Theodor 1889-1968 . . . . **CLC 16**
See also CA 116

Drieu la Rochelle, Pierre(-Eugene)
1893-1945 . . . . **TCLC 21**
See also CA 117; DLB 72

Drinkwater, John 1882-1937 . . . . . . **TCLC 57**
See also CA 109; DLB 10, 19, 149

Drop Shot
See Cable, George Washington

Droste-Hulshoff, Annette Freiin von
1797-1848 . . . . **NCLC 3**
See also DLB 133

Drummond, Walter
See Silverberg, Robert

Drummond, William Henry
1854-1907 . . . . **TCLC 25**
See also DLB 92

Drummond de Andrade, Carlos
1902-1987 . . . . **CLC 18**
See also Andrade, Carlos Drummond de
See also CA 132; 123

Drury, Allen (Stuart) 1918- . . . . **CLC 37**
See also CA 57-60; CANR 18

Dryden, John
1631-1700 . . . **LC 3, 21; DA; DC 3; WLC**
See also CDBLB 1660-1789; DLB 80, 101, 131

Duberman, Martin 1930- . . . . **CLC 8**
See also CA 1-4R; CANR 2

Dubie, Norman (Evans) 1945- . . . . . . **CLC 36**
See also CA 69-72; CANR 12; DLB 120

Du Bois, W(illiam) E(dward) B(urghardt)
1868-1963 . . . . . . **CLC 1, 2, 13, 64; BLC; DA; WLC**
See also BW 1; CA 85-88; CANR 34; CDALB 1865-1917; DLB 47, 50, 91; MTCW; SATA 42

Dubus, Andre 1936- . . . **CLC 13, 36; SSC 15**
See also CA 21-24R; CANR 17; DLB 130

Duca Minimo
See D'Annunzio, Gabriele

Ducharme, Rejean 1941- . . . . **CLC 74**
See also DLB 60

Duclos, Charles Pinot 1704-1772 . . . . . **LC 1**

Dudek, Louis 1918- . . . . **CLC 11, 19**
See also CA 45-48; CAAS 14; CANR 1; DLB 88

Duerrenmatt, Friedrich
1921-1990 . . . . . . **CLC 1, 4, 8, 11, 15, 43**
See also CA 17-20R; CANR 33; DLB 69, 124; MTCW

Duffy, Bruce (?)- . . . . **CLC 50**

Duffy, Maureen 1933- . . . . **CLC 37**
See also CA 25-28R; CANR 33; DLB 14; MTCW

Dugan, Alan 1923- . . . . **CLC 2, 6**
See also CA 81-84; DLB 5

du Gard, Roger Martin
See Martin du Gard, Roger

Duhamel, Georges 1884-1966 . . . . **CLC 8**
See also CA 81-84; 25-28R; CANR 35; DLB 65; MTCW

Dujardin, Edouard (Emile Louis)
1861-1949 . . . . **TCLC 13**
See also CA 109; DLB 123

Dumas, Alexandre (Davy de la Pailleterie)
1802-1870 . . . . **NCLC 11; DA; WLC**
See also DLB 119; SATA 18

Dumas, Alexandre
1824-1895 . . . . **NCLC 9; DC 1**

Dumas, Claudine
See Malzberg, Barry N(athaniel)

Dumas, Henry L. 1934-1968 . . . . . **CLC 6, 62**
See also BW 1; CA 85-88; DLB 41

du Maurier, Daphne
1907-1989 . . . . . . **CLC 6, 11, 59; SSC 18**
See also CA 5-8R; 128; CANR 6; MTCW; SATA 27; SATA-Obit 60

Dunbar, Paul Laurence
1872-1906 . . . . . . **TCLC 2, 12; BLC; DA; PC 5; SSC 8; WLC**
See also BW 1; CA 104; 124; CDALB 1865-1917; DLB 50, 54, 78; SATA 34

Dunbar, William 1460(?)-1530(?) . . . . **LC 20**
See also DLB 132, 146

Duncan, Lois 1934- . . . . **CLC 26**
See also AAYA 4; CA 1-4R; CANR 2, 23, 36; CLR 29; JRDA; MAICYA; SAAS 2; SATA 1, 36, 75

Duncan, Robert (Edward)
1919-1988 . . . . **CLC 1, 2, 4, 7, 15, 41, 55; PC 2**
See also CA 9-12R; 124; CANR 28; DLB 5, 16; MTCW

Duncan, Sara Jeannette
1861-1922 . . . . **TCLC 60**
See also DLB 92

Dunlap, William 1766-1839 . . . . **NCLC 2**
See also DLB 30, 37, 59

Dunn, Douglas (Eaglesham)
1942- . . . . **CLC 6, 40**
See also CA 45-48; CANR 2, 33; DLB 40; MTCW

Dunn, Katherine (Karen) 1945- . . . . . **CLC 71**
See also CA 33-36R

Dunn, Stephen 1939- . . . . **CLC 36**
See also CA 33-36R; CANR 12, 48; DLB 105

Dunne, Finley Peter 1867-1936. . . . **TCLC 28**
See also CA 108; DLB 11, 23

Dunne, John Gregory 1932-. . . . . **CLC 28**
See also CA 25-28R; CANR 14; DLBY 80

Dunsany, Edward John Moreton Drax Plunkett 1878-1957
See Dunsany, Lord
See also CA 104; DLB 10

Dunsany, Lord. . . . . **TCLC 2, 59**
See also Dunsany, Edward John Moreton Drax Plunkett
See also DLB 77, 153

du Perry, Jean
See Simenon, Georges (Jacques Christian)

Durang, Christopher (Ferdinand) 1949- . . . . **CLC 27, 38**
See also CA 105

Duras, Marguerite 1914- . . . . . . **CLC 3, 6, 11, 20, 34, 40, 68**
See also CA 25-28R; DLB 83; MTCW

Durban, (Rosa) Pam 1947-. . . . . **CLC 39**
See also CA 123

Durcan, Paul 1944-. . . . . **CLC 43, 70**
See also CA 134

Durkheim, Emile 1858-1917 . . . . . . **TCLC 55**

Durrell, Lawrence (George) 1912-1990 . . . . **CLC 1, 4, 6, 8, 13, 27, 41**
See also CA 9-12R; 132; CANR 40; CDBLB 1945-1960; DLB 15, 27; DLBY 90; MTCW

Durrenmatt, Friedrich
See Duerrenmatt, Friedrich

Dutt, Toru 1856-1877. . . . . **NCLC 29**

Dwight, Timothy 1752-1817. . . . . . **NCLC 13**
See also DLB 37

Dworkin, Andrea 1946- . . . . **CLC 43**
See also CA 77-80; CAAS 21; CANR 16, 39; MTCW

Dwyer, Deanna
See Koontz, Dean R(ay)

Dwyer, K. R.
See Koontz, Dean R(ay)

Dylan, Bob 1941- . . . . . . **CLC 3, 4, 6, 12, 77**
See also CA 41-44R; DLB 16

Eagleton, Terence (Francis) 1943-
See Eagleton, Terry
See also CA 57-60; CANR 7, 23; MTCW

Eagleton, Terry . . . . **CLC 63**
See also Eagleton, Terence (Francis)

Early, Jack
See Scoppettone, Sandra

East, Michael
See West, Morris L(anglo)

Eastaway, Edward
See Thomas, (Philip) Edward

Eastlake, William (Derry) 1917-. . . . . **CLC 8**
See also CA 5-8R; CAAS 1; CANR 5; DLB 6

Eastman, Charles A(lexander) 1858-1939 . . . . **TCLC 55**
See also NNAL; YABC 1

Eberhart, Richard (Ghormley) 1904- . . . . **CLC 3, 11, 19, 56**
See also CA 1-4R; CANR 2; CDALB 1941-1968; DLB 48; MTCW

Eberstadt, Fernanda 1960-. . . . . **CLC 39**
See also CA 136

Echegaray (y Eizaguirre), Jose (Maria Waldo) 1832-1916 . . . . **TCLC 4**
See also CA 104; CANR 32; HW; MTCW

Echeverria, (Jose) Esteban (Antonino) 1805-1851 . . . . **NCLC 18**

Echo
See Proust, (Valentin-Louis-George-Eugene-) Marcel

Eckert, Allan W. 1931- . . . . **CLC 17**
See also CA 13-16R; CANR 14, 45; SATA 29; SATA-Brief 27

Eckhart, Meister 1260(?)-1328(?) . . **CMLC 9**
See also DLB 115

Eckmar, F. R.
See de Hartog, Jan

Eco, Umberto 1932- . . . . **CLC 28, 60**
See also BEST 90:1; CA 77-80; CANR 12, 33; MTCW

Eddison, E(ric) R(ucker) 1882-1945 . . . . **TCLC 15**
See also CA 109

Edel, (Joseph) Leon 1907- . . . . . . **CLC 29, 34**
See also CA 1-4R; CANR 1, 22; DLB 103

Eden, Emily 1797-1869 . . . . **NCLC 10**

Edgar, David 1948-. . . . . **CLC 42**
See also CA 57-60; CANR 12; DLB 13; MTCW

Edgerton, Clyde (Carlyle) 1944- . . . . **CLC 39**
See also CA 118; 134

Edgeworth, Maria 1767-1849. . . **NCLC 1, 51**
See also DLB 116; SATA 21

Edmonds, Paul
See Kuttner, Henry

Edmonds, Walter D(umaux) 1903- . . **CLC 35**
See also CA 5-8R; CANR 2; DLB 9; MAICYA; SAAS 4; SATA 1, 27

Edmondson, Wallace
See Ellison, Harlan (Jay)

Edson, Russell. **CLC 13**
See also CA 33-36R

Edwards, Bronwen Elizabeth
See Rose, Wendy

Edwards, G(erald) B(asil) 1899-1976 . . . . **CLC 25**
See also CA 110

Edwards, Gus 1939- . . . . **CLC 43**
See also CA 108

Edwards, Jonathan 1703-1758. . . . **LC 7; DA**
See also DLB 24

Efron, Marina Ivanovna Tsvetaeva
See Tsvetaeva (Efron), Marina (Ivanovna)

Ehle, John (Marsden, Jr.) 1925- . . . . **CLC 27**
See also CA 9-12R

Ehrenbourg, Ilya (Grigoryevich)
See Ehrenburg, Ilya (Grigoryevich)

Ehrenburg, Ilya (Grigoryevich) 1891-1967 . . . . **CLC 18, 34, 62**
See also CA 102; 25-28R

Ehrenburg, Ilyo (Grigoryevich)
See Ehrenburg, Ilya (Grigoryevich)

Eich, Guenter 1907-1972 . . . . **CLC 15**
See also CA 111; 93-96; DLB 69, 124

Eichendorff, Joseph Freiherr von 1788-1857 . . . . **NCLC 8**
See also DLB 90

Eigner, Larry. . . . . **CLC 9**
See also Eigner, Laurence (Joel)
See also DLB 5

Eigner, Laurence (Joel) 1927-
See Eigner, Larry
See also CA 9-12R; CANR 6

Eiseley, Loren Corey 1907-1977 . . . . . **CLC 7**
See also AAYA 5; CA 1-4R; 73-76; CANR 6

Eisenstadt, Jill 1963- . . . . **CLC 50**
See also CA 140

Eisenstein, Sergei (Mikhailovich) 1898-1948 . . . . **TCLC 57**
See also CA 114

Eisner, Simon
See Kornbluth, C(yril) M.

Ekeloef, (Bengt) Gunnar 1907-1968 . . . . **CLC 27**
See also CA 123; 25-28R

Ekelof, (Bengt) Gunnar
See Ekeloef, (Bengt) Gunnar

Ekwensi, C. O. D.
See Ekwensi, Cyprian (Odiatu Duaka)

Ekwensi, Cyprian (Odiatu Duaka) 1921- . . . . **CLC 4; BLC**
See also BW 2; CA 29-32R; CANR 18, 42; DLB 117; MTCW; SATA 66

Elaine . . . . **TCLC 18**
See also Leverson, Ada

El Crummo
See Crumb, R(obert)

Elia
See Lamb, Charles

Eliade, Mircea 1907-1986 . . . . **CLC 19**
See also CA 65-68; 119; CANR 30; MTCW

Eliot, A. D.
See Jewett, (Theodora) Sarah Orne

Eliot, Alice
See Jewett, (Theodora) Sarah Orne

Eliot, Dan
See Silverberg, Robert

Eliot, George 1819-1880 . . . . . **NCLC 4, 13, 23, 41, 49; DA; WLC**
See also CDBLB 1832-1890; DLB 21, 35, 55

Eliot, John 1604-1690 . . . . **LC 5**
See also DLB 24

Eliot, T(homas) S(tearns) 1888-1965 . . . . . **CLC 1, 2, 3, 6, 9, 10, 13, 15, 24, 34, 41, 55, 57; DA; PC 5; WLC 2**
See also CA 5-8R; 25-28R; CANR 41; CDALB 1929-1941; DLB 7, 10, 45, 63; DLBY 88; MTCW

Elizabeth 1866-1941. . . . . **TCLC 41**

Fagen, Donald 1948- . . . . **CLC 26**

Fainzilberg, Ilya Arnoldovich 1897-1937
See Ilf, Ilya
See also CA 120

Fair, Ronald L. 1932- . . . . **CLC 18**
See also BW 1; CA 69-72; CANR 25; DLB 33

Fairbairns, Zoe (Ann) 1948- . . . . **CLC 32**
See also CA 103; CANR 21

Falco, Gian
See Papini, Giovanni

Falconer, James
See Kirkup, James

Falconer, Kenneth
See Kornbluth, C(yril) M.

Falkland, Samuel
See Heijermans, Herman

Fallaci, Oriana 1930- . . . . **CLC 11**
See also CA 77-80; CANR 15; MTCW

Faludy, George 1913- . . . . **CLC 42**
See also CA 21-24R

Faludy, Gyoergy
See Faludy, George

Fanon, Frantz 1925-1961 . . . . . **CLC 74; BLC**
See also BW 1; CA 116; 89-92

Fanshawe, Ann 1625-1680 . . . . **LC 11**

Fante, John (Thomas) 1911-1983 . . . **CLC 60**
See also CA 69-72; 109; CANR 23; DLB 130; DLBY 83

Farah, Nuruddin 1945- . . . . **CLC 53; BLC**
See also BW 2; CA 106; DLB 125

Fargue, Leon-Paul 1876(?)-1947 . . . **TCLC 11**
See also CA 109

Farigoule, Louis
See Romains, Jules

Farina, Richard 1936(?)-1966 . . . . **CLC 9**
See also CA 81-84; 25-28R

Farley, Walter (Lorimer)
1915-1989 . . . . **CLC 17**
See also CA 17-20R; CANR 8, 29; DLB 22; JRDA; MAICYA; SATA 2, 43

Farmer, Philip Jose 1918- . . . . **CLC 1, 19**
See also CA 1-4R; CANR 4, 35; DLB 8; MTCW

Farquhar, George 1677-1707 . . . . **LC 21**
See also DLB 84

Farrell, J(ames) G(ordon)
1935-1979 . . . . **CLC 6**
See also CA 73-76; 89-92; CANR 36; DLB 14; MTCW

Farrell, James T(homas)
1904-1979 . . . . **CLC 1, 4, 8, 11, 66**
See also CA 5-8R; 89-92; CANR 9; DLB 4, 9, 86; DLBD 2; MTCW

Farren, Richard J.
See Betjeman, John

Farren, Richard M.
See Betjeman, John

Fassbinder, Rainer Werner
1946-1982 . . . . **CLC 20**
See also CA 93-96; 106; CANR 31

Fast, Howard (Melvin) 1914- . . . . . . **CLC 23**
See also CA 1-4R; CAAS 18; CANR 1, 33; DLB 9; SATA 7

Faulcon, Robert
See Holdstock, Robert P.

Faulkner, William (Cuthbert)
1897-1962 . . . . . **CLC 1, 3, 6, 8, 9, 11, 14, 18, 28, 52, 68; DA; SSC 1; WLC**
See also AAYA 7; CA 81-84; CANR 33; CDALB 1929-1941; DLB 9, 11, 44, 102; DLBD 2; DLBY 86; MTCW

Fauset, Jessie Redmon
1884(?)-1961 . . . . **CLC 19, 54; BLC**
See also BW 1; CA 109; DLB 51

Faust, Frederick (Schiller)
1892-1944(?) . . . . **TCLC 49**
See also CA 108

Faust, Irvin 1924- . . . . **CLC 8**
See also CA 33-36R; CANR 28; DLB 2, 28; DLBY 80

Fawkes, Guy
See Benchley, Robert (Charles)

Fearing, Kenneth (Flexner)
1902-1961 . . . . **CLC 51**
See also CA 93-96; DLB 9

Fecamps, Elise
See Creasey, John

Federman, Raymond 1928- . . . . . . **CLC 6, 47**
See also CA 17-20R; CAAS 8; CANR 10, 43; DLBY 80

Federspiel, J(uerg) F. 1931- . . . . **CLC 42**
See also CA 146

Feiffer, Jules (Ralph) 1929- . . . . **CLC 2, 8, 64**
See also AAYA 3; CA 17-20R; CANR 30; DLB 7, 44; MTCW; SATA 8, 61

Feige, Hermann Albert Otto Maximilian
See Traven, B.

Feinberg, David B. 1956-1994 . . . . . . **CLC 59**
See also CA 135; 147

Feinstein, Elaine 1930- . . . . **CLC 36**
See also CA 69-72; CAAS 1; CANR 31; DLB 14, 40; MTCW

Feldman, Irving (Mordecai) 1928- . . . . **CLC 7**
See also CA 1-4R; CANR 1

Fellini, Federico 1920-1993 . . . . . **CLC 16, 85**
See also CA 65-68; 143; CANR 33

Felsen, Henry Gregor 1916- . . . . **CLC 17**
See also CA 1-4R; CANR 1; SAAS 2; SATA 1

Fenton, James Martin 1949- . . . . **CLC 32**
See also CA 102; DLB 40

Ferber, Edna 1887-1968 . . . . **CLC 18**
See also AITN 1; CA 5-8R; 25-28R; DLB 9, 28, 86; MTCW; SATA 7

Ferguson, Helen
See Kavan, Anna

Ferguson, Samuel 1810-1886 . . . . . **NCLC 33**
See also DLB 32

Fergusson, Robert 1750-1774 . . . . **LC 29**
See also DLB 109

Ferling, Lawrence
See Ferlinghetti, Lawrence (Monsanto)

Ferlinghetti, Lawrence (Monsanto)
1919(?)- . . . . **CLC 2, 6, 10, 27; PC 1**
See also CA 5-8R; CANR 3, 41; CDALB 1941-1968; DLB 5, 16; MTCW

Fernandez, Vicente Garcia Huidobro
See Huidobro Fernandez, Vicente Garcia

Ferrer, Gabriel (Francisco Victor) Miro
See Miro (Ferrer), Gabriel (Francisco Victor)

Ferrier, Susan (Edmonstone)
1782-1854 . . . . **NCLC 8**
See also DLB 116

Ferrigno, Robert 1948(?)- . . . . **CLC 65**
See also CA 140

Feuchtwanger, Lion 1884-1958 . . . . . **TCLC 3**
See also CA 104; DLB 66

Feuillet, Octave 1821-1890 . . . . . . **NCLC 45**

Feydeau, Georges (Leon Jules Marie)
1862-1921 . . . . **TCLC 22**
See also CA 113

Ficino, Marsilio 1433-1499 . . . . **LC 12**

Fiedeler, Hans
See Doeblin, Alfred

Fiedler, Leslie A(aron)
1917- . . . . **CLC 4, 13, 24**
See also CA 9-12R; CANR 7; DLB 28, 67; MTCW

Field, Andrew 1938- . . . . **CLC 44**
See also CA 97-100; CANR 25

Field, Eugene 1850-1895 . . . . **NCLC 3**
See also DLB 23, 42, 140; MAICYA; SATA 16

Field, Gans T.
See Wellman, Manly Wade

Field, Michael . . . . **TCLC 43**

Field, Peter
See Hobson, Laura Z(ametkin)

Fielding, Henry
1707-1754 . . . . **LC 1; DA; WLC**
See also CDBLB 1660-1789; DLB 39, 84, 101

Fielding, Sarah 1710-1768 . . . . **LC 1**
See also DLB 39

Fierstein, Harvey (Forbes) 1954- . . . **CLC 33**
See also CA 123; 129

Figes, Eva 1932- . . . . **CLC 31**
See also CA 53-56; CANR 4, 44; DLB 14

Finch, Robert (Duer Claydon)
1900- . . . . **CLC 18**
See also CA 57-60; CANR 9, 24; DLB 88

Findley, Timothy 1930- . . . . **CLC 27**
See also CA 25-28R; CANR 12, 42; DLB 53

Fink, William
See Mencken, H(enry) L(ouis)

Firbank, Louis 1942-
See Reed, Lou
See also CA 117

Firbank, (Arthur Annesley) Ronald
1886-1926 . . . . **TCLC 1**
See also CA 104; DLB 36

Fisher, M(ary) F(rances) K(ennedy)
1908-1992 . . . . **CLC 76, 87**
See also CA 77-80; 138; CANR 44

Fisher, Roy 1930- . . . . **CLC 25**
See also CA 81-84; CAAS 10; CANR 16; DLB 40

Fisher, Rudolph 1897-1934 . . . . **TCLC 11; BLC**
See also BW 1; CA 107; 124; DLB 51, 102

Fisher, Vardis (Alvero) 1895-1968. . . . **CLC 7**
See also CA 5-8R; 25-28R; DLB 9

Fiske, Tarleton
See Bloch, Robert (Albert)

Fitch, Clarke
See Sinclair, Upton (Beall)

Fitch, John IV
See Cormier, Robert (Edmund)

Fitzgerald, Captain Hugh
See Baum, L(yman) Frank

FitzGerald, Edward 1809-1883 . . . . **NCLC 9**
See also DLB 32

Fitzgerald, F(rancis) Scott (Key) 1896-1940 . . . . **TCLC 1, 6, 14, 28, 55; DA; SSC 6; WLC**
See also AITN 1; CA 110; 123; CDALB 1917-1929; DLB 4, 9, 86; DLBD 1; DLBY 81; MTCW

Fitzgerald, Penelope 1916-. . . **CLC 19, 51, 61**
See also CA 85-88; CAAS 10; DLB 14

Fitzgerald, Robert (Stuart) 1910-1985 . . . . **CLC 39**
See also CA 1-4R; 114; CANR 1; DLBY 80

FitzGerald, Robert D(avid) 1902-1987 . . . . **CLC 19**
See also CA 17-20R

Fitzgerald, Zelda (Sayre) 1900-1948 . . . . **TCLC 52**
See also CA 117; 126; DLBY 84

Flanagan, Thomas (James Bonner) 1923- . . . . **CLC 25, 52**
See also CA 108; DLBY 80; MTCW

Flaubert, Gustave 1821-1880 . . . . **NCLC 2, 10, 19; DA; SSC 11; WLC**
See also DLB 119

Flecker, (Herman) James Elroy 1884-1915 . . . . **TCLC 43**
See also CA 109; DLB 10, 19

Fleming, Ian (Lancaster) 1908-1964 . . . . **CLC 3, 30**
See also CA 5-8R; CDBLB 1945-1960; DLB 87; MTCW; SATA 9

Fleming, Thomas (James) 1927- . . . . **CLC 37**
See also CA 5-8R; CANR 10; SATA 8

Fletcher, John Gould 1886-1950 . . . **TCLC 35**
See also CA 107; DLB 4, 45

Fleur, Paul
See Pohl, Frederik

Flooglebuckle, Al
See Spiegelman, Art

Flying Officer X
See Bates, H(erbert) E(rnest)

Fo, Dario 1926-. . . . . **CLC 32**
See also CA 116; 128; MTCW

Fogarty, Jonathan Titulescu Esq.
See Farrell, James T(homas)

Folke, Will
See Bloch, Robert (Albert)

Follett, Ken(neth Martin) 1949- . . . . **CLC 18**
See also AAYA 6; BEST 89:4; CA 81-84; CANR 13, 33; DLB 87; DLBY 81; MTCW

Fontane, Theodor 1819-1898 . . . . . **NCLC 26**
See also DLB 129

Foote, Horton 1916-. . . . . **CLC 51**
See also CA 73-76; CANR 34; DLB 26

Foote, Shelby 1916- . . . . **CLC 75**
See also CA 5-8R; CANR 3, 45; DLB 2, 17

Forbes, Esther 1891-1967. . . . . **CLC 12**
See also CA 13-14; 25-28R; CAP 1; CLR 27; DLB 22; JRDA; MAICYA; SATA 2

Forche, Carolyn (Louise) 1950- . . . . **CLC 25, 83, 86; PC 10**
See also CA 109; 117; DLB 5

Ford, Elbur
See Hibbert, Eleanor Alice Burford

Ford, Ford Madox 1873-1939 . . . . **TCLC 1, 15, 39, 57**
See also CA 104; 132; CDBLB 1914-1945; DLB 34, 98; MTCW

Ford, John 1895-1973. . . . . **CLC 16**
See also CA 45-48

Ford, Richard 1944-. . . . . **CLC 46**
See also CA 69-72; CANR 11, 47

Ford, Webster
See Masters, Edgar Lee

Foreman, Richard 1937-. . . . . **CLC 50**
See also CA 65-68; CANR 32

Forester, C(ecil) S(cott) 1899-1966 . . . . **CLC 35**
See also CA 73-76; 25-28R; SATA 13

Forez
See Mauriac, Francois (Charles)

Forman, James Douglas 1932-. . . . . . **CLC 21**
See also CA 9-12R; CANR 4, 19, 42; JRDA; MAICYA; SATA 8, 70

Fornes, Maria Irene 1930-. . . . . . **CLC 39, 61**
See also CA 25-28R; CANR 28; DLB 7; HW; MTCW

Forrest, Leon 1937- . . . . **CLC 4**
See also BW 2; CA 89-92; CAAS 7; CANR 25; DLB 33

Forster, E(dward) M(organ) 1879-1970 . . . . . **CLC 1, 2, 3, 4, 9, 10, 13, 15, 22, 45, 77; DA; WLC**
See also AAYA 2; CA 13-14; 25-28R; CANR 45; CAP 1; CDBLB 1914-1945; DLB 34, 98; DLBD 10; MTCW; SATA 57

Forster, John 1812-1876 . . . . **NCLC 11**
See also DLB 144

Forsyth, Frederick 1938- . . . . . . **CLC 2, 5, 36**
See also BEST 89:4; CA 85-88; CANR 38; DLB 87; MTCW

Forten, Charlotte L. . . . . **TCLC 16; BLC**
See also Grimke, Charlotte L(ottie) Forten
See also DLB 50

Foscolo, Ugo 1778-1827. . . . . **NCLC 8**

Fosse, Bob . . . . **CLC 20**
See also Fosse, Robert Louis

Fosse, Robert Louis 1927-1987
See Fosse, Bob
See also CA 110; 123

Foster, Stephen Collins 1826-1864 . . . . **NCLC 26**

Foucault, Michel 1926-1984 . . . . **CLC 31, 34, 69**
See also CA 105; 113; CANR 34; MTCW

Fouque, Friedrich (Heinrich Karl) de la Motte 1777-1843 . . . . **NCLC 2**
See also DLB 90

Fourier, Charles 1772-1837 . . . . . . **NCLC 51**

Fournier, Henri Alban 1886-1914
See Alain-Fournier
See also CA 104

Fournier, Pierre 1916- . . . . **CLC 11**
See also Gascar, Pierre
See also CA 89-92; CANR 16, 40

Fowles, John 1926- . . . . . . **CLC 1, 2, 3, 4, 6, 9, 10, 15, 33, 87**
See also CA 5-8R; CANR 25; CDBLB 1960 to Present; DLB 14, 139; MTCW; SATA 22

Fox, Paula 1923-. . . . . **CLC 2, 8**
See also AAYA 3; CA 73-76; CANR 20, 36; CLR 1; DLB 52; JRDA; MAICYA; MTCW; SATA 17, 60

Fox, William Price (Jr.) 1926- . . . . . **CLC 22**
See also CA 17-20R; CAAS 19; CANR 11; DLB 2; DLBY 81

Foxe, John 1516(?)-1587 . . . . **LC 14**

Frame, Janet . . . . **CLC 2, 3, 6, 22, 66**
See also Clutha, Janet Paterson Frame

France, Anatole . . . . **TCLC 9**
See also Thibault, Jacques Anatole Francois
See also DLB 123

Francis, Claude 19(?)- . . . . **CLC 50**

Francis, Dick 1920- . . . . **CLC 2, 22, 42**
See also AAYA 5; BEST 89:3; CA 5-8R; CANR 9, 42; CDBLB 1960 to Present; DLB 87; MTCW

Francis, Robert (Churchill) 1901-1987 . . . . **CLC 15**
See also CA 1-4R; 123; CANR 1

Frank, Anne(lies Marie) 1929-1945 . . . . **TCLC 17; DA; WLC**
See also AAYA 12; CA 113; 133; MTCW; SATA-Brief 42

Frank, Elizabeth 1945-. . . . . **CLC 39**
See also CA 121; 126

Franklin, Benjamin
See Hasek, Jaroslav (Matej Frantisek)

Franklin, Benjamin 1706-1790. . . **LC 25; DA**
See also CDALB 1640-1865; DLB 24, 43, 73

Franklin, (Stella Maraia Sarah) Miles 1879-1954 . . . . **TCLC 7**
See also CA 104

Fraser, (Lady) Antonia (Pakenham) 1932- . . . . **CLC 32**
See also CA 85-88; CANR 44; MTCW; SATA-Brief 32

Fraser, George MacDonald 1925-. . . . **CLC 7**
See also CA 45-48; CANR 2, 48

Gard, Janice
See Latham, Jean Lee

Gard, Roger Martin du
See Martin du Gard, Roger

Gardam, Jane 1928- .... **CLC 43**
See also CA 49-52; CANR 2, 18, 33; CLR 12; DLB 14; MAICYA; MTCW; SAAS 9; SATA 39, 76; SATA-Brief 28

Gardner, Herb .... **CLC 44**

Gardner, John (Champlin), Jr.
1933-1982 ..... **CLC 2, 3, 5, 7, 8, 10, 18, 28, 34; SSC 7**
See also AITN 1; CA 65-68; 107; CANR 33; DLB 2; DLBY 82; MTCW; SATA 40; SATA-Obit 31

Gardner, John (Edmund) 1926- ..... **CLC 30**
See also CA 103; CANR 15; MTCW

Gardner, Noel
See Kuttner, Henry

Gardons, S. S.
See Snodgrass, W(illiam) D(e Witt)

Garfield, Leon 1921- .... **CLC 12**
See also AAYA 8; CA 17-20R; CANR 38, 41; CLR 21; JRDA; MAICYA; SATA 1, 32, 76

Garland, (Hannibal) Hamlin
1860-1940 .... **TCLC 3; SSC 18**
See also CA 104; DLB 12, 71, 78

Garneau, (Hector de) Saint-Denys
1912-1943 .... **TCLC 13**
See also CA 111; DLB 88

Garner, Alan 1934- .... **CLC 17**
See also CA 73-76; CANR 15; CLR 20; MAICYA; MTCW; SATA 18, 69

Garner, Hugh 1913-1979 .... **CLC 13**
See also CA 69-72; CANR 31; DLB 68

Garnett, David 1892-1981 .... **CLC 3**
See also CA 5-8R; 103; CANR 17; DLB 34

Garos, Stephanie
See Katz, Steve

Garrett, George (Palmer)
1929- .... **CLC 3, 11, 51**
See also CA 1-4R; CAAS 5; CANR 1, 42; DLB 2, 5, 130, 152; DLBY 83

Garrick, David 1717-1779 .... **LC 15**
See also DLB 84

Garrigue, Jean 1914-1972 .... **CLC 2, 8**
See also CA 5-8R; 37-40R; CANR 20

Garrison, Frederick
See Sinclair, Upton (Beall)

Garth, Will
See Hamilton, Edmond; Kuttner, Henry

Garvey, Marcus (Moziah, Jr.)
1887-1940 .... **TCLC 41; BLC**
See also BW 1; CA 120; 124

Gary, Romain .... **CLC 25**
See also Kacew, Romain
See also DLB 83

Gascar, Pierre .... **CLC 11**
See also Fournier, Pierre

Gascoyne, David (Emery) 1916- .... **CLC 45**
See also CA 65-68; CANR 10, 28; DLB 20; MTCW

Gaskell, Elizabeth Cleghorn
1810-1865 .... **NCLC 5**
See also CDBLB 1832-1890; DLB 21, 144

Gass, William H(oward)
1924- ... **CLC 1, 2, 8, 11, 15, 39; SSC 12**
See also CA 17-20R; CANR 30; DLB 2; MTCW

Gasset, Jose Ortega y
See Ortega y Gasset, Jose

Gates, Henry Louis, Jr. 1950- ...... **CLC 65**
See also BW 2; CA 109; CANR 25; DLB 67

Gautier, Theophile
1811-1872 .... **NCLC 1; SSC 20**
See also DLB 119

Gawsworth, John
See Bates, H(erbert) E(rnest)

Gaye, Marvin (Penze) 1939-1984 ... **CLC 26**
See also CA 112

Gebler, Carlo (Ernest) 1954- .... **CLC 39**
See also CA 119; 133

Gee, Maggie (Mary) 1948- .... **CLC 57**
See also CA 130

Gee, Maurice (Gough) 1931- .... **CLC 29**
See also CA 97-100; SATA 46

Gelbart, Larry (Simon) 1923- ... **CLC 21, 61**
See also CA 73-76; CANR 45

Gelber, Jack 1932- .... **CLC 1, 6, 14, 79**
See also CA 1-4R; CANR 2; DLB 7

Gellhorn, Martha (Ellis) 1908- .. **CLC 14, 60**
See also CA 77-80; CANR 44; DLBY 82

Genet, Jean
1910-1986 ... **CLC 1, 2, 5, 10, 14, 44, 46**
See also CA 13-16R; CANR 18; DLB 72; DLBY 86; MTCW

Gent, Peter 1942- .... **CLC 29**
See also AITN 1; CA 89-92; DLBY 82

Gentlewoman in New England, A
See Bradstreet, Anne

Gentlewoman in Those Parts, A
See Bradstreet, Anne

George, Jean Craighead 1919- ...... **CLC 35**
See also AAYA 8; CA 5-8R; CANR 25; CLR 1; DLB 52; JRDA; MAICYA; SATA 2, 68

George, Stefan (Anton)
1868-1933 .... **TCLC 2, 14**
See also CA 104

Georges, Georges Martin
See Simenon, Georges (Jacques Christian)

Gerhardi, William Alexander
See Gerhardie, William Alexander

Gerhardie, William Alexander
1895-1977 .... **CLC 5**
See also CA 25-28R; 73-76; CANR 18; DLB 36

Gerstler, Amy 1956- .... **CLC 70**
See also CA 146

Gertler, T. .... **CLC 34**
See also CA 116; 121

Ghalib 1797-1869 .... **NCLC 39**

Ghelderode, Michel de
1898-1962 .... **CLC 6, 11**
See also CA 85-88; CANR 40

Ghiselin, Brewster 1903- .... **CLC 23**
See also CA 13-16R; CAAS 10; CANR 13

Ghose, Zulfikar 1935- .... **CLC 42**
See also CA 65-68

Ghosh, Amitav 1956- .... **CLC 44**
See also CA 147

Giacosa, Giuseppe 1847-1906 ...... **TCLC 7**
See also CA 104

Gibb, Lee
See Waterhouse, Keith (Spencer)

Gibbon, Lewis Grassic .... **TCLC 4**
See also Mitchell, James Leslie

Gibbons, Kaye 1960- .... **CLC 50, 88**

Gibran, Kahlil
1883-1931 .... **TCLC 1, 9; PC 9**
See also CA 104

Gibson, William 1914- .... **CLC 23; DA**
See also CA 9-12R; CANR 9, 42; DLB 7; SATA 66

Gibson, William (Ford) 1948- ... **CLC 39, 63**
See also AAYA 12; CA 126; 133

Gide, Andre (Paul Guillaume)
1869-1951 .... **TCLC 5, 12, 36; DA; SSC 13; WLC**
See also CA 104; 124; DLB 65; MTCW

Gifford, Barry (Colby) 1946- .... **CLC 34**
See also CA 65-68; CANR 9, 30, 40

Gilbert, W(illiam) S(chwenck)
1836-1911 .... **TCLC 3**
See also CA 104; SATA 36

Gilbreth, Frank B., Jr. 1911- .... **CLC 17**
See also CA 9-12R; SATA 2

Gilchrist, Ellen 1935- .. **CLC 34, 48; SSC 14**
See also CA 113; 116; CANR 41; DLB 130; MTCW

Giles, Molly 1942- .... **CLC 39**
See also CA 126

Gill, Patrick
See Creasey, John

Gilliam, Terry (Vance) 1940- .... **CLC 21**
See also Monty Python
See also CA 108; 113; CANR 35

Gillian, Jerry
See Gilliam, Terry (Vance)

Gilliatt, Penelope (Ann Douglass)
1932-1993 .... **CLC 2, 10, 13, 53**
See also AITN 2; CA 13-16R; 141; DLB 14

Gilman, Charlotte (Anna) Perkins (Stetson)
1860-1935 .... **TCLC 9, 37; SSC 13**
See also CA 106

Gilmour, David 1949- .... **CLC 35**
See also CA 138, 147

Gilpin, William 1724-1804 .... **NCLC 30**

Gilray, J. D.
See Mencken, H(enry) L(ouis)

Gilroy, Frank D(aniel) 1925- .... **CLC 2**
See also CA 81-84; CANR 32; DLB 7

Ginsberg, Allen
1926- ...... **CLC 1, 2, 3, 4, 6, 13, 36, 69; DA; PC 4; WLC 3**
See also AITN 1; CA 1-4R; CANR 2, 41; CDALB 1941-1968; DLB 5, 16; MTCW

Ginzburg, Natalia 1916-1991 .... **CLC 5, 11, 54, 70**
See also CA 85-88; 135; CANR 33; MTCW

Giono, Jean 1895-1970.......... **CLC 4, 11**
See also CA 45-48; 29-32R; CANR 2, 35; DLB 72; MTCW

Giovanni, Nikki 1943- ...... **CLC 2, 4, 19, 64; BLC; DA**
See also AITN 1; BW 2; CA 29-32R; CAAS 6; CANR 18, 41; CLR 6; DLB 5, 41; MAICYA; MTCW; SATA 24

Giovene, Andrea 1904-............ **CLC 7**
See also CA 85-88

Gippius, Zinaida (Nikolayevna) 1869-1945
See Hippius, Zinaida
See also CA 106

Giraudoux, (Hippolyte) Jean 1882-1944 .... **TCLC 2, 7**
See also CA 104; DLB 65

Gironella, Jose Maria 1917- .... **CLC 11**
See also CA 101

Gissing, George (Robert) 1857-1903 .... **TCLC 3, 24, 47**
See also CA 105; DLB 18, 135

Giurlani, Aldo
See Palazzeschi, Aldo

Gladkov, Fyodor (Vasilyevich) 1883-1958 .... **TCLC 27**

Glanville, Brian (Lester) 1931- ...... **CLC 6**
See also CA 5-8R; CAAS 9; CANR 3; DLB 15, 139; SATA 42

Glasgow, Ellen (Anderson Gholson) 1873(?)-1945 .... **TCLC 2, 7**
See also CA 104; DLB 9, 12

Glaspell, Susan (Keating) 1882(?)-1948 .... **TCLC 55**
See also CA 110; DLB 7, 9, 78; YABC 2

Glassco, John 1909-1981 .... **CLC 9**
See also CA 13-16R; 102; CANR 15; DLB 68

Glasscock, Amnesia
See Steinbeck, John (Ernst)

Glasser, Ronald J. 1940(?)- .... **CLC 37**

Glassman, Joyce
See Johnson, Joyce

Glendinning, Victoria 1937-........ **CLC 50**
See also CA 120; 127

Glissant, Edouard 1928-........ **CLC 10, 68**

Gloag, Julian 1930- .... **CLC 40**
See also AITN 1; CA 65-68; CANR 10

Glowacki, Aleksander
See Prus, Boleslaw

Glueck, Louise (Elisabeth) 1943- .... **CLC 7, 22, 44, 81**
See also CA 33-36R; CANR 40; DLB 5

Gobineau, Joseph Arthur (Comte) de 1816-1882 .... **NCLC 17**
See also DLB 123

Godard, Jean-Luc 1930-.......... **CLC 20**
See also CA 93-96

Godden, (Margaret) Rumer 1907-... **CLC 53**
See also AAYA 6; CA 5-8R; CANR 4, 27, 36; CLR 20; MAICYA; SAAS 12; SATA 3, 36

Godoy Alcayaga, Lucila 1889-1957
See Mistral, Gabriela
See also BW 2; CA 104; 131; HW; MTCW

Godwin, Gail (Kathleen) 1937- .... **CLC 5, 8, 22, 31, 69**
See also CA 29-32R; CANR 15, 43; DLB 6; MTCW

Godwin, William 1756-1836...... **NCLC 14**
See also CDBLB 1789-1832; DLB 39, 104, 142

Goethe, Johann Wolfgang von 1749-1832 .... **NCLC 4, 22, 34; DA; PC 5; WLC 3**
See also DLB 94

Gogarty, Oliver St. John 1878-1957 .... **TCLC 15**
See also CA 109; DLB 15, 19

Gogol, Nikolai (Vasilyevich) 1809-1852 .... **NCLC 5, 15, 31; DA; DC 1; SSC 4; WLC**

Goines, Donald 1937(?)-1974 .... **CLC 80; BLC**
See also AITN 1; BW 1; CA 124; 114; DLB 33

Gold, Herbert 1924-....... **CLC 4, 7, 14, 42**
See also CA 9-12R; CANR 17, 45; DLB 2; DLBY 81

Goldbarth, Albert 1948-......... **CLC 5, 38**
See also CA 53-56; CANR 6, 40; DLB 120

Goldberg, Anatol 1910-1982 .... **CLC 34**
See also CA 131; 117

Goldemberg, Isaac 1945- .... **CLC 52**
See also CA 69-72; CAAS 12; CANR 11, 32; HW

Golding, William (Gerald) 1911-1993 .... **CLC 1, 2, 3, 8, 10, 17, 27, 58, 81; DA; WLC**
See also AAYA 5; CA 5-8R; 141; CANR 13, 33; CDBLB 1945-1960; DLB 15, 100; MTCW

Goldman, Emma 1869-1940....... **TCLC 13**
See also CA 110

Goldman, Francisco 1955-......... **CLC 76**

Goldman, William (W.) 1931- .... **CLC 1, 48**
See also CA 9-12R; CANR 29; DLB 44

Goldmann, Lucien 1913-1970 ...... **CLC 24**
See also CA 25-28; CAP 2

Goldoni, Carlo 1707-1793 .... **LC 4**

Goldsberry, Steven 1949-.......... **CLC 34**
See also CA 131

Goldsmith, Oliver 1728-1774 .... **LC 2; DA; WLC**
See also CDBLB 1660-1789; DLB 39, 89, 104, 109, 142; SATA 26

Goldsmith, Peter
See Priestley, J(ohn) B(oynton)

Gombrowicz, Witold 1904-1969 .... **CLC 4, 7, 11, 49**
See also CA 19-20; 25-28R; CAP 2

Gomez de la Serna, Ramon 1888-1963 .... **CLC 9**
See also CA 116; HW

Goncharov, Ivan Alexandrovich 1812-1891 .... **NCLC 1**

Goncourt, Edmond (Louis Antoine Huot) de 1822-1896 .... **NCLC 7**
See also DLB 123

Goncourt, Jules (Alfred Huot) de 1830-1870 .... **NCLC 7**
See also DLB 123

Gontier, Fernande 19(?)- .... **CLC 50**

Goodman, Paul 1911-1972.... **CLC 1, 2, 4, 7**
See also CA 19-20; 37-40R; CANR 34; CAP 2; DLB 130; MTCW

Gordimer, Nadine 1923- .... **CLC 3, 5, 7, 10, 18, 33, 51, 70; DA; SSC 17**
See also CA 5-8R; CANR 3, 28; MTCW

Gordon, Adam Lindsay 1833-1870 .... **NCLC 21**

Gordon, Caroline 1895-1981 ... **CLC 6, 13, 29, 83; SSC 15**
See also CA 11-12; 103; CANR 36; CAP 1; DLB 4, 9, 102; DLBY 81; MTCW

Gordon, Charles William 1860-1937
See Connor, Ralph
See also CA 109

Gordon, Mary (Catherine) 1949- .... **CLC 13, 22**
See also CA 102; CANR 44; DLB 6; DLBY 81; MTCW

Gordon, Sol 1923-................ **CLC 26**
See also CA 53-56; CANR 4; SATA 11

Gordone, Charles 1925- .... **CLC 1, 4**
See also BW 1; CA 93-96; DLB 7; MTCW

Gorenko, Anna Andreevna
See Akhmatova, Anna

Gorky, Maxim.............. **TCLC 8; WLC**
See also Peshkov, Alexei Maximovich

Goryan, Sirak
See Saroyan, William

Gosse, Edmund (William) 1849-1928 .... **TCLC 28**
See also CA 117; DLB 57, 144

Gotlieb, Phyllis Fay (Bloom) 1926- .... **CLC 18**
See also CA 13-16R; CANR 7; DLB 88

Gottesman, S. D.
See Kornbluth, C(yril) M.; Pohl, Frederik

Gottfried von Strassburg fl. c. 1210-................ **CMLC 10**
See also DLB 138

Gould, Lois .... **CLC 4, 10**
See also CA 77-80; CANR 29; MTCW

Gourmont, Remy de 1858-1915.... **TCLC 17**
See also CA 109

Govier, Katherine 1948-........... **CLC 51**
See also CA 101; CANR 18, 40

Goyen, (Charles) William 1915-1983 .... **CLC 5, 8, 14, 40**
See also AITN 2; CA 5-8R; 110; CANR 6; DLB 2; DLBY 83

Goytisolo, Juan 1931- .... **CLC 5, 10, 23; HLC**
See also CA 85-88; CANR 32; HW; MTCW

Gozzano, Guido 1883-1916 .... **PC 10**
See also DLB 114

Gozzi, (Conte) Carlo 1720-1806 .. **NCLC 23**

Grabbe, Christian Dietrich
1801-1836 .... **NCLC 2**
See also DLB 133

Grace, Patricia 1937- .... **CLC 56**

Gracian y Morales, Baltasar
1601-1658 .... **LC 15**

Gracq, Julien .... **CLC 11, 48**
See also Poirier, Louis
See also DLB 83

Grade, Chaim 1910-1982 .... **CLC 10**
See also CA 93-96; 107

Graduate of Oxford, A
See Ruskin, John

Graham, John
See Phillips, David Graham

Graham, Jorie 1951- .... **CLC 48**
See also CA 111; DLB 120

Graham, R(obert) B(ontine) Cunninghame
See Cunninghame Graham, R(obert) B(ontine)
See also DLB 98, 135

Graham, Robert
See Haldeman, Joe (William)

Graham, Tom
See Lewis, (Harry) Sinclair

Graham, W(illiam) S(ydney)
1918-1986 .... **CLC 29**
See also CA 73-76; 118; DLB 20

Graham, Winston (Mawdsley)
1910- .... **CLC 23**
See also CA 49-52; CANR 2, 22, 45; DLB 77

Grant, Skeeter
See Spiegelman, Art

Granville-Barker, Harley
1877-1946 .... **TCLC 2**
See also Barker, Harley Granville
See also CA 104

Grass, Guenter (Wilhelm)
1927- ..... **CLC 1, 2, 4, 6, 11, 15, 22, 32, 49, 88; DA; WLC**
See also CA 13-16R; CANR 20; DLB 75, 124; MTCW

Gratton, Thomas
See Hulme, T(homas) E(rnest)

Grau, Shirley Ann
1929- .... **CLC 4, 9; SSC 15**
See also CA 89-92; CANR 22; DLB 2; MTCW

Gravel, Fern
See Hall, James Norman

Graver, Elizabeth 1964- .... **CLC 70**
See also CA 135

Graves, Richard Perceval 1945- .... **CLC 44**
See also CA 65-68; CANR 9, 26

Graves, Robert (von Ranke)
1895-1985 ...... **CLC 1, 2, 6, 11, 39, 44, 45; PC 6**
See also CA 5-8R; 117; CANR 5, 36; CDBLB 1914-1945; DLB 20, 100; DLBY 85; MTCW; SATA 45

Gray, Alasdair (James) 1934- ...... **CLC 41**
See also CA 126; CANR 47; MTCW

Gray, Amlin 1946- .... **CLC 29**
See also CA 138

Gray, Francine du Plessix 1930- .... **CLC 22**
See also BEST 90:3; CA 61-64; CAAS 2; CANR 11, 33; MTCW

Gray, John (Henry) 1866-1934 .... **TCLC 19**
See also CA 119

Gray, Simon (James Holliday)
1936- .... **CLC 9, 14, 36**
See also AITN 1; CA 21-24R; CAAS 3; CANR 32; DLB 13; MTCW

Gray, Spalding 1941- .... **CLC 49**
See also CA 128

Gray, Thomas
1716-1771 ...... **LC 4; DA; PC 2; WLC**
See also CDBLB 1660-1789; DLB 109

Grayson, David
See Baker, Ray Stannard

Grayson, Richard (A.) 1951- .... **CLC 38**
See also CA 85-88; CANR 14, 31

Greeley, Andrew M(oran) 1928- .... **CLC 28**
See also CA 5-8R; CAAS 7; CANR 7, 43; MTCW

Green, Brian
See Card, Orson Scott

Green, Hannah
See Greenberg, Joanne (Goldenberg)

Green, Hannah .... **CLC 3**
See also CA 73-76

Green, Henry .... **CLC 2, 13**
See also Yorke, Henry Vincent
See also DLB 15

Green, Julian (Hartridge) 1900-
See Green, Julien
See also CA 21-24R; CANR 33; DLB 4, 72; MTCW

Green, Julien .... **CLC 3, 11, 77**
See also Green, Julian (Hartridge)

Green, Paul (Eliot) 1894-1981 ...... **CLC 25**
See also AITN 1; CA 5-8R; 103; CANR 3; DLB 7, 9; DLBY 81

Greenberg, Ivan 1908-1973
See Rahv, Philip
See also CA 85-88

Greenberg, Joanne (Goldenberg)
1932- .... **CLC 7, 30**
See also AAYA 12; CA 5-8R; CANR 14, 32; SATA 25

Greenberg, Richard 1959(?)- .... **CLC 57**
See also CA 138

Greene, Bette 1934- .... **CLC 30**
See also AAYA 7; CA 53-56; CANR 4; CLR 2; JRDA; MAICYA; SAAS 16; SATA 8

Greene, Gael .... **CLC 8**
See also CA 13-16R; CANR 10

Greene, Graham
1904-1991 .... **CLC 1, 3, 6, 9, 14, 18, 27, 37, 70, 72; DA; WLC**
See also AITN 2; CA 13-16R; 133; CANR 35; CDBLB 1945-1960; DLB 13, 15, 77, 100; DLBY 91; MTCW; SATA 20

Greer, Richard
See Silverberg, Robert

Gregor, Arthur 1923- .... **CLC 9**
See also CA 25-28R; CAAS 10; CANR 11; SATA 36

Gregor, Lee
See Pohl, Frederik

Gregory, Isabella Augusta (Persse)
1852-1932 .... **TCLC 1**
See also CA 104; DLB 10

Gregory, J. Dennis
See Williams, John A(lfred)

Grendon, Stephen
See Derleth, August (William)

Grenville, Kate 1950- .... **CLC 61**
See also CA 118

Grenville, Pelham
See Wodehouse, P(elham) G(renville)

Greve, Felix Paul (Berthold Friedrich)
1879-1948
See Grove, Frederick Philip
See also CA 104; 141

Grey, Zane 1872-1939 .... **TCLC 6**
See also CA 104; 132; DLB 9; MTCW

Grieg, (Johan) Nordahl (Brun)
1902-1943 .... **TCLC 10**
See also CA 107

Grieve, C(hristopher) M(urray)
1892-1978 .... **CLC 11, 19**
See also MacDiarmid, Hugh
See also CA 5-8R; 85-88; CANR 33; MTCW

Griffin, Gerald 1803-1840 .... **NCLC 7**

Griffin, John Howard 1920-1980 .... **CLC 68**
See also AITN 1; CA 1-4R; 101; CANR 2

Griffin, Peter 1942- .... **CLC 39**
See also CA 136

Griffiths, Trevor 1935- .... **CLC 13, 52**
See also CA 97-100; CANR 45; DLB 13

Grigson, Geoffrey (Edward Harvey)
1905-1985 .... **CLC 7, 39**
See also CA 25-28R; 118; CANR 20, 33; DLB 27; MTCW

Grillparzer, Franz 1791-1872 ...... **NCLC 1**
See also DLB 133

Grimble, Reverend Charles James
See Eliot, T(homas) S(tearns)

Grimke, Charlotte L(ottie) Forten
1837(?)-1914
See Forten, Charlotte L.
See also BW 1; CA 117; 124

Grimm, Jacob Ludwig Karl
1785-1863 .... **NCLC 3**
See also DLB 90; MAICYA; SATA 22

Grimm, Wilhelm Karl 1786-1859 .. **NCLC 3**
See also DLB 90; MAICYA; SATA 22

Grimmelshausen, Johann Jakob Christoffel von 1621-1676 .... **LC 6**

Grindel, Eugene 1895-1952
See Eluard, Paul
See also CA 104

Grisham, John 1955- .... **CLC 84**
See also AAYA 14; CA 138; CANR 47

Grossman, David 1954- .... **CLC 67**
See also CA 138

Grossman, Vasily (Semenovich)
1905-1964 .... **CLC 41**
See also CA 124; 130; MTCW

Grove, Frederick Philip .... **TCLC 4**
See also Greve, Felix Paul (Berthold Friedrich)
See also DLB 92

Grubb
See Crumb, R(obert)

Grumbach, Doris (Isaac) 1918- .... **CLC 13, 22, 64**
See also CA 5-8R; CAAS 2; CANR 9, 42

Grundtvig, Nicolai Frederik Severin 1783-1872 .... **NCLC 1**

Grunge
See Crumb, R(obert)

Grunwald, Lisa 1959- .... **CLC 44**
See also CA 120

Guare, John 1938- .... **CLC 8, 14, 29, 67**
See also CA 73-76; CANR 21; DLB 7; MTCW

Gudjonsson, Halldor Kiljan 1902-
See Laxness, Halldor
See also CA 103

Guenter, Erich
See Eich, Guenter

Guest, Barbara 1920- .... **CLC 34**
See also CA 25-28R; CANR 11, 44; DLB 5

Guest, Judith (Ann) 1936- .... **CLC 8, 30**
See also AAYA 7; CA 77-80; CANR 15; MTCW

Guevara, Che .... **CLC 87; HLC**
See also Guevara (Serna), Ernesto

Guevara (Serna), Ernesto 1928-1967
See Guevara, Che
See also CA 127; 111; HW

Guild, Nicholas M. 1944- .... **CLC 33**
See also CA 93-96

Guillemin, Jacques
See Sartre, Jean-Paul

Guillen, Jorge 1893-1984 .... **CLC 11**
See also CA 89-92; 112; DLB 108; HW

Guillen (y Batista), Nicolas (Cristobal) 1902-1989 ..... **CLC 48, 79; BLC; HLC**
See also BW 2; CA 116; 125; 129; HW

Guillevic, (Eugene) 1907- .... **CLC 33**
See also CA 93-96

Guillois
See Desnos, Robert

Guiney, Louise Imogen 1861-1920 .... **TCLC 41**
See also DLB 54

Guiraldes, Ricardo (Guillermo) 1886-1927 .... **TCLC 39**
See also CA 131; HW; MTCW

Gumilev, Nikolai Stephanovich 1886-1921 .... **TCLC 60**

Gunn, Bill .... **CLC 5**
See also Gunn, William Harrison
See also DLB 38

Gunn, Thom(son William) 1929- .... **CLC 3, 6, 18, 32, 81**
See also CA 17-20R; CANR 9, 33; CDBLB 1960 to Present; DLB 27; MTCW

Gunn, William Harrison 1934(?)-1989
See Gunn, Bill
See also AITN 1; BW 1; CA 13-16R; 128; CANR 12, 25

Gunnars, Kristjana 1948- .... **CLC 69**
See also CA 113; DLB 60

Gurganus, Allan 1947- .... **CLC 70**
See also BEST 90:1; CA 135

Gurney, A(lbert) R(amsdell), Jr. 1930- .... **CLC 32, 50, 54**
See also CA 77-80; CANR 32

Gurney, Ivor (Bertie) 1890-1937 ... **TCLC 33**

Gurney, Peter
See Gurney, A(lbert) R(amsdell), Jr.

Guro, Elena 1877-1913 .... **TCLC 56**

Gustafson, Ralph (Barker) 1909- .... **CLC 36**
See also CA 21-24R; CANR 8, 45; DLB 88

Gut, Gom
See Simenon, Georges (Jacques Christian)

Guthrie, A(lfred) B(ertram), Jr. 1901-1991 .... **CLC 23**
See also CA 57-60; 134; CANR 24; DLB 6; SATA 62; SATA-Obit 67

Guthrie, Isobel
See Grieve, C(hristopher) M(urray)

Guthrie, Woodrow Wilson 1912-1967
See Guthrie, Woody
See also CA 113; 93-96

Guthrie, Woody .... **CLC 35**
See also Guthrie, Woodrow Wilson

Guy, Rosa (Cuthbert) 1928- .... **CLC 26**
See also AAYA 4; BW 2; CA 17-20R; CANR 14, 34; CLR 13; DLB 33; JRDA; MAICYA; SATA 14, 62

Gwendolyn
See Bennett, (Enoch) Arnold

H. D. .... **CLC 3, 8, 14, 31, 34, 73; PC 5**
See also Doolittle, Hilda

H. de V.
See Buchan, John

Haavikko, Paavo Juhani 1931- .... **CLC 18, 34**
See also CA 106

Habbema, Koos
See Heijermans, Herman

Hacker, Marilyn 1942- .... **CLC 5, 9, 23, 72**
See also CA 77-80; DLB 120

Haggard, H(enry) Rider 1856-1925 .... **TCLC 11**
See also CA 108; DLB 70; SATA 16

Hagiwara Sakutaro 1886-1942 .... **TCLC 60**

Haig, Fenil
See Ford, Ford Madox

Haig-Brown, Roderick (Langmere) 1908-1976 .... **CLC 21**
See also CA 5-8R; 69-72; CANR 4, 38; CLR 31; DLB 88; MAICYA; SATA 12

Hailey, Arthur 1920- .... **CLC 5**
See also AITN 2; BEST 90:3; CA 1-4R; CANR 2, 36; DLB 88; DLBY 82; MTCW

Hailey, Elizabeth Forsythe 1938- ... **CLC 40**
See also CA 93-96; CAAS 1; CANR 15, 48

Haines, John (Meade) 1924- .... **CLC 58**
See also CA 17-20R; CANR 13, 34; DLB 5

Haldeman, Joe (William) 1943- ..... **CLC 61**
See also CA 53-56; CANR 6; DLB 8

Haley, Alex(ander Murray Palmer) 1921-1992 .... **CLC 8, 12, 76; BLC; DA**
See also BW 2; CA 77-80; 136; DLB 38; MTCW

Haliburton, Thomas Chandler 1796-1865 .... **NCLC 15**
See also DLB 11, 99

Hall, Donald (Andrew, Jr.) 1928- .... **CLC 1, 13, 37, 59**
See also CA 5-8R; CAAS 7; CANR 2, 44; DLB 5; SATA 23

Hall, Frederic Sauser
See Sauser-Hall, Frederic

Hall, James
See Kuttner, Henry

Hall, James Norman 1887-1951 ... **TCLC 23**
See also CA 123; SATA 21

Hall, (Marguerite) Radclyffe 1886(?)-1943 .... **TCLC 12**
See also CA 110

Hall, Rodney 1935- .... **CLC 51**
See also CA 109

Halleck, Fitz-Greene 1790-1867 .. **NCLC 47**
See also DLB 3

Halliday, Michael
See Creasey, John

Halpern, Daniel 1945- .... **CLC 14**
See also CA 33-36R

Hamburger, Michael (Peter Leopold) 1924- .... **CLC 5, 14**
See also CA 5-8R; CAAS 4; CANR 2, 47; DLB 27

Hamill, Pete 1935- .... **CLC 10**
See also CA 25-28R; CANR 18

Hamilton, Alexander 1755(?)-1804 .... **NCLC 49**
See also DLB 37

Hamilton, Clive
See Lewis, C(live) S(taples)

Hamilton, Edmond 1904-1977 .... **CLC 1**
See also CA 1-4R; CANR 3; DLB 8

Hamilton, Eugene (Jacob) Lee
See Lee-Hamilton, Eugene (Jacob)

Hamilton, Franklin
See Silverberg, Robert

Hamilton, Gail
See Corcoran, Barbara

Hamilton, Mollie
See Kaye, M(ary) M(argaret)

Hamilton, (Anthony Walter) Patrick 1904-1962 .... **CLC 51**
See also CA 113; DLB 10

Hamilton, Virginia 1936- .... **CLC 26**
See also AAYA 2; BW 2; CA 25-28R; CANR 20, 37; CLR 1, 11; DLB 33, 52; JRDA; MAICYA; MTCW; SATA 4, 56, 79

Hammett, (Samuel) Dashiell 1894-1961 .... **CLC 3, 5, 10, 19, 47; SSC 17**
See also AITN 1; CA 81-84; CANR 42; CDALB 1929-1941; DLBD 6; MTCW

Hammon, Jupiter 1711(?)-1800(?) .... **NCLC 5; BLC**
See also DLB 31, 50

Hammond, Keith
See Kuttner, Henry

Hamner, Earl (Henry), Jr. 1923- ... **CLC 12**
See also AITN 2; CA 73-76; DLB 6

Hampton, Christopher (James) 1946- .... **CLC 4**
See also CA 25-28R; DLB 13; MTCW

Hamsun, Knut .... **TCLC 2, 14, 49**
See also Pedersen, Knut

Handke, Peter 1942- .. **CLC 5, 8, 10, 15, 38**
See also CA 77-80; CANR 33; DLB 85, 124; MTCW

Hanley, James 1901-1985 ... **CLC 3, 5, 8, 13**
See also CA 73-76; 117; CANR 36; MTCW

Hannah, Barry 1942- .... **CLC 23, 38**
See also CA 108; 110; CANR 43; DLB 6; MTCW

Hannon, Ezra
See Hunter, Evan

Hansberry, Lorraine (Vivian) 1930-1965 ...... **CLC 17, 62; BLC; DA; DC 2**
See also BW 1; CA 109; 25-28R; CABS 3; CDALB 1941-1968; DLB 7, 38; MTCW

Hansen, Joseph 1923- .... **CLC 38**
See also CA 29-32R; CAAS 17; CANR 16, 44

Hansen, Martin A. 1909-1955 ..... **TCLC 32**

Hanson, Kenneth O(stlin) 1922- .... **CLC 13**
See also CA 53-56; CANR 7

Hardwick, Elizabeth 1916- .... **CLC 13**
See also CA 5-8R; CANR 3, 32; DLB 6; MTCW

Hardy, Thomas 1840-1928 ...... **TCLC 4, 10, 18, 32, 48, 53; DA; PC 8; SSC 2; WLC**
See also CA 104; 123; CDBLB 1890-1914; DLB 18, 19, 135; MTCW

Hare, David 1947- .... **CLC 29, 58**
See also CA 97-100; CANR 39; DLB 13; MTCW

Harford, Henry
See Hudson, W(illiam) H(enry)

Hargrave, Leonie
See Disch, Thomas M(ichael)

Harjo, Joy 1951- .... **CLC 83**
See also CA 114; CANR 35; DLB 120; NNAL

Harlan, Louis R(udolph) 1922- ..... **CLC 34**
See also CA 21-24R; CANR 25

Harling, Robert 1951(?)- .... **CLC 53**
See also CA 147

Harmon, William (Ruth) 1938- ..... **CLC 38**
See also CA 33-36R; CANR 14, 32, 35; SATA 65

Harper, F. E. W.
See Harper, Frances Ellen Watkins

Harper, Frances E. W.
See Harper, Frances Ellen Watkins

Harper, Frances E. Watkins
See Harper, Frances Ellen Watkins

Harper, Frances Ellen
See Harper, Frances Ellen Watkins

Harper, Frances Ellen Watkins 1825-1911 .... **TCLC 14; BLC**
See also BW 1; CA 111; 125; DLB 50

Harper, Michael S(teven) 1938- .. **CLC 7, 22**
See also BW 1; CA 33-36R; CANR 24; DLB 41

Harper, Mrs. F. E. W.
See Harper, Frances Ellen Watkins

Harris, Christie (Lucy) Irwin 1907- .... **CLC 12**
See also CA 5-8R; CANR 6; DLB 88; JRDA; MAICYA; SAAS 10; SATA 6, 74

Harris, Frank 1856(?)-1931 .... **TCLC 24**
See also CA 109

Harris, George Washington 1814-1869 .... **NCLC 23**
See also DLB 3, 11

Harris, Joel Chandler 1848-1908 .... **TCLC 2; SSC 19**
See also CA 104; 137; DLB 11, 23, 42, 78, 91; MAICYA; YABC 1

Harris, John (Wyndham Parkes Lucas) Beynon 1903-1969
See Wyndham, John
See also CA 102; 89-92

Harris, MacDonald .... **CLC 9**
See also Heiney, Donald (William)

Harris, Mark 1922- .... **CLC 19**
See also CA 5-8R; CAAS 3; CANR 2; DLB 2; DLBY 80

Harris, (Theodore) Wilson 1921- .... **CLC 25**
See also BW 2; CA 65-68; CAAS 16; CANR 11, 27; DLB 117; MTCW

Harrison, Elizabeth Cavanna 1909-
See Cavanna, Betty
See also CA 9-12R; CANR 6, 27

Harrison, Harry (Max) 1925- ...... **CLC 42**
See also CA 1-4R; CANR 5, 21; DLB 8; SATA 4

Harrison, James (Thomas) 1937- .... **CLC 6, 14, 33, 66; SSC 19**
See also CA 13-16R; CANR 8; DLBY 82

Harrison, Jim
See Harrison, James (Thomas)

Harrison, Kathryn 1961- .... **CLC 70**
See also CA 144

Harrison, Tony 1937- .... **CLC 43**
See also CA 65-68; CANR 44; DLB 40; MTCW

Harriss, Will(ard Irvin) 1922- ...... **CLC 34**
See also CA 111

Harson, Sley
See Ellison, Harlan (Jay)

Hart, Ellis
See Ellison, Harlan (Jay)

Hart, Josephine 1942(?)- .... **CLC 70**
See also CA 138

Hart, Moss 1904-1961 .... **CLC 66**
See also CA 109; 89-92; DLB 7

Harte, (Francis) Bret(t) 1836(?)-1902 .... **TCLC 1, 25; DA; SSC 8; WLC**
See also CA 104; 140; CDALB 1865-1917; DLB 12, 64, 74, 79; SATA 26

Hartley, L(eslie) P(oles) 1895-1972 .... **CLC 2, 22**
See also CA 45-48; 37-40R; CANR 33; DLB 15, 139; MTCW

Hartman, Geoffrey H. 1929- .... **CLC 27**
See also CA 117; 125; DLB 67

Hartmann von Aue c. 1160-c. 1205 .... **CMLC 15**
See also DLB 138

Haruf, Kent 19(?)- .... **CLC 34**

Harwood, Ronald 1934- .... **CLC 32**
See also CA 1-4R; CANR 4; DLB 13

Hasek, Jaroslav (Matej Frantisek) 1883-1923 .... **TCLC 4**
See also CA 104; 129; MTCW

Hass, Robert 1941- .... **CLC 18, 39**
See also CA 111; CANR 30; DLB 105

Hastings, Hudson
See Kuttner, Henry

Hastings, Selina .... **CLC 44**

Hatteras, Amelia
See Mencken, H(enry) L(ouis)

Hatteras, Owen .... **TCLC 18**
See also Mencken, H(enry) L(ouis); Nathan, George Jean

Hauptmann, Gerhart (Johann Robert) 1862-1946 .... **TCLC 4**
See also CA 104; DLB 66, 118

Havel, Vaclav 1936- .... **CLC 25, 58, 65**
See also CA 104; CANR 36; MTCW

Haviaras, Stratis .... **CLC 33**
See also Chaviaras, Strates

Hawes, Stephen 1475(?)-1523(?) ..... **LC 17**

Hawkes, John (Clendennin Burne, Jr.) 1925- ...... **CLC 1, 2, 3, 4, 7, 9, 14, 15, 27, 49**
See also CA 1-4R; CANR 2, 47; DLB 2, 7; DLBY 80; MTCW

Hawking, S. W.
See Hawking, Stephen W(illiam)

Hawking, Stephen W(illiam) 1942- .... **CLC 63**
See also AAYA 13; BEST 89:1; CA 126; 129; CANR 48

Hawthorne, Julian 1846-1934 ..... **TCLC 25**

Hawthorne, Nathaniel 1804-1864 ...... **NCLC 39; DA; SSC 3; WLC**
See also CDALB 1640-1865; DLB 1, 74; YABC 2

Haxton, Josephine Ayres 1921-
See Douglas, Ellen
See also CA 115; CANR 41

Hayaseca y Eizaguirre, Jorge
See Echegaray (y Eizaguirre), Jose (Maria Waldo)

Hayashi Fumiko 1904-1951 .... **TCLC 27**

Haycraft, Anna
See Ellis, Alice Thomas
See also CA 122

Hayden, Robert E(arl) 1913-1980 . . . . . . **CLC 5, 9, 14, 37; BLC; DA; PC 6**
See also BW 1; CA 69-72; 97-100; CABS 2; CANR 24; CDALB 1941-1968; DLB 5, 76; MTCW; SATA 19; SATA-Obit 26

Hayford, J(oseph) E(phraim) Casely
See Casely-Hayford, J(oseph) E(phraim)

Hayman, Ronald 1932-. . . . . **CLC 44**
See also CA 25-28R; CANR 18

Haywood, Eliza (Fowler) 1693(?)-1756 . . . . **LC 1**

Hazlitt, William 1778-1830 . . . . . . **NCLC 29**
See also DLB 110

Hazzard, Shirley 1931- . . . . **CLC 18**
See also CA 9-12R; CANR 4; DLBY 82; MTCW

Head, Bessie 1937-1986 . . . **CLC 25, 67; BLC**
See also BW 2; CA 29-32R; 119; CANR 25; DLB 117; MTCW

Headon, (Nicky) Topper 1956(?)- . . . **CLC 30**

Heaney, Seamus (Justin) 1939- . . . . **CLC 5, 7, 14, 25, 37, 74**
See also CA 85-88; CANR 25, 48; CDBLB 1960 to Present; DLB 40; MTCW

Hearn, (Patricio) Lafcadio (Tessima Carlos) 1850-1904 . . . . **TCLC 9**
See also CA 105; DLB 12, 78

Hearne, Vicki 1946-. . . . . **CLC 56**
See also CA 139

Hearon, Shelby 1931-. . . . . **CLC 63**
See also AITN 2; CA 25-28R; CANR 18, 48

Heat-Moon, William Least. . . . . **CLC 29**
See also Trogdon, William (Lewis)
See also AAYA 9

Hebbel, Friedrich 1813-1863 . . . . . **NCLC 43**
See also DLB 129

Hebert, Anne 1916- . . . . **CLC 4, 13, 29**
See also CA 85-88; DLB 68; MTCW

Hecht, Anthony (Evan) 1923- . . . . **CLC 8, 13, 19**
See also CA 9-12R; CANR 6; DLB 5

Hecht, Ben 1894-1964 . . . . **CLC 8**
See also CA 85-88; DLB 7, 9, 25, 26, 28, 86

Hedayat, Sadeq 1903-1951. . . . . **TCLC 21**
See also CA 120

Hegel, Georg Wilhelm Friedrich 1770-1831 . . . . **NCLC 46**
See also DLB 90

Heidegger, Martin 1889-1976 . . . . . . **CLC 24**
See also CA 81-84; 65-68; CANR 34; MTCW

Heidenstam, (Carl Gustaf) Verner von 1859-1940 . . . . **TCLC 5**
See also CA 104

Heifner, Jack 1946-. . . . . **CLC 11**
See also CA 105; CANR 47

Heijermans, Herman 1864-1924 . . . **TCLC 24**
See also CA 123

Heilbrun, Carolyn G(old) 1926-. . . . . **CLC 25**
See also CA 45-48; CANR 1, 28

Heine, Heinrich 1797-1856 . . . . **NCLC 4**
See also DLB 90

Heinemann, Larry (Curtiss) 1944- . . **CLC 50**
See also CA 110; CAAS 21; CANR 31; DLBD 9

Heiney, Donald (William) 1921-1993
See Harris, MacDonald
See also CA 1-4R; 142; CANR 3

Heinlein, Robert A(nson) 1907-1988 . . . . . . **CLC 1, 3, 8, 14, 26, 55**
See also CA 1-4R; 125; CANR 1, 20; DLB 8; JRDA; MAICYA; MTCW; SATA 9, 69; SATA-Obit 56

Helforth, John
See Doolittle, Hilda

Hellenhofferu, Vojtech Kapristian z
See Hasek, Jaroslav (Matej Frantisek)

Heller, Joseph 1923- . . . . **CLC 1, 3, 5, 8, 11, 36, 63; DA; WLC**
See also AITN 1; CA 5-8R; CABS 1; CANR 8, 42; DLB 2, 28; DLBY 80; MTCW

Hellman, Lillian (Florence) 1906-1984 . . . . . . **CLC 2, 4, 8, 14, 18, 34, 44, 52; DC 1**
See also AITN 1, 2; CA 13-16R; 112; CANR 33; DLB 7; DLBY 84; MTCW

Helprin, Mark 1947- . . . . . **CLC 7, 10, 22, 32**
See also CA 81-84; CANR 47; DLBY 85; MTCW

Helvetius, Claude-Adrien 1715-1771 . . . . **LC 26**

Helyar, Jane Penelope Josephine 1933-
See Poole, Josephine
See also CA 21-24R; CANR 10, 26

Hemans, Felicia 1793-1835 . . . . . . **NCLC 29**
See also DLB 96

Hemingway, Ernest (Miller) 1899-1961 . . . . **CLC 1, 3, 6, 8, 10, 13, 19, 30, 34, 39, 41, 44, 50, 61, 80; DA; SSC 1; WLC**
See also CA 77-80; CANR 34; CDALB 1917-1929; DLB 4, 9, 102; DLBD 1; DLBY 81, 87; MTCW

Hempel, Amy 1951- . . . . **CLC 39**
See also CA 118; 137

Henderson, F. C.
See Mencken, H(enry) L(ouis)

Henderson, Sylvia
See Ashton-Warner, Sylvia (Constance)

Henley, Beth . . . . **CLC 23**
See also Henley, Elizabeth Becker
See also CABS 3; DLBY 86

Henley, Elizabeth Becker 1952-
See Henley, Beth
See also CA 107; CANR 32; MTCW

Henley, William Ernest 1849-1903 . . . . **TCLC 8**
See also CA 105; DLB 19

Hennissart, Martha
See Lathen, Emma
See also CA 85-88

Henry, O.. . . . . **TCLC 1, 19; SSC 5; WLC**
See also Porter, William Sydney

Henry, Patrick 1736-1799 . . . . **LC 25**

Henryson, Robert 1430(?)-1506(?). . . . **LC 20**
See also DLB 146

Henry VIII 1491-1547 . . . . **LC 10**

Henschke, Alfred
See Klabund

Hentoff, Nat(han Irving) 1925- . . . . . **CLC 26**
See also AAYA 4; CA 1-4R; CAAS 6; CANR 5, 25; CLR 1; JRDA; MAICYA; SATA 42, 69; SATA-Brief 27

Heppenstall, (John) Rayner 1911-1981 . . . . **CLC 10**
See also CA 1-4R; 103; CANR 29

Herbert, Frank (Patrick) 1920-1986 . . . . . . **CLC 12, 23, 35, 44, 85**
See also CA 53-56; 118; CANR 5, 43; DLB 8; MTCW; SATA 9, 37; SATA-Obit 47

Herbert, George 1593-1633 . . . . **LC 24; PC 4**
See also CDBLB Before 1660; DLB 126

Herbert, Zbigniew 1924- . . . . **CLC 9, 43**
See also CA 89-92; CANR 36; MTCW

Herbst, Josephine (Frey) 1897-1969 . . . . **CLC 34**
See also CA 5-8R; 25-28R; DLB 9

Hergesheimer, Joseph 1880-1954 . . . . **TCLC 11**
See also CA 109; DLB 102, 9

Herlihy, James Leo 1927-1993 . . . . . . **CLC 6**
See also CA 1-4R; 143; CANR 2

Hermogenes fl. c. 175- . . . . **CMLC 6**

Hernandez, Jose 1834-1886. . . . . . **NCLC 17**

Herrick, Robert 1591-1674 . . . . **LC 13; DA; PC 9**
See also DLB 126

Herring, Guilles
See Somerville, Edith

Herriot, James 1916-1995 . . . . **CLC 12**
See also Wight, James Alfred
See also AAYA 1; CANR 40

Herrmann, Dorothy 1941- . . . . **CLC 44**
See also CA 107

Herrmann, Taffy
See Herrmann, Dorothy

Hersey, John (Richard) 1914-1993 . . . . **CLC 1, 2, 7, 9, 40, 81**
See also CA 17-20R; 140; CANR 33; DLB 6; MTCW; SATA 25; SATA-Obit 76

Herzen, Aleksandr Ivanovich 1812-1870 . . . . **NCLC 10**

Herzl, Theodor 1860-1904 . . . . **TCLC 36**

Herzog, Werner 1942- . . . . **CLC 16**
See also CA 89-92

Hesiod c. 8th cent. B.C.- . . . . **CMLC 5**

Hesse, Hermann 1877-1962 . . . . **CLC 1, 2, 3, 6, 11, 17, 25, 69; DA; SSC 9; WLC**
See also CA 17-18; CAP 2; DLB 66; MTCW; SATA 50

Hewes, Cady
See De Voto, Bernard (Augustine)

Heyen, William 1940- . . . . **CLC 13, 18**
See also CA 33-36R; CAAS 9; DLB 5

Heyerdahl, Thor 1914- . . . . **CLC 26**
See also CA 5-8R; CANR 5, 22; MTCW; SATA 2, 52

Heym, Georg (Theodor Franz Arthur) 1887-1912 . . . . **TCLC 9**
See also CA 106

Heym, Stefan 1913- . . . . **CLC 41**
See also CA 9-12R; CANR 4; DLB 69

Heyse, Paul (Johann Ludwig von) 1830-1914 . . . . **TCLC 8**
See also CA 104; DLB 129

Heyward, (Edwin) DuBose 1885-1940 . . . . **TCLC 59**
See also CA 108; DLB 7, 9, 45; SATA 21

Hibbert, Eleanor Alice Burford 1906-1993 . . . . **CLC 7**
See also BEST 90:4; CA 17-20R; 140; CANR 9, 28; SATA 2; SATA-Obit 74

Higgins, George V(incent) 1939- . . . . **CLC 4, 7, 10, 18**
See also CA 77-80; CAAS 5; CANR 17; DLB 2; DLBY 81; MTCW

Higginson, Thomas Wentworth 1823-1911 . . . . **TCLC 36**
See also DLB 1, 64

Highet, Helen
See MacInnes, Helen (Clark)

Highsmith, (Mary) Patricia 1921-1995 . . . . **CLC 2, 4, 14, 42**
See also CA 1-4R; 147; CANR 1, 20, 48; MTCW

Highwater, Jamake (Mamake) 1942(?)- . . . . **CLC 12**
See also AAYA 7; CA 65-68; CAAS 7; CANR 10, 34; CLR 17; DLB 52; DLBY 85; JRDA; MAICYA; SATA 32, 69; SATA-Brief 30

Higuchi, Ichiyo 1872-1896. . . . . . . **NCLC 49**

Hijuelos, Oscar 1951- . . . . . . **CLC 65; HLC**
See also BEST 90:1; CA 123; DLB 145; HW

Hikmet, Nazim 1902(?)-1963. . . . . . . **CLC 40**
See also CA 141; 93-96

Hildesheimer, Wolfgang 1916-1991 . . . . **CLC 49**
See also CA 101; 135; DLB 69, 124

Hill, Geoffrey (William) 1932- . . . . **CLC 5, 8, 18, 45**
See also CA 81-84; CANR 21; CDBLB 1960 to Present; DLB 40; MTCW

Hill, George Roy 1921- . . . . **CLC 26**
See also CA 110; 122

Hill, John
See Koontz, Dean R(ay)

Hill, Susan (Elizabeth) 1942- . . . . **CLC 4**
See also CA 33-36R; CANR 29; DLB 14, 139; MTCW

Hillerman, Tony 1925-. . . . . **CLC 62**
See also AAYA 6; BEST 89:1; CA 29-32R; CANR 21, 42; SATA 6

Hillesum, Etty 1914-1943 . . . . **TCLC 49**
See also CA 137

Hilliard, Noel (Harvey) 1929-. . . . . . **CLC 15**
See also CA 9-12R; CANR 7

Hillis, Rick 1956-. . . . . **CLC 66**
See also CA 134

Hilton, James 1900-1954 . . . . **TCLC 21**
See also CA 108; DLB 34, 77; SATA 34

Himes, Chester (Bomar) 1909-1984 . . . . **CLC 2, 4, 7, 18, 58; BLC**
See also BW 2; CA 25-28R; 114; CANR 22; DLB 2, 76, 143; MTCW

Hinde, Thomas . . . . **CLC 6, 11**
See also Chitty, Thomas Willes

Hindin, Nathan
See Bloch, Robert (Albert)

Hine, (William) Daryl 1936- . . . . **CLC 15**
See also CA 1-4R; CAAS 15; CANR 1, 20; DLB 60

Hinkson, Katharine Tynan
See Tynan, Katharine

Hinton, S(usan) E(loise) 1950- . . . . **CLC 30; DA**
See also AAYA 2; CA 81-84; CANR 32; CLR 3, 23; JRDA; MAICYA; MTCW; SATA 19, 58

Hippius, Zinaida . . . . **TCLC 9**
See also Gippius, Zinaida (Nikolayevna)

Hiraoka, Kimitake 1925-1970
See Mishima, Yukio
See also CA 97-100; 29-32R; MTCW

Hirsch, E(ric) D(onald), Jr. 1928-. . . **CLC 79**
See also CA 25-28R; CANR 27; DLB 67; MTCW

Hirsch, Edward 1950- . . . . **CLC 31, 50**
See also CA 104; CANR 20, 42; DLB 120

Hitchcock, Alfred (Joseph) 1899-1980 . . . . **CLC 16**
See also CA 97-100; SATA 27; SATA-Obit 24

Hitler, Adolf 1889-1945. . . . . **TCLC 53**
See also CA 117; 147

Hoagland, Edward 1932- . . . . **CLC 28**
See also CA 1-4R; CANR 2, 31; DLB 6; SATA 51

Hoban, Russell (Conwell) 1925- . . **CLC 7, 25**
See also CA 5-8R; CANR 23, 37; CLR 3; DLB 52; MAICYA; MTCW; SATA 1, 40, 78

Hobbs, Perry
See Blackmur, R(ichard) P(almer)

Hobson, Laura Z(ametkin) 1900-1986 . . . . **CLC 7, 25**
See also CA 17-20R; 118; DLB 28; SATA 52

Hochhuth, Rolf 1931-. . . . . **CLC 4, 11, 18**
See also CA 5-8R; CANR 33; DLB 124; MTCW

Hochman, Sandra 1936-. . . . . **CLC 3, 8**
See also CA 5-8R; DLB 5

Hochwaelder, Fritz 1911-1986. . . . . . **CLC 36**
See also CA 29-32R; 120; CANR 42; MTCW

Hochwalder, Fritz
See Hochwaelder, Fritz

Hocking, Mary (Eunice) 1921- . . . . . **CLC 13**
See also CA 101; CANR 18, 40

Hodgins, Jack 1938-. . . . . **CLC 23**
See also CA 93-96; DLB 60

Hodgson, William Hope 1877(?)-1918 . . . . **TCLC 13**
See also CA 111; DLB 70, 153

Hoffman, Alice 1952-. . . . . **CLC 51**
See also CA 77-80; CANR 34; MTCW

Hoffman, Daniel (Gerard) 1923- . . . . **CLC 6, 13, 23**
See also CA 1-4R; CANR 4; DLB 5

Hoffman, Stanley 1944-. . . . . **CLC 5**
See also CA 77-80

Hoffman, William M(oses) 1939- . . . **CLC 40**
See also CA 57-60; CANR 11

Hoffmann, E(rnst) T(heodor) A(madeus) 1776-1822 . . . . **NCLC 2; SSC 13**
See also DLB 90; SATA 27

Hofmann, Gert 1931-. . . . . **CLC 54**
See also CA 128

Hofmannsthal, Hugo von 1874-1929 . . . . **TCLC 11; DC 4**
See also CA 106; DLB 81, 118

Hogan, Linda 1947- . . . . **CLC 73**
See also CA 120; CANR 45; NNAL

Hogarth, Charles
See Creasey, John

Hogg, James 1770-1835. . . . . **NCLC 4**
See also DLB 93, 116

Holbach, Paul Henri Thiry Baron 1723-1789 . . . . **LC 14**

Holberg, Ludvig 1684-1754 . . . . **LC 6**

Holden, Ursula 1921-. . . . . **CLC 18**
See also CA 101; CAAS 8; CANR 22

Holderlin, (Johann Christian) Friedrich 1770-1843 . . . . **NCLC 16; PC 4**

Holdstock, Robert
See Holdstock, Robert P.

Holdstock, Robert P. 1948-. . . . . **CLC 39**
See also CA 131

Holland, Isabelle 1920- . . . . **CLC 21**
See also AAYA 11; CA 21-24R; CANR 10, 25, 47; JRDA; MAICYA; SATA 8, 70

Holland, Marcus
See Caldwell, (Janet Miriam) Taylor (Holland)

Hollander, John 1929-. . . . . . **CLC 2, 5, 8, 14**
See also CA 1-4R; CANR 1; DLB 5; SATA 13

Hollander, Paul
See Silverberg, Robert

Holleran, Andrew 1943(?)-. . . . . **CLC 38**
See also CA 144

Hollinghurst, Alan 1954- . . . . **CLC 55**
See also CA 114

Hollis, Jim
See Summers, Hollis (Spurgeon, Jr.)

Holmes, John
See Souster, (Holmes) Raymond

Holmes, John Clellon 1926-1988. . . . **CLC 56**
See also CA 9-12R; 125; CANR 4; DLB 16

Holmes, Oliver Wendell 1809-1894 . . . . **NCLC 14**
See also CDALB 1640-1865; DLB 1; SATA 34

Holmes, Raymond
See Souster, (Holmes) Raymond

Holt, Victoria
See Hibbert, Eleanor Alice Burford

Holub, Miroslav 1923- . . . . **CLC 4**
See also CA 21-24R; CANR 10

Homer c. 8th cent. B.C.- . . . . . **CMLC 1; DA**

Honig, Edwin 1919- . . . . **CLC 33**
See also CA 5-8R; CAAS 8; CANR 4, 45; DLB 5

Hood, Hugh (John Blagdon) 1928- . . . . **CLC 15, 28**
See also CA 49-52; CAAS 17; CANR 1, 33; DLB 53

Hood, Thomas 1799-1845. . . . . **NCLC 16**
See also DLB 96

Hooker, (Peter) Jeremy 1941- . . . . . . **CLC 43**
See also CA 77-80; CANR 22; DLB 40

Hope, A(lec) D(erwent) 1907- . . . . **CLC 3, 51**
See also CA 21-24R; CANR 33; MTCW

Hope, Brian
See Creasey, John

Hope, Christopher (David Tully) 1944- . . . . **CLC 52**
See also CA 106; CANR 47; SATA 62

Hopkins, Gerard Manley 1844-1889 . . . . **NCLC 17; DA; WLC**
See also CDBLB 1890-1914; DLB 35, 57

Hopkins, John (Richard) 1931- . . . . . . **CLC 4**
See also CA 85-88

Hopkins, Pauline Elizabeth 1859-1930 . . . . **TCLC 28; BLC**
See also BW 2; CA 141; DLB 50

Hopkinson, Francis 1737-1791 . . . . . . **LC 25**
See also DLB 31

Hopley-Woolrich, Cornell George 1903-1968
See Woolrich, Cornell
See also CA 13-14; CAP 1

Horatio
See Proust, (Valentin-Louis-George-Eugene-) Marcel

Horgan, Paul (George Vincent O'Shaughnessy) 1903-1995 . . . . **CLC 9, 53**
See also CA 13-16R; 147; CANR 9, 35; DLB 102; DLBY 85; MTCW; SATA 13

Horn, Peter
See Kuttner, Henry

Hornem, Horace Esq.
See Byron, George Gordon (Noel)

Hornung, E(rnest) W(illiam) 1866-1921 . . . . **TCLC 59**
See also CA 108; DLB 70

Horovitz, Israel (Arthur) 1939- . . . . . **CLC 56**
See also CA 33-36R; CANR 46; DLB 7

Horvath, Odon von
See Horvath, Oedoen von
See also DLB 85, 124

Horvath, Oedoen von 1901-1938. . . **TCLC 45**
See also Horvath, Odon von
See also CA 118

Horwitz, Julius 1920-1986. . . . . **CLC 14**
See also CA 9-12R; 119; CANR 12

Hospital, Janette Turner 1942- . . . . . **CLC 42**
See also CA 108; CANR 48

Hostos, E. M. de
See Hostos (y Bonilla), Eugenio Maria de

Hostos, Eugenio M. de
See Hostos (y Bonilla), Eugenio Maria de

Hostos, Eugenio Maria
See Hostos (y Bonilla), Eugenio Maria de

Hostos (y Bonilla), Eugenio Maria de 1839-1903 . . . . **TCLC 24**
See also CA 123; 131; HW

Houdini
See Lovecraft, H(oward) P(hillips)

Hougan, Carolyn 1943- . . . . **CLC 34**
See also CA 139

Household, Geoffrey (Edward West) 1900-1988 . . . . **CLC 11**
See also CA 77-80; 126; DLB 87; SATA 14; SATA-Obit 59

Housman, A(lfred) E(dward) 1859-1936 . . . . . . **TCLC 1, 10; DA; PC 2**
See also CA 104; 125; DLB 19; MTCW

Housman, Laurence 1865-1959 . . . . . **TCLC 7**
See also CA 106; DLB 10; SATA 25

Howard, Elizabeth Jane 1923- . . . **CLC 7, 29**
See also CA 5-8R; CANR 8

Howard, Maureen 1930- . . . . . **CLC 5, 14, 46**
See also CA 53-56; CANR 31; DLBY 83; MTCW

Howard, Richard 1929- . . . . . . **CLC 7, 10, 47**
See also AITN 1; CA 85-88; CANR 25; DLB 5

Howard, Robert Ervin 1906-1936 . . . **TCLC 8**
See also CA 105

Howard, Warren F.
See Pohl, Frederik

Howe, Fanny 1940- . . . . **CLC 47**
See also CA 117; SATA-Brief 52

Howe, Irving 1920-1993. . . . . **CLC 85**
See also CA 9-12R; 141; CANR 21; DLB 67; MTCW

Howe, Julia Ward 1819-1910 . . . . . **TCLC 21**
See also CA 117; DLB 1

Howe, Susan 1937- . . . . **CLC 72**
See also DLB 120

Howe, Tina 1937- . . . . **CLC 48**
See also CA 109

Howell, James 1594(?)-1666 . . . . **LC 13**
See also DLB 151

Howells, W. D.
See Howells, William Dean

Howells, William D.
See Howells, William Dean

Howells, William Dean 1837-1920 . . . . **TCLC 7, 17, 41**
See also CA 104; 134; CDALB 1865-1917; DLB 12, 64, 74, 79

Howes, Barbara 1914- . . . . **CLC 15**
See also CA 9-12R; CAAS 3; SATA 5

Hrabal, Bohumil 1914- . . . . **CLC 13, 67**
See also CA 106; CAAS 12

Hsun, Lu . . . . **TCLC 3; SSC 20**
See also Shu-Jen, Chou

Hubbard, L(afayette) Ron(ald) 1911-1986 . . . . **CLC 43**
See also CA 77-80; 118; CANR 22

Huch, Ricarda (Octavia) 1864-1947 . . . . **TCLC 13**
See also CA 111; DLB 66

Huddle, David 1942- . . . . **CLC 49**
See also CA 57-60; CAAS 20; DLB 130

Hudson, Jeffrey
See Crichton, (John) Michael

Hudson, W(illiam) H(enry) 1841-1922 . . . . **TCLC 29**
See also CA 115; DLB 98, 153; SATA 35

Hueffer, Ford Madox
See Ford, Ford Madox

Hughart, Barry 1934- . . . . **CLC 39**
See also CA 137

Hughes, Colin
See Creasey, John

Hughes, David (John) 1930- . . . . **CLC 48**
See also CA 116; 129; DLB 14

Hughes, (James) Langston 1902-1967 . . . . . **CLC 1, 5, 10, 15, 35, 44; BLC; DA; DC 3; PC 1; SSC 6; WLC**
See also AAYA 12; BW 1; CA 1-4R; 25-28R; CANR 1, 34; CDALB 1929-1941; CLR 17; DLB 4, 7, 48, 51, 86; JRDA; MAICYA; MTCW; SATA 4, 33

Hughes, Richard (Arthur Warren) 1900-1976 . . . . **CLC 1, 11**
See also CA 5-8R; 65-68; CANR 4; DLB 15; MTCW; SATA 8; SATA-Obit 25

Hughes, Ted 1930- . . . . **CLC 2, 4, 9, 14, 37; PC 7**
See also CA 1-4R; CANR 1, 33; CLR 3; DLB 40; MAICYA; MTCW; SATA 49; SATA-Brief 27

Hugo, Richard F(ranklin) 1923-1982 . . . . **CLC 6, 18, 32**
See also CA 49-52; 108; CANR 3; DLB 5

Hugo, Victor (Marie) 1802-1885 . . **NCLC 3, 10, 21; DA; WLC**
See also DLB 119; SATA 47

Huidobro, Vicente
See Huidobro Fernandez, Vicente Garcia

Huidobro Fernandez, Vicente Garcia 1893-1948 . . . . **TCLC 31**
See also CA 131; HW

Hulme, Keri 1947- . . . . **CLC 39**
See also CA 125

Hulme, T(homas) E(rnest) 1883-1917 . . . . **TCLC 21**
See also CA 117; DLB 19

Hume, David 1711-1776. . . . . **LC 7**
See also DLB 104

Humphrey, William 1924- . . . . **CLC 45**
See also CA 77-80; DLB 6

Humphreys, Emyr Owen 1919- . . . . . **CLC 47**
See also CA 5-8R; CANR 3, 24; DLB 15

Humphreys, Josephine 1945- . . . . **CLC 34, 57**
See also CA 121; 127

Hungerford, Pixie
See Brinsmead, H(esba) F(ay)

Hunt, E(verette) Howard, (Jr.)
1918- . . . . **CLC 3**
See also AITN 1; CA 45-48; CANR 2, 47

Hunt, Kyle
See Creasey, John

Hunt, (James Henry) Leigh
1784-1859 . . . . **NCLC 1**

Hunt, Marsha 1946- . . . . **CLC 70**
See also BW 2; CA 143

Hunt, Violet 1866-1942 . . . . **TCLC 53**

Hunter, E. Waldo
See Sturgeon, Theodore (Hamilton)

Hunter, Evan 1926- . . . . **CLC 11, 31**
See also CA 5-8R; CANR 5, 38; DLBY 82; MTCW; SATA 25

Hunter, Kristin (Eggleston) 1931- . . . **CLC 35**
See also AITN 1; BW 1; CA 13-16R; CANR 13; CLR 3; DLB 33; MAICYA; SAAS 10; SATA 12

Hunter, Mollie 1922- . . . . **CLC 21**
See also McIlwraith, Maureen Mollie Hunter
See also AAYA 13; CANR 37; CLR 25; JRDA; MAICYA; SAAS 7; SATA 54

Hunter, Robert (?)-1734 . . . . **LC 7**

Hurston, Zora Neale
1903-1960 . . . . **CLC 7, 30, 61; BLC; DA; SSC 4**
See also BW 1; CA 85-88; DLB 51, 86; MTCW

Huston, John (Marcellus)
1906-1987 . . . . **CLC 20**
See also CA 73-76; 123; CANR 34; DLB 26

Hustvedt, Siri 1955- . . . . **CLC 76**
See also CA 137

Hutten, Ulrich von 1488-1523 . . . . **LC 16**

Huxley, Aldous (Leonard)
1894-1963 . . . . . **CLC 1, 3, 4, 5, 8, 11, 18, 35, 79; DA; WLC**
See also AAYA 11; CA 85-88; CANR 44; CDBLB 1914-1945; DLB 36, 100; MTCW; SATA 63

Huysmans, Charles Marie Georges
1848-1907
See Huysmans, Joris-Karl
See also CA 104

Huysmans, Joris-Karl . . . . **TCLC 7**
See also Huysmans, Charles Marie Georges
See also DLB 123

Hwang, David Henry
1957- . . . . **CLC 55; DC 4**
See also CA 127; 132

Hyde, Anthony 1946- . . . . **CLC 42**
See also CA 136

Hyde, Margaret O(ldroyd) 1917- . . . **CLC 21**
See also CA 1-4R; CANR 1, 36; CLR 23; JRDA; MAICYA; SAAS 8; SATA 1, 42, 76

Hynes, James 1956(?)- . . . . **CLC 65**

Ian, Janis 1951- . . . . **CLC 21**
See also CA 105

Ibanez, Vicente Blasco
See Blasco Ibanez, Vicente

Ibarguengoitia, Jorge 1928-1983 . . . . **CLC 37**
See also CA 124; 113; HW

Ibsen, Henrik (Johan)
1828-1906 . . . . **TCLC 2, 8, 16, 37, 52; DA; DC 2; WLC**
See also CA 104; 141

Ibuse Masuji 1898-1993 . . . . **CLC 22**
See also CA 127; 141

Ichikawa, Kon 1915- . . . . **CLC 20**
See also CA 121

Idle, Eric 1943- . . . . **CLC 21**
See also Monty Python
See also CA 116; CANR 35

Ignatow, David 1914- . . . . . . **CLC 4, 7, 14, 40**
See also CA 9-12R; CAAS 3; CANR 31; DLB 5

Ihimaera, Witi 1944- . . . . **CLC 46**
See also CA 77-80

Ilf, Ilya . . . . **TCLC 21**
See also Fainzilberg, Ilya Arnoldovich

Immermann, Karl (Lebrecht)
1796-1840 . . . . **NCLC 4, 49**
See also DLB 133

Inclan, Ramon (Maria) del Valle
See Valle-Inclan, Ramon (Maria) del

Infante, G(uillermo) Cabrera
See Cabrera Infante, G(uillermo)

Ingalls, Rachel (Holmes) 1940- . . . . . **CLC 42**
See also CA 123; 127

Ingamells, Rex 1913-1955 . . . . **TCLC 35**

Inge, William Motter
1913-1973 . . . . **CLC 1, 8, 19**
See also CA 9-12R; CDALB 1941-1968; DLB 7; MTCW

Ingelow, Jean 1820-1897 . . . . **NCLC 39**
See also DLB 35; SATA 33

Ingram, Willis J.
See Harris, Mark

Innaurato, Albert (F.) 1948(?)- . . **CLC 21, 60**
See also CA 115; 122

Innes, Michael
See Stewart, J(ohn) I(nnes) M(ackintosh)

Ionesco, Eugene
1909-1994 . . . . **CLC 1, 4, 6, 9, 11, 15, 41, 86; DA; WLC**
See also CA 9-12R; 144; MTCW; SATA 7; SATA-Obit 79

Iqbal, Muhammad 1873-1938 . . . . . **TCLC 28**

Ireland, Patrick
See O'Doherty, Brian

Iron, Ralph
See Schreiner, Olive (Emilie Albertina)

Irving, John (Winslow)
1942- . . . . **CLC 13, 23, 38**
See also AAYA 8; BEST 89:3; CA 25-28R; CANR 28; DLB 6; DLBY 82; MTCW

Irving, Washington
1783-1859 . . . . **NCLC 2, 19; DA; SSC 2; WLC**
See also CDALB 1640-1865; DLB 3, 11, 30, 59, 73, 74; YABC 2

Irwin, P. K.
See Page, P(atricia) K(athleen)

Isaacs, Susan 1943- . . . . **CLC 32**
See also BEST 89:1; CA 89-92; CANR 20, 41; MTCW

Isherwood, Christopher (William Bradshaw)
1904-1986 . . . . **CLC 1, 9, 11, 14, 44**
See also CA 13-16R; 117; CANR 35; DLB 15; DLBY 86; MTCW

Ishiguro, Kazuo 1954- . . . . . . **CLC 27, 56, 59**
See also BEST 90:2; CA 120; MTCW

Ishikawa Takuboku
1886(?)-1912 . . . . **TCLC 15; PC 10**
See also CA 113

Iskander, Fazil 1929- . . . . **CLC 47**
See also CA 102

Ivan IV 1530-1584 . . . . **LC 17**

Ivanov, Vyacheslav Ivanovich
1866-1949 . . . . **TCLC 33**
See also CA 122

Ivask, Ivar Vidrik 1927-1992 . . . . **CLC 14**
See also CA 37-40R; 139; CANR 24

Jackson, Daniel
See Wingrove, David (John)

Jackson, Jesse 1908-1983 . . . . **CLC 12**
See also BW 1; CA 25-28R; 109; CANR 27; CLR 28; MAICYA; SATA 2, 29; SATA-Obit 48

Jackson, Laura (Riding) 1901-1991
See Riding, Laura
See also CA 65-68; 135; CANR 28; DLB 48

Jackson, Sam
See Trumbo, Dalton

Jackson, Sara
See Wingrove, David (John)

Jackson, Shirley
1919-1965 . . . . **CLC 11, 60, 87; DA; SSC 9; WLC**
See also AAYA 9; CA 1-4R; 25-28R; CANR 4; CDALB 1941-1968; DLB 6; SATA 2

Jacob, (Cyprien-)Max 1876-1944 . . . **TCLC 6**
See also CA 104

Jacobs, Jim 1942- . . . . **CLC 12**
See also CA 97-100

Jacobs, W(illiam) W(ymark)
1863-1943 . . . . **TCLC 22**
See also CA 121; DLB 135

Jacobsen, Jens Peter 1847-1885 . . **NCLC 34**

Jacobsen, Josephine 1908- . . . . **CLC 48**
See also CA 33-36R; CAAS 18; CANR 23, 48

Jacobson, Dan 1929- . . . . **CLC 4, 14**
See also CA 1-4R; CANR 2, 25; DLB 14; MTCW

Jacqueline
See Carpentier (y Valmont), Alejo

Jagger, Mick 1944- . . . . **CLC 17**

Jakes, John (William) 1932- . . . . **CLC 29**
See also BEST 89:4; CA 57-60; CANR 10, 43; DLBY 83; MTCW; SATA 62

James, Andrew
See Kirkup, James

Jones, John J.
See Lovecraft, H(oward) P(hillips)

Jones, LeRoi . . . . **CLC 1, 2, 3, 5, 10, 14**
See also Baraka, Amiri

Jones, Louis B. . . . . **CLC 65**
See also CA 141

Jones, Madison (Percy, Jr.) 1925- . . . **CLC 4**
See also CA 13-16R; CAAS 11; CANR 7; DLB 152

Jones, Mervyn 1922- . . . . **CLC 10, 52**
See also CA 45-48; CAAS 5; CANR 1; MTCW

Jones, Mick 1956(?)- . . . . **CLC 30**

Jones, Nettie (Pearl) 1941- . . . . **CLC 34**
See also BW 2; CA 137; CAAS 20

Jones, Preston 1936-1979 . . . . **CLC 10**
See also CA 73-76; 89-92; DLB 7

Jones, Robert F(rancis) 1934- . . . . **CLC 7**
See also CA 49-52; CANR 2

Jones, Rod 1953- . . . . **CLC 50**
See also CA 128

Jones, Terence Graham Parry
1942- . . . . **CLC 21**
See also Jones, Terry; Monty Python
See also CA 112; 116; CANR 35

Jones, Terry
See Jones, Terence Graham Parry
See also SATA 67; SATA-Brief 51

Jones, Thom 1945(?)- . . . . **CLC 81**

Jong, Erica 1942- . . . . . . **CLC 4, 6, 8, 18, 83**
See also AITN 1; BEST 90:2; CA 73-76; CANR 26; DLB 2, 5, 28, 152; MTCW

Jonson, Ben(jamin)
1572(?)-1637 . . . . **LC 6; DA; DC 4; WLC**
See also CDBLB Before 1660; DLB 62, 121

Jordan, June 1936- . . . . **CLC 5, 11, 23**
See also AAYA 2; BW 2; CA 33-36R; CANR 25; CLR 10; DLB 38; MAICYA; MTCW; SATA 4

Jordan, Pat(rick M.) 1941- . . . . **CLC 37**
See also CA 33-36R

Jorgensen, Ivar
See Ellison, Harlan (Jay)

Jorgenson, Ivar
See Silverberg, Robert

Josephus, Flavius c. 37-100 . . . . . . **CMLC 13**

Josipovici, Gabriel 1940- . . . . **CLC 6, 43**
See also CA 37-40R; CAAS 8; CANR 47; DLB 14

Joubert, Joseph 1754-1824 . . . . **NCLC 9**

Jouve, Pierre Jean 1887-1976 . . . . . . **CLC 47**
See also CA 65-68

Joyce, James (Augustine Aloysius)
1882-1941 . . . . **TCLC 3, 8, 16, 35, 52; DA; SSC 3; WLC**
See also CA 104; 126; CDBLB 1914-1945; DLB 10, 19, 36; MTCW

Jozsef, Attila 1905-1937. . . . . **TCLC 22**
See also CA 116

Juana Ines de la Cruz 1651(?)-1695 . . . **LC 5**

Judd, Cyril
See Kornbluth, C(yril) M.; Pohl, Frederik

Julian of Norwich 1342(?)-1416(?) . . . . **LC 6**
See also DLB 146

Juniper, Alex
See Hospital, Janette Turner

Just, Ward (Swift) 1935- . . . . **CLC 4, 27**
See also CA 25-28R; CANR 32

Justice, Donald (Rodney) 1925- . . **CLC 6, 19**
See also CA 5-8R; CANR 26; DLBY 83

Juvenal c. 55-c. 127 . . . . **CMLC 8**

Juvenis
See Bourne, Randolph S(illiman)

Kacew, Romain 1914-1980
See Gary, Romain
See also CA 108; 102

Kadare, Ismail 1936- . . . . **CLC 52**

Kadohata, Cynthia. . . . . **CLC 59**
See also CA 140

Kafka, Franz
1883-1924 . . . . **TCLC 2, 6, 13, 29, 47, 53; DA; SSC 5; WLC**
See also CA 105; 126; DLB 81; MTCW

Kahanovitsch, Pinkhes
See Der Nister

Kahn, Roger 1927- . . . . **CLC 30**
See also CA 25-28R; CANR 44; SATA 37

Kain, Saul
See Sassoon, Siegfried (Lorraine)

Kaiser, Georg 1878-1945 . . . . **TCLC 9**
See also CA 106; DLB 124

Kaletski, Alexander 1946- . . . . **CLC 39**
See also CA 118; 143

Kalidasa fl. c. 400- . . . . **CMLC 9**

Kallman, Chester (Simon)
1921-1975 . . . . **CLC 2**
See also CA 45-48; 53-56; CANR 3

Kaminsky, Melvin 1926-
See Brooks, Mel
See also CA 65-68; CANR 16

Kaminsky, Stuart M(elvin) 1934- . . . **CLC 59**
See also CA 73-76; CANR 29

Kane, Paul
See Simon, Paul

Kane, Wilson
See Bloch, Robert (Albert)

Kanin, Garson 1912-. . . . . **CLC 22**
See also AITN 1; CA 5-8R; CANR 7; DLB 7

Kaniuk, Yoram 1930-. . . . . **CLC 19**
See also CA 134

Kant, Immanuel 1724-1804 . . . . . . **NCLC 27**
See also DLB 94

Kantor, MacKinlay 1904-1977 . . . . . . **CLC 7**
See also CA 61-64; 73-76; DLB 9, 102

Kaplan, David Michael 1946- . . . . . . **CLC 50**

Kaplan, James 1951- . . . . **CLC 59**
See also CA 135

Karageorge, Michael
See Anderson, Poul (William)

Karamzin, Nikolai Mikhailovich
1766-1826 . . . . **NCLC 3**
See also DLB 150

Karapanou, Margarita 1946- . . . . **CLC 13**
See also CA 101

Karinthy, Frigyes 1887-1938 . . . . . . **TCLC 47**

Karl, Frederick R(obert) 1927- . . . . . **CLC 34**
See also CA 5-8R; CANR 3, 44

Kastel, Warren
See Silverberg, Robert

Kataev, Evgeny Petrovich 1903-1942
See Petrov, Evgeny
See also CA 120

Kataphusin
See Ruskin, John

Katz, Steve 1935- . . . . **CLC 47**
See also CA 25-28R; CAAS 14; CANR 12; DLBY 83

Kauffman, Janet 1945- . . . . **CLC 42**
See also CA 117; CANR 43; DLBY 86

Kaufman, Bob (Garnell)
1925-1986 . . . . **CLC 49**
See also BW 1; CA 41-44R; 118; CANR 22; DLB 16, 41

Kaufman, George S. 1889-1961 . . . . . **CLC 38**
See also CA 108; 93-96; DLB 7

Kaufman, Sue . . . . **CLC 3, 8**
See also Barondess, Sue K(aufman)

Kavafis, Konstantinos Petrou 1863-1933
See Cavafy, C(onstantine) P(eter)
See also CA 104

Kavan, Anna 1901-1968 . . . . . . **CLC 5, 13, 82**
See also CA 5-8R; CANR 6; MTCW

Kavanagh, Dan
See Barnes, Julian

Kavanagh, Patrick (Joseph)
1904-1967 . . . . **CLC 22**
See also CA 123; 25-28R; DLB 15, 20; MTCW

Kawabata, Yasunari
1899-1972 . . . . . **CLC 2, 5, 9, 18; SSC 17**
See also CA 93-96; 33-36R

Kaye, M(ary) M(argaret) 1909-. . . . . **CLC 28**
See also CA 89-92; CANR 24; MTCW; SATA 62

Kaye, Mollie
See Kaye, M(ary) M(argaret)

Kaye-Smith, Sheila 1887-1956. . . . . **TCLC 20**
See also CA 118; DLB 36

Kaymor, Patrice Maguilene
See Senghor, Leopold Sedar

Kazan, Elia 1909- . . . . **CLC 6, 16, 63**
See also CA 21-24R; CANR 32

Kazantzakis, Nikos
1883(?)-1957 . . . . **TCLC 2, 5, 33**
See also CA 105; 132; MTCW

Kazin, Alfred 1915- . . . . **CLC 34, 38**
See also CA 1-4R; CAAS 7; CANR 1, 45; DLB 67

Keane, Mary Nesta (Skrine) 1904-
See Keane, Molly
See also CA 108; 114

Keane, Molly. **CLC 31**
See also Keane, Mary Nesta (Skrine)

Keates, Jonathan 19(?)- . . . . **CLC 34**

Keaton, Buster 1895-1966 . . . . **CLC 20**

Keats, John
1795-1821 . . . **NCLC 8; DA; PC 1; WLC**
See also CDBLB 1789-1832; DLB 96, 110

Keene, Donald 1922- . . . . **CLC 34**
See also CA 1-4R; CANR 5

Keillor, Garrison . . . . **CLC 40**
See also Keillor, Gary (Edward)
See also AAYA 2; BEST 89:3; DLBY 87; SATA 58

Keillor, Gary (Edward) 1942-
See Keillor, Garrison
See also CA 111; 117; CANR 36; MTCW

Keith, Michael
See Hubbard, L(afayette) Ron(ald)

Keller, Gottfried 1819-1890 . . . . **NCLC 2**
See also DLB 129

Kellerman, Jonathan 1949- . . . . **CLC 44**
See also BEST 90:1; CA 106; CANR 29

Kelley, William Melvin 1937- . . . . . . **CLC 22**
See also BW 1; CA 77-80; CANR 27; DLB 33

Kellogg, Marjorie 1922- . . . . **CLC 2**
See also CA 81-84

Kellow, Kathleen
See Hibbert, Eleanor Alice Burford

Kelly, M(ilton) T(erry) 1947- . . . . **CLC 55**
See also CA 97-100; CANR 19, 43

Kelman, James 1946- . . . . **CLC 58, 86**

Kemal, Yashar 1923- . . . . **CLC 14, 29**
See also CA 89-92; CANR 44

Kemble, Fanny 1809-1893 . . . . **NCLC 18**
See also DLB 32

Kemelman, Harry 1908- . . . . **CLC 2**
See also AITN 1; CA 9-12R; CANR 6; DLB 28

Kempe, Margery 1373(?)-1440(?) . . . . . **LC 6**
See also DLB 146

Kempis, Thomas a 1380-1471 . . . . **LC 11**

Kendall, Henry 1839-1882 . . . . **NCLC 12**

Keneally, Thomas (Michael)
1935- . . . . . . **CLC 5, 8, 10, 14, 19, 27, 43**
See also CA 85-88; CANR 10; MTCW

Kennedy, Adrienne (Lita)
1931- . . . . **CLC 66; BLC; DC 5**
See also BW 2; CA 103; CAAS 20; CABS 3; CANR 26; DLB 38

Kennedy, John Pendleton
1795-1870 . . . . **NCLC 2**
See also DLB 3

Kennedy, Joseph Charles 1929-
See Kennedy, X. J.
See also CA 1-4R; CANR 4, 30, 40; SATA 14

Kennedy, William 1928- . . . **CLC 6, 28, 34, 53**
See also AAYA 1; CA 85-88; CANR 14, 31; DLB 143; DLBY 85; MTCW; SATA 57

Kennedy, X. J. . . . . **CLC 8, 42**
See also Kennedy, Joseph Charles
See also CAAS 9; CLR 27; DLB 5

Kenny, Maurice (Francis) 1929- . . . . **CLC 87**
See also CA 144; NNAL

Kent, Kelvin
See Kuttner, Henry

Kenton, Maxwell
See Southern, Terry

Kenyon, Robert O.
See Kuttner, Henry

Kerouac, Jack . . . . . **CLC 1, 2, 3, 5, 14, 29, 61**
See also Kerouac, Jean-Louis Lebris de
See also CDALB 1941-1968; DLB 2, 16; DLBD 3

Kerouac, Jean-Louis Lebris de 1922-1969
See Kerouac, Jack
See also AITN 1; CA 5-8R; 25-28R; CANR 26; DA; MTCW; WLC

Kerr, Jean 1923- . . . . **CLC 22**
See also CA 5-8R; CANR 7

Kerr, M. E. . . . . **CLC 12, 35**
See also Meaker, Marijane (Agnes)
See also AAYA 2; CLR 29; SAAS 1

Kerr, Robert . . . . **CLC 55**

Kerrigan, (Thomas) Anthony
1918- . . . . **CLC 4, 6**
See also CA 49-52; CAAS 11; CANR 4

Kerry, Lois
See Duncan, Lois

Kesey, Ken (Elton)
1935- . . . . . . **CLC 1, 3, 6, 11, 46, 64; DA; WLC**
See also CA 1-4R; CANR 22, 38; CDALB 1968-1988; DLB 2, 16; MTCW; SATA 66

Kesselring, Joseph (Otto)
1902-1967 . . . . **CLC 45**

Kessler, Jascha (Frederick) 1929- . . . . **CLC 4**
See also CA 17-20R; CANR 8, 48

Kettelkamp, Larry (Dale) 1933- . . . . **CLC 12**
See also CA 29-32R; CANR 16; SAAS 3; SATA 2

Keyber, Conny
See Fielding, Henry

Keyes, Daniel 1927- . . . . **CLC 80; DA**
See also CA 17-20R; CANR 10, 26; SATA 37

Khanshendel, Chiron
See Rose, Wendy

Khayyam, Omar
1048-1131 . . . . **CMLC 11; PC 8**

Kherdian, David 1931- . . . . **CLC 6, 9**
See also CA 21-24R; CAAS 2; CANR 39; CLR 24; JRDA; MAICYA; SATA 16, 74

Khlebnikov, Velimir . . . . **TCLC 20**
See also Khlebnikov, Viktor Vladimirovich

Khlebnikov, Viktor Vladimirovich 1885-1922
See Khlebnikov, Velimir
See also CA 117

Khodasevich, Vladislav (Felitsianovich)
1886-1939 . . . . **TCLC 15**
See also CA 115

Kielland, Alexander Lange
1849-1906 . . . . **TCLC 5**
See also CA 104

Kiely, Benedict 1919- . . . . **CLC 23, 43**
See also CA 1-4R; CANR 2; DLB 15

Kienzle, William X(avier) 1928- . . . . **CLC 25**
See also CA 93-96; CAAS 1; CANR 9, 31; MTCW

Kierkegaard, Soren 1813-1855 . . . . **NCLC 34**

Killens, John Oliver 1916-1987 . . . . . **CLC 10**
See also BW 2; CA 77-80; 123; CAAS 2; CANR 26; DLB 33

Killigrew, Anne 1660-1685 . . . . **LC 4**
See also DLB 131

Kim
See Simenon, Georges (Jacques Christian)

Kincaid, Jamaica 1949- . . . **CLC 43, 68; BLC**
See also AAYA 13; BW 2; CA 125; CANR 47

King, Francis (Henry) 1923- . . . . . **CLC 8, 53**
See also CA 1-4R; CANR 1, 33; DLB 15, 139; MTCW

King, Martin Luther, Jr.
1929-1968 . . . . **CLC 83; BLC; DA**
See also BW 2; CA 25-28; CANR 27, 44; CAP 2; MTCW; SATA 14

King, Stephen (Edwin)
1947- . . . . . . **CLC 12, 26, 37, 61; SSC 17**
See also AAYA 1; BEST 90:1; CA 61-64; CANR 1, 30; DLB 143; DLBY 80; JRDA; MTCW; SATA 9, 55

King, Steve
See King, Stephen (Edwin)

King, Thomas 1943- . . . . **CLC 89**
See also CA 144; NNAL

Kingman, Lee . . . . **CLC 17**
See also Natti, (Mary) Lee
See also SAAS 3; SATA 1, 67

Kingsley, Charles 1819-1875 . . . . . **NCLC 35**
See also DLB 21, 32; YABC 2

Kingsley, Sidney 1906-1995 . . . . **CLC 44**
See also CA 85-88; 147; DLB 7

Kingsolver, Barbara 1955- . . . . . . **CLC 55, 81**
See also CA 129; 134

Kingston, Maxine (Ting Ting) Hong
1940- . . . . **CLC 12, 19, 58**
See also AAYA 8; CA 69-72; CANR 13, 38; DLBY 80; MTCW; SATA 53

Kinnell, Galway
1927- . . . . **CLC 1, 2, 3, 5, 13, 29**
See also CA 9-12R; CANR 10, 34; DLB 5; DLBY 87; MTCW

Kinsella, Thomas 1928- . . . . **CLC 4, 19**
See also CA 17-20R; CANR 15; DLB 27; MTCW

Kinsella, W(illiam) P(atrick)
1935- . . . . **CLC 27, 43**
See also AAYA 7; CA 97-100; CAAS 7; CANR 21, 35; MTCW

Kipling, (Joseph) Rudyard
1865-1936 . . . . . . **TCLC 8, 17; DA; PC 3; SSC 5; WLC**
See also CA 105; 120; CANR 33; CDBLB 1890-1914; DLB 19, 34, 141; MAICYA; MTCW; YABC 2

Kirkup, James 1918- . . . . **CLC 1**
See also CA 1-4R; CAAS 4; CANR 2; DLB 27; SATA 12

Kirkwood, James 1930(?)-1989 . . . . . . **CLC 9**
See also AITN 2; CA 1-4R; 128; CANR 6, 40

Kis, Danilo 1935-1989 . . . . **CLC 57**
See also CA 109; 118; 129; MTCW

Kivi, Aleksis 1834-1872 . . . . **NCLC 30**

Kizer, Carolyn (Ashley)
1925- . . . . **CLC 15, 39, 80**
See also CA 65-68; CAAS 5; CANR 24; DLB 5

Klabund 1890-1928 . . . . **TCLC 44**
See also DLB 66

Klappert, Peter 1942- . . . . **CLC 57**
See also CA 33-36R; DLB 5

Klein, A(braham) M(oses)
1909-1972 . . . . **CLC 19**
See also CA 101; 37-40R; DLB 68

Klein, Norma 1938-1989 . . . . **CLC 30**
See also AAYA 2; CA 41-44R; 128; CANR 15, 37; CLR 2, 19; JRDA; MAICYA; SAAS 1; SATA 7, 57

Klein, T(heodore) E(ibon) D(onald)
1947- . . . . **CLC 34**
See also CA 119; CANR 44

Kleist, Heinrich von
1777-1811 . . . . **NCLC 2, 37**
See also DLB 90

Klima, Ivan 1931- . . . . **CLC 56**
See also CA 25-28R; CANR 17

Klimentov, Andrei Platonovich 1899-1951
See Platonov, Andrei
See also CA 108

Klinger, Friedrich Maximilian von
1752-1831 . . . . **NCLC 1**
See also DLB 94

Klopstock, Friedrich Gottlieb
1724-1803 . . . . **NCLC 11**
See also DLB 97

Knebel, Fletcher 1911-1993 . . . . **CLC 14**
See also AITN 1; CA 1-4R; 140; CAAS 3; CANR 1, 36; SATA 36; SATA-Obit 75

Knickerbocker, Diedrich
See Irving, Washington

Knight, Etheridge
1931-1991 . . . . **CLC 40; BLC**
See also BW 1; CA 21-24R; 133; CANR 23; DLB 41

Knight, Sarah Kemble 1666-1727 . . . . . **LC 7**
See also DLB 24

Knister, Raymond 1899-1932 . . . . . . **TCLC 56**
See also DLB 68

Knowles, John
1926- . . . . **CLC 1, 4, 10, 26; DA**
See also AAYA 10; CA 17-20R; CANR 40; CDALB 1968-1988; DLB 6; MTCW; SATA 8

Knox, Calvin M.
See Silverberg, Robert

Knye, Cassandra
See Disch, Thomas M(ichael)

Koch, C(hristopher) J(ohn) 1932- . . . **CLC 42**
See also CA 127

Koch, Christopher
See Koch, C(hristopher) J(ohn)

Koch, Kenneth 1925- . . . . **CLC 5, 8, 44**
See also CA 1-4R; CANR 6, 36; DLB 5; SATA 65

Kochanowski, Jan 1530-1584 . . . . **LC 10**

Kock, Charles Paul de
1794-1871 . . . . **NCLC 16**

Koda Shigeyuki 1867-1947
See Rohan, Koda
See also CA 121

Koestler, Arthur
1905-1983 . . . . **CLC 1, 3, 6, 8, 15, 33**
See also CA 1-4R; 109; CANR 1, 33; CDBLB 1945-1960; DLBY 83; MTCW

Kogawa, Joy Nozomi 1935- . . . . **CLC 78**
See also CA 101; CANR 19

Kohout, Pavel 1928- . . . . **CLC 13**
See also CA 45-48; CANR 3

Koizumi, Yakumo
See Hearn, (Patricio) Lafcadio (Tessima Carlos)

Kolmar, Gertrud 1894-1943 . . . . **TCLC 40**

Komunyakaa, Yusef 1947- . . . . **CLC 86**
See also CA 147; DLB 120

Konrad, George
See Konrad, Gyoergy

Konrad, Gyoergy 1933- . . . . . . **CLC 4, 10, 73**
See also CA 85-88

Konwicki, Tadeusz 1926- . . . . . **CLC 8, 28, 54**
See also CA 101; CAAS 9; CANR 39; MTCW

Koontz, Dean R(ay) 1945- . . . . **CLC 78**
See also AAYA 9; BEST 89:3, 90:2; CA 108; CANR 19, 36; MTCW

Kopit, Arthur (Lee) 1937- . . . . **CLC 1, 18, 33**
See also AITN 1; CA 81-84; CABS 3; DLB 7; MTCW

Kops, Bernard 1926- . . . . **CLC 4**
See also CA 5-8R; DLB 13

Kornbluth, C(yril) M. 1923-1958 . . . . **TCLC 8**
See also CA 105; DLB 8

Korolenko, V. G.
See Korolenko, Vladimir Galaktionovich

Korolenko, Vladimir
See Korolenko, Vladimir Galaktionovich

Korolenko, Vladimir G.
See Korolenko, Vladimir Galaktionovich

Korolenko, Vladimir Galaktionovich
1853-1921 . . . . **TCLC 22**
See also CA 121

Kosinski, Jerzy (Nikodem)
1933-1991 . . . . **CLC 1, 2, 3, 6, 10, 15, 53, 70**
See also CA 17-20R; 134; CANR 9, 46; DLB 2; DLBY 82; MTCW

Kostelanetz, Richard (Cory) 1940- . . **CLC 28**
See also CA 13-16R; CAAS 8; CANR 38

Kostrowitzki, Wilhelm Apollinaris de
1880-1918
See Apollinaire, Guillaume
See also CA 104

Kotlowitz, Robert 1924- . . . . **CLC 4**
See also CA 33-36R; CANR 36

Kotzebue, August (Friedrich Ferdinand) von
1761-1819 . . . . **NCLC 25**
See also DLB 94

Kotzwinkle, William 1938- . . . **CLC 5, 14, 35**
See also CA 45-48; CANR 3, 44; CLR 6; MAICYA; SATA 24, 70

Kozol, Jonathan 1936- . . . . **CLC 17**
See also CA 61-64; CANR 16, 45

Kozoll, Michael 1940(?)- . . . . **CLC 35**

Kramer, Kathryn 19(?)- . . . . **CLC 34**

Kramer, Larry 1935- . . . . **CLC 42**
See also CA 124; 126

Krasicki, Ignacy 1735-1801 . . . . **NCLC 8**

Krasinski, Zygmunt 1812-1859 . . . . **NCLC 4**

Kraus, Karl 1874-1936 . . . . **TCLC 5**
See also CA 104; DLB 118

Kreve (Mickevicius), Vincas
1882-1954 . . . . **TCLC 27**

Kristeva, Julia 1941- . . . . **CLC 77**

Kristofferson, Kris 1936- . . . . **CLC 26**
See also CA 104

Krizanc, John 1956- . . . . **CLC 57**

Krleza, Miroslav 1893-1981 . . . . **CLC 8**
See also CA 97-100; 105; DLB 147

Kroetsch, Robert 1927- . . . . . . **CLC 5, 23, 57**
See also CA 17-20R; CANR 8, 38; DLB 53; MTCW

Kroetz, Franz
See Kroetz, Franz Xaver

Kroetz, Franz Xaver 1946- . . . . **CLC 41**
See also CA 130

Kroker, Arthur 1945- . . . . **CLC 77**

Kropotkin, Peter (Aleksieevich)
1842-1921 . . . . **TCLC 36**
See also CA 119

Krotkov, Yuri 1917- . . . . **CLC 19**
See also CA 102

Krumb
See Crumb, R(obert)

Krumgold, Joseph (Quincy)
1908-1980 . . . . **CLC 12**
See also CA 9-12R; 101; CANR 7; MAICYA; SATA 1, 48; SATA-Obit 23

Krumwitz
See Crumb, R(obert)

Krutch, Joseph Wood 1893-1970 . . . . **CLC 24**
See also CA 1-4R; 25-28R; CANR 4; DLB 63

Krutzch, Gus
See Eliot, T(homas) S(tearns)

Krylov, Ivan Andreevich
1768(?)-1844 . . . . **NCLC 1**
See also DLB 150

Kubin, Alfred 1877-1959 . . . . **TCLC 23**
See also CA 112; DLB 81

Kubrick, Stanley 1928- . . . . **CLC 16**
See also CA 81-84; CANR 33; DLB 26

Kumin, Maxine (Winokur)
1925- . . . . **CLC 5, 13, 28**
See also AITN 2; CA 1-4R; CAAS 8; CANR 1, 21; DLB 5; MTCW; SATA 12

Kundera, Milan
1929- . . . . **CLC 4, 9, 19, 32, 68**
See also AAYA 2; CA 85-88; CANR 19; MTCW

Kunene, Mazisi (Raymond) 1930- . . . **CLC 85**
See also BW 1; CA 125; DLB 117

Kunitz, Stanley (Jasspon)
1905- . . . . **CLC 6, 11, 14**
See also CA 41-44R; CANR 26; DLB 48; MTCW

Kunze, Reiner 1933- . . . . **CLC 10**
See also CA 93-96; DLB 75

Kuprin, Aleksandr Ivanovich
1870-1938 . . . . **TCLC 5**
See also CA 104

Kureishi, Hanif 1954(?)- . . . . **CLC 64**
See also CA 139

Kurosawa, Akira 1910- . . . . **CLC 16**
See also AAYA 11; CA 101; CANR 46

Kushner, Tony 1957(?)- . . . . **CLC 81**
See also CA 144

Kuttner, Henry 1915-1958 . . . . **TCLC 10**
See also CA 107; DLB 8

Kuzma, Greg 1944- . . . . **CLC 7**
See also CA 33-36R

Kuzmin, Mikhail 1872(?)-1936 . . . . **TCLC 40**

Kyd, Thomas 1558-1594 . . . . **LC 22; DC 3**
See also DLB 62

Kyprianos, Iossif
See Samarakis, Antonis

La Bruyere, Jean de 1645-1696 . . . . . . **LC 17**

Lacan, Jacques (Marie Emile)
1901-1981 . . . . **CLC 75**
See also CA 121; 104

Laclos, Pierre Ambroise Francois Choderlos de 1741-1803 . . . . **NCLC 4**

Lacolere, Francois
See Aragon, Louis

La Colere, Francois
See Aragon, Louis

La Deshabilleuse
See Simenon, Georges (Jacques Christian)

Lady Gregory
See Gregory, Isabella Augusta (Persse)

Lady of Quality, A
See Bagnold, Enid

La Fayette, Marie (Madelaine Pioche de la Vergne Comtes 1634-1693 . . . . **LC 2**

Lafayette, Rene
See Hubbard, L(afayette) Ron(ald)

Laforgue, Jules
1860-1887 . . . . **NCLC 5; SSC 20**

Lagerkvist, Paer (Fabian)
1891-1974 . . . . **CLC 7, 10, 13, 54**
See also Lagerkvist, Par
See also CA 85-88; 49-52; MTCW

Lagerkvist, Par . . . . **SSC**
See also Lagerkvist, Paer (Fabian)

Lagerloef, Selma (Ottiliana Lovisa)
1858-1940 . . . . **TCLC 4, 36**
See also Lagerlof, Selma (Ottiliana Lovisa)
See also CA 108; SATA 15

Lagerlof, Selma (Ottiliana Lovisa)
See Lagerloef, Selma (Ottiliana Lovisa)
See also CLR 7; SATA 15

La Guma, (Justin) Alex(ander)
1925-1985 . . . . **CLC 19**
See also BW 1; CA 49-52; 118; CANR 25; DLB 117; MTCW

Laidlaw, A. K.
See Grieve, C(hristopher) M(urray)

Lainez, Manuel Mujica
See Mujica Lainez, Manuel
See also HW

Lamartine, Alphonse (Marie Louis Prat) de
1790-1869 . . . . **NCLC 11**

Lamb, Charles
1775-1834 . . . . **NCLC 10; DA; WLC**
See also CDBLB 1789-1832; DLB 93, 107; SATA 17

Lamb, Lady Caroline 1785-1828 . . **NCLC 38**
See also DLB 116

Lamming, George (William)
1927- . . . . **CLC 2, 4, 66; BLC**
See also BW 2; CA 85-88; CANR 26; DLB 125; MTCW

L'Amour, Louis (Dearborn)
1908-1988 . . . . **CLC 25, 55**
See also AITN 2; BEST 89:2; CA 1-4R; 125; CANR 3, 25, 40; DLBY 80; MTCW

Lampedusa, Giuseppe (Tomasi) di . . . **TCLC 13**
See also Tomasi di Lampedusa, Giuseppe

Lampman, Archibald 1861-1899 . . **NCLC 25**
See also DLB 92

Lancaster, Bruce 1896-1963 . . . . **CLC 36**
See also CA 9-10; CAP 1; SATA 9

Landau, Mark Alexandrovich
See Aldanov, Mark (Alexandrovich)

Landau-Aldanov, Mark Alexandrovich
See Aldanov, Mark (Alexandrovich)

Landis, John 1950- . . . . **CLC 26**
See also CA 112; 122

Landolfi, Tommaso 1908-1979 . . . **CLC 11, 49**
See also CA 127; 117

Landon, Letitia Elizabeth
1802-1838 . . . . **NCLC 15**
See also DLB 96

Landor, Walter Savage
1775-1864 . . . . **NCLC 14**
See also DLB 93, 107

Landwirth, Heinz 1927-
See Lind, Jakov
See also CA 9-12R; CANR 7

Lane, Patrick 1939- . . . . **CLC 25**
See also CA 97-100; DLB 53

Lang, Andrew 1844-1912 . . . . **TCLC 16**
See also CA 114; 137; DLB 98, 141; MAICYA; SATA 16

Lang, Fritz 1890-1976 . . . . **CLC 20**
See also CA 77-80; 69-72; CANR 30

Lange, John
See Crichton, (John) Michael

Langer, Elinor 1939- . . . . **CLC 34**
See also CA 121

Langland, William
1330(?)-1400(?) . . . . **LC 19; DA**
See also DLB 146

Langstaff, Launcelot
See Irving, Washington

Lanier, Sidney 1842-1881 . . . . **NCLC 6**
See also DLB 64; MAICYA; SATA 18

Lanyer, Aemilia 1569-1645 . . . . . . **LC 10, 30**
See also DLB 121

Lao Tzu . . . . **CMLC 7**

Lapine, James (Elliot) 1949- . . . . **CLC 39**
See also CA 123; 130

Larbaud, Valery (Nicolas)
1881-1957 . . . . **TCLC 9**
See also CA 106

Lardner, Ring
See Lardner, Ring(gold) W(ilmer)

Lardner, Ring W., Jr.
See Lardner, Ring(gold) W(ilmer)

Lardner, Ring(gold) W(ilmer)
1885-1933 . . . . **TCLC 2, 14**
See also CA 104; 131; CDALB 1917-1929; DLB 11, 25, 86; MTCW

Laredo, Betty
See Codrescu, Andrei

Larkin, Maia
See Wojciechowska, Maia (Teresa)

Larkin, Philip (Arthur)
1922-1985 . . . . **CLC 3, 5, 8, 9, 13, 18, 33, 39, 64**
See also CA 5-8R; 117; CANR 24; CDBLB 1960 to Present; DLB 27; MTCW

Larra (y Sanchez de Castro), Mariano Jose de
1809-1837 . . . . **NCLC 17**

Larsen, Eric 1941- . . . . **CLC 55**
See also CA 132

Larsen, Nella 1891-1964 . . . . . **CLC 37; BLC**
See also BW 1; CA 125; DLB 51

Larson, Charles R(aymond) 1938- . . . **CLC 31**
See also CA 53-56; CANR 4

Lasker-Schueler, Else 1869-1945 . . **TCLC 57**
See also DLB 66, 124

Latham, Jean Lee 1902- . . . . **CLC 12**
See also AITN 1; CA 5-8R; CANR 7; MAICYA; SATA 2, 68

Latham, Mavis
See Clark, Mavis Thorpe

Lathen, Emma . . . . **CLC 2**
See also Hennissart, Martha; Latsis, Mary J(ane)

Lathrop, Francis
See Leiber, Fritz (Reuter, Jr.)

Latsis, Mary J(ane)
See Lathen, Emma
See also CA 85-88

Lattimore, Richmond (Alexander)
1906-1984 . . . . **CLC 3**
See also CA 1-4R; 112; CANR 1

Laughlin, James 1914- . . . . **CLC 49**
See also CA 21-24R; CANR 9, 47; DLB 48

Laurence, (Jean) Margaret (Wemyss)
1926-1987 . . **CLC 3, 6, 13, 50, 62; SSC 7**
See also CA 5-8R; 121; CANR 33; DLB 53; MTCW; SATA-Obit 50

Laurent, Antoine 1952- . . . . **CLC 50**

Lauscher, Hermann
See Hesse, Hermann

Lautreamont, Comte de
1846-1870 . . . . **NCLC 12; SSC 14**

Laverty, Donald
See Blish, James (Benjamin)

Lavin, Mary 1912- . . . . . . **CLC 4, 18; SSC 4**
See also CA 9-12R; CANR 33; DLB 15; MTCW

Lavond, Paul Dennis
See Kornbluth, C(yril) M.; Pohl, Frederik

Lawler, Raymond Evenor 1922- . . . . **CLC 58**
See also CA 103

Lawrence, D(avid) H(erbert Richards)
1885-1930 . . . . **TCLC 2, 9, 16, 33, 48; DA; SSC 4, 19; WLC**
See also CA 104; 121; CDBLB 1914-1945; DLB 10, 19, 36, 98; MTCW

Lawrence, T(homas) E(dward)
1888-1935 . . . . **TCLC 18**
See also Dale, Colin
See also CA 115

Lawrence of Arabia
See Lawrence, T(homas) E(dward)

Lawson, Henry (Archibald Hertzberg)
1867-1922 . . . . **TCLC 27; SSC 18**
See also CA 120

Lawton, Dennis
See Faust, Frederick (Schiller)

Laxness, Halldor . . . . **CLC 25**
See also Gudjonsson, Halldor Kiljan

Layamon fl. c. 1200- . . . . **CMLC 10**
See also DLB 146

Laye, Camara 1928-1980 . . . **CLC 4, 38; BLC**
See also BW 1; CA 85-88; 97-100; CANR 25; MTCW

Layton, Irving (Peter) 1912- . . . . . **CLC 2, 15**
See also CA 1-4R; CANR 2, 33, 43; DLB 88; MTCW

Lazarus, Emma 1849-1887. . . . . **NCLC 8**

Lazarus, Felix
See Cable, George Washington

Lazarus, Henry
See Slavitt, David R(ytman)

Lea, Joan
See Neufeld, John (Arthur)

Leacock, Stephen (Butler)
1869-1944 . . . . **TCLC 2**
See also CA 104; 141; DLB 92

Lear, Edward 1812-1888 . . . . **NCLC 3**
See also CLR 1; DLB 32; MAICYA; SATA 18

Lear, Norman (Milton) 1922- . . . . . . **CLC 12**
See also CA 73-76

Leavis, F(rank) R(aymond)
1895-1978 . . . . **CLC 24**
See also CA 21-24R; 77-80; CANR 44; MTCW

Leavitt, David 1961- . . . . **CLC 34**
See also CA 116; 122; DLB 130

Leblanc, Maurice (Marie Emile)
1864-1941 . . . . **TCLC 49**
See also CA 110

Lebowitz, Fran(ces Ann)
1951(?)- . . . . **CLC 11, 36**
See also CA 81-84; CANR 14; MTCW

Lebrecht, Peter
See Tieck, (Johann) Ludwig

le Carre, John . . . . **CLC 3, 5, 9, 15, 28**
See also Cornwell, David (John Moore)
See also BEST 89:4; CDBLB 1960 to Present; DLB 87

Le Clezio, J(ean) M(arie) G(ustave)
1940- . . . . **CLC 31**
See also CA 116; 128; DLB 83

Leconte de Lisle, Charles-Marie-Rene
1818-1894 . . . . **NCLC 29**

Le Coq, Monsieur
See Simenon, Georges (Jacques Christian)

Leduc, Violette 1907-1972 . . . . **CLC 22**
See also CA 13-14; 33-36R; CAP 1

Ledwidge, Francis 1887(?)-1917 . . . **TCLC 23**
See also CA 123; DLB 20

Lee, Andrea 1953- . . . . **CLC 36; BLC**
See also BW 1; CA 125

Lee, Andrew
See Auchincloss, Louis (Stanton)

Lee, Don L. . . . . **CLC 2**
See also Madhubuti, Haki R.

Lee, George W(ashington)
1894-1976 . . . . **CLC 52; BLC**
See also BW 1; CA 125; DLB 51

Lee, (Nelle) Harper
1926- . . . . **CLC 12, 60; DA; WLC**
See also AAYA 13; CA 13-16R; CDALB 1941-1968; DLB 6; MTCW; SATA 11

Lee, Helen Elaine 1959(?)- . . . . **CLC 86**

Lee, Julian
See Latham, Jean Lee

Lee, Larry
See Lee, Lawrence

Lee, Lawrence 1941-1990. . . . . **CLC 34**
See also CA 131; CANR 43

Lee, Manfred B(ennington)
1905-1971 . . . . **CLC 11**
See also Queen, Ellery
See also CA 1-4R; 29-32R; CANR 2; DLB 137

Lee, Stan 1922- . . . . **CLC 17**
See also AAYA 5; CA 108; 111

Lee, Tanith 1947- . . . . **CLC 46**
See also CA 37-40R; SATA 8

Lee, Vernon . . . . **TCLC 5**
See also Paget, Violet
See also DLB 57, 153

Lee, William
See Burroughs, William S(eward)

Lee, Willy
See Burroughs, William S(eward)

Lee-Hamilton, Eugene (Jacob)
1845-1907 . . . . **TCLC 22**
See also CA 117

Leet, Judith 1935- . . . . **CLC 11**

Le Fanu, Joseph Sheridan
1814-1873 . . . . **NCLC 9; SSC 14**
See also DLB 21, 70

Leffland, Ella 1931- . . . . **CLC 19**
See also CA 29-32R; CANR 35; DLBY 84; SATA 65

Leger, Alexis
See Leger, (Marie-Rene Auguste) Alexis Saint-Leger

Leger, (Marie-Rene Auguste) Alexis Saint-Leger 1887-1975. . . . . **CLC 11**
See also Perse, St.-John
See also CA 13-16R; 61-64; CANR 43; MTCW

Leger, Saintleger
See Leger, (Marie-Rene Auguste) Alexis Saint-Leger

Le Guin, Ursula K(roeber)
1929- . . . . **CLC 8, 13, 22, 45, 71; SSC 12**
See also AAYA 9; AITN 1; CA 21-24R; CANR 9, 32; CDALB 1968-1988; CLR 3, 28; DLB 8, 52; JRDA; MAICYA; MTCW; SATA 4, 52

Lehmann, Rosamond (Nina)
1901-1990 . . . . **CLC 5**
See also CA 77-80; 131; CANR 8; DLB 15

Leiber, Fritz (Reuter, Jr.)
1910-1992 . . . . **CLC 25**
See also CA 45-48; 139; CANR 2, 40; DLB 8; MTCW; SATA 45; SATA-Obit 73

Leimbach, Martha 1963-
See Leimbach, Marti
See also CA 130

Leimbach, Marti . . . . **CLC 65**
See also Leimbach, Martha

Leino, Eino . . . . **TCLC 24**
See also Loennbohm, Armas Eino Leopold

Leiris, Michel (Julien) 1901-1990 . . . **CLC 61**
See also CA 119; 128; 132

Leithauser, Brad 1953- . . . . **CLC 27**
See also CA 107; CANR 27; DLB 120

Lelchuk, Alan 1938- . . . . **CLC 5**
See also CA 45-48; CAAS 20; CANR 1

Lem, Stanislaw 1921- . . . . **CLC 8, 15, 40**
See also CA 105; CAAS 1; CANR 32; MTCW

Lemann, Nancy 1956- . . . . **CLC 39**
See also CA 118; 136

Lemonnier, (Antoine Louis) Camille
1844-1913 . . . . **TCLC 22**
See also CA 121

Lenau, Nikolaus 1802-1850 . . . . . . **NCLC 16**

L'Engle, Madeleine (Camp Franklin)
1918- . . . . **CLC 12**
See also AAYA 1; AITN 2; CA 1-4R; CANR 3, 21, 39; CLR 1, 14; DLB 52; JRDA; MAICYA; MTCW; SAAS 15; SATA 1, 27, 75

Lengyel, Jozsef 1896-1975. . . . . **CLC 7**
See also CA 85-88; 57-60

Lennon, John (Ono)
1940-1980 . . . . **CLC 12, 35**
See also CA 102

Lennox, Charlotte Ramsay
1729(?)-1804 . . . . **NCLC 23**
See also DLB 39

Lentricchia, Frank (Jr.) 1940- . . . . . . **CLC 34**
See also CA 25-28R; CANR 19

Lenz, Siegfried 1926- . . . . **CLC 27**
See also CA 89-92; DLB 75

Author Index

Lively, Penelope (Margaret) 1933- . . . . **CLC 32, 50**
See also CA 41-44R; CANR 29; CLR 7; DLB 14; JRDA; MAICYA; MTCW; SATA 7, 60

Livesay, Dorothy (Kathleen) 1909- . . . . **CLC 4, 15, 79**
See also AITN 2; CA 25-28R; CAAS 8; CANR 36; DLB 68; MTCW

Livy c. 59B.C.-c. 17 . . . . **CMLC 11**

Lizardi, Jose Joaquin Fernandez de 1776-1827 . . . . **NCLC 30**

Llewellyn, Richard
See Llewellyn Lloyd, Richard Dafydd Vivian
See also DLB 15

Llewellyn Lloyd, Richard Dafydd Vivian 1906-1983 . . . . **CLC 7, 80**
See also Llewellyn, Richard
See also CA 53-56; 111; CANR 7; SATA 11; SATA-Obit 37

Llosa, (Jorge) Mario (Pedro) Vargas
See Vargas Llosa, (Jorge) Mario (Pedro)

Lloyd Webber, Andrew 1948-
See Webber, Andrew Lloyd
See also AAYA 1; CA 116; SATA 56

Llull, Ramon c. 1235-c. 1316. . . . . **CMLC 12**

Locke, Alain (Le Roy) 1886-1954 . . . . **TCLC 43**
See also BW 1; CA 106; 124; DLB 51

Locke, John 1632-1704 . . . . **LC 7**
See also DLB 101

Locke-Elliott, Sumner
See Elliott, Sumner Locke

Lockhart, John Gibson 1794-1854 . . . . **NCLC 6**
See also DLB 110, 116, 144

Lodge, David (John) 1935-. . . . . **CLC 36**
See also BEST 90:1; CA 17-20R; CANR 19; DLB 14; MTCW

Loennbohm, Armas Eino Leopold 1878-1926
See Leino, Eino
See also CA 123

Loewinsohn, Ron(ald William) 1937- . . . . **CLC 52**
See also CA 25-28R

Logan, Jake
See Smith, Martin Cruz

Logan, John (Burton) 1923-1987. . . . . **CLC 5**
See also CA 77-80; 124; CANR 45; DLB 5

Lo Kuan-chung 1330(?)-1400(?). . . . . . **LC 12**

Lombard, Nap
See Johnson, Pamela Hansford

London, Jack. . **TCLC 9, 15, 39; SSC 4; WLC**
See also London, John Griffith
See also AAYA 13; AITN 2; CDALB 1865-1917; DLB 8, 12, 78; SATA 18

London, John Griffith 1876-1916
See London, Jack
See also CA 110; 119; DA; JRDA; MAICYA; MTCW

Long, Emmett
See Leonard, Elmore (John, Jr.)

Longbaugh, Harry
See Goldman, William (W.)

Longfellow, Henry Wadsworth 1807-1882 . . . . **NCLC 2, 45; DA**
See also CDALB 1640-1865; DLB 1, 59; SATA 19

Longley, Michael 1939- . . . . **CLC 29**
See also CA 102; DLB 40

Longus fl. c. 2nd cent. - . . . . **CMLC 7**

Longway, A. Hugh
See Lang, Andrew

Lopate, Phillip 1943- . . . . **CLC 29**
See also CA 97-100; DLBY 80

Lopez Portillo (y Pacheco), Jose 1920- . . . . **CLC 46**
See also CA 129; HW

Lopez y Fuentes, Gregorio 1897(?)-1966 . . . . **CLC 32**
See also CA 131; HW

Lorca, Federico Garcia
See Garcia Lorca, Federico

Lord, Bette Bao 1938- . . . . **CLC 23**
See also BEST 90:3; CA 107; CANR 41; SATA 58

Lord Auch
See Bataille, Georges

Lord Byron
See Byron, George Gordon (Noel)

Lorde, Audre (Geraldine) 1934-1992 . . . . **CLC 18, 71; BLC; PC 12**
See also BW 1; CA 25-28R; 142; CANR 16, 26, 46; DLB 41; MTCW

Lord Jeffrey
See Jeffrey, Francis

Lorenzo, Heberto Padilla
See Padilla (Lorenzo), Heberto

Loris
See Hofmannsthal, Hugo von

Loti, Pierre . . . . **TCLC 11**
See also Viaud, (Louis Marie) Julien
See also DLB 123

Louie, David Wong 1954- . . . . **CLC 70**
See also CA 139

Louis, Father M.
See Merton, Thomas

Lovecraft, H(oward) P(hillips) 1890-1937 . . . . **TCLC 4, 22; SSC 3**
See also AAYA 14; CA 104; 133; MTCW

Lovelace, Earl 1935-. . . . . **CLC 51**
See also BW 2; CA 77-80; CANR 41; DLB 125; MTCW

Lovelace, Richard 1618-1657. . . . . **LC 24**
See also DLB 131

Lowell, Amy 1874-1925 . . **TCLC 1, 8; PC 12**
See also CA 104; DLB 54, 140

Lowell, James Russell 1819-1891 . . **NCLC 2**
See also CDALB 1640-1865; DLB 1, 11, 64, 79

Lowell, Robert (Traill Spence, Jr.) 1917-1977 . . . **CLC 1, 2, 3, 4, 5, 8, 9, 11, 15, 37; DA; PC 3; WLC**
See also CA 9-12R; 73-76; CABS 2; CANR 26; DLB 5; MTCW

Lowndes, Marie Adelaide (Belloc) 1868-1947 . . . . **TCLC 12**
See also CA 107; DLB 70

Lowry, (Clarence) Malcolm 1909-1957 . . . . **TCLC 6, 40**
See also CA 105; 131; CDBLB 1945-1960; DLB 15; MTCW

Lowry, Mina Gertrude 1882-1966
See Loy, Mina
See also CA 113

Loxsmith, John
See Brunner, John (Kilian Houston)

Loy, Mina . . . . **CLC 28**
See also Lowry, Mina Gertrude
See also DLB 4, 54

Loyson-Bridet
See Schwob, (Mayer Andre) Marcel

Lucas, Craig 1951- . . . . **CLC 64**
See also CA 137

Lucas, George 1944-. . . . . **CLC 16**
See also AAYA 1; CA 77-80; CANR 30; SATA 56

Lucas, Hans
See Godard, Jean-Luc

Lucas, Victoria
See Plath, Sylvia

Ludlam, Charles 1943-1987 . . . . . **CLC 46, 50**
See also CA 85-88; 122

Ludlum, Robert 1927- . . . . **CLC 22, 43**
See also AAYA 10; BEST 89:1, 90:3; CA 33-36R; CANR 25, 41; DLBY 82; MTCW

Ludwig, Ken. . . . . **CLC 60**

Ludwig, Otto 1813-1865. . . . . **NCLC 4**
See also DLB 129

Lugones, Leopoldo 1874-1938 . . . . . **TCLC 15**
See also CA 116; 131; HW

Lu Hsun 1881-1936 . . . . **TCLC 3**

Lukacs, George . . . . **CLC 24**
See also Lukacs, Gyorgy (Szegeny von)

Lukacs, Gyorgy (Szegeny von) 1885-1971
See Lukacs, George
See also CA 101; 29-32R

Luke, Peter (Ambrose Cyprian) 1919-1995 . . . . **CLC 38**
See also CA 81-84; 147; DLB 13

Lunar, Dennis
See Mungo, Raymond

Lurie, Alison 1926-. . . . . **CLC 4, 5, 18, 39**
See also CA 1-4R; CANR 2, 17; DLB 2; MTCW; SATA 46

Lustig, Arnost 1926-. . . . . **CLC 56**
See also AAYA 3; CA 69-72; CANR 47; SATA 56

Luther, Martin 1483-1546 . . . . **LC 9**

Luzi, Mario 1914-. . . . . **CLC 13**
See also CA 61-64; CANR 9; DLB 128

Lynch, B. Suarez
See Bioy Casares, Adolfo; Borges, Jorge Luis

Lynch, David (K.) 1946-. . . . . **CLC 66**
See also CA 124; 129

Lynch, James
See Andreyev, Leonid (Nikolaevich)

Lynch Davis, B.
See Bioy Casares, Adolfo; Borges, Jorge Luis

Lyndsay, Sir David 1490-1555 ...... **LC 20**

Lynn, Kenneth S(chuyler) 1923- .... **CLC 50**
See also CA 1-4R; CANR 3, 27

Lynx
See West, Rebecca

Lyons, Marcus
See Blish, James (Benjamin)

Lyre, Pinchbeck
See Sassoon, Siegfried (Lorraine)

Lytle, Andrew (Nelson) 1902- ...... **CLC 22**
See also CA 9-12R; DLB 6

Lyttelton, George 1709-1773 .... **LC 10**

Maas, Peter 1929- .... **CLC 29**
See also CA 93-96

Macaulay, Rose 1881-1958 ..... **TCLC 7, 44**
See also CA 104; DLB 36

Macaulay, Thomas Babington
1800-1859 .... **NCLC 42**
See also CDBLB 1832-1890; DLB 32, 55

MacBeth, George (Mann)
1932-1992 .... **CLC 2, 5, 9**
See also CA 25-28R; 136; DLB 40; MTCW; SATA 4; SATA-Obit 70

MacCaig, Norman (Alexander)
1910- .... **CLC 36**
See also CA 9-12R; CANR 3, 34; DLB 27

MacCarthy, (Sir Charles Otto) Desmond
1877-1952 .... **TCLC 36**

MacDiarmid, Hugh
.... **CLC 2, 4, 11, 19, 63; PC 9**
See also Grieve, C(hristopher) M(urray)
See also CDBLB 1945-1960; DLB 20

MacDonald, Anson
See Heinlein, Robert A(nson)

Macdonald, Cynthia 1928- ...... **CLC 13, 19**
See also CA 49-52; CANR 4, 44; DLB 105

MacDonald, George 1824-1905 ..... **TCLC 9**
See also CA 106; 137; DLB 18; MAICYA; SATA 33

Macdonald, John
See Millar, Kenneth

MacDonald, John D(ann)
1916-1986 .... **CLC 3, 27, 44**
See also CA 1-4R; 121; CANR 1, 19; DLB 8; DLBY 86; MTCW

Macdonald, John Ross
See Millar, Kenneth

Macdonald, Ross ..... **CLC 1, 2, 3, 14, 34, 41**
See also Millar, Kenneth
See also DLBD 6

MacDougal, John
See Blish, James (Benjamin)

MacEwen, Gwendolyn (Margaret)
1941-1987 .... **CLC 13, 55**
See also CA 9-12R; 124; CANR 7, 22; DLB 53; SATA 50; SATA-Obit 55

Macha, Karel Hynek 1810-1846 .. **NCLC 46**

Machado (y Ruiz), Antonio
1875-1939 .... **TCLC 3**
See also CA 104; DLB 108

Machado de Assis, Joaquim Maria
1839-1908 .... **TCLC 10; BLC**
See also CA 107

Machen, Arthur .... **TCLC 4; SSC 20**
See also Jones, Arthur Llewellyn
See also DLB 36

Machiavelli, Niccolo 1469-1527 .. **LC 8; DA**

MacInnes, Colin 1914-1976 ...... **CLC 4, 23**
See also CA 69-72; 65-68; CANR 21; DLB 14; MTCW

MacInnes, Helen (Clark)
1907-1985 .... **CLC 27, 39**
See also CA 1-4R; 117; CANR 1, 28; DLB 87; MTCW; SATA 22; SATA-Obit 44

Mackay, Mary 1855-1924
See Corelli, Marie
See also CA 118

Mackenzie, Compton (Edward Montague)
1883-1972 .... **CLC 18**
See also CA 21-22; 37-40R; CAP 2; DLB 34, 100

Mackenzie, Henry 1745-1831 .... **NCLC 41**
See also DLB 39

Mackintosh, Elizabeth 1896(?)-1952
See Tey, Josephine
See also CA 110

MacLaren, James
See Grieve, C(hristopher) M(urray)

Mac Laverty, Bernard 1942- .... **CLC 31**
See also CA 116; 118; CANR 43

MacLean, Alistair (Stuart)
1922-1987 .... **CLC 3, 13, 50, 63**
See also CA 57-60; 121; CANR 28; MTCW; SATA 23; SATA-Obit 50

Maclean, Norman (Fitzroy)
1902-1990 .... **CLC 78; SSC 13**
See also CA 102; 132

MacLeish, Archibald
1892-1982 .... **CLC 3, 8, 14, 68**
See also CA 9-12R; 106; CANR 33; DLB 4, 7, 45; DLBY 82; MTCW

MacLennan, (John) Hugh
1907-1990 .... **CLC 2, 14**
See also CA 5-8R; 142; CANR 33; DLB 68; MTCW

MacLeod, Alistair 1936- .... **CLC 56**
See also CA 123; DLB 60

MacNeice, (Frederick) Louis
1907-1963 .... **CLC 1, 4, 10, 53**
See also CA 85-88; DLB 10, 20; MTCW

MacNeill, Dand
See Fraser, George MacDonald

Macpherson, James 1736-1796 ...... **LC 29**
See also DLB 109

Macpherson, (Jean) Jay 1931- ...... **CLC 14**
See also CA 5-8R; DLB 53

MacShane, Frank 1927- .... **CLC 39**
See also CA 9-12R; CANR 3, 33; DLB 111

Macumber, Mari
See Sandoz, Mari(e Susette)

Madach, Imre 1823-1864 .... **NCLC 19**

Madden, (Jerry) David 1933- .... **CLC 5, 15**
See also CA 1-4R; CAAS 3; CANR 4, 45; DLB 6; MTCW

Maddern, Al(an)
See Ellison, Harlan (Jay)

Madhubuti, Haki R.
1942- .... **CLC 6, 73; BLC; PC 5**
See also Lee, Don L.
See also BW 2; CA 73-76; CANR 24; DLB 5, 41; DLBD 8

Maepenn, Hugh
See Kuttner, Henry

Maepenn, K. H.
See Kuttner, Henry

Maeterlinck, Maurice 1862-1949 ... **TCLC 3**
See also CA 104; 136; SATA 66

Maginn, William 1794-1842 .... **NCLC 8**
See also DLB 110

Mahapatra, Jayanta 1928- .... **CLC 33**
See also CA 73-76; CAAS 9; CANR 15, 33

Mahfouz, Naguib (Abdel Aziz Al-Sabilgi)
1911(?)-
See Mahfuz, Najib
See also BEST 89:2; CA 128; MTCW

Mahfuz, Najib .... **CLC 52, 55**
See also Mahfouz, Naguib (Abdel Aziz Al-Sabilgi)
See also DLBY 88

Mahon, Derek 1941- .... **CLC 27**
See also CA 113; 128; DLB 40

Mailer, Norman
1923- ...... **CLC 1, 2, 3, 4, 5, 8, 11, 14, 28, 39, 74; DA**
See also AITN 2; CA 9-12R; CABS 1; CANR 28; CDALB 1968-1988; DLB 2, 16, 28; DLBD 3; DLBY 80, 83; MTCW

Maillet, Antonine 1929- .... **CLC 54**
See also CA 115; 120; CANR 46; DLB 60

Mais, Roger 1905-1955 .... **TCLC 8**
See also BW 1; CA 105; 124; DLB 125; MTCW

Maistre, Joseph de 1753-1821 .... **NCLC 37**

Maitland, Sara (Louise) 1950- ...... **CLC 49**
See also CA 69-72; CANR 13

Major, Clarence
1936- .... **CLC 3, 19, 48; BLC**
See also BW 2; CA 21-24R; CAAS 6; CANR 13, 25; DLB 33

Major, Kevin (Gerald) 1949- .... **CLC 26**
See also CA 97-100; CANR 21, 38; CLR 11; DLB 60; JRDA; MAICYA; SATA 32

Maki, James
See Ozu, Yasujiro

Malabaila, Damiano
See Levi, Primo

Malamud, Bernard
1914-1986 ...... **CLC 1, 2, 3, 5, 8, 9, 11, 18, 27, 44, 78, 85; DA; SSC 15; WLC**
See also CA 5-8R; 118; CABS 1; CANR 28; CDALB 1941-1968; DLB 2, 28, 152; DLBY 80, 86; MTCW

Malaparte, Curzio 1898-1957 ..... **TCLC 52**

Malcolm, Dan
See Silverberg, Robert

Malcolm X .... **CLC 82; BLC**
See also Little, Malcolm

Malherbe, Francois de 1555-1628 ..... **LC 5**

Mallarme, Stephane 1842-1898 .... **NCLC 4, 41; PC 4**

Mallet-Joris, Francoise 1930- ...... **CLC 11**
See also CA 65-68; CANR 17; DLB 83

Malley, Ern
See McAuley, James Phillip

Mallowan, Agatha Christie
See Christie, Agatha (Mary Clarissa)

Maloff, Saul 1922- .... **CLC 5**
See also CA 33-36R

Malone, Louis
See MacNeice, (Frederick) Louis

Malone, Michael (Christopher) 1942- .... **CLC 43**
See also CA 77-80; CANR 14, 32

Malory, (Sir) Thomas 1410(?)-1471(?) .... **LC 11; DA**
See also CDBLB Before 1660; DLB 146; SATA 59; SATA-Brief 33

Malouf, (George Joseph) David 1934- .... **CLC 28, 86**
See also CA 124

Malraux, (Georges-)Andre 1901-1976 ...... **CLC 1, 4, 9, 13, 15, 57**
See also CA 21-22; 69-72; CANR 34; CAP 2; DLB 72; MTCW

Malzberg, Barry N(athaniel) 1939-... **CLC 7**
See also CA 61-64; CAAS 4; CANR 16; DLB 8

Mamet, David (Alan) 1947- .... **CLC 9, 15, 34, 46; DC 4**
See also AAYA 3; CA 81-84; CABS 3; CANR 15, 41; DLB 7; MTCW

Mamoulian, Rouben (Zachary) 1897-1987 .... **CLC 16**
See also CA 25-28R; 124

Mandelstam, Osip (Emilievich) 1891(?)-1938(?) .... **TCLC 2, 6**
See also CA 104

Mander, (Mary) Jane 1877-1949... **TCLC 31**

Mandiargues, Andre Pieyre de....... **CLC 41**
See also Pieyre de Mandiargues, Andre
See also DLB 83

Mandrake, Ethel Belle
See Thurman, Wallace (Henry)

Mangan, James Clarence 1803-1849 .... **NCLC 27**

Maniere, J.-E.
See Giraudoux, (Hippolyte) Jean

Manley, (Mary) Delariviere 1672(?)-1724 .... **LC 1**
See also DLB 39, 80

Mann, Abel
See Creasey, John

Mann, (Luiz) Heinrich 1871-1950... **TCLC 9**
See also CA 106; DLB 66

Mann, (Paul) Thomas 1875-1955 .... **TCLC 2, 8, 14, 21, 35, 44, 60; DA; SSC 5; WLC**
See also CA 104; 128; DLB 66; MTCW

Manning, David
See Faust, Frederick (Schiller)

Manning, Frederic 1887(?)-1935 ... **TCLC 25**
See also CA 124

Manning, Olivia 1915-1980 ...... **CLC 5, 19**
See also CA 5-8R; 101; CANR 29; MTCW

Mano, D. Keith 1942- .... **CLC 2, 10**
See also CA 25-28R; CAAS 6; CANR 26; DLB 6

Mansfield, Katherine .... **TCLC 2, 8, 39; SSC 9; WLC**
See also Beauchamp, Kathleen Mansfield

Manso, Peter 1940- .... **CLC 39**
See also CA 29-32R; CANR 44

Mantecon, Juan Jimenez
See Jimenez (Mantecon), Juan Ramon

Manton, Peter
See Creasey, John

Man Without a Spleen, A
See Chekhov, Anton (Pavlovich)

Manzoni, Alessandro 1785-1873 .. **NCLC 29**

Mapu, Abraham (ben Jekutiel) 1808-1867 .... **NCLC 18**

Mara, Sally
See Queneau, Raymond

Marat, Jean Paul 1743-1793........ **LC 10**

Marcel, Gabriel Honore 1889-1973 .... **CLC 15**
See also CA 102; 45-48; MTCW

Marchbanks, Samuel
See Davies, (William) Robertson

Marchi, Giacomo
See Bassani, Giorgio

Margulies, Donald................. **CLC 76**

Marie de France c. 12th cent. -.... **CMLC 8**

Marie de l'Incarnation 1599-1672.... **LC 10**

Mariner, Scott
See Pohl, Frederik

Marinetti, Filippo Tommaso 1876-1944 .... **TCLC 10**
See also CA 107; DLB 114

Marivaux, Pierre Carlet de Chamblain de 1688-1763 .... **LC 4**

Markandaya, Kamala .... **CLC 8, 38**
See also Taylor, Kamala (Purnaiya)

Markfield, Wallace 1926-........... **CLC 8**
See also CA 69-72; CAAS 3; DLB 2, 28

Markham, Edwin 1852-1940 ...... **TCLC 47**
See also DLB 54

Markham, Robert
See Amis, Kingsley (William)

Marks, J
See Highwater, Jamake (Mamake)

Marks-Highwater, J
See Highwater, Jamake (Mamake)

Markson, David M(errill) 1927- .... **CLC 67**
See also CA 49-52; CANR 1

Marley, Bob...................... **CLC 17**
See also Marley, Robert Nesta

Marley, Robert Nesta 1945-1981
See Marley, Bob
See also CA 107; 103

Marlowe, Christopher 1564-1593 ..... **LC 22; DA; DC 1; WLC**
See also CDBLB Before 1660; DLB 62

Marmontel, Jean-Francois 1723-1799 .... **LC 2**

Marquand, John P(hillips) 1893-1960 .... **CLC 2, 10**
See also CA 85-88; DLB 9, 102

Marquez, Gabriel (Jose) Garcia
See Garcia Marquez, Gabriel (Jose)

Marquis, Don(ald Robert Perry) 1878-1937 .... **TCLC 7**
See also CA 104; DLB 11, 25

Marric, J. J.
See Creasey, John

Marrow, Bernard
See Moore, Brian

Marryat, Frederick 1792-1848 .... **NCLC 3**
See also DLB 21

Marsden, James
See Creasey, John

Marsh, (Edith) Ngaio 1899-1982 .... **CLC 7, 53**
See also CA 9-12R; CANR 6; DLB 77; MTCW

Marshall, Garry 1934- .... **CLC 17**
See also AAYA 3; CA 111; SATA 60

Marshall, Paule 1929- .... **CLC 27, 72; BLC; SSC 3**
See also BW 2; CA 77-80; CANR 25; DLB 33; MTCW

Marsten, Richard
See Hunter, Evan

Martha, Henry
See Harris, Mark

Martial c. 40-c. 104 .... **PC 10**

Martin, Ken
See Hubbard, L(afayette) Ron(ald)

Martin, Richard
See Creasey, John

Martin, Steve 1945- .... **CLC 30**
See also CA 97-100; CANR 30; MTCW

Martin, Valerie 1948-............. **CLC 89**
See also BEST 90:2; CA 85-88

Martin, Violet Florence 1862-1915 .... **TCLC 51**

Martin, Webber
See Silverberg, Robert

Martindale, Patrick Victor
See White, Patrick (Victor Martindale)

Martin du Gard, Roger 1881-1958 .... **TCLC 24**
See also CA 118; DLB 65

Martineau, Harriet 1802-1876.... **NCLC 26**
See also DLB 21, 55; YABC 2

Martines, Julia
See O'Faolain, Julia

Martinez, Jacinto Benavente y
See Benavente (y Martinez), Jacinto

Martinez Ruiz, Jose 1873-1967
See Azorin; Ruiz, Jose Martinez
See also CA 93-96; HW

Martinez Sierra, Gregorio 1881-1947 .... **TCLC 6**
See also CA 115

McElroy, Joseph 1930- . . . . **CLC 5, 47**
See also CA 17-20R

McEwan, Ian (Russell) 1948- . . . **CLC 13, 66**
See also BEST 90:4; CA 61-64; CANR 14, 41; DLB 14; MTCW

McFadden, David 1940- . . . . **CLC 48**
See also CA 104; DLB 60

McFarland, Dennis 1950- . . . . **CLC 65**

McGahern, John
1934- . . . . **CLC 5, 9, 48; SSC 17**
See also CA 17-20R; CANR 29; DLB 14; MTCW

McGinley, Patrick (Anthony)
1937- . . . . **CLC 41**
See also CA 120; 127

McGinley, Phyllis 1905-1978 . . . . . . **CLC 14**
See also CA 9-12R; 77-80; CANR 19; DLB 11, 48; SATA 2, 44; SATA-Obit 24

McGinniss, Joe 1942- . . . . **CLC 32**
See also AITN 2; BEST 89:2; CA 25-28R; CANR 26

McGivern, Maureen Daly
See Daly, Maureen

McGrath, Patrick 1950- . . . . **CLC 55**
See also CA 136

McGrath, Thomas (Matthew)
1916-1990 . . . . **CLC 28, 59**
See also CA 9-12R; 132; CANR 6, 33; MTCW; SATA 41; SATA-Obit 66

McGuane, Thomas (Francis III)
1939- . . . . **CLC 3, 7, 18, 45**
See also AITN 2; CA 49-52; CANR 5, 24; DLB 2; DLBY 80; MTCW

McGuckian, Medbh 1950- . . . . **CLC 48**
See also CA 143; DLB 40

McHale, Tom 1942(?)-1982 . . . . **CLC 3, 5**
See also AITN 1; CA 77-80; 106

McIlvanney, William 1936- . . . . **CLC 42**
See also CA 25-28R; DLB 14

McIlwraith, Maureen Mollie Hunter
See Hunter, Mollie
See also SATA 2

McInerney, Jay 1955- . . . . **CLC 34**
See also CA 116; 123; CANR 45

McIntyre, Vonda N(eel) 1948- . . . . . **CLC 18**
See also CA 81-84; CANR 17, 34; MTCW

McKay, Claude . . . . . **TCLC 7, 41; BLC; PC 2**
See also McKay, Festus Claudius
See also DLB 4, 45, 51, 117

McKay, Festus Claudius 1889-1948
See McKay, Claude
See also BW 1; CA 104; 124; DA; MTCW; WLC

McKuen, Rod 1933- . . . . **CLC 1, 3**
See also AITN 1; CA 41-44R; CANR 40

McLoughlin, R. B.
See Mencken, H(enry) L(ouis)

McLuhan, (Herbert) Marshall
1911-1980 . . . . **CLC 37, 83**
See also CA 9-12R; 102; CANR 12, 34; DLB 88; MTCW

McMillan, Terry (L.) 1951- . . . . . **CLC 50, 61**
See also BW 2; CA 140

McMurtry, Larry (Jeff)
1936- . . . . **CLC 2, 3, 7, 11, 27, 44**
See also AITN 2; BEST 89:2; CA 5-8R; CANR 19, 43; CDALB 1968-1988; DLB 2, 143; DLBY 80, 87; MTCW

McNally, T. M. 1961- . . . . **CLC 82**

McNally, Terrence 1939- . . . . . . **CLC 4, 7, 41**
See also CA 45-48; CANR 2; DLB 7

McNamer, Deirdre 1950- . . . . **CLC 70**

McNeile, Herman Cyril 1888-1937
See Sapper
See also DLB 77

McNickle, (William) D'Arcy
1904-1977 . . . . **CLC 89**
See also CA 9-12R; 85-88; CANR 5, 45; NNAL; SATA-Obit 22

McPhee, John (Angus) 1931- . . . . . . **CLC 36**
See also BEST 90:1; CA 65-68; CANR 20, 46; MTCW

McPherson, James Alan
1943- . . . . **CLC 19, 77**
See also BW 1; CA 25-28R; CAAS 17; CANR 24; DLB 38; MTCW

McPherson, William (Alexander)
1933- . . . . **CLC 34**
See also CA 69-72; CANR 28

Mead, Margaret 1901-1978 . . . . **CLC 37**
See also AITN 1; CA 1-4R; 81-84; CANR 4; MTCW; SATA-Obit 20

Meaker, Marijane (Agnes) 1927-
See Kerr, M. E.
See also CA 107; CANR 37; JRDA; MAICYA; MTCW; SATA 20, 61

Medoff, Mark (Howard) 1940- . . . **CLC 6, 23**
See also AITN 1; CA 53-56; CANR 5; DLB 7

Medvedev, P. N.
See Bakhtin, Mikhail Mikhailovich

Meged, Aharon
See Megged, Aharon

Meged, Aron
See Megged, Aharon

Megged, Aharon 1920- . . . . **CLC 9**
See also CA 49-52; CAAS 13; CANR 1

Mehta, Ved (Parkash) 1934- . . . . **CLC 37**
See also CA 1-4R; CANR 2, 23; MTCW

Melanter
See Blackmore, R(ichard) D(oddridge)

Melikow, Loris
See Hofmannsthal, Hugo von

Melmoth, Sebastian
See Wilde, Oscar (Fingal O'Flahertie Wills)

Meltzer, Milton 1915- . . . . **CLC 26**
See also AAYA 8; CA 13-16R; CANR 38; CLR 13; DLB 61; JRDA; MAICYA; SAAS 1; SATA 1, 50, 80

Melville, Herman
1819-1891 . . . . . **NCLC 3, 12, 29, 45, 49; DA; SSC 1, 17; WLC**
See also CDALB 1640-1865; DLB 3, 74; SATA 59

Menander
c. 342B.C.-c. 292B.C. . . . . **CMLC 9; DC 3**

Mencken, H(enry) L(ouis)
1880-1956 . . . . **TCLC 13**
See also CA 105; 125; CDALB 1917-1929; DLB 11, 29, 63, 137; MTCW

Mercer, David 1928-1980. . . . . **CLC 5**
See also CA 9-12R; 102; CANR 23; DLB 13; MTCW

Merchant, Paul
See Ellison, Harlan (Jay)

Meredith, George 1828-1909 . . . **TCLC 17, 43**
See also CA 117; CDBLB 1832-1890; DLB 18, 35, 57

Meredith, William (Morris)
1919- . . . . **CLC 4, 13, 22, 55**
See also CA 9-12R; CAAS 14; CANR 6, 40; DLB 5

Merezhkovsky, Dmitry Sergeyevich
1865-1941 . . . . **TCLC 29**

Merimee, Prosper
1803-1870 . . . . **NCLC 6; SSC 7**
See also DLB 119

Merkin, Daphne 1954- . . . . **CLC 44**
See also CA 123

Merlin, Arthur
See Blish, James (Benjamin)

Merrill, James (Ingram)
1926-1995 . . . . **CLC 2, 3, 6, 8, 13, 18, 34**
See also CA 13-16R; 147; CANR 10; DLB 5; DLBY 85; MTCW

Merriman, Alex
See Silverberg, Robert

Merritt, E. B.
See Waddington, Miriam

Merton, Thomas
1915-1968 . . **CLC 1, 3, 11, 34, 83; PC 10**
See also CA 5-8R; 25-28R; CANR 22; DLB 48; DLBY 81; MTCW

Merwin, W(illiam) S(tanley)
1927- . . . **CLC 1, 2, 3, 5, 8, 13, 18, 45, 88**
See also CA 13-16R; CANR 15; DLB 5; MTCW

Metcalf, John 1938- . . . . **CLC 37**
See also CA 113; DLB 60

Metcalf, Suzanne
See Baum, L(yman) Frank

Mew, Charlotte (Mary)
1870-1928 . . . . **TCLC 8**
See also CA 105; DLB 19, 135

Mewshaw, Michael 1943- . . . . **CLC 9**
See also CA 53-56; CANR 7, 47; DLBY 80

Meyer, June
See Jordan, June

Meyer, Lynn
See Slavitt, David R(ytman)

Meyer-Meyrink, Gustav 1868-1932
See Meyrink, Gustav
See also CA 117

Meyers, Jeffrey 1939- . . . . **CLC 39**
See also CA 73-76; DLB 111

Meynell, Alice (Christina Gertrude Thompson)
1847-1922 . . . . **TCLC 6**
See also CA 104; DLB 19, 98

Meyrink, Gustav . . . . **TCLC 21**
See also Meyer-Meyrink, Gustav
See also DLB 81

Michaels, Leonard 1933- .... **CLC 6, 25; SSC 16**
See also CA 61-64; CANR 21; DLB 130; MTCW

Michaux, Henri 1899-1984 ...... **CLC 8, 19**
See also CA 85-88; 114

Michelangelo 1475-1564............ **LC 12**

Michelet, Jules 1798-1874....... **NCLC 31**

Michener, James A(lbert) 1907(?)- .... **CLC 1, 5, 11, 29, 60**
See also AITN 1; BEST 90:1; CA 5-8R; CANR 21, 45; DLB 6; MTCW

Mickiewicz, Adam 1798-1855 ..... **NCLC 3**

Middleton, Christopher 1926- ...... **CLC 13**
See also CA 13-16R; CANR 29; DLB 40

Middleton, Richard (Barham) 1882-1911 .... **TCLC 56**

Middleton, Stanley 1919-........ **CLC 7, 38**
See also CA 25-28R; CANR 21, 46; DLB 14

Middleton, Thomas 1580-1627........ **DC 5**
See also DLB 58

Migueis, Jose Rodrigues 1901- ..... **CLC 10**

Mikszath, Kalman 1847-1910 ..... **TCLC 31**

Miles, Josephine 1911-1985 .... **CLC 1, 2, 14, 34, 39**
See also CA 1-4R; 116; CANR 2; DLB 48

Militant
See Sandburg, Carl (August)

Mill, John Stuart 1806-1873 ..... **NCLC 11**
See also CDBLB 1832-1890; DLB 55

Millar, Kenneth 1915-1983 .... **CLC 14**
See also Macdonald, Ross
See also CA 9-12R; 110; CANR 16; DLB 2; DLBD 6; DLBY 83; MTCW

Millay, E. Vincent
See Millay, Edna St. Vincent

Millay, Edna St. Vincent 1892-1950 ...... **TCLC 4, 49; DA; PC 6**
See also CA 104; 130; CDALB 1917-1929; DLB 45; MTCW

Miller, Arthur 1915- .... **CLC 1, 2, 6, 10, 15, 26, 47, 78; DA; DC 1; WLC**
See also AITN 1; CA 1-4R; CABS 3; CANR 2, 30; CDALB 1941-1968; DLB 7; MTCW

Miller, Henry (Valentine) 1891-1980 .... **CLC 1, 2, 4, 9, 14, 43, 84; DA; WLC**
See also CA 9-12R; 97-100; CANR 33; CDALB 1929-1941; DLB 4, 9; DLBY 80; MTCW

Miller, Jason 1939(?)- .... **CLC 2**
See also AITN 1; CA 73-76; DLB 7

Miller, Sue 1943- .... **CLC 44**
See also BEST 90:3; CA 139; DLB 143

Miller, Walter M(ichael, Jr.) 1923- .... **CLC 4, 30**
See also CA 85-88; DLB 8

Millett, Kate 1934-............... **CLC 67**
See also AITN 1; CA 73-76; CANR 32; MTCW

Millhauser, Steven 1943-....... **CLC 21, 54**
See also CA 110; 111; DLB 2

Millin, Sarah Gertrude 1889-1968 .. **CLC 49**
See also CA 102; 93-96

Milne, A(lan) A(lexander) 1882-1956 .... **TCLC 6**
See also CA 104; 133; CLR 1, 26; DLB 10, 77, 100; MAICYA; MTCW; YABC 1

Milner, Ron(ald) 1938-....... **CLC 56; BLC**
See also AITN 1; BW 1; CA 73-76; CANR 24; DLB 38; MTCW

Milosz, Czeslaw 1911- ... **CLC 5, 11, 22, 31, 56, 82; PC 8**
See also CA 81-84; CANR 23; MTCW

Milton, John 1608-1674... **LC 9; DA; WLC**
See also CDBLB 1660-1789; DLB 131, 151

Min, Anchee 1957-............... **CLC 86**
See also CA 146

Minehaha, Cornelius
See Wedekind, (Benjamin) Frank(lin)

Miner, Valerie 1947- .... **CLC 40**
See also CA 97-100

Minimo, Duca
See D'Annunzio, Gabriele

Minot, Susan 1956- .... **CLC 44**
See also CA 134

Minus, Ed 1938-................. **CLC 39**

Miranda, Javier
See Bioy Casares, Adolfo

Mirbeau, Octave 1848-1917....... **TCLC 55**
See also DLB 123

Miro (Ferrer), Gabriel (Francisco Victor) 1879-1930 .... **TCLC 5**
See also CA 104

Mishima, Yukio .... **CLC 2, 4, 6, 9, 27; DC 1; SSC 4**
See also Hiraoka, Kimitake

Mistral, Frederic 1830-1914 ...... **TCLC 51**
See also CA 122

Mistral, Gabriela............ **TCLC 2; HLC**
See also Godoy Alcayaga, Lucila

Mistry, Rohinton 1952-........... **CLC 71**
See also CA 141

Mitchell, Clyde
See Ellison, Harlan (Jay); Silverberg, Robert

Mitchell, James Leslie 1901-1935
See Gibbon, Lewis Grassic
See also CA 104; DLB 15

Mitchell, Joni 1943-.............. **CLC 12**
See also CA 112

Mitchell, Margaret (Munnerlyn) 1900-1949 .... **TCLC 11**
See also CA 109; 125; DLB 9; MTCW

Mitchell, Peggy
See Mitchell, Margaret (Munnerlyn)

Mitchell, S(ilas) Weir 1829-1914 .. **TCLC 36**

Mitchell, W(illiam) O(rmond) 1914- .... **CLC 25**
See also CA 77-80; CANR 15, 43; DLB 88

Mitford, Mary Russell 1787-1855.. **NCLC 4**
See also DLB 110, 116

Mitford, Nancy 1904-1973......... **CLC 44**
See also CA 9-12R

Miyamoto, Yuriko 1899-1951 ..... **TCLC 37**

Mo, Timothy (Peter) 1950(?)- ...... **CLC 46**
See also CA 117; MTCW

Modarressi, Taghi (M.) 1931- ...... **CLC 44**
See also CA 121; 134

Modiano, Patrick (Jean) 1945- ..... **CLC 18**
See also CA 85-88; CANR 17, 40; DLB 83

Moerck, Paal
See Roelvaag, O(le) E(dvart)

Mofolo, Thomas (Mokopu) 1875(?)-1948 .... **TCLC 22; BLC**
See also CA 121

Mohr, Nicholasa 1935-...... **CLC 12; HLC**
See also AAYA 8; CA 49-52; CANR 1, 32; CLR 22; DLB 145; HW; JRDA; SAAS 8; SATA 8

Mojtabai, A(nn) G(race) 1938- .... **CLC 5, 9, 15, 29**
See also CA 85-88

Moliere 1622-1673 .... **LC 28; DA; WLC**

Molin, Charles
See Mayne, William (James Carter)

Molnar, Ferenc 1878-1952........ **TCLC 20**
See also CA 109

Momaday, N(avarre) Scott 1934- .... **CLC 2, 19, 85; DA**
See also AAYA 11; CA 25-28R; CANR 14, 34; DLB 143; MTCW; NNAL; SATA 48; SATA-Brief 30

Monette, Paul 1945-1995.......... **CLC 82**
See also CA 139; 147

Monroe, Harriet 1860-1936....... **TCLC 12**
See also CA 109; DLB 54, 91

Monroe, Lyle
See Heinlein, Robert A(nson)

Montagu, Elizabeth 1917- .... **NCLC 7**
See also CA 9-12R

Montagu, Mary (Pierrepont) Wortley 1689-1762 .... **LC 9**
See also DLB 95, 101

Montagu, W. H.
See Coleridge, Samuel Taylor

Montague, John (Patrick) 1929- .... **CLC 13, 46**
See also CA 9-12R; CANR 9; DLB 40; MTCW

Montaigne, Michel (Eyquem) de 1533-1592 .... **LC 8; DA; WLC**

Montale, Eugenio 1896-1981 .... **CLC 7, 9, 18; PC 12**
See also CA 17-20R; 104; CANR 30; DLB 114; MTCW

Montesquieu, Charles-Louis de Secondat 1689-1755 .... **LC 7**

Montgomery, (Robert) Bruce 1921-1978
See Crispin, Edmund
See also CA 104

Montgomery, L(ucy) M(aud) 1874-1942 .... **TCLC 51**
See also AAYA 12; CA 108; 137; CLR 8; DLB 92; JRDA; MAICYA; YABC 1

Montgomery, Marion H., Jr. 1925- .. **CLC 7**
See also AITN 1; CA 1-4R; CANR 3, 48; DLB 6

Author Index

Mukherjee, Bharati 1940- . . . . **CLC 53**
See also BEST 89:2; CA 107; CANR 45; DLB 60; MTCW

Muldoon, Paul 1951- . . . . **CLC 32, 72**
See also CA 113; 129; DLB 40

Mulisch, Harry 1927- . . . . **CLC 42**
See also CA 9-12R; CANR 6, 26

Mull, Martin 1943- . . . . **CLC 17**
See also CA 105

Mulock, Dinah Maria
See Craik, Dinah Maria (Mulock)

Munford, Robert 1737(?)-1783 . . . . **LC 5**
See also DLB 31

Mungo, Raymond 1946- . . . . **CLC 72**
See also CA 49-52; CANR 2

Munro, Alice
1931- . . . . **CLC 6, 10, 19, 50; SSC 3**
See also AITN 2; CA 33-36R; CANR 33; DLB 53; MTCW; SATA 29

Munro, H(ector) H(ugh) 1870-1916
See Saki
See also CA 104; 130; CDBLB 1890-1914; DA; DLB 34; MTCW; WLC

Murasaki, Lady . . . . **CMLC 1**

Murdoch, (Jean) Iris
1919- . . . . . . **CLC 1, 2, 3, 4, 6, 8, 11, 15, 22, 31, 51**
See also CA 13-16R; CANR 8, 43; CDBLB 1960 to Present; DLB 14; MTCW

Murnau, Friedrich Wilhelm
See Plumpe, Friedrich Wilhelm

Murphy, Richard 1927- . . . . **CLC 41**
See also CA 29-32R; DLB 40

Murphy, Sylvia 1937- . . . . **CLC 34**
See also CA 121

Murphy, Thomas (Bernard) 1935- . . . **CLC 51**
See also CA 101

Murray, Albert L. 1916- . . . . **CLC 73**
See also BW 2; CA 49-52; CANR 26; DLB 38

Murray, Les(lie) A(llan) 1938- . . . . . **CLC 40**
See also CA 21-24R; CANR 11, 27

Murry, J. Middleton
See Murry, John Middleton

Murry, John Middleton
1889-1957 . . . . **TCLC 16**
See also CA 118; DLB 149

Musgrave, Susan 1951- . . . . **CLC 13, 54**
See also CA 69-72; CANR 45

Musil, Robert (Edler von)
1880-1942 . . . . **TCLC 12; SSC 18**
See also CA 109; DLB 81, 124

Musset, (Louis Charles) Alfred de
1810-1857 . . . . **NCLC 7**

My Brother's Brother
See Chekhov, Anton (Pavlovich)

Myers, L. H. 1881-1944 . . . . **TCLC 59**
See also DLB 15

Myers, Walter Dean 1937- . . . **CLC 35; BLC**
See also AAYA 4; BW 2; CA 33-36R; CANR 20, 42; CLR 4, 16, 35; DLB 33; JRDA; MAICYA; SAAS 2; SATA 41, 71; SATA-Brief 27

Myers, Walter M.
See Myers, Walter Dean

Myles, Symon
See Follett, Ken(neth Martin)

Nabokov, Vladimir (Vladimirovich)
1899-1977 . . . . . **CLC 1, 2, 3, 6, 8, 11, 15, 23, 44, 46, 64; DA; SSC 11; WLC**
See also CA 5-8R; 69-72; CANR 20; CDALB 1941-1968; DLB 2; DLBD 3; DLBY 80, 91; MTCW

Nagai Kafu . . . . **TCLC 51**
See also Nagai Sokichi

Nagai Sokichi 1879-1959
See Nagai Kafu
See also CA 117

Nagy, Laszlo 1925-1978 . . . . **CLC 7**
See also CA 129; 112

Naipaul, Shiva(dhar Srinivasa)
1945-1985 . . . . **CLC 32, 39**
See also CA 110; 112; 116; CANR 33; DLBY 85; MTCW

Naipaul, V(idiadhar) S(urajprasad)
1932- . . . . **CLC 4, 7, 9, 13, 18, 37**
See also CA 1-4R; CANR 1, 33; CDBLB 1960 to Present; DLB 125; DLBY 85; MTCW

Nakos, Lilika 1899(?)- . . . . **CLC 29**

Narayan, R(asipuram) K(rishnaswami)
1906- . . . . **CLC 7, 28, 47**
See also CA 81-84; CANR 33; MTCW; SATA 62

Nash, (Frediric) Ogden 1902-1971 . . **CLC 23**
See also CA 13-14; 29-32R; CANR 34; CAP 1; DLB 11; MAICYA; MTCW; SATA 2, 46

Nathan, Daniel
See Dannay, Frederic

Nathan, George Jean 1882-1958 . . . **TCLC 18**
See also Hatteras, Owen
See also CA 114; DLB 137

Natsume, Kinnosuke 1867-1916
See Natsume, Soseki
See also CA 104

Natsume, Soseki . . . . **TCLC 2, 10**
See also Natsume, Kinnosuke

Natti, (Mary) Lee 1919-
See Kingman, Lee
See also CA 5-8R; CANR 2

Naylor, Gloria
1950- . . . . **CLC 28, 52; BLC; DA**
See also AAYA 6; BW 2; CA 107; CANR 27; MTCW

Neihardt, John Gneisenau
1881-1973 . . . . **CLC 32**
See also CA 13-14; CAP 1; DLB 9, 54

Nekrasov, Nikolai Alekseevich
1821-1878 . . . . **NCLC 11**

Nelligan, Emile 1879-1941 . . . . **TCLC 14**
See also CA 114; DLB 92

Nelson, Willie 1933- . . . . **CLC 17**
See also CA 107

Nemerov, Howard (Stanley)
1920-1991 . . . . **CLC 2, 6, 9, 36**
See also CA 1-4R; 134; CABS 2; CANR 1, 27; DLB 6; DLBY 83; MTCW

Neruda, Pablo
1904-1973 . . . . . **CLC 1, 2, 5, 7, 9, 28, 62; DA; HLC; PC 4; WLC**
See also CA 19-20; 45-48; CAP 2; HW; MTCW

Nerval, Gerard de
1808-1855 . . . . . **NCLC 1; PC 12; SSC 18**

Nervo, (Jose) Amado (Ruiz de)
1870-1919 . . . . **TCLC 11**
See also CA 109; 131; HW

Nessi, Pio Baroja y
See Baroja (y Nessi), Pio

Nestroy, Johann 1801-1862 . . . . . . **NCLC 42**
See also DLB 133

Neufeld, John (Arthur) 1938- . . . . . . **CLC 17**
See also AAYA 11; CA 25-28R; CANR 11, 37; MAICYA; SAAS 3; SATA 6, 81

Neville, Emily Cheney 1919- . . . . **CLC 12**
See also CA 5-8R; CANR 3, 37; JRDA; MAICYA; SAAS 2; SATA 1

Newbound, Bernard Slade 1930-
See Slade, Bernard
See also CA 81-84

Newby, P(ercy) H(oward)
1918- . . . . **CLC 2, 13**
See also CA 5-8R; CANR 32; DLB 15; MTCW

Newlove, Donald 1928- . . . . **CLC 6**
See also CA 29-32R; CANR 25

Newlove, John (Herbert) 1938- . . . . . **CLC 14**
See also CA 21-24R; CANR 9, 25

Newman, Charles 1938- . . . . **CLC 2, 8**
See also CA 21-24R

Newman, Edwin (Harold) 1919- . . . . **CLC 14**
See also AITN 1; CA 69-72; CANR 5

Newman, John Henry
1801-1890 . . . . **NCLC 38**
See also DLB 18, 32, 55

Newton, Suzanne 1936- . . . . **CLC 35**
See also CA 41-44R; CANR 14; JRDA; SATA 5, 77

Nexo, Martin Andersen
1869-1954 . . . . **TCLC 43**

Nezval, Vitezslav 1900-1958 . . . . . . **TCLC 44**
See also CA 123

Ng, Fae Myenne 1957(?)- . . . . **CLC 81**
See also CA 146

Ngema, Mbongeni 1955- . . . . **CLC 57**
See also BW 2; CA 143

Ngugi, James T(hiong'o) . . . . **CLC 3, 7, 13**
See also Ngugi wa Thiong'o

Ngugi wa Thiong'o 1938- . . . . . **CLC 36; BLC**
See also Ngugi, James T(hiong'o)
See also BW 2; CA 81-84; CANR 27; DLB 125; MTCW

Nichol, B(arrie) P(hillip)
1944-1988 . . . . **CLC 18**
See also CA 53-56; DLB 53; SATA 66

Nichols, John (Treadwell) 1940- . . . . **CLC 38**
See also CA 9-12R; CAAS 2; CANR 6; DLBY 82

Nichols, Leigh
See Koontz, Dean R(ay)

Nichols, Peter (Richard)
1927- . . . . **CLC 5, 36, 65**
See also CA 104; CANR 33; DLB 13; MTCW

Nicolas, F. R. E.
See Freeling, Nicolas

Niedecker, Lorine 1903-1970. . . . **CLC 10, 42**
See also CA 25-28; CAP 2; DLB 48

Nietzsche, Friedrich (Wilhelm)
1844-1900 . . . . **TCLC 10, 18, 55**
See also CA 107; 121; DLB 129

Nievo, Ippolito 1831-1861 . . . . **NCLC 22**

Nightingale, Anne Redmon 1943-
See Redmon, Anne
See also CA 103

Nik. T. O.
See Annensky, Innokenty Fyodorovich

Nin, Anais
1903-1977 . . . . . . **CLC 1, 4, 8, 11, 14, 60; SSC 10**
See also AITN 2; CA 13-16R; 69-72; CANR 22; DLB 2, 4, 152; MTCW

Nissenson, Hugh 1933-. . . . . **CLC 4, 9**
See also CA 17-20R; CANR 27; DLB 28

Niven, Larry . . . . **CLC 8**
See also Niven, Laurence Van Cott
See also DLB 8

Niven, Laurence Van Cott 1938-
See Niven, Larry
See also CA 21-24R; CAAS 12; CANR 14, 44; MTCW

Nixon, Agnes Eckhardt 1927- . . . . . . **CLC 21**
See also CA 110

Nizan, Paul 1905-1940. . . . . **TCLC 40**
See also DLB 72

Nkosi, Lewis 1936-. . . . . **CLC 45; BLC**
See also BW 1; CA 65-68; CANR 27

Nodier, (Jean) Charles (Emmanuel)
1780-1844 . . . . **NCLC 19**
See also DLB 119

Nolan, Christopher 1965-. . . . . **CLC 58**
See also CA 111

Norden, Charles
See Durrell, Lawrence (George)

Nordhoff, Charles (Bernard)
1887-1947 . . . . **TCLC 23**
See also CA 108; DLB 9; SATA 23

Norfolk, Lawrence 1963-. . . . . **CLC 76**
See also CA 144

Norman, Marsha 1947- . . . . **CLC 28**
See also CA 105; CABS 3; CANR 41; DLBY 84

Norris, Benjamin Franklin, Jr.
1870-1902 . . . . **TCLC 24**
See also Norris, Frank
See also CA 110

Norris, Frank
See Norris, Benjamin Franklin, Jr.
See also CDALB 1865-1917; DLB 12, 71

Norris, Leslie 1921- . . . . **CLC 14**
See also CA 11-12; CANR 14; CAP 1; DLB 27

North, Andrew
See Norton, Andre

North, Anthony
See Koontz, Dean R(ay)

North, Captain George
See Stevenson, Robert Louis (Balfour)

North, Milou
See Erdrich, Louise

Northrup, B. A.
See Hubbard, L(afayette) Ron(ald)

North Staffs
See Hulme, T(homas) E(rnest)

Norton, Alice Mary
See Norton, Andre
See also MAICYA; SATA 1, 43

Norton, Andre 1912- . . . . **CLC 12**
See also Norton, Alice Mary
See also AAYA 14; CA 1-4R; CANR 2, 31; DLB 8, 52; JRDA; MTCW

Norton, Caroline 1808-1877. . . . . . **NCLC 47**
See also DLB 21

Norway, Nevil Shute 1899-1960
See Shute, Nevil
See also CA 102; 93-96

Norwid, Cyprian Kamil
1821-1883 . . . . **NCLC 17**

Nosille, Nabrah
See Ellison, Harlan (Jay)

Nossack, Hans Erich 1901-1978 . . . . . **CLC 6**
See also CA 93-96; 85-88; DLB 69

Nostradamus 1503-1566. . . . . **LC 27**

Nosu, Chuji
See Ozu, Yasujiro

Notenburg, Eleanora (Genrikhovna) von
See Guro, Elena

Nova, Craig 1945-. . . . . **CLC 7, 31**
See also CA 45-48; CANR 2

Novak, Joseph
See Kosinski, Jerzy (Nikodem)

Novalis 1772-1801 . . . . **NCLC 13**
See also DLB 90

Nowlan, Alden (Albert) 1933-1983 . . **CLC 15**
See also CA 9-12R; CANR 5; DLB 53

Noyes, Alfred 1880-1958 . . . . **TCLC 7**
See also CA 104; DLB 20

Nunn, Kem 19(?)- . . . . **CLC 34**

Nye, Robert 1939- . . . . **CLC 13, 42**
See also CA 33-36R; CANR 29; DLB 14; MTCW; SATA 6

Nyro, Laura 1947- . . . . **CLC 17**

Oates, Joyce Carol
1938- . . . . . . **CLC 1, 2, 3, 6, 9, 11, 15, 19, 33, 52; DA; SSC 6; WLC**
See also AITN 1; BEST 89:2; CA 5-8R; CANR 25, 45; CDALB 1968-1988; DLB 2, 5, 130; DLBY 81; MTCW

O'Brien, Darcy 1939-. . . . . **CLC 11**
See also CA 21-24R; CANR 8

O'Brien, E. G.
See Clarke, Arthur C(harles)

O'Brien, Edna
1936- . . . **CLC 3, 5, 8, 13, 36, 65; SSC 10**
See also CA 1-4R; CANR 6, 41; CDBLB 1960 to Present; DLB 14; MTCW

O'Brien, Fitz-James 1828-1862. . . **NCLC 21**
See also DLB 74

O'Brien, Flann. . . . . **CLC 1, 4, 5, 7, 10, 47**
See also O Nuallain, Brian

O'Brien, Richard 1942- . . . . **CLC 17**
See also CA 124

O'Brien, Tim 1946-. . . . . **CLC 7, 19, 40**
See also CA 85-88; CANR 40; DLB 152; DLBD 9; DLBY 80

Obstfelder, Sigbjoern 1866-1900. . . **TCLC 23**
See also CA 123

O'Casey, Sean
1880-1964 . . . . . . **CLC 1, 5, 9, 11, 15, 88**
See also CA 89-92; CDBLB 1914-1945; DLB 10; MTCW

O'Cathasaigh, Sean
See O'Casey, Sean

Ochs, Phil 1940-1976. . . . . **CLC 17**
See also CA 65-68

O'Connor, Edwin (Greene)
1918-1968 . . . . **CLC 14**
See also CA 93-96; 25-28R

O'Connor, (Mary) Flannery
1925-1964 . . . . **CLC 1, 2, 3, 6, 10, 13, 15, 21, 66; DA; SSC 1; WLC**
See also AAYA 7; CA 1-4R; CANR 3, 41; CDALB 1941-1968; DLB 2, 152; DLBD 12; DLBY 80; MTCW

O'Connor, Frank. . . . . **CLC 23; SSC 5**
See also O'Donovan, Michael John

O'Dell, Scott 1898-1989. . . . . **CLC 30**
See also AAYA 3; CA 61-64; 129; CANR 12, 30; CLR 1, 16; DLB 52; JRDA; MAICYA; SATA 12, 60

Odets, Clifford 1906-1963 . . . . **CLC 2, 28**
See also CA 85-88; DLB 7, 26; MTCW

O'Doherty, Brian 1934- . . . . **CLC 76**
See also CA 105

O'Donnell, K. M.
See Malzberg, Barry N(athaniel)

O'Donnell, Lawrence
See Kuttner, Henry

O'Donovan, Michael John
1903-1966 . . . . **CLC 14**
See also O'Connor, Frank
See also CA 93-96

Oe, Kenzaburo
1935- . . . . **CLC 10, 36, 86; SSC 20**
See also CA 97-100; CANR 36; MTCW

O'Faolain, Julia 1932- . . . . **CLC 6, 19, 47**
See also CA 81-84; CAAS 2; CANR 12; DLB 14; MTCW

O'Faolain, Sean
1900-1991 . . . . **CLC 1, 7, 14, 32, 70; SSC 13**
See also CA 61-64; 134; CANR 12; DLB 15; MTCW

O'Flaherty, Liam
1896-1984 . . . . **CLC 5, 34; SSC 6**
See also CA 101; 113; CANR 35; DLB 36; DLBY 84; MTCW

Ogilvy, Gavin
See Barrie, J(ames) M(atthew)

O'Grady, Standish James
1846-1928 . . . . **TCLC 5**
See also CA 104

O'Grady, Timothy 1951- . . . . **CLC 59**
See also CA 138

O'Hara, Frank
1926-1966 . . . . **CLC 2, 5, 13, 78**
See also CA 9-12R; 25-28R; CANR 33; DLB 5, 16; MTCW

O'Hara, John (Henry)
1905-1970 . . . . **CLC 1, 2, 3, 6, 11, 42; SSC 15**
See also CA 5-8R; 25-28R; CANR 31; CDALB 1929-1941; DLB 9, 86; DLBD 2; MTCW

O Hehir, Diana 1922- . . . . **CLC 41**
See also CA 93-96

Okigbo, Christopher (Ifenayichukwu)
1932-1967 . . . . . **CLC 25, 84; BLC; PC 7**
See also BW 1; CA 77-80; DLB 125; MTCW

Okri, Ben 1959- . . . . **CLC 87**
See also BW 2; CA 130; 138

Olds, Sharon 1942- . . . . **CLC 32, 39, 85**
See also CA 101; CANR 18, 41; DLB 120

Oldstyle, Jonathan
See Irving, Washington

Olesha, Yuri (Karlovich)
1899-1960 . . . . **CLC 8**
See also CA 85-88

Oliphant, Laurence
1829(?)-1888 . . . . **NCLC 47**
See also DLB 18

Oliphant, Margaret (Oliphant Wilson)
1828-1897 . . . . **NCLC 11**
See also DLB 18

Oliver, Mary 1935- . . . . **CLC 19, 34**
See also CA 21-24R; CANR 9, 43; DLB 5

Olivier, Laurence (Kerr)
1907-1989 . . . . **CLC 20**
See also CA 111; 129

Olsen, Tillie
1913- . . . . **CLC 4, 13; DA; SSC 11**
See also CA 1-4R; CANR 1, 43; DLB 28; DLBY 80; MTCW

Olson, Charles (John)
1910-1970 . . . . . **CLC 1, 2, 5, 6, 9, 11, 29**
See also CA 13-16; 25-28R; CABS 2; CANR 35; CAP 1; DLB 5, 16; MTCW

Olson, Toby 1937- . . . . **CLC 28**
See also CA 65-68; CANR 9, 31

Olyesha, Yuri
See Olesha, Yuri (Karlovich)

Ondaatje, (Philip) Michael
1943- . . . . **CLC 14, 29, 51, 76**
See also CA 77-80; CANR 42; DLB 60

Oneal, Elizabeth 1934-
See Oneal, Zibby
See also CA 106; CANR 28; MAICYA; SATA 30

Oneal, Zibby . . . . **CLC 30**
See also Oneal, Elizabeth
See also AAYA 5; CLR 13; JRDA

O'Neill, Eugene (Gladstone)
1888-1953 . . . . . . **TCLC 1, 6, 27, 49; DA; WLC**
See also AITN 1; CA 110; 132; CDALB 1929-1941; DLB 7; MTCW

Onetti, Juan Carlos 1909-1994 . . . **CLC 7, 10**
See also CA 85-88; 145; CANR 32; DLB 113; HW; MTCW

O Nuallain, Brian 1911-1966
See O'Brien, Flann
See also CA 21-22; 25-28R; CAP 2

Oppen, George 1908-1984 . . . . **CLC 7, 13, 34**
See also CA 13-16R; 113; CANR 8; DLB 5

Oppenheim, E(dward) Phillips
1866-1946 . . . . **TCLC 45**
See also CA 111; DLB 70

Orlovitz, Gil 1918-1973 . . . . **CLC 22**
See also CA 77-80; 45-48; DLB 2, 5

Orris
See Ingelow, Jean

Ortega y Gasset, Jose
1883-1955 . . . . **TCLC 9; HLC**
See also CA 106; 130; HW; MTCW

Ortese, Anna Maria 1914- . . . . **CLC 89**

Ortiz, Simon J(oseph) 1941- . . . . **CLC 45**
See also CA 134; DLB 120; NNAL

Orton, Joe . . . . **CLC 4, 13, 43; DC 3**
See also Orton, John Kingsley
See also CDBLB 1960 to Present; DLB 13

Orton, John Kingsley 1933-1967
See Orton, Joe
See also CA 85-88; CANR 35; MTCW

Orwell, George
. . . . **TCLC 2, 6, 15, 31, 51; WLC**
See also Blair, Eric (Arthur)
See also CDBLB 1945-1960; DLB 15, 98

Osborne, David
See Silverberg, Robert

Osborne, George
See Silverberg, Robert

Osborne, John (James)
1929-1994 . . . . . **CLC 1, 2, 5, 11, 45; DA; WLC**
See also CA 13-16R; 147; CANR 21; CDBLB 1945-1960; DLB 13; MTCW

Osborne, Lawrence 1958- . . . . **CLC 50**

Oshima, Nagisa 1932- . . . . **CLC 20**
See also CA 116; 121

Oskison, John Milton
1874-1947 . . . . **TCLC 35**
See also CA 144; NNAL

Ossoli, Sarah Margaret (Fuller marchesa d')
1810-1850
See Fuller, Margaret
See also SATA 25

Ostrovsky, Alexander
1823-1886 . . . . **NCLC 30**

Otero, Blas de 1916-1979. . . . . **CLC 11**
See also CA 89-92; DLB 134

Otto, Whitney 1955- . . . . **CLC 70**
See also CA 140

Ouida . . . . **TCLC 43**
See also De La Ramee, (Marie) Louise
See also DLB 18

Ousmane, Sembene 1923- . . . . **CLC 66; BLC**
See also BW 1; CA 117; 125; MTCW

Ovid 43B.C.-18(?) . . . . **CMLC 7; PC 2**

Owen, Hugh
See Faust, Frederick (Schiller)

Owen, Wilfred (Edward Salter)
1893-1918 . . . . . . **TCLC 5, 27; DA; WLC**
See also CA 104; 141; CDBLB 1914-1945; DLB 20

Owens, Rochelle 1936- . . . . **CLC 8**
See also CA 17-20R; CAAS 2; CANR 39

Oz, Amos 1939- . . . **CLC 5, 8, 11, 27, 33, 54**
See also CA 53-56; CANR 27, 47; MTCW

Ozick, Cynthia
1928- . . . . **CLC 3, 7, 28, 62; SSC 15**
See also BEST 90:1; CA 17-20R; CANR 23; DLB 28, 152; DLBY 82; MTCW

Ozu, Yasujiro 1903-1963 . . . . **CLC 16**
See also CA 112

Pacheco, C.
See Pessoa, Fernando (Antonio Nogueira)

Pa Chin . . . . **CLC 18**
See also Li Fei-kan

Pack, Robert 1929- . . . . **CLC 13**
See also CA 1-4R; CANR 3, 44; DLB 5

Padgett, Lewis
See Kuttner, Henry

Padilla (Lorenzo), Heberto 1932- . . . **CLC 38**
See also AITN 1; CA 123; 131; HW

Page, Jimmy 1944- . . . . **CLC 12**

Page, Louise 1955- . . . . **CLC 40**
See also CA 140

Page, P(atricia) K(athleen)
1916- . . . . **CLC 7, 18; PC 12**
See also CA 53-56; CANR 4, 22; DLB 68; MTCW

Paget, Violet 1856-1935
See Lee, Vernon
See also CA 104

Paget-Lowe, Henry
See Lovecraft, H(oward) P(hillips)

Paglia, Camille (Anna) 1947- . . . . **CLC 68**
See also CA 140

Paige, Richard
See Koontz, Dean R(ay)

Pakenham, Antonia
See Fraser, (Lady) Antonia (Pakenham)

Palamas, Kostes 1859-1943 . . . . **TCLC 5**
See also CA 105

Palazzeschi, Aldo 1885-1974 . . . . **CLC 11**
See also CA 89-92; 53-56; DLB 114

Paley, Grace 1922- . . . . **CLC 4, 6, 37; SSC 8**
See also CA 25-28R; CANR 13, 46; DLB 28; MTCW

Palin, Michael (Edward) 1943- . . . . . **CLC 21**
See also Monty Python
See also CA 107; CANR 35; SATA 67

Palliser, Charles 1947- . . . . **CLC 65**
See also CA 136

Palma, Ricardo 1833-1919 . . . . **TCLC 29**

Pancake, Breece Dexter 1952-1979
See Pancake, Breece D'J
See also CA 123; 109

Pancake, Breece D'J .... **CLC 29**
See also Pancake, Breece Dexter
See also DLB 130

Panko, Rudy
See Gogol, Nikolai (Vasilyevich)

Papadiamantis, Alexandros 1851-1911 .... **TCLC 29**

Papadiamantopoulos, Johannes 1856-1910
See Moreas, Jean
See also CA 117

Papini, Giovanni 1881-1956....... **TCLC 22**
See also CA 121

Paracelsus 1493-1541.............. **LC 14**

Parasol, Peter
See Stevens, Wallace

Parfenie, Maria
See Codrescu, Andrei

Parini, Jay (Lee) 1948- .... **CLC 54**
See also CA 97-100; CAAS 16; CANR 32

Park, Jordan
See Kornbluth, C(yril) M.; Pohl, Frederik

Parker, Bert
See Ellison, Harlan (Jay)

Parker, Dorothy (Rothschild) 1893-1967 .... **CLC 15, 68; SSC 2**
See also CA 19-20; 25-28R; CAP 2; DLB 11, 45, 86; MTCW

Parker, Robert B(rown) 1932-...... **CLC 27**
See also BEST 89:4; CA 49-52; CANR 1, 26; MTCW

Parkin, Frank 1940-.............. **CLC 43**
See also CA 147

Parkman, Francis, Jr. 1823-1893 .... **NCLC 12**
See also DLB 1, 30

Parks, Gordon (Alexander Buchanan) 1912- .... **CLC 1, 16; BLC**
See also AITN 2; BW 2; CA 41-44R; CANR 26; DLB 33; SATA 8

Parnell, Thomas 1679-1718 .... **LC 3**
See also DLB 94

Parra, Nicanor 1914- .... **CLC 2; HLC**
See also CA 85-88; CANR 32; HW; MTCW

Parrish, Mary Frances
See Fisher, M(ary) F(rances) K(ennedy)

Parson
See Coleridge, Samuel Taylor

Parson Lot
See Kingsley, Charles

Partridge, Anthony
See Oppenheim, E(dward) Phillips

Pascoli, Giovanni 1855-1912 ...... **TCLC 45**

Pasolini, Pier Paolo 1922-1975 .... **CLC 20, 37**
See also CA 93-96; 61-64; DLB 128; MTCW

Pasquini
See Silone, Ignazio

Pastan, Linda (Olenik) 1932- ...... **CLC 27**
See also CA 61-64; CANR 18, 40; DLB 5

Pasternak, Boris (Leonidovich) 1890-1960 ...... **CLC 7, 10, 18, 63; DA; PC 6; WLC**
See also CA 127; 116; MTCW

Patchen, Kenneth 1911-1972... **CLC 1, 2, 18**
See also CA 1-4R; 33-36R; CANR 3, 35; DLB 16, 48; MTCW

Pater, Walter (Horatio) 1839-1894 .... **NCLC 7**
See also CDBLB 1832-1890; DLB 57

Paterson, A(ndrew) B(arton) 1864-1941 .... **TCLC 32**

Paterson, Katherine (Womeldorf) 1932- .... **CLC 12, 30**
See also AAYA 1; CA 21-24R; CANR 28; CLR 7; DLB 52; JRDA; MAICYA; MTCW; SATA 13, 53

Patmore, Coventry Kersey Dighton 1823-1896 .... **NCLC 9**
See also DLB 35, 98

Paton, Alan (Stewart) 1903-1988 ...... **CLC 4, 10, 25, 55; DA; WLC**
See also CA 13-16; 125; CANR 22; CAP 1; MTCW; SATA 11; SATA-Obit 56

Paton Walsh, Gillian 1937-
See Walsh, Jill Paton
See also CANR 38; JRDA; MAICYA; SAAS 3; SATA 4, 72

Paulding, James Kirke 1778-1860.. **NCLC 2**
See also DLB 3, 59, 74

Paulin, Thomas Neilson 1949-
See Paulin, Tom
See also CA 123; 128

Paulin, Tom .... **CLC 37**
See also Paulin, Thomas Neilson
See also DLB 40

Paustovsky, Konstantin (Georgievich) 1892-1968 .... **CLC 40**
See also CA 93-96; 25-28R

Pavese, Cesare 1908-1950 ..... **TCLC 3; PC 12; SSC 19**
See also CA 104; DLB 128

Pavic, Milorad 1929- .... **CLC 60**
See also CA 136

Payne, Alan
See Jakes, John (William)

Paz, Gil
See Lugones, Leopoldo

Paz, Octavio 1914- .... **CLC 3, 4, 6, 10, 19, 51, 65; DA; HLC; PC 1; WLC**
See also CA 73-76; CANR 32; DLBY 90; HW; MTCW

Peacock, Molly 1947-............. **CLC 60**
See also CA 103; CAAS 21; DLB 120

Peacock, Thomas Love 1785-1866 .... **NCLC 22**
See also DLB 96, 116

Peake, Mervyn 1911-1968....... **CLC 7, 54**
See also CA 5-8R; 25-28R; CANR 3; DLB 15; MTCW; SATA 23

Pearce, Philippa .... **CLC 21**
See also Christie, (Ann) Philippa
See also CLR 9; MAICYA; SATA 1, 67

Pearl, Eric
See Elman, Richard

Pearson, T(homas) R(eid) 1956- .... **CLC 39**
See also CA 120; 130

Peck, Dale 1968(?)- .... **CLC 81**

Peck, John 1941- .... **CLC 3**
See also CA 49-52; CANR 3

Peck, Richard (Wayne) 1934- ...... **CLC 21**
See also AAYA 1; CA 85-88; CANR 19, 38; CLR 15; JRDA; MAICYA; SAAS 2; SATA 18, 55

Peck, Robert Newton 1928-.... **CLC 17; DA**
See also AAYA 3; CA 81-84; CANR 31; JRDA; MAICYA; SAAS 1; SATA 21, 62

Peckinpah, (David) Sam(uel) 1925-1984 .... **CLC 20**
See also CA 109; 114

Pedersen, Knut 1859-1952
See Hamsun, Knut
See also CA 104; 119; MTCW

Peeslake, Gaffer
See Durrell, Lawrence (George)

Peguy, Charles Pierre 1873-1914 .... **TCLC 10**
See also CA 107

Pena, Ramon del Valle y
See Valle-Inclan, Ramon (Maria) del

Pendennis, Arthur Esquir
See Thackeray, William Makepeace

Penn, William 1644-1718........... **LC 25**
See also DLB 24

Pepys, Samuel 1633-1703 .... **LC 11; DA; WLC**
See also CDBLB 1660-1789; DLB 101

Percy, Walker 1916-1990 .... **CLC 2, 3, 6, 8, 14, 18, 47, 65**
See also CA 1-4R; 131; CANR 1, 23; DLB 2; DLBY 80, 90; MTCW

Perec, Georges 1936-1982 .... **CLC 56**
See also CA 141; DLB 83

Pereda (y Sanchez de Porrua), Jose Maria de 1833-1906 .... **TCLC 16**
See also CA 117

Pereda y Porrua, Jose Maria de
See Pereda (y Sanchez de Porrua), Jose Maria de

Peregoy, George Weems
See Mencken, H(enry) L(ouis)

Perelman, S(idney) J(oseph) 1904-1979 ... **CLC 3, 5, 9, 15, 23, 44, 49**
See also AITN 1, 2; CA 73-76; 89-92; CANR 18; DLB 11, 44; MTCW

Peret, Benjamin 1899-1959 .... **TCLC 20**
See also CA 117

Peretz, Isaac Loeb 1851(?)-1915... **TCLC 16**
See also CA 109

Peretz, Yitzkhok Leibush
See Peretz, Isaac Loeb

Perez Galdos, Benito 1843-1920... **TCLC 27**
See also CA 125; HW

Perrault, Charles 1628-1703 .... **LC 2**
See also MAICYA; SATA 25

Perry, Brighton
See Sherwood, Robert E(mmet)

Perse, St.-John .... **CLC 4, 11, 46**
See also Leger, (Marie-Rene Auguste) Alexis Saint-Leger

Perutz, Leo 1882-1957 . . . . **TCLC 60**
See also DLB 81

Peseenz, Tulio F.
See Lopez y Fuentes, Gregorio

Pesetsky, Bette 1932- . . . . **CLC 28**
See also CA 133; DLB 130

Peshkov, Alexei Maximovich 1868-1936
See Gorky, Maxim
See also CA 105; 141; DA

Pessoa, Fernando (Antonio Nogueira)
1888-1935 . . . . **TCLC 27; HLC**
See also CA 125

Peterkin, Julia Mood 1880-1961 . . . . **CLC 31**
See also CA 102; DLB 9

Peters, Joan K. 1945- . . . . **CLC 39**

Peters, Robert L(ouis) 1924- . . . . **CLC 7**
See also CA 13-16R; CAAS 8; DLB 105

Petofi, Sandor 1823-1849 . . . . **NCLC 21**

Petrakis, Harry Mark 1923- . . . . **CLC 3**
See also CA 9-12R; CANR 4, 30

Petrarch 1304-1374 . . . . **PC 8**

Petrov, Evgeny . . . . **TCLC 21**
See also Kataev, Evgeny Petrovich

Petry, Ann (Lane) 1908- . . . . . . **CLC 1, 7, 18**
See also BW 1; CA 5-8R; CAAS 6; CANR 4, 46; CLR 12; DLB 76; JRDA; MAICYA; MTCW; SATA 5

Petursson, Halligrimur 1614-1674 . . . . **LC 8**

Philips, Katherine 1632-1664 . . . . **LC 30**
See also DLB 131

Philipson, Morris H. 1926- . . . . **CLC 53**
See also CA 1-4R; CANR 4

Phillips, David Graham
1867-1911 . . . . **TCLC 44**
See also CA 108; DLB 9, 12

Phillips, Jack
See Sandburg, Carl (August)

Phillips, Jayne Anne
1952- . . . . **CLC 15, 33; SSC 16**
See also CA 101; CANR 24; DLBY 80; MTCW

Phillips, Richard
See Dick, Philip K(indred)

Phillips, Robert (Schaeffer) 1938- . . . **CLC 28**
See also CA 17-20R; CAAS 13; CANR 8; DLB 105

Phillips, Ward
See Lovecraft, H(oward) P(hillips)

Piccolo, Lucio 1901-1969 . . . . **CLC 13**
See also CA 97-100; DLB 114

Pickthall, Marjorie L(owry) C(hristie)
1883-1922 . . . . **TCLC 21**
See also CA 107; DLB 92

Pico della Mirandola, Giovanni
1463-1494 . . . . **LC 15**

Piercy, Marge
1936- . . . . **CLC 3, 6, 14, 18, 27, 62**
See also CA 21-24R; CAAS 1; CANR 13, 43; DLB 120; MTCW

Piers, Robert
See Anthony, Piers

Pieyre de Mandiargues, Andre 1909-1991
See Mandiargues, Andre Pieyre de
See also CA 103; 136; CANR 22

Pilnyak, Boris . . . . **TCLC 23**
See also Vogau, Boris Andreyevich

Pincherle, Alberto 1907-1990 . . . **CLC 11, 18**
See also Moravia, Alberto
See also CA 25-28R; 132; CANR 33; MTCW

Pinckney, Darryl 1953- . . . . **CLC 76**
See also BW 2; CA 143

Pindar 518B.C.-446B.C. . . . . **CMLC 12**

Pineda, Cecile 1942- . . . . **CLC 39**
See also CA 118

Pinero, Arthur Wing 1855-1934 . . . **TCLC 32**
See also CA 110; DLB 10

Pinero, Miguel (Antonio Gomez)
1946-1988 . . . . **CLC 4, 55**
See also CA 61-64; 125; CANR 29; HW

Pinget, Robert 1919- . . . . **CLC 7, 13, 37**
See also CA 85-88; DLB 83

Pink Floyd
See Barrett, (Roger) Syd; Gilmour, David; Mason, Nick; Waters, Roger; Wright, Rick

Pinkney, Edward 1802-1828 . . . . . **NCLC 31**

Pinkwater, Daniel Manus 1941- . . . . **CLC 35**
See also Pinkwater, Manus
See also AAYA 1; CA 29-32R; CANR 12, 38; CLR 4; JRDA; MAICYA; SAAS 3; SATA 46, 76

Pinkwater, Manus
See Pinkwater, Daniel Manus
See also SATA 8

Pinsky, Robert 1940- . . . . **CLC 9, 19, 38**
See also CA 29-32R; CAAS 4; DLBY 82

Pinta, Harold
See Pinter, Harold

Pinter, Harold
1930- . . . . . **CLC 1, 3, 6, 9, 11, 15, 27, 58, 73; DA; WLC**
See also CA 5-8R; CANR 33; CDBLB 1960 to Present; DLB 13; MTCW

Pirandello, Luigi
1867-1936 . . . . . **TCLC 4, 29; DA; DC 5; WLC**
See also CA 104

Pirsig, Robert M(aynard)
1928- . . . . **CLC 4, 6, 73**
See also CA 53-56; CANR 42; MTCW; SATA 39

Pisarev, Dmitry Ivanovich
1840-1868 . . . . **NCLC 25**

Pix, Mary (Griffith) 1666-1709 . . . . **LC 8**
See also DLB 80

Pixerecourt, Guilbert de
1773-1844 . . . . **NCLC 39**

Plaidy, Jean
See Hibbert, Eleanor Alice Burford

Planche, James Robinson
1796-1880 . . . . **NCLC 42**

Plant, Robert 1948- . . . . **CLC 12**

Plante, David (Robert)
1940- . . . . **CLC 7, 23, 38**
See also CA 37-40R; CANR 12, 36; DLBY 83; MTCW

Plath, Sylvia
1932-1963 . . . . . **CLC 1, 2, 3, 5, 9, 11, 14, 17, 50, 51, 62; DA; PC 1; WLC**
See also AAYA 13; CA 19-20; CANR 34; CAP 2; CDALB 1941-1968; DLB 5, 6, 152; MTCW

Plato 428(?)B.C.-348(?)B.C. . . . **CMLC 8; DA**

Platonov, Andrei . . . . **TCLC 14**
See also Klimentov, Andrei Platonovich

Platt, Kin 1911- . . . . **CLC 26**
See also AAYA 11; CA 17-20R; CANR 11; JRDA; SAAS 17; SATA 21

Plick et Plock
See Simenon, Georges (Jacques Christian)

Plimpton, George (Ames) 1927- . . . . . **CLC 36**
See also AITN 1; CA 21-24R; CANR 32; MTCW; SATA 10

Plomer, William Charles Franklin
1903-1973 . . . . **CLC 4, 8**
See also CA 21-22; CANR 34; CAP 2; DLB 20; MTCW; SATA 24

Plowman, Piers
See Kavanagh, Patrick (Joseph)

Plum, J.
See Wodehouse, P(elham) G(renville)

Plumly, Stanley (Ross) 1939- . . . . . . **CLC 33**
See also CA 108; 110; DLB 5

Plumpe, Friedrich Wilhelm
1888-1931 . . . . **TCLC 53**
See also CA 112

Poe, Edgar Allan
1809-1849 . . . . . **NCLC 1, 16; DA; PC 1; SSC 1; WLC**
See also AAYA 14; CDALB 1640-1865; DLB 3, 59, 73, 74; SATA 23

Poet of Titchfield Street, The
See Pound, Ezra (Weston Loomis)

Pohl, Frederik 1919- . . . . **CLC 18**
See also CA 61-64; CAAS 1; CANR 11, 37; DLB 8; MTCW; SATA 24

Poirier, Louis 1910-
See Gracq, Julien
See also CA 122; 126

Poitier, Sidney 1927- . . . . **CLC 26**
See also BW 1; CA 117

Polanski, Roman 1933- . . . . **CLC 16**
See also CA 77-80

Poliakoff, Stephen 1952- . . . . **CLC 38**
See also CA 106; DLB 13

Police, The
See Copeland, Stewart (Armstrong); Summers, Andrew James; Sumner, Gordon Matthew

Polidori, John William
1795-1821 . . . . **NCLC 51**
See also DLB 116

Pollitt, Katha 1949- . . . . **CLC 28**
See also CA 120; 122; MTCW

Pollock, (Mary) Sharon 1936- . . . . . . **CLC 50**
See also CA 141; DLB 60

Polo, Marco 1254-1324 . . . . **CMLC 15**

Pomerance, Bernard 1940- . . . . **CLC 13**
See also CA 101

Ponge, Francis (Jean Gaston Alfred) 1899-1988 . . . . **CLC 6, 18**
See also CA 85-88; 126; CANR 40

Pontoppidan, Henrik 1857-1943 . . . **TCLC 29**

Poole, Josephine . . . . **CLC 17**
See also Helyar, Jane Penelope Josephine
See also SAAS 2; SATA 5

Popa, Vasko 1922- . . . . **CLC 19**
See also CA 112

Pope, Alexander 1688-1744 . . . . **LC 3; DA; WLC**
See also CDBLB 1660-1789; DLB 95, 101

Porter, Connie (Rose) 1959(?)- . . . . . **CLC 70**
See also BW 2; CA 142; SATA 81

Porter, Gene(va Grace) Stratton 1863(?)-1924 . . . . **TCLC 21**
See also CA 112

Porter, Katherine Anne 1890-1980 . . . . . . **CLC 1, 3, 7, 10, 13, 15, 27; DA; SSC 4**
See also AITN 2; CA 1-4R; 101; CANR 1; DLB 4, 9, 102; DLBD 12; DLBY 80; MTCW; SATA 39; SATA-Obit 23

Porter, Peter (Neville Frederick) 1929- . . . . **CLC 5, 13, 33**
See also CA 85-88; DLB 40

Porter, William Sydney 1862-1910
See Henry, O.
See also CA 104; 131; CDALB 1865-1917; DA; DLB 12, 78, 79; MTCW; YABC 2

Portillo (y Pacheco), Jose Lopez
See Lopez Portillo (y Pacheco), Jose

Post, Melville Davisson 1869-1930 . . . . **TCLC 39**
See also CA 110

Potok, Chaim 1929- . . . . **CLC 2, 7, 14, 26**
See also AITN 1, 2; CA 17-20R; CANR 19, 35; DLB 28, 152; MTCW; SATA 33

Potter, Beatrice
See Webb, (Martha) Beatrice (Potter)
See also MAICYA

Potter, Dennis (Christopher George) 1935-1994 . . . . **CLC 58, 86**
See also CA 107; 145; CANR 33; MTCW

Pound, Ezra (Weston Loomis) 1885-1972 . . . . . . **CLC 1, 2, 3, 4, 5, 7, 10, 13, 18, 34, 48, 50; DA; PC 4; WLC**
See also CA 5-8R; 37-40R; CANR 40; CDALB 1917-1929; DLB 4, 45, 63; MTCW

Povod, Reinaldo 1959-1994 . . . . **CLC 44**
See also CA 136; 146

Powell, Adam Clayton, Jr. 1908-1972 . . . . **CLC 89; BLC**
See also BW 1; CA 102; 33-36R

Powell, Anthony (Dymoke) 1905- . . . . **CLC 1, 3, 7, 9, 10, 31**
See also CA 1-4R; CANR 1, 32; CDBLB 1945-1960; DLB 15; MTCW

Powell, Dawn 1897-1965 . . . . **CLC 66**
See also CA 5-8R

Powell, Padgett 1952- . . . . **CLC 34**
See also CA 126

Powers, J(ames) F(arl) 1917- . . . . **CLC 1, 4, 8, 57; SSC 4**
See also CA 1-4R; CANR 2; DLB 130; MTCW

Powers, John J(ames) 1945-
See Powers, John R.
See also CA 69-72

Powers, John R. . . . . **CLC 66**
See also Powers, John J(ames)

Pownall, David 1938- . . . . **CLC 10**
See also CA 89-92; CAAS 18; DLB 14

Powys, John Cowper 1872-1963 . . . . **CLC 7, 9, 15, 46**
See also CA 85-88; DLB 15; MTCW

Powys, T(heodore) F(rancis) 1875-1953 . . . . **TCLC 9**
See also CA 106; DLB 36

Prager, Emily 1952- . . . . **CLC 56**

Pratt, E(dwin) J(ohn) 1883(?)-1964 . . . . **CLC 19**
See also CA 141; 93-96; DLB 92

Premchand . . . . **TCLC 21**
See also Srivastava, Dhanpat Rai

Preussler, Otfried 1923- . . . . **CLC 17**
See also CA 77-80; SATA 24

Prevert, Jacques (Henri Marie) 1900-1977 . . . . **CLC 15**
See also CA 77-80; 69-72; CANR 29; MTCW; SATA-Obit 30

Prevost, Abbe (Antoine Francois) 1697-1763 . . . . **LC 1**

Price, (Edward) Reynolds 1933- . . . . **CLC 3, 6, 13, 43, 50, 63**
See also CA 1-4R; CANR 1, 37; DLB 2

Price, Richard 1949- . . . . **CLC 6, 12**
See also CA 49-52; CANR 3; DLBY 81

Prichard, Katharine Susannah 1883-1969 . . . . **CLC 46**
See also CA 11-12; CANR 33; CAP 1; MTCW; SATA 66

Priestley, J(ohn) B(oynton) 1894-1984 . . . . **CLC 2, 5, 9, 34**
See also CA 9-12R; 113; CANR 33; CDBLB 1914-1945; DLB 10, 34, 77, 100, 139; DLBY 84; MTCW

Prince 1958(?)- . . . . **CLC 35**

Prince, F(rank) T(empleton) 1912- . . **CLC 22**
See also CA 101; CANR 43; DLB 20

Prince Kropotkin
See Kropotkin, Peter (Aleksieevich)

Prior, Matthew 1664-1721 . . . . **LC 4**
See also DLB 95

Pritchard, William H(arrison) 1932- . . . . **CLC 34**
See also CA 65-68; CANR 23; DLB 111

Pritchett, V(ictor) S(awdon) 1900- . . . . **CLC 5, 13, 15, 41; SSC 14**
See also CA 61-64; CANR 31; DLB 15, 139; MTCW

Private 19022
See Manning, Frederic

Probst, Mark 1925- . . . . **CLC 59**
See also CA 130

Prokosch, Frederic 1908-1989 . . . . **CLC 4, 48**
See also CA 73-76; 128; DLB 48

Prophet, The
See Dreiser, Theodore (Herman Albert)

Prose, Francine 1947- . . . . **CLC 45**
See also CA 109; 112; CANR 46

Proudhon
See Cunha, Euclides (Rodrigues Pimenta) da

Proulx, E. Annie 1935- . . . . **CLC 81**

Proust, (Valentin-Louis-George-Eugene-) Marcel 1871-1922 . . . **TCLC 7, 13, 33; DA; WLC**
See also CA 104; 120; DLB 65; MTCW

Prowler, Harley
See Masters, Edgar Lee

Prus, Boleslaw 1845-1912 . . . . **TCLC 48**

Pryor, Richard (Franklin Lenox Thomas) 1940- . . . . **CLC 26**
See also CA 122

Przybyszewski, Stanislaw 1868-1927 . . . . **TCLC 36**
See also DLB 66

Pteleon
See Grieve, C(hristopher) M(urray)

Puckett, Lute
See Masters, Edgar Lee

Puig, Manuel 1932-1990 . . . **CLC 3, 5, 10, 28, 65; HLC**
See also CA 45-48; CANR 2, 32; DLB 113; HW; MTCW

Purdy, Al(fred Wellington) 1918- . . . . **CLC 3, 6, 14, 50**
See also CA 81-84; CAAS 17; CANR 42; DLB 88

Purdy, James (Amos) 1923- . . . . **CLC 2, 4, 10, 28, 52**
See also CA 33-36R; CAAS 1; CANR 19; DLB 2; MTCW

Pure, Simon
See Swinnerton, Frank Arthur

Pushkin, Alexander (Sergeyevich) 1799-1837 . . . . **NCLC 3, 27; DA; PC 10; WLC**
See also SATA 61

P'u Sung-ling 1640-1715 . . . . **LC 3**

Putnam, Arthur Lee
See Alger, Horatio, Jr.

Puzo, Mario 1920- . . . . **CLC 1, 2, 6, 36**
See also CA 65-68; CANR 4, 42; DLB 6; MTCW

Pym, Barbara (Mary Crampton) 1913-1980 . . . . **CLC 13, 19, 37**
See also CA 13-14; 97-100; CANR 13, 34; CAP 1; DLB 14; DLBY 87; MTCW

Pynchon, Thomas (Ruggles, Jr.) 1937- . . . . . **CLC 2, 3, 6, 9, 11, 18, 33, 62, 72; DA; SSC 14; WLC**
See also BEST 90:2; CA 17-20R; CANR 22, 46; DLB 2; MTCW

Qian Zhongshu
See Ch'ien Chung-shu

Qroll
See Dagerman, Stig (Halvard)

Quarrington, Paul (Lewis) 1953-.... **CLC 65**
See also CA 129

Quasimodo, Salvatore 1901-1968 ... **CLC 10**
See also CA 13-16; 25-28R; CAP 1; DLB 114; MTCW

Queen, Ellery.................. **CLC 3, 11**
See also Dannay, Frederic; Davidson, Avram; Lee, Manfred B(ennington); Sturgeon, Theodore (Hamilton); Vance, John Holbrook

Queen, Ellery, Jr.
See Dannay, Frederic; Lee, Manfred B(ennington)

Queneau, Raymond
1903-1976 .... **CLC 2, 5, 10, 42**
See also CA 77-80; 69-72; CANR 32; DLB 72; MTCW

Quevedo, Francisco de 1580-1645.... **LC 23**

Quiller-Couch, Arthur Thomas
1863-1944 .... **TCLC 53**
See also CA 118; DLB 135, 153

Quin, Ann (Marie) 1936-1973....... **CLC 6**
See also CA 9-12R; 45-48; DLB 14

Quinn, Martin
See Smith, Martin Cruz

Quinn, Simon
See Smith, Martin Cruz

Quiroga, Horacio (Sylvestre)
1878-1937 .... **TCLC 20; HLC**
See also CA 117; 131; HW; MTCW

Quoirez, Francoise 1935-........... **CLC 9**
See also Sagan, Francoise
See also CA 49-52; CANR 6, 39; MTCW

Raabe, Wilhelm 1831-1910 .... **TCLC 45**
See also DLB 129

Rabe, David (William) 1940-... **CLC 4, 8, 33**
See also CA 85-88; CABS 3; DLB 7

Rabelais, Francois
1483-1553 .... **LC 5; DA; WLC**

Rabinovitch, Sholem 1859-1916
See Aleichem, Sholom
See also CA 104

Racine, Jean 1639-1699............ **LC 28**

Radcliffe, Ann (Ward) 1764-1823.. **NCLC 6**
See also DLB 39

Radiguet, Raymond 1903-1923 .... **TCLC 29**
See also DLB 65

Radnoti, Miklos 1909-1944 .... **TCLC 16**
See also CA 118

Rado, James 1939-............... **CLC 17**
See also CA 105

Radvanyi, Netty 1900-1983
See Seghers, Anna
See also CA 85-88; 110

Rae, Ben
See Griffiths, Trevor

Raeburn, John (Hay) 1941-........ **CLC 34**
See also CA 57-60

Ragni, Gerome 1942-1991 .... **CLC 17**
See also CA 105; 134

Rahv, Philip 1908-1973 .... **CLC 24**
See also Greenberg, Ivan
See also DLB 137

Raine, Craig 1944-............... **CLC 32**
See also CA 108; CANR 29; DLB 40

Raine, Kathleen (Jessie) 1908- ... **CLC 7, 45**
See also CA 85-88; CANR 46; DLB 20; MTCW

Rainis, Janis 1865-1929.......... **TCLC 29**

Rakosi, Carl...................... **CLC 47**
See also Rawley, Callman
See also CAAS 5

Raleigh, Richard
See Lovecraft, H(oward) P(hillips)

Rallentando, H. P.
See Sayers, Dorothy L(eigh)

Ramal, Walter
See de la Mare, Walter (John)

Ramon, Juan
See Jimenez (Mantecon), Juan Ramon

Ramos, Graciliano 1892-1953 ..... **TCLC 32**

Rampersad, Arnold 1941-.......... **CLC 44**
See also BW 2; CA 127; 133; DLB 111

Rampling, Anne
See Rice, Anne

Ramsay, Allan 1684(?)-1758 .... **LC 29**
See also DLB 95

Ramuz, Charles-Ferdinand
1878-1947 .... **TCLC 33**

Rand, Ayn
1905-1982 ...... **CLC 3, 30, 44, 79; DA; WLC**
See also AAYA 10; CA 13-16R; 105; CANR 27; MTCW

Randall, Dudley (Felker)
1914- .... **CLC 1; BLC**
See also BW 1; CA 25-28R; CANR 23; DLB 41

Randall, Robert
See Silverberg, Robert

Ranger, Ken
See Creasey, John

Ransom, John Crowe
1888-1974 .... **CLC 2, 4, 5, 11, 24**
See also CA 5-8R; 49-52; CANR 6, 34; DLB 45, 63; MTCW

Rao, Raja 1909-.............. **CLC 25, 56**
See also CA 73-76; MTCW

Raphael, Frederic (Michael)
1931- .... **CLC 2, 14**
See also CA 1-4R; CANR 1; DLB 14

Ratcliffe, James P.
See Mencken, H(enry) L(ouis)

Rathbone, Julian 1935- .... **CLC 41**
See also CA 101; CANR 34

Rattigan, Terence (Mervyn)
1911-1977 .... **CLC 7**
See also CA 85-88; 73-76; CDBLB 1945-1960; DLB 13; MTCW

Ratushinskaya, Irina 1954-........ **CLC 54**
See also CA 129

Raven, Simon (Arthur Noel)
1927- .... **CLC 14**
See also CA 81-84

Rawley, Callman 1903-
See Rakosi, Carl
See also CA 21-24R; CANR 12, 32

Rawlings, Marjorie Kinnan
1896-1953 .... **TCLC 4**
See also CA 104; 137; DLB 9, 22, 102; JRDA; MAICYA; YABC 1

Ray, Satyajit 1921-1992........ **CLC 16, 76**
See also CA 114; 137

Read, Herbert Edward 1893-1968.... **CLC 4**
See also CA 85-88; 25-28R; DLB 20, 149

Read, Piers Paul 1941- ...... **CLC 4, 10, 25**
See also CA 21-24R; CANR 38; DLB 14; SATA 21

Reade, Charles 1814-1884 .... **NCLC 2**
See also DLB 21

Reade, Hamish
See Gray, Simon (James Holliday)

Reading, Peter 1946- .... **CLC 47**
See also CA 103; CANR 46; DLB 40

Reaney, James 1926-............. **CLC 13**
See also CA 41-44R; CAAS 15; CANR 42; DLB 68; SATA 43

Rebreanu, Liviu 1885-1944 .... **TCLC 28**

Rechy, John (Francisco)
1934- .... **CLC 1, 7, 14, 18; HLC**
See also CA 5-8R; CAAS 4; CANR 6, 32; DLB 122; DLBY 82; HW

Redcam, Tom 1870-1933 .... **TCLC 25**

Reddin, Keith..................... **CLC 67**

Redgrove, Peter (William)
1932- .... **CLC 6, 41**
See also CA 1-4R; CANR 3, 39; DLB 40

Redmon, Anne.................... **CLC 22**
See also Nightingale, Anne Redmon
See also DLBY 86

Reed, Eliot
See Ambler, Eric

Reed, Ishmael
1938- ... **CLC 2, 3, 5, 6, 13, 32, 60; BLC**
See also BW 2; CA 21-24R; CANR 25, 48; DLB 2, 5, 33; DLBD 8; MTCW

Reed, John (Silas) 1887-1920 ...... **TCLC 9**
See also CA 106

Reed, Lou........................ **CLC 21**
See also Firbank, Louis

Reeve, Clara 1729-1807 .... **NCLC 19**
See also DLB 39

Reich, Wilhelm 1897-1957........ **TCLC 57**

Reid, Christopher (John) 1949-..... **CLC 33**
See also CA 140; DLB 40

Reid, Desmond
See Moorcock, Michael (John)

Reid Banks, Lynne 1929-
See Banks, Lynne Reid
See also CA 1-4R; CANR 6, 22, 38; CLR 24; JRDA; MAICYA; SATA 22, 75

Reilly, William K.
See Creasey, John

Reiner, Max
See Caldwell, (Janet Miriam) Taylor (Holland)

Reis, Ricardo
See Pessoa, Fernando (Antonio Nogueira)

Remarque, Erich Maria 1898-1970 . . . . **CLC 21; DA**
See also CA 77-80; 29-32R; DLB 56; MTCW

Remizov, A.
See Remizov, Aleksei (Mikhailovich)

Remizov, A. M.
See Remizov, Aleksei (Mikhailovich)

Remizov, Aleksei (Mikhailovich) 1877-1957 . . . . **TCLC 27**
See also CA 125; 133

Renan, Joseph Ernest 1823-1892 . . . . **NCLC 26**

Renard, Jules 1864-1910 . . . . **TCLC 17**
See also CA 117

Renault, Mary . . . . **CLC 3, 11, 17**
See also Challans, Mary
See also DLBY 83

Rendell, Ruth (Barbara) 1930- . . **CLC 28, 48**
See also Vine, Barbara
See also CA 109; CANR 32; DLB 87; MTCW

Renoir, Jean 1894-1979 . . . . **CLC 20**
See also CA 129; 85-88

Resnais, Alain 1922- . . . . **CLC 16**

Reverdy, Pierre 1889-1960 . . . . **CLC 53**
See also CA 97-100; 89-92

Rexroth, Kenneth 1905-1982 . . . . . . **CLC 1, 2, 6, 11, 22, 49**
See also CA 5-8R; 107; CANR 14, 34; CDALB 1941-1968; DLB 16, 48; DLBY 82; MTCW

Reyes, Alfonso 1889-1959 . . . . **TCLC 33**
See also CA 131; HW

Reyes y Basoalto, Ricardo Eliecer Neftali
See Neruda, Pablo

Reymont, Wladyslaw (Stanislaw) 1868(?)-1925 . . . . **TCLC 5**
See also CA 104

Reynolds, Jonathan 1942- . . . . **CLC 6, 38**
See also CA 65-68; CANR 28

Reynolds, Joshua 1723-1792 . . . . **LC 15**
See also DLB 104

Reynolds, Michael Shane 1937- . . . . **CLC 44**
See also CA 65-68; CANR 9

Reznikoff, Charles 1894-1976 . . . . **CLC 9**
See also CA 33-36; 61-64; CAP 2; DLB 28, 45

Rezzori (d'Arezzo), Gregor von 1914- . . . . **CLC 25**
See also CA 122; 136

Rhine, Richard
See Silverstein, Alvin

Rhodes, Eugene Manlove 1869-1934 . . . . **TCLC 53**

R'hoone
See Balzac, Honore de

Rhys, Jean 1890(?)-1979 . . . . **CLC 2, 4, 6, 14, 19, 51**
See also CA 25-28R; 85-88; CANR 35; CDBLB 1945-1960; DLB 36, 117; MTCW

Ribeiro, Darcy 1922- . . . . **CLC 34**
See also CA 33-36R

Ribeiro, Joao Ubaldo (Osorio Pimentel) 1941- . . . . **CLC 10, 67**
See also CA 81-84

Ribman, Ronald (Burt) 1932- . . . . **CLC 7**
See also CA 21-24R; CANR 46

Ricci, Nino 1959- . . . . **CLC 70**
See also CA 137

Rice, Anne 1941- . . . . **CLC 41**
See also AAYA 9; BEST 89:2; CA 65-68; CANR 12, 36

Rice, Elmer (Leopold) 1892-1967 . . . . **CLC 7, 49**
See also CA 21-22; 25-28R; CAP 2; DLB 4, 7; MTCW

Rice, Tim(othy Miles Bindon) 1944- . . . . **CLC 21**
See also CA 103; CANR 46

Rich, Adrienne (Cecile) 1929- . . . . **CLC 3, 6, 7, 11, 18, 36, 73, 76; PC 5**
See also CA 9-12R; CANR 20; DLB 5, 67; MTCW

Rich, Barbara
See Graves, Robert (von Ranke)

Rich, Robert
See Trumbo, Dalton

Richard, Keith . . . . **CLC 17**
See also Richards, Keith

Richards, David Adams 1950- . . . . . . **CLC 59**
See also CA 93-96; DLB 53

Richards, I(vor) A(rmstrong) 1893-1979 . . . . **CLC 14, 24**
See also CA 41-44R; 89-92; CANR 34; DLB 27

Richards, Keith 1943-
See Richard, Keith
See also CA 107

Richardson, Anne
See Roiphe, Anne (Richardson)

Richardson, Dorothy Miller 1873-1957 . . . . **TCLC 3**
See also CA 104; DLB 36

Richardson, Ethel Florence (Lindesay) 1870-1946
See Richardson, Henry Handel
See also CA 105

Richardson, Henry Handel . . . . **TCLC 4**
See also Richardson, Ethel Florence (Lindesay)

Richardson, Samuel 1689-1761 . . . . **LC 1; DA; WLC**
See also CDBLB 1660-1789; DLB 39

Richler, Mordecai 1931- . . . . **CLC 3, 5, 9, 13, 18, 46, 70**
See also AITN 1; CA 65-68; CANR 31; CLR 17; DLB 53; MAICYA; MTCW; SATA 44; SATA-Brief 27

Richter, Conrad (Michael) 1890-1968 . . . . **CLC 30**
See also CA 5-8R; 25-28R; CANR 23; DLB 9; MTCW; SATA 3

Ricostranza, Tom
See Ellis, Trey

Riddell, J. H. 1832-1906 . . . . **TCLC 40**

Riding, Laura . . . . **CLC 3, 7**
See also Jackson, Laura (Riding)

Riefenstahl, Berta Helene Amalia 1902-
See Riefenstahl, Leni
See also CA 108

Riefenstahl, Leni . . . . **CLC 16**
See also Riefenstahl, Berta Helene Amalia

Riffe, Ernest
See Bergman, (Ernst) Ingmar

Riggs, (Rolla) Lynn 1899-1954 . . . . **TCLC 56**
See also CA 144; NNAL

Riley, James Whitcomb 1849-1916 . . . . **TCLC 51**
See also CA 118; 137; MAICYA; SATA 17

Riley, Tex
See Creasey, John

Rilke, Rainer Maria 1875-1926 . . . . **TCLC 1, 6, 19; PC 2**
See also CA 104; 132; DLB 81; MTCW

Rimbaud, (Jean Nicolas) Arthur 1854-1891 . . . . . **NCLC 4, 35; DA; PC 3; WLC**

Rinehart, Mary Roberts 1876-1958 . . . . **TCLC 52**
See also CA 108

Ringmaster, The
See Mencken, H(enry) L(ouis)

Ringwood, Gwen(dolyn Margaret) Pharis 1910-1984 . . . . **CLC 48**
See also CA 112; DLB 88

Rio, Michel 19(?)- . . . . **CLC 43**

Ritsos, Giannes
See Ritsos, Yannis

Ritsos, Yannis 1909-1990. . . . . **CLC 6, 13, 31**
See also CA 77-80; 133; CANR 39; MTCW

Ritter, Erika 1948(?)- . . . . **CLC 52**

Rivera, Jose Eustasio 1889-1928. . . **TCLC 35**
See also HW

Rivers, Conrad Kent 1933-1968. . . . . . **CLC 1**
See also BW 1; CA 85-88; DLB 41

Rivers, Elfrida
See Bradley, Marion Zimmer

Riverside, John
See Heinlein, Robert A(nson)

Rizal, Jose 1861-1896. . . . . **NCLC 27**

Roa Bastos, Augusto (Antonio) 1917- . . . . **CLC 45; HLC**
See also CA 131; DLB 113; HW

Robbe-Grillet, Alain 1922- . . . . . . **CLC 1, 2, 4, 6, 8, 10, 14, 43**
See also CA 9-12R; CANR 33; DLB 83; MTCW

Robbins, Harold 1916- . . . . **CLC 5**
See also CA 73-76; CANR 26; MTCW

Robbins, Thomas Eugene 1936-
See Robbins, Tom
See also CA 81-84; CANR 29; MTCW

Robbins, Tom . . . . **CLC 9, 32, 64**
See also Robbins, Thomas Eugene
See also BEST 90:3; DLBY 80

Robbins, Trina 1938- . . . . **CLC 21**
See also CA 128

Roberts, Charles G(eorge) D(ouglas) 1860-1943 .... **TCLC 8**
See also CA 105; CLR 33; DLB 92; SATA-Brief 29

Roberts, Kate 1891-1985 .... **CLC 15**
See also CA 107; 116

Roberts, Keith (John Kingston) 1935- .... **CLC 14**
See also CA 25-28R; CANR 46

Roberts, Kenneth (Lewis) 1885-1957 .... **TCLC 23**
See also CA 109; DLB 9

Roberts, Michele (B.) 1949-........ **CLC 48**
See also CA 115

Robertson, Ellis
See Ellison, Harlan (Jay); Silverberg, Robert

Robertson, Thomas William 1829-1871 .... **NCLC 35**

Robinson, Edwin Arlington 1869-1935 .... **TCLC 5; DA; PC 1**
See also CA 104; 133; CDALB 1865-1917; DLB 54; MTCW

Robinson, Henry Crabb 1775-1867 .... **NCLC 15**
See also DLB 107

Robinson, Jill 1936-.............. **CLC 10**
See also CA 102

Robinson, Kim Stanley 1952- ...... **CLC 34**
See also CA 126

Robinson, Lloyd
See Silverberg, Robert

Robinson, Marilynne 1944-........ **CLC 25**
See also CA 116

Robinson, Smokey................. **CLC 21**
See also Robinson, William, Jr.

Robinson, William, Jr. 1940-
See Robinson, Smokey
See also CA 116

Robison, Mary 1949-............. **CLC 42**
See also CA 113; 116; DLB 130

Rod, Edouard 1857-1910 .... **TCLC 52**

Roddenberry, Eugene Wesley 1921-1991
See Roddenberry, Gene
See also CA 110; 135; CANR 37; SATA 45; SATA-Obit 69

Roddenberry, Gene................ **CLC 17**
See also Roddenberry, Eugene Wesley
See also AAYA 5; SATA-Obit 69

Rodgers, Mary 1931-............. **CLC 12**
See also CA 49-52; CANR 8; CLR 20; JRDA; MAICYA; SATA 8

Rodgers, W(illiam) R(obert) 1909-1969 .... **CLC 7**
See also CA 85-88; DLB 20

Rodman, Eric
See Silverberg, Robert

Rodman, Howard 1920(?)-1985..... **CLC 65**
See also CA 118

Rodman, Maia
See Wojciechowska, Maia (Teresa)

Rodriguez, Claudio 1934-.......... **CLC 10**
See also DLB 134

Roelvaag, O(le) E(dvart) 1876-1931 .... **TCLC 17**
See also CA 117; DLB 9

Roethke, Theodore (Huebner) 1908-1963 ...... **CLC 1, 3, 8, 11, 19, 46**
See also CA 81-84; CABS 2; CDALB 1941-1968; DLB 5; MTCW

Rogers, Thomas Hunton 1927- ..... **CLC 57**
See also CA 89-92

Rogers, Will(iam Penn Adair) 1879-1935 .... **TCLC 8**
See also CA 105; 144; DLB 11; NNAL

Rogin, Gilbert 1929-.............. **CLC 18**
See also CA 65-68; CANR 15

Rohan, Koda .... **TCLC 22**
See also Koda Shigeyuki

Rohmer, Eric..................... **CLC 16**
See also Scherer, Jean-Marie Maurice

Rohmer, Sax .... **TCLC 28**
See also Ward, Arthur Henry Sarsfield
See also DLB 70

Roiphe, Anne (Richardson) 1935- .... **CLC 3, 9**
See also CA 89-92; CANR 45; DLBY 80

Rojas, Fernando de 1465-1541 ...... **LC 23**

Rolfe, Frederick (William Serafino Austin Lewis Mary) 1860-1913...... **TCLC 12**
See also CA 107; DLB 34

Rolland, Romain 1866-1944....... **TCLC 23**
See also CA 118; DLB 65

Rolvaag, O(le) E(dvart)
See Roelvaag, O(le) E(dvart)

Romain Arnaud, Saint
See Aragon, Louis

Romains, Jules 1885-1972.......... **CLC 7**
See also CA 85-88; CANR 34; DLB 65; MTCW

Romero, Jose Ruben 1890-1952 ... **TCLC 14**
See also CA 114; 131; HW

Ronsard, Pierre de 1524-1585 .... **LC 6; PC 11**

Rooke, Leon 1934-............ **CLC 25, 34**
See also CA 25-28R; CANR 23

Roper, William 1498-1578.......... **LC 10**

Roquelaure, A. N.
See Rice, Anne

Rosa, Joao Guimaraes 1908-1967 ... **CLC 23**
See also CA 89-92; DLB 113

Rose, Wendy 1948-......... **CLC 85; PC 12**
See also CA 53-56; CANR 5; NNAL; SATA 12

Rosen, Richard (Dean) 1949-....... **CLC 39**
See also CA 77-80

Rosenberg, Isaac 1890-1918....... **TCLC 12**
See also CA 107; DLB 20

Rosenblatt, Joe .... **CLC 15**
See also Rosenblatt, Joseph

Rosenblatt, Joseph 1933-
See Rosenblatt, Joe
See also CA 89-92

Rosenfeld, Samuel 1896-1963
See Tzara, Tristan
See also CA 89-92

Rosenthal, M(acha) L(ouis) 1917-... **CLC 28**
See also CA 1-4R; CAAS 6; CANR 4; DLB 5; SATA 59

Ross, Barnaby
See Dannay, Frederic

Ross, Bernard L.
See Follett, Ken(neth Martin)

Ross, J. H.
See Lawrence, T(homas) E(dward)

Ross, Martin
See Martin, Violet Florence
See also DLB 135

Ross, (James) Sinclair 1908-....... **CLC 13**
See also CA 73-76; DLB 88

Rossetti, Christina (Georgina) 1830-1894 ..... **NCLC 2, 50; DA; PC 7; WLC**
See also DLB 35; MAICYA; SATA 20

Rossetti, Dante Gabriel 1828-1882 .... **NCLC 4; DA; WLC**
See also CDBLB 1832-1890; DLB 35

Rossner, Judith (Perelman) 1935- .... **CLC 6, 9, 29**
See also AITN 2; BEST 90:3; CA 17-20R; CANR 18; DLB 6; MTCW

Rostand, Edmond (Eugene Alexis) 1868-1918 .... **TCLC 6, 37; DA**
See also CA 104; 126; MTCW

Roth, Henry 1906-........... **CLC 2, 6, 11**
See also CA 11-12; CANR 38; CAP 1; DLB 28; MTCW

Roth, Joseph 1894-1939.......... **TCLC 33**
See also DLB 85

Roth, Philip (Milton) 1933- ...... **CLC 1, 2, 3, 4, 6, 9, 15, 22, 31, 47, 66, 86; DA; WLC**
See also BEST 90:3; CA 1-4R; CANR 1, 22, 36; CDALB 1968-1988; DLB 2, 28; DLBY 82; MTCW

Rothenberg, Jerome 1931-....... **CLC 6, 57**
See also CA 45-48; CANR 1; DLB 5

Roumain, Jacques (Jean Baptiste) 1907-1944 .... **TCLC 19; BLC**
See also BW 1; CA 117; 125

Rourke, Constance (Mayfield) 1885-1941 .... **TCLC 12**
See also CA 107; YABC 1

Rousseau, Jean-Baptiste 1671-1741 ... **LC 9**

Rousseau, Jean-Jacques 1712-1778 .... **LC 14; DA; WLC**

Roussel, Raymond 1877-1933 ..... **TCLC 20**
See also CA 117

Rovit, Earl (Herbert) 1927-......... **CLC 7**
See also CA 5-8R; CANR 12

Rowe, Nicholas 1674-1718........... **LC 8**
See also DLB 84

Rowley, Ames Dorrance
See Lovecraft, H(oward) P(hillips)

Rowson, Susanna Haswell 1762(?)-1824 .... **NCLC 5**
See also DLB 37

Roy, Gabrielle 1909-1983....... **CLC 10, 14**
See also CA 53-56; 110; CANR 5; DLB 68; MTCW

Rozewicz, Tadeusz 1921- . . . . **CLC 9, 23**
See also CA 108; CANR 36; MTCW

Ruark, Gibbons 1941- . . . . **CLC 3**
See also CA 33-36R; CANR 14, 31; DLB 120

Rubens, Bernice (Ruth) 1923- . . . **CLC 19, 31**
See also CA 25-28R; CANR 33; DLB 14; MTCW

Rudkin, (James) David 1936- . . . . . . **CLC 14**
See also CA 89-92; DLB 13

Rudnik, Raphael 1933- . . . . **CLC 7**
See also CA 29-32R

Ruffian, M.
See Hasek, Jaroslav (Matej Frantisek)

Ruiz, Jose Martinez . . . . **CLC 11**
See also Martinez Ruiz, Jose

Rukeyser, Muriel
1913-1980 . . . . **CLC 6, 10, 15, 27; PC 12**
See also CA 5-8R; 93-96; CANR 26; DLB 48; MTCW; SATA-Obit 22

Rule, Jane (Vance) 1931- . . . . **CLC 27**
See also CA 25-28R; CAAS 18; CANR 12; DLB 60

Rulfo, Juan 1918-1986 . . . . **CLC 8, 80; HLC**
See also CA 85-88; 118; CANR 26; DLB 113; HW; MTCW

Runeberg, Johan 1804-1877 . . . . . . **NCLC 41**

Runyon, (Alfred) Damon
1884(?)-1946 . . . . **TCLC 10**
See also CA 107; DLB 11, 86

Rush, Norman 1933- . . . . **CLC 44**
See also CA 121; 126

Rushdie, (Ahmed) Salman
1947- . . . . **CLC 23, 31, 55**
See also BEST 89:3; CA 108; 111; CANR 33; MTCW

Rushforth, Peter (Scott) 1945- . . . . . **CLC 19**
See also CA 101

Ruskin, John 1819-1900 . . . . **TCLC 20**
See also CA 114; 129; CDBLB 1832-1890; DLB 55; SATA 24

Russ, Joanna 1937- . . . . **CLC 15**
See also CA 25-28R; CANR 11, 31; DLB 8; MTCW

Russell, George William 1867-1935
See A. E.
See also CA 104; CDBLB 1890-1914

Russell, (Henry) Ken(neth Alfred)
1927- . . . . **CLC 16**
See also CA 105

Russell, Willy 1947- . . . . **CLC 60**

Rutherford, Mark . . . . **TCLC 25**
See also White, William Hale
See also DLB 18

Ruyslinck, Ward 1929- . . . . **CLC 14**
See also Belser, Reimond Karel Maria de

Ryan, Cornelius (John) 1920-1974 . . . **CLC 7**
See also CA 69-72; 53-56; CANR 38

Ryan, Michael 1946- . . . . **CLC 65**
See also CA 49-52; DLBY 82

Rybakov, Anatoli (Naumovich)
1911- . . . . **CLC 23, 53**
See also CA 126; 135; SATA 79

Ryder, Jonathan
See Ludlum, Robert

Ryga, George 1932-1987 . . . . **CLC 14**
See also CA 101; 124; CANR 43; DLB 60

S. S.
See Sassoon, Siegfried (Lorraine)

Saba, Umberto 1883-1957 . . . . **TCLC 33**
See also CA 144; DLB 114

Sabatini, Rafael 1875-1950 . . . . **TCLC 47**

Sabato, Ernesto (R.)
1911- . . . . **CLC 10, 23; HLC**
See also CA 97-100; CANR 32; DLB 145; HW; MTCW

Sacastru, Martin
See Bioy Casares, Adolfo

Sacher-Masoch, Leopold von
1836(?)-1895 . . . . **NCLC 31**

Sachs, Marilyn (Stickle) 1927- . . . . . **CLC 35**
See also AAYA 2; CA 17-20R; CANR 13, 47; CLR 2; JRDA; MAICYA; SAAS 2; SATA 3, 68

Sachs, Nelly 1891-1970 . . . . **CLC 14**
See also CA 17-18; 25-28R; CAP 2

Sackler, Howard (Oliver)
1929-1982 . . . . **CLC 14**
See also CA 61-64; 108; CANR 30; DLB 7

Sacks, Oliver (Wolf) 1933- . . . . **CLC 67**
See also CA 53-56; CANR 28; MTCW

Sade, Donatien Alphonse Francois Comte
1740-1814 . . . . **NCLC 47**

Sadoff, Ira 1945- . . . . **CLC 9**
See also CA 53-56; CANR 5, 21; DLB 120

Saetone
See Camus, Albert

Safire, William 1929- . . . . **CLC 10**
See also CA 17-20R; CANR 31

Sagan, Carl (Edward) 1934- . . . . **CLC 30**
See also AAYA 2; CA 25-28R; CANR 11, 36; MTCW; SATA 58

Sagan, Francoise . . . . **CLC 3, 6, 9, 17, 36**
See also Quoirez, Francoise
See also DLB 83

Sahgal, Nayantara (Pandit) 1927- . . . **CLC 41**
See also CA 9-12R; CANR 11

Saint, H(arry) F. 1941- . . . . **CLC 50**
See also CA 127

St. Aubin de Teran, Lisa 1953-
See Teran, Lisa St. Aubin de
See also CA 118; 126

Sainte-Beuve, Charles Augustin
1804-1869 . . . . **NCLC 5**

Saint-Exupery, Antoine (Jean Baptiste Marie Roger) de
1900-1944 . . . . **TCLC 2, 56; WLC**
See also CA 108; 132; CLR 10; DLB 72; MAICYA; MTCW; SATA 20

St. John, David
See Hunt, E(verette) Howard, (Jr.)

Saint-John Perse
See Leger, (Marie-Rene Auguste) Alexis Saint-Leger

Saintsbury, George (Edward Bateman)
1845-1933 . . . . **TCLC 31**
See also DLB 57, 149

Sait Faik . . . . **TCLC 23**
See also Abasiyanik, Sait Faik

Saki . . . . **TCLC 3; SSC 12**
See also Munro, H(ector) H(ugh)

Sala, George Augustus . . . . **NCLC 46**

Salama, Hannu 1936- . . . . **CLC 18**

Salamanca, J(ack) R(ichard)
1922- . . . . **CLC 4, 15**
See also CA 25-28R

Sale, J. Kirkpatrick
See Sale, Kirkpatrick

Sale, Kirkpatrick 1937- . . . . **CLC 68**
See also CA 13-16R; CANR 10

Salinas (y Serrano), Pedro
1891(?)-1951 . . . . **TCLC 17**
See also CA 117; DLB 134

Salinger, J(erome) D(avid)
1919- . . . . . . **CLC 1, 3, 8, 12, 55, 56; DA; SSC 2; WLC**
See also AAYA 2; CA 5-8R; CANR 39; CDALB 1941-1968; CLR 18; DLB 2, 102; MAICYA; MTCW; SATA 67

Salisbury, John
See Caute, David

Salter, James 1925- . . . . **CLC 7, 52, 59**
See also CA 73-76; DLB 130

Saltus, Edgar (Everton)
1855-1921 . . . . **TCLC 8**
See also CA 105

Saltykov, Mikhail Evgrafovich
1826-1889 . . . . **NCLC 16**

Samarakis, Antonis 1919- . . . . **CLC 5**
See also CA 25-28R; CAAS 16; CANR 36

Sanchez, Florencio 1875-1910 . . . . . **TCLC 37**
See also HW

Sanchez, Luis Rafael 1936- . . . . **CLC 23**
See also CA 128; DLB 145; HW

Sanchez, Sonia 1934- . . . **CLC 5; BLC; PC 9**
See also BW 2; CA 33-36R; CANR 24; CLR 18; DLB 41; DLBD 8; MAICYA; MTCW; SATA 22

Sand, George
1804-1876 . . . . . . **NCLC 2, 42; DA; WLC**
See also DLB 119

Sandburg, Carl (August)
1878-1967 . . . . **CLC 1, 4, 10, 15, 35; DA; PC 2; WLC**
See also CA 5-8R; 25-28R; CANR 35; CDALB 1865-1917; DLB 17, 54; MAICYA; MTCW; SATA 8

Sandburg, Charles
See Sandburg, Carl (August)

Sandburg, Charles A.
See Sandburg, Carl (August)

Sanders, (James) Ed(ward) 1939- . . . **CLC 53**
See also CA 13-16R; CAAS 21; CANR 13, 44; DLB 16

Sanders, Lawrence 1920- . . . . **CLC 41**
See also BEST 89:4; CA 81-84; CANR 33; MTCW

Sanders, Noah
See Blount, Roy (Alton), Jr.

Sanders, Winston P.
See Anderson, Poul (William)

Scorsese, Martin 1942- .... **CLC 20, 89**
See also CA 110; 114; CANR 46

Scotland, Jay
See Jakes, John (William)

Scott, Duncan Campbell
1862-1947 .... **TCLC 6**
See also CA 104; DLB 92

Scott, Evelyn 1893-1963........... **CLC 43**
See also CA 104; 112; DLB 9, 48

Scott, F(rancis) R(eginald)
1899-1985 .... **CLC 22**
See also CA 101; 114; DLB 88

Scott, Frank
See Scott, F(rancis) R(eginald)

Scott, Joanna 1960- .... **CLC 50**
See also CA 126

Scott, Paul (Mark) 1920-1978.... **CLC 9, 60**
See also CA 81-84; 77-80; CANR 33; DLB 14; MTCW

Scott, Walter
1771-1832 ...... **NCLC 15; DA; PC 12; WLC**
See also CDBLB 1789-1832; DLB 93, 107, 116, 144; YABC 2

Scribe, (Augustin) Eugene
1791-1861 .... **NCLC 16; DC 5**

Scrum, R.
See Crumb, R(obert)

Scudery, Madeleine de 1607-1701..... **LC 2**

Scum
See Crumb, R(obert)

Scumbag, Little Bobby
See Crumb, R(obert)

Seabrook, John
See Hubbard, L(afayette) Ron(ald)

Sealy, I. Allan 1951- .... **CLC 55**

Search, Alexander
See Pessoa, Fernando (Antonio Nogueira)

Sebastian, Lee
See Silverberg, Robert

Sebastian Owl
See Thompson, Hunter S(tockton)

Sebestyen, Ouida 1924- .... **CLC 30**
See also AAYA 8; CA 107; CANR 40; CLR 17; JRDA; MAICYA; SAAS 10; SATA 39

Secundus, H. Scriblerus
See Fielding, Henry

Sedges, John
See Buck, Pearl S(ydenstricker)

Sedgwick, Catharine Maria
1789-1867 .... **NCLC 19**
See also DLB 1, 74

Seelye, John 1931-................ **CLC 7**

Seferiades, Giorgos Stylianou 1900-1971
See Seferis, George
See also CA 5-8R; 33-36R; CANR 5, 36; MTCW

Seferis, George .... **CLC 5, 11**
See also Seferiades, Giorgos Stylianou

Segal, Erich (Wolf) 1937- .... **CLC 3, 10**
See also BEST 89:1; CA 25-28R; CANR 20, 36; DLBY 86; MTCW

Seger, Bob 1945-................. **CLC 35**

Seghers, Anna .... **CLC 7**
See also Radvanyi, Netty
See also DLB 69

Seidel, Frederick (Lewis) 1936-..... **CLC 18**
See also CA 13-16R; CANR 8; DLBY 84

Seifert, Jaroslav 1901-1986..... **CLC 34, 44**
See also CA 127; MTCW

Sei Shonagon c. 966-1017(?) ...... **CMLC 6**

Selby, Hubert, Jr.
1928- .... **CLC 1, 2, 4, 8; SSC 20**
See also CA 13-16R; CANR 33; DLB 2

Selzer, Richard 1928-............. **CLC 74**
See also CA 65-68; CANR 14

Sembene, Ousmane
See Ousmane, Sembene

Senancour, Etienne Pivert de
1770-1846 .... **NCLC 16**
See also DLB 119

Sender, Ramon (Jose)
1902-1982 .... **CLC 8; HLC**
See also CA 5-8R; 105; CANR 8; HW; MTCW

Seneca, Lucius Annaeus
4B.C.-65.............. **CMLC 6; DC 5**

Senghor, Leopold Sedar
1906- .... **CLC 54; BLC**
See also BW 2; CA 116; 125; CANR 47; MTCW

Serling, (Edward) Rod(man)
1924-1975 .... **CLC 30**
See also AAYA 14; AITN 1; CA 65-68; 57-60; DLB 26

Serna, Ramon Gomez de la
See Gomez de la Serna, Ramon

Serpieres
See Guillevic, (Eugene)

Service, Robert
See Service, Robert W(illiam)
See also DLB 92

Service, Robert W(illiam)
1874(?)-1958 ...... **TCLC 15; DA; WLC**
See also Service, Robert
See also CA 115; 140; SATA 20

Seth, Vikram 1952-.............. **CLC 43**
See also CA 121; 127; DLB 120

Seton, Cynthia Propper
1926-1982 .... **CLC 27**
See also CA 5-8R; 108; CANR 7

Seton, Ernest (Evan) Thompson
1860-1946 .... **TCLC 31**
See also CA 109; DLB 92; JRDA; SATA 18

Seton-Thompson, Ernest
See Seton, Ernest (Evan) Thompson

Settle, Mary Lee 1918- .... **CLC 19, 61**
See also CA 89-92; CAAS 1; CANR 44; DLB 6

Seuphor, Michel
See Arp, Jean

Sevigne, Marie (de Rabutin-Chantal) Marquise de 1626-1696 .... **LC 11**

Sexton, Anne (Harvey)
1928-1974 .... **CLC 2, 4, 6, 8, 10, 15, 53; DA; PC 2; WLC**
See also CA 1-4R; 53-56; CABS 2; CANR 3, 36; CDALB 1941-1968; DLB 5; MTCW; SATA 10

Shaara, Michael (Joseph, Jr.)
1929-1988 .... **CLC 15**
See also AITN 1; CA 102; 125; DLBY 83

Shackleton, C. C.
See Aldiss, Brian W(ilson)

Shacochis, Bob .... **CLC 39**
See also Shacochis, Robert G.

Shacochis, Robert G. 1951-
See Shacochis, Bob
See also CA 119; 124

Shaffer, Anthony (Joshua) 1926-.... **CLC 19**
See also CA 110; 116; DLB 13

Shaffer, Peter (Levin)
1926- .... **CLC 5, 14, 18, 37, 60**
See also CA 25-28R; CANR 25, 47; CDBLB 1960 to Present; DLB 13; MTCW

Shakey, Bernard
See Young, Neil

Shalamov, Varlam (Tikhonovich)
1907(?)-1982 .... **CLC 18**
See also CA 129; 105

Shamlu, Ahmad 1925- .... **CLC 10**

Shammas, Anton 1951-............ **CLC 55**

Shange, Ntozake
1948- .... **CLC 8, 25, 38, 74; BLC; DC 3**
See also AAYA 9; BW 2; CA 85-88; CABS 3; CANR 27, 48; DLB 38; MTCW

Shanley, John Patrick 1950-....... **CLC 75**
See also CA 128; 133

Shapcott, Thomas W(illiam) 1935- .. **CLC 38**
See also CA 69-72

Shapiro, Jane..................... **CLC 76**

Shapiro, Karl (Jay) 1913- .. **CLC 4, 8, 15, 53**
See also CA 1-4R; CAAS 6; CANR 1, 36; DLB 48; MTCW

Sharp, William 1855-1905 .... **TCLC 39**

Sharpe, Thomas Ridley 1928-
See Sharpe, Tom
See also CA 114; 122

Sharpe, Tom...................... **CLC 36**
See also Sharpe, Thomas Ridley
See also DLB 14

Shaw, Bernard................... **TCLC 45**
See also Shaw, George Bernard
See also BW 1

Shaw, G. Bernard
See Shaw, George Bernard

Shaw, George Bernard
1856-1950 .... **TCLC 3, 9, 21; DA; WLC**
See also Shaw, Bernard
See also CA 104; 128; CDBLB 1914-1945; DLB 10, 57; MTCW

Shaw, Henry Wheeler
1818-1885 .... **NCLC 15**
See also DLB 11

Simpson, N(orman) F(rederick) 1919- . . . . **CLC 29**
See also CA 13-16R; DLB 13

Sinclair, Andrew (Annandale) 1935- . . . . **CLC 2, 14**
See also CA 9-12R; CAAS 5; CANR 14, 38; DLB 14; MTCW

Sinclair, Emil
See Hesse, Hermann

Sinclair, Iain 1943- . . . . **CLC 76**
See also CA 132

Sinclair, Iain MacGregor
See Sinclair, Iain

Sinclair, Mary Amelia St. Clair 1865(?)-1946
See Sinclair, May
See also CA 104

Sinclair, May . . . . **TCLC 3, 11**
See also Sinclair, Mary Amelia St. Clair
See also DLB 36, 135

Sinclair, Upton (Beall) 1878-1968 . . . . . . **CLC 1, 11, 15, 63; DA; WLC**
See also CA 5-8R; 25-28R; CANR 7; CDALB 1929-1941; DLB 9; MTCW; SATA 9

Singer, Isaac
See Singer, Isaac Bashevis

Singer, Isaac Bashevis 1904-1991 . . . . **CLC 1, 3, 6, 9, 11, 15, 23, 38, 69; DA; SSC 3; WLC**
See also AITN 1, 2; CA 1-4R; 134; CANR 1, 39; CDALB 1941-1968; CLR 1; DLB 6, 28, 52; DLBY 91; JRDA; MAICYA; MTCW; SATA 3, 27; SATA-Obit 68

Singer, Israel Joshua 1893-1944 . . . **TCLC 33**

Singh, Khushwant 1915- . . . . **CLC 11**
See also CA 9-12R; CAAS 9; CANR 6

Sinjohn, John
See Galsworthy, John

Sinyavsky, Andrei (Donatevich) 1925- . . . . **CLC 8**
See also CA 85-88

Sirin, V.
See Nabokov, Vladimir (Vladimirovich)

Sissman, L(ouis) E(dward) 1928-1976 . . . . **CLC 9, 18**
See also CA 21-24R; 65-68; CANR 13; DLB 5

Sisson, C(harles) H(ubert) 1914- . . . . . **CLC 8**
See also CA 1-4R; CAAS 3; CANR 3, 48; DLB 27

Sitwell, Dame Edith 1887-1964 . . . . **CLC 2, 9, 67; PC 3**
See also CA 9-12R; CANR 35; CDBLB 1945-1960; DLB 20; MTCW

Sjoewall, Maj 1935- . . . . **CLC 7**
See also CA 65-68

Sjowall, Maj
See Sjoewall, Maj

Skelton, Robin 1925- . . . . **CLC 13**
See also AITN 2; CA 5-8R; CAAS 5; CANR 28; DLB 27, 53

Skolimowski, Jerzy 1938- . . . . **CLC 20**
See also CA 128

Skram, Amalie (Bertha) 1847-1905 . . . . **TCLC 25**

Skvorecky, Josef (Vaclav) 1924- . . . . **CLC 15, 39, 69**
See also CA 61-64; CAAS 1; CANR 10, 34; MTCW

Slade, Bernard . . . . **CLC 11, 46**
See also Newbound, Bernard Slade
See also CAAS 9; DLB 53

Slaughter, Carolyn 1946- . . . . **CLC 56**
See also CA 85-88

Slaughter, Frank G(ill) 1908- . . . . . . **CLC 29**
See also AITN 2; CA 5-8R; CANR 5

Slavitt, David R(ytman) 1935- . . . . **CLC 5, 14**
See also CA 21-24R; CAAS 3; CANR 41; DLB 5, 6

Slesinger, Tess 1905-1945 . . . . **TCLC 10**
See also CA 107; DLB 102

Slessor, Kenneth 1901-1971 . . . . **CLC 14**
See also CA 102; 89-92

Slowacki, Juliusz 1809-1849 . . . . . **NCLC 15**

Smart, Christopher 1722-1771 . . . . **LC 3; PC 12**
See also DLB 109

Smart, Elizabeth 1913-1986 . . . . **CLC 54**
See also CA 81-84; 118; DLB 88

Smiley, Jane (Graves) 1949- . . . . **CLC 53, 76**
See also CA 104; CANR 30

Smith, A(rthur) J(ames) M(arshall) 1902-1980 . . . . **CLC 15**
See also CA 1-4R; 102; CANR 4; DLB 88

Smith, Anna Deavere 1950- . . . . **CLC 86**
See also CA 133

Smith, Betty (Wehner) 1896-1972 . . . **CLC 19**
See also CA 5-8R; 33-36R; DLBY 82; SATA 6

Smith, Charlotte (Turner) 1749-1806 . . . . **NCLC 23**
See also DLB 39, 109

Smith, Clark Ashton 1893-1961 . . . . **CLC 43**
See also CA 143

Smith, Dave . . . . **CLC 22, 42**
See also Smith, David (Jeddie)
See also CAAS 7; DLB 5

Smith, David (Jeddie) 1942-
See Smith, Dave
See also CA 49-52; CANR 1

Smith, Florence Margaret 1902-1971
See Smith, Stevie
See also CA 17-18; 29-32R; CANR 35; CAP 2; MTCW

Smith, Iain Crichton 1928- . . . . **CLC 64**
See also CA 21-24R; DLB 40, 139

Smith, John 1580(?)-1631 . . . . **LC 9**

Smith, Johnston
See Crane, Stephen (Townley)

Smith, Lee 1944- . . . . **CLC 25, 73**
See also CA 114; 119; CANR 46; DLB 143; DLBY 83

Smith, Martin
See Smith, Martin Cruz

Smith, Martin Cruz 1942- . . . . **CLC 25**
See also BEST 89:4; CA 85-88; CANR 6, 23, 43; NNAL

Smith, Mary-Ann Tirone 1944- . . . . . **CLC 39**
See also CA 118; 136

Smith, Patti 1946- . . . . **CLC 12**
See also CA 93-96

Smith, Pauline (Urmson) 1882-1959 . . . . **TCLC 25**

Smith, Rosamond
See Oates, Joyce Carol

Smith, Sheila Kaye
See Kaye-Smith, Sheila

Smith, Stevie . . . . **CLC 3, 8, 25, 44; PC 12**
See also Smith, Florence Margaret
See also DLB 20

Smith, Wilbur (Addison) 1933- . . . . . **CLC 33**
See also CA 13-16R; CANR 7, 46; MTCW

Smith, William Jay 1918- . . . . **CLC 6**
See also CA 5-8R; CANR 44; DLB 5; MAICYA; SATA 2, 68

Smith, Woodrow Wilson
See Kuttner, Henry

Smolenskin, Peretz 1842-1885 . . . . **NCLC 30**

Smollett, Tobias (George) 1721-1771 . . **LC 2**
See also CDBLB 1660-1789; DLB 39, 104

Snodgrass, W(illiam) D(e Witt) 1926- . . . . **CLC 2, 6, 10, 18, 68**
See also CA 1-4R; CANR 6, 36; DLB 5; MTCW

Snow, C(harles) P(ercy) 1905-1980 . . . . **CLC 1, 4, 6, 9, 13, 19**
See also CA 5-8R; 101; CANR 28; CDBLB 1945-1960; DLB 15, 77; MTCW

Snow, Frances Compton
See Adams, Henry (Brooks)

Snyder, Gary (Sherman) 1930- . . . . **CLC 1, 2, 5, 9, 32**
See also CA 17-20R; CANR 30; DLB 5, 16

Snyder, Zilpha Keatley 1927- . . . . . . **CLC 17**
See also CA 9-12R; CANR 38; CLR 31; JRDA; MAICYA; SAAS 2; SATA 1, 28, 75

Soares, Bernardo
See Pessoa, Fernando (Antonio Nogueira)

Sobh, A.
See Shamlu, Ahmad

Sobol, Joshua . . . . **CLC 60**

Soderberg, Hjalmar 1869-1941 . . . . **TCLC 39**

Sodergran, Edith (Irene)
See Soedergran, Edith (Irene)

Soedergran, Edith (Irene) 1892-1923 . . . . **TCLC 31**

Softly, Edgar
See Lovecraft, H(oward) P(hillips)

Softly, Edward
See Lovecraft, H(oward) P(hillips)

Sokolov, Raymond 1941- . . . . **CLC 7**
See also CA 85-88

Solo, Jay
See Ellison, Harlan (Jay)

Sologub, Fyodor . . . . **TCLC 9**
See also Teternikov, Fyodor Kuzmich

Solomons, Ikey Esquir
See Thackeray, William Makepeace

Solomos, Dionysios 1798-1857 . . . **NCLC 15**

Author Index

Solwoska, Mara
See French, Marilyn

Solzhenitsyn, Aleksandr I(sayevich) 1918- ...... **CLC 1, 2, 4, 7, 9, 10, 18, 26, 34, 78; DA; WLC**
See also AITN 1; CA 69-72; CANR 40; MTCW

Somers, Jane
See Lessing, Doris (May)

Somerville, Edith 1858-1949 ...... **TCLC 51**
See also DLB 135

Somerville & Ross
See Martin, Violet Florence; Somerville, Edith

Sommer, Scott 1951- .... **CLC 25**
See also CA 106

Sondheim, Stephen (Joshua) 1930- .... **CLC 30, 39**
See also AAYA 11; CA 103; CANR 47

Sontag, Susan 1933-... **CLC 1, 2, 10, 13, 31**
See also CA 17-20R; CANR 25; DLB 2, 67; MTCW

Sophocles 496(?)B.C.-406(?)B.C..... **CMLC 2; DA; DC 1**

Sordello 1189-1269............. **CMLC 15**

Sorel, Julia
See Drexler, Rosalyn

Sorrentino, Gilbert 1929- .... **CLC 3, 7, 14, 22, 40**
See also CA 77-80; CANR 14, 33; DLB 5; DLBY 80

Soto, Gary 1952-........ **CLC 32, 80; HLC**
See also AAYA 10; CA 119; 125; CLR 38; DLB 82; HW; JRDA; SATA 80

Soupault, Philippe 1897-1990 ...... **CLC 68**
See also CA 116; 147; 131

Souster, (Holmes) Raymond 1921- .... **CLC 5, 14**
See also CA 13-16R; CAAS 14; CANR 13, 29; DLB 88; SATA 63

Southern, Terry 1926- .... **CLC 7**
See also CA 1-4R; CANR 1; DLB 2

Southey, Robert 1774-1843 .... **NCLC 8**
See also DLB 93, 107, 142; SATA 54

Southworth, Emma Dorothy Eliza Nevitte 1819-1899 .... **NCLC 26**

Souza, Ernest
See Scott, Evelyn

Soyinka, Wole 1934- .... **CLC 3, 5, 14, 36, 44; BLC; DA; DC 2; WLC**
See also BW 2; CA 13-16R; CANR 27, 39; DLB 125; MTCW

Spackman, W(illiam) M(ode) 1905-1990 .... **CLC 46**
See also CA 81-84; 132

Spacks, Barry 1931-.............. **CLC 14**
See also CA 29-32R; CANR 33; DLB 105

Spanidou, Irini 1946- .... **CLC 44**

Spark, Muriel (Sarah) 1918- .... **CLC 2, 3, 5, 8, 13, 18, 40; SSC 10**
See also CA 5-8R; CANR 12, 36; CDBLB 1945-1960; DLB 15, 139; MTCW

Spaulding, Douglas
See Bradbury, Ray (Douglas)

Spaulding, Leonard
See Bradbury, Ray (Douglas)

Spence, J. A. D.
See Eliot, T(homas) S(tearns)

Spencer, Elizabeth 1921- .... **CLC 22**
See also CA 13-16R; CANR 32; DLB 6; MTCW; SATA 14

Spencer, Leonard G.
See Silverberg, Robert

Spencer, Scott 1945-.............. **CLC 30**
See also CA 113; DLBY 86

Spender, Stephen (Harold) 1909- .... **CLC 1, 2, 5, 10, 41**
See also CA 9-12R; CANR 31; CDBLB 1945-1960; DLB 20; MTCW

Spengler, Oswald (Arnold Gottfried) 1880-1936 .... **TCLC 25**
See also CA 118

Spenser, Edmund 1552(?)-1599 .... **LC 5; DA; PC 8; WLC**
See also CDBLB Before 1660

Spicer, Jack 1925-1965 ...... **CLC 8, 18, 72**
See also CA 85-88; DLB 5, 16

Spiegelman, Art 1948- .... **CLC 76**
See also AAYA 10; CA 125; CANR 41

Spielberg, Peter 1929- .... **CLC 6**
See also CA 5-8R; CANR 4, 48; DLBY 81

Spielberg, Steven 1947- .... **CLC 20**
See also AAYA 8; CA 77-80; CANR 32; SATA 32

Spillane, Frank Morrison 1918-
See Spillane, Mickey
See also CA 25-28R; CANR 28; MTCW; SATA 66

Spillane, Mickey................ **CLC 3, 13**
See also Spillane, Frank Morrison

Spinoza, Benedictus de 1632-1677 .... **LC 9**

Spinrad, Norman (Richard) 1940-... **CLC 46**
See also CA 37-40R; CAAS 19; CANR 20; DLB 8

Spitteler, Carl (Friedrich Georg) 1845-1924 .... **TCLC 12**
See also CA 109; DLB 129

Spivack, Kathleen (Romola Drucker) 1938- .... **CLC 6**
See also CA 49-52

Spoto, Donald 1941-.............. **CLC 39**
See also CA 65-68; CANR 11

Springsteen, Bruce (F.) 1949- ...... **CLC 17**
See also CA 111

Spurling, Hilary 1940-............ **CLC 34**
See also CA 104; CANR 25

Spyker, John Howland
See Elman, Richard

Squires, (James) Radcliffe 1917-1993 .... **CLC 51**
See also CA 1-4R; 140; CANR 6, 21

Srivastava, Dhanpat Rai 1880(?)-1936
See Premchand
See also CA 118

Stacy, Donald
See Pohl, Frederik

Stael, Germaine de
See Stael-Holstein, Anne Louise Germaine Necker Baronn
See also DLB 119

Stael-Holstein, Anne Louise Germaine Necker Baronn 1766-1817 .... **NCLC 3**
See also Stael, Germaine de

Stafford, Jean 1915-1979... **CLC 4, 7, 19, 68**
See also CA 1-4R; 85-88; CANR 3; DLB 2; MTCW; SATA-Obit 22

Stafford, William (Edgar) 1914-1993 .... **CLC 4, 7, 29**
See also CA 5-8R; 142; CAAS 3; CANR 5, 22; DLB 5

Staines, Trevor
See Brunner, John (Kilian Houston)

Stairs, Gordon
See Austin, Mary (Hunter)

Stannard, Martin 1947- .... **CLC 44**
See also CA 142

Stanton, Maura 1946- .... **CLC 9**
See also CA 89-92; CANR 15; DLB 120

Stanton, Schuyler
See Baum, L(yman) Frank

Stapledon, (William) Olaf 1886-1950 .... **TCLC 22**
See also CA 111; DLB 15

Starbuck, George (Edwin) 1931-.... **CLC 53**
See also CA 21-24R; CANR 23

Stark, Richard
See Westlake, Donald E(dwin)

Staunton, Schuyler
See Baum, L(yman) Frank

Stead, Christina (Ellen) 1902-1983 .... **CLC 2, 5, 8, 32, 80**
See also CA 13-16R; 109; CANR 33, 40; MTCW

Stead, William Thomas 1849-1912 .... **TCLC 48**

Steele, Richard 1672-1729.......... **LC 18**
See also CDBLB 1660-1789; DLB 84, 101

Steele, Timothy (Reid) 1948-....... **CLC 45**
See also CA 93-96; CANR 16; DLB 120

Steffens, (Joseph) Lincoln 1866-1936 .... **TCLC 20**
See also CA 117

Stegner, Wallace (Earle) 1909-1993 .... **CLC 9, 49, 81**
See also AITN 1; BEST 90:3; CA 1-4R; 141; CAAS 9; CANR 1, 21, 46; DLB 9; DLBY 93; MTCW

Stein, Gertrude 1874-1946 ...... **TCLC 1, 6, 28, 48; DA; WLC**
See also CA 104; 132; CDALB 1917-1929; DLB 4, 54, 86; MTCW

Steinbeck, John (Ernst) 1902-1968 ...... **CLC 1, 5, 9, 13, 21, 34, 45, 75; DA; SSC 11; WLC**
See also AAYA 12; CA 1-4R; 25-28R; CANR 1, 35; CDALB 1929-1941; DLB 7, 9; DLBD 2; MTCW; SATA 9

Steinem, Gloria 1934-............. **CLC 63**
See also CA 53-56; CANR 28; MTCW

Suarez Lynch, B.
See Bioy Casares, Adolfo; Borges, Jorge Luis

Su Chien 1884-1918
See Su Man-shu
See also CA 123

Suckow, Ruth 1892-1960 .... **SSC**
See also CA 113; DLB 9, 102

Sudermann, Hermann 1857-1928 .. **TCLC 15**
See also CA 107; DLB 118

Sue, Eugene 1804-1857 .... **NCLC 1**
See also DLB 119

Sueskind, Patrick 1949-.......... **CLC 44**
See also Suskind, Patrick

Sukenick, Ronald 1932-..... **CLC 3, 4, 6, 48**
See also CA 25-28R; CAAS 8; CANR 32; DLBY 81

Suknaski, Andrew 1942- .... **CLC 19**
See also CA 101; DLB 53

Sullivan, Vernon
See Vian, Boris

Sully Prudhomme 1839-1907...... **TCLC 31**

Su Man-shu .... **TCLC 24**
See also Su Chien

Summerforest, Ivy B.
See Kirkup, James

Summers, Andrew James 1942-..... **CLC 26**

Summers, Andy
See Summers, Andrew James

Summers, Hollis (Spurgeon, Jr.)
1916- .... **CLC 10**
See also CA 5-8R; CANR 3; DLB 6

Summers, (Alphonsus Joseph-Mary Augustus) Montague 1880-1948 .... **TCLC 16**
See also CA 118

Sumner, Gordon Matthew 1951-.... **CLC 26**

Surtees, Robert Smith
1803-1864 .... **NCLC 14**
See also DLB 21

Susann, Jacqueline 1921-1974....... **CLC 3**
See also AITN 1; CA 65-68; 53-56; MTCW

Suskind, Patrick
See Sueskind, Patrick
See also CA 145

Sutcliff, Rosemary 1920-1992 ...... **CLC 26**
See also AAYA 10; CA 5-8R; 139; CANR 37; CLR 1, 37; JRDA; MAICYA; SATA 6, 44, 78; SATA-Obit 73

Sutro, Alfred 1863-1933........... **TCLC 6**
See also CA 105; DLB 10

Sutton, Henry
See Slavitt, David R(ytman)

Svevo, Italo .... **TCLC 2, 35**
See also Schmitz, Aron Hector

Swados, Elizabeth 1951- .... **CLC 12**
See also CA 97-100

Swados, Harvey 1920-1972 .... **CLC 5**
See also CA 5-8R; 37-40R; CANR 6; DLB 2

Swan, Gladys 1934- .... **CLC 69**
See also CA 101; CANR 17, 39

Swarthout, Glendon (Fred)
1918-1992 .... **CLC 35**
See also CA 1-4R; 139; CANR 1, 47; SATA 26

Sweet, Sarah C.
See Jewett, (Theodora) Sarah Orne

Swenson, May
1919-1989 .... **CLC 4, 14, 61; DA**
See also CA 5-8R; 130; CANR 36; DLB 5; MTCW; SATA 15

Swift, Augustus
See Lovecraft, H(oward) P(hillips)

Swift, Graham (Colin) 1949-.... **CLC 41, 88**
See also CA 117; 122; CANR 46

Swift, Jonathan
1667-1745 ...... **LC 1; DA; PC 9; WLC**
See also CDBLB 1660-1789; DLB 39, 95, 101; SATA 19

Swinburne, Algernon Charles
1837-1909 ...... **TCLC 8, 36; DA; WLC**
See also CA 105; 140; CDBLB 1832-1890; DLB 35, 57

Swinfen, Ann .... **CLC 34**

Swinnerton, Frank Arthur
1884-1982 .... **CLC 31**
See also CA 108; DLB 34

Swithen, John
See King, Stephen (Edwin)

Sylvia
See Ashton-Warner, Sylvia (Constance)

Symmes, Robert Edward
See Duncan, Robert (Edward)

Symonds, John Addington
1840-1893 .... **NCLC 34**
See also DLB 57, 144

Symons, Arthur 1865-1945 .... **TCLC 11**
See also CA 107; DLB 19, 57, 149

Symons, Julian (Gustave)
1912-1994 .... **CLC 2, 14, 32**
See also CA 49-52; 147; CAAS 3; CANR 3, 33; DLB 87; DLBY 92; MTCW

Synge, (Edmund) J(ohn) M(illington)
1871-1909 .... **TCLC 6, 37; DC 2**
See also CA 104; 141; CDBLB 1890-1914; DLB 10, 19

Syruc, J.
See Milosz, Czeslaw

Szirtes, George 1948-............. **CLC 46**
See also CA 109; CANR 27

Tabori, George 1914-............. **CLC 19**
See also CA 49-52; CANR 4

Tagore, Rabindranath
1861-1941 .... **TCLC 3, 53; PC 8**
See also CA 104; 120; MTCW

Taine, Hippolyte Adolphe
1828-1893 .... **NCLC 15**

Talese, Gay 1932-................ **CLC 37**
See also AITN 1; CA 1-4R; CANR 9; MTCW

Tallent, Elizabeth (Ann) 1954- ..... **CLC 45**
See also CA 117; DLB 130

Tally, Ted 1952-................. **CLC 42**
See also CA 120; 124

Tamayo y Baus, Manuel
1829-1898 .... **NCLC 1**

Tammsaare, A(nton) H(ansen)
1878-1940 .... **TCLC 27**

Tan, Amy 1952- .... **CLC 59**
See also AAYA 9; BEST 89:3; CA 136; SATA 75

Tandem, Felix
See Spitteler, Carl (Friedrich Georg)

Tanizaki, Jun'ichiro
1886-1965 .... **CLC 8, 14, 28**
See also CA 93-96; 25-28R

Tanner, William
See Amis, Kingsley (William)

Tao Lao
See Storni, Alfonsina

Tarassoff, Lev
See Troyat, Henri

Tarbell, Ida M(inerva)
1857-1944 .... **TCLC 40**
See also CA 122; DLB 47

Tarkington, (Newton) Booth
1869-1946 .... **TCLC 9**
See also CA 110; 143; DLB 9, 102; SATA 17

Tarkovsky, Andrei (Arsenyevich)
1932-1986 .... **CLC 75**
See also CA 127

Tartt, Donna 1964(?)-............ **CLC 76**
See also CA 142

Tasso, Torquato 1544-1595 .... **LC 5**

Tate, (John Orley) Allen
1899-1979 .... **CLC 2, 4, 6, 9, 11, 14, 24**
See also CA 5-8R; 85-88; CANR 32; DLB 4, 45, 63; MTCW

Tate, Ellalice
See Hibbert, Eleanor Alice Burford

Tate, James (Vincent) 1943- ... **CLC 2, 6, 25**
See also CA 21-24R; CANR 29; DLB 5

Tavel, Ronald 1940-.............. **CLC 6**
See also CA 21-24R; CANR 33

Taylor, C(ecil) P(hilip) 1929-1981... **CLC 27**
See also CA 25-28R; 105; CANR 47

Taylor, Edward 1642(?)-1729.... **LC 11; DA**
See also DLB 24

Taylor, Eleanor Ross 1920-......... **CLC 5**
See also CA 81-84

Taylor, Elizabeth 1912-1975 ... **CLC 2, 4, 29**
See also CA 13-16R; CANR 9; DLB 139; MTCW; SATA 13

Taylor, Henry (Splawn) 1942-...... **CLC 44**
See also CA 33-36R; CAAS 7; CANR 31; DLB 5

Taylor, Kamala (Purnaiya) 1924-
See Markandaya, Kamala
See also CA 77-80

Taylor, Mildred D. .... **CLC 21**
See also AAYA 10; BW 1; CA 85-88; CANR 25; CLR 9; DLB 52; JRDA; MAICYA; SAAS 5; SATA 15, 70

Taylor, Peter (Hillsman)
1917-1994 ..... **CLC 1, 4, 18, 37, 44, 50, 71; SSC 10**
See also CA 13-16R; 147; CANR 9; DLBY 81, 94; MTCW

Taylor, Robert Lewis 1912-........ **CLC 14**
See also CA 1-4R; CANR 3; SATA 10

Tchekhov, Anton
See Chekhov, Anton (Pavlovich)

Teasdale, Sara 1884-1933.......... **TCLC 4**
See also CA 104; DLB 45; SATA 32

Tegner, Esaias 1782-1846......... **NCLC 2**

Teilhard de Chardin, (Marie Joseph) Pierre
1881-1955 .... **TCLC 9**
See also CA 105

Temple, Ann
See Mortimer, Penelope (Ruth)

Tennant, Emma (Christina)
1937- .... **CLC 13, 52**
See also CA 65-68; CAAS 9; CANR 10, 38; DLB 14

Tenneshaw, S. M.
See Silverberg, Robert

Tennyson, Alfred
1809-1892 .. **NCLC 30; DA; PC 6; WLC**
See also CDBLB 1832-1890; DLB 32

Teran, Lisa St. Aubin de .... **CLC 36**
See also St. Aubin de Teran, Lisa

Terence 195(?)B.C.-159B.C....... **CMLC 14**

Teresa de Jesus, St. 1515-1582...... **LC 18**

Terkel, Louis 1912-
See Terkel, Studs
See also CA 57-60; CANR 18, 45; MTCW

Terkel, Studs .... **CLC 38**
See also Terkel, Louis
See also AITN 1

Terry, C. V.
See Slaughter, Frank G(ill)

Terry, Megan 1932-.............. **CLC 19**
See also CA 77-80; CABS 3; CANR 43; DLB 7

Tertz, Abram
See Sinyavsky, Andrei (Donatevich)

Tesich, Steve 1943(?)-.......... **CLC 40, 69**
See also CA 105; DLBY 83

Teternikov, Fyodor Kuzmich 1863-1927
See Sologub, Fyodor
See also CA 104

Tevis, Walter 1928-1984 .... **CLC 42**
See also CA 113

Tey, Josephine.................... **TCLC 14**
See also Mackintosh, Elizabeth
See also DLB 77

Thackeray, William Makepeace
1811-1863 .... **NCLC 5, 14, 22, 43; DA; WLC**
See also CDBLB 1832-1890; DLB 21, 55; SATA 23

Thakura, Ravindranatha
See Tagore, Rabindranath

Tharoor, Shashi 1956- .... **CLC 70**
See also CA 141

Thelwell, Michael Miles 1939- ..... **CLC 22**
See also BW 2; CA 101

Theobald, Lewis, Jr.
See Lovecraft, H(oward) P(hillips)

Theodorescu, Ion N. 1880-1967
See Arghezi, Tudor
See also CA 116

Theriault, Yves 1915-1983......... **CLC 79**
See also CA 102; DLB 88

Theroux, Alexander (Louis)
1939- .... **CLC 2, 25**
See also CA 85-88; CANR 20

Theroux, Paul (Edward)
1941- .... **CLC 5, 8, 11, 15, 28, 46**
See also BEST 89:4; CA 33-36R; CANR 20, 45; DLB 2; MTCW; SATA 44

Thesen, Sharon 1946-............. **CLC 56**

Thevenin, Denis
See Duhamel, Georges

Thibault, Jacques Anatole Francois
1844-1924
See France, Anatole
See also CA 106; 127; MTCW

Thiele, Colin (Milton) 1920- .... **CLC 17**
See also CA 29-32R; CANR 12, 28; CLR 27; MAICYA; SAAS 2; SATA 14, 72

Thomas, Audrey (Callahan)
1935- .... **CLC 7, 13, 37; SSC 20**
See also AITN 2; CA 21-24R; CAAS 19; CANR 36; DLB 60; MTCW

Thomas, D(onald) M(ichael)
1935- .... **CLC 13, 22, 31**
See also CA 61-64; CAAS 11; CANR 17, 45; CDBLB 1960 to Present; DLB 40; MTCW

Thomas, Dylan (Marlais)
1914-1953 ... **TCLC 1, 8, 45; DA; PC 2; SSC 3; WLC**
See also CA 104; 120; CDBLB 1945-1960; DLB 13, 20, 139; MTCW; SATA 60

Thomas, (Philip) Edward
1878-1917 .... **TCLC 10**
See also CA 106; DLB 19

Thomas, Joyce Carol 1938-........ **CLC 35**
See also AAYA 12; BW 2; CA 113; 116; CANR 48; CLR 19; DLB 33; JRDA; MAICYA; MTCW; SAAS 7; SATA 40, 78

Thomas, Lewis 1913-1993 .... **CLC 35**
See also CA 85-88; 143; CANR 38; MTCW

Thomas, Paul
See Mann, (Paul) Thomas

Thomas, Piri 1928-............... **CLC 17**
See also CA 73-76; HW

Thomas, R(onald) S(tuart)
1913- .... **CLC 6, 13, 48**
See also CA 89-92; CAAS 4; CANR 30; CDBLB 1960 to Present; DLB 27; MTCW

Thomas, Ross (Elmore) 1926- ...... **CLC 39**
See also CA 33-36R; CANR 22

Thompson, Francis Clegg
See Mencken, H(enry) L(ouis)

Thompson, Francis Joseph
1859-1907 .... **TCLC 4**
See also CA 104; CDBLB 1890-1914; DLB 19

Thompson, Hunter S(tockton)
1939- .... **CLC 9, 17, 40**
See also BEST 89:1; CA 17-20R; CANR 23, 46; MTCW

Thompson, James Myers
See Thompson, Jim (Myers)

Thompson, Jim (Myers)
1906-1977(?) .... **CLC 69**
See also CA 140

Thompson, Judith .... **CLC 39**

Thomson, James 1700-1748...... **LC 16, 29**
See also DLB 95

Thomson, James 1834-1882...... **NCLC 18**
See also DLB 35

Thoreau, Henry David
1817-1862 ...... **NCLC 7, 21; DA; WLC**
See also CDALB 1640-1865; DLB 1

Thornton, Hall
See Silverberg, Robert

Thurber, James (Grover)
1894-1961 ... **CLC 5, 11, 25; DA; SSC 1**
See also CA 73-76; CANR 17, 39; CDALB 1929-1941; DLB 4, 11, 22, 102; MAICYA; MTCW; SATA 13

Thurman, Wallace (Henry)
1902-1934 .... **TCLC 6; BLC**
See also BW 1; CA 104; 124; DLB 51

Ticheburn, Cheviot
See Ainsworth, William Harrison

Tieck, (Johann) Ludwig
1773-1853 .... **NCLC 5, 46**
See also DLB 90

Tiger, Derry
See Ellison, Harlan (Jay)

Tilghman, Christopher 1948(?)-..... **CLC 65**

Tillinghast, Richard (Williford)
1940- .... **CLC 29**
See also CA 29-32R; CANR 26

Timrod, Henry 1828-1867 .... **NCLC 25**
See also DLB 3

Tindall, Gillian 1938-.............. **CLC 7**
See also CA 21-24R; CANR 11

Tiptree, James, Jr. .... **CLC 48, 50**
See also Sheldon, Alice Hastings Bradley
See also DLB 8

Titmarsh, Michael Angelo
See Thackeray, William Makepeace

Tocqueville, Alexis (Charles Henri Maurice Clerel Comte) 1805-1859..... **NCLC 7**

Tolkien, J(ohn) R(onald) R(euel)
1892-1973 .... **CLC 1, 2, 3, 8, 12, 38; DA; WLC**
See also AAYA 10; AITN 1; CA 17-18; 45-48; CANR 36; CAP 2; CDBLB 1914-1945; DLB 15; JRDA; MAICYA; MTCW; SATA 2, 32; SATA-Obit 24

Toller, Ernst 1893-1939 .... **TCLC 10**
See also CA 107; DLB 124

Tolson, M. B.
See Tolson, Melvin B(eaunorus)

Tolson, Melvin B(eaunorus)
1898(?)-1966 .... **CLC 36; BLC**
See also BW 1; CA 124; 89-92; DLB 48, 76

Tyler, Anne
1941- . . . . **CLC 7, 11, 18, 28, 44, 59**
See also BEST 89:1; CA 9-12R; CANR 11, 33; DLB 6, 143; DLBY 82; MTCW; SATA 7

Tyler, Royall 1757-1826. . . . . **NCLC 3**
See also DLB 37

Tynan, Katharine 1861-1931 . . . . **TCLC 3**
See also CA 104; DLB 153

Tyutchev, Fyodor 1803-1873 . . . . . **NCLC 34**

Tzara, Tristan . . . . **CLC 47**
See also Rosenfeld, Samuel

Uhry, Alfred 1936- . . . . **CLC 55**
See also CA 127; 133

Ulf, Haerved
See Strindberg, (Johan) August

Ulf, Harved
See Strindberg, (Johan) August

Ulibarri, Sabine R(eyes) 1919- . . . . . **CLC 83**
See also CA 131; DLB 82; HW

Unamuno (y Jugo), Miguel de
1864-1936 . . . . **TCLC 2, 9; HLC; SSC 11**
See also CA 104; 131; DLB 108; HW; MTCW

Undercliffe, Errol
See Campbell, (John) Ramsey

Underwood, Miles
See Glassco, John

Undset, Sigrid
1882-1949 . . . . **TCLC 3; DA; WLC**
See also CA 104; 129; MTCW

Ungaretti, Giuseppe
1888-1970 . . . . **CLC 7, 11, 15**
See also CA 19-20; 25-28R; CAP 2; DLB 114

Unger, Douglas 1952- . . . . **CLC 34**
See also CA 130

Unsworth, Barry (Forster) 1930- . . . . **CLC 76**
See also CA 25-28R; CANR 30

Updike, John (Hoyer)
1932- . . . . . . **CLC 1, 2, 3, 5, 7, 9, 13, 15, 23, 34, 43, 70; DA; SSC 13; WLC**
See also CA 1-4R; CABS 1; CANR 4, 33; CDALB 1968-1988; DLB 2, 5, 143; DLBD 3; DLBY 80, 82; MTCW

Upshaw, Margaret Mitchell
See Mitchell, Margaret (Munnerlyn)

Upton, Mark
See Sanders, Lawrence

Urdang, Constance (Henriette)
1922- . . . . **CLC 47**
See also CA 21-24R; CANR 9, 24

Uriel, Henry
See Faust, Frederick (Schiller)

Uris, Leon (Marcus) 1924- . . . . **CLC 7, 32**
See also AITN 1, 2; BEST 89:2; CA 1-4R; CANR 1, 40; MTCW; SATA 49

Urmuz
See Codrescu, Andrei

Ustinov, Peter (Alexander) 1921- . . . . **CLC 1**
See also AITN 1; CA 13-16R; CANR 25; DLB 13

Vaculik, Ludvik 1926- . . . . **CLC 7**
See also CA 53-56

Valdez, Luis (Miguel)
1940- . . . . **CLC 84; HLC**
See also CA 101; CANR 32; DLB 122; HW

Valenzuela, Luisa 1938- . . . **CLC 31; SSC 14**
See also CA 101; CANR 32; DLB 113; HW

Valera y Alcala-Galiano, Juan
1824-1905 . . . . **TCLC 10**
See also CA 106

Valery, (Ambroise) Paul (Toussaint Jules)
1871-1945 . . . . **TCLC 4, 15; PC 9**
See also CA 104; 122; MTCW

Valle-Inclan, Ramon (Maria) del
1866-1936 . . . . **TCLC 5; HLC**
See also CA 106; DLB 134

Vallejo, Antonio Buero
See Buero Vallejo, Antonio

Vallejo, Cesar (Abraham)
1892-1938 . . . . **TCLC 3, 56; HLC**
See also CA 105; HW

Valle Y Pena, Ramon del
See Valle-Inclan, Ramon (Maria) del

Van Ash, Cay 1918- . . . . **CLC 34**

Vanbrugh, Sir John 1664-1726 . . . . . . **LC 21**
See also DLB 80

Van Campen, Karl
See Campbell, John W(ood, Jr.)

Vance, Gerald
See Silverberg, Robert

Vance, Jack . . . . **CLC 35**
See also Vance, John Holbrook
See also DLB 8

Vance, John Holbrook 1916-
See Queen, Ellery; Vance, Jack
See also CA 29-32R; CANR 17; MTCW

Van Den Bogarde, Derek Jules Gaspard Ulric Niven 1921-
See Bogarde, Dirk
See also CA 77-80

Vandenburgh, Jane . . . . **CLC 59**

Vanderhaeghe, Guy 1951- . . . . **CLC 41**
See also CA 113

van der Post, Laurens (Jan) 1906- . . . **CLC 5**
See also CA 5-8R; CANR 35

van de Wetering, Janwillem 1931- . . **CLC 47**
See also CA 49-52; CANR 4

Van Dine, S. S. . . . . **TCLC 23**
See also Wright, Willard Huntington

Van Doren, Carl (Clinton)
1885-1950 . . . . **TCLC 18**
See also CA 111

Van Doren, Mark 1894-1972. . . . . **CLC 6, 10**
See also CA 1-4R; 37-40R; CANR 3; DLB 45; MTCW

Van Druten, John (William)
1901-1957 . . . . **TCLC 2**
See also CA 104; DLB 10

Van Duyn, Mona (Jane)
1921- . . . . **CLC 3, 7, 63**
See also CA 9-12R; CANR 7, 38; DLB 5

Van Dyne, Edith
See Baum, L(yman) Frank

van Itallie, Jean-Claude 1936- . . . . **CLC 3**
See also CA 45-48; CAAS 2; CANR 1, 48; DLB 7

van Ostaijen, Paul 1896-1928 . . . . . **TCLC 33**

Van Peebles, Melvin 1932- . . . . . . **CLC 2, 20**
See also BW 2; CA 85-88; CANR 27

Vansittart, Peter 1920- . . . . **CLC 42**
See also CA 1-4R; CANR 3

Van Vechten, Carl 1880-1964 . . . . . . **CLC 33**
See also CA 89-92; DLB 4, 9, 51

Van Vogt, A(lfred) E(lton) 1912- . . . . . **CLC 1**
See also CA 21-24R; CANR 28; DLB 8; SATA 14

Varda, Agnes 1928- . . . . **CLC 16**
See also CA 116; 122

Vargas Llosa, (Jorge) Mario (Pedro)
1936- . . . . **CLC 3, 6, 9, 10, 15, 31, 42, 85; DA; HLC**
See also CA 73-76; CANR 18, 32, 42; DLB 145; HW; MTCW

Vasiliu, Gheorghe 1881-1957
See Bacovia, George
See also CA 123

Vassa, Gustavus
See Equiano, Olaudah

Vassilikos, Vassilis 1933- . . . . **CLC 4, 8**
See also CA 81-84

Vaughan, Henry 1621-1695 . . . . **LC 27**
See also DLB 131

Vaughn, Stephanie. . . . . **CLC 62**

Vazov, Ivan (Minchov)
1850-1921 . . . . **TCLC 25**
See also CA 121; DLB 147

Veblen, Thorstein (Bunde)
1857-1929 . . . . **TCLC 31**
See also CA 115

Vega, Lope de 1562-1635. . . . . **LC 23**

Venison, Alfred
See Pound, Ezra (Weston Loomis)

Verdi, Marie de
See Mencken, H(enry) L(ouis)

Verdu, Matilde
See Cela, Camilo Jose

Verga, Giovanni (Carmelo)
1840-1922 . . . . **TCLC 3**
See also CA 104; 123

Vergil
70B.C.-19B.C. . . . . **CMLC 9; DA; PC 12**

Verhaeren, Emile (Adolphe Gustave)
1855-1916 . . . . **TCLC 12**
See also CA 109

Verlaine, Paul (Marie)
1844-1896 . . . . **NCLC 2, 51; PC 2**

Verne, Jules (Gabriel)
1828-1905 . . . . **TCLC 6, 52**
See also CA 110; 131; DLB 123; JRDA; MAICYA; SATA 21

Very, Jones 1813-1880. . . . . **NCLC 9**
See also DLB 1

Vesaas, Tarjei 1897-1970. . . . . **CLC 48**
See also CA 29-32R

Vialis, Gaston
See Simenon, Georges (Jacques Christian)

Vian, Boris 1920-1959 . . . . **TCLC 9**
See also CA 106; DLB 72

Walser, Martin 1927- . . . . **CLC 27**
See also CA 57-60; CANR 8, 46; DLB 75, 124

Walser, Robert
1878-1956 . . . . **TCLC 18; SSC 20**
See also CA 118; DLB 66

Walsh, Jill Paton . . . . **CLC 35**
See also Paton Walsh, Gillian
See also AAYA 11; CLR 2; SAAS 3

Walter, Villiam Christian
See Andersen, Hans Christian

Wambaugh, Joseph (Aloysius, Jr.)
1937- . . . . **CLC 3, 18**
See also AITN 1; BEST 89:3; CA 33-36R; CANR 42; DLB 6; DLBY 83; MTCW

Ward, Arthur Henry Sarsfield 1883-1959
See Rohmer, Sax
See also CA 108

Ward, Douglas Turner 1930- . . . . **CLC 19**
See also BW 1; CA 81-84; CANR 27; DLB 7, 38

Ward, Mary Augusta
See Ward, Mrs. Humphry

Ward, Mrs. Humphry
1851-1920 . . . . **TCLC 55**
See also DLB 18

Ward, Peter
See Faust, Frederick (Schiller)

Warhol, Andy 1928(?)-1987 . . . . **CLC 20**
See also AAYA 12; BEST 89:4; CA 89-92; 121; CANR 34

Warner, Francis (Robert le Plastrier)
1937- . . . . **CLC 14**
See also CA 53-56; CANR 11

Warner, Marina 1946- . . . . **CLC 59**
See also CA 65-68; CANR 21

Warner, Rex (Ernest) 1905-1986. . . . **CLC 45**
See also CA 89-92; 119; DLB 15

Warner, Susan (Bogert)
1819-1885 . . . . **NCLC 31**
See also DLB 3, 42

Warner, Sylvia (Constance) Ashton
See Ashton-Warner, Sylvia (Constance)

Warner, Sylvia Townsend
1893-1978 . . . . **CLC 7, 19**
See also CA 61-64; 77-80; CANR 16; DLB 34, 139; MTCW

Warren, Mercy Otis 1728-1814. . . **NCLC 13**
See also DLB 31

Warren, Robert Penn
1905-1989 . . . . **CLC 1, 4, 6, 8, 10, 13, 18, 39, 53, 59; DA; SSC 4; WLC**
See also AITN 1; CA 13-16R; 129; CANR 10, 47; CDALB 1968-1988; DLB 2, 48, 152; DLBY 80, 89; MTCW; SATA 46; SATA-Obit 63

Warshofsky, Isaac
See Singer, Isaac Bashevis

Warton, Thomas 1728-1790. . . . . **LC 15**
See also DLB 104, 109

Waruk, Kona
See Harris, (Theodore) Wilson

Warung, Price 1855-1911. . . . . **TCLC 45**

Warwick, Jarvis
See Garner, Hugh

Washington, Alex
See Harris, Mark

Washington, Booker T(aliaferro)
1856-1915 . . . . **TCLC 10; BLC**
See also BW 1; CA 114; 125; SATA 28

Washington, George 1732-1799. . . . . . **LC 25**
See also DLB 31

Wassermann, (Karl) Jakob
1873-1934 . . . . **TCLC 6**
See also CA 104; DLB 66

Wasserstein, Wendy
1950- . . . . **CLC 32, 59; DC 4**
See also CA 121; 129; CABS 3

Waterhouse, Keith (Spencer)
1929- . . . . **CLC 47**
See also CA 5-8R; CANR 38; DLB 13, 15; MTCW

Waters, Frank (Joseph) 1902- . . . . . . **CLC 88**
See also CA 5-8R; CAAS 13; CANR 3, 18; DLBY 86

Waters, Roger 1944- . . . . **CLC 35**

Watkins, Frances Ellen
See Harper, Frances Ellen Watkins

Watkins, Gerrold
See Malzberg, Barry N(athaniel)

Watkins, Paul 1964- . . . . **CLC 55**
See also CA 132

Watkins, Vernon Phillips
1906-1967 . . . . **CLC 43**
See also CA 9-10; 25-28R; CAP 1; DLB 20

Watson, Irving S.
See Mencken, H(enry) L(ouis)

Watson, John H.
See Farmer, Philip Jose

Watson, Richard F.
See Silverberg, Robert

Waugh, Auberon (Alexander) 1939- . . **CLC 7**
See also CA 45-48; CANR 6, 22; DLB 14

Waugh, Evelyn (Arthur St. John)
1903-1966 . . . . . . **CLC 1, 3, 8, 13, 19, 27, 44; DA; WLC**
See also CA 85-88; 25-28R; CANR 22; CDBLB 1914-1945; DLB 15; MTCW

Waugh, Harriet 1944- . . . . **CLC 6**
See also CA 85-88; CANR 22

Ways, C. R.
See Blount, Roy (Alton), Jr.

Waystaff, Simon
See Swift, Jonathan

Webb, (Martha) Beatrice (Potter)
1858-1943 . . . . **TCLC 22**
See also Potter, Beatrice
See also CA 117

Webb, Charles (Richard) 1939- . . . . . . **CLC 7**
See also CA 25-28R

Webb, James H(enry), Jr. 1946- . . . . **CLC 22**
See also CA 81-84

Webb, Mary (Gladys Meredith)
1881-1927 . . . . **TCLC 24**
See also CA 123; DLB 34

Webb, Mrs. Sidney
See Webb, (Martha) Beatrice (Potter)

Webb, Phyllis 1927- . . . . **CLC 18**
See also CA 104; CANR 23; DLB 53

Webb, Sidney (James)
1859-1947 . . . . **TCLC 22**
See also CA 117

Webber, Andrew Lloyd . . . . **CLC 21**
See also Lloyd Webber, Andrew

Weber, Lenora Mattingly
1895-1971 . . . . **CLC 12**
See also CA 19-20; 29-32R; CAP 1; SATA 2; SATA-Obit 26

Webster, John 1579(?)-1634(?) . . . . **DC 2**
See also CDBLB Before 1660; DA; DLB 58; WLC

Webster, Noah 1758-1843 . . . . **NCLC 30**

Wedekind, (Benjamin) Frank(lin)
1864-1918 . . . . **TCLC 7**
See also CA 104; DLB 118

Weidman, Jerome 1913-. . . . . **CLC 7**
See also AITN 2; CA 1-4R; CANR 1; DLB 28

Weil, Simone (Adolphine)
1909-1943 . . . . **TCLC 23**
See also CA 117

Weinstein, Nathan
See West, Nathanael

Weinstein, Nathan von Wallenstein
See West, Nathanael

Weir, Peter (Lindsay) 1944- . . . . **CLC 20**
See also CA 113; 123

Weiss, Peter (Ulrich)
1916-1982 . . . . **CLC 3, 15, 51**
See also CA 45-48; 106; CANR 3; DLB 69, 124

Weiss, Theodore (Russell)
1916- . . . . **CLC 3, 8, 14**
See also CA 9-12R; CAAS 2; CANR 46; DLB 5

Welch, (Maurice) Denton
1915-1948 . . . . **TCLC 22**
See also CA 121

Welch, James 1940- . . . . **CLC 6, 14, 52**
See also CA 85-88; CANR 42; NNAL

Weldon, Fay
1933- . . . . **CLC 6, 9, 11, 19, 36, 59**
See also CA 21-24R; CANR 16, 46; CDBLB 1960 to Present; DLB 14; MTCW

Wellek, Rene 1903- . . . . **CLC 28**
See also CA 5-8R; CAAS 7; CANR 8; DLB 63

Weller, Michael 1942- . . . . **CLC 10, 53**
See also CA 85-88

Weller, Paul 1958- . . . . **CLC 26**

Wellershoff, Dieter 1925-. . . . . **CLC 46**
See also CA 89-92; CANR 16, 37

Welles, (George) Orson
1915-1985 . . . . **CLC 20, 80**
See also CA 93-96; 117

Wellman, Mac 1945- . . . . **CLC 65**

Wellman, Manly Wade 1903-1986 . . **CLC 49**
See also CA 1-4R; 118; CANR 6, 16, 44; SATA 6; SATA-Obit 47

Wells, Carolyn 1869(?)-1942 . . . . . . **TCLC 35**
See also CA 113; DLB 11

Wells, H(erbert) G(eorge) 1866-1946 .... **TCLC 6, 12, 19; DA; SSC 6; WLC**
See also CA 110; 121; CDBLB 1914-1945; DLB 34, 70; MTCW; SATA 20

Wells, Rosemary 1943-............ **CLC 12**
See also AAYA 13; CA 85-88; CANR 48; CLR 16; MAICYA; SAAS 1; SATA 18, 69

Welty, Eudora 1909- ...... **CLC 1, 2, 5, 14, 22, 33; DA; SSC 1; WLC**
See also CA 9-12R; CABS 1; CANR 32; CDALB 1941-1968; DLB 2, 102, 143; DLBD 12; DLBY 87; MTCW

Wen I-to 1899-1946 .... **TCLC 28**

Wentworth, Robert
See Hamilton, Edmond

Werfel, Franz (V.) 1890-1945 ...... **TCLC 8**
See also CA 104; DLB 81, 124

Wergeland, Henrik Arnold 1808-1845 .... **NCLC 5**

Wersba, Barbara 1932-............ **CLC 30**
See also AAYA 2; CA 29-32R; CANR 16, 38; CLR 3; DLB 52; JRDA; MAICYA; SAAS 2; SATA 1, 58

Wertmueller, Lina 1928- .... **CLC 16**
See also CA 97-100; CANR 39

Wescott, Glenway 1901-1987....... **CLC 13**
See also CA 13-16R; 121; CANR 23; DLB 4, 9, 102

Wesker, Arnold 1932- .... **CLC 3, 5, 42**
See also CA 1-4R; CAAS 7; CANR 1, 33; CDBLB 1960 to Present; DLB 13; MTCW

Wesley, Richard (Errol) 1945-....... **CLC 7**
See also BW 1; CA 57-60; CANR 27; DLB 38

Wessel, Johan Herman 1742-1785 .... **LC 7**

West, Anthony (Panther) 1914-1987 .... **CLC 50**
See also CA 45-48; 124; CANR 3, 19; DLB 15

West, C. P.
See Wodehouse, P(elham) G(renville)

West, (Mary) Jessamyn 1902-1984 .... **CLC 7, 17**
See also CA 9-12R; 112; CANR 27; DLB 6; DLBY 84; MTCW; SATA-Obit 37

West, Morris L(anglo) 1916-..... **CLC 6, 33**
See also CA 5-8R; CANR 24; MTCW

West, Nathanael 1903-1940 ..... **TCLC 1, 14, 44; SSC 16**
See also CA 104; 125; CDALB 1929-1941; DLB 4, 9, 28; MTCW

West, Owen
See Koontz, Dean R(ay)

West, Paul 1930- .... **CLC 7, 14**
See also CA 13-16R; CAAS 7; CANR 22; DLB 14

West, Rebecca 1892-1983 .. **CLC 7, 9, 31, 50**
See also CA 5-8R; 109; CANR 19; DLB 36; DLBY 83; MTCW

Westall, Robert (Atkinson) 1929-1993 .... **CLC 17**
See also AAYA 12; CA 69-72; 141; CANR 18; CLR 13; JRDA; MAICYA; SAAS 2; SATA 23, 69; SATA-Obit 75

Westlake, Donald E(dwin) 1933- .... **CLC 7, 33**
See also CA 17-20R; CAAS 13; CANR 16, 44

Westmacott, Mary
See Christie, Agatha (Mary Clarissa)

Weston, Allen
See Norton, Andre

Wetcheek, J. L.
See Feuchtwanger, Lion

Wetering, Janwillem van de
See van de Wetering, Janwillem

Wetherell, Elizabeth
See Warner, Susan (Bogert)

Whalen, Philip 1923- .... **CLC 6, 29**
See also CA 9-12R; CANR 5, 39; DLB 16

Wharton, Edith (Newbold Jones) 1862-1937 ...... **TCLC 3, 9, 27, 53; DA; SSC 6; WLC**
See also CA 104; 132; CDALB 1865-1917; DLB 4, 9, 12, 78; MTCW

Wharton, James
See Mencken, H(enry) L(ouis)

Wharton, William (a pseudonym) .... **CLC 18, 37**
See also CA 93-96; DLBY 80

Wheatley (Peters), Phillis 1754(?)-1784 .... **LC 3; BLC; DA; PC 3; WLC**
See also CDALB 1640-1865; DLB 31, 50

Wheelock, John Hall 1886-1978 .... **CLC 14**
See also CA 13-16R; 77-80; CANR 14; DLB 45

White, E(lwyn) B(rooks) 1899-1985 .... **CLC 10, 34, 39**
See also AITN 2; CA 13-16R; 116; CANR 16, 37; CLR 1, 21; DLB 11, 22; MAICYA; MTCW; SATA 2, 29; SATA-Obit 44

White, Edmund (Valentine III) 1940- .... **CLC 27**
See also AAYA 7; CA 45-48; CANR 3, 19, 36; MTCW

White, Patrick (Victor Martindale) 1912-1990 .. **CLC 3, 4, 5, 7, 9, 18, 65, 69**
See also CA 81-84; 132; CANR 43; MTCW

White, Phyllis Dorothy James 1920-
See James, P. D.
See also CA 21-24R; CANR 17, 43; MTCW

White, T(erence) H(anbury) 1906-1964 .... **CLC 30**
See also CA 73-76; CANR 37; JRDA; MAICYA; SATA 12

White, Terence de Vere 1912-1994 .... **CLC 49**
See also CA 49-52; 145; CANR 3

White, Walter F(rancis) 1893-1955 .... **TCLC 15**
See also White, Walter
See also BW 1; CA 115; 124; DLB 51

White, William Hale 1831-1913
See Rutherford, Mark
See also CA 121

Whitehead, E(dward) A(nthony) 1933- .... **CLC 5**
See also CA 65-68

Whitemore, Hugh (John) 1936-..... **CLC 37**
See also CA 132

Whitman, Sarah Helen (Power) 1803-1878 .... **NCLC 19**
See also DLB 1

Whitman, Walt(er) 1819-1892 ..... **NCLC 4, 31; DA; PC 3; WLC**
See also CDALB 1640-1865; DLB 3, 64; SATA 20

Whitney, Phyllis A(yame) 1903-.... **CLC 42**
See also AITN 2; BEST 90:3; CA 1-4R; CANR 3, 25, 38; JRDA; MAICYA; SATA 1, 30

Whittemore, (Edward) Reed (Jr.) 1919- .... **CLC 4**
See also CA 9-12R; CAAS 8; CANR 4; DLB 5

Whittier, John Greenleaf 1807-1892 .... **NCLC 8**
See also CDALB 1640-1865; DLB 1

Whittlebot, Hernia
See Coward, Noel (Peirce)

Wicker, Thomas Grey 1926-
See Wicker, Tom
See also CA 65-68; CANR 21, 46

Wicker, Tom .... **CLC 7**
See also Wicker, Thomas Grey

Wideman, John Edgar 1941- .... **CLC 5, 34, 36, 67; BLC**
See also BW 2; CA 85-88; CANR 14, 42; DLB 33, 143

Wiebe, Rudy (Henry) 1934-... **CLC 6, 11, 14**
See also CA 37-40R; CANR 42; DLB 60

Wieland, Christoph Martin 1733-1813 .... **NCLC 17**
See also DLB 97

Wiene, Robert 1881-1938......... **TCLC 56**

Wieners, John 1934-............... **CLC 7**
See also CA 13-16R; DLB 16

Wiesel, Elie(zer) 1928- .... **CLC 3, 5, 11, 37; DA**
See also AAYA 7; AITN 1; CA 5-8R; CAAS 4; CANR 8, 40; DLB 83; DLBY 87; MTCW; SATA 56

Wiggins, Marianne 1947-.......... **CLC 57**
See also BEST 89:3; CA 130

Wight, James Alfred 1916-
See Herriot, James
See also CA 77-80; SATA 55; SATA-Brief 44

Wilbur, Richard (Purdy) 1921- .... **CLC 3, 6, 9, 14, 53; DA**
See also CA 1-4R; CABS 2; CANR 2, 29; DLB 5; MTCW; SATA 9

Wild, Peter 1940-................ **CLC 14**
See also CA 37-40R; DLB 5

Wilde, Oscar (Fingal O'Flahertie Wills) 1854(?)-1900 .... **TCLC 1, 8, 23, 41; DA; SSC 11; WLC**
See also CA 104; 119; CDBLB 1890-1914; DLB 10, 19, 34, 57, 141; SATA 24

Wilder, Billy .... **CLC 20**
See also Wilder, Samuel
See also DLB 26

Wilder, Samuel 1906-
See Wilder, Billy
See also CA 89-92

Wilder, Thornton (Niven) 1897-1975 ...... **CLC 1, 5, 6, 10, 15, 35, 82; DA; DC 1; WLC**
See also AITN 2; CA 13-16R; 61-64; CANR 40; DLB 4, 7, 9; MTCW

Wilding, Michael 1942-........... **CLC 73**
See also CA 104; CANR 24

Wiley, Richard 1944-............. **CLC 44**
See also CA 121; 129

Wilhelm, Kate .... **CLC 7**
See also Wilhelm, Katie Gertrude
See also CAAS 5; DLB 8

Wilhelm, Katie Gertrude 1928-
See Wilhelm, Kate
See also CA 37-40R; CANR 17, 36; MTCW

Wilkins, Mary
See Freeman, Mary Eleanor Wilkins

Willard, Nancy 1936-........... **CLC 7, 37**
See also CA 89-92; CANR 10, 39; CLR 5; DLB 5, 52; MAICYA; MTCW; SATA 37, 71; SATA-Brief 30

Williams, C(harles) K(enneth) 1936- .... **CLC 33, 56**
See also CA 37-40R; DLB 5

Williams, Charles
See Collier, James L(incoln)

Williams, Charles (Walter Stansby) 1886-1945 .... **TCLC 1, 11**
See also CA 104; DLB 100, 153

Williams, (George) Emlyn 1905-1987 .... **CLC 15**
See also CA 104; 123; CANR 36; DLB 10, 77; MTCW

Williams, Hugo 1942-............. **CLC 42**
See also CA 17-20R; CANR 45; DLB 40

Williams, J. Walker
See Wodehouse, P(elham) G(renville)

Williams, John A(lfred) 1925- .... **CLC 5, 13; BLC**
See also BW 2; CA 53-56; CAAS 3; CANR 6, 26; DLB 2, 33

Williams, Jonathan (Chamberlain) 1929- .... **CLC 13**
See also CA 9-12R; CAAS 12; CANR 8; DLB 5

Williams, Joy 1944-.............. **CLC 31**
See also CA 41-44R; CANR 22, 48

Williams, Norman 1952- .... **CLC 39**
See also CA 118

Williams, Sherley Anne 1944- .... **CLC 89; BLC**
See also BW 2; CA 73-76; CANR 25; DLB 41; SATA 78

Williams, Shirley
See Williams, Sherley Anne

Williams, Tennessee 1911-1983 ..... **CLC 1, 2, 5, 7, 8, 11, 15, 19, 30, 39, 45, 71; DA; DC 4; WLC**
See also AITN 1, 2; CA 5-8R; 108; CABS 3; CANR 31; CDALB 1941-1968; DLB 7; DLBD 4; DLBY 83; MTCW

Williams, Thomas (Alonzo) 1926-1990 .... **CLC 14**
See also CA 1-4R; 132; CANR 2

Williams, William C.
See Williams, William Carlos

Williams, William Carlos 1883-1963 .... **CLC 1, 2, 5, 9, 13, 22, 42, 67; DA; PC 7**
See also CA 89-92; CANR 34; CDALB 1917-1929; DLB 4, 16, 54, 86; MTCW

Williamson, David (Keith) 1942-.... **CLC 56**
See also CA 103; CANR 41

Williamson, Ellen Douglas 1905-1984
See Douglas, Ellen
See also CA 17-20R; 114; CANR 39

Williamson, Jack................. **CLC 29**
See also Williamson, John Stewart
See also CAAS 8; DLB 8

Williamson, John Stewart 1908-
See Williamson, Jack
See also CA 17-20R; CANR 23

Willie, Frederick
See Lovecraft, H(oward) P(hillips)

Willingham, Calder (Baynard, Jr.) 1922-1995 .... **CLC 5, 51**
See also CA 5-8R; 147; CANR 3; DLB 2, 44; MTCW

Willis, Charles
See Clarke, Arthur C(harles)

Willy
See Colette, (Sidonie-Gabrielle)

Willy, Colette
See Colette, (Sidonie-Gabrielle)

Wilson, A(ndrew) N(orman) 1950- .. **CLC 33**
See also CA 112; 122; DLB 14

Wilson, Angus (Frank Johnstone) 1913-1991 .... **CLC 2, 3, 5, 25, 34**
See also CA 5-8R; 134; CANR 21; DLB 15, 139; MTCW

Wilson, August 1945- .. **CLC 39, 50, 63; BLC; DA; DC 2**
See also BW 2; CA 115; 122; CANR 42; MTCW

Wilson, Brian 1942-.............. **CLC 12**

Wilson, Colin 1931- .... **CLC 3, 14**
See also CA 1-4R; CAAS 5; CANR 1, 22, 33; DLB 14; MTCW

Wilson, Dirk
See Pohl, Frederik

Wilson, Edmund 1895-1972 .... **CLC 1, 2, 3, 8, 24**
See also CA 1-4R; 37-40R; CANR 1, 46; DLB 63; MTCW

Wilson, Ethel Davis (Bryant) 1888(?)-1980 .... **CLC 13**
See also CA 102; DLB 68; MTCW

Wilson, John 1785-1854.......... **NCLC 5**

Wilson, John (Anthony) Burgess 1917-1993
See Burgess, Anthony
See also CA 1-4R; 143; CANR 2, 46; MTCW

Wilson, Lanford 1937-....... **CLC 7, 14, 36**
See also CA 17-20R; CABS 3; CANR 45; DLB 7

Wilson, Robert M. 1944-......... **CLC 7, 9**
See also CA 49-52; CANR 2, 41; MTCW

Wilson, Robert McLiam 1964-..... **CLC 59**
See also CA 132

Wilson, Sloan 1920-.............. **CLC 32**
See also CA 1-4R; CANR 1, 44

Wilson, Snoo 1948-............... **CLC 33**
See also CA 69-72

Wilson, William S(mith) 1932-..... **CLC 49**
See also CA 81-84

Winchilsea, Anne (Kingsmill) Finch Counte 1661-1720 .... **LC 3**

Windham, Basil
See Wodehouse, P(elham) G(renville)

Wingrove, David (John) 1954-...... **CLC 68**
See also CA 133

Winters, Janet Lewis .... **CLC 41**
See also Lewis, Janet
See also DLBY 87

Winters, (Arthur) Yvor 1900-1968 .... **CLC 4, 8, 32**
See also CA 11-12; 25-28R; CAP 1; DLB 48; MTCW

Winterson, Jeanette 1959-......... **CLC 64**
See also CA 136

Wiseman, Frederick 1930-......... **CLC 20**

Wister, Owen 1860-1938 .... **TCLC 21**
See also CA 108; DLB 9, 78; SATA 62

Witkacy
See Witkiewicz, Stanislaw Ignacy

Witkiewicz, Stanislaw Ignacy 1885-1939 .... **TCLC 8**
See also CA 105

Wittgenstein, Ludwig (Josef Johann) 1889-1951 .... **TCLC 59**
See also CA 113

Wittig, Monique 1935(?)-.......... **CLC 22**
See also CA 116; 135; DLB 83

Wittlin, Jozef 1896-1976 .... **CLC 25**
See also CA 49-52; 65-68; CANR 3

Wodehouse, P(elham) G(renville) 1881-1975 ... **CLC 1, 2, 5, 10, 22; SSC 2**
See also AITN 2; CA 45-48; 57-60; CANR 3, 33; CDBLB 1914-1945; DLB 34; MTCW; SATA 22

Woiwode, L.
See Woiwode, Larry (Alfred)

Woiwode, Larry (Alfred) 1941-... **CLC 6, 10**
See also CA 73-76; CANR 16; DLB 6

Wojciechowska, Maia (Teresa) 1927- .... **CLC 26**
See also AAYA 8; CA 9-12R; CANR 4, 41; CLR 1; JRDA; MAICYA; SAAS 1; SATA 1, 28

Yourcenar, Marguerite
1903-1987 .... **CLC 19, 38, 50, 87**
See also CA 69-72; CANR 23; DLB 72; DLBY 88; MTCW

Yurick, Sol 1925- .... **CLC 6**
See also CA 13-16R; CANR 25

Zabolotskii, Nikolai Alekseevich
1903-1958 .... **TCLC 52**
See also CA 116

Zamiatin, Yevgenii
See Zamyatin, Evgeny Ivanovich

Zamora, Bernice (B. Ortiz)
1938- .... **CLC 89; HLC**
See also DLB 82; HW

Zamyatin, Evgeny Ivanovich
1884-1937 .... **TCLC 8, 37**
See also CA 105

Zangwill, Israel 1864-1926........ **TCLC 16**
See also CA 109; DLB 10, 135

Zappa, Francis Vincent, Jr. 1940-1993
See Zappa, Frank
See also CA 108; 143

Zappa, Frank..................... **CLC 17**
See also Zappa, Francis Vincent, Jr.

Zaturenska, Marya 1902-1982.... **CLC 6, 11**
See also CA 13-16R; 105; CANR 22

Zelazny, Roger (Joseph) 1937- ..... **CLC 21**
See also AAYA 7; CA 21-24R; CANR 26; DLB 8; MTCW; SATA 57; SATA-Brief 39

Zhdanov, Andrei A(lexandrovich)
1896-1948 .... **TCLC 18**
See also CA 117

Zhukovsky, Vasily 1783-1852 .... **NCLC 35**

Ziegenhagen, Eric .... **CLC 55**

Zimmer, Jill Schary
See Robinson, Jill

Zimmerman, Robert
See Dylan, Bob

Zindel, Paul 1936- ... **CLC 6, 26; DA; DC 5**
See also AAYA 2; CA 73-76; CANR 31; CLR 3; DLB 7, 52; JRDA; MAICYA; MTCW; SATA 16, 58

Zinov'Ev, A. A.
See Zinoviev, Alexander (Aleksandrovich)

Zinoviev, Alexander (Aleksandrovich)
1922- .... **CLC 19**
See also CA 116; 133; CAAS 10

Zoilus
See Lovecraft, H(oward) P(hillips)

Zola, Emile (Edouard Charles Antoine)
1840-1902 ...... **TCLC 1, 6, 21, 41; DA; WLC**
See also CA 104; 138; DLB 123

Zoline, Pamela 1941- .... **CLC 62**

Zorrilla y Moral, Jose 1817-1893.. **NCLC 6**

Zoshchenko, Mikhail (Mikhailovich)
1895-1958 .... **TCLC 15; SSC 15**
See also CA 115

Zuckmayer, Carl 1896-1977........ **CLC 18**
See also CA 69-72; DLB 56, 124

Zuk, Georges
See Skelton, Robin

Zukofsky, Louis
1904-1978 .... **CLC 1, 2, 4, 7, 11, 18; PC 11**
See also CA 9-12R; 77-80; CANR 39; DLB 5; MTCW

Zweig, Paul 1935-1984......... **CLC 34, 42**
See also CA 85-88; 113

Zweig, Stefan 1881-1942 .... **TCLC 17**
See also CA 112; DLB 81, 118

Literary Criticism Series Cumulative Topic Index

This index lists all topic entries in Gale's *Classical and Medieval Literature Criticism, Contemporary Literary Criticism, Literature Criticism from 1400 to 1800, Nineteenth-Century Literature Criticism,* and *Twentieth-Century Literary Criticism.*

Topic Index

TCLC Cumulative Nationality Index

TCLC-60 Title Index

ISBN 0-8103-9305-0
90000
9 780810 393059